GREECE – 431 B.C.
at the start of the
PELOPONNESIAN WAR

Neutral Greek States   Sparta and Allies   Athens and Allies

GREEK ORDERS OF ARCHITECTURE

ornamentation richness

slenderness grace

Corinthian
A modification of the Ionic, appearing in the 4th century B.C.

simplicity strength solidity

Ionic
First used in cities of Ionia, about 6th century B.C.

Doric
Oldest form.
Appeared in late 7th century B.C.
Used by ancient Dorians.

BLACK SEA

THRACE

Sea of Marmara

MACEDONIA

Pella

Thasos

Chalcidice

PHRYGIA

PERSIAN

EPIRUS

THESSALY

Thracian Sea

Lemnos

AEGEAN

Corcyra

Dolopia

Lesbos

LYDIA

EMPIRE

ONIAN SEA

AETOLIA

Leucas

Locris

Euboea

Scyrus

SEA

Chios

Delphi

Boeotia

Eretria

Cephalonia

Thebes

Attica

Zacynthus

Achaia

Samos

Andros

Elis

Corinth

Athens

Miletus

IONIA

Olympia

Delos

Halicarnassus

Messenia

Cyclades

Naxos

Sparta

Laconia

Rhodes

Olympia
—site of Olympic Games

Cythera

CRETAN SEA

Carpathos

Cnossus

CRETE

0   100   200
miles

Kotschar

damnus

sium

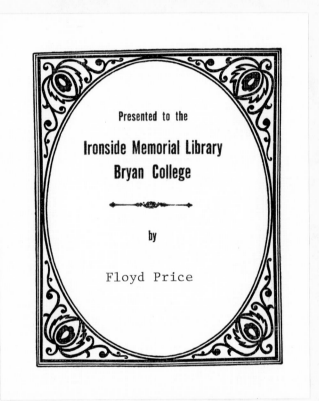

The Heritage of the Past

From the Earliest Times to 1715

HOLT, RINEHART AND WINSTON

New York — Chicago — San Francisco
Toronto — London

STEWART C. EASTON

Alternate Edition

The Heritage of the Past

FROM THE EARLIEST TIMES TO 1715

9

This book is an alternative edition of a text of the same title, *The Heritage of the Past,* which covers the civilizations of the world from the earliest times to the close of the Middle Ages. The preparation of this alternative edition was undertaken at the request of a number of colleges which found it impossible to devote a full semester to the period prior to 1500, and therefore needed a text with a later finishing date. In order to make the subject manageable, the chapter on the Far East in the earlier edition has been omitted altogether, and the material on the Ancient Orient, Greece, and Rome has been compressed into a space approximately a third of that allotted to it in the earlier edition.

In the process the book has necessarily acquired a different emphasis. The course for which the present edition is designed tends to stress the historical antecedents of the present rather than the values of past civilizations in themselves, although the latter are not altogether neglected. The medieval chapters in the earlier edition adopted the approach used in the present volume, the Middle Ages being regarded as the earliest period of our own Western civilization. So they remain substantially as they were originally written, and the same approach has been used for the writing of the new chapters

dealing with the period 1500 to 1715. The foundations of the modern Western world, economic, institutional, and intellectual, are handled in a topical manner. In the process much purely historical material which is interesting but not especially significant for the understanding of the modern world has been purposely omitted.

It has been my experience that students gain much more from a course which appeals to their understanding rather than too exclusively to their capacity for memorizing. Most college students have a real desire to comprehend. Too often their elementary college courses do not ask enough of them, but leave them at the end still seriously undernourished. This text asks rather a lot of the student. It is longer than most in the field, and assignments will necessarily be longer than customary. Some chapters are certainly difficult. But the historical process is not simple. The political structure of the Middle Ages, for instance, cannot be adequately understood without a grasp of a good deal of significant detail, especially in the matter of the relations between the king and the nobility. If this has never been understood properly by the student, then the struggle between king and parliament which forms the basis for modern political democracy will never be appreciated at its full value. Nor can the modern scientific outlook be comprehended without some understanding of the medieval effort to establish the place of reason in a world dominated by faith. I am well aware that the last chapter in this book may well be found difficult by students, but I do not think that a brightly written chapter on the achievements of the seventeenth century in the realm of science would be an adequate substitute for the effort to comprehend the new *manner* of thinking about the world on which the achievements themselves are based. As I have said, however, I am convinced that most college students want to comprehend and are quick to resent oversimplification.

A word should be said on the illustrations and maps. Almost every illustration has been chosen for the light it will throw on the text. The publisher has designed the book in such a way that, with rare exceptions, a picture will be found on the same page as the point illustrated. The illustrations, though they may incidentally be decorative, were not included for decorative purposes. They are an integral part of the text, which in some sections, as for instance that on medieval architecture, cannot be well understood without them. The maps have been specially designed to give important information supplementary to that in the text. They are all drawn to an exact scale. While in many cases serving to illustrate definite topics and movements—as, for instance, in the maps showing the penetration of Western Europe by the barbarians in the fifth century A.D., and the original map showing the territory held by Pope Innocent III in his capacity of feudal lord—the maps also mention important cities and natural geographical features by name. Every place mentioned in the text has been included in one map or another, and the index indicates on which map each such place is to be found. The maps strive to hold a balance between useful information and impressionism. The student should be able to grasp the general picture at once, and then study later the details for the purpose of acquiring essential information.

I am greatly indebted to the cartographer, Mr. Vincent Kotschar, for his brilliant work in designing the maps to bring out the points that I felt needed to be made. In the selection of fitting illustrations I am indebted especially to Mrs. Mildred McGill of The Metropolitan Museum of Art, and to Miss Mary M. Kenway of the Pierpont Morgan Library, as well as to the many other persons and institutions by whose courtesy the illustrations have been permitted to appear.

I cannot praise too highly the enthusiastic cooperation of my publisher at every phase of the work. Several colleagues of the Department of History of the College of the City of New York read portions of the manuscript at different stages of the work and made useful comments and suggestions. Particular mention should be made of Mr. Vito Caporale, who read the medieval chapters in the present edition, and whose comment and encouragement were of the greatest help. I am also indebted to Madeline R. Robinton, Associate Professor of History, Brooklyn College, for suggestions pertaining to Chapter 15, and to Dr. Marshall Dill, Jr., for a detailed critique of what are now Chapters 6 to 15. The abbreviated Chapters 1 to 5 and the new Chapters 16 through 22 were given a very careful reading and criticism by Sidney R. Packard, Professor of History, Smith College, and David L. Dowd, Associate Professor of History, University of Florida, both of whom made a number of most important suggestions which materially contributed to such merit as the book may now possess. Valuable suggestions were received also from Professor John R. Williams, Dartmouth College, and Dr. Richard S. Dunn and Dr. Edward Lurie, University of Michigan, who reviewed the outline and prospectus for the present edition.

If the book is now readable and free from grievous error it is because of all those who have contributed specific suggestions, and of countless historians stretching back as far in time as Herodotus; what remains in error is entirely my own responsibility. In particular for the interpretations which are scattered everywhere throughout the book I offer apologies to those historians whose ideas I have adopted wholesale and retail without their consent and to those others who will, as is the way of historians, disagree with them. If any of the latter are required by the exigencies of their profession to teach from this text I offer them my sympathies and trust that they may receive some compensatory enjoyment from revealing to their students the dark secret that historians, even those who write textbooks, are not thereby rendered infallible.

STEWART C. EASTON

January, 1957

Contents

III Classical Civilization of the West

IV The Centuries of Transition

V Civilization of the Middle Ages in Europe

22 The Rise of the Scientific Outlook   775

Appendix: Major Rulers and Regimes in the Modern Period   804

Index   807

Illustrations

Maps

The Heritage of the Past

From the Earliest Times to 1715

I | Before History

The Black Bull, a prehistoric fresco from the Lascaux Caves, Dordogne, France. From L'art préhistorique; peintures, gravures, et sculptures rupestres, *1951.* (COURTESY LES ÉDITIONS BRAUN ET CIE, PARIS, NEW YORK)

1

The Foundations of an
Organized Society

*The economic, political, and cultural foundations of a society • The rise and
fall of civilizations • Theories of history: Marx, Spengler, Toynbee • The
necessity of objectivity and imagination in historical study*

► ## The economic, political, and cultural foundations of a society

THE ECONOMIC REQUIREMENTS OF A SOCIETY

Every human being as an individual has certain cultural and religious needs, as a member of a society he has to regulate his relations with other human beings, and as a producer and consumer he must take his part in economic affairs. These three necessities in his life have always been reflected in human societies. Our first task must therefore be to consider the cultural, political, and economic foundations upon which social institutions have rested.

While each society is in some degree unique, the difference between societies is most visible in the field of culture, in which the creativeness of the individual human being finds the greatest opportunity for expression. In culture, taken in its widest sense, the possibilities for creativeness are infinite; whereas the economic needs of human beings are ultimately limited by their far from infinite ability to consume material goods and in historical societies by the availability of adequate resources and techniques. It is essential for the historian to indicate

how each society organized to produce these material goods, and to show how far its failure to produce enough for all the needs of the human beings in it seriously limited their leisure to engage in cultural pursuits and affected its political organization in a crucial manner. But the economic activities in themselves have been so similar in all the societies considered in this book that it has not been thought necessary to go into much detail unless a particular society made important innovations. In a premachine society such as existed from the Neolithic period to the modern Industrial Revolution, the overwhelming majority of mankind was forced to labor for long hours under difficult conditions to make a bare subsistence. Only since the Industrial Revolution, when man was presented with the necessity of organizing the production and consumption of material goods on a scale hitherto unheard of, did the human efforts to do this become a subject worthy of detailed study in itself.

The basic economic requirements of human beings may be limited to three—food, shelter, and clothing. In the earliest societies known to us, their pursuit consumed such an enormous proportion of available human energies that there was little left for other activities. Food could be obtained from animals and wild plants, which were hunted or harvested in accordance with the skills and techniques available to the society. Such an economy may be termed a natural one— man was dependent entirely upon what was provided for him by nature, especially if he clothed himself in animal skins and lived in caves. When nature failed him, he moved on to a more favorable location, where he continued to live in a natural economy.

At the next stage of development, called the Neolithic Revolution, man ceased to be totally dependent upon nature and began in some degree to control it. He learned to breed and tend animals, so that they were always available to him for food when he needed them, and he taught them to work for him and supplement the labor of his own hands. He also learned to plant crops and harvest them, laying down seeds in some spot cleared for the purpose and in which such plants did not grow by nature. He learned to build himself a home where none had been provided by nature, and he even discovered how to grow special crops such as flax from which he could make himself clothing.

Having thus learned in some degree to control and harness nature, man at last found himself both with leisure to produce luxuries which made life more pleasant and comfortable, and with a surplus of crops beyond the consuming needs of his society. These surpluses of manufactured luxuries, and of crops for human consumption, he was able to offer in exchange for goods produced by other men outside his immediate group. This *trade* was ultimately supplemented and fed by the products of *industry*. Industrial production is characterized by a more intensive division of labor under which some members of the society, freed from direct agricultural work, specialize in manufacturing a varied assortment of articles to be consumed at home or to be traded in exchange for foreign products. An economically advanced society is characterized by the diversity of products manufactured, and by effective or-

ganization of production to take advantage of specialized skills, and minimize the waste of human energies in unnecessary labor.

THE POLITICAL REQUIREMENTS OF A SOCIETY

Protection through government and law

It used to be thought that man in a state of nature was forced to compete with all other human beings for his very subsistence, or, in the famous words of Thomas Hobbes, that his life was "solitary, poor, nasty, brutish, and short." We have no record of such a way of life, either in early times, or among present-day "primitive" men. And it no longer seems as probable to us as it did in the nineteenth century, under the influence of the biological ideas of Darwin, that human survival was a matter of success in the constant struggle for existence, if this struggle is conceived of as a struggle between human beings. It now seems more probable that survival has always been due to successful cooperation between human beings to resist the always dangerous forces of nature.

The first political necessity for men has always been, and remains still, protection— whether from animals, natural hazards, or hostile human beings; and protection must necessarily mean that some human beings band together under some kind of accepted political organization. The first requirement of any government is that it should possess power to enforce its will upon individuals, forcing them to behave in accordance with its dictates. This power may be either military or moral or both; but a government cannot survive without one kind or the other. It follows that a government must be acceptable either to a majority of the people or to a minority who possess enough moral or military power to coerce the majority. No government, whether by one man or by many, can survive without some support and acceptance.

A government, to ensure its acceptance by any of the people, cannot behave in an arbitrary and unpredictable manner. It must make clear what its policy is to be in matters of daily concern to the people. This need for certainty is satisfied by the establishment of law, which explains to the people what is expected of them, and decrees penalties for the behavior it defines as unacceptable. Law is essentially the regulation of the public behavior of human beings in an organized society, and it is enforced by the power of the government, as long as the government is able to maintain its authority.

From very early times men have considered that laws should be made in accordance with an abstraction called justice. But, as there has never been any agreed conception of justice at any time in history, individuals in each society have arrived at their own conceptions of justice by their own thought, and have tried to modify the law accordingly. Justice has remained a valuable ideal, but in fact it has been the enforceable law which has prevailed rather than the abstract and unenforceable ideal. Most lawgivers in early societies claimed that they received the law from the gods and that their laws were therefore in accordance with the ideal of justice; hence they decreed severe penalties for anyone who should attempt, from his feeble human thinking, to change them. In ancient Egypt there was no written law at all until a very late date. The Pharaoh was supposed to "know the hearts of men," and since he was in constant touch with divine powers, he could judge cases in the light of his intuitive and immediate perception of justice.

Evolution of political institutions—From clans and tribes to the national state

In every society there has always been some form of government, since authority has always been necessary, however small the social unit. A natural social unit is the family; and it may be that in some far-off age the self-sufficient family may also have been the political unit, with one member exercising an authority recognized and accepted by the other members. This state of affairs, however, presupposes the self-sufficiency of the one family, and such self-sufficiency is unlikely at any time or in any place. The clan, or union of a small number of families, sometimes closely connected by blood relationship, with perhaps a recent common ancestor, is known as a historical unit, with the leaders of the component families exercising the functions of government. A larger unit is the tribe, composed of several clans. When tribes or clans are gathered together in one area, the government may be made up of the heads of families, or perhaps of a tribal chieftain, acceptable to the other heads by virtue of his birth into one leading family, or because of his own personal, military, or other qualities.

When these tribal units emerge into the light of history there is usually such a chieftain occupying the position of the head of the tribal government, advised by other minor chiefs or heads of families, and sometimes by the whole body of adults, who form an assembly whose advice is called for on special occasions, and whose consent is necessary for important decisions. Such a government is a Primitive Democracy, of the kind we shall find in Mesopotamia at an early date, and traces of which are found among other peoples, such as the primitive Greeks, Romans, and Germans of the West. In other societies we find at an early time the institution of kingship, with the ruler having already been granted the power to govern without the formality of consultation with his subjects. Larger units of government are city-states; empires, which sometimes rule over wide areas subdued by warfare; and, in our own times, national states. Common to all these forms of government are systems of law and officials who carry out the policies of the government under authority delegated by it. From the very primitive to the most advanced and modern forms of government the essential function is always the provision of protection to the governed; and though modern governments have undertaken multifarious subsidiary tasks, essentially they perform these tasks instead of the people themselves because the people have requested or allowed them to do so—tasks supposedly for their benefit which, in their view, can best be performed by common rather than private effort and under direction from above. The modern political and economic theory known as socialism emphasizes the importance of the role of the government in providing for the people what they are unable to provide for themselves.

Historical forms of government— Monarchy, oligarchy, democracy

The essential requirement of government is, then, that it be effective, and that its authority should be accepted in the area entrusted to it. Many forms of government may fulfill these criteria, and many forms are known to history; human inventiveness may yet devise new combinations. But three main classifications are usually recognized—monarchy, or rule by one; oligarchy, or rule by a few; and democracy, or rule by the people. Each of these may exist in pure or mixed forms. Monarchy may consist of rule by a king or a single ruler under some other title and his chosen advisers, with the responsibility ultimately resting with the ruler, or it may be a rule limited by the legal or moral necessity for him to consult his advisers, by whom he may be overruled. The latter is a limited or constitutional monarchy, and within this classification there are many degrees of limitation, down to the point where the "advisers" rule, and the king is merely a respected figurehead and symbol of unity, as in England. An oligarchy may be elected, or it may be entitled to rule by hereditary right; and it may have to consult the people in certain matters and submit to being overruled on occasion. A democracy may be direct, as in Athens, or representative as in modern states, the representatives subject to re-election or recall. The form of government, then, is always subject to change and modification in accordance with the needs of the time and the wishes of the people governed; but, whatever the form, and whatever the label—some modern labels are devised purely with the aim of confusing—a government's functions are those described in the preceding section.

THE "CULTURE" OF A SOCIETY

The common elements of all cultures—The accumulated heritage from the past

In every society it is the free activity of men—their thoughts, their feelings, and their actions—which molds its characteristic institutions, and gives it its characteristic way of looking at life. Together the social organization, political institutions, economic activities, law, science, art, religion, and thought are called the culture of a society. The cave paintings of the Old Stone Age and the mass-production economic technique of the twentieth century are equally an expression of the cultural creativeness of these particular societies. They are the work of men living in the society, making use of the physical environment provided for them by nature. Their creativeness is limited by the natural conditions, but not determined by them. The men of the Old Stone Age could hardly have progressed at a single leap to the mass-production technique of the twentieth century or to its representative political government, since the thoughts of men had first to traverse all the intermediate stages, and the institutions of their society had to be modified in accordance with these newer thoughts. Men had first to live in settled communities, and develop institutions fit for such communities; they had to make the necessary technical inventions, means of communication, transportation, and production, and again slowly develop social institutions which could release and take advantage of natural human inventiveness.

But it is not necessary for each society to start again from scratch, inventing its techniques from the beginning. It can take advantage of the achievements of its predecessors. Once the Neolithic Revolution had taken place and agriculture was seen to be an improvement over the ancient food gathering, this fundamental invention became a part of the permanent possession of mankind, and any new society could build on the foundations laid by Neolithic man. Cultural progress, therefore, is cumulative. The thoughts of mankind have been, as it were, built into the world—and the world has been changed by them, forever. Only if every literate human being were suddenly killed, and all knowledge of human deeds in the last seven thousand years were lost, would it be necessary for mankind to return to the conditions of the Old Stone Age and start again.

The uniqueness of each culture

Yet, although each society does build on the foundations laid by its predecessors and exploits its cultural heritage, it is also, in a sense, unique. The men of ancient Egypt developed a political institution, the divine kingship, which they were unwilling to abandon, yet which was not copied by other societies; they developed an art which had little influence on subsequent art in other countries, and yet has been considered by many to be a perfect expression of the Egyptian attitude toward life. This attitude toward life seems to be the unique element in every society, which gives it its characteristic form. While the ancient Egyptians denied the fact of change, regarding it as illusory, and had therefore no interest in progress, we in the twentieth century not only recognize the fact of change, but try to take advantage of it and help it on by our own efforts. We set ourselves goals which we try to achieve; then, having achieved them, we set ourselves ever more distant goals and strive toward them. We make our ideas into ideals, into the achieving of which we put the whole strength of our wills.

But no society before ours had any such conception of progress. Many societies looked back to a Golden Age in the past which they longed to recapture, and even the Greeks, whose ideas in so many ways were similar to ours, lacked that sense of the importance of building for the future which is characteristic of modern Western civilization. It is necessary, therefore, in studying civilization as it was manifested in a particular society, to try to discover its own characteristic attitude toward life and to view its cultural achievements in the light of this attitude, while at the same time noting those cultural advances which it made and passed on to its successors as part of the total cultural heritage of mankind.

The diffusion of culture

Cultural advances first made within a particular society may be taken up by other societies and spread throughout the entire world. But they must be able to find their proper place in the receiving society, they must find a fertile ground for reception and propagation. The divine kingship of Egypt would not have fitted into the contemporaneous society in Mesopotamia, and even if the Mesopotamian peoples had known of it, they would hardly have tried to graft it onto their existing native institutions. On the other hand, the Christian and other religions have been diffused through many countries where they supplied answers to the problems which the inhabitants of those countries had been trying to solve and where they fitted in with the psychological predisposition of those peoples. The system of representative government developed in medieval England was gradually diffused throughout Europe and, especially since World War I, has spread into many countries of the world which desired to accept a form of government that had apparently proved itself to be effective in the war itself. But in other places it has so far failed to take root because of the tenacity of existing institutions.

Technical inventions do not, as a rule, meet with the same opposition as religious or political innovations, and can be passed from one society to another with less disturbance. There are thousands of examples of such diffusion of inventions from the earliest times to the present. Probably the idea of food growing and the domestication of animals spread throughout the world from some center in the Near East, though the possibility of the separate invention of such a fundamental idea cannot be ruled out. The invention of writing was almost certainly diffused from the ancient land of Sumer, though the earliest receivers, the Egyptians, modified and improved upon the Sumerian practice, using their own pictures and symbols, and developing new writing materials available to them but not to the Sumerians. It is not known by how many millenniums the use of language preceded the written symbols, but the languages of peoples in historic times have many resemblances to each other which can only be explained by diffusion from one people to another. Philologists have classified several families of languages, which they have called by such names as Semitic, Hamitic, and Indo-European, and by examining them have even tried to reveal laws under which the changes take place between one language and another after diffusion, in accordance with certain well-defined principles.[1] Other inventions such as printing, gunpowder, and the cultivation of the silkworm can be traced in some detail by the historian from their first use in one country to their full development in another.

Each society, then, receives by diffusion some of its cultural heritage, and it adds to what it has received the characteristic products of its own genius. It may even invent unnecessarily for itself things which have already been developed elsewhere, unknown to it, which it could have received by diffusion if it had had wider cultural contacts. On the other hand, not all knowledge available to any one people has been preserved or transmitted to others. The ancient Sume-

rians knew all the basic forms of architecture, but the Egyptians and Greeks did not make use of them; medieval European technical knowledge—as, for instance, of the rotation of crops—was in many ways markedly inferior to that of several earlier peoples. The Renaissance Italians had to reinvent many commercial aids known to the Hellenistic world. Each civilization does not accept the entire cultural heritage of its predecessors and build on it; it accepts only what fits its own environment and its own way of living. Even our immense technical achievements, valuable as we may think them—and likely to bring great material benefits if adopted by the peoples we consider backward—may not be universally acceptable. History has yet to show to what extent Western technology will be accepted by a people like, say, the Hindus, who do not share our view of the relation between the material and the spiritual and the relative importance to be assigned to this world and the hereafter. To receive and use what we are willing to transmit to them, perhaps their whole scheme of values must be altered, and their civilization may fall into decay rather than adopt such an alien scheme of values as ours.

▶ The rise and fall of civilizations

THEORIES OF HISTORY—MARX, SPENGLER, TOYNBEE

In recent centuries the attention of the historian has been especially concentrated on the rise and fall of the many civilizations that have been known in the past. Why, he asks, has a civilization or a society known some sudden period of great creativeness, and why, then, does life seem to have gone from it, and the cultural leadership of mankind, which it held for a brief season, to have passed from it into other hands? Many have been the answers propounded, but none has gained universal assent. It may indeed be that no answer can ever be given in material terms and that no explanation will ever be satisfactory because in fact there *is* no explanation of universal validity. Karl Marx tried to show that the economic conditions of an epoch determine the cultural

---

[1] At one time the different peoples who spoke one or another of these groups of languages were given the same classification. They were called Semitic, Hamitic, and Indo-European peoples, and certain physical characteristics were assigned to them. But recent discoveries have tended to show many similarities among the languages of these peoples, and other more ancient languages have been uncovered which seem to fit into none of these categories (as, for instance, the ancient Sumerian language itself). Informed opinion among philologists has therefore been modified, and at the present time there is a tendency to believe that there were earlier languages as yet unknown to us from which these families themselves sprang. The racial classifications have also been increasingly abandoned as equally unsatisfactory. Though we shall still use the words "Semitic," "Hamitic," and "Indo-European" in this book, the possibility is not ruled out that all these peoples in the not so very distant past came from some earlier root stock or stocks, in spite of a few markedly different physical characteristics which can be noted in historic times.

achievements of a civilization, but he failed to give sufficient attention to the diversity of human institutions and achievements in spite of very similar economic conditions at many different stages of history. Hence the Marxist historians have always suffered from the temptation to make the facts fit the theory, tending to neglect those facts which are not in conformity with it. In Marxian theory, then, the fall of a civilization is determined by changes in economic conditions. Oswald Spengler tried to show that the life of a society followed certain laws of growth and decay analogous to those to be found in the plant world, and thus its whole life cycle is predestined.

Arnold Toynbee has tried to explain the arresting of progress as a failure to respond creatively to a challenge presented by certain difficulties which had to be faced by the society. Toynbee, of course, thus assumed that a society ought to evolve, and make progress; and that if it failed to do so, it was in some way not fulfilling its proper tasks. It is doubtful if this is a fair assumption, as there is no inherent reason why a society should wish to progress, and should not be simply content with its present way of life, as apparently the ancient Egyptians were. The desire to progress is a typically modern and Western ideal, and should not be assumed as part of the make-up of earlier peoples; though perhaps when we look back upon the history of mankind from our vantage point we are not unjustified in observing that they *did not* make progress, even if there is no reason why they should have wished to do so. The value of Toynbee's approach is a moral one. He wishes to remind us that change is always with us, whether we will it or not, and as human beings we have to learn how to deal with it by being willing and ready to change ourselves and our outlook in order to cope with the ever new situations that confront us.

THE NECESSITY FOR OBJECTIVITY AND
IMAGINATION IN HISTORICAL STUDY

The moralist's approach to history, however, is not one to be wholeheartedly recommended. It obscures too much, and it tends to prevent a true appreciation of the past. The student of history should strive to see each society and civilization first of all in its own terms, and should try to appreciate its outlook and attitude toward life, carefully refraining from moral judgments based on experience in our own society—should see, for instance, whether to be a slave was the same thing in ancient Egypt, in fifth-century Athens or Sparta, and in the nineteenth-century Southern states of America. The student of history might well conclude that it was a totally different thing to be the slave of an Egyptian Pharaoh in the days before individual freedom and self-realization had become an ideal. Nor should he, with the Marxists, overhastily transfer his knowledge of Western European class struggles into the ancient world, and assume, for example, that the breakdown of Egyptian government after the Old Kingdom was in any way the equivalent of the French or Russian Revolutions. He should try to avoid being taken in by the use of the same word to describe events which occurred in totally different cultural contexts.

Such a procedure requires the exercise of historical imagination, and this can only be acquired by study, life experience, and hard effort. But the effort is well worth while, for it enlarges the horizons and develops that perspective which can be of the utmost value in ordinary affairs.

Second, the student should also try to see the indebtedness of one civilization to another, trace the process of cultural assimilation and transmission, and see how each people has stood upon the shoulders of its predecessors. Such understanding may lead him to a sense of responsibility toward his own heritage from the past, and to the determination to pass this heritage on to posterity substantially unimpaired, and if possible increased.

The general form of this book has been designed to show the separate characteristics of each society and civilization considered, and also to reveal the cumulative heritage of mankind and how all the achievements of mankind in our society have their roots far back in the past; and how impossible it would have been for us to have reached our present heights if the slow tedious work of developing the intellectual and physical tools had not been done for us by those giants who went before us, who had so little to work with and such a long road to travel.

When we tend to neglect this debt and overestimate ourselves and our achievements, it is perhaps wise for us to stop for a moment, think, and remember once more that "we are the heirs of all the ages."

▶ Suggestions for further reading

The three most famous modern interpretations of history are those of Toynbee, Spengler, and Marx, referred to in the text. There has in recent times been much criticism of Toynbee's thesis, and of his use of a rather arbitrary selection of historical facts to support his theories. Many of the facts themselves are not above suspicion. Nearly all specialists have complained of the deficiencies of Toynbee's scholarship in their own particular fields. Nevertheless, these criticisms do not really touch the heart of the matter. However doubtful Toynbee's thesis is, it has unquestionably acted as stimulus to further study and further attempts at synthesis. In this writer's view, all students of history should at least dip into his major work, Arnold J. Toynbee, *A Study of History*, ten vols. (London: Oxford University Press, 1935–1954), if only to see what all the controversy is about. The ten-volume edition is to be preferred above the single-volume abridgment of the first six volumes by D. C. Somervell (New York: Oxford University Press, 1947), since the latter, well though the project has been carried out, makes Toynbee appear far more dogmatic than he really is because of the necessary abridgement of his supporting evidence.

The footnotes, which in the larger project have proved a source of delight to many readers, are likewise necessarily omitted in the abridgement.

Most of the material concerning the beginnings of history and the general statement of the challenge and response theory appear in Volume 1 of the six-volume work. Spengler's cyclical theory of history is contained in his monumental work *The Decline of the West* (tr. C. F. Atkinson, special one-volume edition; New York: Alfred A. Knopf, Inc., 1939), but this book is very difficult to read and is not recommended for beginning students. It is probably better to use an effective digest of his theories, such as H. S. Hughes, *Oswald Spengler; A Critical Estimate* (New York: Charles Scribner's Sons, 1952).

The theories of Karl Marx are to be found scattered through many of his works, but not in easy or convenient form. An extremely interesting criticism of the historical theories of Toynbee, Spengler, and Marx, as well as those of other philosophers of history, is presented in Karl R. Popper, *The Open Society and Its Enemies* (rev. ed.; Princeton, N.J.: Princeton University Press 1950), and is well worth reading, though it is hardly less opinionated and dogmatic than the work of the men it criticizes.

Among other recent works on the meaning and purpose of history the following are highly recommended: H. J. Muller, *The Uses of the Past* (New York: Oxford University Press, 1952), Herbert Butterfield, *History and Human Relations* (New York: The Macmillan Company, 1952), and Carl G. Gustavson, *A Preface to History* (New York: McGraw-Hill Book Company, Inc., 1955).

A stimulating little book on the way in which culture and ideas are diffused, with valuable and thought-provoking illustrations from all periods of history, is Gilbert Highet, *The Migration of Ideas* (New York: Oxford University Press, 1954).

2

Prehistoric Man

Difficulties of studying prehistory • The first beginnings of man • Paleoanthropic man • Lower Paleolithic period • Neanderthal man • Upper Paleolithic period • Neolithic Revolution • The beginnings of metallurgy

---

▶ Difficulties of studying prehistory

It is now believed that a creature recognizable as man has walked the earth for more than half a million years. He has not always lived in the same areas of the earth, for at different times the movements of glaciers and changes of climate have made some regions uninhabitable. But at no time was the whole earth uninhabitable in the last half million years, and immense periods of time have separated the great glacial epochs from each other. Yet it is, at the most, ten thousand—probably not more than eight thousand—years ago that man first began to grow his own food and domesticate the useful animals.

This presents to us at once the great question—why so long? Could prehistoric man not have taken this supreme step earlier, and started on the road to civilization many thousands of years before 8000 B. C.?

To this fundamental question it is impossible to give an answer. The truth is that we know very little indeed about prehistoric man, and the unremitting labors of archaeologists and anthropologists, fruitful though these have been, have only scratched the surface of our almost total ignorance. Besides, no two experts are ever in agreement on all points in their interpretation of the meager data available.

It is necessary to stress this point because all that will be said in this chapter is still in the realm of opinion. It is possible that in two hundred years none of it will be acceptable to our less ignorant descendants. No one should think that prehistory or even ancient history stands still. On the contrary, the older the history the more it can gain from archaeology, and from the discovery and reinterpretation of documents and inscriptions unknown or neglected before. Every discovery of a new fossil of early man is important, every discovery of a cave, or every excavation of an early camp site may alter in fundamental points some of our reconstructed history of early man, whereas even the discovery of a hitherto unknown manuscript or a painting of Leonardo da Vinci would not alter in any important respect our knowledge of the general history of the Italian Renaissance.

▶ The first beginnings of man

THE EVOLUTION OF MAN AS A SPECIES

The evolutionary theory of the origin of man has been greatly modified since Darwin first propounded it in crude form in the middle of the nineteenth century. There are still many inconvenient facts, especially in the animal world, which seem very difficult to explain on the basis of natural selection. But, for the present, the total theory is still widely accepted in the Western world, outside of Russia, and it explains reasonably well what we know of early man. According to this theory those species of living organisms which were best fitted to survive in their environment did survive, and were gradually modified in form by the process of mutation, a process which can be observed in the laboratory in the case of certain animals. The ancestors of man were not those most specialized and suitable for a particular environment. On the contrary, they were more "generalized" and adaptable. From time to time new mutations appeared in the species, and those creatures that could survive best in a changed environment did so, and propagated, while the older, less adaptable species died out. The huge animals became overspecialized and incapable of adaptation, perhaps in a modified environment, and so became extinct; while the smaller, unspecialized creatures, forced to adapt themselves or perish, developed mutations with survival value. Thus, it is hypothesized, the ancestors of man first came on to dry land from the ocean, lived for countless aeons in trees, and at last descended to the earth and began to walk upright, in the process increasing their brain capacity. And finally we had the first real men, the protoanthropi, of whom the oldest so far discovered is the so-called Java man, or *Pithecanthropus erectus*.

THE NATURE OF THE EVIDENCE FOR THE ACTIVITIES OF EARLY MAN

Before we deal with the early men known to us from archaeology it should be stated clearly that it is not permissible to use evidence from people who are living today under primitive conditions and assume at once that they are living in the same way as our ancestors of the Old Stone Age. It is not impossible that these contemporary "primitive" men, though they now use tools recognizably similar to those discovered in ancient deposits, have lost certain knowledge their ancestors once possessed, and so their culture would then represent a decline from some higher stage. On the other hand, they may have made some slight progress in ten thousand years, though not as much as civilized man. We can only use our knowledge of these contemporaries of ours to create an imaginative picture of what Old Stone Age men were like, and of the life they lived. But it remains an imaginative picture, which may or may not be true to reality, and cannot be used as evidence in any way the equal of the inferences we may make from the actual remains discovered by archaeologists.

We have just said that the archaeologist has to make inferences. By this it is meant that he unearths objects, not written records; and the objects tell no clear story by themselves. We have before us, say, a dead body painted with ocher in a corner of a cave, and there are tools beside the body, and perhaps food. We infer some kind of primitive religion from the juxtaposition of these objects, but we cannot be certain of the existence of this religion. It has been suggested that such finds prove that a belief was held in a future life, in which the soul is supposed to return to earth to use the tools he used once in life and to eat the food left for him; or alternatively he needs these things for his use in a future life. But such an inference as this can never be proved true, and, as a result, archaeologists are frequently at odds with each other, and wide agreement is rare. Perhaps the tools were considered to be a part of the man's personality; perhaps they were believed to bring bad luck upon anyone who used them after he was dead. The food might be a simple remnant of a funeral feast partaken of by the survivors. The ocher may have been a primitive cosmetic, and the smearing of the corpse a ceremony of no more significance than the attentions lavished upon the American dead by "morticians" in the twentieth century. The objects alone tell us little beyond the fact that such or such objects were in use. All the rest is inference.

► **chronological chart**

Ages of Prehistory

Type of Man	Cultural Epoch	Geological Epoch	Approximate Date (B.C.)
Pithecanthropus (Java man)	Lower Paleolithic (Food gathering)	Pleistocene Age	500,000
Sinanthropus (Peking man)	Lower Paleolithic (Food gathering)	Pleistocene Age	500,000
Neanderthal	Lower Paleolithic (Food gathering)	Pleistocene Age	150,000
Neanderthaloid (Rhodesian and Palestinian)	Lower Paleolithic (Food gathering)	Pleistocene Age	150,000
Cro-Magnon Grimaldi	Upper Paleolithic (Cave paintings ca. 20,000 B.C.)	(Würm glaciation)	50,000
	Mesolithic (Domestication of dog)	Holocene (recent age)	12,000
	Neolithic Revolution (Food growing—Middle East and Europe)	Holocene (recent age)	8000–5500
	Followed by: Copper Age		ca. 4500
	Bronze Age		ca. 3500
	Iron Age		ca. 1800

All the above dates are in dispute, and no consensus is to be found among scholars. Only the authentically different and widely distributed early men have been included, as in the text.

THE PROTOANTHROPI, OR FIRST MEN
(*ca.* 500,000 B.C.)

It is one of the hazards of the profession of paleontology (the study of fossils) that the description "erectus" should have been given prematurely to the first Java man discovered, on the basis of a skull and thighbone found in the same deposit and supposed to belong to the same creature. Later scientists with impressive and unusual unanimity have doubted that these fossils belonged together, since the thighbone seems too delicate ever to have been related to such a massive skull. Three more pithecanthropi have since been discovered in the same area, but, alas, not a thighbone. Scientists continue to believe that the pithecanthropi were indeed men; but the evidence on which the supposition was based has been dissipated, and his erect stature, like so much information on prehistoric men, is now based only upon an act of faith.

These four protoanthropi are dated on the best authority as about 500,000 B.C. Al-

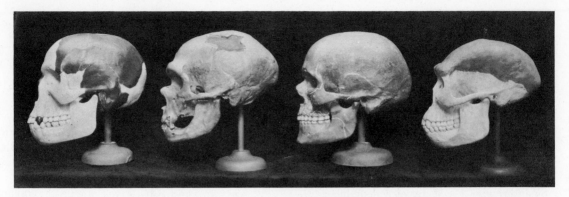

Skulls of prehistoric men; from left to right, "Piltdown," Neanderthal, Cro-Magnon, Pithecanthropus. Restoration by J. H. McGregor. Unfortunately, Dr. McGregor made these restorations before it was proved that Piltdown man was a fake. (COURTESY AMERICAN MUSEUM OF NATURAL HISTORY)

most contemporary is a considerable series of "men" found in hills and caves in China, near Peking (Sinanthropi, or Peking men). There are only superficial differences between the China and Java protoanthropi, and thighbones have fortunately been found for the Chinese variety. From these we know that these Peking men did stand erect, and there is further interesting, if not quite conclusive, evidence that they were cannibals. Peking man seems also to have possessed fire and primitive "chopping tools" of stone and bone. Both Java and Peking men had brain cavities about twice as large as those of gorillas, very thick skulls, enormous eyebrow ridges, and no chins.

After these two species of early men there is a long break. For a good many years it was believed that an English fossil known as "Piltdown man" was almost as ancient as Java and Peking men. His fate, however, was decided in 1953, when it was finally revealed through chemical analysis that he was simply a fake. The illustration of "Piltdown man" included in the text should be looked upon therefore as a melancholy example of the fallibility of experts in this highly speculative field of human inquiry. These reconstructed heads, so familiar to readers of textbooks, may be no more accurate resemblances to actual prehistoric men as they were known to their contemporaries than was "Piltdown man" himself.

▶ **Paleoanthropic man—Lower Paleolithic period—Neanderthal man (ca. 150,000 B.C.)**

The next recognizably different kind of man to be considered, therefore, is Neanderthal man. Neanderthal is a paleoanthropus. He is not yet styled *Homo* as distinct from *Anthropus* because it is not believed that modern *Homo sapiens* (or thinking man) derives directly from him. He became extinct some time in the comparatively recent past after a long career dating from perhaps as long ago as 450,000 B.C. to about 70,000 B.C. The first Neanderthal fossil was found in a cave of the Neander Gorge near Düsseldorf in Germany in 1856, and thus received his name. But in the past century many specimens of his type have been found throughout Europe, and similar types, with only superficial differences, have been unearthed as far away as Rhodesia in South Africa. Very important finds have also been made in Palestine, together with blade tools of a kind superior to anything known to have been used by other Neanderthal men. It would seem, therefore, that Neanderthal man inhabited this planet for a far longer total period than any other type, and over the hundreds of thousands of years during which he was the chief representative of the human species he may well have wandered over the whole earth.

Physically, Neanderthal man was the owner of a brain already of a size not greatly inferior to our own. But at the same time he had a curvature of the thighbone even more marked than that of his predecessors, the protoanthropi. He used chipped bone, he flaked flint tools, and he used fire. A kind of all-purpose tool, something between a pick and an ax, and no doubt serving the purpose of both, was in use (called by the French a *coup de poing*, from the fact that it resembles a human fist). Many of the Neanderthal finds have been in caves, where these men lived for at least part of the year. Some of the skeletons seem to have been laid away with care, in the bottom of the caves, with food and implements beside them, suggesting formal burial practices, if not a belief in immortality.

The period when Neanderthal man roamed the earth is generally called the Lower Paleolithic Age—lower because in fossil deposits the lower remains are earlier, and Paleolithic (Old Stone) because all implements were made of either bone or stone. The classification by implements has become conventional, but it is not satisfactory unless one wishes to speak only of the tools used. The development in tools from the Paleolithic to the Neolithic (New Stone) Age was far less important than the epoch-making change from food gathering to food producing which characterized these periods.

The whole of the Lower Paleolithic period is placed within the geological age known as the Pleistocene. During this time most authorities recognize four glaciations for Europe and America. The glaciers

Tools of prehistoric men, showing various phases of development, and revealing why some of these tools were called "coups de poing" [blows of fist]. (COURTESY AMERICAN MUSEUM OF NATURAL HISTORY)

stretched down as far south as France, making the climate bitterly cold within their range. When they receded, the climate was as warm as, or perhaps even warmer than, now. It is possible that even at the present time we are in an interglacial period, since it is only about 50,000 years since the last glaciers (Würm glaciation) began to recede, not a long time for an interglacial period. They had perhaps not receded to their present position until almost the end of the Upper Paleolithic Age.

▶ Upper Paleolithic period

HOMO SAPIENS—CRO-MAGNON AND GRIMALDI (*ca.* 50,000 B.C.)

We date the Upper Paleolithic period from about 50,000 B.C., with the beginning of *Homo sapiens,* or modern man (neoanthropi, as distinct from paleoanthropi and protoanthropi). There are many remains dating from this period which can be fairly accurately dated, and successive phases of Upper Paleolithic culture have been agreed upon. The people of this age in Europe, apparently of Caucasian stock, are called Cro-Magnon. Contemporary with them are Grimaldi men found in Southern Europe, which had physical characteristics similar to those of present-day Negroes. Further south in North Africa are other remains of people with Caucasian features, as have the inhabitants of these areas today. It is considered unlikely that a full Negro race was present in Southern Europe in Upper Paleolithic times and then disappeared without a trace. Since naturally no hair or skin has survived, it is impossible to say whether Grimaldi man was actually a Negro.

Cro-Magnon man lacked the protruding eyebrow ridge of his predecessors, and, curiously enough, he had a larger brain than present-day man's. The average height of the specimens examined is five feet ten inches. It is, of course, again possible that only the finest specimens have survived. But the physical examination of Cro-Magnon man conclusively proves that the advances made by Neolithic man were not due to the evolution of a physically superior people. Nor can we say anything about the functioning of the brain from the mere measurement of the skull capacity. He would indeed be a hardy male who would dare to put forward such a hypothesis today when it is known that the average female skull capacity in our time is some 10 per cent smaller than the male's!

Cro-Magnon's experiments in improved living, however, are impressive by any standard. In toolmaking he began to make a more sophisticated use of bone. There were bone knives, pins, needles, fishhooks, and harpoons as well as sharp bone heads for spears. He made beads of bone for ornament, and later also used horn and ivory. The needles suggest that he (or his wife) sewed and stitched garments. But above all he used paints, not only for covering dead bodies, which are often smeared with red ocher, but for the first real art.

THE CAVE PAINTINGS OF CRO-MAGNON MAN

Cave paintings have been discovered in southern France and northern Spain which were undoubtedly made by men in Upper Paleolithic times. The paintings, in which several colors were used, are mostly of animals, though there are a few also of human beings. Controversy has raged fiercely about these paintings ever since they were discovered, and indeed there are many problems connected with them.

Paintings were sometimes superimposed upon one another; they are often on the walls near the roof of the caves. They obviously were not made to be admired by human beings. How did the artists obtain enough light to be able to make their paintings in such dim, almost inaccessible corners? No primitive torch could give our own artists enough light to duplicate them, even if they could manage, as these early artists manifestly could, to do without living models. There are paintings which are so far from the ground that elaborate scaffolding must have been erected, as the floor does not seem to have sunk since Paleolithic times.

All Paleolithic men lived by hunting and

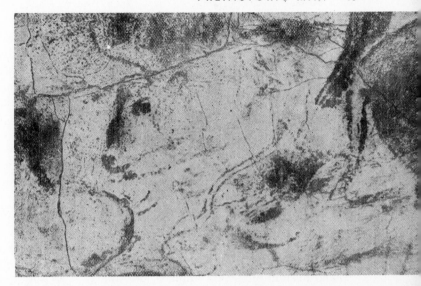

This photograph shows one of the cave paintings at Altamira, Spain, as it actually appears. Notice that the same portion of the wall is occupied by several animals, and that it is difficult to distinguish between them. The neat pictures of individual animals sometimes shown are copies made by modern artists who have separated the animals from their surroundings. At Altamira the pictures are made in color.

Charcoal drawings, not colored, from Cave of Las Monedas (also Spanish). The vast majority of the known examples of cave art are either drawn in charcoal or scratched with sharp stone implements.

food gathering. They were dependent for their subsistence on their manual skills and their observation. Living in caves or crude huts, they necessarily moved from place to place as hunting grounds became exhausted or as the climate changed. They lived in the same world as the animals, but had not yet learned to make use of them except for food.

THE DOMESTICATION OF THE DOG (MESOLITHIC AGE, *ca.* 12,000 B.C.)

The first great advance to be observed in the archaeological record is the domesti-

cation of the dog. This occurs in the period conventionally known as the Mesolithic (Middle Stone) Age, a period arbitrarily intervening between the Paleolithic and the Neolithic. Geologists speak of the Mesolithic Age as the beginning of the geologically recent or Holocene Age. The glaciers were receding, pine, birch, and willow were gradually creeping northward. The older tundra gradually became more thickly forested and the larger animals moved away or became extinct. Smaller game had to be hunted, requiring a greater expenditure of labor. Cave art died away, and it seems that tools became smaller. But the dog came to live with man, perhaps even then as an aid to hunting the smaller game. The bow and arrow also are first authenticated in the Mesolithic.

▶ The Neolithic Revolution

TRANSITION TO FOOD GROWING
(*ca.* 8000–5500 B.C.)

This age of comparative quiet shades over into the age when occurred what is certainly man's greatest advance to this day—the advance that has made all later civilization possible. The Neolithic Revolution, as it has been called, was characterized by the domestication of several animals, but above all by the first conscious breeding of plants.

When man lived by food gathering and hunting, he was dependent upon his environment. His sole influence upon this environment consisted in his depredations. He could not repair any damage he did to it; his only remedy was to move away. In this respect his life was like that of the animals. If it were not for his art we should be tempted to say that he was still only one of the animals, less specialized and able to make use of tools beyond their capacity, but not yet fully able to use his superior mind to take control of his environment. This now became possible with the conscious growing of plants. It was a social and intellectual revolution rather than a technical one. Man could have continued, as certain tribes still existing today have continued, to make his living only by food gathering. But he did not. For hundreds of thousands of years he had lived in the same old way, never settling down permanently, building no cities, producing no surplus for a leisured population. Now all these activities became possible.

It is not yet certain when and where the revolution began, nor is it known whether it sprang from a single center and was diffused through other areas. Obviously such a fruitful idea, once it had been thought out, was capable of application by all other peoples in a similar stage of development. Planting sites have been uncovered in many different parts of the world, but opinion is divided on which had priority. Even the dates of the sites uncovered are in dispute.

It is, however, fairly certain that the revolution first occurred in the Near East or possibly in Egypt, and it was many centuries before it spread to Europe.

The obvious possibilities in food growing must have been realized early. All the excavations of Neolithic sites have been of villages or hamlets, small communities presumably living in cooperation. We know nothing about the system of landholding, but certainly a more definite organization was necessary than there had been in the nomadic food-gathering times. In the periods of the year when the crops had been harvested or when they were in the ground, the family must nevertheless remain close to its fields. It could not leave for distant places, as in the past. Crops had to be stored and guarded, and the beasts had to be tended. So the result was that more permanent houses of wood and mud were built. Man finally came up above ground, where he has lived ever since—even though occasionally he has had to go below ground for protection, and may be forced to do so again.

One of the best-preserved sites is in Europe, considerably later than the Near Eastern developments, but still Neolithic, giving us a fair picture of Neolithic culture as it probably also existed elsewhere. More than a hundred sites have been examined of Swiss lake dwellers who built their houses on piles above water, lakes, and rivers, as well as occasionally in the same style above dry land. The refuse from these houses, dropped into the water and so preserved for future generations, is of the utmost interest. Many different species of plants, vegetables, and fruits were in use, and there were several different kinds of stone tools with wooden handles. These Neolithic peoples who had learned to spin, used cloth. But by this time the Bronze Age was already in full swing in the Near East, and the first large-scale settlements, the heralds of an urban civilization, had come into being, together with a host of superior inventions.

Lake dwellings of Neolithic man (Switzerland)—a model constructed by the American Museum of Natural History. Refuse thrown to the ground from these houses constitutes an important source of information about the lives of Neolithic men in Europe. (COURTESY AMERICAN MUSEUM OF NATURAL HISTORY)

POTTERY

During the Neolithic period pottery first came into wide use. Almost all known Neolithic communities used it. This was a real invention, probably spread by diffusion from the community that invented it. It had to be discovered that potter's clay can be made to hold its form indefinitely after it has been baked at a fairly high temperature (about 600°C.). The ancient potter molded the clay to whatever shape he (or, as is generally believed, she) desired, then fired it, making this shape permanent. But before good vases or utensils could be made, the raw material had to be carefully selected, purged of impurities, and, in some cases, supplemented with sand or a similar substance. All these processes were rather complicated, and no doubt took many centuries to perfect. In Neolithic times there is no evidence of the use of the potter's wheel which in later historic times must have revolutionized the ceramic industry, making possible large-scale production. Crude wheeled vehicles were known as early as 3500 B.C. in Mesopotamia, and it is at about this time that the first pieces of wheel-turned pottery are also known to have appeared. But whether the wheel was invented for use in ceramics or for transport is not yet known.

STONE MONUMENTS—MENHIRS, CROMLECHS, DOLMENS

One feature of the Late Neolithic Age in Europe has given rise to controversy at least since the twelfth century A.D., though

Aerial view of Stonehenge (England). Note how this view emphasizes the fact that these megaliths make up a temple. Beneath the stones at the outer edge of the circle are remains of burials. (COURTESY BRITISH INFORMATION SERVICES)

recent research with scientific techniques has given us new clues. Any visitor to Brittany, Wales, or Salisbury Plain in England is sure to have seen menhirs, large single pillars of stone, and the circles of such stones, which are called cromlechs. Stone slabs or blocks, with other slabs serving as a roof, making a kind of chamber of stones, are not uncommon; these are known as dolmens. The controversy has concerned the purpose of these monuments (which are collectively called megaliths, "large stones"), and most authorities agree that the stones are in some way connected with the very ancient and natural religion of sun worship.

Far the most impressive of all the Neolithic monuments is Stonehenge on Salisbury Plain in England. This is a circle of megaliths, and is clearly an ancient temple. Close to this temple are burial pits which probably antedate the stone circle itself. The bodies were cremated and the remains buried in these pits.

SIGNIFICANCE OF THE NEOLITHIC REVOLUTION

It will by this time be clear that the Neolithic Revolution was perhaps the most important event in the history of man since he first began to live on dry land. The next great revolution of comparable importance took place only in the nineteenth century, when man first began to use extensively the power of machinery rather than the labor of his own hands and back. From Neolithic times to the Industrial Revolution a condition of universal plenty was never possible, even if men had been able to achieve the social organization required. Every human being can do only a limited amount of work himself in a day. He can produce only a limited surplus which cannot keep any very large number of people fed and clothed who are not themselves engaged in actual production. The leisured classes in such circumstances must always be strictly limited in number. Improvement in transportation and organization can distribute very widely the surplus of the many producers. But this total surplus can never be very great. This inconvenient fact has conditioned all civilizations between the Neolithic and Industrial revolutions. A small class of leisured people, with their needs and even luxuries provided for, have been the leaders in civilization. In our own times, with the machine harnessed to provide almost unlimited power, plenty for all has at last, and for the first time, become theoretically possible.

Before the Neolithic Revolution man was condemned to live from hand to mouth. He had no means of preserving his food, which had to be killed and eaten as he needed it. He took whatever crops were provided for him by his environment. With the Neolithic Revolution it was possible for some favored people to be spared the manual labor of farming because each farmer could now produce a small surplus over and above his immediate needs. Moreover, it was possible even for the farmer himself to spend a part of his year without filling every hour of the day in manual labor. He could spend at least some of his time in thinking and in cultural activities not immediately connected with his bodily sustenance; and many producers could spare enough so that an occasional man need not work with his hands at all. All that was needed now was better organization of production, an improved social order, and the technological equipment and understanding for the production of a new range of materials and manufactures.

▶ The beginnings of metallurgy

THE BRONZE AGE (*ca.* 3500 B.C.)

The earliest development of towns and cities will be considered in the next chapter. With these, and the development of the first written records, we shall have passed out of prehistory into the light of history. But the period that, according to convention, follows the Neolithic Revolution still antedates the first known cities and is characterized by the development of the first use of metals.

Metalworking presupposes a higher degree of social organization than a wholly agricultural hamlet or small village. We shall probably never know either who first thought of the use of bronze, or how the invention was made. Bronze, of course, does not appear in nature. It is composed of copper and tin, which must both be smelted to produce bronze. Copper ore can be used in its natural state and can be roughly molded by beating and by other Stone Age methods. It can thereafter be used without treatment by heat. But copper is never found with tin in a natural state, and tin ore, in addition to being very rare, especially in the Near East where, as far as we know, it was first used, does not look as if it contained any metal at all. What kind of luck was necessary before the idea of bronze could be worked out is difficult to imagine. But the fact is undoubtedly there, awaiting explanation.

Copper tools were known before bronze, but not long before. Gold was known at the same time, but then, as now, it was primarily used for ornaments, and no doubt "placer-mined" out of river gravels. In some places, therefore, a Copper Age is recognized before the long-lived Bronze Age, which only slowly gave way to the Age of Iron.

THE IRON AGE (*ca.* 1800 B.C.)

It was at least 2,000 years after the Bronze Age that the Age of Iron began. By this time towns and cities and a considerable urban culture had existed for many hundreds of years. Iron in meteoric form had probably been occasionally molded and beaten into tools before this. Iron ornaments were known long before the first use of terrestrial iron, and their meteoric origin is to be recognized by the high component of nickel always found in this kind of iron. Although iron is so much more common than tin or copper, the process of making steel, the most usable form of the metal, is complex and was not discovered until wrought iron had been in use for many centuries. The processes of extracting tin and copper and bronze founding do not require the extremes of heat necessary for wrought iron nor the long-continued hammering by the blacksmith. There is no reason, as has been pointed out, why a bronze caster should ever discover the use of iron, as his methods would not uncover it. Iron ore would seem quite useless to a bronze worker. Hence when iron ore was finally smelted and beaten into wrought iron by the muscular activity of the smith, the invention was probably made quite independently of the bronze workers, and made by a people who used or invented the bellows without which the heat necessary for ironworking could not be produced. The Greeks later attributed the invention to a people called the Chalybes in the region now called Armenia, later incorporated into the Hittite Empire. The Hittite kings' monopoly of the product excited the cupidity and envy of their neighbors, and there are records of occasional gifts of iron made by them to friendly potentates.

Once iron had been invented, however, its progress was assured. It was readily available, and could be used not only by kings, heroes, and nobles, but by common men. It could be used on farms as well as in palaces. Derided as it no doubt was, it was destined to replace bronze for all but decorative purposes until this day.

▶ Suggestions for further reading

One of the best short accounts of the present state of our knowledge of prehistoric man will be found in R. J. Braidwood, *Prehistoric Man* (2nd ed.; Chicago: Natural History Museum, 1951), a book which its publishers hitherto have kept up to date. A good popular work on the achievements of archaeologists is C. W. Ceram, *Gods, Graves and Scholars* (New York: Alfred A. Knopf, Inc. 1951), which is generally reliable. But far fuller and extremely entertaining is Herbert Wendt, *In Search of Adam* (Boston: Houghton Mifflin Company, 1956), which manages to pack a very considerable amount of erudition on man's search for his ancestors into a manageable compass and make it so palatable that it was chosen as a selection by the Book of the Month Club. Two useful interpretations readily available are V. G. Childe, *Man Makes Himself* (New York: New American Library of World Literature, 1951), and V. G. Childe, *What Happened in History* (Harmondsworth, Middlesex: Penguin Books, 1946). *Man Makes Himself* was written as long ago as 1936 and is therefore seriously out of date in some respects. But it is still the most effective short treatment of the probable stages of development of prehistoric man and of his transition to a settled life. Almost all writers on the subject owe a considerable debt to Childe, even though some of his theories are no longer acceptable. *What Happened in History* is a supplement to the earlier book and should be read in conjunction with it. Sir Leonard Woolley's little book, *Digging Up the Past* (Harmondsworth, Middlesex: Penguin Books, 1931), is a useful introduction to the work archaeologists actually do, by one of the leading pioneers in the field.

There is one outstanding book on cave art, which is unfortunately very expensive and not readily available except in good libraries. But it is well worth making the effort to find it and examine not only the interesting text but the hundreds of fine photographs taken in the caves themselves. This is H. Breuil, *Four Hundred Centuries of Cave Art* (tr. M. E. Boyle; Montignac, France: Centre d'études et de documentation préhistoriques, 1952).

Any standard book on anthropology will contain much supplementary information on all phases of the activity of prehistoric man. Specially recommended is A. L. Kroeber, *Anthropology* (rev. ed.; New York: Harcourt, Brace & Co., Inc., 1948), especially pages 1–13, 43–58, 78–123, 622–678, 689–732.

II East of the Mediterranean— the Foundation of Civilization

A modern photograph of the pyramids at Gizeh at the time of the inundation of the Nile. From this picture it can be seen why the ancient Egyptians were likely to choose the period of the inundation for transporting the building materials required for the pyramids. (PHOTO BY FUZANI)

3

The Heritage of the
Ancient Near East

Egypt: The Old Kingdom, First Intermediate Period, the Middle Kingdom, Second Intermediate Period, the New Kingdom • Egypt's legacy to later civilizations • Mesopotamia: the Sumerians and their successors, the Assyrian Empire, the Chaldean Empire, the Persian Empire • The influence of Mesopotamia • The Hebrews: Reasons for studying, Kingdoms of Israel and Judah, religious achievement

---

▶ Egypt

THE OLD KINGDOM (*ca.* 3000–2200 B.C.)

It has already been indicated in the last chapter that the Neolithic Revolution first occurred in the ancient Near East, probably in northwestern Iran. The earliest Neolithic communities known to us are to be found in this region, and it is in Mesopotamia that we can first justly speak of civilization, with the beginnings of that kind of culture that can grow only in cities, where there is enough labor available for specialization and enough leisure for strictly cultural pursuits. We should therefore properly start this history of civilization by dealing with the urban culture of Mesopotamia and the city states that fostered it.

Yet in a chapter to be devoted mainly to the achievements of three peoples, the Egyptians, the peoples of Mesopotamia, and the Hebrews, the latter two have such a clear connection between them that it seems preferable to study Egypt first, in spite of the fact that cultural diffusion, as far as it can

be traced, is from Mesopotamia to Egypt rather than the other way round, and Mesopotamia rather than Egypt may more justly be looked upon as the "cradle of civilization."

Egypt was undoubtedly one of the great civilizations of the world, if only because it persisted so long. At least 2,500 years separate the First Dynasty of Egypt from its inglorious end at the hands of the conquering Persians in 525 B.C. During the whole of that period there was little outward change. The fundamental concepts which underlie the Egyptian outlook, as it is reflected in its institutions and way of life, persist throughout the period. It takes a close and discerning eye to detect those changes that were occurring under the surface, a change from a fundamental optimism to a resigned pessimism, from a concern with this life to an overwhelming concern with the hereafter, from the unquestioned supremacy of the Pharaoh as king-god to a rule by the Pharaoh as titular god by courtesy of an all-powerful priesthood.

► chronological chart

Egypt

Neolithic Age	*ca.* 6000–3000
Old Kingdom: Dynasties I–VI	*ca.* 3000–2200
Unification of Upper and Lower Egypt	*ca.* 3000
Great Pyramid of Khufu	*ca.* 2600
Pyramid Texts	2350–2175
First Intermediate Period: Dynasties VII–XI	*ca.* 2200–2000
Reconquest of north by Theban princes	2050–2000
Middle Kingdom: Dynasty XII	*ca.* 2000–1792
Coffin Texts	2150–1700
Second Intermediate Period: Hyksos Invasion—Dynasties XIII–XVII	*ca.* 1800–1550
Reconquest of Egypt by Theban princes	1580–1550
New Kingdom: Period of Empire—Dynasties XVIII–XX	1570–1090
Conquest of Syria and part of Mesopotamia	1468
Book of the Dead (present form)	*ca.* 1400 onward
Religious revolution of Akhenaton	*ca.* 1377–1360
Restoration by Tutankhamon	*ca.* 1360
Rameses II (captivity and exodus of Israelites?)	1301–1234
Battle of Kadesh and treaty with Hittites	1297
New Kingdom: Post-imperial period—Dynasties XXI–XXX	*ca.* 1090–525
Conquest by Assyria	*ca.* 670
Conquest by Persia	525
Conquest by Alexander the Great	332

Mesopotamia

Neolithic Age	*ca.* 6000–4500
Early Copper Age	*ca.* 4500–3000
Invention of writing	*ca.* 3500
Early Sumerian cities (Bronze Age)	3000–2400
Temple communities	
Semitic conquests of Mesopotamia	
Akkadians (Sargon)	2400–2200
Guti	2200–2000
Independence of Sumerian cities	2300
Amorites	2000–1750
Hammurabi Code	1800
Kassites	1750–910
Assyrian Empire	
Conquest of Babylon	910
Conquest of Samaria and deportation of Ten Tribes	721
Conquest of Egypt by Esar-Haddon	670

Fall of Nineveh to Medes, Chaldeans, and Scythians 612
Battle of Carchemish—End of Assyrian Empire and annihilation
of Assyrians 606

Chaldeans and New Babylonians
Conquest of Jerusalem by Nebuchadnezzar 586
Reign of Nabonidus 555–538
Fall of Babylon to Persians 538

Persian Empire
Zoroaster the Prophet *ca.* 600
Cyrus of Persia accepted as king by Medes 549
Conquest of Lydia by Cyrus 547
Conquest of Babylon 538
Conquest of Egypt (Cambyses) 525
Reorganization of Persia by Darius I 522–486
First Persian expedition to Greece (Darius) 490
Second Persian expedition to Greece (Xerxes) 480–479
Persian influence in Greece 410–338
Conquest of Persia by Alexander the Great 330

Hebrews

Wanderings of Hebrew patriarchs (?) 2000–1700
Family of Jacob migrates to Egypt (?) 1700
Exodus of Hebrews from Egypt (?) 1260
Period of Judges in Israel 1225–1020
Saul, king of Israel 1020–1004
David 1004–965
Solomon 965–926
Division of kingdom of Israel 926
Fall of Samaria to Assyrians 721
Fall of Jerusalem; Exile in Babylon 586
Return of Jews to Jerusalem 538
Building of the new temple 520–516
Conquest of Palestine by Alexander the Great (part of
Ptolemy I's domain) 332
Palestine conquered by Antiochus III of Syria 198
Revolt of Maccabees against Antiochus IV 167
Conquest by Romans under Pompey, ruled by family of
Herods, clients of Romans 63
Direct rule by Romans A.D. 6–41
Jewish revolt against Romans 66–70
Destruction of Jerusalem by Titus 70
Jerusalem rebuilt under name of Aelia Capitolina; Jews not
permitted to live in it; Judaea remains Roman province 135

Dates (except those for the last four entries) are before Christ.
Earlier dates are disputed; others may be a year out.

Chief authority used: G. E. Wright and F. V. Filson, eds., *Westminster Historical Atlas to the Bible* (Philadelphia: Westminster Press, 1945), and J. A. Wilson, *The Burden of Egypt* (Chicago: The University of Chicago Press, 1951), pp. vii–viii.

*Predynastic Egyptian jar, decorated with ga-
zelles and ostriches. Note the considerable skill
of the artist at this very early stage of Egyptian
history.* (COURTESY THE METROPOLITAN MUSEUM
OF ART)

These changes can only be briefly indicated in a single chapter devoted to the pre-
Greek world.

Ancient Egypt is worth studying for its
own sake, in part because of its strangeness,
its fundamental ideas so alien to ours, but
which nevertheless served to give it a stability our own dynamic Western civilization
has hitherto lacked. It is worth studying not
because it bequeathed so much to later civilizations but precisely because it did not. The
Hebrews derived their cultural heritage almost entirely from the Mesopotamian civilization. They answered questions propounded
by the Mesopotamian peoples in a manner
which has been found satisfactory by subsequent peoples and has been incorporated
even into our own Western tradition by way
of Christianity. The Hebrews always believed they had, in their own phrase, "spoiled
the Egyptians," but they had not. Egyptian
civilization continued to satisfy the Egyptian
people. It had a survival value unique in
history; and yet few achievements can be
attributed to it that were thought by later
peoples to be worth their while to imitate.
Why the paradox? Was it because Egyptian
conditions are peculiar to Egypt and thus its
inventions are not transferable elsewhere?

Why is the institution of the infallible king-
god, the key institution of Egypt, so different
from other Oriental despotisms?

Egypt has in ancient and modern times
been called the "gift of the Nile." The Nile
is a predictable river. It overflows regularly
every year, bringing with it not only the
life-giving water, but fertile silt which continually enriches the soil of Egypt. Some
years the flow is not as high as in others, but
always there is an inundation, which appeared to the Egyptians to be the work of
heavenly powers. Specifically these powers
were believed to reside in the Pharaoh. He
did not predict the rise of the Nile, he *caused*
it. This was by no means the limit of his
heavenly powers. He knew the hearts of men,
he had access to the wisdom of the spiritual
world, he knew—to use the Egyptian untranslatable term—*Ma'at*, the harmony of the
universe, which can be expressed on earth
not only as harmony but in everything that
is harmonious and in accordance with reality,
notably in truth and justice. Thus as early
as we know it the government of Egypt was
a divine monarchy, and the king during his
lifetime was a Horus, son of Osiris, while
from a different point of view he could also
be regarded as the son of Re, the sun-god.
After death he became an Osiris, powerful
also in the afterlife, to which he conducted
his servants who had been faithful to him on
earth, while his successor became a Horus
in his turn.

Possessed of authority, perception, and
knowledge of heavenly and earthly truth,
the king-god was far above man. He made
no code of laws; his word, based on his
perception, was law. His ministers knew how
to judge because he knew their hearts when
he chose them for their positions. The whole
land of Egypt belonged to him, though in
practice in the Old and Middle Kingdoms
he appears to have taken no material advantage for himself of such ownership. He
"made disclosures" rather than asked for
advice.

It does not seem that the people of
Egypt groaned under such despotism; indeed
there is something to be said for this kind of

The New Kingdom Pharaoh Thutmose III destroying his enemies. Note the gigantic size of the Pharaoh and the conventional puniness of his enemies.

rule as providing a framework for a certain kind of freedom. There is no doubt that men felt themselves free to rise as far as their talents would take them. When all are equally low in comparison with the monarch, amongst his servants there is a kind of equality of opportunity as well as equality of status. And from extant inscriptions written by servants of the monarch we can observe a certain pride of achievement, even though the success is correctly ascribed to the favor of the Pharaoh earned by their deeds on his behalf.

We have been accustomed to think of the building of the Pyramids during the Old Kingdom as the work of hundreds of thousands of slaves, since that is the tale given us by the much-read Herodotus, the Greek traveler, who made inquiries from the Egyptian priests more than two thousand years

later. Yet there is no contemporary evidence for slavery in the Old Kingdom. Slavery became extensive only in the later New Kingdom during the age of foreign conquests. Far more probable is the theory that the Pyramids, started during the lifetime of the Pharaoh and completed only after his death, were an act of faith, a labor devoted to ensuring the ascent of the Pharaoh to the heavenly world after his death (we know from the Pyramid texts that this was one of their functions), thus enabling him to continue his beneficent work for the Egyptian people even after he had joined his fellow gods in the heavens. The Pyramids of the Old Kingdom, built with jeweler's precision, with the four corners of the base oriented exactly toward the four points of the compass, were likewise a wonderful make-work for the thousands of skilled and unskilled

The stepped pyramid of Zoser at Sakkarah (IIIrd Dynasty). This shows the earliest form of a pyramid. (PHOTO BY LEKEGIAN)

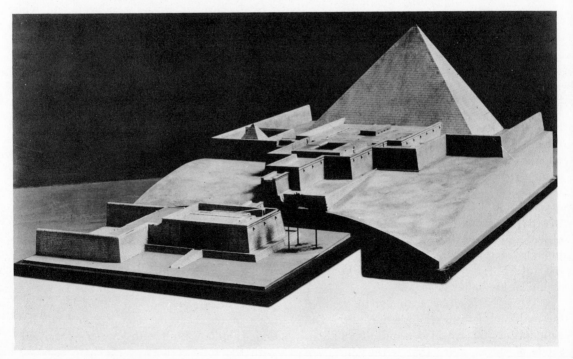

Model of the Great Pyramid complex, constructed by The Metropolitan Museum of Art. Note the impressive mortuary temples leading up to the pyramid itself. (COURTESY THE METROPOLITAN MUSEUM OF ART)

laborers who had little to do at a time when the annual flood was at its height, when the materials could be floated on barges right up to the base of the Pyramid.

In the Old Kingdom of Egypt it would seem that the people enjoyed themselves, that they expected the afterlife to be just like this one, secure in the knowledge that if they had served well in this life the Pharaoh would ensure their continued service in the hereafter. There seems to have been no special attention paid to ceremonial burial with support from spells and charms, so characteristic of the later period of Egypt and which we associate so particularly with the Egyptians. In short, since the Nile did indeed bless the people of Egypt and provide them with an easy living and reasonable prosperity for all at a time when there was no overpopulation, when there were no for-

eign invaders, and Egypt was a secure and self-sufficient community, it is not surprising that all Old Kingdom art breathes an air of confidence and self-satisfaction. And it is perhaps not so surprising also that all the great creative achievements of Egyptian civilization, the hieroglyphic writing and alphabet (rarely used but certainly known to the priests), the Pyramids, the characteristic art forms, and the divine monarchy were all the work of the Old Kingdom. And the belief in the eternal stability of the world, the fundamental changelessness of a static universe, likewise was formulated and accepted at this time; and not all the vicissitudes of later eras ever served altogether to dispel this belief.

FIRST INTERMEDIATE PERIOD (*ca.* 2200–2000 B.C.)

But change at last did come into this changeless land. A Pharaoh named Pepi II lived to an advanced age and apparently lost his grip on the government. Already before his death some of the nobles of Upper Egypt became virtually independent, while foreigners infiltrated into Lower Egypt from the sea and the desert. For almost two hundred years the divine monarch controlled only a small part of Egypt. The old capital of Memphis in Lower Egypt and the later capital of Thebes in Upper Egypt were alike lost to the titular Pharaoh, who now ruled only a small territory around Heracleopolis.

What is of interest to us in this period is the effect it had upon the people who experienced it. From documents of the period we learn that it was widely said that *Ma'at* (order and harmony) had disappeared from the world, everything was topsy-turvy and upside down. The land, said a priest, "spins around like a potter's wheel." There is no evidence that it was a planned revolution, although its effects were revolutionary in the deepest sense. Possibly the nobles, now independent, rejoiced, but as far as we can judge the people were shocked. When a divine government fails, what is to take its place?

During this time the nobles began to

MEDITERRANEAN SEA

Nile Delta

Memphis · Heliopolis

the Pyramids

LOWER EGYPT

Sinai Pen.

LIBYA

Akhetaton (Tel-el-Amarna)

Abydos

Karnak (Luxor) · Thebes

UPPER EGYPT

(1st cataract)

DESERT

RED SEA

Nile R.

REGION OF FERTILITY

NUBIA

ANCIENT EGYPT

⊙ Capital

100 50 0 100
Miles

appropriate to themselves texts that had previously been used only for the dead Pharaoh. They began to use the royal funerary customs for themselves, and soon we find what are called "coffin texts" rather than Pyramid texts. The Egyptians, who had scarcely believed that foreigners were human beings at all, now realized to their cost that these foreigners had to be dealt with as if they were. We possess a dialogue between one of the Pharaohs of this time and a minister, in which the minister presumes even to criticize his master for not having given sufficient attention to his land in spite of his heavenly knowledge. And the Pharaoh can only agree that he ought to have known and done better.

But at last the anarchy was over. A prince of Thebes in Upper Egypt reunified the country under his control and established Thebes as the capital. The writers breathed a sigh of relief. *Ma'at* had been restored to the land. And so the great Middle Kingdom began, under the leadership of the great Pharaoh Amenemhat I.

THE MIDDLE KINGDOM (2000–1792 B.C.)

The change to the people of Egypt may not have been noticeable. The Middle Kingdom under its one dynasty (the 12th) restored order. The intermediate period was forgotten and *Ma'at* prevailed again. Again there was peace and prosperity in the land. The Middle Kingdom is the period of much of the best craftsmanship of Egypt. It was certainly the period when social ideas advanced to the highest point that was ever known in the country. The effect of the troubles on the monarchy was a curious one. The Pharaoh was revered as a king-god as before. All the ceremonial and ritual of the divine monarchy was retained. But the Pharaoh himself, as it would appear, may well not have believed the myth any longer. How should he, after the failure of the monarch in the two previous centuries? We see from the texts a new concern for social justice, the Pharaoh regarding himself as a shepherd of the people rather than their unquestioned master. The royal sculpture, as has been pointed out, now depicts these monarchs as careworn individuals rather than majestic supermen.

In the Middle Kingdom also texts appear stressing that the afterlife with the blessed will be a reward for good deeds performed upon earth. But at the same time far more attention was already being paid to ceremonial funerary practices for as many of the people as could afford them. There is a great necropolis at Abydos where nobles and commoners are buried together. Clearly it was no longer believed, as in the Old Kingdom, that the Pharaoh had the power to take those of his servants with him into the afterworld who had served him well. The people evidently began to believe, as they so clearly believed in the New Kingdom, that they had to look out for their own personal immortality, and could no longer rely upon their divine monarch for this service.

SECOND INTERMEDIATE PERIOD AND THE NEW KINGDOM (1792–525 B.C.)

Rise of Egyptian Empire

This period of prosperity and peace was rudely broken by a new series of invasions by a people known to history as the Hyksos, whose origins are obscure. This conquest was a real conquest by foreigners, not by native Egyptians; and though the Hyksos rulers usurped the Egyptian throne and tried to behave in every way like their Egyptian predecessors, it is clear that they were never accepted as legitimate rulers, however well they in fact ruled the land. Over parts of Upper Egypt their rule was only nominal, however, and in due course it was again a prince of Upper Egypt, Ahmose I, who drove them out and reestablished the divine monarchy. The rest of the period of Egyptian independence is called the New Kingdom, though in fact many of the rulers in later centuries were also foreigners who usurped the throne.

The new rulers of Egypt, determined that never again should there be any such conquest as that of the Hyksos, finally decided on an expansion of their own. Under

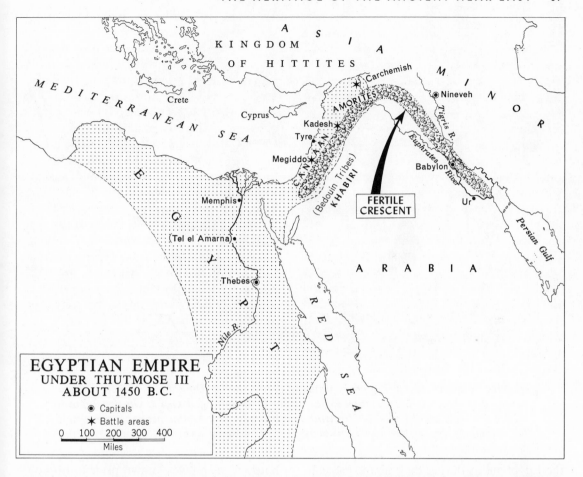

EGYPTIAN EMPIRE
UNDER THUTMOSE III
ABOUT 1450 B.C.
⊙ Capitals
✶ Battle areas
0   100   200   300   400
Miles

Thutmose III the Egyptians conquered Palestine and Mesopotamia as far as the Euphrates. The results for Egypt were far from an unmixed blessing. The Egyptians came into contact with foreigners, destroying forever their sense of isolation and self-sufficiency, and prisoners of war were brought into Egypt and put to work on the great monuments built by the victors. It was during the New Kingdom that the Israelites were enslaved and made to "build bricks without straw." As always when there are many slaves in a country the wages of free labor declined catastrophically, and there was a distinct cleavage between rich and poor that had been missing before.

The religious and political revolution of Akhenaton

It was not unnatural that this period should have seen the rise of the priesthood to increased power. Not only did the imperial war-god Amon-Re receive the patronage of the warrior Pharaohs, but the popular religion of Osiris which was concerned with individual resurrection in the hereafter became stronger than ever before. This popular religion maintained its hold to the very end of Egyptian independence, so that it was possible for Herodotus to describe the Egyptians as the "most religious of peoples." It may be surmised that the conditions of the present life on earth were such that a blessed afterlife seemed more than ever desirable and worth making sacrifices on earth to attain. The priesthood was not slow to respond. They were willing to mummify the bodies of all who could pay for the service, and they sold spells and charms to accompany the dead man on his journey into the afterworld. Especially in the late period of the empire, when all was not going so well with

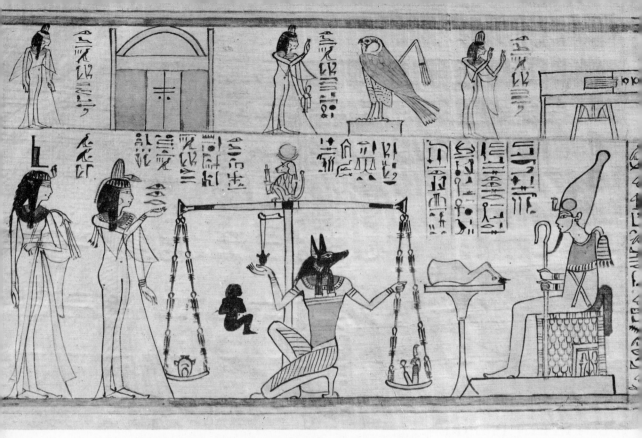

Funerary papyrus of an Egyptian princess of the XXIst Dynasty. The heart of the deceased is shown being weighed in the scales before the god Osiris. On the opposite side of the scale are the symbols for truth and life. The god Anubis performs the weighing ceremony. (COURTESY THE METROPOLITAN MUSEUM OF ART)

the Egyptians as during their first expansion, there is noticeable a great increase in superstition and fear of the dangers of the afterlife. No longer, as in the Old Kingdom and for a long time thereafter, was there a confident expectation of a continuance of the good life after death. On the contrary there was a fear of monsters, a fear of being made to walk upside down or doing forced labor, a fear that the soul would not properly separate from the body, and above all a fear that one would not know the right answers to the inquisitors; and a "declaration of innocence" had to be obtained which would pacify them. All these things would be supplied to the purchaser by the priests.

It is not surprising then that a religious reformer should have arisen, who tried to take away some of the power of both the imperial war-god Amon-Re and Osiris and their priesthoods. This was the Pharaoh Akhenaton (*ca.* 1377–1360 B.C.), or Amen-

hotep IV, as he was known prior to his apostasy. This imperial reformer was strong enough to change the imperial religion to the worship of the sun-disk, the Aton, and suppress the old religion of Amon-Re for at least his lifetime. He believed in the one god Aton, pictured always as the sun itself. Thus his religion, like the new art of his period, was naturalistic. The Pharaoh and his family are portrayed as human beings with ordinary human passions and pleasures, an extraordinary change from the traditional formalism of Egyptian art. The Pharaoh built himself a city which he named after his god, and there he took his courtiers and those who were willing to follow him, while the priesthood bided its time. Akhenaton seems also to have attempted to suppress or at least keep within bounds the growth of the popular Osirian religion, though here we have little evidence to show how far he was successful.

The Pharaoh Akhenaton worshiping. Note how he himself offers worship to the sun god Aton, whose rays enfold him, while his family, at a lower eminence, appear to be worshiping the Pharaoh rather than Aton. (COURTESY CAIRO MUSEUM)

Decline and fall of the New Kingdom

Unfortunately for his successors Akhenaton was so deeply absorbed in his political and religious reform that he neglected to secure his empire. There are extant a large number of letters written to him by his generals, demanding that he bestow on the empire some of his attention. But he paid no heed, and when he died peacefully at an early age, almost all classes in the empire were against the regime, and it seems probable that only the special sanctity of the throne prevented an armed revolt. The new Pharaoh, seeing the way the wind was blowing, quickly came to terms with the priesthood. The old religion was restored and the name of Akhenaton blotted from the Egyptian records. Soon afterward an army general succeeded to the throne.

Thereafter it was difficult for the monarchs to keep the empire intact. Rameses II, a great builder and, in his own opinion, a great warrior, exhausted the resources of Egypt in wars against the rising Hittites in the north (a war concluded by the first extant treaty in history), and in his building program. Soon thereafter the Egyptians were confined within their own borders. Several foreign monarchs occupied the Egyptian throne, there was a short-lived conquest of Egypt by the rulers of Assyria, and finally in 525 B.C. a conquest by the Persians. Two hundred years later it was again won by Alexander the Great, whose successors, the Ptolemies, were Macedonians, as was Cleopatra, the last of their line. Finally it fell to the Romans. As the Hebrew Ezekiel had prophesied, no more princes of the land of Egypt arose (until the twentieth century A.D.).

Copy of an original painting from the time of Akhenaton. Note the fresh naturalism of the bird and plants typical of this period. (COURTESY THE METROPOLITAN MUSEUM OF ART)

THE VALUES OF EGYPT—HER LEGACY TO LATER
CIVILIZATIONS

The Greeks considered Egypt the repository of all ancient wisdom, and they accorded to her a respect which was perhaps
undeserved. While we may now admire the
civilization of the Egyptians, it sometimes
makes us impatient that they made so little
progress, that the great achievements of the
Old Kingdom were not treated as the beginning of an ascending path, a fine start to be
built upon rather than a Golden Age of
glory to be looked back upon and forever
imitated. It was a civilization that looked
backward and decayed, as distinct from the
picture familiar to us of a Western civilization that looks forward and strives forward,
but is chaotic and unstable—which is even
now able to destroy itself and all its works
by the destructive use of a science perfected
through that very desire to progress which
is the essential feature of this civilization.
If we assume that it is an inborn characteristic of man to wish to advance, it is perhaps
as well to realize that it was not a characteristic of the ancient Egyptians. Toynbee,
in studying Egyptian civilization, was hard
put to it to discover his challenges and re-
sponses and succeeded in devising a pattern
satisfactory to him only by doing grave violence to the facts of Egyptian history, as has
already been pointed out by many historians.
The Marxian interpretation of history finds
little confirmation in Egypt. We are thus left
with a phenomenon which seems ultimately
to be explained only in terms of itself—that
the Egyptians, unlike ourselves, neither
wished to advance nor succeeded in doing so
after a brilliant start. Yet their civilization
endured for twenty-five centuries.

▶ Mesopotamia

THE SUMERIANS

Primitive democracy—The temple community

Mesopotamian civilization, on the other
hand, was far from stable. This instability
parallels, and may in part be explained by,

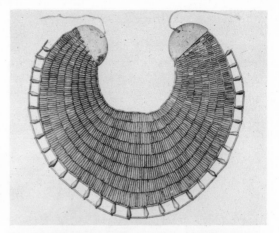

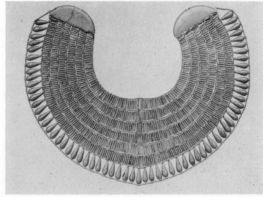

*Two collars of beads. The one at the top dates
from the XIth Dynasty, the one at the bottom
from the XVIIIth. More than seven hundred
years separate these two collars, yet the design
is the same, suggesting something of Egyptian
conservatism.* (COURTESY THE METROPOLITAN
MUSEUM OF ART)

the difference between the rivers of Mesopotamia and the Egyptian Nile. The Tigris
and the Euphrates did not overflow regularly, though it was possible to use them for
irrigation. The climate was far from equable.
Sometimes there were severe rainstorms and
hailstorms, which destroyed the crops; sometimes it was so hot as to be almost unbear-
able. The country, which was marked by
no obvious boundaries, lay wide open to
invasion from all sides, and history reveals
a constant flow of conquerors who ruled the
land between the two rivers. But, as in
Egypt, the basic components of the culture
and the vast majority of its inventions were

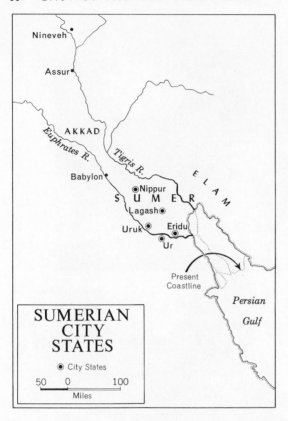

SUMERIAN
CITY
STATES

◉ City States

50   0   100

Miles

and its temple. When for purposes of defense or for other reasons a number of cities united, then a true king or *lugal* ruled over them, without disrupting the local administration that had preceded their advent. The ensi therefore may be considered best as the ruler of a city-state, while the lugal ruled either a league of city-states or one city-state dominating a number of smaller ones. Even in the largest of the Sumerian governmental entities and in all the regimes that succeeded them the ruler continued to exercise what was in theory a stewardship in relation to the gods. In theory it was always the gods who ruled in Mesopotamian countries, while the king was only their representative or steward on earth. The Mesopotamian ruler was never a god himself, as in Egypt, though there are some texts extant which suggest that certain kings did attribute to themselves divine qualities.

Scientific and literary achievements

The Sumerians are almost certainly the inventors of writing, although it was the Egyptian method of writing on papyrus with picture signs that was taken over by later peoples, rather than the more cumbersome method of cutting wedges into clay and baking the clay, used by the Sumerians and later peoples in Mesopotamia. The Sumerian cuneiform signs, however, did evolve from pictures in the same way as the Egyptian script, although quite early the Sumerian pictures became so stylized as to be unrecognizable as pictures. The Sumerians developed also the characteristic *ziggurat* form for their temples, and this was used by the later Babylonians, Assyrians, and Chaldeans. The most famous *ziggurat* is the temple of Marduk described by Herodotus in the Babylon of his day, famous for its Hanging Gardens. The Sumerians were skilled architects and knew all the basic architectural forms used by later peoples—the dome, the arch, and the vault. Building largely in brick, they displayed much ingenuity in learning to use this material in different ways to solve their architectural problems. Finally the Sumerians are noted for their mathematical system,

provided by the first people to settle in the land from without. These were the Sumerians, a people whose origins are still obscure, known to themselves simply as the "black-headed people."

When they first become known to history they lived in self-governing communities in the lower part of the valleys of the Tigris and Euphrates rivers. There is evidence that government of these states evolved from what may be called a primitive democracy, or rule by elders with the consent of the people, to temple communities where the city-god was the official owner and ruler of the city but governed through an official called a *sangu,* or steward, who managed the god's property and performed the functions both of priest and king. When the small temple communities, perhaps described best as large villages, coalesced into larger units, then this official became an *ensi,* presumably with several sangus under him and each responsible for his own smaller community

These two pictures show the mound of Tepe Gawra in Assyria at different stages of excavation. Tepe Gawra, in the words of Dr. Speiser, the director of the excavation project, "furnishes the longest continuous record of superimposed occupations known to science." The latest of the settlements was abandoned at least 3,500 years ago, and the great majority of the settlements date from the third and fourth millenniums B.C.; over half are demonstrably prehistoric. (COURTESY OF E. A. SPEISER)

no doubt developed because of their commercial needs, which was based on the number 60 rather than 10 (our own decimal system), but was a true positional system like ours and unlike the systems of the Greeks and Romans. The mathematical tradition thus begun by the Sumerians persisted throughout Mesopotamian history. Successors of the Sumerians divided the circle into six units of 60 degrees, and the great astronomical achievements of the later Chaldeans, which provided the raw material for Hellenistic science, were solidly based on the work done so early in history by the Sumerians.

The Sumerian city-states also developed the first written law known to us. The famous Hammurabi Code granted to the Babylo-

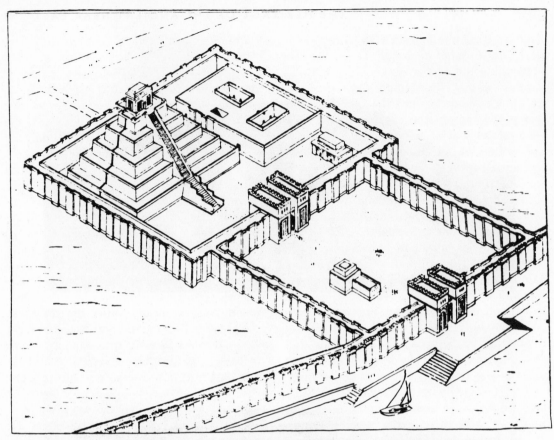

Model of the Ziggurat of Nippur, taken from a tentative reconstruction by Hilprecht and Fisher. All Ziggurats are to some degree hypothetical, and scholars and archaeologists disagree on the details since all that we possess, after all, are the collapsed ruins of the buildings, and artifacts whose position in the completed structure has to be conjectured.

Ruins of the Ziggurat of Assur from the south.

nians by the Amorite king Hammurabi at a much later date is drawn from various Sumerian codes known to us only in fragmentary form. These fragments, however, are quite enough to show that already long before Hammurabi the customs of the different states had been crystallized into law and appropriate penalties and means of enforcement had been devised.

The fundamental myths of the peoples of Mesopotamia also derive from the Sumerians. The creation story, known to us best in the Hammurabi version, dates from Sumerian times, although only a few fragments remain from the earlier period. In the Hammurabi version Marduk, the supreme Babylonian god, destroys Tiamat, the goddess of chaos, then creates the world and man, who is created solely for the purpose of working for the gods and thus setting the gods free from labor. The Flood story, to be found in the Epic of Gilgamesh and copied by the Hebrews with alterations, was likewise Sumerian. It may therefore be appropriate to deal here with the Sumerian attitude to life as evidenced in these stories and other extant Sumerian literature, rather than describe this attitude as it appears in the later Babylonian and Assyrian literature. The details may be changed amongst these later peoples, but the framework laid down by the early Sumerians persists, and there is no fundamental change before the conquest of Mesopotamia by Cyrus the Persian and its incorporation into the huge Persian Empire.

Attitude to life

Sumerians and their successors—If a generalization may be made of the Mesopotamian attitude to life it may be said that it was basically pessimistic, as distinct from the initial optimism of the Egyptians. The Creation story shows that man's purpose in the universe is solely to serve the gods, to set the gods free from the labor they had hitherto performed. Man has no rights against the gods, who may be as arbitrary and unjust as they wish. Man has no recourse against them and no rights. The gods

therefore expect men to do their will. Unfortunately, however, they had not troubled to inform men of just what was desired of them. It was the primary duty of the king, as we have seen, to act as the representative of the gods on earth, primarily of the city-god to whom the city owed especial allegiance. The king, therefore, had the responsibility of finding out what the gods required of their people. There is a very interesting cylinder seal extant on which are recorded the efforts of an *ensi* of Lagash, named Gudea, to discover just what kind of temple should be built to the city-god and his spouse. Gudea had first been informed of the god's wishes in a dream, but he made a considerable effort to check his interpretation by various means. When the state was too large for the king to be expected to carry out such a task himself, it became necessary to have a professional priesthood, whose chief task it was to examine whatever signs were available to determine the will of the gods and communicate it to the king, who himself would usually have to perform the particular tasks demanded. Thus grew up various practices of divination, such as examining the livers of freshly killed chickens kept for the purpose, watching the flight of birds, interpreting dreams, and, finally, observing the movements of the heavenly bodies, which had the great advantage that they could be predicted a long time in advance. This latter of course gave rise to astrology and ultimately, as a by-product, to true astronomy.

Even the great kings of Assyria, terrifying and powerful conquerors as they appeared to others, were nevertheless constrained to obey the orders of the gods. Their only recourse against the priesthood was to query their interpretations, which it was possible to some extent to do, since the various interpretations were written down in books which could be consulted as well by the king as by the priests. There are texts extant of state letters of the Assyrian monarchs to their priests in which it is asked whether the interpretation is correct that the king must undergo a ritual shaving or stay in a reed hut in the desert for a time. The king, in Mesopotamian thought, besides being their monarch was a kind of scapegoat for the people. Ritual atonement had first of all to be performed by him, and sometimes by him alone on behalf of the people. All such notions stemmed from the belief that the king was a representative of the gods on earth, his power was not absolute but limited by a necessary submission to the will of the gods, and both he and his people were expected to make their primary duty in life the carrying out of the gods' behests. All such ideas are to be found again in Hebrew thought, significantly changed but, in spite of the change, easily recognizable.

Relation between man and gods—The Epic of Gilgamesh, the first of the great poems of quest (cf. the Odyssey, Parzifal) throws more light on the Sumerian attitude toward the gods. Though many themes are intermingled in the poem, the central theme is the search for the plant of immortality by Gilgamesh the king of Uruk. Faced with the death of a beloved friend, Gilgamesh asks himself why do men die, and is there any way of attaining immortality without death? At last he finds the plant of immortality, only to have it stolen by a serpent, so that thereafter the serpent has immortality (sheds its skin), while man does not. There is no reason given, as there is no true reason why the god Enlil should have wished to destroy mankind in the Flood, a subsidiary story also to be found in the Epic of Gilgamesh. The same question of why man must die is asked by Gilgamesh in another poem which is authentically Sumerian, though only known in a fragment. Here Gilgamesh is told that the gods have given him valor and renown in the world, but this is to be his only solace. There is no immortality. Unlike the Egyptians who pictured the afterlife as similar to life on earth, the Mesopotamian afterlife is pictured as a dreary existence for shades. This conception of the afterlife is faithfully reflected in the Hebrew picture of Sheol.

All Mesopotamian thought accepts the idea that man is rewarded or punished on earth in accordance with his earthly deeds.

He does not, like the Egyptian, have to buy spells or charms. The king and all the people are expected to know what the gods desire and to perform what is required of them. The gods do not require deeds that are ethical, as the Hebrew prophets insisted; they do not ask, like Micah, for man "to do justly and to love mercy and to walk humbly with thy god." They have certain duties to perform, and it is the task of the king and priests to discover what those duties are. Appropriate sacrifices and rituals must be performed. If they are not performed the gods will punish, even though the people were never given any clear indication what, actually, was demanded. Thus, in essence, they are punished for their ignorance. The Hebrews likewise thought that God required the keeping of the Law, the performance of certain rituals, behavior according to certain recognized norms of conduct. The Hebrews likewise were punished if they did not obey the commands of God. But there was a great difference between the attitude of God and the attitude of the Mesopotamian gods. The latter kept men in ignorance, and treated as slaves those who were not expected to know the reasons for their punishment; whereas the Hebrew God was a loving father who instructed his children and tried to bring them up in the way they should go. Thus again we see how the Mesopotamian peoples raised the problem but did not solve it. Their assumption was that the gods made demands of man and expected obedience; they did not attain to the Hebrew thought that God laid down eternal laws of behavior and punished disobedience to them—still less that God asked ethical behavior from man over and beyond the prescribed dictates of the Law.

The Mesopotamian peoples also were bedeviled by the fact that there were so many gods, whose demands of man might be contradictory. There was no supreme god, although the god Marduk of Babylon sometimes in the texts approaches this position. There were not only the great gods, representing nature forces, but there were local gods for particular cities and even personal gods, possessed of little power but sometimes able to intercede on behalf of their worshipers. A late prayer points up the dilemma in no uncertain terms when the penitent asks that the fury of not only his own god and goddess be quieted toward him, but also the fury of all the gods whom he "knows or does not know," and for all the transgressions which he "knows or does not know." And the last Chaldean king of Babylon is shown to us as trying to make an image which will be a composite of all the gods in an apparent last desperate effort to achieve some kind of unity. This incident, of course, is referred to in the famous passage in the Book of Daniel where the three Hebrews alone in the city refuse to worship this image and are cast into the "burning fiery furnace." (Daniel: 3)

SUCCESSORS OF THE SUMERIANS

Amorite conquest

The Sumerian city-states submitted to their first conquest when a certain Sargon of Agade unified them from the north (ca.

2400 B.C.) and introduced them to the Semitic language of Akkadian which was ultimately to supersede the older Sumerian. After Sargon's death, however, the Sumerian cities regained their independence, though intermittently they had to submit to another northern tribe known as the Guti. However, about 2000 B.C. a more permanent conquest ensued, with the capture of the village of Babylon by the Amorites, a desert people. Babylon was elevated into the capital of the whole territory, and later Amorite rulers made what had been the land of Sumer into a considerable empire stretching far to the north of the territory of the old city-states. Thereafter it is more accurate to speak of the Babylonian Empire, by which term the whole of the Mesopotamian civilization is more commonly known.

Hammurabi Code

General characteristics—Hammurabi is the famous of the Amorite kings of Babylon. He derived his fame largely from the Code

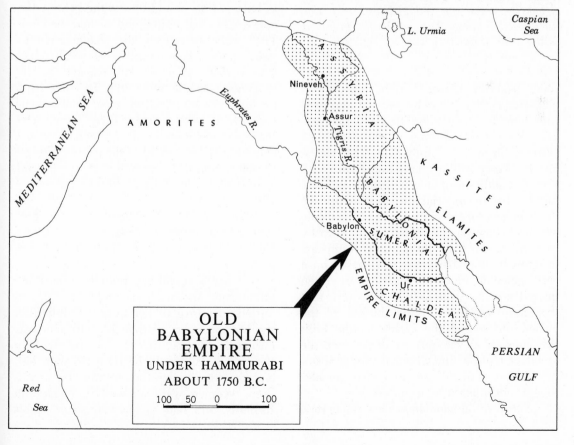

OLD
BABYLONIAN
EMPIRE
UNDER HAMMURABI
ABOUT 1750 B.C.
100   50   0   100

A stela showing Hammurabi receiving his code of laws from the sun god Shamash, who was also the god of justice. The code itself is inscribed on the stela. (COURTESY THE LOUVRE)

which bears his name, though, as has been suggested earlier, it was by no means original with him. It seems clear that the king regarded his Code as one of the means of unifying his motley empire. The Code therefore is a composite of many Sumerian codes with the addition of new material specially suitable for an imperial structure. No doubt this accounts for the unevenness of the Code, which in some parts is enlightened, even by modern standards, while in others it appears to us to be both barbarous and based on a very peculiar kind of logic. Most often quoted are the sections which require that if a house collapses killing the son of the owner, the son of the architect who built the house shall be put to death, not the architect himself, for whom it might in our day be considered an excessive penalty though not inherently an unjust one.

Nature of Babylonian justice—But certain features of Babylonian society do emerge clearly from the Code. Justice was unequal. The population was divided into three classes, nobles, free commoners, and serfs and slaves. Crimes against nobles were dealt with more severely than those against the lower classes; but nobles themselves were also in many cases dealt with more severely if it was they who committed the crime. Property seems to have been rated above human life—crimes against property being usually treated more severely. Even accidental homicide was regarded as a crime against the victim's family and compensated accordingly. Murder was not a crime against the state but against the person. Aliens were treated liberally, women held a relatively high position, and there were extensive regulations for industry and trade, as might be expected in a commercial civilization. Noteworthy is the fact that private tenure of land seems to have been the rule, unlike the system described for the Sumerian city-states. Peasants were sharecroppers or serfs as before; but, in addition to the priests, the government and nobles now owned the land. This probably reflects the changed conditions under a conquering house of invaders who would not necessarily respect the arrangements made by deities for their sustenance, even while they accepted the general divine order decreed by them. The sharecroppers were protected by law against eviction before the end of the contract year—as before under the regime of the gods—and against obligation to pay full rent if the crop failed.

Social provisions—There are many provisions governing marriage in the Code. Evidently it was a legal contract in Babylonia. Though the wife was the legal property of her husband and brought a marriage gift to him, she had some rights, being permitted to return to her father if ill-treated by her husband. Although marriage was ordinarily for life, divorce was permissible; the bridal gift would be returned with her, and she would keep the custody of the children. Women were allowed to engage in business, and had as many business rights as the men. However, if the husband fell into debt the wife could be sold as payment for it. There are severe penalties for adultery and other sexual offenses.

Significance and influence—If we knew more about the earlier law codes and, as said earlier, if we knew how it was administered, we could comment with more confidence upon the significance of this Code and how far it represented an advance upon earlier thinking. But the correspondence of Hammurabi shows at least that he took his duties very seriously. Quite trivial disputes he investigated himself, and there are several instances of his sending back cases for retrial, as well as handing down decisions himself. There can be little doubt that the parts of the Code which stem from Hammurabi and Babylon represent a codification of existing practices in the commercial civilization of Babylonia. It cannot, however, be described truly as the first secular legislation. It is significant that it was represented as having divine sanction and as being unalterable, and that it was enforced by the authority both of the ruler and the gods. Legislation that was truly secular, and subject to change by duly authorized legislators, did not arise until the time of the Romans. Even the Greeks entrusted their basic legislation to individuals, and those who proposed to modify these laws ran the risk of severe penalties if the proposals were turned down.

It is certain that both the Hammurabi Code and the whole Mesopotamian legal tradition had a marked influence upon the Hebrew law of a far later epoch, especially upon those parts of the Hebrew codes which seem to be the most ancient. Here no fewer than thirty-five provisions out of fifty are similar. Even the language in both has marked resemblances. The probable explanation is the influence the legal tradition had upon Canaanites and other peoples of Palestine rather than any direct borrowing by the Hebrews. The Hebrews would naturally adopt some of the customs of the Canaanites; and if, as seems probable, there were already Israelites in Palestine before the exodus

of the captives from Egypt, during the reunion of the two branches of the people after the exodus each would absorb customs and laws from the other.

THE ASSYRIAN EMPIRE (910–606 B.C.)

Not long after the reign of Hammurabi Babylonia again fell upon evil times, the city of Babylon falling to the barbarian Kassites who held it precariously until its conquest in 910 B.C. by the Assyrians, whose empire deserves more than a passing mention. The Assyrians had long been resident in northern Babylonia, and at times had been subjected to Babylonian rule. Toward the end of the first millennium B.C., however, a number of Assyrian rulers began to establish a military tradition, and to train their not very numerous people for war to the partial exclusion of their previous agricultural and pastoral pursuits. It was not long before the trained Assyrian army began to expand and conquer its neighbors. The Assyrian rulers adopted a policy of extreme frightfulness for which they have been known in all subsequent times, in part because their final defeat and extinction as a people invites the easy attention of the moralist. At the height of their power the Assyrians had conquered as far south as Egypt, forced Judah to pay tribute, and had deported the peoples of northern Israel, exchanging them for other peoples from their extensive empire (the "lost ten tribes of Israel").

Their conquests and methods, however, so aroused their neighbors, as well as the half subdued peoples in their empire, that a coalition was formed against them. This coalition they could defeat in battle but not without some unavoidable losses which they could not afford. In the end Nineveh, their capital, was captured (612 B.C.)—celebrated in the Bible by the book of the prophet Nahum—and the Assyrians were exterminated. Though the Babylonians survived, there has been no trace of any Assyrian people as a people since that time. In spite of their fate, however, the Assyrians undoubtedly did prepare the way for later, better organized, and more humane empires in the

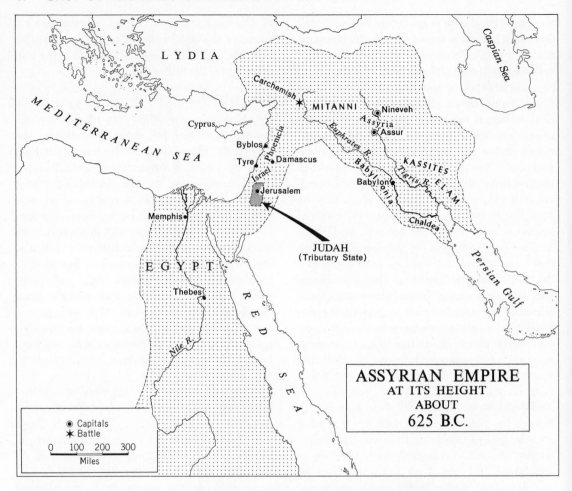

ASSYRIAN EMPIRE
AT ITS HEIGHT
ABOUT
625 B.C.

territory they had conquered. They did improve communications, if only to ensure the collection of the tribute they imposed on their victims; and, very important to us, they collected in the great library of Assurbanipal in Nineveh cuneiform documents from all over the Near East, which were left undisturbed for modern archaeologists, who discovered them in the middle of the nineteenth century, since no ancient people dared to lay sacrilegious hands upon the "cursed" site of Nineveh.

THE CHALDEAN EMPIRE (612–538 B.C.)

When the coalition succeeded in destroying Nineveh the lion's share of the reconquered territory fell to the Babylonians, who founded a new empire, usually called

the Chaldean Empire. Babylon was rebuilt, with a new temple of Marduk, as mentioned in an earlier section. Trade recovered and the whole empire attained to a prosperity that it had not known before. It was during this period that the leaders of Judah were carried away captive into Babylon, with such important results for the future of Judaism. The greatest intellectual achievement of the Chaldean Empire was the revival and development of mathematics and astronomy, although the latter science was strictly subordinated to astrology. Correct observations were made of the stars and their movements, however, and correct predictions could be made with the aid of mathematics. The attitude of the Chaldean people toward their gods and toward life in general does not seem to have undergone any significant change. There was a great deal of personal piety, and there were many questionings of the purposes of the gods and of what they expected of man. There are a number of penitential psalms, but no significantly new thought on any of these matters. A change in Babylonian religion had to wait until the Persian monarchs introduced the higher religion of Zoroastrianism, with its altogether different theology, its advanced ethical teachings, and its idea of a future life.

THE PERSIAN EMPIRE (549–330 B.C.)

Conquest and organization of Near East

Following the breakup of the Assyrian Empire the territory to the east of Babylonia fell into the hands of a people called the Medes, who expanded into the east and incorporated the Persians for a time into their empire. However, an enterprising and able Persian prince named Cyrus in 549 B.C. revolted from the Medes, and after a brief struggle was accepted by them as king. Then the unified Medes and Persians swept westward, conquering Babylonia and Asia Minor. Successors of Cyrus eventually added Egypt also to the empire. Thus arose the first of the great oriental empires to be compared in any way with the empire of Alexander or the Romans. This Persian Empire was thoroughly organized by Darius I, who also sent an expedition against Greece which was defeated at the battle of Marathon in 490 B.C. A subsequent larger expedition sent by his son Xerxes met the same fate, and thereafter the Persians were content for a time with a toehold in Thrace and then with interference in the internal affairs of Greece through the use of money and diplomacy.

Though rather ramshackle in its composition, the Persian Empire did bring the benefits of peace and some degree of civili-

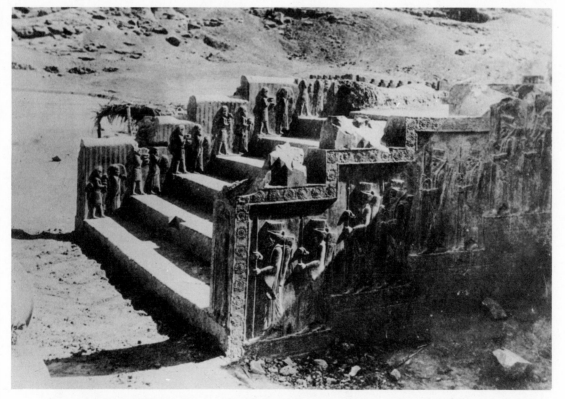

One of the rich finds of the University of Chicago expedition, near Persepolis, was this sculptured relief on a stairway. Persepolis, the Versailles of ancient Persia, was burned by Alexander the Great during a drunken debauch. (WIDE WORLD PHOTO)

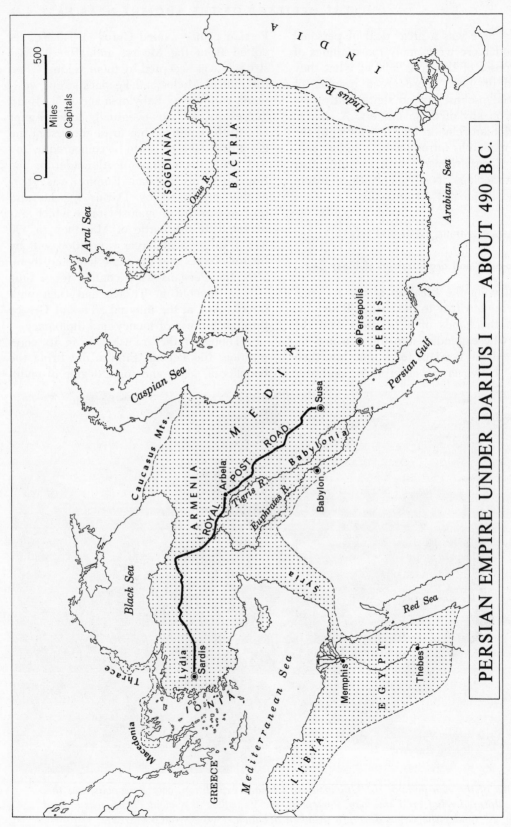

PERSIAN EMPIRE UNDER DARIUS I — ABOUT 490 B.C.

500

Miles
⊙ Capitals

Aral Sea

SOGDIANA

Oxus R.

BACTRIA

INDIA

Indus R.

Caspian Sea

Caucasus Mts.

Black Sea

ARMENIA

M E D I A

Arbela

ROYAL · POST · ROAD

Tigris R.

Euphrates R.

B a b y l o n i a

Babylon

Susa

Persepolis

P E R S I S

Persian Gulf

Arabian Sea

Lydia

Sardis

ROYAL

Syria

Red Sea

Thrace

Macedonia

GREECE

Mediterranean Sea

LIBYA

Memphis

E G Y P T

Thebes

46

zation to the peoples who composed it. The empire was organized into satrapies under satraps or governors responsible to the monarch. The satraps in later times exercised a considerable degree of independence, but they could always be deposed by the monarch when necessary. The Persians as a rule did not attempt to interfere with local customs, and even the Persian religion seems to have been accepted rather than imposed. The monarch had at his disposal a band of picked nobles called the Immortals, who constituted a force of shock troops. The huge motley army of Xerxes which invaded Greece in 480 B.C. was apparently something unusual for Persia, accounting for the many years spent in preparing the expedition. The difficulty of organizing such an army, with its component parts belonging to different races and speaking different languages, was also no doubt largely responsible for the weakness of the defense offered to the conquering Macedonian Alexander the Great in the late fourth century B.C.

Zoroastrianism

The religion brought by the Persians into their empire has little relation to what they found there. The prophet Zoroaster, its supposed founder, is a rather mysterious figure, and may have lived, if he lived at all, as late as the sixth or seventh century B.C. or many centuries earlier. In any case he should not be thought of as having inaugurated an altogether new religion. Perhaps he performed something of the work of Buddha in India, in that he clarified the ethics of the existing religion and to some degree systematized its theology. Zoroastrianism was deeply concerned, as the older religions were not, with the problem of good and evil, ethical good and evil, and not merely with the failure to observe prescribed ritual practices or to understand what the gods required of man and his integration within the order of the universe.

The world had been created by Ahura-Mazda, the god of light. But though he would ultimately triumph, he was not omnipotent, and was engaged in a constant struggle with the god of darkness, Aingra-Manu, or Ahriman, who was the embodiment of all wickedness, treachery, and deceit and possessed of almost equal powers. Each of these gods had his attendant host of spirits ceaselessly working for him. It was man's duty—within limits he had free choice—to aid the god of light in his struggle with the god of darkness and help to overcome him. The Persian kings all claimed their position by the grace of Ahura-Mazda and conceived it as their duty to support the rule of light upon earth, administer justice, and rule according to righteousness. The priests of Zarathustra, usually called the Magi, kept alive the sacred fire, the symbol of Ahura-Mazda in their temples.

Zoroastrianism contained a definite and clear belief in a future life. In the process of time the good powers would overcome the evil, and then a messiah would be born to prepare the end of the world. The last great day would then come when Ahriman would be finally vanquished, and the souls of the dead would be judged according to their deeds, the justified would at once enter Paradise, while the wicked would be cast into Hell with their master Ahriman. There they would serve him until they too would be redeemed in a far distant future. There can be little doubt that the Christian story of the Wise Men of the East who visited the infant Jesus in Bethlehem to worship him was intended to show that the priests of Zarathustra had recognized in him the Messiah whom they awaited.

The sins which lead to damnation are catalogued: pride, gluttony, sloth, and other of the Christians' "deadly sins," as are also the virtues: keeping contracts, obeying rulers, tilling the soil, showing mercy, giving alms, and not doing to others what one did not wish done to one's self. Early Zoroastrianism, unlike the later religions which developed from it and stressed the evil nature of the material world, did not approve of asceticism, self-inflicted suffering, and excessive fasting or grief.

Successors of Zoroastrianism—Mithraism, Manichaeism, medieval heresies

The elements of this new revealed religion which affected later Judaism and Christianity are obvious; and it may be said that many of its best features found their fruition elsewhere than in those religions which developed directly from it. In Mithraism, which in the Roman Empire presented such competition to Christianity during the first centuries of the Christian Era, there is far more stress laid on Mithras the Redeemer, as also upon the evil nature of the world, than in Zoroastrianism, with the resultant emphasis on the corrupt nature of mankind and the means of overcoming it in self-mortification. By the time of the rise of Manichaeism in the third century A. D. the world has been altogether corrupted by the god of darkness, with all its terrible consequences; and matter itself is conceived of as evil. From this teaching came the beliefs of the Cathari and Albigensians in medieval Europe. But these religions and their influence upon Christianity will be kept for a brief discussion in a later chapter.

CONCLUSION—THE INFLUENCE OF
MESOPOTAMIA

We have now traced the history of Mesopotamia until the coming of the Greeks. The greatest direct contribution of these peoples to Western civilization was probably their science, which became mingled with Greek science and so was passed on to the West after the conquests of Alexander. The art of writing was discovered by them, they did important work in mathematics, and they laid the foundations of astronomy. Indirectly their work was of the greatest importance for the Hebrews, since they gave them their basic law, and from them sprang the whole tradition of submission and obedience to the gods who ruled the universe. The Persians added an ethical emphasis which affected both later Hebrew thought and Christianity, with their conception of the Last Judgment and rewards and punishments in the next world, and new thoughts on the nature of

good and evil. The Assyrians provided a great object lesson on the dangers of undiluted imperialism which was appreciated and profited from by the Persians and Greeks who followed them.

In bulk the contribution of Mesopotamia does not begin to compare with the legacy to the West of the Greeks and Romans, though it probably surpasses the legacy of Egypt; but in the depth of its influence it is surpassed by few civilizations. Without the pioneer work of the Mesopotamian peoples in science and religion the lives of all later peoples would have been substantially different. And Mesopotamia itself did not cease to be a center of civilization, but again rose to power and influence under the Parthians, the Sassanid Persians, and the Muslim Abbasids. But by this time the independent civilizations of the West were growing up and the civilizations of the Near East had only a minor influence upon them. When Harun-al-Rashid of Bagdad and Charlemagne of Aachen exchanged courtesies in the eighth century A.D., each knew almost nothing of the other. The East and West had embarked on their independent journeys.

▶ The Hebrews—The kingdoms of Israel and Judah

REASONS FOR STUDYING HEBREW HISTORY

The third Near-Eastern civilization that merits detailed discussion, even in a brief one-chapter survey, is distinguished from the two already dealt with by the fact that its achievements lie entirely within the realm of religion and religious literature. The Hebrews produced no great art, no distinctive method of government; they had no material inventions whatever to their credit. Yet their influence on later peoples has far surpassed that of Egypt or the Mesopotamian civilization. Hebrew religious thought is still believed to be truth by a sizable percentage of twentieth-century men and women. Aside from Judaism itself, both Christianity and Islam have adopted a considerable portion of the Hebrew religious

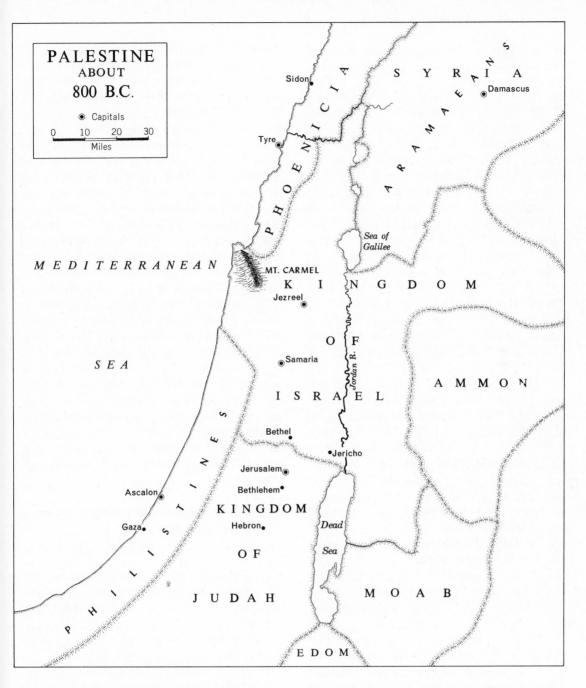

PALESTINE
ABOUT
800 B.C.

◉ Capitals

0   10   20   30
Miles

SYRIA

Sidon

Damascus

Tyre

PHOENICIA

ARAMAEANS

MEDITERRANEAN

Sea of
Galilee

MT. CARMEL

KINGDOM

Jezreel

SEA

OF

Samaria

AMMON

ISRAEL

Bethel

Jericho

Jerusalem

Ascalon

Bethlehem

KINGDOM

Gaza

PHILISTINES

Hebron

Dead

OF

Sea

JUDAH

MOAB

EDOM

insights as their own. In such a chapter as this the Hittites, who for many centuries possessed a great empire in Asia Minor and surrounding lands, may be dismissed, along with the Lydians, who succeeded them in western Asia Minor and are credited with the invention of coinage, and also the Phoenicians and Aramaeans, who performed a notable service as traders by sea and land respectively. The Hebrews, however, require

a more than perfunctory consideration, even though their history as such could be paralleled by many other minor peoples, and though their independence lasted for a paltry few centuries.

Hebrew history would not be worth considering at all if it were not for the fact that it is familiar to millions of Westerners through the medium of the Bible, and for the remarkable fact that the Hebrews were the first people who systematically recorded their history and strove to give it meaning. Events that merely happened were for the first time given an important significance by the priestly chroniclers of the Hebrews. They were significant because God was the ruler of history. If the Hebrews were defeated in battle by the Egyptians then it was because God had willed it, and the deed was a reply to an act of disobedience on the part of the Hebrews. If two men were swallowed up in an earthquake it was because they had sinned against the Lord. This effort to interpret what we might call natural events, or events to be explained wholly by natural causes, was unique at the time, though the method had a future; it was believed to be a proper method of historical interpretation until very recently, and still forms the basis for many philosophies of history even in our own century.

The facts of Hebrew history are still and probably will forever be in dispute. On the whole the Bible has been confirmed as good history by archaeological research more than it has been refuted. Nevertheless the fact remains that the historical method of the chroniclers leaves a great deal to be desired since it is so highly selective. Reigns of which we should like to have heard more have been passed over in a few words because there was nothing of especially religious significance to be recorded. The sojourn of a relatively small number of Hebrews in Egypt was religiously of supreme importance, and hence, from a purely historical point of view, is given a disproportionate amount of space.

However, history as such is not what we look for in the Bible. The interpretation is, to us, of supreme importance too. The historical background against which Hebrew religion developed is of importance, but it is not for us the crucial thing. So the history itself may be given in a few bald lines.

HISTORY OF HEBREW KINGDOMS

Hebrew civilization may be said to start with Abraham, according to the Biblical record. He it was who began the religion of

Yahweh in Palestine. His grandson Jacob led a number of Hebrews into Egypt at the time of a famine in Palestine. Outstaying their welcome, this band of Hebrews was enslaved by a later Pharaoh and made to work on his building program. In due course a leader arose among them named Moses, who was able to revive in the people a renewed belief in their ancestral God, Yahweh, and against the persistent opposition of the Pharaoh led them out into the wilderness, where they remained for forty years. During this period Moses gave them the Law of Yahweh, which, again after some opposition, he was able to make prevail as the Law of the whole people. Trained as warriors and held together by their religion and their Law, the people of Israel were led by Joshua into the land of Canaan (Palestine), which after a long time they finally succeeded in subduing against the opposition of the existing inhabitants. The kingdom was unified under the rulership of a warrior-king named David, who had been chosen and anointed as king by the prophet-priest Samuel (ca. 1000 B.C.). The unified kingdom of Israel and Judah survived for only one generation after David. David's son Solomon tried to live like an Oriental monarch on resources suitable for a minor kingdom, and he built the first temple at Jerusalem with the aid of the Phoenician monarch, with whom he had an alliance. The cost was heavy, for he had to permit Israelites to work at forced labor for King Hiram of Phoenicia. This resulted in a rebellion on his death, and thereafter the kingdom was split. The larger and agriculturally better favored northern kingdom of Israel (or Ephraim) was in a politically precarious position, surrounded by stronger nations. The only recourse for Israel was to enter into alliances with one or the other of them, necessitating the toleration or even acceptance of the gods of the foreign princess who sat on the throne. This brought down upon the kings of Israel the wrath of the priests and prophets who claimed that Yahweh was being neglected. It is significant that in the priestly account not one king of Israel did "that which was right in the sight of the Lord." The system of alliances finally collapsed with the rise of Assyria, which succeeded in defeating all the neighbors of Israel, and in 721 B.C. besieged and captured Samaria, the northern capital. Thereafter the people of the northern kingdom were scattered, and an alien people, not worshipers of Yahweh, were brought into the country by the Assyrians to take their place.

Judah meanwhile had to some degree maintained its worship of Yahweh, and the temple at Jerusalem in Judah remained the center of the Hebrew religion. Moreover the country was poor and did not excite the cupidity of its neighbors to the same degree as Israel. Thus it was permitted to survive by the Assyrians on condition of paying tribute, and not until the Chaldean Empire arose on the ruins of Assyria did Judah have to submit to the yoke of the foreigner. The last few kings of Judah were Babylonian puppets, but under constant pressure from the priests were unable to maintain an acceptable attitude toward their master in Babylon. As a result of constant rebellions the Babylonians finally decided to take the leaders of Judah as captives into Babylon. They destroyed the temple and put an end to Hebrew independence (586 B.C.). The exiles in Babylon, however, did not despair. They were held together by priests and prophets, and when the Persians at length put an end to Babylonian independence the Hebrews, or Jews as they may now be called, were allowed to return to Palestine and rebuild their temple. This condition of limited self-government under Persian auspices was rudely shattered when Alexander the Great conquered the Near East. One of his successors tried forcibly to Hellenize the Jews, causing a revolt of the orthodox led by the family of the Maccabees. The revolt succeeding, the Jews again had a period of independence until they were conquered by the Romans, who created the province of Judaea in 6 A.D. A later revolt in the seventh decade of the century led to the final destruction of the temple and the scattering of the people.

Until the twentieth century there was never again an independent state of Israel or Judah.

RELIGIOUS ACHIEVEMENT OF THE HEBREWS

Monotheism

The Hebrews are, of course, credited above all with the formulation of monotheism, the worship of one God; and this monotheism has been transmitted both to Christianity and to Islam, so that it is the fundamental religious belief of the West. But it is not always recognized that they are also responsible for the precise definition of the nature of sin; and their thought upon the question of sin and punishment has permeated Western thought as deeply as has the concept of monotheism itself. The evolution of Hebrew thought on these two subjects will therefore be treated in some detail in this chapter.

The Hebrews did not come all at once to their idea of a transcendent God ruling the universe. In the period of the desert wanderings we find them given the commandment that they are to have no other gods besides Yahweh, but there is as yet no suggestion that other gods do not exist. He is their special God, their protector and rock of defense, who will keep his promises to his chosen people; but as yet nothing more. It is only in relatively late times that the great prophets picture him as the God of the universe, with all peoples alike subjected to him, and the gods of other peoples as nothing but idols of wood and stone. They were perhaps driven to this conclusion through their belief that God used foreigners to punish his own people, and thus must control these foreigners also.

In early times also it is clear that the Hebrews believed in a rather primitive anthropomorphism, that Yahweh could walk the earth and talk to men, and that he needed an earthly habitation. By the time of the end of the kingdom of Judah the priests were emphasizing that God could neither be seen nor heard by human beings, but that he was a spirit, infinitely remote from man, though caring for him like a father, dwelling in heaven and not on earth. Ultimately both these concepts—the unity and the spiritual nature of God—were fully accepted by the Jews, and it was in this form that the Hebrew ideas about God were transmitted to posterity.

The supreme consequence of the Hebrew concept is in the field of morality. Because God is a person, he can take part in human affairs, guiding them, rewarding and punishing his children, thus upholding the moral order.

The Hebrew God, being one, not a force of nature but a transcendent being, separate from the world, could act as ruler and governor, first of his chosen people and then of the whole world. He could issue a law which instructed the people as to exactly what he expected of them, could define disobedience to the law as sin, and could take steps to see that he was obeyed. The law thus removed any doubt in the sinner's mind as to what he was expected to do, and what was forbidden him, and held out the hope that if he fulfilled these duties toward God he would be prosperous and happy. We shall see in the next section how the Hebrews were forced to modify this simple concept in the light of their actual experience.

Ethics and morality

Hebrew monotheism, then, with its consequent belief that God rewarded and punished men in accordance with their deeds, has been of incalculable importance in the religious and psychological history of mankind. Nevertheless, the traditional Hebrew concept of morality, enforced by God in his capacity as judge, even tempered by mercy shown by him as a loving father who "rebukes and chastens" his children, is ultimately a sterile one, negative because it does not (indeed, cannot) prescribe goodness, and because it does not touch the more difficult matter of human ethics, or the art of right action.

This aspect too did not escape the best Hebrew thinkers. Some of the prophets saw that the commands of the Law limited morality within a too rigid framework. When Micah spoke of the task of man as to "do justice, love mercy, and walk humbly with thy God," he extended the boundaries of those actions favored by God to cover less circumscribed activities. And Jeremiah had an inkling of the need for escape from the bondage of the Law when he made this promise in the name of the Lord: "Behold I will make a new covenant with the house of Israel . . . . I will put my law in their inward parts and in their hearts will I write it . . . . And they shall teach no more every man his neighbor and his brothers, saying, 'Know the Lord'; for they shall all know me from the least to the greatest of them."[1]

Divine activity in the world

The third great development in Hebrew thought concerns the total activity of God in the world. In early times the whole concept of God expressed in Hebrew writings was as protector of the Children of Israel, his chosen and peculiar people. But if he was all-powerful, then he did not have to fight with other nations; he would deliver them into the hands of Israel. What, then, did this deduction mean, from the point of view of other nations? Was he not their God also? Once this problem was posed, and it did not arise so long as Yahweh was only one God among many, the answer must follow. But it did arise when the logical consequences of his supreme power were considered. If his power were not supreme, then he had to fight on behalf of Israel against the gods of their enemies. If he was supreme, then he was their *enemies'* protector too; or else they were unfortunately left without a true God at all, which would be unjust. There was no way out of the dilemma; the other nations must somehow fit into the world order. It was all very well to denounce Assyria and Egypt, call their gods false gods, and prophesy destruction for them. But could any prophet with a

[1] Jeremiah 31:31–34.

sense of justice allow such a one-sided arrangement and say it was the work of a just God?

The answer might be, and was, given in terms of Israel's mission. God was using the foreign nations for purposes of his own, for the disciplining of Israel. He could have prevented the Assyrians from oppressing Israel, as he prevented them from taking Jerusalem in the time of Hezekiah; or he could use them to punish Israel's sin, as when the northern kingdom was deported. But to the more thoughtful among the prophets even this seemed rather a cavalier treatment of foreign nations. Were they not judged and punished for their sins; or did only Israel's sins count?

The question was no sooner posed in this manner than it must be answered in the only way possible. If Yahweh were indeed the God of the whole earth, then all the peoples were responsible to him equally, even if Israel had special tasks and special responsibilities as the only people of the earth to whom he had revealed himself and his Law. But the Assyrians were responsible when they broke the ordinary unrevealed natural law, and could be punished for it.

And so we have the Book of Jonah, which tells how the prophet was sent to Nineveh to urge the Assyrians to repent. It is nothing short of astounding how daring this thought was that a prophet from the despised nation of Israel should go up to the capital of the mightiest world empire at the height of its power and prophesy its destruction (if it did not repent). And the writer shows that Jonah was well aware of his temerity. For at first he did not dare to go, but took a ship going in the opposite direction. Then the Lord sent a storm upon the ship and did not calm it until the sailors had cast Jonah into the sea. Here he was swallowed by a whale, and not released from the belly of the whale until he had repented and promised to fulfill his mission. So at last he went up to Nineveh and preached. And, lo and behold, the Assyrians did repent, and the Lord spared them.

A medieval impression of Jonah praying to God for deliverance from the belly of the whale. Evidently the illustrator's knowledge of zoology left something to be desired! From a manuscript, Pseudo-Rudolf von Ems, Weltchronik, ca. 1400. (COURTESY THE PIERPONT MORGAN LIBRARY. Ms. 769, folio 223)

But the story does not end here. Jonah is angry because God has forgiven the Assyrians, thus making him a false prophet. So he sulks in the sun by the gate of the city. A gourd grows to protect him from the sun, and then, at God's command, the gourd withers, showing him by this sign that God has everything in his power, and that Jonah himself would not survive against God's will. And the book ends with the stern rebuke, "Should I not have compassion on Nineveh, that great city, in which are more than a hundred and twenty thousand people who know not their right hands from the left, and also many cattle?" Their ignorance saved them, for they had not been chosen and so had not known of God; when at last they were warned and heard, then God turned from his original purpose.

It should not be thought from this emphasis on the logical thought of the Hebrews that there was anything cold or abstract about their religion or their God. On the contrary, their whole thinking represented God as a person impossibly high above man, but recognizably akin to him, and with the feelings of man. It was thus possible not only to worship God but to love him, and God loved man in return. Man was in a real sense to the Hebrews the son of God, who must occasionally be corrected, but always with a fatherly hand. "Those I love I rebuke and chasten," says the writer of the Proverbs. But the emphasis was not always in the chastening. "I taught Ephraim to walk, I took him in my arms . . . with human bonds I drew him, with cords of love. How shall I give you up, Ephraim, how shall I let you go, Israel? My heart turns within me, all my tenderness is kindled. I will not perform my fierce anger. I will not turn about to destroy Ephraim. For I am God and not man."[2]

Sin and punishment

It has already been suggested that later Hebrew thought was disturbed by the discrepancy between the promises made by God to his people seen by the Hebrews as a special Covenant between God and his chosen people—and the experience of life on earth as they knew it. If they obeyed the Law they should have been rewarded, and if they ceased to obey it, then they should have been punished. But only rarely did this happen; and it was the apparent happiness of the ungodly, and the undoubted occasional suffering of the manifestly righteous that probably persuaded the later Hebrews to adopt the idea of a future life where justice would be vindicated.

It does not seem that the Covenant itself was ever seriously questioned. But later thinkers realized that it could not comprise the whole duty of man, nor could the simple theory of rewards and punishments on earth for keeping or breaking it suffice for them. More thought was needed on this central problem of the relationship between God and man, and much of the profoundest thought of mankind went into the effort to understand it—which thought, embodied in the Old Testament, became part of the imperishable heritage of Western man.

God had created man, not as a slave

of God, but in the image of God. He had made man only a little lower than the Elohim (one of the Hebrew words for God, but sometimes translated by the timorous who do not appreciate the grandeur of the Hebrew aspiration, as "angels"); he was God's special favorite among all living creatures, a child of God. And God was for man a Rock of Defense. If this were so, and God was all-just, all-righteous, and all-powerful, demanding equal righteousness from man, how could he sometimes seem not to care, and deliver man over to destructive forces of nature or to his earthly enemies? Was this the protection to which he was entitled by the Covenant?

The answer varied in different stages of Hebrew civilization, and according to whether the fate of the Hebrew people or the individual man was being considered. But both problems were thoroughly explored.

The most prevalent early view, the one expounded by the priestly writers when they considered the history of the people of Israel, was that in fact the people had not obeyed the Law and were rightly punished for disobedience. The individual kings were also punished for leading Israel into sin.

According to the priestly tradition, then, the sins of the people of Israel and Judah were responsible for the destruction of these independent kingdoms; but Judah, because it was the home of David, to whom God had made special promises, would not be destroyed forever, because of God's mercy and because of his oath to David. God therefore was able to act unilaterally on behalf of his people out of his mercy, though the people had not in fact deserved it. The people sinned and deserved punishment; God sometimes spared and sometimes condemned them.

The great prophets, deeper thinkers than the priests, and gradually moving away from the strict tradition of the Law as comprising the sum total of human duties, would not accept the traditional answer; and some of them came to the thought that the sufferings of the people were not the result of sin, but a preparation, a testing, for an even

[2] Hosea 11:3–8.

higher destiny. At the time of the fall of Jerusalem to Babylon, and during the exile, this thought alone seemed to fit the circumstances. It was not only because of God's mercy that the remnant was saved; it was because God had need of them. Not all of them, but those who had continued to worship him in spite of all their disasters. From the idea of suffering as the due recompense for sin, it became instead a discipline, a purification in the fire, so that those who survived were fitted for this great destiny. And so ultimately, fully in accord with this thought, followed the idea of a messiah who should redeem the world, sometimes conceived of as an earthly king who would inaugurate the rule of righteousness on earth, and sometimes as a suffering servant, "the man of sorrows and acquainted with grief," who would take upon himself the sorrows of the world. In both cases the mission of the whole Hebrew people had been to prepare themselves to be ready to receive the Messiah, forming an elect body of righteous men to leaven the great masses of wicked humanity in the new age.

It did not, however, need a prophet to give the answer to the other parallel problem, the sufferings of the individual. To the logical mind, if the man who keeps the Law suffers, there must be some reason. Conversely, if the man who fails to keep the Law is not punished, why not? Here there are more possibilities, and the Hebrews explored all but one—the possibility of a future life of rewards and punishments—very thoroughly. And this last possibility as soon as it was suggested was abandoned by all the thinkers included in the canonical books of the Old Testament. Moreover, even when it was accepted by some Jews, it did not attain the dignity of a revelation, and was still not accepted by the priestly party at the time of Christ.

We see a suggestion of the problem very early; and already in the Law there is a typically primitive answer. The sins of the fathers are visited upon the children, an answer scornfully rejected by the prophets Ezekiel and Jeremiah: "The fathers have eaten sour grapes, and the children's teeth are set on edge." It is posed frequently in the Psalms: "Why do the ungodly flourish like a green bay tree?" Look to the end of their life, suggests one answer. Their good fortune will change. But manifestly this is not always the case. The fullest answer is offered by the book of Job, which is entirely devoted to the problem. Job is presented as a righteous man, afflicted without any known reason. His friends carry on an extensive dialogue with him, trying to persuade him to admit that he has sinned, but in vain. Finally Job appeals to God himself to give him an answer, but the only answer he receives is that man cannot understand the ways of God. This, indeed, is the final answer of the ancient Hebrews. It is beyond the capacity of man to fathom the wisdom of God, and it is purposeless to question his judgments. He must, like the Psalmist, rely on faith in God's justice, and seek the only answer in the sanctuary of God.

The canonization of the Law

It should be emphasized that the bulk of Hebrew thought on the relationship between man and God was achieved by prophets and independent thinkers rather than by the priests. But in the last days of the kingdom of Judah a book of the Law was "found" in the temple and became the basis of a thoroughgoing religious reform carried out by King Josiah and the priests. This book is almost certainly the one called Deuteronomy, and from it we can see that as yet there has been no great change in the concept of sin and punishment held in earlier times, no emphasis on righteousness beyond the dictates of the Law. God will prosper the people if they keep his Law. "If you will but heed the commands that I am giving you today, to love the Lord your God, and serve him with all your mind and heart, he will give you rain for your land in due season . . . and he will produce grass in your fields for your cattle, and you will eat your fill."[3] This is the tone of the

[3] Deuteronomy 11:13–15.

whole book, as was indeed to be expected in a religious reform carried out by the aid of the priesthood. The emphasis was on the tribulations that had come upon the people because they had not kept the Law, and the material rewards that would be their lot if they returned to it.

A short time afterward the kingdom was conquered by the Chaldeans, and some of the leading Jews were taken captive and brought to Babylon. There, in spite of great prophets to lead them who laid little emphasis on the Law, they were held together as a people by the Law, and on their return to Palestine under Persian auspices it was the priests who supervised the return and rebuilt the temple. As can be clearly seen especially from the book called *Ecclesiasticus,* or the *Wisdom of Sirach,* the Law had become the cement binding together both the Hebrew religion and the Jewish nation. The Law in its now conclusive form was sufficient for all human purposes. The Torah or Pentateuch (the first five books of the Old Testament) was canonized as the revealed word of God. It was not earthly but divine; and it was unchangeable. It remained for Jesus Christ and his followers to return the emphasis to the *spirit* of the Law as suggested by Jeremiah, and allow scope for human ethics beyond it.

The influence and importance of the Hebrew religion

The importance of the whole Hebrew religion to the world is incalculable. Once the problems of man's relationship with God and the resultant ethics had been wrestled with and certain conclusions reached, the world would never be the same again. One may deny the original premises[4] and ask for the evidence for the existence of any God at all; one may say that the Hebrews projected their own highest aspirations into their imagination of a supreme ruler of the universe. But one cannot deny the aspirations nor that the conclusions, as far as they go, follow from the premises. Not only did Christianity, the predominant religion in the

[4] The author of Ecclesiastes, a canonical book, even puts this point of view forward himself!

West, base itself upon Hebrew thinking, but Islam also adopted the idea of the single transcendent God and much of Hebrew social thought. The teachings of the Old Testament became the standard of conduct and even provided some of the law for the Protestant reformers in the sixteenth century, especially for those who followed the teachings of Calvin. And the Jews themselves have preserved their heritage and their belief in the promised land even thirty centuries after the death of Moses, and over nineteen hundred years after they ceased to exist as a separate nation. But more important than all this may have been their belief that man is answerable to God for his deeds on earth, that there is a divine sanction over man's activity. Whether we forget this, or believe with Aristotle that man cannot be happy unless he is good and that no divine sanction is necessary, since man must seek for happiness, we cannot deny that the concept has profoundly influenced all subsequent civilization, and that few men in the West have not at some time in their lives been forced to consider the possibility of its truth.

▶ Suggestions for further reading

Since the history and achievements of three separate civilizations have been so greatly compressed in this chapter, and few students can feel satisfied that they have obtained an adequate knowledge of them, the reading suggestions will be fuller than elsewhere in this book. For his account and interpretation of all three civilizations the author is himself indebted to a marked degree to the work of the Oriental Institute in Chicago. The student is advised to consult on Egypt the original works published by the University of Chicago Press. The most complete is by the former director of the Institute, J. A. Wilson, *The Burden of Egypt* (Chicago: The University of Chicago Press, 1951). Egyptian kingship is studied in the first half of Henri Frankfort, *Kingship and the Gods* (Chicago: The University of Chicago Press, 1948). Egyptian religion is studied by the same author in a little book which offers many stimulating insights, Henri Frankfort, *Ancient Egyptian Religion* (New York: Columbia University Press, 1948). Various scholars of the Oriental Institute collaborated in a pioneer work, Henri Frankfort *et al., The Intellectual Adventure of Ancient Man* (Chicago: The University of Chicago Press, 1946), but the chapter on Egypt, written by J. A. Wilson, is greatly inferior to the same author's later complete book, *The Burden of Egypt.* However, the 1946 symposium is reprinted in convenient form in a Pelican book, Henri Frankfort *et al., Before Philosophy* (Harmondsworth, Middlesex: Penguin Books, 1951), and it should certainly be read if *The Burden of Egypt* is not available. The Mesopotamian chapters written by Thorkild Jacobsen in *The Intellectual Adventure of Ancient Man* present the evidence for the general pessimistic outlook of the various Mesopotamian peoples, while the position of the Mesopotamian kings is studied in greater detail in Henri Frankfort, *Kingship and the Gods.* The first-mentioned of these two books is reprinted, as far as the material on Mesopotamia is concerned, in *Before Philosophy.* Use has also been made of W. A. Irwin's essay on the Hebrews in *The Intellectual Adventure of Ancient Man,* which essay, however, was not reprinted in the Pelican *Before Philosophy.* This is a very provocative piece of work, in which the author looks again with fresh eyes upon the real contribution of the Hebrews to human thought.

EGYPT

There are no first-rate, up-to-date histories of ancient Egypt in English. In spite of certain deficiencies, the best are still J. H. Breasted, *A History of Egypt* (2nd ed.; New York: Charles Scribner's Sons, 1909), and A. Baikie, *A History of Egypt from the Earliest Times to the End of the XVIIIth Dynasty* (New York: The Macmillan Company, 1929). The first-named of these works was an outstanding pioneer effort in its day, but it has never been revised in the light of modern discoveries, although the older edition is still kept in print. Baikie's book was a painstaking work and made use of the best sources, but it was written by one who was not himself an expert in the field. A notable attempt to bring Breasted up to date for the period of the Egyptian Empire was Georg Steindorff and K. C. Steele, *When Egypt Ruled the East* (Chicago: The University of Chicago Press, 1942). This work is especially valuable for its first-rate illustrations, which really do illustrate the text and are not mere decorative appendages.

The pyramids are carefully considered in another Pelican book, I. E. S. Edwards, *The Pyramids of Egypt* (Harmondsworth, Middlesex: Penguin Books, 1947). Here the author gives most of the known facts about the pyramids, explaining how they must have been built, while indicating the numerous problems still to be solved. The Pyramid Texts are translated in a recently published work, S. A. B. Mercer, *The Pyramid Texts in Translation and Commentary* (New York: Longmans, Green & Co., Inc., 1952), Vol. 1, but on the whole these difficult texts are not recommended for beginning students. A useful account of Egyptian life is to be found in A. Moret, *The Nile and Egyptian Civilization* (New York: Alfred A. Knopf, Inc., 1927). A vivid account of the recent finding of a IIIrd Dynasty pyramid, by the directing archaeologist M. Zakaria Goneim (*The Lost Pyramid,* New York: Rinehart & Company, Inc., 1956), will bring home very clearly to the reader both the kind of work involved in these necessarily slow and careful excavations and the drama, suspense, occasional elation, and frequent disappointment that accompany it.

By far the best collection of easily available source material in translation is J. B. Pritchard, ed., *Ancient Near Eastern Texts Relating to the Old Testament* (Princeton, N.J.: Princeton University Press, 1950). Though the size of the collection is limited by the requirements of the subject matter, the editor has interpreted his mandate generously, and most of the best-known and interesting Egyptian documents are included, in spite of a rather remote connection with the Old Testament.

MESOPOTAMIA

There are, likewise, no really satisfactory histories of Mesopotamia in ancient times. Perhaps the best for a beginning student, and sufficient to give him a general orientation in the subject, is G. S. Goodspeed, *A History of the Babylonians and Assyrians* (New York: Charles Scribner's Sons, 1921). Better histories of Assyria and Persia are, however, available. The standard work on Assyrian history is A. T. Olmstead, *History of Assyria* (New York: Charles Scribner's Sons, 1923), which may appear to some to be too favorable to imperialism, though the author defends his thesis by claiming that other empires have been just as bloody if more hypocritical. The book is very well written, and the author's enthusiasm for his subject is visible on every page. A suitable antidote may be found for his point of view in the brilliant attack of Arnold J.

Toynbee on Assyrian imperialism in *A Study of History* (London: Oxford University Press, 1935), IV, 468–488. Here Toynbee offers the thesis that Assyrian specialization in militarism brought about the utter destruction of the state, and cites its downfall as a horrible example of suicidal warfare unredeemed by any success in the creative arts of civilization. Albert Olmstead's posthumously published *History of the Persian Empire* (Chicago: The University of Chicago Press, 1948) takes into account modern archaeological investigations, and is as brilliantly written as his *History of Assyria*. But it has several important defects, which would probably have been remedied if he had lived to revise it himself. Especially is he not sufficiently critical of his sources in dealing with Zoroastrianism. Curiously enough, a high priest of modern Parseeism has written a much more convincing and critical account of Zoroastrianism, which is probably the best work on the subject up to the present time, M. N. Dhalla, *History of Zoroastrianism* (New York: Oxford University Press, 1938). The most readable and analytical account of the organization of the Persian Empire is Clément Huart, *Ancient Persian and Iranian Civilization* (New York: Alfred A. Knopf, Inc., 1927), though modern archaeological investigation will probably need to add important details to this work, and change it in some particulars.

On the early civilization in Mesopotamia a useful short work is Henri Frankfort, *The Birth of Civilization in the Near East* (Bloomington, Ind.: Indiana University Press, 1951), while a standard pioneer work, many times reprinted, is Charles Leonard Woolley, *The Sumerians* (Oxford: The Clarendon Press, 1929), though it is to some degree marred by certain overhasty conclusions. The Hammurabi Code, together with much other important material, is printed in J. B. Pritchard, ed., *Ancient Near Eastern Texts Relating to the Old Testament*, with numerous valuable footnotes giving the comparable passages in the Old Testament lawbooks. The best commentary on the Code is S. R. Driver, *The Babylonian Laws* (New York: Oxford University Press, 1952), Vol. I, but much of this book will be found too difficult by the beginning student. Many of the original documents showing the relationship between the Assyrian kings and their priests are printed in R. H. Pfeiffer, *State Letters of Assyria* (New Haven, Conn.: American Oriental Society, 1935). An up-to-date account of the daily life in Mesopotamia,

excellently illustrated, based on the latest archaeological investigations, is contained in G. Contenau, *Everyday Life in Babylon and Assyria* (tr. K. R. and A. R. Maxwell-Hyslop; New York: St. Martin's Press, 1954).

Books on the various special achievements of the Mesopotamian peoples which may prove useful are I. J. Gelb, *A Study of Writing* (Chicago: The University of Chicago Press, 1952); Howard Eves, *An Introduction to the History of Mathematics* (New York: Rinehart & Co., Inc., 1953); and Otto Neugebauer, *The Exact Sciences in Antiquity* (Princeton, N.J.: Princeton University Press, 1952). The last-named book contains an entire re-evaluation of the contribution of the Babylonians to science, which is difficult and technical, but very well worth while for any student interested in the origins of science who has the required technical ability to understand it.

HEBREWS

On the Hebrews there is an enormous amount of material available, and the main difficulty is to select what is most valuable for the beginning student. The Pelican book by W. F. Albright, *The Archaeology of Palestine* (Harmondsworth, Middlesex: Penguin Books, 1949), is an excellent survey of the various peoples who inhabited Palestine from the earliest times, written entirely from the point of view of an archaeologist, leaving the reader, for the most part, to reconcile this material with the Old Testament records. The best general history of the Hebrews, a carefully planned, judicious, readable study, which takes full account of the history of the other peoples with whom the Hebrews were in contact, and uses all the material available at the time of writing, is T. H. Robinson and W. O. E. Oesterly, *A History of Israel* (2 vols.; Oxford: The Clarendon Press, 1932). Shorter, but more up to date, is a masterly survey, including the findings of the latest scholarship, Cyrus H. Gordon, *Introduction to Old Testament Times* (Ventnor, N.J.: Ventnor Publishers, Inc., 1956).

Two well-organized books by Adolphe Lods gives a very thoughtful, interesting account of the religious, intellectual, and social history of the Hebrews, using primarily, but not exclusively, the Old Testament records: *Israel from Its Beginnings to the Middle of the Eighth Century* (tr. S. H. Hooke; New York: Alfred A. Knopf, Inc., 1932) and *The Prophets and the Rise of Judaism* (tr. S. H. H. Hooke; New York: E. P. Dutton & Co., 1937). A brief (117 pages) but stimulating interpretation of the work of the Hebrew prophets from a social point of view is W. C. Graham, *The Prophets and Israel's Culture* (Chicago: The University of Chicago Press, 1934).

The pioneer work on the Old Testament documents which was constantly reprinted until most of it had been generally incorporated into other men's work, but still worth reading, is S. R. Driver, *Introduction to the Literature of the Old Testament* (9th ed., rev.; New York: Charles Scribner's Sons, 1914). On the distinctive contribution to human thought made by the Hebrews, in addition to the chapter by Irwin mentioned above, from another point of view, the English historian Butterfield examines the Hebrew attitude toward history and traces the influence of Hebrew ideas on the meaning of history in several superb chapters in H. Butterfield, *Christianity and History* (New York: Charles Scribner's Sons, 1950). A good survey of the influence of Hebrew thought is to be found in W. G. De Burgh, *The Legacy of the Ancient World* (Harmondsworth, Middlesex: Penguin Books, 1953), I, 50–95.

Finally, of course, as much of the Old Testament should be read as possible, including the Apocrypha, but preferably in some modern translation such as J. M. P. Smith and E. J. Goodspeed, eds., *The Complete Bible: An American Translation* (Chicago: The University of Chicago Press, 1939). In the author's view, it is a great mistake for the student anxious to ascertain and understand the meaning of the Bible, to read it in the early seventeenth-century translation known as the King James version, in spite of the extreme beauty of the archaic diction. The familiar words, no longer in current usage, serve to obscure the true meaning, and prevent too often the serious attempt to understand the subject matter. Moreover, in most editions of the King James version the insistence on the use of verses printed separately in a quite arbitrary manner, rather than paragraphs designed according to the required sense, is an additional hindrance.

III Classical Civilization of the West

This photograph of the Parthenon as it appears today suggests the commanding position of this unique temple on the Acropolis at Athens. (COURTESY ROYAL GREEK EMBASSY)

4

The Heritage of Greek Civilization

Aegean civilization • The Homeric Age • Age of colonization • The polis, political and social unit • Athens and Sparta • Intercity relations: Persian Wars, Athenian imperialism, Peloponnesian War • The searching mind of the Greek • Art, architecture, sculpture • The expansion of Greece: Philip of Macedon, Alexander the Great • The Hellenistic Age: Thought, science, art • Greek influence on Rome

---

▶ ## The Aegean civilization

One important civilization, contemporary with ancient Egypt and Mesopotamia, has not hitherto been mentioned. As early as 3000 B.C. a maritime civilization had been founded on the island of Crete. As we have seen, the Egyptians tended to be self-sufficient, and did not care to venture beyond the borders of their country in early times. This left open possibilities for any enterprising people who wished to do so to bring foreign products to Egypt and in turn trade Egyptian exports. For almost two millenniums the Cretans provided this service for the Egyptians, and in the process colonized many islands of the Aegean Sea and a few important centers on the mainland. Almost all our knowledge of this Aegean civilization comes from archaeology. Only within the last few years has the riddle of the Cretan language yielded to investigation. Even now the Cretan script of earlier times has not

been fully deciphered, though, now that the key has been found by deciphering a later mainland version of the script, it seems certain that in due course it will be deciphered.

Even the history of the island civilization is not yet fully agreed upon. It seems probable that the Cretans first brought some of the benefits of civilization to the native peoples of Greece. Then, somewhere in the second millennium B.C. much of Greece was conquered by a people called the Achaeans who presumably moved into Greece from the north, perhaps from central Europe. These Achaeans learned from the Cretans. They also gave better attention to their military forces, centered in particular around the city of Mycenae, of which Agamemnon was king in the time of the Trojan War. Somewhere around 1400 B.C. the Achaeans attacked Crete and conquered it, perhaps because the Cretans had allowed themselves to become unwarlike in the course of their always successful trading. Thereafter they

► chronological chart

Aegean Civilization
    Early Bronze Age in Crete   before   B.C. 3000
    Minoan civilizations in Crete   3000–1400
    Mycenaean civilization on mainland   before   1600

Period of invasions
    Conquest of Crete by Achaeans (?)   ca. 1400
    Early period, Achaeans, Ionians, Aeolians, etc.   1300–1100
    Conquest of Crete by Dorians   ca. 1200
    Fall of Troy to Achaeans and others   ca. 1184
    Dorian invasions   1200–1000
    Settlements in Asia Minor (Aeolians, Ionians, Dorians)   1000–900

Homeric Age in Greece
    Homeric poems   ca. 850
    Hesiod   ca. 700

Expansion of Greece   800–600
    Colonization of Sicily and southern Italy   760–700
    Black Sea (Euxine) settlements   756–747
    Byzantium colonized by Megara   660
    Great age of Miletus   750–550

Sparta
    First Messenian War (first enslavement of Messenians)   736–716
    Second Messenian War   650–630
    "Lycurgan" reforms   610?
    Peloponnesian League   560

Athens
    Rule of Areopagus and archons (abolition of kingship)   ca. 683
    Draconian Code   621
    Solonian reforms   594
    Regime of Pisistratus   561–527
    Constitution of Cleisthenes   508
    Ascendancy of Pericles   457–429

Intercity relations
    First Persian invasion—Battle of Marathon   490
    Second Persian invasion—Salamis and Plataea   480–479
    Organization of Confederation of Delos   477
    Persians defeated at Eurymedon   467
    Treasury of the Confederation removed to Athens   454
    Peloponnesian War   431–404
    Knights of Aristophanes—Ascendancy of Cleon   425

Intercity relations (*continued*)

Athenian expedition to Syracuse	B.C.	415–413
Battle of Aegospotami—Defeat of Athenians		404
Regime of Thirty and Ten "tyrants"		404–403
Restoration of the democracy		403
Trial and execution of Socrates		399
Spartan hegemony of Greece		404–371
Battle of Leuctra—Defeat of Spartans by Thebans		371
Freedom of Spartan helots and organization of Arcadian League		370
Hegemony of Thebes		371–362

Hellenistic Age

Philip II becomes king of Macedon (Macedonia)	359
Battle of Chaeronea	338
Congress of Corinth and foundation of Hellenic League	338–337
Murder of Philip	336
Alexander crushes revolts in Greece	335
Alexander invades Asia—Battle of Granicus	334
Battle of Issus	333
Expedition to Egypt and submission of Egyptians	332–331
Battle of Gaugamela (Arbela)	331
Murder of Darius—Alexander becomes Great King	330
Indian campaign of Alexander	327–324
Death of Alexander	323
Ptolemy I Soter seizes Egypt	321
Civil War between the generals	322–301
Seleucus I founder of Seleucid dynasty in Asia	305–280
Battle of Ipsus—Final division of Alexander's kingdom	301
Foundation of Museum of Alexandria	286
Eumenes I founds independent kingdom of Pergamum	263
Attalus III of Pergamum bequeaths kingdom to Rome	133
Syria made a Roman province by Pompey	64
Cleopatra (VII) on Egyptian throne	51

ruled Crete for the next two hundred years until they too were overwhelmed by the Dorians, a new wave of barbarians who penetrated into southern Greece, remained there, and then sent an expedition over to Crete. This proved to be the end of Cretan civilization, and what may justly be called a dark age fell upon Greece, which will be briefly dealt with later.

Since what we know mostly about Crete is its art and architecture, the result of the work of early twentieth-century archaeologists, all that can be said with certainty about its civilization is what may be inferred from its material remains, and from casual references in later Greek writings and some contemporary Egyptian documents and inscriptions. We know about the Cretan love of sports and life in the open air, we know about their attention to luxury and much about their domestic way of life. Although there is marked Egyptian influence in some Cretan work, nevertheless on the whole the Cretans appear to us rather as precursors of the mainland Greeks than as in any way an offshoot of Egyptian culture. There can be little doubt that they prepared the way for the later civilization of Greece by giving the

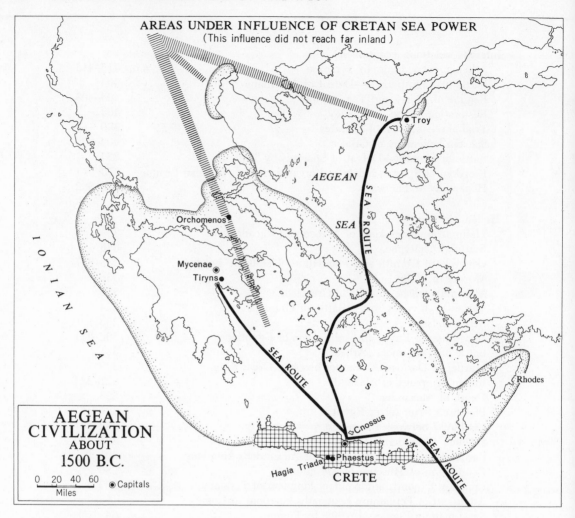

AREAS UNDER INFLUENCE OF CRETAN SEA POWER
(This influence did not reach far inland)

AEGEAN
SEA

IONIAN SEA

Orchomenos

Mycenae
Tiryns

CYCLADES

Troy

SEA ROUTE

SEA ROUTE

SEA ROUTE

Rhodes

Cnossus

Hagia Triada   Phaestus

CRETE

SEA ROUTE

AEGEAN
CIVILIZATION
ABOUT
1500 B.C.

0 20 40 60
Miles   ● Capitals

Aegean world its first acquaintance with foreign civilization by way of maritime trade. When their script is finally deciphered and the extensive written material read it will be easier to assign them their true place in the history of civilization.

▶ The Homeric Age in Greece

From the middle of the second millennium, as has been said, barbarians began to penetrate into Greece from the north. Apart from the Achaeans the leading groups were the Ionians (who may have been in Greece even before the Achaeans), the Aeolians, and the last group of invaders, the Dorians. The Dorians used iron, and this may in part

account for their easy conquest of the bronze-using Achaeans and Cretans, since bronze was an expensive metal and its use was necessarily confined to a small group of warriors. Much of the history of Greece from the beginning of these conquests is obscure, illuminated only by the Homeric epics, the *Iliad* and the *Odyssey*. These poems, still considered by many to be the greatest works of Western literature, are surrounded by mysteries which will probably never be solved. It is not known who wrote them, when they were written, whether they were both written by the same poet, or whether they are not merely traditional poems edited by a man whom later ages have called "Homer."

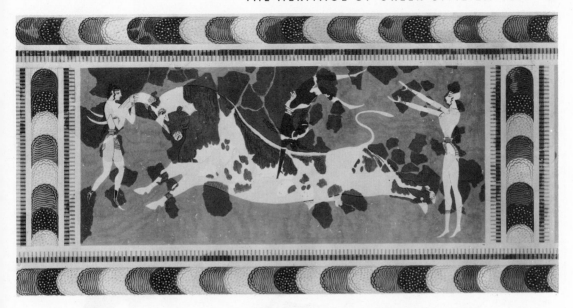

Reproduction of a Cretan fresco from the palace at Cnossus, showing the sport of bull leaping. Evidently the man uses the bull's horns as an aid in leaping over the bull, to be caught by his female partner on the other side. (COURTESY THE METROPOLITAN MUSEUM OF ART)

These problems need not concern us here. All that needs to be said is that these epics purport to tell the history of a part of the war between a group of allies from the mainland of Greece and the city of Troy (the *Iliad*), and the story of the wanderings of Odysseus after the fall of Troy. It is probable that the *Iliad* and the *Odyssey* took their final shape about 800 B.C. The conditions, described by Homer, therefore, may be taken to have a general application to those in the period of the invasions and for a few hundred years afterward. Society was aristocratic, but the freemen obviously were allowed their say in the council and assemblies; the kings and chiefs held their position by heredity, but they were far from absolute and there is certainly no trace whatever of anything resembling the divine monarchy of Egypt. Agamemnon, leader of the Trojan expedition, holds some special prerogatives by virtue of his position, and, though he is a lesser warrior than Achilles, he is nevertheless strong enough to force Achilles to give up his captive slave-girl after the god Apollo

Reproduction of a fragment of a Cretan fresco, showing the head of a young girl. Note the elaborate hair styling, with a modern-looking "spit curl." (COURTESY THE METROPOLITAN MUSEUM OF ART)

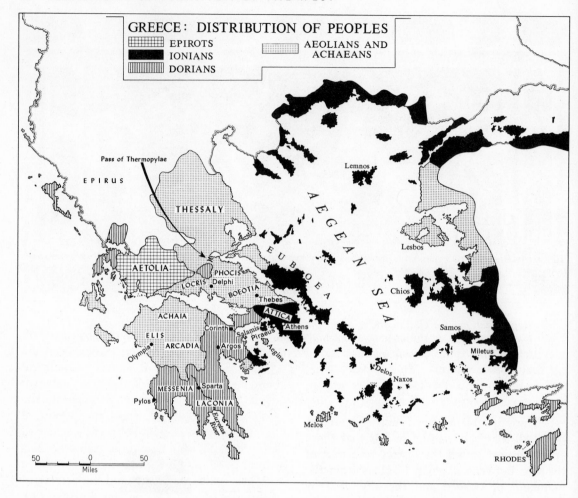

GREECE: DISTRIBUTION OF PEOPLES

EPIROTS
IONIANS
DORIANS
AEOLIANS AND ACHAEANS

Pass of Thermopylae

EPIRUS

THESSALY

AETOLIA

LOCRIS   PHOCIS   Delphi

BOEOTIA

Thebes

ATTICA

ACHAIA

Athens

ELIS   Corinth   Salamis   Piraeus

ARCADIA   Argos   Aegina

Olympia

MESSENIA   Sparta

Pylos   LACONIA

Eurotas River

AEGEAN SEA

EUBOEA

Lemnos

Lesbos

Chios

Samos

Miletus

Delos   Naxos

Melos

RHODES

50   0   50
Miles

had forced him to give up his own prize. Yet Agamemnon can use no sanctions against Achilles when the latter refuses to fight any longer in the war. For the rest, it is clear that Greece was not yet overpopulated and there are numerous descriptions of feasts which would have been unheard of in a later age, when Greece was too poor to support her population save on the most meager of diets. The chieftains themselves knew how to plow and did not regard agriculture as menial work; indeed farming and sheep-herding were clearly the main occupations of the era. It would seem also that the Greeks were not yet skilled in the making of industrial products, and the chief method of distribution of surplus goods was by barter, aided by war and plunder.

▶ Age of colonization

Not long after the Homeric Age and perhaps even during the lifetime of the poet, all the peoples of Greece, with a few notable exceptions, took part in a considerable movement of colonization. The movement was probably the result of land hunger and pressure of population on the scant resources of the country. The Greek colonies, unlike those of the earlier peoples such as the Phoenicians, were not mainly for the purposes of trade. They were rather settlements of citizens, sent out usually with the full blessings of the mother state, to build homes for themselves beyond the seas, and, if possible, to produce a surplus of agricultural products which could then be exchanged

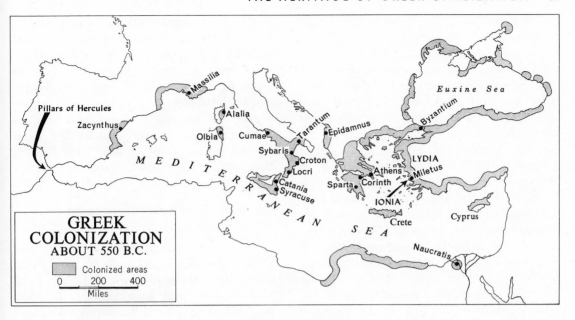

GREEK
COLONIZATION
ABOUT 550 B.C.

☐ Colonized areas

0   200   400

Miles

for the goods of the mother country. No jurisdiction over these colonies was asserted by the mother country. The colonies were free to set up their own form of government. It was regarded as an offense against common decency to wage war against the mother country, but even so nothing could be done about it, and there are later instances in Greece of important colonies siding against their founders on the mainland in a general war. As a result of this movement colonies grew up on the borders of the Black Sea, in the coastal areas of Africa bordering on Egypt, and as far away from the homeland as eastern Spain; in addition, the coastal areas of Asia Minor and much of southern Italy were largely peopled by Greeks. It was not unusual for such colonies to be more powerful and prosperous than the often small city-states from which they had sprung.

▶ The Greek city–states

THE POLIS—CHARACTERISTIC GREEK POLITICAL
AND SOCIAL UNIT

The very word "political," used in the above heading, comes from the Greek word *polis,* the Greek unit of government par excellence. If the achievements of Greek culture are to be understood it is necessary to consider briefly what this unit consisted of, and how it may be said to have favored the special development of man as a political being, which was one of the great achievements of Greek civilization. Historically the polis probably derives from the period of the invasions when a strong point was necessary to hold off marauding enemies. This strong point was the *acropolis,* and round it were the cultivated fields and the centers of trading necessary to keep the fortress supplied. The developed polis then was not only the central strong point, the nucleus of the city, but all the territory around until the boundaries of the neighboring polis were reached. Thus the polis is a city-state in the true sense of the word, a city plus its environment, over which the government of the city exercised jurisdiction. The military leaders in early times necessarily administered the government, but when the invasions ceased to present such a pressing problem, the peaceful farmers and traders naturally expected to be consulted and perhaps to take some responsible part in the government. Each polis, however, had its own interests and liked to exercise its own self-government. Another polis might be absorbed in war, and no doubt in early times many budding *poleis* (plural of polis) were incorporated into the territory of larger neighbors; but such mergers could, as a rule, be accomplished only by war. Each polis strove fiercely to maintain its complete independence and autonomy, and all the citizenry were prepared to defend their polis at a moment's notice against any attempted encroachment.

The number of citizens in a polis naturally varied according to its size. In the smaller polis doubtless everyone knew everyone else, and in a sense this was always the ideal. The polis was at least as much an enlarged family as it was an official governmental unit. Aristotle once remarked that a man who could live without a polis "must be either a beast or a god," that is, he must be either subhuman or superhuman. In his view it was the ideal field of development for man. Man is a creature, he says elsewhere, "whose nature it is to live in a polis." It gave him a sense of belonging and a secure status. If he emigrated to another polis he would be accorded only the status of a *metic,* or resident alien. He did not possess full political rights since he could not be expected to know enough of the aims and ideals of his new polis to participate effectively in its political life.

THE LEADING CITIES—ATHENS AND SPARTA

A study in extremes

In the study of Greek political life, a study which has been considered worth while only for about a century, in contradistinction to the study of the Roman Republic which has never failed to find interested scholars, even in the Middle Ages, it is fascinating to observe how extreme the two leading cities are as examples of a particular kind of society. Sparta was the perfect type of what the philosopher Henri Bergson called the "closed society," whereas Athens was the almost perfect type of the "open society." Athens was ruined by her democratic excesses, her too extreme freedom, whereas Sparta became a classic case of arrested development, all her forms so rigid that there was no possibility of a peaceful

evolution in a necessarily changing world. The student can therefore study these two societies with profit not only for their inherent interest, but for the lessons they have to teach of the danger of excess—a danger which the Greeks themselves fully appreciated. The leading ideal of Greek thinkers was *sophrosyne,* or moderation; but from all that we can discover from their history, they may have continued to seek but did not find it.

Political and social development of Sparta

Lest we be astonished that the Spartans should have developed a society and institutions that seem to demand so much of human nature and go so contrary to what we think of as natural human impulses and instincts, it should be explained at once that there were sound historical reasons for the development of a militarized state. The Spartan nobles, evidently hungry for land, committed an aggression upon their neighbors, the equally Dorian Messenians. After winning the First Messenian War and imposing severe terms on their enemies, the Spartans soon had to defend themselves against an attempt by the Messenians to recovery their position. During this war the Spartan homeland was in very grave danger, and only a providential death of the general of the leading ally of the Messenians saved the Spartans from conquest. Recovering from their early defeats they succeeded once more in conquering Messenia. Then, instead of being content with territorial changes of a minor nature, they decided to enslave the whole Messenian population. This meant that the Spartans were now in the sorry position of having to keep down a considerable population, possibly one outnumbering their own, and force them to work for their new masters. And these people were not alien barbarians but Dorian Greeks, in every respect the equal of their masters save that they had been defeated in battle. Thus the Spartans, in order to force their victims, who were called *helots,* or state slaves, to work, had themselves to be prepared constantly to put down a revolt; and such revolts were not few, although conditions in the country prevented easy coordination between the scattered helots.

Although nothing is known for certain of the famous lawgiver of Sparta who has passed down to history as Lycurgus, and we know neither if nor when he lived, the laws are authentic enough. They probably considerably antedate the Messenian Wars, since long before these culminating wars the Dorians of Laconia (whose chief city was Sparta) had had to fight hard to conquer their territory, and the system of state slavery had already been established. Now, however, it was more thoroughly systematized, and the constitution that will be described later on in this chapter was the one in operation by the end of the seventh century B.C.

There were three classes of people in Sparta at this time, the free-born, who were called Spartiates, the *perioeci,* and the helots. The perioeci were not Spartan citizens; they could not become professional soldiers nor intermarry with Spartans; they possessed no political rights. Their task was to handle all the economic affairs of the Spartans, especially dealings with foreigners. Sometimes in case of war they could serve with the Spartan infantry. The helots, as the property of the state, possessed certain elementary rights. They could not be put to death save by the authority of the state, and they possessed a certain amount of personal freedom as long as they farmed well and provided their particular master with enough for his subsistence. In times of grave danger they could serve in the Spartan army, though they were naturally regarded as untrustworthy. It was, however, possible to earn their freedom from helotry by such means. The helot, therefore, was in a sense lent by the Spartan state to the free citizens as a source of permanent labor, relieving them from having to undertake menial work themselves, thus leaving them free for a totally military life.

The professional military class devoted itself to nothing but war and preparations for war. This class was rigidly selected.

Children who were weak and puny at birth were simply exposed to die. Education for boys consisted of all forms of athletics, military instruction, and physical exercise. Boys were made to go barefoot and ill-clad in winter, to sleep without coverings, and to prepare all their own meals. Girls fit to be mothers of Spartans had to undergo a similar regime of athletics and games, and were taught courage, endurance, and patriotism. Boys lived at home with their mothers till they were seven years old. Then they went into military training in groups under the charge of older boys, and lived in barracks. At the age of twenty marriage was compulsory, but the husband continued to live in barracks, and could visit his wife only on rare occasions. According to Plutarch, it was hoped that this continence would serve to procreate more healthy children, and in any case protected the Spartiate from a possible weakening caused by contact with home comforts. From the labor of his helots each adult had to supply his share of the food eaten at the public mess. If a Spartiate for any reason could not supply his share, he lost status and became an inferior citizen, with reduced political and social rights. To prevent contamination with foreign ideas and people, aliens were rarely admitted to the city; and those who received permits were periodically expelled. To prevent the accumulation of wealth the Spartans maintained a heavy iron currency which was not exchangeable anywhere else.

This logical "Lycurgan" system fulfilled its purpose. The helots were kept under control for more than two hundred years, and Sparta possessed an army which was able to play a noble part in defeating the Persians. Its heavy infantry was unbeaten by any Greek city in battle until the rise of Thebes in the fourth century, and was the most highly disciplined and efficient body of troops in Greece. However, it should be understood that the main purpose of this army was for internal control, and not for foreign imperialist adventures. Spartan heroism, however, was proverbial, and undoubtedly real. The social sanctions ensured it, for

Two views of a Spartan kylix (terracotta). The painted interior depicts the apotheosis of Hercules. This piece shows that by 580 B.C., the date of the kylix, the Spartans were still able to produce works of craftsmanship comparable to that of the other Greeks. (COURTESY THE METROPOLITAN MUSEUM OF ART)

no Spartan dared go home in disgrace; he dared not even leave the battlefield to take news home.

The other Greeks, with their high ideal of civic virtue and duty, recognized that on this score the Spartans were their superiors. Civic duty, though in Sparta it was of a military nature, was nevertheless imposed by the polis and accepted by the citizens. This condition, to them, was not slavery, because obedience to laws was the whole ideal framework of the polis, as obedience to divine laws was a similar duty for the individual. The other Greeks did not think the Spartans lived under a tyranny, but under a regime chosen for them by Lycurgus, and accepted by them. The Athenian would not have accepted such laws for a moment, nor would

he have put up with the Spartan food and frugality, which were the object of frequent jests among citizens of other states, frugal as they were themselves by our standards.

It was the privilege of the Spartans to choose their laws and to obey them; and to all appearances they did obey them. We do not hear of Spartans leaving their city to enjoy the delights of Athens or Corinth until after the Spartan victory in the Peloponnesian War (404 B.C.). It was perhaps the heroic nature of their extreme and narrow ideal and the heroic way in which they lived up to it that excited the admiration of their neighbors; whereas the philosophers admired the way they used their laws to form character and the logical nature of the laws themselves. The vulgarity, boasting, and propaganda of modern fascist states distinguish them effectively from Sparta. It was the Spartan's pride that he was a man of few words; and the word "laconic" has passed into our language. And a "Spartan" regime means, not an imperialist, fascist, communist, or oligarchic state, but a regime of simplicity and abstinence.

Athens—Political evolution

As soon as we come to study Athens we are at once made aware of a marked difference between the two peoples. The Athenians themselves, of course, were fully aware of it, and on the whole they tended to attribute it to the fact that they were Ionians while the Spartans were Dorians. The Athenians were experimental, they were willing to take a chance that change might mean improvement, and their ruling classes at a crucial moment in Athenian history did not fight to stave off change and maintain their privileged position, but preferred to allow the political forms of their state to evolve. Once this initial step had been taken they may well have been sorry, since not only did the immediate change take place, but the Athenians went forward to the most complete democracy the world has yet seen, and in the process the aristocrats lost all their privileges and had to submit to rule by the majority, which did not mean themselves. It is worth devoting some attention to this process, since it tells us much about the Athenian people and why to this day we remember their civilization as one of the greatest in world history.

The land of Attica, which comprised the polis of Athens, was not a territory rich in resources. Yet it was large in comparison with most of the Greek city-states, and Athens had taken but little share in the great colonizing movement of the eighth and seventh centuries. But the Athenians were trying to grow wheat and be self-sufficient on land that was for the most part totally unsuited for it. The result was that the peasants who made up the bulk of the population by the middle of the seventh century were having a great deal of difficulty in making a living. Moreover the majority probably did not own their own land and had to supply a considerable proportion of their crop to their landlords, who also controlled the effective machinery of the state. The result was that they fell into debt, borrowed money for their new crops, and ultimately had no security to offer but their own persons. They were then sold into slavery abroad. This caused the agitation that might have been expected and there were no doubt murders and much ravaging of property. It should be added that the landowners used wheat, which was readily salable everywhere, as payment for their industrial imports, in spite of the fact that there was too little wheat at home to fill the needs of the people, even with fair distribution. So the peasants, who produced the wheat, went hungry.

Probably for the reason that trade was seriously affected by the disturbances, the peasants found an ally in the traders, who put pressure upon the landowners for reforms. The first effort at reform was merely to produce a code of law so that the peasants could be properly tried before being punished (constitution of Draco, 621 B.C.), but in the early part of the sixth century the aristocrats at last agreed to allow one of the wise men of Greece, Solon, to try his hand at a political and economic reform, which he was peculiarly well fitted to do since he had both landowning and trading interests. Solon realized that the basic difficulty in Athens was the unsuitability of its main crop and the lack of industry in the city. To solve this twofold problem he forbade the export of wheat, encouraged the growing of vines and olives instead of wheat, and invited skilled artisans into Athens with the promise of full citizenship. Thus it would become possible for dispossessed peasants to make an alternative living in the city. It meant also that Athens thereafter would be dependent upon imports of grain to make up the deficiency in production, and that therefore, like some modern economies, she would have to export manufactured goods to pay for them. Solon also inaugurated a far-

Ostraka, or ballots, used for ostracism (forced exile by popular vote) in Athens in the fifth century B.C. Note the names of prominent Athenian statesmen written on them: Kimon, Themistokles, (A)risteid(es), Perikles, Miltiades. (COURTESY AMERICAN SCHOOL OF CLASSICAL STUDIES AT ATHENS)

reaching reform of the law courts, and instituted an assembly and council made up of propertied classes, but with far wider representation than the old exclusive aristocratic council of the Areopagus.

Solon's reforms were evidently too drastic to be carried out without some degree of compulsion. This was supplied by an enlightened autocrat named Pisistratus, who managed to rule Athens by political manipulation for upward of thirty years and nevertheless die peacefully in his bed. By the time of his death most of the economic problems had been solved, the most recalcitrant of the aristocrats were in exile in Sparta, Athens was a leading exporter of pottery and specialized agricultural products, and she was the possessor of a fine navy. She was now ready for a further dose of democracy.

The occasion for political reform was provided by the autocratic behavior of Hippias, son of Pisistratus, who never recognized the basis of consent by which his father operated. This gave the exiled aristocrats a chance of success if they returned. Led by Cleisthenes they came back to Athens with a Spartan army, but were unable to agree among themselves. When Cleisthenes suddenly decided to become a democrat and desert his erstwhile companions, the victory was won for democracy and Cleisthenes was instructed to draw up a new and suitable constitution. By a piece of skilled gerrymandering he prevented the rise of another dictator like Pisistratus, while he gave the Athenians their first real democracy.

The pivot of the Athenian constitution was the Assembly of all male citizens, without property qualification, which had to be called into session at least ten times a year, and was absolutely sovereign except for certain safeguards which need not be entered into here. In addition to the Assembly, which decided on all important questions, a Council of 500 was elected, soon afterward if not in the time of Cleisthenes, by lot from a list of eligible citizens who had not sat in the Council in at least the ten previous years. This Council, divided into committees of fifty, each the chief committee for a tenth of the year, acted as the executive of the state, looking after all the details of administration. Later there was instituted a board of ten generals who had further executive duties to perform. From their number the Assembly chose the actual war leaders in case of hostilities. The government therefore was a full democracy of a town-meeting type not unlike that of the early American colonies. It was based on the theory that government by amateurs is best, that each citizen was as qualified as the next one in the somewhat elementary duties of government, and that full participation and interest in the affairs of the state can alone make a democratic government work. The only representative principle in this government is to be found in the board of generals. A general could be elected and re-elected as long as the people had confidence in him. It was customary for each general to represent one of the ten tribes, but it was also possible for some noted citizens, such as Pericles in later years, to be elected at large by all the citizens. It was generally understood who was the leading citizen at any given time, and such a man would usually have the privilege of addressing the Assembly first and putting forward his suggestions. The Council was expected to prepare other legislation for the Assembly and to give it a preliminary discussion.

For a century this government worked on the whole very effectively, largely because of the aristocratic leaders of ability whom the people were willing to follow. It deteriorated badly during the Peloponnesian War when the ruling majority too often forgot the interests of the state and showed themselves excessively docile in the hands of warmongering demagogues. Nevertheless, even after its comparative failure at this time, the people restored it as soon as they were able after their defeat and occupation by Sparta, and a form of government quite recognizable as a descendant of that of Cleisthenes remained in Athens until its conquest by Macedonia in the late fourth century B.C.

▶ Intercity relations

THE PERSIAN WARS

Only a few years after Cleisthenes had established the new Athenian constitution all the peoples of Greece were to be put to a severe test. The expanding empire of Persia took over the Greek city-states in Asia Minor, which appealed to their friends on the mainland for help. Athens sent a small expedition which soon returned after some successes. The Persian king, Darius I, was furious with this interference, however, and sent an expedition of his own against Athens and such other states as would not submit and send earth and water as a token of humility before the great monarch. The result was the campaign of Marathon (490 B.C.) in which the Athenians almost alone defeated the great expedition, which was beset by ignorance of the territory and hopes of treachery from Athenian aristocrats which did not materialize until too late. Darius' son Xerxes prepared a much larger expedition which was to proceed both by land and sea. The Greeks knew of the preparations but found it extremely difficult to concert any policy. Athens was obviously best fitted for leadership by sea and Sparta by land. Matters were further complicated because some of the northern cities submitted rather than defend themselves.

The outcome was the heroic defeat of the Spartans at Thermopylae, followed by the capture and sack of Athens, mitigated by the great sea victory of Salamis won by the Athenian and allied navy (480 B.C.). In spite of the loss of their city the Athenians fought on, and the following year a grand alliance led by Sparta was able to defeat the Persian land forces at the battle of Plataea, while the Athenian and allied navy defeated the Persian navy at Mycale (479 B.C.). Thereafter Greece was free from attack by Persia, though from the end of the fifth century through the fourth until the conquest of Persia by Alexander, Persian influence was strong in Greece, and Persian money played a not inconspicuous part in the final defeat of the Athenians in the Peloponnesian War.

THE CONFEDERATION OF DELOS— ATHENIAN IMPERIALISM

After the war was over the Athenians decided that the only way to prevent a renewed attack was to form a league of defense, composed of herself and as many of the Aegean islands as she could persuade to join her. Sparta was also invited into the league (called the Confederation of Delos), but firmly and politely declined. Originally it was a free league, although obviously Athens was the leading partner. Some of the islands provided money, and a few of the larger ones provided ships. The money was used by the Athenians to build ships, but the sailors were trained in Athens and the commanders were Athenian. It is therefore not surprising that the instrument thus forged proved to be too tempting for the Athenians, and under the leadership of Pericles it began to be used for purposes for which it had not been intended. After a defeat had been sustained in the eastern Mediterranean where the navy had no business to be, Pericles turned the debacle to good account by having the treasury, hitherto located in Delos, one of the smaller islands sacred to Apollo, transferred to Athens. When the league decided not to permit anyone to leave it, the free league had clearly become an Athenian empire.

THE PELOPONNESIAN WAR

In addition to using the fleet as he saw fit, and using the surplus of the treasury for beautifying Athens, Pericles then began to interfere in the internal affairs of the islands, encouraging the setting up of democratic

Bust of Pericles, the Athenian statesman. (COURTESY BRITISH MUSEUM)

governments favorable to Athens in place of the older oligarchies which had been traditional. For a time also he carried on some minor wars on the mainland of Greece until a few setbacks decided him to pursue his ends by the more diplomatic means of trying to bring over states allied to Sparta into his league. Ultimately the fear induced in Sparta and in the leading Peloponnesian trading state of Corinth caused them to launch a preventive war, to be known henceforth as the Peloponnesian War, since the historians of the war are Athenian. Honors in this war were fairly equally divided for the first half, which was concluded by a temporary peace. The Spartans could not be seriously defeated by land (though they did suffer some severe losses in Athenian minor expeditions), nor could the Athenians be defeated by sea; and as long as they held command of the sea they could not be starved. However, when the peace was broken and the war renewed, the Athenians overreached themselves and through bad judgment in the campaign lost the whole of a great expedition sent to Syracuse in Sicily. Thereafter the Athenians were on the defensive. They had lost more

0 20 40 60 80 100
Miles
◉ Capitals

Euxine Sea

Propontis

MACEDONIA

Bosporus

Chalcidice

Hellespont

EPIRUS

THESSALY

Lesbos
•Mitylene

Corcyra

AEGEAN SEA

Acarnania

Euboea

Locris
Delphi• Phocis
Boeotia •Thebes
Achaea •Decelea
Corinth◉ •Megara• •Athens
Argos◉ Aegina
P E L O P O N N E S U S
Messenia ◉Sparta
Pylos• Laconia

Chios

Samos

•Miletus

Naxos

Cos

IONIAN SEA

Melos

CRETE

431 B.C.
GREECE AT THE
BEGINNING OF THE
PELOPONNESIAN WAR
ATHENS AND ALLIES
SPARTA AND ALLIES
NEUTRAL

than they could recover, a number of the islands revolted, and the Persians saw their chance to finish off their ancient enemy by giving aid and comfort to Sparta. The last Athenian fleet was destroyed at Aegospotami in 405 B.C., and Athens was forced to surrender for lack of supplies, now cut off by the victorious Spartans. Though the Athenians made a partial recovery in the fourth century, they were forever afterward plagued by poverty and never built up a first-class state again.

Throughout the great fifth century,

Athens had been able to maintain her position as a first-class power in the Greek world only because of the tribute money that she had at her disposal from the islands in the league. She was always faced with a large visible unfavorable balance of trade due to her overpopulation and general under-employment. But the carrying trade and the balance of money from the islands not actually used for the allied navy were able to make up this deficit. To the use of this money we undoubtedly owe the incomparable artistic achievements of the fifth century.

Both Sparta and Athens, and indeed all Greece, suffered severely from the internecine struggle of the Peloponnesian War. Not only had many thousands of men been killed, but a great deal of the territory had been ravaged, and, perhaps worst of all, the custom had arisen of looking to Persia for support in the fratricidal struggles between the city-states. And Persia had no interest in them except to keep as many states as possible weak and disunited. No great thing was achieved by the war, party struggles and bitterness were exacerbated, and the necessary unity of Greece was postponed until such time as they were conquered by the outsider Philip of Macedon in the second half of the fourth century. If Athens, Sparta, and Corinth had learned to live together, or if Athens had been willing to let her league be really free and perhaps ultimately federal, then the work of Philip of Macedon would have been impossible. It was the Peloponnesian War that made his ultimate rise, or the rise of another like him, inevitable.

▶ ## Daily life in Athens

The whole social life of Athens, and indeed that of all other Greek cities, reflects, above all, the extraordinary poverty of material resources, which was not only accepted philosophically by the Greeks but regarded as the natural and even desirable order of things. The ordinary man remained a frugal liver, both in imperial times and in the fourth century. Even what he considered luxuries would be to the imperial Roman very little indeed. Everything must be judged by Greek standards. When Pericles boasts that luxuries from the whole world stream into Athens we must set this against the background of the known national income, and the known social life as shown by the inscriptions, by the artistic remains as well as by the literature. All Greeks wore clothes of the utmost simplicity at all times, an undergarment fastened with a safety pin, and an outer garment draped about their

This model of the Agora shows Athens in the second century A.D. rather than in the period covered by the text. Many changes were made during the period of domination by the wealthy Hellenistic monarchs; however, the model will serve to give some idea of the layout of the Agora. Although the buildings of the fifth century B.C. were less sumptuous and costly and the arrangement was less orderly, the style of architecture was not greatly different. (COURTESY AMERICAN SCHOOL OF CLASSICAL STUDIES AT ATHENS)

person. The same garment served as a blanket. Beds were usually planks, without springs. The average house, unlike the temples, was made of sun-dried brick, and houses were built close together. The walls were not decorated, the furniture was crude and utilitarian. When Pericles insisted that Athenian homes were beautiful and elegant, he may have been speaking the truth, because the artistic decorations that the Greek knew so well how to make may have been in use. If so, we know nothing of such decorations; but the furniture in the house of the most fashionable young man of Athens in his day, a list of which we do possess, is singularly unimpressive. The houses themselves were adequate for living in, but bear no comparison at all with those of pre-Greek Minoan Crete.

The reason for this utter lack of luxury in the private homes of the Athenians is simple enough. The Greek lived primarily in the open air. More hours of the day were spent in the gymnasium, the agora, or the streets than in his house. When it was dark he went to bed, and at dawn he usually rose and went into the street, without breakfast. We hear nothing from any source of any great mansions of the Roman type in classical times, nor of palatial private gardens and pleasure grounds. Rich men contributed their wealth to the polis, and did not use it so much for their own pleasure; but even their riches were small enough by Roman or Cretan standards. There were no gargantuan feasts; food was scarce and lacked variety. Meat was rarely eaten.

The truth seems to be, hard as it may be for us to believe, that the Greek really did not care for luxury, or not enough to give up his leisure to gain it; and it was frowned upon by public opinion. A contrast sometimes made between Athenian luxury and Spartan simplicity is extremely relative. Both lived simply; but the Spartan cultivated simplicity, wearing only one garment in winter and going barefoot, whereas the Athenian had sandals. The Athenian was able to decorate his city superbly because he cared for it rather than for his home; and to the service of his gods and his city he devoted all his unparalleled artistic talents.

The kind of freedom that resulted from this doing without is one that is unique in history, and can never be repeated. But if one delights in free talk, assemblies, festivals, plays, the development of the mind and the body, self-government, and civic glory, the logical thing to do is to avoid cluttering oneself up with possessions useless to this kind of life. But the loss of the city life—not necessarily even the city itself, for this could be rebuilt—would be irreparable. In the rest of this chapter we shall see how they used this freedom.

▶ The searching mind of the Greek

GENERAL CHARACTERISTICS OF
GREEK THOUGHT

All knowledge, said the Greeks, begins in wonder—wonder about the world, and wonder about man. The Hebrews asked only one question about man: his relation to his God. The Greeks asked not only this question but all other questions. They were the greatest people for questioning that the world has yet seen, or at all events until our own time. When Aristotle came to write his *Politics* he felt obliged to ask a great many fundamental questions before he dared to generalize. He had amassed material on 158 constitutions, constitutions evolved by generations of men struggling with the problem of how men could best be governed. None of the constitutions was perfect; all had failed in some respects. But the people themselves had discovered the defects, and by asking why and considering the alternatives they had tried to remedy them. So Aristotle conceived it to be his task to classify these constitutions, to see if he could evolve a system that would have the most merits and the fewest weaknesses even if it would not be ideal. Plato, on the other hand, was looking in his *Republic* for an ideal state. So it was necessary for him to inquire first on what principles an ideal state could be built, and then try to find institutions through which it could be expressed. This took him a long way. For, having discovered that it must be based on justice, he then had to find out what justice was. Neither Plato nor Aristotle ever thought for a moment that it was not the duty of man to improve his institutions, as the ancient Egyptians had thought. And it is this willingness to seek new knowledge and to stake their lives upon the result of ever-continuous experiment based on the best thinking of which they were capable that distinguishes the Greeks from their predecessors.

The Greeks wondered about the physical world. What was the underlying stable substratum in a world where everything appeared to be in flux—was it water, air, fire, or atoms? Clearly everything changed in appearance; but they did not doubt that this change was only an apparent change. Underneath was a unity. When Thales saw the Egyptian notebooks which told of the measurements of the angles and sides of a triangle, his mind leaped ahead to the universal idea underlying all these particulars. And he is credited with the famous pons asinorum theorem—in *all* triangles, the angles subtending equal sides are equal to one another.

They wondered about man—his nature, the seen body, and the unseen soul that gave life to it. They assumed the existence of the soul, but they tried to find the relationship between soul and body. How does man acquire knowledge? What is the nature of the mind that knows it? What are the laws of thinking? How does one idea connect with another? What is an idea? What are the activities proper to man? What is morality?

In all these questions except the last, the Greeks were pioneers in human thinking; and even in the last they were different from the Hebrews in that at least the later Greeks accepted nothing, not even the gods, as final arbiters. While they might admit that the fear of the Lord was the beginning of wisdom, this to them would only be one more reminder that they were men and not gods. The last thing a classical Greek would do would be to enter the sanctuary and there receive a comfort which would save him the necessity of questioning further.

WONDER ABOUT THE WORLD—COSMOLOGY

The first thinkers to speculate about the nature of the world and the universe were not Athenians, nor indeed did the Athenians show much interest at any time in physical speculation. Their almost exclusive interest was in man. The early cosmologists hailed from Ionia, and the problem they set themselves to inquire into was the fundamental problem, which, expressed literally, was: out of what does everything come? What is the primal substance underlying all visible physical phenomena, however much the form or appearance of objects changes? The Ionians assumed that there was such a substance. Thales suggested water; Anaximenes, air; Heraclitus, fire. Naturally they could not prove which, if any, of these substances was the primary one, although no doubt they had observed such phenomena as the three visible stages of water.

The Eleatic school of thinkers in southern Italy gave consideration to the same problem. Parmenides came to the conclusion on theoretical grounds that there could be no such thing as nothing. The whole idea, for him, was inconceivable. Thus there could be no such thing as a real change, since this would involve the appearance of something new that had not been in existence before. Essentially all phenomena must be the same, with the consequence that all visible change must be illusory. This criticism having been accepted by all later thinkers, the question was shifted, and now became a quest for what caused the visible changes in phenomena. Out of all this speculation ultimately arose the Greek atomic theory explained in detail by Democritus of Abdera. All things, said he, are made up of filled space and empty space, atoms and the void. The atoms were not infinitely small but simply very small (like our molecules). Each atom had its own characteristics, a characteristic shape and a characteristic movement, which gave rise to the qualities observed in objects by men: sweet and sour, hard and soft, and all the infinite variety that we perceive.

The importance of all this speculation

was not, of course, in its results, but in the fact that it is altogether new in its objectives and in the kinds of explanation that it offers. The gods are not brought in to explain phenomena; it is assumed that the basis of all things is material. Man had, in his mind, removed himself from his universe and stopped to look at it. He had taken the first steps along a road the ending of which is not yet in sight but which, along the way, has led to modern science and a transformed world.

WONDER ABOUT MAN AND HIS PLACE IN THE UNIVERSE—THE ATHENIAN CONTRIBUTION

The relationship between man and gods—Greek tragedy

It has become customary to call the cosmologists whose work we have been considering the "pre-Socratic" philosophers. Philosophers or not—and we prefer to think of them as early theoretical scientists—the term pre-Socratic suggests an important truth, that Socrates, though he never wrote a line, is the key figure in the history of Greek thought. The philosophers who follow him build upon his work, while the thinkers before him, notably the great Athenian tragic dramatists, Aeschylus and Sophocles, seem to live in an altogether different world, with different assumptions and different insights. Yet it was not Socrates himself whose thought was so crucial. He was the first thinker who tried to repair the damage done to traditional thinking by the Sophists, but the intellectual revolution itself was the achievement of the Sophists. Thus in this chapter we shall deal with the pre-Sophists and their framework of ideas first, show how the Sophists destroyed this framework with their criticism, and finally how the great thinkers Socrates, Plato, and Aristotle repaired the damage as far as it could be repaired, and set the world on a new path of thinking that has persisted since their time. As this intellectual revolution can lay claim to be the most important such revolution in the history of mankind, and is the most distinctive contribution of the Greeks to the intellectual heritage of mankind, most of the rest of this chapter will be devoted to it.

The great question, for the Greeks as for the Hebrews, was, What is the relation between the earthly and the spiritual man—what is the relation between man and the gods? This may well be the question we in our Western civilization should be asking ourselves, but too often we have forgotten it, still under the spell of the Sophists who claimed that it was unanswerable. The central thought of early Greek civilization was that man lives within a framework of destiny, which the Greeks called *Moira*. This idea suffuses the work of Homer; it is implicit in the *Odyssey* and extremely explicit in parts of the *Iliad*. In Homer it is made clear that man's deeds on earth, however pleasing they may have been to the gods, will not avail to save him from his destined destruction. Hector, it is explicitly stated, has always fulfilled his religious obligations toward Zeus and the other gods; his moral character has been impeccable; and yet he must fall a victim to the spear of Achilles, who is on all counts his moral inferior. Zeus himself is ruled by the superior power of Moira. He weighs the lot of Hector and the lot of Achilles in the balance; when it is shown by this test that Hector is the one who must die in the duel between the two heroes, then Zeus has to forbid further divine help to him and turns him over to his godly and earthly enemies. Hector himself, elsewhere in the poem, recognizes that he is no match for Achilles and that he will die. Andromache, his wife, cannot persuade him to escape the duel, not with all the love she bears him and he bears her. It is his duty as a man to engage in the conflict, a duty toward himself, or what the Greeks called *arete*. Man can therefore, in the view of Homer, not escape his fate. There is a realm of necessity which is the framework within which his deeds must be performed, and his only task within this framework is to bear himself nobly and with dignity as befits a true man.

This thought is the core also of early Greek tragedy. The tragedian's task was not to entertain but to teach the people. The tragedy was performed at the Dionysiac festival; it was a part therefore of Greek religion. Aristotle in a famous definition of the purposes of tragedy explains that it must be "of some magnitude" (concerning matters of moment), must present "an imitation of life," and must by inspiring compassion and awe lead to a "catharsis" of these and other emotions. The process of taking part in the performance of tragedy was therefore a cleansing one. For this purpose Aeschylus and Sophocles always showed noble actions performed by heroes who were not fully realistic but were to some degree idealized. In every tragic hero there was some nobility, even though he may have greatly erred (all Greek "sin" is error; there is no other word in the Greek language for sin but error). Prometheus in Aeschylus' play, *Prometheus Bound*, has disobeyed the gods in pursuit of a higher task for mankind, so he is punished, though it was ultimately within the needs of destiny that man should receive the Promethean gift. The whole house of Agamemnon has been pursued by a cruel destiny that was not of Agamemnon's original making. In the Oedipus trilogy of Sophocles it is expressly shown that Oedipus has been destined to kill his father and marry his mother, and all the puny human efforts to avoid this fate succeed only in deepening the tragedy. Both Aeschylus and Sophocles thought profoundly on these problems. Sophocles in his last play, *Oedipus at Colonus*, suggests as a solution that the sufferings of Oedipus ultimately have been worth while because the land in which he is buried is to be blessed. But, in the thought of these dramatists, as in that of Homer, there is no explanation of why men suffer that can be universally applicable. Human suffering is the work of Moira or the gods, and man has but a limited freedom. It is right for the people to be instructed in these things, to admire and revere the nobility of man in the face of his suffering, and to accept the decrees of the gods and learn humility and fortitude. As Sophocles says in the last words of the *Antigone*, only in old age can man learn wisdom and acceptance.

This was the world of the Athenians before the age of Pericles. In Aristophanes, the great comic poet, who lived in a later and far different age, we can find a nostalgic yearning for the past. His "old men who fought at Marathon" were to him the repository of all the ancient virtues, virtues no more to be seen in his own decadent era. This charge of decadence has been a time-honored complaint of conservatives. But in looking back with the perspective of more than two thousand years we can see that there was something in the substance of Aristophanes' complaints, that indeed there had been an overturning of the old thoughts and the old values, and that these would never reappear. The criticism done by the Sophists was crucial; the world would never be the same again.

Criticism of traditional beliefs— The Sophists

The central thought of the Sophists was stated powerfully and succinctly by one of the earliest of them. Protagoras' dictum, "Man is the measure of all things, of things that are, that they are; of things that are not, that they are not," when taken as seriously and as comprehensively as his successors took it, proved to be the lever which lifted Greek traditional thought off its hinges. Everything hereafter must be looked at from the point of view of man. The gods may exist but they do not reveal themselves to us; therefore they may be disregarded. Laws were made by men and for men; the gods do not sanction laws and do not punish those who offend against them. The individual is more important than the community; he has only one life, let him make the most of it and not lose it stupidly. There is no "natural" difference between the slave and the free; it is just an unfortunate but temporary condition due to historical circumstances.

Such thoughts fell upon fertile ground during the days of the Athenian Empire and the Peloponnesian War. Who can really refute the saying of Thrasymachus the Sophist that "justice is the interest of the stronger," or might makes right? "Of men we know, and of gods we can be fairly sure, that they take power whenever they can," say the Athenian ambassadors to the Melians who try to opt for neutrality in the war. In essence they say, "We are stronger than you, so you may as well submit, and don't believe that the gods will save you. We have as good reason as you to believe they are on our side, not yours." Plato himself, in the *Laws*, has an Athenian stranger remark that the troubles of Athens all stem from their acquired belief that man, not God, is the measure of all things. Alcibiades defends his action in betraying the Athenians to the Spartans by saying that it is only "natural" for an exile to look after his own self and to do everything he can to get back to his old city, even by betraying it to the enemy and returning in the wake of the conquerors.

Euripides, pupil of the Sophists, cannot accept altogether the thought that there are no gods; he is too well aware of the inexplicable fate of man, he is too sympathetic with human suffering, and he cannot, like the Hellenistic individualists of a later era, merely attribute suffering or success to chance. But for him the gods are unjust, man is not noble and does not often suffer in well-trained resignation and fortitude. So he does not care to show his heroes as heroes in the old sense; he presents them as fallible human beings. His study of Agamemnon in the *Iphigenia in Aulis*, his best and most mature tragedy, is a psychological masterpiece; but Agamemnon is no hero. He is a weak and unfortunate man, ruled by ambition, caught in an impossibly difficult dilemma. So Euripides puts real men and women on the stage; tragic destiny and heroic human acceptance disappear; and all possibility of catharsis is lost. Faith had been a casualty in the warfare, and it was never to be replaced during the rest of Greek civilization.

Reconstruction of religious thought— Search for ethical standards—Socrates

The Socratic Method—It was left for Socrates, himself a Sophist in many ways, to try to show that the Sophists had neglected

Socrates. This statue suggests the reason why Alcibiades, in Plato's Symposium, *compares Socrates with Marsyas the satyr, the Greek model of ugliness. Yet the artist has also contrived to show the deep seriousness of the master engaged in a problem which requires concentration of thought.* (COURTESY BRITISH MUSEUM)

an important part of human experience—the inner self. Accepting, in the main, the Sophistic criticism that man has always relied upon traditional thought rather than the best thought of which he is capable, Socrates set out to discover what it is that man really does know and how he comes to know it. Plato tells us how the oracle at Delphi made the categorical statement that Socrates was the wisest man in Greece, and how Socrates, trying to confirm or disprove this statement, searched Greece looking for a wiser man than himself. Finding none, he came to the conclusion that he alone was wise because he alone knew that he knew nothing. This profound paradox is the heart of Socratean thought. It is, of course, already implied in the dictum of Protagoras; and in so far as Socrates stresses the ignorance of those who profess to know, and the unproved nature of all traditional thinking, he is one with the Sophists. But he goes further than they; and this marks his constructiveness as a thinker. We must not indeed take received opinion on trust; but man *can* know through self-examination.

In order to discover this truth, which every man knows inwardly, it is necessary to bring knowledge to birth. For this purpose Socrates developed a method of question and answer, ever since associated with his name, by which it is gradually discovered first what is *not* true; and thereafter the truth is built up stage by stage, allowing no definition to stand until it has been examined, and no questionable statement to pass without criticism. When the process has finished, the questioner will then find that he really knows something, however little, that he was not aware of knowing before. Socrates thus calls himself the "midwife" of knowledge in that he has brought knowledge to birth through the labor of the dialectic (the technical term given to the Socratic method).

Clearly this method is above all applicable to the realm of ethics; and the greater part of the Platonic dialogues where Socrates seems to be himself and not the mere mouthpiece of his pupil is devoted to inquiry into the nature of the good, and how it can be pursued by man. Furthermore, can virtue (*arete*) or moral excellence be taught? If the code of right behavior is not to be dictated by tradition, received opinion, and the supposed will of the gods, then it must emanate from man. An individual ethic based on man's own best knowledge must replace the traditional one. It is Socrates' belief that if we rid ourselves of all prejudice and previous thinking on the subject, then by constant criticism followed by constructive thought we can obtain an idea of the good which will be the same for all; because the human being is so constituted that he *can* know the good. And, knowing it, he can follow it; for no one who truly knows the good would deliberately choose to follow the evil. This is a typically Greek notion, and is attractive to all rationalists. The greatest medieval rationalist, Thomas Aquinas, goes with Socrates as far as *knowledge* of the good is concerned; but, being a Christian, he also stresses the infirmity of the human *will*, which, being evil as the result of original sin, cannot carry out without divine grace what the intellect indicates as the good. And most medieval Christians would not even allow a true knowledge of the good without grace. It follows, therefore, that virtue is knowledge and ignorance is the root of moral evil; from which conclusion Socrates and his pupil Plato drew out the full consequences.

Socratean ethics—In dealing with the Sophists, Socrates deliberately points out the inadequacy of their aim of teaching "useful knowledge." He asks pertinently, "Useful for what?" and has no difficulty in showing that the only truly human aim is the pursuit of the good, to which all else is subordinate. He denies their premise that knowledge is relative; but he admits that it must be tentative. No one knows, or can know, the final truth about anything (Plato excepts mathematics); and the frequency with which Plato shows him as dissatisfied with his preliminary destructive criticism, and the tentative conclusions that fill the vacuum he has created by it, suggests the real humility before knowledge which entitled him to the accolade of Apollo of Delphi, god of wisdom.

In spite of his apparently individualistic ethics, Socrates was a profoundly social being and lover of his polis. He had a high opinion of the truth that lay behind the religious traditions of Greece, though he always interpreted them in his own way, as spiritual rather than physical truths. It was not his task to destroy the law and government of his polis, even though they were based on tradition; he fully accepted the right of the democracy to put him to death under its laws. These laws provided the whole framework for his social life; they were not unchangeable and their ethical content might no doubt be improved. But if it happened that he was the victim of the laws in their present state, then it still behooved him as a citizen to abide by them.

Within himself he only answered to the call of his own inner knowledge. He understood very fully that others might be moved by tradition and prejudice; but this was no excuse for him to follow their example. Very gravely and accurately he describes the activity of the human conscience which never tells him what to do but only what not to do. And he calls this his "daimonion," his little god—as indeed for him it was, since it took the place of the sanctions of the gods and the traditional piety associated with them.

Trial and execution—His teachings may have been too heady for many who were not of the highest moral fiber. Alcibiades, traitor and loose liver, was one of his pupils; so was Critias, oligarchic leader of the Thirty Tyrants who instituted and carried out a bloody proscription of the democratic leaders —though it is not altogether reasonable to blame the master for the human frailties of his pupils. We can see in the Platonic dialogues how easily Socrates' method lends itself to misconstruction, and how quickly an enemy could take his gently objective criticism as personal disbelief. In the *Meno*, for instance, Socrates has been showing that no virtuous man has been able to teach virtue to his son. Anytus, one of his accusers at his trial, at once jumps to the conclusion that Socrates is maligning these men instead of using them to prove his philosophical point. In the political conditions of the restoration of the democracy after the oligarchic revolution, it was difficult to believe that any man could be searching for philosophical truth. Yet Socrates continued in the only activity that for him made life worth living.

In 399 B.C. his enemies brought him to trial before the people's jury on a charge of atheism and corrupting the youth. It was a clever charge, for it was, in appearance, true. Socrates took part in all the festivals and performed all his religious observances, but he did speak of his daimonion, a strange god, and he did teach—indeed the whole of his teaching led inevitably to the conclusion —that a new dispensation had come when man was to be free, to rule himself, not be ruled by the gods. And in so far as this was his instruction to his pupils, then he "corrupted the youth."

The account of his trial in Plato's *Apology* shows his moral courage and his confidence that his own path was right. He defends himself against the charges only by affirming them. Convicted by a small majority and asked for a suggestion as to what punishment he deserves, with the same serene confidence he tells them that he ought to have a pension and be supported at the city's expense for the rest of his life. This irony is too much for human endurance, and by a larger vote the jury condemns him to death. Instead of going into exile as his friends urge, an exile which would undoubtedly have been winked at, he accepts his sentence, not in stoical resignation but with dignity, tenderness for his friends, and good humor. While he awaits the fatal hemlock he discourses on immortality, still with the same calm reason that he had shown during his life. There is, he believes, an inner self in man, his divine part; this, being of the same nature as the divine, cannot die, and will dwell forever with the gods. But he will soon know. He shows no fear and no regrets. And so he drinks the hemlock; and by the manner of his dying he truly ensured his immortality on earth. For it was a turning point in the life of his pupil Plato, then a young man of about twenty-eight years of age.

Constructive philosophy—Idealism of Plato

The heart of Plato's teaching stems from the original conception of Socrates that the human being can know the good; and that, knowing it, he can do it. What Plato seeks to discover is *how* he can know it, and *what* it is exactly that he knows. And by using the dialogue form he shows us the whole process by which he arrived at his conclusions; hence the endless stimulation that Plato has afforded to all subsequent mankind. All that we must do is hitch up to his thought at one place, and either follow him to the same conclusions, or, by casting aside some of his thoughts as based on assumptions which we will not accept, proceed to arrive at different conclusions.

Assuming, then, that man can know the good, with what faculty does he know it, and what is the object of this faculty? To this Plato answers that man is possessed of the power of thinking (*Nous*), and that this spiritual element in man can recognize the spiritual element akin to it—the Idea. And this Idea is not in the physical world, but in the spiritual world, forever hidden from every faculty in man save the Nous. Following this thought further, he concludes that everything we see in front of us is a *particular*, a single example of something, the Idea or archetype of which is really spiritual, and not to be found on earth. We see, for instance, a single plant; but the Idea of the plant is in the spiritual world. From this it is but a short step to the value judgment that the earthly example is necessarily an inferior copy of the ideal plant—that the spiritual reality is more beautiful, more worthy of contemplation than anything on earth.

The next step is to consider how we can recognize this earthly copy as indeed a copy of an Idea. And to this Plato's answer is that the soul, with its active faculty, the Nous, existed before incarnation on earth in a human body. Before it descended to earth

it glimpsed these Ideas, which were implanted forever in the soul. Thus knowledge of the universal behind the particular appearance on earth is simply *recognition*. This, it will be seen, completely accounts for man's possession of innate knowledge, which Socrates had shown man did possess.

It is clear that this "idealist" philosophy gives an enormous scope to the philosopher. He is not compelled to examine the phenomena in front of him but may reason a priori; indeed, since it is only human thinking that can perceive the Ideas, there is no other method of reasoning than a priori. Thus by reasoning, the moral and political philosopher must try to discover for himself the ideal good, and not the practicable good.

The *Republic* is the Platonic masterpiece of this kind of reasoning. But by this it should not be thought that Plato had no practical ends in view. He tells us specifically that he has. No political state of which he has knowledge has been *thought* out; all are defective. But in his view these defects need not be inevitable. For if men know the good they will not deliberately prefer the evil unless they have been warped beyond cure. Since "virtue" may be taught, men can be educated to admire the best, and not choose a second-best polity to live in.

His method, then, is to discover what is the bond which holds society together (justice), and then try to arrive at a definition of justice. He comes to the conclusion that justice in the citizen and in the state is identical, and that if each man is given a position in the social order which enables him to do that for which he is best fitted, and he performs this task properly, then the ends of both the citizen and the state will be fully served, and the society will be a just one. Plato then proceeds to inquire into how human potentialities can best be realized in a social framework, and what will be the nature of the social institutions required.

Given his premises, the whole work, built up on these lines, is logically impeccable. Its value in all ages has been its suggestiveness, and the joy of following the thought of a truly creative mind, willing to pursue the argument wherever it will lead, without deference to conventional Greek notions, as, for instance, on the inequality of women. It is not native conservatism or a preference for oligarchy—though these may have been present, they are irrelevant—that forces him to the conclusion that the enlightened despotism of a board of professional guardians (philosopher kings and queens) is the only possible "best" government. These alone have been able to discover the good, and they must be dedicated utterly to its pursuit, without the warping of judgment which would arise from the possession of either material goods or family. With such a body of truly scientific professionals there would be no need for laws or for the exercise of power; for at all grades in the society each man would have received the education, and hold the position, for which he was best fitted.

It has often been pointed out, justly, that Plato makes a number of assumptions which are extremely questionable—for instance, that public and private virtue are identical, and that a state made up of good individuals will be able to function harmoniously as a state. But it will usually be found that these assumptions are the result of his fundamental belief that no one, knowing the good, would deliberately choose to do evil. If the state is a just one, its duties will be just and good; the individual, if he is good, will desire to do this duty. Duty and inclination must coincide. If they do not, then either the state needs to be corrected or the individual needs to be improved—by development and adjustment, not by repression and force.

Plato may also be accused of neglecting the psychology of man, as it *must* have been known to him from experience. What was the use of theorizing about an ideal state when he knew of its impossibility in real life? Again the answer must be that by showing men the ideal good which was, for him, having regard to his assumptions, not impossible of realization but only extremely difficult, he was pointing out a direction for the aspirations and endeavors of man. And that

it was not his last thought on the subject is shown by his later works, the *Statesman* and *Laws*, in which he outlines the "second-best state," the state ruled by laws, laws which are directed to the ethical improvement of man, but cannot be as scientifically impeccable as the personal guidance of the philosopher kings. And elsewhere he shows that he is not unaware of human psychology. He recognizes the irrational part of man, but does not consider it incurable. The desires are controlled by reason, which, in the light of its knowledge of the good, will give man the power of evaluating his desires at their true worth.

As with the state, so with man. The harmonious functioning of all the parts that go to make up the full man, this is self-realization under the guiding power of the Nous. It is a psychology the truth of which would be vehemently denied by both Christians and Freudians, who both deny the power of the mind to control the will unaided. Perhaps to these the psychology of Plato would seem naïve; but it was the fullest and most complete expression of the Greek ideal of harmony and *sophrosyne,* and of the Greek belief in the efficacy of human thinking. If it is a glorification of the one specifically human power, this to the Greeks would have been a recommendation. Oedipus to the Greeks was not a complex but a human being, proud and erring but undefeated; and they were glad to be considered of his company.

Philosophy becomes science—Aristotle

The universality of his genius—Aristotle was the son of a Chalcidian physician in the service of Philip of Macedon. He studied at the Academy of Plato and was unquestionably his most brilliant pupil. He was tutor of Alexander, son of Philip, for several years, returning to Athens and opening a school himself (the Lyceum), where he taught for twelve years. Forced into exile on the death of Alexander, he died a year later in 322 B.C. at the age of sixty-two.

Thus Aristotle stands at the end of the Classical Age of Greece before the great emigration to Asia that followed the conquests of Alexander; and in a very real sense he completed it. Though he left one or two things undone which were repaired by Theophrastus his pupil and successor (for instance, a work on plants and another on human character) and he contributed nothing to Greek mathematics, which followed an independent course, in other respects he took all the varied speculations of his Greek predecessors, brilliant and disorganized as they were, and by the giant force of his capacity for system, order, and classification, discharged them from his hands as sciences, a body of work that could be communicated to others in comprehensible form. Once he had laid down the principles of scientific inquiry, the work would not have to be done again. He was the first true scientist in the history of mankind; and few who have really studied his work would dispute his title to be the greatest the world has yet known. And now that we have passed beyond recovery into a world of specialists, there never will be anyone again who will be able to lay claim to the universality of his learning. Any one of half a dozen of his mental achievements would have entitled him to an undying fame. The sum total is almost beyond belief.

*The laws of thinking—Logic—*If this seem excessive praise, let us consider for a moment a few of Aristotle's achievements. Basing his observations upon Plato's theory of ideas, he formulated the laws of thinking, the relation between the universal and the particular, the formal procedure required for arriving at conclusions and correct reasoning, giving in passing a different solution to the problem of the origin of the universal. Disturbed by the way in which objects are described without including all their features, he formulated a method for describing them inclusively (the "categories of being"). Stimulated perhaps by Socrates' remark that he himself knew that his will prevented him from going into exile and not "his bones and sinews," as Anaxagoras would have claimed, he formulated a system for dealing accurately with causation and had to invent a

new vocabulary for the purpose. Faced with a mass of biological data, he evolved a system of classification into genus and species which has been followed with modifications ever since.

*The foundation for classification of phenomena—Genus and species—*Aristotle is usually praised in these days rather patronizingly for his excellent and careful observation and description of the animal world, and his early recognition of facts which modern science with its greater knowledge and improved instruments has shown to be true —as if anyone with the time and the patience could not observe correctly! And he has been criticized for premature guesses on the basis of insufficient information, for his doctrines of purpose, for his denial of the atomic theory, and in general for having held back medieval scientists from more correct theories while they elaborated on his incorrect ones instead. But insufficient attention has been paid to the gigantic mental effort required to create order out of chaos, and to make the world *intelligible*, which was his primary purpose. No one before his time had seen the need for a method of inquiry, or classification of knowledge. Philosophers had speculated, and looked for universal principles, every now and then carrying out a few desultory experiments but always jumping to theoretical conclusions of little value beyond their aesthetic appeal. But to watch Aristotle at work trying to determine how to deal with zoology with no previous guide, as in the first book of his *Parts of Animals,* is to see the enormous difficulties that faced him in the struggle to put the material in order; and to read any part of the *Metaphysics* is to realize his extraordinary ability to handle the most difficult abstractions of thought with the utmost delicacy and sureness—in which again he had no predecessor. Plato charms us because of his artistry and imagination, and because there is no word that we cannot understand, no thought that we cannot follow. He flatters our ignorance, making us believe we are not as ignorant as we are; in reading Plato we all imagine ourselves philosophers. But Aristotle is hard work, and he makes no concessions to us; even when we think we have grasped one of his thoughts it quickly eludes us again. Then suddenly it becomes clear and fruitful and applicable in a hundred other ways, and we possess a tool for understanding the world.

In following the Aristotelian method as we have all followed it since his time without acknowledgments, our work has been made easy. But it was not easy for him. He had first to invent the tools of analysis, and then with these to set to work on all the phenomena of knowledge available to the Greek world. Both parts of his work he largely accomplished. His nephew went with Alexander on his expedition, and Alexander himself sent back data that he thought would be of interest to his old tutor. His students collected material for him, and he analyzed and classified it, no doubt with their assistance. For his *Politics* he analyzed and digested the constitutions of 158 different states, this analysis enabling him to classify the different kinds of states on the basis of evidence. He viewed the plays of his own age and the tragic drama of the great era, and in his *Poetics* classified the results, together with his findings in general terms of the requirements of tragedy. He did the same thing for the animal world in his three great works in zoology, the *History of Animals, Parts of Animals,* and *Generation of Animals;* and so on. Certainly in some cases he generalized and theorized too soon; but only very rarely did he fail to offer good reasons for the theories and for his acute criticisms of his predecessors. And never did his analysis fail. His successors could have built always upon his foundations, and revised his theories when necessary.

Summary of work of Aristotle—His place in the history of thought—It was a tragedy that Aristotle of all men should have been regarded as an authority and the last word on any subject, he who was the most ready of all the ancient investigators to base his theories on the observed facts. And it is now the prevalent opinion that when at last the late medieval scholars did begin to work on

his findings at the University of Padua without accepting him as infallible, then they only had to revise his groundwork, and criticize some of his conclusions on the basis of their improved knowledge of the facts, and it was possible for Galileo, who studied at Padua, to lay the basis for modern science. Aristotle was not abandoned, save by the ignorant; but adapted, improved upon, and commented upon until at last he emerged as the great pioneer he was, but no longer "the master of those who know," which he was not.

If we examine the conclusions reached by Aristotle in all the numerous fields of inquiry to which he gave his attention, we shall find that they were almost always inspired by common sense, which has not been regarded as a useful tool in modern exact science with its powerful mathematics and instruments of research. Almost none of the findings of modern science, from the electron to the Copernican theory, from the physics of Einstein to the corpuscular-wave theory of light is validated by common sense or direct sense observation. For this reason Aristotle's conclusions in the physical sciences have to be interpreted very spaciously and charitably if they are to be in any way acceptable, while his conclusions in the social sciences may be as valid as in the days they were written.

Both Plato and Aristotle had an advantage over later thinkers in that the known world was small, and the whole range of knowledge was not very great. So it was still possible for one man to try to encompass it. Frequently throughout the work of Aristotle we find him making the statement that any science or art ought to cover the whole of a subject; and it is true that he makes the attempt. But not only this; he tries also to cover the whole of *all* subjects, using his key of logical analysis and systematic organization. This no successor has ever been able to do, and few have tried—though, as we shall see, it was the aim of Roger Bacon in medieval times. But even he did not find it necessary to go over a subject again once Aristotle had "completed" it; though toward the end of Bacon's life he suggested that a corps of specialists should be organized for the purpose of producing the necessary compendium. It is certain that no single person will ever try again.

This work of Aristotle was therefore unique, a last and most complete expression of the Greek desire for an orderly and harmonious whole, one of the greatest intellectual monuments in the history of mankind. If the highest praise is to be given, let us say that his work is worthy of the Greek genius.

▶ Influence of Greek thought—
Significance of Greek search
for new truth

The great thinkers dealt with so far have occupied so much of the space in this chapter because they were the men whose thoughts provided the substratum for all the thinking of later Western man. The revolution ushered in by the Sophists has never been completed and perhaps never will be. At times, especially in the Middle Ages, men have preferred to take the traditional religiously inspired picture of the world as true and have not questioned its validity. This attitude has seldom led to new knowledge. The attitude of resignation in the face of divine will has sometimes prevailed in Western civilization, but always to the detriment of scientific inquiry. It might be more comfortable and give greater security to the individual to live in a world in which everything is known, and knowledge is contemplated, not enlarged; but such a world would be static. The world of the Sophists, in which one idea is as good as another, is a difficult world to live in, and it cannot be long endured. But the answer may well be that we need another Socrates to help us seek out the good, rather than despairing of finding it and resigning ourselves to the ethical nihilism which too often appears to present the only alternative to the acceptance of the teachings of tradition. The Greeks were the first to escape from the bonds imposed by their ancestors and strike out on a new path, the

end of which could not and cannot now be seen. It is this above all that is meant by the Greek spirit. Greek art, perfect in its way as it is, has only been imitated by the West, copied but not equaled. For though we have inherited the Greek view of life and carried it on with our own genius to new realms unsuspected by the Greeks, the Greek feeling for man as a union of soul and body in equilibrium was peculiar to themselves, and we of the West can only dimly sense this view when we touch the few authentic masterpieces that have been preserved to us, and wonder at their perfection.

▶ Greek Art

ART AS EXPRESSION OF THE GREEK SPIRIT

We have remarked earlier that the Greek ideal was *sophrosyne,* or moderation, although as a people the Greeks markedly lacked this virtue. In the realm of art, however, their search was not doomed to the same failure as in the necessarily imperfect world in which they had to live, and their volatile passions could not be involved in this ideal world as deeply as in the political world of live men and women. In art man is a creator. His materials are at hand but as yet without form. It is for the artist to give form to them. The soul, in Greek thought, is the *form* of the body; it shapes the inchoate mass, the mere raw physical material which decays at death into its original primal matter. So, for the Greek artist, the task is to give form to matter, to give it a soul which makes it live. And it is a curious feature of Greek above all other art that this illusion of life is indeed given to the dead material, marble. This feature can be perceived best in Greek sculpture, but even the Greek temple does not seem to be altogether dead. We can analyze these temples and see that by such and such technical means certain illusions were created, but the miracle remains, and we have not been able to achieve the same results, even with our greatly advanced technical ingenuity.

The Greeks of the Classical Age did not

Model of the Parthenon, now a semi-ruin, constructed by The Metropolitan Museum of Art. Note the Doric columns. (COURTESY THE METROPOLITAN MUSEUM OF ART)

Church of La Madeleine (Paris), constructed in the reign of Napoleon I, showing the persistent copying of Greek design. Clearly this church is modeled after the Parthenon, though Corinthian—more ornate—columns were preferred.

think of art as useful, nor did they set out to create self-consciously something "artistic." Indeed they did not possess a word for what we speak of as "artistic." Their only word for art was *techne*, which means craft. Every product of the Classical Age in Greece is, by our standards, artistic; form and substance are united in a harmony that can be recognized at once. Form is given to the material in accordance with the nature of the material and the purpose for which the object is to be used. This quality seems to have been an almost instinctive achievement of the Greek craftsman; and though it is very possible that the barbarian princes and Persian nobles who often bought these works did not appreciate what they had acquired, it would have been impossible, working in the Greek artistic tradition, for the craftsman to have made a shoddy and inferior product, even for barbarians.

The same honesty is observed when we consider the temples. The most famous of Greek temples, the Parthenon at Athens, was filled with sculptures that could never be seen by mortal eye, high up in the part of the temple where the statue of the goddess Athena was housed. Yet this sculpture was as honestly and truly wrought as anything in the visible parts of the temple. The building of a temple was the highlight in the life of the Athenian craftsman. We know that Greek artisans all received the same low wage each day they were at work for the city, just enough to maintain their wives and families for that one day. It was considered the highest honor to work for the polis; even those who scorned private employment as unworthy of free men welcomed the opportunity. The temple was a home for the god to whom it was dedicated and whose statue inhabited it. The god thus honored gave protection to the city. The great temple of the Erechtheum at Athens was completed in the darkest days of the Peloponnesian War, with resources which the city could ill spare. Thus the Greek craftsmen, like the medieval craftsmen who built the Gothic cathedrals as an expression both of civic pride and of their devotion to God, gave the best that was in them with complete honesty. The result is what no man would deny as being true art.

Two slabs from the Parthenon frieze known as the Elgin marbles after the English lord who carried them off to England. Note the mastery of the riders in the Panathenaic procession, and the absence of any sense of the strain which is noticeable in some of the realistic sculpture of the Hellenistic Age shown on later pages. The riders are caught in a moment of eternity rather than individualized as riders taking part in one particular procession at one particular moment. The frieze was designed by Phidias and carried out at his direction though by different craftsmen. (COURTESY BRITISH MUSEUM)

The famous Hermes of Praxiteles, the only almost complete statue extant from the fourth century B.C. Note how the god is given truly human features, which should be contrasted with the less differentiated features of the participants in the Panathenaic procession shown in the Parthenon frieze (Elgin marbles).

Marble relief of a Maenad. Classical period, fifth century B.C. (COURTESY THE METROPOLITAN MUSEUM OF ART)

ARCHITECTURE AND SCULPTURE

The Greek temple is not an imposing building from the point of view of size, and it makes use of the simplest structural forms known to man. Essentially it was composed of the *cella*, a rectangular chamber, the dwelling place of the statue of the god; the columns surrounding the cella and forming a porch; the lintel which rested on the columns and supported the roof; the gabled roof itself; and the pediment, the triangular section under the roof. The style of the temple is determined by the column. Three types were used by the Greek architects:

Doric, Ionic, and Corinthian, though the last named was too ornate for classical Greek taste and came into use only after the expansion of Greece into the Oriental world. In the sculpture of the age of Pericles, the era of the Parthenon, the Greek ideal of man as a harmony of body and soul was brought to perfection. The figures in the Parthenon friezes were ideal figures, perfectly proportioned. There is no striving after effect; each muscle is perfectly rendered, whether in tension or repose. The effect is one of dignity and restrained movement. The horses are prancing, the young riders are in perfect control; a moment appears to have been captured in stone, not an event but a moment of eternity, as if the riders will go on prancing and the young riders will sit their horses forever.

Yet a word of warning should be given. All Greek sculptures were painted, and what we now see in the whiteness of marble must have looked utterly different in classical times, so that it is hard for us to imagine either the Parthenon or the city of Athens as they appeared to the Greeks who lived there, with statues on every corner gleaming and shining in full color in the Greek sunlight. We may think it crude of the Greeks to disguise and embellish their lovely masterpieces, which needed no such adornment.

But this is the way the Greeks were, and who are we to criticize them? Can we be so sure that we have learned sophrosyne?

▶ The expansion of Greece—The Hellenistic Age

RISE OF PHILIP OF MACEDON

We have briefly alluded earlier in this chapter to the Greek loss of independence to Philip of Macedon. This remarkable monarch came to the throne of his semibarbaric

GREECE
AT TIME OF
CONQUEST BY PHILIP
338 B.C.

→ Campaign of Philip

★ Battle
◉ Capital

0   25   75
Miles

country in 359 B.C. He built himself a small but powerful army, which he trained in new military tactics; he financed his operations by the acquisition of some gold mines through a piece of cunning manipulation; and then he set out to use these assets to conquer all Greece. He never fought a battle if he could win by diplomatic means what he needed, but he was not hesitant to use his army when it appeared to be the best means of achieving his goals. He recognized the venality and poverty of the Greek poleis of his day and their ruling politicians. He did not scruple to buy their support and sow as much discord as he could among the cities. Demosthenes, the Athenian statesman, was aware of the danger to Greek liberties early in Philip's career, and did his best to rouse the Athenians from their fatal torpor. But he was only partially successful. The aid given to threatened cities that should have been Athenian allies was always too inconsequential to save them. Thebes, the leading power of Greece, always thought that Philip was her friend until the last moment when it was too late. So by piecemeal conquest Philip made himself the master of Greece and achieved a final decisive victory on the battlefield of Chaeronea in 338 B.C. His terms, except for Thebes, were light. He aimed at conquest of Asia; Greece was to be for him only the first step. He desired to go to Asia as the chosen leader of the Greek people, whether they supported him with arms or not. But before he could organize the Asiatic expedition Philip was murdered. He was succeeded by his son, known to history as Alexander the Great.

THE CONQUESTS OF ALEXANDER THE GREAT
(336–323 B.C.)

The military career of Alexander is the most astonishing in all history. He rapidly quelled a revolt in Greece which marked the beginning of his reign, then organized for himself the expedition that his father had planned. Meagerly financed, and hardly supported at all by the Greek cities, which hoped for his speedy defeat and their own liberation from Macedonian rule, he nevertheless succeeded in destroying the huge Persian Empire and succeeding to its rule. He added Egypt to his possessions without more than token fighting. He advanced into India and defeated an army that included elephants, which he had never seen before. Improvising tactics and policy as he went along, never at a loss for an expedient, possessed of a personality that overawed the toughest of generals and quelled incipient revolt among his followers when they objected to his policy of fraternization with Persians after their defeat, and yet singularly lacking in sophrosyne in spite of a personal education at the hands of Aristotle, Alexander and his life and works became legendary soon after his early death. Even now books about him pour from the press and movies celebrate his deeds. For the purposes of this history it is enough to say that the world was altogether changed by his work. Of no other man can it be said with equal justice that he laid his mark upon all the civilizations that followed him in the lands where he had fought, and upon all those civilizations to the West which in turn took over from them.

Alexander's original purpose was to avenge the expedition of Xerxes. This duly accomplished by the defeat and death of the Persian monarch, he then proceeded to invite immigration from Greece and to become himself the Great King of Persia. As Persian king it was his duty to care for his Persian subjects as for his Macedonians. He thus took Persian nobles into his service, and encouraged intermarriage between Greeks and Persians. Though he roused opposition amongst his Macedonians, who felt they should have been specially privileged, his policy prevailed. He founded cities throughout the newly conquered lands, and imported Greek institutions suitable for the polis, which, as he had no doubt been instructed by Aristotle, was the most perfect form of social entity. And, once the initial distrust had worn off, the immigrants from poor overpopulated Greece began to pour into the country, giving the rather outclassed Persians a dose of Greek efficiency which galvanized the ancient Orient into unaccustomed life.

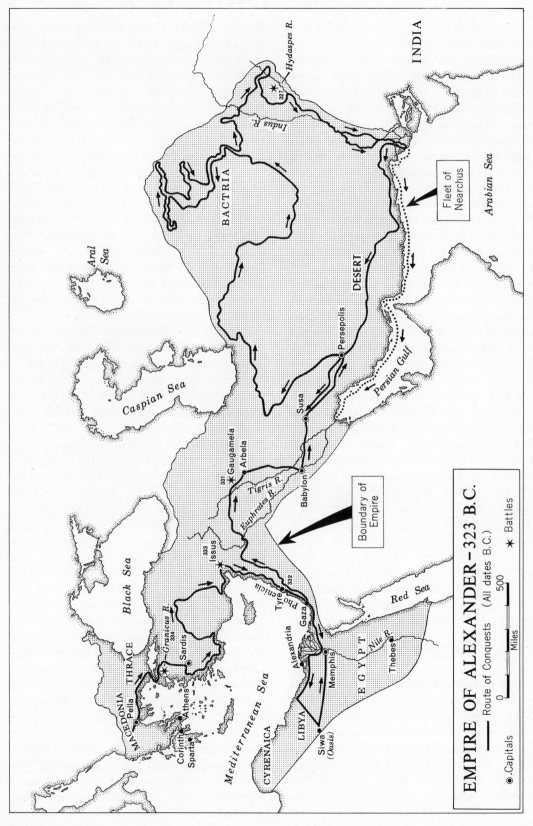

EMPIRE OF ALEXANDER – 323 B.C.

—— Route of Conquests   (All dates B.C.)

● .Capitals   ★ Battles

Fleet of Nearchus

Boundary of Empire

INDIA

Arabian Sea

Hydaspes R.

Indus R.

BACTRIA

DESERT

Persian Gulf

Aral Sea

Caspian Sea

Persepolis

Susa

Gaugamela

Arbela

Tigris R.

Euphrates R.

Babylon

331

Black Sea

Issus

333

Granicus R.

334

Sardis

MACEDONIA

Pella

THRACE

Corinth

Athens

Sparta

Mediterranean Sea

CYRENAICA

LIBYA

Siwa
(Oasis)

Alexandria

Gaza

Tyre

332

Phoenicia

EGYPT

Memphis

Nile R.

Thebes

Red Sea

Miles

0   500

THE SUCCESSORS OF ALEXANDER

Alexander died at the early age of thirty-three, and his generals struggled for the succession. After thirty years of civil war amongst the generals the territory was finally divided amongst the survivors. Ptolemy Soter took Egypt, the prize of the empire, though not the largest section; Seleucus took most of the Asiatic mainland, leaving a small but prosperous kingdom in Asia Minor for Attalus; while Greece and Macedonia fell to a general named Antigonus. The mainland of Greece, from having been overpopulated, now was denuded of its most enterprising sons, and its history need concern us no further. Egypt became a model of efficient government and expanding economic activity under monarchs who fully appreciated and exploited the old fiction that the Pharaoh of Egypt owned all the land and that all his subjects were royal tenants. The Seleucid monarchs in Asia were faced with many minor wars, but on the whole were able to make of their empire a fairly efficient unit, and pursued a cultural policy based directly upon the original plans of Alexander. Pergamum in northern Asia Minor became a prosperous commercial state noted for the fine buildings, palaces, and temples paid for by royal bounty and the enterprise of individual merchants.

THE HELLENISTIC AGE—MINGLING OF GREEK AND ORIENTAL

The age that followed the death of Alexander is called the Hellenistic Age, as distinct from the earlier Hellenic Age, prior to the conquests, when the center of culture was on the mainland. The Hellenistic period is marked especially by a mingling for the first time of Greek and Oriental culture. To this the Orientals contributed primarily their religions, while the Greeks contributed their philosophy. Within the new cities, populated for the most part by immigrant Greeks, some of the forms of the old polis were maintained. The governments were made up of assemblies and councils as in Athens; but full self-government and freedom to act could not be

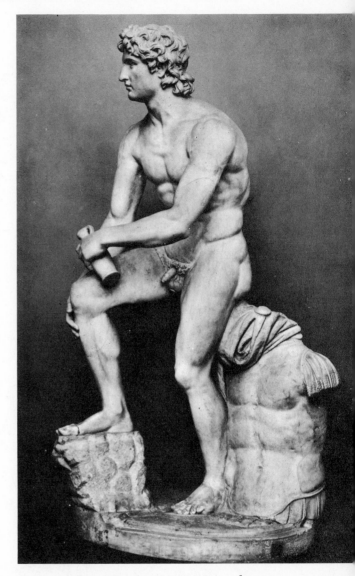

Statue of Alexander the Great, artist unknown.

granted to them since foreign policy necessarily remained in the hands of the monarchs. Thus to a large extent the forms were a façade. But not altogether; for the most part the cities possessed at least a kind of municipal self-government, a tradition which was of great value to the Romans when they incorporated this part of the world into their own empire. Persians in the Seleucid Empire were able to participate in the new culture and contributed to it. The Greek language prevailed, though no longer so pure as in the days of Pericles. All the educated classes

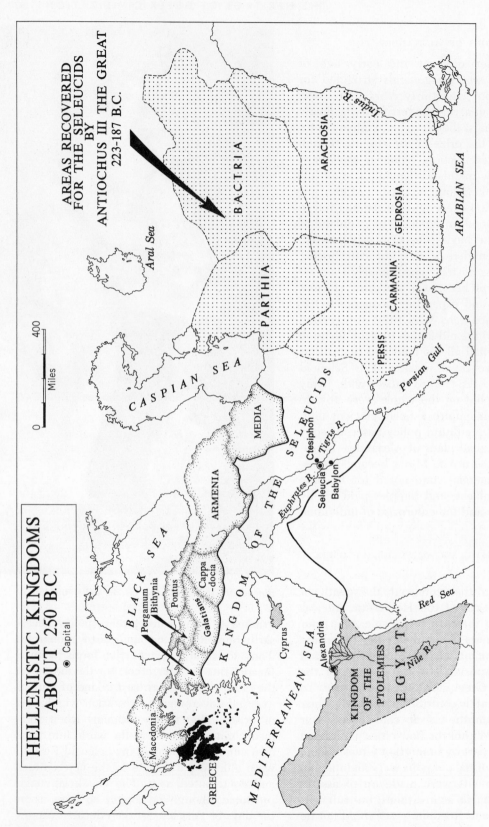

HELLENISTIC KINGDOMS
ABOUT 250 B.C.

◉ Capital

AREAS RECOVERED
FOR THE SELEUCIDS
BY
ANTIOCHUS III THE GREAT
223-187 B.C.

400

Miles

0

CASPIAN SEA

Aral Sea

BACTRIA

PARTHIA

ARACHOSIA

Indus R.

GEDROSIA

CARMANIA

PERSIS

ARABIAN SEA

Persian Gulf

MEDIA

ARMENIA

SELEUCIDS

Tigris R.

Ctesiphon

Babylon

Euphrates R.

Seleucia

OF THE

KINGDOM

Pergamum

Bithynia

Pontus

Cappa-docia

Galatians

BLACK SEA

Macedonia

GREECE

MEDITERRANEAN SEA

Cyprus

Red Sea

Alexandria

KINGDOM
OF THE
PTOLEMIES

EGYPT

Nile R.

Ruins of the temple of Zeus at Pergamum as they appear at the present time. The size of the ruins will give some indication of the scale of the work of the Hellenistic monarchs of this commercial state. (COURTESY TURKISH INFORMATION OFFICE)

could speak the *koine,* as it was called, the common tongue of the wider *koinon* or community of the Hellenes which composed the whole Hellenistic world.

On the whole it was a prosperous world. The Greeks on the mainland had always been fertile in inventions and expedients. They had invented many financial tools which could now be put to use in a land where there was wide scope for them. But there was far more slavery than in the Hellenic Age, and while there were more rich men there were also far more poor ones. Moreover, the ancient security of the polis had been entirely lost. Socrates would have felt completely out of place in a Hellenistic city. No one would have known him, no one would have had time to talk. Each man had to look after his business or be defeated by a competitor; no age of the ancient world so much resembles ours as the Hellenistic

Age. The result was that a great many of the immigrant Greeks felt they had lost their roots. No imitation polis in Asia could take the place of the old, secure polis, where everyone had status as a citizen and everyone participated in government and held all the responsibilities of the active participator with his full share of responsibility. Cosmopolitanism (the world-polis) could exercise no hold upon his heart and mind. So all men had to become individualists, seek to make what they could for themselves. The Sophist teaching at last came to full fruition. Each man was an individual, he had to look after his own interests first, and leave the government to Ptolemy or Seleucus.

HELLENISTIC PHILOSOPHIES—INDIVIDUALISM

In a world where not all men could succeed, it was not surprising that there should be a marked growth of religions.

Since these will be dealt with at the beginning of the more detailed chapter on Christianity, nothing need be said of them here save that they no doubt performed an important function of giving hope in a better world to those who could not succeed in this. A similar function was performed by the new individualistic philosophies that are characteristic of the Hellenistic Age. Stoicism, Epicurism, even Cynicism, all stem from the desire to attain what the Greeks called *ataraxia*, or a state of "being unmoved," an inner tranquillity of soul. The Cynics scoffed at worldly wealth and tried to acquire wisdom, this wisdom to consist primarily in the understanding of the uselessness of possessions. The typical early Cynic was Diogenes, who lived in a tub and cultivated rudeness and self-sufficiency. The movement, obviously not designed to attract a numerous following, was largely absorbed in the long-lasting and extremely important philosophy of Stoicism, which grew in scope as the centuries passed, much of it being woven into Christian ethics and much into Roman law. The purpose of the Stoic is to become indifferent to all earthly joys and pleasures, not to care whether success is attained or not, and to rest secure in the consciousness of one's own rectitude and obey only one's conscience. There is a Divine Reason which rules in the world, and man also shares in this reason. All men are equal in their ability to discover and obey the dictates of reason; there is no natural inequality, but all men are equally doomed to suffering and all are equally able to rise above it by cultivating the life of the soul and reason. Stoics therefore were the first Greeks to speak out against slavery; and it is an interesting fact that the two best-known Stoic writers, both remembered long after the Hellenistic world had been replaced by the Roman Empire, are Marcus Aurelius the Roman emperor, and Epictetus, born a crippled slave.

Epicurism was likewise an attempt to deal with the conditions of the Hellenistic world. Do not strive for success, said the Epicureans, for it is unlikely to be attained, and desiring what cannot be attained leads to unhappiness. The goal of the Epicurean was happiness, but happiness attained by simple pleasures and curtailing the desire for more. Epicurus himself lived a simple life, eating frugally and gently discoursing on philosophy with his disciples. He believed in the atomic theory of Democritus and that the gods, if they exist, play no part in the affairs of men but dwell peacefully at ease in some remote part of the universe. The affairs of men are ruled by chance and the fact might as well be accepted. The conclusion was that one should make the most of life as it is and not seek to change it by excessive (and unsuccessful) activity. It is ironical that the philosophy of Epicurus, who himself taught a gentle asceticism, should have been so transformed by the Romans that the word Epicurean, in Roman as in our own time, should have been associated primarily with gluttony—although it must be admitted that a purely hedonistic philosophy is capable of this transformation. Epicurus may have said "eat, drink, and be merry, for tomorrow we die"; but it was always possible to forget the last four words and leave the first five naked.

HELLENISTIC SCIENCE

The Hellenistic world is noted for its science, the first really practical science attained by the Greeks. The occasion for study was provided for them above all by the Museum of Alexandria, a great research center founded by the Ptolemies and maintained by them with funds gained through the successful management of the estate of Egypt. Here scholars of all kinds were subsidized. Their work did not have to be useful so long as it redounded to the prestige of their master. Here the works of the great literary masters of the mainland were edited and their manuscripts multiplied. Here the Greek astronomers met with the vast records of astronomical data collected in previous centuries by the Babylonian priests and astrologers. Faced with such data the Greek theorists soon began to explain, whereas the Babylonians had been content to record and use for astrological purposes. Hipparchus discovered (or possibly restated the Chaldean theory of) the precession of the equinoxes, and was able to explain satisfactorily all the known data on the supposed movement of the sun around the earth and to predict correctly on the basis of his theories. Here Aristarchus propounded the opposite theory that the earth moved around the sun but was unable to convince his contemporaries. Here Euclid and Archimedes worked as mathematicians, and Eratosthenes calculated the diameter of the earth. Finally Hero explained the vacuum and invented a machine using the principles later incorporated in the modern steam engine. Medicine also was not neglected, the theories of the earlier Hippocrates, father of secular medicine, being studied and carried further. The great library of Alexandria, containing more than half a million books, was unique in that age and for more than fifteen hundred years afterward.

HELLENISTIC ART—NEW REALISM

Finally, a word should be said on Hellenistic art. The tendency in Hellenistic architecture was away from classical simplicity. The buildings were larger and the columns more ornate, with the Corinthian coming into fashion toward the end of the epoch. Hellenistic sculpture tended toward realism. There was no loss of technical ability, but there is sometimes, as in the "Laocoön," a rather marked straining after effect. A dying Gaul with blood flowing, and a market woman straining under her heavy burden, are well-known works of this age. But so also is the perfect "Aphrodite" of Melos, and the "Winged Victory" of Samothrace, suggestive of movement in every line, and far removed indeed from the rather static splendor of the Parthenon friezes. There was a great growth of portrait sculpture, for it is clear that art had now, like

Goddess Aphrodite of Hellenistic period discovered at Smyrna. The statue was broken when found, but most of the parts were retrieved and assembled as shown here.
(COURTESY TURKISH INFORMATION OFFICE)

Opinion has varied remarkably at different times on the merits of the Laocoön, a late Hellenistic group showing the priest Laocoön and his two sons grappling with snakes. The impression of strain and power has appealed to many as one of the finest expressions of Hellenistic realism, while others have found the whole composition theatrical and forced and, from the Greek point of view, "bad art."

The Nike (Victory) of Samothrace, a statue (now in the Louvre) in the form of the prow of a ship. Note how the Nike suggests speed and movement, unlike the static figures of the Parthenon. (COURTESY THE LOUVRE)

The Aphrodite of Melos (so called because the statue was discovered on the island of Melos) is widely regarded as the finest statue of a woman ever made. The artist is unknown, but the figure probably dates from the second century B.C. No photograph can do justice to this masterpiece. Located in the Louvre, it is displayed to perfection—especially at night, when it is most effectively lighted. (COURTESY THE LOUVRE)

Hellenistic realism. This statue of an old market woman, discovered at Rome, dates from the second century B.C. and was perhaps looted from Greece by the Romans. (COURTESY THE METROPOLITAN MUSEUM OF ART)

everything else, become a business, and Greek artists had to find their patrons apart from the polis.

▶ Summary—Greek influence on subsequent Roman civilization

When the Hellenistic world was conquered by the Romans, in a very real sense it may be said that the Greeks made a cultural conquest of Rome at the same time. It was contact with the Greek cities of southern Italy that inspired the first Roman poetry and the first Roman art; and the Near East was always both the most prosperous and the most highly cultured part of the Roman Empire. The second language of every culti-

vated Roman was Greek, and Greek rather than Latin was spoken in all the eastern domains of Rome. But the Hellenistic world did not and could not supply good government to the peoples of the East, and they did not enforce peace. So when the unified Romans, with their distinctive gifts in the fields of government and law, were forced into contact with the Greeks of the Hellenistic world through the never-ending internecine squabbles of their rulers, their policy of divide and rule was made to order. They conquered this world by force and diplomacy. But they did not Latinize it. It remained Greek, and became Greek in government again with the fall of Rome. Not until the Muslims took over the Near East in the seventh century A.D. was Greek influence ousted. And even then the Muslims took over much of Greek thought, ultimately transmitting it to a revived Western civilization. But this story will be told in a later chapter.

▶ Suggestions for further reading

On the Aegean civilization undoubtedly the most comprehensive work is still G. Glotz, *The Aegean Civilization* (New York: Alfred A. Knopf, Inc., 1925), although in detail some of Glotz's views are no longer acceptable. A. R. Burn, *Minoans, Philistines, and Greeks* (New York: Alfred A. Knopf, Inc., 1930), is an interesting attempt to write a chronological history of the Aegean world from records available in 1930, and is certainly a fair summary of the work done by archaeologists up to that time. The book, however, is also an illustration of the difficulties inherent in the writing of any history without access to contemporary written records. Sometimes Burn blandly assumes the truth of highly disputed hypotheses and states them as facts without mentioning that they are hypotheses. The coming decipherment of Cretan records, now confidently hoped for, may make all these earlier books obsolete. But meanwhile Burn is still worth reading, if only for the attempted synthesis of legendary, semimythical, and archaeological material.

The best account of Minoan art is probably J. D. S. Pendlebury, *The Archaeology of Crete* (London: Methuen & Co., Ltd., 1939), which is well illustrated, though somewhat technical for the general reader.

In studying classical Greek civilization there is no substitute for the reading of as many Greek works as possible in translation, and secondary sources should always take second place to the Greek writers themselves. Some useful works of interpretation will be suggested in this and the following chapters, but attention will also be drawn to those translations which seem best fitted for the student. In reading Homer, one should remember that the *Iliad* and the *Odyssey* are magnificent heroic poems; and I am unsympathetic to the modern tendency to be observed, for instance, in the Penguin and Mentor editions destined for a large public, to treat them as if they were merely tales, almost the equivalent of modern novels. On the other hand, self-consciously archaic language goes to the other extreme and is often irritating to the modern student. My personal choice, as the most satisfactory verse translation of the *Iliad,* is R. Lattimore, *The Iliad* (Chicago: The University of Chicago Press, 1951) and an excellent recent translation in prose is A. H. Chase and W. G. Perry, Jr., *The Iliad* (Boston: Little, Brown & Co., 1950). For the *Odyssey* the student may select any that suits his fancy; I will make no recommendation.

In general, the translations published in the Loeb Classical Library (Cambridge, Mass.: Harvard University Press) are the most accurate and reliable, though they are sometimes pedestrian. All classical Greek works are available in this series, though of course other editions exist. New translations of Herodotus and Thucydides have recently appeared in the Penguin Classics series, which are both modern in diction and, as far as I have checked, accurate. These are almost certain to supersede the older nineteenth-century translations, which were difficult to read: Herodotus, *The Persian Wars,* tr. Aubrey de Selincourt, and Thucydides, *The Peloponnesian War,* tr. Rex Warner (Harmondsworth, Middlesex: Penguin Books, 1954). These works, written in prose, do not suffer so much as the *Iliad* and *Odyssey* from colloquialism. For the understanding of material in this chapter the treatise of the aristocrat known as the Old Oligarch should be read. It is to be found in G. W. Botsford and E. G. Sihler, *Hellenic Civilization* (New York: Columbia University Press, 1915), pp. 222–239, although the nineteenth-century translation, even when revised by Sihler, leaves a good deal to be desired in certain places and is distinguished by excessive and unnecessary circumlocution. Some of the biographies of Plutarch should also be read, especially those of Themistocles, Pericles, Cimon, Alcibiades, Aristides, and Nicias. Aristotle, *Constitution of Athens* (tr. K. von Fritz and E. Kapp; New York: Hafner Publishing Co., 1950), is a succinct account by the great philosopher of the political history of Athens, and should not be missed.

Two classics among the secondary sources are G. L. Dickinson, *The Greek View of Life* (22nd ed.; London: Methuen & Co., Ltd., 1949), and A. Zimmern, *The Greek Commonwealth* (5th ed., rev.; Oxford: The Clarendon Press, 1931), though both are perhaps excessively favorable to the Athenians. Zimmern contains a great deal of important economic and financial material not easily found elsewhere, though a more strictly economic work of considerable merit is J. Toutain, *The Economic Life of the Ancient World* (New York: Alfred A. Knopf, Inc., 1930). A very good short survey of Greek life, which includes a specially interesting section on women in Athens, is H. D. F. Kitto, *The Greeks* (Harmondsworth, Middlesex: Penguin Books, 1951). A suitable antidote for the general praise of the Athenians prevalent in most books may be gained by examining the section on freedom and tyranny in the ancient world, written by the present author in K. Setton and H. Winkler, eds., *Great Problems in European Civilization* (Englewood Cliffs, N. J.: Prentice-Hall, Inc., 1954), Chapter 1, in which differing opinions of both ancient and modern authors are placed side by side. The chapter on the Athenians in F. D. Marsh, *Modern Problems in the Ancient World* (Austin, Texas: The University of Texas Press, 1943), may also be profitably examined, as also the classic study of Greek imperialism, W. S. Ferguson, *Greek Imperialism* (Boston: Houghton Mifflin Company, 1913). Comprehensive studies of the Greek city are G. Glotz's two works, *The Greek City* (New York: Alfred A. Knopf, Inc., 1930) and *Ancient Greece at Work* (New York: Alfred A. Knopf, Inc., 1936). A brilliant study of Sparta as the classic case of an arrested civilization is to be found in A. Toynbee, *A Study of History* (London: Oxford University Press, 1935), III, 50–79. The primary sources upon which all studies of Sparta are based are Xenophon, *Constitution of the Lacedaemonians,* and Plutarch, *Lycurgus,* which may be read in any edition available.

On the conquests of Alexander, Plutarch's Life of Alexander is worth reading, in spite of the invariable moralist's bias in this author's work. But the best primary source is Arrian, whose work is to be found in F. R. B. Godolphin, ed., *The Greek Historians* (New York: Random House, Inc., 1942). Biographies of Alexander are numerous. Most of them, if not all, are to a greater or lesser degree marred by the particular prejudices of their authors. This is natural in the case of such a romantic figure about whose inner thought we really know almost nothing. C. A. Robinson, Jr., *Alexander the Great* (New York: E. P. Dutton & Co., Inc., 1947), is certainly not free from visible defects, and some of the author's assumptions are not really to be sustained by the evidence; but on the whole it is a simply written, well-balanced work by a fine classical scholar, and is to be recommended. A thoughtful study of Macedonian imperialism is to be found in P. Jouguet, *Macedonian Imperialism and the Hellenization of the East* (New York: Alfred A. Knopf, Inc., 1928).

There are two really outstanding studies of the Hellenistic world which should be attempted by any students interested in this crucial period of history. These are M. I. Rostovtzeff, *Social and Economic History of the Hellenistic World,* a long but well-written study which is not as formidable as it looks (Oxford: The Clarendon Press, 1941), Vols. 1 and 2, and W. W. Tarn, *Hellenistic Civilization* (3rd ed.; London: Edward Arnold & Co., 1952). At the other extreme from these two detailed studies is the masterly brief exposition of the nature of Hellenistic civilization by W. L. Westermann in *Encyclopaedia of the Social Sciences* (New York: The Macmillan Company, 1930), I, 31–41.

In the field of Greek cultural and intellectual history there is such a wealth of material available that I am necessarily reduced to offering a number of collections where the student may pick and choose for himself according to his interests, and to mentioning a few secondary works which proved of special interest to me and provide good introductions to the vast subject. Strongly recommended are T. F. Higham and C. M. Bowra, eds., *The Oxford Book of Greek Verse in Translation* (Oxford: The Clarendon Press, 1938), and W. J. Oates and Eugene O'Neill, Jr., eds., *The Complete Greek Drama* (2 vols.; New York: Random House, 1938). The introduction to the latter volume by O'Neill is especially valuable. F. R. B. Godolphin, ed., *The*

Greek Historians (2 vols.; New York: Random House, Inc., 1942), is a comprehensive work, but the Penguin translations of Herodotus and Thucydides referred to earlier may be preferred. M. C. Nahm, ed., *Selections from Early Greek Philosophy* (3rd ed.; New York: Appleton-Century-Crofts, Inc., 1947), with a useful introduction by the editor, collects in one volume a substantial number of the fragments of the writings of the pre-Socratic philosophers which are difficult to find together elsewhere in English. Until very recently the most easily available complete translation of the works of Plato, that of Benjamin Jowett, led many students astray in their attempts to understand exactly what Plato had said. In spite of the real excellence of Jowett's work as a whole, much fault could be found in detail. Now, however, a new edition of Jowett's work has just been issued, substantially revised where necessary by a number of distinguished scholars. This new edition, B. Jowett, *The Dialogues of Plato,* revised by D. J. Allan and H. E. Dale (4 vols.; Oxford: The Clarendon Press, 1953), should certainly be used when available. The standard edition of the works of Aristotle, on which most other editions have been based, is that of W. D. Ross, who also edited an abridged version for students, *The Student's Oxford Aristotle* (6 vols.; London: Oxford University Press, 1942). There are many convenient anthologies containing some of the more important works of Aristotle. Among the most useful is R. McKeon, ed., *Introduction to Aristotle* (New York: The Modern Library, 1947).

On Greek tragedy, contrary to much modern opinion, I am inclined, as may have been noticed, toward the view of Nietzsche, which emphasizes the relation of tragedy to Greek religion, and I regard it as having been destroyed by the rationalism of the Sophists. This view has been eloquently expounded in Nietzsche's *The Birth of Tragedy,* which is excellently translated by Clifton Fadiman, in C. Fadiman, ed., *The Philosophy of Nietzsche* (New York: The Modern Library, 1927). For a careful analysis of the extant plays, with a standpoint differing substantially from mine, the reader is referred to H. D. F. Kitto, *Greek Tragedy* (Garden City, N.Y.: Doubleday & Co., Inc., 1954), an Anchor book. A well-organized history of philosophy which gives, on the whole, a very fair summary of all Greek thought is W. T. Jones, *A History of Western Philosophy* (New York: Harcourt, Brace

& Co., 1952), Vol. 1. An evaluation of Greek thought, paying special attention to the problems with which Greek thinkers were wrestling, which has always seemed to me to be one of the very best books of its kind, is J. M. Warbeke, *The Searching Mind of Greece* (New York: Appleton-Century-Crofts, Inc., 1930). A fine, though highly controversial, criticism of Thucydides as a prose tragedian is the old classic, F. M. Cornford, *Thucydides Mythistoricus* (London: Edward Arnold & Co., 1907). A vivid and easily available picture of Hellenic culture is provided in Edith Hamilton, *The Greek Way to Western Civilization* (New York: The New American Library of World Literature, Inc., 1948). On political theory a very convenient and thoughtful summary is given in the first six chapters of G. H. Sabine, *A History of Political Theory* (New York: Henry Holt & Co., 1937). Another good summary of the special nature of the Greek contribution to the history of thought, emphasizing its relation to the Hebrew thinkers and Roman and Christian thinkers, including also a few pages on the Hellenistic contribution, is to be found in the Pelican book already recommended at the end of Chapter 3, W. G. De Burgh, *The Legacy of the Ancient World* (Harmondsworth, Middlesex: Penguin Books, 1953), I, 96–224. The extant writings of Stoic and Epicurean philosophers may be read in W. J. Oates, ed., *The Stoic and Epicurean Philosophers* (New York: Random House, Inc., 1940). The political thought of the Stoics is dealt with in a thoughtful and convincing manner in G. H. Sabine, *A History of Political Theory* (New York: Henry Holt & Co., 1937), pp. 123–158.

For many years B. Farrington's work on Greek (especially Hellenistic) science, *Greek Science: Its Meaning for Us* (Harmondsworth, Middlesex: Penguin Books, 1944), was the only nontechnical work on Greek science available easily. It was therefore widely read, in spite of the author's explanations, which seemed to many to be highly oversimplified. Now, however, there has recently appeared a very full, careful, and scholarly work, the product of many years' research, which should supersede Farrington, even for the general reader who will no doubt skip some of the more technical parts of this new book: G. Sarton, *A History of Science* (Cambridge, Mass.: Harvard University Press, 1952), Vol. 1. O. Neugebauer's book, recommended also at the end of Chapter 3—*The Exact Sciences in Antiquity* (Princeton, N.J.: Princeton University Press, 1952), is also excellent, especially in the sections on Hellenistic science and the contributions made to it by the earlier Babylonian science.

Finally, a special study of Egypt in the Hellenistic Age and the influence of Hellenism on native Egyptian culture is well worth study as a pioneer work in a very interesting field, H. I. Bell, *Egypt from Alexander the Great to the Arab Conquest* (Oxford: The Clarendon Press, 1948).

5

From Republic to Empire—The
Evolution of Roman Civilization

Republic and empire, a contrast • Evolution of the republic • Unification of Italy: Sammite and Pyrrhic Wars • Expansion beyond Italy: Punic Wars, invasion of Greece and Near East • Provincial system • Collapse of the republic: Sulla, Pompey, Julius Caesar • Civil war and foundation of the empire • Augustus and his successors • Influence of the imperial idea and of law • Roman culture

---

▶ Republic and Empire—A contrast

The study of Rome within the compass of a single chapter presents a peculiarly difficult problem. The history of Rome falls into two distinct parts: the first, ending in 31 B.C., is the history of the republic, governed under forms which can be considered democratic but which permitted an oligarchy to rule for almost the whole period; the second is the history of the Empire, under a monarch, with the forms of the monarchy at first disguised and then obvious to all. Most of the territory acquired by the Roman people and later called the Roman Empire was won during the republic; in the imperial period this territory was thoroughly reorganized and converted into the efficient institution which so much impressed the Christians and which affected so profoundly the whole civilization of the Western world.

The republic is a classic instance of the inability of institutions which grew up to take care of one set of conditions to function effectively when these conditions have alto-gether changed. The Roman Republic was utterly unable to administer its empire either efficiently or for the benefit of the governed; it collapsed in a civil war amid a welter of blood. Yet the gradual progress toward empire, the policies by which the numerically few Roman people won such a large expanse of territory, the way in which the democratic forms were attained, the manner in which these forms worked and were ultimately lost, are subjects of perennial interest to all students of history and government. The story of the republic therefore is far more interesting than that of the rather static Empire, which was evolving toward nothing, though it provided a framework for the gradual civilizing of peoples who until then had known little of the blessings of civilization. To understand the republic a considerable amount of intricate detail has to be mastered, as always when a complex governmental system is studied. This detail is out of place in a single chapter devoted to Rome and cannot therefore be given. All that will be attempted is a brief account of the evolu-

► chronological chart
Roman Civilization

THE EARLY MONARCHY

Traditional date of founding of Rome	B.C.	753	Servius Tullius B.C.	578–534
Traditional first four kings of Rome		753–616	Tarquinius Superbus (Etruscan king)	534–510
Tarquinius Priscus (Etruscan king)		616–578	End of Etruscan domination	509

THE REPUBLIC

Internal history

First secession of plebs—Election of tribunes and establishment of Concilium plebis (plebiscites binding on plebs)	B.C.	494
Establishment of Comitia tributa (Assembly of Tribes)	ca.	460
Twelve Tables		450–449
Valerio-Horatian Laws (legislation by plebs binding on state if accepted by Senate)		448
Intermarriage permitted between plebeians and patricians		445
Suspension of consulship, substituted by military tribunes, open to plebeians		444–367
Licinian-Sextian Laws—Consulship opened to plebeians		367
Censors to give preference to ex-magistrates in drawing up list of senators		310
Loss of senatorial veto on all legislation		287
Tiberius Gracchus elected tribune		133
Tribunate of Gaius Gracchus		123–122
Death of Gaius Gracchus		121
Marius elected consul		107
Reorganization of army on volunteer basis by Marius		106
Sullan Constitution		83–80
Pompey given extended command against Mithridates		66
Return of Pompey to Rome		62
First Triumvirate		60
Caesar appointed to command in Gaul		58
Return of Caesar to Italy		49
Caesar as dictator		46–44
Murder of Caesar		44

External history

Battle of Lake Regillus—Roman victory over Latin League	B.C.	496
Treaty with Latin League—Promulgation of Latin rights		493
Rome leader of Latin League—Gradual expansion		490–430
Conquest of Veii (southern Etruria)		396
Invasion of Italy by Gauls—Sack of Rome		387–386
War with Latin League		340–338
Defeat of Latin League—Roman Confederation		338
Samnite Wars		327–290
War with Pyrrhus and Magna Graecia		281–272
First Punic War		264–241
Sicily becomes first Roman province		227
Second Punic War		218–201
Wars with Macedonia		200–197; 171–168
Defeat of Antiochus III (king of Syria) at Magnesia		190
Third Punic War		149–146
Destruction of Carthage and sack of Corinth		146
Macedonia becomes Roman province		146
Jugurthine War		112–106
Marius defeats Cimbri and Teutones		102–101
Social War in Italy		90–88
Sulla undertakes war with Mithridates		87
Wars with Mithridates (Lucullus)		75–66
Slave War in Italy		74–71
Conquest and reorganization of Asia by Pompey		66–62
Caesar conquers Gaul		58–51
Crassus defeated and killed in Parthia		53

THE PRINCIPATE

tion of republican institutions and a description of the government as it functioned at the height of the republic. All detailed explanations of why this should have come about will have to be studied in a larger work.

▶ **From kingship to democracy— The evolution of the Republic to 287 B.C.**

STRUGGLE OF PLEBEIANS FOR EQUAL RIGHTS

The traditional date of the founding of Rome was 753 B.C. This date, however, is not accepted by historians, who are well aware that there was a settlement on the site of Rome at least as early as 1000 B.C. Traditionally the first king was Romulus, a person of whom nothing is known beyond what later and unreliable legend tells us. However, it is certain that during the seventh and sixth centuries B.C. Rome was ruled by a monarchy, and the last of these monarchs was an Etruscan named Tarquin the Proud. It is also certain that the Etruscans, a people whose origins are still obscure but who probably came from Asia Minor, dominated Rome for the last period of the kingship, and Roman legend always speaks of the expulsion of the kings as the beginning of Roman independence under republican forms (about 509 B.C.). All through the period of the republic the name of king was detested by the Romans in memory of this famous expulsion of men presumed to be tyrants.

The position of the king was taken by two *consuls,* each holding office for a year, chosen exclusively from the noble or patrician class. In early Rome there was a formal and definite class distinction between patricians and nonpatricians, who were called plebeians. Patricians held their position by birth, and it was not possible to rise into the patrician class, since intermarriage between the two classes was prohibited. Thus, traders, small farmers, artisans and all other free men who did not belong to the noble families were lumped together into the plebeian order. In the class struggles that followed the establishment of the republic, it is natural that the wealthier and better-placed members of the plebeian order should have taken the lead in fighting for reforms, and it should not be thought that the ordinary peasant or small farmer was likely to be especially interested in breaking down the class distinction or repealing the laws against intermarriage. His daughter was unlikely to marry into the aristocracy, whatever the laws might permit.

Since early Rome was engaged in constant wars, the plebeians who took their share in the fighting had a potent weapon at their disposal for extracting concessions from the patricians. As the result of a strike (about 494 B.C.) of the army when it had been called out for campaign duty, the first concessions were granted. The plebeians were allowed to have two officers of state called tribunes, with the power of vetoing any acts of the consuls. These men were to be elected by the plebeians themselves, assembled into a council for the purpose. About 449 B.C., probably also as the result of another strike or threatened strike, the law was codified in such a manner that plebeians could expect due process in case of being brought to trial, and they could only be punished for infractions of these definite laws (Twelve Tables). A few years afterward plebeians were permitted to intermarry with patricians. Some time during the years between the first and the second strikes the Assembly of the plebs, which chose the tribunes, was permitted to pass legislation binding on the plebs alone, and the Assembly itself was reorganized to permit the entry of patricians. In 448 B.C. this reorganized Assembly, most of whose members were, of course, plebeians, was permitted to pass laws which were then submitted to the patrician body, the Senate, and if accepted by the latter, the laws were considered binding on the whole people. Apart from legislation, however, the Senate continued to dominate the state, and the veto that they exercised prevented the plebeians from having any real say in the government. It was, however, a good beginning, and the struggle continued, with ever-increasing victories for the plebeians.

The most important disadvantage now suffered by the plebeians was their exclusion from the highest office in the state, the consulship. The patricians were reluctant to give way on this, and for a time, rather than admit plebeians to an office of such prestige, they abolished the office altogether. However, in 367 B.C. they gave way, relying upon the fact that they controlled the electoral machinery and could thus ensure that no plebeians would in fact be elected. The attempt to hold up plebeian election by such means was, however, a failure. The plebeians who controlled the legislature so often forced the bill on the Senate that one of the consuls *must* be a plebeian that the Senate at last withdrew its veto, and thereafter one of the consuls always was a plebeian. Gradually by the same means all the offices of state were opened to plebeians until at last all that the Senate had remaining was the veto on legislation. A third general strike in 287 B.C. forced the removal of the veto, and thereafter all legislation passed by the Assembly (*Comitia tributa*) was binding on the state, whether or not the Senate approved it.

CONTINUED STRENGTH OF ARISTOCRATS IN DEMOCRATIC FRAMEWORK

Thus by 287 B.C. there was formal equality within the state, and all offices were open to all citizens. Yet the people did not in fact rule. The august Senate, now made up not only of patricians, but of all those citizens who had held important office in the state, managed to rule indirectly for almost 150 years after it lost its veto. This feat was achieved by the effective process of disarming all likely opposition through admitting tribunes (of whom there were now ten, each with a veto) to the Senate and allowing them to call it into session. Thus all proposed legislation was first debated in the Senate. All through the republic's history the Assembly could only vote yes or no, but could not debate. The tribunes were welcomed into aristocratic houses and families and, allied with the nobles, often adopted their viewpoint. The Senate also controlled the treasury and all foreign policy. It had almost a monopoly of talent within its ranks. Finally, as if this were not enough, various senatorial factions controlled political machines which ensured that the urban masses of Rome could at all times be outnumbered in voting by senatorial clients and landowners, unless the farmers themselves came into Rome in person to vote on some issue that was of special interest to them, as happened in 133 B.C. at the time of the Gracchan Revolution.

▶ External history to 272 B.C.—The unification of Italy

SYSTEM OF DEALING WITH CONQUERED
ITALIANS—ALLIED RIGHTS

As has already been noted, the Romans were engaged in constant wars, originally for survival against their neighbors and then for the control of the whole peninsula of Italy. In the early years of their independence they were greatly helped by the Latin League, a league of smaller city-states to the south of Rome. And although the league at times resented and feared Roman domination and fought against the Romans, the latter were never left altogether without allies, even though a great deal of prestige was lost on one occasion when the Celtic people called the Gauls descended from the north and were able to sack Rome itself (387–86 B.C.). The secret of the Roman success probably lies in the fact that they never agreed that they had been beaten in all their history. They never were forced to conclude a loser's peace. When they made treaties without winning a war it was only to resume the war as soon as opportunity permitted. For centuries there was nothing in Rome worth plundering. A foreign invader could take nothing worth his while. And without exterminating the whole Roman people there was no way of concluding a war or making a peace settlement that could be expected to endure.

But, perhaps more important than their stubbornness and refusal to admit final defeat, the treaty system invented by the Romans was a crucial element in their success. If any enemy surrendered to the Romans he could usually expect good terms. The Romans seldom destroyed their enemies, but preferred to make it possible for themselves to live at peace with them afterward. Although treaties existed long prior to the Romans (the most famous early treaty known to us was between Rameses II of Egypt and the Hittites) it was the Romans amongst the ancient peoples who developed the art of treaty-making in the most systematic manner. Already early in the period of the republic they showed their talent for law and government that was their most conspicuous gift as a people, compensating thereby to a large extent for their lack of almost all the cultural graces which we associate with the Greeks.

The ability to make effective treaties rests on their concept of citizenship. Citizenship, to a Roman, was vested in a person, and did not depend on his place of residence. Thus citizenship could be granted as well as inherited. Moreover, Roman citizenship included certain specific and definite rights. So it was possible to grant an enemy recently defeated in battle either full citizenship, or some of the rights of citizens. The main rights of citizens were three: the right to trade, the right to intermarry, and the right to vote. The last-named right included many other subsidiary rights, and was reserved for the full Roman citizen. When the Italians who possessed for centuries only Latin rights, or half citizenship, felt at the beginning of the first century B.C. that they needed the right to vote, with all its appurtenances, for their own protection, the Romans resisted the claim, and a severe war had to be fought before it was granted. But in the earlier centuries the Latin allies were content with rights other than the right to vote, and it was customary for the Romans to grant these, thus associating the allies with the success of the Romans and giving them some share in the proceeds of their victories. When the Romans began to expand beyond Latium into the southern part of Italy they invented a new right, the right of an ally, which entitled the possessor to protection by Rome against external enemies. By the use of this right the Romans took over, in effect, the

The Appian Way, the most famous road in Italy, built by the censor Appius Claudius during the fourth century B.C. (COURTESY ITALIAN STATE TOURIST OFFICE)

foreign policy of the ally, who could no longer make war on his own account, and was bound to come to the aid of the Romans if they engaged in a war. Since the Romans then frequently did proceed into a war which was none of the making of the ally, as a rule they gained more than they lost by the arrangement. However, as will be seen, the treaty could work the other way also and drag the Romans into a war which they would have preferred to avoid.

SAMNITE AND PYRRHIC WARS

From the latter part of the fourth century B.C. the Romans engaged in hostilities with a people originally more powerful than themselves and their Latin allies together. These people, the Samnites, proved very dangerous to them, especially since some of the Latin allies deserted to the Samnites

in the course of the wars, feeling that Rome was becoming too powerful and ought to be restrained. Several times the Romans were severely defeated, but their persistence paid off in the end, and by 290 B.C. the Samnites, who found themselves in the course of the war compelled to set up a confederation of their own comparable to that of the Romans, submitted. This war, however, brought the Romans into direct contact with the Greeks in southern Italy, a people with a far superior culture, who made their living largely by maritime trade. Like most Greek cities they were constantly quarreling with one another, and the presence of such a strong power as Rome in central Italy exercised an overwhelming influence in a quarrel between any two of them. It was not long before Rome was called in when one of the smaller Greek cities found itself at war with a bigger

UNIFICATION
OF ITALY

DATES (B.C.) INDICATE
FINAL CONQUEST
BY ROMANS

◎ Capital   ★ Battle

0   50   100
Miles

Po R.

CISPADANE GAUL

A D R I A T I C   S E A

ETRURIA
280

UMBRIA
290

PICENUM
302

Tiber R.

Veii
396

AEQUI
303

Rome

LATIUM
338

SAMNIUM
290

Cumae

CAMPANIA

Naples
338

Beneventum

APULIA
312

Brundisium

Tarentum

T Y R R H E N I A N

S E A

Heraclea

MAGNA GRAECIA
272

Thurii

Rhegium

Messina

S I C I L Y

Syracuse

one. In turn the larger city, Tarentum, called
in the aid of a Greek king from the mainland.
This new entry brought Carthage, the north
African maritime power which controlled
most of Sicily at the time, to the aid of the
Romans, since Pyrrhus, the Greek king, had

his eye on Sicily and had been interfering
there prior to his being summoned by Tarentum. There ensued a war in which Pyrrhus,
in spite of being aided by elephants, found
himself unable to undertake successfully a
two-front war. He was finally expelled both

from Italy and Sicily, and the Romans added the Greek cities to their confederation as allies, with allied rights.

▶ The expansion of Rome beyond Italy

THE PUNIC WARS

It was not long before war broke out again, this time between Rome and Carthage. This was altogether natural, and could have been predicted. Prior to the conquest of the Greek cities in Italy the Romans had not been interested in maritime trade. But these cities had been carrying on a running fight with the Carthaginians, who jealously guarded their empire and permitted only very restricted trading rights to others. It was too tempting an opportunity for the Greek cities to resist, knowing that the Romans were compelled to aid them if they should get into open hostilities. The expected incident soon occurred, and though the Roman Senate did not desire to honor its obligations, pressure by the wealthy classes and the consuls who wished for military commands succeeded in overcoming its opposition, and the first Punic War followed. Again the Romans had the greatest difficulty in winning this war. They were unaccustomed to the sea and they did not trust the newly conquered Greek cities who could have helped them. More men in this war were drowned at sea than were ever killed in battle. But, as always, sheer persistence won the day; Carthage was defeated and forced to concede that part of Sicily that had been under its control. The island of Sardinia followed soon afterward.

But Carthage was far from subdued, and under a gifted general named Hannibal decided to pursue the Romans in their own stronghold of Italy. Roman leadership at first was completely unable to cope with the well-trained Carthaginian army which crossed the Alps (218 B.C.) and annihilated two Roman armies sent against it. Hannibal did not, however, succeed in taking Rome, and made no serious attempt to do so. His fine army, marooned in southern Italy and cut off from sources of reinforcement, wasted

away while the Romans adopted harassing tactics. At last the Romans found a first-rate general too, and sent an expedition to Africa to take the Carthaginian homeland. Hannibal was forced to return, and was decisively defeated. Once again the Romans had won the last battle.

EXPANSION OF ROMANS INTO GREECE AND THE NEAR EAST

Meanwhile the Romans had found it necessary to protect their allies in eastern Italy, which meant policing the Adriatic Sea. Finding it impossible to do this effectively without a base on the Greek mainland, they proceeded to take such a base, thereby involving themselves with Macedonia, which resented the presence of an alien power on Greek soil. The Macedonians allied themselves with the Seleucid monarch of Asia, and the Romans were forced to deal with him too. Several times they defeated the Macedonians, and apparently tried not to incorporate either Macedonia or southern Greece into their expanding empire. Once a Roman consul theatrically proclaimed the liberation of all Greece, to the accompaniment of ecstatic cheers. But none of these countries could remain free permanently. One faction would quarrel with another and invite Rome in to settle the question. In the end the Romans stayed, and by the middle of the second century B.C. there were enough Romans with a vested interest in the empire, which by this time extended into the Near East, to be able to persuade the Senate and people to engage in new wars even when there was little excuse for them. This effect of the empire upon the government and people of Rome will be considered in a later section.

▶ The provincial system

PROBLEM OF ADMINISTERING LANDS OUTSIDE ITALY

When the Romans were ceded territory beyond Italy it was necessary to decide what kind of administration the new lands should be given. It did not seem feasible to extend

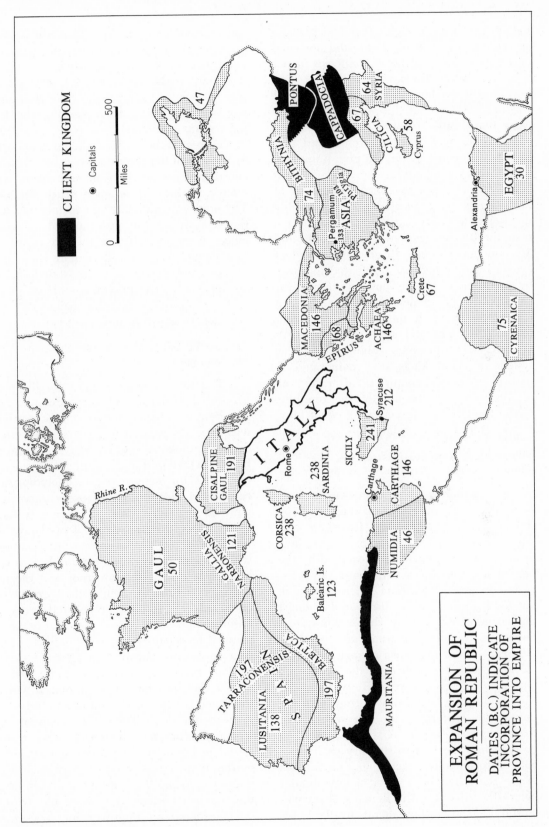

EXPANSION OF
ROMAN REPUBLIC

DATES (B.C.) INDICATE
INCORPORATION OF
PROVINCE INTO EMPIRE

CLIENT KINGDOM

Capitals

Miles

0   500

GAUL
50

GALLIA NARBONENSIS
121

SPAIN
TARRACONENSIS
197

BAETICA
197

LUSITANIA
138

Rhine R.

MAURITANIA

CISALPINE
GAUL 191

CORSICA
238

SARDINIA
238

Baleáric Is.
123

ITALY

Rome

NUMIDIA
46

Carthage

CARTHAGE
146

SICILY
241

Syracuse 212

EPIRUS

MACEDONIA
146

168

ACHAEA
146

Crete
67

CYRENAICA
75

PONTUS

BITHYNIA
74

CAPPADOCIA

67

ASIA
133

Pergamum

PHRYGIA
105

CILICIA
58

Cyprus

SYRIA
64

Alexandria

EGYPT
30

47

117

the system of allied rights that had been so successful in Italy itself. Rome did not need or desire the help of these territories in her wars, nor would Roman rights at that time have meant anything to their peoples. What was needed was that the provinces, as they came to be called, should contribute financially to the well-being of Rome, and that their governments should not give Rome any trouble and should not have any independent policy of their own. Manifestly, too many of these lands were incapable of governing themselves to Roman satisfaction—as we have seen, the Romans tried to let the Greeks and Macedonians continue to govern themselves even after they had been defeated in battle by the Romans. Where, however, there was an effective government in the hands of a respectable monarch, the Romans were content to leave him in charge provided he fulfilled certain necessary obligations. This system of client kings was maintained in parts of the Roman Empire till after the time of Augustus and the end of the republic. Herod the Great of Judea was a client king, as was Herod Agrippa later.

GOVERNMENT AND ADMINISTRATION IN THE PROVINCES

For territories where there was no king available the Romans devised the provincial system. Each province had its rights and duties clearly defined in a provincial law, dictated by the Romans but accepted by the provincials, sometimes with some difficulty, as in the case of Sardinia where no legal-minded leaders could be discovered amongst the barbarian inhabitants. Under this system there was a Roman governor, appointed by the Senate from the ranks of men who had recently held high office in the state. His term of office was one year. He was assisted by a moderately large body of troops for the purpose of keeping order and seeing that there was no rebellion. A stated tax had to be paid into the Roman treasury each year, but, unfortunately, except in rare cases where there had been efficient government before the advent of the Romans, there was no suitable body of bureaucrats available for

the collection of the tax. Thus the system grew up of farming the taxes out to private enterprise. In some of the provinces, including Sicily at the beginning, the tax contract was let to local bankers who were restrained by local patriotism from fleecing the taxpayers too mercilessly. In other provinces, however—and they formed the large majority by the end of the second century B.C.—the tax contracts were let to Roman bankers who were restrained by no such gentle feelings. The only safeguard the provincials had was the honesty of the governor whose good offices were necessary if the tax collectors (*publicani*) were to collect more than their due—a fixed percentage was stated in the law governing the province—and the possibility of prosecuting the collectors and perhaps the governor in Roman law courts.

FAILURE OF PROVINCIAL SYSTEM UNDER THE REPUBLIC

The two safeguards were not likely to be, and were not in fact, very effective. The governor, who held office for only a year and who expected at most two years as governor during his official career, was not allowed by law to take part in any trade or commerce himself. With living expenses, including the expense of election, rising every year, and with no regular source of income beyond what he could squeeze out of his lands, he was thus subject to extraordinary temptation, which, as far as we can ascertain, he did not often resist. Thus the governor and the tax collector flourished, while the provincials could only look to the courts for redress. And, unfortunately for them, the courts were manned by senators who were unlikely to be so austere as to betray their class by a conviction, especially not when there was a chance that they too might be placed within the reach of the same temptation and wish to succumb to it. Toward the end of the second century B.C. the courts were transferred to the equestrian order, a new order in the Roman state made up primarily of businessmen and the middle class. This, from the provincial point of view, could hardly be considered an improvement. The most notable conviction for extortion in the early first century was that of one Rutilius Rufus who had in fact himself scrupulously avoided any extortion, and had indeed clamped down upon the businessmen who had attempted it during his regime. The courts, interested only in discouraging honesty in governors, handed down a conviction in spite of the lack of reliable evidence. Rutilius was thereupon invited to take up his residence and live free for the rest of his life in the province he was supposed to have so mercilessly exploited!

Although the provincial system demonstrated the unfitness of the republic to rule an empire without drastic changes, it was not in itself an important factor in the collapse of republican institutions, as has sometimes been claimed. The governors in charge of provinces possessed too small military might to present a threat to the republic. As we shall see, it was the long-term commands of proconsuls with jurisdiction over far more than a mere province, in command of less meager forces than a governor had at his disposal, that finally put an end to the republic and ensured one-man rule.

▶ Consequences of Roman expansion

ENRICHMENT OF GENERALS, LANDOWNERS, AND BANKERS

In order to explain the many-sided effect of the expansion upon Rome some preliminary explanations are necessary. The Roman army had originally been made up of both patricians and plebeians, but no man who was entirely without property could serve. The whole army was conscripted for particular campaigns, and the soldiers expected to return to civilian life as soon as the campaign was over. This system worked well enough for some centuries, but when the campaigns took the soldiers ever farther afield, many of the returnees found that their property had been taken over by local landowners, who could not be easily dislodged. Moreover, after the wars with Carthage, and especially after the Second Punic War when Hannibal occupied a considerable section of

Italy, the small farmer found that he had too little capital available to bring his land back into cultivation. The result was that the large landowner with access to capital continually increased his holdings at the expense of the small farmer, who often lost his land with very little compensation. So, when the farmer was conscripted into the army he began to look upon his land as likely to be lost in any case. He therefore was willing to stay for a longer period in the army, provided he could compensate himself with war booty. Thus he began to gain a vested interest in continued warfare, especially warfare against countries which possessed sufficient movable property for his needs. The commanders of these armies likewise felt that they should make some material gains from the war. Commands were short-lived and the commanders had expenses as high as provincial governors; indeed they looked forward to being provincial governors after their term of command in the army. Thus they too began to gain a vested interest in profitable warfare.

The middle classes, especially the bankers and contractors, found that tax collecting, and the purchase of provincial tax contracts, was a profitable business. The more provinces that fell to the Roman sword the richer the pickings for them. The populace of Rome, on the other hand, saw little good in it. The city was thronged with dispossessed farmers, and Rome never was able to provide much work, save in small industry such as shield-making and the manufacture of goods for local consumption. Imported goods were better and cheaper; and many imports had been merely taken as campaign booty. There were no taxes, to be sure; but it is doubtful whether most of the poor would have paid taxes in any case, since they possessed so little property or income. Their only gain was a subsidized price for grain, a very small consideration to be set against the low wages earned in competition with skilled imported slaves and for far too few jobs. But these men still had the vote, and the full consequences of their latent political power had not yet been exploited. This was

Ruins of the temple of Mars in the Roman Forum. (COURTESY ITALIAN STATE TOURIST OFFICE)

to come during the Gracchan Revolution, when at last they found two leaders who were willing to stand up against the senatorial monopoly of power.

POLITICAL EFFECTS IN ROME

The Gracchan Revolution

Tiberius Gracchus became tribune of the plebs in 133 B.C., pledged to a program of land redistribution in Italy, breaking up the large estates and giving them to the illegally dispossessed farmers. As soon as he introduced his legislation he was faced with a veto from one of his nine colleagues. This was one of the traditional safeguards of the senatorial party (called the Optimates); hitherto it had always been possible to bribe at least one tribune. But Tiberius did not

take this lying down, as no doubt his predecessors had done. He called upon the people to depose the tribune. This they did, though it was illegal. The legislation duly passed, there came the question of putting it into force, and this needed money. Providentially just at this moment a Hellenistic king, dying without heirs, bequeathed his kingdom to the Roman people. Tiberius and his Assembly gratefully accepted the gift, while the Senate, the traditional repository of all monies, had to accept the situation with the best grace possible. This was not illegal, but it was highly inflammatory. Finally, Tiberius decided that he must be reelected in order to put the bill into effect. No tribune, however, could succeed himself. The Optimates therefore countered with their command of the armed forces. A band of supporters of the constitution, led by the high priest, murdered Tiberius on election day and with him three hundred of his supporters. The land law, however, was put into effect, and much of the Italian land was indeed redistributed.

Ten years later Gaius, the younger brother of Tiberius Gracchus, was elected tribune. In the meantime re-election of a tribune had been made legal. Gaius therefore could look forward to several years of leadership in the Assembly if he could hold the confidence of the people. This time the Optimates had a better card to play. They had one of themselves elected tribune as one of the colleagues of Gaius. This man proceeded systematically to outbid his colleague, having no intention of carrying out his promises. His task was made easier by the fact that Gaius was studiously moderate and not all of his proposals were equally popular with the people. The third year that he stood for office, with only half of his legislative program enacted into law, he was defeated. Fearing for his life, he surrounded himself with a bodyguard, whereupon the Senate, after a few inflammatory incidents had been provoked, called upon the consul to restore order, in effect declaring martial law. Gaius was either murdered or committed suicide, and more than three thousand of his followers were killed. The popular revolution had failed, but the Senate had declared its bankruptcy.

The rise of the soldier of fortune— Preparation for one-man rule

The senatorial oligarchy supported by the monied interests had successfully curbed the possible establishment of a popular democracy in Rome; but it was unable to defend itself against the military. Only if the army was loyal and civilian rule was unthreatened could the Senate, which had few armed forces at its disposal, hope to rule Rome. It had been highly dangerous, as well as ruinous to its prestige, to invoke extralegal powers to suppress the revolt of the Gracchi, however much provocation it had been given. Power was soon to pass from its hands into the hands of the soldier

of fortune with an effective political machine.

Few could probably have foreseen the result of an important but necessary reform of the method of recruiting the army, which was put into effect about 108 B.C. A minor war had been in progress in Africa for some years, which had been going unfavorably for Rome. It was rumored that the generals had been bribed by the enemy, a not altogether unlikely possibility, indeed boasted of by the young African prince who led the enemy. An officer named Marius began to attack his superiors and boast that he could finish off the war if given the command. Instead of being court-martialed as in our own day, he was permitted to go back to Rome to stand for election as consul. An efficient political machine ensured his election, and when the Senate hesitated to give him the African command, the Assembly conferred it upon him by law. In order to win the war he reorganized the army, making it into a volunteer army, recruited from any who wished to join. Naturally the Roman proletariat regarded this as an opportunity to win booty and perhaps pensions at the end of their military service. From being made up of the propertied classes with a stake, however small, in the Roman state, the army was now made up of propertyless men to whom Rome had been a poor mistress, to whom they felt they owed little. Their loyalty lay with the general who had trained them and led them to victory and booty, and whose influence could force the Senate to grant them pensions and property when they were too old to fight. From this time onward power was to lie with those generals who had had commands long enough for them to win the loyalty of their troops.

▶ Collapse of the Roman Republic

LAST ATTEMPT AT RECONSTRUCTION
BY SULLA

The full results of this policy were not visible for many years to come. Marius himself was a very feeble politician, and he still stood in some awe of the Senate. Not until his last years did he recognize the chance he had missed, when he saw his junior officer in the African campaign, a general named Sulla, dictate to the Roman Senate and people just how they were to behave while he was away on campaign in Greece. It is true that as soon as Sulla had left, Marius recaptured Rome with a rabble army, but he lived for only one month afterward. When Sulla returned from Greece triumphant, the supporters of Marius were given short shrift, while Sulla himself became dictator. If he had wished he could have become the first emperor of Rome.

But Sulla did not so wish. Instead he preferred to make an effort to reform the constitution, taking away from the people and their Assembly much of their power, weakening the office of tribune, which had been so much abused, in such a manner that no ambitious man would wish to hold it, and reorganizing the Senate into what should have been a really effective body. Then he retired quietly to his estates, dying soon afterward. His constitution failed because no one, not even the Senate itself, apparently really wished to try to make it work. As soon as the next crisis arose, the Senate was willing to abdicate its responsibility and give extended powers to the nearest capable military man. At this time a continuous war was being waged in Asia against the most formidable enemy the republic ever had to face, King Mithridates VI of Pontus, so that short-term commands were obviously unfeasible.

POMPEY—THE POPULAR GENERAL

Pompey was the beneficiary of this situation. First elected by the Assembly to a long-term command against pirates in the Mediterranean Sea, and having made short work of these, he was then given a further long-term command in the East. There he replaced a senatorial general whose tight-fisted treatment of his troops had caused them to go on strike to the detriment of the campaign against Mithridates. Pompey, who cared nothing for money, soon settled this situation and proceeded to conquer not only Pontus but also several other countries ripe to be added to the ever-expanding empire.

This took him several years, but during the period he kept his political machine at home well oiled, and everyone in Rome knew that when he returned home he could assume whatever power he wished. There was no power in Italy or elsewhere that could possibly withstand his victorious army.

RISE OF CAESAR—
THE FIRST TRIUMVIRATE (60 B.C.)

When, however, he did at length return home, he showed no signs of desiring anything but pensions for his troops and the ratification of his acts in the East. The Senate, taking this for a sign of weakness, refused these moderate demands. Pompey, nonplussed, looked around for some political help, as he now held no office himself. He discovered it in the person of Julius Caesar, a rising military man who had just returned from a campaign in Spain and was the consul-elect, and also in the person of a banker named Crassus who had financed Caesar's career. Caesar's price was a long-term command in Gaul, Crassus remaining content with financial concessions. Pompey accepted the terms. Caesar accordingly introduced a resolution in the Senate giving Pompey the pensions and ratifications that he needed. When these requests were turned down, Pompey called upon a few troops who were still waiting patiently for their pensions and so could be relied upon, whereupon the Senate thought better of its refusal. For the next ten years the triumvirate of Pompey, Caesar, and Crassus did as they liked. Crassus, though aging, thought he would like a command in the East before he died, and was given it. He was killed in a stunning defeat by the Parthians. Caesar made a thorough job of conquering Gaul, although when he began his career there seemed to be no special necessity to add this province to the empire, as it was giving no particular trouble. Pompey stayed close to Rome, aging also, and taking no active command. Secure in the laurels he had won, he did not realize until too late that Caesar was building up precisely the same kind of loyal military following that he had once possessed himself.

CIVIL WAR AND THE DICTATORSHIP
OF CAESAR

The showdown came when Caesar prepared to return to Rome. The Senate had decided that Pompey was less dangerous to the republic than the ambitious Caesar, and had succeeded at last in enlisting his support. But when Caesar crossed the Rubicon and illegally entered Italy with his army, it was found that there were no troops in Italy capable of withstanding him, in spite of all the commands that Pompey in theory still held. Pompey and his senatorial supporters therefore crossed over into Greece, where Pompey still had a considerable reputation. But bad management of their campaign played into Caesar's hands, and Pompey was decisively defeated at the battle of Pharsalia in 48 B.C. He fled to Egypt and was murdered shortly afterward. Caesar followed him, making the acquaintance of Cleopatra, Queen of Egypt, in the process. Having settled the affairs of Egypt to his satisfaction, he proceeded to mop up various pockets of resistance in North Africa and Spain, and returned to Italy to celebrate a magnificent triumph. He began to prepare a campaign against Parthia to avenge Crassus and recover the lost Roman eagles, while he set in motion numerous administrative reforms to take care of the most pressing problems. However, he had barely started on this work when he was murdered by a group of senators and disgruntled officers in 44 B.C.

None of the reforms initiated by Julius Caesar really touched the heart of the problem, which was in its essence political rather than administrative. Above all, the position of the ruler had to be regularized, and some substitute found for the rule by Senate and people which had so conspicuously failed. Caesar could think of nothing better than to make himself permanent dictator, a title which in Rome always accompanied a temporary position held only in times of extreme danger. He thought of becoming king, but realized after a few trial balloons had been sent up that the people would not tolerate such a title. Kings had been execrated too long in Rome for a king to be acceptable now. Caesar was able to put into effect some much-needed reforms in the provinces before his murder, and he set up an important public-works program to give some occupation to the proletariat. He improved the tax system and took steps to ensure a regular supply of officials for public service in the free municipalities of the empire.

It was a good beginning and a considerable achievement for two years of absolute power. But it seems that Caesar could understand only the tangible needs of the empire, and he lacked that sense for the intangibles that characterized his successor and made the latter's work so much more fruitful and lasting. Caesar's attempt to "reform" the Senate consisted in packing it with military men and even provincials, which succeeded only in degrading it in its own eyes. The move might have been a wise one if he had really been interested in making this august and ancient body work. After all, it had ruled Rome for almost five hundred years, and though at the end it had fallen on evil times, surely it was not an institution that could simply be treated with disdain and given nothing to do but debate and confer titles on its master. There can be little doubt that the tactlessness with which he treated the Senate was the chief reason for the conspiracy against his life. So, for lack of the art of a true statesman, Caesar must remain as a first-class military man and an administrator of genius (Pompey, in this field, incidentally, must be counted as his equal), but not as the real founder of the empire that he might have been—though without his preliminary work the empire could hardly have been founded by his successor and heir.

▶ The foundation of the Roman Empire

THE SECOND TRIUMVIRATE AND
THE TRIUMPH OF AUGUSTUS

The conspirators who murdered Caesar had no idea of what steps to take next. They appear to have assumed that the government would revert to the Senate and people as heretofore. But the republic was dead beyond any possibility of revival. Caesar's army had, for the most part, been disbanded, but it was still a potent political and military force. And Caesar through his will continued to exercise an influence even after his death. Mark Antony as consul commanded an army of Caesar's veterans, and Lepidus, Caesar's official second in command, had a legion at his disposal. Moreover, in his will Caesar, in addition to bequeathing large sums to his troops, had made his great-nephew, Octavian, a young man of little public experience, his heir, with the potent title of Caesar, which he was to exploit to its full value. Antony might have been murdered by the conspirators, but was spared. As soon as he had ridden out the immediate storm, he was able to rouse Rome against them, and they were forced to flee abroad, to try to raise troops against Antony. But Antony made a serious mistake in not giving the troops their donative promised by Caesar. This enabled the young Octavian to gain credit and support from the legions in southern Italy, with which he entered Rome, to be given the command against Antony by the Senate. Antony, faced with one of the conspirators in southern Gaul and with Octavian and the consuls in central Italy, was defeated by the latter and retired to the north, allowing Octavian to return to Rome in triumph. Again the Senate repeated its earlier mistake against Pompey and slighted the young man, refusing him high office in the state on technical grounds.

It was the Senate's last chance. Octavian with his legions proceeded to join Antony, and with Lepidus they formed the Second Triumvirate. All the triumvirs took vengeance on their political enemies with wholesale proscriptions. In part this helped them to raise enough money from confiscated estates to put an army in the field sufficient to defeat the remnants of the conspirators who were arrayed against them in Greece. When they had been disposed of at the battle of Philippi (42 B.C.), Antony and Octavian were supreme. Lepidus could safely be disregarded, and it only remained to come to an agree-ment about the respective roles that each should play. Antony as the senior partner was given the command against the East, while Octavian stayed behind in Italy with a number of minor campaigns to settle.

The uneasy alliance continued for more than ten years. But Antony played into Octavian's hands by acting like an Oriental monarch, and especially by his relations with Cleopatra, regarded by everyone in Rome as a dangerous Oriental princess who had fascinated Antony and charmed him away from his loyalty to Rome. Octavian fostered this point of view by an unexampled use of propaganda, gradually undermining Antony's position so effectively that when the break came little actual fighting had to be done. Octavian had built up an important political party of his own, and had chosen at least one highly efficient general. So the battle of Actium in 31 B.C. was a foregone conclusion. Most of Antony's troops deserted when Cleopatra insisted on going into battle with him. Thereafter there was no power left in the Roman world to challenge Octavian. Four years later the Senate conferred upon him the title of Augustus by which he was henceforth to be known.

THE SCOPE OF THE PROBLEMS

The magnitude and scope of the problems facing the young ruler (he had been born in 63 B.C. and was thus thirty-two at the time of the battle of Actium) can hardly be overestimated. The old Roman Republic had clearly failed to live up to the responsibilities of empire, and had collapsed from its own weaknesses. Yet some form of government must replace it which was capable of enduring. And this government, whatever it might be, must also be able to keep under control the vast territories which had fallen to Roman arms during the previous three centuries. Rome had a responsibility to them also. It was impossible simply to decree their freedom and independence, even if the idea had ever occurred to Augustus. Their earlier forms of government had been destroyed beyond recall and could not be restored by a mere imperial fiat. In the last century of the republic the governors of the provinces had been political appointees of the Senate, anxious only to make their fortunes and return to Rome. By corruption and extortion they had advanced themselves; moreover, they were in league with the equestrian class of Rome which had milked the provinces for the sake of its own financial interests. The provinces had suffered abominably from this regular regime, and in many cases had been driven into bankruptcy by the more recent civil wars and irregular extortions by would-be rulers of Rome. There was little encouragement to honesty or efficiency, qualities rarely found in the governors. Was it possible for Augustus to reward these qualities and so improve the provincial system that they would become the rule rather than the exception?

We have seen that the enrollment of volunteer armies by Marius had led directly to the fall of the republic, since the troops relied upon their generals for pay and pensions, and their loyalty was given to these generals rather than to Rome. Moreover the various armies had swollen to such an extent in the civil wars that there were probably at least half a million men under arms at the time of the battle of Actium. Augustus had to consider what was the real purpose of an army in the Roman Empire, where the various legions should be stationed, how they were to occupy themselves during peacetime, how they could be persuaded to be loyal to Rome rather than to generals; and yet at the same time the armies must continue to have those professional military virtues, the absence of which in the earlier armies had compelled Marius to introduce long-term volunteer service.

Behind the great political and administrative problems was the ever-present social and economic background. Rome was not a great manufacturing city, not even a trading center of importance comparable to its size and population. There were far too many people in Rome unable to make a living and requiring public support. Yet these men were citizens and possessed the right to vote. The votes of this urban proletariat had always been for sale to the highest bidder in the last century of the republic. Could they be made

into a self-respecting citizenry by any means available to a capable administrator? How could the numerous slaves live side by side with a free citizenry without depressing wages? In spite of the fertility of much of the soil, Italy had never really recovered from the depredations of Hannibal nearly two centuries earlier. The small estates had been swallowed by senators and capitalists and made into large specialized agricultural units worked usually by slaves under overseers. Moreover, the small landholders who survived suffered from chronic insecurity of tenure, their properties often being sequestrated for the benefit of veterans. And throughout the length and breadth of Italy, especially near Rome, rich men built their villas, too often neglecting the land itself and its cultivation.

The cleavage between rich and poor had undermined the old Roman traditional virtues, and the search for ever-increasing luxury among the upper classes had replaced the stern frugality of the earlier republic. Family life in the upper classes had almost disappeared, with divorce to be had for the asking and marriage used for political and financial advancement. The birth rate among the free Romans had naturally been declining. Was it possible to arrest this process, at least the decay of public morality, even if the ancient virtues had disappeared forever?

These were a few of the problems with which Augustus had to contend. If he did not solve them all, at least he perceived their existence, and made an attempt to solve them. And the organization of an empire which endured for many centuries, the most enduring indeed that the Western world has yet seen, is almost entirely his work. The essential administrative structure was built by him, though the conquests themselves were bequeathed to him by the Roman conquerors of the republic.

THE WORK OF AUGUSTUS

The establishment of a legitimate government

The most difficult problem of all was undoubtedly the reorganization of the government: and it was the most fundamental. Not even a provincial reorganization, the establishment of an equitable system of taxation, nor the enlargement of the conception of Roman citizenship, would have been of any permanent value without a governmental system which was capable of controlling the empire and which was at the same time acceptable to the people. Any dictatorship or arbitrary military rule can be cut short by assassination, as Caesar's own career had shown. It was a measure of the genius of Augustus that he made his government both acceptable and legitimate. Though he did not solve permanently the method of succession, this may only be because, as will be discussed later, the problem may well be insoluble within the framework of absolute monarchy.

According to the tradition believed by the Romans, Rome had existed as a city for more than seven hundred years. For almost five hundred it had been free and self-governing. Though occasionally defeated in individual battles, it had never lost a war and had never been compelled to sign a peace with an undefeated enemy. For five hundred years magistrates had been elected and the noblest of the citizens had sat in the Senate and given their advice to the magistrates. It was a body of incomparable prestige, even though in the last century, often through its own incompetence, it had been forced to bow to arbitrary military men with armies at their backs. And the people of Rome had accepted its supremacy and shared in the glories won by their arms under its leadership. Though Rome was not a state, the Romans were truly a people, and Roman citizenship was prized by everyone who possessed it; and those who did not possess it valued it and sought to win it for themselves. During all these years the name of *rex* or king had been detested. The Romans no less than the Greeks regarded it as an office fit only for barbarians.

Yet Augustus realized that he must be king in fact, even though he did not hold the title. It would never have occurred to him—nor indeed would it have been possible

—to have ruled the empire with its many different peoples of varying degrees of culture, through any kind of representative government. The empire was too vast and heterogeneous for any such experiment. But if the government had been returned to Senate and people as under the republic, the same weaknesses would have led to the same breakdown of government. Only a monarch could hope to hold it together.

Augustus solved his dilemma by one of the great creative compromises of history, a species of legal fiction which bridged the gulf between the fallen republic and the monarchy which had to come. In time the republic was forgotten, the monarchy supplanted it, and the necessity for the fiction disappeared. But in the competent hands of Augustus, who understood it, the reasons for it, and the behavior required of him to maintain it, the fiction worked. Though thinking Romans of course knew that he was the sole ruler and that his power was ultimately based on the army and the treasury, nevertheless to the mass of the people the republic still survived. They felt at home in the new Roman state. The magistrates were still elected by the same procedure as before, though no candidate would even have run for office without the approval of Augustus; the Senate and the Assemblies still met for debate and legislation; and though there was now a Princeps, or first citizen, a title and office unknown to the republic, he was not obtrusive, he scrupulously respected all the old republican forms, and his public and private life were beyond reproach in the best tradition of the early days of the Roman Republic.

Augustus confined the offices held by himself personally to the minimum required for his possession of the reality of power. He had a permanent proconsular military power (*proconsulare imperium*) conferred upon him, giving him supreme command of the army; he was granted a permanent civil power as previously exercised by the tribunes (*tribunicia potestas*), which gave him the power to introduce legislation and veto it. He became chief priest (*Pontifex Maximus*), giving him authority in religious matters; but, characteristically, he did not assume this office until the death of Lepidus, who had been ousted from his position as triumvir in 36 B.C. and consoled for his loss of power by appointment to this honored position. Occasionally Augustus allowed himself to be elected consul in the early years of his rule, feeling that he needed the civil as well as the military power inherent in this office. But consuls, praetors, aediles, and even tribunes were elected as before to perform the specific duties of these offices under the guidance of the Princeps.

Augustus tried his best to maintain the dignity of the Senate. He encouraged it to give him advice, and he presided over it personally as *Princeps Senatus*. The judicial functions of the Senate were maintained and even increased under his rule. By setting aside certain provinces to be ruled by ex-magistrates under the direct control of the Senate and not of himself, he made it worth while moving through the full sequence of offices (*cursus honorum*) to the exalted position of consul. The Senate also had its own treasury. From the equestrian order Augustus recruited a body of public officials, paid out of the imperial treasury (*fiscus*) but with the same duties as tax gatherers and tax assessors that they had performed in their own interests under the republic. Under later emperors these men became part of the imperial civil service.

When it was proposed that he should be worshiped as a god (his adoptive father had already been deified), he refused the honor, but permitted his Genius to be worshiped instead. According to old Roman belief every man had a guiding Genius, and the Genius of the head of a family guided the fortunes of that family. In allowing a cult to be set up to his Genius, Augustus was therefore directing Roman worship toward the state of which he was now the controlling Genius. Later this indeed became the worship of the living emperor as god, a state cult to which all had to subscribe or be condemned for treason. But Augustus in his lifetime never claimed to be a god except in the Hellenistic

Bust of Augustus at the prime of his manhood. (COURTESY BRITISH MUSEUM)

world, which had for centuries been accustomed to a divine monarchy.

Unsolved problem of the succession

The greatest difficulty inherent in his position as sole ruler, the difficulty of the succession, Augustus never solved. Perhaps the problem is incapable of solution and is one of the inherent defects of absolute monarchy. The possibilities are strictly limited. The Roman ruler had to be an exceptionally capable man. If hereditary succession were to be used the chances of any ruler's having a capable son are not especially good. If such a son possesses good natural talents, the experience of being brought up in the household of an absolute ruler is likely to damage his character, as was so often to be found in the history of the Roman Empire. If the choice were to pass into the hands of a civilian body such as the Senate, then political considerations might become predominant, and in any case the army might not

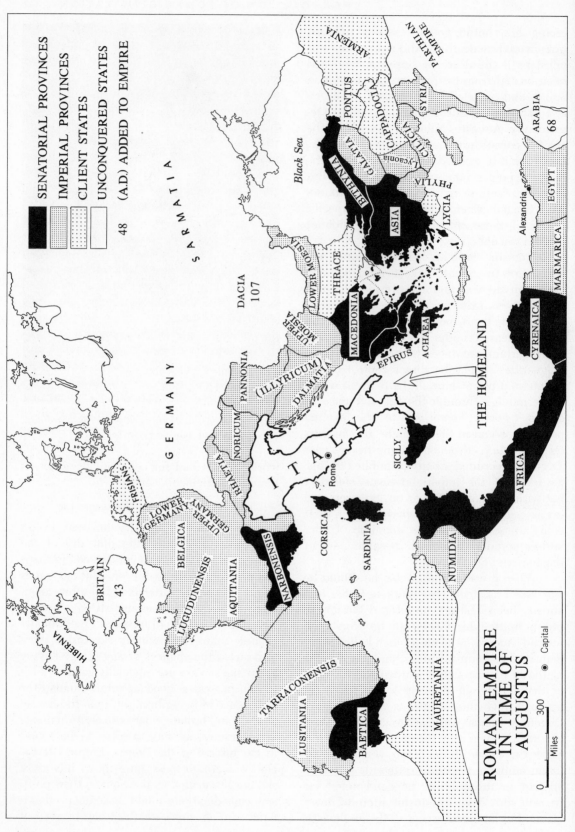

ROMAN EMPIRE
IN TIME OF
AUGUSTUS

● Capital

0   300
Miles

Legend:
- SENATORIAL PROVINCES
- IMPERIAL PROVINCES
- CLIENT STATES
- UNCONQUERED STATES

48 (A.D.) ADDED TO EMPIRE

HIBERNIA

BRITAIN
43

FRISIANS

GERMANY

SARMATIA

LOWER GERMANY

UPPER GERMANY

BELGICA

LUGUDUNENSIS

AQUITANIA

NARBONENSIS

RHAETIA

NORICUM

PANNONIA

(ILLYRICUM)

DALMATIA

DACIA
107

UPPER MOESIA

LOWER MOESIA

THRACE

Black Sea

BITHYNIA

PONTUS

GALATIA

CAPPADOCIA

ARMENIA

PARTHIAN EMPIRE

CILICIA

Lycaonia

SYRIA

ASIA

PHYLIA

LYCIA

ARABIA
68

MACEDONIA

EPIRUS

ACHAEA

I T A L Y

Rome

THE HOMELAND

SICILY

SARDINIA

CORSICA

TARRACONENSIS

LUSITANIA

BAETICA

MAURETANIA

NUMIDIA

AFRICA

CYRENAICA

MARMARICA

EGYPT

Alexandria

128

accept the choice; and it was certain that there would be disgruntled candidates ready to make trouble for the new incumbent. Moreover, there would be a period of transition between the death of the old monarch and the election of the new which could be dangerous for the empire.

It was necessary for all to know who the new ruler was to be before the old one died. With the old ruler's son designated as the heir, this could be attained. The other possibility was for the ruler to choose his successor and transfer enough power to him in his own lifetime that there would be no competitive power in the empire strong enough to prevent his succession. In fact, this is what usually happened in the empire unless the incumbent came to an untimely death before he had made arrangements. But Augustus, who had no male heirs in the direct line who survived him, preferred to use the principle of adoption. Tiberius, who was his stepson, was also adopted as his son and forced to marry his daughter, after divorcing a previous wife. Later a number of childless emperors adopted their successors, choosing the most effective men they could find. During this period (A.D. 96–180), known as the age of the "Good Emperors," the empire reached its greatest heights of prosperity and good government. But the last of these, Marcus Aurelius, had a son Commodus, whom he did not wish to pass over. Thus the claims of paternity and the claims of good government came into conflict. Commodus was one of the worst of the emperors, as it turned out, and his reign was a disaster from which Rome never really recovered.

The reorganization of the provinces

The reorganization of the provinces was a further example of Augustus' efficient use of such opportunities as existed. He saw at once that it was not necessary to keep armies in every province, as had been the custom in the later years of the republic. Those that had long been pacified and had no frontiers to be defended against barbarians needed no more than enough troops to ensure local discipline. Such provinces (see the map for details) he entrusted to the Senate, which was given the power of appointing governors and administering the tax monies. These provinces, as under the republic, were reserved for ex-magistrates, and constituted a reward for those who had progressed through the *cursus honorum*. In addition the arrangement gave the Senate some real work to do and served to maintain its prestige as a body. And though Augustus exercised a final supervisory jurisdiction over these provinces, he left them largely to themselves. Those provinces, however, which needed legions of trained troops, and whose frontiers had continually to be defended against enemies, were under his direct control, which he exercised through the appointment of salaried legates, personally responsible to him, who could hold their positions as long as they proved efficient. This arrangement gave them the opportunity to gain a real knowledge of their provinces and to win the loyalty of their troops, but in later times it proved a serious danger to the state in the event of a disputed succession to the throne. Egypt, as the richest province, the primary source of the grain supply for Rome and Italy, was given a special status in keeping with its history as well as its present importance. As in the past, the ruler was divine and the owner of all the land. Augustus, therefore, was a Pharaoh in Egypt, with all the privileges of this office, although he did not perform his duties as king-god there himself, but entrusted them to a prefect of equestrian rank, responsible to himself. The country, however, was farmed as an imperial estate rather than as a province with a certain degree of self-government, and its revenues accrued directly to the ruler. No one of senatorial rank was permitted within the territory without the permission of the Princeps. Finally, a number of kingdoms on the outskirts of the empire were permitted self-government under their kings, who became clients or vassals of Rome.

The provinces of the Roman Empire had always been made up of more or less self-governing municipalities, city-states on the Greek model, together with a number of other communities whose position had been defined by treaty, usually without full self-government. Augustus encouraged as much local administration as was compatible with the imperial relationship, thus saving the burden of direct administration. The corrupt tax system of the republican period was not abolished by Augustus, probably for lack of any alternative method of collection. His successors, especially Claudius and Hadrian, developed a regular civil service which gradually supplanted the tax companies. Meanwhile the abuses of the system were checked through more efficient supervision by the Princeps, even in the senatorial provinces. Penalties for extortion were severe, and even senatorial governors were far too much under control to be able to lend the efficient aid to the tax farmers that had been the custom under the republic in its last years. And the nucleus of the later civil service was formed with the inclusion of treasury officials in the staff of the governors.

The entire system of provinces was reorganized thoroughly by Augustus, with new boundaries, chosen for the sake of efficient administration and defense (see map). In the process a number of minor conquests had to be undertaken to round out many territories which had been acquired haphazardly by the republic according to the needs of the moment. Augustus always hoped to make the northern boundary the Elbe rather than the Rhine, as shorter and more easily defensible. Such a boundary, however, would have necessitated the conquest of a large part of Germany. Though progress with this conquest was made in the earlier years of his reign, his armies suffered a severe defeat toward the end of his life, and the conquest was abandoned. The Rhine became the northwestern frontier, while Augustus maintained the Danube in the East, refusing to move into Dacia to the north of the Danube (the modern Rumania) on the grounds that it was indefensible. This policy was maintained until Trajan A.D. 98–117, who not only took Dacia but engaged in extensive wars in the East, the spoils of which had to be abandoned by his successors, as

Augustus had predicted. The empire was held together by the great Roman roads, which were constantly extended throughout the imperial period and over which the imperial post traveled, bringing news to the emperor and his instructions in return.

The provincial system proved to be the most enduring of the reforms of Augustus. Whatever happened at Rome, the life of the provinces went on much as usual, under good rulers and bad alike. Only when the burden of taxation was heavily increased and prosperity declined in the third century A.D. with the continuous civil and foreign wars was the strength of the provinces slowly sapped. But while the Roman peace (*Pax Romana*) gave them a respite from war they had never previously enjoyed, their prosperity increased and with it the ability to pay the taxes which ensured the continuance of that rule.

Augustus himself, as has been said, was an Italian rather than a Roman, and always regarded Italy as the center of his dominions, the homeland with special privileges, with Rome as first the capital of Italy and then of the empire. The inhabitants of Rome, however, were no longer exempt from all taxation as had been the case under the republic for all Roman citizens. But their taxes always remained lighter than those of the provinces. Every native freeborn Italian was a Roman citizen with all the privileges attached to the position. The provincials could achieve Roman citizenship, but Augustus regarded it as a privilege to be earned and not a right to which they were entitled by birth. This policy was gradually abandoned by his successors until in A.D. 212 citizenship was granted to every free inhabitant of the empire.

The reform of the army

By virtue of his proconsular power the Princeps was naturally commander in chief of the army. Augustus, drawing upon the experience of his predecessors and especially of his adoptive father, laid down a permanent basis for recruitment and for the composition of the army, which survived in its essentials throughout the whole empire. The regular troops or legionaries were drawn from Italians and the most Romanized provincials, who received citizenship on enlistment if they did not already possess it. They served for twenty years, receiving a regular salary and a pension on retirement. In addition to these were auxiliary troops who received citizenship only on retirement. These were also salaried men, but drawn from the less Romanized provinces, and serving primarily within these provinces. Their officers also were originally drawn from the same territory, but later, after it had been shown that these troops were capable of rebellion in the interests of their own provinces, Italian officers were substituted. The armies were by no means always engaged in active warfare, although the legions might at any time be transferred to a danger spot on a distant frontier. During the first two centuries, however, the general practice was for the legionaries to live in camps behind permanent fortifications which were built by themselves. There were strategic roads to be built, ditches and moats to be dug, walls to be erected, and many of the troops necessarily became skilled artisans as well as soldiers, not unlike the modern corps of army engineers. These men, holding Roman citizenship, speaking Latin, imbued with Roman tradition, enjoying even on the frontiers the comforts of Roman civilization, such as warm baths, naturally mingled with the peoples among whom they were stationed, and served therefore as an important instrument for the Romanization of the empire. The army, however, in its own estimation, was rarely well enough paid in proportion to its value to the state. Its chronic dissatisfaction and its sporadic insistence on bonuses gave ambitious generals the opportunity to make lavish promises in exchange for support of their candidacies to the throne.

Social and economic policy

Rome had never been an important industrial center, and even as a commercial city its usefulness was impaired by its lack of a good harbor. The muddy Tiber had constantly to be dredged to keep the harbor of Ostia at its mouth open for commerce at all. Puteoli, where Paul landed on his journey to Rome, became the regular seaport for Roman trade, and developed into a great city, largely peopled by Greeks and other foreigners, who remained the leaders in maritime commerce as under the republic. But in spite of the absence of large-scale industry, there were innumerable small manufacturing shops in Rome and throughout Italy. For centuries Italy was the chief manufacturer for the Western world, though its products were far surpassed in quality by those of Alexandria and the East. Nevertheless, the Italian balance of trade was always unfavorable, if Rome is included with Italy, since Rome remained a parasite on the economy.

Augustus did not take any active interest in the economy as such. Except for Egypt, industry in the Roman Empire was overwhelmingly in private hands. There was no state industry, nor monopolies of the kind that later developed in the Eastern Roman Empire of Constantinople. But indirectly the establishment of the Pax Romana, with its network of roads and safe transportation, increased prosperity for all classes throughout the empire. And Augustus used the tax money that came from the provinces to pay for an enormous program of public works, chiefly temples and other public buildings, gardens, and baths; and in this the majority of those emperors who had the money available and were not too heavily engaged in unproductive warfare followed his example. These public works provided a market for numerous products made by small industry throughout the empire, and direct work for the large army of unemployed in Rome itself. The provincial municipalities also engaged in similar programs on their account, and it became a matter of civic pride for wealthy citizens to improve their cities with gifts of parks, gardens, temples, and other public buildings.

The unemployment problem

For the poor of the city of Rome, who were grossly underemployed, he found no

Reconstruction, by the Metropolitan Museum of Art, of a bedroom from the southern Italian city of Boscoreale, which was buried by the famous eruption of Vesuvius in A.D. 79. Note the frescoes on the three walls. The room is furnished with authentic pieces from the same city dating from the period of the eruption. (COURTESY THE METROPOLITAN MUSEUM OF ART)

remedy beyond his public works programs and a continuance of the republican practice of providing them with cheap or free food. In addition he, and more particularly the later emperors, provided lavish public spectacles to keep them amused. This program was called by the later satirist Juvenal "bread and circuses." Since the elections were arranged and laws were now really made indirectly by the Princeps, the Roman people, so powerful in the last century of the republic when their votes were necessary for the election of magistrates and army officers, lost their power. Riots could be dangerous on occasion, but they could now be easily suppressed. On the other hand, all the rulers were anxious to keep the people as contented as possible, and tried to provide for their needs. Augustus, recognizing the irresponsibility that went with their unemployment and dependence on imperial handouts, tried to give them some status in the community and in their own eyes by incorporating them formally into an order, the plebeian as distinct from the equestrian and senatorial orders. But since they had no real duties in addition to their privileges, it is probable that the gesture remained an empty formality. We are not told what the plebeians themselves thought about it.

The city in the time of Augustus was efficiently policed, and a fire brigade was established, first under elected officials and then under appointees of the Princeps.

In agriculture Augustus strove to increase the number of small farmers. He gave security of tenure to those who had farms already, and he made an effort to instill a real love of the Italian countryside into the free peasantry. In this effort he was ably assisted by the poet-farmer Vergil, whose *Georgics* are a long paean of praise of the rural life. But the tendencies of the time were against Augustus. It was difficult to arrest the growth of large farms and estates which could be more economically worked than the small unit. The exodus of farmers to the cities which had been such an important feature of the last years of the republic continued. Not all the praise of the rural life could prevail against the hard necessities of making a living. Though there was, as has been seen, chronic underemployment in Rome, at least the citizen could scrape a living somehow, and free bread and circuses were available, as nowhere else. Not until the Industrial Revolution in modern times did it become possible to work farms efficiently with a small labor force, and at the same time keep millions employed in the large cities through the production of machine-made goods and the provision of multifarious services. The problem of Rome itself was almost certainly insoluble by Augustus, however great his power and intelligence.

Estimate of the achievement of Augustus

It is difficult to find in the records of all history a greater political and administrative genius than the first Princeps of Rome, the "architect of empire," Augustus Caesar, and there are few who have approached him. He has suffered in comparison with his great-uncle, who was undoubtedly a more impressive personality with more spectacular and captivating qualities. He has also suffered from his biographers in ancient times, who could not appreciate at their true worth his farsightedness and understanding of the real problems involved in the transition from republic to monarchy, and who paid too much attention to minor failures.

He was conservative, cherishing the old virtues and the old institutions, and appreciating their value; and he devised means to continue what seemed good in them. He did not try to set back the clock in his governmental reforms, nor yet leap forward rashly into impossible experiments forbidden by the nature of the times. The most difficult and rare art of the statesman is to see the limits of the possible and pursue only the possible. And his monument was the Roman peace and the Roman Empire, which endured for hundreds of years in the framework which he had invented. The empire did not collapse after his death as did Charlemagne's, nor fall to pieces by military overextension as did Napoleon's.

Augustus had a tremendous job to accomplish in which all his predecessors had failed; and yet once he had achieved supreme power he substituted, almost without friction, a legitimate and acceptable civil government for civil warfare and domestic anarchy. There is a tale that a man was brought before him who had attempted a conspiracy against him. Augustus reasoned with the man, asking him how he proposed to replace him, and succeeded in convincing him of the impossibility of any alternative. Thereupon he forgave the would-be murderer and even promoted him in the public service. Perhaps Augustus was fortunate in that he was still a young man and had many years of life in front of him to make full use of the opportunity with which he had been presented. But he was never a healthy man, and it is one of his titles to greatness that he was able to overcome the handicap. He lived without ostentation, and never let anyone believe that he had any other ambition than to be first citizen in a restored and transformed republic. He is the most eminent disproof in history of the famous dictum of Lord Acton that "all power corrupts, and absolute power corrupts absolutely."

▶ The successors of Augustus

TIBERIUS AND THE DECLINE OF THE SENATE

It is not necessary in a book of this compass to go into detail on the achievements of the successors of Augustus. The reign of Tiberius (A.D. 14–37) was marked by excellent provincial administration but a growing disharmony between the Princeps and the Senate. Tiberius most certainly lacked his stepfather's tact, and he was already a morose and disillusioned elderly man when he became Princeps. It was not surprising that the senators for the first time now realized the potentialities for an *imperial* tyranny that had been masked under the principate of Augustus. And many of them began to look back nostalgically to the lost republic, viewing it through rose-colored glasses since few of them had actually experienced it. Brutus and Cassius, the tyrannicides, became their heroes, for they had defended with their lives the dignity of senators. Throughout the reign of Tiberius there were constant intrigues over the succession, even while his son, later poisoned by the orders of his favorite, the praetorian prefect Sejanus, was still alive. Betrayed by the one man he had trusted, Tiberius countered the opposition to him with new laws against treason, and new rewards for informers, setting a precedent followed by too many of his successors. There were many real conspiracies against him, but, more than anyone else Sejanus, master of Rome when Tiberius retired to Capri for a little peace in his old age, betrayed him; and though Tiberius was strong enough to crush this conspiracy, the aftermath of treason trials and executions was always remembered against him by later historians and posterity.

The position of the Senate was indeed unenviable. It had had a long tradition of power under the republic, and its position even at its worst was always one of dignity. Augustus had given the senators work to do, but there was no doubt that all real power had been taken from them, and they were deeply offended. Tiberius would preside over the Senate; and though even the anti-imperial historian Tacitus admits that, at least in the early part of his reign, he encouraged the senators to speak freely, most of them were careful to catch every sign of approval or disapproval, so that they would not be found on the wrong side, in opposition to the Princeps, with all the danger that this entailed. This subservience wounded them in their dignity. They were forced out of fear to agree, and their true opinions were not valued. As long as any republican tradition remained, as it did at least until the death of Nero, A.D. 68, they were bound to regret their lost freedom, human dignity, and respect. Not all the outward dignity of a special toga could compensate them. Only the Stoics in the reigns to come provided any real resistance to the rulers, since they had a philosophy to sustain them, and at the last a sword to fall upon; and it was no accident that the tyrannous emperors especially singled out the Stoics as their enemies and treated them accordingly.

THE JULIANS, FLAVIANS, AND THE "GOOD EMPERORS"—RECURRING PROBLEM OF THE SUCCESSION

At last Tiberius died, and was succeeded by Caligula (A.D. 37–41), a young man of no ability and no experience who soon became insane, his insanity revealing itself in an undisguised tyranny and sadistic cruelty. When he was murdered in a praetorian conspiracy he was succeeded by Claudius (A.D. 41–54), an able administrator and student of history who effected many valuable reforms in the provincial administration but was unable to keep order in his own house, being ruled by his successive wives. He was murdered by his last wife, who thus succeeded in securing the succession for her son Nero (A.D. 54–68), who was only the stepson of Claudius. Nero lost no time in getting rid of his stepbrother, who was a real son of Claudius, but for five years he allowed his praetorian prefect Burrus and his tutor Seneca to exercise the actual rule of the empire. Thus the first five years of

Nero's administration became proverbial for excellent administration at home and abroad. Then Nero began to show himself as the misfit he was on the throne, a second-rate artist, anxious only for the plaudits of the crowds for his theatrical performances, and careless of his administration. The people loved him for his spectacular games and gladiatorial shows, but he degraded the imperial dignity, emptied the treasury, and won only contempt and enmity from the upper classes, contempt which culminated in conspiracies against his life. Thereafter no one in Rome was safe from his vengeance, and especially not his former friends. His tyranny in his last years equaled that of the madman Caligula. When he was overthrown by an open revolt and perished at the hands of a freedman when he lacked courage to take his own life, no provision had been made for the succession and no direct heir remained of the Julian house (called Julian after Julius Caesar). First the commander of the Spanish legions took the throne, then the praetorian prefect, then the commander of the German legions, none surviving the year (A.D. 69). Finally the commander of the Eastern legions, a plebeian general of rural ancestry, gained the throne and restored order.

Vespasian (69–79) ruled sensibly and restored some of its earlier dignity to the principate. He was succeeded by his two sons (the Flavian dynasty), one of whom died after two years, while Domitian, the second son (81–96), a suspicious tyrant but a good administrator, fell victim to a conspiracy. This was the end of the hereditary principle for nearly a century. For the first time no obvious candidate was available for the throne, and the choice fell into the hands of the Senate, which selected Nerva (96–98), a mild, elderly man whose most important act was the adoption of the best general in the empire as his son. Thus the adoptive principle superseded the hereditary, and the result was the period known as the era of the "Good Emperors." Each of the four emperors who reigned between 98 and 180 was a good administrator, and Trajan (98–

117) was a great general, though it is not certain that his policy of enlarging the empire was altogether a wise one. The province of Dacia, north of the Danube, acquired by him, in addition to territories in Asia had to be abandoned before most of the rest of the empire, but not before it had been civilized by the Romans. The old Roman province of Dacia, the present-day Rumania, still has a language based upon Latin. Hadrian (117–138) was one of the ablest of the Roman emperors as an administrator. He it was who systematized the civil service, the most competent body of bureaucrats outside China in the ancient world, recruiting its members almost exclusively from the equestrian order, which was now entirely dependent upon himself. Hadrian also gave impetus to the study and codification of the Roman Law by abolishing the edicts of the annually elected praetors (see the next section). By Hadrian's time it was recognized that the word of the emperor was the true source of law for the empire, and it may be said that with Hadrian disappeared

Bust of the Emperor Antoninus Pius. Note the Greek influence and the careful attention to detail characteristic of this period, as shown in the treatment of hair and beard. (COURTESY THE METROPOLITAN MUSEUM OF ART)

the remnants of the old republican tradition. Antoninus Pius (138–161) further improved the law and provided a long reign of almost unbroken peace. Marcus Aurelius (161–180), the Stoic writer of the *Meditations,* was compelled to spend most of his reign defending the empire against barbarian tribes who were threatening the frontiers, but maintained the record of his predecessors in the administration of the empire.

All these emperors were chosen by their predecessors and adopted as their sons. The Augustan title of Princeps, though still formally used, no longer seems appropriate for these absolute rulers. Unfortunately, as has already been mentioned, Marcus Aurelius was not, like the others, childless, and chose as his successor his worthless son Commodus (180–193), whose reign marked the beginning of the serious decline of the empire, as will be narrated in a later chapter. But, whatever the principle of succession used, there was no thought now of restoring the antique republic. The monarchy as an institution had proved itself; the republic was a fit subject only for historical study.

▶ **The provinces in the first two centuries**

Life in the provinces was rarely affected by the disturbances in the capital. The chief annoyance undoubtedly was the arbitrary increases in taxation necessitated by the spendthrift habits of some of the early emperors, especially Caligula and Nero. Imperial governors usually remained over from one regime to another, and senatorial governors continued to be appointed as before unless the emperor was especially interested in the appointment. The Roman peace was maintained in almost the whole empire without a break. The only power in the first two centuries that presented any danger was the Parthian Empire in the Near East. But it was already on the decline in the second century, and Trajan inflicted several severe defeats upon it, altering the Augustan settlement in this region by annexing several new provinces. But his suc-

cessor recognized the great difficulty of holding them, and the fact that the expense involved could ill be afforded. For this reason he returned some of the new provinces to client kings. Not until the reign of Marcus Aurelius was the Roman peace seriously threatened by the first movements of barbarians against the frontiers; and even this was of no moment to the interior provinces, save for increases in taxation to pay for the wars.

The first two centuries of the empire were characterized by an increasing centralization of the government, above all through the growth of the bureaucracy or imperial civil service. Hadrian brought every official under direct imperial control, including those in Italy, even in some cases nominating the governors of senatorial provinces, who were in any case by now the prisoners of the bureaucracy provided for them by the emperor. The municipalities also lost some of their responsibilities. Though the "Good Emperors," including Hadrian, were not personally tyrants, and indeed kept on very good terms with the Senate, being themselves drawn from the senatorial class, their policies tended toward an increasing absolutism which was ultimately recognized by the formal changes in the nature of the monarchy brought about by Diocletian at the end of the third century A.D. It should be added, however, that the Senate no longer provided any opposition to the absolutist tendency, for it had been itself enrolled by previous emperors, and the old qualification of nobility of birth alone had long ago disappeared. The tyrants Caligula, Nero, and Domitian had paid careful attention to see that it should.

The Romanized provinces by the end of the second century had become the real heart of the empire, though Rome, of course, remained the capital. The rank and file of the legions was made up exclusively of provincials, and the officers now came as much from the Romanized provinces as from Italy. One of the reasons why Trajan's wars in the East were ultimately so dangerous to Rome was that the most thoroughly Romanized

provinces, Gaul and the two Spanish provinces, provided so many of his troops, who
too often did not return to their homelands;
if they were not killed in the East they were
likely to settle there. All the emperors after
Nero had had long experience in the provinces and recognized their importance;
Trajan and Hadrian were both Spaniards.
The Italian patriotism of Augustus was therefore slowly replaced by the wider patriotism
of the citizen of the Roman Empire itself.
This reality was ultimately recognized in the
famous edict of the Emperor Caracalla in
212, which granted Roman citizenship to
every freeman of the empire.

▶ Influence of the Roman imperial idea

The Roman Empire, then, by the end
of the second century had become fully
established and accepted as the natural order
of things. Internal opposition had disappeared, and the idea of the Roman Empire
now had such a hold on the hearts and
heads of men as no empire in the past had
ever achieved, with the possible exception
of the Chinese Empire under the Hans.
There was some excuse for the belief that
it was eternal, that it had even been willed
by the gods. It was in this atmosphere of
eternity and impregnability that the foundations of the Christian Church were laid, and
this Church, the spiritual successor of the
Roman Empire, was deeply influenced by it.

The achievements of the empire had
already been enormous. It had always given
tolerable and often excellent administration
and an equitable law to a vast area, and it
had given this area a peace it neither knew
before nor has known since. If liberty was
missing, this was a lack not felt by the people
of the time. No one alive had known it from
experience. It survived, at most, as a philosophical ideal. In the remainder of this
chapter we shall see the other contributions
to the cultural heritage of the world made by
this hard-headed, efficient, practical, but
hardly inspired people who first unified and
ruled the Western world.

▶ General characteristics of Roman culture

CONTRAST WITH CREATIVENESS OF THE GREEKS

It is one of the ironies of history that,
in spite of our admiration for the Greeks,
Western civilization has always been nourished far more by Roman ideas and institutions than by Greek. With the recovery of
Greek literature in recent centuries and the
opportunity to study some of the masterpieces of Greek art in the original we have
been able to make a comparative estimate of
Greek and Roman contributions; and few
would today claim the Romans to have been
qualitatively superior in any single field of
cultural endeavor to which the Greeks turned
their attention. Roman architecture made use
of far more forms than the Greeks had found
necessary for their simpler needs, Roman
engineering solved practical problems that
were outside Greek experience. But though
we are impressed by the grandeur of the
Pantheon in Rome and admire the excellence
of Roman roads, bridges, and aqueducts, it
is to the Athenian Parthenon that we go for
an ideal of architectural beauty. Yet our own
public buildings are copied from the Romans,
we are inclined to use the Corinthian rather
than Doric or Ionic capitals, and our columns, like Roman columns, too often support
nothing and are merely superfluous decorations. But remove a Greek column and the
building will collapse. To us the Greek world
is remote, to be admired but not imitated,
whereas the Romans are close to us. We feel
we understand them. They are people like
ourselves. To enter the Greek world requires
an effort of the imagination; but the Romans,
nearly as far away from us in time, can be
understood, it seems, without any such rare
and difficult mental activity.

It would appear that even to the Romans
themselves the Greeks were a people apart.
They admitted that in every branch of cultural activity the Greeks were their teachers
and masters, and they did their best to
imitate them. But they never seriously tried
to think in the way the Greeks had thought.

The Pantheon at Rome, a much-imitated building, where the deified emperors were buried. Note the combination of dome and Corinthian columns. (COURTESY ITALIAN STATE TOURIST OFFICE)

One such imitation—the Low Library at Columbia University, New York. (COURTESY COLUMBIA UNIVERSITY)

This famous Roman aqueduct, the Pont du Gard in France, gives some idea of Roman engineering skill and the gigantic size of Roman public works of the imperial period. Such construction is even more impressive when one realizes it was carried on with only the most primitive machinery.

It is impossible to conceive of any Roman with whom we are acquainted taking time out to consider the fundamental problem of the early cosmologist, what it is that is stable in a world of changing appearances. No Roman could speculate like Plato or reason like Aristotle. The more simple ideas of these masters they could understand, at least in part. But whenever they tried to explain what they had read—and many Romans, notably Cicero and Seneca, made a real effort to cope with the problems of philosophy— the result always appears as oversimplification, not touching the root of the matter, in some way debased. The truth seems to be, however it may be explained, that the Roman mind simply *could* not think in the Greek manner. Not that such thinking died out in the Roman period. The Greeks, Claudius Ptolemy the astronomer and Galen the physician are recognizably Greek in their thinking, though they lived in the second century of the Roman Empire.

PRACTICAL NATURE OF THE ROMAN GENIUS

The great Roman contribution to world culture therefore lies not in the field of thought, but in the application of thought in the ordinary world of men. In this way they served as a complement to the Greeks. They reaped the harvest of whatever had been thought before them, putting it to practical use. Where the Greeks had been concerned with ethical speculations, the Romans translated these into practical everyday morality; where Democritus had speculated on the constitution of matter, and Epicurus had drawn the conclusion that in such a cosmology there was no need for gods, the Roman Lucretius makes a passionate attack on religion and superstition as the prime causes of human suffering; where human morality is conspicuously missing in the adventures of Odysseus as told by Homer, the Roman Vergil in his *Aeneid* emphasizes the filial devotion of his hero, and the glorification of Rome and its destiny —the purpose of the voyage of Aeneas— breathes in every line of the poem.

► Roman law

GENERAL CHARACTERISTICS

The Romans, then, were the greatest transmitters of culture the world has yet seen, though to a lesser degree the Arabs later performed the same function. But the Roman spirit is nevertheless imprinted on every line the Romans wrote, every idea they took up and put to use. They should not be regarded as mere copiers. Moreover, when the Greeks left no model, the Romans showed themselves quite capable of developing new forms of their own, as in satire, epigram, letter writing, and perhaps even fiction. If anyone had ever had the temerity to translate a Roman work into Greek, it would at once have been recognized as Roman handiwork. So, though we can recognize the merits of these minor achievements it seems best in a brief chapter to devote ourselves to a fuller study of the really great achievement of the Romans, their law, the development of which we are fortunately able to trace almost from the earliest times, owing to the extant writings of so many great jurists, and to the firsthand description of the working of republican courts derived from such men as the practicing lawyer Cicero.

As was seen earlier, the first codified law of Rome was the Twelve Tables, drawn up by a committee of ten in 449 B.C. under the stimulus of the second secession of the plebs. Primitive as this law was, it remained the basic statute law of the Romans. In addition, statute law was made from time to time by the Assembly. These laws, however, covered primarily constitutional and criminal law, which have only limited importance. They were applicable only to Rome herself and her citizens. Since no principles were involved they were incapable of wider application.

THE RIGHTS OF THE ROMAN CITIZEN— JUS CIVILE

But the Romans did have a new and quite original conception of citizenship, which covered certain well-defined rights, discussed earlier. The rights belonged to the man who was a citizen, they were inherent in his person, wherever he might happen to be. This is the first time these particular rights, which in earlier times accrued to a man only by birth, were believed to be vested in a *person.* In Athens the city gave certain privileges to its citizens, but there was no kind of contract between them and the city, and naturally they possessed no privileges unless they were living in the particular city which gave them. But the Romans guaranteed certain definite rights to their citizens, and these they retained even when abroad. These rights collectively were known as *jus,* and a Roman citizen was entitled to have any case tried under the *jus civile,* or civil law.

Now this law was rarely affected by statutes (*leges*) passed by the Assembly. It was built up ordinarily in early times by the priests, who stated on authority what the law was. This task then passed to a special official called the *praetor urbanus* (city praetor). The praetor, however, was an elected official, probably a would-be general rather than a jurist. It was hardly possible for him to state what the law was, or to decide all cases personally, and it was not his duty to do so. He had as assistants judges who came from noble families, and who were in charge of the actual trial. But even these judges were not as a rule trained lawyers, though they had more experience than the annually elected praetor.

When, therefore, a civil case was brought to trial, it was necessary for the parties to the case to have some knowledge of what the law was likely to be in their case. So it gradually came about that the praetor every year on assuming office made a public statement of the law that he would use while in office. This was called the *edictum,* and it was made up largely of the instructions that he proposed to give to the judges. These instructions were called *formulae.* And the edict was made up, for the most part, of decisions that had been made by his predecessors in office.

It will be seen, then, that in this way a collection of decisions would be built up which would really have the force of law, even though no statutes had been made on the subject. Statute law would, of course, be taken into consideration by the praetor, but even this he could interpret, as our judges and higher courts interpret law today. And this interpretation would probably be incorporated in the edict of the next praetor and so be binding for the future, unless a praetor for good reasons decided to depart from it— as our judges may also on occasion depart from interpretations of their predecessors.

THE RIGHTS OF FOREIGNERS—JUS GENTIUM

This, then, was the system for public and private law for Roman citizens, and it lasted for a considerable length of time. But cases also arose where one party to a lawsuit was a Roman citizen and one was not, and where two resident noncitizens might engage in litigation with each other in the Roman courts. If the case concerned a foreigner's personal status, it would clearly be impossible to settle it through the *jus civile,* applicable only to citizens. So in 242 B.C. a *praetor peregrinus* or foreign praetor, whose task was to look after such cases, was elected for the first time. Thus the idea arose that foreigners also had rights, and the new law under which they were judged was called the *jus gentium,* or law of peoples. Both praetors now issued annual edicts covering the cases for which they were responsible.

INTERPRETATION OF THE LAW—BEGINNINGS OF JURISPRUDENCE

As the Roman state grew in importance and undertook more and more responsibilities, and legal decisions of wide significance had to be made by unqualified persons, an innovation was made which proved to be the real foundation of Roman jurisprudence. It became the custom for certain skilled lawyers, who had also held high office in the state, to assist the praetors in drawing up their edicts and in answering questions put by judges. They could also give advice to litigants. These men were not paid, nor did they hold any official position, but undertook the work from a sense of duty and for the prestige involved. Since these *juris prudentes* (men skilled in the law, hence our word "jurisprudence") were appealed to for advice, especially in cases where the law was doubtful, they became specialists in interpretation, and theirs was now the chief responsibility in the building up of new law for the future. It was among these men that the conception of equity (*aequitas*) grew up as a principle which could override a strict interpretation of the law. In time, especially under the empire, certain individuals among them became known for the excellence of their opinions, as certain Supreme Court Justices of the past may still be quoted and accepted in the United States even though they have been long dead.

INFLUENCE OF PHILOSOPHY—JUS NATURALE

Many of these *juris prudentes* were strongly influenced by Stoicism, with its conception of the natural law of divine reason (*jus naturale*), which became a commonly accepted ideal, a kind of ideal law in accordance with which all statute law should be made and all legal decisions should be rendered. The strongly humanitarian viewpoint of the Stoics thus became incorporated into Roman law.

Under the early principate the same system was maintained. But naturally the edict of the praetor and the opinions of the *juris prudentes* had to take account of the new influence of the princeps; and with the increasing absolutism of the emperors the decisions in public law tended to reflect the increasing importance of the state. There was also far more statute law in the empire than under the republic. The Assembly declined as a lawmaking body after Augustus, but the Senate now became for the first time since 448 B.C. a real legislative body, though its laws were naturally in accordance with the emperor's wishes. The emperors after Augustus also issued decrees which had all the force of law. Under Hadrian the praetors' edicts were codified into a perpetual edict, leaving the *juris prudentes* and their interpretations of still greater importance than before. After Hadrian many of them began to hold official positions in the imperial service, often serving as advisers to the emperor, who now felt in need of skilled legal assistance. The law continued to develop, often in accordance with newer Greek and Oriental philosophical ideas.

By this time there was virtually no distinction between the *jus civile* and the *jus gentium,* since the vast majority of the inhabitants of the empire by the time of Hadrian, and all by A.D. 212, were Roman citizens. It was the principles of the *jus gentium,* which had always been more universal and thus more in accordance with philosophical principles, as well as more in accordance with contemporary requirements in law, which prevailed. In the last stage of the empire, the great codification of the law began. Creativeness declined under the absolutist emperors, and the opinions of the great *juris prudentes* of the past were taken as actual law, and a number of dead jurists were named whose opinions must prevail. In the event of a tie, the opinion of the supposed greatest, Papinian, was to be decisive.

THE GREAT CODIFICATION OF THE LAW
AND ITS INFLUENCE

The Theodosian Code of A.D. 438 was a collection of imperial edicts binding in the Eastern and Western Empires. This was followed in the sixth century by the great definitive code of Justinian, drawn up by Trebonian and a group of distinguished jurists in Constantinople. This code, known as the *Corpus Juris Civilis,* had four parts: the Code, which consisted of the imperial edicts of all the emperors (*constitutiones*); the Digest, which contained the decisions of the great *juris prudentes;* the Institutes, primarily a manual on legal principles for use in schools; and the Novels, a series of new laws which Justinian found necessary to complete the whole structure. Naturally the Digest was the most important part of the code for posterity, since these opinions,

based on the best thought of the greatest jurists in accordance with their conceptions of the natural law, were to a large extent free from limitations of time and place. This law code, however, differed from earlier ones in that Christian influence had now been admitted to it. Religious crimes, such as heresy, were included, but on the whole the Christian influence was a gain, especially the legislation on slavery.

The influence of Roman law is almost incalculable. It is not so much that codes of law in many modern countries are still largely Roman, nor that the canon law of the Church is almost exclusively Roman; but that this civilizing work was done by the Romans once and for all, and there was no need ever to do it again. The primitive laws of the barbarian invaders of the empire were so far behind Roman law in principles and sheer intellectual grasp of the problems involved in any law code that all took freely from the Romans, and no code in the Western world has not been influenced by it. It was used as a political tool to help the development of the national state by medieval monarchs. It was so patently superior to feudal law that when the king's justice was modified Roman, and the local law was feudal, every litigant, if he had the choice, would prefer the king's justice. When Napoleon needed a new law code for France in the early nineteenth century, it was to Roman law that he went for a model.

And, as we shall see in a later chapter, the great tradition of the *juris prudentes* was carried on by the jurists of the University of Bologna from the eleventh century onward. Indeed, the university itself only came into existence as a law school with the rediscovery of the *Corpus juris civilis* of Justinian, which had been lost in the ages of barbarian domination of Europe.

▶ Roman art

ARCHITECTURE—CULT OF THE GRANDIOSE

Since far more Roman remains exist in Europe today than Greek, a few words should be devoted to Roman art, architec-

A Roman theater at Arles, in southern France, as it appears today.

ture, sculpture and engineering, which owed much to the Greeks during the period of the Republic, but became to a large degree emancipated during the Empire.

After the Punic Wars, Greek influence became predominant in Rome, and during this period Roman buildings, public and private, were usually copies of those in Hellenistic cities. But even in this copying the Romans knew what they liked, which was invariably the ornate and the grandiose. The Corinthian column was preferred to the more severe Ionic and Doric, and the post and lintel construction was abandoned as unsuitable for large buildings constructed for practical needs, for which the dome, vault, and arch were more suitable. Gradually the Greek forms which the Romans, like ourselves, felt to be "artistic," became merely decorative on Roman buildings. They solemnly inserted useless columns, supporting nothing, they carefully fluted their columns although the fluting served now no practical purpose. The volutes at the top of the columns became more and more luxuriant and decorative, the Corinthian and Ionic

capitals now being welded into a new composite.

When the spoils of war began to flow into Rome during the last century of the republic, private houses, often built by successful bankers and generals, became larger and more ostentatious, and still for the most part constructed by Greek architects, and often furnished with Greek works of art looted during the successful campaigns. Pompey built the first permanent Roman theater out of his spoils, Julius Caesar from his Gallic booty built a new Forum and repaved the old. Roman taste at this time, as usual with the new rich, ran to the extravagant and splendid, with elaborate ornamentation and statuary (copied from the Greek, of course) in wild profusion.

With the advent of Augustus, Roman architecture came into its own, and we begin to hear of Roman architects and engineers, even though Greek influence was still strong and perhaps predominant. The rebuilding of Rome by Augustus, and the construction of vast new temples in accordance with his religious policy of trying to restore the old

*Aerial view of the Colosseum at Rome, built by the Flavian emperors for the display
of such public entertainment as gladiatorial fights.* (COURTESY ITALIAN STATE TOURIST
OFFICE)

gods to honor, influenced provincial cities
also to take advantage of the new prosperity
and rebuild their cities. In the imperial
period every city of any importance had its
baths, and even the smaller cities were able
to build theaters, amphitheaters, and basili-
cas which were used for public business and
to house the law courts. The best known of
the Roman amphitheaters is the Colosseum,
constructed by the first two Flavian emperors, much of which is still standing today,
a huge round structure with a great arena
for the spectacle. Underneath the arena is a
network of passages, enabling performers—
beasts and men—to reach any part of the
arena as required. The basilica is a typical
Roman structure, the plan of which, with
nave, aisles, and clerestory windows, was
adapted by the Christians for their early
churches. The cross-vaulting of the Romanesque cathedrals seems to have been a

Roman invention, and allowed far greater
size to the buildings.

SCULPTURE—REALISM

Like architecture, Roman sculpture was
first influenced by the Etruscans and then by
the Greeks. Indeed, the Romans had such a
high opinion of Greek (almost exclusively
Hellenistic) sculpture that to the end of the
empire many sculptors were employed
simply at making copies of Greek statuary
for the Roman market. But aside from these
copies there is a pronounced difference between Roman and even Hellenistic sculpture,
which is in full keeping with the Roman
character as we know it. The Romans liked
their sculpture to be realistic, thus completing what was only a tendency in the
Hellenistic world. In this preference they
followed the Etruscan tradition also. The
Romans therefore developed the art of real-

The Arch of Constantine in Rome, a triumphal arch for which he is said to have pillaged materials from other such monuments. The workmanship is greatly inferior to that of earlier works of the same kind, though its size remains impressive. (COURTESY ITALIAN STATE TOURIST OFFICE)

istic portraiture far more than the Greeks. When the Greeks, even Hellenistic Greeks, carved a portrait they were always conscious of the harmony between body and mind or soul, between life itself and the material it informed. So the Greeks preferred to carve the whole body, of which the head and face were only a part. When, at the request of the Romans, who usually desired merely a portrait bust, Greek artists took to portrait sculpture, they remained aware of the mind which lay behind the mere features, and thus strove to reveal character through the features and the harmony of the whole composition. The details thus fitted into place as part of the whole, but were not insisted upon, and perhaps the Greek sculptor did

not care too much whether he caught the actual features to be observed on the model. This tendency is what is usually meant when we speak of the idealism of Greek sculpture.

The Romans, on the other hand, as always, were preoccupied by the outer appearance, which they carved exactly as they saw it, including lines of anxiety and unruly hair, which in most cases had no relation at all to what the Greek was trying to portray. For a period in the early empire the two tendencies fully harmonized, the realistic detail being combined with the psychological penetration of the Greek. Then the tendency again disappeared, and this time it was the Greek spirit alone which triumphed, late imperial and other portraits

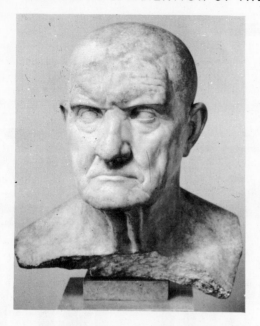

A Roman of the first century B.C. Note how the Romans strove to express character in their subjects' faces. It would appear from their literature that the Romans indeed believed character showed in a man's face. This may account for the prevalence of the bust over the full-sized statue. (COURTESY THE METROPOLITAN MUSEUM OF ART)

often being only suggestive of the subject rather than realistic likenesses. In noting the insistence of the Romans on this detail in the portrait busts, one is reminded of the way in which Tacitus describes the senators watching the emperor Tiberius for any change of facial expression, trying to discover what he was thinking from the outward appearance. It is clear that the Romans believed that the outward face was the true expression of a man's individuality, lines of anxiety and the set of the eyes included, and they probably did not wish any detail to escape them, however apparently unimportant. Hence this emphasis on what we call realism.

In technology the Romans made progress beyond their masters. Even in early republican days they developed a new technique for making roads, the best ones paved with stone, while secondary roads were surfaced with gravel. They built their roads up carefully from a depth of several feet below the surface of the surrounding country, using small stones and even concrete. It seems to have been by accident rather than through any scientific knowledge that the Romans discovered how to make a real concrete composed of lime and a volcanic ash which happens to contain the necessary ingredients. This discovery enabled the Romans to construct their public buildings out of a readily available material instead of using only the always expensive marble, which was then freed for use as a veneer.

The Romans knew how to construct strong bridges through the extensive use of the arch; they made tunnels through difficult mountain terrain; and they understood, but rarely used, the principle of the siphon for their baths and aqueducts. The many Roman remains, not only in Italy but throughout Europe, are an ample testimony to the strength of the materials used and the effectiveness of the Romans as engineers.

▶ **The Empire at the close of the second century**

In this chapter we have traced briefly the history of Rome from the establishment of the republic to the reign of Commodus. There can be no doubt that for the peoples of the empire the rule by emperors and bureaucracy was a great improvement over anything they had known when they were ruled by Senate and people. The empire had given them peace and the opportunity for prosperity. Roman officials, as yet, were for the most part honest and uncorrupted. A considerable amount of self-government was permitted, and the Romans tried to interfere as little as possible. When the English eighteenth-century historian Gibbon asserted that this was probably the period in world history when more people were contented and secure than at any other time, there may well be some truth in his remark. It is true that the emperor Marcus Aurelius had to spend a large part of his reign in unwelcomed campaigns against German barbarians, but few Romans or provincials probably recognized the permanent and ever-growing danger that these barbarians were to represent to the security of the empire, still less that in the fullness of time they would destroy it.

In the next chapter, where the more detailed part of this book begins, Christianity, which in so many ways succeeded to the Roman heritage, will be considered, and in the following chapter the fall of the empire will receive careful attention. But it would have been a singularly inspired prophet who could have predicted either the fall or the legatee at the close of the second century.

▶ Suggestions for further reading

There is one excellent modern source book which gives many pertinent extracts from the primary sources, including inscriptions. This is N. Lewis and M. Reinhold, *Roman Civilization* (New York: Columbia University Press, 1951). Aside from these readings, the Loeb Classical Library translations may be used, and the student is urged to try at least some of the letters and speeches of Cicero, and the political work of Polybius. Though Livy as a historian has to be treated with caution, the student should read at least a few of the earlier books of this writer. If he does so, it might be interesting to examine the way in which a Renaissance Italian historian and statesman interpreted Livy, by looking into Niccolo Machiavelli's comments on Livy, recently published in a cheap edition: N. Machiavelli, *The Prince and the Discourses* (New York: Carlton House, n.d.). Plutarch's biographies of such Romans as Marcus Cato, Cato the Younger, Crassus, Marius, Sulla, Cicero, Caesar,

Pompey, and Marcus Brutus may also be consulted.

In Roman constitutional history there is one outstanding summary which is a masterpiece of compression and clarity. It is, however, difficult to obtain except in good libraries, since it was published in South Africa. This is J. K. Wylie, *Roman Constitutional History from the Earliest Times to the Death of Justinian* (Cape Town, South Africa: African Bookman, 1948). If this is not available, perhaps the best book is F. F. Abbott, *History and Description of Roman Political Institutions* (Boston: Ginn & Company, 1911). Very clear, but sometimes suppressing some of the difficulties, is L. Homo, *Roman Political Institutions* (New York: Alfred A. Knopf, Inc., 1929).

These lists do not, as a rule, recommend textbooks for further study. But an exception should be made for a really outstanding piece of clear exposition which will serve admirably to fill out some of the gaps in the text. This is R. Geer, *Classical Civilization* (2nd ed.; Englewood Cliffs, N.J., Prentice-Hall, Inc., 1950), Vol. 2, *Rome*.

For the last century of the Roman Republic there is available an excellent study which deals with all the factors that entered into the decline and final fall of the republic—F. R. Cowell, *Cicero and the Roman Republic* (New York: Chanticleer Press, 1948). This book is graced also with a number of colored charts which well repay study, once the technique has been mastered. A clear and interesting essay on the fall of the republic is also to be found in F. D. Marsh, *Modern Problems in the Ancient World* (Austin: University of Texas Press, 1943). A pioneer study, sometimes truculent and ill-tempered, highly destructive of earlier romantic traditions about the great men of the last age of the republic and the early empire, but solidly based in the most recent scholarship, is R. Syme, *The Roman Revolution* (Oxford: The Clarendon Press, 1939). No serious student of the Roman Republic, however, can afford to neglect this work, even though he is cautioned to treat it with some reserve. A well-balanced and judicious account which may serve to complete the study of this period is F. D. Marsh, *The Foundation of the Roman Empire* (2nd ed.; London: Oxford University Press, 1927).

Every student should make the effort to read at least some part of the great history of Tacitus, which is conveniently printed in the

Modern Library series in the standard translation, M. Hadas, ed., *The Complete Works of Tacitus* (tr. A. J. Church and W. J. Brodribb; New York: The Modern Library, 1942). The *Annals* covers the Julian Age; and the *Histories* covers especially the period of anarchy following the death of Nero and the re-establishment of the principate under Vespasian. Other worthwhile authors are Juvenal, some parts of Seneca, Lucan, and, with caution, Suetonius. These may be read in the Loeb Classical series.

For the differing views on Augustus and Tiberius, the present author's chapter on "Freedom and Tyranny in the Ancient World," in K. Setton and H. Winkler, eds., *Great Problems in European History* (Englewood Cliffs, N.J.: Prentice-Hall, Inc., 1954), will serve to introduce the problem and give some idea of the varying views of contemporaries and posterity. The last half of R. Syme, *The Roman Revolution* (Oxford: The Clarendon Press, 1939), already referred to, and J. Buchan, *Augustus* (Boston: Houghton Mifflin & Company, 1937), should be read, preferably in conjunction, since they represent opposite points of view. F. D. Marsh, *The Reign of Tiberius* (London: Oxford University Press, 1931), is a masterly attempt to rehabilitate the second princeps, who the author feels has been much maligned by Tacitus.

Almost all the information the beginning student will wish to know on the actual workings of the early empire are to be found in the pages of M. I. Rostovtzeff, *The Social and Economic History of the Roman Empire* (New York: Oxford University Press, 1926), though the reader should be warned that not all scholars agree with his conclusions. The book is also excellently illustrated. For the more conservative opinion, the old classic, T. Mommsen, *The Provinces of the Roman Empire* (2nd ed.; New York: Charles Scribner's Sons, 1909), is still worth consulting. For a briefer picture of the Roman Empire, including its cultural achievements, a valuable work is M. P. Charlesworth, *The Roman Empire* (Home University Library; London: Oxford University Press, 1951).

The standard book on Roman society of the early imperial period is S. Dill, *Roman Society from Nero to Marcus Aurelius* (London: Macmillan & Co., Ltd., 1904), which may be supplemented by a more lively account by J. Carcopino, *Daily Life in Ancient Rome* (tr. E. O. Lorimer; New Haven, Conn.: Yale University Press, 1940). A useful survey, which contains also much cultural material, is F. G. Moore, *The Roman's World* (New York: Columbia University Press, 1936).

The most noble poem in the Latin language, the *Aeneid* of Vergil, is available in many translations. A new translation in an inexpensive edition, which steers a safe path between modern and archaic language and is highly recommended, is K. Guinagh, *The Aeneid of Vergil* (New York: Rinehart & Co., Inc., 1953). Other Latin authors who should be read are Lucretius, Horace, and Ovid, in addition to those mentioned at the end of the two previous chapters. There are many good translations available, especially two Classics Club editions of the two first-named poets.

On Latin literature there are two outstanding works by J. W. Duff, one of them recently reprinted. There is no other history of Latin literature which will begin to compare with these masterpieces: J. W. Duff, *A Literary History of Rome to the Close of the Golden Age* (ed. A. M. Duff; New York: Barnes & Noble, Inc., 1953), and J. W. Duff, *A Literary History of Rome in the Silver Age from Tiberius to Hadrian* (New York: Charles Scribner's Sons, 1927).

An interesting effort to isolate the "Roman Spirit" and distinguish it from the "Greek Spirit" and Greek influence is provided in C. Grénier, *The Roman Spirit in Religion, Thought, and Art* (tr. M. R. Dobie; New York: Alfred A. Knopf, Inc., 1926), but, in general, books on Roman culture have, perhaps naturally, tended to fall far below the level attained by books on the achievements of the Greeks. R. Geer, as he did with the political life of the Romans, has done an excellent job in presenting Roman achievements in a brief compass, with first-rate illustrations, in his text book, *Classical Civilization* (2nd ed.; Englewood Cliffs, N.J.: Prentice-Hall, Inc., 1950), Vol. 2, *Rome*.

On Roman law, J. Declareuil, *Rome the Law-Giver* (tr. E. A. Parker; New York: Alfred A. Knopf, Inc., 1927), is a masterly presentation of Roman law which stresses and explains its uniqueness and importance, but the book is not easily obtainable. Otherwise the books on Roman law are too technical for the general student. A brief survey is given in R. H. Barrow, *The Romans* (Harmondsworth, Middlesex: Penguin Books, 1949), pp. 209–217, and in Geer's book, just mentioned, pp. 347–357. Barrow's book is otherwise recommended for its excellent first chapter on ancient Roman religion and traditions, but elsewhere it is too thin to be even adequate as a survey.

On the city of Rome itself mention should be made of the well-written and well-illustrated G. Showerman, *Eternal Rome* (New Haven, Conn.: Yale University Press, 1924), Vol. 1, which tells much of the history of Rome from the point of view of the city of Rome, an original idea well sustained and carried out.

Since, above all, Rome was famed for its buildings and engineering feats, many of which still survive today, the interested student should consult W. J. Anderson and R. P. Spiers, *The Architecture of Greece and Rome* (New York: Charles Scribner's Sons, 1927), Vol. 2, *Rome*, which should be available in all good libraries.

Finally, mention should be made of the *Meditations* of Marcus Aurelius, available in many editions and translations. This little book, though written in Greek and therefore not forming part of Latin literature, was written by a Roman emperor, and tells much not only of the emperor himself but of Stoic philosophy as it was understood in the Silver Age.

IV The Centuries of Transition

Church of the Holy Wisdom (Hagia Sophia, Sancta Sophia) at Constantinople, built by the Emperor Justinian. This building embodied altogether new principles of architecture. Especially difficult was the erection of the huge dome. The angle of this photograph sets off the commanding position of the church, which is often obscured from other directions by the modern Turkish buildings. The minarets close to the church are later additions dating from the period when the church was used by the Muslim Turks as a mosque. In the foreground is the Mosque of Sultan Ahmed, one of the minarets of which appears just in front of the camera. (COURTESY TURKISH INFORMATION OFFICE)

6

The Rise of Christianity

Religious conditions in the Roman Empire at the beginning of the Christian Era • The life and death of Jesus Christ • The early Christian Church • The organization of the Church • The establishment of Christian doctrine • The persistent ideal of poverty and holiness: monasticism

---

▶ **Religious conditions in the Roman Empire at the beginning of the Christian Era**

THE GREEK BACKGROUND

In order to understand the setting for the new faith that is to be considered in this chapter, a faith that was destined to supersede the numerous religions current in the Roman Empire, it is first necessary to consider the religious conditions in the Augustan Age, especially in the Hellenistic world in which Christianity arose. We have already noticed briefly the political changes that occurred in Greece after the conquests of Alexander. When the Greek city-states lost their independence, the old civic pride, and with it civic religion, had declined; but the Greeks had not lost their vitality and creativeness, nor their intellectual curiosity. The whole Hellenistic world had become the field for their activities, and under their stimulus a momentous change had come over the native Oriental peoples. No people in the whole Near East had remained untouched by the Greek spirit, and

Greek restlessness had communicated itself to the others.

But the whole vast field of political activity which had taken so much of the energy of the Hellenes in the days of independence was now closed to them. The Hellenistic monarchical system had altogether replaced democracy, and when these monarchies themselves succumbed in turn to the Roman expansion, there was still no outlet for political aspirations save for individuals in Roman service. Roman influence in the Hellenistic world, however, was primarily in government and military affairs. The Romans usually protected and ruled this world efficiently enough, but the cultural influence was all in the other direction. The Greeks absorbed the Romans into their culture, which continued to expand ever further westward as the Romans provided the means.

Deprived of what had been the joy of his life in earlier times, the restless Greek engaged in commercial activity, transforming the economy of the Near East; he introduced his language, his art, his literature, his philosophy, his sports, and his whole way of life wherever he went. But still he was not satisfied. Something essential had gone from his life, and for all the great show of activity too often he felt his existence was empty. The gods were pleasant myths to be explained away and Chance ruled now; but though she could be wooed, she could hardly be loved or worshiped. Nor could philosophies hold the allegiance of the Greeks. The Skeptics were busy showing that all philosophies were based on untenable assumptions and that the truth could not be known. The vacuum could only be filled by a religion which appealed to the heart, giving a meaning to the aimless life of the now cosmopolitan and rootless Greeks.

First came a revival of the native Greek mysteries of Eleusis and Samothrace, which, as Plutarch tells us, left the initiate feeling as if he had indeed had an experience of divinity. These mysteries had always demanded much of their devotees, but in return had assured them of immortality, through the undergoing of certain trials which purified the soul. And throughout the Hellenistic world the Oriental religions all experienced a revival, the cults of Cybele and Isis and of Mithra offering impressive ceremonial, festivals, ritual, and initiation, as well as purification and redemption of the soul with the aid of a mediator who sacrificed himself for the salvation of men. At last the Orient ceased to accept from the Greeks without giving in return. Now the culture became truly Greco-Oriental, with the Romans as outside conquerors, resisting or succumbing to the allurements of this culture, but always alien in the Hellenistic world.

THE JEWISH BACKGROUND

But there was one Oriental people which held itself aloof, for the Jews had already received their separate promises. The Jewish religion had absorbed elements from the other Oriental teachings, and the more orthodox Jews now believed in the future life, and they believed in the Satan and demons of Persian Zoroastrianism and Mithraism; but they also held fast to their more ancient law and ritual which, with the ascendancy of their priesthood, had become

ever more strict and rigid. They remained monotheists, believing that all other gods than Yahweh were either demons, idols, or nonexistent. And above all they were looking for a Messiah who would come to redeem the faithful people of Israel; for him they must remain apart, a chosen people, the only righteous ones on earth, the only ones ready to greet him when he came. The center of the Jewish religion was the holy city of Jerusalem, which had retained a precarious independence under the Maccabees, only to fall to the arms of Pompey, and thereafter submit, first to a client king, Herod of Idumaea, and then to the direct government of Rome under an equestrian procurator. The Romans had never been able to understand the Jews. From sad experience they knew that they could not drive them into making any compromises with polytheism, not even the formal acknowledgment of the divinity of the emperor. So at last they accepted the fact and let them alone, giving them religious privileges withheld from any other subjects of Rome, for the Romans felt that the Jewish faith did not constitute any real danger. It seemed impossible that such a small and exclusive sect could expand so far that it could undermine the loyalty of the vast population of the empire.

But the Jews in Jerusalem were by no means the only Jews in the Hellenistic world. Elsewhere, in every city of importance, there was a Jewish colony which sent representatives to the great festivals at Jerusalem, willingly acknowledged the temple there as the headquarters of their religion, and from their greater wealth often sent donations for the poorer Jews of the religious capital. The widely scattered Jews of the Diaspora (Dispersion) lived in Greek cities, and were subject to the all pervading influence of Greek culture. They could not all be so strict in their religious observances as their brethren of Jerusalem. Though they studied and loved the Hebrew Law, they also studied Greek philosophy at Greek schools; they were familiar with all the intellectual currents of the Greek world. Such a one was Saul of Tarsus, who was to became the first great Christian missionary.

Even in Jerusalem itself not all the Jews had kept themselves free from Greek influence. In the days of Antiochus Epiphanes, there were Jewish collaborators, and though these had lost power in the time of the Maccabees, others were still ready to collaborate with the Greeks and Romans when the Jews lost their independence. It was necessary for these men to play a very careful game with the Romans, for the ultimate benefit, as they no doubt felt, of the whole Jewish people. These men provided the high priest at the time of the Crucifixion, and probably a majority of the Jewish Council (Sanhedrin or Synedrion), which was entrusted by the Romans with local government, subject only to the general supervision of the Roman procurator.

But these Hellenized Jews (Sadducees) who accepted realistically the Roman rule differed in one important respect from their fellow Jews the Pharisees. They did not believe in the resurrection of the body and in immortality.

With many fervent men and women looking for a Messiah, and with no certainty of when he would come, nor how he would reveal himself, it was natural that there were many who claimed to be the Messiah. These men gathered around themselves fanatical bands of disciples, who were too often determined that their Messiah should prevail, if necessary by force. But all failed, and by the time of the birth of Jesus there was none who had been able to command the faith and allegiance of all the Jews. The Sadducees had found it necessary to suppress these would-be Messiahs, for they were held responsible by their masters for all riots. Other Jews, like the Essenes, had gone into the desert, purifying themselves by ascetic practices, but they too were waiting for the Messiah to reveal himself. And again others, like the Pharisee Hillel, had begun to teach the people that the true religion was a religion of the heart, one that emphasized love for one's neighbor, rather than only an affair of religious observances and ritual.

Such, then, was the atmosphere in Judaea and Palestine when Jesus was born.

▶ The life and death of Jesus Christ

THE NATURE OF THE SOURCES

We do not know as much as we should like about the early history of Christianity, and the actual life and work of its founder, for reasons not unlike those already discussed in connection with the Hebrews. And though the traditions about Jesus Christ grew up far closer in time to his actual life than the traditions about Moses, and indeed some of the writers may have known him on earth and participated in his work, the chief difficulty remains that these men were not concerned with writing a history so much as with presenting a picture which would captivate the minds and hearts of their readers. The four Gospels (the Greek word is "evangelion," meaning "good news," hence the writers were called Evangelists), which tell of the life of Jesus all present this unique personality in terms sufficiently alike for us to recognize the authenticity of the general portrait. But each Evangelist selects from Jesus' life and teachings those elements which the writer personally has felt to be essential. The portrait is thus colored by the understanding and purpose of the Evangelist himself. Matthew and Luke record the birth, and, very briefly, the childhood of Jesus, while Mark is apparently only interested in the mission of Christ. Mark therefore begins his Gospel with the baptism in the river Jordan, where this mission received its public divine approval—one of the few incidents described by all four Evangelists. John also writes only of the mission of Christ, but every word in his Gospel is deeply concerned with the divinity of Christ and the inner meaning of the impulse of love that he came on earth to proclaim.

None of the Evangelists shows any signs of having done any historical research, nor would it seem to have occurred to any of them to do so. While Matthew and Luke make brief mention of an important event in the life of Jesus at the age of twelve, both are silent on the years between this event and the baptism at the age of thirty; and this period can only be filled, if at all, by the use of much later legends, which may have some basis of truth behind them.

Apparent contradictions in the accounts have always been difficult for commentators to explain, as, for instance, the different genealogies of Jesus which appear in Matthew and Luke, and the voyage to Egypt described by Matthew, which seems inconsistent with the Luke narrative. Yet these Gospels are all that we possess in the way of external record, and from them must be constructed such consecutive history as we can. The personality of Jesus Christ shines out so clearly from all four narratives that there has never been any real question as to their general truth and authenticity.

After the death of Christ the records become more plentiful. For the years immediately after his death the book of the Acts of the Apostles, probably also written by Luke, comes much closer to being a historical narrative than do the Gospels. Contemporary with this book are the letters of the apostle Paul to the churches which he founded. Most of these are certainly authentic. In the early second century we have the first mention of Christians from Roman sources, and from the middle of the second century there are enough Christian records for a consecutive account to be framed with some accuracy. But most of first-century Christianity and even the question whether St. Peter was the first bishop of Rome and was martyred there are not yet entirely historically established.

The Evangelist St. John writing his gospel. The eagle, always associated with St. John, symbolized, according to the inscription, the evangelist's yearning toward the heights. From a book of gospels (Anglo-Frankish), ca. 850. (COURTESY THE PIERPONT MORGAN LIBRARY, Ms. 862, folio 144)

► chronological chart

The life and death of Jesus Christ
Birth of Jesus	(probably) B.C.	4
Mission of Jesus Christ	(probably) A.D.	26–30
Crucifixion of Jesus Christ	(probably)	30

The early Christian Church
Missionary journeys of Paul	ca. 34–60
Paul appeals to Roman emperor	60
Fire of Rome—Massacre of Christians	64
Pliny's correspondence with Trajan about Christians	111–112
Rescript by Marcus Aurelius against Christians	169
General persecution of Christians by Emperor Decius	249–51
"Diocletian" persecution	303–13
Constantine succeeds to throne	312
"Edict of Milan"	313
Council of Nicaea	325
Conversion and death of Constantine	337
Conversion of Goths to Arianism (Bishop Ulfilas)	340–348
Julian the Apostate	361–363
Theodosius I forced to do penance for massacre at Thessalonica	390
Proscription of pagan religions by Theodosius	392
Death of Augustine (*City of God, ca.* 425–430)	430
Invasion of Italy by Attila the Hun	452
Western bishops subjected to Pope Leo I by Emperor Valentinian III	455

Monasticism
Rule of St. Basil	ca. 360
St. Patrick's mission to Ireland	432
Rule of St. Benedict	529
Irish monasticism of St. Columba	533–597
Columba founds monastery of Iona and Scottish Church	563
Missionary work of St. Columban in Europe	590–615
Pope Gregory I the Great	590–604
Conversion of England to Catholic Christianity	597
Synod of Whitby—Submission of Irish Church	664

The story, therefore, that follows will necessarily be drawn from the Gospels and the other books of the New Testament, with the reminder that it may not be fully accurate, and it cannot be independently verified by any means now available to us.

THE GOSPEL ACCOUNT

Jesus was born in Bethlehem of Judaea, as prophesied by the Hebrew prophet Micah. He was born through the influence of the Holy Spirit to Mary, whose husband was Joseph of the lineage of King David. Mary had been informed by an angel that the child was to be born, and was to be a "son of the Most High." Thus far the story parallels that of Mithra, who was born by a similar divine dispensation.

While only a few days old Jesus was visited by representatives of the Oriental religions in the form of three wise men or kings, who followed a star to the cattle barn where he was lying (Matthew), and by humble shepherds to whom the birth had been revealed by a choir of angels (Luke). After a journey to Egypt to escape from persecution by King Herod, who had heard of the visit by the wise men (Matthew), Jesus returned to Nazareth, where he was brought up in the Jewish faith. At the age of twelve he was taken to Jerusalem by his parents, who found him after some days in the temple disputing with the Jewish rabbis. The Evangelist records that his parents were astonished at his learning, thus making it clear his knowledge of the Jewish Law had been acquired by divine dispensation, and not through their instruction. When they found him he returned with them to Nazareth, where in due course he took up his father's trade of carpentry.

Thereafter there is a break in the narrative until all four Evangelists record a visit to an Essene prophet, John the Baptist, who has been preaching the imminent coming of the Messiah, and urging the people to change their way of thinking in preparation for this event.[1] John has already declared that he himself is not the Messiah. When he sees Jesus coming he immediately recognizes him as the one who should come, "the latchet of whose shoes I am unworthy to unloose," and baptizes him in the river. A voice is heard from heaven saying, "This is my beloved son in whom I am well pleased," and the Holy Spirit is seen descending from heaven in the form of a dove.

This is the beginning of the Messianic mission of Christ (the word "Christus" means the "anointed one"). For the next three years he preaches to the people and heals the sick, giving many signs of his Messiahship.[2] Sometimes he teaches straightforwardly, attacking above all the strict Pharisees, whose religion is mere outward show. At other times he hides his true mes-

sage within parables, sometimes adding, even as he gives one interpretation, the words, "Let him hear who has ears to hear." He chooses twelve men to be his special aides, and these are called apostles; around him gather many more who come to listen to him. Those who decided to follow him are called disciples.

Throughout Christ's teaching there is always the emphasis that true religion comes from the heart, and that "the Law and the prophets" are comprised in two commandments, the love of God and the love of one's neighbor. Though these teachings, with their evident wealth of hidden meanings, have inspired Christians ever since, nevertheless it is not the teachings of Christ so much as his life and death and whole personality as revealed by the Gospels that have been taken by the Christian Church and Christian believers as the truest evidence for the divine origin of his mission and for the divinity of his person. The Gospels thus gave Christianity some of its human appeal over such competing religions as Mithraism and the Egyptian mystery religions in that the central figure of Christianity was a man who had actually lived on earth, and had been seen and could be remembered by his followers. The teachings have been expressed by others almost equally well, and there is nothing profoundly *new* in them. But the inspiration of the death and resurrection has been constantly renewed in countless Christian hearts in all the centuries since.

The Gospel accounts are in substantial agreement with each other on the death and resurrection of Jesus Christ. After three years of preaching and healing he had aroused the resentment of many Jews who had not been convinced by his signs or his teachings. But it was one of Christ's own apostles, Judas Iscariot, who betrayed him to the leading Jews, who thereupon sent a guard to take him prisoner. Christ made no attempt to defend himself, and indeed forbade his disciples to use any violence against the guard. He had already warned them that he would be put to death and raised from

[1] The Greek word "metanoeite" used means literally "change your outlook" or "change your way of thinking." This conveys a different sense from the word "repent," by which it is usually translated.

[2] The Greek word "semaion" or "sign" was translated into Latin in the authoritative Latin Bible of St. Jerome as *miraculum;* hence our word "miracle," which probably gives the wrong impression of these symbolic acts.

The crucifixion of Jesus Christ painted by the Dominican Friar, Fra Angelico (fourteenth century). (COURTESY THE METROPOLITAN MUSEUM OF ART)

the dead after three days, but they had not understood him. When therefore they saw that he was captured and would not defend himself, they deserted him. The leading apostle, Peter, even went so far as to deny publicly that he had ever known Christ, thus again fulfilling a prophecy of his master.

Christ was then examined by the High Priest, and admitted that he was the Son of God. The High Priest and Council, declaring that this admission was a blasphemy, wished to put him to death in accordance with Jewish law, but to do so they needed confirmation of the sentence from the Roman procurator, Pontius Pilate. Pilate then questioned him, but finding that his offense seemed to be only a religious

one, was anxious to release him. However, when the Jews insisted that Christ wished to make himself "King of the Jews," Pilate became afraid, no doubt remembering that Tiberius was on the throne, and had recently passed severe laws against treason. He therefore confirmed the sentence and Christ was crucified. A rich follower claimed the body, and buried it in the tomb prepared for himself.

At this point it must have seemed to anyone alive at the time that Christ's mission had failed. The new Messiah had been put to death, and his followers, mostly men and women of the lower classes and of no influence, had deserted him. Like other Jewish Messiahs, of whom there had been many, he would be forgotten.

▶ The early Christian Church

THE CONVERSION OF ST. PAUL AND THE NEW
MISSIONARY IMPULSE

This time, however, there was a strikingly different outcome. On the third day after his death Peter, John, and a woman follower of Jesus named Mary Magdalene went to the tomb and found it empty. Then they saw their master once more alive in the body, and he showed himself to his disciples several times. This experience gave them new hope and energy, and after they had seen the resurrected Christ received into heaven, they all awaited the last fulfillment of his promise—the coming of the Helper or Holy Spirit who, according to the promise, could only come to them after Christ had died and had been resurrected. One day, when the apostles had gathered together in an upper room and after they had chosen by lot a twelfth apostle to replace Judas Iscariot, who had, in remorse, hanged himself, there was suddenly "the sound of a rushing mighty wind," and they were all filled with the Holy Spirit, and began to prophesy, and speak each in the tongue of the land of his origin. The onlookers thought them drunk, but with new inspiration they began to preach the resurrection of Christ and to make converts. One of the disciples, Stephen, addressed an assembly of Jews, accusing them of always having maltreated, rejected, and put to death their prophets. The Jews, goaded beyond their endurance, stoned him to death, making him the first Christian martyr (Greek for "witness"). Apparently the Roman officials looked the other way and did not interfere.

Present at the stoning was Saul of Tarsus, a Roman citizen, an orthodox Hellenized Jew of the sect of the Pharisees, who at once saw the danger from these new fanatical believers in a Messiah who had failed and died without fulfilling the mission expected of him. Saul therefore, with a band of determined helpers, proceeded to lead an expedition of extermination against the Christians, presumably with the aid, or at least the connivance, of the authorities. Having done his best in Jerusalem, he set out on a journey to Damascus in Syria to continue the persecution of converts in the north. On the road to Damascus he had an experience in which the crucified Christ appeared to him in a vision. This experience gave him an absolute conviction from which he never afterward wavered, leading him to regard and speak of himself as an apostle called out of due time. At first, however, he was paralyzed and struck blind; his servants brought him to Damascus, where his faculties were restored by a Christian. From this moment Saul, whom the records thereafter call Paul, was as strongly for the Christians as he had previously been against them. After a period of retirement during which he was apparently coming to an understanding of his experience on the road to Damascus, and the realization of his mission he went to Jerusalem, where he was naturally received with some distrust by his late enemies. But, even without any real authorization from the body of Jewish Christians who had now formed a church in Jerusalem as headquarters of the new religion, he set out on a missionary journey, during the course of which he took the epoch-making decision to baptize Greeks and other non-Jews as Christians without making them become Jews first, sparing them the Jewish rites and ritual which Peter had been insisting on in Palestine.

Returning to Jerusalem, Paul reached a compromise with Peter that Gentiles outside Palestine need not become Jews, while the church in Jerusalem would continue with the requirement. Then Paul set out again, making converts everywhere, especially among the Greeks to whom he, with his Greek education, was able to speak in their own language and in their own terms. At Athens itself, finding an altar dedicated "To the unknown God," he showed the Athenians who this God was, and why he hitherto had been unknown to them. With rare organizing ability and drive, he founded churches in all the places he visited, and kept in touch with them afterward by correspondence. His letters, the earliest authentic Christian documents, expounded the new Christian theology, which seems to have been almost entirely his own work, and answered the numerous questions put to him. In all the cities Paul visited in Asia Minor and Greece, his most determined opponents were always the Jews.

OPPOSITION OF THE JEWS TO CHRISTIANITY

It cannot be stated categorically why the Jews were so determinedly hostile as a body to the Christians, although individual Jews were of course converted, especially in the Hellenistic cities. The Jewish leaders, Pharisees and Sadducees alike, had instigated the proceedings which led to the Crucifixion, but only a few took an active part in this event. The usual explanation is that the Jews were looking for a Messiah of an entirely different kind from Jesus Christ, one who would give them temporal power and not merely redeem them through suffering. Their prophet Isaiah had devoted his matchless eloquence to a description of a "suffering servant," a "man of sorrows and acquainted with grief,"—but it was not certain that this prophecy referred to an actual man, a Messiah. It might only refer to the people of Israel as a whole. Moreover, by no means all Jews had yet accepted the idea of a future life. If there was no such future life and no heavenly kingdom, then clearly such a Messiah as Christ was worse than useless, since his religion tended to create a schism within Jewry which could not be tolerated. All through Hebrew history there had been such schisms, and in Jewish belief these had been punished by Yahweh. They had, indeed, been responsible in part for Yahweh's continual postponement of the fulfillment of his promises. The temptation offered by Christianity, therefore, was just one more test of their faith. And even those Jews who took account of political rather than religious realities could see that Christianity represented a grave danger to the privileged status of their religion in the Roman Empire. They realized that the Romans would look upon Christianity as a Jewish sect—but potentially dangerous not only because of its exclusive monotheism but because of its zeal for conversion from which the Jews themselves had usually been free.

Christ had been a Jew, thoroughly grounded in the Law and the prophets. But he had claimed that the Law itself had to be newly interpreted, not in the manner of the rabbis, but through breathing a new spirit into it. Many were impressed by the authority with which he spoke, even daring to criticize Moses—"Moses said to you, but I say." Now St. Paul, claiming a similar authority as an apostle, was even more explicit. The Law, he wrote in a letter, is a schoolmaster to bring us to Christ. The Law had been given to the Hebrews because at that time they did not know right from wrong, nor did they know how God was to be worshiped and what he required of them. Now, however, under the new dispensation of Jesus Christ, they were no longer children, needing to be kept under discipline, but "sons," with their knowledge of right and wrong coming from within, through faith and love. Therefore, although Hebrew thought, formerly an exclusive possession of the Jews, was spread throughout the whole Western world by Christianity, the orthodox Jews took no pride in this dissemination of their heritage, for if this heritage was to be a possession of the world, then their mission as a chosen people was over.

ST. PAUL AS THE FOUNDER OF
CHRISTIAN THEOLOGY

On the whole Paul met with little opposition from Greeks and Romans unless, as at Ephesus, he offended the priesthood of a powerful Greco-Oriental mystery cult. But regularly the local Jewish community tried to prevent him from preaching. Several times he was thrown into prisons by the Roman authorities for causing riots, but in general it was the Romans who protected him. When at last he returned to Jerusalem, opposition to him was so strong that he was first taken into protective custody by the Romans.

Then, when he was about to be punished for his part in the riots, he used his right as a Roman citizen and appealed to Caesar (Nero). The local governor was thus forced to send him to Rome, where he was allowed a limited freedom even before his trial came up. We know nothing further of his life for certain, but tradition has it that he was beheaded during the first organized persecution of Christians in Rome about A.D. 65.

St. Paul was the real founder of Christianity as a universal religion. If the other apostles, who wished to confine Christianity to the Jews, had been successful it hardly seems possible that it could have survived. Paul also deserves to be considered as one of the most influential thinkers of history. It was no mean feat to transform what was, after all, to external eyes nothing beyond the life and death of a great prophet, into a system of theology, logical, clear, and compelling, which has stood the test of time, and is still the fundamental theological doctrine of all Christian churches, Catholic and Protestant alike.

Christ, according to Paul, had been the Son of God—a God-man—though he was also fully a man by virtue of his incarnation into a human body. Every man born into the world suffers from the sin of Adam. ("As in Adam all die, so in Christ shall all be made alive.") Man would have been doomed only to hell if it had not been for the voluntary sacrifice of Christ upon the cross, which redeemed mankind through his blood, and made possible man's salvation and reception into a blessed immortality in heaven. For Paul the necessity for man was to believe in Christ, which faith effected an inner transformation of his whole being, freeing him from the bonds of original sin, and enabling him to be good also on earth. Thus man was not saved through good works, but the good works were the fruit of his faith. The symbol of the washing away of the original sin of Adam was baptism, by which a man of his own free will declared his faith in Christ, and was received into the Church.

It should be added that, although Paul founded churches as communities of Christians who had all accepted Christ and been baptized, it was not the reception into the Church which was decisive for salvation, but the inner act of "putting on the whole armor of Christ," allowing Christ to live within the inner self—the symbol for which was the baptism in water, which symbolically washed away the sins of the convert. Only in later days with the growth of the Church did the belief come to be accepted that the Eucharist and the other sacraments were necessary to salvation, and that the transubstantiation, the miracle of the turning of the bread and wine into the body and blood of Christ, was the supreme need of all human beings. The baptism then became a rite to be performed in infancy, and not an affirmation of faith by a believer; from childhood, then, a Christian was cleansed from original sin and was thus eligible for Heaven even though he never lived to participate in the other sacraments.[3]

THE APPEAL OF CHRISTIANITY IN THE ROMAN WORLD

Christianity, as it emerged from the mind and heart of St. Paul, was eminently fitted to make the deepest appeal to religious men and women throughout the world. It promised salvation in the hereafter to all who would accept Christ, and this acceptance was simply an act of faith. Thus, in spite of its complex theology, perhaps never understood by more than a small minority of its adherents, it was basically simple. It was no respecter of persons. The meanest slave was eligible for salvation, and to him it also offered the fullest compensation for his hard life on earth—which was merely a testing ground for the hereafter. No distinction was made between men and women, and there were no difficult trials and initiation ceremonies to be undergone by the convert. And in early days there was a belief in the imminent second coming of Christ to judge the world, so that the faithful Christians might not even see death. No religion

[3] It should be pointed out that there are other varying interpretations of the teachings of St. Paul, and that what has been said here is still in dispute among theologians.

in the world of the time, not even the mystery religions, could offer as much to its converts—community fellowship, a sense of mission and urgency, a promise of a blessed immortality, and a systematic theology and philosophy which could satisfy even the Greek mind when later it set to work on it. And if at first Christianity lacked gorgeous ceremonial, this was later added in full measure by the Church. And in the recorded sayings of Christ it had a fund of ethical and moral teachings which could satisfy even the Roman feeling for active morality.

Yet it did not appeal in early times to the upper classes among either the Romans or the Greeks; indeed, for centuries it was primarily a religion of Greeks and Orientals, with comparatively few Roman converts, no Roman pope for two centuries, and hardly a single Roman martyr. The Romans, even when they were correctly informed about it, regarded it as a religion for slaves and foreigners, and it was difficult for them to accept as a redeemer a man who had belonged to a despised people and had suffered a slave's death in a remote part of the empire. His origin and manner of dying offended their class consciousness and pride of race, while the Greek intellectuals considered his teachings at first as philosophically negligible. In time, however, as the Greeks learned more about the religion, many of them began to take an active role in the formulation of Christian theology, and, especially in the early days of the Byzantine Empire, they entered passionately into theological controversy.

Physical conditions in the Roman Empire, however, were ideally suited for the spread of Christianity. The establishment of the Pax Romana made it possible for missionaries to travel in perfect safety from one end of the empire to the other, and the strategic Roman roads provided an ideal means of communication. The common languages of Greek and Latin could be understood everywhere. And Roman protection was extended to all without discrimination, at least until the new religion was proscribed as a subversive organization. And, as we

have seen, any missionary like Paul who happened to be also a Roman citizen had special privileges in addition to the general protection extended by the Roman Empire to all its subjects.

ROMAN MEASURES AGAINST CHRISTIANITY TO THE CONVERSION OF CONSTANTINE

In general, as we have seen, the Romans were tolerant of all religions, and gave hospitality in their shrines to the gods of all their subject peoples. They would have been entirely willing to include Christ among these divinities. But the Christians refused to acknowledge the existence of the other gods, or else categorically condemned them as demons. And this intolerance made the Christians refuse even to pay formal obeisance to the dead emperors as gods. This refusal was, to the Romans, not a religious but a political offense, and when it became dangerous it had to be severely punished. The Jews had long been known to possess similar subversive views, but since they made no attempt to convert, and did not make themselves conspicuous, they were generally tolerated except by such a mentally unbalanced emperor as Caligula. But the Christians kept themselves apart in small communities, with simple ceremonies such as common meals during which they celebrated the last supper of Christ and his disciples. Few Romans could believe that Christian practices were really as simple and harmless as they appeared, and it was easy for their enemies to say that they performed hideous rites in secret. Even the eating of bread and the drinking of wine, which in the early days of the religion they seem to have regarded simply as symbolic of the body and blood of Christ, brought accusations of cannibalism upon them. And since many of their early communities held all goods in common, they were accused of undermining society.

So when Nero, after a serious fire had broken out in Rome (A.D. 64), was himself accused of setting it, it was not too difficult for him to turn the accusation against the Christians, inspiring the first important persecution. Tacitus, who recorded the fact of the accusation, did not think the Christians set the fire, but he did regard them as "haters of the human race," and for this reason worthy of punishment. The Roman citizens among those condemned, traditionally including Paul, were beheaded, while of the remainder most were killed by wild beasts in the arena, the Roman method of execution which economically served for entertainment as well as satisfying the needs of justice. St. Peter also probably perished in Rome at this time, but, according to tradition, by being crucified upside down. Yet even in this persecution, as at all times in Roman history, anyone who recanted, and was willing to prove he was no Christian by formally acknowledging the divinity of the emperors, was spared.

The laws against Christians remained on the statute books, but were only sporadically enforced. Pliny, governor of Bithynia in the early second century, asked his master Trajan if he should enforce them, and was told that he was not to seek Christians out, but that he must punish them if they were brought before him for trial and either confessed or refused to recant. In the reign of Marcus Aurelius (A.D. 177) forty-eight Christians were executed in Lyons, but this seems to have been done by the Roman authorities at the demand of a mob, presumably drawn from adherents of competing religions. This massacre was followed by a decree against all subversive religions which were likely to lead to riots. In the middle of the third century the emperors Decius and Valerius, in an attempt to halt the anarchy of the time and revive loyalty to the throne, issued a number of decrees ordering the Christians to take part in the official state worship. But though there were some martyrdoms and recantations, the laws were soon abandoned with the deaths of their authors, and the decrees were even officially rescinded by their successors.

In the early fourth century, just before the acceptance of Christianity by Constantine, a new series of decrees were issued by Diocletian and Galerius, which were this time put energetically into effect. Diocletian's new oriental absolutism (to be described in the next chapter), with the monarch a god on earth, obviously could not tolerate the state within a state that the Christian sect had now become. But though many Christians fell away from the Church at this time, the faithful remained steadfast, and it was soon seen that the religion was too powerful to be exterminated merely by force. In 311 Galerius issued an Edict of Toleration, and the following year Constantine won his battle of the Milvia Bridge under the sign of the cross. In 313 he and the Eastern Emperor Licinius jointly prepared the so-called Edict of Milan,[4] granting equal toleration to all religions in the empire.

Constantine, though not baptized a Christian until he was on his deathbed, took an active interest in the religion, presiding over the important Council of Nicaea, which defined the doctrine of the Trinity. During the fourth century, under imperial protection, except for two years under Julian the Apostate, the Christian religion in spite of considerable opposition to it throughout the empire, made rapid progress, even in rural areas where the old gods had never altogether lost their appeal. When at the end of the century (A.D. 392) Theodosius I decreed that henceforth Christianity was to be the only religion in the empire, the countryside perforce had to submit and adopt at least the forms of Christianity. But it would probably have been difficult for any observer to detect much difference. Instead of pagan deities, Christ was enthroned; instead of the pagan shrine, a church was erected. But it is clear that these folk knew little enough of the teachings or theology of Christianity, and the festivals and ceremonies of paganism for the most part were incorporated directly into the new official religion.

[4] Most modern opinion holds that there was no actual Edict of Milan. The matter was discussed by the two emperors, and Licinius later issued an imperial rescript on the subject from his headquarters in the East. Constantine had already made clear his own position.

The organization of the Church

IN THE PROVINCES

As the Church grew, so naturally did the complexity of its organization. St. Paul himself, as we have seen, kept in touch with all the congregations he had founded, giving them advice and visiting them when he could. As yet there were no priests or Church officials of any kind, and the simple ceremonies and meetings did not require the services of men set aside for purely religious duties. The affairs of the churches were managed by elders, active men in the congregation who took the initiative in matters of religion. But as ever more congregations were organized and it was realized that they might drift apart both in doctrine and in practices if left to themselves, it became clear to the leaders that some kind of more elaborate organization was necessary to keep them united. Living, as they did, within the Roman Empire, there was obviously one particular pattern of organization that could best be imitated, the organization of the empire itself. Within the congregations three hierarchies differentiated themselves in the process of time: deacons, whose task was to give help to Christians in their ordinary daily affairs and especially to take care of the administration of charity; presbyters, who looked after religious affairs of the church; and then an individual leader, called an overseer or episcopus, from which comes our word "bishop."

In early times neither presbyters nor bishops were in any way superior to the ordinary layman, nor did they go through any special ceremony when they were elected to their position. But by the end of the second century, with the elaboration of the ceremonial of the Church, and the growth of the belief that its services were needed for salvation, these clergy became set apart as a class of real priests who were *ordained* by the bishops. And this ordination, like baptism and the Eucharist, had now become a *sacrament*, while the ceremony of ordination

had now become a ritual conferring special sanctity upon the holder. For several centuries more it was the congregations who chose their bishops; but once chosen, these men had full monarchical power within their churches. As time went on, it became necessary to have archbishops whose seats were usually in the Roman capitals, or chief cities, of the provinces and who were in charge of all the churches in their respective provinces. These men were called *metropolitans*. The bishops in the whole empire met from time to time in ecumenical (universal) councils, presided over by the metropolitans or by the Bishop of Rome (later called *Pope*[5]), to consider doctrinal problems and to discuss matters which concerned the Church as a whole.

IN ROME—THE BISHOP OF ROME—
PETRINE SUPREMACY

The bishop of Rome had a peculiar position as the head of the Church in the capital city of the empire. Probably as early as the second century A.D. the Roman congregation was the largest in the empire. The Church in Rome, according to tradition, had been founded by the apostle Peter, who had been martyred and buried there. He thus became the first bishop of Rome. Though there is as yet no certain documentary evidence of this fact, there is no reason why it should not be true; at all events, it was generally believed by the middle of the second century A.D., since lists of the bishops of Rome were compiled about this time, and the first name on the list was always that of Peter. The tradition was also confirmed by a passage in the Gospel of St. Matthew, in the course of which Christ himself had said to Peter: "Thou art Peter (Greek for *rock*), and upon this rock I shall found my Church." Then he had given to Peter "the keys of heaven" and told him, "Whatever you bind on earth shall be bound in the

[5] The Latin word *papa* merely means "father," a title given by courtesy to other priests than the pope. It is not known for certain when the word "pope" was first applied exclusively to the bishop of Rome.

heavens, and whatever you loose on earth shall be loosed in the heavens."[6]

But it was a long time before St. Peter's position was supposed to confer any supreme authority upon his successors. Other bishops claimed to be the equal of the bishops of Rome, and it was usually the reputation and personality of individual bishops which gave them whatever authority they might possess in spiritual matters. Ambrose, bishop of Milan in the fourth century, was clearly the most influential bishop of his day, and was able to force the emperor himself to do penance for a massacre he had committed. Augustine, the great bishop of Hippo, tells us in his *Confessions* that he himself would never have accepted the authority of the Church if it had not been that he discovered from this passage in Matthew that the Church had been founded by Christ, who had delegated authority to Peter. Peter then had delegated this authority to his successor, and so on down to Augustine's own time. This gradually became the accepted doctrine of the Church. This theory of the Petrine succession, as it is called, is still the basis for the authority claimed by the Catholic Church.

As long as an emperor ruled in Rome, the bishop's authority was naturally limited to his spiritual domain. But when Honorius, Emperor of the West, removed his court to Ravenna at the end of the fourth century, the bishop was left as the chief dignitary in Rome, and at times he performed the functions of a Roman ruler in the city. One great pope, Leo I, negotiated with Attila the Hun, and succeeded in diverting him from the city, and the same pope negotiated for the safety of its inhabitants during the sack of Rome by the Vandals. As the Roman provincial administration gradually collapsed in the fifth century, under the impact of the barbarian invaders, the bishops in many of the provinces took over from the helpless Roman governors, and tried to protect the interests of the people as best they could. They now started to look to the pope (as we may now call the Bishop of Rome) as their chief guide in political policy as well as for spiritual leadership. Pope Leo I was given official recognition by Emperor Valentinian III of Ravenna, who conferred upon him full authority over all the bishops in the empire, an authority which he did not hesitate to use, demanding implicit obedience from them and pronouncing final decisions in matters of doctrine.

▶ The establishment of Christian doctrine

THE QUESTIONS NOT ANSWERED BY ST. PAUL

St. Paul, as already mentioned, was the founder of Christian theology; but his teachings, usually given in response to definite questions put to him by his churches, were very far from satisfying the inquiring minds, especially of his Greek audience. Early in the history of the Christian Church his authority was accepted as that of an apostle chosen by the resurrected Christ to explain the nature of his relationship to God the Father and other mysteries of the religion; and by A.D. 170 his letters, together with letters of the other apostles, the four Gospels, the Acts of the Apostles, and most of the present books of the New Testament were accepted as canonical or inspired books. These are the basic books of Christianity, and nothing else written by any later Christians has quite the same authority. Other men might add to this theology, but these men were not apostles;[7] they had never known Christ personally on earth, and there was no inherent reason why one man's ideas on the subject should be better than any other man's. Yet clearly all the questions that could be asked had not been answered by Christ, Paul, or the other apostles. And it was equally

---

[6] This is the literal translation of the Greek (Matthew 16:19). It should be added that some scholars have rejected the whole passage as spurious, while Protestant theologians deny the interpretation placed upon it by the Roman Catholic Church, since there is no reference to the word "sin" always associated with it in Catholic doctrine. The Greek merely says *"whatever you bind, . . ."* (ὅ ἐὰν δήσῃς).

[7] Neither, of course, was Paul one of the original apostles. But he claimed to have been personally chosen as an apostle by the resurrected Christ, and his authority was accepted by the second century A.D. by all Christians.

clear that some questions really did need answering. Moreover, many men came into Christianity after earlier experience in the mystery religions, and they were not all ready to abandon what they had been taught before conversion.

While most Romans, as was to be expected from such an unphilosophical people, were more interested in the organization of the Church and its day-to-day activities, the Greeks and Orientals were by no means content simply to believe. They wanted to *understand*. At the heart of Christian theology, however, there is a mystery. The religion was monotheistic, like its predecessor Judaism. But yet at the same time there is a Trinity of Father, Son, and Holy Spirit—a belief which later led the Muslims to attack the Christians as tritheists (having three Gods). This central Christian mystery was, of course, accepted by most Christians as a mystery not to be resolved by reason, and some of the early Christian teachers instructed their congregations not to think about the matter at all. Tertullian, for instance, an African bishop, stated openly that the more absurd an idea appeared to be to the unaided human reason, so much the more meritorious it was in the eyes of God to believe it, since such faith involved a purposeful humbling of the rational faculty, and humility had been enjoined upon his followers by Christ himself. But questionings would not be stilled, especially among Greek converts to Christianity. What was the true relationship between the Father and the other persons of the Trinity? How did the Father-God beget a Son? Where was the Son of God before he became a man? If he was really a God, then did he suffer when he was crucified?

In the first four Christian centuries there was endless division between different Christian thinkers on these problems. At the one extreme were the Gnostics, who insisted that Christ was a spiritual being whose physical body was only a phantom, while at the other extreme were the Arians (followers of Arius of Alexandria), who claimed that Christ was only sent from God, possessed divine substance, but was in no sense coequal with God. In the middle was Athanasius, whose opinion was finally accepted as orthodox (literally—correct opinion), and who stated substantially the present doctrine of the Catholic Church on the nature of the Trinity.

But questions concerning doctrine were by no means the only ones to be considered in the first few centuries of the Christian Era. When it became a settled belief that the sacraments of the Church (to be more fully explained in a later chapter) were necessary for salvation, the question naturally arose as to whether the faithful partaking of the sacraments was alone necessary for salvation. If a man sinned and yet partook of the sacraments, would he be saved? Paul had already been forced to deal with the question of whether faith alone without good works was sufficient for salvation. An affirmative answer might be taken as permission to sin, as Paul's opponents insisted. If God knew in advance who was to be saved, and God by definition must be all-knowing, then how could man be said to have free will? If everything had been predetermined, then man was not a free being at all, but only a kind of puppet in the hands of God. Would it not be better, argued Pelagius, to say that man must work his way into heaven by his deeds? Then, Augustine retorted to Pelagius, what became of God's saving grace? How could man force God to save him if God were omnipotent? If God's son had sacrificed himself for the sins of the world—and this was the central teaching of Paul's theology—then salvation must be a gift of God. What was man's own share in his own salvation?

DOCTRINAL HERESIES

By the time of the conversion of Constantine many of these differing opinions had already been stated publicly by their proponents, but there was no evident way of establishing the truth. Constantine himself, however, anxious to put an end to the strife, called a council at Nicaea (A.D. 325), over which he presided. Here the bishops of the empire assembled and a statement of beliefs, or a creed, was agreed upon. Majority opinion was against Arius, whose teachings had been making considerable headway in recent times. The result was that Arius himself was banished and Christians were forbidden to preach his doctrines on the nature of the Trinity.

However, this proscription of Arianism was not final. During the same fourth century some of the emperors of Constantinople preferred the simpler teaching of Arius and had Arianism proclaimed as the true doctrine. This temporary ascendancy of Arianism had momentous consequences, for it was during this period that many of the barbarian peoples were converted to Christianity, and it was the Arian *heresy* (from the Greek word for choice) that was accepted by them in preference to the teaching which Athanasius had proclaimed and ultimately became orthodox. The popes in Rome had never accepted Arianism at all—a fact which probably contributed to the later acceptance of the pope as final arbiter in matters of faith and doctrine.

The heresies, however, were far from suppressed, and struggles over doctrine constantly broke out during the next centuries, especially in Constantinople. The chief Church official in Constantinople, the patriarch, who was appointed by the emperor, frequently differed from the pope in Rome. Backed by all the prestige of the empire, the patriarch and his master frequently adopted theological positions at variance with those of the pope, while the latter considered himself, and was considered generally in the West, as having a spiritual authority far above that of the servant of an emperor who might be only a successful warrior of no learning whatever. In the eleventh century there was a final split between the Eastern and Western Churches, ostensibly over a theological question, but complicated by a real question of jurisdiction between the Churches of the East and West which will be discussed more fully in Chapter 8. The split between the Churches persists up to the present time, though for a period in the thirteenth century they were briefly united

by force when Constantinople was captured by a party of crusaders from the West. The Coptic Church of Abyssinia parted company with both the Eastern and Western Churches on a theological question as early as the fifth century A.D. and is still independent.

NEW AUTHORITATIVE DOCTRINE—THE CHURCH FATHERS

Gradually the doctrine of the Petrine supremacy became accepted in the West, and by the end of the fifth century few would have questioned the right of the pope to declare the true doctrines of the Church by virtue of his authority as the successor of Peter. By virtue of this authority he could state which of the early Christian writings had to be accepted as containing correct teachings, which among them were in the direct tradition of the apostles themselves and thus had access to directly inspired information, if not themselves inspired. Thus grew up the authority of the so-called "Apostolic Fathers" of the Church, both Greek and Latin, whose teachings were to be regarded as orthodox. Certain creeds were adopted as correct formulations of Christian faith; the Latin Vulgate version of the Bible, translated by St. Jerome, became the authoritative Latin text; and in later times such doctrines as Purgatory and the immaculate conception of Mary the mother of Jesus became accepted as part of Church doctrine, though not appearing in the Bible itself.

The earliest of the Latin Fathers of the Church was Ambrose (339?–397) Bishop of Milan, a powerful churchman who was especially important because of his insistence on the right of the clergy to discipline offenders, a right of cardinal importance in the attempt of the Church to maintain the unity of Christendom. He was also a preacher of great persuasiveness who was instrumental in converting many leading pagans, and bringing them into active work in the Church. One of his converts was Augustine. In his sermons St. Ambrose, like Pope Gregory the Great in a later century, gave a great deal of practical advice which was accepted as authoritative in the life of the early Church. St. Jerome (*ca.* 340–420), another Latin Father, translated the authoritative version of the Bible, and wrote many tracts on theology. He was a supporter of the orthodox position on the Trinity, and attacked and refuted heresy.

But by far the most influential of these Latin Church Fathers was St. Augustine (354–430), who was made bishop of Hippo in North Africa by his congregation, and then devoted his life not only to the duties of his bishopric but to evolving a theology which became in its essentials the accepted doctrine of the Church, even though some of his most extreme views were not stressed owing to their momentous consequences for human free will. Augustine has left us in his *Confessions* a complete account of his intellectual and spiritual struggles before his conversion, which are of the greatest importance for our understanding of the conflicting intellectual currents of the time. Always conscious of his own guilt and sinfulness, like Martin Luther, who resembled him in so many respects, he could only believe in a real conversion of the heart. But for a long time he could not bring himself to accept Christianity, which he was inclined to despise because it left too many questions unanswered. Tempted by the dualistic doctrine of Manichaeism, he never really freed himself from it, believing most fervently in the power of evil, which he had experienced within himself. Then he immersed himself in the last great pagan philosophy of Neoplatonism,[8] which also taught the evilness of matter, and

the necessity of overcoming all material desires for the purpose of attaining a mystical union with God. This also finds its place in Augustine's theology; and there is an extraordinarily moving passage in the *Confessions* where he describes such an experience, which came to him as the result of his conversion.

The real question, therefore, for Augustine, it will be seen, was what need there was for a Church as mediator between man and God, and why there should be a Church at all. Indeed, Martin Luther, a deep student of Augustine, did break away from the Catholic Church, while not deviating from St. Augustine save in this one matter. The human will, said Augustine, following St. Paul, is not free, and the human being is bound by original sin. He cannot even acquire any true knowledge merely out of himself. But Christ's sacrifice had redeemed mankind, and thereafter it had become possible for man to receive grace, as a heavenly gift. Grace alone can enable man to know the truth, and to do good. And he accepts the Church teaching that grace can be obtained only if a man truly believes and receives the sacraments. The Catholic Church alone can administer these sacraments. Where did the Catholic Church receive this power? Directly from Christ to St. Peter, as we have seen, and so through the succession of popes.

This, however, does not mean that man is necessarily saved by faith or by receiving the sacraments, for God has infinite foreknowledge and infinite power. Augustine therefore comes to the conclusion that God has predestined some men for salvation and some to damnation. Man can never know for certain whether he is saved, since this is entirely in God's hands, and within his knowledge alone. In logic this position is irrefutable, and Thomas Aquinas and the medieval scholastics were forced to wrestle with the problem again. But predestination was never stressed in the Catholic Church, and not until John Calvin in the sixteenth century was it stated in this extreme form again. The remainder of the doctrine—the

[8] This philosophy, whose founder was an Egyptian named Plotinus, was derived from Plato, but it is a far more systematic idealism than that of the Greek. Fundamentally it is an attempt to bring mysticism within the scope of philosophy, and is both a philosophical explanation of the experience of the human soul when it finds union with God (called by Plotinus the One), and an "otherworldly" ethic which emphasizes the desirability of this union. It is impossible in a brief space to do any justice to the philosophy, which had an immense influence on both Christian and Muslim thought, though a few further remarks will be devoted to it in later chapters, especially in connection with the philosopher John Scotus Erigena in Chapter 13.

powerlessness of human thinking and willing, and the necessity for grace—became part of orthodox Christian thought.

Augustine was also a pioneer in another field of thought at least as influential as his theology. An earlier Christian Father, Eusebius, had written an *Ecclesiastical History* which interpreted all the events of his own and earlier times in the light of the Old Testament, and especially of Hebrew prophecy. But Augustine went much further, and in his *City of God* wrote a history designed to show that with the coming of Christ an entirely new phase had opened. Attacking the pagans who claimed that the sack of Rome by Alaric was due to the desertion of the old gods by their worshipers, Augustine declared that this was part of God's scheme. Rome belonged to the "City of Man," which was only temporary and must pass away, to give place to the "City of God" on earth, which will endure forever, the beginnings of which had already been made under the Hebrew theocracy, and now from the coming of Christ must be continued by the Christian Church. And Augustine with great passion and power describes God's whole plan for the world, the creation and fall of man and the old dispensation, followed by man's redemption in the new age and the building of the City of God. It need hardly be pointed out how much this conception owes to the Hebrew interpretation of history, already discussed in an earlier chapter.

In Augustine's own thought it is clear that the perfect City of God can never exist on earth; but it is the ideal to which all Christians should aspire, and the beginnings of the building can be made in the here and now. Christians in subsequent ages, however, took it to be the ideal of Chistendom, a working plan for all Christians to follow, justifying the extirpation of heresy as treason to the City of God, and later justifying also the extermination of infidels as a fulfillment of God's plan for the unity of all men on earth in the Christian religion. The *City of God* was perhaps, after the Bible, the most influential book in the medieval world.

▶ The persistent ideal of poverty and holiness—Monasticism

From very early times there was opposition to the Church as an organized institution, and especially in the East, where Roman organization had not been so greatly admired as by its inheritors in the West. These dissenters could point to the teachings of Christ himself on poverty and its spiritual value, and to his advice to the young man who asked him what was necessary to salvation. Christ had replied that he should sell all his goods and follow him, "but the young man went away sorrowful because he had great possessions." These men were deeply influenced by Oriental thought, and indeed by the mystery religions, which taught that the true path of salvation was by purification on earth and an inward acceptance of the Divine. They did not believe in the machinery of salvation, as propounded by the Church, regarding it as too complex and too legal, too much in the nature of a Roman contract to be the real path to salvation. Yet at the same time they fervently believed in Christ and the central truths of the Christian religion as taught by Christ himself. Determined on self-purification, some went alone into the desert, fasted and prayed and inflicted tortures upon themselves, trying to mortify their evil nature. Others lived in small communities, holding their possessions in common, and aiding each other in their self-mortifying practices. These ascetics were regarded by all the people as holy men, so that it was difficult for the official Church to say that they were heretics.

But they did present a real problem for a Church which had chosen a different path, one that entailed organization, material resources, and political power. Their lives were a standing reproach to such a Church gradually becoming immersed in worldliness. Both in the East and in the West, however, the Church proved flexible enough to accept popular opinion of these hermits and anchorites, sometimes canonizing them as saints, even the famous St. Simeon Stylites, who lived on a pillar for more than thirty years without even space to lie down. But it did attempt also to organize them. By the end of the fourth century the moderate Rule of St. Basil was adopted, which prescribed an orderly, regular life for these monks, as they were called. They no longer lived in the open air or in the desert or in caves, but in a communal dwelling house or monastery, in which each did a share of the work required for their subsistence. Most monks of the Eastern Church still live under the fourth-century Rule of St. Basil.

In the West asceticism of the kind possible in Egypt and the East was more difficult, as the climate in most parts is not conducive to a solitary outdoor life throughout the year. But the ascetic practices found favor with those who wished to devote their whole lives to prayer and worship, and we know of many solitary hermits and hermits already living in communities in the time of St. Jerome, who spent much of his eloquence in defending the practice. It met severe opposition from those who objected to the monks on the ground that they were too often merely escaping their social responsibilities; and when women also began to organize themselves into monasteries or nunneries

Jerome had to take up the cudgels on their behalf also. St. Martin of Tours (316–397), who spent most of his life destroying the last remnants of paganism in France after the decree of Theodosius forbidding the practice of any religion but Christianity, was criticized sharply by his superiors for his own personally ascetic regimen, although he never was a monk. But in time the monasteries became institutionalized, both for men and for women; and it became a recognized sign of holiness that a man or woman should submit to mortification of the flesh while on earth, even if such people did not live according to a recognized Rule. If they lived by a Rule they were called "regular" clergy, or sometimes just "religious," since they devoted their whole lives to religion. They were distinguished from the "secular" clergy, whose duties lay in the outer world.

At the beginning of the sixth century an acceptable Rule which was applicable to all Western monasteries was drawn up by St. Benedict, who had begun his religious career as a hermit. When, however, his fame as a holy man began to attract many followers, he changed his manner of living and founded the monastery of Monte Cassino, instituting an orderly regimen which was blessed by

The monastery of Monte Cassino, in southern Italy, as it was before it was destroyed during World War II. It is now being rebuilt.

Pope Gregory the Great. The monks at Monte Cassino and all those who lived by the Benedictine Rule had to take vows of poverty and obedience to the abbot, the head of the community. They had to cut off all ties with their families and their previous lives before entering the monastery. Periods were set aside each day for prayer and worship; the rest of the day was to be spent in manual labor, either in the fields, which were cultivated with great care and made to yield all the food required by the community, or in the monastery itself. No monk was permitted to own anything at all; everything was to be handled by the abbot, whose word was law within the monastery. Monks slept in a common dormitory and ate in a common dining room.

By the eighth century the Benedictine Rule was adopted by the vast majority of monasteries in the West except the Irish, and for centuries it was the model life for the religious, and faithfully observed by those who had chosen it. Even when abuses began to creep in, all those who undertook reforms returned to the Benedictine Rule or some modification of it, as the ideal Rule for a religious community. There was no doubt that in spite of its initial reservations the Church was wise to permit and ultimately take the lead in organizing these communities of monks. For if it was necessary to institutionalize the Church, and the papacy had no doubts on this necessity, then it was also necessary to take care of those deeply earnest men and women who wished to devote all their lives to their religion, and to live a communal life of poverty that seemed to them more in accordance with the teachings of Christ. As long as the monks continued to live holy lives they were a standing example of the virtues of Christianity; they troubled no one, and at the same time they absorbed into their communities all those who might have attacked the Church for its institutionalism and worldliness. It is surely no accident that those later medieval heresies which stressed poverty and asceticism as the true Christian ideal never arose while the monasteries were still truly religious communities and practiced poverty and abstinence; but that when they no longer fulfilled this function and the monks became notorious for laxity in morals, idleness, and luxurious habits, such a heresy as that of the Poor Men of Lyons obtained numerous adherents and for a long time constituted a real threat to the Church, calling forth a St. Francis and a St. Dominic to set the example once more of saintly lives spent in the earliest tradition of Christianity.

The Irish monasteries alone did not conform to the Benedictine Rule and some monasteries founded by Irish missionaries persisted for a long time on the Continent. The reason for this situation is to be found in the manner in which the Irish had been converted to Christianity. Ireland had been a land of clans, with a very primitive system of government; it had never been conquered by the Romans. St. Patrick, who had been attracted by Oriental monasticism before going to Ireland, succeeded in converting many of the savage chieftains and with them their clansmen. Instead of setting up a church on the Roman model, he allowed the clan to become the congregation. There were no priests except monks, and these did not live in the same isolation from their fellow men as in Western Europe, since they had also to perform the same functions as the secular clergy. They undertook the task of converting the other clansmen who had remained heathen while at the same time they lived in monasteries, practicing austerities, and gaining a great reputation for both piety and learning. Remaining for centuries unconnected with the Church in Rome, they were unaware even of many of the newer teachings of the Church. The result was that they developed a Christianity that was never institutionalized in the Roman manner, and they retained a fervor, especially in missionary activity, that had begun to disappear from Europe. St. Columba converted some Celtic tribes in Britain before they had yet been visited by official emissaries of the Church, St. Columban penetrated into Gaul and made converts in places where Christianity had as yet no foothold and founded monasteries there; another Irishman founded the great monastery of St. Gall in what is now Switzerland. Moreover, once the first monks had gained a knowledge of Greek, it continued to be taught in the monasteries, and was never allowed to die out in Ireland. The only great philosopher of the Dark Ages in Europe, John Scotus Erigena, was an Irishman.

But this progress was rudely checked in Britain. Pope Gregory I (the fourth and last of the officially recognized Latin Fathers of the Church), of whom more in the next chapter, at the end of the sixth century sent a missionary to Britain named Augustine, who succeeded in converting the South. As this Catholic Christianity progressed northward it came into contact with the communities converted from Ireland, which had quite unknowingly adopted a different form of ecclesiastical usage. Both sides agreed to accept the decision of a synod at Whitby (664), presided over by the king of Northumbria. The question hinged upon the Petrine supremacy. The Irish could point to no such authority as that of the pope, descended from St. Peter. Their failure was decisive. The Roman Church received the award, the new English Church was organized after the Roman manner and the monasteries accepted the Benedictine Rule; in time even the Irish themselves accepted the inevitable, and adopted the discipline and organization of the central Church in Rome.

▶ Suggestions for further reading

Every student should of course read as much of the New Testament as possible—the Gospels for the story of the life and death of Jesus Christ, the Acts of the Apostles for the only near-contemporary account of the foundation of the Christian religion and the missionary journeys of St. Paul, and the epistles of various apostles for the first efforts to build a Christian theology and to deal with the practical problems that came up in the first century A.D. in the light of Christian ethical teachings. For translations to be used, see Chapter 3, where the Old Testament translations are considered.

Study of the development of early Christian doctrine is made difficult by the personal beliefs of the authors of books on the subject. Naturally, Catholics and Protestants interpret both history and doctrine from divergent points of view. There is probably no work available which would satisfy all parties. Moreover, Christian doctrine was never simple, and any books that attempt to make it simple are likely to be misleading. One of the best is certainly G. P. Fisher, *The History of Christian Doctrine* (New York: Charles Scribner's Sons, 1923), but the student should have a real interest in the subject if he is to read the book fruitfully. It cannot be skimmed through. A very simple account, entirely accurate but limited in scope, of the rise of Christianity, with no visible bias, is E. R. Goodenough, *The Church in the Roman Empire* (Berkshire Studies in European History; New York: Henry Holt & Co., Inc., 1931). This book, which barely attempts, however, to define or deal with Christian doctrine, achieves what it sets out to do, that is, to give a clear and simple account of the facts, about as well as it can be done.

There are many books which give the primary sources for early Christian history. One such book, easily available, is H. S. Bettinson, ed., *Documents of the Christian Church* (New York: Oxford University Press, 1947). Very valuable for its collection of primary documents on the growth of the papacy and the gradual acceptance of the bishop of Rome as the head of the Church is J. T. Shotwell and L. R. Loomis, eds., *The See of Peter* (New York: Columbia University Press, 1927).

Many students will no doubt have obtained a great deal of their information about early Christianity from novels, or from movies made from these novels. Most works of this sort are neither historically accurate, in so far as we possess the facts, nor anything but misleading. In general, they are sentimental rubbish. An exception might be made, however, for the sympathetic, non-Christian works of Shalom Asch. In particular, *The Apostle* (tr. M. Samuel; New York: G. P. Putnam's Sons, 1943), which tells, although necessarily with fictional embellishments, of the life and work of Paul, is a real aid to the effort to re-imagine the atmosphere of the first Christian century. Asch sticks closely to the known facts, and his additions and interpretation are believable.

The epoch-making and influential work of Augustine should certainly be studied, especially the *Confessions* (which throw a revealing light on the great bishop himself and on the struggles an intellectual pagan had to make before he could bring himself to accept Christianity, a religion which was, as yet, rather anti-intellectual) and the *City of God*. Far the best available translation of the former is *Confessions of St. Augustine* (tr. F. J. Sheed; New York: Sheed & Ward, 1943). Several translations of the *City of God* are available, but none is entirely satisfactory. Much of the book is repetitious, but since it remains probably the most influential work in the field of political thought, it should be attempted. Easily available is the *City of God* (tr. and ed. M. Dods, 2 vols.; New York: Hafner Pub. Co., Inc., 1948). For a good though brief commentary on the political thought of Augustine, the student is referred to Chapter 10 of G. H. Sabine, *A History of Political Theory* (New York: Henry Holt & Co., Inc., 1937).

Finally, attention should be drawn to a masterly study of the problems involved in the conversion of Constantine to Christianity, and of the political and religious issues of the time, in Setton's chapter, "The Triumph of Christianity," in K. Setton and H. Winkler, eds., *Great Problems in European Civilization* (New York: Prentice-Hall, Inc., 1954); here a judicious selection from primary and secondary sources is made which permits the reader to make up his own mind on the matter.

(See also under Duckett in the Readings for Chapter 7.)

7

The End of the Roman Empire, and the Establishment of Successor States

The beginning of the end • Re-establishment of discipline: totalitarianism • External dangers to the empire • Barbarian conquest of Italy • Barbarian kingdoms of the West • The end of an era

► The beginning of the end

THE MILITARY AUTOCRACY OF SEPTIMIUS SEVERUS (193–211)

The murder of Commodus in 192 was the signal for the opening of a period of outright domination of the Roman emperor by the army, which was to last till the fall of the empire. The first half of this period, up to the accession of Diocletian, was characterized by the increasing disintegration of the civil government under a series of military usurpers whose chief, and sometimes only, ability lay in the military sphere. The empire itself was, on the whole, successfully defended against external pressure on the boundaries, but at tremendous cost to its internal stability. The second half was characterized by the development of a totalitarian state under a civil administration backed by a usually obedient professional mercenary army, directed by an absolute emperor. Without going into the question at this stage of whether wiser policies on the part of the emperors could have prevented this sequence, which culminated in the fall of the empire and the survival of a truncated East-

ern Empire under absolutist government, it is clear that it was the policies of the early third-century emperor, Septimius Severus, that set the process in motion.

He himself owed his position to his military ability alone, which was sufficient to enable him to defeat several other contenders. African by birth but Roman in education, and with a Syrian wife, he had no personal or sentimental attachment to Rome and her institutions. He frankly despised the Senate, and showed no understanding of the political and economic basis of the empire. Certainly the pretense that the government was a principate with himself as first citizen, that it was a partnership between ruler and people, had long been outmoded. And it was demonstrably true that the ruler was made and unmade by the various armies of the state. But the armies still had to be fed, paid, and clothed; and if their requirements were not to be always forcibly taken directly from the people that provided them, then some basis of consent must be retained. Moreover, since the empire's prosperity, such as it was, was based to such a large extent upon the production of the cities, and it was the cities which provided the bulk of the tax money for the troops, it was not wise to destroy the urban middle classes for the sake of the army, the peasants, and the urban proletariat. Whether the policies of Severus had any such intention or not, their result was to set in motion the process which led inexorably to the impoverishment and ultimate destruction of the middle classes and the independent municipalities which had provided the solid substructure of the older empire.

To pay for his increased army it was necessary both to increase taxes and to take more active steps to see that they were paid. Severus therefore kept a very strict watch upon all provincial governors, brought many provincials into the imperial service, and in this respect his administration was superior to those of his immediate predecessors. His object, however, was not in any way to lighten the burdens of the provinces and municipalities, but to see that his treasury was full. For this purpose he initiated the policy of making municipal magistrates personally responsible for the collection of the taxes. If they were not paid in full, the magistrates themselves had to make up the difference. To see that all sources of income were tapped and that all officials were kept to their duty, he inaugurated a secret police to report directly to himself on any failure to fulfill obligations and to warn him of any tendencies toward treason. On the other hand, he won the approval of the proletariat by increasing its dole from the state, and passed other special legislation which protected its interests.

THE ASCENDANCY OF THE PEASANT ARMY

But the real danger of the policy of Severus was in the favoritism he showed to his legions. Their pay was considerably raised, and many concessions were made to them which had the effect of impairing their usefulness to the state, while incidentally lowering their efficiency. Married soldiers were allowed to live with their wives in towns behind the lines, auxiliary divisions were given permanent lands, and social clubs

in the army were encouraged. This policy made the troops relatively immobile and unfit for service on an endangered frontier. It also made them less willing to fight and less amenable to discipline. Time after time in the third century we hear of mutinies and of the assassination of military leaders when they called upon the troops to fight in defense of the frontiers or tried to instill some discipline into them. Moreover, Severus now made it possible for all provincial soldiers to rise to the position of centurion, which carried with it equestrian rank. Since this was the class favored both by Severus and by his successors for all posts in the imperial bureaucracy, the result was that a military career became the best means of entry to the highest positions in the state, and civilian rule was gradually replaced by military. The very highest offices in the imperial service brought their holders within the senatorial aristocracy, which carried special privileges. Thus the senatorial order became increasingly filled with successful soldiers who acquired large tracts of land and settled down, unencumbered by taxation, having in their progress from the ranks avoided any payment of taxes whatever, and having acquired a vast contempt for those more productive members of society upon whom fell the whole burden of their upkeep. Thus the army became a privileged career, and the military caste, pampered and favored by Severus and all the third-century emperors, became a state within the state, entirely irresponsible, and giving its support only to those rulers who perpetuated its position and catered to its demands.

By opening to soldiers from the ranks the way even to the crown itself, the emperors might have attracted into the army men from the upper and middle classes. But, though Italians and provincials of equestrian rank did continue to provide some of the officers, the bulk of the army was recruited, by design, from the peasantry. It has even been suggested that this was a deliberate policy to increase the class struggle between the peasantry and the urban middle classes. It would seem more probable, however, that the conscript army could only find recruits in sufficient number from the peasantry, and that the concessions made to them were of the kind more likely to appeal to a largely illiterate and semicivilized peasantry which had always found it difficult to make a living from the land. The result of the whole policy, as doubtless intended, was to undermine the position of the upper classes and infiltrate them with uncouth but able soldiers; but it was probably not foreseen that the army itself would become progressively barbarized, nor that it would prefer its privileged life behind the lines to defending the state. The soldiers preferred to follow only those leaders who promised them the most at the least cost to themselves in military activity. So many emperors were assassinated by rebellious troops during fifty years of the third century that only one of eighteen such "emperors" died peacefully in his bed.

FIFTY YEARS OF ANARCHY—THE "BARRACK EMPERORS" (235–284)

There is no need to dwell on the lives, activities, and sudden deaths of these "barrack" emperors. No real rule of succession was observed, though on a few occasions fathers were in fact succeeded by sons who had made appropriate donatives to the legions; frequently there were several competing emperors supported by their own troops but not accepted by any others. On several occasions the Germans penetrated into Gaul, once even passing the Alps and only meeting ultimate defeat in northern Italy. For ten years there was a separate kingdom of Gaul with complete independence. Without effective central administration, tax collecting was by the rough-and-ready method of requisition of supplies and forced levies of money. Almost the whole of Roman Asia acquired a virtual independence for a time (267–273) under the leadership of a desert city named Palmyra, and its queen, Zenobia. The middle classes and active peasants were progressively impoverished; it hardly seemed worth while to plant crops or to engage in any commercial activity when so little could be kept from the insatiable maw of the army.

Near the frontiers the Germanic barbarians at times were able to enter the empire and plunder at will.

But at last a succession of emperors from Illyria was able to re-establish discipline in the armies. And though the greatest of these, Aurelian, was himself murdered (275) after enjoying only five years of supreme power, it was not before he had restored Asia to the empire, defeated the Parthians, brought Gaul back to her allegiance and unified the old Roman Empire almost within her ancient boundaries, though the province of Dacia added by Trajan had been lost forever.

▶ Re-establishment of discipline— Totalitarianism

THE ESTABLISHMENT OF ABSOLUTE GOVERNMENT—DIOCLETIAN AND HIS ASSOCIATES

When Diocletian (285–305) became sole ruler of the empire in 285, having vanquished his only serious rival, he was faced with problems beyond the capacity of any ruler to solve. The years of anarchy had impoverished the middle classes to such an extent that desperate measures to ensure their continued service to the state and payment of taxes had already been put into effect; the industrial and agricultural workers were already being regimented in a similar manner. Trade had been meeting increasing difficulties, not only because of the insecurity of transport but because of constant depreciations of the currency. The Illyrian emperors had been driven to the expedient of inviting warlike barbarians to serve in the imperial armies for pay, and even in the ranks of the officers barbarians were rapidly becoming as frequent as Roman citizens. But at least these barbarians were usually willing to serve; and, being professional soldiers, they fought better than the peasantry of the earlier part of the century and were better disciplined, not having yet grown to look upon the army as a privileged existence, entitling them to live indefinitely off the civilian economy without giving services in return. On the other hand, they owed no

► chronological chart

Roman Empire

Murder of Roman Emperor Commodus	192
Reign of Septimius Severus	193–211
Edict of Caracalla—Extension of Roman citizenship to virtually all free inhabitants of the empire	212
Murder of Emperor Alexander Severus	235
"Barrack Emperors"	235–284
Palmyra declares independence under Queen Zenobia	267
Capture of Zenobia and sack of Palmyra by Aurelian	273
Murder of Aurelian	275
Accession of Diocletian	284
Diocletian chooses Maximian as colleague (Augustus)	285
Appointment of two "Caesars"	293
Edict limiting prices of goods and labor	301
Persecution of Christians	303–311
Abdication of Diocletian and Maximian	305
Galerius emperor of the East, Constantius of West	305
Death of Constantius in Britain, Constantine saluted as emperor	306
Death of Galerius	311
Battle of Milvian Bridge, death of Maxentius	312
Constantine emperor of West, Licinius of East	312
"Edict of Milan"	313
Execution of Licinius	324
Constantine sole emperor	324–337
Council of Nicaea	325
Foundation of Constantinople	330
Conversion and death of Constantine	337
Advance of Huns into empire, defeating Goths	372
Goths permitted across Danube by Emperor Valens	376
Battle of Adrianople—Death of Valens	378
Stilicho the Vandal becomes imperial master of troops	400
Honorius moves Roman capital to Ravenna	ca. 400
Sack of Rome by Alaric and Visigoths	410

Roman Empire (cont'd)

Aetius becomes master of the troops under Valentinian III	430
Aetius defeats Visigoths in Gaul	436
Rise of Attila to power among Huns, moves west	445
Battle of Chalons—Partial victory of Aetius over Attila	451
Aetius defeats some Franks, remainder permitted into Gaul	451
Attila invades Italy	452
Death of Attila	453
Murder of Aetius by Valentinian III	454
Sack of Rome by Vandals under Gaeseric	455
Puppet rulers in Rome	455–476
Odoacer deposes last emperor ("Fall of Rome")	476

England and France

Roman legions leave England	407–442
Franks penetrate into Gaul	431 onward
Aetius defeats some Franks, remainder permitted into Gaul	451
Clovis consolidates Franks into kingdom	481–511
Merovingian kingdom	481–754
Conversion of Clovis and Franks to Roman Catholicism	486
Invasions of England by Angles, Saxons, and Jutes	5th and 6th centuries
Mission of St. Augustine of Canterbury to England	596–597
Conquests of Angles, Saxons, and Jutes completed by	615
Influx of Celtic Christianity into England from Iona	633 onward
Synod of Whitby—Triumph of Roman Catholicism over Celtic Christianity	664
Charles Martel "mayor of the palace" in France	714–741
Pepin crowned king of the Franks (Pepin the Short)	754

Goths, Vandals, and Lombards

Conversion of Goths to Arian Christianity	340–348
Advance of Huns into Europe, defeating Goths	372
Goths permitted across Danube by Emperor Valens	376
Battle of Adrianople—Gothic victory —Death of Valens	378
Vandals advance into Gaul	406
Vandals cross Pyrenees into Spain	409
Sack of Rome by Alaric and Visigoths	410
Visigoths move into Spain	415
Vandals move into Africa	429
Vandal kingdom of Africa	429–534
Aetius defeats Visigoths in Gaul	436
Sack of Rome by Vandals under Gaeseric	455
Visigothic kingdom of Spain	466–711
Odoacer deposes last Roman emperor	476
Invasion of Italy by Theodoric the Ostrogoth	488
Murder of Odoacer—Theodoric king of Italy	493
Theodoric the Ostrogoth king of Italy	493–526
Execution of Boethius	524
Vandal kingdom of Africa reconquered by Justinian	533–548
Reconquest of Italy by Justinian	535–554
Southeastern Spain conquered from Visigoths by Justinian, but lost soon afterward	554
Invasion of Italy by Lombards	568
Gradual conquest of northern and central Italy by Lombards	568–605
Conversion of Visigoths in Spain to Roman Catholicism	587
Pope Gregory i, the Great	590–604
Conversion of Lombard ruler to Roman Catholicism	ca. 650

loyalty whatever to the empire. Serving for experience and pay alone, they were loyal to their paymaster the emperor, but to no one else.

Finally, there was no acceptable method of succession to the throne, and no apparent way of preventing usurpation by the strongest commander.

Diocletian was in no sense an innovator. But he was a distinterested ruler, with no personal ambitions—he abdicated later in accordance with a plan he devised for a succession without bloodshed—and he had many years of life in front of him in which to accomplish his reforms. His general plan was to accept conditions as they were and to create formal institutions in keeping with them, and, by instituting a strong government, try to preserve the empire at least from the anarchy of the previous fifty years. In this he was, on the whole, successful, in spite of the failure of his new principle of succession. The empire did survive in form for nearly another two hundred years, and a substantial part of it, the later Byzantine Empire, ultimately gained a new lease of life and survived for a further thousand years.

In a word, his plan was to make of the whole empire one centrally administered state of the kind now called totalitarian.[1] This necessitated the final abolition of the principate in theory as well as in fact. But Diocletian also realized that the administration of the empire and the defense of its boundaries against the increasingly dangerous barbarians were far too much for one man. He therefore invited Maximian, another Illyrian general, to act as his colleague in the empire, sharing the title of Augustus. Maximian and he then chose two seconds-in-command, with the title of Caesar. The two Augusti were to retire after twenty years in office, to be succeeded by the two Caesars, each then naming a pair of Caesars who would in turn succeed them. Unfortunately

---

[1] The system has often been called "oriental absolutism," but the latter is a very vague term, since the Orient has known many different degrees of absolutism, while the analogy with modern totalitarian states, with their emphasis on guns instead of butter, is clear.

not all these potentates were as disinterested as himself, nor were the sons of the Augusti willing to be discarded in favor of generals of greater experience, even under parental pressure. The scheme actually never worked at all except when Diocletian was able to compel the Augusti to keep to their agreement, and civil wars continued until Constantine (312–337) established for good the hereditary principle, in spite of the danger that the empire might fall into childish or incompetent hands.

The division of the empire into two parts, however, survived the abdication and death of Diocletian, though without the refinement of the two added Caesars. And the scheme of the two Augusti and the two Caesars proved effective enough in his own lifetime to enable him to put into effect the necessary administrative reforms that made the empire into a totalitarian state. The frontiers were guarded, a number of minor revolts were quelled, and the expanding Persian Empire was held in check.

REORGANIZATION OF ARMY AND PROVINCES UNDER IMPERIAL CONTROL

The army was considerably enlarged, friendly barbarians were allowed to settle in frontier districts with an obligation to military service, companies of barbarians, sometimes even under their own chiefs, were welcomed, while the more warlike sections of the empire provided further conscripted recruits; if not of high quality their discipline and training were better than they had been for years. Diocletian also organized a force of picked men who could be moved from one part of the empire to another as danger threatened, helping to stiffen the resistance of the resident legions. The army was under the direct command of the emperor and his associates, who were all experienced generals, so that there was less opportunity for local armies to revolt and try to set up a new emperor.

The number of the provinces was increased by subdivision to 101, with every governor an appointee of one of the emperors, and subject to control by vicars who

had about seven provinces each (dioceses), who in their turn were responsible to four prefects, personal representatives of the four rulers. The vicars, however, had the right of direct appeal to Diocletian, as senior emperor, against decisions of the prefects. Thus was established a graded hierarchy responsible to the emperor and his associates alone.

Diocletian and Maximian as Augusti now took divine titles although they did not call themselves actual gods. They withdrew as much as possible from direct participation in public life, instituting an elaborate court ceremonial of an Oriental kind, including prostration and kissing the hem of the emperor's robe when the privilege of an audience was granted. The persecution of Christians which accompanied the elevation of the monarchy has been discussed in the last chapter. Many new temples were built to the old gods, while there was an insistence on greater observance of the imperial cult.

REGIMENTATION OF PUBLIC AND PRIVATE LIFE

The imperial bureaucracy and its task

It was clear at once that the expenses of the new administration could not be less than the old. The increased burden of the army and the building program could be met only by increased and more efficiently collected taxes. And this collection must also entail an increase in the unproductive army of imperial bureaucrats whose task it was to see that the taxes were paid. Diocletian's solution was simply to use his army and his bureaucrats, including secret police and paid informers, to ensure the collection, and hope to keep up the necessary agricultural and industrial production by all the legal weapons available to him, enforced by his officials and his army.

Compulsory agriculture—The *coloni*

The armies during the period of anarchy had been accustomed to requisition supplies. Diocletian now took away the arbitrary and casual requisitioning and made it regular and legal. Having little idea of the productive value of the various lands in his empire, he assessed them in accordance with

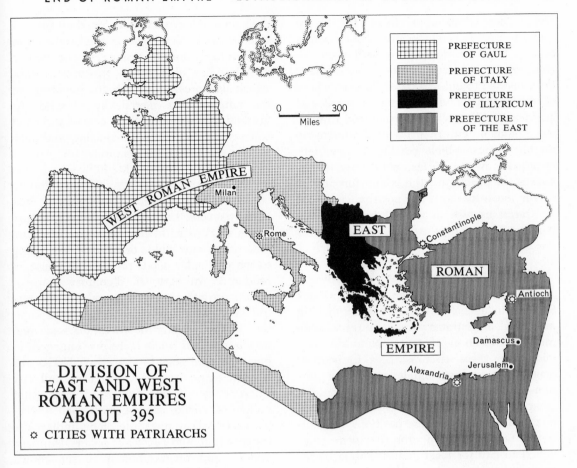

DIVISION OF
EAST AND WEST
ROMAN EMPIRES
ABOUT 395
✿ CITIES WITH PATRIARCHS

the numbers of cultivators employed and the land under cultivation, irrespective of the fertility of the soil and the probable yields, which were more difficult to measure. This tax was then collected by his officials, regardless of the actual ability to pay or the hardship payment entailed upon individual farmers. Since many farmers tried to escape their obligations and left the land, by the time of Constantine they were forced to remain on it, whether they were owners, tenants, or sharecroppers. If they left they were still liable for the tax on the land they had left, and if found they were returned to it. Though still theoretically freemen, they were practically serfs. These farmers were called *coloni*. Manumitted slaves were now free only in name also. They remained tied to their masters and bound to work for them. If they did not pay their masters due "reverence," a phrase which could be made to cover

any refusal to obey instructions, they could be returned to their status of slaves.

The privileged landowners

On the other hand, the large landowners who still employed some slaves, and had always a number of *coloni* on their lands, were often able to avoid taxation altogether, as they were in many cases too powerful for the imperial officials to dare to antagonize them. During the period of anarchy these landholders had often been able to increase their estates when the small farmers had fallen irretrievably into debt or had had their livestock driven off by the rapacious armies. From this time onward the large landowners were the only people to profit by the imperial policy, and many of them, who had been soldiers or imperial officials themselves, had obtained legal immunity from taxation. Assisted by slaves and *coloni* who were completely dependent upon them, they were rarely forced by even the strongest emperors to pay taxes commensurate with their income, for a squadron of troops would have been needed to enforce the collection. Many of the luxurious villas of these privileged aristocrats still survive, especially in France, some of them with their own manufacturing establishments which produced a variety of goods, even luxuries, with large store-houses for provisions, the whole fortified as if for security against possible imperial emissaries as well as against invading barbarians. These villas are the forerunners of the medieval manors.

Compulsory state service—The *curiales*

We have already seen that Septimius Severus inaugurated the system of making municipal magistrates personally responsible for the collection of taxes. Naturally few wished in these circumstances to become magistrates, however much prestige the position might bring them. Diocletian made it compulsory for men of a certain property qualification to hold these positions. In addition to taxes to the emperor, they were compelled to pay for local games, public buildings, and their repairs, and were personally responsible for seeing that all such work was carried out satisfactorily. Constantine laid the burden of this taxation upon the whole body of people eligible for these offices, who were called *curiales*, once a title of honor but now a badge of municipal serfdom.

The only way for the *curiales* to escape their onerous position would have been to rise to the senatorial class and receive tax immunity. But this also was made impossible by decree in the century after Diocletian. If they left their class, then their children would have to undertake the curial obligation instead. If they tried to escape by joining the army, they were summarily returned to their previous duties. And, forced to find means to pay the taxes and other obligations, they naturally tried to obtain as much as they could from their own tenant cultivators or *coloni;* thus the class struggle was intensified more than ever. With no chance of escaping

their involuntary servitude, faced on the one side by the imperial officers and on the other by a bitterly hostile peasantry, and with a complete lack of incentive, this middle class, which had previously been the backbone of the empire, was mercilessly crushed. Its gradual disappearance was one of the chief causes for the economic decline and ultimately the fall of the empire.

Compulsory industry—The *collegia*

The regimentation in industry was equally severe. As early as the second century urban workers had been encouraged to form themselves into guilds or *collegia,* according to the particular goods produced or services rendered. An early third-century emperor organized into monopolies under state control all collegia suplying goods to the capital. The same control was exercised over merchants and manufacturers engaged in purveying supplies to the army. Under the Illyrian emperors and Constantine, all city workers were finally organized into castes under strict state control, with each worker bound to follow the trade of his father. We know of hereditary castes of bakers, shippers, millers, and others, but it is not known whether all industry was thus regimented or if any escaped. None, however, escaped the ubiquitous tax collectors.

Thus with *coloni, curiales,* and artisans all forbidden to change their occupations and unable to improve their status, the entire class structure of the state was stratified, and the totalitarian empire firmly established. The only way of avoiding one's obligations was to bribe the tax collectors; and we hear of numerous cases of such corruption in the following two centuries. But even bribery amounted to nothing more than an irregular alternative to taxes, and could only modify the impositions for a brief period.

CONSTANTINE AND THE PERFECTING OF TOTALITARIANISM

Economic and military policy

After his prescribed twenty years of rule Diocletian celebrated a jubilee in 305, and

A reconstruction of the huge palace which the Emperor Diocletian built for his retirement after he abdicated. The palace is at Split, Yugoslavia. (COURTESY YUGOSLAV STATE TOURIST OFFICE)

then retired, dying much later in 313. His colleague Maximian, however, was not yet tired of power. Diocletian at last persuaded him to relinquish it, but Maximian preferred to hand it over to his sons rather than to the properly appointed Caesars. An intermittent civil war then broke out which was concluded by a great victory in 312 won by Constantine, son of a man who had been Caesar while Diocletian was still on the throne. Diocletian, who survived these brief wars, contented himself with exhortations issued from his huge fortress-palace at Salona (now Split, in Dalmatia). For a further twelve years after Constantine's succession to the empire in the West the new emperor tolerated an Eastern colleague, Licinius, in charge of the empire in the East. Then they came to blows, in part because of the latter's studied policy of persecuting Christians and trying to restore the old religion. Constantine prevailed and in 324 became sole emperor.

The policies of Constantine were in full accord with those of Diocletian, but after over thirty years of experience it was now possible to see in what respects they had failed. Constantine concluded only that they had not yet been carried far enough. He increased the imperial bureaucracy still further and clamped the machinery of repression still tighter. By the end of his reign the totalitarian state was complete, and the hereditary caste system no longer had any loopholes in it. Each man was securely fixed in the position in which he had been born; and his obligation to fulfill his quota of work and provide a surplus for the ever more insatiable needs of the army was absolute. The police and the bureaucracy were ubiquitous in ferreting out any source of income, returning escapees to their duty, and requisitioning food and supplies when money was unavailable.

Though Constantine reformed the coinage it is clear that there was not enough precious metal available even to keep the wheels of trade and industry revolving, much less to provide the agricultural workers with hard cash. As we now know, some of it had left the empire altogether for distant places such as India, which had always had a favorable trade balance with the empire. Increasingly taxes were paid in kind, and there was a gradual return to a barter economy and self-sufficiency on the large estates. The surplus of raw materials thus collected by the emperors presented a further problem, which was solved in the classic totalitarian manner. The emperors set up industrial establishments of their own with conscripted hereditary workers manufacturing for the needs of the emperor and the army. These factories were under the control of imperial bureaucrats, and formed the pattern for the great imperial monopolies of the later Byzantine Empire.

Constantine completed the barbarization of the army by carrying Diocletian's policies to their logical conclusion. The old frontier legions which had been at least recruited from Roman citizens, even though they had been little enough influenced by Roman civilization, were now degraded to a local militia, and troops still drawn from the citizen body were made inferior in status to the German mercenaries. The real army was a mobile field army, recruited from the neighboring barbarians, chiefly the Germanic tribes in the West, and the Sarmatians on the Danube. The elite corps of cavalry, the crack troops of the empire, were entirely composed of German mercenaries. It was possible for the foreign mercenaries to reach the highest position in the army and become *magistri militum,* or masters of the troops. From the time of Constantine onward, and especially in the fifth century, we find German masters of the troops far more powerful than their puppets who wore the purple and were still called emperors. As a rule the barbarian leaders did not aspire to the throne themselves—a possible reason for the choice of barbarians for the supreme military position. But this army, at least in the hands of Constantine, was the most efficient instru-

ment the Romans had possessed in centuries for its two primary purposes—the defense against unauthorized barbarian immigration and armed attacks into the empire, and the enforcement of discipline upon the civilians who paid for its upkeep. Always increasing as defense needs grew more imperious, it devoured the substance of the civil population, laying its heavy, unproductive hand upon all enterprise until the Roman empire collapsed from within under the impact of foreign peoples with a population almost certainly far short of theirs. But the army at least served to introduce many of the most able barbarians to the civilization of the empire, which trained them and gave them military experience—which many of them used in later years against the empire itself.

New Rome on the Bosporus

The most significant act of the reign of Constantine, however, was the founding of a new capital near the incomparable site of ancient Byzantium on the Bosporus at the entrance to the Black Sea. This city, called Constantinople, quickly grew to surpass Rome. The eastern provinces of the empire, though equally ground down by taxation, never sank to the level of the more agricultural West. Some cities continued to thrive and trade continued, if less luxuriantly than in the past. It was certainly for this reason that Constantine founded his new capital in the midst of this area. The western provinces hardly served to support themselves and their defense, while the defense needs in the East were not so vast. Moreover, the provinces themselves provided some surplus for luxuries appreciated by the now entirely Orientalized court of the first Christian monarch.

Constantinople was also a port, which Rome had never been; it could be made impregnable by sea and strongly fortified by land. Not very far from the capital was the river Danube, more easily defended than the distant Rhine. Time and again the barbarians threatened the Danube, and on some occasions they crossed it and reached almost to

Constantinople. But faced with the formidable bastion of the city itself, they realized they could hardly conquer it with their crude weapons. When, therefore, the emperors suggested to them that the West was an easier target, Alaric, Theodoric, and other barbarian leaders took the hint, and Constantinople was left in peace. Not until the barbarian "crusaders" from the West took it in 1204 against what was little more than a token defense did it ever succumb to an external invader.

For the adornment of his new capital Constantine sent for the best artists and craftsmen of the empire. But their talent proved to be far from adequate to the opportunity. Constantine then proceeded systematically to pillage Greece. The ancient Greek shrines were made to yield up their sculpture of the glorious age of Hellenic art. Trophies of the battle of Salamis, marble columns from temples to the Greek gods, possibly even the Olympian Zeus of Phidias, by all accounts the noblest sculpture the world has yet seen, priceless manuscripts from Alexandria and other Hellenistic cities were brought into Constantinople, where they survived for many more centuries, cheek by jowl with the inferior, badly built, and artistically tasteless artifacts of the age of Constantine. The bulk of these works was destroyed in the early thirteenth century by Latin "crusaders" ignorant of art and interested primarily in the precious metals of which so many of these works of art were made. What was not stolen at this time was largely destroyed by fires set by both the "crusaders" and their victims.

Constantine himself ruled over the united empire, and he ensured the succession of his sons to the throne. But he realized it was too vast for efficient rule by one man; and, having two sons, he divided it. Thereafter, though in theory they were each co-emperors of the whole, the empire was in fact divided between two emperors, one resident in Constantinople, the other with an official residence in Rome, but more often living in Milan, Trier, or Ravenna, an impregnable city in the marshes of north-

eastern Italy where, amid the invasions of the Goths, the emperor felt safe enough to neglect the interests of the empire with impunity.

► External dangers to the empire

BARBARIAN INFILTRATION

The Germanic tribes, general characteristics

We have already had occasion to refer to the infiltration of barbarians into the Roman Empire. Naturally this description of the invaders is not the preferred term in Germany and Northern Europe where the whole process, which occupied several centuries, is known as the *Völkerwanderung*, or the migration of peoples. Without attempting to pronounce on the native excellences of these peoples, it is clear that they were imperfectly versed at this time in the practices of civilization which had grown up in cities, of which these peoples had none.

Julius Caesar and Tacitus among the Roman historians had described the manners and customs of the German peoples in their day—Caesar briefly from the point of view of an alien conqueror; Tacitus actuated, in part at least, by a desire to contrast the noble savage with the effete and decadent Romans of the capital at the beginning of the second century. These accounts, valuable as they are, need to be treated with some caution. Tacitus himself had probably never been in Germany, and his picture, convincing though his incomparable style makes it, is only based on information received from others. Nevertheless the facts of his *Germania* coincide in essentials with later records based on the firsthand observations of later times.

In physical characteristics the Germans were, as a group, taller than the Roman peoples from the Mediterranean area; many of them had reddish or blond hair which they wore long. The country which they inhabited was infertile, swampy, and heavily forested; to the Germans, therefore, life was a constant struggle for survival. Their chief joy in life appears to have been fighting, and many of them knew no other occupation. Though by the fourth century they had moved from "savagery" to "barbarism," and cultivated some crops, their chief occupation remained hunting and food gathering. They possessed large numbers of domestic animals, especially pigs and cattle with which they supplemented their food supply. Their agricultural practices were wasteful. When one piece of land was exhausted they moved on to another. However, like the Dorian peoples who invaded and conquered Greece, they had the use of iron, and the weapons of at least the leading warriors were made of that metal. Both in their manner of living and in many features of their political and social organization they strongly resembled the North American Indian as he was known to the Americans of the colonial era.

As in all primitive societies, their basic unit was the family, and a number of families composed a clan or tribe. The clan had a hereditary chieftain who was the leader in war and peace. There was also a tribal assembly of all free men who met in council to decide policies suggested by the chief. If they agreed they showed their assent by clashing their shields. In later times many tribes would unite under a king; as a rule when the Romans came in contact with them it was with the king they had to negotiate, and the kings and the tribes consolidated under them with whom they had to fight. The only distinctive organization not to be found in the other primitive peoples studied in earlier chapters was the *comitatus*, or league of companions. In a fighting people it was to be expected that powerful warriors would sometimes arise who held no hereditary position. These men would attract around themselves others who looked to them for leadership. Such organizations were encouraged by the Germans. They fought together, and if necessary died together. The leader looked first to the needs of his men, and they in turn were bound to him by the strongest ties of loyalty. In this institution we evi-

dently have the germ of the later feudal relationship between lords and the vassals who were tied to them by an oath of fealty, and owed military service to them.

Such law as these peoples possessed was based upon the tribal relationships. It was the duty of a family or tribe to avenge the death of its members or exact monetary compensation for it. The tribal council might act as arbiter but without considering so much factual evidence as the number and quality of the oaths taken by supporters of both sides. In cases of doubt, single combat might be prescribed, the loser thus being proved guilty; or, in the case of men of inferior status and women, an ordeal would be called for, from which if the victim emerged without serious damage he could safely be presumed to be innocent.[2]

The men of the German tribes spent most of their lives in fighting or looking after the animals, the women stayed home and looked after the household, while the slaves, who had some personal freedom though tied to the land, looked after such crops as the tribes possessed. Not being closely attached to any piece of land, it was not difficult for whole tribes or nations to migrate, either in search of better pastures or crop land or from simple restlessness. None of the Germanic peoples had moved very far from the nomadic life; while other barbarian peoples who now began to endanger the empire were still truly nomads, who pushed the more settled peoples before them, and, as a result, set an even larger migration in motion.

These migrations of people are as old as history. We have already noticed the Achaean, Ionian, and Dorian invasions of Greece. In the fourth century B.C. the Celts migrated all over Europe and into Asia, and

[2] It has been thought by some that the institution of compurgation (joint swearing) by "oath-helpers," mentioned here, was the origin of the modern jury, especially since twelve was the number of oath-helpers most commonly used. However, it is generally believed that the jury system in England originated in the medieval French practice of sending out officials to inquire into various matters of interest to the kings, about which evidence was taken on oath.

were defeated by the Romans only with great difficulty, not before Rome itself had been thoroughly sacked. At the turn of the first century B.C. the Germanic Cimbri and Teutones had penetrated far into Italy, and could not be defeated until the Romans had reorganized their army. The rulers of the early Roman Empire after a few abortive efforts, decided that it was impossible to civilize and conquer the barbarians beyond the borders of the empire, and contented themselves with building fortifications to defend its boundaries. For several centuries this defense was successful.

When at last new groups of barbarians began to threaten again, the danger came from Eastern Europe rather than from the land known to the Romans as Germany. But the threatening peoples were still Germanic in origin. By this time they were a far more formidable enemy than the earlier primitive Germanic tribes, having learned new methods of warfare from contact with less primitive peoples. Many of them now fought on horseback and used the lance and improved armor. These were the Goths, Vandals, Burgundians, and Alemanni. They in turn were followed by native Germanic groups who had never migrated to Eastern Europe, and were armed with pikes and battle-axes, with wooden shields carried on their left arms, fighting on foot and lacking mobility, but powerful in defense, and terrifying when they appeared in large numbers. These peoples were the Franks, and the Angles and Saxons who conquered Britain. Among them only the leaders rode on horseback; and they lacked the ability to produce the superior military equipment used by their less primitive predecessors.

Behind the Germanic groups were the Sarmatians, a warlike people who gave much trouble to the Byzantine Empire with their raids into the Balkans, but who for the most part remained in southern Russia; and the Slavs, who at this time lived in a more primitive manner than any of the other groups, but whose capacity for resisting and absorbing conquerors enabled them to survive when most of the more warlike groups

had disappeared. These Slavs moved into eastern Germany and Central Europe in the wake of the migrating Germanic peoples, and stayed there, many of them to this day, as well as infiltrating into the Balkans. Behind all these peoples, again, were the Asiatic Huns who relentlessly moved westward, pushing the other peoples in front of them.

The Goths

Relations with the empire—A great island of civilization into which they were not permitted to penetrate naturally exercised a powerful fascination on those barbarian peoples who were closest to the Roman frontiers. Within the empire were settled towns, law and order, luxuries, and a way of living entirely alien to them but nonetheless attractive for that. The disciplined legionaries of Rome were always more than a match for them save in exceptional circumstances, and they hesitated to try conclusions with them unless pressure from the rear forced them to violate the Roman boundaries in spite of themselves. On the other hand, they fiercely defended themselves against attacks from the Roman side. While they may have at all times expressed contempt for the civilized Romans on the other side of the barrier, great numbers of them seem to have hungered for a different kind of life, and not only for the plunder of a successful raid. When the Roman emperors found that they could no longer rely upon the empire and the citizen body to defend their boundaries, and especially during the half century of anarchy when individual Roman generals seeking the supreme power would take troops wherever they could find them, then it was natural to turn to these barbarians whose trade it was to fight, who were strong and warlike, though lacking the training which would enable them to defeat the Roman legionaries.

So from the third century we find individual barbarians and whole tribes being enrolled into the army, receiving training, and acquiring some knowledge and understanding of Roman civilization. They were not, of course, at first loyal to Rome or to the empire, impersonal entities quite alien to their experience, which was always of men rather than institutions. Few indeed can ever have grasped the idea of the Roman Empire. But they did take to disciplined military life, and did not lose their warrior spirit; and they were far more loyal to their new leaders than most of the Roman peasants who had been conscripted into the army, were scarcely more literate than the barbarians, lacked warlike spirit, and yet looked upon themselves as a privileged caste.

It was, therefore, natural for the Roman soldier-emperors to look more and more to the barbarians, especially to the Goths, and, in the East, to the Sarmatians, for the real core of their armies. As long as they needed troops there were unlimited numbers of barbarians available to them, who served for pay, who obeyed orders, who did not want to set themselves up as emperors, and who in their simplicity would put up with more hardships than would the citizen conscripts. Thus arose the military policy of the late emperors, especially Constantine. They were managers of a totalitarian state which had to be kept down by an iron rule, and whose citizens had to be forced to work and to pay taxes. Many of these emperors no doubt believed in the Roman Empire, believed that no price was too high to pay for its formal preservation. And few indeed probably realized what the result would be: that instead of the Romans civilizing the barbarians and making them into good civilized servants of the empire, it was the empire that would be barbarized by the Goths and their successors, and that the whole superstructure of an imperial universal state would collapse from within, when the real cement that held it together, the free municipalities and the economy and culture based on them, finally crashed and gave way. The Romans, as has been said, were not an imaginative people, and few were their thinkers who perceived the inevitable end even when it was almost upon them.

The policies adopted by the emperors were dictated by the immediate circum-stances of each case. There never was a settled, agreed policy for keeping the barbarians in check. The earliest Goths were recruited for the army as individual soldiers, perhaps a comitatus, or even a tribe. When in later times large bodies of barbarians clamored for entry into the empire, with their wives and children, they were allowed to come in as *coloni,* were given land to cultivate which they were not permitted to leave, and agreed to give military service for the privilege. When in the late fourth and fifth centuries the boundaries became increasingly difficult to defend, whole tribes and even nations with their kings violated the frontier openly and settled down in land that had been Roman territory. When the emperors got around to it they legalized the position by giving these peoples the status of allies, *foederati,* bound by treaty to Rome and expected to defend their newly acquired lands against the next comers. This they often did, the Goths having little friendship for the Franks, and even the West Goths (Visigoths) little enough for the East Goths (Ostrogoths), and vice versa. And all united, as we shall see, against the Huns. Other groups applied for permission to come in as allies in advance, and were allowed in, upon the signing of a treaty; but these in many cases found the Roman officials unbearably patronizing and predatory, reluctant to carry out the terms to which their masters had agreed.

Gradual barbarization of the Romans— It was to be expected that once the boundaries were defended by barbarians, some at least of their kinsmen would be admitted without formalities, and that gradually the frontier provinces would become predominantly barbarian. As a privileged caste also the soldiers would have little respect for the Roman citizens who were living in virtual slavery under constant threat from themselves, the emperors, and the imperial bureaucracy. If they were not paid promptly they could always loot a few cities, for which they had little respect but much envy. The Romans, whose cities had been destroyed by the Goths, could not hope to recover in the circumstances of the fifth century. Thus, gradually, and especially after the invasion of the Huns which forced ever more peoples over the imperial boundaries, the peoples of the empire became themselves barbarized, sometimes joining the hordes and plundering their neighbors, protected only by some of the assimilated barbarians who now regarded themselves as Romans and by those few landholders who could still maintain their independence in spite of barbarian infiltration.

Conversion of the barbarians to Christianity—One softening influence, however, should be noticed. For much of the fourth century Bishop Ulfilas (*ca.* 311–383), of partly Gothic ancestry himself, but educated in Constantinople, had been working in the Gothic vineyard. He gave the Goths their first writing, including a Gothic Bible, and converted great numbers of the West Goths, who passed the new religion on to many of the East Goths and Vandals who were in close contact with them. The type of Christianity, however, to which he converted them was Arianism, which had been the accepted doctrine in Constantinople during the good bishop's period of study, and which in any case was far more likely to be acceptable to the simple barbarians than the more mysterious teachings of orthodox Christianity. Thus all the earlier barbarian peoples who invaded the Roman Empire were converted to Arian Christianity, ultimately bringing upon themselves difficulties when an orthodox pope and an orthodox emperor used their heresy as an excuse for the invasion of Italy and the destruction of the East Gothic kingdom. The organization of the Arian Church in the areas inhabited by these peoples was also of material help during the most severe period of the barbarian invasions when the imperial government broke down. In Gaul, later Frankland, however, most of the bishops remained orthodox, giving great help to the orthodox Frankish King Clovis at the end of the fifth century in the establishment of his authority over most of the territory which had been Gaul.

THE BARBARIAN INVASIONS

The advance of the Huns (372–451)

While the first stage of the entry of the barbarians into the West is marked by slow infiltration, with the agreement, if not always active support of the emperors, the second stage consists of true invasions, not intentional on the part of the invaders, but forced by the westward advance of a central Asiatic people, the Huns. These people, according to the records of their enemies, were a group of short, squat, strong warriors who came riding into Europe on horses, which they seldom left, being believed by the Goths even to sleep on them. Their numbers do not seem to have been overwhelming; but they could move very rapidly, giving the appearance of great numbers. They were yellow-skinned, beardless, and to the Westerners incredibly ugly, and terrifying. They showed no mercy.

Involuntary advance of the barbarians into the empire

The Goths and other Germanic peoples were unable to hold their own against the assaults of the Huns. Most of the Ostrogoths were penned in near the Black Sea, while others escaped to the Carpathian mountains. Large numbers of the Visigoths, pushed by the Huns, congregated on the Danube, the boundary of the empire, and petitioned the Eastern emperor to allow them to cross into safety. The emperor, Valens, faced with such massive immigration, was uncertain what policy to adopt. At last he made up his mind to accept them as *foederati;* but as soon as the Goths were in Roman territory the imperial officials proceeded to plunder them, carrying off some of their people as slaves, and refusing to supply the remainder even with food. The fiercely independent and numerically superior Goths finally took matters into their own hands and made their way towards Constantinople, plundering and ravaging as they went. The emperor called to the West for aid. But his young nephew Gratian, who had succeeded to the throne in 375, was fully occupied with a campaign against the Alemanni. After a few successes won by his generals, Valens became more confident and rejected the advice of his nephew, who urged him to wait for the arrival of his own force. Taking the field himself, Valens was disastrously defeated in the battle of Adrianople, and was killed shortly afterwards while trying to make his escape (378). His successor promptly made terms and tried to carry out the original treaty. But the Goths were now firmly ensconced in the empire, with their own kings and leaders, a constant menace to the emperors, sometimes paid salaries and serving in the imperial armies, sometimes taking the law into their own hands, wandering up and down Europe.

But the Eastern emperor held two trump cards denied to the emperor in the West. The heart of his territory was defensible. His important towns were strongly fortified, and Constantinople itself was impregnable to barbarian arms. And the emperor, commanding the resources of the only remaining prosperous area in the empire, had access to ready money. The combination of these two was sufficient to enable the Eastern Empire to survive the worst that the barbarians could do. The emperor was willing to take them into the army and pay them well; and they could not, on the other hand, hope to conquer him unless he should be as foolhardy as Valens. There can be no doubt also that the Oriental splendor of the imperial court made a deep impression on the barbarians and convinced them that the emperor possessed power greater than he actually had at his disposal. At all events, it was possible for him to convince the ambitious barbarians that pickings were easier elsewhere.

The barbarian invasions in the West— Visigoths, Vandals, Franks, Burgundians, Bretons—So it was upon the now greatly enfeebled empire in the West that the Goths concentrated their attacks, opposed for a few years by a Vandal general in the service of Rome, then on his death marching into Italy and sacking Rome, as will be described in more detail in the next section devoted to the fortunes of Italy. From Italy they moved into Gaul and thence into Spain, where in 419 they were allowed to form their own kingdom as allies of the empire. They were later driven from Gaul by the Franks.

At the beginning of the fifth century the Vandals, themselves driven relentlessly by constant pressure from the westward advance of the Huns, moved into Gaul without meeting much opposition, plundering and burning as they went. From the fact that the Roman prefect a few years earlier had been transferred to southeastern Gaul it seems clear that the empire had given up hope of defending the Rhine and the North. It took three years (406–409) for the Vandals to eat up the resources of Gaul ("the whole of Gaul burnt like a torch," as a contemporary poet described it) and cross over into Spain. After a few years in Spain, they were driven by the Roman armies and their Gothic allies into the extreme south. Here they found in Gaiseric a great leader who, through the treachery of the Roman governor in Africa, was allowed to cross the strait of Gibraltar into Africa, where he founded a kingdom (429). This kingdom was later recognized by the Roman emperor as another ally. But by this time the emperor exercised hardly even a nominal sway over his numerous barbarian allies.

Behind the Vandals came the Franks and the Burgundians. The last great Roman general, Aetius (magister militum, 430–454), permitted the Franks to stay in northern Gaul, again as allies; while the Burgundians moved, also with his assent, into southern Gaul along the valley of the Rhone, and into the area now known as Savoy. Taking advantage of the general movement, a group of Celts, severely harassed by the activities of another Germanic group, the Saxons, who had sent expeditions to Britain from about 440, passed over from their home in Britain into northwest Gaul, the land now called Brittany.

The lifting of the Hun menace

In the early fifth century the Huns, who had been largely responsible for the barbarian movement in the first place, united under the leadership of a chieftain named

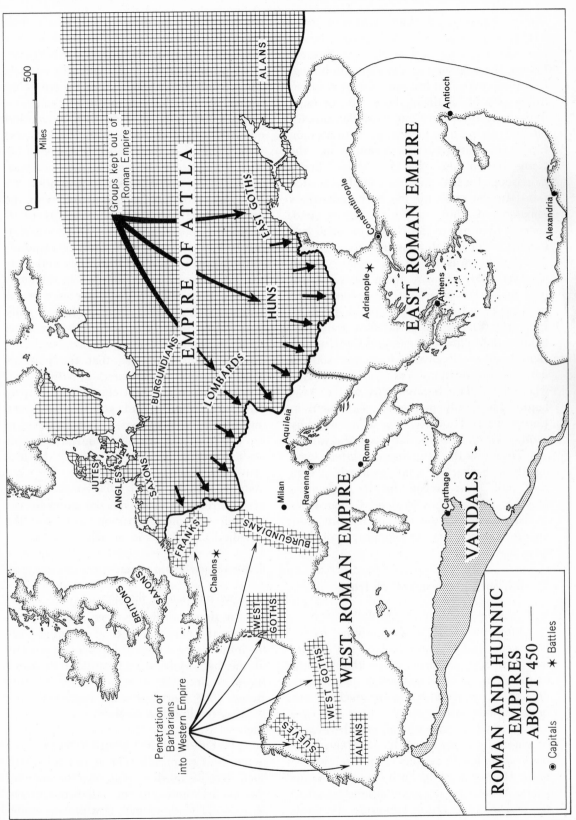

500

Miles

0

Groups kept out of Roman Empire

EMPIRE OF ATTILA

ALANS

EAST GOTHS

HUNS

BURGUNDIANS

LOMBARDS

EAST ROMAN EMPIRE

Antioch

Constantinople

Adrianople ✴

Athens

Alexandria

JUTES

ANGLES

SAXONS

BRITONS

SAXONS

FRANKS

Chalons ✴

BURGUNDIANS

WEST GOTHS

WEST ROMAN EMPIRE

Aquileia

Milan

Ravenna

Rome

Carthage

VANDALS

Penetration of Barbarians into Western Empire

WEST GOTHS

SUEVES

ALANS

ROMAN AND HUNNIC
EMPIRES
—ABOUT 450—

● Capitals   ✴ Battles

191

Attila, and resumed their westward drive (445). For some time they had hovered near the frontiers of the Eastern Empire, forcing the emperors to pay them an annual tribute. But when at last one of them refused, Attila, possibly realizing he could not hope to do more than carry out sporadic raids for plunder, or perhaps acting on a suggestion from some Eastern traitor, decided, like the Goths before him, that the West offered more scope for his enterprise, and he invaded Gaul. In the crisis all the barbarian tribes remembered their duty to Rome, and, spurred by terror of the Hun, they stood and fought under the Roman imperial general Aetius. This was the battle usually called Chalons (451). It was not a clear-cut victory for either side; but Attila deemed it prudent to retreat to a prepared position, from which he began to threaten Italy. But he died the following year, and the Hunnish confederation dissolved, remnants settling down in Europe but others returning to Asia, where later they became part of the Avar horde. Their only permanent settlement in Europe was in Hungary, later to be settled by another group of barbarians, the Magyars.

Thus was the Hun menace lifted, leaving those barbarians who for nearly a century had been forced by the relentless pressure of the Huns to defend themselves at the expense of the Roman Empire, now able for the first time to take charge of their own destinies.

▶ Barbarian conquest of Italy

NOMINAL IMPERIAL RULE FROM RAVENNA

After the death of Constantine, as we have seen, the Western half of the empire had its own co-emperor, but, without access to the more prosperous part of the Roman dominions, it fell into a swift decline. For brief periods during the century the East and West were again united, and the façade of empire was successfully maintained for most of the fourth century until the pressure of the Huns started the barbarian movements again. When the dangers became acute at the end of the century, Honorius, the west-

ern emperor, moved his capital to Ravenna (ca. 400), leaving the pope as the real ruler of Rome. Thereafter most of the emperors were either children, feeble-minded, or both. They lived in a hothouse atmosphere of intrigue, surrounded by eunuchs, courtiers, clergy, and women. But they were still officially rulers of the empire, and it was with them that the barbarians negotiated. Secure in their stronghold of Ravenna, which, fully fortified and surrounded by marshes, could not be conquered with the resources available to the barbarians, many of these emperors behaved with an astounding lack of foresight and sense of responsibility. Beset by fears of treachery and even ignorant of what was going on in their territories, they still imagined themselves the potentates that earlier emperors had actually been. They treated the barbarians, including their own generals, too often with a lordly disdain. The result was that the generals were forced to take matters into their own hands, and do the best they could to preserve the empire. And yet the emperors, on at least two occasions, rewarded them, in the one case with execution, and in the other with assassination. By the end of the fifth century the last of these successors of Constantine was deposed by the barbarian general of the day, who merely assumed the kingship without opposition. This was the so-called fall of Rome in 476.

ROME UNDER PAPAL RULE

The position of the pope

In Rome itself the pope was the real, but not the nominal, ruler of the city. Only his influence was able to temper the ferocity of the barbarians who invaded Italy three times during the century, twice sacking Rome. The imperial generals were away from Italy, defending the northern provinces. On each occasion it was the failure of these generals that allowed the barbarians to enter the defenseless peninsula. The popes organized such defense as there was, negotiated with the enemy, and superintended the reconstruction. The old Senate, now only a municipal council of Rome, gave occasional aid; even consuls continued to be elected, but they were not allowed to exercise any real power. The only well-organized and effective body in Rome was the clergy, under the authority of the pope.

Sack of Rome by Alaric (410)

The first attack came from Alaric the Visigoth, who had marched over from the Danubian provinces. The barbarian imperial general Stilicho twice defeated him; but the emperor Honorius suspected his general's loyalty, and had him executed. The Goth was thus given a free passage into Italy. No army was there to meet him, the emperor remaining safely defiant in Ravenna when Alaric asked him for land in Italy for the settlement of his people. The Roman citizens offered Alaric a ransom for their city, but he wanted land, not cash. Exasperated with the stubbornness of Honorius, Alaric then appointed an emperor of his own, a Roman noble. But when this gentleman also was either unwilling or unable to grant his demands, Alaric and his troops lost patience and sacked Rome for three days. But the Gothic king died within a year, and the emperor patched up a treaty with his successors. The Visigoths moved off to greener pastures.

The invasion of Attila (452)

For forty years Rome survived, and was partly reconstructed under papal direction. It was now little more than a defenseless provincial city, no longer the seat of empire, and grievously depopulated; but it still housed the spiritual head of Christendom.

After his check at Chalons Attila looked around for an area for his next year's campaigns, and Italy looked like an easy conquest. It is said that he hoped for a marriage into the imperial family, a suit not altogether discouraged by the lady herself, who was tired of her nunnery and wrote him letters whose content can only be guessed. But Attila could gain no satisfaction from her brother, the emperor at Ravenna. He therefore took matters into his own hands, invaded

Italy, and approached the gates of Rome. Here the pious legends say that he was checked by Pope Leo I, who appeared with all the regalia of his office, and a procession of acolytes bearing candles. The barbarian was dismayed—or perhaps bought off with the remains of the treasures of the Church. At all events he retired to winter quarters in the north of Italy, gave up hopes of a bride from the imperial family, and satisfied himself with a beautiful barbarian princess. He died shortly afterward and his empire vanished with him.

Sack of Rome by Vandals (455)

But the barbarians were not yet through with Rome. Only three years later, at a moment when Aetius, the Roman victor of Chalons, had just been assassinated by the emperor Valentinian III (a murder quickly avenged by friends of the general), Gaiseric, the terrible king of the Vandals, sailed from Carthage with a fleet of barbarians bent on plunder. Sailing unmolested up the Tiber in their shallow-bottomed boats, the Vandals entered Rome. Again Pope Leo interceded, but was able to win nothing but the lives of the citizens. The Vandals then sacked the defenseless city for two weeks. When their ships left, laden with booty, Rome was little but a desolate ruin, her temples pillaged, her palaces sacked and burned, and everything of any value that had not been hidden from the barbarians was on the way to Africa.

THE BARBARIANS IN ITALY—THE END OF IMPERIAL RULE ("FALL OF ROME," 476)

For another twenty years the imperial rulers in Ravenna exercised a nominal sway over Italy. But the real rulers were the barbarian chieftains who bore Roman titles and commanded the army, which was still Roman in name. Emperors were made and unmade at will until one of the generals, Odoacer by name, finally decided to put an end to the solemn farce. The last emperor, a child rejoicing in the name of Romulus, the little Augustus (Augustulus), was formally deposed, his imperial insignia confiscated and sent to Zeno, the crafty emperor of the East, as a token that there was no further emperor in the West. Though he proclaimed himself king of Italy, Odoacer thus showed himself willing to acknowledge the overlordship of the Eastern emperor, who was theoretically still lord of the whole united empire. Doubtless Odoacer thought him sufficiently far away and sufficiently occupied to be of no danger to his Italian sovereignty. Thus was the fall of Rome, which had stood for almost a thousand years in proud independence, consummated by the simple act of a barbarian general, without fighting, and with little noticeable change even in the form of the government. For a long time the imperial officials had been powerless, with the clergy alone keeping their Roman-inspired organization intact. Even under Odoacer, the Senate still sat as the municipal council of Rome, a position of honor but no authority; and even consuls continued to be solemnly elected. But all real power was now in the hands of the army and its generals. The army itself was made up of various Germanic tribesmen under the leadership of Odoacer himself, whose origin is unknown. He has been thought by some scholars even to have been a Hun, though he was originally called Herulian. High positions in the state were reserved for the barbarian rulers. Relations with the papacy were correct but not cordial, for these barbarian peoples were all heretical Arians and thus unacceptable to orthodox Christians. Not until Justinian's reconquest of Italy, to be described later, was the papacy to be freed from its difficult position as an island of orthodoxy within a sea of heresy.

OSTROGOTHIC KINGDOM OF ITALY— THEODORIC (493–526)

But Odoacer was not to enjoy his new crown in peace. His army, though loyal to him, had no united body of tribesmen behind it. It was a formidable enough body of military men, but not strong enough to defend itself against a powerful united people. And such a people under Theodoric, prob-

ably the greatest of all barbarian generals and administrators, this army was now to be called upon to meet.

We have seen that the Ostrogoths (East Goths) had early submitted to Attila, and had been penned into a territory near the Black Sea. When this menace was lifted the Ostrogoths began to stir again and look for land for settlement. They made a treaty with Constantinople under which they became allies of the empire, and a young prince named Theodoric was sent to the capital as hostage. Thus he was educated in Constantinople, learned to understand and respect Roman institutions and even Roman law, and gained military experience. When his father died and he became king of a section of the Ostrogothic people he continued friendly relations with Zeno, emperor at Constantinople, was made a Roman citizen, and a master of the Byzantine troops. But later, when Theodoric consolidated all the Ostrogoths under his rulership, the emperor began to worry, and thought it would be safer to divert Theodoric and his people to the West, where he had no objection to the expulsion of Odoacer. Theodoric, taking the hint, led his people over into Italy and drove his opponent into Ravenna, from which, however, he found it impossible to dislodge him. Resorting to treachery under cover of peace negotiations, Theodoric was able to murder his rival, and became sole ruler of Italy, with a united Ostrogothic people behind him (493).

His reign of thirty-seven years was a remarkable example of the importance of good government to the prosperity of a country, even one as ill-used as Italy had been in the last centuries. Unencumbered by an imperial heritage, facing no enemies who could not be easily handled, keeping Constantinople at a safe distance and without cause for complaint against him since he scrupulously acknowledged the overlordship of the emperor, Theodoric gave a government to the Italians such as they had not known for centuries. The Goths were assigned land in Italy, apparently by the simple expedient of dispossessing a few large pro-

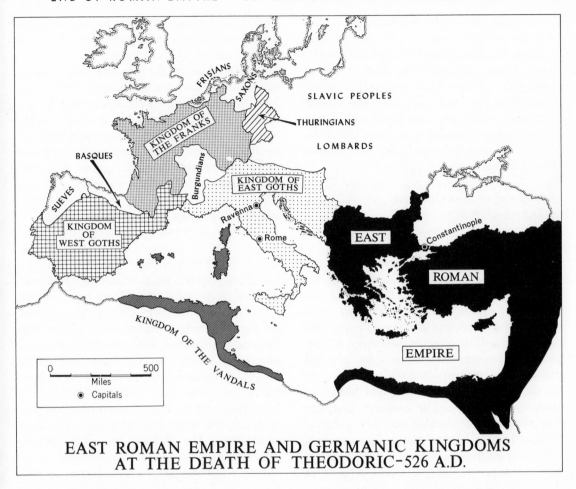

EAST ROMAN EMPIRE AND GERMANIC KINGDOMS
AT THE DEATH OF THEODORIC-526 A.D.

prietors and repopulating land that was not being worked for lack of cultivators, while those who were not in the army settled down as farmers. The Roman administration of government and justice was maintained, the Senate remained, on the whole, loyal to the king, and taxes were drastically reduced, as there was no longer such need for them. Agriculture and commerce revived; even private enterprise began to appear. Theodoric dredged the harbors, rebuilt aqueducts, and restored the cities as far as he could with his limited means. No longer having a vast empire to maintain, and with a greatly reduced population to support, Italy became the self-supporting territory that she has always had it in her power to be. The pope continued to maintain correct relations with the king though he was an Arian; and Theodoric in

return made no attempt to convert his ortho-dox Roman subjects to Arianism.

There was even a brief revival of culture, with the two great scholars Boethius and Cassiodorus the chief ornaments. Boethius, foreseeing correctly the certain loss of all Greek culture in the West under the barbarian monarchy, spent much of his life translating the logical works of Aristotle into Latin, and writing textbooks based on the dying Greek knowledge, but suitable for the barbarians and barbarized Romans who alone would remain to study them. Unfortunately he became suspected of treasonable designs against the throne, and was cast into prison. Here he wrote the *Consolations of Philosophy*, which has been read ever since, and was especially popular in the Middle Ages. Ultimately he was executed by order of Theodoric. His shade, however, may have been compensated by the knowledge that his textbooks and translations did indeed survive to become the chief intellectual diet of generations of medieval students. Cassiodorus, however, long outlived the Gothic king, supervising the translating and copying of manuscripts in a monastery which he founded on his own estate. He also wrote a *History of the Goths*.

RECONQUEST OF ITALY BY THE BYZANTINE EMPIRE

Italian policy of Justinian

Theodoric's kingdom, however, did not survive his death. It was evidently only his personality that held it together. Civil war disrupted the kingdom, the succession, as so often in the Germanic kingdoms, being disputed between several contestants; in 535, Justinian, the emperor of the East, decided that the time was ripe for the restoration of the old Roman Empire, as it had been and always ought to be. The emperor Justinian was also a strong zealot for the orthodox faith as long as he was allowed to interpret it himself. In the laudable aim of extinguishing Arianism, he had the moral support of the papacy in Rome, and whatever more tangible support it could give him—at least until the popes recognized that Justinian's authoritarianism extended to the field of religion also.

Destruction of Ostrogothic kingdom— Economic and strategic consequences

In a long-drawn-out and ruinously expensive war, Justinian's generals, Belisarius and Narses, reconquered Italy piecemeal. Behind them came the imperial bureaucracy and the tax collectors from whom the fortunate Italians had been free for a generation. The Ostrogothic nation resisted to the last, and was virtually destroyed, Italy was devastated; twenty years of warfare in which neither side showed any mercy was the final crippling blow to a country which had been able to recover from so many in the past. From this she never recovered for centuries.

Justinian, leaving an *exarch,* an imperial official, to rule Italy from Ravenna on his behalf, and a pope grateful for his orthodoxy but disliking intensely his autocratic manner of dealing with spiritual matters which he had acquired in his own capital, turned his attention to other affairs. He died soon afterward, having saddled his empire with a territory almost useless for exploitation, and incapable of self-defense against any barbarian horde that wished to enter.

INVASION OF ITALY BY LOMBARDS (568) —PARTITION OF ITALY

The Lombard conquests (568–605)

This was not long in coming. Justinian had not been in his grave three years before the Lombards, another Germanic people, but by far the least civilized of any that had hitherto penetrated into Southern Europe, nominally Arians also, but in fact nearer to heathenism, swept into northern Italy, where there was no one left to oppose them. This time they made no compromises with the emperor, nor were they interested in Roman civilization. The Italians lost their estates, which were simply sequestrated by the Lombards. Northern Italy was consolidated under their rule in seven years, and they began to push southward. The exarch of Ravenna maintained his stronghold, still theoretically the ruler of Italy under the emperor; but neither he nor the rest of Italy could obtain any support from the various emperors of Constantinople, who were fully engaged elsewhere. Nor did the emperors give any aid to the other isolated areas in Italy under their nominal rule. And there was no such partly civilized king as Theodoric over the Lombards. They were united only for conquest and plunder. Thereafter their separate leaders (dukes) took what they could, and maintained it as their own private possession. By 605 all Italy except Ravenna, Naples, Rome, and parts of the extreme south were in the hands of the barbarians.

Remnants of Byzantine rule

What remained to the empire from the

warfare of Justinian was the isolated and useless Ravenna, and the south. Rome acknowledged the overlordship of Constantinople on the principle that a distant overlord is better than a local one, especially if he is powerless to intervene. Since such acknowledgment carried with it no obligation to obedience, the popes were content to make it for centuries to come. And the pope of Rome was now at last in fact its temporal lord also. He was the spiritual lord of all Christendom, the owner of many scattered estates in Italy which had been given to the Church in the troubled times, and the defender of Rome against the barbarian Lombards from whom he had managed to keep his city intact.

Position of the papacy—Gregory I (590–604)

This was the work of one man, one of the greatest of the popes, a Roman by descent, a saint, and a gifted administrator and diplomatist, Gregory I, the Great.

It is possible that the Lombards, vastly superior in numbers as they were, could have taken Rome by force if they had united against it. But they seem to have respected the person of the pope, and perhaps the sanctity of the city, in spite of the fact that they were only nominal Christians, and a heretical sect at that. At all events, they never made any serious effort to do so, perhaps in part because of their internal disunity. Thus for centuries the popes were able to exist, often isolated and always precariously, until they were rescued in the eighth century by the orthodox Frankish kings. Gregory, who had at an earlier stage in his life been an official agent of the papacy in Constantinople, knew how useless it was to look for help from this quarter. He therefore accepted the position, and negotiated directly with the Lombards, while the emperor continued to bid him resist, and for many years refused to accept his arrangements. Ultimately the empire recognized the conquests; and Gregory through the negotiations was allowed to keep his city and the territory around it.

Such a position, in spite of its precariousness, had certain manifest advantages. As a temporal ruler the pope continued to owe a nominal allegiance to Constantinople, an allegiance which could not be enforced, but still gave him legal title to his position, and perhaps served to keep the Lombards away from his city. As a spiritual and temporal leader he had just shown himself as a true shepherd of his people, thereby greatly enhancing his prestige. He began to improve his position still further by directing missionary enterprises, especially the successful mission of St. Augustine to England (596), and a further mission to Spain, where the Visigothic king was at last converted from his Arianism to orthodox Catholicism. Gregory took careful thought for the position of the clergy in Christendom, and wrote several works giving them guidance and practical advice on the care of souls. His instructions to bishops remain the fundamental work on the subject, explaining in a simple manner the different kinds of cases with which they would be called upon to deal, and how the instruction varied in each case. As explained already, he also fully supported the work of St. Benedict in his reform of the monasteries.

Perhaps the most important of Gregory's work was his insistence that all the clergy of Europe should obey the papacy and receive instructions from it. He was not too successful in France, where the appointment of the clergy was largely in the hands of the Merovingian kings, but the bishops nevertheless listened to him with respect, and later popes could quote Gregory as authority for their own claims. Newly converted Spain and England accepted the overlordship of the papacy from the first. And wherever there were orthodox clergy in Italy, they too accepted his supremacy. Though Gregory could not actually alter the domination of the Church by the state in Constantinople, he constantly repeated his claim that all the Eastern bishops and the Patriarch of Constantinople were subordinate to the Holy See by virtue of the Petrine supremacy. In all these things he gave a lead to the popes

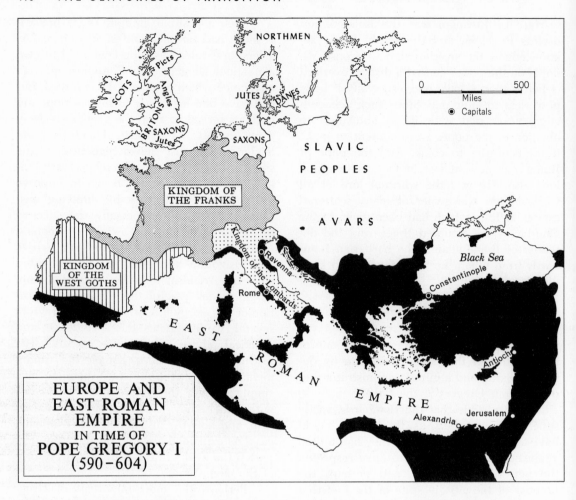

EUROPE AND
EAST ROMAN
EMPIRE
IN TIME OF
POPE GREGORY I
(590–604)

who followed him. For, though the practice of appointing bishops by lay rulers was never abandoned in France and Germany, and discipline could hardly be enforced, the clergy nevertheless did look to the papacy for guidance in spiritual affairs when they felt the need for it; and this dependence largely remained even when the papacy fell into weak hands, and when Constantinople and the Eastern Empire drifted entirely away from papal rule.

▶ Barbarian kingdoms in the West

THE ASCENDANCY OF THE FRANKS

Conquest of Gaul by Clovis (481–511)

When we last mentioned the Franks, they were following the Vandals into the land that was then called Gaul but thereafter was to be known as Frankland or France. Meeting little opposition from the few remaining Romans, the Franks first set up several kingdoms in the north under separate kings. But in 482 a young prince named Clovis became the ruler of one small kingdom clustered around the modern Tournai. Able and ambitious, he began to expand his kingdom to the south by judicious murders, treachery, and open warfare. France at the time was peopled by Visigoths, Burgundians, Alemanni, as well as the old Gallo-Romans, including a Gallic noble who called himself king of Rome. Defeating this pretender first, Clovis then drove the Alemanni back across the Rhine into Germany (to which they gave their name, Allemagne in the French language) and incorporated their kingdom into his; then he turned south and drove the Visigothic remnants into Spain to join their fellow tribesmen; and at last, having disposed also of his fellow Frankish kings, he consolidated a kingdom not much smaller than the present-day France (481–511).

Conversion of Clovis to orthodox Catholicism

Clovis, as it happened, had a Christian wife, Clotilda, who was orthodox and not Arian; after his victories he allowed himself to be converted by her clerical adviser and with him his Franks, thus being the first barbarian group to deviate from the otherwise universal Arianism. Publicly baptised at Rheims by a Catholic bishop, by this act he gained the support of the entire clergy of France, who now rallied to his aid. This was no mean help, since they controlled what was left of the old Gallo-Roman administration, while the remainder of the old Gallo-Roman population, also orthodox Christians, offered Clovis at least their moral support. From this time onward the Frankish monarchy remained the papal favorite among secular powers, and it was to the Franks that the papacy looked for help and military aid when it became involved with the Lombard kings, in preference to the official overlord of Italy away in Constantinople who was too prone to lapse into heresy and was inclined to treat papal claims to supremacy with disrespect.

The Merovingian kingdom

After the death of Clovis, his kingdom, according to Germanic custom, was divided between his four sons, who spent most of their lives fighting against each other, though they united against all non-Frankish outsiders, consolidating their total dominions by the addition of almost all the remainder of modern France. The Merovingian kingdom (418–754, so called after Meroveus, grandfather of Clovis) was sometimes under the rule of one member of the family and sometimes subdivided. But until the eighth century at least one of his descendants occu-

pied the throne, though in later years the authority of the kings was only nominal and the real power was in the hands of hereditary officials, chief stewards, who are usually, and incorrectly, called mayors of the palace (*major domus*). Ultimately, as we shall see, one of these officials deposed his titular master with papal approval and became king of the Franks himself.

It is difficult to generalize about the state of the country in Merovingian times. Some of Gaul had been thoroughly Romanized, and remained so, even under alien monarchs. On the whole, it can be said that the Latin element tended to prevail. The French language has barely four hundred words of Germanic origin, all the remainder being of Latin origin. Much of Roman law and even Roman governmental system remained, especially in the center and the south, while in the north German customs prevailed. On the other hand, the barbaric habits of the kings; their addiction to murder, wholesale and retail; their lack of care for commerce and trade so long as they were able to have the Oriental luxuries, especially of dress and ornament, in which they delighted; their general propensity to treat their territories as if they were private estates to be exploited for their own gain; and their failure to control the rapacity of local, semi-independent chiefs called counts—all these tended to push the unhappy country further into barbarism, which historians have politely called a fusion between German and Gallo-Roman culture. This fusion undoubtedly existed, and the result, after many centuries, was the modern kingdom of France, but far more Latin than Germanic—in this showing once again how the superior culture tends to absorb the lesser, if the lesser, like the Frankish culture of this period, has less to offer. The best that can be said for the Merovingian monarchy is that, by providing government of a sort and by not interfering too drastically with institutions they were incapable of understanding and with a culture that meant nothing to them, they preserved France for a brighter future when the Dark Ages which had fallen

TERRITORY OF THE FRANKS
UNDER THE MEROVINGIAN KINGS
614 A.D.

0   100   200   ◉ Capitals

Miles

on all Europe at last should come to an end.

As in all other matters the Merovingian kings were dictatorial and arbitrary in their policy toward the Church. They insisted on making all higher appointments themselves, or at least in supervising them. The result was that the choice was not always suitable, and morality does not seem to have been one of the more important qualifications for office. However, there were many good choices among the bad, and there can be little doubt that, on the whole, the bishops were several degrees better than the counts, with whom they shared the authority within

the territories under their control. While we hear of bishops who publicly boasted of their adulteries, who adopted the trade of highwaymen in addition to their spiritual duties, who daily used to drink themselves into a stupor and celebrate Mass without taking the trouble to recover their sobriety, of bishops who went to war in full armor and of at least one who admitted to regicide, the record would be incomplete without mention also of many who spent their lives looking after the poor and humble and defending them against the secular power, many who administered justice faithfully, and many who were true shepherds of their

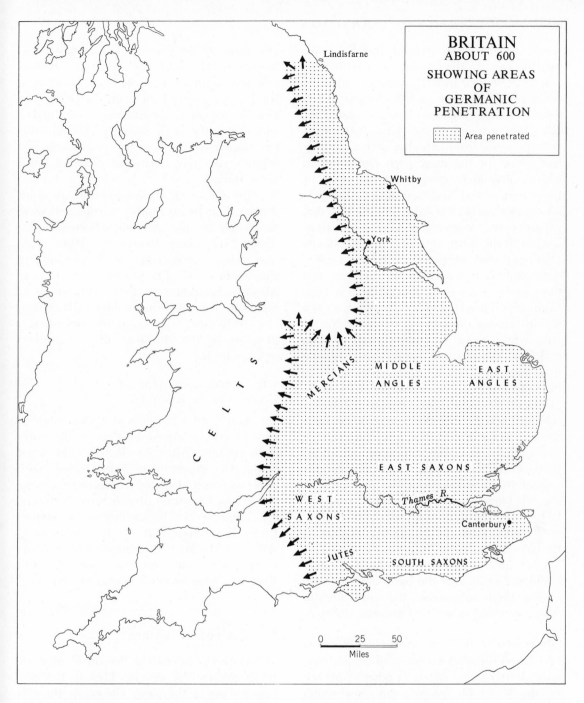

BRITAIN
ABOUT 600

SHOWING AREAS
OF
GERMANIC
PENETRATION

:::::: Area penetrated

Lindisfarne

Whitby

York

CELTS

MERCIANS

MIDDLE
ANGLES

EAST
ANGLES

EAST SAXONS

Thames R.

WEST
SAXONS

Canterbury

JUTES

SOUTH SAXONS

0   25   50
Miles

flocks. The bishops and clergy were a reflection of the times in which they lived and of the monarchs who appointed them.

THE ANGLO-SAXON KINGDOM OF ENGLAND—
INVASION (440–615)

In the early fifth century the Roman legions in Britain revolted, and finally left the country to its fate (442). The northern walls which had protected the country from the Celtic Picts were promptly overrun by these invaders, while other Celts from Ireland, called the Scots, came over by sea. Saxons from Germany, and later a people called Angles, usually collectively known as Anglo-Saxons, together with some Jutes from Denmark, invaded Britain from the east, driving the Celtic population, including the recent arrivals from Ireland and Scotland, into the west of the country, and setting up kingdoms of their own, the Angles and Jutes in the north and east, and the Saxons in the south. These conquests were completed by 615. The original Celts, who had never fully accepted Roman culture, though they had been, for the most part, converted to Christianity, fled into the extreme west of the country, and relapsed into barbarism, retaining their Celtic language to this day (Welsh); they were not reclaimed into England until the fourteenth century. The Celts (Britons) who remained in England were thoroughly Germanized by the invaders, and the country became in all essentials a Germanic one. This Anglo-Saxon realm was even able to survive the fierce raids of the Northmen, who invaded repeatedly from the late eighth to the eleventh century, and at one time gave England, as the country came to be called, one of the greatest of its kings (Cnut). The Irish and Roman Churches soon competed for converts among the English, as described in the last chapter, the Roman Church finally obtaining one of its most constantly faithful clergy and people, subject to discipline from the papacy. The English kings made no attempt to defy the Church or interfere with clerical appointments until after the Norman Conquest in the eleventh century. This was the most successful and permanent of the Germanic kingdoms, of all that the barbarians invaded during these migrations the only country which survived as a truly Germanic entity.

THE VISIGOTHIC KINGDOM OF SPAIN (507–711)

The Visigothic kingdom of Spain, conquered after many efforts in other directions by the Visigothic people, remained under Gothic control until the beginning of the eighth century, with the exception of a small area in the south which was conquered by Justinian in 554 and held by the Byzantines for a few years. Being the most civilized of the German barbarians, they fused more easily with the Romanized Spaniards than did the Franks with the Gallo-Roman peoples of France. This was especially true after the conversion of the Visigoths to Catholic Christianity in the late sixth century. Roman law was maintained as well as elements of the Roman government, with the Goths providing the ruler, though they remained a small minority in the country. The Spanish language has very few words of Germanic origin, remaining almost as close to Latin as is Italian.

But the Goths declined in military ardor during their two centuries of rule, and were no match for the invading Muslims under Tarik (711), even though the latter were only one comparatively small unit among the numerous Muslim armies. As soon as the Muslims brought over their first reinforcements the kingdom succumbed without serious resistance. The consolidation of this kingdom by the Muslims will be described in Chapter 9.

THE VANDAL KINGDOM IN AFRICA—ITS
EXTINCTION BY JUSTINIAN

The Vandal kingdom in Africa, founded by Gaiseric, survived only until the early sixth century. After the death of the great leader the government disintegrated, with civil war and disputed successions among the chiefs. One such dispute gave Justinian, the Emperor of Constantinople, the opportunity to interfere and add this Arian kingdom to orthodox Christendom. This was accomplished in one expedition under the brilliant Byzantine general Belisarius (533).

► The end of an era

With the fall of the Roman Empire we reach the end of an era. Though the successor-state in the East, known as the Byzantine Empire, survived for almost a thousand years longer, this civilization was so different from the old Roman Empire that it will be discussed separately in the next chapter, together with its own offshoots.

The achievements of Greco-Roman civilization were far from lost, even in the West; but the destruction of its political system and the decline of its culture as a living creative force threw Europe into a condition of political, social, and cultural degradation which used to be called the "Dark Ages." If these centuries are not believed by modern scholars to be as dark as earlier historians thought them, the term remains not altogether inappropriate. It was a period of fermentation which ultimately proved to have in it the potentiality for new life and creativity; but while the fermentation was in process life was dark indeed, and no one could have foretold what would arise from it. Other countries which have had great cultures in the past have never emerged from their stagnation, and it was possible that Europe might have followed their example.

The conditions which made possible the Greek and Roman achievements had disappeared, as it proved, forever. The Roman Empire had survived as long as it had because it was able to make use of the old city-state culture which was the distinctive achievement of the Greeks. The empire had succeeded in the one field in which the Greeks had failed; it had provided a political framework under which the ruinous intercity warfare was no longer possible. But the later empire had destroyed the basis for its own government when, by relentless pressure, it undermined the ability of the cities to survive as independent entities. It was not possible to force them to produce in the same way as they had produced under their own impetus; and though the peasant has always been ready to work his land under the most tyrannous oppression, either by landlords or by monarchs, Europe was too vast to treat as if it were an Egypt, and no emperor could be strong enough to keep every landlord in Europe directly subject to him and obedient to his orders. So no basis remained for absolute government; the army could not be maintained with the cities refusing to work, and with the peasants out of the control of the absolute monarchs. The army was merely an instrument for compulsion, and it could not itself produce.

With the destruction of the cities, land alone remained; and for the next few centuries the rule of Europe was in the hands of landlords, sometimes nominally subject to monarchs, but actually exercising almost independent control of comparatively small areas which were not beyond their capacity to rule. With the subsequent rise of cities it again became possible for monarchs to unite with them and subject the landlords to control; but it has never been possible up to this time to exercise this dominion in areas as large and with as wide and varied a culture as the territory ruled by the Roman Empire.

This is not to say that this fact was ever understood by contemporaries. To the people who could remember, or whose institutions had been formed by the Roman Empire, it seemed that the natural form of government was a huge universal state ruled by an emperor who, at least according to Christian thought, was responsible to God, or perhaps to God's spiritual representative on earth, the pope. If this no longer suited the new condition of Europe, then it must be imposed by force. Charlemagne, as we shall see, succeeded by the force of his personal genius in subjecting most of the landlords to discipline in his day and compelling them to acknowledge his authority. But all they had to do was to sit out his lifetime and throw off his out-of-date despotism as soon as he was dead. In this they were backed by all the effective force of the times.

The papacy, seeking a similar restoration of the empire in a different form, would probably have liked an emperor, obedient to itself in spiritual matters but exercising supreme authority in the secular sphere. This arrangement would have been more convenient, but the basis for such an authority was nowhere to be found. The emperor of Constantinople before the division of the Eastern and Western Churches refused to accept the overlordship of the papacy, even in spiritual matters. And the Holy Roman Empire was usually only a shadow empire, unable to maintain undisputed authority even within Germany, and could not even aspire, after Charlemagne, to the rulership of Europe.

So the papacy had to fall back upon the dream of a spiritual dominion, its ruler trying to dictate to the separate governments of Europe in spiritual matters, the only universal authority in a Europe split into many separate and warring states. But in the Middle Ages, when the Church fulfilled so many functions now considered the prerogative of secular governments, it was impossible to draw a dividing line between the realms of each. The secular governments, trying to establish their own power within their states, could not tolerate what came to seem foreign intervention in domestic matters, and conflict ensued between them and the spiritual authority exercised from Rome. And the latter, in an age of declining faith and increasing interest in worldly matters, was, at the last, unable to substantiate its claims.

So there was no restoration of the Roman Empire, either by secular or religious powers. It had served its purpose in history. Its achievements had been many; it had given to the Western world its first long experience of peace, it had spread Greek culture, with its ability to deal with abstract thought, its thirst for experimentation and explanation, and its tendency to think of life in terms of this world; and it had itself introduced mankind to the idea that each human being has rights which should be embodied in a law which ought to be just, clear, and not arbitrary, and as far as possible in accordance with what man could discover about the Divine Reason. It had given hospitality to an Oriental religion which gave man hope of a blessed hereafter, and explained this life as a proving ground for a world to come; and it has been contended that it also laid the impress of its own thought on the ancient Hebrew idea of man's atonement for sin by making it into a contract between man and God with salvation as the reward; and it certainly gave the organization of this Church as a gift to the religion. And it provided a language for this Church which could be understood throughout Europe, and has remained its chosen language to this day.

If little that was authentically Roman survived outside the Church in the Dark Ages Roman and Greek rationalism was not lost forever. When the human mind awakened again—when, with Anselm, it was first found necessary to *prove* the existence of God—the process was set in motion that led to modern Western civilization. And the work of the Greeks and Romans, gradually recovered and assimilated, had no mean share in it.

▶ ## Suggestions for further reading

There have been so many studies on the fall of the Roman Empire that it is impossible to make a really satisfactory choice. Each book is inclined to stress some factors to the exclusion or minimization of others, as, indeed, this text itself has been forced to do. In the author's opinion the most adequate account within a reasonable space is F. Lot, *The End of the Ancient World and the Beginnings of the Middle Ages* (tr. P. and M. Leon; New York: Alfred A. Knopf, Inc., 1931). This book offers a useful synthesis of causes for the decline and fall, with a very thoughtful evaluation, and the whole is presented with an admirable clarity. H. St. L. B. Moss, *The Birth of the Middle Ages, 395–814* (Oxford: The Clarendon Press, 1935), offers a good brief general picture of Roman civilization in the last centuries of the Roman Empire, and gives much essential information on the barbarian invasions and the establishment of the barbarian kingdoms, with a clarity not usually found in books about this confusing period. From the point of view of a classical scholar primarily interested in the culture of this period, Miss E. S. Duckett gives an admirable survey, country by country, of the new barbarian kingdoms and the interaction of the Romans and barbarians, its effects upon the old Roman culture. There is a particularly sympathetic account of Boethius, and a picture of the world of Pope Gregory i which should be read in connection with the material at the close of Chapter 6. This book is E. S. Duckett, *The Gateway to the Middle Ages* (New York: The Macmillan Company, 1938). Utilizing in particular the Latin writings of this period, Miss Duckett succeeds in giving a very fresh and interesting account, with many quotations not easily found elsewhere. Dill's masterpiece, long a classic in this field, should also not be missed, especially the long quotations from the writers of the fifth century which show so clearly the decadence of the time and the surprising ignorance of the Romans that their Empire was on the verge of collapse: S. Dill, *Roman Society in the Last Century of the Western Empire* (2nd ed., rev.; London: Macmillan & Co., Ltd., 1921). Finally, the heritage of Rome and what it meant to the world are well handled in C. Dawson, *The Making of Europe* (New York: The Macmillan Company, 1932), which is described more fully under Chapters 8 and 10.

All students should read *Germania,* the fundamental study of the German barbarians by the Roman historian Tacitus, available in many different editions. One easily available edition is M. Hadas, ed., *The Complete Works of Tacitus* (tr. A. J. Church and W. J. Brodribb; New York: Modern Library, Inc., 1942).

For students interested in the Merovingian kingdom of Gaul there is a very complete study by Dill also in this field, *Roman Society in Gaul in the Merovingian Age* (New York: The Macmillan Company, 1926). This book appears to be slightly misnamed, since it does not exclusively deal with, nor even especially emphasize, the remnants of Roman culture in Gaul, as might be expected. It is, nevertheless, an exhaustive study of Merovingian society, as far as it can be described from the numerous literary sources extant, and there is as yet nothing in English which will supersede it, though in France there has been much study in recent times of the extant nonliterary sources which will in time round out the picture more fully. A competent survey of Anglo-Saxon England, adequate for the general student, will be found in the Pelican book, D. Whitelock, *The Beginnings of English Society* (Harmondsworth, Middlesex: Penguin Books, 1952).

8

The Byzantine and Slavic Worlds

The Byzantine Empire • Byzantine relations with Eastern Europe: Bulgar and Slav invasions; the Russians • The disputed territories of Eastern Europe: Hungary, Bohemia, and Moravia; Prussia, Poland, and Lithuania

---

▶ Introductory

The last great successor-state of the Roman Empire, the empire we call Byzantine after the ancient name of its capital Byzantium, survived, as we have seen, the fall of the empire in the West, and for many centuries was the only civilized power in all Europe. The cultural radiation from this center spread not only over the lands in the eastern Mediterranean that had formed part of the old Roman Empire, but also over lands inhabited previously only by barbarians, altogether untouched by any civilizing influences from Rome.

It is still of great importance to us today that the eastern Slavs were converted to Christianity by missionaries from Constantinople, and that they knew their first taste of luxury at the Byzantine court. These peoples were unmoved by papal decrees from Rome, and they lived far beyond the bounds of the Holy Roman Empire. Some Slavs moved west, were absorbed by Western Christianity, and came within the orbit of the emperors of the West; but the vast majority either raided into Southeastern Europe, ultimately settling in the Balkan peninsula within the orbit of Constantinople,

or remained in their own vast steppes in Eastern Europe, defending themselves against Christian knights from the West or Mongol and other invaders from the East. No attempt will be made in this chapter to recount the full history of either the Byzantine Empire or of the numerous Slavic peoples introduced to civilization by it. Only as much will be given as is necessary to provide the essential medieval background for the study of the Slavic peoples in the period after 1500.

▶ The Byzantine Empire

THE SOURCES OF BYZANTINE STRENGTH

Economic basis

As we have seen in the previous chapter, the Eastern Roman, or Byzantine Empire survived the fall of the West not so much through the excellence of its rulers as through the fact that it had been able to take control of the most prosperous part of the empire. The fall of the West, which had been deprived of its main economic resources, can almost be considered as a necessary consequence of the recovery of the East.

The totalitarian heritage of the later

empire, the severe taxation, the huge imperial bureaucracy, and the mercenary army were retained in the Eastern Empire. But there were significant differences. Far less money was needed for the defense of its much shorter boundaries, the capital of the empire was also its greatest industrial city and port, and there was a constant flow of trade between this capital and many other large cities in the empire. Most of the best agricultural land of the old empire was in the new, including the granary of Egypt. The East, moreover, was not burdened with the huge estates, virtually exempt from taxation, which had been such a source of weakness in the old empire. The people were highly civilized, with a far smaller admixture of unassimilable barbarians; they were, on the whole, far more enterprising, especially in commerce, than the Romans; and there was no such serious proletarian problem as in the previous capital, since there was far more profitable work to be done. In a word, the new imperial unit was more manageable than the old, and, high though the taxation was, except in periods of external danger it fell upon an economy that could bear it.

It was primarily the strength of its economy that enabled the Eastern Empire to survive—with a brief interlude of Latin occupation—for almost a thousand years; for the inefficiency and extravagance of so many of its rulers and the corruption of its bureaucracy would have ruined a less resilient economy many times over. Yet in spite of intrigues over the succession, numerous foreign wars, rule by dissolute women and incompetent and irresponsible men, the state never went bankrupt in all its history; and several times it was able to produce an effective ruler from most unpromising sources, just when to an outsider it would have seemed that all was lost.

Administrative system

The Byzantines called themselves Romans (though they wrote the word in the Greek language), but the language and culture were overwhelmingly Greek, with strong Oriental influence. Looked at from a Greek point of view, the Eastern Empire was the restoration of a united Hellenistic monarchy after a three-hundred-year interlude of barbaric Roman occupation. But the Roman rule had also left its influence in the one field in which the Romans had been creative—in law and government. The Byzantine administrative system had been directly inherited from the later post-Diocletian empire, and it did not change its nature. The people of the empire were all equally the subjects of the monarch; they had no rights against him except the protection afforded by the law. He could raise and lower the taxes, his word had the force of law, and he could enforce obedience through his bureaucracy and his army. The cities had only such self-government as the emperor wished to allow them. The backbone of the state was no longer the free municipalities. City magistrates were imperial officials, who collected taxes on the basis of imperial needs. So there was nothing of the Roman Republic or the Augustan principate in the new empire; the system of Diocletian and Constantine prevailed.

The Roman law, with its Stoic admixture and its concept of natural law and equity, remained the law of the Byzantines, as has already been explained. But already, long before the fall of the West, Greek and Oriental thought had been incorporated in it. Under Theodosius, Justinian, Leo III, and the other legal reformers and codifiers, it now became more Christianized, but it was still recognizably Roman law.

In spite of the authoritarianism of the administration, it cannot be said that the peoples of the empire felt themselves to be slaves. The government was neither liked nor disliked. It was a fact to be accepted, and made the best of. Political factions came into existence, satisfying the Greek love of politics. But they were not divided on matters of principle. All accepted the inevitability of the absolutist regime; there were no attempts at revolution, or the restoration of any kind of republic or free institutions. The factions supported rival contenders for the throne, but not the overthrow of the monarchy itself.

For the rest, the Byzantine world, like the Hellenistic world, offered many incentives to enterprise and hard work, either in the imperial service or in commerce and industry. Many fields of activity were left open to the private citizen in this empire so honeycombed with prosperous cities. If one became rich, one paid heavy taxes; but at least, with the surplus, life could be made more pleasant. There were luxuries to be bought, there were innumerable forms of entertainment, new and old, especially horse and chariot racing in the Hippodrome at Constantinople. And, for the pious and those who felt the emptiness of a pleasure-seeking life, there was now the Christian religion, as there had not been in the Hellenistic world.

RELATIONS BETWEEN CHURCH AND STATE

The position of the patriarch

The chief official in the Church of Constantinople was called the patriarch. He was an imperial nominee, subject to dismissal by the emperor at any time. This fact, however, does not mean that he was totally subservient to the emperor during his term of office.

It would take us too far afield in this survey to go at length into this important question of how it happened that an imperial nominee, the patriarch of Constantinople (later called the Ecumenical, or universal, Patriarch) could obtain such power as he undoubtedly possessed after his appointment. But a few indications must be given, since they are essential for the understanding of the relationship between the Byzantine Empire and the Slavs, who were rarely within the political boundaries of the empire, but came within its cultural and religious sphere of influence—an influence which has had momentous consequences even to the present time.

The emperor, as has been said, could replace a stubborn patriarch with a more pliable official. But if a patriarch thus ousted could keep the support of his clergy and monks, even the most powerful emperor would soon find himself in trouble, for he could not dispense with the services of the clergy for very long. On several occasions in Byzantine history a patriarch who stood up to the emperor commanded greater support, even in the imperial household, than the emperor himself. Such was the case at all stages in Byzantine history. Furthermore, in later centuries the patriarch often was actually in a far stronger position than the emperor, because the patriarch commanded the allegiance of believers outside the empire, whereas the emperor was often hard put to it to maintain his political authority within the boundaries of his supposed empire. He had to fight Turks and other barbarians as well as occasional Westerners, while the spiritual domain of the Ecumenical Patriarch might stretch on the one side far into Russia and on the other beyond the Danube into Central Europe.

The fact that the patriarch, with such a vast territory subject to his spiritual rule, was nevertheless appointed by and subject to dismissal by the emperor entailed some remarkable consequences, especially in the borderlands between the spheres of influence of the Western Church and the Eastern. A monarch who was politically independent of Constantinople would think twice before accepting the Eastern rite, when acceptance must mean that the emperor in Constantinople, who was often his political enemy, could exercise some control upon him through the patriarch. There was always the thought that membership in the Eastern Orthodox Church entailed some degree of political subservience to the emperor.

Yet, on the other hand, if these distant peoples chose to submit in religious matters to Rome instead of to Constantinople, there were other disadvantages of a different kind, not political but religious. The Roman Church insisted on the use of Latin, a language incomprehensible to most of the Slavs, whereas the Orthodox Church not only permitted but encouraged the use of a liturgy in the Slavonic vernaculars. Moreover, by the ninth century, the Orthodox Church differed in a very important dogma (on the "proces-

► chronological chart

The Byzantine Empire

Foundation of Constantinople	330	Byzantine emperor killed in battle by Bulgarian khan, Krum	811
Theodosius the Great last emperor of East and West	379–395	Krum at the gates of Constantinople	813
Reign of Justinian	527–565	Thirty years' peace with Bulgars signed	817
Corpus juris civilis of Justinian	533	End of iconoclastic controversy; image worship restored	843
Conquest of North Africa	533–543	First appearance of Varangians at Constantinople	860
Conquest of Italy	535–554	Mission of Sts. Cyril and Methodius to Slavs	863–885
Great Persian War	540–562	Renewal of wars with Bulgarians	889
Fifty years' peace with Persia— Justinian to pay tribute	562	Reign of Basil II the Bulgar-Killer	976–1025
Loss of Italian possessions to Lombards (except Rome, Ravenna, and Naples)	568–571	Bulgaria incorporated into Byzantine Empire	1018
Reign of Heraclius	610–641	Final schism between Rome and Constantinople	1054
"Flight" of Mahomet from Mecca to Medina	622	Reign of Alexius Comnenus	1081–1118
Persian Wars of Heraclius	622–630	The First Crusade	1096–1097
Conquest of Syria by Muslims under Khalid	635–641	Latin Conquest of Constantinople (Fourth Crusade)	1204
Conquest of Egypt by Muslims	639–655	Latin Kingdom of Constantinople	1204–1261
Blockade of Constantinople by Muslims	673–678	Reconquest of Constantinople by Michael VIII	1261
Thirty years' peace concluded between Byzantines and Muslims	678	Rise of the Ottoman Turks in Asia Minor	1326
Conquest of Carthage by Muslims	698	Serbs under Stephen Dushan at the gates of Constantinople	1355
Second siege of Constantinople by Muslims	717–718	Siege of Constantinople by Turks under Bayazid I	1391–1397
Reign of Leo III (the Isaurian)	717–740	Defeat of Turks by Tamerlane at battle of Angora	1402
Beginning of the iconoclastic controversy	726	Council of Florence—Agreement by Byzantine emperor to religious union with Rome	1439
Promulgation of *Ecloga* by Leo III	739	Siege and Capture of Constantinople by Ottoman Turks	1453
Conquest of exarchate of Ravenna by Lombards	751	Marriage of Ivan III, Grand Duke of Moscow, to Zoë, niece of last emperor of Constantinople—Ivan takes title of Tsar, and adopts Byzantine court ceremonial	1472
Defeat of Lombards by Pepin the Short, king of the Franks	754–756		
Donation of Pepin of Lombard (Byzantine) lands to pope	756		
Reign of Charlemagne in the West	768–814		
Peace between Byzantines and Charlemagne (Byzantines retaining southern Italy, Venice, and Dalmatia)	803		

Bulgaria

Movements of Bulgars to the south of the Danube	650 onward
Tervel, Bulgarian khan, advances to gates of Constantinople—Byzantine emperor agrees to pay tribute	712
Bulgarians subjugated by Byzantines	*ca.* 775
Battle of Marcellae, defeat of Byzantines by Bulgars, refoundation of Bulgarian state under Kardam	792
Krum, Bulgar khan, at gates of Constantinople	813
Foundation of Preslav, Bulgarian capital	821
Reign of Boris I	852–888
Conversion of Bulgars to Christianity	865
Reign of Tsar Symeon—Constant wars with Byzantines	893–927
Reign of Tsar Peter	927–969
Raids on Bulgaria by Magyars and Patzinaks	934–962
Invasion of Bulgaria by Sviatoslav and Russians	967
Defeat of Russians and Bulgarians by Byzantines—End of Bulgarian Empire	969–972
Reign of Tsar Samuel	976–1014
Re-establishment of Bulgarian kingdom	976–989
Reign of Byzantine emperor Basil II (the Bulgar-Killer)	976–1025
Battle of Balathista—Defeat and death of Tsar Samuel	1014
Bulgaria incorporated into Byzantine Empire	1018
Bulgaria in Byzantine Empire	1018–1185
Refoundation of Bulgarian kingdom by John and Peter Asen	1185
Defeat of crusaders (Fourth Crusade) by King Kaloyan, and capture of Latin emperor, Baldwin I	1205
Peace with Latin kingdom of Constantinople	1213
Reign of John Asen II	1218–1241
John proclaims independence of Bulgarian Church	1232
Ottoman Turks cross into Europe	1345
Shishman, Bulgarian king, becomes vassal of Turks	1372
Battle of Kossovo—Bulgarians, with allies, totally defeated by Turks	1389
Incorporation of Bulgaria into Turkish Empire	1393

Serbia

Conversion of Serbs to Eastern Christianity	end of 10th century
Expansion of Serbs at expense of Byzantines	1280 onward
Reign of Stephen Dushan	1331–1355
Subjection of almost whole Balkan peninsula by Stephen	1331–1344
Stephen proclaims himself Emperor of Serbs, Greeks, Bulgars, and Albanians	1346
Death of Stephen en route to Constantinople	1355
Battle of Kossovo—Defeat of Serbs and allies by Turks—Serbia vassal of Turks	1389
George Brankevitch, despot of Serbia, escapes vassalage of Turks	1436–1444
George recognized by Turks as independent	1444
Turks conquer and incorporate Serbia in empire	1459

Poland and Lithuania

Conversion of Mieszko I of Poland to Christianity	966
Boleslav I organizes a Polish state	992–1025
Boleslav becomes king of Poland	1025
Heathen reaction in Poland and persecution of Christians	1034–1040
Casimir I restores Christianity	1054
Teutonic Knights' efforts to convert Lithuanians	1230 onward
Teutonic Knights raid into Poland	1326–1333
Olgerd, Duke of Lithuania, defeated by Teutonic Knights	1360
Jadwiga elected queen of Poland	1384
Marriage of Jadwiga to Jagiello, Duke of Lithuania	1386
Lithuania converted to Christianity by Jagiello	1387 onward
Lithuania separated from Poland under Grand Duke Witold	1398
Battle of Tannenberg—Defeat of Teutonic Knights by Jagiello	1410
Poland and Lithuania again united by Casimir IV of Poland	1447
Wars against Teutonic Order	1454–1466
Second Peace of Thorn—Teutonic Order vassal of Polish crown	1466
Constitution of Radom—National Diet becomes supreme legislature of Poland	1505
Diet passes laws establishing serfdom in Poland	1511

Russia

Traditional date of rule in Novgorod of Rurik	860
First recorded appearance of Varangians in Constantinople	860
Novgorod and Kiev under rule of Prince Oleg	880–912
Russians (Varangians) extract trade concessions from Constantinople	911
Conversion of Grand Duchess Olga of Kiev to Christianity	957
Rule of Sviatoslav as Grand Duke of Kiev	964–972
Expeditions of Sviatoslav into Byzantine Empire and against Byzantines	965–971
Reign of Vladimir i as Grand Duke of Kiev	978–1015
Conversion of Russians to Christianity	990
Disintegration of Duchy of Kiev, forming especially the territory of Novgorod in north and Grand Duchy of Moscow	1054 onward
Conquest of Kiev by Andrei Boguliubski, prince of central Russia	1169
Foundation of Livonian Knights	1202
Teutonic Knights commissioned to conquer Prussia	1226
Union of Livonian and Teutonic Knights	1237
Mongol conquest of most of Russia	1237–1240
Mongol conquest of Kiev	1240
Defeat of Swedes and others by Alexander Nevski of Novgorod at battle of the Neva	1240
Defeat of Teutonic Knights at battle of Lake Peipus by Alexander Nevski	1242
Ivan i Grand Duke of Moscow (vassal of Mongols)	1325–1341
Battle of Kulikovo—Defeat of Mongols by Russians	1380
Ivan iii, the Great, Grand Duke of Moscow	1462–1505
Conquest of Novgorod by Ivan iii	1470
Marriage of Ivan to Zoë, niece of last emperor of Constantinople	1472
Incorporation of territory of Novgorod and dissolution of the Hansa in Novgorod	1494
Expansion of Russians into Lithuania and incorporation of some Lithuanian territories	1503
Ivan iv, the Terrible, becomes Tsar of Russia	1547

Croatia

Croats under Frankish domination from	9th century
Tomislav becomes king of Croatia, accepting crown from pope	924
King Peter defeated by Ladislas i of Hungary	1091
Croatia and Hungary in dynastic union	1102

Hungary, Bohemia, and Moravia

Hungarians raid into Europe	end of 9th century
Gradual conversion of Hungarians to Eastern and Western Christianity	972–997
St. Stephen i crowned king of Hungary with crown sent by pope —Forcible conversion to Roman Catholicism	1001
Conquest of Croatia and Bosnia by St. Ladislas i	1091
Invasion of Hungary by Mongols	1241
End of native (Arpad) Hungarian dynasty (thereafter kings were mostly foreign potentates)	1301–1308
Sigismund king of Hungary (Luxembourg House)	1387–1437
John Hunyadi (frontier lord in Hungary) defeats Turks	1437
Hunyadi leads crusade against Turks	1456
Reign of Mathias Corvinus, son of Hunyadi	1458–1490
Mathias king of Bohemia as well as Hungary	1470
Turks advance into Hungary	1521
Battle of Mohacs—Defeat of Hungarians and allies by Turks	1526
Most of Hungary vassal state of Turks	1540 onward

Mongols

Reign of Jenghiz Khan	1206–1227
Reign of Ogodai Khan	1229–1241
Reign of Batu Khan	1242–1255
Reign of Kublai Khan	1260–1294

sion of the Holy Spirit") from the Western Church, and the clergy from the West were very stubborn in their insistence upon the correctness of the Western interpretation— sanctified, of course, by the authority of the incumbent of the Chair of Peter.[1]

Furthermore, the Patriarch of Constantinople, whatever his pretensions to the designation Ecumenical, was always theoretically subject to the spiritual leadership of the successor of Peter, the pope in Rome. But at the same time these very popes acknowledged the theoretical overlordship of the emperor as the true heir of Constantine, in matters not concerned with religion, even though the emperor seldom had much effective power in Italy, and never in Rome itself. This relationship was more convenient for the pope than for the emperor since the latter, after the time of Justinian (sixth century), was not interested in exercising any rights over the pope, while the pope frequently called upon the emperor for military assistance against his enemies the Lombards (and was, as frequently, refused). But when, in the ninth century, a western European outpost of Slavs petitioned the emperor to send missionaries to convert them to Chris-

tianity, and the emperor duly obliged by sending them St. Cyril and St. Methodius, the pope (Nicholas I) decided that the new Moravian converts should belong to the Western Church, though he allowed them, at first, to use a Slavonic liturgy. The emperor gracefully accepted the decision, but his clergy were not so happy about it, since the territory was lost from their jurisdiction, while the emperor had never hoped to add such a distant land as Moravia to his empire. On the other hand, when, for political and economic reasons, as well as religious, an earlier emperor, Leo III (717–740), and his successors forbade the use of images in churches (the iconoclastic controversy, dealt with in more detail below, page 219) and a series of popes defied them, the emperors refused to accept papal dictation, and the patriarchs were forced to obey their immediate masters in Constantinople rather than their spiritual superiors in Rome.

In the last centuries of the Byzantine Empire the Orthodox Church was often more powerful than the emperors. The Church continually interfered with the imperial policy of maintaining correct relations, as far as possible, with the papacy. The final split in 1054 between the Orthodox Church and the papacy, ostensibly over the theological question of the procession of the Holy Spirit (whether the Holy Spirit descended from the Father or from the Father and the Son), was deliberately provoked by the Patriarch Michael, in spite of the fact that the emperor had a political alliance with the papacy at the time which he was anxious to preserve. The emperor found himself unable to discipline his recalcitrant official, who was supported by the clergy and people, who were fanatically anti-Western and anti-papal.

A patriarch excommunicated an emperor in 1262 for blinding a defeated enemy. The emperor deposed him, but the patriarch, who was living safely in a fortified monastery some distance from the capital, refused to consider himself deposed, even though the emperor appointed a successor to him in Constantinople. Even in the last century of the empire, when it was in mortal danger

[1] Illustrative of the difficulties involved in conversion is the case of the Bulgarian khan, Boris I (853–888), who was too close to Constantinople for comfort, and would have preferred, on political grounds, to accept the overlordship of the distant pope, which carried with it no stigma of political servitude, and would have permitted him to carry out inroads on the Byzantine Empire without fear of spiritual reprisals. But, on religious grounds, both he and his people preferred the Eastern rite and the Eastern dogma. He switched allegiance several times, and was given the free right to choose by the Byzantine emperor, Basil I, who was evidently fairly sure of the khan's final choice, and confident that the Western clergy would overreach themselves. As the emperor had foreseen, the Western clergy made a sufficient nuisance of themselves by insisting on the Latin Liturgy and on their own version of the procession of the Holy Spirit, so that the Bulgarian khan at last threw in his lot with the emperor and patriarch even though he was aware that this gave the emperor the opportunity to intervene in Bulgarian affairs. The position became so intolerable to the Bulgarians that the younger son of Boris, Symeon, who had originally been a monk in Constantinople, made a serious effort to obtain the imperial crown for himself, at least, in part, for the satisfaction of appointing his own patriarch.

The monastery of Mt. Athos occupies a commanding site. From close up it is very similar to the monastery of Monte Cassino shown in Chapter 6. (COURTESY ROYAL GREEK EMBASSY)

from the Ottoman Turks, the Orthodox clergy refused to recognize the union with the papacy which had been contrived by the diplomacy of the emperor in the hopes of obtaining aid from the West.

When at last Constantinople fell to the Turks in 1453 the Orthodox Church and its clergy survived. The Turks adopted a tolerant policy toward the Christians, and believed they could make use of the clerical hierarchy. They made the Christian patriarch the official leader of all Christians in the Turkish dominions, with all minor patriarchs in the East subordinate to him. He had at last become an "Ecumenical" Patriarch, and the patriarchate had survived the empire itself.

The nature of the Byzantine religion

The strength of the Byzantine religion, however, did not depend on the nature of Church government in the empire, as is seen by the continued creativity of Byzantine religious art, and even to some degree in the endless theological controversies in which the Greeks took a passionate interest. Byzantine religion was always more mystical, less formal and rational, than in the West, and thus less dependent upon the quality of its priesthood. The gorgeous ceremonies and rituals performed in the Byzantine churches, with their magnificent interiors, ablaze with light and rich with incense, were the heart of the Byzantine religion, as was the extreme veneration of holy pictures, and icons, which had tempted the iconoclastic emperors to suppress their use for a time (see page 219). Finally, those who wished for a deeper religious life and revolted against the materialism and pleasure seeking of the Byzantine world could always go into the monasteries, especially the great religious center of Mt. Athos, which were less orderly and more ascetic than those of the West, with less emphasis on community living, but at least as much devoted in their prime to earnest pursuit of the spiritual life.

THE REIGN OF JUSTINIAN (527–565)

Conquests—Africa, Spain, Italy

Until the sixth century the Roman influence was strong and the Latin language was still known. But after the long reign of Justinian, with the loss of contact with Italy and strained relations with the papacy, this influence quickly disappeared; soon even the law code of Justinian had to be translated into Greek. The reign of Justinian is notable for the last effort, by a Roman of Illyrian descent, to re-establish the old Roman Empire as a totality. He came to the throne in 527, after having already been the power behind his uncle's throne for some years previously, and reigned till 565. Justinian was a man of great energy combined with an interest in giving close attention to detail, thoroughly imbued with the imperial spirit of the later Roman Empire, but with no real grasp of the problems of his time. He was immensely successful in his own lifetime but he left a heritage to his successors which was disastrous for his empire and might well have wrecked it altogether.

His conquest of North Africa, Italy, and part of Spain has already been noticed. The Spanish province was quickly retaken even by the enfeebled Visigoths; most of Italy, weakened by the destruction of the Ostrogoths and impossible for the successors of Justinian to defend, fell a prey to the Lombards; and though Africa survived for a while, it collapsed at the Muslim assault in the next century almost without a struggle.

Persian and Balkan policy

But the cost to the Eastern Empire of these expeditions can hardly be calculated. Not only were the taxes increased in the worst later Roman manner, to the point where distress became widespread, in spite of commercial and industrial prosperity, but Justinian was forced to weaken the defense of his eastern frontiers and even give large donations to the newly vitalized Persian Empire to stave off invasion. Moreover, remnants from the Hunnish invasions and numerous Slav peoples, who had hitherto been held back by more warlike groups of barbarians, began to approach and threaten his northern boundaries.

Justinian, indeed, perceived this danger. He built a considerable number of forts to defend the Balkans, but these ultimately proved useless when inadequately defended by troops. He invited barbarian chiefs to his Oriental court at Constantinople, impressing them with his splendor and giving them sumptuous gifts. He tried all the arts of diplomacy—and in Greek hands these were not inconsiderable—to foster dissension among the various tribes. But it is questionable whether these were as effective as an army, and there is no doubt that the barbarians, while accepting his hospitality, were hardly too simple to perceive that these riches could also be enjoyed through conquest. If Justinian had not been so obsessed with his Roman dream he would have seen that his eastern hinterland and the Danube frontier were far more vital to his empire than anything the West could offer. Indeed, if there had been any attempt by his successors to defend his conquests, nothing could have saved even Constantinople itself in the seventh century.

Administrative and legal reforms, economic policy

However questionable Justinian's military policy may have been, his administrative capacity is undoubted. We have already mentioned in Chapter 5 in the section deal-

Summit of the dome of the Church of the Holy Wisdom in Constantinople (See also picture of the Church facing page 174). (COURTESY TURKISH INFORMATION OFFICE)

ing with Roman Culture his great codification of the Roman law, always associated with his name. He also pruned the imperial bureaucracy for greater efficiency in tax collecting at less expense, he fixed regular salaries for all his officials, and inaugurated a more regular method of recruiting them. He established state industrial monopolies in various luxury goods, including silk, the secret of which was stolen from the Chinese during his reign. The mulberry trees necessary for the cultivation of silkworms were planted on an imperial estate. Justinian also issued new and effective regulations for traders in the great cities of his empire. All these measures contributed to the absolute power of the emperor, and all survived his reign, forming the basis of the Byzantine administrative system which survived so many dangers in the following centuries substantially unimpaired.

Religious and cultural policy— Consequences

In his dealings with the Church, Justinian was equally autocratic. He refused to accept the claims of the pope to spiritual supremacy, and he insisted on dictating Church policies, and even giving decisions on theological questions wherever his power extended. His concern for the right opinions of his subjects was reinforced by a measure that none of his predecessors had considered necessary. He closed the last pagan center of learning, the School of Athens, which had been continuously in existence since the time of Plato and Aristotle, where the classical philosophies were still taught and where commentaries on Aristotle, which later medieval Christian scholars found of the utmost value, were still being written. Simplicius, one of the best of the Aristotelian

Main façade of the Byzantine Church of St. Marks in Venice. (COURTESY ITALIAN STATE TOURIST OFFICE)

commentators, and his companions were warmly welcomed, however, by the king of Persia, who gave them a home, as his predecessors had given a home to philosophical heretics driven out in earlier years. But philosophy apparently was a hothouse growth in Persia, and the exiles were not happy, preferring even silence in their own land. Yet the Persian efforts nevertheless bore a surprising fruit in later years; for the Muslims, coming upon the Persian academy of Gondisapur, founded by the distinguished Persian emperor Sapur I, were fired by enthusiasm for the Greek philosophy and science, especially medicine, taught there. So by devious routes, through Avicenna and Averroës and numerous other scholars, the works of Aristotle came to the West through Syriac, Arabic, and sometimes Hebrew versions until they became absorbed in medieval scholasticism.

Justinian also spent enormous fortunes on his capital of Constantinople, building the great church of the Holy Wisdom (Hagia Sophia) in a new style of architecture, owing much to Roman experience but incorporating new designs perfected by two architects of genius who discovered how to rest a round dome gracefully on a square opening. This great church, the largest in Christendom, became the model for what is known as the Byzantine style in architecture, examples of which are to be found throughout Eastern Europe from Venice to Moscow.

THE DISASTROUS LEGACY OF JUSTINIAN

Loss of western provinces

By permitting his finance minister to use every unscrupulous device he could discover for gaining new sources of income, as well as by really improving the system of tax collection, Justinian managed to survive these unprecedented expenses without bankruptcy; and though at his death its treasury was empty, the Eastern Empire had enough resilience to make a partial recovery which carried it through the next forty years. Yet the country was too poor and too greatly weakened in the face of new threats to be able to make any effort to defend the western provinces so recently won at such cost. The decision not to accede to the desperate requests of Gregory the Great and other Italian emissaries was undoubtedly a wise one, even though, as we have seen, it forced Gregory to make his own terms with the invading Lombards, and made the papacy from this time on virtually independent of its imperial overlord in Constantinople.

Wars with Persia and the Avars— Heraclius (610–641)

Justinian had kept the Persians quiet by his gifts, but these were discontinued by his successors. The Persians, taking advantage of the murder of an emperor and a disputed succession, invaded the richest territories of the empire, and within a few years the Avars swept over the Danube, Illyria, and the Balkans. The Persians made light of such imperial armies as attempted to defend the eastern provinces, conquered Syria, invaded Egypt, and marched almost to the gates of Constantinople, shearing from the empire almost the whole of its Asiatic hinterland on which it was dependent. To make matters almost hopeless for Constantinople, the Persian emperor Chosroes made a treaty with the Avars which would enable him to put Constantinople under fire from two sides. The Byzantine emperor Heraclius (610–641), who had previously been governor of Africa and who had seized the throne

of Constantinople from another usurper, tried vainly to stem the double attacks, while he feverishly attempted from what remained to him to build up new resources for the defense. At last, when the Avars were almost at the gates of Constantinople, and the Persians were across the Bosporus at Chalcedon, Heraclius gave up hope, and determined to return to the safer refuge of Africa.

At this juncture, the patriarch, a militant priest named Sergius, undertook to breathe new life into his master. With a combination of threats and pious exhortations he shamed Heraclius into remaining, and together they prepared to put Constantinople into a condition to withstand the inevitable siege. When the city was strong enough, Heraclius himself left by sea to take the Persians in the rear, while Sergius superintended the defense of the city against the Avars. The maneuver was successful. The Persian emperor had to turn back to face his unexpected assailant, and Heraclius, after inflicting several defeats upon him, marched into the interior of Persia and succeeded in capturing the capital, Ctesiphon. The war between the two fairly evenly matched adversaries went on for years, exhausting both parties equally. The new empire of Chosroes was ruined, at enormous cost not only to himself but to the Byzantines. The story is told that Chosroes, encamped by the banks of a river, received a letter from an unknown Arab named Mahomet, commanding him to acknowledge that there was only one God, whose name was Allah and whose prophet was Mahomet himself. The emperor is said to have torn up the letter and thrown it into the river. When Mahomet heard of it, he prophesied that "thus God would tear the kingdom and reject the prayers of Chosroes." At all events, this incident (ca. 628) was shortly to be followed by an invasion of Persia by the followers of Mahomet, though Chosroes himself was not alive to endure it. His name is held in abhorrence by all pious Muslims for his blasphemous act in rejecting the appeal from the Prophet.

At last Heraclius defeated the Persians

Most Byzantine icons were destroyed during the iconoclastic controversy by order of the emperors. This picture shows a fifteenth-century Russian icon, with Christ enthroned. Painted in oil on wood, these pictures received a reverence from pious worshipers that the Byzantine emperors claimed was close to idolatry. (COURTESY THE METROPOLITAN MUSEUM OF ART)

and made a treaty which restored all the imperial territories so recently wrested from the empire. Returning to Constantinople he found that the Avars likewise had been driven back by the efforts of Patriarch Sergius. The Byzantine Empire had been given a new lease of life, but at appalling cost. The Avars, an Asiatic people akin to the Turks, and the Slavs who had followed in their wake, had occupied the Balkans and had overrun Illyria, the home of so many great Roman and Byzantine emperors, from which they would never again be dislodged. In the southeast, Mahomet and his successors were gathering their strength for a new assault on the empire. All that remained to Heraclius were the seacoasts of Greece, Macedonia, and the Adriatic, together with the few remaining territories reconquered less than a century before by Justinian. The Danube frontier was lost; and though the land around Constantinople and the heartland of the empire in Asia Minor (Anatolia) remained,

they did not have time to recover from the ravages of the wars before the Muslims fell upon them.

The first attacks by the Muslims were carried out by sea, after Syria and Palestine, together with important islands in the Mediterranean and the Aegean, had fallen to them. Year after year the Muslims returned to the attack, but Constantinople proved impregnable. The Byzantines used "Greek fire," some unknown explosive compound, with devastating effect. In 677, the Muslims gave up the attempt until after they had conquered Asia Minor. In 717, when this conquest had been completed, they attacked Constantinople by land on the European side, and by sea. But again they were unsuccessful, the defense being carried out by one of the greatest of the Byzantine emperors, Leo III, the Isaurian, who at last drove the Muslims back to the line of the Taurus Mountains in southeast Asia Minor. It was the last great effort of the Muslims until the inroads of the Turks in the eleventh century, and by that time the West was able to lend aid to save the empire (the First Crusade).

THE REIGN OF LEO III (717–740)

The restoration of the empire

The work of Leo III has sometimes been regarded as a second foundation of the empire. The policy of Justinian had been abandoned, once and for all. There would be no further expansion into the West, and much of what had formerly belonged to the Byzantine Empire was lost to the Muslims forever. Most of the Christians in this part of the world had embraced Islam, and the minor patriarchs in the Muslim Empire only continued to exist by the permission of the rulers of Islam. But the lands now controlled by Leo the Isaurian were compact and manageable, and an economic base for an empire, even if the empire was perforce much smaller than before, still existed. Constantinople recovered her prosperity under the reigns of Leo and his son, who between them ruled over fifty years, the tax system was reformed from top to bottom, and the army was put on a new basis stressing military efficiency and permanent professional service. A new revised law code (the *Ecloga*) was promulgated, a more humane and Christian code than that of Justinian, which remained the dominant law code in the empire, with minor revisions, until its final destruction.

The iconoclastic controversy

Brief reference has already been made to an action of fundamental importance in the relations between the Eastern and Western Churches, the condemnation of images by the Byzantine emperors, an action known as iconoclasm. The first prohibition of images was made by the emperor Leo III in 725. Until this time images and icons, as well as naturalistic representations of Christ, had been very popular in Constantinople, and numerous monks had made their living by manufacturing them. Leo claimed that this practice was gross superstition, a survival of ancient pagan practices, and equivalent to idol worship. In this stand he was probably supported by most Greek theologians, who objected to any representation of the divine in human form, and it is probable that the Muslims and Jews, who both forbade the use of "graven images," had influenced the emperor against icons. (Leo was not himself a Greek, but a Syrian.) Nevertheless there was naturally a great outcry from the monks who made their living out of the images, and the people who used them no doubt gave little support to the emperor's policy. Leo retorted that the monks were idle and should be busy cultivating the land, and he did not mind at all if the monasteries were closed and their inhabitants turned to more useful occupation. His soldiers were then instructed to break all the images they could find.

The pope, who was the theoretical leader of the whole Christian Church, defended the use of images, claiming that they were aids to true devotion, but was unable to deflect the emperor from his policy; a fact which deeply embittered relations between Rome and Constantinople. Leo's successors for more than a century, with one exception, the empress Irene, continued the edicts against the images (the Iconoclastic Emperors), and councils were called in Constantinople to support the edicts. Several of the emperors, realizing that the chief opposition centered in the monasteries, persecuted the monks and closed the monasteries. During this period the popes had as few dealings as they could with Constantinople, calling in the Franks, as we shall see, to protect them against the reviving Lombards in the middle of the eighth century.[2] The struggle was brought to an end at last in 843, when the regent Theodora of Constantinople called another council which restored the use of images. Iconoclasm was dead, and the monks had triumphed. But even so there were no more sculptured icons in the Byzantine Em-

[2] It is curious, however, to note that the idea of imperial overlordship over the West was still so strong, even during the Iconoclastic Controversy, that Pope Stephen II did first appeal to Constantinople, and its "super-iconoclast" Constantine V, for help against the Lombards, though he must have been relieved at the failure of his efforts.

pire; flat images took their place. By this time Charlemagne had been crowned emperor in the West (800); there has always been doubt if the pope would have dared to defy Constantinople by crowning an emperor in the West if there had not been a long heritage of strife between popes and eastern emperors during the Iconoclastic Controversy.

▶ **Byzantine relations with Eastern Europe**

BULGAR AND SLAV INVASIONS

The last chapter described at some length the invasions of the barbarians who delivered the *coup de grâce* to the old Roman Empire; the later invasions of Northmen and Magyars will be dealt with in Chapter 10. Mention now needs to be made of another great people who followed behind these warlike spearheads, and who inherited many of the lands vacated by those who finally settled in the empire. The origin of the Slavs is still not known, nor is it known for certain when they settled in Europe east of the Elbe. By the sixth century A.D. the most westerly groups of Slavs were already in that part of eastern Germany later known as Bohemia and Moravia. They had not yet been converted to Christianity. Unlike the bulk of their contemporaries, they seem to have been a peaceful people who possessed no political unity and were content to work for whatever masters dominated the lands they inhabited. Forced by pressure of Asiatic nomads, Slavs were also infiltrating into the Balkan peninsula, again settling there peacefully until the nomad warriors caught up with them and on some occasions forced them into open hostilities with the Byzantine Empire. Nevertheless, it was the Slavic culture and language that survived, an impressive demonstration of the formidable superiority of endurance over mere militancy. The Avars swept into the Balkans and were absorbed, while those offshoots from the Avars who remained north of the Balkans were defeated by Charlemagne (see Chapter 10) and disappeared from history. The

Bulgars from Western Asia, originally a people akin to the Turks and with a Turki language, made fierce inroads into the Balkans also, and became serious competitors of Constantinople itself, which they almost captured on several occasions; but though they gave their name to a country which still exists today, their culture and language became entirely Slavic, and today, despite their origin, the Bulgars are a Slavic people. And though Rurik, a Viking Swede, founded the state of Russia in the ninth century, the sea of Slavs again absorbed the handful of Swedes, and Russians today also are Slavs.

The Byzantine Empire was in no position before the end of the tenth century to resist this penetration into the Balkans had it wished to do so. The European hinterland of the empire became Slavic to the Adriatic Sea. The Slavs learned from Constantinople the arts of civilization, and the powerful radiation from Constantinople so attracted them that almost all the eastern Slavs joined the Byzantines and their patriarch in the escape from papal discipline in the eleventh century. And, in the end, with their Byzantine teachers, the eastern Slavs fell to the Ottoman Turks, from whose domination they escaped only in the nineteenth and twentieth centuries. A brief summary of the medieval history of these Slavic peoples will serve to remind the student that Serbs and Bulgars as well as Greeks have roots as nations in the distant past, and that they did not spring full-grown from the decaying body of the Ottoman Empire in the nineteenth century.

THE CONVERSION OF THE SLAVS TO CHRISTIANITY

A brief mention should be made at this point about the conversion of the western Slavs to Christianity. About 862 Rostislav, Prince of Moravia, asked that missionaries be sent to his country to instruct his people in Christianity. It may be supposed that the decision was not taken suddenly. The Slavs in Central Europe had been in contact with Christianity on their western boundaries for a considerable time, and the German clergy

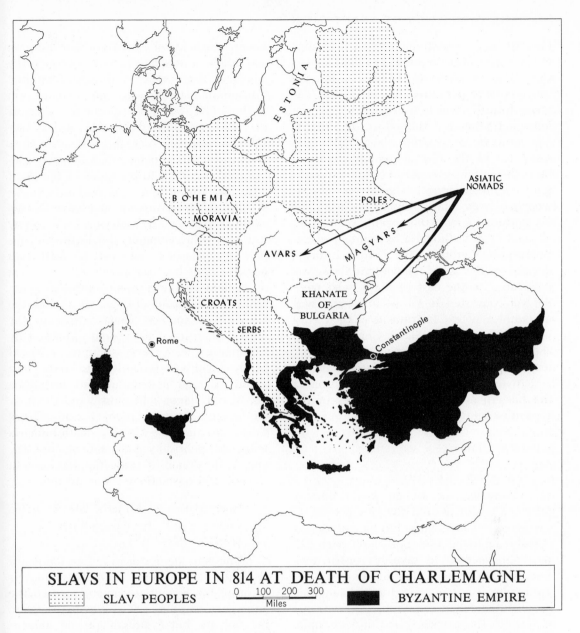

SLAVS IN EUROPE IN 814 AT DEATH OF CHARLEMAGNE

:::::: SLAV PEOPLES	0 100 200 300 Miles	■ BYZANTINE EMPIRE

had been making efforts to convert them, at least since the reign of Charlemagne (768–814). But the Moravians could not resist all blandishments from the Christians indefinitely, and it must have seemed safer to Rostislav to receive instruction from distant Constantinople rather than from the comparatively local German clergy. The Byzantines took the request seriously, and two missionaries, St. Cyril and St. Methodius, set out, bearing with them a new Slavonic alphabet (called Cyrillic after St. Cyril, though probably it was not his own inven-

tion) based on the Greek letters, into which the Bible and the Byzantine Liturgy could be translated for the use of the Slavs, who had not yet a written language. The mission was successful, but it naturally aroused the opposition of the German clergy, who complained to Rome. The two saints were summoned to Rome by the reigning pope, Nicholas I, who had already successfully asserted his authority over Constantinople.

They were received graciously by the pontiff, but both Nicholas and his successors insisted that the new Christian principalities (the Moravian, Bohemian, and Slovak tribes of the Slavs) must be subject to the German clergy and, of course, to the papacy; but the converts were permitted the use of the Slavonic Liturgy, which was provided in the following years by Methodius. This privilege, however, was withdrawn in 885 at the insistence of the German clergy, and the Slavs thereafter were forced to use the Latin tongue for their services. The Slavonic clergy, who had been ministering to the needs of the converts for more than twenty years, were allowed to go to Bulgaria by courtesy of the Byzantine emperor, and the Slavonic Liturgy, devised for the use of the western Slavs, was introduced to the eastern Slavs, who were not yet converted to Christianity, and was no doubt a potent instrument in their conversion. The western Slavic Churches, thus rudely thrust into the bosom of the West, remained under papal rule in later centuries and to this day, even after the division of the Eastern and Western Churches in the eleventh century.

RISE OF BULGARIA

Conversion of Bulgars

Meanwhile the Bulgar khan, Boris I (853–888), also desired that his people be converted to Christianity, but he, for reasons already suggested (see note 1 on page 212 above), preferred to take his instructions from distant Rome. But the pressure of geography was too great for him, and his people ultimately became subject in religious matters to the patriarch at Constantinople, though at times the Bulgarian Church was virtually independent. At first the Bulgars had to use the Greek Liturgy of Constantinople, though, as has been seen, after 885 they were permitted to use the Slavonic tongue, which by this time had become the vernacular of the whole Bulgarian people, including the non-Slavic ruling class.

First wars with Constantinople

When Boris abdicated and went into a monastery (888), to be succeeded by his two sons in turn, the Bulgars reversed his policy of peace with the Byzantine Empire, and made a serious effort to conquer the whole of the empire in Europe, including Constantinople. Symeon, the younger son of Boris (893–927), who in the last years of his reign proclaimed himself to be Tsar (Slavonic form of "Caesar") and not a mere khan, ravaged the peninsula with a formidable army right up to the gates of the great city; and toward the end of his reign he attempted to secure the succession of the empire for himself by marrying his daughter to the reigning emperor. But in the end his policies collapsed, he lost to barbarian nomads lands held across the Danube (part of modern Rumania), while the Serbs, another Slavic people to the west, and the Croats, yet another Slavic people to the northwest, resisted continuously, backed by Constantinople. Symeon's empire collapsed before it had been properly consolidated into a unity, though his reign marked the golden age of old Slavonic literature, and the Tsar encouraged the translation of many Greek works into Slavonic. After his death Bulgaria remained politically independent, but the immediate dream of being the successor in Europe of Constantinople was over.

Incorporation of Bulgaria into Byzantine Empire—Basil the Bulgar–Killer (Basil II, 976–1025)

The war was resumed before the death of Symeon's son Peter (927–969). On this occasion the Byzantine emperor invited the pagan Russians under Sviatoslav to discipline the Bulgars, but Sviatoslav proved unmanageable. He destroyed the Bulgarian Empire altogether, but then turned on Constantinople. The Byzantine emperor John I at last defeated him in 972 and assumed the Bulgarian throne. But soon afterward the Bulgar remnants in western Bulgaria discovered a leader (Tsar Samuel, 976–1014) and returned to the attack. The result was a devastating war which lasted for forty-three years, during which countless atrocities were committed, and a large part of the population of both empires, including the best troops of the Byzantines recruited in Anatolia, were killed.

The Byzantine emperor who conducted this war to the death gained the honorific title of Basil the Bulgar-Killer from his successes, and after the war was over he gave a mild peace to the survivors. For a time the Byzantines ruled triumphantly from the Euphrates to the Adriatic, and included parts of Italy under their sway. But within fifty years the Seljuk Turks began moving into Anatolia, disastrously defeating a motley imperial army at Manzikert (1071), and the oppressed subjects of Constantinople began to convert en masse to Islam and to the less oppressive Turks.

Restoration of the Bulgarian kingdom

In 1186 the Bulgars rose again under a new dynasty, and the Byzantines, fully oc-cupied elsewhere, were unable to prevent the restoration of the kingdom. When the Latin crusaders took Constantinople in 1204 (see Chapter 11), the Bulgars at once con-quered almost the whole Balkan peninsula except Greece from the crusaders. But again the Bulgars were unable to hold their pos-sessions for long. In the early fourteenth century they were subdued, first by their fellow Slavs, the Serbs, to the west, and then by the Ottoman Turks at the decisive battle of Kossovo in 1389, which extinguished the independence of all the Slavs in the peninsula until the nineteenth century.

SERBIA AND CROATIA

Brief mention has already been made of Serbia. This Slavic country in the north-

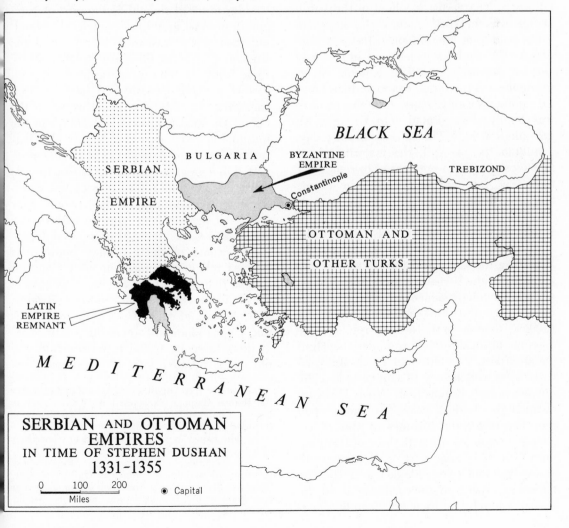

SERBIAN AND OTTOMAN EMPIRES
IN TIME OF STEPHEN DUSHAN
1331-1355

0   100   200
Miles

⊙ Capital

western part of the Balkan peninsula was converted, like Bulgaria, to Orthodox Christianity in the ninth century. In the twelfth and early thirteenth centuries the various Serbian princes united under a monarch, and the kingdom, free of foreign control, was ruled by the descendants of Stephen Nemanja for two centuries. In the fourteenth century, when the Greek empire of Constantinople had been restored (see Chapter 11) after the Latin interlude, the Serbian king, Stephen Dushan (1331–1355), made a bid for the control of the whole Balkan peninsula once more. But he, like so many of his predecessors, was unable to capture Constantinople, and shortly after his death his great kingdom, which extended from the Danube to the Gulf of Corinth, began to fall apart. The Serbians joined in the battle of Kossovo in 1389 against the Ottoman Turks, and their king, Stephen Lazar, whose defeat and death are celebrated in so many Serbian poems, was killed. Nominal independence was permitted to the Serbian kings for another seventy years until the country was finally incorporated into the Turkish dominions in 1459. The patriotic Serbs today, a militant people still, the majority group in Yugoslavia, have not ceased to remember their few days of glory under the heroic Stephen Dushan.

The Croatian Slavs to the north of Serbia were converted to Christianity in the ninth century, but, unlike the Serbs, from the beginning they accepted the leadership and authority of the Roman Church. After a short period of independence Croatia was conquered by the Magyars from Hungary (1091), though permitted to retain some measure of local autonomy under the Hungarian crown. The Ottoman Turks absorbed Croatia, as well as most of Hungary, in 1526, but never fully subdued it. When Hungary escaped the Turkish yoke, Croatia escaped too. Thereafter the fortunes of this Slavic people were bound up with those of Hungary until Croatia became part of the new south Slavic kingdom (Yugo-Slavia) in 1918. The Croatians, owing to their allegiance to the Roman Church and their long-standing con-

nection with the West through rule by Hungary (later Austria-Hungary) have always considered themselves superior to the Serbs and other south Slavs, and the feeling is reciprocated by the latter. The medieval schism between these Slavic peoples has still not been healed today in spite of the existence of the state of Yugoslavia.[3]

THE RUSSIANS

Conversion to Christianity

The vast bulk of the Slavic peoples are Russians. As has already been noted, the Russians obtained their name from the Swedish Vikings,[4] those Varangians (dealt with also briefly in Chapter 14) who settled in western Russia, first at Novgorod, and then at Kiev. The descendants of Rurik, the Viking captor of the old Slavic port of Novgorod, became grand dukes of Kiev, extending their power eastward over most of the Russian plain. By the early tenth century these Russians, who were by this time completely a Slavic people, had not yet been converted to Christianity. However, the Grand Duchess Olga of Kiev, mother of the formidable Sviatoslav, for whom she was regent for many years, was formally converted in a great ceremony at Constantinople about 957.[5] On her return to Kiev she seems to have tried to convert her people (for which act she was later honored with canonization as a saint), but was unsuccessful, perhaps because of the necessary political as well as religious connection with Constantinople that would have followed. Sviatoslav thus made his fierce inroads into the Balkans as a pagan, and even Olga's grandson Vladimir I (St. Vladimir) spent his early years as duke fervently trying to restore fully the old pagan religion with its blood sacrifices.

[3] Present-day Yugoslavia of course includes also the Roman Catholic Slovenes, but as Slovenia was never an independent state, its history has not been included in this chapter.

[4] The name "Russian" is believed to come from "Ruotsi," the Finnish word for Swedes.

[5] Constantinople conferred upon the duchess the title of "archon-ess," thus, as Gibbon puts it, "Whimsically borrowing the title of an Athenian magistrate with a female termination, which would have astonished the ear of Demosthenes."

0   100   200
Miles
◉ Capitals

Novgorod

LITHUANIA

PRUSSIA

POLAND

RUSSIA

Kiev

Dnieper R.

HUNGARY

C U M A N S

K H A Z A R S

BLACK SEA

Constantinople

**RUSSIA BEFORE
MONGOL INVASIONS
ABOUT 1200**

But either because of the efforts of the Greek missionaries in Russia, or because he wished to marry a Greek princess for the prestige the alliance would give him and for the sake of improved trade relations with Constantinople, Vladimir allowed himself at last to be converted, and, with as much fervor as he had hitherto supported them, proceeded to make a public destruction of the images of the old gods. The Russians were obdurate and it was a long time before all Vladimir's subjects were duly baptized; but from their conversion onward they were the most faithful and orthodox of Christians. Kiev and Novgorod became cities of churches, especially Kiev, which for a time became second only to Constantinople as a great and prosperous city in the whole of Europe. Furs, honey, hides, wax, and slaves were the principal articles exported. But from its commanding position on the Dnieper, Kiev was also a port of transit and transshipment for goods destined from Scandinavia to Constantinople, thus altogether by-passing feudal Europe. In the middle of the twelfth century the rule of the grand duchy of Kiev was at its height. Then, in the early thirteenth century it was all destroyed, and Kiev was a

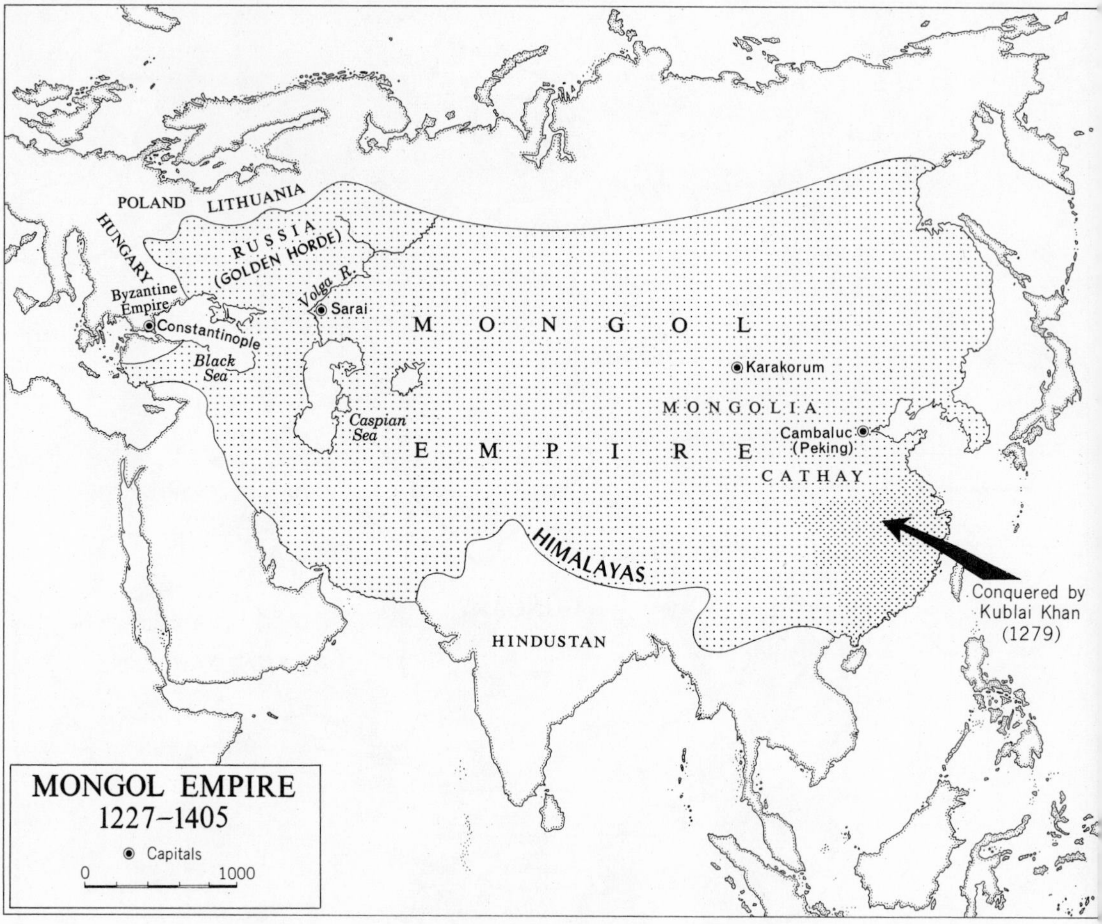

POLAND   LITHUANIA

HUNGARY

RUSSIA
(GOLDEN HORDE)

Volga R.

Byzantine
Empire

Constantinople

Black
Sea

Sarai

Caspian
Sea

M O N G O L

Karakorum

MONGOLIA

E M P I R E

Cambaluc
(Peking)

CATHAY

HIMALAYAS

HINDUSTAN

Conquered by
Kublai Khan
(1279)

**MONGOL EMPIRE
1227–1405**

⊙ Capitals

0   1000

blazing ruin; and the whole of Russia was cast back into a barbarism which prevented the country, for all its large and diligent population, from taking its place until recent times with the nations of Europe.

The Mongol invasions

The fall of Kiev was the result of the invasion of the Mongols (or Tatars). Sporadic invasions of nomadic Mongols from Central Asia had occurred in the twelfth century. Then in 1206 a great Mongol ruler arose, Jenghiz Khan, who united the scattered Mongol tribes into what was perhaps the most formidable band of warriors the world had yet seen. This Mongol khan was the first such leader since Attila the Hun. Jenghiz Khan and his successors carved out for themselves the largest empire in terri-

torial extent so far seen in the world's history. By the time of the death of Jenghiz in 1227 northern China had been taken, together with almost the whole of Central Asia; even Russia had been briefly raided. The death of Jenghiz, however, meant a short respite for Europe since all the sons of the khan had to return to Asia for the election of his successor.

The successors of the great Jenghiz, however, were hardly less formidable than he. During the reign of Ogodai Khan and later during that of his cousin Batu, Europe was invaded in force—Poland, Silesia, and Hungary being overrun; and in each case Europe, which was unable to provide an army capable of resisting the Mongols, was saved only by the death of the khan. After the death of Ogodai, the Mongols returned,

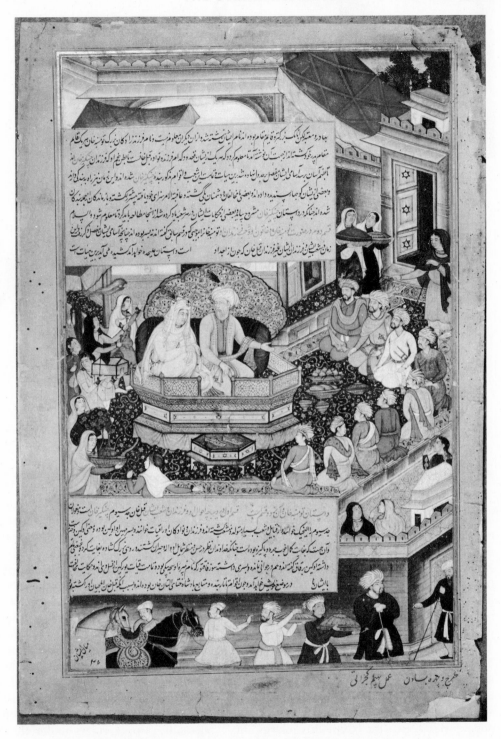

When the great Khans died, their sons had to return to the capital of Karakorum to receive their inheritance. This picture is taken from a manuscript illustration in a sixteenth-century book, and shows Jenghiz Khan dividing his kingdom, prior to his death, between his sons. (COURTESY THE METROPOLITAN MUSEUM OF ART)

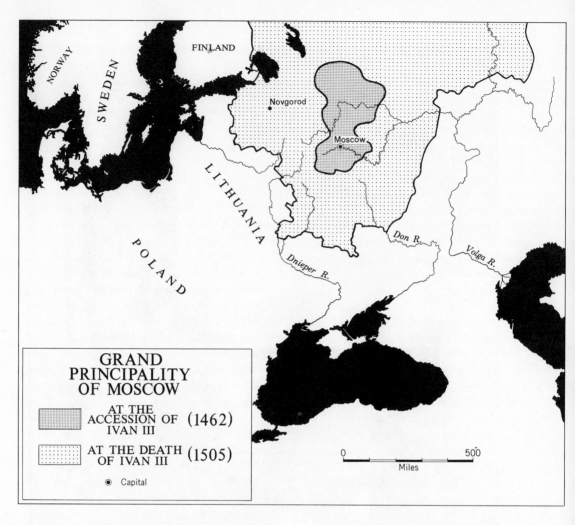

GRAND
PRINCIPALITY
OF MOSCOW

AT THE
ACCESSION OF (1462)
IVAN III

AT THE DEATH (1505)
OF IVAN III

● Capital

and the Golden Horde of Batu Khan encamped on the banks of the Volga in southern Russia, having captured and ruthlessly
sacked every important city in Russia save
Novgorod, which at this time escaped into
the Western orbit, becoming later an independent Hanseatic trading city, while the
rest of Russia groaned under the Mongol
yoke. The Golden Horde remained as an
Asiatic occupying army for two centuries,
demanding and receiving tribute from the
Russian princelings. The Mongols, after some
hesitation, were converted to Islam, but, in
accordance with traditional Muslim religious
policy, permitted the Orthodox clergy in
Russia to remain independent. The clergy,
unlike the secular lords, were not made to
pay tribute, and they thus were enabled to
reach a unique position of power and influence under the Mongol occupation.

The western provinces of Russia, as we
shall see in the next section, gradually freed
themselves from the Mongols, and the earlier
great cities in what is now the Ukraine,
which never recovered from the pillage and
ruin inflicted on them by their conquerors,
ceased to be a part of Russia. It therefore
fell to one of the minor principalities,
Moscow, to become the leader in the new
state. In due course its ruler, Grand Duke
Ivan I (1325–1341) became the chief collector of taxes for the Mongols, with the duty
of forcing the other principalities to pay
them. This position made the grand dukes
virtually puppet rulers under the Mongols;
but when the power of the latter at last
declined it was they who were in the best
position to assert leadership. With the whole-
hearted assistance of the clergy, who constantly preached liberation from the Golden

228

Horde, the grand duke won an ephemeral victory in 1380, but slavery was reimposed in two years. At the beginning of the fifteenth century, Tamerlane, another Mongol ruler bent on world conquest, severely defeated the Golden Horde, weakening its power so that it could no longer control its Russian vassals. Ivan III, the Great (1462–1505), Grand Duke of Moscow, united the greater part of modern European Russia under his absolute autocratic sway, incidentally reabsorbing the independent city of Novgorod. Then he took other important cities in the west from the kingdom of Poland-Lithuania to be described in the next section.

"Holy Russia"

In 1472 Ivan married the niece of the last emperor of Constantinople, a symbolic act of which he proceeded to take full advantage. Moscow under Ivan and his successors proclaimed itself the true successor of Constantinople, the "third Rome," with a Church that had remained consistently "Orthodox," a powerful and efficient clergy, under ducal control, with a "metropolitan" who was the protector of all Orthodox Christians everywhere and the natural successor of the Patriarch of Constantinople, now the puppet of the Turks. The Muscovite court was Byzantine, the architecture of the great Russian cities was Byzantine, and the religion was Byzantine. As far as was possible in such a vast domain, the government and administration were Byzantine. When Ivan the Great proclaimed himself sovereign of all Russia, he ruled the only territory in Eastern Europe comparable with that of the Turks. If the Ottoman Turks had inherited the body of Constantinople, Ivan the Great had surely inherited the soul. And if today the Russians still do not possess the body, it has not been for want of trying.

▶ ## The disputed territories of Eastern Europe

HUNGARY, BOHEMIA, AND MORAVIA

As we shall see in Chapter 10, Hungary in South Central Europe, was settled by the conquering Magyars in the period after the death of Charlemagne.[6] For a long time they remained pagan, but were converted to the Roman Church at the beginning of the eleventh century by St. Stephen I (1001–1038). Stephen was granted the title of "apostolic king," by Pope Sylvester II (Gerbert), who sent him a crown, preserved as a sacred symbol of Hungarian independence until 1945, even during the time Hungary was in subjection to foreign powers. For centuries the Hungarian kings had difficulty in maintaining a position much superior to that of the great nobles, who preferred a feudal state; and many of the kings had to submit to feudal domination. Hungary was continually drawn into the politics of Central Europe, and its throne was frequently occupied by kings who also possessed foreign thrones, and were often enough not Hungarian at all. Living in the eastern borderlands of Europe, the Hungarians frequently also had to bear the brunt of invasions from the East. The Mongols occupied the whole country for a year (1241) until the usual retirement on the death of the khan, and the Hungarians had to defend Europe also against the onset of the Ottoman Turks. Together with the Serbs and other Slavs, the Hungarians were defeated by the Turks at the battle of Kossovo in 1389. In spite of several victories in the fifteenth century which postponed the evil day, at last they were defeated by the Turks at the battle of Mohacs in 1526, and were condemned to partition between the Austrians and the Turks, since the country was not strong enough to survive as an independent nation. Though the Turkish part was recovered at the end of the seventeenth century it was only to fall to the Hapsburgs of Austria, who remained the rulers of Hungary until 1918.

Farthest to the west of all the Slavic peoples were those of Bohemia and Moravia.

[6] Hungary, of course, is not a Slavic country, but it has always possessed a large Slavic minority, especially in Slovakia, which was a part of Hungary from the tenth to the twentieth centuries, was incorporated into Czechoslovakia in 1919, and was nominally independent for a short time under the regime of Hitler.

These territories were already settled by Slavs in the sixth century, who were called Czechs and spoke the Slavonic dialect of Czech. At the time of the mission of St. Cyril and St. Methodius, already described, the two countries were united under Moravian rule, and both were converted to Christianity. After a brief period of struggle they accepted the ecclesiastical rule of Rome. Thereafter their history lay with the West. In the tenth century Bohemia became dominant over Moravia under St. Wenceslas I (died 935), king of Bohemia, and Bohemia itself became the vassal of the Holy Roman Empire, after Otto I had repelled from Moravia the invasions of the Magyars (Chapter 10). German influence grew constantly in the country, the towns prospered, and the country became Westernized and altogether out of touch with the eastern Slavs, similar to them in language, but not in culture.[7] At times Bohemia was the largest of all the territories of the Empire, though its king remained the vassal of the emperor. On several occasions the king of Bohemia was also emperor, and with the Golden Bull (1356) the king of Bohemia was formally recognized as an elector of the Empire. The later history of Bohemia and its final subjugation by the Hapsburg monarchy will be considered in Chapter 19. A few brief references to seventeenth-century Hungary will also appear in the same chapter.

PRUSSIA, POLAND, AND LITHUANIA

In East Central Europe, east of the boundaries of the Holy Roman Empire, and extending far up the Baltic Sea, were the Baltic peoples of Prussia and Lithuania, the Slavs of Poland, and the Finnish people of Livonia. The Poles had become Christians in the tenth century under their Duke Mieszko I (962–992) of the Piast family, which reigned, later as kings, in Poland until 1370. But the Prussians and Lithuanians

remained obstinately pagan until the Teutonic Knights were invited by a Polish prince to help him with a campaign against the Prussians. The Teutonic Knights were a crusading order of militant "monks" dedicated, like the other orders to be mentioned in Chapter 11, to a life of fighting. After the failure of the Third Crusade they returned to Europe, settling in Hungary until they were called upon for action against the Prussians. A group of these Knights joined another missionary order (Livonian Brothers of the Sword) and proceeded to conquer and convert Livonia (present-day Estonia and most of Latvia). Cities were founded in the newly converted land which became flourishing members of the Hanseatic League; but by far the greater part of the territory was given to German nobles, who thus extended the feudal system into these Baltic borderlands, creating a permanent German aristocracy which has only been expelled by the Russians since World War II. The Livonian Knights, unable to move further east after a defeat at the Neva by the Russians under Alexander Nevski (1242), amalgamated with the Teutonic Knights and together the two orders proceeded systematically to subdue and convert the Prussians. Under their Grand Master Hermann of Salza, the Knights made considerable conquests, settling, however, as feudal lords in the new territories, and owing only nominal allegiance to the popes, to the discomfiture of the Poles who claimed the territories. Prussia was thoroughly Germanized, and the earlier Slavic population almost exterminated.

When the Knights pressed on into Pomerelia, to the northwest of the kingdom of Poland, the Poles tried to organize resistance, but did not have any great success until the Teutonic Order fell into decay, in part owing to excessive material prosperity. Then in 1386 the heiress to the Polish crown, Princess Jadwiga, married Jagiello, Grand Duke of Lithuania, who thereupon became King Ladislaus II of Poland, and a huge if short-lived kingdom was thus created which stretched from the Baltic to the Black Sea.

[7] The (Sudeten) Germans whom Hitler discovered to be oppressed by the Czech majority in 1938 had lived in Bohemia peacefully side by side with the Slavic Czechs since medieval times.

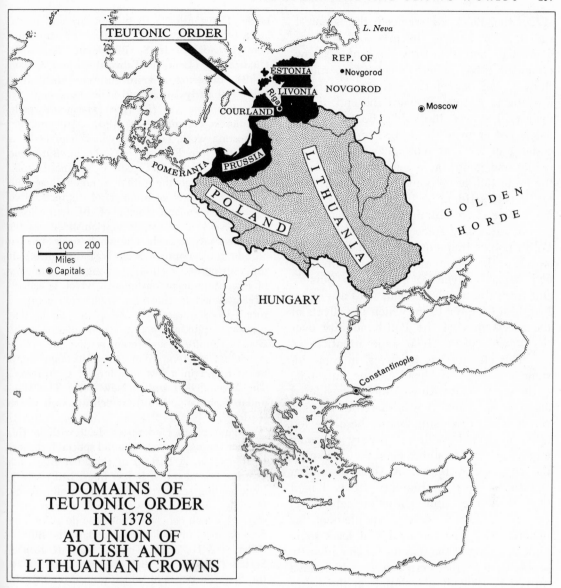

TEUTONIC ORDER

DOMAINS OF
TEUTONIC ORDER
IN 1378
AT UNION OF
POLISH AND
LITHUANIAN CROWNS

Up to this time Lithuania had remained stubbornly impervious to the best efforts of Christian missionaries. Her dukes had created a huge, ramshackle state, much of it carved out of western Russia, which the dominant Mongols were unable to defend. After the union with the Polish crown the new king at last accepted Roman Christianity for himself and his people, with the exception of the Russian and Ukrainian people in his state, who were already Christians but of the Orthodox faith. This new state had resources formidable even for the militant Teu-

tonic Knights, upon whom it inflicted an overwhelming defeat at the battle of Tannenberg (1410). Thereafter, however, with the freeing of the Russians and the ascendancy of the duchy of Moscow, the eastern provinces of Poland-Lithuania fell away, following their coreligionists into obedience to the metropolitan of Moscow. In 1569 the Lithuanians merged with Poland in the Union of Lublin to protect themselves from the inroads of Ivan iv, the Terrible, the Tsar of Russia.

During the Jagiello dynasty (1386–

1572) the Poles experienced the greatest age in their history, the arts and sciences flourished, and the University of Cracow (founded 1364), where Nicolas Copernicus studied, was one of the leading centers of learning in Europe. Toward the end of the dynasty, however, the nobles began to gain much power over the kings, forcing Alexander i in 1505 to reorganize the Diet of nobles and gentry as a legislature. Lacking the protection of the king, the peasants were reduced to serfdom by the nobles. The later kings were elected by the Diet, but had little power, especially since the jealousy of the Polish nobles frequently resulted in the bestowal of the throne on foreigners with their own separate dynastic interests to pursue. But this subject will be dealt with at greater length in Chapter 19, in which the effects of the ascendancy of the Polish nobility over the crown will be given some attention.

This chapter has taken us, in some instances, a long way ahead in time, and some of the states dealt with will not be considered again in this book. It was therefore thought worth while discussing briefly here the too often neglected medieval history of some important modern states, even though within the compass of this book such discussion has to be very perfunctory. It is hoped that the maps and chronological charts (pp. 209–211) will serve to complement this material and give the reader at least some understanding of the reasons for the minority problems in southeastern Europe which have proved so difficult of solution in the twentieth century.

▶ **Suggestions for further reading**

In recent years there has been a great revival of interest in Byzantine studies. Many societies and specialized magazines have come into existence which deal exclusively with Byzantine history and art.

There are several good surveys of Byzantine civilization as a whole. Excellent is N. H. Baynes, *The Byzantine Empire* (Home University Library; London: Oxford University Press, 1925), many times reprinted, which covers the various fields of Byzantine activity topically and has a large bibliography. Rather fuller, but still eminently readable, is S. Runciman, *Byzantine Civilization* (London: Edward Arnold & Co., 1933). Covering a more restricted field is a survey of early Byzantine civilization, in P. N. Ure, *Justinian and His Age* (Harmondsworth, Middlesex: Penguin Books, 1951). An extremely interesting work, not all of which has yet been translated into English, is C. Diehl, *Byzantine Portraits* (New York: Alfred A. Knopf, Inc., 1927), in which the author, a noted Byzantine specialist, selects a number of representative Byzantine men and women of different classes and presents a rather impressionistic character and life study of each. The whole serves to give an admirable impression of Byzantine society at different periods of time. A thoughtful summary of Byzantine accomplishments, which is especially intended to show the civilization centered round Constantinople as a separate civilization in its own right, and neither a continuation of the Roman Empire in a different setting nor even a specially Greek empire in spite of its language, is to be found in a few chapters of C. Dawson, *The Making of Europe* (New York: The Macmillan Company, 1932), which are well worth reading.

On the other countries dealt with in this chapter there are two very good special histories: S. Runciman, *A History of the First Bulgarian Empire* (London: G. Bell & Sons, Ltd., 1930), by a leading scholar in this difficult and almost unknown field, a lively and well-written piece of work which concludes with the death of Tsar Samuel and the final victory of Basil the Bulgar-Killer; and H. W. V. Temperley, *A History of Serbia* (London: G. Bell & Sons, Ltd., 1917), the first 106 pages of which are devoted to the history of Serbia as far as the Turkish conquest. This latter book is free from the excessive nationalist bias which has marred other more recent books on modern Yugo-Slavia, though the book is, rather naturally, keenly sympathetic to Serbia's struggle against the central European powers, which was at its height in 1917. Within its limits the book is as accurate as could be expected at that time. For the Turks an old work, E. S. Creasy, *History of the Ottoman Turks* (2nd ed.; London: Richard Bentley and Son, 1878), has never been superseded, while there is a valuable modern study of the whole Balkan Peninsula in F. Schevill, *The History of the Balkan Peninsula* (rev. ed.; New York: Harcourt Brace & Co., Inc., 1933).

With the growing interest in Eastern Europe which has resulted from World War II, a number of books have appeared in recent times which have dealt with the early history of these peoples in a way comprehensible to the West. J. Roucek, ed., *Central-Eastern Europe, Crucible of World Wars* (New York: Prentice-Hall, Inc., 1946), attempts to do on a larger scale what Chapter 8 of this text has attempted, that is, to give a severely compressed historical background which may serve as a necessary minimum of knowledge for the general student, and thus to provide an introduction to be filled in by fuller study. Such a fuller study is given in a really outstanding account of this difficult and little-known history, in O. Halecki, *Border Lands of Western Civilization* (New York: The Ronald Press Company, 1952). This book will give the student a fine introduction to the history of Poland and Lithuania and other border countries, including the expansion of Russia at the end of the medieval period. The information contained in this book is to be found only with the greatest difficulty elsewhere, and, as far as the author knows, Halecki's book is the one thorough work in English on the subject.

For the early history of Russia the standard book is G. Vernadsky, *A History of Russia* (4th ed., completely rev.; New Haven, Conn.: Yale University Press, 1954).

9

The Muslim Empire

*Arabia before Mahomet • Mahomet and Islam • Progress of Islam in the time
of Mahomet • Expansion of Islam • The nature of Muslim culture • Decay of
Muslim civilization: the Turks*

► Arabia before Mahomet

THE ARAB PEOPLE

It was noticed briefly in the last chapter that the Persian Emperor Chosroes, while engaged in war with the Byzantines, received a letter from an unknown Arab informing him of the existence of a new prophet, whose message, accepted by millions to whom Christianity made no appeal, was to change the world hardly less profoundly than Christianity's own founder. And even before Heraclius was dead he already knew that his long and exhausting war with Persia had been fruitless; for the prophet of Mecca and his followers were surely to enter into his heritage.

The peninsula of Arabia had hitherto played little part in history. A small area in the north had been a Roman province; but the great desert lands of the south had supported only Bedouin, nomad tribesmen who wandered from oasis to oasis with their flocks, warlike, hospitable, illiterate but with a remarkable natural shrewdness and understanding, fiercely loyal to their tribes, families, and chiefs (sheiks), but quick to take offense and as quick to avenge a slight as an injury. The sheiks were independent chief-

tains, owing homage to no man, and their country was without political organization of any kind; the few families who made up a tribe were part of no larger unit.

Along the coasts of Arabia, however, the land was more fertile, and a few cities had grown up. Jidda was the seaport, Mecca and Yathrib were trading cities, with their bazaars selling the products of the country—meat, dates, nuts, palm oil, and other foodstuffs, luxuries imported by sea and caravan as well as made by local industry. And from these cities set out camel caravans to the north, south, and through the desert to the east, manned by shrewd Arab traders and Jewish merchants. The cities, like the Bedouin tribesmen, were dominated by local families. One of the greatest of these was the Kuraish, which dominated Mecca, the chief commercial and religious center of the country. Though often warring among themselves, the Kuraish, with their many collateral branches, could be relied upon to unite when family interests were threatened.

Probably such a people as this would never have been united by political means; no king had yet arisen among them as in the other states with a similar early society that we have studied. Loyalty from such a people could not be commanded or enforced. But what could and did unite them and make of them one of the greatest fighting forces the world has yet seen was a new and dynamic religion whose early successes, often against overwhelming odds, must have seemed to doubters proof indeed of its divine origin.

RELIGION BEFORE ISLAM

Before the days of Mahomet, Mecca was already a religious center. A stone, believed to have fallen from heaven (a meteorite?) around which a temple, the Kaaba, had been built, was the chief object of veneration. Arabs from distant lands came to pay homage at it, to the financial advantage of the trading community. Idols and other sacred objects were worshiped. Both in the holy city of Mecca and elsewhere there seem to have been many varieties of sacrifice offered both to deities and to deified forces of nature. But, as far as we can tell, no synthesis of beliefs or religious practices existed which would justify our calling it in any way a religion. And this was surprising since Judaism and even Christianity were known to the Arabs from traders and wandering missionaries, who must have been astonished at their lack of interest when they had so little positive religion of their own. And yet, as we shall see, the religious spirit was there, quiescent, waiting for the words of inspiration that would kindle it. This task was the lifework of Mahomet.

▶ Mahomet and Islam

RELIGIOUS EXPERIENCE OF MAHOMET

Mahomet (the name is spelled in even more different ways than Shakespeare's) was born in Mecca in 570 of one of the poorer and less influential branches of the leading Kuraish family. His childhood was spent in the shadow of poverty, it would appear. But when he was twenty-five he began to work for a widow Khadija, older than he, a business woman of ability and in comfortable circumstances, whom he later married. By her he had his only child, Fatima. From this time on Mahomet prospered as a trader, leading his wife's caravans, once as far as Syria, and until the age of forty gave no indication that he would

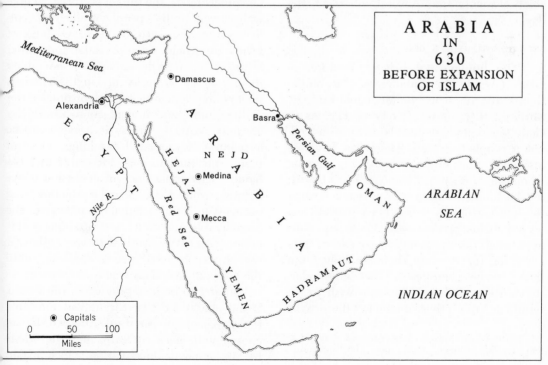

ARABIA
IN
630
BEFORE EXPANSION
OF ISLAM

Mediterranean Sea

Damascus

Alexandria

EGYPT

Nile R.

Red Sea

HEJAZ

Medina

Mecca

YEMEN

ARABIA

NEJD

Basra

Persian Gulf

OMAN

HADRAMAUT

ARABIAN SEA

INDIAN OCEAN

Capitals
0   50   100
Miles

later preach a new religion. But it seems clear that he must have pondered long on what he knew of the other religions of the Near East and often have thought of the religious backwardness of his native land. And it is said that for a month each year he went into the desert, and there his thoughts became clearer, and he prepared himself so that at last, when the revelation came to him, he was ready. The revelation was that there was only one God, Allah, and that he, Mahomet, had been chosen to be God's prophet. Islam therefore stands firmly on the revelations to Mahomet, as Judaism stands upon the revelations to Moses. It is consequently a religion that calls for faith, with all the dynamism that such a religion entails. And although Islam contains much from the older religions, commingled with observations growing out of the customs of the desert tribes, it should not be regarded as a religion that was simply tailored by the keen intellect of Mahomet to fit the circumstances of his country. Students of history should avoid such an easy assumption, which is sometimes made when we speak of *syncretistic* religions, or those which draw their chief elements from several others of the day.

RELATION TO OTHER RELIGIONS

The fundamental belief, therefore, in Islam (Arabic for "submission") is monotheism of the strict Judaic kind. For the Muslim,[1] there is no Trinity of Persons in God. Mahomet did not claim to be a god, but a prophet of God. There had been, in his belief, other prophets before him, among whom he numbered Moses and Jesus Christ; but he himself was to be the last, revealing the whole truth as it had been partially revealed to his predecessors. There was thus no reason for despising these earlier religions, or for denying their teachings; but they were not complete, and not fully understood. Islam therefore does not wish to exterminate the other religions; those who

converted to Islam showed that they were a chosen people insofar as they had been able to accept the higher revelation, and for this reason in a Muslim country would be entitled to special privileges. Those who preferred to keep their second-class religions could do so, but they must then expect to be treated as second-class citizens in a religious state. As "people of the Book," believers in other religions were permitted to keep their Books. Only those who had no Book and no religion were to be converted by force. This attitude always remained the religious policy of Islam, which was reflected in its political policies. A holy war (*jehad*) could only be proclaimed against heathen, or when Islam was forced to defend itself against other religions which attacked it. A holy war, enjoined upon the faithful only in certain well-defined circumstances, could never be arbitrary, or for the sake of simple conquest; the true religion must be endangered first by the enemy.

THE KORAN—HADITH, ULEMA

Mahomet from the time he began his mission received many revelations from, as he proclaimed, the angel Gabriel. These were given to the people orally, but collected after his death in the sacred book of Islam—the Koran. Each revelation (or sura) is separate, and the compilers assembled them only in the order of length. There is thus no logical, chronological, or other order in the Koran, and if read consecutively by an unsympathetic critic, it appears to be a medley of unrelated teachings, most of them concerned with everyday life and behavior. This appearance of confusion is the natural result of the fact that Mahomet did not trust to his own judgment to answer the innumerable questions put to him in his earlier years. When asked for an authoritative answer, he meditated in the desert until the answer came. This was then a new revelation later to be incorporated in the Koran. It may be added that throughout the book the language is beautiful, the words are chosen with masterly care, and the whole betrays a poetic imagination which makes

---

[1] The word "Muslim," also Anglicized as "Moslem" or "Mussulman," means one who "surrenders himself to God."

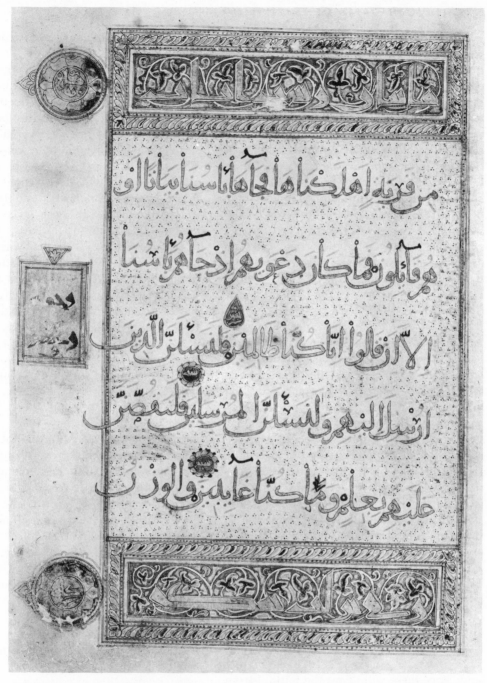

Leaf from a thirteenth-century Koran. (COURTESY THE METROPOLITAN MUSEUM OF ART)

it not unworthy to stand beside the Hebrew Scriptures. And it has never been difficult for any believing Muslim to accept it as inspired, in spite of occasional contradictions between various instructions to the faithful, which are explained as a progressive understanding of his mission by the Prophet, who, after all, was not divine but partook of some of the frailties of mortals.

The Koran contained all the positive teaching given by Mahomet in his lifetime; but, as with Christianity, not all points of Islamic theology had been cleared up by the Prophet himself. And since the Koran was also a guide to ethics and ordinary worldly activity, it early became necessary to have authoritative rulings on knotty points of doctrine. Moreover, Mahomet had also given oral instructions to his disciples which were not direct revelations like the suras in the Koran but were almost equally authoritative. Thus were added to the teachings of the holy book itself the *Hadith,* or traditions, which derived directly from the Prophet; and a number of learned men, the *ulema,* became recognized as the interpreters of the sacred text and the Hadith. These ulema still exist today with the same tasks in orthodox Muslim communities, even though there is no priesthood.

ORGANIZATION AND DOCTRINES OF ISLAM— SIMPLICITY, APPEAL TO JEWS

In Islam there has never been any recognized priesthood. Each community may have an *imam,* who leads the prayers while there is also a *muezzin* who summons the faithful at sundown to turn toward Mecca and pray. The prayers are regularly prescribed, as are also fast days; and a whole month, Ramadan, is set aside during which no Muslim may break his fast between sunrise and sundown. In addition, there are moral duties to be performed, such as giving alms to the poor, showing hospitality to strangers; and there are injunctions against pride and worldliness and taking advantage of the difficult position of one's neighbor. There are laws of ritual cleanliness to be observed, following the general pattern of the Jewish codes: the pig is unclean, and there are ritual washings to be performed. No wine or strong drink must be taken, and there must be no images or idols of any kind, since these will divert the faithful from the strictest monotheism, persuading them to believe that other beings beside Allah have godlike attributes. The articles of belief are few and equally simple. There is a resurrection of the body and Paradise for the righteous, and an unending suffering in Gehenna for the wicked; both places are eloquently described in the Koran. There are also angels

of God and evil beings, emissaries of the Devil.

Thus the religion is essentially simple. It does away with the complexity of Christianity, with its Trinity and doctrine of the Redemption, and concentrates on the few essentials which proved acceptable to the simple people to whom these were preached. The simple elements of Jewish ritual were alone retained, while the whole of Jewish legalism was abandoned. And the ancient desert morality at its best—such virtues as simplicity, straightforwardness, hospitality to friends and even enemies—was enshrined now as moral law, binding on the faithful, so that little change was needed from what was already practiced. The religion, there can be little doubt, was intended to appeal to Jews as well as to the heathen, and much of early Hebrew legend is incorporated in the Koran as fact. Although in the process of time many Jews within this culture were indeed converted, on the whole Islam did not succeed in weaning them from their Law. In early times there were many wars against Jewish communities, but the communities were not destroyed; and within a Muslim state Judaism was tolerated in the same way as Christianity. And Mahomet, who always regarded Jerusalem as a holy city, and indeed chose it himself as the place from which he ascended to Heaven, ultimately did not adopt it as the chief, but only the second, holy city in Islam, the place of supreme honor being reserved to his birthplace Mecca.

▶ Progress of the religion in the time of Mahomet

OPPOSITION IN MECCA

Mahomet's first convert appears to have been his wife. But progress was very slow in the early years of his mission when its appeal was exclusively religious. He was unable to obtain the support of his own Kuraish family, who were apparently afraid for the future of the lucrative tourist trade

► chronological chart

Islam in the time of Mahomet

Birth of Mahomet	570
"Flight" of Mahomet to Medina from Mecca	622
Organization of the commonwealth of Islam in Medina	622–630
Return to Mecca of Mahomet	630
Death of Mahomet	632

Expansion of Islam

Caliphate of Abu Bekr	632–634
Caliphate of Omar	634–644
Conquest of Syria	634–641
Conquest of Persia	635–641
Conquest of Egypt	639–644
Conquest and slow subjugation of North Africa	643–711
Ommeyad caliphate founded by Moawiya	661
Blockade of Constantinople	673–678
Peace with Constantinople	678
Civil wars between rival sects and dynasties	680–699
Conquest of Transoxania and part of Turkestan	705–712
Conquest of Punjab	708–715
Conquest of Spain	711–715
Invasions of southern France	715–732
Battle of "Tours"	732
Conquest of Georgia	727–733
End of the Ommeyad caliphate	750
Abbasid caliphate	750–1258
Independent Ommeyad dynasty under Abdu-r-Rahman in Spain	755
Caliphate of Harun-al-Rashid	785–809
Ommeyad caliphate in Spain (Cordova)	756–1031
Fatimid dynasty of Egypt	968–1171
Capture of Bagdad by Seljuk Turks	1055
Capture and sack of Bagdad by Mongols, execution of last Abbasid caliph	1258

to Mecca, since there was as yet no suggestion that Mecca would continue to be a holy city. Naturally Mahomet's uncompromising monotheism offended all those who had a vested interest in the old religion; and there are always difficulties in the way of accepting as a prophet a man one has known all one's life. It was not surprising, then, that most of the earliest converts were gained in a city other than his birthplace, the city of Yathrib. Mahomet then made up his mind to leave his birthplace for Yathrib, and his followers began by political intrigue to prepare for him there a position of honor. When all was ready, he left Mecca, having been preceded by all his Meccan converts, and was given command of the whole city, the name of which was shortly afterward changed to Medina, the "City of the Prophet." This migration was the famous Hegira, of 622, from which year the Muslim Era is counted.

PROGRESS IN MEDINA

The date is truly an epochal one, since from this time Islam began to forge ahead as a religious and political movement. The support of the Bedouins of the desert was enlisted, while the Jews in Medina whom Mahomet had been hoping to gain as converts finally refused to join him and were rewarded with confiscation of their property for the benefit of the faithful. In addition, Mecca was now an idolatrous enemy, a fit target for a holy war, in which the Bedouins engaged with enthusiasm, since one of their most pleasurable and profitable occupations was the raiding of caravans. The Meccans tried to defend themselves, but were beaten on several occasions by the growing army of Muslims. Finally Mahomet judged the time ripe for the forcible conversion of the people of his birthplace. He gathered an army of about ten thousand men and marched on the city.

VICTORIOUS RETURN TO MECCA—CONVERSION OF ARABIA

The Kuraish looked at this vast army, far larger than anything they could hope to muster, and decided that it was better to make terms and follow the Prophet to victory rather than resist him. Mahomet entered Mecca in triumph, destroyed the idols and all remnants of the old religion, but maintained the sacred Kaaba and the stone from heaven, which remained for Islam the most holy place of pilgrimage. Thus the commercial interests of the Meccans and the religious imperatives of Islam were both respected.

Meanwhile, the religion had also been spreading. The Bedouins accepted it without murmur, and the people of Mecca and Medina and the other Arabian cities at least outwardly conformed. It now became allied with Arab expansionism, and its future was assured by its early successes. Mahomet himself died two years later (in 632), when Arabia itself was only half converted, and without making clear provisions for a successor. There was no central government for

Arabia; and at this point few could have predicted the astonishing career that awaited the new religion under the leadership of the successors of the Prophet. In fact, there never was a stable central government for Arabia, as the Bedouins cherished their independence too closely. But after a series of minor wars a loose overlordship of Medina was accepted, and the Bedouins were perfectly willing to follow the military leadership of the faithful in their attacks upon foreign countries.

▶ Expansion of Islam

THE SUCCESSION TO THE PROPHET—ALI, MOAWIYA, OMMEYADS, ABBASIDS

At the time of Mahomet's death in 632 little thought seems to have been given as to how Islam was to be propagated and by whom. Mahomet himself had always acted as the absolute and infallible leader, and his followers had been able to rely upon his revelations. Now there were to be no more revelations, and it was not yet known whether his spiritual mantle would fall upon his family or upon his disciples. And to this day there is still a major schism in Islam on this very point. Mahomet's daughter Fatima had married his own cousin. Clearly this man was the nearest male heir in the immediate family. But Ali, the cousin, was overshadowed as a warrior by many of the other followers, and it did not seem probable that he could give the leadership required. So the followers passed him over and chose the elderly father-in-law of the Prophet, Abu Bekr, who survived only two years (632–634). The second leader (called caliph, a religious and political title) was the great warrior Omar, who ruled for ten years and added Syria and Persia to the growing empire. The next to be chosen belonged to the Ommeyad family, one of the most important of the Meccan families, whose leaders had been faithful to Mahomet from the first. But while all these caliphs reigned, opposition had been gathering around the person of Ali, the son-in-law and cousin of Mahomet, who wished to keep the caliphate in the family of the founder and keep intact the Koran as the only inspired book, without the Hadith or traditions.

On the murder of the Ommeyad caliph by supporters of Ali, war broke out between the latter and the Ommeyad family, with its new head, Moawiya; and though Ali was proclaimed caliph, he was murdered not long afterward. Moawiya then became caliph (661). The followers of Ali became a dissident sect within Islam, the Shiites, which remained the leading group in Persia and later in Egypt. Other descendants of Ali and Mahomet from time to time set themselves up as independent caliphs, and the next great dynasty of the Abbasids was predominantly Shiite in contrast to the orthodox Muslims called Sunni. The Shiites still persist today, especially in Persia and Afghanistan.

The dynasty of the Ommeyads (661–750) removed the capital of the religion and empire to Damascus in Syria, and it was during their caliphates that Islam expanded farthest. In 750 the descendants of Abbas, a cousin of Mahomet, overthrew the Syrian Ommeyads and established the Abbasid dynasty, with the new capital at Bagdad in Mesopotamia. This dynasty, which officially ruled till 1258, saw the Oriental courts of such potentates as Harun-al-Rashid and Al-Mamun, which fell heir to the ancient traditions of Persia, and Persian influence was predominant throughout. For the last few centuries of the Abbasid rule in Bagdad the caliph was the prisoner of his Turkish mercenaries, who overran his territories and ruled in his name. These were the Seljuk Turks, whose conquest of Jerusalem led to the Crusades.

THE FORCES BEHIND EXPANSION—
OVERPOPULATION, RELIGION, INSPIRED
LEADERSHIP, TOLERATION

The successful expansion of Islam should not be credited altogether to the nature of the religion, which, as we have seen, was far from fanatical in its beginnings, and never was inherently expansionist. This was not the first time in history that the Semites of the desert penetrated into the richer lands of the north. The usual explanation for this new drive is given as the increasing desiccation of the desert and the drying up of oases on which the Bedouins had been dependent. There is, however, no evidence for this, though of course it is possible. There can be no doubt that the Bedouins had always been condemned to a low standard of living in view of the meager resources of their country. And being trained in the hard school of the desert and naturally warlike, with nothing to lose, they would follow any successful and inspired leadership. If the unifying and dynamic force of Islam had not been provided just at that time there is no reason to suppose that they would have erupted out of the desert to conquer a world empire at that particular moment. But the spark was provided by Mahomet and his religion; and the brilliant success of the initial enterprises against weak and divided opposition brought ever-increasing numbers of converts to swell the expanding armies. The Arabs from the desert alone could never have conquered such an empire, but they did provide the effective leadership for all the heterogeneous forces that joined them and embraced their religion.

It is quite untrue to picture these invading Muslims as a fanatical horde bent on attaining Paradise at the cost of their lives and ready to die in battle for this immediate reward. The Koran did indeed promise such a reward, but it is not to be supposed that this was the passage in the sacred text that claimed their exclusive attention. The Koran had also told them what policy to adopt toward the unbelievers; and this policy was worth far more to the faithful than any fanatical self-sacrifice. Briefly, as noted before, the unbelievers could keep their religion, could even keep their churches and their synagogues and their priesthood; but they had to pay dearly for the privilege. Anyone who converted to Islam was freed of all taxes, though, of course, he accepted voluntarily the obligation to give alms to the poor as prescribed by the Koran. The taxes were borne by the unbelievers, and until the era of conquest was over no faithful Muslim had to pay any. Moreover, the Muslims were not at all interested in destroying the civilization of the peoples they conquered. On the contrary, they had the most endearing trait of being extremely interested in the native cultures and wishing only to learn from them and contribute to them what they could—in this respect putting to shame many of the conquerors of history and imitating only the greatest, Alexander the Great. It was this quality of cultural tolerance which made the Muslims and the civilization they created the most influential transmitters of culture that the world has yet seen, superior to the Romans in that these new imperialists took also from the best that India and the Far East could give. Only when the barbarous Turks entered into the Muslim heritage, after it had been in decay for centuries, did Islam become fanatical and destroy more than it created and preserved.

The governments of Syria and Bagdad were Oriental despotisms of a familiar kind, owing much to the example of Constantinople. Their courts were centers of luxury and culture; but both were, on the whole, more creative than Constantinople, with its ancient Greek heritage on which it too exclusively relied. The subjects of the caliphates of Syria and Bagdad were kept under central control as far as it was possible for the monarchs to establish such control. But the Bedouin tribes of Arabia, whose dynamism had been responsible for the upsurge of Islam in the first place, were unwilling to submit to any kind of central rule. Nor were the warlike tribes in Africa. So the despots made only sporadic efforts to enforce their authority over these tribes, which, for the most part, remained independent under local leadership, retaining to this day the religion of Islam, but never more than nominal subjects of the Muslim political empires. Islam as a religion was congenial to them and did not interfere with their way of life; but the political system of the Muslim Empire interfered with their traditional independence, and it is not surprising that they rejected it.

WEAKNESS OF OPPOSITION TO MUSLIM EXPANSION—THE BYZANTINE AND PERSIAN EMPIRES

At the outset of their career the Muslims found an inspired general, Khalid, the "sword of Allah." Though his armies were small in comparison with those of his enemies, they were determined; and Syria was oppressed by Byzantine taxes, having been only recently recovered by the Byzantine from the Persians. The Syrian armies hardly put up more than token resistance, and the population, itself Semitic like the Arabs, positively welcomed the relief from Byzantine tyranny and was, for the most part, entirely willing to submit to the formality of conversion with its privileged status. Another army marched on Persia, where it met the same situation. Persia, too, had been exhausted by the recent wars, the Persian religion had long ago fallen into decay, and the king had for a long time been unable to make his authority felt against his nobles. It took only three battles to conquer the Persians and thereafter many of the Persians joined the army of conquest. The victorious Muslims spread out to the East, carrying their religion with them. They usually had to fight against the great cities, but opposition was not prolonged, and at last they reached the limits of the ancient Persian Empire and the confines of China and India. Here they halted, and their expansion took a different form.

Aided by the Persian converts, they built fleets and sailed the Persian Gulf down into the Indian Ocean, trading and engaging in missionary activity for Islam wherever they went. Part of India was converted, and almost the whole of what is today called Indonesia, and the Malay Peninsula. They established colonies even in the chief cities of China itself. These areas were never part of the political empire of the Muslims, though as Muslims the inhabitants looked to the caliph as their religious leader. The vast majority of these converts made in the Far East have remained Muslims to this day.

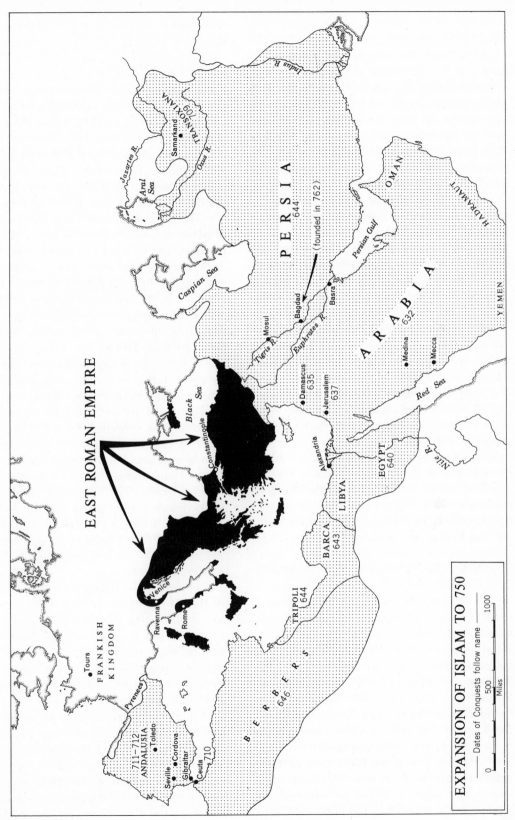

EAST ROMAN EMPIRE

TRANSOXIANA 709

Samarkand

Jaxartes R.
Aral Sea
Oxus R.

Caspian Sea

PERSIA 644

(founded in 762)

Baghdad

Basra

Mosul
Tigris R.
Euphrates R.

OMAN

HADRAMAUT

Persian Gulf

ARABIA

YEMEN

Black Sea

Constantinople

Damascus 635

Jerusalem 637

Medina 632

Mecca

Red Sea

Alexandria

EGYPT 640

Nile R.

LIBYA

BARCA 643

TRIPOLI 644

B E R B E R S 646

Venice

Ravenna

Rome

Tours

FRANKISH KINGDOM

Pyrenees

Toledo

711–712
ANDALUSIA

Seville

Cordova

Gibraltar

Ceuta 710

EXPANSION OF ISLAM TO 750

——— Dates of Conquests follow name

0   500   1000
Miles

THE CONQUEST OF NORTH AFRICA (639–711)

Egypt and North Africa still belonged in name to the Byzantine Empire when the Arabs began their career of conquests. But the Byzantines, with their limited resources, were unable to hold them against this new menace. Egypt succumbed quickly, leaving its rich lands in the possession of the Muslims and cut off forever from Constantinople, which never recovered fully from the loss. Carthage, the old capital of the Vandal kingdom, in the hands of the Byzantines since Justinian, resisted the outlying bands of Arabs which attacked it for a few years until the Arabs could bring up sufficient reinforcements. Then it, too, was lost to Constantinople, while the Arabs pressed on to the West.

Here, however, they met solid resistance from the Berbers, desert people like themselves, just as fiercely independent, and with a tradition as warlike as that of the Bedouins. But at last the Berbers were defeated, accepting Islam at first reluctantly, and then with a fanaticism that outmatched that of their conquerors. Perhaps, too, they were not uninfluenced in their decision to embrace Islam by the prospects it held out for further plunder. At all events, it was the Berbers who formed the bulk of the expeditions into Spain, which succeeded in adding that country also to the dominions of the Ommeyads.

THE CONQUEST OF SPAIN AND THE EXPEDITIONS
INTO FRANCE

In 711 the Berbers, led by a general named Tarik and a small number of seasoned Arabs, moved across the Pillars of Hercules and captured the Rock of Gibraltar, which received its new name from the Arab leader (Jebel Tarik). Conditions in Spain since the Visigothic conversion to Orthodox Christianity had deteriorated until the Church had become the chief power in the realm, far more important than the Visigothic kings, who had lost most of their authority and could not at this late stage regain it in time to muster an effective defending army. Moreover, the heretical Christians and Jews, persecuted by the Orthodox Christian Church, positively welcomed the Muslims, who were, of course, willing to tolerate them; and it is said that much of Tarik's army was composed of refugees from ecclesiastical persecution. The Muslims, therefore, met with little more than token resistance except from the Basques in the north, who indeed fought them with such stubbornness that during their whole rule in Spain the Muslims never troubled to conquer their small strips of Basque land.

Having disposed of Spain, the victorious Muslims moved on into France. But here progress ceased to be so easy. The Arabs were a long way from home, and had to rely on the Berbers for reinforcements; the latter seem to have been content with Spain, and were also engaged in revolting against the Arab rulers in Africa, whose authority they resented. So the Arab army in France was not strong enough to conquer the country against the much more determined resistance of the Franks under the Merovingian "mayor of the palace," Charles Martel. Defeated at the so-called battle of Tours in 732 ("so-called" because it seems to have been fought near Poitiers, many miles away), the Muslim armies moved to southwestern France, where they remained until finally being driven from the country in 759. Not many years afterward Charlemagne, by then king of the Franks, launched a counteroffensive and established the Spanish March, a frontier state in Northern Spain which served as the outpost for the reconquest of Spain by the Christians in a later century. Since the expedition to France could hardly have conquered the country against Frankish resistance even under a lesser captain than Charles Martel, the battle of Tours is perhaps not so epoch-making as it has sometimes been described. Its significance rather lies in what it meant in the way of prestige for the family of Charles Martel and the leadership in Europe that it gave to the Franks. However, the Muslims had at last been checked and the limits for their expansion determined. In Spain the usual tolerance was shown to the Christians, but in a Muslim

CALIPHATE
OF
CORDOVA
IN
10th CENTURY

⊙ Capitals

0   50   100

Miles

country they were cut off from contact with the papacy. They developed a form of worship quite distinct from papal Catholicism, with their own separate Liturgy, called the Mozarabic Liturgy. The spirit of this Christianity was curiously Muslim in its attitude toward heresy and its taste for secular literature; and it did not take altogether kindly to the Christian crusaders, emissaries of the papacy, who returned in a later century to enforce orthodox Catholicism upon them again. But after the conquest of Toledo by the Christians in the eleventh century the Arabized Spanish Christians entered with enthusiasm into the work of translating Aristotle and the Arabic commentators into Latin for the benefit of their new masters.

THE MUSLIM FAILURE AGAINST CONSTANTINOPLE

The greatest prize in the civilized world was, of course, Constantinople; but the Muslims of this age never succeeded in conquering it. This was reserved for their Turkish successors as late as 1453. With the aid of a fleet built in Egypt and using the old Byzantine naval base of Alexandria, the Muslims took the Byzantine bases of Cyprus and Rhodes in the Eastern Mediterranean, and they were able with their fleet to pass the

Hellespont and besiege Constantinople by sea. They also overran Asia Minor in the early eighth century. But they could not take the impregnable city at any of their many attempts, being unable, as we have seen, to overcome the Byzantine secret weapon, Greek fire, which seems to have been a kind of primitive flame thrower with an explosive compound which set fire to the enemy's ships and, according to the descriptions, would even burn on the water. Soon afterward the Muslims withdrew from Asia Minor also, and Eastern Europe was saved. Two centuries later the Byzantines recovered much of what had been lost, including the command of the Eastern Mediterranean, but for a period the whole sea was a Muslim lake.

CONQUEST OF THE MEDITERRANEAN—
CONSEQUENCES

The eastern Mediterranean was conquered early, as has been seen, in accordance with the Muslim plan for conquering Constantinople and maintaining safely the possession of Syria. Crete was the next to fall. But it was another century before the Muslims of a new strong state in modern Algeria and Tunis began to move across the Mediterranean, taking Malta and Sicily. They advanced into southern Italy, capturing from the Byzantine Empire the last of the conquests of Justinian. And though this was again restored to the Macedonian dynasty of Constantinople (ninth and tenth centuries), Sicily remained a Muslim land until its conquest by the Normans in the late eleventh century.

This conquest of the Mediterranean cut off all sea trade between Constantinople and the kingdom of the Franks. For a long time before the actual conquests Muslim pirates had made trade difficult, working out of the North African ports. Some important ports had retained sea trade with the East long after the fall of the Roman Empire, trade which, in turn, had kept up some prosperity in the cities of France and in neighboring lands. With the important sea-borne luxury trade cut off by the Muslims, who did not view the Christian lands in Europe with any favor, and were in any case fond of piracy, European towns were hard hit, although some trade in later centuries was carried on with the Muslims themselves, especially from the Italian port of Amalfi. Not until the Byzantines reconquered the eastern Mediterranean and Venice began to trade with them was the West again able to enjoy in quantity the superior goods of the East. Sicily remained an outpost of Muslim culture and was able to exercise a considerable cultural influence upon the Normans who conquered it. It was from Sicily and Spain that, from the eleventh century onward, the European Christians gained their first real knowledge of Muslim culture, which became so influential in the next centuries. In the East during the Crusades these Christians were in contact only with the Seljuk Turks, far behind both Spain and Sicily in the arts of civilization.

THE SPECIFICALLY ARAB CONTRIBUTION TO THE
EXPANSION OF ISLAM

In general it may be said that the higher civilizations conquered by the Arabs absorbed their masters, thus following the rule that we have observed already. And indeed the Arabs made no effort to impose such culture as they had upon their new subjects. The Persian and Byzantine systems of government, with their bureaucracies and their absolutism, were taken over intact by the Arabs. A similar system with modifications, under a dynasty of Ommeyad caliphs, independent of the Abbasid caliphs of Bagdad, prevailed in Spain. Elsewhere the Arabs were rarely complete masters in their own realm and made use of what was at hand, not developing any new bureaucracy where none existed already. But the Arabic religion was accepted everywhere, if in a heretical form in some parts of the empire, and Islam spread in the Far East without benefit of conquest. The religion of Islam was a truly native product, with its desert origin plainly marked upon it. But the subtle minds of the Persian theologians transformed even this religion, developing a true theology out of it, while continuing to maintain the integrity of the Koran and its divine inspiration. The other great contribution, in addition to the dynamism and leadership provided, was the incomparable Arabic language. The Koran may not be translated into any other language, according to the law of Islam. And the Koran must be read by all the faithful. Therefore it was necessary to learn Arabic, which became, as Greek had once been, the common language of the whole empire and of the whole area converted to the religion of Islam. It is true that the original language was greatly altered in its transmission through these lands. But it proved capable of meeting the demands made upon it. Words when necessary were imported from Greek, and words were invented to express the conceptions never needed in the lands of the desert. Arabic, with its delicate signs used so beautifully in decorative work designed in Muslim lands, has remained one of the great languages of the world, strengthened and enlarged through the centuries, but retaining still the marks of its Arab origin.

▶ ## The nature of Muslim culture

ATTITUDE OF THE MUSLIMS TOWARD LEARNING

As has already been said, the Arabs, unlike the Romans, were genuinely interested in learning. As a practical people, the Arabs were chiefly interested in science. But there were also many learned philosophers in the new Muslim Empire, though their influence was probably not as great as the quality of their work would have justified. Philosophy never seems to have become a regular subject of instruction in their universities, perhaps because of the difficulties that have always arisen when philosophy and revealed religion must be reconciled. The Muslims took from the people in their empire what interested them, and neglected the remainder. They did not, for instance, show any interest in Greek literature and poetry, probably because there was already a long Arab tradition in these fields and the work in the ancient Hellenic tradition did not lend itself to translation in the Arabic. Moreover, Greek

religion, which suffused Greek literature, would not be acceptable to confirmed believers in the Koran. No Roman work except the law seems to have come into their hands at all, showing that, with the exception of Spain, Latin knowledge had died out in the territories which they controlled.

In every field that they touched the Muslims added something of their own. Though they regarded Aristotle as the real master of philosophy, calling him simply "The Philosopher," they nevertheless tried to understand him, and the great Muslim philosophers took his work as the starting point and added commentaries, trying to explain and enlarge his often brief and cryptic remarks. They took the great synthesis of Greek scientific knowledge written by Claudius Ptolemy in the second century A.D. as the point of departure for their own science, and then added numerous observations to it, especially in the fields of optics and astronomy. And, being in contact with Hindu thought also, they added the mathematical knowledge of the Hindus to the work of Euclid and the great Greek geometricians, and they advanced trigonometry beyond the point that Ptolemy had reached in his fundamental work. These instances are only given here to suggest the kind of work that the Muslims performed; a later section will give more detail on their specific contributions. The Muslims were the heirs of all the ages up to their own time; and though little that is really new can be credited to them, they preserved the Greek and Persian heritages, added something of Hindu achievements, and even took a fundamental invention from China, paper. And this they handed on to the Western civilization intact and improved. And though much in Western civilization owed little to the Muslims, and their influence should not be exaggerated, nevertheless in theoretical and applied science their influence was crucial, as the large number of scientific words incorporated into Western languages sufficiently demonstrates, most of them words in daily use such as "algebra," "alcohol," "zenith," and "zero"; while Muslim commercial invention and innovations made possible the voyages of discovery, the exploitation of which led directly to the modern world.

Philosophy

If one reads through the work of a medieval thinker, such as Roger Bacon, who was interested in Muslim thought, one is at once struck by the very considerable number of Muslim philosophers whom he quotes as authority. But the two philosophers whose names appear most frequently are Avicenna and Averroës, as the Latins called them. Both men wrote extensive commentaries on Aristotle, but also did much serious thinking of their own.

Avicenna was a Persian who lived in the early eleventh century, and is known chiefly for his great *Canon* of medical knowledge. As a philosopher he was very popular with medieval scholars, since his ideas, which were almost as much Platonic as Aristotelian, were more easy to reconcile with religious teachings than were those of Aristotle. Plato's theories on the creation of the world, as given, for instance, in his dialogue the *Timaeus,* are not too far from those of medieval Christians, whereas Aristotle does not seem to have believed in a creation of the world by God at all. Astrology, a subject of absorbing interest to many medieval scholars, is also more easily fitted into a Platonic framework. Avicenna, when apparently commenting on Aristotle, introduces a considerable number of the ideas of Plato and the Neoplatonists, and his work did not arouse as much opposition in Christendom as that of Averroës, who was a more strict Aristotelian. Perhaps the most interesting original work of Avicenna concerns the nature of the human soul, where he uses his considerable knowledge of human physiology to supplement his philosophical considerations on the nature of the soul and its relation to the body.

Averroës was a Spanish Muslim who lived in the twelfth century, at a time when Spain was in the process of being conquered by the Christians, and the last defense was being put up by semicivilized Muslim immigrants from Africa. These fanatical Muslims disapproved of the work of Averroës, and it is said that they drove him from his native city of Cordova; they cared neither for his Aristotelian philosophy nor for its implications for Islam. So it happened that Averroës was never as highly regarded in the Muslim world as in the Christian, where his works were translated and appeared in Paris some forty years after his death. Averroës wrote what many consider even today as the best of all commentaries on Aristotle, and his reputation was such that medieval scholars called him simply "The Commentator." Very faithful to the original spirit, his writings are extremely objective and openminded, following the Master according to no preconceived ideas as to how he should be interpreted, in this differing from the medievals, who wished to reconcile him with Christian thought. Averroës came to some conclusions rather startling to medieval Christians, for instance, that Aristotle did not believe in the creation of the world. This would not have been so serious—and indeed Thomas Aquinas agreed that this was the correct interpretation of Aristotle—but Averroës also seemed to deny individual immortality. For him there was one great world soul into which all individual souls merged after death, thus admitting collective but not individual immortality. Whether this could be deduced from Aristotle is questionable; but at all events it was a theory which naturally offended both Christians and Muslims. Averroës, in defending his theory, was forced to the conclusion that there were different degrees of truth, the truth of religion to be accepted on faith, and the truth of philosophy which could be ascertained by the natural reason of man, and these sometimes appeared to be contradictory. This point of view was later in the medieval world known as Averroism, after the great Muslim philosopher. His theories caused considerable trouble at the University of Paris in the second half of the thirteenth century, and were later the basis for much original speculation in many fields at the University of Padua, which bore fruitful results in the scientific renaissance in Italy of the fifteenth and sixteenth centuries.

Science

Theoretical—Mathematics, physics, astronomy—The Muslims, curiously enough, are remembered in the field of mathematics chiefly for the "Arabic" numerals. These numerals, however, were not invented by the Arabs, nor, in fact, are the actual signs used of such supreme importance. Any signs whose meaning would be universally accepted would suffice, but, of course, preferably not letters, which were used as numbers by both Greeks and Romans. The signs themselves are modified from the Hindu. The importance of the numerals, however, lies in their combination with the zero, which may or may not also be Hindu. Spengler has argued interestingly that the Greeks, with their conception of geometry as the chief mathematical science and their tendency to regard all geometrical figures as actual substantial segments, bounded by lines, could never come to a conception of anything that was not, in some sense, a body; whereas the Hindus with their urge toward self-obliteration in nothingness, and their conception of the world as really nothing, an illusion, would naturally arrive at the idea of zero. So he insists that the Greeks could subdivide 1 an infinite number of times but never could conceive of zero being ever reached. However this may be, it is not as yet possible from records to determine whether the Hindus or the Muslims had priority in the invention of the zero. But at all events the epoch-making work in which the nine numerals and the zero are used, with the decimal positional system that had been known in a different form to both Babylonians and Egyptians, was written by one Al-Khwarizmi (flourished 810, from whose name comes our word "algorism"), and were later introduced to the Western world by Leonardo of Pisa at the beginning of the thirteenth century. The same Muslim mathematician wrote a basic textbook in algebra, which seems to have

been largely a Muslim invention (the word "algebra" is also Arabic), combining work done by the later Greek mathematicians and Hindus. The symbols used in algebra in the Western world were the work of a sixteenth-century Italian, Vieta. The elements of musical notation and the measurement of time values in music are also to be credited to Muslims, especially Al-Farabi (died 950). In the field of trigonometry, impressive work was also done by many Muslims using the basis laid by Ptolemy in his fundamental work on the subject.

In the field of physics the single great philosopher of the Arabic people, Al-Kindi (ninth century), wrote over two hundred works, especially in meteorology and optics. But he also worked out a complex theory concerning lines of force, or what the medievals called the "multiplication of species," based primarily upon optical observations. The physicist Al-Hazen (Al-Haitham, *ca.* 965–1039), wrote extensively on optics, including the reflection and refraction of rays, and put forward a theory of the manner in which the human eye is able to perceive objects which has many merits; it was accepted by most medievals who gave their attention to the subject, and perhaps is not altogether disproved today, though it is not presently in fashion. The great medieval bishop Robert Grosseteste was deeply indebted to Al-Hazen as was Roger Bacon.

The Muslims were greatly interested in astronomy, and many of their scientists wrote on the subject. But though they made many observations, they did not add much to the theoretical side of this science, since Ptolemy was regarded still as the great authority. Ptolemy's work was early translated under the title of the *Almagest* (Al-Majisti), by which it was known to the medievals when it was translated at the beginning of the thirteenth century. More Muslims were probably interested in the less scientific aspect of astronomy, preferring to draw astrological horoscopes for which, it would appear, there was a considerable demand in the Muslim world. Their astrology was also the basis for the medieval work in this field, which oc-

*An Arabic astrolabe. This instrument, which was suspended by the ring at its
top, was used to take bearings by the stars. The crosspiece, called the alidade,
was directed toward a particular star, and the navigator or astronomer took his
bearing by sighting along it. By the fourteenth century it was customary to use
two alidades and thus take a double bearing and calculate exactly the position
of the ship.* (COURTESY THE OWNER, MR. BARNEY OF NEW YORK. PHOTO BY
MORTON A. BERGER)

cupied the minds of enormous numbers of people till at least the late sixteenth century, though it was never approved of by the Church. The Muslims also perfected an astronomical instrument of great value, the astrolabe, with which to observe the movements of heavenly bodies.

Practical science—Medicine, chemistry, agriculture, geography—It has already been mentioned that heretic Christians, driven from Constantinople, founded an academy of medicine under Persian auspices before the Muslim invasions. These Hellenized Christians were soon persuaded to turn their accumulated learning into the Arabic language, and by the early ninth century the Muslims had at their disposal the whole body of Greek medical writings, including all the work of the school of Hippocrates and Galen. The Persians of Bagdad were the best physicians, and studied especially the diseases of the eye, which were so common in the Near East. But they were very careful observers of all diseases, and the greatest of their practicing physicians, Rhazes (Al-Razi), wrote more than a hundred separate medical works including a twenty-volume compendium of all the medical knowledge of the time. These books were in use in the Muslim world until as late as the nineteenth century. The most comprehensive of all the Muslim medical books was the *Canon* of Avicenna, who has already been referred to as a philosopher. In this work, in addition to careful descriptions, there is much very intelligent theory, having regard to the material at his disposal. It is not surprising that Jews and Muslims were greatly sought after in the Western world, whose own medicine even by late medieval times was a terrifying compound of superstition and quackery.

Muslim chemistry is not always judged fairly, owing to the prevalent belief in the transmutation of elements, the search for a universal catalyst (the philosopher's stone), and the diversion of intellectual and practical effort to these unprofitable pursuits. And in the practice of this science of alchemy there was much that we should call excessively mystical, even in the hands of the Muslims. But if we have lost our wonder at the marvelous transformations possible in the world of chemistry, this is not because there is nothing wonderful in it but because we have been so accustomed to think of all scientific wonders as commonplace. The fact remains that in their experimentations the Muslims discovered how to isolate many important chemicals, including sal ammoniac, saltpeter, and a number of oxides, and learned how to prepare sulfuric and nitric acids. There can be no doubt at all that Muslim alchemy laid the basis for modern chemistry by performing this pioneer work, whatever the objectives of their experimentation.

The Muslims made considerable progress in agriculture, especially in the science of irrigation. They improved the irrigation system in Egypt by carrying the Nile water further from the river and up slopes to higher ground; in Spain they brought water from the higher regions down to the plains which had always been arid. It is possible that Spain was never so well cultivated at any time in her history as under the Ommeyads. Vineyards were planted, and scientific methods of terracing were used, perhaps learned from the Far East. Cordova was noted for beautiful landscape gardening made possible by irrigation.

Muslim voyages into areas previously unknown to the West and the Near East made possible a great increase in geographical knowledge, and an improvement in map making. The best-known geographer, Al-Idrisi (1099–1154), was employed by the Normans in Sicily in the twelfth century, thus introducing the best geographical knowledge of the day into the West. The Muslims also introduced, if they did not invent, the crucial mariner's compass. The actual inventor is unknown.

Art

Architecture—The most characteristic Muslim structure is the mosque, which differs essentially from the Christian church or the Greek temple in that no provision had to be made for the celebration of the

Interior of Sultan Ahmed Mosque in Constantinople. (COURTESY TURKISH INFORMATION OFFICE)

Exterior of Mosque of Selim at Edirne (Adrianople). Note certain elements of similarity between this typical mosque and the Church of Hagia Sophia, which influenced so much of Muslim architecture. From the minarets the muezzin called to prayer. (COURTESY TURKISH INFORMATION OFFICE)

sacraments, nor was there, of course, any god to be housed in it. The Muslims, keeping strictly to the law against "graven images," allowed no representation in their mosques of either human beings or animals, thus limiting sculpture to flowers and leaves, but above all to geometrical patterns which reached a high degree of intricacy and beauty of design (arabesques). On the other hand, since the Koran must be read publicly, a pulpit was necessary; a place must be provided for the ritual washing; and from the mosque the muezzin called to prayer. For the last-named function the Muslims added to their mosques the graceful minaret, so characteristic a feature of all Muslim ecclesiastical architecture— which was, as usual, copied by other peoples who did not use it for any such purpose.

In other hands the minaret, when used, became mere decoration, like the Roman and Renaissance columns which supported nothing. The campanile, or bell tower, of Christian churches, however, was often imitated from the design of the Muslim minaret. The Muslims used many different forms of the arch, especially developing the horseshoe arch, almost a signature of Muslim architecture. For decoration the Muslims, like the Byzantines, excelled in mosaic, the use of colored glass, stone, and other materials fitted into a decorative design. This seems to have been a Persian invention taken over by both Byzantines and the later Muslims. The dome, brought to perfection by the architects of Justinian, was almost universal in Muslim architecture.

Applied arts—Muslim craftsmen were

Decorated introductory page of a sixteenth-century Persian book. The geometrical patterns are called arabesques; they were much used by the Muslims, who were forbidden by their religion to use so many forms approved of in other religions. (COURTESY THE METROPOLITAN MUSEUM OF ART)

A Moorish temple in Tetuán, Spanish Morocco, features a horse-shoe arch typical of Moorish architecture. (COURTESY THE SPANISH STATE TOURIST DEPARTMENT)

Arabesque decorations on a fourteenth-century Persian tombstone. Note the similarity between these decorations and those on the book shown previously. (COURTESY THE METROPOLITAN MUSEUM OF ART)

The Persians have always been noted for the exquisite design of their rugs. Here is a sixteenth-century example. (COURTESY THE METROPOLITAN MUSEUM OF ART)

noted throughout the world for the excellence of their handwork, their only competitor being the Byzantine Empire. The process known as damascening, the inlaying of gold and silver on cheaper metals, was called after the city of Damascus and was a Muslim invention. Persian carpets are still famous today. The tooling of leather was a specialty (morocco, cordova), and swords and rapiers of Toledo steel were valued by Christian knights as the finest weapons in the medieval world. The designing of silks, brocades, muslins, and other materials was brought to high perfection and many of the materials used still keep their Arabic names (damask, muslin).

Literature

When we think of Arabic literature we think almost automatically of the *Rubáiyát* of Omar Khayyam and the *Arabian Nights*. The former, written by a Persian mathematician, gives expression to the refined hedonism and polite fatalism of late Muslim Persia, and is, of course, known to the West through its very free translation by Edward Fitzgerald, so that the poem is better known perhaps in English-speaking countries than in its native Persia, where Omar was only one of many great poets. The *Thousand and One Nights* reflects the society of Bagdad in the time of Harun-al-Rashid, who appears in many of the tales in person. Arabs had always been fond of storytelling, even in the days before Mahomet, and this is one of many collections which was to exercise a considerable influence upon medieval and even modern storytellers. Boccaccio especially was influenced by the mode; though as a rule he wrote on contemporary themes, nevertheless many of his stories made use of those of his Arabic predecessors. The minstrels of Spain had a decisive influence on Provençal medieval poetry associated with the troubadours, and for a long time the whole civilization of Provence, so ruthlessly destroyed in the Albigensian Crusade, was indebted to the Muslim culture of Spain.

Throughout Muslim civilization there were always historians of talent, culminating, long after the civilization was in full decay, in the first great secular philosophy of history written by Ibn Khaldun (1332–1406), the great merits of which are only in very recent times beginning to be discovered, having been reintroduced to the Western world in part by the efforts of Toynbee, whose work lies in a similar field. Ibn Khaldun wrote a penetrating study of the causes for the success of the original Arab invasions, which is as full of remarkable generalizations as the works of Thucydides, though, for the most part, it is concerned with the nature of nomad peoples and their peculiar ethos, and why they were able to conquer the sedentary peoples with so much ease. He came to the conclusion that it was impossible for such conquests to survive unless the conquerors were held together by a religion, in spite of the fact that the nomads possessed an *esprit de corps* (*'asabiyah*) and unity of purpose denied to the sedentary peoples. The study of the growth and decay of the Muslim Empire leads him to make further generalizations about the rise and fall of all empires in terms of the degree of *'asabiyah* of the people and the corruption of the bourgeoisie by luxury and lack of opportunity for dangerous living. Ibn Khaldun's experience and knowledge of history were limited in scope, and it would be impossible for us to sustain his generalizations on the basis of our fuller knowledge. But Thucydides also had an equally limited experience and knowledge, and it is with the great Greek historian that Ibn Khaldun may not unfairly be compared. It is enough to say that it is by no means certain that, having regard to the material available to each, the Muslim historian would come off second best.

▶ Decay of Muslim civilization

Muslim civilization was unable to recover from the political disasters that overtook it from the eleventh century onward. The Seljuk Turks from Central Asia took over the Abbasid Empire of Bagdad, as we have seen (1055–1258). These Turks remained imperfectly civilized, although there was still enough cultural resilience in Islam for Islamic civilization to hold its own for some centuries. Then an even more barbarous group, the Ottoman Turks, took over from their Seljuk brethren. They consolidated much of eastern Europe and the Near East into a new political unit known as the Ottoman Empire, already briefly discussed in the previous chapter. Though in some respects the Turks took over the worst features of the Byzantine Empire, with corrupt and despotic provincial governors and oppressive taxation, in other respects the government was distinctively oriental. The sultan was an absolute ruler and his officials and soldiers were his slaves. An important contingent in his army was the corps of Janissaries, Christians who had been forced into his service when children, and later converted to Islam and trained as warriors. Soon after the subjugation of the Byzantine Empire the Turkish sultan became the caliph, called the "Commander of the Faithful."

But they laid a dead hand upon Islam. They themselves were strict Muslims, and under their rule the fatalism that was always implicit in Islam became increasingly the dominant attitude among Muslims. Some of the great cities survived, but grievously depopulated, while the implacable hostility of the Christians, whose civilization was growing as Muslim civilization declined, also served to prevent the cultural interpenetration that might have infused new life into the ancient Muslim civilization. Only in the present century have there appeared signs of a cultural renascence in Islam, though now under the spur of nationalism.

▶ Summary and conclusion

The achievements of Muslim civilization have sometimes been minimized and sometimes exaggerated, especially by scholars who have enjoyed contrasting medieval European backwardness, lack of science, and superstition with Muslim enlightenment. The Muslims were not on the whole great creators and innovators, but they were incomparable imitators and assimilators. For many centuries they acted as the sole bridge between East and West. They studied Greek science, neglected and almost unknown in the West of the day, and they studied and translated Greek philosophy. They did not add much to Plato and Aristotle beyond commentaries, but they added a great deal to Hellenistic science from their own thinking and observations. And they were able to make use of Hindu speculation and discoveries hitherto unknown in Europe. Their medicine, both theory and practice, was renowned in Europe, and the first European medical school at Salerno was originally staffed by Muslims.

They were an extremely mobile people, and their traveling merchants carried more than news and gossip and geographical information over the thousands of miles of their trade routes. They carried Persian techniques and manufacturing processes into Spain and Sicily and so ultimately into Christian Europe. They navigated the seas and brought the perfected astrolabe, quadrant, and mariner's compass to the West. Their storytellers provided the basis for much of medieval European literature. If the West had had to discover for itself all that the Muslims taught it, Western civilization might have been delayed for centuries.

But it is hardly fair to judge the Muslims by what they gave to the West, great though our debt is to them. Anyone who visits southern Spain today and sees the ruins of the great works of the Muslims, who looks at the arid lands which were made to blossom by Muslim genius and are now desolate, does not need to be reminded that this was a great civilization in its own right, and that the peoples who worshiped the one God Allah, whose prophet was Mahomet, do not need to fear comparison with the greatest there have been—even though their genius has been overshadowed in recent centuries by the expansionism and 'asabiyah of the Christians, and of the Western civilization which has flourished as it has, at least in part by virtue of its own heritage from the Muslims.

▶ Suggestions for further reading

It is very difficult to find western studies of Islam which are free from the besetting sin of the West, that is, underestimating or even despising Islam as an inferior and derivative religion, in spite of the undoubted fact of its survival as a living force after so many centuries. Likewise, accounts written by believing Muslims are inclined to take the western attitude into consideration and to assume the form of apologetics if addressed to the western world. Perhaps the most successful attempt at objectivity is the admirable short survey in the Home University Library, by H. A. R. Gibb, *Mohammedanism, a Historical Survey* (London: Oxford University Press, 1949). Another recent survey by a noted Arabist is A. Guillaume, *Islam* (Harmondsworth, Middlesex: Penguin Books, 1954). A series of lectures by a well-known oriental scholar, T. W. Arnold, *The Caliphate* (Oxford: The Clarendon Press, 1924), gives a succinct account of the relation between Muslim political life and Muslim religion. It is difficult to extract this information from the fuller books available on the subject, in spite of its great importance. Another series of lectures, by a well-known legal writer, D. S. Margoliouth, *The Early Development of Mohammedanism* (London: Constable & Co., Ltd., 1926), explains in a clear and concise manner the relationship between Islamic law and the teachings of the Koran. It goes without saying that some parts of the Koran itself should be read, though none of the translations known to the author is really adequate, and it is perhaps truly untranslatable into any western tongue.

In general, the series of books with such titles as the *Legacy of Greece* and the *Legacy of Rome* are not recommended for the beginning student, as they are either too full of unknown names, too technical in content, or too compressed to be really useful. An exception must be made, however, for T. W. Arnold and A. Guillaume, eds., *The Legacy of Islam* (Oxford: The Clarendon Press, 1931), in which many sections are admirably done; the material is difficult, if not impossible, to find elsewhere in English except in highly specialized works. The chapters on geography and commerce, and especially those on the minor arts in which the Muslims excelled, are highly recommended. Those on law and literature are also first-rate and do not suffer from excessive profusion of names, in spite of being reasonably comprehensive. It is still difficult to find in English any accounts of Mus-

lim science that are at all adequate. An old nineteenth-century work which was extremely influential in drawing attention in the West to our astonishing neglect of this subject is still worth looking into, although it is extremely pugnacious and although the author was deliberately overstating his case, especially against the medieval thinkers who had, in his now outmoded view, neglected and even persecuted science. This is J. W. Draper, *History of the Intellectual Development of Europe* (2 vols., rev. ed.; New York: Harper & Brothers, 1899), especially Vol. I, Chap. 13, and Vol. II, Chap. 2. On the whole, in spite of certain inadequacies, the two books by DeLacy O'Leary, *Arabic Thought and Its Place in History* (rev. ed.; New York: E. P. Dutton & Co., Inc., 1939), and *How Greek Science Passed to the Arabs* (London: Routledge & Kegan Paul, Ltd., 1949), are probably the best introduction for the English-speaking student. The thumbnail sketches of the great Muslim scientists given in G. Sarton, *Introduction to the History of Science* (Baltimore: The Williams and Wilkins Company, 1931), Vols. I and II, are always well considered, and if further study is desired, this great historian of science refers to as many works as were available in 1931. Lynn Thorndike, *A History of Magic and Experimental Science* (New York: The Macmillan Company, 1923), Vols. I and II, offers a fuller account of a number of outstanding Muslim scientists.

V Civilization of the Middle Ages in Europe

Manorial tenant touching his cap to his lord.
From a Book of Hours *(Flemish),* ca. *1515.*
(COURTESY THE PIERPONT MORGAN LIBRARY. Ms.
399, folio 4)

10

Political and Social Structure of the Early Middle Ages

The Frankish kingdom in the eighth century • The Papacy in the eighth century • The Carolingian Empire • The successors of Charlemagne • Renewed invasion by barbarians in the ninth century • The feudal system • The manorial system: economic basis of feudalism

▶ The Frankish kingdom in the eighth century

In Chapter 7 we saw that the Merovingian kingdom of the Franks had fallen under the control of stewards of the king's household (mayors of the palace), a position which had become hereditary. Charles Martel, one of these mayors, had succeeded in uniting the Franks under his command against the Muslims, defeating them, with the aid of the Lombards from northern Italy, in 732 at the battle of "Tours." The prestige gained by this victory enabled Charles to maintain his ascendancy over both the feeble kings and the warring lords of his realm. He also added to his kingdom by further victories against various Germanic peoples which had hitherto never been brought under Frankish control and were still pagan. He worked closely with the great English missionary and church organizer St. Boniface, who himself admitted that his work of conversion could hardly have proceeded without the aid of the sword of Charles.

When Charles died, leaving his position and lands to his two sons in accordance with Frankish custom, his work might have come to a sudden end. Fortunately one of these sons abdicated his position and went into a monastery, leaving the kingdom, of which Charles had been king in everything but name, to Pepin the Short (Pepin III) (752–768).

It should be recognized that it was a work of the utmost difficulty to keep together the Frankish kingdom, which, in the centuries since Clovis, had sometimes been split into as many as three separate kingdoms, each under a Merovingian king and his mayor. Furthermore there were many powerful nobles scattered throughout the country whose allegiance to the crown was, as a rule, only nominal, and who exercised almost complete control within their dominions. All through the Merovingian age there had been a gradual growth of feudalism, a decentralized form of social and political organization under which military protection was provided locally by landowners. The rise of feudalism, in other words, was a process of decentralization, in the course of which real power slipped into the hands of noble landowners, who alone were in a position to provide protection. Such protection, of course, was the theoretical prerogative of the king, but too often he was not in a position to assert it. Since, however, the process of feudalization was held up to some degree under the effective rule of the Carolingian family (so called from Charlemagne, or Carolus Magnus, its greatest representative), it can be better discussed after the collapse of the Carolingian Empire.

Charles Martel had been content with the real power in France, and had not troubled himself about the title of king. One of his ancestors had tried prematurely to dispose of the reigning Merovingian monarch and had been killed by the outraged nobles, who evidently preferred a puppet to a real monarch; so Charles may have thought it wiser not to stir up gratuitous trouble for himself. But Pepin, his son, wanted to regularize his position. The Merovingian monarchs had held their office by descent from Clovis, who had been supported by the papacy after his conversion to Christianity, and had been crowned king by an archbishop. It occurred, therefore, to Pepin that the act which he proposed of setting aside this legitimate king could best be sanctioned by the pope as head of Christendom; and Pepin was prepared to pay a high price for this sanction. Hence he did not at once proclaim himself king, preferring to send the

pope a message gently inquiring whether it was fitter for the one who held the power to be king, or the one who held the title but no power. This message, ostensibly a request for a ruling from the head of Christendom on a question of abstract justice, had evidently been carefully prepared by Pepin and his advisers, probably including St. Boniface; in a masterful manner it gave the pope time to think over all the implications, while at the same time it did not require him to interfere in a political matter outside his competence, thereby perhaps setting an unwelcome precedent.

▶ **The Papacy in the eighth century**

RELATIONS WITH CONSTANTINOPLE

The iconoclastic controversy

It is necessary here to consider the position of the papacy at this time in some detail, since from this request of Pepin onward the pope was deep in European politics. The favorable answer he gave to Pepin had momentous results for the Church, setting in motion the train of events which ultimately precipitated the contest between the Church and the State for the successorship of the Roman Empire.

As explained in Chapter 7, Pope

▶ **chronological chart**

Frankish kingdom and Carolingian Empire		Papacy	
Merovingian kingdom	486–751	Lombard conquest of Italy	568
Charles Martel becomes Mayor of Palace	714	Leo III of Constantinople forbids use of images	726
Battle of "Tours"—Victory of Charles over Muslims	732	Iconoclastic controversy	726–843
Pepin the Short elected king by Frankish nobles	752	Aistulf becomes king of Lombards	749
Donation of Pepin to papacy	756	Pope Stephen II crowns Pepin king of Franks	754
Muslims retreat over Pyrenees	759	Charlemagne crowned emperor by Pope Leo III	800
Accession of Charlemagne	768	Otto the Great crowned emperor by pope	962

Carolingian Empire

Charlemagne defeats Lombards and assumes title of king	773–774
Battle of Roncesvalles—Defeat of Charlemagne's army under Roland in Spain	778
Charlemagne completes conquest of Saxons	785
Charlemagne conquers Bavarians	787–788
Charlemagne conquers Avars	795–796
Charlemagne crowned emperor by Pope Leo III	800
Establishment of the Spanish March	801
Introduction of system of *missi dominici*	802
Treaty with Constantinople— Recognition of Charlemagne by Nicephorus, Byzantine emperor	803
Death of Charlemagne	814

The successors of Charlemagne

Louis the Debonair (814–840) agrees to the division of his kingdom among his three sons	817
Louis makes second division of kingdom to include youngest son, Charles the Bald	838
Death of Louis—Succession of Lothair as emperor	840
Oaths of Strasbourg	842
Treaty of Verdun	843
Division of Empire at death of Lothair	855
Charles the Fat, emperor and king of East and West Franks (West Franks 884–887)	881–887
Paris defended by Odo against Northmen	886
Deposition of Charles the Fat	887
Robert, Count of Paris and brother of Odo, elected king of France	922
Death of Robert	923
Hugh Capet king of France	987
Henry the Fowler king of Germany	919–936
Accession of Otto the Great	936
First expedition of Otto to Italy	951–952
Second expedition of Otto to Italy	961–964
Otto the Great crowned emperor by pope	962

Invasions of Magyars

Magyars cross Carpathians into Central Europe	*ca.* 895
Magyars defeated by Henry the Fowler	933
Battle of Augsburg—Magyars defeated by Otto I	955
Magyars accept Christianity (missionaries from East and West)	974 onward
St. Stephen I king of Magyars (Hungary)—Completion of conversion of Hungarians to Roman Catholic Christianity	997–1038

Invasions of Northmen

First invasions of England by Northmen (Danes)	787
Continuous invasions of England	856–875
Foundation of Novgorod by Swedes	862
Alfred the Great, king of England— Danes checked	871–900
Colonization of Iceland by Northmen	874
Siege of Paris by Northmen	886
Foundation of Kiev by Swedes	about 900
Rollo becomes Duke of Normandy	911
Colonization of Greenland by Northmen	981
Sweyn (Sven) Danish king of England	1013–1014
Canute (Cnut) king of England	1017–1035
Normans conquer southern Italy from Byzantines	1042–1068
Invasion of England by Harold Hardrada of Norway	1066
Defeat and death of Harold Hardrada at Stamford Bridge (September)	1066
Invasion of England by Duke William of Normandy—Battle of Hastings (October)	1066
Normans conquer Sicily from Muslims	1072–1091
Norman sack of Rome (Robert Guiscard)	1084
Norman kingdom of Sicily	1091–1266

Gregory I and his successors acknowledged the temporal overlordship of the Byzantine Empire, while refusing to admit that the emperor had any right to interfere in spiritual matters. Nevertheless, as we have seen in Chapter 8, the emperors continued to appoint their own patriarchs in Constantinople, and regarded themselves as head of both church and state in their own realms, which included the extreme southern part of Italy, where they usually exercised effective jurisdiction. Relations between pope and emperor were rarely cordial, especially when the emperors set themselves up as theologians; but there were few open quarrels until the emperor Leo III took a step of such importance in a field clearly outside his competence as a mere temporal ruler that the Pope felt himself obliged to make vehement protest, and mobilized all his forces to resist. This, of course, was the iconoclastic controversy, already described, set in motion by the decrees of Leo in 725.

The papacy, which never had any sympathy with the iconoclastic movement, did everything in its power to stop it, ultimately even excommunicating all iconoclasts. But the emperors, with the exception of two women who held the throne, were for a century iconoclasts, and the whole movement deeply embittered the papacy against the Byzantine Empire.

Thus it happened that in 751 when, as has been noted, Pope Zacharias was in difficulties with the Lombards, and his request for aid went unheeded by the emperor Constantine V, one of the strictest of the iconoclasts, the pontiff was certainly relieved to find an alternative and more acceptable champion in Frankland.

THE DANGER FROM THE LOMBARDS

For thirty years the papacy had been in danger from a revived Lombard kingdom in northern and central Italy. The Lombards since their conversion to Catholic Christianity were no longer so barbarous as at the time of their invasion of Italy in the years following 568. Indeed, they had been largely assimilated with the Italians and were already adopting the modified Latin which ultimately became the Italian language. They presented, however, a serious danger to the temporal power of the papacy, which had been reasonably undisturbed during the period of Byzantine overlordship. Yet, as we have seen, the papacy could hardly expect much help from Constantinople when the throne was occupied by an iconoclast, even though the request was formally made, on this as on several other occasions. There was only one direction to turn—and the pope had already turned there soon after the battle of "Tours." But Charles Martel had refused, not wishing to fight the Lombard king who had done yeoman service on his behalf at that battle.

With the accession of a new Lombard king, Aistulf, who conquered Ravenna, the last foothold of the Byzantine Empire in northern Italy, and was evidently preparing a march on Rome itself to round out a complete conquest of northern and central Italy, the papal position was serious indeed. It was at this opportune moment that Zacharias received Pepin's request for a ruling on the Merovingian kingdom. This request must have seemed like an answer to prayer.

PAPAL ACCEPTANCE OF FRANKISH HELP

Of course the papacy could have become, as it finally did in 1870, a purely spiritual power, with no claim to earthly rulership over any territories whatever. But, as earlier chapters have shown, for centuries it had actually ruled over Rome and the area around Rome, as well as over various scattered lands in Italy. These secured to it an income which, if not sufficient for its needs, was at least safe, and could be collected without difficulty. In that age when communications were always threatened, when obedience to the papacy was by no means universal, when local prelates could hold up donations to the papacy made by the faithful, it would have seemed madness to rely upon anything except the effective possession of land for the expenses of the Holy See. To have allowed Rome to be captured by the Lombards, however faithful to the Church they might be, would have been to put the papacy in perpetual danger from a secular power, and would have made even spiritual independence impossible. Lombards could have forced whatever appointments from the papacy they wished. If the popes must be dependent upon any secular power, then it would surely be better to have that power a distant one, allowing at least intervals of independence when direct force was unavailable.

Zacharias must have known at once that it would be possible to persuade Pepin now to undertake the task refused by his father. He therefore sent back the message that he who held the power should also have the title. Pepin took the hint, was formally elected king by his nobles, sending the young incumbent to a monastery. Then, a few weeks later, the new king was crowned, probably by St. Boniface himself (752). The throne was in the eyes of all a gift from the Church; in return the throne was expected to constitute itself protector of the Church. The Frankish kingdom had always been a useful support for the papacy since the days of Clovis; now, in the hour of danger, it was to take its full position of leadership.

It was two years before the Lombards made any dangerous move. Then, when they suddenly became threatening, Pope Stephen II himself voyaged over the Alps and anointed Pepin with the sacred oil, a supreme gesture, for Pepin was the first king ever to be anointed by a pope. Pepin cooperated with an assault on the Lombards which was completely successful. After his victory he presented the pope with symbolic keys, and gave him the overlordship not only of papal lands taken by the Lombards, but of the exarchate of Ravenna taken by the Lombards from the Byzantine Empire. Pepin himself took the title of *patricius* of Rome, a late imperial title given to successful generals. This made him the official protector of the Papal States.

DONATION OF PEPIN—PSEUDO DONATION OF CONSTANTINE

The pope, by this donation of Pepin, was now the temporal monarch of a compact kingdom in central Italy which cut a swath across the Lombard possessions and for centuries made the unification of Italy impossible under any secular ruler. The popes held onto this kingdom, with brief intervals when some of it was temporarily conquered, for over eleven hundred years.

The pope may have had some misgivings about the cavalier manner in which the Byzantines had been robbed of their territory. It seems probable, therefore, that it was about this time that the famous forged document known as the Donation of Constantine was made known. This curious document purported to have been written by the great emperor Constantine I, the founder of Constantinople. The emperor, so the document stated, having been healed of leprosy by the pope, embraced Christianity and decided to leave Rome forever, giving it, together with all his western dominions, to the pope and his successors. While the forgers were about it, they took the opportunity to emphasize that, in Constantine's view, the pope was to be "highest and chief of all priests in the whole world," superior to the throne of the emperor, and with rule over all the other sees in Christendom. "The sacred see of Peter shall be gloriously exalted above our empire and earthly throne." Anything less likely to have come from Constantine the Great, the father of all Caesaropapists, and perhaps the most authoritarian of all Roman emperors, can hardly be imagined; but this pious forgery was believed by the faithful to be genuine until Lorenzo Valla, a fifteenth-century humanist, showed conclusively that its Latin was not the Latin of the Age of Constantine. But for many centuries to come numerous popes were to quote it as authority for their claims.

Pepin was succeeded in 768 by his two sons. But one died early, leaving Charles, known as Charles the Great or Charlemagne (or, in Latin, Carolus Magnus), as sole ruler (768–814). When the Lombards attacked the papal possessions again, the new pope again called to the king of the Franks for aid. Charles descended swiftly on Italy, deposed the king of the Lombards, took all the remaining Lombard possessions, and became king of the Lombards himself. He confirmed the Donation of Pepin, but also made it clear that his new Italian possessions belonged to the Frankish Empire, with the pope holding the Papal States under his authority. Of the relationship between the pope and the secular ruler as Charlemagne conceived it, we shall have occasion to speak in a later section.

▶ **The Carolingian Empire**

THE IMPERIAL DREAM

The feudal reality

By all odds, Charlemagne, son of Pepin, is the most considerable figure of the Dark Ages, whose name became legendary within a few years of his death. As a conqueror and administrator he was the equal of all but the very greatest in history. And yet the bulk of his work died with him. He set back the growing tide of feudalism for a few generations, he forced the heathen Saxons into the fold of Christianity, and by his imperial patronage of education he helped to reawaken the desire for learning which had for centuries been slowly dying on the continent of Europe. These achievements, great as they may appear in relation to those of others in the Dark Ages,[1] are small in comparison with his fame. For it was not given to any in his own day to realize the general futility of his policy; and only with the hindsight of the historian can the inevitable failure of his out-of-date Roman imperial dream be judged.

[1] The term "Dark Ages" is by no means acceptable to all scholars, but for various reasons it seems to the present writer to be justifiable. It is used in this book to designate the period of time between the fall of the Roman Empire and the eleventh century.

It is sometimes said that the destruction of his work was simply a consequence of the fact that the Germanic practice of dividing an inheritance among all the sons was not abandoned in favor of handing it intact to the eldest (primogeniture). But, even if this reform had been possible, a question begged by holders of that view, the causes of Charlemagne's ultimate failure lie deeper. It was not possible to impose an imperial system upon a decentralized agricultural society, as has already been pointed out in the chapter on the fall of Rome. The strong hand and watchful eye of Charlemagne, combined with his imperial prestige, might compel the landowners into obedience for a time; but the real power was theirs, not his. They possessed the means for enforcing law in their realms; all the wearer of the crown could do was try to make them enforce it on his behalf and in accordance with his wishes, something they would only do as long as it suited them. Charlemagne's army was drawn from his own lands, the lands over which he was the effective chief. Outside these he was dependent upon what the landowners were willing to provide him. He could hold their loyalty while he was alive; in some cases it had been he who first gave them their land out of his conquests and endowed them with the rank necessary to make their rule legitimate. They would be grateful to him, loyal to him while he lived, but their separate interests were diametrically opposed to those of any monarchy, and their gratitude could not be expected to extend to his successors.

So monarchy or empire could not be a solution to the political ills of the time; it could not be superimposed upon a feudal structure and survive. In the later years of the Merovingian kingdom civil wars were incessant—and not simply due to the quarrels between rival kings. Rival lords quarreled too, joining one king or another according to their separate interests, but involved in the quarrel only because of local gains they hoped to make. After the death of Charlemagne the civil wars returned, more virulent and destructive than ever. The new national states had to be born before these civil wars could be quelled by superior power imposed by monarchs.

Caesaropapism—Supremacy of secular over spiritual power

But Charlemagne was a Christian as well as a secular ruler. And his biographer tells us that one of his favorite books was Augustine's *City of God*. There can be no doubt that he was greatly impressed by it, and what he gained from it is clearly to be seen in his policy. He conceived of a great Christian Empire, including, if possible, Constantinople, whose empress Irene he desired to marry. At all events the empire was to comprise the whole of his lands in the West, with himself exercising the temporal power; while the pope, approved of by him if not his own nominee, would exercise the spiritual power, and the emperor would see that the pope's commands were enforced.

Unfortunately the popes had a different version of the same dream. Their theory was exactly the opposite to that of Charlemagne. The pope, wielding the spiritual power, was naturally above the temporal, as the soul is superior to the body, and eternal life is superior to the temporal life on earth. As we shall see, this assertion of papal superiority ultimately brought the papacy into an irreconcilable conflict with the Empire, which forced it to use temporal as well as spiritual weapons. With these it was able to ruin the Empire, but in doing so it destroyed its own basis for even the universal spiritual dominion it had been offered by Charlemagne. Charlemagne was

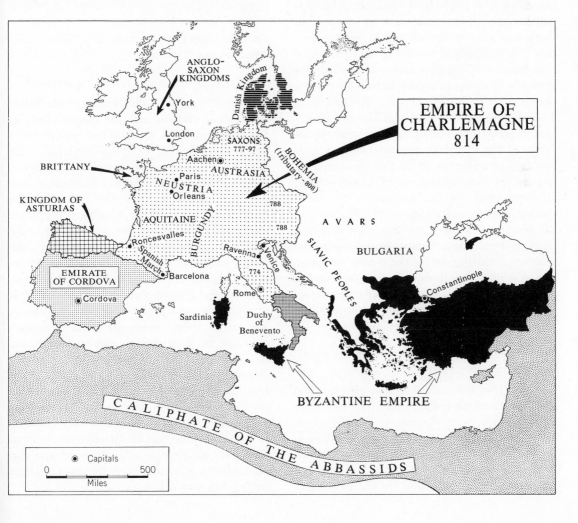

the only really effective Caesaropapist in the West, as his empire was the nearest approach to a restored Roman Empire. But the dream died hard, and many war-filled centuries were to pass before it was abandoned.

THE CONQUESTS OF CHARLEMAGNE

The Saxons

Although Charlemagne was engaged in almost continuous war throughout his reign, his main efforts were devoted to the conquest of the heathen Saxons. This Germanic people seems to have remained faithful to the ancient pagan gods, worshiping them to the accompaniment of many rites repulsive to the Christians. They resisted Charlemagne with cunning as well as force, frequently agreeing to a peace and submitting to conversion, and then breaking it as soon as his back was turned. It took thirty-two years of hard campaigning, fearful proscriptions of the Saxon leaders, massacres, and wholesale transfer of the population, before they were finally subdued and allowed the Christian churches to be organized in Saxony. If any Saxon refused to be baptized, or even broke some of the Christian customs such as fasting in Lent, he was to be put to death, according to the regulations of Charlemagne. Unfortunately for his successors, the campaigns were so exhausting to the Franks and so deeply embittered the Saxons that when new waves of barbarians broke upon the Empire from the north, these new enemies, the Vikings, found their task much easier than it would probably have been if the two peoples had not wasted their resources and man power in their fratricidal strife.

Other conquests—Bavaria, the Avars, the Spanish March

Bavaria was conquered and absorbed into the Frankish Empire, and the Avar state in Hungary was destroyed. Charlemagne also attempted the conquest of Muslim Spain, but was unable to make much headway, his rear guard being attacked and cut to pieces on one occasion by the independ-ent Christian Basques at Roncesvalles. The death of the Frankish commander Roland was immortalized in the earliest French epic, the *Chanson de Roland*. However, Charles was able to take some territory on the other side of the Pyrenees, which he organized into the Spanish March, later to be a bridge-head for the conquest of Spain.

To defend his new empire Charles made all his frontier territories into Marches, the defense of which he assigned to newly created Counts of the March (margraves, marquises), who became entirely independent in their new homes under his successors, though most of them were effective enough in their primary task of defending the empire against external enemies. He also founded monasteries in the newly conquered territories to assist in their conversion and purification.

THE ORGANIZATION OF THE CAROLINGIAN EMPIRE

Personal versus institutional government

Charles gave much thought to the internal organization of his vast empire; but, as has been indicated, it could not endure without his personality to guide it. Unlike the Romans, the Germanic peoples had no experience of, and no natural inclination for, rule by impersonal institutions based on an impersonal law. In an impersonal system, when an official dies there is another to take his place at once, and the institution continues to function. All our institutions today are of this character. When even the President of the United States dies, his office is at once assumed by his successor, and taxes are still collected, rents are paid, diplomats continue in their posts; essentially nothing is changed. This impersonality was the strength of the Roman system, and, as we have seen, the provincial administration continued even under the worst of emperors and during years of civil war. The Church was the only system of the Roman type in the Frankish Empire, and it could and did continue to function without great change under different rulers.

But the Germanic system was personal, and it was many centuries before institutions took over from persons. Government was based on a personal relationship between the governor and the governed. Loyalty was a personal thing, symbolized by oaths of allegiance and fealty. There might be a loyalty to a family, set apart as especially sacred, such as the families of chiefs and kings, but the relationship was still personal. The knight or noble held his sword at the disposal of the king, but not of the institution of kingship. Hence the extreme importance of having a king from a particular line; when the line failed, the necessary loyalty of the subject too often failed with it.

Another interesting contrast between the Frankish and Roman conceptions is the importance given in Frankish life to the officers of the household who performed personal and direct services for the monarch, and were thus in close daily association with him. As we have seen, Charlemagne's own family rose to power through holding the office of chief steward of the Merovingian king. The emperor's own chief official was the chamberlain or governor of the palace; next in line came the seneschal, who managed his goods and estates; the marshal, who was in charge of his stable and came to have command of the army; and the butler, who had charge of his wine cellar and vineyards. These tasks were considered by the Germanic peoples as the greatest honor the king could bestow, and the positions were of the highest importance and prestige. At Rome such tasks would have been considered beneath the dignity of nobles and reserved for freedmen and slaves. The German tradition, however, was maintained in Europe, and to this day such positions as the king's chamberlain and the queen's ladies in waiting in England are reserved for the highest nobility.

Administrative regulations of Charlemagne—Capitularies

Charlemagne was a very energetic man, and we are fortunate to possess his instructions (*capitularies*) to his officials, by which he tried to govern his vast realm. But few

hold more than a passing interest, since no one considered himself bound by them once Charles was no longer there to enforce them. Many of them are concerned with the management of the emperor's many estates, and go into the greatest detail in such matters as the furnishings for the rooms in his manor houses and palaces, methods of keeping accounts and taking inventory, useful no doubt as showing the best custom of the time and probably followed by many managers of large estates. He issued regulations for the conduct of courts, and stated who should attend them. He divided his empire into counties, marking the boundaries of the jurisdiction of each court. He codified the laws for the different peoples of the empire who had as yet no written codes, though the Germanic basis was, of course, retained.

The *missi dominici*

To see whether his interests were being properly looked after, Charles sent out two officials whose task it was to inquire whether justice was being properly done and to listen to complaints. These men, called *missi dominici*, or royal messengers, were armed with his own personal authority. One was always a cleric, usually a bishop, while the other was a layman. It is possible that in this system, though it died out with Charles, lay the germ of the idea of itinerant justices, first sent out in England by the Norman King Henry I, probably following Norman custom of the day. Out of these circuit judges developed the English system of regular assizes, the basis for the administration of criminal law in England to this day.

CROWNING OF CHARLEMAGNE AS ROMAN EMPEROR—SIGNIFICANCE

Toward the end of his reign Charles reached the height of his prestige on being crowned Charles Augustus, Emperor of the Romans, by the pope. Einhard, his biographer, says that he was so averse to receiving the title at the hands of the pope that he would not have gone to the church that day if he had known what to expect, although it was the day of a great festival.

A medieval illustrator's idea of the coronation of Charlemagne. From Christ-Herre Chronik, ca. *1400.* (COURTESY THE PIERPONT MORGAN LIBRARY. Ms. 769, folio 340)

This remark has given much trouble to scholars, many of whom have found themselves unable to believe that Charles knew nothing about the event until it happened, and have doubted whether the reluctance was anything more than a piece of assumed modesty. To understand his position it is necessary to consider in some detail the circumstances of the crowning.

Pope Leo III had been subjected to many indignities at the hands of his council and local nobles. They justified themselves by accusing him of perjury and adultery. Finally escaping from them, Leo made his way over the Alps to Germany and threw himself upon the mercy of Charles himself, pleading for protection. His accusers followed him there to repeat the charges in front of the king. Charles, as we have seen, regarded himself as protector of the whole Church; with his ideas on the proper function of the papacy as the regulator of the spiritual life of Christendom, he thought it of the utmost importance that the pope's authority should not be questioned except by the protector. So he placed the suppliant under his protection and sent him to Rome to await his arrival, when he would hear the case in front of a council. On reaching Rome at the end of the year 800, Charlemagne had evidently decided that

it would be a dangerous precedent if a pope were to be condemned by any council. He therefore allowed Leo to declare his innocence under oath, according to German law; then, regarding him as acquitted, he reinstated him as pope. Two days later, on Christmas Day 800, Leo anointed Charles Emperor of the Romans, at a time when Charles was unable to escape, during the Christmas service in the cathedral.

Now it seems at first sight inconceivable to us that Leo would not have consulted Charles in advance, when he was so obviously in the king's power. But at the Christmas festival Charles was in no position to refuse the pope's honor, because for once it was the pope's day; he was in charge of the service and not the king. It is possible that Charles would some time have proclaimed himself emperor, and would have called upon the pope to crown him, thus avoiding any appearance of granting the pope the right to make emperors, with the corresponding right of refusing to make them. But Charles would hardly have chosen that particular moment, when it looked to the whole congregation that the pope was conferring a dignity upon the emperor of his own free will. From Leo's point of view, it would seem that he could strengthen his own position by anointing the emperor without permission, for Charles could not repudiate him without repudiating the crown at the same time. And since he wanted the crown, that alternative was closed. Henceforth the emperor must support the pope against the latter's personal enemies, or admit that he had been crowned by unworthy hands.

The coronation had the effect that Leo had probably foreseen. Once the precedent had been established, it was accepted throughout Christendom that the pope had the right to crown the emperor; and many popes used this power as a lever to extract concessions from imperial candidates before agreeing to perform the ceremony. In a later time the papacy used the precedent to prove that the Church alone possessed from God the power to crown emperors and kings, and

The coronation chair of Charlemagne at Aachen. (COURTESY GERMAN TOURIST INFORMA-
TION OFFICE)

was thus superior to them, even claiming that Leo had, by virtue of his spiritual authority, transferred the crown from the unworthy head of the notoriously dissolute Empress Irene of Constantinople to the loyal son of the Church who ruled the Western world from Aachen. That Charles had understood the implications of his coronation is confirmed by the action that he took the year before his death in having his own son crown himself emperor rather than accept the crown at the hands of a pope.

Having accepted his title, Charles now realized it would have to be made legitimate, for, after all, there was another theoretical emperor of the Romans at Constantinople. And as Irene was deposed in 802 he could no longer hope to unite the empires by marriage. Charles hastened to make a treaty with her successor. In exchange for some of his eastern territories his title was recognized, and the Roman Empire was duly established as it had been after Constantine, an emperor in the East and one in the West dividing the actual rule, while the empire itself was, as always, theoretically one and indivisible.

This monumental piece of archaism, this desire to return to a past which could never be restored, is a tribute to the hold that the old Roman Empire still had on the minds of men, and speaks volumes for the political conservatism of both the clerical and lay leaders of the time. It also demonstrates the power of an idea to create and mold institutions; but its sequel also demonstrates in an unexceptionable manner a further truth which has not lost its validity—that an idea cannot prevail unless it is in accordance with the political, social, and economic realities of the time. For Charles's empire almost immediately disintegrated after his death, and not all the efforts of his successors could put it together again.

"THE CAROLINGIAN RENAISSANCE"

The educational work of Charlemagne will be left to a later chapter. All that is necessary to say here is that, in conformity with his policy of using clerics in his govern-

ment, these must at least be able, unlike the emperor himself, to read and write. The monasteries under the Benedictine Rule did not emphasize learning, though the monks received the rudiments of education, and many spent their spare time copying manuscripts. It was possible for students to go to a monastery to study, but it was inconvenient. Though the monasteries were usually far from the important centers, for the next few centuries they continued to hold their own until they were to a large degree replaced by the cathedral schools, which will be dealt with in Chapter 13. Charles encouraged the monasteries to devote more time to teaching and study, but he also founded an important school of his own which was attached to his palace at Aachen (Aix-la-Chapelle). Since at that time he was the only patron of learning on a large scale, this school served to attract scholars from all over the empire and from outside it. In particular he skimmed the scholarly cream from England, the country which was at the time most advanced in scholarship. This movement is sometimes grandiloquently called the "Carolingian Renaissance." It was certainly a step in the right direction, though on a very small scale, and entirely dependent upon the patronage of the monarch. The real medieval renaissance had to wait for a few more centuries, as we shall see. But such as it was, the Carolingian Renaissance will be discussed in the chapter on medieval culture.

▶ **The successors of Charlemagne**

THE DIVISION OF THE EMPIRE

Charles had not been long in his grave before the Empire began to break up into semi-independent segments, as was to be expected. Since he had only one surviving son, the Empire passed intact to him, with the title of Emperor, which as has been seen, he had Louis assume without benefit of the papacy. Louis, however, called the Debonair, later allowed himself to be recrowned by the pope, and immediately afterward took steps to regulate the succession. He was no longer a young man, and he had three grown-up sons, Lothair, Pepin, and Louis. In a solemn assembly in 817, attended by churchmen and the nobility, he declared that the Empire was to go to the eldest, Lothair, while the two younger sons were to have two territories of their own, one in the east containing Bavaria and the Eastern March, and one in the west, Aquitaine and the Spanish March, with the title of king which they could pass on to their successors. Both, however, were to be subordinate to Lothair, were forbidden to carry out an independent policy, and were to contribute to his expenses from their own revenues. This scheme, evidently an attempt under clerical influence to mitigate the Germanic system of dividing an inheritance into equal parts, was approved by all present at the assembly who swore to uphold it. Then Louis proceeded to spoil it all by marrying for the second time. The new empress, a self-willed young Bavarian girl, apparently chosen by the emperor in the ninth-century equivalent of the modern beauty contest, provided him with another heir, who was later to be known as Charles the Bald. The young empress then insisted on a kingdom for her son, too, a request which her fond husband found it impossible to refuse. But the bishops insisted that he keep to his arrangements, the elder sons also had something to say on the matter, and the nobles began, rather naturally, to fish in the troubled waters. But Louis and his empress were adamant.

In the course of a confused twenty years Louis was deposed, publicly confessed his sins and was restored; intermittent civil war broke out in different parts of the realm; and Charles the Bald grew up to manhood, presumably losing his hair in the process. Meanwhile one of the emperor's sons, Pepin, had died; but the arrangement of 817 had long ago been abandoned. Louis himself died in 840. The Empire was divided between his surviving sons; but, though Lothair still retained the title of Emperor, he no longer had the supreme position guaranteed to him twenty-three years before.

Discontented with the division, the two younger brothers made an alliance against him, making an oath to be faithful to each other, each swearing in the vernacular language of the other. These Strasbourg Oaths (842) are of fundamental importance for the study of the evolving language of the period, since Charles swore in German and Louis in Gallicized Latin. The purpose of taking the oath in different languages seems to have been to enable the soldiers on each side to understand the nature of the alliance, for the two brothers themselves must have spoken a tongue they both could understand.

Louis and Charles succeeded in inflicting such a defeat on Lothair that he quickly came to terms, embodied in the Treaty of Verdun in 843. Under this arrangement Lothair kept his title of Emperor, but the territory of Charlemagne was divided into three parts, more or less equal in area, but with no regard to the defensibility or compactness of the segments. The emperor took both capitals, Rome and Aachen, and his territory was a comparatively narrow strip stretching all the way from the modern Netherlands almost to Naples in Italy (see map). The kingdom of Charles the Bald included everything to the west of Lothair's land, and the kingdom of Louis everything to the east. It has been suggested that the areas were chosen in this way in order to include the greatest possible variety of agricultural resources, since all the European varieties of climate are represented in each segment; it has also been suggested that it was divided according to the number of estates directly controlled in each by the Carolingian family. Possibly it was a combination of both these considerations. Nevertheless, it was a disastrous settlement on account of the lack of natural and defensible boundaries, and because it paid no attention to growing national differences. Ancient Gaul had to yield up part of its territories to Lothair, and it lost its Rhine boundary. The monstrous territory of Lothair, its northern part later to be called Lotharingia and still retaining the name of Lothringen (French, Lorraine), was to be disputed between

DIVISION OF
CHARLEMAGNE'S KINGDOM
AT TREATY OF VERDUN–843

0   100   200   ● Capitals
Miles

France and Germany even into the present century. The Italian part, separated from the German by the Alps, had to be reconquered by many generations of Germans under their emperors; for the tenacious efforts of the emperors and the popes to hold on to their territories in Italy was to prevent the formation of any national state of Italy until the nineteenth century. A case can be made out for this settlement as the most important treaty in the whole history of Europe, since it was signed at a period when the national

state was not yet born, but the gestation process was already far advanced. This arbitrary division of the Treaty of Verdun forced the nations into a mold not designed by nature, and which the ensuing wars were never able to change once and for all. The monarchs did not take the results of such subsequent wars as final, citing the ancient treaty as their authority for renewed efforts to change them. It is perhaps not altogether fruitless to speculate how different the future of Europe might have been if Louis the

Debonair had not been so debonair and had eschewed beauty contests, and if he had thus been survived by two sons instead of by three.

Lothair was able to hold his kingdom together till his death in 855, dividing it again in his will—the eldest son Louis taking Italy and the title of Emperor, while the others took the northern and southern halves of the remainder. Upon the premature death of Lothair II, king of Lotharingia, his uncles Charles the Bald (France) and Louis, perhaps better called by the German equivalent Ludwig, since he was the ruler of Germany, fought for the territory of Lotharingia. First one gained it, and then the other, thus setting an example for later kings who disputed the possession of the fair lands of Lorraine. Sundry premature deaths succeeded in uniting the whole territory for a brief period under Charles the Fat of Germany, but his cowardice in the face of the Viking invasions persuaded the nobles to depose him, bringing the Empire in the west to an inglorious end in 888. Thereupon the western kingdom was given to Odo, the defender of Paris, while the Germans gave their half to a more valiant nephew of Charles. The imperial title, such as it was, was frequently disputed by several claimants, none of whom was accepted by the others. By the early tenth century it had ceased to be of any importance, no ruler of any distinction even bothering to claim it.

THE EMERGENCE OF THE FRENCH MONARCHY

But out of this anarchy emerged Odo as king of the Franks; and though the Church and Frankish nobles returned after his death to another Carolingian, the family of Odo was strong enough to reinstate his brother by 922. His grandson was the first of the continuous line of French kings, Hugh Capet (987–996), who was thus no descendant of Charlemagne, laid no claim to any imperial title, and possessed little but his own county of Paris. His claim to the throne rested on the valor of his great-uncle Odo, and the choice of his grandfather as king was the work of the nobles of France who elected him. This was the Capetian dynasty that was to unite France and provide, with the aid of the collateral branches of Valois and Bourbon, monarchs of legitimate descent until the French Revolution, and still provides a pretender to the French throne whose title, like that of Hugh Capet, is still the Count of Paris.

RESTORATION OF THE EMPIRE AS A GERMAN PRESERVE

The title of Emperor was extinguished when the last of the descendants of Charlemagne, Ludwig the Child, died in 911. The German nobles would hardly have looked to the last Carolingian now on the French throne (Charles the Simple) to set up as an emperor over them. They were by now entirely independent, and intended to remain so. But habit was strong and they returned to their ancient practice of electing a king as a kind of leader of the independent tribal duchies. After the death of the first of these they turned to the most powerful lord, Duke Henry (Henry the Fowler) of Saxony (919–936). He justified the choice by leading the Germans against the invading Magyars and thoroughly defeating them. He was also successful in incorporating the whole of Lorraine within his territory. When he died he left the throne to Otto I, who was formally elected without opposition.

But without any dangerous enemies abroad, Otto's lords became rebellious, and, while still quite young, Otto had to decide how he was to make himself an effective king and not be a king in name only, a king to be overthrown by rebellion as soon as his lords combined against him. He was by far the strongest lord in Germany, as far as his lands were concerned, and his feudal army was perhaps the equal of any two that could be brought against him. But he could not fight them all alone if they united against him. He needed powerful allies, and there was just one place open to him. This was the Church.

The Church had certain manifest advantages as an ally. It possessed the best administrators in the realm, it had an efficient working organization, and it was controlled by the higher clergy under the nominal, but not in this age effective, control of the papacy. What was necessary if the Church organization were to be used for the benefit of the kingdom of Germany was that Otto as king should make all the appointments, without the approval of the papacy. The obvious way to accomplish this was to constitute himself, like Charlemagne, the protector of the papacy, and control the appointment even of the popes themselves. The higher clergy in Germany were drawn from the feudal families, but their position could not be inherited, in part owing to the canon law against the marriage of the clergy, which was not too strictly observed, and because in any case all appointments lapsed at the death of the incumbent. Otto here was in a strong position. He had the right to appoint all the higher clergy in his realm, and they needed the land which he alone could give them, since they had no other regular source of income.

Thus was inaugurated the policy of what was later called lay investiture, which, though it was not new with Otto, was carefully systematized by him. The bishops were tied to him by feudal tenure, required to provide both military and financial aid from their territories. Certainly the Ottonian bishops were not noted for their piety, but he was careful to appoint competent and loyal administrators, his first appointments, indeed, being made from his own very competent family. Many of these clerics actually went to war themselves on his behalf, some of them becoming noted warriors, no doubt the envy of Otto's brother rulers in Europe. In short, the German Church, though partially independent, like other feudal magnates, usually lent its aid to the monarch, helping him to keep the lay feudal nobles in their place.

In 951 the first opportunity occurred to interfere in Italy. The Lombards had revived their kingship, but it was ineffectual, and the greater part of Italy had become the prey of rival lords. Taking advantage of a dispute over the Lombard crown, Otto made short work of the pretender, married the widow of the previous king, and became king of the Lombards himself, a title, it will be remembered, once held by Charlemagne. Recalled to Germany by renewed pressure from the Magyars, he was summoned for aid by a pope (John XII) in 961 against, as usual, the Lombards. This time after his customary victory over the Lombard nobles he forced the pope to crown him emperor, later to be called the Holy Roman Emperor. At the same time he extracted a formal promise, from a council called for the purpose, that his confirmation was to be required for all elections to the papacy.

The Roman nobles who for many years had been accustomed to this privilege, usually electing one of the feeblest of their own number, objected; and as soon as Otto had left they proceeded to elect a pope of their own. Otto returned, ousted the Roman choice and put in his own nominee. When this one, too, was driven out the new emperor lost his patience, returned with yet another army, and inflicted a sanguinary punishment on the rebels. Thereafter Rome was quiet. The emperor had established the right to approve of the election of popes, he was likely to be untroubled by papal interference with his choice of the German clergy, and he was now the accepted overlord of Germany and Italy. And the Roman dream of Charlemagne had once more been revived, to the irreparable damage, as we shall see, of both countries.

The papacy still possessed its estates in Italy, now under the overlordship of the German emperor, but it had lost what authority it had over the German clergy, being no longer able to choose the appointees or invest them. A pope could not even hold his own office without imperial approval. He was as much a servant of the secular power as were ever the popes under Charlemagne. Yet, from the papal point of view, there was one advantage, slight as it was, that Otto had over Charlemagne. He was no theologian, and his appointees were not chosen for their piety. The Empire was thus vulnerable on religious grounds; a movement for the reform of the clergy would have the support of true Christians throughout Germany and the Christian world, and might even be fortunate enough to find some day a successor of Otto the Great who was himself a Christian before he was an emperor. And already, even in the darkest hour of the papacy, when the Holy See itself was a plaything of the Roman nobles, the reform movement had been set in motion which was ultimately to lead to the re-establishment of the authority of Church and papacy, and to the destruction of the Empire itself. This movement and its consequences will be described in the next chapter.

▶ **Renewed invasions by barbarians in the ninth century**

MUSLIM PIRACY AND MAGYAR RAIDS

We have been discussing the political changes in Europe, but the other causes and results of the long anarchy have yet to be considered.

Soon after the death of Charlemagne, Europe was again threatened by barbarian invaders; and this time there was no effective centralized monarchy to hold them

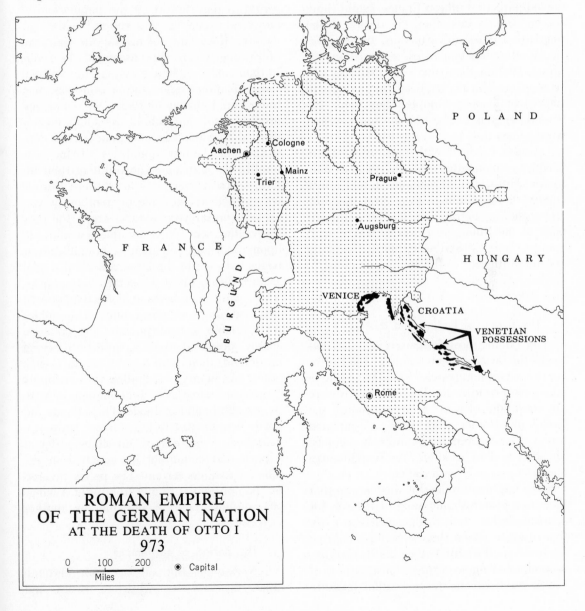

ROMAN EMPIRE
OF THE GERMAN NATION
AT THE DEATH OF OTTO I
973

0   100   200
Miles

⊙ Capital

back. The Germanic peoples had become sufficiently civilized for them to be able ultimately to absorb the invaders; but their defense against them was scattered, and for more than a century at least the Northmen could move into most parts of Europe without meeting serious resistance. The Muslims, working out of Tunis, terrorized the Mediterranean, occupied much of southern Italy until driven out by the "Macedonian" dynasty of Constantinople, which in the tenth century suddenly sprang into renewed activity; and for extended periods the Muslims also occupied parts of southern France, establishing centers from which they could prey upon unguarded cities and caravans, paying particular attention to parties of Christian pilgrims. Though they succeeded, as has been seen, in finally cutting off all Mediterranean trade from Constantinople, they were the least dangerous of the new invaders within Europe itself.

Magyars (dealt with in more detail in Chapter 8), another Asiatic people akin to the Huns, made repeated inroads into Europe, finally settling down, after they had on occasions penetrated even as far as the left bank of the Rhine, as a ruling class of warriors in Hungary, and accepting Christianity and the authority of the Roman Church.

THE NORTHMEN

The period of looting and destruction

By far the most dangerous and destructive of the invasions were made by the Northmen, a seafaring people from Scandinavia and of Germanic origin. These invasions were not migrations of peoples, at least not in the beginning. Rather were they well-planned forays of freebooters led by individual chiefs, sometimes called sea kings. The Scandinavian countries can only with difficulty support an extensive agriculture, and it was natural that their inhabitants should take to the sea for a living, and there is evidence that in early times they confined themselves to their role as traders. But from the ninth century, no doubt having seen the defenselessness of Europe, and driven by population pressure

on their limited resources, they expanded all over Northern Europe, including parts of Russia, where a Swedish inland state was set up which lasted for centuries; while in the West they settled the Faroes, Iceland, and southern Greenland; discovered America; and occupied parts of western Scotland and the Isle of Man.

In boats which would hold sixty warriors and using both sail and oars, these bands of still heathen Northmen, clad in chain mail and using the sword and the battle-ax, crossed to England, where for centuries they terrorized the population, at one time occupying and ruling most of the country; then they advanced to the mainland of Europe, where they ascended the rivers in their boats, pillaging and sacking without discrimination. When the season was over they would return to their own countries, leaving desolation behind them. They early learned that the Christian monasteries possessed the largest quantities of movable wealth, so these bore the brunt of their attacks. Almost every city in Western Europe was sacked at one time or another; it was useless for farmers to raise crops for they knew that soon the Northmen would fall upon them and rob them. Agriculture was neglected save in the large defended feudal estates; the only remedy seemed to be prayer, which was for a long time ineffective, though repeated daily in the Litany. The nobles were unable to unite against the common enemy, occupied as they were with trying to defend their own estates against each other, and in any case finding it exceedingly difficult to defeat such a mobile enemy with their earth-bound methods. The Vikings did not bother to wait to fight; if any army approached, it was easy to go off by water at a pace that could not be matched in the difficult roadless terrain. The policy favored by the nobles was simply to buy the Vikings off, sending them, if possible, in another direction.

The period of settlement

Normandy—But at last, not through great victories by Christian arms, but

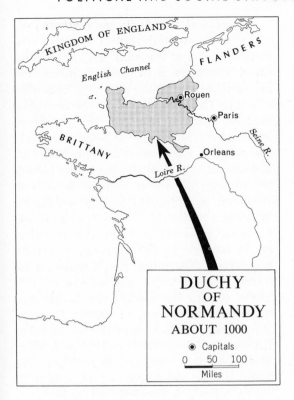

DUCHY
OF
NORMANDY
ABOUT 1000
⊙ Capitals
0   50   100
Miles

exchange for permission to live peaceably on his territory. As no one but these Northmen now owned it, Charles was glad to oblige. And though the actual homage ceremony was turned into a farce by the proud Northmen, Rollo did become the vassal of the French king, he and his descendants accepted Christianity, and a new state within the Frankish kingdom was formed.

England under the Northmen (Danes)— From the early ninth century the Northmen, called Danes by the English, began to send expeditions to England in force, sacking the principal towns throughout the south and east of England, including London. They defeated one king of the divided country after another until Alfred (871–900) king of Wessex (southwest England, West Saxons) began to build up an army of resistance, and ultimately to advance into the territory to the east, which had been altogether subdued by the invaders. At last he was able to sign a peace with them, under which he granted them the eastern lands of England which they had already acquired, on condition that they recognized him as king of all England, agreed to be his vassals (a similar arrangement to that made between Rollo and Charles the Simple), and formally accepted Christianity. The land was to be known henceforth as the Danelaw.

Neither party, however, was prepared to accept the division as permanent. The Danes encouraged continuous migration from their homeland, while the successors of Alfred, fired by his resistance, prepared to reconquer it. That work was completed in the first half of the tenth century, only to be endangered again when Ethelred (the Unready) became king of England while a new Danish pagan monarch made preparations for conquering not only the Danelaw but all England. Once again Ethelred started paying Danegeld (Winston Churchill in recent years used the same term to describe the appeasement of Hitler); whenever he ceased paying it the Danish king Sweyn (Sven), who had by now added the resources of Norway to his realm, descended upon England in force. At last he conquered the whole, and his son Canute

through the lack of further resources to plunder, the Northmen began to settle down, to bring their families with them, and to carve out territories where they would live permanently. They still sent out forays from their new homes into surrounding lands, but less regularly. And the Christians had begun to learn how to deal with them. The defenses of the riverside cities were strengthened, defensive castles were built by the nobles, and on a few occasions some great warrior would inflict a local defeat upon them. We have seen how Paris was defended by its count Odo; and though the emperor Charles the Fat raised the siege by paying unnecessary ransom (Danegeld) as usual, and directing the Vikings toward Burgundy, his cowardice cost him his throne, this very fact showing that the Franks now felt themselves strong enough to handle the invaders.

In 911 Rollo (Hrolf), who had taken possession of a part of northern France, later called Normandy, offered his allegiance to Charles the Simple, king of the Franks, in

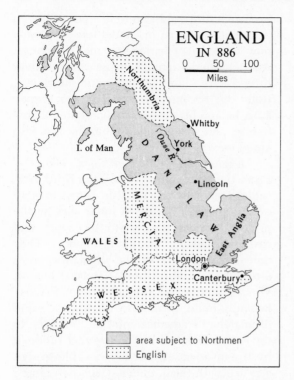

ENGLAND
IN 886

0　50　100
Miles

Northumbria

Whitby

I. of Man　Ouse R.　York

D A N E L A W

Lincoln

MERCIA

East Anglia

WALES

London

Canterbury

W E S S E X

▨ area subject to Northmen
▨ English

(Cnut), now a Christian, ruled over an England that was part of a large Scandinavian Empire (1017–1035).

After the death of King Canute's sons, who also sat briefly on the English throne, the Scandinavians allowed the succession to pass to an Englishman, a descendant of King Alfred the Great (Edward the Confessor, 1042–1066). When Edward died, however, leaving no direct heirs, the Norwegian king of the day, Harold Hardrada, decided that he would like to be king of England as well as of Norway, and launched an expedition against the nominee of the English lords, Harold the Saxon, son of Godwin. At the same time Duke William of Normandy, himself also a descendant of the Vikings, but lord of a far more civilized realm than the Norway of that era, claimed the English throne. The issue was decided by battle. Harold the Saxon defeated and killed Harold Hardrada, king of Norway, at Stamford Bridge, but succumbed in turn to the Norman knights under Duke William at the battle of Hastings (1066). Thus was founded the Norman monarchy of England, to be discussed at greater length in Chapter 15.

The kingdom of Sicily and southern Italy —Late in the eleventh century a further venturesome band of Normans, tired of peaceful life in Normandy, went in search of new land and adventures in Italy, under the leadership of Robert Guiscard (the Sly). The Byzantine Empire, which at that time ruled southern Italy, was having trouble at home with Turks and other peoples from the steppes of Asia. Robert had little difficulty in carving himself the duchies of Apulia and Calabria from Byzantine domains. The papacy, looking for allies against the German emperor, recognized the conquest, and Robert was willing to do homage to the pope in return for recognition. Thereafter the Normans, reinforced from home, began to expand into Sicily, winning the island from the Muslims by 1091. The nephew of Robert Guiscard was crowned in the ancient Muslim capital of Palermo on Christmas Day 1130 as King of Sicily, Apulia, and Calabria. Thus was founded the great Norman kingdom of "Sicily" of which we shall have occasion to speak later.

The Northmen—An estimate

The Northmen, Vikings, or Normans, were an extraordinary people. They came into a semicivilized world as wild heathen barbarians, the terror of all. Yet once they decided to accept the religion and civilization of the kingdoms they had so recently plundered, they showed a genius for government and administration hardly equaled by any other people in history. For centuries the kingdom of *Sicily* was the most tolerant, enlightened, cultured, and far the best governed state in Europe, though based on a decaying Muslim civilization. The Normans breathed new life into this Muslim culture, not destroying but assimilating it. With their ancient talent for seafaring and trade, they made full use of the commanding strategic position of Sicily in the Mediterranean Sea and developed the Sicilian capital of Palermo into the greatest and richest city in Europe outside Constantinople.

Normandy, the first territory granted to this gifted people, became quickly one of

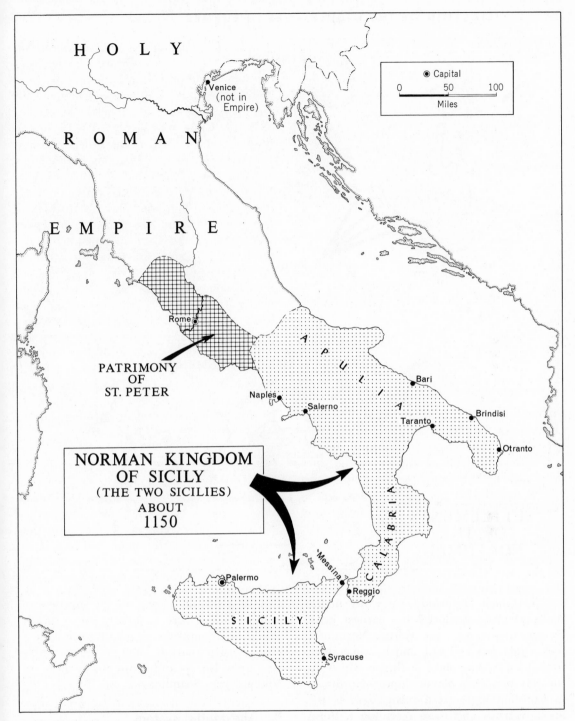

HOLY

ROMAN

EMPIRE

Venice
(not in
Empire)

Rome

PATRIMONY
OF
ST. PETER

Naples

Salerno

A P U L I A

Bari

Taranto

Brindisi

Otranto

NORMAN KINGDOM
OF SICILY
(THE TWO SICILIES)
ABOUT
1150

C A L A B R I A

Messina

Palermo

Reggio

S I C I L Y

Syracuse

Capital

0   50   100
Miles

the best organized parts of France, the
Norman rulers adapting to their use many
of the ancient institutions of France which
had not been effectively used since the
eighth and ninth centuries, when France had
been a part of Charlemagne's empire. *England* became a great nation primarily because

Duke William of Normandy and his successors on the English throne were able to
give it a strong feudal government, much
stronger than that of their Anglo-Saxon predecessors, while at the same time they put
to use what was best in the Anglo-Saxon
heritage.

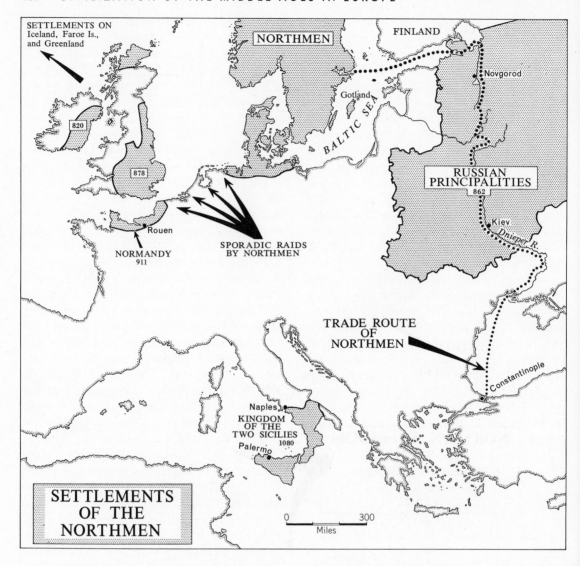

SETTLEMENTS ON Iceland, Faroe Is., and Greenland

NORTHMEN

FINLAND

Gotland

BALTIC SEA

Novgorod

820

878

RUSSIAN PRINCIPALITIES 862

Rouen

NORMANDY 911

SPORADIC RAIDS BY NORTHMEN

Kiev

Dnieper R.

TRADE ROUTE OF NORTHMEN

Constantinople

Naples
KINGDOM OF THE TWO SICILIES 1080
Palermo

SETTLEMENTS OF THE NORTHMEN

0   300
Miles

Northmen in *Iceland,* far away in the north Atlantic, produced the earliest great European literature, the Eddas. Northmen, meanwhile, led by Rurik and his successors, founded a trading state in *Russia* which ultimately became a Slavic empire; Northmen in Constantinople were recognized as the finest warriors and were recruited to form the emperor's bodyguard. Normans distinguished themselves in the Crusades, and were usually the acknowledged leaders; they were responsible for the Norman style of architecture (a modified form of Romanesque), and their monuments are still to be seen today dotted through the English and northern French countryside. It is difficult

to find a people among all the invaders of Europe who were evidently so naturally gifted or so versatile, or who have left their characteristic mark in such an unmistakable way upon European institutions as these ex-Vikings from Scandinavia.

▶ **The feudal system**

THE NATURE OF FEUDAL AUTHORITY—
ARBITRARY LOCAL POWER MODIFIED BY CUSTOM
AND MORAL SANCTIONS

Having seen the anarchy of the period after the death of Charlemagne and the breakup of his Empire, we now need to examine in more detail what it was that filled this political vacuum. Power, as always, continued to exist; but it was now widely diffused, and no longer exercised by a responsible government. Put briefly, the power relapsed into the hands of landowners who each possessed a private army supported from his own resources. But the power was not exercised in a completely arbitrary manner; there was a network of customary and legal sanctions upon its exercise which, though perhaps not as strong as sanctions exercised by monarchs who had armies and bureaucracies at their disposal to enforce their will, were nonetheless adequate to keep powerful landowners from doing everything that their fancy dictated.

We have already seen that in Egypt what has been loosely called a Feudal Age replaced the Divine Monarchy of the Old Kingdom. We know too little about this remote period to be able to state what sanctions there were upon the arbitrary power of Egyptian landowners. All we know is that the landowners appear to have assumed power after the breakdown of the monarchy. In the absence of such essential information we cannot call the age truly "feudal" in the way that the early Middle Ages were feudal. If we wish to be accurate, we must say that the only truly feudal age known to us is this medieval period, characterized by the holding of *feuda,* or fiefs.

The relationship between lord (suzerain)[2] and vassal, between the bestower and receiver of the fief, is the heart of the medieval feudal system; and the duties imposed on each party to the transaction by feudal law and custom are the chief sanctions on the arbitrary use of their power by either. A vassal had the power to go to war against his suzerain, and, indeed, only too frequently he did so; but, if he did, unless the suzerain had failed to perform his own duties, the vassal not only broke the feudal law and could be called to account for it in the feudal court of his lord, but also broke an oath of fealty which he had taken. And this itself,

in an age when an oath was taken upon the Cross or upon holy relics, and was considered sacred, was enough to brand him as a false knight and hold him up to infamy.

So the sanctions in the feudal system were both material and moral, as under any effective law. The difficulty was that too often the law could not be enforced, and it never could be enforced without war; hence a man might brave the moral sanctions if his material interests were involved and he thought he had a chance in the ensuing war. It was thus an ineffectual system rather than an arbitrary or immoral one; and since it was also an unequal one in that the peasants and lower classes had few rights, and those unenforceable without military power to back them, it was not one that would obtain the assent of more than a small minority. It was only likely to endure as long as the effective power could be kept within the small class of nobles. Later medieval and modern history can be viewed largely as the attempt to destroy the privileges of the upper class and replace them with a more equitable system giving more rights to ever-increasing numbers of people. The national state, under a monarch backed by a middle class which hardly existed in earlier medieval times, provided such a system, however imperfectly; and the establishment of national states in several European countries, coincident with the destruction of the greater part of the feudal system, will form a fitting climax to this account of the Western heritage from ancient times. With the establishment of national states modern political history really begins.

THE ORIGIN OF FEUDALISM

The Roman heritage

To trace back into the past the origins of such a mass of irrational customs and laws as the feudal system is not a very profitable task, though many scholars have devoted their lives to it without coming to any agreed conclusions. It would seem tolerably certain that feudalism derives from both Roman and Germanic sources. We have already seen that in late Roman society, when

[2] The word "suzerain" is used in this chapter to denote the superior lord in a lord-vassal relationship, although the word has in certain countries a definite technical meaning not applicable to all such overlords.

the barbarians were invading and the ordinary small landholders found difficulty in surviving without military protection, these latter would ask the nobility to protect them in exchange for what services they could give. This practice was called *patrocinium*, or patronage. As a rule military services were not required so much as cultivation of land, whether such land was given to the farmer by the lord or already belonged to him. This relationship between patron and client is entirely a late Roman feature, and has little to do with the patron-client relationship in earlier days, when the client was usually of the same social class but inferior in worldly goods.

During the period of the Merovingian kings there was as much danger to a small independent man as in the late Roman Empire. So we find in the early Middle Ages an established practice of *commendation* by a poor and landless man, who asked for protection from a noble in a better situation. The more powerful nobles could gather large bands of followers in this way; the greater they were, the more men would commend themselves to them, for the safer would be the protection. Some of these were lesser nobles themselves and not farmers, but for some reason they had lost their land. In these cases the patron after commendation would take them into his service as military followers.

Another heritage from Roman times was similar. A free farmer who suffered from insecurity or had fallen into debt could yield up his land either to his creditor or to some noble, and ask for it back again as a tenant. This was called *precarium*, or requesting. Another form of precarium was simply the prayer by a landless farmer for some land to cultivate in exchange for goods and services. Since the noble had far too much land to cultivate himself, it was to his advantage to give it out to a good tenant. So the precarium helped him to take care of his needs, and was mutually advantageous. The Church, in particular, found the system valuable. It was forbidden to alienate Church lands altogether, but a precarious tenancy permitted it to have its lands cultivated without losing them; and in feudal times it had enough sanctions of its own peculiar kind at its disposal for it to be as well able as the secular lord to protect its tenants.

The precarium by the eighth century had largely been replaced by the *beneficium*, or benefice, which was practically the same thing under a different name. Both were tantamount to leases of land for a limited period; but the later benefices rarely took land from freeholders and gave them back, for there was little such land available by this time. Benefices were given frequently by the great nobles to their officials and assistants in lieu of a money income. They were also given to lesser nobles who could provide great nobles with troops paid for out of the proceeds of the benefice. The Carolingian kings gave out such benefices freely, in many cases including an *immunity* from taxation and the performance of feudal services; then the land was held as a virtual freehold.

The Germanic heritage

The development from Roman times seems to be fairly clear. But in the system described above there seems to be an obvious parallel with the German custom of *comitatus* already noticed. Here, it will be remembered, the old warrior bands of Germans used to join the troop of an independent chieftain to whom they were bound by ties of honor and fealty and for whom they were ready to fight and die. It would seem that in the early feudal period before Charlemagne, Roman custom was predominant, and that the precarious system noted above arose in response to the definite needs of the time. But the necessity, under Germanic influence, became converted into a virtue; and all the ancient sanctions of the comitatus were gradually invoked to tie the lesser landholder and benefice holder to his lord. The moral sanctions now became established instead of sanctions that were only legal and instead of the ordinary ties of self-interest as between landlord and tenant. The vassal, as he shortly came to be called, owed loyalty and allegiance to his lord, a virtue conspicuously missing in late Roman and Merovingian times. This development corresponded with the increasing militarization of the whole society and with the rise of a class of nobles whose interest ceased to be in land. Though of course he had to own land, the noble gave out most of it again to vassals in exchange primarily, not for goods and ordinary menial and farming services, but for military service under his command.

It is now in this post-Carolingian period that feudalism based on the possession of fiefs comes to the fore. A fief was really only a hereditary benefice;[3] but almost invariably the obligation upon the vassal or fief holder was to supply warriors. Knights who could ride on horseback and provide their own equipment were the most valued. Anyone who could not do this was unlikely to be given a fief. Hence fief holders finally became warriors belonging to the class of the nobility, or churchmen with such warriors under them, who could perform the same service.

RELATIONSHIP BETWEEN LORD AND VASSAL

The theoretical relationship—Practical complications—Subinfeudation

The developed feudal system thus contained the lord or suzerain who held his land, originally or theoretically, by gift from the king, who was in theory the owner of all the land. This suzerain let out most of his land to vassals in exchange for military and certain other stipulated services to be described later; but he retained some land as a demesne from which he obtained the subsistence required for himself, his family, his personal landless military retainers, and his servants. The land received as fiefs by his vassals could also be subdivided, and let out again as fiefs to yet other vassals who would perform for them the same services as they themselves performed for their suzerains. This was a method of passing

on some of the military obligations to others, and was called *subinfeudation*. At times the greater lords tried to check excessive subinfeudation, since by it they tended to lose control of their subtenants, who owed them no direct allegiance, and could be reached only through their own personal vassals.

At this stage the process is not too complicated. Diagrammatically it would look like this:

King
↑
Suzerain 1
↑
Vassal 1 (himself a suzerain in relation to Vassal 2)
↑
Vassal 2
. . . . .

But unfortunately it was not in practice so simple. Any vassal could hold any number of fiefs from different suzerains; and sooner or later it would happen that, say, Vassal 2 in the above diagram would have let out part of his land as a fief to Suzerain 1, and would thus be in the relationship of a vassal to the vassal of this suzerain (Vassal 1), and yet be a suzerain in relation to the suzerain of his own suzerain! If this appears complicated, it is only a reflection of the actual state of feudal society, and may be illustrated in a more complex diagram (arrows indicate the direction of the services rendered).

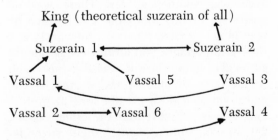

(part of Suzerain 2's land is held as a fief from Suzerain 1, and another part in a different locality he has let out to the same suzerain)

---

[3] A fief was not necessarily even land. Some honor or right could be held as a fief, entailing the usual obligations of a vassal.

Puzzle: What happens when Suzerain 2 decides he will cease performing feudal services for Suzerain 1, and what will Vassal 3 do when called out by his respective suzerains?

The answer to the puzzle is that, if a vassal was anxious to do the right thing, he would give his own personal service to one lord while allowing his own vassals to perform the remainder of his service. But clearly this would not hold good if he were called out by two lords at the same time who happened to be at war with one another.

It can be easily seen from these diagrams and examples that there was endless occasion for feudal wars. These could hardly have been avoided even if the feudal aristocracy had not in any case regarded war as a positive pleasure, their one great vocation in life, while they were content to hand over the management of their estates, from which they obtained their subsistence, to baseborn hirelings.

The legal structure—The feudal court

In order to enforce these rights the lord would periodically hold a court to which he summoned all his vassals. If any vassal did not appear without sufficient excuse, or if his equals in the court condemned him for failure to perform his proper feudal services, his fief could be forfeited. If he was accused by another vassal in his lord's court, he could claim the right to single combat with his accuser. If he lost, he was presumed to be guilty.

The enforcement of the decree, however, was another matter. There was no means for driving him from a fief which he held in actual possession save by war. It was thus of importance that all the vassals should sit on the court, since it was they also who would have to enforce the decree. If the guilty vassal had no greater lord to protect him, it was probable that the other vassals, fighting in unison under their suzerain, would succeed in compelling him to yield up the fief. It need hardly be emphasized how rough and ready such justice was; nor need it surprise us that many of the lesser

nobility in later centuries supported the efforts of the kings to establish a king's justice, containing elements of Roman law, in preference to the feudal variety.

The duties of the lord toward his vassal

The lord, of course, provided the vassal with his land in the first place. But it was also his duty to protect this land and the vassal from other lords or invaders. In this he was, in theory, only protecting his own land. It was also his duty to protect the vassal in other ways. If, for instance, a vassal were summoned to the king's court for an offense, as became possible when the kings began to hold courts for the administration of justice, it was the lord's duty to defend him. In theory, if the lord did not fulfill his obligation to protect the vassal, the contract was terminated, and the vassal no longer owed him allegiance. We find Pope Gregory VII later using this as an excuse for his deposition of the German Emperor, and it is the basis for the much later idea of the supposed Social Contract, under which, as expounded by the English theorist John Locke, the people were released from their allegiance to the king if he did not maintain their "natural rights."

The duties of the vassal toward his lord

The first duty of the vassal to his lord was allegiance, symbolized in the (Frankish) ceremony of homage. On being given or on inheriting a fief the vassal would kneel, place his two hands within those of his lord and declare himself his man. If the lord accepted the homage he kissed him as a sign of recognition of his vassalage. Since in theory a fief was not hereditary, an heir on coming into his father's estate had to do homage for his fief, which could, in theory also, be refused. In practice, the eldest son of a vassal inherited the fief of his father, and merely had to do homage for it, perform certain special services, and pay special dues, the equivalent of an inheritance tax. If a vassal died without male heirs, then the fief theoretically escheated to the suzerain, even if there was a surviving daughter.

But in practice this daughter inherited it, though the suzerain took her under his protection and saw that she was provided with a suitable husband, who then undertook the duties of the vassal. If there were no heirs, male or female, then the land did escheat, that is, it returned to the suzerain. The fief was not subdivided between many sons, but passed down intact to the eldest (primogeniture), who could, of course, let it out by subinfeudation if he desired.

The chief duty for most fief holders was to provide a stipulated number of knights, mounted warriors, calculated in accordance with the size of the fief. The custom, however, varied in different parts as indeed, did all the feudal arrangements. These warriors were bound to serve only for a definite, quite limited period, a fact which made long campaigns difficult. The period, as a rule, was forty days in each year. However, the lord could promise booty or other rewards and then have his vassals follow him voluntarily, as, for instance when William the Conqueror invaded England on the understanding that there would be new fiefs for all. In later medieval periods the military service could be commuted for a sum of money called *scutage*. This arrangement was more convenient for towns, in particular, if they happened to form part of a fief; and the money was often more appreciated by the lord than military service, since it enabled him to hire mercenaries who could serve for a longer period of time. The Church also on occasion paid scutage instead of military service, since it had more easy access to money than to warriors. Nevertheless, most ecclesiastical fiefs had some military service to perform, which was usually done by subinfeudation to lords who were willing to undertake the service.

The vassal had the duty of providing hospitality to his lord when he visited him. As this visit might be very expensive if the lord arrived with a large retinue, it was limited by custom and sometimes was commuted for a regular sum of money. The vassal also, as we have seen, had to attend the lord's court when requested.

When the lord was in financial difficulties, as for instance if he were trying to raise money to go on a crusade, the vassal could be called upon for a gift, known as an *aid*. At other times the aids were given for the ransoming of the lord, for the knighting of his eldest son, and for the marriage of his eldest daughter. These again were limited by custom according to the size and value of the fief.

A further sum of money was provided by the vassal on certain specified occasions, which was known as a *relief*. When an heir inherited his fief, it was customary to pay a relief, which might amount to as much as a whole year's revenue. When the lord himself died and was succeeded by his heir a relief was also paid. Finally when a vassal wished to transfer his fief to someone else, the equivalent of a sale, then he had to give a relief to the lord in exchange for his permission to the transfer. All these reliefs were fixed by custom, and when the money economy began to take the place of the earlier commodity economy the reliefs usually took the form of money payments. An heiress who wished to marry without the consent of the suzerain might persuade him to give it by offering him a sum of money. One of the best, if most irregular, sources of income for a lord was from the fief of a minor, or of an unmarried girl, whom he looked after till he or she came of age. The child for the time gave up what would have been his rights had he been of age to become a vassal, and the lord took the income from his estate. The lord did not have to reimburse the child for any losses that were sustained by such a child during his infancy.

It should be emphasized that the lord did not live off the income provided him by his vassals, which was quite limited and only given at irregular intervals. He lived off the income from his demesne, which contained his personal manors run by his servants. These will be dealt with in a later section. Every vassal belonged to the feudal nobility himself, and he always possessed a demesne of his own unless he were a personal retainer living with his lord, a situation which became rare in the later feudal age. The primary purpose of the feudal system was to provide warriors for protection and prestige. It was the manorial system, the private demesnes of these feudal lords, which provided the economic base for the feudal system. The feudal nobility therefore was a military aristocracy which incidentally owned land, rather than a landed aristocracy, which occasionally had to defend its property by military means, but at other times lived quietly, attending to its rural concerns. With the exception of the lord himself, the managers of the estates were of a different class from the nobility, were hired by them, and were treated as social inferiors. Most of the lords felt themselves too superior, and were too busy with their military affairs, to pay much attention to their estates. If this had not been so, they would not have given out so much of their land in financially unrewarding fiefs; they would, like the later Roman nobles, have lived in the lap of luxury from the intelligent exploitation of huge estates worked by laborers who could not rebel and could not leave the land.

The special position of the feudal king

In view of the later importance of kings a few words are necessary here on the anomalous position they occupied during the feudal age. Theoretically, as we have seen, the kings owned all the land, and every noble in a given country owed allegiance to his king. But, as a matter of historical fact, the greater nobles, perhaps the majority of them, had never even received their land from a king in the first place, but had taken it for themselves during the period of disintegration following the breakup of the Carolingian Empire. And the king exercised very little power over them. The king's effective power was only what he derived from his own feudal estates, which were often, as in the case of France, by design of the nobles smaller in extent than those of many of the lords who owed nominal allegiance to him. The French lords, in choosing their king

from the Capetian family, had probably agreed on the choice for the simple reason that he was less powerful than they, and thus likely to present little threat to their power.

The king's position was naturally different in each country, according to the local conditions found there. The German king, who was usually also at the same time the Holy Roman Emperor, was elected from among the German nobles; and, though there was a tendency to keep the office within certain families for long periods at a time, it never did become formally a hereditary position, and his power, as elsewhere, was derived from the estates of his house. After he had been elected king by the chief nobles, and later by certain of the higher clergy of his realm, he had only prestige in addition to what he had before, with two important exceptions. He had in his hands the appointment of the bulk of the higher clergy, a patronage that an astute monarch could manipulate to great advantage, and land left without heirs altogether would escheat to him and not to any other noble. His prestige and title gave him the first refusal of the command in any all-German or all-European war, such as the Crusades. When the emperors tried to make good their claim to Italy, and sent a regular "Roman expedition" of German warriors over the Alps, their leadership was not challenged. For the rest, the only real feudal tie between the nobles and their elected monarch was the oath of allegiance which they took to him after election; and, as we shall see, the right claimed by the papacy to absolve from oaths by virtue of its spiritual power was also used as a political instrument for the deposition of an emperor. When Gregory VII wished to depose Henry IV of Germany, a prerogative naturally contested bitterly by this emperor, he solemnly absolved all the German nobles from their oaths of allegiance so that they could elect another emperor.

In England after the conquest by Duke William of Normandy, the kings of his line actually did own all the land, since it had been acquired by conquest. They gave it out as fiefs, with certain restrictions on the raising of private armies which will be discussed in a later chapter on the rise of the English national state. It is only important here to notice that in England the theory corresponded to the actual facts, with incalculable advantages for the monarchy.

The position of the French king, however, is of the most interest, since the Capetian kings used their theoretical powers and their prestige to such good effect that they were ultimately able to unify France under their rule. Hugh Capet and his successors actually owned only a small compact area around Paris. They owned this as counts, and their armies were only such as could be drawn from this comparatively small territory. Yet, as kings, they were socially of a higher rank than any of the more powerful lords in their realm. They were solemnly anointed as kings by the archbishop of Rheims, and made to swear a coronation oath under which they promised to defend the humble, help the oppressed, preserve peace, maintain justice, and perform a number of other functions which were fantastically outside the scope of their real powers. But in theory they were expected to do this, and in their efforts they could usually count on the full support of the Church and the ecclesiastical officials, who had nothing, as a rule, to gain from the lawlessness created by the independent nobles. In addition the king held in his hands much of the best patronage of the Church, especially in northern France.

The king as theoretical owner of all the land in the territory vaguely called France was owed allegiance by all the lords in his realm. His prestige was such that most nobles, at all events those of French origin, usually did perform the act of homage once in their lives; it cost them nothing, since the king was not in a position to take away their fiefs, and they did not have to give him anything substantial unless he was in a position to compel them. He was theoretically entitled to the usual military service from them, and could summon them to his court for the administration of justice. None of these rights was worth much as long as the kings were unable to enforce them. But in a society which laid so much store by custom and loyalty they were not negligible. And the king had one immense advantage which was ultimately to prove crucial; if any lord did not obey the summons issued by him, then the lord was in the wrong. The king had the feudal law on his side if he went to war with the rebellious noble, and he had the right to call upon all the other lords in the kingdom to aid in punishing the rebel. Naturally the other nobles would consult their own interests in deciding whether or not they would obey the king; but it happened frequently enough that these interests would best be served by joining him and dispossessing the rebellious vassal. Philip Augustus used this power with extreme skill and effectiveness against his English vassal, John, king of England, who considered it beneath his dignity to attend the court of a man he considered his inferior and who owned far less land even in France than John himself. When John refused to obey his summons Philip called upon the other French nobles to dispossess him; and since John was regarded as an interloper in France and commanded few French sympathies, Philip was able to take away the bulk of his lands and bestow them on his own followers as fiefs; but with the great difference that Philip was now their real overlord and not merely a theoretical one.

Finally the king had all the social prestige belonging to his title. His wife would be queen, unlike the wife of any other noble, a position naturally sought after by heiresses; and their lands would serve to extend the feudal estates of the monarch while land without heirs would escheat to him. The king was often chosen as the most fitting protector of minors and of young women who had not yet found a suitable husband. And, like the German emperor, the French king[4] was the natural leader for a crusade or other foreign war if he wished to go. It

---

[4] Later chapters in this volume will deal briefly with other states than Germany and France, as well as go into more detail on the French monarchy.

can be seen, therefore, that in shrewd and able hands the position of king, in spite of his relative poverty, had certain manifest advantages over the rest of the feudal nobility; and perhaps it will no longer seem so strange that from these small beginnings the French monarchy was ultimately able to unify France and effectively control that feudal nobility which had elected him in the first place with far different expectations.

THE LIFE OF THE FEUDAL LORD

The feudal castle—Structure and purpose

The primary task of the feudal noble, as we have seen, was the provision of protection for his dependents. If he failed in this duty not only would he lose his retainers but he would also lose his very land to more warlike enemies. Especially during the invasions of the Northmen this duty was far from easy to fulfill. With only a small band of retainers he could not hope to meet an army in open combat, and there might be occasions when he could look for no help from either his lord or his fellow vassals. His only recourse, then, was to wall himself in, and keep the invading warriors out. Thus his home had to be fortified as strongly as his resources would permit.

The early castle was primitive enough. As a rule there had to be a moat or fosse, as an outer protection against invaders. Over the moat there had to be a bridge which could be raised and lowered at will. Invaders who tried to cross were at a disadvantage, for the defenders were able to discharge their weapons at them while keeping as far as possible out of sight themselves. Any house that could satisfy these conditions could be called a castle, although the earliest examples were only wooden affairs, not very large, with dark rooms and with slits for windows. Gradually, with the improvement of technique, the castles began to be

An impressive feudal castle in southern France (Les Baux en Provence) now in ruins. The castle commanded an extensive valley and was considered impregnable until it was captured in the time of Cardinal Richelieu. The village around it, which used to house some five thousand people, is now populated by a bare fifty.

This castle at Obidos (Portugal), only slightly restored, is now a government hotel. A picture of the town of Óbidos, which still has its medieval walls intact, appears in Chapter 14.

built of stone and to be larger and larger. A castle that was meant to withstand a siege had to contain within its walls storehouses for food, sufficient weapons and missiles and the means for making them, and shelter for all the defenders and their horses. While this was the minimum needed for purposes of defense, the castle was also the home of the lord and his family, and therefore needed some amenities. Later castles, therefore, were quite elaborate structures, serving for defense but also for display. Every castle maintained its inner portion in addition to the donjon or keep, a wooden or stone tower protected by its own portcullis (a grating made of strong bars of wood or iron, sharp pointed, which could be dropped suddenly in case of an attack) a drawbridge, and a moat. Here the last stand would be made in case of assault. The outer battlements were protected from attackers by walls which had smaller towers on them at intervals from which the defenders could discharge their missiles, and pour down boiling oil and other dangerous substances as well as rocks upon the besiegers, who were at a distinct disadvantage down below. Before the days of gunpowder and the cannon ball it was very difficult to storm a castle. Scaling ladders had to be used to reach the battlements, and

all the time that the besiegers were trying to place them in position and climb them the defenders were more or less immune from attack, and could use all the resources at their disposal to destroy the battering rams, the siege machines, and the other paraphernalia used against them. The usual way to take a castle in earlier days was to sit down in front of it and starve the defenders into submission. Hence the importance of making the castle as nearly self-sufficient as possible and thus continually increasing its size. There might be enough room even for the peasants of the noble to escape to the castle in the event of an attack.

In the later Middle Ages, when feudal warfare had been brought under some control, the castle became more of a home, the central point for the administration of the fief. Here the lord usually lived, surrounded by his officials and administrators, who stayed there permanently; but the lord himself, if he owned many estates, could live in one of his lesser manor houses if he preferred it. He had access to whatever luxuries were available, a diet largely of meat, cooked on open fires of charcoal or roasted on a spit above the fire, washed down by plenty of wine. Furnishings in the castle were primitive until trade with the East was opened

A medieval deer hunt. From Book of the King Modus *(French), ca. 1460.* (COURTESY THE PIERPONT MORGAN LIBRARY. Ms. 820, folio 12)

up after the Muslims had been driven from the Mediterranean; especially after the Crusades, rugs and tapestries became more frequent, and in the later Middle Ages fine tapestries were also manufactured in the West. But the castle rooms always remained rather dark and cheerless, though the great hall had dignity and spaciousness which in some degree compensated; and on the occasion of a feast, with minstrels and musicians and storytellers plying their arts, a feudal noble could feel that he had at hand everything that truly made life worth living.

Amusements of the feudal nobility

The chief amusement of a noble was warfare, in which he took a delight that was never altogether assuaged. If he could not indulge in this, then, in later ages, he made mock fights, called jousts or tournaments. In these elaborate imitations of the real thing all danger was not removed. Neither single combat between horsemen armed with the lance, nor mock battles between groups of knights on horseback lacked danger for the participants. In early times the armor consisted only of a shirt of mail reaching to the hips, and a helmet. But in later ages, when in fact the armored horseman was becoming an anachronism, vanquished by the crossbow, the longbow, and finally gunpowder, the armor became more elaborate and well made than ever, with the horse and its rider protected in every possible place. The result, of course, was that an unfortunate horseman became also immobile, and a fall from his horse might even have dangerous consequences. But it was when the feudal tradition was dying, and there was less serious warfare, that the tournaments reached their

Falconers show off their birds to a queen. From Book of the King Modus *(French), ca. 1460.* (COURTESY THE PIERPONT MORGAN LIBRARY. Ms. 820, folio 55)

Game of backgammon—not too dissimilar to our own game. From a miniature, Hugo von Trimberg, Der Renner, *fifteenth century.* (COURTESY THE PIERPONT MORGAN LIBRARY. Ms. 763, folio 134)

Woodcut from a Caxton printed book, showing a game of chess. From Jacobus de Cessolis, The Game and Play of Chess, *ca. 1482.* (COURTESY THE PIERPONT MORGAN LIBRARY)

This medieval miniature shows the Israelite general Joab entertaining Abner, whom he is planning to murder. As in all these miniatures, the picture faithfully represents the illustrator's contemporary experience, and the feasting scene depicted here is no doubt authentically medieval. From a Picture Bible *(French), ca. 1250.* (COURTESY THE PIERPONT MORGAN LIBRARY. Ms. 638, folio 37)

height. And if the dates of the armorial collections in our museums are ever examined, it will be noticed how many of the most decorative are fourteenth- and fifteenth- and even sixteenth-century manufactures, while the battle of Crécy in 1346 had already shown that the feudal chivalry of France was no match for the yeomanry of England armed with the longbow.

If they could not fight men, the nobles hunted animals. Every noble learned to hunt, not for food—though this was important too—but for pleasure and for the chance to exercise his skill in what became, and has remained, a ritual and a cult, reserved only for the feudal nobility. Above all in the later Middle Ages hunting with the falcon became the highest of skills; Emperor Frederic II

devoted a remarkable and scientific book to the *Art of Hunting with Birds,* in which he explains the ritual of hunting and goes into considerable detail on the different kinds of falcon and how they should be bred. Few activities of the noble were more damaging to his peasants, since all game was protected and there were very stringent and strictly enforced laws on the preservation of forests and woodlands. Moreover, the peasant was not allowed to touch even a rabbit himself, while the hunt was likely to destroy his standing crops if it passed through them. The practice of hunting has persisted in Europe long after other feudal vestiges have disappeared, and it has always remained the hallmark of a class. One does not need to be reminded of the late Marshal Goering's visits to Poland or the passion of the Archduke Francis Ferdinand for the chase (the prince who was murdered at Sarajevo), or the importance of August 12 in England and Scotland before the world wars (the opening of the grouse season) to realize how persistent this feudal prerogative has been.

Among less sanguinary sports could be mentioned games of dice, such as backgammon, and the mock battle of chess, introduced into the West at the end of eleventh century. An amusement seldom found among the feudal nobility, however, was reading. As a class nobles were not noted for their literacy, though there were some famous exceptions, notably Emperor Frederic himself.

The noble lady

The wife of the feudal lord, even though she had probably been married for her family connections and possible estates, nevertheless had a most important and no doubt insufficiently appreciated part to play in feudal society. The entire household arrangements of the castle fell within her province. And this, in an economy that tried to be self-sufficient, was no small task. She had to supervise the making of clothing and furnishings, she had to apportion tasks among the women of her entourage, and not infrequently she had to undertake the administrative duties of her husband as well. If he went on a crusade she had to manage the fief; if he were killed on campaign she had to undertake all his duties until she found herself a new husband or one was found for her by a relative or her husband's suzerain; or she would have to negotiate with her lord so that he gave her permission to remain a widow. She had to visit the peasants and tenantry on the estate, acting as Lady Bountiful, occasionally nursing the sick herself, or at least making arrangements for nursing care. In her spare time she plied her needle in embroidery and decorative work. Finally, at a pinch, she must be prepared to defend the castle in the absence of suitable males and to direct the lesser-born warriors on the battlements.

If a noble lady did not find a husband she could go to a convent; if she did not bear a child to her lord, preferably a male, then there was usually not too much difficulty in finding some cleric who would declare that the marriage was within the prohibited degrees and thus null and void from the beginning. This annulment was not hard to reconcile with a clerical conscience, since so many members of the privileged nobility were indeed closely related to each other. Marriage to a first cousin was considered too close, and it was likewise forbidden to marry various relatives who were related only by marriage.

In the later Middle Ages a movement sprang up, under the inspiration of some of the greatest of these ladies, especially Eleanor of Aquitaine, which made use of more romantic conceptions of womanhood than were current in real life. These tended to raise the ideal of womanhood, if not the status of women. This new ideal, called *chivalry*, will be discussed, however, in a later section of this chapter.

THE POSITION OF THE CHURCH IN THE FEUDAL SYSTEM

The Church as captive of the system

In the discussion of the relationship between the German emperor Otto I and his clergy, reference has already been made to the way in which the appointment of the higher clergy fell into the hands of the secular powers. In general, throughout Europe in the early Middle Ages the king and the nobility were the patrons of the Church and made all appointments, right down to the parish priests, who had the actual task of ministering to the spiritual needs of the people. The local higher clergy might have some say in the appointments, but since they too were drawn from the noble class this choice would probably not have been much improvement over the appointments made by the noble lords themselves. The quality of the clergy under these conditions was not likely to be high. Most appointments were made to relatives, to friends, or to those who could afford to buy them. The reason for this system of patronage was simply that the clergy, like everyone else, had to live. And they could live only if they were assured of a continuing income. This they could only gain from the possession of land; and the possession of land meant that they had to fulfill the feudal obligations that went with it. Otto I may have intentionally tried to recruit potential warriors into the Church hierarchy, but other rulers and nobles certainly chose their appointees from those who were noted for competence rather than for piety.

So the Church itself became part of the feudal system, with the higher clergy drawn from the feudal class and performing feudal duties in addition to their tasks as clerics. On the other hand, the Church did have one manifest advantage in a rude age; it had at its disposal all the powers of compulsion wielded by the nobility. The clergy could discipline their flocks, even if they had to bow to their own feudal overlords; and they had their own courts in which to try offenders against ecclesiastical law and regulations. They could enforce their decisions either by exacting spiritual punishments (penances) or by handing over offenders to the secular authorities. And on the whole, with certain notorious exceptions, it would seem that their influence was exercised in a more humane manner than the nobles used theirs; moreover, their influence on the nobility was not negligible, and probably greater than it would have been had they belonged to a different and more despised class.

Attitude of Church toward feudal system

For the papacy, as we shall see, feudalism was an enemy, to be controlled and if possible destroyed; but this point need not be labored further here. The papacy was naturally opposed to any decentralized system into which its own monarchical framework could not fit. Above all the clergy disapproved of the unlimited warfare of the feudal classes and tried their best to restrain it. They had no power to compel obedience; all they could use was moral suasion and the fact that the lords themselves were professing Christians. The first effective effort in this direction was the proclamation by councils throughout Europe of several "Peaces of God" which tried to protect certain classes of the people from the rapacity of the nobles. Merchants were to be protected, and, above all, the churches, the monasteries, and their inhabitants. Curses were also called down upon those who robbed the poor. These Peaces, proclaimed in 989 and on several occasions thereafter, had some effect, since certain Christian nobles took oaths not to do any of the forbidden things, at least for part of the year.

A further effort was made in the early eleventh century with the "Truce of God." Under threat of excommunication[5] private warfare was forbidden from sundown on Wednesday to sunrise on Monday, and for certain specified periods of the year. The hope was that the peasants would at least be able to undertake their planting and harvesting work without molestation. Again the edict was not everywhere, or perhaps even in most places, observed; but it had some effect, since at this time the kings were gaining more power and prestige, and it was to their advantage also to curb feudal warfare, except in their own interests. These efforts, at all events, showed that the Church was alive to some of the tasks required of it as a spiritual institution. The Church also made serious efforts as far as it could to mitigate the evils of the warfare when it could not stop them, and many cases are known of charitable efforts to help and protect the poor, orphans, and other unprotected members of feudal society. The warfare, however, was satisfactorily curbed only when the papacy was able to direct the more warlike spirits against the Muslims in Spain and Palestine; such warfare against infidels could be approved of wholeheartedly for the sake of its good cause.

It has already been noted how the French clergy gave continuous support to the king in his efforts to deal with his nobles.

[5] This and other Church penalties will be explained in the next chapter.

A jongleur and a medieval lady. Chansonnier Provençal *(Paduan), thirteenth century.* (COURTESY THE PIERPONT MORGAN LIBRARY. Ms. 819, folio 57)

This support was given even by some of the clergy who were appointed by other lords than the king. When there was a chance to support the king they did, but it was too difficult to quarrel with one's overlord for such clergy to be ready to take the risks involved in following a feeble king. When, however, the French kings began to increase in power, they had no more faithful supporters than the higher clergy.

Chivalry

As the Middle Ages approached their height a curious movement arose, partly literary in origin, which began to glorify the feudal ideals and separate them from the practices of the day, which were far from "noble" in our sense of the word. And this movement in turn had its effect upon the feudal practices, softening them and making them in fact more "noble," in this sense, than they had been. This movement was the cult of chivalry.

We have seen that in the ancient Germanic comitatus, loyalty was the highest virtue, and the personal relationship between the vassal and his lord was always sustained by the pledge of allegiance and

Two knights do battle for a demoiselle, who is seen watching the combat. From a miniature, Tristan, ca. 1450. (COURTESY THE PIERPONT MORGAN LIBRARY. Ms. 41, folio 49)

loyalty. This element naturally appealed to the minstrels and poets, even while too many actual feudal nobles by no means observed the pledge. The troubadours of southern France, the minnesingers in Germany, and the trouvères of northern France all combined to sing the praises of this virtue, but at the same time they also began to raise the ideal itself. Gradually a whole code of honor was evolved for the noble, and thus the ideal of knighthood was born.

There had always been much ceremony attached to becoming a knight when the age of twenty-one was reached. But in earlier times the ceremony had been performed by any noble, and though it was a formal act, there were no special preparations for it and no code of honor to be sworn to and solemnly observed beyond those involved in the ordinary duty of vassal to lord. But in later times it was only the king or great nobles who could perform the ceremony, and the youth had to undergo severe trials, purifications, and rituals, and then had to swear an oath of fealty upon the Gospels or upon holy relics. His training had to start at the age of seven, when he went as page to the court of a noble, usually the suzerain of his father, where he learned to serve and took training in the manners of his class. At fourteen he began to be trained in military duties, sports, and hunting, and perhaps in some of the social graces. From a youth he was among women as well as men, especially during the period from seven to fourteen; and it gradually came to be accepted that he should form a romantic attachment to the lady of the court, or one of her attendants, who was to be his ideal and for whom he was to perform deeds of gallantry. He was always to observe perfect courtesy toward her, including the courtesy of loving and cherishing her above all women. When he went out into the world it was the custom for the knight to defend her honor, and challenge any word spoken against her. He also had to keep faith, speak the truth at all times, protect the weak, and practice numerous other virtues.

It is clear that the Church had a hand in this, although the hand was concealed. It is a feudal and class ideal, but it is not exclusively this. The Church had gradually allowed into its worship a special reverence for Mary, the mother of Jesus, which had never been present in earlier Christianity. But she became the great religious ideal of the Middle Ages, an ideal of the heavenly feminine, called Our Lady, and a mediator between the sinner and Christ with whom she intercedes on his behalf. It seems clear that the connection between the new ideal of chivalry and courtesy toward womanhood and this new element in Christianity is close. And it is also clear that it must have raised the status of women in this particular society, even though the Christians elsewhere showed no more regard for women than before. It was not surprising that Eleanor of Aquitaine, Marie de France, and their twelfth- and thirteenth-century followers among the women writers and poets took up the cause with enthusiasm. And the whole romantic ideal of Western civilization, which does not yet seem to have spent its force, is its heritage.

▶ The manorial system—Economic basis of feudalism

THE MANOR AS AN ECONOMIC UNIT

Origin of manor

In the feudal system ultimately the entire noble class was supported by the labor of the peasantry, the sole producers in feudal society outside the few towns. In this section the organization of the peasantry for production will be discussed, and how it was possible for a small class of hereditary nobles to compel the enormous majority of human beings in the society to produce a surplus large enough for them to live as economic parasites, whatever valuable political and cultural services they may have performed.

Since the agricultural unit was the manor, the system is usually called the manorial system. As usual in medieval institutions, both Roman and Germanic origins can

Farm animals. From a miniature, Petrus Crescentius, ca. *1460.* (COURTESY THE PIER-
PONT MORGAN LIBRARY. Ms. 232, folio 212)

Sowing and reaping on a medieval manor. From a Book of Hours *(Flemish), ca. 1515.*
(COURTESY THE PIERPONT MORGAN LIBRARY. Ms. 399, folios 9 and 10)

be traced. The large agricultural estate of the Roman Empire was called a villa. Attached to the villa were slaves and *coloni,* both working the land, the *coloni* in theory freemen, but in later Roman times forbidden by law to leave the land. The medieval manor had rarely any actual slaves, but the serfs were unable to leave the land, and were thus the equivalent of the *coloni.* There were also freemen on the manors who found it, as a rule, impossible to leave the land for lack, in early times, of anywhere else to go, and who were tied by debt and other obligations to the lord of the manor. These freemen were called in most places *villeins,* from the Latin *villa.* Medieval estates were sometimes the very same that had been villas in Roman times. Probably more estates, however, had originally been villages worked by communities of freemen who had been forced by the need for protection to seek it from some feudal lord, who had thereupon reduced the status of the freemen to virtual or actual serfdom.

302

Relation of feudal to manorial system

As we have seen, most feudal lords gave away the greater part of their land to vassals in exchange for military service. But all lords, whether owning large or small estates, were compelled to keep some land which was cultivated for their own use. From this land they obtained the bulk of their income, since the feudal incidents and reliefs were comparatively small in total and only reached them at irregular intervals. The income from their own estates or manors was, on the contrary, entirely regular, and under their own control, either directly or through officials appointed by and responsible to themselves. And only from the proceeds of their manors could they pay for the soldiers they were forced to furnish for their lords, together with the various feudal payments described above. It was therefore necessary for every lord to keep in his hands as many manors as was necessary for the purpose. A wealthy lord, with large obligations, might have a considerable number of manors, quite beyond his ability to supervise personally even if he had the competence. These manors would be supervised by bailiffs and stewards, who in every respect drew their authority from him, and carried out his orders as his representative.

Manorial self-sufficiency

The lord's demesne—Every manorial estate had on it a manor house inhabited by the lord or his officials, a certain amount of arable and pasture land, and probably some forest land. There was probably also a parish church, whose priest lived in his own house, and was appointed to his position by the lord. There was a village where the peasants lived, and other workers required by the estate but who did not work on the land. Such men would be blacksmiths, wheelwrights, shoemakers, and other specialized workers.

A portion of the land, fixed by custom, like everything else on a manor, was set aside as the lord's personal demesne. It was seldom more than a third of the whole property and might be as little as a sixth. This land was worked for him by the peasants under the direct supervision, as a rule, of one of their number chosen by the other peasants, and according to the instructions of the lord or steward. When they were working on the lord's land the supervisor had authority to beat the peasants if they did not work hard enough. All the produce from the lord's demesne belonged to the lord and constituted the major source of his income.

The land of the peasants—The remainder of the manorial land was worked by the peasants for their own account, whether they were freemen or serfs, and was subject to taxation, which will be discussed in detail in a later section. Each peasant had a certain acreage allotted to him varying from a half dozen to about thirty acres each. But the acres were not all together, making up a self-contained farm. They were in strips, each strip containing about an acre, and each of the length that a team of oxen could plow before it needed

to take a rest (from which comes the measure "furlong"—furrow long). A peasant's strips were separated from each other, sometimes by quite a considerable distance, perhaps in order to give each peasant his fair share of the best and the worst land. Among these strips were also the strips belonging to the lord which had to be cultivated by the peasants without profit.

The strip system, however, was not so uneconomical in medieval as it would be in modern times, for the cultivation was done on a cooperative basis. No peasant was likely to own enough oxen to pull through soil that was at all stubborn the very primitive plow that was in use. Usually a team of eight of these scrawny, ill-fed animals was necessary to pull it. Thus the strips would all be cultivated together, though the produce of each strip went to the individual owner. The meadow and pasture land was kept for hay, necessary to keep the animals fed over the winter; when the hay crop had been taken off, the land then became common property, and all the peasants might pasture their animals on it. Likewise, when the crops had been harvested from the arable land the stubble could be used as rough pasture for the beasts. Pigs were allowed to gather what nourishment they could from the forest land, which remained in the hands of the peasantry after the lord had set aside what he needed for his own use. Since the strips were divided from each other only by a rough path or perhaps a double furrow, this system is known as the open-field system.

A scientific rotation of crops, though known to the ancient Greeks and Romans, was unknown to the medieval peasant. But it was recognized that the fertility of the soil needed to be renewed, and that the manure from the few domestic animals was insufficient for the purpose. The only method known to the peasants was the practice of letting the land lie fallow. In some parts of the country a full half of the arable land was allowed to lie fallow every year, being plowed twice in the month of June, the only use for the land for that year being for rough pasture in the fall. Elsewhere it was found that only a third of the land need lie fallow and that two crops could be safely taken off in succession before the fallow. Naturally the frequency of fallow depended upon the fertility of the soil, but in most areas of Europe if in one year a spring crop was planted and in the next year a fall crop, sufficient fertility was maintained. These systems are known as the two-field and three-field systems, and they remained the common practice until the agricultural discoveries of the seventeenth century which led to the agricultural revolution of the eighteenth and nineteenth.

The peasant lived in the village in a small thatched hut which had a small plot of land attached to it which he could use as he wished. In this he grew vegetables, and kept a few chickens or geese which could pick up enough feed to sustain life and yield a few eggs a year. He lived on black bread, fresh vegetables if he was thrifty enough to grow them, porridge,

This medieval illustration of the building of a biblical city again reflects authentic medieval practice. From a Picture Bible *(French), ca. 1250.* (COURTESY THE PIERPONT MORGAN LIBRARY. Ms. 638, folio 3)

cheese, and very occasionally meat or fish, and wine. The staple field crops to which he had access were rye and wheat, planted in the fall, and barley, oats, beans, peas, and sometimes spring rye, planted in the spring and harvested in the fall of the same year. Rye was the cereal used most for the peasant's bread, wheat for his lord's.

Subsidiary workers on the manor—Many of the menial tasks were done for the lord by free peasants and serfs. In the lord's mill millers were needed, and bakers for the lord's household. These men might receive full-time employment from the lord, or they might also have a few strips to cultivate. The blacksmith, carpenter, mason, and the rest had their houses in the village and might combine their other specialized work with agricultural labor. The aim of the lord was naturally to be as self-sufficient on his manor as possible, for money was scarce and there were some items which must be imported, such as salt, spices, and all the luxuries for which he could pay. Moreover, it was only the surplus of the manor that provided him with such money as he had, and therefore it was not to his interest to keep more peasants working on the land than could be profitably employed. It was better to use any surplus labor on the manufacture of goods that could be exported and bring him some cash income. Indeed, one of the reasons for the later improvement of the status of the peasantry was the taste for luxury acquired by the lord, which forced him to improve his system of production; this often meant hiring free laborers, organizing them more efficiently, and allowing the manufacturing part of the village to become specialized into a town.

Status of the peasant—In practice, the peasant was not altogether without rights though in theory his lord could do almost anything he wished with him. The lord could if necessary enforce his own rights in the manorial court, presided over by himself or his steward. Here also could serfs obtain justice against other serfs, and villeins

This medieval blacksmith is no ordinary smith, but St. Eloy, patron of all blacksmiths. When the Devil tormented him, he tweaked the Devil's nose. When the horse would not stand still to be shod, the saint cut off his hoof, shod it, and put it back. From Bonifacius Calabrensis, Of the Care of Horses (Italy), ca. 1400. (COURTESY THE PIERPONT MORGAN LIBRARY. Ms. 735, folio 3)

against villeins.[6] But no class had any rights against a higher class.

The sons and daughters of a serf remained serfs. In a "mixed marriage" between a serf and a freeman, the new status was determined by the custom of the manor, subject to the decision of the lord in the particular case. As a rule it was the freeman who reverted to the status of the serf rather than the other way round. On the other hand, a serf was protected against eviction by the very fact that he was the property of his lord. Individually he could not be sold if he

were a cultivator of the land, though there are instances of the sales of sons of serfs, and occasionally of serf cultivators who had probably in some way offended their lord and were punished in this way, contrary to the usual custom. The serf was not allowed to marry except with the permission of the lord, for which permission he paid a small fee; if he wanted to marry outside the manor he might be refused permission. If it were granted the fee would be larger, and probably the woman would also have to pay a fee to her lord for the privilege.

The same regulations applied to the children of the serf. Though we know of cases where peasants' sons attained to high rank in the Church, perhaps including the great

[6] A villein by derivation means simply a villager. Customarily it is used to designate a peasant who was theoretically not a serf, but was at the same time not wholly free, owing to his lord special manorial services not owed by the real freeman.

Pope Gregory VII, permission had first to be obtained from the lord and a fee paid. If the serf left the land without permission he could be brought back by force if the lord could catch him, which was not always easy. And if he were able to stay away for a year and a day without recapture the lord's right lapsed, and the serf became free. Hence arose the saying that "town air makes free," for many a serf escaped from his bondage to the towns and was never recaptured.

The parish priest on the manor—As a rule the Church division of a parish (a term still used in many countries) corresponded exactly to the area covered by a manor. There was thus one priest required for each manor, whose duty it was to provide for the spiritual needs of the peasantry and the lord. Appointed by the lord, he was as much his servant as any of his officials; and he had some of the rights of the lord within his parish. He had a separate house and small plot of ground of his own; he was also provided with a certain number of the strips which had to be cultivated by the peasants in the same way as the lord's. His income was provided by a tax of one tenth (tithe) of the income of every peasant in the parish. However, the better priests, often themselves drawn from the ranks of the peasants, lived very close to the people; and the priest's services at every important crisis in the peasants' lives to administer the sacraments, as well as his regular visits and giving of

Dances in the street. From a Book of Hours *(French), ca. 1474.* (COURTESY THE PIERPONT MORGAN LIBRARY. Ms. 677, folio 137)

spiritual comfort, were appreciated. Sometimes, but not always, he had had at least the rudiments of education and could impart these to the younger peasants, thus preparing them for a wider life either in the Church or in the towns. His church was provided for him by the lord, with the aid, of course, of the labor of the peasants.

Amusements of the peasantry—The peasant's life was hard, and, as we shall see, a very large percentage of the fruits of his labor was yielded up to the lord. But there were certain compensations of a simple kind. He did not have to work, and was indeed forbidden to work on Sundays, and on the festivals of a considerable number of saints. On these festival days there was always dancing in the village—in the parish hall if there was one, if not, in the streets or even in the church itself. Two or three times a year most lords entertained their peasantry, especially at harvest time or after bringing the hay in, after sowing and at the great festivals, especially Christmas, when the peasants decorated the manor house and were allowed to enjoy themselves in it afterward. In wine country there was always a vintage festival. Sometimes jugglers and acrobats came through the village and performed for the villagers either in the manor house or in the parish hall. In the later Middle Ages fairs became common to which the peasants could take their produce and enjoy themselves in the towns for the day.

Though these occasional joys did not compensate for the hardness of the peasants' work and the scantiness of their reward, they did mitigate their lot. We should remember also the fact that every peasant had a secure place, however humble, in his society, that he belonged to the same religion as his neighbors and had to cooperate with them every minute of his life. He was dependent upon them as they upon him. When one considers all that this means for psychological security, it can be more easily understood why, even in our own century, those who were compelled by circumstances to come to America have not always made their peace with it until the second generation.

THE INCOME OF THE LORD OF THE MANOR

From his demesne land

The lord's land was cultivated by his peasants, and he took the produce from it. Though the lord in theory could make unlimited demands upon the labor of his peasants, custom usually regulated the limit placed on it in fact. The regular work was called *week work*, and limited as a rule to not more than three days a week. The time depended naturally upon the size of the lord's land and the number of peasants available. At certain times the peasant could be called upon for additional work, as at harvest time. This was called *boon work*, and included such extra duties as bringing in firewood and hay for the lord. Finally, the peasant was made to do forced labor on the estate such as digging ditches and making roads, while his wife and children might be called upon for housework in the manor. This labor was called *corvée*. The amount of *corvée* required was again regulated by custom as well as by the need of the lord, and depended upon the status of the peasant, whether he was a serf or technically a freeman. The building and repairing of a castle were a very heavy burden on the peasant, but they were done by *corvée*.

From the peasants' land— Different forms of taxation

The lord was not content with having his peasants work his own land for his benefit. In numerous ways he levied toll upon what the peasant produced from his own land. The levies were not arbitrary, but fixed by custom; this, however, did not prevent them from being very heavy, and there was nothing except the probable resistance of the peasants, perhaps by armed revolt, to prevent the lord from increasing them.

There was usually a head tax paid annually by all serfs, and there was a direct tax upon the property of every peasant, known as tallage (French *taille*). There were many "gifts" to be made at specified seasons of the year, and there was a special tax to be paid when a serf inherited his land. The last two were similar to feudal aids. These taxes were seldom excessive, and could be regarded as the equivalent of rent, while the tilling of the lord's land could be regarded as a form of sharecropping—though a modern sharecropper does not have to pay rent too!

But far more annoying and probably more costly in actual cash or produce paid out were the payments that had to be made for the use of various facilities provided by the lord, whether the peasants wished to use them or not. The lord, for instance, provided a bake oven, and the peasant was not permitted to make one for himself. He had to use the lord's bake oven and pay a fee for the privilege. He was not permitted to grind his own wheat, but had to use the lord's mill and the services of his millers, who usually cheated him. He was made to buy wine whether he wanted it or not, use the lord's winepress, and use the lord's bull for breeding; moreover, the lord erected toll houses on his roads and bridges which everyone had to use. These nuisance taxes were called *banalités* and were extremely difficult to get rid of. The French nobles never gave them up till the French Revolution, and they were largely responsible for the fact that the conservative peasants helped to foment it. And always the lord could enforce the payment of fines for breaking his regulations, and impose fines for any other breach of the peace or misdemeanor brought to him for trial.

It is impossible to say what percentage of the actual produce of his manor went into the lord's pocket by one device or another, but it was certainly a large one, and kept the peasants from accumulating much that they could call their own. And it sufficiently accounts for the ability of the feudal nobility to engage in their pleasant pursuits in spite of the low-producing nature of the manorial economy.

THE PEASANT'S INCOME

What he had left over after paying all taxes and fines belonged to the peasant. Though it was not much, there would be something if the land were fertile and he and his wife were good managers. He could convert his produce into cash at the fairs, and we do know that enough agricultural produce found its way into the towns to feed the townsmen, though some of it also came from the lord's demesne and what he had collected in kind from the peasantry. There might be enough in the peasant's sock or mattress to pay a small amount to the priest to educate his son or to pay the apprentice's fee for his son to learn a trade in a town. But seldom do we hear of any luxury in the peasant's home. It would, in any case, have only invited unpleasant attention from his lord.

THE ATTITUDE OF THE CHURCH TOWARD THE PEASANT

The theory of the Church was no different from the theory of the lord as far as the serf was concerned. He was a piece of property. Yet he was also a human soul, and as likely to go to heaven as his lord. The Church believed that the needs of the peasant's soul could be taken care of by the priest with his sacraments, but that Divine Providence had arranged that each man should be born into a certain position in life in which he should remain. Life was not supposed to be a bed of roses, but a hard testing ground in preparation for the world to come. There were three estates in the world, two privileged and the third unprivileged whose duty it was to work for the two privileged classes. The two upper classes or estates were the clergy and the nobility. The townsman or bourgeois belonged to the third estate, along with the peasant. No distinction was made between the bourgeois and the peasants in medieval theory; it was the bourgeois themselves who assumed the title of the third estate as referring only to themselves in later years, when these estates became the first French approach to a Parliament.

Yet there were individual churchmen who recognized the parasitic position of the nobility, and some preached thundering sermons against their exploitation of the peasantry. Jacques de Vitry, a thirteenth-century clergyman, famous for his sermons, once caustically pointed out that "what the peasant takes a year of hard labor to produce the noble consumes in an hour." But in general the clergy recognized that everything that could be said of the nobles could equally be said of themselves, and that it was as well not to disturb the established order. Monasteries and higher clergy were also lords of the manor, and exploited peasants themselves, often more severely than the worst of lords because they were more efficient. It was only reformers and parish priests who seriously tried to improve the lot of the manorial peasants, and their efforts in an entrenched system had little effect. The Church was hardly at all responsible for the ultimate improvement of the peasant's lot through emancipation.

EMANCIPATION OF THE PEASANT

It has already been explained that if a serf stayed away from his manor for a year and a day he had earned his freedom. This was perhaps the principal loophole through which he finally escaped his servitude. With the growth of towns there was some other place for him to go. When Crusades were called the lords were under great pressure from the Church and public opinion to allow them to leave. Few returned alive from the Crusades, especially the First Crusade, when large numbers of peasants were massacred in trying to make their way overland to Palestine. Those who did survive naturally did not return to the manors.

The lord's desire for luxuries beyond what an ordinary manor could provide under its generally inefficient management was also an aid to the peasants. More efficient management meant fewer serfs and large numbers were freed, especially from the thirteenth century onward. In later times it was found that sheep farming earned larger dividends. This gave rise to the enclosure movement which turned many former manors into estates run by few laborers, though at the cost of great hardship to peasants who found themselves deprived by legal means of their strips. When the kings began to establish their authority over the feudal nobility they found themselves in constant need of mercenary soldiers. These again came from the ranks of the peasantry, and no lord could pursue and bring back a peasant who had joined the king's army.

The manorial system itself survived for many centuries, but greatly transformed. The servile status and the legal power of the lords over their peasants disappeared first, and in most Western countries did not survive the thirteenth century. Tenant farmers and small proprietors took the place of serfs, the former still bound by the ancient customs and the ancient taxes, and still forced on occasions to do *corvée* and to pay the *banalités*. But when the taxes were raised the peasants soon learned that they had the power to revolt. And though the revolts were usually mercilessly suppressed, reforms did come in time, for the lords as well as the peasants were the losers by them.

More than anything else it was probably the inefficiency of the early manorial system that condemned it; with the growth of towns and the commercial revolution a more efficient use had to be made of the land, and this could be provided neither by the warrior class of feudal nobility nor by the manorial system which nourished it.

▶ Suggestions for further reading

Books on the political and social structure of the early Middle Ages are numerous. There are several good chapters on the early centuries in Dawson's book, already referred to, *The Making of Europe* (New York: The Macmillan Company, 1932). There is a fine survey in short compass in a book in the Home University Library series, which, though written in 1911, was considered worthy of a reprint in 1948: H. W. C. Davis, *Medieval Europe* (London: Oxford University Press, 1948). This little book studies especially those medieval topics likely to be of most interest to the beginning student, though everything in it has clearly behind it the lifetime learning of a great scholar on the medieval period. Another short popular survey by a noted scholar is S. Painter, *Medieval Society* (Ithaca: Cornell University Press, 1951). A more extensive survey, not entirely up to date but very thoughtful and well organized under topics of interest to the student, is G. B. Adams, *Civilization during the Middle Ages* (New York: Charles Scribner's Sons, 1914). A much fuller book, no doubt used as a text but readable in itself, fully up to date, and with proper attention paid to Byzantine history and to the relations of Constantinople with the West, is J. L. La Monte, *The World of the Middle Ages* (New York: Appleton-Century-Crofts, Inc., 1949).

On medieval society of this period there is a very interesting recent book based on the actual observations of Alexander Neckam, a medieval traveler and indefatigable student; H. T. Holmes, *Daily Living in the Twelfth Century* (Madison: University of Wisconsin Press, 1952). Numerous books by G. G. Coulton, all based on original research which will bring the student close to the actual writings of the period, are available. Probably the best to use is *Medieval Panorama* (New York: The Macmillan Company, 1943), which should, however, be judiciously skipped. The student will easily discover for himself the parts which are really familiar to the author, and worth reading, and he can neglect chapters which are thin and derivative. Coulton, in spite of a lifetime's research, was not able to keep up with all the work done by other medieval scholars. He is always at his best in

social history. The same author's *The Medieval Village* (Cambridge, England: Cambridge University Press, 1926) is a full study of certain aspects of village life, particularly in England, based on original records and literature; it shows clearly the relationship between the various classes in rural society. While Eileen Power's classic *Medieval People* (9th ed.; London: Methuen & Co., Ltd., 1950) contains some elements that are undoubtedly fictional, it is based on solid research and brings vividly to the imagination various medieval individuals and the milieu in which they lived.

Although this particular book, J. B. Ross and M. M. McLaughlin, *The Portable Medieval Reader* (New York: The Viking Press, Inc., 1949), is not perhaps quite up to the standard of some of the others in its admirable series, and although some of the selections are of minimal interest, there are enough good selections to make it well worth reading, with some skipping. An imaginative picture of a French seigneury is given in W. S. Davis, *Life in a Medieval Barony* (New York: Harper & Brothers, 1923), which, in spite of its derivation from different sources, all, of course, authentically feudal, will give the student a good impression of the actual nature of feudalism in the Middle Ages. A special study of chivalry is to be found in S. Painter, *French Chivalry, Chivalric Ideas and Practices in Medieval France* (Baltimore: Johns Hopkins University Press, 1940).

11

The Growth of the Papacy
to Innocent III

The church in the tenth century • The Cluniac reform • Conflict between the papacy and secular powers • Unification of Christendom against the Muslims • The Crusades • Reaction to the worldliness of the Church • Reaction of the Church to the rise of heresy • The issue of apostolic poverty

---

▸ The Church in the tenth century

ECCLESIASTICAL ORGANIZATION IN EUROPE— LAY INVESTITURE

It will have been realized from the last chapter how completely the Church had become integrated into the feudal system. Throughout Europe the emperor, kings, and chief nobles appointed the bishops and the archbishops; the clerical assistants in the episcopal sees (cathedral chapters), who were responsible for the administration of the diocese, were appointed by the bishops, while the parish priests, chosen by local lords, usually from their own free peasantry, were ordained priests by the bishops whenever the latter found time for it, without too closely inquiring into the qualifications of the priests. There was no way in which the papacy could interfere in the process, though in theory all the high clergy were at least subject to confirmation from the Holy See. If the rulers desired to sell the offices of the Church or give them to their friends and relatives, no papal wrath could stop them; if the bishops accepted fees illegally for the performance of their ordinary duties, if they

inflicted fines as penance and put the proceeds into their own pockets, perhaps to pay the sum exacted from them by the kings in exchange for their appointment, no one could insist on their obedience to the laws of the Church which forbade such practices. If the parish priest had no qualifications for his office, knew no Latin, permitted gaming and dicing in his church, was unable to celebrate the Mass with due order and dignity, and betrayed the secrets of the confessional for private gain—if his manorial lord did not discipline him, no one else would. All these practices were common, and there was not much that anyone in high authority in the Church could do about it.

THE PAPACY IN THE FEUDAL SYSTEM

The papacy itself was in no position to institute reforms. When the pope was not chosen by the local Italian nobles and people, he was chosen by the emperor. If he offended the emperor, he could be deposed; if he offended the local nobles, they also could depose him by force unless the emperor objected. The revenues of the Papal States in Italy were collected through the papal

► chronological chart

The Cluniac reform and its consequences

Foundation of monastery of Cluny	910
Growth of Cluniac influence	910–1050
Otto the Great crowned emperor	962
Henry III emperor	1039–1056
Henry III appoints four successive reform popes	1046–1054
Schism between Eastern and Western Churches	1054
Domination of papacy by Hildebrand (later Gregory VII)	1054–1085
Death of Henry III, accession of boy Henry IV	1056
Synod of the Lateran—Popes to be elected by College of Cardinals	1059
Synod of Melfi—Condemnation of clerical marriage	1059
Treaty of Melfi—Robert Guiscard invested with southern Italy by pope Nicholas II	1059
Saxon rebellion against Henry IV	1073–1075
Gregory VII becomes pope	1073
Synod of Rome—Decrees against simony, clerical marriage, and lay investiture	1075
Henry IV quells rebellion of Saxon nobles	1075
Dictatus papae by Gregory VII	1076
Synod of Worms, called by Henry IV, deposes Gregory	1076
Penance of Henry IV at Canossa	1077
Renewed Saxon wars in Germany	1077–1080
Defeat and death of Rudolph of Swabia	1080
Second deposition of Henry IV by Gregory VII	1080
Henry invades Italy	1081
Sack of Rome by Normans	1084
Death of Gregory VII	1085
Proclamation of First Crusade by Urban II	1095
Compromises over lay investiture in England and France	1107
Concordat of Worms	1122

Rise of Hohenstaufen family

Conrad III first Hohenstaufen emperor	1138–1152
Frederic I (Barbarossa) emperor	1152–1190

Rise of Hohenstaufen family (cont'd)

Frederic states claims on Italian cities at Diet of Roncaglia	1158
Formation of Lombard League	1159
Destruction of Milan by Frederic	1162
Battle of Legnano—Defeat of Frederic by Lombard League	1176
Peace of Constance	1183
Marriage of Henry (son of Frederic) to Constance of Sicily	1186
Death of Frederic Barbarossa on Third Crusade	1190
Henry VI emperor	1190–1197
Capture of Richard I of England by Henry and payment of heavy ransom	1192–1194
Birth of Frederic Hohenstaufen (Frederic II)	1194
Death of Henry VI	1197
Civil War in Germany	1197–1212
Pontificate of Innocent III	1198–1216
Frederic Hohenstaufen becomes king of the Romans	1212
Frederic crowned emperor	1220

The Papacy and England

Conquest of England by Normans with papal approval	1066
Compromise over lay investiture	1107
St. Thomas Becket becomes Archbishop of Canterbury	1162
Constitutions of Clarendon	1164
Murder of St. Thomas Becket	1170
John King of England	1199–1216
Innocent III appoints Stephen Langton Archbishop of Canterbury	1207
Innocent lays interdict on England	1208
Innocent excommunicates John	1209
Innocent deposes John and invites Philip Augustus to execute the sentence	1213
John submits, doing homage to Innocent for throne	1213
Battle of Bouvines—Victory of Philip over allies of John	1214
Magna Carta	1215
Deaths of John and Innocent	1216
Louis, son of Philip Augustus, abandons efforts to gain English crown	1217

bureaucracy; but this also was composed of local nobles who could direct them into more suitable pockets than the pope's.

In such circumstances few would have ventured to predict that in little more than a century a pope would have brought an emperor to beg his forgiveness in the snow, still less that in two and a half centuries Pope Innocent III would be successfully disciplining every monarch in Europe. Such an achievement therefore deserves a careful analysis in itself as a political event of the first magnitude. Moreover, the swift collapse of papal power that followed Innocent's triumphs may also reveal the necessary limitations on the exercise of political authority by a power whose claims were spiritual, and whose sanctions depended on moral rather than on military and political force.

THE THEORY OF SALVATION

The means of salvation

In our modern age, when Christianity has been split into numerous sects, when a large number of people are religious skeptics, and when power rests firmly in the hands of secular authorities, it is clear that the moral reform of the individual can only be enforced, if at all, by secular authority through legislation. A Church can only hope to induce moral reform by persuasion and by the threat of cutting off such ecclesiastical comforts as it can supply. In the Middle Ages, however, Catholic Christianity was a religious monopoly, and there is no evidence that anyone in the whole of Christendom in the tenth century doubted its main teachings, so far as they were understood. The central teaching understood by all was that there was a God in Heaven, a Devil in Hell, and that after death human beings went to either Heaven or Hell according to a verdict given by God in his capacity as judge. The supreme aim of man's life on earth was to win a favorable decision at this last judgment. And it was universally believed that the purpose of the Church was to help man win the decision and thus attain Heaven.

Largely on the authority of Pope Gregory I a further important doctrine had been propounded for the belief of the faithful, though it was not widely understood: the doctrine that there was an intermediate place between the earth and Heaven through which those who were destined for Heaven would pass. This was called Purgatory, the place where sins were purged through punishment, leaving a purified soul to pass on to Heaven. It was only a temporary abode, but the period passed in it varied according to the sins committed on earth. The Church could also help mitigate the punishment in purgatory.

The role of the Church in the attainment of salvation

The sacraments—According to the theory of salvation put forward by Augustine in the fifth century, modified by Gregory I, and generally accepted as the true teaching of the Church, man was saved only through grace, bestowed as a heavenly gift by God, a gift made possible only by the sacrifice of Christ. Grace, however, was given to man only through the medium of the sacraments of the Church, which had been founded by Christ for this purpose.

There were seven sacraments: baptism, by which the newborn child was redeemed from original sin, with godparents accepting Christianity on his behalf; confirmation, when a child of about twelve accepted Christianity for himself; the Eucharist, the most sacred and important of the sacraments, offered daily, in which through the miracle of transubstantiation bread and wine were made into the body and blood of Christ; matrimony; penance; and extreme unction, which prepares the Christian for death and wipes away what is left of his sins. The seventh sacrament (holy orders) was the ceremony by which a layman was made into a priest, setting him apart from ordinary men, and enabling him to celebrate the Eucharist and grant absolution from sin.

Penance—Indulgences—The sacrament of penance needs a few words of explanation because of its role in the disciplining of the

Christian by the Church, and the consequent power conferred by it on the clergy. In theory the Church could not guarantee salvation; all that was sure was that salvation could not be won without the aid of the Church—a distinction not always clear to the unschooled Christian. But the Church could save the Christian sinner from having to suffer the consequences of his sin in Purgatory—provided always that God had chosen to grant him salvation and an entry into Heaven. Christ and his saints, according to Church doctrine, had made full satisfaction to God for the sins of every man on earth, and thus a treasury of merits had been accumulated which was at the disposal of the Church for helping repentant sinners through Purgatory.

If a sinner repented truly and confessed his sins to a priest, then it was the duty of the priest to absolve him. This was the sacrament of penance. But the consequences of the sin still remained, and in the absence of any intervention by the Church, full punishment for it would be exacted in Purgatory. But the Church could remit the punishment by assigning some temporal punishment on earth, in the form of the repetition of a certain number of prayers, the undertaking of special fasts, the performance of a useful social work such as building a bridge, or even a pilgrimage to some sacred place such as Rome or Jerusalem. Such an act would relieve the sinner of some period of punishment in Purgatory. The statement of this remission of punishment was called an *indulgence*. A plenary indulgence, which was the chief inducement offered to crusaders, remitted the whole time of punishment in Purgatory. If, therefore, God had chosen to save a sinner who had been given a plenary indulgence, then he would enter Heaven at once without having to spend any time in Purgatory.

It is clear that this complex theory would not be understood by the ordinary ignorant layman. It is not, therefore, to be wondered at that only too often the sinner who possessed an indulgence regarded it as a safe passport to Heaven; and it is also not too surprising that the temptation to abuse the sacrament of penance and sell the indulgences for money was sometimes too much for a Church that had many uses for money. It was the flagrant abuse of the indulgence in the sixteenth century that was the principal factor in the rebellion of Martin Luther against the Church which began the Protestant Reformation.

The withholding of the sacraments—The disciplinary powers of the Church—Since the receiving of the sacraments was necessary for salvation, the most severe penalty that could be meted out to a Christian was to withhold them, a penalty known as excommunication. Complete excommunication, which could be pronounced by the higher clergy or by the pope, meant that the offender was severed from all services performed by the Church. No Christian might have any dealings with him on pain of excommunication himself, he could not attend services of the Church or receive any sacraments, and he could not be buried in holy ground. If the state accepted the excommunication it would sometimes withdraw the benefits of secular law from him also, making him an outlaw. He then could be killed with impunity, and by the Church action he was necessarily condemned to Hell. If excommunication was to be lifted by the Church the offender would be expected to make a complete submission, and undergo severe penance.

As a supplement to excommunication when directed at a monarch or an independent feudal lord, the Church could also declare an interdict upon his whole territory. This was a kind of excommunication en masse of a whole population, and its purpose was to bring the pressure of public opinion to bear on the offending ruler. In a land laid under an interdict the Church performed none of its duties at all—though exception might be made by special dispensation for some of the essential sacraments such as baptism and extreme unction. When it is remembered how many duties the Church performed in the Middle Ages that we now regard as functions of the state, it

can readily be seen how effective this weapon might be in the hands of a Church obedient to its leaders.

Clearly neither of these disciplinary powers, however, would have any effect at all if the local clergy did not cooperate. When, as in the tenth century, the clergy were nominated by local lords, they could not be used; and probably no cleric could even be found who would read a bull of excommunication of a high noble or a monarch.

In addition to these weapons, the pope, who alone could pronounce an interdict, claimed the right to depose a king, who, theoretically, could not hold office from the moment of his excommunication; and the oath of allegiance made to him by his subjects became automatically void. Naturally this right was never admitted by the rulers, who themselves claimed to hold their power from God and not from the Church. The pope's ability to make his decree effective depended entirely upon the conditions in the country concerned—as, for instance, whether there was any rival for the throne, or whether any foreign king could be induced with papal support to overthrow the offending and deposed monarch.

THE CHURCH AS REGULATOR OF CHRISTIAN MORALITY—CANON LAW

The Church had always claimed jurisdiction throughout Christendom in all matters which concerned faith and morals. In the early centuries of Christianity authoritative creeds—statements of what Christians must believe—had been drawn up by councils. But gradually it was recognized that a single authority must be accepted in such matters, and this, after many centuries of doubt as to where the authority lay, was granted by consent in the Western world to the pope. From time to time popes also promulgated new dogmas which must be believed by the faithful. Those who refused to subscribe to these beliefs could be charged with heresy, and handed over to the state for punishment. If they did not recant they could be put to death by burning (without the shedding of blood, forbidden to church-men). Before the establishment of the Inquisition in the thirteenth century heresy trials were in the hands of the bishops. By such means the Church attempted to guard the purity of the faith.

In the realm of morals, which covered a very wide field and which the Church in the days of its power sought to make ever wider, the authority was the canon law, the rules laid down by the early councils, combined with decrees made by various popes. These were codified by Gratian in the twelfth century.

Canon law stated that all clerics, both regular and secular, and even those in minor orders—assistants of the higher clergy, even, later, students at universities—were subject only to the jurisdiction of the Church and were not to be tried for any offense whatever by the temporal powers. It claimed that all crimes against religion, whoever committed them, were to be tried by the Church. This included not only heresy, simony, and blasphemy, but sorcery, adultery, and sexual crimes, usury, and even the illegal fighting of duels. If these were not punished by the state of its own accord—and in the early Middle Ages many of the chief offenders were rulers and nobles in high position who did not even recognize these acts as crimes—then the Church claimed the right to try the offenders instead.

Finally, canon law regulated all civil cases connected in any way with one of the sacraments, as, for instance, marriage settlements and divorces, wills, and civil contracts which concerned inheritance. The canon law, observing Roman principles and taking into account such things as motives, not recognized as important under feudal law, did serve to mitigate some of the evils of feudal law, as well as adding to the power of the Church.

Again, however, it must be emphasized that the Church was able to regulate such matters only if the State permitted it to do so. In general, the Church was allowed to have its way in matters that were not of too great

moment to the rulers, and the higher courts were always crowded with legal business at a time when feudal law was only rudimentary, and incompetent to deal with much that occupied the Church. The Church, however, was rarely allowed much say in the matter of feudal inheritance; but when a quarrel was precipitated with Henry II, a strong king of England, over his efforts to establish a uniform law for clerics and laymen alike, it was the Church, not the king, who won the victory.

THE REQUIREMENTS FOR THE ESTABLISHMENT OF PAPAL AUTHORITY IN EUROPE

From the above it can be seen what relation the claims of the Church had to the reality of its power in the tenth century. It remains to be considered what were the essential changes that must be made if the pretended power were to become real. First, and underlying all the remainder, it must re-establish its moral supremacy in Europe, so that Christians throughout the whole area could see that the Church was not just an oppressive secular institution demanding tithes and feudal dues and contributions, but a body with a true spiritual mission and able to help in the saving of souls. It must renew the faith of the people both in Christianity itself and in the mission of the Church.

Second, and as a consequence of this, it must attract to itself as a body sufficient voluntary financial support to enable it to carry out its duties and maintain some independence from the feudal lords. Voluntary support would only be forthcoming if the people believed in its efficacy for salvation. And the Papal States, the best immediate source of income, must be thoroughly subjected to the pope and firmly administered.

Third, the papacy must free itself from the domination of the German emperor and the Roman nobles and people, thus enabling it to carry out a consistent policy, dependent not on imperial or local desires, but upon what it considered best for the Church. The most obvious way was for a pope to name, or have a large share in naming, his successor.

Fourth, the control of appointments to the higher clergy must be taken out of the hands of the feudal lords and kings and put under the control of the papacy. If the higher clergy were papal appointees, then the lower clergy would likewise become responsive to papal policy through these nominees. This meant, of course, the suppression of such practices as the sale of Church offices (simony), the bestowal of them on relatives (nepotism), and incelibacy, since a church office might become hereditary if a clergyman had sons to succeed him.

This tremendous program was substantially carried out in the next few centuries. Its instrument, as so often in the reforms of the Church in the Middle Ages, was found in the monastic system, which had for a long time ceased to play any important part in the public life of the Christian world, but was now to show itself capable of a self-renewal that was as unexpected to the papacy as it was welcome. And in the end, as it happened, it was the monastic reform that took over the papacy instead of the papacy's taking over and exploiting the reform.

▶ The Cluniac reform

THE CLUNIAC SYSTEM

In 910, a Duke William of Aquitaine, desiring to have Masses said for his soul, and dissatisfied with the existing monasteries, although they had for a long time been striving to reform themselves, left land for a new monastery or abbey to be established at Cluny in eastern France (Burgundy). This abbey, under a distinguished churchman, was to be entirely free from either royal or feudal jurisdiction and subject only to the papacy. It was to be a reformed monastery, returning to the strict Benedictine Rule.

Under its first abbot, Odo, and a subsequent series of remarkable abbots, it did indeed return to the Benedictine Rule, but with certain innovations. There was not so much stress on manual labor or even on scholarly pursuits—though many of the abbots and monks were in fact as learned as any in

Christendom—as there was stress on a strict return to canon law in such matters as chastity and celibacy and the proper election to Church offices. It is clear that such a program was intended from the beginning to be influential in the reform of the whole Church, and from the beginning it attracted all those serious Christians in Europe who hoped for and wanted to work for Church reform.

Soon the mother abbey began to expand and found daughter-houses and the bequests of land began to come in; for it need hardly be stressed that if a noble was thinking of giving an estate to the Church for the benefit of his soul the most likely place to find clergy competent for the purpose would be at Cluny, where the monks were chaste, where they spent many hours of the day interceding for the souls of the living and the departed; he would not be likely to bequeath it to his brother whose appointment to the office of bishop he had influenced, or to a monastery noted only for the excellence of its food and liquor. The same principle as in the foundation of Cluny itself was observed in the foundation of the daughter abbeys called *priories;* the land must be unencumbered by feudal privileges, and each priory must be obedient to the abbey at Cluny. This obedience was enforced through the priors of each of these houses, who were appointed by the abbot of Cluny and regularly visited by him.

CONSEQUENCES OF CLUNY REFORM

Growth of elite and educated clergy

The first important consequence of the reform was that at last a monastery attracted not only monks who wished to escape the world but ambitious and sincere clergymen who wished to reform it. They knew that at Cluny they would receive training for the job that was to be done—above all ecclesiastical reform. It was much easier to obtain appointment from a king or a lord and enjoy personally the fruits of office; but it was the dedicated men who went to Cluny. Under the supervision of the abbot who had uncontrolled authority—for real control by the tenth-century papacy was unthinkable—ability would have a better chance of being recognized than anywhere else. Once monks were trained, they could preach safely without being made to submit to feudal dictation; even though they ran the risk of being manhandled by the lords and their henchmen, public opinion would be on their side. Above all, there was a practical and realizable goal to be striven for, and if the movement grew, the results of their work would be visible to all.

For all these reasons there can be no question that the Cluny monasteries for nearly two centuries, until excessive worldly success undermined their original high purpose, received the pick of the crop of those who sincerely wished for the reform of Christianity and the elevation of the Church to a position of honor and independence. And, as we know from the influence of the low-born Hildebrand, Cluny was able to call upon all ranks of society for its members and not only upon the feudal nobility, as in the higher positions within the secular clergy.

Independence from lay control

The secret of the success of the reform movement lay in its independence from lay control. Set down as an independent body in the heart of the feudal system, it was in the highest degree revolutionary, threatening to overthrow the entire established order without fear of reprisals, except crude and violent ones which could only hurt individuals but not the system. The king could not dismiss them; he could not take away their land and revenue for it was not his; even the imperial control of the papacy did not help, for the abbot of Cluny could no more be made to obey a pope than a feudal bishop or archbishop. So a corps of elite clergy was gradually recruited, of great potential danger to the secular clergy and to the prized patronage of the monarch—and they could do nothing about it.

Growth of Christian spirit among the laity

Even more dangerous to the nobility and to the monarchs, had they been able to real-

ize it, was the fact that for the first time in centuries there was a genuine spiritual revival that affected all classes of society. Here were some clergymen who were personally moral and chaste, who preached with fervor and conviction, and who said just what most people had been thinking about the Church for a long time—that it was unspiritual, interested only in its own comfort, careless of the spiritual needs of the people, unchaste, simoniac, and not fit to be considered the Church of God. Though the opinion of the serfs on the manor might not be important, and unless they were close to a Cluny priory they would know nothing of the reform, other men of importance, even among the feudal nobility, did not approve of the practices of the secular clergy. Such men were often in a position to influence the appointment of bishops. Reformers at all times in history have been able to make a genuine appeal to disinterested persons; and no Christian could afford to stand against reform if he really believed in Christianity and the importance of the Church—unless his personal interests in this world were too deeply involved to pay an equal attention to the next.

So it began to happen that some noblemen who had the gift of bishoprics chose to appoint reformers from Cluny to these offices. The first foothold in the secular world had been won. It remained for the reformers to develop a complete program for the Church and to use their influence to put it into effect.

CLUNY AND THE ESTABLISHMENT OF PAPAL AUTHORITY

Release of the clergy from secular control—Reform of abuses in appointment, simony, nepotism, incelibacy

The second stage of the Cluniac reform involves the reform of the papacy itself. Since this is associated with the name of Pope Gregory VII (1073–1085), it is sometimes called the Gregorian Reform, though it was a natural consequence of the Cluniac reform and involved no change in policy.

As mentioned earlier, the main line of the attack on secular control of the clergy was

The monastery of Montmajour (twelfth century), in southern France.

directed verbally against the abuses in appointment, against simony, nepotism, and incelibacy. This had for a long time little effect. The secular clergy had been accustomed to living openly with their wives or concubines, and considered the monkish demand for celibacy inhuman. Most rulers also were not willing to give up their patronage so easily, though there were some notable exceptions who greatly advanced the cause of the reform.

But slowly and carefully the ground was prepared and at last it was possible for the popes, several of them from Cluny, to decree that only the pope was entitled to appoint the higher clergy. There must be no more appointments to church positions by the laity. Thus was precipitated the quarrel between rulers and the papacy over lay investiture.

It was a demand for more than the popes could hope to gain. The clergy required an income, and income could at this time only be obtained from land. The Church had no land to give to its clergy. Hence the feudal lord must give the land, and the Church was willing to allow him to invest with the symbols of sovereignty, which right it could hardly take away. But the reformers nevertheless went boldly ahead and demanded the abolition of lay investiture altogether.

Release of papacy from secular control —Election by cardinals

It was not possible for the papacy itself to be independent until it could free itself from control by the emperor. The reformers therefore waited patiently for a suitable opportunity to throw off the shackles. This presented itself when a child (Henry IV) was elected emperor. The papacy then announced (1059) that the pope henceforth would be elected by the College of Cardinals. The cardinals were originally assistants in the papal court of Rome and the heads of certain Italian churches. In time they came to be chosen from all the clergy of Christendom, and the title became an honorary one, carrying great prestige and power because of the cardinal's role in the election of a pope, but held in conjunction with any other office in the Church he might possess. The importance of the announcement at this time was that cardinals could be appointed only by the pope, and they held office for life. Thus continuity of policy could be maintained. The papal appointees of the previous few reigns chose the next incumbent; and the emperor had nothing to do with it.

Role of the papal legates—By-passing of the secular clergy

A third feature of importance and fundamental to the program was the growth of a new position in the Church, the papal legate. The legate was a personal representative of the pope and had precedence over any clergyman in the country to which he was sent. The local clergy and nobles might not like these ambassadors, but they could neglect them only if they also intended to defy the pope. And legates could proclaim the announcements of the pope in the churches of their diocese, they could read the bulls which the local clergy might have wished to suppress, and they could excommunicate or lay an interdict upon the country by the direct authority of the pope himself; by means of the legates the pope could make a direct appeal to public opinion over the heads of the clergy.

The reform movement could not now fail for want of publicity given to the decrees of the pope in the countries for which they were intended.

THE EMERGENCE OF A STRONG PAPACY UNDER CLUNIAC INSPIRATION—HILDEBRAND (GREGORY VII)

From the middle of the eleventh century all the popes were serious reformers, the first being chosen, against his feudal interests, by the German emperor, Henry III, who approved of the reform for religious reasons. The power behind the papal throne from 1054 onward was a monk named Hildebrand, who did not himself take the chair as

Gregory VII till 1073. But as assistant to one pope after another he was largely responsible for policy. When Henry III died, his son was only a child, and during the regency of the child's mother the popes were able to prevent the Germans from playing any active part in papal affairs. This, then, was the opportune moment for proclaiming the new procedure for election. Some German bishops protested, but the dowager empress did not make an issue of it.

Since the first and most long-drawn-out struggle with the secular authorities by the papacy was with the German emperors, a full section will be devoted to this conflict, which will reveal the nature and efficacy of the weapons at the disposal of both sides and will show clearly how and in what circumstances the pope was able to make his authority effective. Subsequent sections will treat more briefly the effectiveness of these same weapons against the other secular powers until the age of Pope Innocent III.

► Conflict between the papacy and secular powers

THE STRUGGLE WITH THE EMPIRE

Ecclesiastical policy of the successors of Otto I

Realization of need for papal reform— Otto the Great, who, as we have seen, became emperor some fifty years after the foundation of Cluny (962), was anxious to be another Charlemagne, keeping effective control of the papacy and permitting no pope to reign who did not support his policy. But his grandson Otto III (983–1002), who came to the throne at a very tender age, was sincerely in favor of ecclesiastical reform, even at the cost of his imperial interests. And by this time Cluny had become a power to be reckoned with in Europe. Otto appointed two popes who, though not themselves educated at Cluny, were strong believers in reform, the second being the finest scholar in Christendom, Gerbert of Aurillac (Pope Sylvester II), whom we shall have occasion to meet in a later chapter. After Otto III's pre-

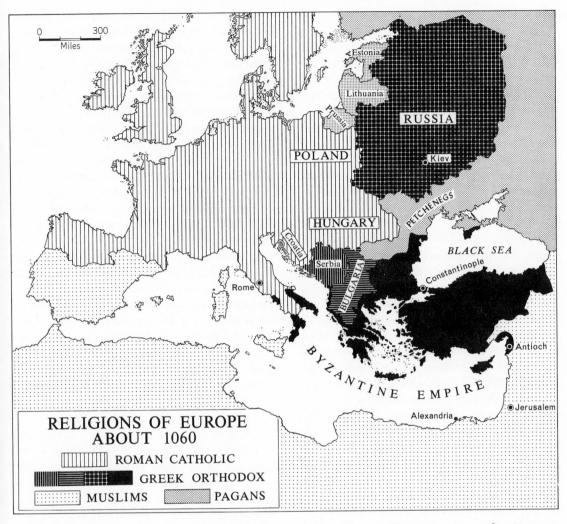

RELIGIONS OF EUROPE
ABOUT 1060

ROMAN CATHOLIC

GREEK ORTHODOX

MUSLIMS   PAGANS

mature death the emperors returned to the policy of Otto I, permitting only subservient popes.

This continued until a new dynasty took possession of the imperial throne (the Salian or Franconian). The second of these rulers, Henry III (1039–1056), became seriously interested in the Cluniac reform. Not realizing how dangerous the reform was to his royal interests in Germany, he supported several reforming popes; moreover, he tried to prevent simony in his own dominions and refused to practice it himself. As a result, by the time of his death in 1056 the papacy was greatly strengthened, to such an extent that it was now prepared to go ahead with its program on its own, even if to do so meant coming into conflict with the empire. But the new emperor, Henry IV, was only six years old, and the regency was in the hands of a French noblewoman, his mother, who was herself in favor of the reform. Nevertheless, perhaps in preparation for the inevitable struggle, the papacy during this period took the opportunity to provide itself with some reliable lay support by recognizing the Norman conquests in southern Italy (see Chapter 10 above), making the Normans theoretically vassals of the papacy. This in itself was a challenge to the empire, which still maintained a claim to the whole of Italy; but Henry IV was too young to know anything about it, and his mother did not care.

Reaction under Henry IV—Restoration of abuses in ecclesiastic appointment—As soon as he grew up Henry IV saw the dangers involved in the reform policies of his father and mother and tried to reverse them. But throughout his reign he was always in trouble with the German nobles, who constantly rebelled against him. He wished for a united Germany under his leadership, and full control of his own clergy and the nobility. He saw at once that he needed his clergy to help control the nobles in the manner of Otto the Great; and he also needed money, most easily obtained by simony, for the purpose of keeping always at hand a body of faithful servants who would help him when necessary to crush the feudal nobility, especially the Saxon lords, who resented the fact that they no longer provided the emperors.

It was thus very difficult to retain control of Italy as well, nor could Henry usually find the time to curb the reformers. Indeed, it was necessary for him even to recognize the reforming popes, in spite of the fact that, in his view, they had been illegally elected since 1059, when election was handed over to the College of Cardinals without his permission. But in Germany he continued to ignore the fulminations of the reformers. He did nothing about clerical marriage, he continued to sell church offices for money for his campaigns; and of course he made all clerical appointments without reference to the popes. He thought he could afford to wait to deal with the papacy; when it suited him he could always repudiate his recognition of the popes since 1059, and claim they had all been illegally elected, including any pope who tried to discipline him.

Weakness of feudal empire in relation to absolute papacy

To understand the sequel, it is necessary to consider briefly the weaknesses of the empire in all its dealings with the papacy. Though since Otto I the crown had always descended from father to son, when the Saxon line of Otto had died out the nobles had chosen Henry IV's grandfather after the old Germanic custom; the hereditary principle had been by no means established. When the crown passed to the Salian line the Saxons in particular felt slighted; and there were always disgruntled nobles who felt that it should have passed to their own families. The only tie between the emperor and these nobles was the oath of allegiance they made to him when he was elected. Although he was theoretically ruler of the whole Empire, his real power was based only on his feudal possessions, whose lords owed him direct allegiance as vassals, and on his control of such bureaucracy as there was, at this time only his own servants and the higher clergy and their staff. He could not therefore voluntarily relinquish his hold on the clergy, as this would mean losing a large part of his effective power.

An elected monarchy meant always the presence of a large number of possible alternatives to a ruler, unlike the situation in a national state where the hereditary monarchy has been fully accepted. And the oaths by which the nobles were bound to the emperor could be dissolved by the Church for good reason, thus safeguarding such conscience as the dissident nobles might possess.

The pontificate of Gregory VII

Views on papal supremacy—The disadvantages of the imperial position had never been lost on the monk Hildebrand who, after probably refusing the position at least once, at last ascended the papal throne in 1073, with the title of Gregory VII, just at a moment when Henry had become involved in a serious Saxon rebellion. Henry could therefore neither give effective support to his German clergy nor devote any energy to dealing with the pope far away in Italy. It was the moment for decisive action by the papacy, and the new pope was certainly the man for the job.

Gregory, as we shall hereafter call him, left behind him many writings from which it is possible to determine with certainty his views on the relative positions of Church and State. Two famous forgeries supplied him with theoretical support, though there is no reason to believe that Gregory doubted their authenticity himself. These were the Donation of Constantine, already referred to, under which the first Christian emperor had given to the papacy overlordship over the whole Western world and full authority over its clergy, and the so-called Isidorian Decretals (False Decretals), a document first published in the ninth century. This went into details of the papal control of the clergy, and made the explicit declaration that the Church was superior to the State, as a more holy institution than the evil and unholy secular authority.

This was precisely the position taken by Gregory. He regarded himself as the spokesman for God on earth, beyond the judgment of anyone on earth, responsible to God for the good behavior of his clergy, and entitled to demand obedience from any secular power in the world. At the beginning of his reign he expressed these principles in a document known as the *Dictatus papae,* and proceeded to use to the full every instrument of power that had been built up by himself and his predecessors. He wrote letters to kings all over Christendom informing them of the authority of his office, and commanding them to acknowledge it, and even pay him tribute. His legates went forth with instructions to kings and nobles, proclaiming them regardless of any objections from the local clergy. But his real task, as he knew, was to establish his authority over the highest power in Christendom, the emperor. If this could be done, then lesser men would fall into line.

Prohibition of lay investiture—He began by excommunicating and deposing from office certain of the German higher clergy who had refused to obey his decrees against simony, nepotism, and unchastity. He followed this up in 1075 with a decree prohibiting lay investiture altogether, thus, of course, making simony forever impossible unless the pope himself sold the offices (not an unheard of thing in later centuries). Unfortunately 1075 was just the year that Henry IV finally succeeded in putting down his Saxon rebellion, leaving him at last free to deal with the papacy. He retained the excommunicated German clergy in office, continued to invest new German bishops, and finally named an archbishop and several bishops in Italy itself.

Excommunication and deposition of Henry IV—Gregory reacted confidently. His legates were instructed to threaten Henry with excommunication if he persisted in lay investiture. Henry then summoned the German clergy, who owed their appointments to him and who in any case resented the high-handed actions of the pope. Under the direction of the emperor they wrote an offensive letter to Gregory, addressing him as Brother Hildebrand and informing him that they had never considered him as pope and owed no obedience to him. Henry added a still more offensive note of his own, calling him "no Pope, but false monk," and calling upon him to descend from his throne "and be damned to eternity."

These amenities over, Gregory, who was entirely confident of success, explained the position to his own overlord, St. Peter, telling him that for rebellion against his Church he was depriving Henry of his kingdom, releasing all Christians from their allegiance to him, and excommunicating him (1076). He also excommunicated the chief prelate in Germany and his schismatic bishops.

Rebellion in Germany—The dilemma of Gregory at Canossa—Gregory's confidence was based on his understanding of the political situation in Germany. The majority of the German clergy, he felt sure, would return to him if he succeeded in defeating their protector. He knew of Henry's unpopularity with his feudal lords, the result of his determined effort to make Germany into a real monarchy; and he must have guessed that a German noble named Rudolph of Swabia would be elected in Henry's place by the lords, although he afterwards claimed that Rudolph's election was made without his knowledge or approval. As Rudolph later gave Gregory very explicit guarantees not to engage in many of Henry's reprehensible practices, and as he would undoubtedly owe his crown to papal support, Gregory certainly must have thought that his intervention in Germany would lead to satisfactory political results.

Gregory was also sure that the solemn excommunication, the first to be used against such an exalted personage, was bound to create a profound sensation, quite sufficient to turn both nobles and people against their ruler; and that the people, forbidden to have any dealings with an excommunicated person, would probably obey, since it endangered their salvation too. Against all this what had Henry to rely on? A wavering clergy, and his own personal vassals, but little else.

Yet Gregory in his calculations forgot one thing, which was to be his undoing. He forgot that he was also a priest, and that his authority was not the equivalent of secular authority. He could not afford to be branded in the eyes of Christendom as a priest who forgot his religious duties in pursuit of political ends.

The effect of the excommunication was all that he had hoped and foreseen. The German clergy, thoroughly frightened, put up no defense of their monarch, while the German nobles took him into custody, saying that if he did not make his peace with Gregory within a certain time, they would no longer recognize him as king. When he refused to make his peace, the nobles invited Gregory to come to Germany in person to preside over the new election. Henry had only one chance; and it seems that he had recognized the Achilles' heel of the pope as Gregory himself had not. He escaped from custody, crossed the Alps in dead of winter, and made his way to the castle at Canossa where Gregory was staying with Countess Matilda, a faithful supporter, on his way to Germany to preside over the election. Clad only in a coarse woolen garment and barefooted, he stood outside the castle in the snow, begging forgiveness. And this was the one thing that Gregory as a priest could not refuse.

It was one of the cruelest dilemmas in history. If he forgave Henry, all his work went for nothing. The clergy and most of the nobles would return to Henry, the rebellious nobles would certainly be victimized, and a civil war would be inevitable. Gregory could not extract any promise from him that he could not break as soon as he regained his power; and he could never excommunicate or discipline him again with a similar

effect. Only a first excommunication could hope to draw the attention of all Europe, and gain the publicity which would make it effective.

Yet he could not refuse. The sight of the highest ruler in Christendom begging for forgiveness in the snow had already shocked all Europe who knew of it, and especially the Countess Matilda and her entourage who witnessed it. Even if he did not fulfill his Christian duty of forgiving an apparently repentant sinner, he must lose the moral support of Christendom and thus endanger the whole reform and undermine its theoretical foundations. So, in the final analysis, he had no choice.

But it seems from his correspondence that the cruelty of the dilemma and his difficult decision unnerved him, and robbed him of the decisiveness he had shown throughout his life. It would seem possible for Gregory to have given Henry some drastic penance, as, for instance, sending him on a pilgrimage to Jerusalem, which would have removed him from Germany. This idea does not seem to have occurred to Gregory. And while relieving Henry of the ban of excommunication Gregory did not say whether he was to be restored to his throne or not, thus leaving Rudolph and the nobles in an impossible position. All he did was extract an oath from Henry that he would not hinder Gregory's own journey to Germany, and would "give satisfaction in the matter of the German clergy." Rudolph wrote an agonized letter to Gregory asking for instructions, but did not receive a straightforward answer. Gregory merely said that he had not restored Henry to the throne, but he did not say that he was still deposed and that the nobles should bestow the crown elsewhere.

Recovery of Henry iv—*Flight of Gregory* —Henry returned to a divided Germany. Legates were busy trying to repair the situation, and preparing for the election of a new king. But Henry immediately assumed his old authority, and nobles and clergy began to return to him. By 1080 Gregory had made up his mind, but by this time the position had deteriorated beyond retrieving.

He excommunicated and deposed Henry again. Rudolph and the rebellious nobles took up the challenge, but they were too few and they had lost their moment. Before the end of the year Henry had crushed them and killed Rudolph. He was now ready to deal with Gregory. At a council of German clergy called by Henry, Gregory was formally deposed, and an antipope was proclaimed in his place.

Gregory now only had one resort while Henry was collecting an army to invade Italy and make his deposition effective. He called upon his Norman vassals to protect Rome. They could not answer at once, however, and Henry arrived first, in 1084. He had himself crowned by his antipope, while Gregory fled.

Sack of Rome by Normans—Death of Gregory VII—No sooner had Henry left for Germany than the Normans appeared, furious with the Roman nobles and people for having yielded Rome to the Germans without a fight. Using this as an excuse, they thoroughly sacked Rome, and took Gregory back with them to Monte Cassino. He died shortly afterward at Salerno, his whole policy apparently a failure; he was detested by the Germans for his interference in imperial affairs, and by the Romans for having invited the barbarous Normans into the city to sack it. And there was an antipope still officially on the papal throne.

Consequence of this attempt at control of secular power by the papacy—This important episode in the rise of the papacy to power has been dealt with in such detail because it reveals so clearly both the strength and the weakness of the papal claim to temporal authority. At a crucial moment the pope could not disregard the fact that he was head of Christendom and not a secular ruler. And his position as arbiter in the affairs of Europe depended on his ability to make use of German disunity. When he was no longer able to make use of it, he had to depend on an army which consulted only its own interests. Pope Innocent III, who in a later century brought papal power to its height, was likewise dependent on a similar German disunity for the free hand he was allowed in his reign, as we shall see; and his ability to discipline English and French rulers was dependent upon the fact that they were at war with each other. The successors of Innocent could no longer hope to divide and rule at all. The papal support was not worth enough troops unless the contending forces were fairly equal. These successors had to enlist the support of towns and independent feudal lords with armies; but in so doing they lost their moral authority, and were treated as the secular lords whose weapons they were using.

This, stripped of theories and pretensions, is the inner story of the rise and fall of the papacy as a universal state within the territory of Europe; and it could already have been predicted in the time of Gregory VII from a close observation of the significant details of his victory and defeat.

Diversion of interest to Crusades under papal leadership

Though Gregory himself was defeated and died in exile, his work did not die with him. Henry in Germany was still excommunicated and, in the eyes of the papacy, still dethroned; and rebellions continued against him for the rest of his life. Finally his son was elected king by the nobles with papal support, and Henry died a year later, really without a throne. The new king once interfered in Italy to ensure his imperial coronation, but the College of Cardinals continued to elect the popes without hindrance, establishing enough precedent for the practice to make it impossible for an emperor later to question its legality. But meanwhile papal interest had shifted to the Crusades, which increased their authority in a different way, as related in a subsequent section.

Concordat of Worms—Compromise on lay investiture

The popes and the new emperor, Henry V, continued to negotiate on the matter of lay investiture, usually in a more cooperative manner. One pope, Paschal II, even admitted the logic of the situation—that if the popes wished to control the clergy they should not rely upon lands bestowed by the emperor but should make other arrangements to support them. This admission naturally raised an outcry from the clergy, who had no desire to lose their fiefs and become dependent on charity. At last a compromise was arranged, embodied in the Concordat of Worms of 1122. Under this settlement the emperor invested the clergy with land and secular authority, symbolized by the scepter; while the pope invested them with spiritual authority, symbolized by ring and staff. Thus each had a veto on the other's appointments, a clear gain for the papacy, for it now gained something it had never previously held, while the emperor lost his right to make nominations without reference to the papacy. As long as the popes remained reformers, simony and incelibacy could be held in check, since they could always refuse to invest any priest who did not fulfill their moral and religious requirements.

The rise of the Hohenstaufen family to the imperial throne—Renewal of conflict

Basis for increased power of the Empire —In the later twelfth century the struggle between Empire and papacy changed its character. A new family, the Hohenstaufens, took over the German kingship; and by a shrewd policy of divide and rule within Germany its leading representative was able to gain the support of enough great feudal lords to keep his power intact through his lifetime and hand it over, fortified by the great prestige of his name and successes, to his son. The second great family in Germany, the Welfs of Saxony, at first conciliated and then ruthlessly suppressed by Frederic Barbarossa of the Hohenstaufens, remained an outstanding competitor for a century. The names of these two families became so well known in Europe that, even in Italy, the Welfs were always regarded as anti-imperial, and the name "Guelph" (corruption of Welf) was used for all anti-imperialists in Italy; while the imperialist supporters were called Ghibellines from the corrupted name of the

imperial estates of the Hohenstaufen family (Waiblingen).

The first Hohenstaufens were supporters of the papacy and the cause of religious reform. But perhaps the greatest king of the line, Frederic I Barbarossa (1152–1190) was interested in the papacy and reform only when they collided with his ambitions. His main task in life was the establishment of a real Holy Roman Empire (the title seems to be his), with full control not only of Germany but of Italy. For most of his life he was able to keep the support of his German clergy and make use of their services for his imperial aims. But the basis of his power was feudal and military. He and his son and grandson were able to bring the Holy Roman Empire to the height of its medieval strength.

Italian policy of Frederic Barbarossa— It was certain that these ambitions would come in conflict with the papal secular interests in Italy, especially since Frederic coveted Rome itself. And the whole reign of Frederic Barbarossa was occupied in a skillful rear-guard action by the papacy, now with one ally and now with another against what seemed until the end to be overwhelming military power.

Northern Italy in the last hundred years had become dotted with prosperous towns, in part as a result of the Crusades. These towns had originally been feudal possessions under the nominal overlordship of the emperor, and ruled directly either by his nobles or by higher clergy who were often hardly distinguishable from the nobility. While the nobility in these towns felt their interests to be bound up with the feudal system and the emperor (Ghibelline party), the bourgeois and the lower classes deeply resented any feudal interference whatever (Guelphs). And when Frederic began to insist that feudal dues be paid to him, an extra burden which had been laxly enforced, if at all, in earlier days, some of the towns overthrew their local feudal overlords altogether, bringing imperial wrath and armies down on their heads. The papacy at first sided with the nobles, especially when bishops and archbishops were attacked; then, quickly realizing where its own interests lay, preferred to support the towns against the emperor.

Frederic precipitated the conflict by stating imperial claims in an extreme form at the Diet of Roncaglia in 1158, including the collection of dues and direct administration of the towns through imperial nominees. Many of the Italian towns, including Milan, made armed resistance to the decrees with papal support. Frederic razed Milan, marched on Rome, denied recognition to Pope Alexan-

der III, and installed an antipope. But Alexander himself escaped, and with support from Venice, the Normans, and, of course, the Italian towns, re-entered Rome as soon as Frederic was gone. He then helped organize the Lombard League of Italian towns, including a new Milan, rebuilt by the efforts of the league.

When Frederic in 1176 was able to give full attention to Italian affairs again, he was met by the united resistance of the league, and his German army was heavily defeated

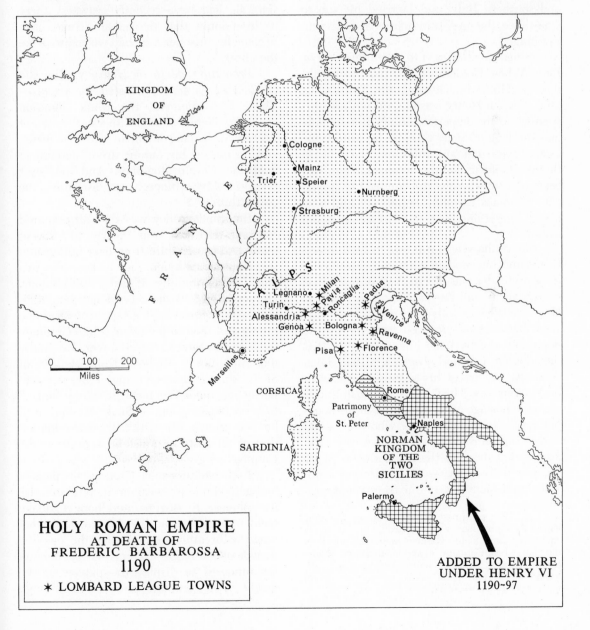

KINGDOM OF ENGLAND

FRANCE

Cologne
Mainz
Trier
Speier
Nurnberg
Strasburg

A L P S
Legnano • Milan
Pavia
Turin • Roncaglia
Alessandria • Padua
Genoa • Bologna • Venice
Ravenna
Pisa • Florence
Marseilles

CORSICA
Rome
Patrimony of St. Peter
Naples

SARDINIA
NORMAN KINGDOM OF THE TWO SICILIES

Palermo

0   100   200
Miles

HOLY ROMAN EMPIRE
AT DEATH OF
FREDERIC BARBAROSSA
1190

★ LOMBARD LEAGUE TOWNS

ADDED TO EMPIRE
UNDER HENRY VI
1190–97

at Legnano, the first major defeat of feudal cavalry by infantry. Frederic at once came to terms with Alexander, recognizing him as the lawful pope, and a few years later signed the Peace of Constance with the towns (1183). By this treaty he retained his less important rights, carrying prestige but little power, while virtual sovereignty was granted to the towns (as described in more detail in a later chapter). But, perhaps of more importance for the future, Frederic also made peace with the Norman kingdom of Sicily and southern Italy, and married his son to Constance, the niece and heiress of the reigning king.

Menace of Henry VI to papal interests in Italy—When Frederic Barbarossa suddenly died in 1190 while leading the Third Crusade,[1] his son Henry was elected without opposition to the imperial throne. But he was also the king of Sicily through his wife Constance, who had just inherited the Sicilian throne. Sicily under the Norman kings had been made into a powerful compact kingdom, with revenues carefully organized, and supplying everything that the German Empire lacked.

Henry, however, was not to be allowed to resume his Sicilian kingdom peacefully, for a pretender was on the throne, supported by the Welfs and the local Sicilian nobility. He marched into Italy, meeting little resistance, had himself crowned emperor by the pope, and received the fortunate news that the king of England, Richard I, had been captured by one of his vassals on the way back from the Third Crusade. Using this valuable hostage as an argument in his negotiations, he forced the Welfs, who were allied to the English royal house, to give way. And just at that moment the pretender in Sicily providentially died, so that Henry's campaign into Sicily became a triumphant procession.

[1] In later centuries Frederic became a heroic legendary figure who was not dead, but lay in an enchanted sleep in the German mountains awaiting the day when Germany again needed him. Nineteenth-century German nationalists revived the legend and it played no small part in the rise of modern German nationalism.

At this point Henry, in control of a temporarily submissive Germany and a united kingdom of Sicily, thus held the Italian peninsula in a pincer grip. There was nowhere for the pope to turn to for allies except the towns, which were now engaged in bickering among themselves, with Guelphs and Ghibellines struggling for control of the individual cities and attacking each other according to whichever party gained control. While Henry VI had apparently no immediate plans in Italy and no quarrel in progress with the papacy since he had been recently crowned, there is little doubt that the papacy could have become his prisoner if he had wished to make the effort.

Premature death of Henry VI—Internal conflict in Empire promoted by papacy—Then, in a moment, the whole situation changed. Henry died at the early age of thirty-two, leaving a son of three in Sicily, and no one of his family strong enough to hold the Empire together. And one year later, in 1198, Innocent III ascended the papal throne.

Innocent's policy was thus all prepared for him. His task was clearly to prevent Sicily and the Empire from ever falling into the same hands again, and to keep the two chief German families at each other's throats. He accomplished the second not very difficult task by throwing his support first to one family and then to the other, while Germany fell into the throes of a civil war. He kindly took the infant Frederic Hohenstaufen of Sicily, son of Henry VI, under his personal patronage, made him his ward, and promised to keep the kingdom of Sicily for him until he was grown up—with the determination that at all costs he must be kept from the Empire.

In the century since Gregory, the papacy had gained no new weapon; it could exercise its influence to disrupt, and hope to make incidental gains from the discord. Nevertheless, the breathing space after the extreme danger of the reign of Henry VI was enough for Innocent to display the papacy at the height of its temporal power; even though to hindsight its foundations were no stronger than the temporary division among the natural opponents of papal prerogatives in the secular realm.

PAPAL POLICY IN FRANCE—RELATIONS WITH CAPETIAN KINGS

Lay investiture

Papal prohibition of lay investiture was not confined to Germany, but was directed against all monarchs equally. Philip I, the French king in Gregory VII's time (1060–1108), like all the poverty-stricken kings of his line, regarded simony as one of his necessary sources of income. He had to be excommunicated three times before he finally submitted; his own feeble position as one of the less powerful of French feudal lords made him vulnerable to papal attack. The question was not of sufficient importance to him to make him wish to endanger the careful work his family was engaged in—trying to expand its feudal domain into a real kingdom. A compromise was agreed to under which the investiture by ring and staff was dropped by the king; but he was permitted to postpone appointments until a suitable candidate was found whom he was ready to confirm, and his right to confirm such candidates was guaranteed by the papacy. This was substantially what was agreed to for Germany at the Concordat of Worms in 1122 as already described.

Philip Augustus and Innocent III

The later Capetian kings chose their clergy wisely and with a regard for their ability rather than for their birth, including the indefatigable Abbot Suger, who was the virtual ruler of the kingdom while his master was on a crusade. Such men, owing their positions altogether to the monarchs, served them far more faithfully than the nobles who were always seeking the advancement of their families and the expansion of their lands.

Philip Augustus (1180–1223), the real unifier of France, a master of political strategy, understood very clearly the strengths and weaknesses of his position. In his dealings with the papacy he showed also that he knew the limitations of its power, and how far he could safely go with Innocent III. In 1193 he repudiated his wife, Ingeborg of Denmark, without papal permission, later marrying another wife. Innocent commanded him to take back Ingeborg and give up his second wife; when Philip refused he laid an interdict upon the country. Thereupon Philip submitted; he was heavily engaged in taking the English king John's possessions in France and could not afford to have the pope and the English king in alliance against him. Innocent continued to object to Philip's conquests of John's territories, but Philip paid no further attention to him, and in due course the pope himself became embroiled with John over the appointment of the Archbishop of Canterbury.

Now Philip's submission paid off. The pope began to support him; and when at last he deposed John, Philip was his chosen successor for the throne of England. Nothing more was said about Philip's conquests in France. If John had not submitted to the pope Philip might well have gained his throne—or at least have been able to bargain with him for all his French possessions in exchange for it. Philip also refused to take part in the Albigensian Crusade proclaimed by the pope against heretics in southern France, although the territory was not yet part of his domains, and denied that the pope had any right to call the crusade at all. In short, outside the minor matter of the divorce, which did not concern his kingdom, Philip pleased himself in France, without caring what Innocent desired, but he was not above making use of Innocent when it seemed profitable to do so. The kingdom thus unified by Philip was to prove itself invulnerable to serious attacks by the papacy at the end of the thirteenth century, the first of the national states to win a complete and enduring victory, as will be seen in the next chapter.

Struggle with the Norman kings over lay investiture

When Duke William of Normandy wished to conquer England at the height of the reform movement, he took the precaution of sounding out the papacy first. He was rewarded with a banner and confirmation of his claim to the throne. The pope was able to justify this action since Harold, the Saxon nominee to the English crown, had sworn an oath that he would not claim it, and so could be regarded as perjured.

But when William had conquered England, he was determined to make his rule absolute, with no interference from any outsiders, however exalted. Papal bulls could not be published in England, the pope himself would not be recognized without the king's consent. William chose and invested with both temporal and spiritual power all the higher clergy, and paid no attention whatever to decrees which forbade such a practice. At the same time he appointed Lanfranc, one of the greatest churchmen of the day, as Archbishop of Canterbury. Lanfranc, who had been an abbot under William in Normandy, was in full sympathy with the greater part of the reform. Not needing the cash, William did not engage in simony, and clerical celibacy was enforced. Though Gregory VII admonished him on lay investiture, the main purpose of the reform was in any case accomplished; papal control of the clergy was not so necessary if the king would truly control them himself. In any case, Gregory's hands were full with Germany, and he had absolutely no power over William in his compact country entirely subordinated to himself—and Gregory knew it.

William Rufus, however, son of the Conqueror, had no Lanfranc at hand, was not interested in the welfare of the Church, and was unable to control his nobles as effectively as his father had. Declaring he would be head of the Church himself, he refused to appoint any successor to Lanfranc. Since this was the period of difficulty after the death of Gregory VII, no action could be taken, until William, of his own accord, stricken by an illness, gave the position to another abbot from Normandy, St. Anselm. But on the recovery of the king, Anselm found his position impossible and left the country, while William continued his lay investiture to which Anselm had objected. Even under William's successor, Henry I, Anselm continued to object, and refused to accept the king's appointees. After Anselm was absent from England several times to plead the case at Rome and gain papal support, his position was vindicated in part. The pope negotiated an agreement with Henry in 1107 under which the king gave up the right to invest with ring and staff, but could receive homage from his appointees on granting them their land.

Henry II and St. Thomas Becket—Royal jurisdiction over the clergy

This question of lay investiture in England having been settled by the usual compromise, during the period of anarchy that followed the death of Henry I the Church became as independent of the king as the feudal nobility; and Henry II felt impelled to reduce both to obedience. He was more successful with the nobles than with the Church. He believed his chance had come when he appointed St. Thomas Becket, his own chancellor, a man who had hitherto been entirely dependent on his favor, as Archbishop of Canterbury. Thomas, Henry thought, would help him with a matter that was of increasing consequence to him, the attempt to make a uniform English law code, and the establishment of the king's justice over feudal and ecclesiastical law.

But Thomas understood very well the nature of his own power as archbishop, that it was conferred upon him by the pope, even though the king had chosen him in the first place and prevailed upon the pope to accept him. And he no longer felt himself the king's servant, but the servant of the Church. When Henry in 1164 issued the Constitutions of Clarendon, declaring that in future all clerks in holy orders accused of secular

The murder of Thomas Becket by the knights of King Henry II of England. From the Ramsey Abbey Psalter *(English), 1285–1300.* (COURTESY THE PIERPONT MORGAN LIBRARY. Ms. 302, folio 4)

crimes were to be tried in the king's courts, Thomas protested; he then went abroad and for several years waged a verbal war with his monarch. Finally in 1170, returning with a bull of excommunication in his pocket ready to be used if necessary, he was murdered at the altar of his cathedral in Canterbury by a party of Henry's knights who had taken a wrathful outburst of the king's to be an order.[2] Public opinion was outraged, Henry had to do penance and allow the monks of Canterbury to scourge him, and was forced to withdraw his Constitutions. The Church had won, though not on this occasion at the initiative of the pope. It was, however, the backing that St. Thomas Becket received from the Papacy that enabled him to stand up against his master who had appointed him.

[2] T. S. Eliot's famous play, *Murder in the Cathedral*, concerns this incident.

Quarrel between John and Innocent III— England a fief of the papacy

Henry's younger son John, as we have seen, embroiled himself with Innocent III; and again the struggle was over the appointment of the Archbishop of Canterbury. John, in desperate need of funds to sustain his unpopular war with Philip Augustus of France over the French possessions of his house, seems to have thought he could lay his hands on the possessions of the Church with impunity. At all events, his challenge of Innocent III seems to have been deliberate, since the appointment itself was of little real consequence, not at all proportionate to the stubbornness with which John tried to get his way. On the death of the previous archbishop there had been a difference of opinion between John and the clergy of Canterbury, who had the right to select a candidate for the king's approval. The king's friends at Canterbury chose one candidate, and his opponents another. Both sides appealed to the pope, who decided to appoint neither, preferring an English cardinal, Stephen Langton, with better qualifications than either of the two suggested candidates. The clergy of Canterbury were converted to the papal viewpoint, and all that was needed was John's assent. This he refused; and Innocent, again using first his bludgeon weapon against the whole people, laid an interdict upon England, later also excommunicating John himself. John then proceeded to confiscate Church property, paying no attention to the interdict or his excommunication. But the country, suffering from the interdict which lasted five years, from John's futile wars in defense of his possessions, and from the refusal of the clergy to assist even in the burial of the dead, was in the utmost misery; and the feudal lords, who had no interest in John's wars in France, and objected strenuously to his illegal collection of taxes, were only looking for a chance to overthrow him.

Finally Innocent used his last weapon, made possible only by the willingness of Philip Augustus of France to cooperate. He deposed John and offered the kingdom to the French monarch, who began to make preparations for an invasion. The English nobles thought it a good opportunity to desert John, and made ready to welcome Philip and his son. At this point John submitted to Innocent, giving him the whole country as a fief, doing him homage, and agreeing to pay him heavy feudal dues as his vassal.

But this was the limit of Innocent's success. Now anxious to protect his vassal, he found that he had encouraged the nobles to revolt, and they were no longer willing to acquiesce in John's arbitrary rule. When John joined the Holy Roman Emperor in an alliance against Philip Augustus and both were defeated at the battle of Bouvines in 1214, the barons were able to bring John to the point of renouncing his arbitrary rule, and signing Magna Carta, dealt with in more detail in a later chapter. This infuriated Innocent, who had by this time called off Philip Augustus, was not at all interested in the grievances of his vassal's nobles, and naturally wished to control them himself through John. He forbade John to observe the Charter (in any case John had no intention of doing so if he could help it). Innocent also forbade the nobles to insist on its enforcement on pain of excommunication. But the nobles were beyond Innocent's reach; they were not afraid of his spiritual weapons, and even Innocent's own appointee to Canterbury joined them. They were all duly excommunicated. The nobles then personally asked Philip Augustus to come over and take the throne. Louis, his son, had already arrived in England when John and the pope both died in the same year, and the invasion was abandoned, while the nobles hastened to try to obtain control over John's young son, who was not yet of age.

Like Innocent's other victories, this long quarrel showed to the world the real weakness of papal power underneath the apparent glittering success. He had not been able to control the English nobles, and had helped to break the power of the English monarchy only to hand it over to a far less easily controlled nobility. By using the interdict he had aroused an enmity in the English people which was never to be overcome. Both nobles and people resented bitterly the aids which the king had to pay as a vassal under feudal law; even a monk like Matthew Paris complained throughout the next reign of the rapacity of papal tax collectors. And within half a century, as a direct result of pious Henry III's efforts to fulfill faithfully his duties as a vassal, the English people had their first Parliament, an instrument of government that was quite beyond the understanding or control of an autocratic papacy. This Parliament, in a later century, was to create a new English Church under the direction of a monarch who was no longer frightened of papal displeasure.

▶ Unification of Christendom against the Muslims—The Crusades

THE BACKGROUND FOR THE FIRST CRUSADE

Papal interest

We must now return to the close of

the eleventh century and take up the history of a movement that first added power to the papacy and then, like the struggle with the secular powers, escaped its control and helped aid those forces working against all religious authority. It will be understood that the Crusades could be described under any of a number of possible headings, and that they have been inserted in this chapter because they will be dealt with here especially from the point of view of their consequences for the growth of papal power.

In 1095, while the reformed Cluniac papacy was still in power and the investiture struggle was not yet settled, Pope Urban II called for the First Crusade in a masterly and impassioned speech. The Seljuk Turks, a warlike and semicivilized group of Muslims, had taken control of the decaying Abbasid dynasty of Bagdad and had gradually encroached on the territories still officially under Abbasid control. Unlike, however, the enlightened caliphs of Bagdad, they showed no respect for Christians, no understanding of the value of the pilgrimage trade to Jerusalem, and still less for the venerable empire of Constantinople. The Byzantines were also threatened by further invasions of Asiatic barbarians from the northeast.

Ordinarily the papacy would have had little sympathy for Alexius Comnenus, the emperor of Constantinople. For forty years the Eastern Empire had been altogether cut off from the papacy, and had set up its own Greek Orthodox Church, which held, among other things, as we have seen, a different opinion from the Western Church on the matter of the procession of the Holy Spirit. But Western Christians did revere Jerusalem, and pilgrimages to the Holy City were a recognized form of penance as well as a means of acquiring merit. So when the Turks started to rob and harass the pilgrims, even refusing them entry to the Holy City, this action was a serious matter for the Church, and tended to make the papacy more ready than usual to listen to the request sent by Alexius for help.

A crusade was not a new thing. For years, under the auspices of the Church, the nobility of Europe had been nibbling away at Muslim domination of Spain, but the sporadic expeditions had never become a mass movement; they did not hold the religious appeal that an all-out war with infidels would provide. The papacy had just been able to assert its spiritual supremacy by bringing the emperor to Canossa. But it could use still more prestige in its struggle with the secular powers; there could be no more glorious way of gaining it than by preaching and supplying the spiritual leadership for an expansion of Christendom into the East and capturing the very center of the religion, the Holy City where Christ had died and been resurrected.

It was also true that there was, from the papal point of view, too much feudal warfare in Europe. The Truce of God could never be fully enforced. The nobles loved fighting; it was their chief business in life. Could some of this excess vigor be used in a holy cause? It might be that some would not return, and that churchmen, as noncombatants, would look after their possessions while they were away. If Jerusalem and Syria were indeed conquered, then who should be the new overlord but the papacy who inspired the conquest? And perhaps Alexius, in exchange for suitable help, would consent to bring his Church once more under papal authority and back to doctrinal orthodoxy.

All these things must have passed through Urban's mind while he played upon the religious feelings of the people, upon the martial feelings of the nobility, and while he promised a plenary or full indulgence for all their sins to those who died for the cause, and when he gave permission to Peter the Hermit to preach a crusade throughout Christendom.

Interest in crusade of other classes in society—Cities, nobility, kings, peasants

The maritime cities, especially Genoa and Venice, had been going ahead rapidly since the Muslims had been driven from the Mediterranean; but the Byzantines kept a tight hold on the Aegean. Timely aid or pressure from the West might persuade them to be less monopolistic with their trade. New trade with Muslims was, of course, reprehensible, but surely possible. And crusaders would not care perhaps to march through Europe when ships could be put at their disposal, for a price. The Venetians and Genoese welcomed the crusade and began to build ships, which they would be delighted to provide in such a noble cause. If the crusaders were successful they could take the Muslim luxuries without payment—a considerable boon to trade which had always been kept to small proportions for the lack of suitable Western goods to export. And if they failed, they still had to pay for transportation, in advance. So how could they lose?

The feudal lords looked first at their own lands, and then thought of Syria and Jerusalem. Europe was getting a little small and overcrowded, and it was very poor. Travelers' tales said the East was rich. The great lords thought it would be a fine thing if the smaller lords went and did not come back; the smaller lords dreamed of fiefs without overlords, and wondered whether they could raise funds for the expedition, and if so from whom. The Normans remembered their Viking ancestry; it had been a long time since they had been permitted a good looting, except those few who had been allowed to sack Rome a few years ago. Europe was becoming a very tame place; perhaps they should not have settled down so quickly. Their cousins had taken Sicily from the Muslims and built themselves a kingdom. Why not a larger and more glorious kingdom in the even more wealthy East? And they all thought what a pleasure it would be to be allowed to fight a holy war, sanctified by the Church, killing infidels and being forgiven one's own sins into the bargain.

The kings thought what a blessing it would be if there were fewer feudal lords in the country. A wide-awake monarch ought to be able to pick up a few lands here and there. He would be glad to act as trustee and protect his theoretical vassals and perhaps even make them into real ones. At all events it was wiser to stay at home where there was much work to be done. Let the crusaders have their glory and if they won some fiefs in Palestine, so much the better. Perhaps they would stay there.

But beyond and above all these private considerations the religious zeal was unmistakable. Many in the full flood of enthusiasm went against their material interests. With scarcely the vaguest idea even of where Jerusalem was, still less of what they would find there, never having seen an infidel, they received absolution from the Church, donned the sacred emblems which showed they were crusaders, and set out by land determined to recover the Holy Sepulcher, without thought of the lands they had mortgaged and left behind them or the dangers which lay in front of them. Afterward it became necessary for the popes to use coercion, and leadership fell into the hands of kings who went because it was expected of them. But no one was coerced for the First Crusade; and it was the only crusade that was successful.

THE FIRST CRUSADE

An army of peasants was the first to be ready. Unable, even if it had occurred to them, to afford the expense of a sea passage, they marched in a disorderly rabble through Europe, led by Peter the Hermit himself. Unable to take along any food for themselves, they lived off the country they passed through, to the great annoyance of the owners who were forced to defend their territories, at high cost to the peasant army. Many died of starvation and exposure. The remnant reached Constantinople in advance of the nobility and was given hasty passage across the Bosporus. In Asia Minor the Turks quickly took care of them; few escaped, though Peter the Hermit was one who did.

Slightly less disorderly were the armies of the feudal nobles and their vassals who followed, also by land, for the few ships available could not transport so many, nor could the nobility afford the cost of sea transport in an economy which contained so little money. But these lords could defend themselves going through Europe, and they were not quite so numerous as the earlier

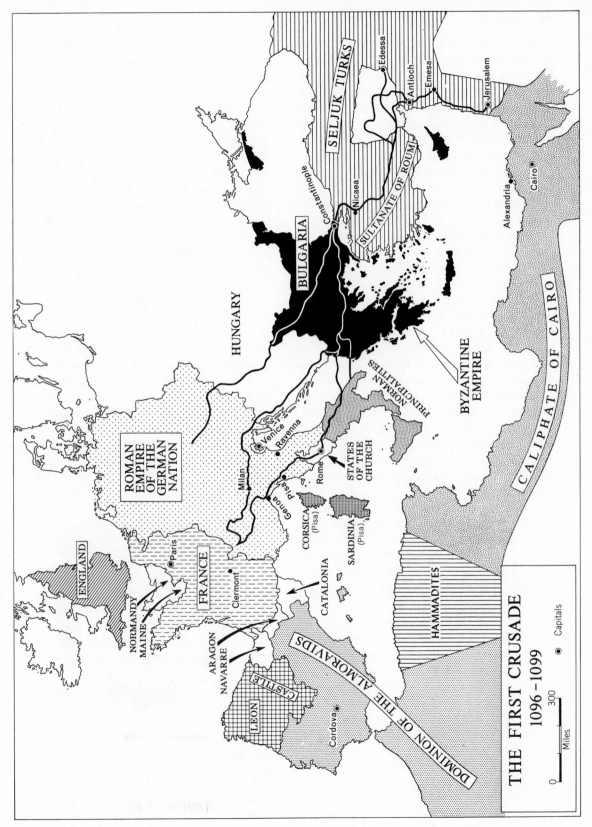

THE FIRST CRUSADE
1096-1099

ENGLAND

NORMANDY
MAINE

FRANCE

Paris

Clermont

ROMAN
EMPIRE
OF THE
GERMAN
NATION

HUNGARY

BULGARIA

SELJUK TURKS

Constantinople

Nicaea

SULTANATE OF ROUM

Edessa

Antioch

Emesa

Jerusalem

Alexandria

Cairo

CALIPHATE OF CAIRO

BYZANTINE
EMPIRE

NORMAN
PRINCIPALITIES

Venice
Ravenna

Milan

Genoa
Pisa

Rome

STATES
OF THE
CHURCH

CORSICA
(Pisa)

SARDINIA
(Pisa)

CATALONIA

ARAGON

NAVARRE

LEON

CASTILE

Cordova

DOMINION OF THE ALMORAVIDS

HAMMADITES

Miles

0   300

● Capitals

335

peasantry. Yet their passage was described by contemporaries as worse than a plague. Reaching Constantinople, they shocked Emperor Alexius by their barbarous manners. But, knowing himself powerless to resist them, and realizing that they might easily turn against his own city, he kept them as satisfied and peaceful as he could, courteously putting up with extreme indignities until he could get rid of them. But he did succeed in extracting an oath from them that they would return to him all his possessions in Asia Minor that they reconquered from the Turks, which he may have promised to give them back again as fiefs in the Western manner, though this is not certain.

At last he was able to move them across the Bosporus, and they captured Nicaea for him. Moving further into Asia Minor, the crusaders began to complain that Alexius was unfairly forbidding them to plunder as was their right, even though the cities were Greek and had been only temporarily occupied by the Turks. Finding it increasingly difficult to keep them in any kind of control, Alexius at last left them, content with what they had reconquered for him and free for a while from any danger of further Turkish inroads.

The crusaders, ignorant of the route to Palestine, and having no central leadership, began to split into small bands. One lord was invited into Edessa by its Christian ruler. He accepted and left the expedition. But at last, after many hardships, most of them reached Antioch, where they found a Genoese fleet with supplies, with the help of which they captured the city, giving it to another crusader for a fief. Then they proceeded down the coast and with only a minor battle captured Jerusalem from the Muslim garrison. They did not know that the Seljuk Empire had broken up some three years before the crusade, and that the reason they had been so successful was that the cities were manned only by Turkish governors without any prospect of reinforcement from Asia.

On capturing Jerusalem the crusaders went berserk, massacring the infidels, a harmless group of almost defenseless Egyptians, until they were up to the waists in corpses, and in Solomon's temple they rode up to their knees in blood, chanting praises to God at the same time for delivering the Holy Sepulcher into their hands. Such of Palestine as was conquered was organized into fiefs on the feudal model, owing allegiance to the papacy, with a Latin Kingdom of Jerusalem being organized soon afterward to take in all territory south of Edessa. For permanent defense various crusading orders of fighting monks were established, and castles were erected throughout the country to keep away the Muslims should their power show signs of reviving.

Every year the fleets of Venice, Genoa, and Pisa brought out reinforcements and supplies, taking back superior Oriental goods in return, which began to move into European markets. Lacking religious zeal, these merchants encouraged fraternization and peaceful relations with the infidels; and in due course the crusaders began to relax their severity, adopt Muslim customs and dress, and lord it over their realms like Oriental princelings, leaving defense to the new crusading orders and to mercenary armies locally recruited from the Oriental population.

A Knight Templar, a member of one of the orders organized to guard the Holy Land after the first crusade. In the particular manuscript from which this minature is taken, various occupations are shown, and a representative of each is seen being taken away by Death. From Hours of the Virgin, ca. 1450. (COURTESY THE PIERPONT MORGAN LIBRARY. Ms. 359, folio 128)

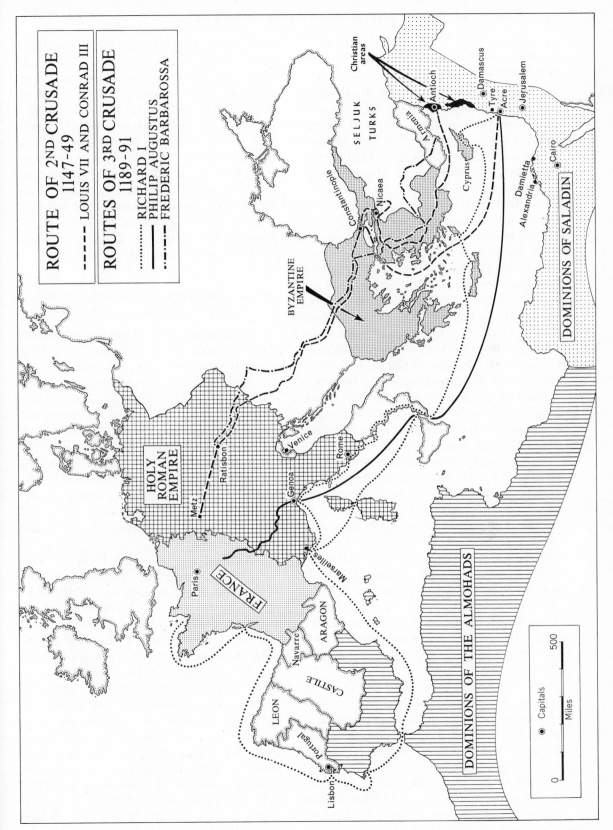

ROUTE OF 2ND CRUSADE
1147-49
—·—·— LOUIS VII AND CONRAD III

ROUTES OF 3RD CRUSADE
1189-91
············ RICHARD I
———— PHILIP AUGUSTUS
———— FREDERIC BARBAROSSA

● Capitals

0   Miles   500

FRANCE

HOLY ROMAN EMPIRE

Paris
Metz
Ratisbon
Genoa
Venice
Rome
Marseilles

LEON
Portugal
Lisbon
CASTILE
Navarre
ARAGON

DOMINIONS OF THE ALMOHADS

BYZANTINE EMPIRE

Constantinople
Nicaea
Aleppo

SELJUK TURKS

Armenia
Cyprus

Christian areas
Antioch
Damascus
Tyre
Acre
Jerusalem

Damietta
Alexandria
Cairo

DOMINIONS OF SALADIN

RECOVERY OF MUSLIM POWER—SECOND AND THIRD CRUSADES

The conquest by such an ill-organized and disunited army had only been possible because of the temporary collapse of Muslim power due to invasions that the Muslims themselves had to sustain from Asiatic Mongols. As soon, however, as Muslim power recovered, the crusaders, so far from home and utterly dependent on European reinforcements, were unable to survive. When Edessa, the independent fief to the northeast of the kingdom, fell in 1144 another crusade was called. This was led by the Holy Roman Emperor, Conrad III, and the French king, Louis VII, who had been shamed into the effort by the preaching of St. Bernard. Again the expedition went by land, and again thousands of lives were lost before Palestine was reached. The Muslims waged guerrilla warfare against the crusaders; finally the kings decided their presence was needed nearer home, and proceeded to return. The crusade never approached close to Edessa, and the rest of Palestine was not yet threatened.

However, the Muslims were already beginning to recover their initiative. The Syrian cities that remained to them were united under one rule, and Saladin, the nephew of the new Syrian ruler, was sent to Egypt to hasten the end of the tottering Fatimid dynasty in Cairo, and if possible take the crown himself. He was successful in this mission, reorganized Egypt, and in 1187 recaptured Jerusalem, which he treated in a conspicuously gentle manner, permitting all those who had money to ransom themselves, and letting those who were too poor to pay ransom go free.

A new crusade was called in Europe to recover Jerusalem. Emperor Frederic Barbarossa agreed to go with an army of Germans. The expedition this time was well organized, but Frederic himself was drowned in crossing a river and most of his army returned home (1190). Richard I (the Lion Heart) and Philip Augustus of France, sworn enemies at home, were both coerced into going, especially Philip, who was no warrior,

and had pressing interests in France where he was trying to take possession of Richard's lands. The armies had little success, in part because of the quarreling of the leaders. When Philip thought he had done enough for honor, he went home, leaving Richard, who was a warrior and liked fighting, to bear the brunt alone. The city of Acre was captured from the Muslims, but otherwise nothing of importance was accomplished. After making a truce with Saladin, which left Jerusalem in the latter's hands, Richard returned home to be captured and held for ransom by the new emperor, Henry VI.

PAPAL PERSISTENCE IN CALLING CRUSADES—THE FOURTH "CRUSADE" TO CONSTANTINOPLE

Pope Innocent III could not view these disasters with equanimity. He refused to recognize the obvious reality that the interests of Europe had turned away from crusading. The feudal nobility were now almost as much interested in obtaining luxuries as in fighting, and their religious zeal was at a low ebb. The upper classes of Europe had begun to know prosperity for the first time since the Roman Empire, and commercial interests were increasing in influence. But Innocent, not to be outdone by his predecessors, used all his authority to get a new crusade started.

No king was willing to leave his territories at the time. Philip Augustus and John of England were engaged in war with each other and turned a deaf ear to his pleas; Innocent himself had seen to it that there was also no Holy Roman Emperor worthy of the name at the moment. The feudal lords pleaded poverty; but Innocent was inexorable. Finally a number of lords agreed to go, after making financial arrangements with the Venetians. But when it was time to go they still had not raised the price. At this point the Venetians graciously permitted them transportation expenses to be paid out of the proceeds of the expedition, and Dandolo, the aged and blind Doge of Venice, added that the city would even provide fifty ships of its own.

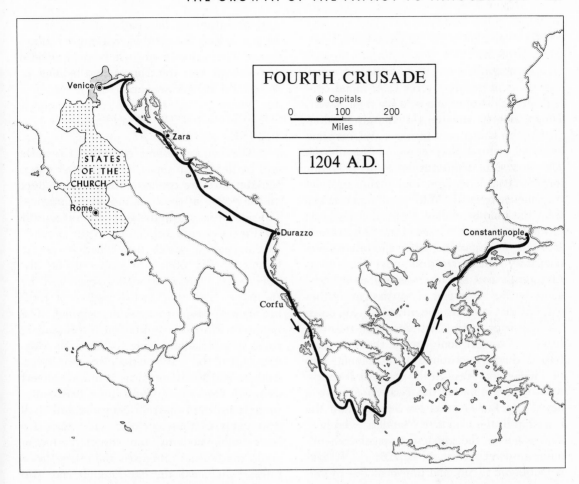

As they started down the Adriatic Dandolo suggested to the crusaders that it would be to the benefit of all if they captured a city for him which had once belonged to Venice, but had been recently lost to the Hungarian king. Obligingly the crusaders turned aside and took Zara on the Dalmatian coast. After looting and sacking the city, they then destroyed it. Innocent, horrified at this crime against a perfectly good Christian city, excommunicated the whole body of crusaders; then, suddenly thinking better of it, he released them from the ban, and allowed them to proceed.

The ships started off again. But now a further temptation assailed them. A Byzantine pretender to the throne of Constantinople who had some real claim to it asked them to lend him some aid. If they succeeded in restoring him, he would pay off all the debts owed by the crusaders to Venice. Seeing no opportunity for similar rewards in Palestine, which by now was no longer so wealthy as in earlier days and offered few opportunities for loot, the fleet proceeded to Constantinople, restored the pretender to his throne, and awaited payment. No serious resistance was offered to the Crusaders save by the imperial guard of Swedes.

The new emperor was slow in paying, but at last he gave the bulk of the promised sum. But the Venetians cornered most of it, leaving the crusaders only a pittance for all their trouble. So when a rebellion broke out against the newly installed monarch, they regarded themselves as freed from all obligations to the Byzantines, and proceeded to besiege the city. Unable to withstand both a fleet and an army, the city soon fell, and was looted by the crusaders and the Venetians for three days. Completely ignorant of the value of anything in the city except precious metals, they broke up priceless works of art simply for their metal content; they destroyed mosaics for their jewels. They wantonly violated the church of Santa Sophia, breaking up the altar and carrying away everything they could lay hands on. The looting of Constantinople in 1204 lost forever most of the precious manuscripts of the ancient world. With the manuscripts went the unique works of classical Hellenic art pillaged from Greece by Constantine. The loss is irreparable, since the other great repository of manuscripts, the Library at Alexandria, had already been pillaged many centuries before during a fourth-century theological riot and by the invading Muslims.

The bulk of the crusaders then returned home laden with booty, while the Venetians busied themselves founding a colonial empire which included all the choicest seaports. And on the ruins of the Eastern Empire a new Latin Empire was organized under the rulership of the Count of Flanders, who held it as a fief of the papacy. It passed an unmeritorious existence till in 1261 the Greeks reconquered it. But the power of the Byzantine Empire was never fully restored after 1204, and it fell a victim to the Ottoman Turks two centuries later without being able to put up much resistance.

Innocent III did penance for the crusaders' victory, but thanked God that the Eastern and Western Churches had at last been united again. And, nothing daunted, he proclaimed another crusade at the Lateran Council of 1215. The king of Hungary agreed to go, but thought the best procedure was to go by way of Egypt. He captured Damietta, but promptly lost it and returned home. A crusade called in 1212 for the reconquest of Spain from the Muslims had better success. By 1236 the Muslims were driven out of Cordova, their capital, and the greater part of the country was in Christian hands.

Before his death Innocent had also forced his youthful protégé, Frederic of Sicily, to take the vow as a crusader. The crusade on which he finally went, after delaying as long as possible, will be described in the next chapter since it is symptomatic of the decline of the Church and belongs to the period after Innocent.

CONSEQUENCES OF THE CRUSADES FOR THE PAPACY

The economic results of the Crusades will be dealt with separately in a later chapter. Here we are concerned with their effect on the power of the Church and the papacy.

There is no doubt that the success of the First Crusade redounded to the prestige of the papacy, which had called it, as the failure of the others to some extent discredited it. The overlordship exercised by the popes over the Latin Kingdom of Jerusalem was never more than nominal. The papacy was unable to prevent the crusaders from tolerating and fraternizing with Muslims, once the early fanaticism was over. And very little attempt was made to convert the Muslims themselves to Christianity. Many crusaders married Muslims and took over many of their customs. They were far more influenced by the superior Muslim civilization even in its decay than they themselves influenced the Muslims. It has also been suggested that contact with the Greek Orthodox Church and with the various heretical groups that had been living peaceably in Palestine for centuries under Muslim rule made them realize that Western Catholicism was not as universally accepted as they had been led to believe, but actual evidence is necessarily missing for this assumption. There can be no doubt that the inability of Innocent to control the crusaders who sacked Constantinople was a blow to his prestige for which even the temporary forced union between Greek and Roman Churches was but a slight compensation, though the failure did not prevent his subsequent success in dictating to the kings of Europe.

The times had changed. The true crusading spirit had disappeared from all but a few remaining knights-errant such as St. Louis IX of France. The commercial spirit symbolized by the Fourth Crusade showed that men now had other interests than salvation. Indulgences had been cheapened by indiscriminate gifts of them to crusaders, the purity of whose deeds and motives was questionable. The political activities and worldliness of the Church were not escaping the notice of the more earnest Christians. And, as we shall see in the next section, the faith of the people, which was ultimately the only basis upon which all papal claims must rest, a truth which had been recognized by Gregory VII but forgotten by Innocent, had been put to a severe test by the actions of the papacy. Within the Church and outside it a movement had been growing since the eleventh century which called for a return to an earlier and more ideal Christianity.

▶ Reaction to the worldliness of the Church

REFORM OF MONASTERIES—ST. BERNARD

The Cluny movement, as we have seen, started as a reform of the monasteries and a return to the strictness of the Benedictine Rule. But the peculiar nature of the political framework of the Cluniac system, which fitted it for use as a means for increasing papal power, militated against its persistence as a thoroughgoing reform movement. Monks ambitious for power in the Church joined it, as well as sincere Christians who wished for a life of strict purity and religious observance; and before the end of the eleventh century the need was already becoming apparent for yet another monastic reform to take care of those Christians who still sought a purely religious life separated altogether from worldly concerns. The chief leader, though not the earliest, in the demand for reform was a man who had started life as a Burgundian noble, known to posterity as St. Bernard of Clairvaux (ca. 1090–1153).

There had already been an increase in the number of hermits living alone in small communities, and one order of extreme austerity had been founded, with its center in a forbidding district of southern France. The Carthusian Order, named for the district of La Grande Chartreuse, really preserved its original purity, and claims today that it is the only order that has never been reformed since it never has needed reformation. But St. Bernard's work was within the regular monastic system itself.

A little before his time the Cistercian Order had been founded by an abbot of a Benedictine monastery who had been unable to reform his own house. But it received a new impulse when Bernard entered it and became abbot of a daughter monastery of the Cistercians at Clairvaux. An ascetic and a mystic, St. Bernard believed that the only truly Christian life was to be found in communion with God. With a profound contempt for this world, its luxuries, and its knowledge, which, in his view, drew man away from his true task and delivered him into the hands of the Devil, he opposed with his matchless eloquence the whole trend of his age toward the secularization of Christianity and toward an increasing interest in earthly life. St. Bernard carried to an extreme the tendency of the early Western Christian Church to despise earthly power, possessions, and wisdom. The only purpose of life on earth was to prepare for salvation. Bernard attacked the secular clergy as grasping and interested only in power and display, to the neglect of its religious duties; he attacked the monks for laxity, loose living, and gluttony. He even attacked the Church builders for the excessive decoration of their churches, and he attacked Abélard for his pride in believing that the unaided human mind was capable of understanding and contributing to the knowledge of religious truth.

Such a man could have been dangerous to the Church, for his eloquence spared no man. In a later century, indeed, he might, like Savonarola, have used it against the Church itself. But in his own time the zeal for reform was widespread, and the papal chair was still occupied by men who had not yet become wholly politicians and diplomats. Christians in high places and low submitted to the lash of his tongue because in his day they still believed that what he said was true. And for forty years he was the most influential man in Christendom, the acknowledged keeper of the conscience of medieval Christianity.

For a time his Cistercian Order maintained its austerity; but, as with all the other successful orders which did not keep themselves altogether separated from the world, the wealth that flowed into it from the faithful undermined its discipline. Many of the Cistercian abbeys pioneered in good farming, and, as wool producers, entered industry; but by the fourteenth century their reputation as holy men and the tradition of St. Bernard had long been swallowed up by the commercial and secular interests of the age.

THE GROWTH OF HERESY

The nature of twelfth-century heresy

As early as the eleventh century attacks on the worldliness of the Church and the failure of the Church to heed them had driven occasional reformers into an uncompromising position which could only mean actual separation from organized religion. There were no other Churches to join; only one great Church, authoritarian and dogmatic, which had to be accepted or rejected. And the penalty for rejection, or heresy, was death if the heretic refused to change his views. Many such heretics no doubt found their way into the reformed monasteries where they could spend their lives in personal worship and outward conformity. If no such monastery appealed to them, then there was no other recourse than heresy.

When we have had occasion to deal with heresy in earlier chapters, the heresies, in the main, concerned questions of theology; at a time when Christian theology had not yet crystallized into dogma, or beliefs necessary for salvation promulgated by authority, such heresy was to be expected until the authority was universally accepted. Twelfth-century heresy is of a different kind. With a few minor exceptions it was anticlerical in origin, it was above everything against the established Church; and though in some cases a different doctrine was preached, the doctrine was subsidiary to the

anticlericalism, and usually grew out of it. The common element in all twelfth-century heresy was the belief that true Christianity consisted in leading a life more consistent with the life of Christ as it had been portrayed in the Gospels. It was, then, a reaction against the apparently non-Christian life of the Church and its clergy.

If this Church and its sacraments were really necessary for salvation, then there could be no escape from it, however irreligious it appeared to be. The difference between the heretic and the reformer was the simple fact that the heretic was willing to "throw out the baby with the bathwater"; he was forced into the position of denying the power of the Church to save souls, and into claiming that a Christian life on earth was the principal requirement for salvation rather than sacraments and rituals. As we have seen, even among the ancient Hebrews this question had arisen, and it could never be settled; it was the chief difference between the priestly and prophetic traditions— as it was to be later the core of the Protestant divergence from Catholicism. The twelfth-century heretic could find clear Scriptural justification for his view; the Church, by careful interpretation of the Scriptures, could also find justification. But the tradition of most of the Christian Fathers leaned far more heavily in favor of the view of the Church. So the heretics threw over the Christian Fathers and their interpretation, and were thus driven into heretical statements in doctrine which could be used in evidence against them. Certain key beliefs of the Catholic Church they could not accept in good conscience; and by their insistent denials of these it was possible for the secular clergy, and later the Inquisition, to condemn them.

The Cathari or Albigensians—Revived Manichaeism

The only important early medieval heresy that had any serious pretensions to being a separate religion, with an intellectual ancestry stretching back into the past, was of Oriental origin. The Cathari or, as they were called from the area where their successes were greatest, the Albigensians, believed, like the Persian Manichaeans, that there were two great forces in the world, good and evil, light and darkness, of equal power. Darkness was equated with matter and light with spirit. The true believer should devote his life to the attempt to purify himself from everything that partook of the nature of darkness, including a rather arbitrarily determined list of foods, and he should avoid sexual union. The possession of private property and all forms of authority, spiritual and secular alike, were repudiated, and the Cathari refused to go to war for any purpose whatever. The Church, with its wealth and materialism, was an instrument of the powers of darkness, as was also the God of the Old Testament, in contrast to the God of the New Testament, and to Christ, whom they accepted as the emissary of the power of the light. They rejected Hell, saying that the soul of the unbeliever was simply punished by entering the body of an impure animal, until it learned by the experience of impurity to appreciate the necessity of being purified. They did not believe in capital punishment and they refused to take oaths; and as they naturally preached celibacy and continence, it is hardly surprising that they were detested by Church, State, and the general public equally, the latter looking upon them with a frenzied superstitious hate that was later to be of the greatest assistance to the Inquisition.

Such an austerity of practice, however, was not required of all Cathari equally. There was a lower class of "believers," and an upper class of ascetics, known as the *perfecti*. But all were expected to purify themselves as they felt death approaching, and to receive the sacred laying on of hands, called the *consolamentum*. This ceremony could be performed only once, and if it was performed while the believer was still in good health, he was thus transformed into one of the *perfecti*, and was expected thereafter to undergo the full austerities of the religion. If he received it when dying he was expected to undergo the extreme initiation rite of the *endura,* a ritual suicide through complete abstention from nourishment.

The surprising thing about this apparently unattractive religion is its popularity, and the way it spread throughout southern France and northern Italy. Indeed, in Languedoc—Albi is one of its leading cities—by the end of the twelfth century with its own ministers drawn from the *perfecti*, its own ceremonies, and its own church organization, it had almost entirely ousted Catholic Christianity, and it was protected by the local feudal lord. And this in the area in France which in its day was also the most civilized, with a flourishing literary and musical culture, the land of the troubadours.

It seems unlikely that the nobles were entirely convinced of the truth of the Catharist doctrine, but they went along with the Cathari in their dislike for the Church. And for the lower grades of the believers it was probably enough to be able to worship in their own communities, to follow a simple life with rewards in prestige or in the next life for any austerities they might wish to practice in this, without inquiring any more than did ordinary Christians into the more esoteric beliefs they were supposed to hold.

The "Poor Men of Lyons"—Waldensians

Another important heretical group was composed of the Waldensians, or "poor men of Lyons," called after their founder, one Peter Waldo, who had discovered in the Gospels that Christ had owned no property but given all his goods to the poor. Waldo followed his example; then, gathering around him a number of disciples, began to preach poverty. This was precisely the same initial impulse that started St. Francis of Assisi on his mission; and at the beginning Waldo, who was obviously a Christian, met with a kindly reception from Pope Alexander III, who allowed the "poor men" to teach and take vows of poverty, provided they obtained permission from the local clergy. This, however, they neglected to do, since their opinion of the local clergy was a low one, and they did not attempt to conceal it. When they were condemned by a Church council they became more outspoken; and it was an easy step to say that there need be no clergy at all, that the only true Christian life was one of renunciation and poverty, and that all the Church customs and ceremonies not specifically mentioned in the Bible did not have to be observed.

In the growing towns, whose spiritual needs were seriously neglected till the thirteenth century, there had always been loose, semi-organized groups of the poorer classes who had had to find their Christianity for themselves; and for lack of more authoritative instruction in the matter had simply taken the Gospels and the life of Christ and his disciples as suitable examples for daily living. These medieval prototypes of modern dissident groups in society had always been regarded as dangerous by Church and secular authorities alike, and had been visited with varying degrees of persecution. The Waldensians, with their missionary fervor, naturally drew members of such groups to them, and the movement began to become really dangerous to the Church, especially when those in northern Italy started to form their own churches with simple ceremonies, and to appoint their own clergy and organize their own schools. In spite of continuous persecution, the Waldensians were never suppressed altogether in Italy; and though in time they became part of the Protestant movement a Church of Waldensians still exists today as a separate Protestant sect.

▶   **Reaction of the Church to the rise of heresy, and the issue of apostolic poverty**

FAILURE OF THE MONASTIC ORDERS

The issue of poverty was a very real one to an organized Church. Although at one time a pope was forced into the position of declaring that it was a heresy to teach that the apostles possessed no common property but lived in absolute poverty, it was not an opinion easily quelled by authority when the Gospels were the heart of Christian teaching, and were available to anyone who could read Latin, and soon to any who could read

at all. The time-honored answer had been to permit all those who sought for a life of poverty and religious devotion to go into a monastery apart from the world. But by the early thirteenth century there was hardly a monastic order that could fulfill the requirements of so many sincere seekers. Moreover, why must the choice be so narrow? That a Christian wished to worship his God simply, with a minimum of ritual, freely, without being forced to believe what he did not believe, trying to follow the example of Christ and his apostles as far as he could, did not necessarily mean that he wanted to quit the world and go into a monastery.

Yet the Church, if it were to exist at all, could not do without money and property; within the feudal system it could not maintain itself without feudal dues. Was it to refuse money genuinely bequeathed to it? If the Church did not supply an expensive organization, what organization would there be? Who would administer the sacraments which it had declared were necessary for salvation? Either it had to abdicate what it believed to be its responsibility to satisfy the objections of a small number of dissidents, or it had to devise a policy for dealing with the dissidents. For it is clear that it could never reform itself enough to satisfy them and still remain an organized Church.

SUPPRESSION OF HERETICS

The Albigensian Crusade

To Innocent III it must have seemed that the only policy that held any hope of success against the Albigensians was repression. The vast majority lived in a limited area under the overlordship of the Count of Toulouse, who was reputed to be sympathetic to them and in any case made no effort to suppress them. The secular clergy in the diocese had tried to convert them back to orthodox Catholicism for years without success, but their weapons were feeble since they lacked the support of the local nobility; even public opinion was not on their side. Their arguments, based on the authority of the Church, fell on deaf ears, for the Cathari accepted no such authority. The Cistercian monks did not take easily to missionary work. A Spanish bishop, assisted by a group of Cistercians and a young and ardent missionary named Dominic who was in the retinue of the bishop, obtained permission from Innocent in 1205 to attempt the reconversion of the territory. It was clear to these missionaries that much of the heresy was due to simple ignorance of Christianity, an ignorance that they tried to relieve. They met, however, with but indifferent success. The Cistercians did not like the work, and the bishop could not spend too much time away from his diocese. Yet, if they had been given time, and the effort had been better organized they might have made some impression on the Cathari. Perhaps Innocent did not know enough of the work to give it proper support, or perhaps he did not have enough missionaries available with the right kind of enthusiasm, and he did not recognize St. Dominic's outstanding talents. At all events he lost patience with the Albigensians, and in 1208 proclaimed a "crusade" against them.

Philip Augustus, king of France, refused his approval to the project; he thought that any proceeding against heretics should be dignified and orderly. The Count of Toulouse should be convicted of heresy if guilty, and he, the king, should then be allowed to sequester his fiefs, although it was not certain that he was in fact the count's overlord. Philip did not seem to be convinced of the extreme danger of the beliefs of the Albigensians. But neither he nor anyone else was able to prevent the pope from proclaiming the crusade and promising the territories of the heretics to the faithful crusaders.

So Innocent went ahead with the second "Crusade" of his eventful pontificate (the first, of course, went to Constantinople), this time against heretics in Europe; and noble lords bent on the plunder of the fairest area in France answered his call, no better organized than usual until a number of small bands united under the leadership of their most capable general, Simon de Montfort. However, generalship in the highest degree was not necessary, for the majority of the Cathari,

not given a chance, like other heretics, to recant and thus save their lives, and mindful, no doubt, of their belief in nonresistance and fortified by the thought that this was the *endura,* the last test of their faith and purity, received the *consolamentum* and prepared to die. The nobility who had protected them, and who now found themselves menaced by covetous nobles in quest of their fiefs, resisted stoutly, aided by some of the less stoical heretics; but the bulk of the Cathari was simply massacred in one of the easiest and most horrible campaigns in history. Innocent, as usual, repented too late of what he had initiated, and tried to call off the crusaders. But they paid no attention to him, and the war which started as a crusade ended as a war of conquest. Raymond, the Count of Toulouse, protector of the heretics, received assistance from his feudal overlord, the good Catholic Peter II of Aragon, who was killed in a battle which followed (1213). Simon de Montfort and his crew finally defeated the heretics and their protectors, he himself became overlord of the territory, and did homage to Philip Augustus for it.

But Raymond's son was able to collect an army. Joined by his father he found the crusaders bickering over the spoils, and was able to defeat and kill Simon de Montfort and recover the fiefs of his family. At this point the French king intervened, and in 1229 a compromise was patched up. Raymond's son, the victor over Simon de Montfort, who had become Count of Toulouse on the death of his father, undertook to help in eradicating the last of the heretics, and the newly organized papal Inquisition, under the successors of the same St. Dominic who had earlier tried to convert them, was able to complete the work to the satisfaction of the orthodox. The most advanced civilization in France had been destroyed, the entire land was desolate, a desolation from which it has never fully recovered to this day; but the heresy had been extirpated. It continued to influence northern Italy, where it joined forces with other anticlerical groups. But on the whole the crusade must be considered a success, since its original purpose had been achieved. A university was founded under the auspices of Pope Gregory ix at Toulouse to instruct the surviving inhabitants in the truths that had hitherto been neglected in that area.

RECONVERSION—THE MENDICANT ORDERS

Dominicans

Already before the Albigensian Crusade Dominic had approached Innocent iii with a request that he be allowed to form a new order. The Pope listened politely but temporized. He was not sure that a new order was desirable, especially not one whose members were vowed to poverty. But he did not forbid Dominic from going ahead, and the young man returned to the scene of his labors, remaining there through the first stages of the crusade, ministering to the wounded and dying, often at serious risk to his life. Returning to Rome he was now able to obtain official recognition for his greatly enlarged group of companions, and a Rule was drawn up, confirmed by Pope Honorius iii in 1220. The new order, called the Order of Preachers, but commonly known as Dominicans, with its companion, the Order of Lesser Brothers, or Franciscans, was a radical departure in Christianity; and though both orders derived from the original initiative of the founders, the Church was soon able to see their value, and give them unusual honors and very full support, which brought upon them the envy and enmity of the pillars of medieval conservatism, the secular clergy and the universities.

The towns had been seriously neglected, as we have seen, for centuries. The parish priest had far more difficulty in the towns than on a compact manor in keeping in touch with his flock, and the higher clergy had too many other duties to give the townspeople much attention. The monasteries were, as a rule, founded in country districts, and had no influence in the cities. But these new orders of friars (brothers), as they were called, went out preaching to the people directly in the market place or in the local church. The Dominicans early became noted for their

learning, and were able to give instruction in a manner hitherto unknown. As missionaries, first within Christianity and then to heathen countries, their influence and activity were enormous. Convents were founded throughout Europe where the friars could live, and which they could use as their headquarters for missionary activity. But unlike the monasteries, the convents were modest institutions. Very little land was required nor was regular income needed from feudal dues, since they lived at the beginning entirely from begging (hence they were called mendicant orders). And from the first they were directly subject to the papacy through their chief officer, called a Minister General, who ruled authoritatively through Provincial Ministers in each country.

The Franciscans

The personality and teaching of St. Francis—The Franciscan Order was founded by St. Francis of Assisi, the son of a merchant in good circumstances who was able to provide Francis with a life of modest luxury. But Francis was suddenly converted from this life of ease by reading the Gospels. At once he gave all his possessions away save the coarsest and simplest of clothing, took, in his own words, Lady Poverty for his bride, and began to preach.

If there has ever been a true Christian saint since the founding of Christianity, then St. Francis was he. By his example and utter sincerity and by the simplicity of his life, he won the hearts of all those who listened to him, and quickly a band of disciples grew up around him. It was not only that he was kind to everyone, even the outcasts of society, the sick and the maimed and the lepers whom no one would touch; the quality of love seemed to shine out from him in a way that no one could resist or wished to resist. But behind this genuine simplicity there was also a rare intuitive understanding of the life around him. He knew that it was impossible for the Church ever fully to accept him, he knew what dangers and temptations his order would have to meet, he knew to how few it is given really to lead such a life of absolute poverty as his. He did not want to organize his order formally, he did not want it to have rules and regulations which would inhibit the spontaneous outpouring of love in which lay his own special genius. He did, however, see Innocent; but it was only natural that the pope should be hesitant, his shrewd diplomatic mind grasping the dangers that such a movement held for his Church, dangerous enough with Dominic, but a hundred times more so with a leader like Francis. It is said that Innocent had a dream in which he saw the Church supported by only these two orders, a dream later enshrined in a famous fresco of Giotto. Whether he heeded the dream or not, he temporized again, and it was his successor who drew up the Franciscan Rule and confirmed the order. Francis himself refused to be Minister General, and insisted on appointing the most worldly of his band to the position, because, as he said, it was right for himself also to be subject to discipline as a Christian duty.

Francis disapproved of learning as unnecessary in a pure gospel of love, and the preaching of his order in his lifetime corresponded to his own. The task of Franciscans was rather to help and heal, to teach by example and not by precept, to go about among the poor bearing the Gospel and praising God for his blessings, and encouraging them to do likewise.

The struggle within the Franciscan Order on the question of poverty—It was inevitable that after the death of Francis there should be a schism within his order. No organized body, but only rare individuals, could live up to such an ideal. Money poured in upon the order, which was not permitted by its Rule to keep it. The appointment of a papal procurator to handle the funds of the order did not solve the problem, and in the eyes of the uncompromising followers of St. Francis, this subterfuge was a betrayal. With the resounding success of both the Dominican and Franciscan Orders and the support given them by the papacy, privileges showered in upon them, and ever more and more recruits to the Franciscan Order. The life of primitive

An almost contemporary (ca. 1265) *miniature of St. Francis of Assisi preaching to the birds. From a* Psalter *(Franco-Flemish).* (COURTESY THE PIERPONT MORGAN LIBRARY. Ms. 72, folio 139)

simplicity had to be abandoned; and the begging of the friars before long became a scandal to those who knew of the order's wealth. Friars of both orders began to seek learning, and the influence of the papacy was able to gain them chairs in theology even at Paris, to the fury of the secular professors who, resenting this unfair competition, unleashed a torrent of scurrilous pamphlets on their way of life and their hypocrisy, replied to in kind by the leading friars. In the convents of both orders learning was approved, and preaching to the people ceased to be universal; friars were permitted to hear confessions, and before the end of the century a friar was pope.

The Dominicans, to whom in any case poverty had never been such an essential part of their movement, accepted the inevitable; the Franciscans split into two. For a while most of the Ministers General were men who had known St. Francis and knew what poverty had meant to him; and those dissident Franciscans who objected to the ownership of property whether by brothers or by the order itself were protected by them. But by the end of the thirteenth century it was clear that the order was doomed if it could not heal the schism. The path that was probably inevitable from the first was chosen. The Conventuals, who accepted the compromise on absolute poverty and who were in a majority within the order, expelled the Spirituals, who wished to retain strict poverty and were ultimately treated as heretics by the Conventuals. By the early fourteenth century the Spirituals had been formally declared heretical,[3] and some were handed over to the Inquisition, while many more languished in Franciscan prisons. Their movement persisted for a long time, being used by secular powers against the Avignon papacy when they wished to castigate its pride and luxury. Ultimately the remnants found refuge in Protestantism.

The friars, however, left an indelible mark upon later medieval Christianity. Much of the art of the early Italian Renaissance was influenced by them, especially by the Franciscans. The human side of Christianity, already visible in the veneration of the Virgin Mary, and the late medieval cult of the Mother and Child, was now emphasized in both art and literature more than ever before. There can be no doubt that there was a real renewal of religious life in all ranks of society in the thirteenth century which can be in large measure put to the credit of the friars who first brought religion to the mass of the people. And the missionary enterprises which multiplied from the thirteenth century onward, reaching to China

and throughout the known world, were a result of this spirit.

PERMANENT COURT FOR DISCOVERY AND SUPPRESSION OF HERETICS—THE INQUISITION

Great though the influence of this last pre-Reformation reform was, it was not sufficient to extirpate heresy altogether. In the early thirteenth century Pope Gregory IX established a regular Inquisition into the beliefs of supposed heretics, which was entrusted first to the Dominicans, and later to both orders. The purpose of the Inquisition was to fix a procedure for this detection and punishment of heretics. The inquisitor, a papal appointee, paid periodical visits to the various cities within his jurisdiction and called on heretics to declare themselves, and upon the faithful to denounce those suspected of heresy. If a heretic confessed and recanted, he was usually let off with a comparatively light penance imposed by the Church. If he refused to recant, then torture was permitted, as in Roman times with slaves, and as in the medieval secular state, to compel the confession. Testimony was taken, but the defendant was not allowed a lawyer nor was he permitted to know the names of his accusers and the nature of the evidence. If two witnesses of good character agreed, then he could be condemned.

The purpose, however, was always to obtain a confession and to persuade the heretic to recant, in which case, if he had been a long time making up his mind to confess, he might receive a severe, but not a capital, punishment. Except when in later years the Inquisition became a tool of the secular powers who used it to confiscate the property of heretics, this provision was usually carried out, and there were far fewer death sentences imposed than penances. If the heretic refused to recant, he was handed over to the secular authorities to be put to death, customarily by burning. If a heretic recanted and then relapsed into heresy he was regarded as incorrigible, and likewise handed over to the secular authorities.

The Inquisition has gained its evil reputation largely from the later so-called Span-

---

[3] By this time, indeed, they had accepted certain prophetic teachings which could be considered formally heretical, although the Spirituals themselves denied that they were.

ish Inquisition, used by the Spanish rulers as a political weapon. The medieval Inquisition never claimed so many victims, and on the whole it seems to have preferred not to impose the death penalty. Its secret procedure laid it open to many abuses, and it does not accord with modern Western ideas of justice. The crime against which it was exclusively used lent itself especially to inquisitorial methods, as has been rediscovered in the present century. Heresy was regarded in a way not unlike political crimes of modern times, as treason to Christendom; now such crimes are treason to a totalitarian state.

The Church, however, was not all-powerful in the medieval period; it could not impose the death penalty itself, and monarchs could and did refuse to have the Inquisition within their dominions. It was never introduced into England or Scandinavia, though Queen Mary I of England burned some three hundred Protestants for heresy and treason without the benefit of the Inquisition. Only when the secular authorities agreed could the death penalty be exacted. They must therefore share the opprobrium for the Inquistion in this case with the Church. That they backed it up as much as they did is because they too regarded heresy as treason, and heretics as rebels against the established order.

▶ **Summary: The papacy at the height of its apparent power—Innocent III**

THE ELEMENT OF GOOD FORTUNE DURING THE PERIOD OF HIS PONTIFICATE

In the last section we have, for the sake of convenience, included events after the death of Innocent III which could equally well have been dealt with as part of the decline of the Church and not of its growth to power, which was the central study of this chapter.

When Innocent called the fourth Lateran Council in 1215, and all the potentates of Christendom came or were represented, while he gave instructions and promulgated dogma, it might have been thought by a contemporary that Christendom was close to becoming a true theocracy, ruled by the representative of God upon earth. It has been the purpose of this chapter to trace the growth of the Papacy to this commanding position, while revealing the cracks in the imposing edifice, and the hollow nature of most of the papal pretensions.

On the surface Innocent had been extraordinarily successful, using to the full the power accumulated in his office by his predecessors. He had reduced the kings of England and France to obedience; not only England but half the smaller countries of Europe were his feudal vassals. He had curbed the power of the Empire, he was on the way to extirpating the Albigensian heretics, and in his time, though not by his efforts, the Eastern and Western Churches had been reunited.

But not one of these triumphs was really significant. The two kings were not in fact properly controlled. They had given way when it suited them, and another time they could resist the same weapons. The quarrel between England and France had been the pope's opportunity, as the premature death of Emperor Henry VI had been his opportunity in Central Europe. He had crushed the Albigensians because he offered land to the nobles; not because they were the obedient Christian executors of his wishes. He had been unable to prevent the Venetians and crusaders from sacking Constantinople, though he had been willing enough to take advantage of their victory. In short, whatever the appearances, the secular powers held all the sources of power in their hands, and they only needed a more favorable moment to throw off the illusory yoke of the pretended theocracy.

SHORTCOMINGS OF INNOCENT'S METHODS AND UNDERSTANDING

Innocent III betrayed no real understanding of this state of affairs; though if he had, there was still little that he could do about it save the last thought that would have occurred to him—to become a spiritual power alone, the moral arbiter of Europe

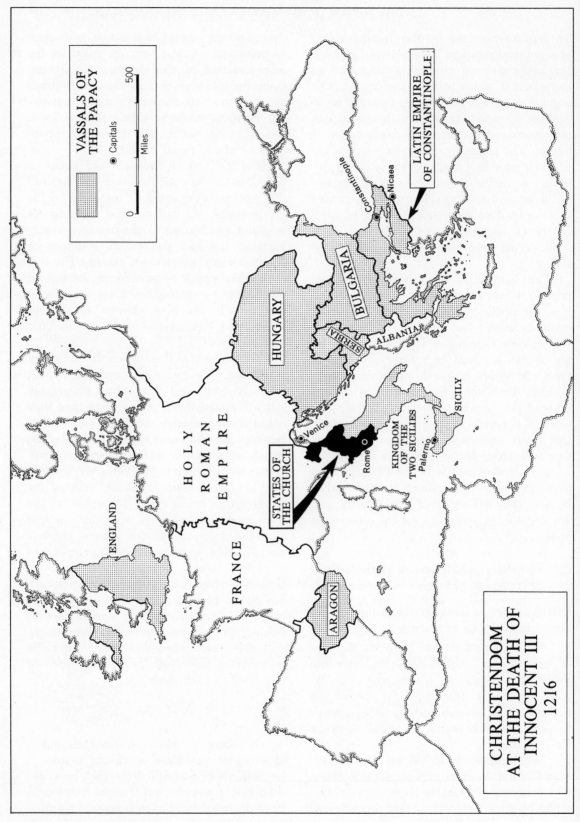

CHRISTENDOM
AT THE DEATH OF
INNOCENT III
1216

VASSALS OF
THE PAPACY

● Capitals

Miles

0   500

LATIN EMPIRE
OF CONSTANTINOPLE

Constantinople

● Nicaea

BULGARIA

HUNGARY

SERBIA

ALBANIA

SICILY

HOLY
ROMAN
EMPIRE

STATES OF
THE CHURCH

Venice

Rome

KINGDOM
OF THE
TWO SICILIES

Palermo

ENGLAND

FRANCE

ARAGON

and not its dictator. When a hint of this other way was revealed to him by St. Francis, he looked hastily in the other direction.

He had no understanding of the growth of commercialism in the century before his day; his eyes were on the past glories of the crusades, and not upon the present reality that the crusading spirit had disappeared from Europe. His political interferences without exception led in the longer run to exactly those results most dangerous to his office and authority, as when he made the English king his vassal; he failed to understand the basis of heresy in a justified anticlericalism, and preferred to wipe heretics out with the sword.

The heritage he left to his successors was a long struggle with the secular powers which could never be won, a universal Church with ambitions beyond its power to achieve, and a tradition of authoritarian dictation which made an ultimate schism inevitable.

By not understanding the nature of the City of God he helped to make it forever impossible.

▶ Suggestions for further reading

A fine study of the position of the Church in the life of medieval man is to be found in the first article by F. M. Powicke in C. G. Crump and E. F. Jacob, eds., *The Legacy of the Middle Ages* (Oxford: The Clarendon Press, 1926), in which the necessary conflict between Christian ideals and the organized Christian Church is lucidly explained. Good histories of this period in English are very scarce, and most of them are rather old. In recent times most of the published works have dealt with special subjects and are unsuitable for the beginning student. Perhaps not too specialized is Lucy M. Smith, *The Early History of the Monastery of Cluny* (Oxford: The Clarendon Press, 1920). J. A. Foakes-Jackson, *Introduction to the History of Christianity, A.D. 590–1314* (London: Macmillan & Co., 1921), has a fairly good section on the Middle Ages, while A. Lagarde, *The Latin Church in the Middle Ages* (New York: Charles Scribner's Sons, 1915), is a clear, competent, and fair-minded account of the things the student most

needs to know about the medieval church. There is, however, an excellent short survey which overlaps the material of this Chapter 11, and Chapter 12: S. Packard, *Europe and the Church under Innocent III* (Berkshire Studies in European History; New York: Henry Holt & Co., Inc., 1927). Much material will also be found in the classic J. Bryce, *The Holy Roman Empire* (new ed., rev. and enlarged; New York: The Macmillan Company, 1926). This book, originally written before the end of the nineteenth century, cannot be too highly recommended for its important insights into the nature of the Holy Roman Empire as an attempt to revive the long-defunct Roman Empire during times unsuitable for any such attempt; and the remarks on the Church as an alternative institution, with aspirations toward a universal spiritual dominion, should also be studied with care, though the viewpoint of Bryce may be one-sided. A standard history, not yet outmoded, giving a clear enough record of the facts, is T. F. Tout, *The Empire and the Papacy, 918–1273* (8th ed.; London: Rivingtons, 1941).

Finally, another of Toynbee's brilliant studies, in which the distinguished historian studies the medieval papacy as an example of what he calls "the nemesis of creativity," or an institution that was so successful that it moved beyond its competence and thus met its own destruction, is to be found in his *A Study of History* (London: Oxford University Press, 1939), IV, 512–584.

The best short history of the Crusades is another Berkshire Study, R. A. Newhall, *The Crusades* (New York: Henry Holt & Co., Inc., 1927), in which the Crusades are kept in the proper perspective and not made responsible for all the changes in medieval life that occurred in the twelfth and later centuries. Newhall, however, manages to encompass a great many topics within his allotted space, and though of course none of them is dealt with at all fully, there are quite enough facts for the needs of the beginning student. A fuller account of the Crusades is S. Runciman, *A History of the Crusades* (2 vols.; Cambridge: Cambridge University Press, 1951–1952).

On the heresies the standard book is still the old H. C. Lea, *A History of the Inquisition in the Middle Ages* (3 vols.; New York: The Macmillan Company, 1908–1911), which, although in some respects outmoded by later scholarship and perhaps unduly anticlerical, has many fine passages and gives a full account of this aspect of the work of the Church. One passage in J. B. Ross and M. M. McLaughlin, *The Portable Medieval Reader* (New York: The Viking Press, Inc., 1949), will be found specially useful for the study of heresy, since it comes straight from the manual of inquisitorial procedure drawn up by an inquisitor himself (pp. 202–216). The standard life of St. Francis is P. Sabatier, *The Life of St. Francis of Assisi* (New York: Charles Scribner's Sons, 1901), many times reprinted, but it suffers from a little too much piety toward the founder of the Franciscan Order, though generally reliable as to fact. Another shorter account is to be found in a very eloquent chapter of H. O. Taylor, *The Medieval Mind* (4th ed., 2 vols.; Cambridge, Mass.: Harvard University Press, 1949). The life of St. Dominic is studied in a work by a Dominican scholar, P. Mandonnet: *St. Dominic and His Work* (St. Louis, Mo.: B. Herder Book Company, 1944).

12

The Decline of the Church as a World Power

Internal efficiency of the ecclesiastical system under Innocent III • Resumption of the struggle with the Empire • The papacy and the national states • The papacy at Avignon and the Great Schism • The papacy at the close of the Middle Ages

---

▶ ## Internal efficiency of the ecclesiastical system under Innocent III

THE PAPAL COURT (CURIA)

At the conclusion of the preceding chapter an attempt was made to show in what way Innocent III misjudged the temper of his times, as well as the flaws in understanding which underlay his policy toward the secular powers. It should, however, be emphasized that the internal structure of the ecclesiastical system was far from weak. Though the papacy was not to be able to force a theocracy upon Western Europe, the struggles of the eleventh and twelfth centuries had succeeded in giving it an efficient bureaucracy far ahead of any administrative system in the secular world of the time. Though the clergy might be chosen by the secular powers with papal approval, nevertheless after their appointment they were by various means kept under the control of the papacy, which had indeed become a true international state within the various state structures of Europe.

At the head was the pope himself. Immediately subject to him was the papal court or Curia, made up of clerks, secretaries, lawyers, and other officials, several of whom held the honorary title of Cardinal. The Curia itself was divided into departments concerned with such matters as the administration of justice and revenue. The popes had striven long and hard to establish their court as the supreme appeal court for all cases tried under canon law, and in this effort they had been largely successful. Canon law had been codified by the middle of the twelfth century, and was generally accepted throughout Europe; the pope and his court were indeed continually appealed to for decisions in numerous cases covering contracts, wills, and such other matters that the still primitive royal and feudal courts could not handle satisfactorily. The popes and clergy constantly fought for the right to judge all clerics, whatever their crimes; and as a rule the kings did not trouble to argue with Church officials, but let them have their own way. Only with the increasing use of the civil law, based, like canon law, on the ancient Roman codes, and the growth of the legal profession within the national states, did the kings begin seriously to resent clerical interference.

REVENUE SYSTEM

The tax-collecting system of the papacy had gradually been systematized. The Church was constantly receiving legacies, it had its regular income from the Papal States, it collected feudal dues from kings and nobles who held land as vassals from the pope, and it subjected the clergy to general taxes for the crusades, even when there were no crusades actually in progress. The popes could also require aids from the clergy similar to those demanded by feudal lords in time of emergency, and there were regular charges for indulgences and other penances. The higher clergy, when appointed to positions in the Church, usually had to pay a percentage of the first year's dues (annates) for the privilege of confirmation by the pope. The custom also arose in the thirteenth century of appointing prelates to benefices which involved no duties for themselves, the duties being farmed out to lesser clergy at a fraction of the salary. Many prelates held several benefices of this kind which they used simply as sources of income and which were shared, at least to some degree, with the pope. Moreover, as the papacy gradually took into its hands ever more and more appointments, the sums derived from patronage became one of the most important sources of income available to it. It was, of course, pointed out by opponents of the papacy that such practices amounted to simony, but the accusation made little noticeable difference in their prevalence.

ATTITUDE OF THE CLERGY TO PAPAL EXACTIONS

To collect all these varied sums the popes had to use skilled administrators; and it was no accident that throughout the thirteenth and fourteenth centuries the majority of the popes, including Innocent III himself, were thoroughly conversant with both civil and canon law. Even when the influence of the popes in external affairs declined and when they could no longer force secular powers to obey them, they continued to administer their estates effectively; indeed, control reached its height when they

left Rome in the fourteenth century and took up their residence at Avignon. And as they put ever greater pressure on their clergy for ever more money, the clergy had no way of protecting themselves except by recourse to the kings. There are many instances of kings supporting the clergy against papal exactions and claims, while the clergy in return backed the kings in their policy. But the process continued until the Protestant Reformation, the success of which in several countries was primarily due to the desire on the part of kings and princes to tax the Church themselves, rather than let all the funds go to support the foreign potentate at Rome.

From the thirteenth century on, this domination of the papacy by lawyers and the ever-increasing concern for money go far toward explaining the failure of the papacy to make its moral influence felt, demonstrating at the same time how changed was the whole spirit of the age, and to what an extent commercial interests had usurped the place of religious.

► Resumption of the struggle with the Empire

INNOCENT III'S EFFORTS TO DIVIDE AND RULE IN GERMANY

When Emperor Henry VI of the Hohenstaufen family died so opportunely in 1197, the way lay open, as we have seen, for papal interference with the new election of an emperor. Henry's son Frederic, a child of three, could be ignored, and Innocent took the child under his protection while supporting in Germany the Welf candidate, Otto of Brunswick. The Hohenstaufen family, however, would not permit the throne to escape from its hands without a fight, and chose a king of their own, Philip of Swabia, the brother of Henry VI. The result was a destructive civil war which lasted for fourteen years. Innocent proceeded to enlarge the Papal States by conquest until they reached the Adriatic, and forced recognition of his conquests from Otto of Brunswick in exchange for papal support. Otto also had to give up any control over the

► chronological chart

Resumption of struggle between Empire and papacy

Pontificate of Innocent III	1198–1216
Civil War in Germany	1197–1212
Murder of Philip of Swabia	1208
Otto of Brunswick crowned emperor	1209
Frederic II becomes king of the Romans	1212
Frederic II crowned emperor by Honorius III	1220
Sixth (Frederic's) Crusade	1227–1229
Excommunication of Frederic by Gregory IX	1227
Papal mercenaries (Soldiers of the Keys) wage war against Frederic's territories in Italy	1228–1229
Frederic negotiates ten-year truce with Muslims	1229
Peace of San Germano between Frederic and Gregory IX	1230
Defeat of Lombard League by Frederic at Cortenuova	1237
Second excommunication of Frederic by Gregory IX	1239
Capture of prelates on way to Rome by Frederic	1241
Death of Gregory IX	1241
Two-year interregnum in papacy	1241–1243
Innocent IV elected pope	1243
Innocent escapes to France	1244
Synod of Lyons—Deposition of Frederic by Innocent IV	1245
Lombard cities defeat Frederic at Parma	1248
Death of Frederic II	1250
Conrad IV emperor	1250–1254
Manfred regent, later king, of Sicily	1250–1266
Interregnum in Empire	1254–1273
Charles of Anjou invades Italy	1266
Battle of Benevento—Defeat and death of Manfred	1266
Conradin, last Hohenstaufen prince, executed	1268
Rudolf of Hapsburg elected emperor	1273
Sicilian Vespers	1282
Peter III of Aragon conquers Sicily and becomes king	1282

The pontificate of Boniface VIII

Abdication of Pope Celestine V	1294
Pontificate of Boniface VIII	1294–1303
Wars between Philip IV of France and Edward I of England	1294–1298
Philip IV assesses French Church for a war levy	1294
Boniface issues bull *Clericis laicos*	1296
Philip forbids export of precious metals from France	1297
Papal jubilee	1300
Philip summons States-General	1302
"Battle of the Spurs"—Defeat of Philip by Flemish	1302
Boniface issues bull *Unam sanctam*	1302
Death of Boniface VIII (Anagni)	1303
Clement V elected Pope	1305

The papacy at Avignon and the Great Schism

"Babylonian Captivity" of papacy	1305–1376
Philip IV confiscates property of Knights Templars	1307
Defensor Pacis of Marsiglio of Padua	1324
William of Occam at court of Emperor Ludwig IV	1328–1346
Golden Bull	1356
The Great Schism	1378–1417
Wyclif translates Bible into English	ca. 1378
Wyclif denies transubstantiation	1380
Foundation of the Brethren of the Common Life	ca. 1380
Council of Pisa	1409
Pope John XXIII	1410–1415
Sigismund emperor (king of Bohemia 1419–1437)	1410–1437
Council of Constance	1414–1418
Deposition of Pope John XXIII	1415
John Hus burned at Constance	1415
Pope Martin V returns to Rome	1417
Hussite Wars	1420–1433
Council of Basel	1431–1449
Taborites defeated by Utraquists in Bohemia	1434
Pontificate of Nicholas V (humanist)	1447–1455
Pontificate of Alexander VI (Borgia)	1492–1503
Savonarola master of Florence	1494–1498
Pontificate of Leo X	1513–1521
Ninety-five theses of Martin Luther	1517

appointment of the higher clergy of the German Church.

Unfortunately for himself, Innocent could not control the course of the civil war; and when it appeared that the Hohenstaufens would win, he suddenly changed sides, accepting Philip of Swabia as his preferred candidate until Philip was suddenly murdered in 1208. Then Innocent had to return to Otto, whom he crowned emperor. Otto, however, seems to have lost the respect he owed to the head of Christendom, for no sooner had the new emperor been crowned than he withdrew his recognition of Innocent's conquests in central Italy and began a campaign to recover them, even seizing part of the kingdom of Sicily that had been reserved for Frederic of Hohenstaufen.

Innocent, at last realizing that he would be used by Otto in accordance with his own needs, played his trump card. He brought forth Frederic, who was now seventeen years old and a typical Hohenstaufen in appearance, and supported his claim to the throne of Germany. Frederic made a triumphal procession to Aachen, supported by Innocent's obedient if bewildered clergy and conquering all hearts by his charm (they called him the Boy of Apulia), and was duly elected king of the Romans.[1] Otto returning to Germany had first to face the army of Philip Augustus of France, which thoroughly defeated him at the battle of Bouvines in 1214. This finished Otto, who was solemnly excommunicated and deposed at the Lateran Council held next year by Innocent. In due course Frederic was elected emperor and crowned at Rome in 1220 by Innocent's successor.

BANKRUPTCY OF INNOCENT'S GERMAN POLICY

Innocent providentially died before he was able to see the disastrous effects of his

---

[1] This was a title given to the elected German king before he was crowned emperor. Occasionally the emperors had the title bestowed upon their sons during their own lifetime in the attempt to ensure the succession for them. Theoretically, it is clear that the two titles were considered divisible, and not necessarily embodied in the same person.

policy. For Frederic was king of the Romans, and he had a clear title to the throne of Sicily, though at this moment it still needed to be reconquered. But beyond a promise he had made to Innocent there was nothing whatever to prevent Frederic from reuniting Germany with Sicily, and there was no other claimant who had any legitimate title at all. Thus the original purpose of the prolonged civil war in Germany fostered by Innocent had been frustrated. The only change effected by Innocent's efforts had been the destruction of the house of Welf at Bouvines. Frederic therefore came into a heritage which was in fact more secure than it would otherwise have been, allowing him to concentrate on his Italian and Sicilian possessions, without fear, for a long time, of any trouble in Germany. On the death of Innocent he proceeded at once to take possession of Sicily and reorganize it into a compact kingdom with a government entirely subservient to himself and unequaled in efficiency in the Western world.

THE REIGN OF FREDERIC II

Character and policy of Frederic

Frederic himself was a remarkable man. Half German, half Norman, in ancestry, brought up in Sicily, after the death of his mother, by various protectors who left him largely to himself, he became probably the best-educated man in the entire Western world, with a fluent knowledge of German, Latin, Greek, and Arabic. A freethinker, he seems to have been little influenced by traditional Christian thought, and was indeed far closer to the less dogmatic Islam of his day than to Christianity. He took nothing on trust; he had a considerable respect, for instance, for Aristotle, but condemned the philosopher's occasional remarks on subjects, such as falconry, with which he was imperfectly acquainted. Frederic questioned the immortality of the soul, which he claimed had not been proven; and indeed he was credited with an experiment in this direction himself. He had an enormous interest not only in birds, on which he wrote

LIMITS OF
PATRIMONY OF
ST. PETER
CLAIMED
BY PAPACY

Patrimony
of St. Peter

KINGDOM
OF
THE
TWO SICILIES

SICILY

HOLY ROMAN EMPIRE
IN THE TIME OF FREDERIC II –
1212-50
★ LOMBARD LEAGUE CITIES

0   100   200
Miles   ⊙ Capitals

a valuable treatise, but in animals, and he traveled through Europe with a private menagerie, to the astonishment of his contemporaries, who were not at all sure that he was not in league with the Devil. It is not difficult to see what excellent openings he afforded Christian propagandists when they were instructed to discredit him.

As a monarch he believed in complete absolutism. While he admitted the superiority of spiritual over temporal power, saying that on moral questions he would sub-

mit to rebuke even from the humblest priest, he denied the right of the papacy to dictate to him in his own secular realm, believing that he had received his rights as an emperor from God and not from the pope. As an administrator he was surpassed by no ruler in medieval times, and approached only by his own Norman predecessors in Sicily. He understood the importance of trade and industry for his Sicilian kingdom; like the early modern mercantilist kings, he encouraged his merchants, worked hard for their prosperity, and then taxed them in exchange for his assistance. He established monopolies in the Byzantine manner when private enterprise failed to fulfill his demands. He built a fleet to protect his trade which was the equal of the fleet of any Italian city of his day. He understood very well the power of money, and how necessary it was to secure a regular income if he were going to keep and extend his empire. He was able to keep armies in the field all his life with the aid of his Sicilian revenues; and the core of his army was a band of Muslims from Sicily, immune from influence by his great enemy the papacy. He established his Muslims, to the great offense of his enemies, in a special town of their own in southern Italy, from which Christians were excluded. It was not surprising that in his own day he was called "stupor mundi," the wonder of the world, by earnest Christians who had never seen such a strange combination of qualities in one man.

It seems to have been his fixed intention to extend his effective rule over all Italy and unite it to his southern kingdom, while leaving Germany, of which he was the titular ruler, largely to its own devices. His policy in Germany was always conciliatory to the great nobles, whom he left, together with the German Church, virtually independent of him. As early as he could he had his eldest son crowned king of the Romans, a title which gave him effective rule in Germany. But the son intrigued against him and finally joined his enemies, the Lombard towns in Italy. Frederic defeated and imprisoned this son, giving the crown to a younger son who cooperated with the nobles according to his father's policy, and never made any serious attempt to control them.

But Frederic's efforts to make the Italian towns submit to him met with resistance not only from them but also from the papacy. All his life he tried to come to a working agreement with the popes, but was never successful except for brief periods when his power was too great to resist. Even when a former friend of his was chosen pope, under his influence, the new pope at once ceased to be his friend, driving Frederic to the observation, "It is impossible for a pope to be a Ghibelline." The papal treasury was as extensive as his own, and the popes used it to hire mercenary troops and pay subsidies to the Italian towns who did not wish to submit to the emperor. For almost the whole of his reign Frederic fought against both papacy and towns, to the accompaniment, for the first time in medieval history, of a torrent of pamphlets addressed both to public opinion and to the other rulers in Europe. The papacy insisted on its right to discipline monarchs, while Frederic declared that the popes were endangering the tranquillity of Europe, sowing dissension for no purpose. The popes constituted as great a danger to the other monarchs as to himself, Frederic told his fellow rulers; indeed he was fighting their battle for them. On the whole, except for the pious English king, who was also a vassal of the papacy but lacked authority in his own country, the monarchs stayed benevolently neutral toward the emperor but gave him no active support.

Frederic's "Crusade"

Even before Frederic had shown the direction his policy would take, the papacy initiated the struggle which was to last till Frederic's death in 1250. The mild successor of Innocent, Pope Honorius III, had crowned Frederic emperor and had not attempted to prevent him from taking his Sicilian throne; but Honorius had gently though firmly reminded him also of his promise to go on a crusade. Because of the pressing nature of his Sicilian interests, Frederic had continually postponed this enterprise, a promise for which had been exacted from him by Innocent. But he made Honorius a firm promise that he would go at the latest by 1227; if he failed to do so, then he would submit to excommunication. However, in 1227 Honorius died, to be succeeded by stern old Gregory IX, then about eighty years of age, but vigorous and stubborn, and apparently determined that his principal mission as pope was to destroy the Hohenstaufens and break their power forever. At all events, his policy was constantly provocative, he never accepted sincerely any of Frederic's olive branches, which were offered frequently in earlier years, and his propaganda against the emperor, with its Biblical imagery, was scarcely if ever equaled even in an age noted for its invective.

Frederic duly started on his crusade in 1227, but at once fell ill and returned. Gregory, choosing to regard this illness as a piece of diplomatic hypochondria, promptly excommunicated him. On his recovery, in spite of the ban, Frederic sailed for Palestine, where he invited the overlord of the country, the sultan of Egypt, to negotiate with him. The sultan was very affable to this enlightened Westerner, who spoke Arabic so fluently; and he was careful not to offend the presumed susceptibilities of a man whom he regarded as a representative of Christianity, even giving instructions to the local muezzins in Jerusalem to refrain from calling the faithful to prayer while he was there. Frederic, however, told the sultan that he was anxious to observe Muslim customs in their own land, and he made a number of jokes about Christians which astounded the Muslim chroniclers of his visit. The business part of the crusade was quickly settled. Frederic could have Jerusalem except for the area around the sacred Mosque of Omar, and he could have Nazareth, Bethlehem, and a valuable strip of coast. Frederic had recently married the heiress to the old Latin Kingdom of Jerusalem, so that he was entitled to be its king. Unable to persuade the Christian patriarch in Jerusalem to crown an excommunicated emperor, he had to crown himself. Then after arranging for a ten-year truce he returned home, having accomplished by a skillful piece of negotiation and goodwill what fifty years of military crusades had failed to win.

It might be added here that Frederic's settlement lasted for fifteen years, after which the Muslims again captured the city. Two more crusades went from the West led by St. Louis IX, king of France. But on the first occasion Louis was captured in Egypt and had to ransom himself; on the second

he died and his army returned home. This was the end of the attempts to recapture the Holy City, though crusades were still called against the Turks in later centuries to stem their advances into Europe.

Gregory IX in Rome and all the faithful were scandalized by Frederic's achievement. First of all, the emperor was excommunicate, so the crusade was not sanctioned by the papacy. Furthermore, Frederic's behavior was not the traditional way to treat infidels, who were fit only for the treatment accorded them on the glorious First Crusade. That he had succeeded where Christian armies had failed added insult to injury. The pope therefore had raised an army of mercenaries in the emperor's absence, and it was ravaging Frederic's southern Italian territories, which no longer belonged to him as an excommunicated emperor and thus were forfeited to his papal overlord.

Frederic, however, made short work of the papal armies and proceeded to threaten the Papal States themselves. The pope was forced to negotiate and lift the excommunication. Frederic now became for a short time Gregory's "beloved son," and returned to Sicily, which at last he had time to organize, founding also the University of Naples for the primary purpose of training officials for his court.

Frederic's attempted conquest of Italy— Papal resistance

Then the emperor began to reveal his plans for Italy. Ever since the Peace of Constance in 1183 the Lombard towns had enjoyed virtual independence. The emperor was still their overlord, and they owed him certain duties. But these had not been offered in the time of Innocent, and they refused to give them now to Frederic. The emperor wanted, moreover, to have the substance of power in northern Italy that had been claimed by his grandfather, Frederic Barbarossa, before his defeat by the Lombard League. When Frederic tried to assert his claim, the towns revived the league but were disastrously defeated by the emperor. He then announced his full plan to revive a

Roman Empire in Italy with its center at Rome, as in the old days, and with every town ruled by a Ghibelline government subservient to him. This plan Gregory could hardly submit to, for it meant the probable extinction of the Papal States, and the cutting off of his important revenue from them. He encouraged the towns to resist and again excommunicated Frederic, accompanying that act with a barrage of propaganda, replied to in kind by the emperor, who suggested a league of monarchs against the papacy. While the tide was still with him, Frederic organized the now prostrate towns into his kingdom and began to make inroads into the Papal States.

Gregory replied by summoning a council of prelates from all Christendom to come to Rome for the solemn deposition of the emperor. Frederic retaliated by sending his fleet to the northern Mediterranean and capturing a boatload of high dignitaries of the Church, who were then imprisoned by the emperor in one of his castles. At this moment Gregory could stand no more and gave up the ghost, being already well over ninety and with his dignity shocked beyond repair. Frederic, now having the bulk of the electors to the papacy under his personal protection, naturally insisted that their new choice be a pope favorable to himself. The good cardinals, hoping to be freed, hit on the idea of choosing a man who was apparently on the point of death. But the Grim Reaper was first on the scene and the cardinals were left again to make a choice. This time they made no mistake, and elected an old friend of Frederic's, a Genoese jurist who assumed the ominous title of Innocent IV (1243–1254).

The papacy of Innocent IV—Deposition and death of Frederic

No sooner had Innocent escaped the imperial clutches than he began to show himself as anti-Hohenstaufen as his predecessors. While appearing to negotiate with Frederic he shrewdly played for time, then suddenly escaped to France where he called a council which solemnly deposed the emperor, in spite of a remarkable defense by an imperial secretary. Carefully staying out of Italy, Innocent proclaimed a crusade against Frederic; sent legates throughout Europe to stir up tumult, and especially to raise rebellion in Germany, where they gained some support from anti-Hohenstaufen nobles; and encouraged the friars to preach against the emperor in unmeasured terms. A conspiracy against Frederic's life was fomented, and of course the Italian towns were subsidized and resumed their warfare. Frederic's delight in the chase was to prove his ruin. While besieging a town in northern Italy, he carelessly left his army and baggage for a while to go hunting, and the citizens made a sortie and cut the army to pieces. Though this defeat was not fatal to him, it was a severe blow to his prestige, and other towns, hitherto neutral, turned out their Ghibelline governments and joined the fight against him. Nevertheless, Frederic continued to receive support from Ghibelline parties, and would probably have recovered his position if he had not suddenly died the next year at the age of fifty-six.

THE END OF THE HOHENSTAUFENS AND THE COLLAPSE OF THE EMPIRE

The struggle was not yet over. The Empire went to Conrad IV, already king of Germany, while Sicily went to an illegitimate son of Frederic as regent for his half brother. But Conrad died soon afterward, and Manfred, his half brother, could not inherit the Empire. However, it was not possible to take Italy from him without reinforcements; he had secured complete control of Sicily and recovered most of his father's strength throughout the peninsula. At this point, Pope Clement IV, a Frenchman, called in Charles of Anjou, a soldier of fortune, feudal lord of a large part of France, and the brother of Louis IX, and gave him the Sicilian kingdom. Charles gathered an army and invaded Italy, Manfred was killed in battle, and Conrad's thirteen-year-old son, the last of the Hohenstaufens, took over the inheritance. But he too was defeated by Charles, and beheaded at Naples with the approval of the pope. Thus was the male line of the Hohenstaufens extinguished; but Manfred's daughter Constance married the king of Aragon in Spain, who was ultimately to take over the Sicilian heritage.

Charles conquered much of Italy and Sicily. But his armies desolated both countries, discrediting his whole enterprise and the papacy which had sponsored it. The anti-French feeling in Sicily was so strong that one night in 1282 every Frenchman in the entire island was massacred (Sicilian Vespers). Charles and his successors never recovered the country, which passed to Peter of Aragon, who maintained his kingdom even when the unrelenting popes called a crusade against him. Sicily remained in Spanish hands for several centuries in spite of claims by the descendants of Charles of Anjou, and in the fiftheenth century southern Italy was joined to it to make the kingdom of the Two Sicilies, which survived until modern times.

In Germany the extinction of the Hohenstaufen family was followed by an interregnum until 1273. The nobles were anxious to bestow the throne only upon minor princes in order to prevent any future ascendancy of any one family like the Hohenstaufens or Welfs. In 1273 they chose Count Rudolf of Hapsburg, a noble of Swiss origin; but even he was able to use the prestige of his position and the right to take possession of vacant fiefs, which traditionally belonged to the monarchy, to add considerably to his power and territory. The electors then turned to a minor prince from the Rhineland of the Luxembourg family. But he was even more successful in turning the monarchy to his advantage, retaining the throne within his family with a few breaks until it too died out, leaving the Hapsburgs the leading family in the country, and without a serious rival. Thereafter the title became a perquisite of the Hapsburgs (except for three years from 1742 to 1745) until the Empire was formally ended by Napoleon.

The Empire never presented any further threat to Italy, and only a few emperors even troubled to go to Rome to be crowned. Occasionally an emperor crossed the Alps intending to add Italy to his possessions, but invariably he had to return with little accomplished. High hopes were held of Henry VII of Luxembourg, especially by the passionately Ghibelline poet Dante, who thought even the rule of a German emperor was preferable to the eternal quarrels of the petty governments of the cities. But the hopes were never realized, and Italy did not know unity till the nineteenth century. Germany also became a country of semi-independent principalities, ruled by local lords, until the Hohenzollern family of Brandenburg came to prominence in the eighteenth century and united Germany, with the exception of Hapsburg Austria, in the nineteenth century.

▶ The papacy and the national states

EUROPEAN REACTION TO PAPAL POLITICS

The papal policy in the thirteenth century was clearly based upon little but considerations of power and the secular interests of the Papal States. The popes were, of course, secular rulers, and as such the interests of the Papal States were the equivalent of national interests to be maintained with all the power available to their rulers. But the papacy claimed to be so much more than this; and only by virtue of its position as spiritual leader of Europe did it have at its disposal the services of the ecclesiastical bureaucracy, the clergy, and the religious orders. These latter groups were dragged along behind the papal chariot to their own irreparable damage. The Empire had been destroyed, for what the victory was worth; but it had not been destroyed by the united forces of an outraged Christendom, nor even by the authority of the pope, entitled as God's vicegerent on earth to see that the monarchies of the world were in worthy hands, but by the naked swords of Charles of Anjou and his feudal vassals and by papal mercenaries whose wages were paid out of the gifts and tithes of faithful Christians.

Naturally in an age of dawning self-consciousness when the Church no longer had the monopoly of learning, when the peoples of the West were beginning to criticize their rulers on legal as well as on moral grounds, sincere Christians were deeply distressed by the wars and desolation for which many did not hesitate to blame the Church. While some looked for a new reform, and left-wing Franciscans criticized the papacy openly for its neglect of the teachings of Christ, others began to prophesy doom. It was a century of prophecy and of looking for some redeemer who would sit on the papal throne and usher in a new golden age of righteousness. When Gregory x, after a short interregnum that followed the death of Clement iv, was elected pope, it was hoped by the would-be reformers and evangelists that he was the chosen one, for a prophecy of "Merlin," a magician of Celtic legend, seemed to refer specifically to him, and he was known to have read the prophecies. But though Gregory ended the interregnum in the Empire, he did nothing else of note, and his successors returned to the old policy, continuing to support Charles of Anjou and making no reforms at all. At last the situation was so serious that an aged hermit with a reputation for sanctity was brought out of his retreat and forced onto the papal throne under the title of Celestine v. But the cardinals only intended him to be a venerable figurehead under whom they could continue to neglect reform. The leading cardinal, Benedetto Gaetani, a noble from a lesser Italian family, a skilled jurist with a very great knowledge of the canon law, made things so difficult for the elderly pope that he resigned the papacy, an unheard-of act, commemorated for all time by Dante as the "Great Refusal." Though Celestine was later canonized as a saint, all chance of reform was gone, and Gaetani succeeded to the papacy under the title of Boniface viii. His tenure of the office was to be epochal.

THE PAPACY OF BONIFACE VIII

Controversy with English and French monarchies over taxation of clergy

It was not long before Boniface embroiled himself with the kings of England and France, both of whom were in extremely strong positions in comparison with the papacy, which had been steadily losing prestige for half a century; even the clergy of Europe who had been appointed by the papacy resented bitterly the heavy taxation laid upon them for papal wars in which they had no interest, and disliked intensely the strict authoritarian control imposed upon them. Since they could no longer be relied upon for unconditional support, the pope was left with little but his pretensions and his bureaucracy.

Philip iv, the Fair, of France (1285–1314) was not slow to take advantage of the situation. His interests were exclusively national, he was not afraid of excommunication or any other penalties the pope might impose, regarding them only as a minor nuisance; and he was quite sure that he held a sufficiently powerful weapon to bring any pope to terms. Philip, engaged in war with Edward i of England (1272–1307) and in need of funds for the mercenary armies which he now employed exclusively for the expansion and consolidation of his kingdom, decided that the best place to turn was to the Church. Under canon law it was forbidden to tax the Church; it could be asked for feudal aids in time of emergency, but did not have to submit to regular taxation. Any taxation beyond these aids and voluntary gifts had to receive the approval of the pope.

Philip and Edward both decided to lay ordinary taxes upon the clergy for state expenses. The French clergy, who were already hard enough hit by papal taxes, appealed to Boniface to help against this double taxation. Boniface then issued a bull known as the *Clericis laicos* (1296), in which he reiterated the long-established principle that the state had no right to tax the clergy without the consent of the pope, adding that kings who did so would be automatically excommunicated.

Edward gave an answer to be expected of the greatest lawmaker in English history. He withdrew the protection of his law from the clergy, who came to terms at once, with the exception of the Archbishop of Canterbury, who could safely be ignored since his only protector could be the pope, whom Edward was prepared to antagonize. In addition Edward prohibited proceeds of certain papal taxes from leaving the country.

Philip took the war right into the enemy's camp, hitting him where it was bound to hurt most. He laid an embargo upon all gold, silver, and bills of exchange leaving France, an embargo which in a national state as well consolidated as France was in Philip's reign, could be effectively enforced. Boniface, at the urgent plea of his bankers, was forced to reverse his position, permitting the French king to tax the clergy in case of emergency, then, under further pressure, agreeing that the king himself could decide when such an emergency existed. Since Philip could ask no more complete submission than this, he withdrew the embargo.

Renewed controversy with Philip— Immunity of clergy from prosecution

But the quarrel was not yet over. In the year 1300 Boniface proclaimed a jubilee, and invited pilgrims to Rome, offering special indulgences to any who might come. The jubilee was a resounding success. Collections were beyond all expectation, and Boniface, now well on in his seventies, was so pleased with the loyalty to Rome shown by the good Christians of Europe that his always latent delusions of grandeur got the better of him, and he felt competent once more to withstand the worst that the French king could do.

A bishop in southern France was accused of treason by Philip, who collected evidence against him and proposed to try him in the king's court. The French clergy pointed out that an appeal to Rome should be allowed. Philip agreed, thinking his evidence was sufficiently damning to convince even Boniface. But the pope, objecting bitterly to the whole procedure and the indignities the bishop had already suffered, countered with the withdrawal of his concessions on the taxation of the clergy, reminded Philip that even a king was subject to discipline from the Holy See, and added

that he was calling a council for the following year in which the clergy of Christendom, including the French, would sit in judgment upon the king's crimes, and make suggestions as to how the government of France was to be reformed.

Naturally this was too much for Philip, and the bull was probably never published in France. Instead of replying personally, Philip summoned to a special assembly representatives of the three estates of the realm, all of whom were in theory his vassals, the real innovation being that for the first time the burgesses of the towns were recognized as his vassals, subject to feudal duties.[2] This assembly—the prototype of the later States-General, with its three estates of clergy, nobility, and the remainder, including towns —voted, under Philip's direction, to protest to the pope; and each estate sent its own message, thus demonstrating to the pope that even his own clergy were against him in France. At the same time Philip unleashed a propaganda warfare against Boniface, including an edited copy of the recent bull.

But in the same year Philip was heavily defeated in battle by the Flemish burghers at the so-called "Battle of the Spurs" (or Courtrai, 1302), and Boniface, misjudging the importance of one battle to a king whose country was so well organized, thought the time had come to make an example of Philip. He therefore issued the bull *Unam sanctam* (1302), in which he reiterated his claim that both the spiritual and temporal powers were in the hands of the pope, and followed this up with the startling declaration that "we state, define, and pronounce that it is altogether necessary for salvation for every human being to be subject to the Roman pontiff." He then demanded complete submission from Philip under the threat of excommunication.

Philip's patience was exhausted. Boniface's claim to the papacy was in some doubt owing to the resignation of his predecessor, and the most was made of this fact in Philip's propaganda. Moreover, the pope was accused of heresy and other crimes, for which

[2] In theory, of course, it was the town itself that was the vassal, not its inhabitants.

Philip proposed to bring him to trial, after calling a council for the purpose. Meanwhile he sent one of his jurists, a man named Nogaret, to Italy to take possession of the person of the pope and bring him to France, where he was to stand trial. Nogaret, allying himself with some Italian opponents of the pope, forced his way into Boniface's presence as he was resting in a palace in his own birthplace of Anagni. Meanwhile Boniface had prepared a last bull, excommunicating the king, releasing Philip's subjects from obedience to him, and forbidding him to make any further Church appointments. The bull, however, was never published, for Nogaret and his accomplices arrived first. The aged pope, dressed in his robes of office, remained adamant, refused to abdicate, and invited them to murder him if that was what they wished. As a murder would spoil all their plans, they were uncertain what to do next, and in their dilemma they were suddenly set upon by the townsmen of Anagni and driven from the city. The pope, however, survived only a month, dying at Rome, whither he had been taken by the solicitous citizens (1303).

THE PAPACY FALLS INTO FRENCH CONTROL

After this violent end to the struggle between France and the papacy, it was clear that no pope's life would be safe without protection. The Italian nobles who had taken a leading part in the affair, having tasted an easy victory for which no punishment was to be inflicted, might endanger the life of any other pope who went contrary to their wishes, and no real protection was possible any longer in Rome. Moreover, the French were now determined to have a pope who was favorable to their interests. With some difficulty, and after one brief effort to escape the choice, the cardinals finally accepted the inevitable and elected a Frenchman, the Archbishop of Bordeaux, technically a vassal of the English king, as pope under the title of Clement v. As pope, however, Clement had no further need to rely on any English support, but delivered himself completely into French hands, after a few unsuccessful attempts to preserve his dignity and integrity by refusing his consent to some of Philip's more outrageous demands.

But ultimately Philip gained all that he could have desired. He was absolved of all complicity in the death of Boniface, and Nogaret also was absolved after a decent interval; Boniface's famous bulls were withdrawn, and the king's claim that a national state was of divine origin was accepted. Clement also gave permission to Philip to dissolve and confiscate the property of the Knights Templars, a crusading order which had become wealthy and owned too much property in France to please the avaricious king. The Templars were accused of horrible crimes, and many of them were tortured and forced to confess, whereupon they were put to death. Theoretically their property was bestowed by the pope on another order, the Knights Hospitalers; but in fact Philip saw that the Hospitalers received but a small portion of the original Templar property.

Engaged in this work on behalf of Philip for much of his reign, Clement v never found the opportunity to go to Rome, and the papacy took up residence in a city which was within the territorial borders of France, though not actually the property of the French king. Here, at Avignon, under the protection of the French monarch, the popes built a huge papal palace still extant, and gradually concentrated in their hands all the power that had been theirs at Rome, with the additional advantage that they no longer had to fear physical violence. Indeed, Avignon was nothing but a papal city, devoted entirely to papal business, unlike Rome, which had been a world capital and had importance entirely apart from the papal Curia. During the period spent by the popes at Avignon (1309–1376), ecclesiastic centralization was completed, and the power of the popes over the churches throughout Europe through the control of appointments and collection of revenue through the bureaucracy was never greater, in spite of the prestige lost by the papacy as a whole, the envy of other nations over the preponderance of French clergy in high positions, and the very general feeling throughout Europe that the proper place for the See of Peter was in Peter's city of Rome.

▶ The papacy at Avignon and the Great Schism

THE PERFECTION OF THE BUREAUCRACY—THE CHURCH AS A FINANCIAL INSTITUTION

The period which follows was called by contemporaries the "Babylonian Captivity of the Church." If one considers only the fact that the papacy was under the protection of the French king, and followed consistently pro-French policies, the term is accurate enough. But, as has been suggested, such was not the whole story. For the power of the papacy over its own clergy was at its height, and, in spite of the loss of much revenue from the abandoned Papal States, new sources were tapped which more than compensated. Papal revenue was higher than the revenue of any king in Europe except the French, and sometimes, as during the Hundred Years' War between England and France, it was undoubtedly higher. By the close of the Avignon period the popes had in their hands the right of appointment to every clerical office in Europe that was worth any income of importance. They did not insist on the appointment also of parish priests only because the income would scarcely repay the cost of collection. It became established that the first year's revenue from any clerical appointment went to the papacy (annates), and the popes even insisted on collecting fees paid to bishops for visitations in the regular course of their duties. Wherever the clergy turned, a papal tax collector was at hand, and they had no protection against him, except such as kings might give for their own purposes, which were hardly disinterested. Edward III of England legislated against papal appointment of foreign clergy to English benefices, since such appointments resulted in money

The Palace of the Popes at Avignon, used during the "Babylonian Captivity" and the Great Schism.

leaving the country, and for the same reason he refused to allow cases under canon law to be appealed to the pope. But the result was a compromise under which the king was able to share in the proceeds, giving no relief to the clergy themselves. Since no one prevented the pope from exercising his prerogatives, the clergy had to submit on pain of losing their offices; but they ceased to perform duties the proceeds of which went to the pope, with further consequences for the prestige of the Church as a spiritual institution. Graft and simony of all kinds were rife, tax collectors kept their share before handing on the remainder to their masters at Avignon, and few offices of the Church would now be performed without appropriate financial recognition. In short, under the highly efficient and by no means captive lawyers who administered the papacy from Avignon, the Church became almost wholly captive to the commercial interests of the time, developing an absolutism which no secular state approached for many centuries to come, taking care of the needs of its own clergy and bureaucrats, but ceasing to perform those essential services for which the money was paid. It was therefore only a matter of time before monarchs would arise who would sequestrate the wealth of the Church and appropriate it to their own secular uses.

THE SUPREMACY OF THE POPE

Unabated claims of the papacy in secular affairs

Over the last few centuries the popes had elaborated the doctrines of the *plenitudo potestatis*, or fullness of power, of the papacy to justify whatever action they might take, either against their own clergy or against the state. We have seen how Boniface VIII asserted the doctrine and with what effects. But his experience did not prevent the Avignon popes from continuing to assert it, continuing to excommunicate monarchs (not, however, including the French), and even attempting to depose them. One such comedy was staged against Emperor Louis

IV, who replied with a deposition of the pope. Neither was, of course, able to make good his claims. But the emperor could suffer inconvenience from an excommunication, while the pope could suffer nothing whatever from an emperor, even though the latter went so far as to proclaim a nominee of his own as pope (such nominees are usually called antipopes). The whole trouble arose from a claim that the election of the emperor had to be approved by the pope, and the successful candidate crowned by him. Louis's successor, Charles, was willing to make a few minor concessions to gain papal approval, but the same emperor also issued a bull of his own, known as the Golden Bull of 1356, which stated clearly how the emperor was in future to be elected (by three archbishops and four designated German princes). The pope was altogether omitted from the document. Emperors were, in fact, elected according to the regulations of the Golden Bull until the end of the Empire in 1806.

Opposition by theorists to doctrine of papal supremacy

As we shall see in the next chapter, all the known works of Aristotle had been now translated into Latin, and were studied at the universities; the great Greek had been partly responsible for a truly revolutionary change in the medieval attitude toward human and earthly activities. For two centuries the proponents of the rights of reason had been gaining ground at the expense of those who, like St. Bernard, had despised reason and exalted faith. The rationalists had not hesitated to turn their weapons against the Church itself, which was, after all, an edifice erected on faith. Reason did not necessarily dictate the supremacy of the spiritual over the temporal unless it was believed, on faith, that the whole purpose of man on earth was to seek salvation in another world. Aristotle had regarded man as competent to decide himself what was the best form of earthly government, and that this should be decided on other grounds than that God willed it. Aristotle's *Politics* was a mine of suggestions as to the nature, purpose, and possible forms of government, and it was difficult indeed for a rational political thinker steeped in the *Politics* to think of earthly society in the stereotypes propounded so long by the Church without opposition. It should be possible to discuss human society without such preconceptions, and medieval students of Aristotle saw no reason why they should not make the attempt.

A Franciscan, who naturally had a distaste for the Church as a secular organization, was one of the earliest critics of the absolutism of the pope. William of Occam denied the papal claims to temporal authority altogether, and thought the papacy should not be so supreme as it was, even in spiritual matters. Protected by Emperor Louis IV, who was glad of any ammunition against the Avignon papacy, William in his later years at the emperor's court argued subtly and effectively against papal claims, and especially attacked the right of pope and clergy to interpret the Bible in any manner they saw fit. William thought that all believing Christians had a similar competence, and that there could be no supreme authority in this field. For this reason a Church council would obviously be a better instrument than the pope in the realm of dogma.

But far more radical was Marsiglio of Padua, who with the aid of a Parisian master, John of Jandun, produced a remarkable work called the *Defender of the Peace* (*Defensor Pacis*). Fully conversant with the politics of his day and protected also by Louis, Marsiglio made a sweeping attack on all the pretensions of the Church, including the Petrine supremacy, treating the Church as clearly inferior to the secular monarchy, with certain special and useful duties assigned to it in the sphere of religion, but incompetent outside that field. Marsiglio wished the monarchy itself to be under the control of the people, and kings were subject even to deposition in certain circumstances. The monarch was to be the servant of the people and act in accordance with the advice of the best people in his country. The clergy,

according to Marsiglio, only had the task of administering the sacraments and preaching. However important such work might be, it did not confer upon them any special authority, especially not in secular affairs. The pope was merely the servant of the people, as indeed the pope always officially claimed to be. As for the Church, which, according to Marsiglio, was composed of the whole body of the faithful, neither clergy nor laity should govern it but a combination of both clergy and laity in the form of a council, whose wishes should be respected by all, the laity, the clergy, and the pope himself. Marsiglio therefore called for the appointment of a representative council, which should strive to reform the pope and clergy and alter the institutions of the Church in conformity with their true function.

Other thinkers, such as the Frenchman Pierre Dubois, attacked the wealth of the Church and denied its right to possess it. He suggested that it would be to the advantage of all if the French king simply confiscated the wealth of the Church and used it for establishing his overlordship over Europe, after which he could perhaps recover the Holy Land.

THE GREAT SCHISM (1378–1417)

The two papacies—Reasons

The papacy at Avignon had been able to maintain its position in part thanks to the electoral procedure. The first French pope to rule from Avignon had taken care to pack the electoral college with French cardinals, who continued to choose Frenchmen as popes. The Italians, however, who had been accustomed for so many centuries to Italian popes, did not take the change quietly, but continued to agitate for the return to Rome; and in due course the cry was taken up by all those who felt that the Eternal City was the only suitable seat for a pope. At length one of the French popes, persuaded thereto by a saintly nun, St. Catherine of Siena, did decide he would return, though the College of Cardinals was still crowded with French prelates, without whose vote no Italian cardinal could hope to be elected. Gregory XI ruled as pope in Rome for one year, from 1377 to 1378, and then died, leaving a vacancy which had to be filled by someone whom the French cardinals would approve. The people and nobles of Rome were clamorous for an Italian after all these years, and the cardinals, who were holding their election in Rome, feared for their lives if they failed to obey. They therefore chose an Italian archbishop, Urban VI, who had no sympathy whatever, as it turned out, with the Avignon papacy, and wished to make sweeping reforms of the whole system. Thereupon the French cardinals retired to a safe post, declared the Italian's election had been carried out by intimidation, and proceeded to elect a Frenchman who went to Avignon with his cardinals and resumed work where it had been left off a year before.

So now there were two popes, and no one knew which was the true one; for it was clear that the cardinals had indeed been intimidated, though certainly not for the first time, and the action of the Italians seemed to many to have been the only way of breaking the French monopoly. Europe divided in its recognition. Germany was split between the emperor, who favored the Italian, and many of the princes and cities, which supported the Frenchman. France naturally supported Avignon, while England, constantly at war with France, equally naturally took the other side. The only thing that was certain was that the situation was a great scandal to every Christian, and that it must be put to an end as soon as possible.

The rise of the conciliar movement

Effort by the cardinals—Council of Pisa —The University of Paris and other more or less disinterested parties tried all means available to them for reaching a compromise. There were now two Colleges of Cardinals as well as two popes; attempts were made to amalgamate the colleges and to extract promises from individual cardinals that if they were elected pope next time they would heal the schism. Conciliators tried to bring the popes together for an interview, and they

tried to get each pope to abdicate in favor of a third. The University of Paris then put forward the claim, already advanced, as we have seen, by theorists, that a council should be called with full authority over both parties, not only to heal the schism, but to put in hand a radical reform of the whole Church. A majority of the cardinals of each pope, heedless of the fact that they had been excommunicated and anathematized by the other, finally left their respective masters and called a general council at Pisa which met in 1409 and assumed the full direction of the Church. Needless to say, the two popes refused to recognize the authority of the council, which, however, ignored them. At the second attempt, the first choice having died, the council chose a third pope, a highly unsuitable candidate, and deposed the other two. The new pope, John XXIII, an Italian ex-pirate, was unable to establish himself in full authority in spite of the backing of the council, and distinguished himself chiefly by sending out indulgence sellers to support his position. So now there were three popes, and the schism was no nearer to being healed than before.

Theory of the supremacy of the council over the Church—The Council of Pisa had been called by cardinals in the exercise of their obvious duty. But it had failed, and the secular rulers began to play a more important part. It was at this time that every publicist of importance seems to have written on the subject of whether a council had the right to overrule the papacy, and many were the explanations as to how the council could have acquired this right. Using theories that had originally been intended to apply to the state, defenders of the council claimed that the papacy was a limited monarchy, subject to regular control by a body representing all Christians, and that this body received its authority from Christ. Such theories, however, were hardly likely to appeal to kings and emperors, who were only interested temporarily in councils as a means of ending the schism. Once the schism was ended, as we shall see, the monarchs deserted the conciliar movement, and made little effort to

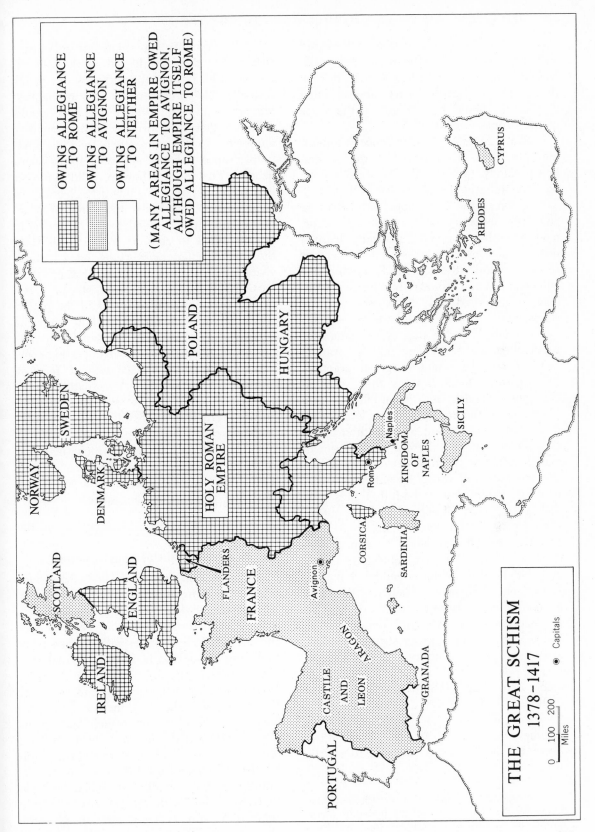

THE GREAT SCHISM
1378–1417

OWING ALLEGIANCE
TO ROME

OWING ALLEGIANCE
TO AVIGNON

OWING ALLEGIANCE
TO NEITHER

(MANY AREAS IN EMPIRE OWED
ALLEGIANCE TO AVIGNON,
ALTHOUGH EMPIRE ITSELF
OWED ALLEGIANCE TO ROME)

NORWAY
SWEDEN
DENMARK
SCOTLAND
IRELAND
ENGLAND
FLANDERS
FRANCE
PORTUGAL
CASTILE
AND
LEON
ARAGON
GRANADA
POLAND
HUNGARY
HOLY ROMAN
EMPIRE
CORSICA
SARDINIA
Avignon
Rome
Naples
KINGDOM
OF
NAPLES
SICILY
RHODES
CYPRUS

● Capitals

0 100 200
Miles

prevent the popes from resuming their old authority, from which the rulers personally had little to fear, much less to fear, in fact, than from the revolutionary doctrine that absolutism should be curbed by the voice of the people in council.

The Council of Constance—Emperor Sigismund, the last member of the Luxembourg family to wear the imperial crown, took the initiative in calling the next council, having forced the Pisan pope, John XXIII, to issue the necessary proclamation. An enormous assembly of prelates and laity, learned doctors, and princes assembled in 1414 at Constance under the general direction of the emperor. But each country had its own problems to be settled with the papacy, and the rulers were as much interested in preventing a monopoly of the papacy by Italians or Frenchmen, and in making private arrangements for improvement of papal practices in their own territories, as they were in the thoroughgoing reform of the Church proposed by the radicals. The clergy were interested in reforming all but those practices which benefited themselves. Agreement was therefore found to be extremely difficult, and the system of voting by nations allowed new national interests to be fully represented and gave much opportunity for political maneuvering. John XXIII realized at once that the council was likely to depose him as well as the other two schismatic popes, and that he did not have enough influence in the council to save himself. He therefore escaped, but was recaptured, put on trial for an assortment of sins, and deposed. The Italian pope, seeing further struggle useless, exchanged his now empty title for a lucrative appointment, while the French pope alone remained obdurate, retiring to a castle in Spain where, as Gibbon asserts, he spent his leisure "excommunicating his enemies three times a day." The schism over,[3] the next thing to do was to fill the vacant see.

[3] It should be added that the Church today recognizes the Roman popes of this period of schism as the true canonically elected successors of Peter, since the dissident cardinals had no authority to depose Urban VI, the first of these Roman popes.

The council's intention was to ensure that a new pope would reform the Church and would submit to the authority of regular councils. The problem was how to be certain that any pope after election would submit either to reform or to the conciliar authority. Furthermore there was no unanimity upon what kinds of reforms were needed. The council, however, did agree on its choice of pope, unanimously electing an Italian noble, who took the name of Martin V. Then it proceeded to try to persuade him to agree to reforms. But by this time the meeting had been going on for three years, and many of the most distinguished participants had gone home. Martin V believed that arrangements could be made which would not detract greatly from his authority, and that once he had taken possession of Rome he could abandon his commitments to the council without fear of reprisals. After satisfying the nations individually by giving up some of his income, he was permitted to dissolve the now thoroughly weary Council and return to Rome (1418). The only promise which the pope could not escape was an agreement to call a council at regular intervals, the first to be held five years after Constance.

RETURN OF THE PAPACY TO ROME

Re-establishment of papal control

The schism was over and there was once more a single pope, ruling from Rome. The papacy under Martin V was apparently only interested in reasserting control over the neglected Papal States and securing revenue from them, and in asserting papal prerogatives as in the days before the councils. Martin at once issued new regulations for the collection of the papal income, and tightened the administration, which had naturally become lax during the schism. He did not, however, dare to refuse to call the council after five years; but few were present, as interest in the conciliar movement seemed to have lapsed with the settlement of the schism. Martin was able to dismiss the council without difficulty, on the promise to call a new one in 1431.

Council of Basel—Collapse of conciliar movement

Contrary to expectations, the Council of Basel was well attended, and the issues between pope and council over the control of the Church were bitterly fought. Before deliberations were completed, the new pope, Eugenius IV, dissolved the council, a dismissal which it refused to accept; and the council chose an antipope who lasted for some years. The Hussite Wars, described in the next section, were raging, and a further question which required the pope's attention was the matter of how to negotiate with the Greek Church, which had offered to unite with Rome in exchange for protection against the advancing Turks. The pope by skillful diplomacy split the council on the latter issue, enabling him to follow the policy of his predecessor, Martin V, in making private agreements with the secular powers over the scope of papal taxation. The French, in the person of Charles VII, asserted full authority over the French Church, prohibiting many taxes and judicial appeals to Rome except in extreme circumstances, while the emperor was content with the handing over to his patronage of a number of important Church benefices. Deprived of the support of the monarchs, the Council, which had dragged on for eighteen years, finally dissolved itself in 1449.

The conciliar movement had failed largely because no one of sufficient power was interested in seeing it succeed. The monarchs were interested in gaining financial concessions from the papacy, and in sharing in the proceeds of papal taxation. They were not interested in seeing a council supreme over the pope, though they were quite glad to use the councils as a tool for extracting concessions. The papacy naturally did not wish to lose or share its supreme control over the Church, which it considered had been entrusted to it by Christ. In the event, the papacy had lost some of its income, and some of its power over clerical appointments, which now had to be shared with the kings. But it had recovered the Papal States, and, though its supposed supremacy over secular powers was shown to be unenforceable, this was a small loss in comparison with its accepted supremacy over the Church.

On the whole the outcome of the councils was a triumph for the monarchs, though the papacy had emerged, if not with prestige, at least with its position intact and its revenues substantially unimpaired. But the conciliar movement had probably made the Protestant Reformation inevitable; the Church had shown itself unwilling to undertake reform of its own accord. The next great council was to be a serious one, and seriously devoted to reform. But it would not be held for another century, and it was the Protestants who, by their successes, forced it upon the papacy. It could hardly be considered as a spontaneous initiative on the part of a papacy earnestly devoted to a reform which it considered necessary.

Violent anticlericalism among all classes

There can be no doubt from the unanimity of the literary evidence that the failure of the clergy to perform their proper spiritual offices and their ostentatious luxury made them a favorite target for ridicule and contempt. As early as the end of the thirteenth century, *The Romance of the Rose* of John de Meun was accusing the clergy of avarice, pride, and laziness. In the fourteenth century Chaucer ridiculed with more gentleness the monk and the pardoner; Boccaccio's stories carry their sharpest sting when directed at the clergy and monks. When the peasants revolted in England at the end of the fourteenth century, many of their grievances were concerned with the exactions of the clergy. It was a common saying that no peasant's daughter was safe while priests lived in celibacy, and, especially in the period after the Black Death in the middle of the fourteenth century, there were violent outbursts against the way in which the clergy (with certain honorable exceptions, especially among the Franciscans) had escaped the plague and had done nothing to help the stricken. Clergy were accused of blasphemy and of selling themselves to the Devil in addition to their more obvious and usual sins, which were visible to all. It was not surprising that in many parts of Europe there was a widespread attempt to come to a simpler and purer religion outside the jurisdiction of the Church altogether, though relatively few of the seekers after righteousness actually broke with the Church and ventured into heresy.

The rise of mysticism

There has always been a mystic element in Christianity, and among many believers there has been a profound desire to enter into a more personal relationship with God than the mere adherence to formal beliefs and participation in the ritual of the Church. In earlier centuries this tendency found its expression in monasticism, especially of the Oriental kind, which sought for inner experience through mortification of the flesh. But in most monasteries of the fourteenth and fifteenth centuries there was no longer a place for such practices. The theory of mysticism—that it is possible for the soul to find union with God though still in the body— had been expressed in a very complete form in the Neoplatonic philosophy of Plotinus, a late pagan philosopher. It was now revived, though unquestionably through a desire to explain his own personal experiences, by the Dominican Meister Eckhart, who lived in the second half of the thirteenth and into the fourteenth century. His disciples, John Tauler and Henry Suso, also from the German Rhineland, wrote in the same vein. The distinctive feature of Christian mysticism was the effort to imagine as a deep inner personal experience the sufferings of Christ and to identify one's self with them. This interest belongs to the whole temper of the fourteenth and fifteenth centuries, an age when the Black Death decimated the population of Europe, when the Great Schism to some portended the final collapse of Christianity, when France was visited with the desolation of the Hundred Years' War. It was no accident that so much of the painting of the period depicts the *Pietà*, the death of Christ upon the Cross, with his mourning mother and with the gaping wounds realistically portrayed, and that some of the more ascetic mystics should have come to believe that purification through suffering was the true path to perfection (e.g. St. Catherine of Siena).

But the mystics were not content only to seek mystic perfection for themselves. They founded schools where the inner life was cultivated and where the initiation ceremonies of esoteric Christianity were taught. Such a school was the Friends of God in the Rhineland. In the Netherlands, John Ruysbroeck described the mystics' exercises and their trials and the states of consciousness through which they pass. Such men naturally could not be expected to think of salvation in some future life as the sole aim of mankind, and thus they gave less importance to the sacraments than did the Church as a whole. The Church therefore was doubtful whether it should approve or condemn; but in the end it decided at least not to disapprove, and Eckhart, though not canonized, received the title of Blessed, and other mystics later actually became saints.

The most practical and popular mysticism was to be found in the Brethren of the Common Life, founded by Gerard Groote at Deventer in the Netherlands. The members of this group did not organize themselves into a monastery nor did they take vows; but they lived together in a community, and meditated, prayed, and taught the people. They were especially noted for their schools, which for a time were unquestionably the best in Europe, and they published many books on the devotional life, the most famous being the *Imitation of Christ*, a simple personal imagination of the true Christian life, based upon the life and teachings of Christ as found in the Gospels. This work, attributed to Thomas à Kempis, has remained since its writing the second bestseller in the Christian world and has never been out of print since its first publication. The work of the mystics had a direct effect upon the early Protestant thinkers, especially Luther, and Erasmus received his early education with the Brethren of the Common Life. Luther's own struggle with the Devil and his earnest desire to submit himself totally to Christ betray the mysticism of his nature, and he admitted the effect especially of Suso upon his own life.

▸ The heretics

WYCLIF AND THE LOLLARDS

John Wyclif may properly be put among the heretics in part because of the work of the last six years of his life, when he wrote most of his attacks upon the teachings of the Church, and in part because heretics undoubtedly made use of his writings. But he was known for most of his life as an ardent anticlerical, and a critic of the Church as an institution. He is first met with as an influential master at Oxford, protected by the English king with whose views on the Church he was, of course, in sympathy. But though Wyclif supported the theory that the Church had no right to own any property at all but should live on voluntary offerings, which would be given in accordance with the services it performed, and though he attacked papal collection of taxes in England, his views were firmly based not upon the reasonings of Aristotle, but upon the teachings of the Scriptures, as he interpreted them. His most notable work of all perhaps was his first translation of the Bible into English, which already has some of the majestic cadences later incorporated into the famous King James version. Like the Spiritual Franciscans, his contemporaries, he castigated the worldliness of the Church, and thought that the only true Christianity was to be found in the system of the early Christian Church, and in imitation of the life of Christ.

In his later years he became ever more radical, so much so that the University of Oxford found his presence altogether too compromising; whereupon he retired to his parish at Lutterworth and continued to write. Now he denied that the Catholic Church was a true Church at all, and the Church became, for him as for the later John Calvin, the body of all those predestined to be saved; and each man could be his own priest, as in the teachings of Luther. The

Church could not ordain true priests, for only Christ could choose these, and they made known their priesthood by the manner of their life. Since above all the Church and priesthood were not necessary as an intermediary between man and God, he was led to reject all the sacraments except marriage, and to deny that any miracle took place in the Mass; and he attacked the whole pomp and glory of the Church as likely to lead man away from God, not toward him. He trained a company of preachers called Lollards who were to go out and spread his doctrines, and these indeed went through Europe preaching, and creating a profound impression, especially, as we shall see, in Bohemia.

Wyclif, though lacking the personality and the organizing ability of the Protestants Luther and Calvin, was undoubtedly in his last years a full Protestant of the later age, and there is hardly a teaching of either Luther or Calvin which is not to be found in his writings, though he did not carry them to their full conclusions in the same degree as these successors. But the time was not yet ripe for such teaching in England. Many of his Lollards seems to have taken part in the famous Peasants' Revolt of 1381, three years before Wyclif's death, and in any case his teachings were blamed in part for the uprising. Such an uprising was bound to bring down upon it all the forces of law and order; and though Wyclif himself died peacefully, still protected by the crown, many of his Lollards were put to death on the order of a later monarch in England, and the papacy was sufficiently influential to have his remains disinterred and buried in unconsecrated ground, after the bulk of his teachings had been condemned at the Council of Constance.

JOHN HUS AND THE BOHEMIAN WARS

It is difficult to disentangle the actual heresy in Bohemia from the manifestations of Czech patriotism which undoubtedly made use of religious unrest; but it is certain that the whole of Bohemia in the fourteenth and fifteenth centuries seethed with hatred of the Church, and that all heresies of the day found refuge there. Among the peasants the Waldensian teachings had taken root, elements of the persecuted Cathari found a home there, and there were considerable numbers of people of all classes who expected an immediate end of the world; for it had been prophesied in the Bible that there would be trials and tribulations before the last day and that the Antichrist would appear. To these earnest souls it seemed that the degradation of the Great Schism and the terrors of the Black Death heralded the end of the world, and many were the suggestions made as to who the Antichrist was.

The Bohemian Church was itself an offshoot of the German Church, and German clerics had always held a preferred position in Bohemia in spite of the fact that they were a minority in the country. Moreover, Bohemia was also generally under the rule of Germans, who were detested by the Slavic Czech population. But Emperor Charles IV, king also of Bohemia, chose, for reasons connected with his feudal interests, to support Czech nationalism; and he gave Prague, the Bohemian capital, an archbishop and a university which was to become the center of Czech nationalism. The Bohemian Church, under its new archbishop, was very strongly opposed to papal exactions, which were for the first time forced upon this rather isolated church by the papacy at Avignon. Supported by the new Bohemian king, Wenceslas IV (1378–1419), who was also emperor until he was deposed in 1400, a young theologian named John Hus came to prominence as an antipapal preacher.

But Hus was also a follower of Wyclif in all except his most radical teachings. He insisted that the Bible was an authority superior to the teachings of the Church, he condemned ecclesiastical simony and wealth, and he advocated the confiscation of Church property. And with such teachings even the Bohemian Church could hardly be expected to agree. It wished to be free from papal exactions, but it was far from prepared to live on nothing but voluntary donations. So

Hus had to rely solely on royal support, which was withdrawn from him when King Wenceslas was deposed from his position as emperor and was succeeded by his brother Sigismund, whom we have seen as the organizer of the Council of Constance, and who was also the king of Germany and Hungary. Such a monarch naturally was disturbed by Czech nationalism, for which Hus was the spokesman. Though without royal support Hus continued to preach, and was excommunicated by the Pisan pope, John XXIII, for attacking the theory and practice of indulgences. When the indulgence sellers, sent by the notorious pirate-turned-pope, arrived in Prague there was such a commotion that Hus retired for a while from the university.

Two years later the Council of Constance met, with the avowed intention of ending the Great Schism, and at the same time checking the spread of heresy. Hus did not consider himself in any way heretical, in spite of his interest in the work of Wyclif, and had no objection to defending himself before the council, provided his person was protected by the secular powers who controlled the conference. He and his disciple Jerome of Prague asked for and received a safe-conduct to and from Constance from Emperor Sigismund. But the council, determined to check the spread of heresy and in particular of the Lollards—one of the few items on the agenda on which all parties were agreed—explained to the emperor that if Hus were convicted of heresy his safe-conduct did not hold good, as heretics were not entitled to such consideration. The emperor cravenly gave way and Hus was brought to trial. A list of supposed errors from his teachings was drawn up, many of them held by Wyclif and not by himself, and he was told he must recant them all, whether he had held them or not. Hus refused to recant all the errors the council chose to impute to him; but he did go so far as to admit some of the teachings, though denying they were errors. On what authority, he asked, did the council presume to treat them as errors? He could accept no

HUSSITE WARS
(1420-1436)

EXPANSION OF
HUSSITES INTO
NEIGHBORING LANDS

⊙ Capital

0   100   200
Miles

teaching as an error unless it could be shown to be so by the authority of Scripture. This position, of course, was heresy, so at last the council had the evidence. In spite of the safe-conduct, Hus was condemned to death and burned in 1415 outside the city of Constance. Jerome of Prague, after recanting, withdrew his recantation and was also burned as a relapsed heretic.

Hus martyred was more powerful than he had ever been in his lifetime. He became at once what he has remained ever since, a Czech national hero, condemned to death for having stood up for the rights of Czechs against a German dominated council. The council, Sigismund, and the new pope all proclaimed the followers of Hus in Bohemia as heretics, and crusades were called against them. If they had not been heretics before, they soon became heretics, even the more conservative among them. Sigismund was driven from Bohemia for violating the safe-conduct, national armies were formed, and Bohemia became entirely independent within the next few years, carrying the offensive over into Germany. The Council of Basel, frightened by the passions let loose, withdrew from the position taken at Constance, and offered to negotiate the differences. The original program contained provisions for the confiscation of the property of the clergy, freedom of speech in preaching, and an important change in the practice of giving the Communion. The conservatives (Utraquists) were willing to compromise on all except the last, and thus made their peace with the Catholics, while the more radical group composed of the peasants and lower classes had a full program of social reform which gained them no sympathy with the more powerful Utraquists. These radicals were called Taborites.

The Taborites and Utraquists then engaged in a ruinous civil war, which was suppressed by a coalition between Catholics and Utraquists. The remnants of the Taborites survived only as individuals until the opportunities offered by the Lutheran movement brought them into prominence again as Anabaptists and other radical reformers. The Utraquists, however, did not keep to their alliance with the Catholics; and after several attempts at compromise formed an independent Hussite Church which rejected altogether the Petrine supremacy. The papacy was never able to suppress the several branches of the Hussite Church, which were in due course absorbed into the Protestant Reformation.

▶ **The papacy at the close of the Middle Ages**

Before the end of the Council of Basel a new secular movement had come into being in Italy, which soon claimed the interest of a succession of popes. This movement, commonly called the Renaissance, or the revival of classical humanism and secularism, will be dealt with in Chapter 16, and is generally studied under modern history, since in many respects it represents a trend distinctively modern and not medieval. It is sufficient to say here that start-

ing with the papacy of Nicholas V, who ascended the papal throne before the end of the Council of Basel, the majority of the popes found a new interest in life in the patronage of humanists, searchers for ancient manuscripts, and artists who succeeded in escaping from the medieval style into one more naturalistic and less stiffly symbolic at least than those painters prior to Giotto.

The popes thus began to pay even less attention to ecclesiastical matters than before. They were not so much interested in asserting their authority as seeing to it that they had enough funds for their vast building projects and other hobbies. The tax system was maintained as before; but as long as it was kept adequately supplied with money, the papacy did not try much interference with secular affairs. When Savonarola, a Dominican friar, purged the city of Florence and preached violent sermons against the luxury of the papacy, Alexander VI, the notorious Borgia, at first merely yawned, and took no action until he was forced to. The disgruntled and exiled nobles took care of Savonarola with the assistance of a bull of excommunication, and the papacy was not greatly disturbed.

When the art-loving Medici, Leo X, took the papal throne in the early sixteenth century, he is said to have remarked: "Let us enjoy the papacy since God has given it to us." Leo was nevertheless forced to bestir himself against Martin Luther, but not too much. It was left to his successors under Spanish influence to bring about the Catholic Reformation, so long overdue, and for the Council of Trent (1545–1563) to set the Catholic Church firmly upon the foundations on which it has rested till the present day.

▶ **Suggestions for further reading**

For this chapter, unlike the preceding one, there are several excellent books, embodying the latest scholarship. An excellent introduction, which gives all the information necessary to understand both the decline of the medieval Church and the decay of medieval society and its transition to the modern era, is to be found in E. P. Cheyney, *The Dawn of a New Era, 1250–1453* (4th ed.; New York: Harper & Brothers, 1936). There are several chapters in this book which deal specifically with the decline of the Church and the rise of the later heresies, but the whole is well worth reading for the background, and it is written in an easy style which the student will find agreeable. Another work, not as formidable as its bulk would indicate, is A. C. Flick, *The Decline of the Medieval Church* (2 vols.; New York: Alfred A. Knopf, Inc., 1930). Although the official subject of this book is specifically the Church, like Cheyney's, it has a tremendous amount of useful information regarding all phases of life at this time, which is organized in a masterful manner around the decline of the Church as the key medieval institution. There is a third extremely useful book, by J. Huizinga, *The Waning of the Middle Ages* (New York: Doubleday Anchor Books, 1954), which is already something of a classic; it should be read by students who are especially interested in cultural history. The author, while ostensibly studying culture, especially in the Low Countries, nevertheless manages to paint a remarkable picture of the gradual decay of the whole medieval spirit, which he connects with the new cult of death (itself in part the result of the Black Death), and which will serve as a partial comment on the two pictures in the text which portray the Knight Templar and the money-changer being carried away by death (Chapters 11 and 14). While few would accept Huizinga's entire thesis, the book cannot be neglected by serious students of the period.

There is an excellent biography of Frederic II by a renowned scholar: E. Kantorowicz, *Frederic II* (New York: Richard R. Smith, Inc., 1931), which, for its picture of the last stages of the struggle between the Empire and the papacy, is greatly superior to the many popular biographies of this remarkable personage. The student is also referred to Packard's study of Innocent III and the Church, and to Toynbee's study of the growth and decline of the medieval church referred to at the close of the previous chapter. These books deal also in part with the period covered by the present chapter.

Finally, there is a useful Pelican book by A. R. Myers, *England in the Late Middle Ages* (London: Penguin Books, 1952), which has a valuable chapter on religious and educational movements in England, presenting an important sidelight on the decline of the Church as it affected England; and there are several good chapters (Chaps. 13–16) on the conflict between Church and State during this period, in Sabine's book, already referred to several times in these notes, *A History of Political Theory* (New York: Henry Holt & Co., Inc., 1937). Here will be found a fuller discussion on Marsiglio and William of Occam than that given in the text above.

13

Medieval Culture

General characteristics of medieval culture • Learning and education in the Dark Ages • The triumph of reason in theology • Medieval science • Education in the Middle Ages • Medieval. art: architecture, music • Medieval literature

---

▶ ## General characteristics of medieval culture

THE MIDDLE AGES AS THE FORMATIVE PERIOD OF MODERN WESTERN CIVILIZATION

In the plan of this book separate sections have been devoted to the culture of the various peoples considered, and no difficulty has been experienced in adopting this procedure. Clearly it is justifiable when it is possible to perceive in the perspective of history the total achievement of a particular civilization in the realm of culture. These earlier civilizations have all come to an end, and their legacy has been absorbed by their successors. But medieval civilization is merely the earlier period of our own Western civilization. There is no pronounced break between medieval and modern times, and historians in general have simply agreed to accept the quite arbitrary date of around 1500 as the end of the Middle Ages, while the beginning may be placed about the time of the fall of the Roman Empire.

The achievements of medieval people are the achievements of our own immediate ancestors. Most of our institutions date back to medieval times; the modern university

is in the direct line of descent from the medieval university. The gowns still worn for graduation at our universities are now only decorative, but served to keep the medieval student warm; in the older English universities they are used to distinguish the student from the townsman, and must be worn every evening and for all academic activities in the daytime. The English Parliament and English law have evolved since medieval times; but they have never been destroyed and replaced by something else, as happened to the institutions of Greece and Rome.

The history of our own particular civilization should therefore start with the invasions of the barbarians, should continue with the civilizing of these barbarians and cover the gradual absorption of the legacy of their predecessors, and should then give their characteristic original achievements. If we stop short at any particular year, this is bound to be an arbitrary procedure, dictated by convenience. However, since this book ends with the year 1715 and does not continue to the present day, we shall try to show the beginnings of Western culture and to impose upon medieval culture a finiteness which it does not possess, since it did not come to a recognizable end.

A generation ago this procedure would not have seemed as arbitrary as it does now; for a curious phenomenon was then believed in, called a "Renaissance," or rebirth, which was supposed to have taken place in Italy and then been diffused over the rest of Europe, marking a radical change from everything medieval. Everything post-Renaissance, according to this view, could be clearly marked as "modern," or different in kind from what was labeled "medieval." Descriptions of this phenomenon were primarily distinguished by an ignorance of exactly what the medieval peoples did accomplish, an ignorance which is only gradually, even today, being dispelled by the efforts of many devoted medievalists; and the "Renaissance" can now be seen more clearly in perspective as a partly reactionary movement, especially in its insistence on a return to Greek and Roman antiquity and in its neglect of science, and partly as a releasing from medieval inhibitions, especially in the field of art. But a secular attitude to life, usually cited as the distinctive feature of the Renaissance, was far from being a Renaissance phenomenon; the development of this attitude was a long process, with its roots back in time at least as early as the Crusades.

As we shall see when we come to study the Renaissance, the curious feature of the thinkers of that time was that they reacted more violently against their immediate past than is customary. Believing themselves to be heralds of a new era, they consistently derided the achievements of their immediate ancestors, labeling their new and distinctive architecture—perhaps the greatest original artistic achievement of our civilization, and certainly the greatest architectural innovation until the twentieth century—as "Gothic" (barbarian), and their philosophy as mere playing with words. Men of the Renaissance pictured their forebears as living in total bondage to an authoritarian Church, unable and unwilling to think for themselves, with every slightest deviation from orthodoxy punishable with a horrible death at the hands of the Inquisition.

This stereotype of the Middle Ages was accepted for so many centuries, and is, even now, dying so hard, that we do not regard medieval times frequently enough as the formative period of our own age, nor examine closely enough the immense obstacles that had to be overcome by the barbarians in a society that had collapsed as completely as the old Greco-Roman civilization. It was centuries before the static manorial feudal society was undermined deeply enough for an urban society to develop, and, as we have seen, civilized arts have hitherto never appeared in a rural society. But the medieval people did finally develop an urban civilization and an urban culture, and the cities which they founded have continued into our own times without serious breaks, excepting a few affected by external causes such as the Black Death.

What should be studied therefore in medieval culture is the struggle of the people to absorb what was left of the heritage of older civilizations, and the new creative effort to strike out on a line of their own afterward, to emancipate themselves from the static conception of life natural to a rural existence, to discover the power of reason and free themselves from the bondage to authority, and to see how in doing this they made possible the enormous scientific and political advances which have been the main glory of Western civilization as a whole. We shall understand their achievement better if we emancipate ourselves from the outworn stereotype that medieval civilization was a thing in itself that began with the barbarian invasions and ended with the Renaissance, that it was an age of faith and acceptance of authority, and that reason did not begin until at least the seventeenth century, that the all-embracing Church stifled the efforts of men to improve their lot on earth by assuring them that the next life alone was of importance. It is true enough that the last was the official teaching of the Church, but it is not true that the teaching stifled initiative and freedom of thought, nor that it succeeded in turning men exclusively to preparation for the hereafter.

The story of medieval culture is, in a sense, extraordinarily dramatic if viewed sympathetically, with a realization of the enormous obstacles to freedom of thought which were progressively overcome; if we try to see the objectives of medieval thinkers and scientists and writers, and realize how consistently they were striving to relate their actual experience to the picture of life on earth and in the hereafter presented to them by the conservative elements in their society; and how the human mind showed itself unable to tolerate restrictions which it ultimately recognized to be artificial. Progress in the Middle Ages was slow, and perhaps the total of its achievements was small in comparison with achievement in the centuries since. But preparatory and formative periods must necessarily last longer and show less spectacular results than the later flowering. It was many centuries after the Dorian invasions that the Greeks came to the height of their powers. There is no flower until the roots have taken hold; and the roots of Western civilization lie far back in the Middle Ages when the struggle was being fought between reason and faith, between freedom and authority, between the miracle and the natural law, between the pull of the past and the urge toward the future.

CONTRAST BETWEEN EARLY AND LATER
PERIODS OF MIDDLE AGES

Medieval culture falls into two periods. The period that has already been characterized as the Dark Ages is really entitled to the adjective. Outside the fold of the Church there was almost no education at all; and even within the Church only a very small percentage of men and women were even literate. In some of the monasteries manuscripts from the ancient world were diligently copied; but, as we know from the errors in copying, too often the contents were not understood. Charlemagne never learned to read or write; and when he wished to make a modest beginning toward a revival of learning in his empire, the scholars that he found, though the best in Europe in his day, would never have been considered anything but mediocre in any more enlightened age. Outside Ireland, Greek had been forgotten. There is but one creative European thinker known in more than three centuries, and he was an Irishman; yet this dark time was also the period of the flowering of the Muslim civilization. When, in the late tenth century, Gerbert became known as the most learned man in the West, and was finally elected pope as Sylvester II, we are told that he had studied every branch of knowledge available in his day. But the sum total is pitiful indeed. Except for those few who could understand Arabic and had access to Muslim works, the only reading available was the Bible, some of the works of the Christian Fathers, a few inaccurate and highly simplified encyclopedias, and some elementary textbooks.

Then, almost suddenly, the Western mind seemed to awake and ask questions, and the Dark Ages were over. On the one side, it began to learn to reason, and to apply reason to what it had hitherto received as dogma, bestowed by authority; and, on the other side, certain individuals began to become aware of the wider world of Muslim culture and become interested, and at once began to contrast this knowledge with the abysmal ignorance of the West. Bringing back knowledge to their homelands, they stimulated others to the same quest. Then, as the Western mind began to sharpen its tools for reasoning, it began also to demand more sustenance. And to satisfy this hunger, one after another the works of Aristotle were translated, an enormous fund of knowledge, gradually assimilated over a period of centuries. Bewildered and impressed by this knowledge, the Westerners in their humility at first thought him almost superhuman, and with the attitude of faith and reverence customary to them they thought he had known everything, and all they had to do was to recover for themselves what he had known, and elaborate on it. Then came the realization that Aristotle too had made mistakes; he was a master mind, but not omniscient. So they understood that it was Aristotle's task to train them in method, but not to give them the finished answers. Not many men had understood this, perhaps, by the close of the Middle Ages; but it was nevertheless the work done by Aristotelians at the Universities of Paris and Padua that, as is now known, prepared the way for Galileo, modern mechanics, and all modern science which is based on it—as it was the thorough reworking of Aristotle by St. Thomas Aquinas that was able to make the teachings of Christianity conform to the requirements of natural reason.

THE LATIN LANGUAGE AND THE VERNACULARS

Through both periods the language of learning was Latin, preserved from the wreckage of the Roman Empire by the Church, but predominant also among the laity in those countries which had been civilized by Rome and adopted her language. This Latin was not, however, the language of the Classical Age, but one that was both more flexible and more simple, lacking the formal elegance of the classical tongue but compensating for this by supplementing it with many new constructions unknown to Cicero. This medieval Latin had developed from the language spoken in the late centuries of the empire. Severe classicists naturally call it a degenerate form; but at least it was a living language, as shown by the very considerable medieval literature in Latin which can in no sense be considered as the work of secluded monks or clerics. From this Latin came the Romance languages, the vernaculars of France, Spain, Italy, and Portugal. It lived side by side with the vernaculars for centuries, but increasingly came to be an official language which was learned at school, a means of communication among learned men of every country. Latin remains, of course, today the language of the Roman Catholic Church, understood by priests throughout the world,

whatever their country of origin. The educated class of the Renaissance, however, in their dislike of their predecessors, despised medieval Latin as barbarous, preferring themselves to return to a style and diction nearly fifteen hundred years out of date. The influence of these so-called humanists in the world of the fifteenth and sixteenth centuries was such that it became fashionable for all educated men to deride the medieval Latin, and they successfully killed it; while the style of Latin they favored, cut off from common speech, was unable to take its place as a living language. Latin became, like classical Greek, a dead language, to be studied at school as a discipline, but separated forever from the common man, and no longer possible as the universal European language it had been in the Middle Ages.

Medieval literature, then, is partly in Latin and partly in the vernaculars, either those of Germanic origin or the Romance languages. Medieval philosophy and science, intended to appeal to educated men in every country, continued to be written only in Latin during the Middle Ages, and much was written in Latin in subsequent centuries even by masters of the vernacular such as Francis Bacon and René Descartes. Newton wrote his epoch-making *Principia* in Latin. But poetry and stories, intended for a more mixed audience, were written increasingly in the vernacular throughout the Middle Ages. The masterpieces of Dante and Chaucer, the tales of Boccaccio and the love lyrics of Petrarch, the great Icelandic, Norse, and German sagas, the French *chansons de geste* are all written in the languages of their countries, and indeed helped to form those languages. Especially is this true of the *Divine Comedy* of Dante, which made the old Tuscan dialect the real literary language of Italy to this day.

THE VARIETY OF MEDIEVAL CULTURE AND OUR DEBT TO IT

From what has been said above it will be seen that it is impossible to characterize medieval culture as being of such or such a kind, for it lacked uniformity. If we say the medievals lacked intellectual curiosity, as we said of the Romans, exceptions at once spring to the mind, and we can see that acceptance of the given world without questioning it was a passing phase. If we say that they were not interested in new knowledge so much as in pondering the old, reading new meanings into it without adding to it, then this attitude too disappeared as reason began to supplant blind faith. If we say they wanted to reconcile all knowledge with the teachings of Christianity, the suggestion of intellectual dishonesty implied in this statement is unfair. Thomas Aquinas undoubtedly believed in Christianity, but he knew that if it was true it *could* not conflict with what reason told him. He did not dishonestly shirk the difficulties, and he honestly tried to resolve them. He was not trying to explain away the findings of his reason in order to bolster an unsound theology. Indeed, he was extremely scrupulous in avoiding the temptation of trying to prove by reason things which he did not think could be proved by it. Naturally as a medieval Christian he believed in the creation of the world out of nothing by God; but he was careful to show that Aristotle had not believed in it, and that his reasoning was justified. The story of the creation was one of the matters which could not be proved, and so must remain in the realm of faith.

Medieval thought, like all thought, was concerned with the problems of the time, and it reflects an honest and not unsuccessful attempt to deal with them within the framework of its presuppositions and assumptions. But, more important, as these assumptions ceased to appear valid, new thinkers arose who grappled with new assumptions and new knowledge. This eagerness for new knowledge is the mark of a living culture, which, in this case, has continued to live and move forward, even into our own time. If the medieval answers no longer seem valid, this is because the compass of our knowledge has been so greatly extended. But it was the medievals

who first in our civilization fought for the rights of reason, the medievals who trained us in logic and analysis and gave us our tools of inquiry, and the medievals who formed the very language in which we continue to express ourselves and who gave the world the first great masterpieces in every Western European tongue. And since it was also the medievals who taught the world to use representative assemblies to limit the powers of monarchs, it is perhaps time that the word "medieval" cease to be used as a term of abuse for all that we like to think of as reactionary.

▶ Learning and education in the Dark Ages

READING MATERIAL OF THE DARK AGES

It has already been noted that when the Western world relapsed into the Dark Ages with the disintegration of the Roman Empire one man in Italy foresaw the complete loss of Greek learning and tried to remedy it insofar as it was possible for one man to do so. This was Boethius, who was executed by the Ostrogothic king in the early sixth century. It was his intention to translate from Greek into Latin as many of the indispensable Greek works of learning as he could. He translated two elementary logical works of Aristotle, the *Categories* and *Concerning Interpretation,* together with an important introduction to the *Categories* by a Neoplatonist. But either he tired of his huge project or circumstances made him realize that it was impossible. For instead of continuing his translation he proceeded to write textbooks on arithmetic, geometry, and music. These works were considered authoritative, and were standard at all schools and universities until translations were again available from the Greek. Contemporary with Boethius was the learned abbot Cassiodorus, who directed his monks to collect and copy all the manuscripts of Latin and Greek they could lay hands on. Undertaking leadership in this work himself, he made his monastery an outstanding center for study. Although such work had not originally been prescribed by the Benedictine Rule, many monasteries followed his example, and it became a regular Benedictine activity to copy manuscripts, although in later centuries it is clear that the monks knew very little of what they were translating. Nevertheless, very many manuscripts are only known to us from these monasteries, and as a work of preservation of the past, these translations proved of the greatest value for future generations.

As has already been mentioned, the chief sources of sustenance for a would-be scholar in the Dark Ages were the encyclopedias, scrapbooks compiled from earlier learning by earnest teachers. The best known and most successful of these was a work called *Etymologies,* by St. Isidore, Bishop of Seville in the early seventh century. The book is full of misinformation and even contradictory statements, culled from various sources. It purports to explain the origin of different words in use; but most of the etymologies are fantastic and completely unreliable. Isidore was aware of the growing decadence of all learning, and tried very nobly to remedy the almost universal ignorance. He discourses on almost all the subjects he can think of, sacred and profane, very occasionally with some accuracy. But since much of his work was taken from Pliny's *Natural History,* itself a book of much pretension but feeble in accurate information, he could hardly be expected to have done much better. Such as it was, the *Etymologies* served as a manual of universal knowledge for many centuries.

Later in the same century an English scholar, the Venerable Bede, a Benedictine monk, devoted the whole of a long life to trying to improve the standard of Christian education by his writings. Most of his work, though well written for his age, showing a good knowledge of Latin and some, even, of Greek (probably under Irish influence), repeats earlier writers on such subjects as the work of God in creating the world in six days, and shows little originality, but greater accuracy and understanding than

Isidore. But Bede also wrote one truly original work, the *Ecclesiastical History of England,* in which he showed himself as a first-rate historian, especially remarkable in his age, carefully checking his statements and explaining the nature of his sources. Bede also wrote a book on chronology which had an important influence in that from it was later taken the method of dating years before and after the birth of Christ (B.C. and A.D.); though modern scholars believe he made an error in his calculations by which Jesus was held to be born four years after he really was.

THE CAROLINGIAN RENAISSANCE

Royal support for learning

It has already been noted in an earlier chapter that Charlemagne made a serious effort to revive learning in his empire, especially by the founding of his palace school at Aachen. Scouring the Western world for scholars, he succeeded in finding a few, led by Alcuin of York, whom he made superintendent of the school. Alcuin himself wrote many textbooks for the use of his students, and commentaries on the Scriptures, none of which is of very high standard. But the school itself was a notable initiative, and its influence spread to the rest of the kingdom of the Franks and stimulated learning in the monasteries. One product of the palace school was Einhard, the biographer of Charlemagne, whose work is certainly the most interesting of its time, though unfortunately he chose to copy in too many respects the Roman biographer Suetonius, whose lives of the Caesars have been criticized earlier. Einhard was almost the only man among all the teachers uncovered by Charlemagne who was not himself a churchman.

Two important consequences stemmed from the educational work of Charlemagne. One was the improvement of the handwriting of the scribes, and the development of a script known as Carolingian minuscule, a very neat script, highly legible, though small, from which came the "Roman" letters

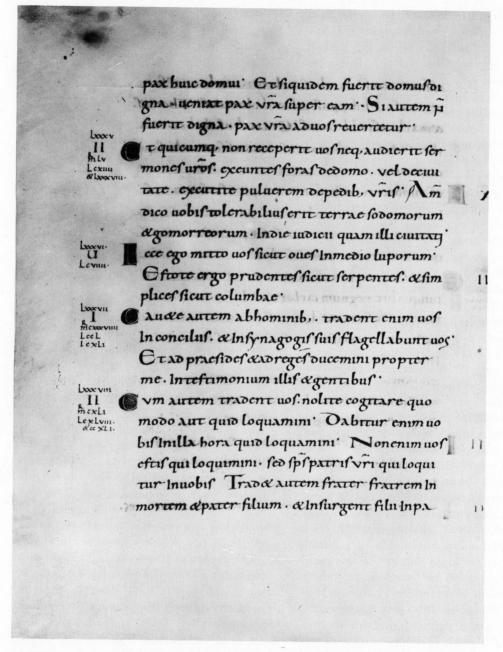

*Example of the new manuscript writing which came into vogue during the Carolingian Renaissance and which is the precursor of our ordinary cursive writing. Previously all writing had been done in capital letters. From a late ninth-century manuscript, Evangelia IV (Switzerland ?). (*COURTESY THE PIERPONT MORGAN LIBRARY. Ms. 1, folio 29*)*

used in most European writing thereafter, replacing, except in Germany, the "Gothic" script. From this script came ultimately those letters which are commonly used today, and which were adopted by printers when printing was finally brought into use in Europe. The other consequence was the gradual development of schools attached to monasteries and cathedrals, where clergy and public officials could obtain such education as was available.

Curriculum of the Carolingian schools

From an early date it was accepted that education should consist of the so-called seven liberal arts. Boethius had subdivided this into the *trivium* and the *quadrivium* (the triple and quadruple paths to knowledge). These were as follows: *Trivium,* grammar (including literature), rhetoric, and logic; *Quadrivium,* arithmetic, geometry, astronomy, and music. This curriculum was now made standard in the Carolingian schools, and many were the learned disquisitions written for centuries to come on the mystical significance of the fact that there were seven and only seven liberal arts. When these had been mastered, the way lay open for study of the supreme knowledge of Theology.

It is clear that an education could be good or indifferent according to what was available in these fields. And unfortunately in the Carolingian age this was precious little. When we reach the high Middle Ages we shall find that really serious progress could be made within this framework of the seven liberal arts, especially with a little juggling, as, for instance, when Aristotle's *Ethics* was classed as rhetoric, for no better reason than that it did not fit in anywhere else.

Under grammar, which of course meant Latin grammar, were studied first of all the grammarians, Donatus and Priscian, elementary but adequate when supplemented by literature, extracts from which were given in the texts themselves. The student could progress to other Latin literature if he wished, but not much was available in the Carolingian age. Under rhetoric, the student could use a textbook of Alcuin, and he could study the sermons and homilies of the Fathers, especially Gregory the Great. He would not be able to understand any of the great Latin classical orators, as their language would be foreign to him and the subjects of no practical importance in

the Carolingian age. Under logic or dialectic, he could read the works translated by Boethius referred to above. But we have no evidence that anyone in the Carolingian age mastered the principles of logic and was able to make use of it for argument. This art came much later in the Middle Ages. Until the Western mind was capable of handling logical problems, even the best textbooks would be as useful as a book on calculus to students without mathematical training.

Under the quadrivium, there were three textbooks of Boethius in the fields of arithmetic, geometry, and music. The first was very feeble because of the difficulty experienced by Greeks and Romans alike from the absence of a positional notation and from the use of letters as numbers. Euclid seems to have disappeared from the curriculum, presumably as being too difficult, and Boethius' geometry was extremely elementary. Music had been treated by the Greeks as a branch of mathematics, and it was the mathematical ratios between the notes of the scale that should have been taught under the quadrivium. But there is little evidence that the subject was seriously taught at all. In astronomy nothing was available at all, as far as we know, and the subject was included in the curriculum only because it traditionally belonged there. Astronomy became a real subject only at the beginning of the thirteenth century, when Ptolemy's *Almagest* was translated from the Arabic and reached the universities.

Carolingian education therefore became what it primarily was, and was no doubt intended to be—a training in language and literacy. Without the indispensable tools of reading and writing, there could have been no progress; and the establishment of schools was at least a beginning.

ALFRED THE GREAT IN ENGLAND

Alfred the Great, who reigned over England for thirty years at the end of the ninth century (871–899) has already been mentioned as the defender of his country against the Danes. Alfred himself was also no mean scholar, and in the intervals of his public activities he translated several important Latin works into Anglo-Saxon, including Boethius' *Consolations of Philosophy* and the *Pastoral Rules* of Pope Gregory the Great. He was also responsible for the beginning of the *Anglo-Saxon Chronicle,* a most important source for early English history, which was maintained by his successors until well after the Norman Conquest. Alfred, too, founded a court school, gathered scholars about him, and tried to revive learning, especially among the clergy, after the manner of Charlemagne. Other Anglo-Saxon literature, especially heroic poetry, had already been flourishing for a long time before Alfred, notably the oldest English epic, *Beowulf*.

RESUMPTION OF THE DARK AGES AFTER THE
DEATH OF CHARLEMAGNE

The chaotic conditions in Europe after the death of Charlemagne were not conducive to the spread of learning and education. Some of the monastery and cathedral schools continued to spread a little light in a dark world. But, curiously enough, in the century after Charles's death appeared the one great creative thinker of the whole period, John Scotus Erigena, an Irishman who for a time lived at the court of Charles the Bald in France. Thoroughly familiar with Greek, and especially with Neoplatonist philosophy, he translated the work of one Dionysius (usually called Pseudo-Dionysius), supposed to have been St. Dionysius the Areopagite mentioned in the Acts of the Apostles, a disciple of Paul, but who clearly lived many centuries later than the time of Paul. In this work was introduced to the West a knowledge of the activities of higher beings above man but lower than God, called Intelligences or Hierarchies, who were God's assistants in the task of creation and continued to play a most important part in the created universe afterward. This book had a remarkable success in the later Middle Ages, being commented on both by Albertus Magnus

and by Thomas Aquinas. John Scotus Erigena, familiar, of course, with the Pseudo-Dionysius, developed a complete metaphysical system, patterned after that of the Neoplatonists, in which he shows how all created beings emanate from the Absolute or God through various stages of being. Man's task, therefore, is to return to the Absolute through mystical contemplation, as also recommended by the Neoplatonists. Erigena has a few words also to say on authority, which he says is weak if not approved by reason, an attitude which foreshadows the later discussions on the subject which will be the heart of the struggle between the Church and the philosophers to be dealt with in the next section. Erigena was far ahead of his time, and few in his day could have understood what he was trying to express. But his book was known and read widely in the later medieval period of the twelfth and thirteenth centuries, and was for a time banned as unfit for Christian use.

At the end of the tenth century another remarkable man appeared who again seems to have had no rivals in his own day and few for a long time afterward. This was Gerbert of Aurillac, who later became Pope Sylvester II (999–1003). As scholar and teacher he was outstanding, introducing new material into the curriculum from his studies in Barcelona and elsewhere in Spain, where he apparently picked up the Arabic numerals, though without the zero. As a mathematician he not only enlarged the understanding of the mathematical basis of music, but was able to demonstrate his teachings by the use of special inventions of his own. He taught some serious astronomy, and constructed spheres to show the planets and constellations. He was also most proficient with the abacus. Furthermore, into the grammatical field he introduced more Latin authors than had ever been used before, and he seriously studied such of Aristotle's logic as was then known through Boethius.

The work of Gerbert was not lost, however; and for this reason he perhaps belongs

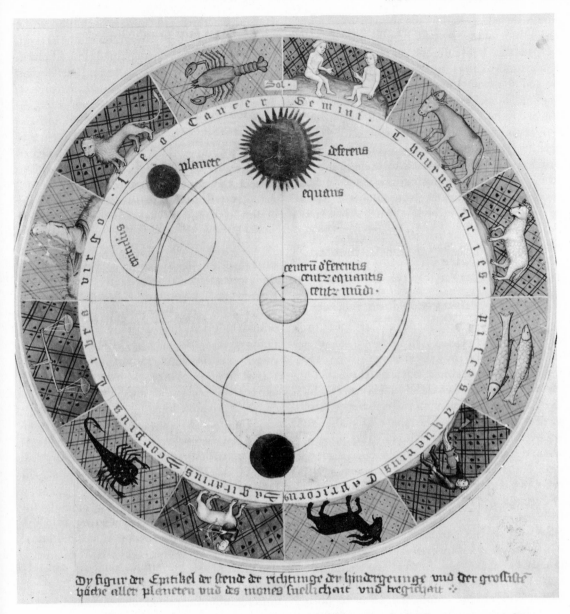

A sphere depicting the signs of the zodiac, the earth, the deferent and equant circles in which the sun and moon's epicycles move, and the epicycles of the planets. In the original, which is an illustration from the famous medieval textbook The Sphere, *by John of Sacrobosco, the signs of the zodiac are upon alternating green and rose-red grounds in the outer circle. The sun and planets are shown in gold, and the moon in silver.*
(COURTESY THE PIERPONT MORGAN LIBRARY. Ms. 722, folio 18)

at the beginning of the next section as the pioneer in the real revival of learning of the Middle Ages. Pupils taught by him continued to be interested in Muslim science, and others, especially at the Cathedral School of Chartres, undertook a close study of the classical Latin authors, while still others profited by his teaching of logic to apply it to some fundamental philosophic questions. Yet the sum total of knowledge acquired by Gerbert—for which he gained such great renown in his lifetime that he was accused of selling his soul to the Devil in exchange for it—was small indeed; but by contrast with his contemporaries as the Dark Ages drew to their close, he was indeed a giant. However, he was the only one of his century. And though he was a learned scholar, and a practical and inventive man with a claim to be considered a scientist, he does not seem to have been a great creative thinker, nor to have put forward any of the profound problems which were to be discussed throughout the later Middle Ages.

▶ The triumph of reason in theology

THE EARLY PHASE

Berengar of Tours—Logic and authority

As has been suggested earlier, perhaps the most outstanding contribution of medieval thinkers to civilization was the reversal of the position taken by the African Fathers of the Church, and especially by Tertullian, that it was morally superior, and more meritorious in the eyes of God, to believe something that to the ordinary mind seemed inherently improbable than to believe something that seemed reasonable. In other words, faith was a moral virtue; and one should not try to lessen the opportunity for exercising it by trying to prove by reason what should be accepted by faith. Tertullian even went so far himself as to make the famous remark that he believed a thing *because* it was absurd. The Scriptural authority for this predominance given to faith was the saying of Christ to the apostle Thomas, "Blessed are they who have not seen and yet have believed." Even as late as the thirteenth century we find Pope Gregory ix telling students in theology that there was no merit in believing what could be shown to be true by natural reason, and urging them to eschew natural reason accordingly.

Moreover, there was also a danger that a Christian would forget that man could not really know of himself; only grace freely bestowed by God enabled man to know.

He might thus fall into the sin of pride, intoxication with his own powers of reasoning, of which St. Bernard accused Abélard, and fall into all kinds of error. The human mind was a weak and imperfect instrument, created for man's undoing, as evidenced by the story of the Tree of Knowledge and the Fall of Man; the attempt to gain earthly knowledge unaided was one of the wiles of the Devil. To the medieval Christian the sins of the mind, and especially intellectual pride, were far more deadly than any sins of the flesh.

Thus there was a formidable barrier of theological opinion to be overcome by medieval thinkers if they were to free themselves for a true pursuit of knowledge. Reason had to be given at least equal rights with faith, and the powerlessness of the human mind to find truth had to be denied before medieval man could be freed. Because of the fundamental importance of this struggle a whole extended section will be devoted to it; and since the struggle was naturally strongest in the realm of theology, we shall try to show how rationalism invaded and took over theology, a strategic position which, in spite of appearances, it still holds today in the theology of the Roman Catholic Church.

One of the first to announce boldly the rights of reason was Berengar of Tours in the eleventh century, who had studied logic[1] at Chartres and thus come to the conclusion that it could not be ignored, even in theological discussion. Logic, he said, is nothing but the power of reasoning, and it was by virtue of his reason that man could be said to be made in the image of God. When authority and reason conflict, he added, then it is reason that must be followed. Armed with his new tool, he brashly attacked the doctrine of transubstantiation. There is no apparent difference to any of the senses in the bread and wine after the sacrament of the Eucharist, he said, and therefore no miracle has taken place. This

[1] The medievals used the word "dialectic," but the more familiar synonym will be used here, since it has substantially the same meaning.

was a remarkable use of logic, which incidentally begs all the questions involved in the difference between spiritual and physical substance and the adequacy of the senses to distinguish between them, and it was unlikely that Berengar would be permitted to announce such doctrines. He was commanded to recant or be declared a heretic. He recanted, but it was hardly a notable defeat for reason itself, for Berengar's use of it was scarcely convincing even to would-be skeptics.

St. Anselm of Bec and Canterbury (1034?–1109)—Proofs for the existence of God

Toward the end of the eleventh century it occurred to St. Anselm not to question the existence of God, but to see whether it was possible by logical demonstration to *prove* this existence, and so confound all atheists and unbelievers. He made his position quite clear by explaining that no Christian should doubt any revealed truth of his religion, but that this truth should be capable of being made intelligible to man. Some truths were above reason and should be accepted unconditionally; but without losing his faith a Christian might nevertheless seek to understand as far as his fallible reason could take him. Anselm and all medieval Christians believed that there could be no contradiction between reason and the truths of revelation; but the opening of the whole subject to discussion was a dangerous path, as was realized by some thinkers even in the eleventh century. For the time might come when an irreconcilable conflict might occur. What, then, was to be done? Abandon what reason seemed to demonstrate, or what the Christian revelation had taught for centuries? For Anselm faith came first ("I do not seek to understand in order that I may believe, but I believe in order that I may understand"); but this position was soon to be reversed by other Christians, as faithful and sincere as himself.

Using his logic, Anselm tried to prove the existence of God. His argument that every mind can conceive of the greatest possible being, and that this Being, to be really greatest, must also have existence, which is known as the "ontological" argument for the existence of God, need not detain us. But it is of the utmost significance that at this moment in the eleventh century a Christian saint and archbishop should have thought it either possible or valuable to be able to prove the existence of God, and it shows that the era was passing in which it was morally superior to believe without seeking for proof. Anselm also undertook to prove why it was necessary for Christ to become a man (*Cur Deus homo?*) and gave a clear systematic theory of the atonement of the Son of God for the sins of mankind, which had hitherto been missing from Christian theology.

But Anselm also played his part in a controversy which split the schools of his time and was the first great problem to be thrashed out thoroughly by the new logicians. The controversy concerned the nature of abstract ideas, or what the medievals called "universals" as distinct from "particulars," and the issue resolved itself into the differences between "realists" and "nominalists."[2] According to Plato and Platonists, the universal idea had permanent reality, and all earthly phenomena were only relative and inferior copies of this heavenly reality. Goodness, for instance, was a heavenly archetype, which must be sought for but could never be attained by human

[2] It has been pointed out by historians of medieval philosophy that the nominalism of this period may better be described as "antirealism," and that real nominalism, recognizable as similar to modern nominalism, does not exist before William of Occam in the fourteenth century. The author has not considered the problem of sufficient importance to give an extended and adequate explanation in this text, preferring to give a fuller treatment to the other great problem of medieval thinkers, the relation between faith and reason, which, in his view, is more valuable for the student as well as more comprehensible to the reader not versed in technical philosophy. If the reader requires a more comprehensive treatment, a textbook on philosophy may be consulted, as, for instance, the short but lucid account in W. T. Jones, *A History of Western Philosophy* (New York: Harcourt, Brace & Company, 1952), pp. 422–430, 519–520.

beings. On earth there may be relatively good men who had approached the perfect idea of goodness but had not attained it nor could they. The "realists" of medieval times claimed that only the universal ideas were real. The Church, as a whole, for instance, really existed as a perfect idea; individual churches were only part of this great whole and gained whatever sanctity they had from being part of the universal ideal Church. The nominalists retorted that the universal ideas were only names given for the sake of convenience, but that they had no real existence. By examining plants we came to the understanding of what a plant was, as such. But this did not mean that the ideal plant which all earthly plants approximated had any actual existence.

Clearly the subject has theological implications. If universal man, or "humanity" exists, then God might have justification in punishing all men for the sin of Adam, who was a part of humanity. If, on the other hand, only individual men exist, then each should be judged on his own merits and all men do not have a share in the sin of Adam. The Holy Trinity, according to strict nominalists, must consist of three Gods; and the Trinity itself was only a convenient term for describing the three. This view of the Trinity was indeed a position taken by the most eminent nominalist of the eleventh century, Roscellinus, who was severely taken to task for heresy by Anselm, who insisted that all men are in species one man, and likewise the three members of the Trinity are each perfect God and one God, partaking of the universal Godhead.

Abélard—"I seek to understand in order that I may believe."

With the great teacher and critic Peter Abélard (1079–1142), the first phase of the struggle for the rights of reason was completed. A man of clear incisive thinking, potentially a skeptic though remaining formally true to his Christian faith, he made a contribution of the utmost significance to medieval thought. Few men in the whole history of thought have been so influential as he, in spite of the fact that he was in no way a creative thinker. But his penetrating logic and clear exposition attracted thousands of students to his lectures, and started them working in a direction from which there was never to be any return.

A brief mention may first be made of his contribution to the controversy on universals. Universals are not true realities, he declared; but they are more than mere names. The common element in things is discovered by the mind, and this element has its own reality, though a mental one, called by Abélard a concept. Humanity is a perfectly legitimate concept, derived from our perception of the common elements between human beings; but it is not more real than the individual human beings, and human beings are not real merely because they partake in the universal idea of humanity. This position, called conceptualism, is very similar to the position taken by Aristotle, which was not known to Abélard. Aristotle's position, however, was known to Thomas Aquinas a century later when he stated a similar point of view as "moderate realism." According to the latter view, the ideas are abstracted from the phenomena by the active intellect, a spiritual faculty of man which can only perceive the ideal or spiritual element in things. This, for St. Thomas Aquinas, is the immortal part of man, and man's ability to abstract the universal ideas is the central element in the Thomistic proof of human immortality. The active intellect, being spiritual, can never die.

Abélard studied for a period with Anselm of Laon and with William of Champeaux, both confirmed realists in the controversy, but did not think very highly of either of them, since they were not his equal in logical prowess. Then he began to teach, and from the first he was followed by hordes of infatuated pupils. Driven out of Paris after an unfortunate love affair with Héloïse followed by tragedy, he escaped to a monastery for a while, then returned to teaching but got into trouble with the Church because of his divergent views on the Trinity. Even in a desolate rural retreat students followed him. The significance of this extraordinary popularity was that he was teaching them to think, and to doubt. His most famous book, called *Sic et Non* (*Yes or No?*), is typical of his method, and permits us to understand what his students found so fascinating. He thought it was the duty of a Christian to use his reason even on the substance of theology. He was the first to point out clearly that the Fathers of the Church who were accepted as authorities had themselves been in doubt, and that there were contradictory opinions on theological subjects even among these authorities. Abélard did not conclude that the Fathers did not know what they were talking about, but rather that there were reasonable grounds for doubting where the truth lay. What he proceeded to do, therefore, was to list a number of important theological questions, and then draw up the various opinions that the Fathers had held about them. Sometimes the contradictions could be reconciled, but more often the only thing to do was to accept the best authority. But, above all, the student must work out the answer for himself, for only by doubting could there be any inquiry, and only by inquiry could one come to truth.

This was already a reversal of the position taken by St. Anselm. Abélard wished to arrive at belief through the process of doubting and trying to understand. Faith no longer was primary, and indeed, implicitly, was an enemy to understanding. Abélard had firmly planted the seed of honest and disinterested inquiry, and suggested that the way to resolve a problem was to think about it, not to see what some great man in the past had thought about it whose opinion had afterward been accepted as authoritative by the Church. Only after one had tried to reason it out for one's self should one have recourse to some predecessor, whose other work had entitled him to be considered as an authority in theology.

REACTION OF THE CHURCH TO THE METHOD OF ABÉLARD

Abélard was unfortunate in that in his own generation he was opposed by so severe a critic and such a sworn foe of human reason as the mystic St. Bernard, of whom we have already spoken in an earlier chapter. Bernard at once saw the danger and pursued Abélard bitterly all his life. If human reason were to triumph, there would be no mystery left. "He thinks himself able by human reason to understand God, completely," Bernard charged. He accused Abélard of pride and arrogance in thinking that man with his puny mind could ever comprehend the mysteries of faith, and he did not hesitate to accuse him of heresy in questioning authority, and arriving at conclusions contrary to those held by the Church. By his influence he was able to have Abélard condemned to silence, but it is doubtful if he could have sustained the conviction at Rome whither Abélard was going to defend himself when he died.

But Bernard was already behind the times, and the victory lay with his opponent. One of Abélard's own pupils, Peter Lombard, Bishop of Paris, using his master's method, became the teacher of generations of churchmen; his book of the *Sentences* became the standard text for theology for centuries and is still not altogether outmoded today. The great Pope Alexander III was also one of Abélard's pupils. Fundamentally any opponent of Abélard must take the untenable position that Christianity is contrary to reason. For if it is not contrary, then reason can only serve to support faith, and help to convert the doubting or the unbelievers.

Nevertheless, for centuries there was opposition to the use of even Peter Lombard's book of the *Sentences*. In the process of discussing theological questions by the use of reason, there was a natural tendency to escape from essential Christianity as it was revealed in the Gospels. Well on into the thirteenth century we find complaints that theological students were wasting their time studying logic and learning to resolve knotty points of doctrine, rather than learning to preach the way of salvation and the teachings of Christ. We find Roger Bacon, with his fundamentally mystical outlook, praising Robert Grosseteste, Bishop of Lincoln, for neglecting the *Sentences* in favor of Scriptural exegesis; we find, as already mentioned, Pope Gregory ix telling the theological students at Paris to refrain from studying philosophy on the grounds that it cramped their style as preachers, and reproducing the hoary old argument that it is better to believe what cannot be proved than try to prove what should be accepted on faith. It is not, however, recorded that the students paid him any attention, and the *Book of the Sentences* continued to be used in the schools, nor, indeed, did Gregory suggest that it should be given up.

THE DEVELOPED SCHOLASTIC METHOD OF PETER LOMBARD

Systematic theology in the hands of Peter Lombard became, following his master Abélard, a discussion of important theological questions. The teacher would propound a question, as, for instance, whether God created the world out of nothing himself or through "intelligences." The discussion therefore always starts with *Utrum*—Whether. The following step is to take the authorities who have spoken in favor of the proposition—*Quod sic videtur*, For it seems so. The arguments will be listed clearly, and perhaps disposed of, at once, if there is an inherent contradiction. Then the arguments on the other side will be taken. *Sed contra*—But, on the other hand. Finally the master will try to reconcile the difficulties in his own *Solutio*, which carries no authority beyond the weight of the particular master's name. These solutions are the master's *Sententiae* or Opinions (hence, the title of Peter's book, the *Sentences*). It became the custom at the universities where theology was taught for every student to dispute publicly on these questions, and to

give his opinions. Thus from many masters of theology in the thirteenth century we possess *Commentaries on the Sentences*, which are usually a publication of their opinions given on disputed questions during their period of study, and thus represent something close to the doctoral dissertations of our own day.

The method is intellectually of the utmost honesty, for no one was allowed to propound opinions in this public manner which relied on anything except the best that reason could offer. Though authorities were used, the master's solution had to be his own or at least one that appealed to reason and itself reconciled the conflicting opinions. It was not, in the last analysis, the weight of authority that decided the question for the successors of Peter Lombard, but the best opinion available at the time; and this is how all questions are decided in a free world.

One of the most interesting and symptomatic discussions which was carried on for nearly a century was on the subject whether theology is a science. By science was meant something which could be known by natural reason, whether theology, in fact, was different from other branches of knowledge, whether it had axioms from which could be deduced further knowledge, and if so what was the origin of these axioms. Alexander of Hales preferred to call it a *sapientia*, or wisdom, rather than science, while others claimed that the data of Biblical revelation were the axioms, and were implanted in the human mind in the same way as geometrical truths. God implanted geometrical axioms in the human mind at birth, while he revealed theological truths to the apostles, the prophets and evangelists, and the Fathers of the Church.

The discussion is not interesting so much for itself as for the evident need on the part of theologians to feel that they were being "scientific" and reasonable, rather than blindly believing; and it suggests parallels in our own day of theologians who still wish to prove that their teachings are in accordance with "science" as represented by modern psychology or the doctrine of biological evolution.

GRADUAL RECOVERY OF ARISTOTLE AND MUSLIM SCIENCE

Effects on theology

In the early twelfth century, medieval thinkers were already becoming aware of the superiority of Muslim knowledge to the very scanty materials of knowledge available in the West. After the conquest of Sicily there were many contacts made with Muslim scholars by Western inquirers, and at the medical school of Salerno in Italy several important Muslim treatises were in use as well as some of the scientific work of Aristotle translated from the Arabic. But with the gradual conquest of Spain, and in particular the capture of Toledo in 1085, a new phase in the assimilation of Muslim learning began. In the middle of the twelfth century, Raymond, Archbishop of Toledo, fascinated by the wealth of Muslim and Greek works of learning available in his archdiocese, began to authorize translations of the more important works. It was difficult at first to find translators who knew both Latin and Arabic; hence the services of many Jews were bespoken, and a number of Latins painfully acquired sufficient familiarity with Arabic to be able to make translations, not all of high quality, but serving until something better was possible. Among the first works to be translated, especially by Gerard of Cremona, dean of the translators (died 1187), who in his lifetime is said to have translated no fewer than seventy-three works from the Arabic, was Aristotle, who thus entered the West via Syriac, Arabic, and sometimes Hebrew. Translations of a few works were available directly from the Greek, but, on the whole, this first phase of translating was mostly from the Arabic. Translating became the rage for a while, and books were poured forth into the eager Latin world, starved for material for half a century.

It was more than a century before the whole corpus of the immense work of Aristotle was available, and such a huge body of work could only be gradually assimilated by Western scholars. But they were assisted by the commentaries, first of Avicenna, who was more acceptable to Christians in part because of his Neoplatonist tendencies already familiar in the West; and then by those of Averroës from about 1230. Often enough, it would appear, the Western scholars did not trouble to read Aristotle himself, but preferred the commentaries which explained to them more simply what the difficult Aristotle had said, as we may be more inclined to read commentaries on Karl Marx rather than the formidable *Das Capital*, or commentaries on Kant rather than the *Critique of Pure Reason* of the master himself.

The Church at first took little official notice of the influx of Aristotelian thought, perhaps because it was sponsored by such an eminent churchman as the Archbishop of Toledo. But then suddenly very strange teachings began to be heard at the newly founded University of Paris in the first decade of the thirteenth century, apparently deriving from Aristotle. And it was remembered that Aristotle was a pagan and knew nothing of Christianity, and, what was worse, he had been commented on by Muslims, actual unbelievers and opponents of Christianity. The first two heresies heard of at Paris in the early thirteenth century in reality had no connection with the teachings of the Greek philosopher; and it was difficult indeed to show that the materialism of Amaury of Bénes or of David of Dinant could have derived from him. Nevertheless when a number of professors were condemned for teaching the heresy of Amaury, and David of Dinant's books were likewise condemned to be burned, Aristotle was caught up in the same holocaust, and the reactionary and stubborn Archbishop of Sens, within whose archdiocese the University of Paris was situated, formally forbade the teaching of the natural scientific work of Aristotle at the university, together with his *Metaphysics*.

This was a serious blow to the scholars,

from whom was withheld the very work which they most wanted to study; for after the long famine in intellectual fodder there was now for the first time a surfeit. They were not, however, formally forbidden to read the works for themselves, though reading was a poor substitute for hearing a master discourse on Aristotle and explain him. It is almost certain that nothing had yet been found in Aristotle which actually conflicted with Christian teaching, and there is no specific complaint of any portion of his work. But this was soon to come. Aristotle's views on creation were clearly not those of the Church, and he was rather ambiguous on the immortality of the soul. And, of course, as a good Greek pagan, he was, in general, extremely secular in his views, and naturally Divine Providence did not appear in his scheme, although his teleological view of the universe was not hostile to it.

When Pope Gregory ix in 1231 confirmed the ban on the same works forbidden in 1209 by the Archbishop of Sens, he set up a commission of three to expurgate them for Christian consumption. Until this was done there must still be no public lecturing on him. It would seem that the pope had not read Aristotle himself or he would have seen the futility of the task. For Aristotle's method could be used by anyone, and similar conclusions would be drawn from the same premises. The true difficulty lay in the naturalistic, secular attitude of the Greek master, which was so contrary to Christian habits of thought. Specific teachings were of minor importance in comparison with this fundamental danger. At all events one member of the committee died soon after his appointment, and the others seem never to have tackled their task.

For some time the ban seems to have been observed fairly strictly in spite of the certainty that the students were bitter against it; and they were made to content themselves with a far more intensive study of logic, made possible by the translation of the advanced work of Aristotle, and a more intensive study of grammar. Then came the long struggle between Pope Innocent iv and Emperor Frederic ii, and discipline at the university seems to have been relaxed. At all events, suddenly, in spite of the ban, we find Aristotle being taught in all his completeness and without any action being taken against the faculty. But now there was a really grave danger. For Michael Scotus had been rash enough to translate the Commentaries of Averroës from the Arabic, and these contained the real stuff of heresy. For Averroës thought that Aristotle had disbelieved in personal immortality, and that the active intellect of individual men was merged with the active intellect of all humanity at death; there was thus no personal immortality but only a collective immortality as part of the one great world mind. In 1250 the pope took cognizance of this teaching. But now, instead of simply banning it, he asked the greatest theological authority of the day, Albertus Magnus, to defend the Christian teaching against those who were proclaiming the doctrine of Averroës. Albert, in fact, was not much of a theologian, but he did his best. The teaching, however, continued, causing a serious schism in the Faculty of Arts at the university twenty years later, when a far more formidable theologian, Thomas Aquinas, with devastating logic tore the arguments of Averroës apart, insisting at the same time that Aristotle had never held such a pernicious doctrine. It was actually difficult to see what Aristotle had in fact taught, for he seems to make different points in two of his works. It was certainly possible to deduce from his remarks the conclusions that Averroës had drawn. But when Siger of Brabant and others at the university persisted in supporting the Averroistic conclusions it was not unnatural for the Church to think of Siger as a heretic. But, even so, he was only banished from his teaching position, and otherwise seems to have gone unpunished save for a mild exile in Italy. From the burning of 1209 right through the century there is no case of the use by the Church of its Inquisition against academic heresies or potential heresies.

The work of Albertus Magnus and Thomas Aquinas in reconciling Aristotle and Christianity

With the rise of the Averroists, it was already clear by the middle of the thirteenth century that Aristotle and his kind of thinking were potential dynamite to Christianity. It had begun to seem that what could be discovered by pure natural reason was not in conformity with Christianity in several important respects; and a horrible formula attributed to Averroës began to find currency in academic circles, that there was a double truth—the truth of Christian revelation and the truth of natural philosophy. If this notion were ever accepted, then it must mean that faith would be subjected to a severe strain, and might come ultimately to be rejected by many.

There was one possible answer to this crisis, but it could be given only by a man of great learning and industry, competent in science and theology, fully aware of the teachings of Christianity while at the same time able to understand and, if necessary, criticize Aristotle. For the work that required to be done was an intensive study of everything that Aristotle wrote that was available in the West, followed by the demonstration, chapter by chapter, either that Aristotle was making statements which could be shown to be untrue or unproved, or that what he said in no way contradicted the teachings of Christianity. This huge enterprise was carried through to completion by the German scholar Albertus Magnus, Albert the Great (1206–1280), the only man in history who received the title of "the Great" for his scholarship.

Albert, in his introduction to his commentaries on Aristotle's *Physics*, explained that he had undertaken his task because in his order, the Dominican, many brothers had been criticizing both Aristotle and philosophy in general while remaining entirely in ignorance of what they consisted. Philosophy, in Albert's view, was of the greatest aid to the study of theology and Christianity, because it showed how reasonable were all Christian beliefs if rightly understood. Aristotle was by no means infallible, and he was not to be regarded as a supreme authority, beyond questioning; and there were many things of which he was ignorant, even in the field of natural science. Nevertheless, in science he was a great master whose views should always be treated with respect; he simply was unfortunate in that he was born too soon to have the benefit of Christian revelation. Aristotle could not therefore be blamed for not understanding that a Divine Providence ruled over the world, but at the same time there was nothing in his biology which disproved such an idea; on the contrary, rightly understood, Aristotle's observations in themselves tended to suggest precisely this.

Albert planned, both as a scientist and reconciler of Aristotle and Christianity, to write a commentary on every subject that Aristotle himself had treated, and supplement it from his own observations. In addition he would write other books on subjects such as mineralogy which Aristotle had neglected, but which he himself had studied. The commentaries that Albert wrote are not detailed verbal commentaries of the kind made by his successor and pupil Thomas Aquinas, but rather digressions on the general subject treated by the master. They are thus not strictly philosophical, but far closer to what we call science. Albert, indeed, was a self-taught man, and had never studied either philosophy or theology very thoroughly; he was always too busy organizing schools within the Dominican Order, engaging in public activity on behalf of the Church, and even for a while serving as Bishop of Ratisbon. He was thus inclined to gloss over some of the philosophical difficulties, and to assume that Aristotle had agreed with the Christian position when a more careful examination would have revealed that he did not, as with the question of the creation of the world out of nothing by God—which Albert, certainly incorrectly, attributed to Aristotle. His work therefore was in no sense definitive, and in itself would not have been completely convincing to a better-trained philosopher. But it was a magnificent pioneer work in what has since come to be called scholasticism, or the reconciliation of philosophy and Christianity.

St. Thomas Aquinas, a much younger contemporary of Albert, had his early education at the University of Naples, and then went to Paris to study theology. There he met Albertus Magnus, and apparently became fascinated with the work he was doing. Instead of finishing his courses at Paris, he chose to accompany Albert to Cologne, whither Albert was called on business for his order, and continued his studies there with his master. Evidently he recognized that this work of reconciliation was of supreme importance for the whole future of philosophical studies and of Christianity; being better trained than Albert, and having a more acute philosophical mind, he was able to bring his master's work to fruition in such a way that, for those who accepted his main premise that there was no contradiction possible between true philosophy and equally true Christianity, and that reason could and should be applied to the understanding of the Christian religion, his work really was definitive and never had to be performed again. For this reason the Catholic Church today regards the work of Thomas Aquinas as supreme, and requires its study by all theologians; since Pope Leo XIII in the nineteenth century it has been accepted as the official teaching of the Church.

Thomas's procedure differed from that of his master in that he wrote a careful and complete textual commentary on every book of Aristotle, from a philosophical point of view, neglecting those works which were not concerned with philosophy. His purpose is to explain exactly what Aristotle said, the consequences that could be deduced

from it, and why every statement should be accepted or rejected. In one of his masterpieces, the *Summa contra Gentiles,* Thomas builds up with subtle logic that is hardly refutable, provided the premises be accepted, an entire structure of natural theology, or theodicy, endeavoring to show how much of theology can be determined by natural reason alone. Using Aristotle's *Physics* and the master's theory of motion he essays to prove by metaphysical arguments the existence of God, on the grounds that everything that is moved requires a mover, leaving a necessary First Mover, which is God. Using Aristotle's *Metaphysics,* he tries to show that everything on earth requires a cause; tracing these causes back he arrives at a First Cause, which must be God. Again using the *Metaphysics,* with much elaboration from his own thinking, he declares that everything on earth and in the universe was not *necessarily* there; it might have not been there. In other words, everything created is contingent, an accident, as distinct from a necessity. The presence of all these contingent things requires the presence also of one Necessary Being, and this is God. He therefore goes on to define God as the Self-subsistent Being.

Having reached this conclusion, he then proceeds to deduce those attributes of God which it cannot be doubted he must possess, building a tremendous logical structure, perhaps the supreme achievement in the history of human thought of a purely rational nature, without reference to observable facts in the world but entirely spun out of the unaided human reason. This was natural theology, and it only needed to be supplemented by knowledge which the human reason could not reach unaided. This God had supplied to man by revelation, the inspired words of the Scriptures. It was impossible, for instance, for man to arrive at the mystery of the Holy Trinity for himself; such knowledge had to be revealed by God. But Thomas wished to grant as much as possible to the reason, and reason should also be used to try to make intelligible those things which had been revealed.

Man could not, according to St. Thomas, arrive for certain by natural reason at the conclusion that the world was created out of nothing by God; but once this had been revealed to him by the Scriptures, then it was possible and proper for man to try to understand for himself the means of creation, and to see that it was reasonable. So the triumph of reason was complete. Revelation was necessary as a supplement, and this required faith from man, which faith was at once to be supplemented by reason. Medieval thought had moved a very long way indeed from St. Bernard in not much more than a century.

Opposition to Thomism—Duns Scotus and William of Occam

Thomas Aquinas in his own day never attained quite the reputation acquired by his master Albertus Magnus, who outlived his pupil by several years. And during the period of Thomas's greatest production, the period of the *Summa Theologica* which undertook to explain the whole drama of salvation and the part played in it by the Church, the University of Paris was no quiet place, full of students anxious for knowledge, but a center of the most violent polemics, first between the regulars and seculars (those clergy who belonged to an order and those who did not), and then within the Faculty of Arts on the doctrine of the double truth and collective or individual immortality (Averroism). Thomas rarely visited Paris during those years, though he defended his Dominican Order against the attacks of the seculars, and he wrote a strongly worded attack on Averroism. It is very probable that his greatest works were not known to the university at this time in any detail, though their general tendency was understood. Finally the squabbles at the university became so severe that the Bishop of Paris, Stephen Tempier, took a hand and drew up a huge list of errors being apparently publicly taught or discussed, including not only those which could be attributed to the Averroists but a considerable number which emanated un-

doubtedly from St. Thomas himself. And though Thomas had himself died three years earlier and could therefore undertake no defense, his aged master, Albertus Magnus, hurried to Paris to see what could be done. The whole rational movement was clearly under fire from the irate bishop, who must have acted under orders from Rome. And when the University of Oxford a few months later followed the example of Paris and condemned a similar series of errors, the danger of a collapse of the whole work of the century was imminent; for the Church had officially taken no action up to this time ever since the original condemnation of Aristotle, and the weight of its authority, backed by many Franciscans and probably the bulk of the secular clergy, could have been decisive.

But Thomas, Albert, and the movement they represented fortunately were not unrepresented at Rome. Devoted Dominicans, determined that the two great lights of their order should not be suppressed, kept the ear of successive popes, evidently impressing upon them how great an aid to faith the work of their masters could be. Gradually they swung the papacy in their direction, and in 1328 they succeeded in having Thomas Aquinas canonized as a saint, and his works from that time on became authoritative (every article is a miracle, declared the pope in his bull authorizing the canonization).

But the Franciscans, especially those at Oxford, who, as we shall see, early took an interest in science, were far from content; and two considerable theologians and philosophers, at the end of the thirteenth century and during the next, denied the whole possibility of attaining truth by the means advocated by St. Thomas Aquinas. Like most Franciscans, they believed in divine illumination of the human mind, and, following St. Augustine, insisted on the mind's incompetence, especially in the field of religion. Duns Scotus (died 1308) denied categorically that it was possible to prove the existence of God, the immortality of the soul, and such truths of religion by reason. The only possible approach to the truths of religion was by faith and meditation. William of Occam (died 1349) took substantially the same line, denying the ability of human reason in heavenly matters but emphasizing it in earthly things. William revived the old doctrine of nominalism in a new form, insisting that the great universal ideas and abstractions of Thomas had no real validity, and that the ideas were only names which described objects of experience in a convenient way. Ideas therefore are applicable only to things of the sense world revealed by experience, and it is only in this realm that reason and its logic are competent. William's influence in his own century was considerable, and those nominalists who followed him, especially at the University of Paris, for a time became interested in a number of scientific questions, for which they hoped to find answers by reason, and to some degree neglected theology.

But it will be noted that these men only denied the competence of logic and reason in religion; they did not deny its competence altogether as St. Bernard would have done, nor did they suggest that its use was likely to lead to the deadly sin of pride. The form of their criticism therefore is the surest sign that reason had at last emerged as the greatest of human faculties, limited indeed, but powerful as an instrument for discovering the truth about the created world. The way lay open for the scientific achievements of Western civilization.

▶ Medieval science

GENERAL CHARACTERISTICS OF ARISTOTELIAN
SCIENCE, AS INTERPRETED BY THE MEDIEVALS

It may be safely said that there was really no medieval science of any importance before the recovery of Aristotle, and that the theory of medieval science was always Aristotelian, as interpreted by Muslim Neoplatonists, within a framework of Christian ideology. Modern science is distinguished from medieval, indeed, by its very lack of a comprehensive general theory. We have minor limited theories in the special sciences, but none to cover the whole field of science. Vaguely we believe that science ought to be useful to mankind in rather obvious ways, such as prolonging life, minimizing pain, increasing pleasure; and we believe, equally vaguely, that it is a good thing to have more knowledge and understanding about the world we live in.

The medievals started from the opposite standpoint. They believed they knew why we are on earth in the first place, the relationship of the soul to the body, the relationship of man to the universe, the purposes served by the animals and plants; they had all the answers to those questions which we think it illegitimate to ask because science is incompetent to deal with them. So-called laws of nature, discovered by induction, were not interesting to them because nature itself as a conception was unacceptable. God was the lawgiver, and laws of nature were God's laws, which were entirely under his control, and he could interfere as often as he wished. At any moment a miracle might happen which would invalidate a law. A relic of a saint, or a suitable prayer offered in the right quarters, might be able to cure a dangerous disease in a moment, or rain could appear out of a cloudless sky. What was the use of trying to discover the mundane causes of a disease or of studying the science of meteorology?

Every medieval scientist had to struggle with these commonly accepted assumptions of his age; hence it was a great step forward when Albertus Magnus proclaimed that God works through natural causes which can be investigated, implying that in the ordinary course of affairs God does not interfere, but allowing him freedom to do so if he wishes. Adopting such an attitude, and performing serious investigation, it would not be too long before a scientist noticed the extreme rarity of miracles, and went ahead without paying too much attention to their possibility.

But it was not so easy to escape from

the leading strings imposed by the more respectable philosophy and science of the Greeks and the Muslims. Astrology was not to the medievals an unscientific aberration as it is to modern scientists, if not to the layman. It was based on the understanding (derived from Plato via Avicenna) that the relationship of man to the universe is as the microcosm (or little world) to the macrocosm (the great world). Man, in Plato's phrase, is a lesser world. Everything in the heavens is reflected in man. A planet seen in the heavens is also present in concentrated form in the organs of man—Saturn, for instance, in his spleen, and Venus in his kidneys. The plant also is directly connected with the planets, the blue-colored flower with Saturn, the yellow with Jupiter, the red with Mars. Thus a knowledge of the heavens is essential for a true understanding of man himself, and is not just a separate science to be studied for its own sake. Astronomy might be a branch of mathematics, but it was also a part of psychology and medicine. A knowledge of the movements of the planets, and their position in the heavens, would therefore be of the utmost importance for man since, in the medieval phrase, superiors (in the heavens) ruled inferiors (on earth); and not only man but all his doings were subject to the decrees of the heavens, which themselves, according to those who remembered their Christianity, expressed the will of God (Neoplatonists and Avicenna had indeed speculated as to whether the stars were not, in fact, gods).

Moreover, every man at birth was an exact image of the cosmos at the moment of his birth; and if the cosmos could be read at that moment, then the physiology and psychology of the man could be exactly determined. Hence the importance of ascertaining the exact hour of birth and casting a horoscope. Up to this point medieval thinkers were in agreement. But there was considerable dispute on how all this affected the free will of man, and whether what was called judicial astrology was equally true and permissible. For it might also be pos-

sible to determine the path of life for man; and, as the heavens were perfect and unchangeable, this looked as if the path of man's life was likewise unchangeable and determined from his birth. After the great age of rationalism in the thirteenth century was over, judicial astrology, appealing to the superstitions of mankind then as now, became ever more popular. Philosophers produced a theory that the movements of the planets paralleled the life of man but did not determine it, thus saving free will; and horoscopes continued to be cast for centuries with only sporadic opposition, at one time being the major interest of the majority of scientists of the day, who found, like Paracelsus, that at the least the casting of horoscopes provided them with a living, allowing them leisure to engage in other and more worth-while pursuits.

Biology was dominated throughout the medieval period by Aristotle, whose biological theories could be made to conform to the Christian idea of Divine Providence. Aristotle had produced a very comprehensive set of observations, most of them extremely accurate. But he had not been content with this; he had also tied them together with a remarkable theory whose central observation was that "nature does nothing in vain." Nothing in the living world exists which does not have a purpose that can be understood by the unaided human mind. The phenomena themselves needed to be investigated for the purpose of adding to human knowledge (Aristotle had begun his *Metaphysics* with the dictum that "all men by nature desire to know"), but once they had been investigated, they could be understood in terms of purposes. If it were seen that a mistletoe grows on an oak tree, then the *how* of this phenomenon did not need to be investigated, though of course it could be if desired. Aristotle himself might very well have also investigated how it is nourished and maintains itself, and what effect it has on the tree. But for purposes of understanding the mistletoe, one must only ask why it is there. And the answer might be, in natural terms, that it relieves the tree of some of its evil humors, or alternatively, and more probably, that it sucks the life out of the tree; or, in human terms, it might exist as an example for man of the evils of parasitism, and thus a moral example for man. Or it might exist because mistletoe is necessary for man and the tree was as convenient a place as any for nature to put it. But of one thing the medieval man could be certain: it must serve some real purpose in the total economy of nature which included man. Roger Bacon was once called upon to answer the question whether plants feel. In Aristotelian terms the answer, to us insoluble, was not difficult. The purpose served by feeling, he replied, is to enable one to move either toward or away from an object exciting it (sympathy and antipathy). A plant is stationary and cannot move. Therefore feeling would be unnecessary to a plant, and nature would have given feeling to it in vain. But nature does nothing in vain. Therefore the plant cannot feel. Q.E.D.

It is clear that the supposed understanding of purposes in nature would conduce to reverence for the Divine Providence which had ordered all things in this beneficent way; but it would not tend to encourage investigation of how they actually worked, and it would certainly inhibit our modern practice of manipulating natural things for human ends. As long as this attitude remained, there could be no practical and applied science.

But medieval practice in time became much better than its theory. We do not find any thinker in medieval times urging the usefulness of knowledge and encouraging scientists to investigate for the purpose of alleviating man's lot on earth, though Roger Bacon does emphasize its usefulness for theology and for helping kings to defeat their enemies. It was a later Bacon, Francis, who in the seventeenth century really for the first time sounded the clarion call for scientific investigation for the improvement of man's ordinary life. But we do find medieval scientists encouraging experiments, if only in the hopes of proving theories which

they could never have proved since they were demonstrably false. We do find a number of experiments being made, though as a rule in an unplanned manner. We find the spirit of criticism growing, and serious efforts to escape from the authority of Aristotle, and we find it gradually becoming natural not to take things for granted without testing by experience. We find, in short, the native curiosity of man escaping from the fetters imposed upon it by a premature belief that everything that was worth knowing was already known. It can hardly be claimed that the Middle Ages were among the great ages of science, but, as in other fields, they were preparing quietly and diligently for the future.

THIRTEENTH-CENTURY SCIENCE—ALBERTUS MAGNUS (1206–1280), ROGER BACON (1214–1292?)

It is impossible in a book of this scope to discuss the work of the several hundred scientists in medieval times whose names, and some of whose work, are known to us. For the most part these men were engaged in assimilating some aspect of Muslim science to which they added little that was original; or they were compilers of other people's work, presenting it in a form likely to interest their contemporaries. In the twelfth century such works were already appearing, giving accounts of what their authors had been able to glean from Muslim material, a few making attempts to be selective and reasonably critical, while the majority merely seem to have inserted what was likely to be interesting and fascinating. The most complete and in many respects the best, and certainly for us the most useful of these encyclopedias, was the *Speculum Majus* of Vincent of Beauvais (1190?–1264?), a Dominican friar, which contains the bulk of what was known of scientific information in the thirteenth century and makes extensive use of the Muslim material. But the two really great names in the thirteenth-century science deserve rather more attention, since in their different ways they represent what was best in science of their time. Moreover, Bacon in himself so often combines at the same time the best and the worst that a more extended study of his work will reveal the scientific shortcomings of the period as well as those tendencies which in later centuries were to create our modern science.

We have already dealt with the purpose of Albert's work—the reconciliation of science and the Christian religion. But it was also remarked that the scientist reveals himself throughout his work, because in fact Albert was a better scientist than he was philosopher or theologian. Though Albert's many volumes are mostly in the form of commentaries on Aristotle, it is the digressions that constitute the value of the work, for in them he adds information that he has personally acquired. He shows in several places that he understands the value of experiment, even though his experiments were not very advanced. He wished to check old wives' tales as well as remarks he had found in Aristotle, as for instance, when he tried to tempt an ostrich with iron but was unable to persuade him to touch it, contrary to a current superstition that the ostrich will eat iron. He is severely critical of many of the statements he has found in other books, once going so far as to say that philosophers are full of lies. And he explains that the method which the student of science must follow is this: he should be critical of everything he is told, and he must try to find the natural causes behind all phenomena. Albert himself was most skilled as a botanist, having been described as the best botanist between the Greeks and the moderns. He has left us many accurate descriptions of flowers and plants, and he does not discourse to the same degree as his contemporaries on the pleasing moral lessons to be obtained from them. He was greatly interested in alchemy, and had studied what he could of the Muslim work in this field, and he has given us his own observations on the properties of rocks and metals—a field neglected by Aristotle. But knowing neither Greek nor Arabic, he was dependent entirely upon what had been translated up to that time, and this included the more fascinating rather than necessarily the more informative of Aristotle's works. But, like most medieval thinkers, Albertus Magnus touched on the majority of fields of study, trying to gain a comprehensive picture of the totality of science, even though, as Bacon observes, he was quite ignorant of both mathematics and optics and therefore could not come to any real understanding of science for want of perceiving how each is dependent on the other.

For this was the heart of Roger Bacon's own efforts. He wanted to have a complete knowledge of all the sciences and was prepared to go to endless trouble in trying to obtain it. He was obsessed with the idea that it was the duty of a Christian, with all the advantages that he had that were denied to infidels and pagans, to become a fully equipped scientist, with up-to-date knowledge in every field; only thus could a man appreciate the way each science contributes to another. He was not the man to be content with a few fragments, or even an intensive knowledge of one or two fields, but he must have a knowledge of them all. It would then be perfect and complete, and a man could contemplate the imposing edifice with aesthetic satisfaction.

Roger Bacon (1214–1292?) reveals himself very clearly in his writings as a man with an insatiable drive toward knowledge, for which he was willing to sacrifice everything and work with single-hearted devotion. But at the same time there was scarcely a single one of his contemporaries whom he did not criticize and profess to despise. When his private means ran out, he became a Franciscan friar, but deeply resented the fact that he was made to do menial tasks instead of writing and carrying out his experiments. But he was determined, whatever the rules of his order, that he would bring his work to the attention of those in authority because he was so certain that he had a message which everyone else was neglecting, a message of supreme importance which justified an appeal directly to the head of Christendom. So he approached one of the leading cardinals through an intermediary, and was rewarded by a mandate to send him his work. But, unable to do so, because of conditions within his order, he delayed, until suddenly the cardinal became Pope Clement IV. Bacon sent another message, asking if His Holiness was still interested, and was rewarded by yet another request. In spite of extreme difficulties due to his own perfectionism and the haste with which he had to work, as well as due to the opposition of his order, he finally dispatched what he called a *persuasio* to the pope, a work intended to persuade him of the urgency of patronizing Bacon's work, and making a number of suggestions for the advancement of science which are of the deepest interest.

This *Opus Majus,* accompanied by a short digest containing some extra information on alchemy, is one of the masterpieces of the Middle Ages—in spite of its great imperfections, perhaps its only scientific masterpiece. From this and from other work Bacon carried out more thoroughly and with more detachment both before and after the *Opus Majus,* it is possible to discover a coherent philosophy of science which is a very strange compound indeed of reactionary and superstitious thinking and brilliant and suggestive observations. Bacon was not primarily an experimenter, though it is clear he was working in conjunction with a number of people who were actually making serious experiments, especially one Peter de Maricourt, who produced an original work on the magnet of evident scientific value. Bacon speaks of the possibility of flying machines and complicated machines for lifting huge weights, and he speaks of gunpowder at some length and other "secret works of nature." But these marvels were merely observed experiments among his contemporaries, and Bacon says nothing of having performed them himself. This is not to say that he performed none; but the only ones he describes of his own are extremely primitive, of the same stature as Albert's efforts to feed iron to an ostrich. But he undoubtedly carried out many observations in astronomy and optics, in which sciences he had probably been interested by Robert Grosseteste, Bishop of Lincoln, a teacher of the Franciscans at Oxford. Grosseteste had studied the work of the Muslims in optics, especially the great Al-Hazen, and in the intervals of a very busy life wrote several books on light which show insight of a high order. Bacon added to what his predecessor had done, and he has much to say that is of interest, especially on the phenomenon of the rainbow, of which he had made repeated observations.

But Bacon was not a great scientist because of his experiments and his observations; his title to fame rests in the thought he gave to scientific problems and the serious attempt he made both to perceive the purpose science should serve and to work out the relationships between the sciences and their relationship as a whole to moral philosophy or ethics; and in his correct understanding of the place experiments should fill in the study of science.

Unfortunately it is difficult to overlook the manifest contradictions in his work, and his thoroughly reactionary attitude toward authority, which was already outmoded in the scholarly world of the thirteenth century. For Bacon did not believe that man finds out knowledge for himself. Over and over again he repeats that science is revealed by God. It was revealed fully to the "sons of Seth" (Seth was the son of Adam) by God, and then again to Solomon. It was not simply some parts of science that were revealed; the whole had been revealed, that universal science which Bacon was himself seeking so ardently. The Greeks had been able to touch some of this wisdom by their contacts with the ancient Hebrews by whom it had been preserved. Plato had access to it, and also Aristotle. Aristotle, by virtue of his character and his saintly life, had had universal science revealed in part to him, and in part he had gained it from the descendants of Solomon. Avicenna, among the Muslims, had received some of it. Bacon therefore considered that the proper task for a scientist in his age was to find out exactly what

Aristotle had said; but what made him really furious with disappointment was that no one now knew just what Aristotle had said. The translations were execrable. The men who had translated him either did not know Greek properly, or did not know Arabic, or did not know Latin. So there was only one thing to do and Bacon did it. He studied Greek and Hebrew (even writing grammars in these languages) to get at the truth of what Aristotle and the ancient writers of the Old Testament had said. There is one passage in Albert which almost certainly refers to Bacon, where he speaks of the fact that even poor translations will give the sense of what Aristotle had said, unless, of course, we think Aristotle was a god and could not make mistakes. But we, for our part, Albert concludes, think Aristotle was a man and could make mistakes as easily as you or I. Because of Bacon's obsession, much of his writing, even when addressed to the pope, is concerned with the errors in translations of Aristotle, urging his patron to subsidize new and better ones; but all for the sad reason that Aristotle had known much revealed truth, and his precious words had been lost or mangled.

Much of Bacon's work is propaganda on behalf of Muslim scientists, who, according to him, are seriously neglected, and could be used by Christians to great advantage if anyone were competent to read them, and if they had been better translated. He urges especially that mathematics should be studied more, as the key to so many other sciences. Astrology, he thinks, is the most practical of sciences, and hardly understood, according to Bacon, at all in the West. It is necessary for medicine, and it would be helpful to kings. But—and here is where Bacon's good scientific sense escapes from his theories—none of what has been given by revelation to Solomon, Aristotle, and the rest, should be taken simply on trust. Nor should anyone believe in astrology from a sole desire to believe. These sciences should be tested thoroughly by planned experiments. In his *Opus Majus* he devotes a whole book to what he calls the science of experi-

ence (*scientia experimentalis*), a term he appears to have picked up from Ptolemy. This, the supreme science (he regards it as a separate science of its own), must be used for proving the theories which derive from the theoretical sciences including the data of revelation, and, of course, mathematics in all its branches. The combination of theory and experience can alone give certitude, and allow the mind to rest in the assurance that it has found truth. And, in turn, the experience itself serves also to confirm the original hypothesis.

It was this last feature that was of especial interest to Bacon. He was a thoroughly religious man, steeped in the Scriptures (and disliking intensely theological studies based on Peter Lombard), and anxious to do all he could to save souls. He believed that successful experiments which went far to prove the truths of Christian revelation might convince even Muslims and heathen, as successful experiments based on astrology or alchemy would serve to show that these sciences were trustworthy and accurate. But above all he insisted, and this is something of which in our atomic age we are sometimes in need of being reminded, that all science must serve a moral purpose. The sciences are indeed related in a kind of hierarchy, with moral philosophy at the summit. The mathematical and observational sciences, according to Bacon, must supply data for the engineer and technologist; but they in turn must consult the moral philosopher to discover if the purpose they are to serve is ethical. Moreover, the special separate sciences must also supply information to each other, making necessary the services of synthesists, who will coordinate the work in these different fields—undoubtedly a desirable plan today, even though extremely difficult in our era of specialization to put into practice.

Bacon, it is clear, had originally thought of himself as occupying the position of chief synthesist; but even he, as he completed his work for the pope and composed his prefatory letter, realized that his ambition was an impossible dream. He would never know enough, and no one ever could know enough again. So he suggests that the pope gather together specialists in every field and encourage them to work with each other. And he outlines the specialties which must be represented, and explains the kind of cooperative outline of scientific knowledge they should try to produce to direct men's attention to the possibilities of science.

Unfortunately, though Bacon's work certainly reached the pope, there is no evidence that Clement ever read it, and he died the following year. Bacon only once briefly referred to his dispatch of these works, but he said nothing of their reception, and it is certain that nothing came of his suggestions. If he was not as consistently scientific in spirit as Albert, if his criticism ran to personalities rather than taking its proper place in the field of ideas, and if he was too anxious to believe to be adequately skeptical where skepticism would have been a virtue, yet for his outstanding insights he deserves an honored place in the history of science, and an especially honored place when one considers the mediocrity in scientific understanding shown by almost all his contemporaries.

A third figure requires more than a passing mention, the great emperor, Frederic II (1197–1250), who has already been dealt with in some detail in an earlier chapter. He is worthy of consideration in this chapter more for his attitude than for his actual accomplishments. Although nearly all the material we have about him comes from his enemies, they frequently referred to his love of experiment and his desire to discover the truth of matters which were usually taken on trust by his contemporaries. He is said to have weighed a dying man before and after his death, to see if there was any change in weight and therefore whether the escaping soul had any material basis; he repeated an experiment attributed by the Greek Herodotus to the king of Egypt, who wanted to find out what was the first human language, and for the purpose shut up newborn babies away from all sound of human speech to see what words they would first utter. The chronicler tells us that the chil-

dren all died, so the experiment was worthless. Another horrible experiment ascribed to him was the killing of two men, one after exercise and one after rest; their intestines were then examined to see which had digested his food more thoroughly. Moreover, Frederic several times sent out questionnaires to distinguished Muslim philosophers asking them their opinions on many different subjects of philosophical interest; further, he asked his court scientist and astrologer, Michael Scot, to give him detailed information about the planets and whether they possessed any inhabitants, where God lived, and what the saints did in heaven. But, in addition to all this inquiry, Frederic also wrote a book on falconry which is our main source for our knowledge of this sport of which medieval nobles were so passionately fond. The book is far more than a description. Frederic was deeply interested in birds, and he had taken the trouble to bring them at great expense from all parts of the world to compare them and to study both their habits and their bodies. He dissected many, and he takes Aristotle to task for several false observations, ridiculing also Aristotle's love of inserting moral rather than physical truths into his work. Aristotle, for instance, according to Frederic, stated that all birds that fly well walk badly and vice versa, this being a pleasantly moral compensation. But Frederic dryly remarks that a crane both flies and walks badly. Elsewhere he makes the equally dry observation that he has not followed Aristotle when he deals with falcons, for "Aristotle seldom or never hunted with birds." Anything more incongruous than the idea of the severe scientist and philosopher Aristotle hunting with falcons, even "seldom," can hardly be imagined!

FOURTEENTH-CENTURY SCIENTISTS—
JEAN BURIDAN, NICHOLAS OF ORESME

There are more scientific names in the fourteenth century even than in the thirteenth, though few of outstanding importance. But at the University of Paris, perhaps under the influence of the nominalists, prolonged attention was paid to a serious problem which arose out of the new use of gunpowder and projectiles. Aristotle's theory of motion was soon seen to be unsatisfactory, and could not adequately explain why a projectile fired from a gun should move at a higher speed when fired than after a few seconds, nor why it should describe a parabola when falling to the earth. A scientist named Jean Buridan suggested the idea of "impetus," a step in the right direction, though the problem was not solved till Galileo solved it by a combination of theory and experiment with inclined planes. Nicholas of Oresme, a bishop, began to question the theory of the movement of the sun around the earth, accepted by nearly all medievals on the authority of the Hellenistic scientist Ptolemy. But, more important, Nicholas liked to use diagrams for the illustration of theological problems. In the process he hit upon the idea of coordinates and curves to show the relation between two variables, thus anticipating by centuries the invention of analytical geometry. At the University of Padua the Averroists, driven forth from Paris at the end of the thirteenth century after the condemnation of their philosophical findings, found a refuge under the protection of Venice. There among much speculation on the immortality of the soul and similar dogmas, they devoted themselves to mathematics, being interested, like the Parisians, especially in the study of acceleration. It was probably at Padua that the first serious work was done in the use of the Arabic numerals, which had been introduced to the West as early as 1202 by Leonardo of Pisa, but had not at first attracted much attention. It was the work done at Padua over several centuries that prepared the ground for the great advances of Galileo which ushered in the age of modern science.

▶ Education in the Middle Ages

THE UNIVERSITY OF PARIS

Organization

We have already dealt with elementary education as it existed under the Carolingians, and we have seen how a great teacher like Abélard might attract thousands of students to his lectures, in spite of the fact that there was no organized instruction and there were no facilities for lectures beyond those rather simple ones offered by the cathedral schools. In Paris, where Abélard had taught, the cathedral school was an important center of learning, and a considerable number of students attended for varying periods during the twelfth century according to the fare offered by the masters. Many of these students were very young, and required some discipline, but there was no effective centrally organized administrative body capable of managing the considerable numbers of students who wished to receive instruction. They spilled over into the city far beyond the immediate confines of the cathedral school of Notre Dame, and had many altercations with the townsmen, who resented the presence of so many foreigners, most of whom, in their view, were unruly, yet who claimed protection by their clerical status from secular interference. After a more serious fracas than usual, the French king, Philip Augustus, in 1200 gave formal recognition to the school as a *studium generale* or university, with certain specified rights of self-government, and official clerical status immune from all but ecclesiastical courts for the entire student body.

The university offered courses in theology, medicine, and civil law at the advanced level, and at the more elementary level, courses in the trivium and the quadrivium, or the seven liberal arts. There was now a recognized faculty for each of these groups of studies. The Faculty of Arts was by far the largest, since many students never progressed beyond the degree of master of arts, which was a prerequisite for all higher degrees. The masters in this faculty were divided according to the country from which they hailed, resulting in four "nations," the French (including Italians and Spanish), the Normans, the Picards (from Flanders and the Netherlands), and the English, (including Germans and other Germanic peoples). These nations united in electing a Rector of the Faculty of Arts who was the virtual governor of the university, although the title officially belonged to the Bishop of Paris, who rarely troubled to exercise his authority. The teaching masters were in general responsible for the organization and discipline of the university.

Curriculum

It has already been explained that medieval education was always formally concerned with only the seven liberal arts, although in earlier times the instruction in the quadrivium was extremely sketchy. This changed with the gradual progress of the study of logic in the twelfth century, and with the recovery of the works of Aristotle and the Muslims. So many new subjects now became available that it was difficult to fit them into the famous and immutable seven, and there was a demand for almost all the new subjects, which the Faculty of Arts was anxious to fulfill. The textbooks were greatly improved, especially in the field of logic, where the advanced works of Aristotle made up a very respectable collection. There was a considerable effort also to study language at a profounder level, and especially one John of Garland in the early thirteenth century wrote several important textbooks on the subject. Aristotle's *Ethics* was squeezed into rhetoric, completing the trivium. Euclid was recovered from the Muslims, greatly improving the study of geometry, which to the trained logical mind of the medieval student presented no further difficulties. Muslim works on trigonometry were soon added. Ptolemy's *Almagest,* in which the great astronomer expounded his geocentric views of the universe, found a natural place under astronomy, together with Muslim works in the same field and Aristotle's discussion of the heavens. But arithmetic still seems to have been neglected, and for centuries little use was made of the Arabic numerals. This still left the vast bulk of the natural scientific work of Aristotle with no official place in the curriculum, even after the ban had ceased to be observed. Yet the works of Aristotle on *Physics,* on *Metaphysics,* and *On the Soul* and his work on coming into being and decaying (*De generatione et corruptione*) were undoubtedly lectured

on, as was also a work on plants by one of his pupils. It is still not known how this bulging curriculum was classified and how it managed to fit into the seven liberal arts, but at all events lectures were given on all these subjects. As will be noticed, the emphasis is still strongly on mental training, and indeed the works of Aristotle are all discussed by the masters in a logical manner, and seldom is there any reference to actual experience by any of them whose work we possess.

The student might go to the university as early as the age of thirteen; if he went at this age he would probably have to study for eight years in the Faculty of Arts, obtaining at the end a master's degree and the right to teach in Paris or in a similar Faculty of Arts. About halfway through his career in this faculty he would receive a bachelor's degree, but this was of little value, and conferred no privileges. At Paris the study which offered the greatest prestige was the study of theology, but the period required for study was extremely long and the courses were arduous. Though there was a minimum of eight years, this was in fact seldom permitted and it became customary to insist on fourteen. And no master of theology could in any case teach theology before the age of thirty-five. As explained earlier, much of a student's theological study consisted in mastering the *Book of Sentences* and in learning how to handle theological problems in the same manner as Peter Lombard. Public disputes were frequent, especially when the student had become a Bachelor of Sentences part way through his career. He would probably have gained a reputation as a disputer long before he came to his final examination in defence of his dissertation. Naturally such a long grind took its toll of casualties. There were never very many masters of theology, and the names of most of them for the thirteenth and fourteenth centuries are known to us.

The other faculties were not held in such high esteem, though in the late medieval period it was probably more profitable, from a worldly point of view, to graduate in civil law, which required only three or four years. Medicine also took about the same time. But Paris was not especially famous for either of these subjects—Bologna was the real center of legal studies, and Montpellier or Salerno for medicine—and as theology was the queen of sciences for the medieval student, and Parisian masters were incomparably greater than those to be found elsewhere, the university in the thirteenth and fourteenth centuries always found enough students, and always maintained its position as the real center of education in Europe.

Student life

The medieval student was not a meek citizen, in spite of his tonsure and his clerical status. He was quarrelsome and did not submit to discipline readily, at least according to contemporary preachers; he was drunken, violent, and decidedly unchaste. He frequented taverns, sang songs of a lewd variety, and composed and recited poems, usually on immoral themes. But preachers do not perhaps offer the best evidence about the lives of the ordinary students, for then, as now, they could make better sermons when there was some sin to be castigated. Perhaps it would be better to listen to Chaucer, whose Clerk of Oxenford was a good student, living quietly, poor, but spending any money he could obtain on books. Probably, then, as now, the student body was mixed. The noisy ones drew attention to themselves and were more noticeable, while the quiet ones stuck to their textbooks, prepared their work, and passed all their exams, and no one but their friends knew them.

In early times there were no buildings to house the students, and few facilities even for lectures. The professors used whatever buildings were available, usually bare church buildings; and sometimes they had to hire halls themselves at their own expense. With luck they might have a desk or a podium; the students had none, and customarily sat on the floor. Books were scarce before the invention of printing and few students possessed them. The master, however, read from his own text slowly, and then commented on it. Paper was also not available in the thirteenth century, and parchment was very expensive. The students as a rule took down what they could on wax tablets, and compared notes afterward with their fellows. They disputed incessantly on the meaning of what the master had said and frequently violently disagreed with him. But the time would come, in all probability, when the master would be expected to give a public disputation, and the opportunity for questioning him directly would not be missed. In some of the extant books of *Questions* published by the various masters, it seems likely that actual students were participating in the discussion, since the objections are such as have always been made by students. It is possible that the masters thought all the objections up themselves, but to the modern reader the masters certainly appear to have had considerable "cooperation" from their students.

UNIVERSITY OF BOLOGNA

Purpose of the university—The study of Roman law

In the late eleventh century, soon after the conquest of Sicily by the Normans, the law code of Justinian was recovered and brought out of the oblivion in which it had rested since the Muslim conquest of the island. This code, which has been described in an earlier chapter, came into the hands of one Irnerius, apparently already a student of law but ignorant of any of the details of the Roman codes. In the Italy of his day there were only the Lombard Code and remnants of the earlier Roman practice; but there could be no systematic study of law until its logical basis had been grasped. Until that time there were only laws, not law. It is clear that Roman law, as applicable to the late Roman or Byzantine Empires, could have little relevance to conditions in Italy in the eleventh century; indeed, even the canon law of the Church, originally Roman, had necessarily been modified over the centuries. However, the fact that Roman law was not at once relevant to eleventh-century conditions did not mean that its ancient logical principles no longer applied. To be sure, these principles must be modified to fit the actual circumstances of the day, but there would always remain the permanent and unchanging principles of jurisprudence, which had been discovered by the Romans and written down in accordance with the best thinking of which a whole line of distinguished jurists and philosophers were capable. Indeed this law, if used widely in Europe, would have a noticeably civilizing effect on the German barbarians, and perhaps be able to wean them from their barbarous methods of determining and executing justice and disposing of property.

Organization of the university— Control by students

Some such thoughts must have been in the mind of Irnerius when he undertook his epoch-making work. The procedure used by him and his successors was to write notes and commentaries on the text of the code, called glosses, suggestions as to how to modify the Roman laws to fit the new circumstances. He began to teach law in the northern Italian city of Bologna, and quickly gathered around him an earnest and enthusiastic group of students, the best of whom became in their turn teachers and writers of glosses. From the beginning it seems that the students were the real controllers of this school at Bologna, hiring and paying the teachers, fining them if they were late, insisting on full value for their money. The students, however, were not young boys as at Paris, but mature men who needed instruction, and were prepared to pay for it, but not willing to tolerate any laxity on the part of their professors. The latter, to protect themselves from their overzealous students, likewise organized themselves into a kind of guild of masters, and, merging with the guild of students who had drawn up their rules for the proper behavior of professors, formed a regular university in the early twelfth century. Both canon and civil law were studied, and the same method was used for each. In the middle of the twelfth century a monk named Gratian codified the canon law, and about a century later several glossators codified the glosses from the greatest of the legal masters since the time of Irnerius, under the leadership of one Accursius. But new glosses in the civil law continued to be made whenever especially gifted teachers appeared.

Diffusion of Roman law

From Bologna masters went throughout Europe organizing Faculties of Civil Law in most of the universities, and as the demand for trained lawyers grew, so ever more students began to study, for the most part not clerics at the time of their study though many later attained high office in the Church. Few popes in the thirteenth or fourteenth centuries had failed to study at least canon law, and the majority of them, at least in the thirteenth century, at Bologna. We have seen how Philip IV of France used a corps of trained lawyers as a means of aiding in his establishment of absolute government and the complete unification of his country. Most kings chose their officials from among trained lawyers, and, with some exceptions, used the logical and equitable Roman law as a means of breaking down the old feudal courts and the feudal system which they upheld. Roman law presupposed an absolute ruler, and the famous Roman dictum that "what pleases the emperor has the force of law" was entirely acceptable to monarchs trying to establish their right to legislate. It was no accident that of the European countries only in England was there serious opposition to it, and the kings who tried to introduce it were forced to abandon the attempt. For, excellent though Roman law might be for absolute kings, it remained the greatest obstacle to parliamentary institutions. The papacy, however, did not approve of its use by monarchs, since it was implicit in Roman law that the ruler owed obedience to no one on earth; indeed, on several occasions the papacy forbade its study. It was no answer to say

MEDIEVAL UNIVERSITIES
(ONLY CITIES WHOSE UNIVERSITIES WERE ESTABLISHED BY 1500 ARE INCLUDED)

0   500

Miles

that the Church itself used it, for the pope did not regard himself as a monarch, and was, in his own view, really supreme on earth. So Roman law continued to flourish, even while earnest theologians were trying to claim, with the English Parliament, that sovereignty resided in the people and not in the monarch.

Although detailed attention has been given here only to the universities of Paris and Bologna, the founding of new universities was continued during the entire medieval period and into modern times. Some idea of the extent of medieval foundations will be gained from a study of the map above. The majority of these universities were organized according to the Parisian model, including the ancient English universities of Oxford and Cambridge.

▶ Medieval art

ARCHITECTURE

Church building, characteristic art of the Middle Ages

Until the late medieval period there was no secular art at all, and all the very

409

considerable artistic achievements of medieval people were in some way connected with their religion. This does not mean that the medieval artist was prevented from exercising his natural gifts freely because the building of churches was almost the sole opportunity for their exercise; on the contrary, the building of churches supplied him with almost unlimited opportunity, especially in sculpture, which was not forbidden by the Christians as it had been by Jews and Muslims. The figures of saints had to follow an approved and customary style, but within this convention it was possible to give life and character to the figures. It was possible to decorate capitals and pillars with scenes from nature, closely observed and accurately rendered, as in the famous "vintage" capitals of the cathedral of Rheims, and in the Romanesque capitals of St. Trophime of Arles shown in the illustration. But in general it must be admitted that the art par excellence of the medievals was church building, and that architecture overshadows all other medieval artistic achievements, although the development of church music runs it a close second.

The development of Romanesque from Roman antecedents

In the Dark Ages there was very little building beyond the mere provision of places of worship. The Germanic peoples had had no experience in building such edifices as churches, and skill and materials were lacking. Such building as there was consisted for the most part of wooden churches, easily destroyed by fire, and later churches built of stone, but with wooden roofs, also easily destroyed by fire, as the Vikings proved. The plan of all medieval churches in early times was derived from the Roman basilica or meeting place, modified to meet the needs of worshipers in a Christian church. The general plan was to have three aisles, the center aisle called the nave, separated from each other by arcades of arches, capitals, and columns. The walls were solid, and light was provided only by small windows set in a clerestory above the nave. At the end of the nave, where the Romans had usually built a semicircular apse in which the presiding officer had his seat, the Christians placed their altar. The apse by religious custom faced the East. In time it became necessary to enlarge this apse in order to contain the choir, and transepts were added by the side of the aisles, bringing the whole church into the form of a Latin cross.

The great difficulty to be overcome, as has been suggested, was the danger of fire on account of the wooden roof. The Romans, however, had not been content with wooden roofs but built them of stone and concrete. The early medievals knew that the Romans had used vaults of different kinds for their roofs, but for many centuries the Christians were unable to build vaults in such a way that the walls were strong enough to hold them. The thrust and weight of the Roman vaults necessitated very strong walls, and if the walls were very massive then it was dangerous to pierce them for windows. We know of many early medieval buildings which indeed did collapse while the architects experimented with different kinds of vaults. Cross vaults were used for the smaller areas to be roofed, while the nave itself had to be roofed, as a rule, with a massive barrel vault. But this doomed the church to shortage of light and only the smallest of windows, owing to the great weight of the roof. In some of the earlier Romanesque churches which had wooden roofs this problem did not arise in such an acute form, and the characteristic gloom of the Romanesque, which some find impressive, was avoided. Moreover, the height of the church was severely limited again by the weight to be supported.

This Romanesque style was capable of modification, therefore, but only within certain well-defined limits. Many of the problems were indeed solved, especially by the Norman builders of the eleventh century, but certain fundamental changes were necessary if a church was to be able to soar to heaven, and be filled with light, as the builders themselves would have wished. It should be emphasized that such changes as

ABOVE

Very early sculptured figure of Christ at Santillana del Mar (Spain).

UPPER RIGHT

Sculptured stone image of St. James the apostle in the cathedral at Santiago de Compostela (Spain, twelfth century), where St. James's bones are said to have been brought after his martyrdom at the hands of Herod Antipas. The city is now a place of pilgrimage, especially in the years when the feast of St. James (July 25) falls on a Sunday.

LOWER RIGHT

Details from the Portico de la Gloria in the cathedral of St. James at Compostela. Note the rounded Romanesque style arch.

UPPER LEFT
The Virgin of Notre Dame de Paris (thirteenth-century Gothic).

ABOVE
Detail of the portal of Notre Dame de Paris.

LEFT
Figures of saints from the Royal Portal of the Cathedral of Chartres (thirteenth-century Gothic).

Early Romanesque interior at Santillana del Mar (Spain), with decorated Romanesque capitals.

The cathedral and the leaning tower of Pisa. The church is built in the style of the old Roman basilica.

Exterior of the Romanesque cathedral of St. Sernin at Toulouse. Note the heavy construction of the Romanesque used before the Gothic pointed arch had been invented to take the stress of the masonry.

Interior of Toulouse cathedral. Note the relative absence of light, and the rounded Romanesque arches.

Decorated sculptured capitals of Romanesque arches at St. Trophime of Arles.

This picture shows the transition between the Romanesque and the Gothic. On the right are Gothic pointed arches, on the left Romanesque (cloister of St. Trophime, Arles).

Exterior of the Gothic cathedral of Notre Dame de Paris. Note the flying buttresses which distribute the weight of the roof, enabling the building to have many windows. The Gothic framework is little but a stone skeleton.

Interior of Notre Dame de Paris. Note the pointed arches and the abundance of light in contrast with St. Sernin at Toulouse.

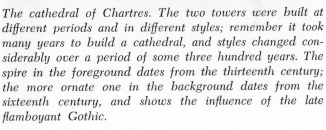

The cathedral of Chartres. The two towers were built at different periods and in different styles; remember it took many years to build a cathedral, and styles changed considerably over a period of some three hundred years. The spire in the foreground dates from the thirteenth century; the more ornate one in the background dates from the sixteenth century, and shows the influence of the late flamboyant Gothic.

The Virgin of Chartres.

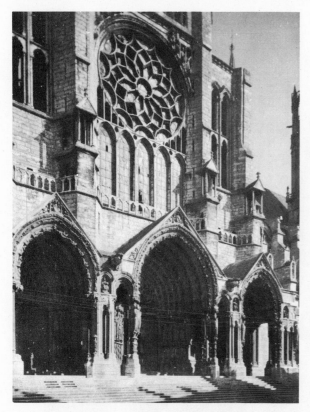

North façade of Chartres cathedral. The famous rose window is above this portal.

was the same religious enthusiasm that was responsible for the success of the First Crusade.

The Gothic style—Pointed arches and flying buttresses

The Gothic style, which solved the outstanding problems of the Romanesque, was developed almost entirely in northern France, though spreading into Germany and elsewhere afterward. The use of the pointed arch, which distributes the weight differently from the rounded arch and the vault, was the key to the new style. It was soon discovered that an entirely different sys-

The north rose window of Chartres cathedral. Many of the Chartres windows were contributed by the various guilds of the city, and some of them depict the mundane occupations of the contributors. A black-and-white picture does not do justice to these windows; imagine sunlight shining through them, bringing out all the brilliant coloring of the glass. Unfortunately, the secret of the medieval processing of the glass has been lost.

took place were figured out by the architects and craftsmen actually on the job. It was impossible in medieval times to work out in advance, as do modern architects, the theoretical stresses to which the various parts of the building would be submitted, and there was much trial and error before the immense difficulties were overcome.

But there was an enormous demand for churches. Every bishop desired to have a great church in his diocese, and an enthusiasm and local patriotism amounting almost to a mania set in during the eleventh and twelfth centuries. The buildings were nearly always raised by cooperative labor, in which every person in the area joined, some yoking themselves to the cart which carried the materials needed for the church and pulling it, while priests chanted and prayed. Throughout the day psalms and canticles were sung, relics of the saints were brought along, and miracles were hourly expected. It

Gothic cathedral of Rheims, before the World War I bombardment destroyed much of the building. (COURTESY FRENCH GOVERNMENT TOURIST OFFICE)

tem of ribbing and support was possible with the pointed arch, which took the weight off the walls and gave the builder freedom to alter the shape of his church as required. The developed Gothic church is nothing but a gigantic skeleton of wall buttresses within the church, flying buttresses outside it, piers and ribbing, all in perfect equilibrium; the walls themselves now cease to be of importance and can be made even of glass. And the best Gothic churches are indeed full of glass, stained glass colored and painted to show whatever scenes the artist wished. And usually over the portal was the great rose window, which was so designed that it lighted the church in a different way at the different hours of the day. Early stained glass was always in solid colors, set into lead frames as a kind of mosaic, with figures suggested by these frames and small, lightly penciled touches. Medieval stained glass was one of the age's greatest achievements, and has never been equaled, even in modern times, with all the advantages of modern technical inventions.

The Gothic church, with its soaring arches aspiring toward heaven, has often been compared with the logical structure of the great medieval *Summae,* those works in which medieval theologians attempted to set forth the whole plan of salvation, tied together by the Aristotelian syllogism; and the comparison is not inept, for the Gothic structures are faultlessly worked out, with perfect balance, each part dependent upon the other, and, in the best examples, free of any unnecessary decoration or striving for effect. The façades of the cathedrals could be and were decorated, and it was here that the sculptor was given a chance to display his mastery, especially in and over the portals, where saints, devils, plants, and animals real and mythological could be shown, and even the Last Judgment. Inside the cathedrals, especially in the wonderful Cathedral of Chartres, the artist was free to fill the windows with scenes from the Old and New Testaments and stories from the lives of saints, with delicate pencil work touching up the solid-colored panes of glass. Even scenes of everyday life are depicted in these windows, scenes often provided by the particular guild represented. The last details of the work, whether inside and visible, or high

Gothic cathedral of Amiens, which gives a good impression of the way in which a medieval cathedral—even if it commanded no outstanding physical site—stood out above all the buildings around it. (COURTESY FRENCH GOVERNMENT TOURIST OFFICE)

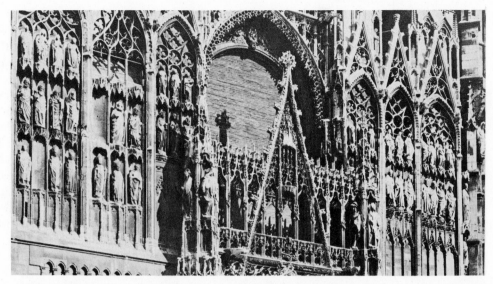

West façade of Rouen Cathedral (fifteenth century). Note the tendency to overelaborate characteristics of the flamboyant Gothic of this period.

Fan vaulting in the King Henry VII chapel at Westminster (1503).

up on the towers where no man could see them once they had been set in position, were almost invariably beautifully and honestly wrought. The medieval craftsman, like the Greek craftsman of the time of Phidias, would not have tolerated anything less than the best he could give in the service of his religion and art.

In a book of this kind it is not worth while to attempt the description of these Gothic masterpieces, since the bare words will do no justice to them, and mean little to those who have not viewed them. The accompanying pictures are inadequate, but they may suggest what the written word cannot, and the special features of the style can be picked out with the aid of the brief remarks printed under each picture. There is no perfect cathedral. Some cathedrals have features that seem to approach perfection, as the fan vaulting in Westminster Abbey, the façade and *chevet* of Notre Dame of Paris, the structural design of Amiens, the incomparable majesty of the site of Rheims, and the interior of Chartres. But in every cathedral there are some dissident elements, the necessary consequence of the long time consumed in the building. The building of a cathedral might take fifty years. Yet the style was living, always growing and evolving, so that the builders who completed the edifice would be working in a different manner from their predecessors when the work was first put in hand. The most familiar of these discords is the pair of spires at Chartres, constructed nearly four centuries apart in time. The twelfth-century spire is simple and chaste, while the sixteenth-century one, a few feet higher, is elaborate and ornate, constructed at a time when Gothic was past its best, and structural simplicity had to some degree been sacrificed to exuberance of decoration—a tendency we have already noted in contrasting Hellenic and Hellenistic art in an earlier chapter.

The Gothic style continues to be a matter of delight and wonder to the modern architect who marvels at the authority which the medieval architect was able to wield over his whole building, subordinating all decoration to the needs of the architecture itself, and who is constantly astonished at what his medieval forebears were able to accomplish with primitive tools, working in stone and with none of the aids he now considers essential, to say nothing of the new materials available in the twentieth century. The artist appreciates the absolute integrity of his medieval ancestor, the truth that he built into his works of stone, and the consummate skill with which he used what was available to him to create beauty, especially in the use of the natural light of the day to shed color and light over the whole interior of the cathedral through the medium of his stained glass windows. Even the modern religious skeptic is made to pause before this revelation in form of a faith that was as fully experienced by the medieval artist as it is alien to himself.

For medieval Gothic really is an expression, caught once and for all time, of a compelling vision whose essence is religious. The purpose of man's life on earth was to aspire toward Heaven. For a brief period medieval man really believed this. Man was a child of God, placed on earth in a particular position of honor or servitude which was none of his fault but merely God's will. He was taught not to envy the great man but to accept his lot, whatever it might be, knowing that after death he and the great man would be equal in the eyes of God and man. Only in the house of God on earth could he know himself as an equal. In the cathedral there was a place for him as there was a place, though a different one, for the noble and the bishop. Together they made up humanity as God had ordained it, and together their souls were lifted up toward the unseen God above. This was the symbolism of the Gothic, the ribs and the vaults and the pointed arches that gave the illusion of height and aspiration toward the great world above where saints and sinners, nobles and serfs, were together before the judgment seat of God, saved through the blood of Christ.

When for the first time in the twelfth and thirteenth centuries it was possible for the medieval man to gain a tiny surplus over and above his daily needs, a surplus of either goods or leisure, the first task, the very first task, that he set himself was the building of a church or cathedral. As the Egyptians in the early part of their civilization built pyramids for the ascent of their king-god to heaven, as the Greeks in the halcyon early days of Pericles built their temples for the gods to live in and protect them by their presence, so the men of the Middle Ages in the springtime of their religious fervor built a cathedral, not for their God to live in, for he was in Heaven, but for a place of assembly for themselves, the congregation of the faithful to worship their God and soar upward in their souls toward him.

It was no wonder that the ages of skeptical "enlightenment" that followed the great age of church building termed the architecture of medieval man Gothic, or barbarian. The vision was too great for them to comprehend. They pretended to feel at home with the classic and the simple, the art forms of this world, not the aspiration toward Heaven and the striving toward infinity that had been the glory of their rude ancestors. Not until the nineteenth century was the supreme achievement of medieval man appreciated; and now we can only visit and wonder, trying to encompass in our imagination what it was that this strange semibarbarian felt in his inner world that could drive him to such a frenzy of creation, to so many hundreds, even thousands, of magnificent buildings, while he lived his ordinary life in unrelieved squalor. The bishop who commanded the task was moved by rivalry with his fellow bishops, the bourgeois who paid out the small profits of his business was moved perhaps by civic pride. But what of the poor unnamed worker, he who dragged the cart, who climbed the scaffolding, who had nothing but his labor to give, for him did the task only represent a day's wage on a public works project? It is hard to think so. And it is certain that there will be no more Gothic cathedrals, that our poor imitations are at once seen as frauds—for even the ignoramus in all matters of art feels no doubt when he comes to distinguish the genuine Gothic from the spurious.

The church we build today is the expression of ourselves. It may have admirable qualities, but it is not an expression of that compelling religious emotion, disciplined by a clear and logical mind, that came to maturity in the twelfth and thirteenth centuries of our era and found its architectural expression in the Gothic cathedral and its literary masterpiece in the *Divine Comedy* of Dante. As the Egyptians after the Old Kingdom built no more pyramids, save a few shoddy efforts by imperial imitators, so shall we build no more cathedrals. But for a few more years we may still hope to see those built by our ancestors, and, seeing them, pause for a few moments in respect for a vision we have lost.

MUSIC

As the great medieval cathedral is not truly itself without the throng of worshipers within, as it is filled with light of many colors streaming through the incomparable stained glass, so also is it only to be recognized truly when filled with song. And of course it is no accident that medieval music, which spread from the cathedral and church into the outer world and ultimately gave birth to the secular instrumental music of our own day, was developed to its fullest within these cathedrals, especially in Notre Dame of Paris, which was famed in medieval times for the excellence of its music. And it is also no accident that the music thus developed fitted in perfectly with the architecture of the buildings themselves.

The voice is the first great musical instrument, and it was the use of the human voice in medieval services of worship that gave birth to the great advance of music in all its forms during the medieval age. Very early in the Middle Ages the voice was used to chant the words of the Latin Liturgy in unison, or what was called *plain song*. In plain song all the voices followed the melody without variation except according to the pitch of the voice, at intervals of a full octave. This Gregorian chant, so called after Pope Gregory I the Great, is still used in church worship, and never died out in spite of the many other forms of song that now supplement it. But by the ninth century other intervals than the octave were used, and the enormous possibilities inherent in these variations were increasingly realized in subsequent centuries. While one voice held the melody, another sang the same melody but at an interval of one fifth (beginnings of polyphony or many sounds). Then other intervals were also found to add beauty and fullness to the total sound, and other altogether different melodies were made to interweave with the whole (the interweaving, note by note, of separate melodies with the basic one was called *counterpoint*). Finally, with the motet, even different words were sung at the same time as the basic melody, which was carried by one of the parts (hence the word "tenor," the "holder" of the melody). Naturally during the process of development, which occupied several centuries, a musical notation had to be adopted which was conventionalized into substantially the same notation that we use today.

The organ, which had originally been invented by the Greeks, and had been developed in the Byzantine Empire, was still rather a primitive instrument when introduced into the West in the ninth century, but it was continually developed into the complex instrument that it was by the end of the fourteenth century. The late medieval organ was able to perform the same kind of interweaving of sound that the human voices had already been trained to make; and ultimately in later centuries of the modern era the various instruments likewise interweave to make the whole which we call the symphony (literally, "coordinated" sound as distinct from merely many sounds, *poly*phony).

In the later days of the medieval period, as the severe Gothic became the overdecorated Gothic, with the decoration in part obscuring the basic design, so did the variations in the musical composition tend to hide the basic melody, thus obscuring the original purpose of setting the words of the Liturgy themselves to music. Cleverness and dexterity became ends in themselves to such an extent that at the time of the Catholic Reformation in the sixteenth century efforts were made to return altogether to the original simple plain song. Here the work, especially of Palestrina, whose period lies outside the scope of this book, was crucial. He was a church composer of such excellence that his partial reform was acceptable even to the conservatives. Without returning to the simple plain song of earlier centuries he was nevertheless able in his work to set the Liturgy in its true place by restoring some much-needed simplicity, firmly placing

church music on the path which it has followed in all essentials since his time.

Secular music was greatly affected by music of the church, although other influences from the Muslim world also contributed to it. Wandering musicians, the troubadours, trouvères (northern France), and jongleurs accompanied their poetry with music, played on the harp, viol, lute, guitar, and similar instruments. Minnesingers in Germany sang their love poems to the accompaniment of their instruments. Probably these singers were little affected by the music of the churches. But popular music such as part songs and rounds were clearly influenced by the development of polyphony in the churches. Each voice took a different part, sometimes different words, sometimes the same words at different times as in such well-known rounds as Three Blind Mice and Frère Jacques. Perhaps the most complex development of part singing was the madrigal, an Italian innovation of the fourteenth century which needed the cooperation of the poets, who made the complex words fit in with each other, and the musician, who set it polyphonically in accordance with the rules of counterpoint. In Germany the artisans formed what today would be called glee clubs, which were often organized by the members of a craft guild. These glee clubs had their own guild laws and rules of organization, and their own degrees of excellence, the master being called a "Master Singer." *The Mastersingers of Nuremberg* of Richard Wagner is a faithful reproduction of the atmosphere and workings of one such guild.

► Medieval literature

LATIN LITERATURE—HYMNS, POEMS

Such an abundance of medieval literature of all kinds is extant that it is impossible here to do more than merely indicate the types, and to devote a little more space to the few acknowledged masterpieces. As has already been explained in the early part of this chapter, the Latin language as used in medieval times was a living tongue, and its use was not confined to works of erudition, though, because it had to be learned, a modicum of education was needed before it could be used as a suitable vehicle for expression. Medieval Latin went easily into poetry, and rhyming was usual. We have the stately hymns of the medieval church, many of which are still in use, either in Latin or in the vernacular. But we also have great quantities of lighthearted verse, much of it composed by students at the universities, singing cheerfully of love and the springtime and similar subjects. There is also much satire, especially on the manners and customs of the clergy. A whole series of these poems are given the name of Goliardic poems probably from the frequent references to a certain Bishop Golias, a mythical character who was supposed to be the poets' patron.

As the Middle Ages drew on, Latin Literature became more confined to the clergy and educated classes, and was the official medium of communication for those who had to appeal to a wider audience than the inhabitants of any single area in Europe. History, memoirs, philosophy, and religious and scientific work continued to be written, for the most part, in Latin, while each area began to develop literature in the vernacular tongues, the medium of expression in everyday life.

VERNACULAR LITERATURE

Heroic epic

Most of the great civilizations known to us produced their first literature in the form of heroic epics, sung and recited perhaps for centuries before they were written down. Western civilization was no exception. All the Germanic peoples had their sagas, dating from very ancient times, long before the advent of Christianity. The content of these is pagan, the deeds of pagan warriors and their gods, though sometimes overlaid with Christian feeling of a later age. *Beowulf,* the great Anglo-Saxon poem, is of the former kind; other examples are the Norse and Icelandic sagas. On the other hand, the

Nibelungenlied, transformed into an operatic cycle by Richard Wagner in the nineteenth century, retains the pagan background, but even in the early Germanic version the ancient warrior ideals have been partly transformed by Christian tradition and chivalry.

Poetry of feudalism

Chansons de geste—This early folk material was succeeded in the eleventh century by at least three distinct types of poetry composed for the entertainment of the feudal nobility, and on subjects of the greatest appeal for them.

The first type is the *chanson de geste,* or tale of heroic deeds, for the most part of northern French origin and headed by a masterpiece, the *Song of Roland,* which concerns the heroic death of Count Roland, one of Charlemagne's knights, at the battle of Roncesvalles against the Muslims. Around the figure of Roland a whole cycle of songs sprang up, even in countries quite unconnected with the hero. The songs also tell of the marvelous deeds of Charlemagne himself, and his other knights. No attempt is made to relate the poems to the actual time of Charlemagne, but all describe the feudal world of the era when they were written and recited.

The troubadours and the poetry of chivalry and courtesy—In southern France, probably under Muslim influence, grew up a school of lyric poetry recited and sung by troubadour minstrels in the noble houses and castles of this area. The troubadours introduced the element of love into their songs, rather than simply a recital of heroic deeds. It was under their influence that the cult of romantic love, still with us, first entered the Western world, since the troubadour by convention addressed his songs to the great lady of the castle, whose charms he extolled endlessly, and for whose smile he was willing to endure any torture. The influence of the troubadours spread into Germany, where they were called *minnesingers* (*minne*—love). In the hands especially of Walther von der Vogelweide (1170?–1230?) the romantic theme is handled with great freshness and delicacy as well as with greater depth than is usual in poetry of this type.

Christian influence—The Arthurian and Grail legends—The third type of poetry is a combination of the *chanson de geste* with the chivalric romance. Instead of the ordinary feudal world of the warrior, we now find portrayed idealized kings and knights, as in the legends of King Arthur, originally of Celtic origin. These knights often perform deeds of heroism for the sake of fair ladies, rescuing them from enchanted castles and such. This world of perfect chivalry is best described in the poetry of Chrétien de Troyes (last half of the twelfth century).

As time went on, the Arthurian legends became suffused with Christian thought and feeling. The culmination of this process is to be found in the legendary search for the Holy Grail, the vessel in which the blood of Christ was caught, or in another version, the vessel used for the Last Supper, or a magic stone. All were equally a symbol of Christian aspiration. The hero who alone can find the Grail is a Christian, not merely a feudal or chivalric hero, whose purity and chastity rather than his deeds as a warrior bring him to his goal. The *Parzival* of Wolfram von Eschenbach (1170?–1220?) is the most fully Christian account of the wanderings of the hero in search of the Grail, while the culmination of the Arthurian legend is to be found in the prose *Morte d'Arthur* of the Englishman Sir Thomas Malory in the fifteenth century.

It has only been possible to touch upon the varieties of medieval poetry as sung and recited among the nobility, in part for reasons of space limitation, and in part on account of the difficulty of making any adequate generalizations when the total bulk is so large and of such varying quality. At their best the heroic sagas are almost, if not quite, the equal of the sagas of the heroic ages of earlier peoples dealt with in earlier chapters; medieval epic at its worst is feeble and derivative, using stock stories from the decadent periods of Greek and Alexandrine literature. On the other hand, the Arthurian legends are ancient Celtic tales which have certainly been transformed out of all recognition by sophisticated poets of a later age, writing for an aristocratic audience for whom they were quite consciously extolling the cult of chivalry.

The fantastic world they depict was no doubt a welcome escape for their audience from the anarchic feudal world of their day. Yet it bears also a direct relationship to it; it is a less harsh world, a world softened by the application in life of Christian ethical teachings. The poets have a secondary purpose beyond mere entertainment; their poems are truly didactic, not spontaneous and descriptive. The virtues they extol are not the heroic and martial virtues of an Achilles; courtesy and gentleness may be rewarded better than mere valor. In the Grail legends and especially in the poem *Parzival*, this tendency comes to full fruition and is entirely explicit. It is instructive to compare such a poem as *Parzival* with the earlier "wandering" epics of Gilgamesh (see Chapter 3) and the *Odyssey*, and to see revealed one aspect of the medieval mind, and the medieval attitude to life. All these poems reflect the preoccupations of their time, as such poems always must. The Sumerian hero Gilgamesh searches for the plant of immortality, but having found it, he loses it again; the gods are arbitrary and unjust, they cheat mankind, and the hero has no recourse but to plunge himself back into life and build a city. Odysseus is stripped of his possessions and loses his companions in a shipwreck. He learns humility by hard experience, and through this experience he regains his lost rights as a king and vanquishes his enemies.

But Parzival in the poem of Wolfram begins as a fool and an ingrate; he leaves his mother without a thought, and she dies of grief. He kills a knight who turns out to be his kinsman, and is so unskilled he cannot even strip the dead knight of his armor. He reaches early the Grail Castle which he is destined some day to rule, but he does not ask the crucial question which would heal the wounded guardian of the Castle. In his subsequent loneliness and suffering he seems to deny even God. Yet this folly is also simplicity; it is culpable, but it can be redeemed and changed through the growth of wisdom. The poem is the story of how through the help of suffering he at last learns wisdom, and is permitted first to meet and become reconciled to his brother, the Oriental pagan prince Feirefiz, then finally to find again the Grail Castle with the help of sages who give him advice and warning. This time he asks the right question and achieves the Grail.

The poem does not seem to be allegorical in essence; it is not a *summa* of salvation like the *Divine Comedy* of Dante, to be described later. The Church plays almost no part in it. It seems to be the pursuit of the Christian ideal through life experience rather than through the mediation of the Church, and in this aspect it is significant. Parzival as a Christian prince is pursuing a Christian ideal. It is not his valor that triumphs. His first victory is not gained through valor, but through foolhardiness and good fortune, and he is defeated in combat by the heathen Feirefiz, who spares his life after Parzival's magical sword has broken. It is the sword of his kinsman whom he killed so wantonly in his youth. In the end it is the purity and simplicity of his human heart and his ability to learn wisdom that make him worthy of the Grail. The wisdom he has learned and the reconciliation with, and ultimate conversion of, his heathen brother lead him to his goal. Thus this German poem already looks forward to a later age of religious thought than Dante's masterpiece, although it was written almost a century earlier; and it was no doubt this element in the poem that made such an appeal to Richard Wagner. Though medieval in setting, *Parzival* transcends the medieval thought of the age when it was written. In the homelessness and loneliness and individual suffering of its hero it seems to picture in advance the modern man, a prototype of Faust rather than of the medieval man who

was led by Vergil and Beatrice on a spiritual journey to the contemplation of God.

Literature of the towns

The fabliaux and their successors— When we enter the world of the growing towns, the life of chivalry and courtesy is left behind, for these qualities are conspicuously missing in popular urban literature. The townsman preferred raw, earthy stories which were concerned with his own experience. He liked, in particular, animal stories and fables, above all the adventures of the cunning Reynard the Fox. The *fabliaux,* especially designed for the taste of townsmen, were undistinguished by literary graces of any kind, and their sense of humor appears to us as extremely primitive. The unfaithfulness, laziness, and untidiness of housewives were pilloried, as were similar sins on the part of monks, friars, and secular clergy. Women and the clergy were the principal butts of the satire of the fabliaux, and the plots hold no surprise. In the same vein as the fabliaux, but at a far higher stage of literary accomplishment, were the fourteenth-century stories of the Italian Boccaccio (1313?–1375) in his *Decameron.* The English popular poet Chaucer (1343–1400), however, stands in a class by himself. The characters in the *Canterbury Tales* are no longer mere types; each is sharply differentiated with wit, humor, and sometimes profound insight. Most of Chaucer's plots, however, are closely related to those of the fabliaux.

It is useless to try to describe Chaucer intelligibly in a few sentences. Always when writing of him, one drops into quotations, the only way to convey his flavor. The *Canterbury Tales,* his masterpiece, though by no means his only poem—he was skilled also as a translator—tells of a pilgrimage made by a group of assorted characters to the tomb of St. Thomas Becket. Each of the characters is introduced to us; then his or her character is hit off with exquisite precision in a series of rhymed couplets, sometimes sympathetic, sometimes malicious. Then Chaucer allows each of them to tell a tale to while away the time on the journey. No other work gives us so full a picture of the ordinary medieval man and woman. When we have taken the journey with them and listened to their tales, we feel that we have indeed met and talked for a time with fourteenth-century human beings; we feel we should recognize them if we met them in life. Though the Middle English of Chaucer is no longer comprehensible to most of us, it slips easily into modern English; and though he has not always been admired as much for his poetical and especially metrical skill as he is today, there has never been a time since his death in 1400 when he has not been read for his narrative ability, his unerring character painting, and the vitality and freshness of his picture of medieval man as he really was in the fourteenth century.

Poetry of social criticism—An earlier contemporary of Chaucer gives us the first piece of serious social criticism of Western civilization, the *Vision of Piers Plowman,* by one William Langland, of whom nothing else is known. In this poem the poor peasant finds his voice. The poem, though couched in the form of an allegory, is a realistic description of the hard lot of the English poor in the fourteenth century, hardships which were later to lead to prolonged revolts, perhaps in part the result of this very poem.

The Romance of the Rose—Perhaps the most popular of all medieval poems was a composite work known as the *Romance of the Rose.* The first part was an allegory, written by William de Lorris (early thirteenth century). It is an ingenious love poem in the conventional style of courteous poetry, but no longer directed only to the noble classes, and clearly influenced by Christian tradition. It tells the story of a youth who is pierced by an arrow sped from the bow of the God of Love, whose heart leaves his own breast to be embodied in the Rose, which is surrounded by thorns and presents a difficult obstacle to be overcome. Jealousy, Reason, Danger, and other abstractions play their part in his efforts to reach the Rose, and after over four thousand lines, when

William's poem breaks off, the unfortunate lover has still not attained his goal. It is at this point that a later writer, John de Meun (second half of the thirteenth century) takes up, and the poem ceases at once to be an idyllic dream and becomes a cynical satire on all contemporary institutions. Hypocrisy (the friars) is given a chance to speak, Reason and the other characters from the earlier poem flay superstition, Nature gives a discourse on medieval science and current history. In short, the poet is able to grasp the opportunity of the unfinished poem to give an invaluable account of medieval life. With the aid of Venus the youth is able to gain his Rose; but this is only incidental to the satire, which has been called a "guidebook to the Middle Ages." But it was a guidebook in an entirely different sense from the greatest of medieval masterpieces which sums up the knowledge and aspiration equally, welding the whole into a perfect synthesis, unique in history, entirely inimitable, and almost untranslatable, the *Divine Comedy* of Dante.

The Divine Comedy—The *Divine Comedy* was not the name Dante Alighieri (1265–1321) gave to his own poem. He himself simply called it the *Comedy,* because it begins in sadness and ends in supreme happiness. But it was early given the epithet "Divine" which has now been incorporated in the title. No poem has ever deserved it more, both for its beauty and for the sublimity of the theme.

It is impossible to do any justice to the poem in a short space; in fact, it cannot properly be described at all. It must be read and experienced, preferably in the original Italian, a language full of vowels and music which Dante himself helped to fix. The Tuscan dialect of the poet indeed became, through his work, the literary language of Italy, and it has in essentials changed very little to this day.

One aspect of the *Comedy* cannot be understood without knowledge of the poet's first work, the *Vita Nuova,* in which he tells how at the age of nine he saw Beatrice, who was herself only eight, and thereafter she remained his ideal though he never knew her well in this earthly life, and she married without being aware of his unspoken feelings. He tells us that he had determined to express one day his love for Beatrice in poetry. It is this human and yet unearthly love that in manhood has transformed the poet's whole inner being, giving especially to the *Paradiso,* the third part of the *Comedy,* an extraordinary intensity of thought and emotion which is recognizably medieval and closely akin to the work of the medieval church builders. It is impossible to separate the poet's sublimated love for Beatrice from the Christian love which has made it possible.

Beatrice is a guide to the poet in his journey through the realm of the spirit to the vision of God, a realm in which the planetary spheres are not only seen but experienced, in which thought is not only apprehended but actually perceived. Yet Beatrice is also a woman before whom Dante is tongue-tied so that at one moment he is unable even to pronounce her name. And she represents also revelation in the sense in which Thomas Aquinas understood it, the visitor from the world of the spirit who adds to what he cannot find for himself. Vergil, the Roman poet, takes Dante as far as the summit of the Mount of Purgatory, but the pagan can go no farther. Reason must be supplemented by Revelation. Vergil was first sent to Dante by Beatrice as he faced the gates of Hell and feared to enter—Divine Grace must aid the natural reason which then, with the help of Revelation, can ascend to the full contemplation of God.

So the poem is profoundly allegorical; and yet at the same time it is real. The journey may have been the ascent of a soul to salvation, but the poet feels and perceives as a human being. The sufferings of the damned are portrayed with gruesome realism, and Dante experiences all the shock and revulsion of a healthy mortal. When Vergil leaves, Dante grieves and wishes him back; he suffers the pangs of loneliness in a deserted Garden of Eden until he recognizes Beatrice, who comes riding to him in her chariot drawn by a gryphon. If the chariot is the Church and the gryphon is the animal symbol of Christ, this symbolism does not intrude. The symbolic or the allegorical and the real are so wonderfully fused that the reader is caught up with his imagination into the experience, and need know nothing of the symbolism until he feels the need of it.

Finally it may be added that the poem has certain important political meanings. Dante was through and through a political man; he played an important part in the affairs of his native Florence, and for a time he was a leading figure in the city's government before being forced into exile by his political enemies. He was a partisan of the Empire in the struggle between the Empire and the papacy. In his work *De Monarchia* (*On the Monarchy*) he makes clear the reasons for this partisanship. He believed that the spheres of Church and State should be separate, but that the State should be a true World State, such as had been known in the early centuries of the Christian Era under the aegis of Rome. The political condition of man is a consequence of sin, and leads to ever more deadly sins. Dante's choice of characters for the dwellers in his three realms of Hell, Purgatory, and Paradise is undoubtedly to some degree determined by his political views. It is significant that the Byzantine emperor, Justinian, noted by historians for his universal law code and for his reconquest of Italy, is greatly exalted in Dante's Paradise, and is seen by the poet as having been permitted by God "the glory of avenging his wrath by the living justice that inspires me"—surely a line hardly equaled for concentrated thought in all literature.

The poem begins on the night preceding Good Friday; during that night the moon is to be at the full. Throughout the next day and night the poet will make his horrifying journey through Hell (the *Inferno*). For twenty-four hours more he struggles to the foot of the Mount of Purgatory (the *Purgatorio*). Then for three days he is on the Mount and at last ascends to Paradise (the *Paradiso*), where there ceases to be any time. It remains the same day (Thursday) as Dante circles the earth in company with the heavenly planets until he is over Italy and the sun is setting in Jerusalem. The journey has taken exactly a week.

In Hell, accompanied by Vergil, he passes by all the various grades of sinners undergoing punishment, till he comes to Satan himself; then he is pulled past the center of gravity by his guide. The worst is over. Those whom he will meet hereafter are souls who are saved but are not yet ready for Heaven. On the Mount of Purgatory there are many terraces, each with its different sinners, and before he even reaches the terraces the poet sees others who have for some reason not yet begun to make the ascent, though in time they will be able to undertake it. In the *Purgatorio* the whole atmosphere is different from that of Hell, where all hope has been abandoned for eternity. Here in Purgatory one first comes to the realization that though the way be long, salvation is ahead. There is hope, indeed certainty, for the sinner in Purgatory. Then at last the Garden of Eden is reached, Vergil leaves the poet, and Beatrice comes for him as his new guide.

Light, music, joy, and love are the glories of Paradise, marvelously conveyed in the liquid Italian, with its many beautiful images; the planets dance and sing as they wheel in the Ptolemaic universe, so deeply experienced by Dante that it seems impossible to doubt that this is the way the universe is in the world of imagination, and Copernicus was wrong. ("Like the clock that calls us to prayer, in which one part draws and impels the other, chiming 'tin tin' so sweetly that the well-disposed spirit swells with love"—"Tin tin sonando con si dolce nota Che il ben disposto spirto d'amor turge.") Here are the great saints, Bernard and Thomas Aquinas, Peter and, at last, the Virgin Mary and a momentary vision of God, which, as soon as it is experienced, cannot be remembered save as an afterglow of something indescribable. But among the blessed this vision is always there. When Dante looks into the eyes of Beatrice, the Light is reflected there, and though he turns about to discover the source of the Light, it eludes him.

In all the great medieval thinkers there is nothing abstract or arid. The Latin of Thomas Aquinas, crystal-clear and sharp, bears the reader along with him, sharing his enthusiasm for the adventures of the mind, the logical thrust and counterthrust corresponding to the thrust and counterthrust of the piers and buttresses of the cathedral, pulled onward toward the summit of the vision, the "intellectual contemplation of God" in which there is nothing cold as Thomas experiences it—the love of the heart leading to the understanding of the Divine (as, also, in Plato's *Symposium*), the love that leads to this ascent having been implanted in man as grace, the gift of God. So also in Dante. "Luce intellettual pien d'amore, Amore del vero pien di letizia, Letizia che trascende ogni dolzore—Light of the mind, full of love, Love of the truth, full of joy, Joy that transcends every sorrow," this is Dante's description of that love which draws mankind to the contemplation of God. Every word in the great poem is full of the profoundest thought, often untranslatable into languages other than Italian, in which feeling and thought are fused as in no other. It lacks the extreme clarity of the cold intellect which is the genius of the French language, and the Italian itself was never again used as it was by Dante, who found in it the perfect vehicle for his experience. The whole knowledge of the world of the senses and the world of the spirit as known to medieval man is in the *Divine Comedy*—the deadliness of sin and the eternal punishment that it entails, the great hope held out to man by God and the means for its attainment, and at last a vision of eternal blessedness with the saints and heavenly hosts in the spaceless, timeless kingdom of heaven.

The medieval drama

A few words should be said of medieval drama, which was in no sense one of the great dramas of the world, but was original and owed nothing to the great drama of the earlier peoples we have discussed. In early medieval times the drama consisted of the re-enacting of Biblical scenes in the churches at times of festival. These re-enactments developed into the mystery play, which also used Biblical subjects, but combined them with legends and tales from the lives of the saints. Mystery plays, too, were performed in church, but quite early were presented in the vernacular since the purpose was to instruct the people. The performers were usually the clergy, though lay actors were also used. An outgrowth of the mystery play is the Passion play, which represented with deep sincerity the crucifixion of Christ. Some of the Passion plays still survive, played by village actors, and joined in by the whole village community. The Oberammergau Passion play, performed in the Bavarian village of that name every ten years, is the outstanding surviving example.

The miracle plays, which became popular by the twelfth century, usually represented some exceptional intervention of a saint or the Virgin Mary in the ordinary lives of men. Finally, with the growth of the towns, came the play we most associate with the Middle Ages, the morality play, originally of a religious nature. By far the best known of these morality plays is the famous *Everyman,* a very free adaptation of which is still played every year in the open air at the Salzburg festival.

As the title of this play implies, the hero is a type rather than an individual. But he is not a type of a particular man; he is a representative of mankind. One of the paradoxes of the Middle Ages, which it has not been possible to stress in this book, is the contrast between the medieval political and religious institutions, which were hierarchical and authoritarian, and the universal belief, implicit, of course, in Christianity, that all human beings are equal in the hour of death. Each man is judged for his sins and saved or condemned as an individual man. The great emperor Frederic II, so arrogant and exalted in his lifetime, put on the garments of a penitent to cross the threshold of death. So the play *Everyman* is concerned with the rich young man who cares nothing for his soul until death appears to warn him of the

few hours he has still to live. When Everyman's bribe to Death is refused, he tries first to persuade his kindred, his friends, and then his Worldly Goods to go with him, but all refuse. Only Good Deeds can help, and Everyman's Good Deeds are so feeble that "she" cannot rise from the ground. But Knowledge takes him to Confession, where he receives absolution and undergoes penance. This revives Good Deeds, but in turn Beauty, Five Wits, Strength, and Discretion leave him. He is accompanied to the edge of the grave by Knowledge; but he must descend into the grave with only Good Deeds, who helps him to ultimate salvation.

The play in its modern adaptation is more dramatically presented, with Death appearing at a feast, which shocks Everyman into a kind of stupor. His companions, failing to understand, then desert him. At the last Everyman is saved by Repentance and Faith. In spite of the simplicity of the theme, it is still possible in the great square in front of the Salzburg cathedral to sense something of the loneliness of the soul in the moment of death which the unknown medieval writer strove to dramatize. And it is seen that there is not, after all, such a great distance from Everyman to Marlowe and Shakespeare, and the tremendous individuals of Elizabethan drama.

The medieval view of man was too simple for Shakespeare. He was not content to say only that man sinned on earth and could be redeemed by repentance and faith. He wished to show how man sins on earth, what was the nature of his sins, and how they bring about their own penalty and judgment on earth. *King Lear, Macbeth, Othello,* all the great tragedies, are as truly morality plays as *Everyman.* But henceforth there is to be no simple answer, no one fate for all mankind, and salvation after death ceases to be the preoccupation of the dramatist. The character, deeds, and motives of man on earth, his relations with other human beings, his actions in the face of his destiny—these were to become the stuff of the drama of Shakespeare, as they are the stuff of life itself as it is known to man.

With the fading of the medieval conviction that all the answers were known, the adolescence of the human being was over.

▶ Suggestions for further reading

If the student is interested in reading primary sources, including the works of any of the writers referred to in this chapter, he should consult an extremely useful book which lists every medieval writer whose works had been translated into English prior to 1946: C. P. Farrar and A. P. Evans, *Bibliography of English Translations from Medieval Sources* (New York: Columbia University Press, 1946).

Of the several hundred books available on different subjects discussed in this chapter the author believes that E. Gilson, *The Spirit of Medieval Philosophy* (New York: Charles Scribner's Sons, 1940), is probably the one that he should choose for an understanding of the subjects considered important by medieval thinkers. The book is extremely well written, and the writer is sympathetic to the medieval viewpoint; also, his work is free from the plethora of names which will confuse most beginning students who attempt the more formal histories of philosophy. Another book that should not be missed is H. O. Taylor, *The Medieval Mind* (4th ed., 2 vols.; Cambridge, Mass.: Harvard University Press, 1949), which devotes a chapter to each of a considerable number of medieval thinkers. The book is slightly uneven, as it is hardly possible for any writer to be completely familiar with all these men and women; but for the most part Taylor's judgments are based on his own readings, and the whole is eloquently written, especially in chapters devoted to writers with whom Taylor feels a special sympathy. A recent historical survey containing a great deal of material on the Byzantine and Muslim civilizations, in addition to strictly medieval thought and culture, is F. B. Artz, *The Mind of the Middle Ages* (New York: Alfred A. Knopf, Inc., 1953). This book also contains the best medieval bibliography easily accessible to a student. In general, the book may be safely used to find additional information on almost everything discussed in this text in the medieval chapters.

On medieval science the writer's own work: S. C. Easton, *Roger Bacon and His Search for a Universal Science* (New York: Columbia University Press, 1952), may be consulted, especially Chapter 9, on the general nature of medieval science. Lynn Thorndike, *A History of Magic and Experimental Science* (6 vols.; New York: The Macmillan Company and Columbia University Press, 1923–1941), may be consulted for reference. Thorndike makes no attempt at a synthesis in these monumental volumes but devotes each chapter to a different scientist. His long chapter on Albertus Magnus is one of the best in the book. An interesting study of several problems handled by medieval scientists is to be found in the early chapters of Herbert Butterfield, *The Origins of Modern Science, 1300–1800* (New York: The Macmillan Company, 1951).

A fine reconstruction of the life of Peter Abélard has been couched in the form of a novel: Helen Waddell, *Peter Abélard* (New York: Henry Holt & Co., Inc., 1933). The author is a fine medieval scholar, and her book captures the medieval spirit probably better than any other.

Two books by Sartell Prentice give a great deal of technical information about the cathedrals in a reasonably simple manner: *The Voice of the Cathedrals* (New York: William Morrow & Co., Inc., 1938) and *The Heritage of the Cathedrals* (New York: William Morrow & Co., Inc., 1939). But a wonderful work of evocation of the spirit that informed the building of the cathedrals, which is still unequaled in its field and is true literature, is Henry Adams, *Mont St. Michel and Chartres* (Boston: Houghton Mifflin Company, 1905), many times reprinted.

A useful recent source book which gives a number of well-chosen selections from medieval literature is C. W. Jones, *Medieval Literature in Translation* (New York: Longmans, Green & Co., Inc., 1950). Among many translations of the *Divine Comedy* this author prefers a very recent inexpensive edition; the poem is simply but accurately translated, in prose, but it is printed in stanzas as if it were poetry: Dante, *The Divine Comedy* (tr. H. R. Huse; New York: Rinehart & Company, Inc., 1954). An excellent book on the wandering poets is H. Waddell, *Wandering Scholars* (New York: Henry Holt & Co., Inc., 1950). Finally, the reader is referred to C. G. Crump and E. F. Jacob, eds., *The Legacy of the Middle Ages* (Oxford: The Clarendon Press, 1926), for a number of excellent articles, not too technical, on medieval art and craftsmanship and other fields of culture, some of which have evidently been written by men with a real enthusiasm for things medieval. The book has also a number of valuable illustrations which make it one of the best in a distinguished series.

14

Commerce and Industry in the Middle Ages

Revival of trade • The rise of the towns • Organization of trade and industry • Medieval economic concepts • Merchant and craft guilds • The rise of medieval capitalism • Breakdown of control over profit seeking • The accumulation of capital • Improvement of business techniques

---

► Revival of trade

TRADE CONDITIONS IN THE DARK AGES

The economic conditions of Europe in the Dark Ages have been touched on briefly in an earlier chapter. During the ninth and tenth centuries the Mediterranean Sea was virtually a Muslim lake, and the ports, such as Marseilles, which had retained some prosperity even after the fall of Rome, now declined into small towns. The great city with which the West wished to trade, by far the greatest city in Europe, was, of course, Constantinople, but only the smallest trickle of trade could get through directly by sea. Such trade as there was had to be carried on, at least in part, by land, by the hazardous route through Eastern Europe, which was itself constantly being invaded by waves of nomads from Asia. Not until Hungary was settled as a country and the Magyars had accepted Christianity was there any reasonable assurance that merchants could reach Constantinople.

There were, however, two exceptions to this general condition. The chief European trade with Constantinople was carried on by the Swedes, who had settled first at

Novgorod, then at Kiev in Russia, as described in Chapter 8. These Russians, or Varangians (they were known by both names), traveled down the great Russian rivers into the Black Sea. The first groups often started out without any trade goods at all, but pillaged some small communities and then used their loot for trade, selling it in Constantinople and the Black Sea cities in the Byzantine Empire. Later they also used the booty taken in the Viking raids in Europe, which was assembled on the Baltic island of Gothland before being distributed through Russia, and even back into the Western cities again. Here they also brought native products from the north, lumber, furs, hides, and similar articles. By the ninth century they had regularized their position in Constantinople, by treaty, and were allotted a special quarter in the imperial capital. But the total of goods that reached Constantinople must have been small enough, and smaller still the Byzantine luxuries that reached the West up the rivers via Gothland. And while the Vikings were still raiding Europe, naturally they did not supply their victims with luxuries from the East. Later, as has been seen, this trade was regu-

An old corner of modern Venice.

The Rialto at Venice (late medieval, early renaissance). (COURTESY ITALIAN STATE TOURIST OFFICE)

The Palace of the Doge (Duke) of Venice. Note the Byzantine influence. (COURTESY ITALIAN STATE TOURIST OFFICE)

larized, and Kiev became an industrial and commercial center of the first importance. The other exception was the city of Venice, on the Adriatic Sea, which was immune to the Muslim ravages as long as it kept to its northern section of the sea. The city, which was built almost on the sea itself, with its thoroughfares in the form of canals and lagoons, had been founded in the sixth century as a refuge for fugitives from the nomad invasions. It was held for a brief period by Charlemagne, though not long enough for him to exercise effective sovereignty over it. So when the emperor in the year 810 was negotiating for the recognition of his title by the Byzantines, he gave up, among other possessions, the city of Venice. Though the Byzantines likewise exercised little effective sovereignty over the city, the connection was valuable for the Venetians, as it permitted them a certain amount of trade with the capital; and, even though the sea voyage to Constantinople was to be impossible for two more centuries, goods could be transported across the Adriatic by sea, whence

the land routes were comparatively short, and passed through territory which was usually under some kind of control by the Byzantines. From the ninth to the eleventh century Venice grew rapidly, and was in fact a republic, self-governed, independent in all but name from Constantinople. When during the eleventh century she aided the Byzantines in a war against the Normans, she was rewarded by being permitted full free trade throughout the Byzantine Empire, a very important advantage over all her competitors in view of the restrictive trade policies adopted by the empire. It amounted to a virtual monopoly for Venice of all trade between Constantinople and the West. Thereafter she was to lead the Western world in sea trade, and rapidly developed overland routes to circulate the Byzantine and Oriental products within Europe.

Aside from these two exceptions, during the whole period of anarchy and desolation in Europe which followed the breakdown of the Carolingian Empire and the Viking raids, trade was on a very small scale in-

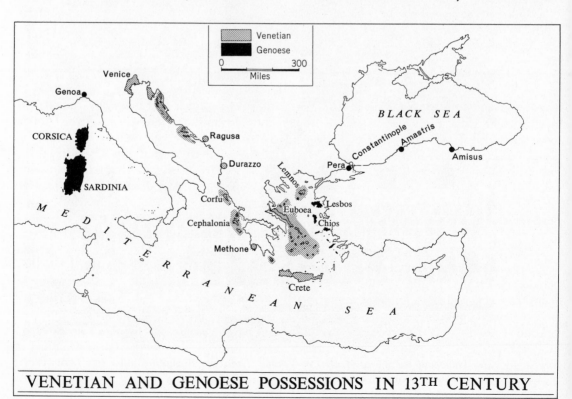

VENETIAN AND GENOESE POSSESSIONS IN 13TH CENTURY

▶ chronological chart

The Great Trading Cities

Foundation of Venice	*ca.*	568
Election of first Doge of Venice		587
Venice recognized as Byzantine territory		810
Foundation of Novgorod, traditionally by Rurik		862
Foundation of Kiev		882
Trading rights granted in Constantinople to Varangians		907
Venetian war with Constantinople—extensive maritime trading rights granted to Venetians		1063
Institution of Great Council of Venice (Venetian oligarchy)		1063
Norman conquest of Sicily		1072–1091
Genoese and Pisans clear western Mediterranean of Muslims		1087
Pisans granted trade privileges by Byzantine Empire		1111
Fourth Crusade—Sack of Constantinople, led by Venetians		1204
War between Venice and Genoa		1253–1299
Battle of Meloria—Defeat of Pisans by Genoese		1284

The Leagues of Towns

Diet of Roncaglia—Frederic I asserts imperial rights over Italian towns	1158
Formation of Lombard League	1159
Battle of Legnano—Defeat of Frederic I by Lombard League	1176
Peace of Constance between Frederic I and Lombard League	1183
Wars between Frederic II and Lombard League	1237–1250
Alliance of Lübeck and Hamburg to protect Baltic trade routes	1244
Privileges granted to German towns in London	1282
Confederation of Cologne—League of Hansa towns against Denmark	1370
Richard II of England renews Hansa privileges	1377
Last assembly of Hanseatic League	1669

deed, and amounted to little more than the exchange of local products, varied by the occasional presence of some courageous small trader who had braved the hazardous overland journey to the East and had been successful.

RISE OF THE ITALIAN SEAPORTS

Rivalry among Genoa, Pisa, and Venice

Meanwhile other Italian cities had been making headway, notably Genoa and Pisa. The Genoese and Pisans, after capturing and keeping for themselves Corsica and Sardinia, aided the Normans in the capture of Sicily (1091), and were given special privileges and quarters in Sicily itself. Before the end of the eleventh century they had also established trading colonies in Northern Africa, and thereafter traded with the Muslims, not allowing religious differences to affect their search for profitable business, even during the Crusades themselves. The western Mediterranean now belonged to these western Italian seaports as much as the Adriatic belonged to the Venetians. The Crusades gave the three cities a command of the whole Mediterranean, although by now they had become rivals poaching upon each other's territory. The Genoese succeeded in eliminating the Pisans by war, but they competed with the Venetians for several centuries afterward. As we have seen, the notorious Fourth Crusade and the subsequent Latin Kingdom of Constantinople gave great advantages to the Venetians, whose project it was. But the Genoese retaliated in 1261 when they helped

Though this minature shows an incident in the life of Sir Galahad, and the persons on the boat are not typical, the ship itself is medieval. From Roman de Tristan *(French), ca. 1450.* (COURTESY THE PIERPONT MORGAN LIBRARY. Ms. 41, folio 259)

restore the Greek emperor to his throne. There was, however, enough trade for both after the Crusades, and the Genoese, in general, continued to exploit the western Mediterranean, retaining valuable footholds in the East, while the Venetians did a greater share of the Oriental trade. The Genoese traded constantly with North Africa, even passing through the Pillars of Hercules (the Strait of Gibraltar) into the Atlantic and sailing a short distance down the Moroccan coast. Both Genoa and Venice were aristocratic merchant republics of which we shall have more to say later.

The nature of sea trade in the Middle Ages

Travel by sea in early medieval times was still far from safe, and wrecks, sometimes assisted by robbers on shore who guided ships onto the rocks by the use of false lights, were very frequent. The ships hugged the coast, as in ancient times, at least until the general use of the mariner's

compass toward the end of the thirteenth century; on the other hand, sea traders could transport several hundred tons of cargo in each vessel and were free from the nuisance and expense of having to pay heavy tolls in order to pass through territory belonging to feudal lords, as did overland travelers. Seafarers still had to contend with pirates, even when the Muslims had been driven from the sea, for the maritime cities did not hesitate to engage in piracy against ships belonging to their rivals. But the same cities that profited so heavily from the voyages of their citizens through customs and excise taxes thought it worth while both to sweep the seas of pirates when possible and to supply armed fleets to protect the merchant vessels. Many medieval fleets sailed in convoy, and their strength was usually too great for any except well-organized pirates.

Both sails and oars were used for propulsion, since medieval sailors learned late how to sail into the wind, and the tiller for steering was not effective till the end of the

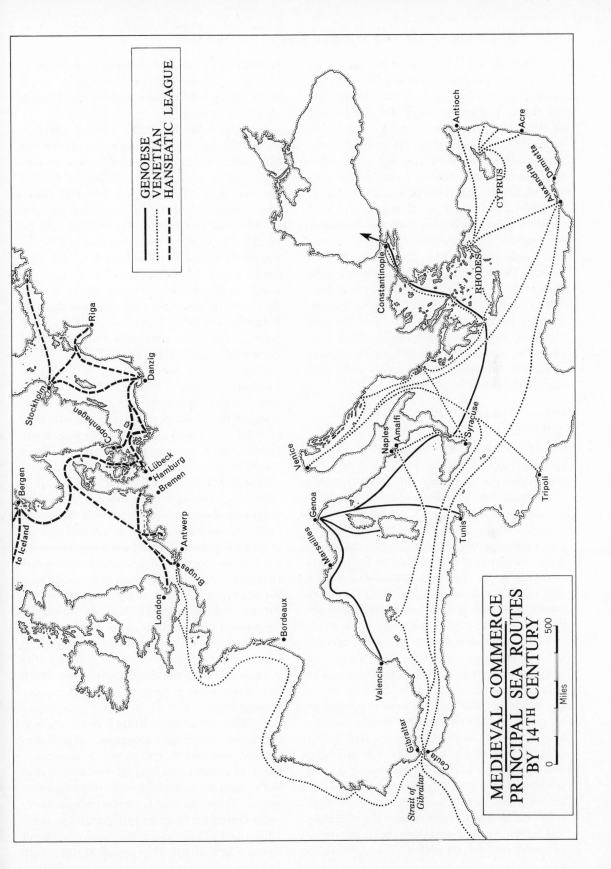

GENOESE
VENETIAN
HANSEATIC LEAGUE

Antioch
Acre
Damietta
CYPRUS
Alexandria
RHODES
Constantinople

Riga
Danzig
Stockholm
Copenhagen
Lübeck
Hamburg
Bremen
Bergen
to Iceland
Antwerp
Bruges
London
Bordeaux

Venice
Naples
Amalfi
Syracuse
Tripoli
Genoa
Marseilles
Tunis

Valencia

Gibraltar
Ceuta
Strait of Gibraltar

MEDIEVAL COMMERCE
PRINCIPAL SEA ROUTES
BY 14TH CENTURY

0   Miles   500

medieval period. The sails were used only for relieving the oarsmen when the wind was behind them. Voyages were made only during the spring and summer, for the hazards of storms and the extreme cold on the overcrowded, cramped ships prevented year-round sailing except on rare occasions when it could not be avoided. Commercial shipping out of Italian ports was confined to the Mediterranean itself until the early fourteenth century, when at last the Venetians inaugurated a service direct to Flanders and the north through the dangerous Bay of Biscay. The northern peoples, however, used the Baltic for trade between the Scandinavian countries, Germany, Flanders, France, and England. Goods imported from the East therefore had to be transferred in the Italian ports for overland transportation, and were stored in warehouses in the ports until such transportation was available.

OVERLAND TRANSPORTATION—ROADS AND RIVERS

It is difficult for us in these days of speedy freight by train, truck, and airplane to imagine the hardships to which a medieval trader had to submit. The invention in the early medieval period of an improved harness, which enabled a horse or mule to pull heavier loads, made vehicular transport possible; but it was still limited by the terrible roads, so that transportation by cart was used, as a rule, only for short hauls between towns in Europe, and not for long-distance haulage from the coast. The roads were full of holes, dusty or muddy according to the season, and had to go over high mountain passes from Italy into Europe. The tolls demanded by the lords through whose territory the roads passed were supposed to be spent on the upkeep of the roads; but the always penurious nobles usually had better uses for the money, and little of it probably found its way into road improvement. A conscientious lord was in no better position to collect tolls than a neglectful one if both were on a main route, since the territory had to be crossed whether the roads were in good or bad condition. The Cistercian

Brothers formed an honorable exception to the general rule, as the building of roads was considered by them and by the Church as an act of piety.

Since vehicular traffic was so difficult, by far the commonest form of transport was the pack train of mules and horses; but as each animal could carry only a very limited amount, it was natural that the chief goods transported would be luxuries, and equally natural that the journey by road should be confined to as short distances as possible. So the goods would be transshipped to the navigable rivers whenever there were any. In barges a far greater quantity could be carried with comparative ease, and for the flat-bottomed medieval boats, even for seagoing boats, rivers were navigable for very much greater distances than now. The navigable waterways were the real heart of European trade, as they are to some extent even today, since water transport remains so much cheaper than transport by land. Towns situated on rivers sprang into existence as trade grew; and it was to the interest of these towns to provide facilities for the traders in exchange for the tolls they collected, and to ensure protection for the traders insofar as it was in their power. As a rule, the towns made themselves responsible for the upkeep of the towpaths along which animals pulled the barges. But the lords through whose territory the rivers ran continued to exact tolls for their use without doing any service in return, and no authority was in a position to prevent this practice, though sometimes the lord took advantage of his position in a constructive manner by encouraging the growth of a town on his property, from which he could draw a more stable and regular income.

Many of the great French rivers, such as the Loire, Seine, and Garonne, became important waterways, fed by roads which left them at certain strategic places and dotted with towns, especially at transshipment points. Other towns grew up where there were important fords or bridges on the overland routes. The greatest concentration of towns was perhaps to be found at the mouth of the Rhine, the longest and most important waterway in Western Europe. These towns in Flanders, and later the Netherlands, were also seaports with a maritime trade with England and the Baltic, so that by the twelfth century they had become extremely important and already prosperous as import and export centers, as well as manufacturing centers, the headquarters of the cloth industry, as we shall see. The great German rivers also provided the Holy Roman Empire with a network of waterways, of which the towns were in later times to take full advantage.

THE NATURE OF OVERSEAS TRADE—THE BALANCE OF TRADE

With all the difficulty and expense of transportation it was to be expected that the goods transported through Europe from the East should be confined to luxuries whose weight and bulk were small in relation to the price obtained. Especially desired were the spices from the East—ginger, cloves, nutmegs, and, above all, pepper. These were used in far greater quantities than now by all who could afford them, to disguise, no doubt, the taste of the meat in the days before refrigeration, and to give some flavor other than salt to meat preserved by the only method known to medieval people. Other small and precious items were medicines, incense, dyestuffs, perfumes, and jewels. Larger items were the Oriental textile specialties such as satin, damask, muslin, gauze, and Oriental carpets, and luxury fruits such as the apricot, orange, and lemon. In late medieval times the West was first introduced to sugar cane, which could supplement honey, the only sweetening hitherto known. Papyrus was still imported from Egypt, since paper appeared only at the end of the medieval period and parchment was probably even more expensive than imported papyrus in spite of the cost of transportation.

In the early Middle Ages, Western Europeans had little enough to give in exchange for all these imports, and raw materials and primary products, which could ill be spared

in Europe itself, were the major export items, together with silver, new sources of which were discovered and exploited during this period. European wine, however, early became an important item of export, though more in European trade than abroad. But in the high Middle Ages the products of medieval craftsmen became known for their quality and were more than the equal of the best that the Orient could offer, especially in its declining days. Textiles of all kinds, but especially woolen and silken materials, tapestries, linen, and exquisite brocades were manufactured and exported, together with armor from central France and glass from Venice, as well as the staple raw materials from the north—lumber, hides, and furs. By the fourteenth century it is certain that the balance of trade was heavily in favor of the West, and gold and silver were shipped with ever greater frequency into Europe, helping the economy immeasurably even before the discovery of new sources in the New World.

OBSTACLES TO A MONEY ECONOMY

Coined money, however, for a long time remained extremely scarce, and very difficult to use for commerce until the close of the Middle Ages. Gold was hardly available at all until the thirteenth century, the only gold coins in use being Byzantine and Oriental. Silver was the generally accepted precious metal, but its use was hampered by the fact that hundreds of nobles had the right to coin it. They would stamp a value on a coin, but there was no guarantee whatever that the silver content would equal its face value, and there was every temptation for a noble to devalue coins to as low a silver content as he could get away with. Moreover those who received the coins could chip and clip them before handing them on. Wherever there was any large-scale exchange of goods, as at fairs and markets, it was absolutely essential to make use of the services of a money-changer, an expert who, for a consideration, could determine the gold or silver content of coins handed to him for valuation. Without the medieval money-changer there could have been no money economy at all, for it was impossible for any but the expert to know the value of a silver coin struck in the West. In the course of time kings and city governments managed to dispossess the nobles of their right to strike coins, and these larger powers thereafter guaranteed the silver and gold content. The Venetian ducat and the Florentine florin, both gold coins, became generally acceptable at face value, and greatly helped in the exchange of goods. But the kings were by no means above devaluing their own coins when short of cash, and they had difficulty in suppressing counterfeiting and the clipping of coins, which remained a profitable enterprise for centuries in spite of the severe punishments meted out to the counterfeiters by rulers if they were caught.

A medieval money-changer being carried away by Death, as in the picture of the Knight Templar shown in Chapter 11. From Hours of the Virgin, *ca. 1450.* (COURTESY THE PIERPONT MORGAN LIBRARY. Ms. 359, folio 144)

INTRA-EUROPEAN TRADE

The market

It has been explained in an earlier chapter that the bulk of the goods produced on the manors was consumed at home. The lord of the manor had his own land worked by the peasants, but as he had a large household to feed, the smaller manors had little surplus. But he also required payment in money from his peasants for many of their manorial dues, and the peasants on most

manors had only one place to go for money —the town. Likewise, if the lord had many manors and wanted to convert his surplus into cash for luxuries, he too had to patronize the town. Every town of any size therefore had a market, usually opened once a week, often, in earlier times, on Sundays, where the manors could send their surplus food to be sold in exchange for money. The townsmen also displayed their wares for the countryfolk, and supplied them with the few things they could afford.

The towns and their markets were always under the protection of some lord, or even the king, except in the case of the rare self-governing towns. The lord gave his permission for a regular market to be held in exchange for market dues paid to him. If the market was the center of a flourishing area with many manors, there would probably be enough surplus food, as well as agricultural raw materials such as flax, so that the merchant could buy in quantity for export. The markets therefore to some extent served as feeders for the export trade as well as centers for the exchange of agricultural and urban goods. The market day was always the most important commercial day of the week, as it still is in English and European towns even though the stores may be open every day for regular purchases. It is on market day that the countryfolk come to town to display and sell their produce directly in stalls, and often side by side with them the townsmen set up their stalls with special bargains, and sometimes especially cheap prices, to attract their rural customers.

The fairs

A market on a much larger scale was the international fair, held in some area where access was easy by either boat or road. Preparations for these fairs might take weeks while the goods were being assembled from all parts of the country, or indeed from many parts of Europe. Transactions were carried out on a considerable scale and needed many special arrangements. Certain lords took a keen interest in these fairs, since they could be made into an excellent source of income if handled honestly and with benefit to all concerned. The greatest European fairs during the twelfth and thirteenth centuries were those held in the plain of Champagne, under the patronage of the counts of Champagne, who were responsible for their management. Safe passage to the fair through the count's territories was guaranteed, and extended as far as possible beyond them. The Church also lent what protection it could. The fairs were under the management of a warden, with a considerable staff under him made up of weighers, measurers, porters, and such, and the fairs were well policed. A special seal of the fair was used to authenticate all purchases made by contract, and, of course, money-changers had to be present to facilitate trade between the participants from various countries with different monies. Moneylenders were also to be found for those who needed quick cash. Storage facilities were provided, and entertainment of all kinds, minstrels, jongleurs, dancers, clowns, and all other amusements which appealed to medieval people. Peasants were usually permitted to make at least one trip to the fairs by their manorial lords; even though they might lack money to make purchases, they could always enjoy themselves at small expense.

At the Champagne fairs different items were sold at different times: textiles, perhaps for two weeks; then leathers and furs for another two weeks; and then domestic animals. The fairs were also held in different seasons of the year at certain fair towns, so that the fair season in Champagne lasted the best part of the year, to the considerable advantage of the worthy count's purse. But the counts of Champagne always kept the dues to a reasonable rate, and their moderation ensured the long-continued success of the fairs in their county. When the king of France interfered at the beginning of the fourteenth century and raised the dues, it was no longer profitable for some of the merchants to display their goods, and the fairs rapidly declined in importance; but by then there were enough large towns where goods could be bought at all times of the

year for the fairs to be no longer the necessity that they had been in earlier times. Nevertheless, many fairs throughout Europe continued, some, such as the famous international fair of Leipzig, to this day. Industry fairs of the twentieth century, such as the British Industries Fair, and occasional large expositions, such as the New York World's Fair of the 1930's, are in the same tradition. The agricultural fairs still held regularly in nearly every state of the United States, by combining amusement and entertainment with business, carry on the medieval tradition.

▶ The rise of the towns

THE POSITION OF THE TOWNS IN THE EARLY MIDDLE AGES

After the fall of Rome and during the decline of the Carolingian Empire there were very few large towns, since the basis for their existence as centers of trade and industry had been lost in the centuries of semibarbarism. The manors were largely self-sufficient, and from most of them there was only a small surplus available for trade, far too little to support the needs of a whole group of specialized workers who would have formed the population of a town. Only a few nobles and higher clergy, with the produce of many manors to draw upon, could guarantee a regular supply of food and at the same time provide a market for the specialized wares of a town; and in those days of poor communications it would be essential to have a surplus regularly moving into a town, or for the townsmen themselves to spend a large part of their time in agriculture. In the earliest medieval towns we find, as a rule, both of these conditions fulfilled. A noble or a bishop with his entourage would live in a town and provide it with its market from the produce of their lands, and the workers themselves who lived there under his protection looked after some of their own food supply, while producing at the same time various specialized wares which could be exchanged for their additional needs. A very few continuously inhabited cities centered in strategic places on trade routes, where communications were relatively good, might be able to make their living from trade and industry alone, exchanging their products for agricultural goods drawn from fairly wide areas; but on the whole the vast majority were of the first kind, the seats of lords or bishops who provided the food and protection needed by the townsmen.

During the period of the invasions such centers of production would naturally attract marauders, for they provided more booty than isolated manors. It was necessary, therefore, that they be protected as efficiently as possible. Almost all medieval towns were to some extent fortified, and surrounded by a wall and moat; and many of them were actually founded during the invasions by great nobles who desired to protect as much of their property as possible, and at the same time to have enough resources within the town to enable it to withstand a siege, the only means of conquest available to the Vikings. Such towns, called burgs, were really enlarged castles, and the artisans were engaged primarily in manufacturing for defense needs. They might be serfs or freemen; but whatever their status they were completely dependent on the lord, whether he was a clergyman or a noble. The fortified nature of the towns and the walls surrounding them made their expansion very difficult. The houses were huddled together and the streets were necessarily narrow to take advantage of all the space available. Only when the invasions were over was it possible to add to them; but such expansion had to be outside the walls. And even when the large-scale invasions were at an end, there was still no secure peace. Thus we find in many medieval cities inner walls surrounding the old town, and then outer walls built in later days to protect the burg itself, and the *faubourg* (outside the burg) or suburbs. By the eleventh century, when the major invasions of the West were over, most European towns were of this kind, either a plain burg, or a burg and *faubourg*. Few of the inhabitants would be engaged full time in trade or manufacture; but the nucleus was there ready for expansion and increased specialization should conditions ever become suitable.

Óbidos, in Portugal, stands at the top of a hill overlooking a valley. Within the walls, which completely surround the village, live a few hundred people; their houses are only slightly modernized from medieval times. This is one of the two European cities which still possess their medieval walls intact (the other being Carcassonne).

THE TOWN AS A FREE CORPORATION

The escape from feudal servitude

The majority of European towns owed their very foundation to feudal lords or to the higher clergy As they began to grow, and especially as merchants engaged exclusively in trade, men who had been free for generations and had never been personally dependent upon feudal overlords, began to settle there permanently, it was natural that they should resent the disabilities placed upon them because the town itself was subordinate to these lords. They began to think themselves capable of making their own defense without calling upon their lord; and yet within the city the lord had certain traditional rights of collecting tolls and rents which seriously interfered with the merchants' freedom and ability to make profits. Lords, in other words, ceased to be worth their keep, from the townsmen's point of view, and at the same time, as their demands for money and luxuries increased, especially after the Crusades, they tended to try to milk the burghers or townsmen for more, while their actual services to them grew less.

So we find from as early as the end of the eleventh century onward efforts made by towns throughout Europe to escape from the galling restrictions of an earlier age. It was not difficult for the burghers to recognize their strong position against the aristocracy. The lords possessed military power and they had the old feudal law on their side. On the other hand, if they used this military power they would destroy the source of their income. They needed regular income, not one single great looting followed by nothing. If they destroyed a town, they would have to rebuild it afterward or forgo their income. If traders refused to trade because conditions were made too onerous, then likewise no tolls could be collected. Most independent lords in these circumstances found it better to compromise with their towns, and draw up a charter stating exactly what the towns had to do for them, what rents and tolls had to be paid, what

scutage or commutation of military service had to be paid, what hospitality and similar feudal services were owed, thus saving themselves from possible total loss if the town fought for and was able to secure complete independence in spite of the theoretical rights of the nobility.

Very great lords, and kings, not being dependent in the same way upon their income from any particular town, could hold out against the demands of the towns and could even afford to inflict punishment upon them. On the other hand, these great lords could provide them with more efficient protection and were thus worth more of what they cost the burghers than was the smaller lord. So we find that in countries where there was an efficient central government under a king the towns maintained only a limited independence and usually did not have their rights confirmed by charters. This was the case with England, and with France after the thirteenth century, where indeed many towns lost their charters after the king had established his supremacy over the whole country. On the other hand, the Italian and German burghers, living in countries where the official ruler exercised only sporadic and never very efficient control, were able to secure and maintain their independence far more effectively. As we have seen, the northern Italian towns united in a league were able to defeat and force concessions out of even such a powerful ruler as Frederic Barbarossa, the Holy Roman Emperor, and were also able to hold their own against his grandson Frederic II.

It was not only the Lombard League which had to fight for its freedom. Throughout Europe many of the higher clergy and the nobility refused to accept the inevitable peacefully, and resisted the rising power of the bourgeoisie with all the force at their disposal. Perhaps the class of people most difficult to handle, from the point of view of the towns, were the simoniacal clergy who had bought their offices, expecting them to carry the overlordship of at least the town in which the bishop had his seat, a bishop who had possibly gone into debt to buy the office and had to repay it from his revenues. Faced with resistance, he could not afford to wait. He could not pass his office on to his children, and, unlike a feudal lord, he had no real proprietorship. But he could always command ecclesiastical sanctions and excommunicate the townsmen, and he would often be backed by the papacy (though not the reformed papacy of the eleventh century, which used the townsmen against the simoniacal clergy). Though the Church did not approve of townsmen, and in particular distrusted their search for profits instead of sanctity and salvation, and was well aware that the atmosphere of a town was not one in which religion was likely to flourish, nevertheless it often had to make use of them against the nobility. So we know of many instances where the town had to fight hard against the bishop and his hired mercenaries, and cases where a victorious bishop looted his own town are not unknown.

The townsmen were often assisted by the division of jurisdiction between the various lords who claimed rights in it—perhaps a king, a count, a bishop, and a smaller lord who was in possession and owned the castle. Such a town was the northern French city of Amiens. In other cases the town was divided into fiefs belonging to several different nobles. It was possible in these circumstances for the townsmen to play one lord against the other, and throw their effective and probably decisive support to the power which was willing to give them their freedom on the best terms.

In the short run, therefore, it can be seen that everything was in favor of the town as against the nobility; in the long run the rise of central governments and national states was likely to doom their independence. They were too weak to stand against a king with all the resources he could command, even from the other cities in his country, their rivals, who would often enough be glad to see them weakened. But for a time there was a real revival of civilization in Europe, especially in Italy and Germany, based upon the growth of city-states. And Italian experience and inventiveness in these states were to prepare the groundwork for the whole of Western commercial and industrial supremacy, which ultimately, under monarchical national governments, was to produce our modern commercial and industrial civilization.

Noble initiative in the foundation of towns—Effect on manorial system

As the feudal lords felt the pressure of an increasing need for money, two methods of increasing their income presented themselves for consideration, both severely disruptive of the old static order, but both promising rich rewards. Here again the Crusades accelerated the process, for the crusading lord needed cash to pay for transportation to the Holy Land, and if he returned safely he had probably acquired a new taste for Oriental luxuries. If, therefore, he possessed a manor which had a suitable strategic position, he could encourage the expansion of the manorial village into a town by establishing a market and allowing his artisans to specialize in some useful and valuable production. From this increased production and from the market he could draw increased revenues at the cost of permitting some measure of freedom to the workers and setting up a center to which his own serfs would hope to go to earn their freedom. He could also bring under cultivation some of his waste swamp or forest land, of which there was an enormous surplus in early medieval times. But to attract workers for this difficult task he could not impose upon them the same disabilities under which his own serfs labored. It was not possible for him to reduce freemen to serfs for the purpose, or nothing would be accomplished. The only method open to him was to give the pioneers a real share in the proceeds of the new territories. Thus came into existence the system of *hôtes,* as the French called them, free peasant proprietors who paid to the lord the equivalent of rent, who were allowed to keep the proceeds of their labor in exchange for the payment of fixed and definite sums of money. The produce of these new lands was naturally sold in the town markets for cash, thus ensuring an increased supply of food for the towns and at the same time contributing to their growth.

Finally, this development also had its effects on the servile system on the old, established manors. There was a constant demand for men and women in the cities. Thus the city authorities tended to extend protection to escaped serfs until they had gained their freedom legally by staying away from their manors for a year and a day. Moreover, as the lords themselves gave privileges to workers on their newly cultivated territories, they found it difficult to enforce the old restrictions on their manors which had been in cultivation for centuries. Over a long period of time in most parts of Europe we find the serf gradually losing his official disabilities, and becoming in effect a small peasant proprietor or tenant or, more probably, a sharecropper, still hampered, it is true, by many restrictions and payments such as the *banalités*, but at least no longer subject to the lord's will in everything, now able to marry and leave the land at will, able to dispose of his own personal property, and able to sell his goods as he wished provided he paid his dues.

Thus the rise of the towns and the decline of the older manorial system reacted upon each other to the general benefit of the lower classes in society, and seriously undermined the primitive feudal system itself.

The government of a commune

Self-governing towns, with or without a charter, are usually called *communes*. The essential element in a commune was its right to be treated as a whole, a corporation, as distinct from its constituent members. The town as a whole undertook obligations toward the lords, and received privileges in return, thus making a distinct break from feudal traditions, where obligations were always binding upon individual persons and not on groups. In order that the town could fulfill these obligations it had to be self-governing, assessing taxes and duties upon

its citizens and paying them in a lump sum to the lord; and though its independence might be limited by the terms of its charter and it thus might not have full control of its foreign relations, within the city itself the governments were substantially autonomous. And when the charter could not be easily enforced, as in the cities of northern Italy, they became for all practical purposes city-states not unlike those of the ancient world. We have seen that when Frederic II (1197–1250), wished to enforce the Peace of Constance (1183), which defined the rights of the Holy Roman Emperor, he had to go to war for the purpose, since the cities had grown accustomed to performing no duties while the imperial throne had been in dispute during the reign of Pope Innocent III (1198–1216).

The towns, as self-governing units, were substantially outside the feudal system, and refused to recognize feudal law or customs as operative within them. The needs of a trading and manufacturing community being entirely different from those of the feudal nobility, the towns developed a much more equitable law which took better account of evidence and was naturally especially concerned with the sanctity and enforcement of contracts. This law, which was close to Roman practice and to some extent influenced by Roman law, was called the *law merchant*.

The government of the towns varied in different parts of Europe; almost the only generalization that can be safely made is that the richer merchants usually had effective control, unless the town was still ruled by its hereditary feudal aristocracy. The commonest early form of government was by a board of elected magistrates, who in time relinquished part of their duties to one or more executive officers, called *consuls* in Italy and southern France, and *aldermen* in England. The Venetian republic remained an oligarchy for centuries, headed by an elected official, the Doge, or Duke. In several Italian towns the violence of party politics within the government resulted in the substitution of government by a manager, a *podesta,* who was appointed, as a rule, from another city, and who was supposed to keep the rival factions in order. Several notable Italians became *podeste* in many different cities during their lifetime, becoming a kind of small professional class of municipal officials. Elsewhere the chief executives of the towns, called *mayors* in England and France and *burgermeisters* in Germany and Flanders, continued to rule with their councils and were eligible for re-election. As early as the twelfth century, efforts were made by the lower classes to take away the monopoly of power from the richer merchants, who were able to use it tyrannically in the interests of their class, and at one time the commune of Milan was ruled briefly by a kind of trade union of workers; but none of these efforts was permanently successful, and it was the individual despot, merchant, or feudal prince, or some adventurer who replaced the city governments with one-man rule, instead of the power of the oligarchy becoming more widely based and democratic.

Intercity rivalry, and factional strife in the cities

The towns in northern Italy competed against each other and were not hesitant about engaging in war in order to get the better of their rivals. Moreover, within the cities were parties which originally had supported the pretensions of the emperors (Ghibellines) as against those who favored the papacy (Guelphs), but who continued to contend under the same names even when the emperors as such had ceased to play any part in Italian affairs. Only rarely did they unite against a common enemy, as against the two emperors, Frederic I and Frederic II; and even then not all the cities were included in the anti-imperial alliance. In each city also there was a substantial minority always in favor of collaboration. So we see in the independent cities of northern Italy the same disruptive influences, treachery, intercity warfare, and virulent party politics that had existed in ancient Greece and had prevented unification of that country except

by external force. But medieval Italy never found its Philip of Macedon, and submitted instead to smaller despots under whom some of the cities attained remarkable heights of culture, especially Florence under the banker princes the Medici. When trade shifted to the Atlantic seaboard in the sixteenth century the Italian towns sank into a lethargy, and their political system became a network of duchies, in which they remained till stirred from it by Napoleon and nineteenth-century liberal nationalism.

Physical features of the medieval town

A medieval town, surrounded by its walls, with suburbs huddling close under them, was a crowded, unsanitary place, only rarely separated from its rural origins, with pigs wandering around the streets, performing the functions of garbage disposal units, and cows and horses often kept in sheds adjoining the houses. Refuse was thrown from the upper stories of the houses onto the streets, to be flushed only by the next rain. It is hardly necessary to add that plagues and epidemics were common; and as most of the houses were made of wood, fire hazards were serious. The streets were narrow, and the upper stories of the houses often projected so far that they almost met across the street. Each city had gates which could be shut in case of attack, and where customs duties could be collected. And, like a medieval castle, the typical city was surrounded with a moat which could only be crossed by a drawbridge. To us these medieval towns, of which many still exist without any very great change as the nucleus of the much larger modern town on the same site, look picturesque; and they were certainly bustling, vital centers of activity, as full of humanity as our own slum areas.

In the larger towns, however, several improvements were made, even within the medieval period. A few adopted regular methods of street cleaning, there were some with good public baths and a pure water supply, and by the late Middle Ages many of the cities had started to build sidewalks made of great paving stones embedded in sand. And in every city of importance there were some good buildings other than the church, more attractive areas where the merchant princes lived in their fortress palaces, and some imposing public buildings, especially in Italy and in the prosperous cities of Flanders.

Population of medieval towns

Estimates of population vary very widely, and there can be no certainty on the figures. By the middle of the thirteenth century, after the destruction of Kiev by the Mongols, there can be no doubt that Palermo, the capital of the Sicilian kingdom, was the largest and most populous city in Europe after Constantinople, with a population estimated as not much short of half a million. Paris was the next, but with considerably less than half the population of Palermo, though it grew tremendously through the century and was perhaps a quarter of a million by its close. Venice probably came third, with a population of not much less than Paris. Probably no other city in Europe reached one hundred thousand, and the average city that could be called large had about fifty thousand. But these figures

A medieval corner of Nürnberg (Germany). (COURTESY GERMAN TOURIST INFORMATION OFFICE)

Medieval section of the imperial city of Nördlingen. Note the similarity of this setting to the houses shown in the medieval miniatures in Chapter 17. (COURTESY GERMAN TOURIST INFORMATION OFFICE)

are still large when the area occupied by a city is considered, for such a population was only made possible through overcrowding and by building the houses as high as, and often higher than, safety permitted.

LEAGUES OF TOWNS

The Lombard League

We have already had occasion to refer to the Lombard League, which was formed to resist the demands and encroachments of the Holy Roman Empire. This league, however, made up as it was of so many rival and constantly quarreling towns with divergent

interests, never became a permanent institution. As soon as the immediate purpose for its existence had disappeared, the league split up into its component parts. The reason for this was the sporadic nature of imperial efforts to keep Italy in subjection. When the emperor and his troops had disappeared over the Alps, the spirit of independence at once revived, and with it the intercity rivalry. But in Germany, where the emperor lived and exercised a rule which was more frequently effective than in Italy, a league came into being, originally for solely commercial purposes. This league was able to develop a real unity which lasted, in spite of local rivalry, for centuries, and probably exercised at all times a more important influence than the emperor himself. This was the league of Hansa towns, usually known as the Hanseatic League.

The Hanseatic League

Quite early in the Middle Ages various groups of merchants engaged in the import and export business from various cities used to unite for the purpose of putting pressure upon various political authorities to gain trading and economic privileges for their class, as, for instance, at the Champagne fairs, and in foreign ports. A subsidiary purpose was to restrict the entry of outsiders into their privileged group. These leagues, called *Hansas*, were essentially made up of

Traces of medieval architecture are still apparent in Lüneburg, which was one of the principal cities in the Hanseatic League. (COURTESY GERMAN TOURIST INFORMATION OFFICE)

individual merchants, and could not expect adequate protection for their special interests from their own city governments.

From the thirteenth century onward, German merchants belonging to a number of important trading cities banded together seriously to obtain concessions by joint action in foreign countries, especially in England, Flanders, and the Scandinavian countries at a time when Germans were also expanding politically into the Slavic countries to the northeast under the auspices of the Teutonic Knights (see Chapter 15, above). Being financially far more secure than ordinary merchants, able to extend credit even to kings, and in possession of a number of products that could not be obtained easily elsewhere and were in great demand, the Hansa merchants were found extremely useful by European rulers and were given special quarters and monopolies in the trading of many kinds of goods by these rulers, even to the detriment of their own nationals. Groups of merchants (Hansas) used to live in these foreign countries, where they proceeded to organize monopolies, even defending themselves against occasional risings by the local peoples. They had their own laws and their own courts. As time went on, these merchants were able to arrange for governments by their own class in their home cities, which they completely controlled, again against frequent opposition from the craft guilds in these cities which resented their ability to dictate prices and conditions of labor through their political power.

The league of merchant cities thus formed never had any formal rules or constitution as such, though congresses were held when necessary to discuss joint problems. The league even went to war for economic purposes on several occasions, using the militia of the Hansa towns and mercenaries, whom they could well afford to pay. By the middle of the fourteenth century almost two hundred towns and villages were directly associated with the League, and Hansa merchants had almost a monopoly of the rich Baltic trade, including trade into northern Russia, and controlled much

of the important wool trade between England and Flanders. Their great financial power in an age of small concentration of capital was their principal strength, and no European ruler could afford to antagonize them. When the king of Denmark in the fourteenth century tried to break their monopoly in the Baltic and take possession of his own herring trade, the league took to arms, and with the aid of the king of Sweden thoroughly defeated him and dictated a peace on terms extremely favorable to itself.

The league endured for several centuries, but it was on the decline by the middle of the. fifteenth. The leadership was always in the hands of the chief city Lübeck, and this was resented by the second greatest city, Cologne, which at one time tried to organize a separatist league of its own. It was impossible to prevent other minor rivalries from growing up between the several cities, and naturally the excluded groups, such as the English and Dutch merchants, struggled against them, especially since the Hansa towns did not even trouble to give reciprocal privileges in their own cities to nationals of the countries where they were installed. The growing realization of the importance of trade to the economy of their countries tempted the monarchs ultimately to try conclusions with the league, and alternative routes for transportation which did not pass through Hansa territories were organized.

It was, of course, impossible in an era of increasing trade for any group permanently to maintain a trade monopoly of this kind over such a wide area, and perhaps it is surprising that the league lasted as long as it did. In any case the discovery of the Americas and so many new sources of trade would have doomed the league even if it had not already been steeply on the decline. Perhaps one continuing result of its success can still be seen in Europe. The Germans to this day are far more fond than any other people of cartels with which they have had a greater success; and the industrial cartel of the nineteenth and twentieth centuries would seem to be a direct descendant of the

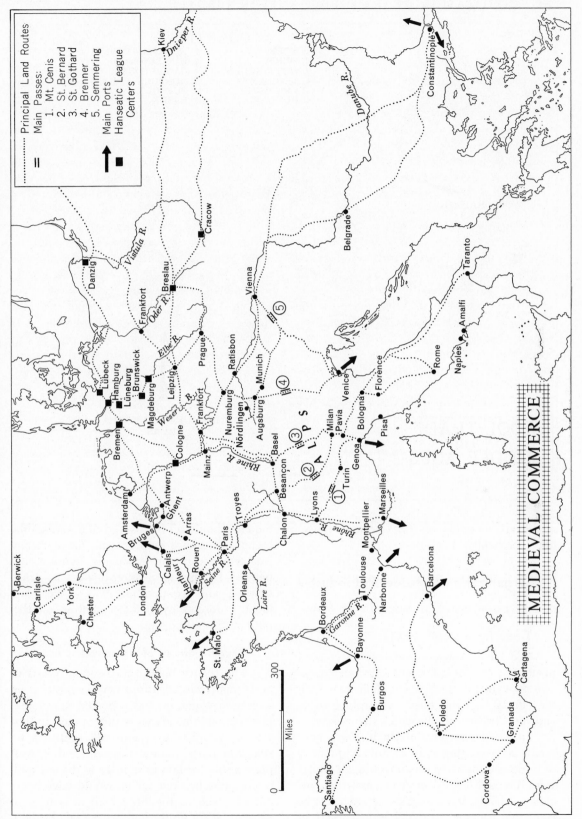

MEDIEVAL COMMERCE

Principal Land Routes
Main Passes:
1. Mt. Cenis
2. St. Bernard
3. St. Gothard
4. Brenner
5. Semmering
Main Ports
Hanseatic League
Centers

Kiev
Dnieper R.
Cracow
Danzig
Vistula R.
Breslau
Frankfort
Oder R.
Lübeck
Hamburg
Brunswick
Lüneburg
Magdeburg
Leipzig
Elbe R.
Bremen
Weser R.
Prague
Cologne
Nuremburg
Frankfort
Ratisbon
R.
Nördlingen
Mainz
Augsburg
Munich
Antwerp
Rhine R.
Basel
Ghent
Amsterdam
Besançon
Arras
Bruges
Troyes
Lyons
Calais
Paris
Chalon
Rhône R.
Berwick
Carlisle
York
Chester
London
Rouen
Orleans
Seine R.
Loire R.
St. Malo
Hatfleur
Bordeaux
Garonne R.
Toulouse
Bayonne
Narbonne
Montpellier
Marseilles
Barcelona
Santiago
Burgos
Toledo
Cordova
Granada
Cartagena

Danube R.
Constantinople
Belgrade
Vienna
Taranto
Amalfi
Naples
Rome
Florence
Pisa
Bologna
Venice
Milan
Pavia
Genoa
Turin

A L P S
① ② ③ ④ ⑤

300
Miles
0

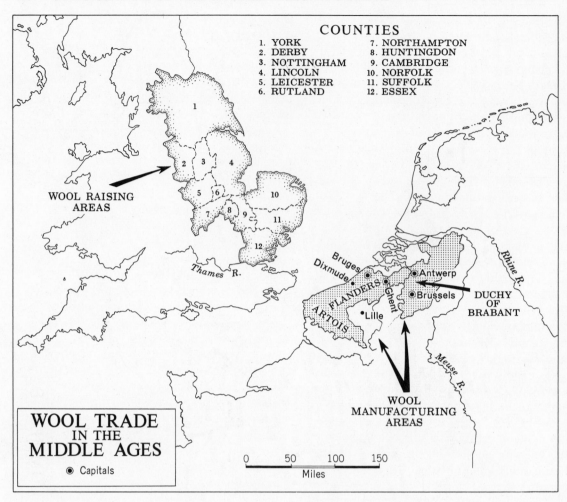

COUNTIES

1. YORK
2. DERBY
3. NOTTINGHAM
4. LINCOLN
5. LEICESTER
6. RUTLAND
7. NORTHAMPTON
8. HUNTINGDON
9. CAMBRIDGE
10. NORFOLK
11. SUFFOLK
12. ESSEX

WOOL RAISING AREAS

WOOL MANUFACTURING AREAS

DUCHY OF BRABANT

WOOL TRADE IN THE MIDDLE AGES

⊙ Capitals

medieval monopoly of the German Hanseatic merchants.

▶ Organization of trade and industry

OBJECTIVES OF MEDIEVAL ORGANIZATION

Trade for a static society

We have now examined an attempted monopoly of foreign trade over an extensive area. In this section we shall deal with the efforts at monopolistic control of trade and industry within the cities themselves.

In a static society in which it was generally believed that only a limited quantity of trade and industry was possible, all efforts were directed toward ensuring first that foreigners should have as little share of it as could be managed, and that the workers in the city should all be assured of a reasonable living and secure employment. Competition was frowned upon, especially unfair competition by means of such devices as price cutting, and cooperation was rather the ideal, enforced by strict regulation on the part of the authorities.

Church defense of a controlled economy

The theory behind the system was that every man was born to a certain position in society in which he was expected to remain. His economic needs were determined by his status. A noble was naturally entitled to consume more than a peasant, and it was permissible for him to indulge in display and to consume luxuries which would have been out of place in the life of an artisan or a peasant. If the latter had aspirations beyond their station, then it was likely that these were dictated by envy or pride, deadly sins condemned by the Church and society. If the common man had a desire for luxury or display, he must be actuated by some form of sensuality, another sin. If he simply wished to accumulate wealth, then he was motivated by avarice; or if he wished to consume too many of the good things of life, then he was a glutton. Finally, if he wished to save enough money for a comfortable old age, then he was slothful and lazy; he wished to avoid work, and this desire, too, was a deadly sin. In view of such restrictions, it was clear that public and ecclesiastical opinion would condemn any enterprise undertaken by the poor and lowborn man for the sake of profit. It was certainly not considered in the Middle Ages that the appetite for gain was a natural principle of human nature, nor that enlightened self-interest was a virtue. Life on earth, in any case, according to the teachings of the Church, should not be too pleasurable; the proper task of man was to prepare for the hereafter and endure whatever came to him in this life without expecting too much of it. Work was a consequence of the sin of Adam. Before the Fall, Adam and Eve had been permitted to live a lazy life in Paradise, but when they were driven out of the Garden of Eden, the Lord God had told the guilty pair that they would have to live by hard work. But the Middle Ages never regarded work as anything but a curse; it was left for the Protestants to glorify work and even write a hymn, every line of which begins with the word "work," concluding with the deathless line, "Work for the night is coming when man works no more!"

The Church likewise objected to the making of profits by merchants, unless the profits were a payment for work honestly performed such as the legitimate charge made for the transportation of goods. Like Karl Marx, the Church held a labor theory of value. The cost of an article plus a reasonable wage was all that the merchant was entitled to. Thus it was possible to calculate a fair and just price for every piece of merchandise. Any price fixed above this was profiteering. It was particularly reprehensible to engross, or try to corner the market, since the increased price represented no honest labor; the practice was morally evil in that it meant taking advantage of the necessities of poor men and charging them highly because the goods which they needed had been made artificially scarce. Forestalling was a similar crime; this was the practice of buying up goods from the peasant before they reached the market, and for the same purpose of pushing up prices. Even coming between the producer and the consumer unnecessarily and buying and selling at a profit was considered wrong, unless there was an obvious need for a middleman's service. The practice was called *regrating*.

Lending money at interest had always been considered wicked by Christians because money was supposed to be sterile, having no value in itself; and, further, to take money for helping others when such a service should be provided free was contrary to Scripture. It was taking advantage of the poor; and indeed, since loans for consumption purposes—the type of borrowing a poor man usually does—were poorly secured, the interest rates for consumer credit were high then, as now. In the early Middle Ages, since it was impossible to do without some form of consumer credit, this business was in the hands of Jews, who were, of course, not bound by ecclesiastical regulations, and who were prevented by various restrictions from making a living in other fields. All lending of money was called usury, whether for high or low rates of interest, and was considered sinful. Secular and clerical authorities constantly condemned and attempted to regulate it. But in an age of growing capitalism it was found impossible to maintain all the artificial restrictions which were suited to a static society. For several centuries, however, the guilds followed faithfully the rules laid down by the Church, with which, indeed, they were fully in sympathy, since they prevented one man from taking unfair advantage of his fellows with consequent unemployment.

THE MERCHANT GUILDS

The earliest form of organization within the towns was the merchant guild, or guild merchant. This was originally a union of merchants and traders, including also the upper class of artisans; and its purpose was to prevent foreign competition and to divide up the home trade equitably between the members. In some cases the merchant guild came into existence before a town even had a charter, and, indeed, it was often the guild which succeeded in extracting the charter from the overlord of the town; in many towns the guild became the actual municipal government afterward. The merchant guild, like the later craft guild, was a closed shop; traders who did not belong to the guild would find themselves excluded from trade within the city.

At the same time it was in the nature also of a fraternal society, taking care of the funerals and other sudden expenses of members, and for a long time it worked closely in conjunction with the Church in other matters, making its own penalties against members who forestalled and engrossed and seeing to it that the widows of deceased members were properly treated, and that prayers were said for the souls of the departed.

The monopolies held in trade matters varied from town to town. Reciprocal privileges could be granted to foreign traders when they seemed to be in the interest of the guild, but severe penalties were always enforced against price cutters; and it was possible to enforce penalties because exclusion from a guild in early times would mean that the offending trader lost his business. And cases are known of the assaulting and beating of offenders.

One interesting example of guild activity is the arrangement made for the export of English wool, which was grown in England and sent abroad to Flanders to be made into cloth. An organization came into existence to collect the wool and ship it to France, where it was stored in the city of Calais, which belonged to the English until the sixteenth century. The ships in which the wool was carried were owned jointly by members of the guild, though each man traded for himself in the collection and distribution of the wool. Such organizations were greatly favored by the English kings, who were able to tax the wool far more easily than if hundreds of separate traders had to be assessed or hundreds of shipments examined. The Merchants Staplers flourished for almost three centuries, until the wool trade declined at the end of the fifteenth century.

As has been said, the early merchant guilds included also representatives of the manufacturers, the crafts. But these soon split off and formed their own analogous associations which will be dealt with in the next section. Thereafter the merchant guilds acted as selling agents for the craft guilds. They always remained both more powerful and more prosperous than the much smaller craft guilds, and it was almost always the merchant guilds rather than the craftsmen which were able to control the government of the town. But by the same token, the merchant guilds declined long before the craft guilds, since with the increase in their trade the individual merchants preferred to carry on business for themselves and compete with their former colleagues, and restrictions were far more hampering to trade than to small-scale manufacture.

Merchant guilds today are common in the Far East, especially among Chinese merchants in such cities as Singapore, where the trade is largely in Chinese hands although the government is alien. All major trading in foreign imports is in the hands of rings, or guilds, and interlopers are forced to be content with relatively small sales. In the West, however, with the increase in the importance of manufacturing, associations of traders alone have only rarely any useful function to perform, though some of the activities such as price fixing are still attempted. It is in foreign markets that the guild still survives under various forms.

Purpose and function

The craft guild was an organization formed to protect the working conditions in a particular industry and also to protect the public. Not all industries were formed into guilds, and the guild organization was not uniform throughout Europe, being strongest in the German and northern towns and weakest in Italy. The regulations of the craft guild were very rigid and very strictly enforced, but always with the same objectives in mind and logically worked out to attain them.

The product had to be sold at a just price, which included the cost of labor and raw materials. It is clear that if any artisan skimped on his material, used inferior workmanship, or cut wages, then the resulting product would be priced too high in relation to its actual value if the price were the same as for goods of standard quality; and of course price cutting was strictly forbidden. Regulations as to the standard of quality were set up by the guild masters in each guild, since only these experts could determine what was the correct quality in their particular craft.

Hours of labor were prescribed and enforced. Nightwork was, as a rule, entirely forbidden, both because it tended to spoil the quality of the work and because the worker who labored for additional hours would in this way be able to get ahead of his neighbors. If one group of workers did overtime, it was clear to the medievals that others would have to do the same, in the same way that one price cutter would force all others to cut their prices too. Improved methods of manufacture were not regarded kindly if introduced by individual craftsmen; it was therefore usual to insist that any such improvements should be agreed to by the guild, which would have the opportunity of spreading the information among all its members.

Advertising of all kinds was forbidden. No salesman could draw attention to his wares in any manner whatever; even a diplomatic sneeze when a customer passed was considered improper and in one place forbidden. Craftsmen had to do their work in shops which were visible from the street so that their practices were at all times open to inspection. Shops were limited in size so that no master could become a regular employer of labor, and thus drive down his costs and perhaps cut prices; and it was forbidden also to attempt to entice away workers from a rival shop.

In brief, the central ideas of the craft guilds were that there was enough work for all if everyone worked for reasonable hours and produced goods of first-rate quality; that every article had a fair price which customers should be able to pay; that the customer who paid this fixed price should be protected from his probable ignorance of the quality of his purchase; and that there was no need to cut this price, since everyone would suffer, and in a limited market no increased business for all would result.

The guilds died very slowly; indeed, some are still in existence today with comparatively small modifications. Their usefulness was impaired when it was discovered that the market was not so limited as had been once thought, and that more goods could in fact be sold if the price were reduced. The guild system was fitted for a truly static society, and unquestionably prevented the terrible abuses which occurred in the early factory system under the Industrial Revolution. Conditions for the medieval worker were incomparably better than those in the early nineteenth century. His living was secured, he did not have to compete for jobs with his fellow workers, and there was a far closer personal relationship between an apprentice and a journeyman and their master than the simple cash nexus of the pay envelope under the industrial system. He did not have to work long hours, and he did not have to work overtime; nor did his wife and family have to aid in the work in order to secure a living wage for the family unit, as in the early nineteenth century.

Moreover, the guild itself was a fraternal society with many social functions to perform. The guilds produced plays, they organized processions on days of festivals, and on the feast day of the saint of a particular guild the latter usually had a colorful pageant. They had fraternal drinking parties, sometimes held in a building of their own, a guildhall. If a guildsman fell sick or died, his fellow members took care of him or paid the expenses of the funeral and tried to assist his widow and family. When a member got into trouble with the law, the guild was expected to defend him and even visit him in jail, and cases between members were settled by arbitration within the guild rather than in the public court. Insults offered to fellow members were punished with fines assessed by the guild.

The guild was able to protect the interests of its members only because of its restraint of competition and the consequence that a price could be fixed which would cover expenses with a sufficient margin. Only when competition can be restrained in this way and when desire or possibility is lacking to increase one's own business at the expense of one's neighbors can a guild of the medieval kind flourish. Unfair practices in later centuries within the guild, refusal to allow qualified journeymen to become masters, and competition between these journeymen and the established masters, with consequent price cutting, helped to break down their organization. But above all the realization that the market was not limited, and the growth of competition and price cutting, undermined them even before the Industrial Revolution which gave most of them the *coup de grâce*. Trade unions to-

The Cloth Hall of Ypres (Belgium), one of the most perfect examples of a medieval commercial building. The hall was destroyed during World War I. (COURTESY BELGIUM GOVERNMENT INFORMATION CENTER)

day still use, however, many guild practices, and their use is increasing even in America, where certain commodities can be sold at a fixed price which allows the unions to demand and receive fraternal benefits paid by the corporations that employ them. And the apprentice system, about to be described, is still applicable in many industries which require skills that can only be acquired over an extended period, although the system itself has naturally been modified to meet conditions brought about by the Industrial Revolution.

Internal organization of the craft guild

The young artisan first entered the guild by becoming apprentice to a master, on payment of a fee. The apprenticeship might last for as long as twelve years according to the nature of the particular craft; the usual period for most crafts was seven years. The boy, however, became an apprentice, when his family signed an indenture. It was the master's task to supervise the boy's morals and behavior as well as his work. He boarded at his master's home, and had to obey his orders in everything. When the apprenticeship was over and the boy was thoroughly trained in his craft, he became a journeyman (dayworker) and was free to leave his master and take work at regular wages wherever he could find it. He could stay on with his master, and perhaps it was the usual custom in early times for him to do so. But in certain trades, especially the building trade, it was of great advantage for the journeyman to work in foreign cities, improving his knowledge of his trade by examining or taking part in the building of churches, cathedrals, and public offices.

In the early Middle Ages, there was no difficulty in the way of a journeyman who wanted to set up himself as a master. While business was gradually increasing there was enough work for all, and the guild had no objections, provided the journeyman had sufficient savings to enable him to purchase the shop and the raw materials and had a wife who could take care of his apprentices. He had to pass an examination before the guild master (or warden), demonstrating his efficiency and his good character and financial standing. The former, however, would be well known from his work as apprentice or journeyman if he remained in the same town. Foreign journeymen were sometimes admitted as masters in early times, though in later times, when the market had become saturated, this practice was abandoned.

All artisans were theoretically members of the guild, though apprentices could not take part in elections or in the management of the guild until they became journeymen. In later times journeymen were also excluded, leaving the guild a monopoly of the masters. As trade increased, and with the decline of serfdom, it was increasingly difficult to maintain the monopoly, but for a long time the masters attempted to maintain it by every means at their disposal. Probably before the middle of the fourteenth century, members of the guilds, apprentices, and journeymen had not felt the guild as a restriction upon their freedom, since there really was enough work for all at a fair price, and an apprentice could look forward to a secure future and ultimately a mastership in his chosen craft. But from this time the situation changed seriously for the worse, and the monopolies had to be broken down if any freedom and security were to be achieved.

The masters had gradually realized the extensive power that had been put into their hands by the system, and with the growing freedom of enterprise and the larger profits gained by the capitalist merchants, the masters evidently felt they should also be entitled to similar rewards, if not through the exercise of increased initiative. They began to try to limit the entries of masters into their respective industries and to keep apprentices and journeymen as their employees whom they could exploit for profit. An ingenious system was invented under which a journeyman had to produce a masterpiece approved by the guild of masters before he could set up for himself, an excellent opportunity for the use of discrimination.[1] The masters began to hand over their businesses only to their sons, and to wait until they were grown up, whether or not they were as skilled as the available journeymen. The masters also used economic pressure against the journeymen by keeping their wages down so that they would not have enough capital to start their own shops. And as the numbers of journeymen increased, it was possible to use the shortage of jobs for this purpose. The masters also charged substantial fees for the privilege of becoming masters, whereas in the earlier days only the capital required for the business was asked of a newcomer. Even among the masters themselves distinctions began to be drawn between wealthy and less wealthy members, and masters of the lower rank were excluded from some of the guild functions, and sometimes had to work for the richer masters not unlike the ordinary journeymen.

The result was inevitable. The journeymen, who were usually just as skilled as the masters, began to band together into journeymen's societies apart from the guild, and set up shops of their own where they could compete with the masters and cut prices. Though in cities where they possessed it the masters used their control of the government to legislate against the journeymen, they were unable to suppress them everywhere. Strikes by journeymen wage earners also became common. But the richer masters were by this time securely entrenched, and having accumulated capital, many of them entered into associations for the promotion of exports similar to the organizations of the merchant guilds. They bought raw materials and had them worked up into export goods by the lesser masters and journeymen. Thus the manufacturing system gradually became capitalistic in the modern manner, and apprentices and journeymen and masters became merely distinguished by their degrees of skill and the wages they could command

[1] The plot of Wagner's opera *The Mastersingers of Nuremberg* is concerned with the production of a "song-masterpiece" in accordance with guild regulations for song writers, the intricacies of which are unknown to the hero of the opera.

for their skill. The guilds, as such, had lost their original purpose; they served to regulate conditions for the apprenticeship, and to some extent could still ensure standards of workmanship. But with the rise of competition the temptation to cut corners, and to debase the standards of craftsmanship and thus sell at a lower price, became irresistible; and with this the monopolistic structure of the guilds could no longer be maintained. Capitalism in industry caught up with capitalism in trade, and the way was open for the Industrial Revolution.

▶ ## The rise of medieval capitalism

BREAKDOWN OF CONTROL OVER
PROFIT SEEKING

From the above discussion it will be seen that the possibility of making profits, as distinct from commanding a living wage in exchange for one's labor, was present from the early thirteenth century in the merchant guilds, and rather later in the craft guilds. But first the social and religious control over the economy had to be broken, and enough money had to be available, or suitable substitutes for coined money developed, so that it would be worth while for the private enterpriser to go ahead and seek profits and the higher standard of living that resulted from profit making. The individual merchant had to escape from the restrictions of the guild merchant, and the individual master had to escape from the necessity of sharing any advances he made with his fellow guild members.

Severe competition among individual traders led naturally to efforts to avoid the traditional cooperation. But few could individually afford, for instance, the cost of a voyage to the Near East, and survive the long wait for financial returns. It was possible for a few traders to get together and plan a joint voyage by pooling their resources. But even this arrangement was difficult unless credit could be acquired. And credit came up at once against the laws of usury, backed not only by the Church but by the State.

The merchants did not attempt a frontal attack on the laws. They gradually learned to circumvent them. And the Church, which was a large property owner itself and often also needed to borrow on the strength of its expected income from ecclesiastical revenues, began to permit certain disguised forms of lending money at interest. One of the earliest forms of borrowing was on the equivalent of a mortgage. A man who owned a piece of property on which a regular rent was paid could sell the land for a limited number of years for a fixed price paid down at one time. He would thus receive a sum of money equal to, say, ten years' revenue, and the sale would be for eleven years. Thus the creditor would collect income for eleven years, although he had advanced money which would be repaid in ten. The eleventh year's income therefore was the equivalent of interest on the original loan. A similar device was used by cities and by the Church itself when short of ready money. All tax farming is based on the same principle. The difference between this device and a mortgage, which for social reasons was frowned upon, was that the borrower did not himself have to repay the loan at all, and his land could not be foreclosed upon since it already belonged for the limited period to the creditor.

A common device was to promise the return of a loan, officially made without interest, at a date by which it was impossible to repay. Then the debtor paid a fine for not keeping his promise. Shylock's famous loan, in Shakespeare's *Merchant of Venice*, was of this nature. A forfeit had to be made, in this case the pound of flesh, as a penalty for not repaying the loan on the due date. Interest was also concealed on agreements for sale when cash was paid in advance. The price agreed upon would take care of the fact that payment, that is, the loan, had been made so early, and would be rather lower than if it had been paid for at the time of delivery. Even if no goods at all were sold, a bill of sale could be made out on the lines indicated above without much fear of discovery.

The Church did not raise such serious objections to usury when the lender risked his capital as when security was good. Theoretically he could be compensated for not having the use of his own money at a time when he needed it. Partnerships of the kinds used so often to finance voyages could conceal the giving of credit and the payment of interest. A merchant could buy himself a share in an enterprise, and when the voyage was successful the share due him could be calculated on the basis of the capital invested plus a return for the use of the money. The same arrangement could also be made to take care of the losses sustained if a ship were sunk. A substantial bonus could be paid if the voyage were successful, while the lender would not even get his money back if the ship were lost. This was, of course, the equivalent of insurance, reinvented by the medieval Italian capitalists, though known also to the ingenious Greeks of an earlier civilization. By the fifteenth century this insurance had become regularized by underwriting, an arrangement by which a number of merchants and financiers agreed in writing to absorb a share of the risks of a voyage in exchange for a bonus if it was successful.

The Church, and many states, continued to legislate against usury, and in the early fourteenth century the Church even tried to bring it within the reach of the Inquisition by announcing that anyone who denied that usury was a sin was a heretic; but by this time business had largely moved out of the reach of spiritual sanctions, and kings profited too much by the prosperity that came from the use of credit to be willing to enforce the laws too strictly. But loans for consumption purposes remained a serious crime, and as they were made in general by professional moneylenders who did not possess as much political power as ordinary merchants, these men could be brought into court and heavily fined for usury, a useful addition to the coffers of penurious kings. And the feeling was never lost that such credit really was an unproductive use of money and took advantage of the hardships of poor men. In time the Franciscans undertook to take care of consumer credit, setting up *montes pietatis* (hills of piety), where the poor man could borrow at very low rates of interest on the security of some small piece of personal property which he handed over for safekeeping until the loan was repaid. This, of course, was the origin of the pawnbroking establishment which soon spread beyond the Franciscan Order.

In addition to the laws on usury, the law on the just price had to be abrogated or circumvented. This, however, was much easier to get around than the laws on usury, since it was impossible to enforce a just price, as no one knew for certain exactly what did constitute a just price. It was only possible to enforce this law ordinarily by purely commercial sanctions, such as refusing to do business with a profiteer; and such sanctions needed a strong merchant guild. Since offenses against the just price would usually be in the direction of an excessively low price, it was not to the interest of anyone except the merchants to enforce the law, though engrossing and cornering the market could be dealt with by kings if they had the power. Even the Venetian government of merchants could not prevent the lowering of prices through the ordinary working of competition and soon ceased to attempt it.

As the older medieval idea that a man's proper business in life was to seek salvation disappeared in favor of the search for wealth and comfort in this life through accumulating riches, even the Church accommodated itself to the reality, emphasizing that the profits should be used for a moral end, such as philanthropic bequests and, of course, gifts to the Church for the souls of deceased merchants. All Churches, including the later Protestant ones, have continued to insist that wealth has its responsibilities, and most Churches have observed the special dangers to a man's soul inherent in both the possession and the pursuit of riches, which can be more easily misused for sinful purposes than the

few possessions of the poor. But at all events by the fourteenth century the capitalist was a respectable member of society to all but ascetic reformers; and such social and religious control over his activities as had operated in the early medieval period was virtually at an end. Only the techniques necessary for business growth and opportunities for the full expansion of trade and profit seeking remained to be discovered.

THE ACCUMULATION OF CAPITAL

Europe had always, even in Roman times, been seriously short of the precious metals, and so far no acceptable substitute had been found. There was very little gold in Europe, and even silver mines could not supply enough to finance all the transactions for which silver was needed. As was noticed above, the balance of trade turned in favor of the West before the end of the thirteenth century, and thereafter gold and silver and precious stones began to move into Europe from the better-supplied Oriental world. The conquest of Constantinople by the crusaders must have added no mean amount to the meager supplies of the West as early as 1204. We have seen also that the flow of gold, especially into Italy, enabled both Florence and Venice to institute gold coinages in the thirteenth century, and florins and ducats circulated all through Europe, being accepted at their face value. As a whole, Europe was developing slowly into a money economy, and even in the manorial system payment in money instead of kind became the rule; and money was always to be found in the local markets. Nevertheless, the chronic shortage remained until the discovery of the Americas, which removed all fear of shortage for the foreseeable future; some African gold resulting from the Portuguese expansion at the end of the fifteenth century, and a few new silver mines, would not have sufficed without the Americas. In the later Middle Ages opportunities for using money were so great that little coin was hidden and accumulated without being used. There was no reason to fear any devaluation; on the contrary, there was every incentive to put coin into circulation at once and allow it to make more money for the owner. In Italy it was not unusual for a sleeping partner, providing capital for a man who was energetic and enterprising but lacked capital, to take up to 75 per cent of the profits of a whole voyage in exchange for a purely financial contribution.

The largest accumulators of capital were the Church and those kings who had an effective control of their finances, such as Philip IV of France. Tax payments to the Church and to the State had to be made in cash and could hardly be made in kind. Nobles and peasants alike had to turn their produce into money before they could pay taxes. But often the kings did not look after their money well, leaving its handling to favorites, many of whom built up enormous fortunes through graft, speculation in land, moneylending, and various financial operations. Both Church and kings frequently had to resort to banking houses for ready cash, secured against future revenues; and the Church for centuries made use of the specialized banking services that came to be offered by Italian bankers, who were known as Lombards, whether they hailed from Lombardy or not. These bankers often acted as collectors of papal revenue, transferring deposits from European countries to Rome for the benefit of the papacy, and taking their share in the process so that over a period of time they were able to accumulate very considerable sums. Nevertheless, these bankers, with so much money tied up in loans to the great, were often very insecure financially because of their lack of liquidity. When King Edward III of England defaulted on his debts to the Italian houses in the middle of the fourteenth century, many of them, including the greatest of all, were ruined.

Banks run by Christians existed in Europe from at least the twelfth century, and the thirteenth century saw a great extension of their activities. On the whole they specialized in business credit of the types referred to above. They lent money for profitable enterprises such as voyages, and they opened branches in every country of Europe, whose cities to this day often have their Lombard Streets, which may be still, as in London, in the center of the financial district. Bankers began to accept deposits and lend out as loans the bulk of what was deposited and on which they charged interest. In due course they tried to attract deposits by paying interest in turn. In this way they kept the limited amount of money in circulation, only retaining a small amount in hand for repayment to depositors. One of the early banking groups was the crusading Order of the Templars, whose strong castles in Europe attracted those who wished to keep their money safe. But the Templars themselves also lent out the money deposited with them, and became so rich that in the early fourteenth century Philip IV of France trumped up charges of sorcery and heresy against them and was able, with the assistance of the pope, to dispossess them.

The deposit banks were, for the most part, moneylenders who lent money for comparatively small business transactions and sometimes for consumer credit. The larger merchant banks, however, specialized in financing large transactions and in lending money to kings and to the papacy. By the fifteenth century many cities had set up banks of their own to facilitate municipal transactions; these accepted small deposits, and were the forerunners of modern deposit banking; some of them, notably the Bank of St. George in Genoa, still exist today. But far greater profits were to be gained from participating in trade voyages and other large-scale commercial transactions than from lending to individuals; for this reason it was the great Italian private banking houses which engaged in activities of this sort that made the really startling profits of these early days of capitalism. And it was almost entirely due to the efforts of these great houses that the important late medieval inventions for facilitating trade were introduced to the Western world. So many commercial techniques were invented that not much remained for the ingenuity of modern times except to perfect them.

IMPROVEMENT OF BUSINESS TECHNIQUES

Perhaps the most important single invention was the *bill of exchange,* which obviated the necessity for the transport of bullion on horseback through Europe, with all the dangers from bandits and robbers entailed, to say nothing of legal regulations against the exporting of gold and silver coins, which almost every ruler tried to enforce. The bill of exchange is simply an agreement to pay in a certain currency at a named date a specified sum of money. The merchant who gave the bill could then make arrangements to suit his own convenience to send the money to the specified place. If he had debtors in the foreign city, he could have them pay the bill, or he could at least shorten the journey for the bullion by sending it from some place where he had a debtor. As a natural evolution of the bill of exchange came the *draft,* which directed the merchant's debtor to pay to some third party a specified sum of money, and the *acceptance,* which made the draft negotiable since the acceptor had agreed to pay. When the Italian merchants developed a world-wide trade with correspondents and customers in all important cities, they seldom needed to send much cash. Transfers of actual bullion were only necessary to settle an unfavorable balance of trade, and before the final transfer was made a vast number of transactions might have taken place. Such devices at least in part compensated for the chronic shortage of gold and silver.

Right at the end of the Middle Ages at the close of the fifteenth century came the most symptomatic invention in the business field, showing clearly that the capitalists had at last understood the goal of their business operations, namely, profit making. This invention, first described by the Italian Pacioli, was double-entry bookkeeping, which divided all business transactions into debits and credits, thus enabling the merchant to learn at any moment the exact condition of his business, and whether or not he was making a profit. This invention, of course, was hardly possible as long as Roman numerals and the abacus were the only tools available for addition and subtraction. By the end of the fifteenth century, however, the Arabic numerals and the positional and decimal system had been accepted so widely that Pacioli's treatise became the standard work in accountancy, and his method was adopted everywhere throughout Europe by progressive businessmen.

The true joint-stock company was not a medieval invention, but the arrangements for financing the voyages of Italian merchants came close to it. Mention has already been made of simple partnerships, under which one partner was likely to provide the capital while the other made the actual voyage. The second partner was thus enabled to accumulate some capital as a reward for his enterprise, and might be able on the next occasion to share also in the financing. In the Middle Ages accumulation of capital was sufficiently rare for money to breed money with extreme rapidity, and the capitalist was paid excessively for the risk he took, frequently, as already mentioned, receiving as much as 75 per cent of the proceeds of the voyage. But if he put up only two thirds and the active partner put up as much as one third, then the profits would be divided equally. Curiously enough, it is in the early Middle Ages that this arrangement, the nearest thing to a joint-stock company, emerged at a time when capital was so rare that for an extensive voyage the risk and the profits would often be shared among a considerable number of merchants, each of whom received in proportion to the shares he had purchased. In later times this plan was regarded as too cumbersome, except perhaps in the case of very large loans to monarchs to which a number of bankers would subscribe. As soon as enough capital accumulated in the hands of individuals, such men then preferred to assume all the expenses, and to profit accordingly. The joint-stock company was only revived in modern times for the same reasons

Matheus.

Liber generationis ihesu xpi filij dauid: filij abraham. Abraham genuit ysaac: ysaac autem genuit iacob. Iacob aut genuit iuda et fratres ei9: iudas aut genuit phares et zara de thamar. Phares aut genuit esrom: esrom aut genuit aram. Aram aut genuit aminadab: aminadab aut genuit naason. Naason aut genuit salomon: salomon aut genuit booz de raab. Booz aut genuit obeth ex ruth: obeth aut genuit iesse. Iesse aute genuit dauid rege: dauid aut rex genuit salomone ex ea q fuit urie. Salomon aut genuit roboam: roboam aut genuit abyam. Abyas aut genuit asa: asa aut genuit iosaphat. Iosaphat aut genuit ioram: ioram aut genuit oziam. Ozias aut genuit ioatham: ioatham aut genuit achar. Achar aut genuit ezechiam: ezechias aut genuit manassen: manasses aut genuit ammon. Ammon aut genuit iosiam: iosias aut genuit iechoniam et fres ei9 i trasmigratione babilonis. Et post transmigratione babilonis iechonias genuit salathiel: salathiel aut genuit zorobabel. Zorobabel aut genuit abiud: abiud autem genuit eliachim. Eliachim aut genuit azor: azor aut genuit sadoch. Sadoch autem genuit achim: achim aut genuit eliud. Eliud aut genuit eleazar: eleazar aut genuit matthan. Matthan aut genuit iacob: iacob aut genuit ioseph uiru marie: de qua nat9 est ihesus: qui uocatur xpc. Omnes itaq generationes ab abraham usq ad dauid: generationes quatuordecim: et a dauid usq ad transmigratione babilonis. generationes quatuorteci: et a trasmigratione babilonis

usq ad xpm. generationes quatuordecim. Xpi autem generatio sic erat. Cum esset desposata mater ihesu maria ioseph: antequam couenirent inuenta e i utero habes de spiritu sancto. Ioseph autem uir ei9 cu esset iustus: et nollet eam traducere: uoluit occulte dimittere eam. Hec aut eo cogitante: ecce angelus dmi apparuit i somnis ioseph dicens. Ioseph fili dauid: noli timere accipere maria coniugem tuam. Qd eni in ea natu est: de spiritu sancto est. Pariet aut filiu: et uocabis nome eius ihesum. Ipse eni saluu faciet ppm suum a peccatis eorum. Hoc autem totu factu est: ut adimpleretur qd dictu esset a domino p propheta dicentem. Ecce uirgo in utero habebit et pariet filiu: et uocabit nome eius emanuel: qd est interpretatu nobiscum deus. Exurgens aut ioseph a somno fecit sicut precepit ei angelus dmi: et accepit coniugem suam. Et non cognoscebat eam donec peperit filium suum primogenitum: et uocauit nomen eius ihesum. Ca. ij. Cum natus esset ihesus in bethleem iude i diebz herodis regis: ecce magi ab oriente uenerut iherosolimam dicentes. Ubi est qui natus est rex iudeox? Uidimus eni stella eius in oriente: et uenim9 adorare eu. Audiens autem herodes rex turbatus e: et omnis iherosolima cu illo. Et congregans omnes principes sacerdotu et scribas ppli: sciscitabat ab eis ubi xpus nasceret. At illi dixerut ei. In bethleem iude. Sic eni scriptu est p prophetam. Et tu bethleem terra iuda: nequaq minima es i principibz iuda. Ex te eni exiet dux qui regat ppm meum israhel. Tunc herodes clam uocatis magis diligenter didicit ab eis tempus stelle q

A page from the earliest European printed work, the Gutenberg Bible. (COURTESY THE PIERPONT MORGAN LIBRARY)

that the Genoese used its earlier form in the thirteenth century—when business transactions became too great to be financed by single men or by small partnerships.

OTHER MEDIEVAL INVENTIONS

The improvements in navigation have already been referred to briefly. The mariner's compass, taken over from the Muslims, was improved by having the needle put on a pivot as in the modern compass. The astrolabe, used for determining latitude, was known in the early Middle Ages, but was perfected for nautical use later. Direct water power was in use in mills for grinding grain, the water falling on a wheel and making it revolve. Milling was the earliest use of the water wheel, but in the later Middle Ages it was used for many other purposes, one of the earliest being for the sawing of wood. The windmill was also employed for various purposes, but windmills were not very widespread by the end of the Middle Ages. Gunpowder, mentioned by Roger Bacon in the thirteenth century as an invention of great possibilities, was used for cannon by the fourteenth, and some time during the next century it was used in hand guns, though the crossbow and the longbow, far more accurate weapons, were not outmoded for a considerable time.

One of the most influential inventions, however, was not made by Europeans but was imported from the East. Paper from rags, originally made in China many centuries earlier, was used also by the Muslims during the height of their civilization, and probably came to the Western world from Spain. Before the advent of rag paper, parchment and papyrus had been used; but their excessive cost had a hampering effect upon all forms of written communication. Once paper had come into the West, business quickly seized upon the invention and used it as an aid in keeping accurate accounts. And it was not long before paper was also used in the printing of books.

The story of the Western invention of printing from movable type is still a matter of dispute. There is no doubt that priority in the invention of printing itself belongs to China. The fundamental idea behind printing lies far back in history in ancient Sumer, where seals were used for impressing clay tablets. The Chinese used wooden blocks, and the earliest printing in the West likewise made use of wooden blocks, a separate block having to be made for each page of a book. This process, however, was scarcely less expensive than copying each page by hand. It is not yet certain whether the idea of these wooden blocks actually came to the West from China by the process of diffusion, or whether it was separately invented in the West. At all events, the crucial invention was the printing from movable metal type, which seems to have originated in Korea, but will forever be associated in the West with the name of John Gutenberg (ca. 1398–1468). Almost every European country had a share in the perfecting of printing with movable metal type, but there can be no doubt that the first great center of printing was Mainz, where Gutenberg was the leading craftsman and inventor in the field. Gutenberg's Mazarin Bible (so called because the first copy to attract widespread attention in modern times was in Cardinal Mazarin's library) is the first printed book known (completed 1456), took several years to print, and is still one of the finest examples of the printer's art ever produced.

The earliest printed books, called *incunabula* if printed before 1500,[2] were made with extreme care. Most of them were religious books which remained for many years in great demand. But before the end of the fifteenth century the Venetians and Flemish in particular started to print the classics of Greece and Rome, and other more popular works. Perhaps no invention in the history of mankind has been more influential and has changed more lives than printing.

Medieval inventions in the field of commerce, industry, and technology may not amount to a very impressive total, but it can surely be claimed that they were crucial.

[2] The word means "cradle books," i.e., books printed in the cradle days of printing.

In this, as in so many other fields of activity, our medieval forebears may clearly be seen to have laid the foundations of the modern world.

▶ Suggestions for further reading

There has been a great deal of controversy in recent years among scholars on the question of the origin of the towns of medieval Europe. On the whole, the thesis of H. Pirenne, in *Medieval Cities, Their Origin and the Revival of Trade* (tr. F. D. Halsey; Princeton, N. J.: Princeton University Press, 1925), is now accepted by the majority of scholars, and it is still probably the best book on medieval cities for the student. A great deal of information, based on a lifetime of historical research, is contained within this small book.

Pirenne was also to the fore with a theory, sustained by some evidence, that trade in the Mediterranean area suffered only a short period of decline when the Muslims controlled the sea, and revived quickly as soon as the Christians again took possession of it. Later scholars, though, have been impressed with the amount of trade still carried on by European cities with the Muslims and so have tended to modify Pirenne's thesis. However this may be, there is a great deal of solid material on medieval trade to be found in his brilliant book, *The Economic and Social History of Medieval Europe* (tr. I. E. Clegg; New York: Harcourt, Brace & Co., Inc., 1937), which is an extract from a much larger work not yet translated from the French. A monumental work, which is a little out of date but a mine of information, is J. W. Thompson, *The Economic and Social History of the Middle Ages, 300–1300,* and *The Economic and Social History of Europe in the later Middle Ages, 1300–1530* (New York: Appleton-Century-Crofts, Inc., 1928–1931). However, for the beginning student it is probably best to read the medieval chapters in any of the standard economic histories of Europe. Excellent is H. Heaton, *Economic History of Europe* (rev. ed.; New York: Harper & Brothers, 1948). The medieval chapters in S. B. Clough and C. W. Cole, *Economic History of Europe* (rev. ed.; Boston: D. C. Heath and Company, 1947), also contain a great deal of useful information not to be found in ordinary histories. There is a Berkshire study by S. Baldwin, *Business in the Middle Ages* (New York: Henry Holt & Co., Inc., 1937), which has its uses, but the author is so anxious to confound opponents and change stereotypes which he feels are still too often accepted that his book seems rather too argumentative for such a short study, and his material appears somewhat arbitrarily selected. Though there is a good deal of useful information in the book, it should not be read by itself without supplementary information from other sources.

R. H. Tawney, *Religion and the Rise of Capitalism* (New York: Penguin Books, 1947), is a classic study in English of the relationship between religious ideas and the growth of trade and commerce. Making effective use of a theory of the German sociologist Max Weber, Tawney undoubtedly overstates his case for the influence of Protestant ethics on the growth of modern capitalism, and his view of the medieval economy as the antithesis of this capitalism is equally overstated. But the theoretical views of the Church on the place of business in society are very clearly shown in the early chapters of this work, even though theory in this case was often far removed from practice.

Nulli vendemus, nulli negabimus, aut differemus, rectum aut justiciam . . .

To no one will we sell, to no one will we deny or delay, right or justice . . .

VI The Beginnings of the Modern State System

Facsimile of Magna Carta. The passage quoted is from Section 40.

15

The Emergence of National
States in Europe

The national state: key political institution of Western civilization • The failure of Germany and Italy to attain national statehood • The English national state • The unification of France • The Spanish national state

---

► **The national state as the key political institution of Western civilization**

CONTRAST WITH CITY-STATE AND EMPIRES

Prior to our own Western civilization the key governmental institution which developed the most advanced political forms was the city-state, whose weaknesses were discussed at length in the chapter on Greece. City-states, unable to solve their problems, and especially unable to refrain from fratricidal warfare, were usually replaced by great empires, of which we have seen many examples in this book. But it is difficult to point to many instances in the ancient world of the true national state, whose inhabitants were bound by ties of loyalty to their fellow nationals, who felt that they had some kind of common kinship merely because they inhabited a certain area of land, larger than a city.

Perhaps the nearest to the modern national state was ancient Egypt, which was considerably more than a mere geographic entity. The Pharaoh of Egypt was a king-god who was responsible for the welfare of Egypt and not that of other countries; he commanded loyalty from his people as their

protector. The Egyptians, in the manner of some modern states, despised the people of Babylonia, who were unfortunate enough to have a "Nile in the sky," and called them "wretched Asiatics." The ancient Hebrews also had a patriotic feeling beyond that of the city-states, and again they had a national God to lead them. But their loyalty was religious and cultural rather than based on the possession of a particular territory, and northerners soon separated from southerners when political and economic conditions suggested a division.

The national state, therefore, is a relatively modern phenomenon, and is not even necessarily the final political form to be evolved by the human race. But its achievements up to this time have been impressive enough, even though it too has failed to solve the problem of fratricidal interstate warfare; which may yet result in the establishment of new empires recognizably similar to those of the ancient world. The national state, possessing within its borders economic resources far greater than those commanded by city-states, has proved superior to the city-state in that it has been able to support comparatively efficient governments manned by professional officials, free from excessive

► chronological chart

The English National State

Reign of Edward the Confessor	1042–1066
Norman Conquest of England	1066
Domesday Book completed	1086
Oath of Salisbury	1086
Reign of Henry I	1100–1135
Interregnum in English monarchy (reign of Stephen)	1135–1154
Marriage of Henry Plantagenet to Eleanor of Aquitaine	1152
Henry II king of England	1154–1189
Assize of Clarendon (grand jury)	1166
Murder of St. Thomas Becket	1170
Richard I held to ransom by Emperor Henry VI	1194
Reign of John	1199–1216
Loss of French lands to Philip	1202–1204
Struggle with Pope Innocent III	1205–1213
Battle of Bouvines	1214
Magna Carta	1215
Provisions of Oxford	1258
Battle of Lewes—Henry III captured by Simon de Montfort	1264
Simon de Montfort's Parliament	1265
Battle of Evesham—Defeat and death of Simon	1265
Reign of Edward I	1272–1307
Conquest of Wales	1276–1284
The Model Parliament	1295
Battle of Bannockburn—Scottish independence	1314
Outbreak of the Hundred Years' War	1337
Battle of Crécy	1346
Battle of Poitiers	1356
Treaty of Brétigny	1360
Reign of Richard II	1377–1399
Great Peasants' Revolt	1381
Renewal of war with France	1383
Constitutional rule of Richard II	1389–1397
Absolute rule of Richard II	1397–1399
Deposition of Richard II	1399
Reign of Henry IV	1399–1413
Henry V claims throne of France	1415
Battle of Agincourt	1415
Treaty of Troyes—Henry V regent of France	1420
Deaths of Henry V and Charles VI of France	1422
Joan of Arc burned at Rouen	1431
Loss of all France except Calais	1453
Wars of the Roses	1455–1485
Henry Tudor, Henry VII of England	1485

The French National State

Reign of Hugh Capet	987–996
Reign of Louis VI, the Fat	1108–1137
Dissolution of marriage between Louis VII and Eleanor of Aquitaine	1152
Reign of Philip Augustus	1180–1223
Reign of Louis IX	1226–1270
Reign of Philip IV, the Fair	1285–1314
Summoning of States-General	1302
End of Capetian monarchy	1328
Hundred Years' War with England	1337–1453
Battle of Poitiers—Capture of King John II	1356
The Jacquerie—Murder of Etienne Marcel	1358
Treaty of Brétigny	1360
Duchy of Burgundy granted by John II to his son Philip	1363
Reconquest of most of territory lost to England	1369–1380
John the Fearless becomes Duke of Burgundy	1404
Intermittent civil war in France between Burgundy and House of Valois (Armagnacs)	1407–1435
Henry V of England invades France	1415
Reign of Charles VII	1422–1461
Joan of Arc at siege of Orléans	1429
Coronation of Charles VII at Rheims	1429
Death of Joan of Arc	1431
Peace of Arras between Charles and Burgundians	1435
Reform of French army	1445–1446
Expulsion of the English	1449–1461
Reign of Louis XI	1461–1483
Charles the Bold, Duke of Burgundy	1467–1477
Edward IV of England bought off by Louis	1475
Battle of Nancy—Defeat and death of Charles the Bold	1477
Unification of France as a national state	1480

Spanish and Portuguese national states

Muslim conquest of Spain	711–719
Christian kingdom of the Asturias reconquered	718–737
Partial conquest of northeastern Spain by Charlemagne	778
Expansion of Christian kingdom of Leon	910–914
Reign of Abdu-r-Rahman III (height of Muslim power)	912–961
Rise of Castile to independence	930–966
Breakup of Ommeyad dynasty into small chiefdoms	1031
Conquest of Leon by Castile	1037
Capture of Toledo by Alphonso VI of Castile	1085
Christian advance into Muslim Spain	1072 onward
Berber dynasties based on Africa in central and southern Spain	1056–1269
Advances by Alphonso VII and Alphonso VIII of Castile	1126–1214
Union of Catalonia and Aragon	1137
Earliest Cortes in Castile	ca. 1188
Battle of Las Navas de Tolosa— decisive defeat of Muslims by Alphonso VIII	1212
Capture of Cordova by Ferdinand III of Castile	1236
Capture of Seville by Ferdinand	1248
Conquest of Sicily by Peter III of Aragon	1282
Portuguese independence secured by decisive victory over Castile	1385
Marriage of Isabella, heiress of Castile, to Ferdinand, heir of Aragon	1469
Isabella succeeds to Castilian throne	1474
Establishment of Spanish Inquisition under royal control	1478
Ferdinand succeeds to throne of Aragon	1479
Fall of Granada, last Muslim stronghold in Spain	1492
Expulsion of Jews from Spain	1492
Expulsion of Moriscos from Spain	1609

dependence upon foreigners and possible enemies for essential supplies; and it has been able to maintain public security better than the empires. But above all the national state has not proved too large to enable individual citizens to feel they have some share in the government. As a consequence of this added sense of responsibility on the part of the public, the modern national government has been able to enforce certain basic human rights in a way that even Roman law could not, since Roman law was not written in Heaven, as the philosophers claimed, but drawn up and administered by servants of the ultimately irresponsible empire.

While a national state must always have a national government in effective control of the whole territory, a government which must be recognized as such by the people of the state, there are otherwise no acceptable criteria for what constitutes a national state. A common language may be an important aid to the establishment of such a state, but multilingual national states such as Switzerland exist; and, conversely, many different states speak the same language. If culture is taken in the widest sense, a common national culture and common ideals are an even greater aid; and it is perhaps arguable that no state has ever been permanently united without them, though, for instance, present-day Yugoslavia has a partly Catholic and a partly Orthodox religious culture.

If the national state is the dominant institution in the world at any given time, as at present, then it is likely that all countries which feel they have enough in common will desire to organize themselves into separate sovereign states. This process can be observed in operation in the twentieth century, though great difficulties have arisen in the attempt to determine into how small units nations should be split. And even in the great national states founded in the Middle Ages, separatist tendencies have still not disappeared; or, if there is not a demand for altogether separate governments, at least there is often agitation for a substantial measure of self-government for the separate parts.

Three major national states, whose history as national entities has been continuous to this day, came into existence in the Middle Ages—England, France, and Spain. The more populous and in some ways more advanced countries, Italy and Germany, did not become national states until the second half of the nineteenth century. Germany was bedeviled by the ghost of the Roman Empire. At a time when both France and England were relatively unimportant, the Germans under the Holy Roman Emperors were trying to establish their dominion over territories where geography made permanent union unlikely. After the imperial dream was over, the German feudal nobles had grasped so much substantial power that for centuries it was impossible to dislodge them; and German towns, as was seen in the previous chapter, constituted a league of states beyond the control of German monarchs for two crucial centuries. No one lord was powerful enough to rule the whole. The emperor was elected by the very nobles to whom he presented a threat, and they were therefore careful to elect only those of their peers who seemed to be least dangerous; if a family made gains while it held the imperial throne, an effort would be made to see that none of its members was elected next time. We shall see in a later chapter how the feudal lords of Germany finally became free of the emperor in the middle of the seventeenth century as a result of the Thirty Years' War. But it took more than half a century of patient work in the nineteenth century by the largest state, masterly diplomacy, a modern army, and three wars, before Germany could be united as a nation.

Italy, at first forced to defend herself against the regular invasions of the emperor, for a while experienced freedom under city-state government, and for two centuries led Europe in commercial development. But the country was divided. Venice always dominated the northeast, the Papal States stretched across the backbone of the country from the Mediterranean to the Adriatic, extremely resistant to any moves looking toward the unity of the country as a whole. The south was under foreign domination, either Spanish or Angevin princes who could usually count on foreign aid to bolster their kingdoms. Several times the possibility of union seemed to open, and Italian writers and publicists from Dante to Machiavelli were well aware that Italy desperately needed unity. But not until Napoleon was the dream almost realized; and with his collapse more than half a century of propaganda, war, and diplomacy was needed to achieve it.

In this chapter, therefore, we shall discuss those states whose development was continuous. In England national unity under a strong monarchy was early achieved, and interest is centered both upon the means by which this early achievement was possible, and upon the efforts made by the nobles to curb the power of the monarchy; in France the central monarchy had difficulty in establishing itself, but once it had done so, the king's power remained intact until the French Revolution in the eighteenth century. Unity in Spain was attained largely through the shared experience of driving out the Muslims, and though partially representative institutions were developed, the kings retained almost absolute power until recent times. The contrast, especially between England and France, will serve to explain much of the modern political history of these countries: the strength of representative government in England based upon so many centuries of tradition, and the weakness of French representative government in a country whose traditions until such recent times were all absolutist and monarchical.

▶ The English national state

THE NATURE OF THE ANGLO-SAXON MONARCHY

The king

As we saw in an earlier chapter, the English king Alfred the Great (871–899) united England against the Danes, and thereafter he and his successors ruled over an England that was no longer split into minor kingdoms. Even when England was altogether conquered by Sweyn and Canute from Scandinavia, the monarchy remained united though England was part of a Scandinavian empire, and English laws and customs remained substantially unchanged. The great council (the *Witan*) of thanes or lords, together with other wise men of the kingdom, still officially elected each king, although the custom had gradually developed for the rule to descend from father to son. The Witan theoretically could have bestowed the crown outside the descendants of Alfred, but the Anglo-Saxon people seem to have expected the council to choose a king from that family, and, as in other countries, a certain sanctity attached to the kingship. The Witan also felt competent to depose a king in certain circumstances, for he possessed no divine right to the office. He swore a coronation oath to support the Church and to maintain justice and mercy.

In late Anglo-Saxon times, before the Norman Conquest, something akin to feudalism had been growing in England, although it is wiser not to use the word to describe the Anglo-Saxon system in view of the real feudalism of the Continental type introduced by the Normans. Though there were as yet far more differences than similarities between the English system and Continental feudalism, the power of the king, as in feudal states, was seriously limited by the independence of the nobility. The king had the right to summon the national army or militia in times of danger. But the period of service was limited; after the service had been completed, the lords and their servants were entitled to return home. The conquest by the Normans was largely due to the fact that the king could not prevent his troops from returning home for harvest and had to rely upon special troops known as *housecarls,* who formed his personal retinue and were dependent upon him. The latter were not, however, the king's personal feudal vassals, as they were in France, and later in England.

The king was also the theoretical head of the justiciary, and certain kinds of lawsuits were always referred to him for decision, in spite of the fact that other law courts existed with their own systems of law. In general, however, almost all law was local, and enforced locally, until the Norman and Plantagenet kings were able to make inroads into local and feudal courts and establish the king's justice as the supreme law of the land.

Anglo-Saxon "feudal" counterparts

The same causes that operated in the direction of increased feudalism on the Continent also operated in Anglo-Saxon England. The old German comitatus, the personal relationship between man and lord, was held to be as sacred in England as elsewhere. The central government was rarely strong enough to control the whole country, and though the king had many rights owed him by villagers in the country, he usually granted these rights to his lords or thanes, and it was the thanes who maintained order and executed justice in their territories. According to an Anglo-Saxon law, every man must either have land which he possessed freehold, or have a lord. This lord must give him the protection that the king, too distant and with too little authority, was unable to provide. Thus the practice of commendation, voluntary elsewhere, was compulsory in England, and in return the lord was entitled to various specified contributions from his men.

On the Continent, commendation, as a whole, usually meant that the land was held by military service. In England, however, there was also a fairly common form of service called a *tenancy in socage,* under which the lord was entitled to various goods and services from his men rather than a specified number of troops. This meant that the lord could not engage so easily in private warfare, since he lacked troops. It also meant that the monarch, when he wished to call out troops, was not hindered by the fact that the men he called had prior obligations toward their feudal overlords. After the Norman Conquest, William I made good use of these ancient English customs to preserve his own position.

By the time of the Conquest, then, there was no fully developed feudal system in England. The relationship between lord and vassal existed, but in primitive form; courts presided over by the lords operated in cases involving themselves and their dependents, while other courts operated for different offenses not concerned with land tenure. The king had certain rights over the common land of England, and these rights had real meaning; but he was not even the theoretical owner of the remainder of the land, as in France. The English thanes owed him military service as a national obligation rather than because they held land from him; they owed it to him as chief warrior who was constantly having to call upon them through the persistence of national danger from the Danes.

The great change made by the Norman Conquest was therefore not the establishment of an entirely different system, but the imposition of order upon a mass of customs which had been gradually growing up, and the speeding up of the feudalization process by a series of able kings, in whose French possessions there was already a well-developed feudal system.

Local government

One of the greatest achievements of the Anglo-Saxons in England was their system of local government, much of which was maintained by the Normans. The country had already been divided into *shires,* later called counties, which differ little from those of the present day. The shires were administered by the bishop, the earl, or the chief lord, and an appointee of the king known as the *shire-reeve* or sheriff. The latter had the important function of looking after the king's business in the shire, especially the mustering of the national militia, and the collection of such taxes as the Danegeld, originally paid to keep the Northmen away, but which was continued, like so many taxes in modern times, long after the immediate necessity had passed away. There was also

a shire court that tried civil and criminal cases which came under its jurisdiction, presided over by the sheriff with the aid of the bishop and occasionally the earl, when necessary. Minor cases were handled in a subdivision of the shire, called a *hundred.* It was in the hundred that the apportionment of taxes to each person was made by men of local knowledge under the guidance of the sheriff.[1] These administrative divisions had given the kings since early times a means of enforcing their will; and because the sheriff in most cases, and the assessors in all cases, were local men, the germ existed for the combination of decentralized government and responsibility to the central government which made representative government possible later, and provided a vehicle by which consent for taxation could be asked and given.

THE NORMAN CONQUEST

The establishment of Continental feudalism

The English king Edward, known as the Confessor, died in 1066 without leaving any obvious heir to the throne, though there was still one direct descendant of Alfred available. But he was a boy, and the times were so troubled that the Witan was ready to pass him over. They therefore chose Harold, the son of the greatest earl of the realm, and a renowned warrior, and he was proclaimed and anointed king.

But there were also two foreign claimants. One, Harold Hardrada, the king of Norway, a close relative of Edward the Confessor, was supported by a traitorous brother of Harold of England, while the other contender, William, Duke of Normandy, claimed that Edward had bequeathed the crown to him, and that Harold had sworn to support him. The issue could only be decided by force of arms.

---

[1] It is not certain that taxes were assessed in these local bodies as early as Anglo-Saxon times. But at all events the later kings, when they wished to have tax assessments made, were able to make use of the administrative division of the hundred for the purpose.

Harold summoned the national militia for service on land and on sea, but the navy had been allowed to deteriorate in the time of Edward and was no match for that of either of the competing foreign kings. The Norwegian king gained a favorable wind first and landed in the north of England. Harold of England, whose army had waited for the attack throughout the summer and was now far under full strength, met the Norwegian army and defeated it at Stamford Bridge. But the victorious army then heard that William had landed in the south. Marching quickly to meet him, Harold's army was almost exhausted when it finally met the feudal barons of the Norman duke, whose numbers had been swelled by recruits of nobles from all over France who had hoped to share in the booty. Harold was defeated and killed in the ensuing battle of Hastings (1066). Duke William then forced the English to choose him as king (1066–1087), and he was duly crowned.

Over the next few years all the lands of England were declared forfeited to the Conqueror. Any English lords who wished to retain their land were compelled to swear allegiance to him and do homage as his vassals. The remainder of the lands were given to William's Norman followers in return for the same recognition of himself as their suzerain. Thus the Conquest made what was elsewhere only a theoretical position real in England. William was the actual lord or suzerain of the entire land of England. Under the Norman kings there was no land whatsoever that was free (or alodial); every land had at least one lord, the king.

The king, however, could not administer such a vast estate himself through his nominees or servants. He retained the greater nobles as his direct vassals, or tenants in chief. But these were permitted, indeed encouraged, to let out the land again to subvassals (subinfeudation), who owed service to the king's tenants in chief as vassals. The service was composed of the usual feudal aids, and these subvassals were said to hold their land, as customary in the feudal system, by knight or military service.

POSSESSIONS OF
WILLIAM I OF ENGLAND
1066–1087

★ Battles

But, in William's eyes, this did not justify the subvassals' fighting on behalf of their lord in his private quarrels. Though private warfare was not altogether quelled, especially under later kings, it was never legal for a vassal to fight for his lord unless the king himself had authorized the calling out of troops. And this he did only in national wars. A subvassal under this system therefore owed military service only to the king; but he was called upon for military service by his own overlord on behalf of the king. Thus the king had the advantage of indirect control over his subvassals, saving him the labor of administration involved, while at the same time he had all the benefits which accrued to a mighty feudal landowner, able to command the military service not only of his own tenants in chief but of every landowner in the country.

The Bayeux tapestry recounts the deeds of Duke William of Normandy and his conquest of England. Here Harold, King of England, is shown as he receives the news that William had landed in Sussex.

Through the sheriffs the king likewise exercised the old Anglo-Saxon privilege of direct taxation of the people without the intervention of the vassals and subvassals, and he retained and extended the power of the king's courts, though feudal lords could hold their courts to deal with matters within their own jurisdiction. No lord could erect a castle except with the king's license, and theoretically every castle in the country belonged to him. It will be seen, therefore, that, with customary Norman intelligence, William made full use of everything that could help him in the existing Anglo-Saxon

Scene of the battle of Hastings, from the Bayeux tapestry. The tide of battle is said to have been turned by a feigned flight on the part of the Normans.

system, while adding to it elements of Norman-French feudalism which could be used with profit to himself.[2]

[2] It may be added that the same combination of Anglo-Saxon and Norman French is to be found in the developed English language. Norman architecture in England is a modification of continental Romanesque architecture incorporating also some elements taken over from the Anglo-Saxons.

Contrast between English and continental feudalism

Under William the great nobles of the realm held their land, as has been said, directly from him as tenants in chief, and they owed military service to him in addition to the usual feudal aids. This secured to the king a regular supply of troops and some money. He also had the right to tax directly through the shires and the hundreds. The lands of the Church were sometimes held by military service, which the ecclesiastical lords had to arrange for as best they could. But in addition in certain cases a church or a monastery would be permitted to hold land by *frankalmoign*. This meant that the religious institution still owed service, but it was service of a religious nature. The clergymen had to say Masses, pray, give alms or some other service suitable to their profession. This mode of service was never very common, but it preserved the façade of feudalism—that all land was held in exchange for some kind of service.

A further service sometimes given in exchange for land was *serjeanty*. Under this arrangement the holder would have to give some special specified service, and his duties were limited to this, perhaps the bearing of the king's shield in battle, or providing him with a suit of armor on occasion.

It was also possible, as has been seen, for tenants to hold land by socage, instead of by knight service. This was an Anglo-Saxon arrangement continued and systematized by William. Instead of owing military service, the tenant owed a specified amount of produce, and definite services such as the *corvée* and working the lord's lands for certain days in the year (as described in Chapter 10 above in the sections on feudalism and manorialism).[3] Naturally the king himself was too great a lord to be able to manage such minor services as these, and he did not have many tenants in chief who held from him by socage. But the king's tenants in chief let out much of their land in this way, and thus were enabled to take care of their own living expenses without having to manage their demesnes themselves or through their agents and stewards, as in

France. Thus while the feudal and manorial systems were connected in France by the fact that each feudal lord had to set aside some manors for his own subsistence out of his total estates and had to make direct arrangements for the farming of these manors, in England a manorial owner owed a certain amount of produce to his lord directly and was responsible for its payment as part of his feudal duties. If he held his land in socage he owed, not the feudal aids which were comparatively small and irregular, but food and produce and labor service which was, of course, not performed by himself but by his villeins and serfs. The result, for the suzerain, was that he was spared the labor of farming his own manors, and could rely upon his vassals in socage for his own subsistence. It was natural, therefore, that he was inclined to favor letting out his land on these terms rather than for military service, of which he could take but little advantage since he could not use for his own advancement the troops provided him under knight service. He was, however, limited in the amount he could let out in socage by the necessity he was under to provide troops for the king.

The holding of land in socage tended to increase under the Norman and Plantagenet kings. But it never took the place of the most common form of landholding in England, the holding by villeinage, which had been fully entrenched even in Anglo-Saxon times. English villeinage is complicated by the fact that some villeins were serfs and tied to the land, while others were legally free and could leave the land at will. But whether serfs or free, the villeins (peasants) held land from their lords and were obligated to provide them with certain goods and services of the same kind as those described under manorialism in an earlier chapter. The difference, of course, between English villeinage and the usual manorial system in Europe was that the villein could manage his land without interference from his lord, thus relieving the lord of onerous responsibilities, while at the same

[3] The student is urged at this point to refresh his memory on the details of feudalism as described in Chapter 10, since an understanding of feudalism is basic for an understanding of the rise of national monarchies.

time helping to provide him with an assured income.

The full establishment of royal authority

The crafty Norman was also quick to take advantage of the system of sheriffs. Bishops and earls were far harder to control than his own appointees. He therefore excluded the former from the government of the shires and hundreds, and made the sheriffs supreme, subject only to dismissal by himself. Hoping to make it entirely clear that the members of the new English nobility were no longer to have the privilege of making private war and that all military service was owed only to himself, in 1086 William summoned to Salisbury all the landowners in the country, whether tenants in chief or only subvassals, and made them swear fealty to himself. They swore that they would be loyal to him even against their direct suzerains. Thereafter every tenant doing homage to his own lord for his fief had to add, "Saving the faith that I owe to my lord the king," which, of course, expressly covered military service, taxation, and legal appeals which were the prerogatives of the crown.

In order to have an exact knowledge of the dues of all kinds owed by every man in the kingdom, whether to himself or to any of his vassals, William sent out clerks into his shire courts where every landholder, whether free or serf, had to appear and under oath answer certain questions about his land, how many people worked on it, how much meadow and forest it contained, how many streams, and who had the various rights involved. All this information was written down in the Domesday Book, a magnificent example of Norman administrative genius altogether unique for that period, and only possible in a country which had developed the necessary local institutions through which the information could be collected. The king now had his hands upon the pulse of the whole realm, but few English kings ever had such power again. The lords, who had been robbed of so much

that belonged to their class elsewhere, did not hesitate to take advantage of any later weakening in the central government, and in so doing ultimately paved the way for the limited monarchy and representative institutions which have been the special glory of the English political genius.

Machinery of government

The king had so many tenants in chief that the customary feudal council made up of the king's vassals would, in England, have been a most cumbersome body. William did call it on occasion, but preferred to work with a committee of these tenants in chief, which took the place of the Witan. The whole body was entitled to be consulted, but few lords desired the privilege, and it became the custom for this smaller council to give advice to the king when he summoned it for the purpose. The whole assembly at this time is known as the *Curia Regis*, or Court of the King, but in practice the Curia was made up of those tenants in chief whose presence William especially desired, and the majority did not attend. William's younger son, Henry I, made this committee a formal institution. William used a small number of regular officials in a full-time capacity. Chief of these was the justiciar, who ruled England in the king's name when, as fairly often happened, he was forced to look after his ducal interests in Normandy. The justiciar also became head of the departments of finance and justice in William's time, though these were separated by his younger son. The chancellor and chamberlain at this time had duties in the king's household. Whenever the king needed any further help he called upon his higher clergy and members of his Curia, whom he authorized to perform special limited tasks in the country, usually in conjunction with the sheriffs. With the feudal system working so efficiently in his behalf, William did not need a great corps of officials in his employ. All that was really needed was competent supervision of the work carried out for him by his tenants in chief in return for the land they had received from him, and this was provided by the few officials that he had.

THE REIGN OF HENRY I

Improved machinery of government

The second son of William the Conqueror succeeded to his throne, leaving Normandy for the eldest. The younger, William Rufus (1087–1100), acquired Normandy from his brother by some sharp tactics, but as king of England he made no innovations beyond tightening his financial hold on the feudal nobility and increasing taxation. When he was killed by an unknown hand while hunting, the youngest son of the Conqueror, Henry Beauclerc, or Henry I (1100–1135) took the throne, and continued to keep his eldest brother from the duchy of Normandy, so that Henry ruled both England and Normandy. Henry, with a thorough understanding of his father's policy and the conditions in England that favored the monarchy, succeeded, in a long reign of thirty-five years, in improving the administration and in strengthening the monarchy still further. Appointing to his personal staff a number of gentlemen who were not of the highest nobility, granting them lands as his direct vassals, and paying careful attention to his ecclesiastical appointments in order to put these into the hands of the best administrators he could find, he created a real council of advisers whose positions were not hereditary and who were thus closely tied to himself. This small council was the governing body of the realm under the king, and the great council of tenants in chief was rarely called together by Henry. Thus was the beginning made in England of the bureaucracy of government officials and heads of departments, which in later times became the king's Privy Council, the executive arm of the English kingdom as long as the king himself was the chief executive. When the king's office became largely honorary, the Privy Council became the Cabinet, still the executive of the country, still containing the heads of the various departments

of state, and still officially responsible to the king—who in theory chooses the chief official, the prime minister.

The considerable secretarial work of the king was entrusted to a special department known as the Chancery, the head of which, an appointee of the monarch, was called the chancellor. As ever, the most important department of government was the Treasury. Henry was both an extremely able and an extremely careful man, especially with his money, as he recognized that much of his power was based on it. It was he who really created the English Treasury, and systematized the collection of the very considerable revenues that accrued to the crown from many different sources, feudal and specifically royal. He was the first English king to make extensive use of scutage (shield money) under which his vassals were excused from military service on payment of a sum of money. Henry thought he could use the money to better advantage than he could the excused man-power, especially since his reign was very peaceful for the times. All his senior officials had care of the Treasury, though the chamberlain was primarily responsible. Twice every year these officials met to scrutinize the accounts, using a table covered by a cloth divided into squares representing the pounds, shillings, and pence received. This cloth gave rise to the word "exchequer," which has ever since been used for the English Treasury.

Legal reforms of Henry I

The law at the beginning of Henry's reign was in a chaotic state owing to the different kinds of law in use: Anglo-Saxon law in the local courts (shires and hundreds), feudal (Norman) law in the feudal courts, canon (Roman) law in the ecclesiastical courts, even merchant law in the towns; and in addition to these were the courts of the king which held jurisdiction in certain cases. Henry, anxious to improve the position of the king's law in relation to the other systems, conceived the project of enforcing a single law which should cover all cases in the kingdom and gradually oust all competitive forms of law.[4] This would mean a tremendous increase of power for the king if it could be carried out. Henry himself did not achieve much more than the beginnings of the project, which could not be imposed simply by decree but must in time receive public acceptance so that people would wish to have their cases tried by the king's law. This law is what is known as the common law, because it was intended to be common to the whole realm.

Henry, as is evident from the claims made by his officials in his behalf, had no clear idea of just what cases would be permitted to come to his courts by local authorities. He therefore made very large, but not easily defensible claims, without any apparent logical system. Every case that had ever been decided by kings was apparently included, but it was not as yet considered exactly what should, in reason and logic, belong to them. The majority of his claims were concerned with the king's rights to taxation and with crimes involving royal property, suggesting the primary motives behind his zeal. His method of enforcing these claims was to appoint a few officials in important shires whose task was to observe the conduct of sheriffs and to see that they executed justice honestly and efficiently; to send notes to sheriffs instructing them to deal with certain cases in their shires which had been brought to his attention, and calling upon them to hold sworn inquests (the germ of the grand jury) under which neighbors were summoned to give

testimony on oath that a crime had been committed; and, finally, to send out some of the members of his Curia of permanent officials with the right to try cases (with jurisdiction over wider areas than the single shires), to examine the conduct of local officials, including the sheriff, and to listen to complaints, while at the same time they had to keep an eye open to see that no one was cheating the king or usurping any of his prerogatives. It may be imagined that these innovations were more satisfactory to the complainant in search of justice than they were to the local officials, whose conduct was thus opened to scrutiny; but it must have accustomed the people to look toward the king for justice, by-passing if possible the local men, and was thus an important factor in the growth of the king's power.

All this, however, was only pioneered by Henry I, and was never regularized and systematized, since he was evidently still experimenting. The work was brought to fruition by his grandson, Henry II, and from his time became incorporated into English administrative procedure. Henry I's own work was halted by the long interregnum and civil war that followed his death.

THE REIGN OF STEPHEN (1135–1154)—CIVIL WAR AND DISINTEGRATION OF CENTRALIZED GOVERNMENT OF THE NORMAN MONARCHS

When Henry died he left only a daughter to succeed him, and it had not yet been settled that a woman could come to the English throne; her son was as yet only two years old. Many of the great nobles favored Stephen of Blois, the son of Henry's sister Adela, the daughter of William the Conqueror, and they thought the disputed crown provided an excellent chance to escape from the rigors of the earlier Norman reigns. Stephen had to make many promises and issue a charter relieving the nobles of some of their burdens before they would consent to his election; many nobles, however, would not accept him at all but took up arms on behalf of Matilda, Henry's daughter, who

[4] In saying that Henry "conceived" this project, it should be understood that the development of common law was a result of the efforts of Henry and his successors, and it must be considered doubtful whether he in fact realized what would be the result of his efforts to improve and to some degree centralize the administration of justice. As so often happens in life, a project started for one purpose, or adopted to meet certain well-defined ends, succeeds in accomplishing other ends altogether unforeseen. The procedural changes initiated by Henry succeeded in giving birth in later centuries to what we call common law, but it is only an inference from his acts to say that he had any intention of creating such law.

was married to a French prince, Geoffrey of Anjou.

The civil war that followed was utterly ruinous to the newly organized and efficient country. The nobles did almost whatever they wished. They built castles without license, they refused to pay their dues to the crown, they forced the peasants everywhere to build castles for them, and they tortured and imprisoned freemen, peasants, and townsmen for their money. All organized government broke down except unrestrained feudalism, and Stephen did not succeed in establishing his authority until almost at the end of the period described as his reign. Meanwhile Matilda's son Henry was growing up, and acquired his father's county of Anjou in France. When Louis VII of France divorced Eleanor of Aquitaine, Henry (surnamed Plantagenet) was able to capture the heiress and marry her though she was several years older than himself, and he thus inherited her vast lands of Poitou and Aquitaine. From his mother he inherited Normandy, which had not fallen to the English king Stephen with the throne of England. With this immense territory, far larger and richer than England, Henry was able to force Stephen to make a treaty with him recognizing his right to the English succession after Stephen's death. Since Stephen died soon afterward, Henry was the undisputed heir to the English throne, and in 1154 he made a determined effort to gain it.

THE REIGN OF HENRY II

Re-establishment of centralized government

It was natural that many of the nobles, with their unlicensed castles and their recovered sovereignty in their own domains, should have intensely disliked the prospect of Henry's arrival. They could not hope to resist him, however, in view of his possession of loyal French troops. The townsmen, of course, would welcome any king who was capable of keeping order, and the people in general would greatly prefer royal order to feudal anarchy. Henry, therefore, was able to make a triumphant procession through England; and though he spent most of his life in his French possessions, he was nevertheless one of the greatest, if not the greatest, of all the kings of England. He had a very considerable understanding of public finance, a necessity in his time; he chose competent public officials; and he was one of the best administrators that ever sat on a throne. He regarded England as a domain which, by efficient administration, could supply him with funds adequate to maintain his Continental possessions, as Frederic II, Holy Roman Emperor and king of Sicily, used Sicily to try to establish his imperial claims. But, though much English money was funneled abroad to pay for military expenditures in France, an incidental by-product was the excellent administration in England, and the expense was probably worth it to the English. When, however, Henry's younger son John tried to use the same policy, lost his Continental wars, and by foolish quarrels with the pope ruined his English administration, the result was Magna Carta, and the diminution of the power of the king. The French possessions of the English monarchy were never anything but a source of weakness to all English kings after Henry II, though the dream of a united France and England was many centuries in dying.

In administration Henry restored the system of his grandfather Henry I. He relieved the chancellor of all financial duties, keeping him as the king's chief official, while the Treasury was reorganized with a professional staff of full-time officials. To make his income more secure and larger, it was, of course, necessary at once to reduce the feudal nobility to submission. It was hardly possible for the nobles to resist a king with such additional sources of strength as his French domains, and they made little resistance when he began to pull down all the unlicensed castles and enforce the payment of the same taxes to which they had been subjected by Henry I, with some additions and heavier scutage. He dismissed almost every sheriff in the realm for activities under Stephen or for inefficiency, though he was

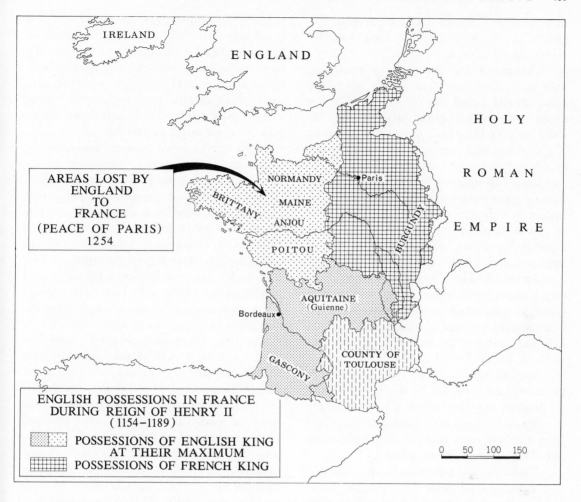

AREAS LOST BY
ENGLAND
TO
FRANCE
(PEACE OF PARIS)
1254

ENGLISH POSSESSIONS IN FRANCE
DURING REIGN OF HENRY II
(1154–1189)
POSSESSIONS OF ENGLISH KING
AT THEIR MAXIMUM
POSSESSIONS OF FRENCH KING

careful to have regular sworn inquests testi-fying to their failings. He instituted the Assize of Arms, which reformed the old militia, ordering all freemen to possess their own arms according to their means, so that they could serve in his army at short notice.

Legal and judicial reforms

Henry's greatest claim to fame, however, rests on his reform of the judicial system on the lines indicated by his grandfather, and the institution of many new arrange-ments which laid the foundation for the entire modern legal system of all English-speaking countries. Influenced by Roman law, which was beginning to be studied in England, he nevertheless retained the bulk of the English law, thus making the English system in some ways superior to the ancient

law of Rome, and capable of very great modification and development. From the beginning Henry seems to have realized that the enforcement of the common law above all earlier systems of law was essential to his power, and this unification was fundamental to all his reforms.

While the sheriff's courts remained, any complainant could apply to the chancery of the king to set a legal case in action within these courts. A writ could be purchased from the chancery for any of a great number of cases, and these at once became cases in which the king was interested, to be settled by the king's law. Writs could even be ob-tained in which the king directed the sheriff to enforce judgments which were the results of lawsuits, thus giving the king also a hand in legal matters previously under the jurisdiction of local courts and accustoming the people to the idea that the king was the source of all justice.

The grand and the petty or trial jury both have their origin in Henry II's reign, although the grand jury of Henry is much closer to the modern grand jury than was his small jury to the modern counterpart. The origin of the trial jury is to be found in the grand and possessory assizes of Henry II. It had been customary, when there was a dispute over the possession of land, to settle the matter in a feudal court, where the wager of battle decided the outcome. If, under Henry's legislation, the man from whom land was demanded wished to appeal to the king he could do so. Then both parties chose two knights, who would then elect twelve other knights who would state on oath before the king's justices which of the parties had the better right to the land. Henry's justiciar Ranulf de Glanville, in one of the earliest English lawbooks, states that the procedure was granted by the king in order to prevent any freeholder who was really entitled to the land from having to endanger it by the uncertain process of judicial combat. This was the grand assize.

Under the possessory assize, if a freeman had been ejected from his land, he could obtain a writ from the chancery calling upon the sheriff to call together twelve men who would certify whether there had been a wrongful ejection or not. In this case the jury had to state a matter of fact, whereas under the grand assize the twelve men were witnesses as to rights. In both cases evidence was used rather than the older method of trial by ordeal or combat; but the procedure applied only to certain specified cases. It was to be a century before a similar procedure was used for the majority of law cases. A beginning, however, had been made.

It is clear that this procedure interfered with feudal prerogatives and feudal courts, which were supposed to deal with disputed questions concerning the possession of property. The nobles, however, were in no position to protest, not even when the king proceeded to legislate changes in the hold-ing of such property, as, for instance, in his insistence on primogeniture and prohibition of the bequeathing of land by will. Once the new procedure had become customary, much of the feudal procedure seems to have died out. The king had won another great victory over the feudal system in the direction of centralized monarchy.

The grand jury's primary function was to ascertain what duties were owed to the king and whether they were being fulfilled. This was the sworn inquest of the earlier Norman monarchs in a different form. The sheriff was instructed by the king's writ to call a body of jurors together who were to swear such matters before the royal justices. But under the Assizes of Clarendon and Northampton (1166 and 1176) the sheriffs were now instructed to bring before the king's justices a group of men who were to swear if any of various specified crimes had been committed in their neighborhood, and to say who, in their opinion, had committed them. The accused would then be subjected to the ordeal or trial by combat. But as time went on, perhaps not at all in the reign of Henry, certain pleas could be made by the accused in front of a sworn jury such as that he had been elsewhere at the time (alibi) or that his accuser had been actuated by malice. He was finally allowed to appeal to a jury of his neighbors on the whole question of guilt or innocence; but it should be emphasized that for a long time the accused did not need to submit to the new procedure but could demand the old trial by ordeal or combat. Nevertheless, even if the accused were successful in the ordeal, the king could order him banished from the realm.

Under Henry I, as has been seen, the king's justices paid visits to the shires to see that justice was done. These visits, however, in Henry I's time seem to have been spasmodic and not regular. Henry II sent out justices regularly into each shire to hear criminal cases brought before them by the grand jury, and he sent out members of his own Curia irregularly to check upon officials, again using the device of the grand jury or sworn inquest. These judges even listened to complaints about the quality of beer sold in a shire, and a check was supposed to be kept on every matter of public importance; but, needless to say, this court was popular with few, and in later years its visits became rare, though it remained a salutary reminder to the people that the king's justice was capable of reaching them in any case of offense against the public interest.

It was as a result of his attempts to make a uniform law code for England that Henry quarreled with the Church in the person of his Archbishop of Canterbury, St. Thomas Becket. Becket had been Henry's chancellor, and the king felt sure that he could rely

ENGLAND IN THE 12TH CENTURY
SHOWING PRINCIPAL TOWNS
0   20   40   60
Miles

upon him as Archbishop to support the royal reforms. But Becket at once upon investiture became a stubborn supporter of all papal claims, and in particular of the right of the Church to try all offenders, whatever their crimes, as long as they were ecclesiastics. Becket refused to accept the Constitutions of Clarendon (1164), the main provisions of which deprived the ecclesiastical courts of the right to try "criminous clerks," or clerics who had committed a crime against the king's law. The recalcitrance of the archbishop ultimately resulted in his murder after the king had in a rage incited some of his knights to the deed. The murder shocked the country. Henry had to do severe penance, and he withdrew part of the Constitutions. The remainder continued in force, allowing the king to make ecclesiastical appointments and preventing the papacy from directly taxing the English Church without the king's consent. In addition, certain important regulations regarding the possession of property by the Church were allowed to stand. The ecclesiastical courts experienced a continuous growth for some time in England after the murder, and Henry was effectively prevented from establishing his jurisdiction in the matters which had customarily been allowed to the Church, as has been discussed in an earlier chapter.

RECRUDESCENCE OF POWER OF FEUDAL
NOBILITY—CHECKS UPON ROYAL POWER

Foreign wars of Richard I and John

Richard I, the Lion-Hearted, who was already in possession of many of his father's lands in France while Henry was still alive, was interested in England primarily as a source of revenue, and spent only six months of his reign (1189–1199) in England. But Richard's financial needs were enormous. Philip Augustus was king of France, and was busily engaged in trying to take the English possessions for himself; while he had only indifferent success against Richard when the English king was present to defend his lands, Philip was usually able to win against Richard's brother John, who was a feeble warrior. Richard, as has been seen in an earlier chapter, spent a large part of his reign on the Third Crusade, an extremely expensive campaign for which his people in England had to pay. Richard's resources thus were squandered all his life on unproductive and unprofitable warfare; and when he was finally captured on his way home from the Crusade, and was forced to pay a huge ransom, the English people found themselves saddled with a debt which it was impossible to pay from regular income.

Nevertheless, his brother John, succeeding to the throne when Richard was killed in 1199, had to carry on the French wars, for which he never possessed adequate funds. Moreover, the English nobles, seeing no profit or likely success under John in this war, were determined to resist the new king's efforts to make the national militia serve in his own personal foreign wars. It was therefore not surprising that John, with no military talent of his own, with a poorly paid mercenary army, and with disgruntled nobles, was unable to make any headway against such an able monarch as Philip Augustus of France, who could not stand up perhaps to Richard in battle but was more than a match for John. Moreover, John fell into most of the traps set for him by Philip, useful legal traps connected with the fact that John, as well as being king of England, was a vassal of the French king for his French lands.

Philip needed to put John in the wrong because as a feudal king himself he could not force his own lords to follow him on lengthy campaigns; under the cover of a legal excuse he could, however, command his lords to execute justice on John and they would be inclined to obey. At all events when John committed a flagrant breach of feudal custom by marrying a wife already promised to one of his French vassals, Philip had no difficulty in having the English king condemned in his feudal court. John, indeed, was so clearly in the wrong under feudal law that he did not bother to attend Philip's court. When, finally, John murdered his own nephew Arthur, who had perhaps a better title to the English throne than had John himself, and who was also a vassal of Philip and supported by him, almost every French noble of importance joined the French king in his attempt to drive John from his French possessions.

It was impossible for John, with his attenuated resources drawn exclusively from England, to defend these possessions. He lost Brittany, Anjou, Maine, Touraine, and even Normandy. Only Poitou, the private possession of John's mother, Eleanor of Aquitaine, remained loyal to the English crown and could not be captured, though under John's successor this too was lost to Louis viii, who had succeeded Philip Augustus in 1223. Only Aquitaine itself, of all the English possessions in France, remained to Henry iii of England (1216–1272), and this really remained in English hands only by courtesy of St. Louis ix of France (1226–1270), who agreed to leave it to Henry in exchange for recognition of French sovereignty over the remainder of the French conquests. Thus England, to her own great advantage, was shorn of most of her French possessions, enabling her kings to concentrate upon English needs until the middle of the fourteenth century, when another series of English kings foolishly renewed the attempt to rule France as well as England.

Internal consequences of foreign policy of Richard and John

Henry ii's bureaucracy was so well organized and it had such a firm hold on the country that for a time the absence of his successors from England made little difference. But the unfortunate English officials were compelled to tighten the screws upon the people for the purpose of extracting enough money for the kings. New taxes were added, much property was confiscated, including the possessions of Jews, who were unable to defend themselves against arbitrary exactions. Offices were sold, especially the office of sheriff. Although the king's Curia appointed new officials to watch the sheriffs and to take over some of their duties, the sheriffs, forced to recuperate their

finances by exactions of their own, got into the habit of selling justice. Gradually the efficiency of the governmental machinery was undermined. Perhaps the only gain for the people in the reigns of these two irresponsible monarchs lay in the numerous charters which were granted to the towns in exchange for money and which gave them for a time a considerable degree of autonomy.

John's financial needs were as great as those of Richard. He had to try to complete the payment of Richard's ransom, which had been paid at the time only at the expense of future revenue; he had his own wars in France to pay for; and finally (as has been seen in Chapter 11), he became involved with Pope Innocent iii over his appointment of an Archbishop of Canterbury, and England had to suffer the rigors of an interdict, which seriously damaged the revenue-producing abilities of the country. To complete the ruin of the king, his own chancery, after the death of his able chancellor Hubert Walter, was made up of men who were no longer of the caliber of the great officials of the previous reigns. In these circumstances, as we have already seen, the English nobles began to abandon John and even look to the French monarchy for help. The English clergy objected to John's efforts to tax them, and even Innocent's acceptance of John as his vassal did not reconcile them to him. The towns were perhaps the hardest hit of all, since their wealth was visible and could be more easily extracted than that of the nobles. But the nobles objected also to John's efforts to force them to serve in France and to his general ill success.

This royal irresponsibility was the background to Magna Carta, which the nobles forced John to sign at Runnymede in 1215. John's only support at this time came from his mercenaries, whose loyalty was dependent upon his ability to pay them, and a very small minority of his nobles. The aid of Innocent iii was entirely useless to him, since Innocent did not command the loyalty of the English Church in the struggle, not even that of the Archbishop of Canterbury, his own nominee for whom he had fought so hard with the king. The Charter therefore was a dictated document, and the nobles were fully aware that it was. They would have been astonished to learn that future generations would come to regard it as the cornerstone of English liberties.

Magna Carta (1215)

In order to understand the importance of the Great Charter a short review of the position of the English king in 1215 may be helpful. The king was still in theory elected; his title had to be confirmed by the assembly of the great nobles of the realm, his tenants in chief. What the nobles could bestow they also could theoretically take away. They could have elected the nephew of John to the throne, and it is possible that they might have done so if Arthur had been of age, and if John's mother, Eleanor of Aquitaine, had not advised her son on the matter of seizing the reins of government and putting pressure on the nobles for an immediate decision. Though the king was overlord of the whole country and every noble owed him allegiance as suzerain, the king himself was bound by feudal custom and law, and was entitled only to feudal aids, which could be commuted by money payments, or scutage. Nevertheless the amount of money paid in scutage was theoretically subject to negotiation between the king and the lord, and could not be raised by unilateral executive action on the part of the king. When, therefore, the king was made to agree in the Charter that he would not levy scutage without the consent of the great council, the nobles were simply protecting their own legal rights. But they were also trying to put to the fore the old council of all tenants in chief, whose functions had been so largely usurped by the king's bureaucracy. This latter body of officials had retained the title of the Curia Regis but was in fact composed of the king's nominees, who, if they were even tenants in chief at all, had probably been given their position by the reigning king who had endowed them with lands from his own royal territories. Though in

later generations the article in the Charter which forced the king to tax only with the consent of the Great Council was interpreted to mean "no taxation without representation," it was in 1215 only the reiteration of a principle which was the existing custom and law of the land.

The nobles made a further effort to prevent the encroachment of the king's legal powers over their own. The king's feudal court was concerned only with matters affecting the king and his relations with his tenants in chief. But all these tenants had their own feudal courts, whose functions had been largely usurped by the monarchy. The nobles did not wish to put the clock back altogether. They recognized the value of some of the king's efforts. But in matters affecting feudal relationships, and a suzerain's rights over his vassal, they would not accept the king's claims. And they especially did not want to abandon their old prerogatives in favor of arbitrary confiscation, buying and selling of justice for the financial benefit of the king and his officials. Thus, when in the Charter the king promised not to imprison or dispossess any free man, nor to outlaw and banish him, except by the legal judgment of his peers, the nobles were trying to reassert the feudal authority of their own courts, and at the same time to prevent the abuses in the king's courts. But again it can be seen how such a promise could later be interpreted to mean that jury trial was to be guaranteed by the monarch.

It cannot be too strongly emphasized that a medieval English king was bound by feudal and local custom and was in no sense absolute, though English monarchs since the Conquest had in fact by administrative action forged much of the machinery of absolutism. In the Great Charter the nobles tried to underline this point, to take away some of the power usurped by the king's small council and give it to the large council of tenants in chief, who held their position by birth as fiefholders in the feudal system, and thus could not be dismissed by the king unless the king were permitted to use his own courts to dispossess them of their land.

When the nobles asserted that the king was below the law, the feudal law, they were only stating what was undoubtedly the legal position of the king in 1215; though parliamentary supporters in later centuries were to enunciate this principle again when they wished to exalt the power of the legislature over the executive, and to insist that the king obey the laws which had been passed by themselves with his approval.

Realizing that the Charter was worth very little without means of enforcement, the nobles inserted one clause which authorized the council of nobles to choose twenty-five of their number who should try first to obtain redress of grievances, and if this failed the clause stated that they should be authorized to organize an armed rebellion against the king. Naturally this was not worth the paper it was written on. It was merely an attempt by the nobles to devise a procedure for taking action against the king, and it did give some color of legality to such action; but no king could be expected to authorize action against himself in the event that he failed to redress grievances. But in the course of the next century there were efforts to force the king to observe the law, and these efforts included armed rebellion. Since the king resisted all such efforts as far as he could, he can hardly be supposed to have felt himself bound by the Charter to authorize them.

THE GROWTH OF PARLIAMENTARY INSTITUTIONS

The Provisions of Oxford and the "Baron's Parliament"

In 1216 John died and was succeeded by his son, a boy of nine. As we have seen already, John made no attempt to observe the Charter in the last year of his reign, and in this he was supported by his feudal overlord the pope. The English lords, called "barons" in the Charter, who had been intriguing with Philip Augustus and had received his son into England as their nominee for king, were largely disarmed by John's death. In the expectation of improved conditions under his son and the regency, which was to rule until he was of age, they returned to their allegiance. Philip abandoned the attempt to win the English throne, and the minority of completely recalcitrant barons were defeated by the regents, who renewed the Charter in the name of Henry III. Frequently throughout the next centuries the king was called upon to swear to observe the Charter, with some clauses omitted, a pledge he usually made on the promise of increased voluntary aids from the nobles. This renewal gradually gave it the fundamental position in the evolution of the English monarchy that it has held in modern opinion.

Henry III was still interested in the recovery of his foreign possessions, and was thus constantly in need of money. Nevertheless he and his advisers did not dare to break the Charter quite openly; on several occasions during his reign Henry summoned his barons and prelates to obtain their voluntary acceptance of his proposals for increased taxation of the clergy and nobility. But his futile foreign policy involved the country in wars with France at the behest of the papacy, and he was too partial to foreigners whenever he had to appoint officials and clergy. So at last the barons lost patience with him. In 1258 a number of feudal lords summoned a "parliament," known as the Mad Parliament, to concert measures for keeping the king under control and restraining his taxation. They proceeded to issue the Provisions of Oxford, a series of reforms which the king was forced to accept. Some of their grievances he was compelled to redress, and he was virtually controlled for a while by this self-constituted committee of greater barons.

Two years later the barons evidently felt that they, too, needed a wider basis of support and authority. They therefore summoned to a special assembly three knights from each shire, who would represent the interests of the lesser lords of the realm who were not tenants in chief of the king. The king issued counterinstructions to the knights to come to meet him instead, thus adding to the confusion. It was impossible for the king to accept indefinitely this kind of dictation from his vassals, and it was clear that civil war could not be long delayed.

When it finally came, in 1264, the barons had discovered a capable leader in the person of Simon de Montfort, son of the leader of the Albigensian Crusade, a French nobleman who had originally been brought to England as one of the king's French favorites. But by this time he had quarreled with the king and identified himself with the baronial interests. Putting himself at the head of an army of barons, he gave battle to the king, who was severely defeated at the battle of Lewes (1264) and taken prisoner. Simon was, for the moment, supreme. But there was no intention of harming the monarch; the sole interest of Simon and the barons was in forcing Henry to yield some of his powers to the feudal aristocracy. The king's own son, later to become Edward I, supported the lords against his father for a time. Simon summoned four knights to be elected to meet the king during 1264, but nothing came of the effort. Then he summoned a full parliament, of lords and higher clergy, though he was careful to choose only those who favored his party, and to these he added representatives from the shires (two knights from each to be elected in the presence of the sheriff) and, for the first time, two representatives from each city and borough. This Parliament of Simon de Montfort was the most representative assembly that had been called since the Conquest, but it came to nothing, for Edward deserted him, returning to his father, and Simon was defeated and killed in the battle of Evesham in 1265. But Edward seems to have remembered the salutary lesson, and it was in his reign that Parliament first became an established institution, giving advice to the king, who was expected to legislate only after having taken careful consideration of such advice. As soon as the war was over Henry conceded many of the desired reforms in the Statute of Marlborough (1267), which to a large extent summed up and confirmed concessions extracted from him during the revolutionary period.

These for the most part concerned the crown's claims to jurisdiction over questions of land tenure traditionally handled by the feudal courts.

The Reign of Edward I (1272–1307)

In 1295 the same Edward, now King Edward I, summoned the most inclusive parliament hitherto called, which was to receive the name of the Model Parliament. But he had already been reigning for twenty-three years (1272–1295) before he found this move necessary, and for years he had been legislating, sometimes with the assent of an advisory body and sometimes not. Indeed, the bulk of his legislation—and he was the first English king who seriously attempted to make statutes which would endure permanently and thus constitute the law of the whole land until repealed—took place before his Model Parliament. To his court the year after his accession came not only the tenants in chief, but knights of the shire and burgesses from the towns, for the primary purpose of swearing fealty to him. Since Edward declared publicly that he had promulgated the great statutes of his reign upon the advice of various great men of the realm, we may presume that he consulted those whose interests were affected before he legislated. But after the Model Parliament it became established as a precedent that statutes would be made only after consultation with a Parliament of this new and comprehensive nature. For more than a century the king continued to draw up the statutes himself with the aid of his council, but the statutes were supposed to be in conformity with what the Parliament had advised him. When members of Parliament complained that the statutes did not in fact conform, it was with a sense of grievance as if the king and council had cheated them; and ultimately they forced him to allow them to make the statutes to which he had only to give his assent.

In this Model Parliament the sheriffs were summoned to cause two knights of each shire, two citizens of each city, and two burgesses of each borough to be elected. The election was to take place in the county court, though it has never been determined for certain what the method of election was at this time and who was eligible to vote. It seems probable that every freeman possessing any property at all in his own right was eligible, though in practice the sheriff regarded the right to vote as belonging to certain properties only. Conjointly with these new additions to the body of the king's advisers, the lords temporal and the lords spiritual were also summoned—the nobility and the clergy; but by no means all the king's tenants in chief were thus honored. To the Parliament of 1296 only forty-eight lords were summoned. The higher clergy, bishops and archbishops, were to attend in force, incidentally considerably outnumbering at this period the nobility in the Parliament; they were supposed to bring with them representatives of the lower clergy, though in practice this procedure was abandoned, as the Church preferred to vote its taxes in ecclesiastical assemblies, and was not interested in the other functions of the Parliament. The higher clergy, however, continued to sit in Parliament by virtue of their positions as barons.

It is important to note that from the beginning the representatives of the Commons (knights of the shire and the townsmen—constituting the third estate) were instructed to receive full powers from their constituents to represent them in all matters. They were not supposed, as in the French States-General, to refer back to their constituencies for further advice and instructions, like ambassadors; and it has remained the theory to this day, and in England largely the practice, that the members of Parliament are national representatives advising the government rather than spokesmen for the local interests which elected them.

It is not known whether the ex officio members of the Parliament and the elected members sat separately from the beginning, but before long they were doing so. The knights of the shire were, of course, landholders and might be presumed to have many interests in common with the larger

barons. But they also had divergent interests as subvassals rather than tenants in chief; though they might also be minor tenants in chief of the king, they usually were not. At all events, these knights decided, and it was a decision of supreme importance for the development of constitutional government, that they would throw in their lot with the townsmen, by whom they were outnumbered, but to whom for centuries they supplied leadership in Parliament. These two groups grew into the modern House of Commons, and both were classified as part of the third estate, while the higher clergy (the first estate) and the higher nobility (the second estate) became the House of Lords.

As a member of either House would have considered it in his time, the primary purpose of having a Parliament was to regulate and minimize the power of the king, especially in matters of taxation. The Parliament presented petitions to the king and could ask for justice even in minor complaints, which the king would refer to the suitable court or department of state. In time these petitions became a means of initiating legislation; the petitions would be discussed and recommendations given, and the king was then expected to act upon them. But the king usually only willingly called Parliament when he needed money and thus gave Parliament the opportunity to go into the whole question of his expenditures. It gradually became accepted that the power of taxation was in the hands of Parliament except for those taxes which belonged to the king from ancient times and were his under feudal law. It was this principle, and its acceptance, that led directly to the limited monarchy at the end of the seventeenth century, and also was ultimately to make the House of Commons superior to the House of Lords, since revenue from the former was far more elastic than anything a few lords and bishops could hope to raise. Only two years after the Model Parliament, at a time when Edward I was in great need of money, and was engaged in controversy with Pope Boniface VIII over the taxing of the clergy, Edward tried to collect money without the consent of his Parliament and to force his barons to serve in a foreign war. The barons took to arms, supported by the merchants whose commodities the king had claimed to be able to tax, and the king was forced to give way, swearing an oath that he would not make such new taxes in the future without the common consent of the realm. His grandson later had to confirm the promise, and it became generally accepted as the law and custom of the land.

Foreign wars of Edward I—Addition of Wales to England—Edward made a serious attempt to unite both Wales and Scotland to his kingdom. After a long and difficult war he was successful in adding Wales, though there were many revolts afterward which were ultimately suppressed. As symbol of the union, he made his son Prince of Wales, a title held by the eldest son of the king to the present time.[5] He intervened in a disputed succession to the crown of Scotland, and was successful in several battles. He was successful largely because, under the Statute of Winchester (1285), he had remodeled the English army, specifying the arms each freeman must bear, and because he relied more upon the bowmen of the English free peasantry and townsmen than upon the feudal nobility, whose fighting was by now seriously out of date. But Edward's son in 1314 lost the battle of Bannockburn to the Scots under Robert I (the Bruce), and thereafter Scotland had full independence until the union of the two crowns under James I (a Scot) in 1603. On the whole Edward I maintained the precarious hold of the English crown on the parts of southern France that remained to it after the defeats of John and Henry III.

Further growth of parliamentary power to the end of Middle Ages

In a book of this kind it is unnecessary to go in detail into the growth of Parliament once it had been established as a going institution entitled to be called regularly for the purpose of petitioning the king, even if

he had no demands to make upon it. Edward II, a weak king (1302–1327) was taken to task by Parliament for the activities of his council, of which more will be said in the next section, and Parliament made certain demands upon him for more regular sessions, to which he agreed, later revoking his decision. The barons took up arms and forced Edward to abdicate, while stating officially in Parliament that he had been deposed, thus arrogating to themselves the right of deposition. However, as they forced him to abdicate after they had deposed him, they do not appear to have been greatly impressed with the legality of their action. Edward III (1327–1377) was in constant need of money for the Hundred Years' War, which was, for the most part, popular with the soldiers and nobility; it was usually successful and loot was available. But the townsmen were not always so contented with the war, and Edward had to find many new sources of revenue. It is at this time that the customs and excise (tunnage and poundage) became a regular imposition, though granted by Parliament for only limited periods and not intended to be a permanent source of revenue for the king. There were a number of other experimental taxes, including income, personal property, and poll taxes. But, as always in the Middle Ages, the new taxes were only temporary grants for definite needs. A permanent source of revenue beyond the king's regular income from crown resources, and the proceeds of his courts of justice, was never acceptable until comparatively modern times. Edward even resorted to loans from Italian bankers, then found himself unable to repay, in spite of their acceptance of the English crown as security.

The reign of Richard II (1377–1399), short as it was, was of considerable constitutional importance. Coming to the throne as a boy of eleven, Richard was at first dominated by his council, which was constantly opposed by the great lords in Parliament who were not in the council. When he finally came of age, he attempted to rule personally, calling Parliament irregularly or not at all, and

[5] The son of the reigning queen of England has, however, not yet been declared Prince of Wales.

trying to use his executive power to collect sufficient money for his needs. But a baronial revolution overthrew him, and the indictment drawn up against him in Parliament declared that he had offended against the laws and customs of the realm by trying to rule and tax without the consent of Parliament, and, again as in the case of Edward II, Parliament deposed him and compelled him to abdicate, choosing as king, under the title of Henry IV (1399–1413), a noble of the House of Lancaster who was clearly not the best heir to the throne. No doubt Parliament was influenced in its choice by the fact that Henry had led the revolt against Richard, who was murdered shortly afterward.

Owing his position to parliamentary support, Henry allowed Parliament to perform all the functions it claimed for itself, and rarely succeeded in imposing his will upon it. He was the only fully constitutional king of the Middle Ages. The House of Commons began to audit the king's accounts, and directed the expenditure of the money it voted to him, and the wording of legislation was now determined by Parliament before a bill reached the king for signature.

Though Henry V (1413–1422) safely succeeded to his father's position, it was not without opposition from another noble house, which had, in its own opinion, a better right to the throne—the House of York. At least in part in order to head off such dynastic opposition, Henry V picked a quarrel with France and plunged his country into a foreign war, in which he was brilliantly successful, winning by the Treaty of Troyes (1420) the consent of the deranged French king to his own succession to the throne of France. Henry, however, died prematurely, and, as we shall see, his son was unable to make good his father's claim to the French crown. As this son, Henry VI (1422–1461) was intermittently insane and never exercised an effective control over it, Parliament in his time was usually supreme.

When Henry VI became permanently insane, the House of York decided to take matters into its own hands. The whole of France except Calais had been lost, mer-

cenaries defeated in France returned to England, where they preyed upon the countryside almost with impunity, while the officials of the government were unable to exercise their functions and were frequently unpaid and corrupt. In these circumstances Richard, Duke of York, claimed that the country required a competent king and that this should be himself, by a hereditary right superior to that of the actual reigning monarch Henry VI. The supporters of the Lancastrian house did not accept his claim and war broke out.[6] Richard was killed. His son and heir Edward (IV) proclaimed himself king in 1461. But his title was not uncontested, and he continued to wage the War of the Roses until his chief opponent, the Earl of **Warwick (the Kingmaker), was killed at the battle of Barnet (1471) and Henry's wife and young son were defeated in the same year at the battle of Tewkesbury. Edward's title to the throne was then formally acknowledged by a subservient Parliament.**

Edward may be considered as the real founder of the absolute monarchy. Henry VII, the first Tudor king, merely followed Edward's policy, with various improvements. Edward called Parliament rarely, and used various indirect means for gaining money for his rule, especially from the townsmen, who did not mind taxation, even severe taxation including forced loans (called benevolences!), provided the War of the Roses did not break out again and ruin everyone. Edward's monarchy was strong, and it was far from constitutional. He had come to power by violence and he did not mind using some violent means to maintain his throne. He no longer had any wars with France on his hands, and his increased revenue obtained from the towns, plus a merciless use of his judicial powers to extract further income, enabled him to be free of Parliament, as Henry VII was able to be when he wished. When Edward died his sons were children, and they were imprisoned and murdered by their uncle, Richard III, who usurped the

---

[6] This war is called the "War of the Roses" because the Lancastrian emblem was a red rose, while that of the House of York was a white rose.

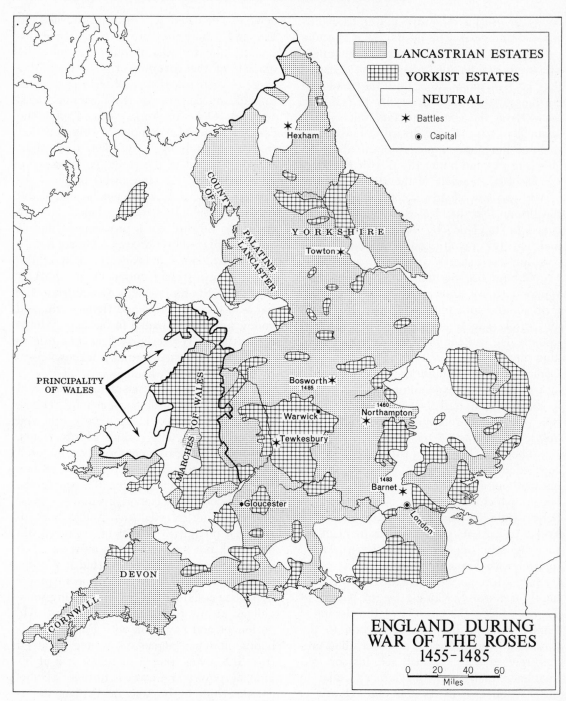

ENGLAND DURING
WAR OF THE ROSES
1455-1485

LANCASTRIAN ESTATES
YORKIST ESTATES
NEUTRAL
★ Battles
⊙ Capital

throne, but reigned for too short a time (1483–1485) and with too little security for any constitutional changes to take place in that period. He called only one Parliament. In 1485 he was killed at the battle of Bosworth, and an outright usurper, with hardly more than a shadow of a claim to the throne through his mother, was accepted as king by Parliament, on the condition, or at least after a promise, that he would marry the heiress of the House of York. Thus began the great Tudor monarchy, and the establishment of an absolutism under which Parliament was clearly an unequal partner in the rule of the country. The subsequent history of England, the ascendancy of the Tudor monarchs beginning with Henry VII, and the final assertion of superior power by Parliament will be dealt with in Chapters 19 and 20.

THE MACHINERY OF GOVERNMENT IN THE LATER MIDDLE AGES

The king's council

We have already seen how the Curia Regis had gradually become a body of officials who held their position by appointment of the monarch. In Edward I's time the council was very large, and almost half of its members did not belong to the feudal nobility. They were well paid by the king for their services, and in his time were far more important than the fledgling Parliament; they drew up all legislation and altered it in accordance with the king's wishes. The king usually consulted at least his chief barons before legislating, and in several cases he also consulted his full Parliament. The Lords and the Commons were both anxious to curb the power of this council and bring it to some extent under their own control, and by this means use it even as a check upon the king himself. When the medieval kings were strong the council obeyed the monarch; when they were weak the nobles usually managed to put some of their number on the council and thus kept the king under their control. In the time of Henry VI the council itself was rent by faction, some favoring the Lancastrians and some the Yorkists.

The Parliament invented a useful device for getting rid of unpopular members of the council. This was impeachment, under which the Commons drew up a complaint and the Lords, in their judicial capacity, tried the particular minister. The procedure, however, was not used very frequently in the Middle Ages, and all the known cases occurred within a period of seventy-three years. Thereafter there were none until the reign of the Stuarts in the seventeenth century. A bill of attainder could also be passed, a bill which went through both houses of Parliament simply decreeing that such or such a man should be punished, usually with death. This deprived the man of any form of trial, and was only used in the Middle Ages during the Wars of the Roses when the ruling faction disposed of the opposition by this means.

Richard II, in his efforts to establish his personal rule and independence of Parliament, appointed commoners to his council almost exclusively as an instrument for keeping the feudal nobility in subjection. In order to legislate as needed he used the council to make decrees or ordinances, a right which he claimed, but which was of doubtful legality at this time. He claimed also another ancient royal right—to dispense with the laws which were already on the statute books. This right had certainly been exercised by kings in the past, and it was doubtful if Parliament could have insisted that the king could not exempt individuals from certain laws, especially when the laws in question had to be executed by him. But in the bill of indictment against Richard at the time of his deposition his claims to be above the law and to be able to make new law were listed among his many offenses.[7]

Under the Lancastrian monarchy, which, as we have seen, was unusually constitutional, Parliament had a considerable hand in the appointment of the council. The majority of its members belonged to the House of Lords, either lords spiritual or lords temporal. However, it was at this time that the nobles in the council, as partisans of the Lancastrian or Yorkist cause, quarreled incessantly with each other, and majority groups in the council virtually ruled England during the reign of Henry VI, whose incompetence and intermittent insanity necessitated rule by a regency for most of his reign.

The council was also a law court for special cases. For much of the later Middle

[7] The charge that the king had illegally dispensed with the laws was also brought against James II in the seventeenth century, and was the principal ground for declaring that he had forfeited the throne ("Glorious Revolution," 1688–1689).

Ages it claimed to be a court of appeal, entitled to call in question decisions of lower courts. It was also a tool of the monarchy as a court under the direct control of the king which was in a position to try important offenders without any means of appeal. It could be, and was, used against the feudal nobility on occasion, and was necessarily objected to by Parliament, which passed a considerable number of laws trying to take away its power and guarantee elementary liberties and jury trials for all offenders. Only a small minority of the council actually sat in judgment as a law court; its procedure was speedy and lacked the formality of the lower courts, and for this reason even Parliament sometimes approved of its use, as, for instance, against rioters and for offenses against wage-fixing legislation approved of by everyone except those affected by it. This committee of the council was revived by Henry VII as the Court of Star Chamber, and in the time of the Stuarts, Parliament resurrected all the legislation of the Middle Ages against the jurisdiction of the council in the effort to show that the laws of England from ancient times did not approve of it.

Justices of the Peace

We have seen earlier that Richard I, or his Curia, first began to appoint assistants to the sheriff who were supposed to watch him and see that the king's peace was maintained. Gradually in the later Middle Ages these guardians of the peace began to be given the bulk of the powers of the sheriffs, and from this time on the sheriff's position became a burden which most men preferred to avoid. It carried little power and small chance of recompense and was an annual position. All it had was dignity. But the guardians of the peace, soon to be called justices, took their place as perhaps the most useful and important of all the instruments of government devised by medieval monarchs. They were at first authorized only to receive indictments against offenders and commit them to trial when the king's justices arrived in their neighborhood. But very soon they were given jurisdiction over minor criminal cases. When Parliament after the Black Death proposed to keep the wages of laborers down to the figure they had commanded before the plague and the shortage of labor that resulted from it, it was to the justices that it turned for enforcement. The kings used them for all minor and even some major cases which affected the king and which were entitled to be tried by royal justice. The justices were empowered first to try minor cases without a jury (summary jurisdiction) and then they were commanded to hold court four times a year (quarter sessions) to try with a jury any offenses except treason, though if the cases were difficult they had to remand to the assizes when the itinerant king's justices visited their area. The justices originally were paid, and the practice continued for several centuries until with the falling value of money their wage was so small, being fixed by statute, that payment was allowed to lapse.

The class from which the justices were drawn was the lower nobility and gentry, only very rarely from the upper nobility. It was a position of great prestige, if little profit. There was for centuries a demand from Parliament that the judges should be elected; but this was never conceded by the kings, not even in modern times. They remained the instrument of the king's rule at the local level. They looked after the king's interest, and had the power of enforcing both his instructions and the statutes made by Parliament, everything from the failure to pay taxes to the suppression of riots. By the sixteenth century all local administration was in their hands. Though in very modern times they have lost some of their power, to this day in England anyone who commits a misdemeanor in any rural area will be haled before a justice of the peace, who may remand him to quarter sessions, where that justice or another will try him in front of a jury and sentence him afterward to his just deserts.

THE WARS WITH FRANCE

As we have seen, the foreign wars waged by English monarchs gave an opportunity to

Parliament to limit their power by withholding funds unless grievances were redressed. In this section we shall consider the wars themselves in a little more detail. The duchy of Aquitaine, comprising Guienne and Gascony, remained in English hands after the first series of wars which ended in 1259. The French kings, once they had almost completed the unification of the territorial area of France, spared no efforts to finish their work. But the English found these provinces economically valuable, especially the export duties on the wine which was the chief product of the area. Few kings troubled to consider whether these duties compensated for the treasure poured out in trying to retain them, because it was not usual for kings to consider such wars in terms of economic loss or gain, whatever the merchants concerned thought of the matter. The English king, as feudal vassal of the French king for this territory, always objected to the ceremony of homage to him which by custom the English king had to perform, and the French king usually made complaints about the improper way in which the English king performed it. A faulty performance of the ceremony gave the former a chance to declare the latter a faithless vassal and call upon his other vassals to take the English king's land. The nobles of the area also could be induced to take complaints to the French rather than the English courts when it suited their interest, and the French king, nothing loath, would often support them.

Moreover, there were frequent quarrels between English and Flemish towns over fishery rights in the North Sea, and their ships sometimes preyed upon each other. But in most respects England and Flanders were in agreement with each other since the English produced raw wool which the Flemish towns manufactured into cloth. The Flemish towns were officially under the rule of the Count of Flanders, a vassal of the French crown, but they resented his rule as strongly as the Italian towns resented their noble masters, all except the ruling oligarchies in these towns. The Count of Flanders would support the oligarchies in the towns and would invite his overlord the French king to support him, while the smaller merchants, those who were dependent upon the English trade, invited the English king, who was vitally interested in doing business with them, to support them. In the early fourteenth century the Count of Flanders, in obedience to the French crown, arrested all Englishmen in his realm, and the English king retaliated by stopping all trade between England and Flanders. Under this kind of pressure the Flemish burghers overthrew the oligarchic governments in their cities and invited the English king to become their overlord in return for a restoration of the old trade between the countries.

At this moment Edward III, a warrior king, discovered that his claim to the French throne was at least as good as the French king's own, crossed over to Flanders, and at Ghent was proclaimed King of France (1340). The first part of the Hundred Years' War which followed went uniformly in favor of the English, whose army was more than a match for the feudal hosts of the French monarchy, and after they had won the naval battle of Sluys (1340) and the land battles of Crécy and Poitiers (1346, 1356) and had

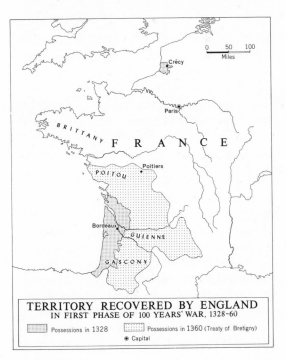

TERRITORY RECOVERED BY ENGLAND
IN FIRST PHASE OF 100 YEARS' WAR, 1328-60

Possessions in 1328   Possessions in 1360 (Treaty of Bretigny)
● Capital

TERRITORIES IN FRANCE
SUBJECT TO ENGLISH INFLUENCE
OR OWING ALLEGIANCE TO ENGLISH CROWN
(AT BEGINNING OF THE WORK OF JOAN OF ARC)
1429

taken the French king prisoner, a treaty was signed giving three counties in the north including Calais to the English, recognizing the English king's right to Aquitaine, and adding the important province of Poitou, but relieving him of the obligation of performing feudal homage for them. Much of this gain was lost by a renewal of the war a short time later, but the successors of Edward III were kept too busy at home to renew the war until the time of Henry v. And by this time France itself was rent by civil war and struggles between two factions for the control of an intermittently insane monarch and his extremely sane queen, Isabel of Bavaria.

Henry v in 1415, allied with the Burgundians, one of the French factions whose position will be explained in the next section, won the battle of Agincourt against tremendous odds, though favored by the French insistence on using the armor which was traditional but a deathtrap against the English yeomen archers. This time it was impossible for the French to recover, and the Burgundian duke, aided by Isabel of Bavaria, arranged the Treaty of Troyes (1420) under which Henry was to inherit the throne of France after the death of the mad king, was to become Regent of France, and was to marry the daughter of the French king. This was the nearest the English ever reached to the full throne of France; but at the same time the success of the English claim was dependent upon the continued support of the Burgundians since the treaty could never be enforced against a united France. Henry's claim to the French throne through his wife and the ancient claim of Edward III could never be the equal of that of the king's reigning son, in spite of the fact that for the moment the latter happened to be at odds with the powerful Burgundians.

But in any case the English cause was ruined by the premature death of Henry v in the same year as the death of the mad king Charles vi of France. The heir of Henry was a child, while the heir of the French king possessed only part of the south of France, being excluded from the remainder by the Burgundians and the English. As long as the Burgundians supported the boy Henry vi of England, the English were able to hold northern France and their remaining possessions in the south. Together they pursued the war against the Dauphin⁸ Charles (vii) with some vigor, while the latter sank into a despondency from which it needed a miracle to rescue him. Harassed by lack of funds through the inability to collect any taxes of substantial value, cut off from his capital, which was in Burgundian hands, the Dauphin seemed to have little in his favor except that the Duke of Burgundy had no title to the French crown and did not claim it, and the English king who had was only

a boy—while his regents, beset by faction as they were, could not organize the country without far more funds than the English Parliament allowed its Lancastrian monarchs, even though these greatly exceeded the resources of Charles the Dauphin.

But the miracle came in the person of Joan of Arc, who not only succeeded in arousing Charles, who always seems to have believed in her, but in awakening a kind of nascent patriotism and anti-English sentiment which was to prove of great value as an aid to the diplomatic ability shown later by Charles vii. The English and Burgundians were driven from their siege of Orléans, by the personal efforts of the Maid of Orléans, as she was called thereafter. Then, with a sure instinct for the dramatic patriotic gesture, she insisted that Charles go to Rheims to be crowned king as his ancestors had been crowned before him. Thereafter Charles and his counselors concentrated on the attempt to dislodge the Duke of Burgundy from his English alliance, an effort which was ultimately successful, though not till after the capture and death of Joan, as will be seen in the next section. Although the Burgundian dukes had to be paid a high price and played almost no part in the expulsion of the English, Charles vii was able to obtain funds from the States-General and to reorganize his army. In the later years of his reign he was uniformly successful, gaining, very surprisingly, the title of Charles the Victorious —surprisingly for one who had started in such an unpromising manner—and ultimately expelling the English in 1453 from all their possessions in France except Calais. The dream of Joan of Arc and her prophecy for Charles himself had been fulfilled.

▶ The unification of France as a national state

THE CAPETIAN MONARCHY TO
PHILIP AUGUSTUS

The rise of the French national state does not require such detail as was needed for the English. France never became a limited monarchy till after the Revolution, and

---

⁸ This title, held by the French king's eldest son, corresponds to that of the Prince of Wales in England.

much of the history of the unification is the attempt of the monarchy to rid itself, first of control by French nobles whose possessions were greater than those of the king himself for many centuries, and then of recurrent English invasions in support of English feudal possessions in the country. When we have seen how unification was finally achieved, we must examine the machinery of absolutism, and the few abortive attempts by the States-General and the Parliaments to limit the power of the king, and why they failed to do so.

We have already described the position of the Capetian monarchy in the early Middle Ages. The king was the feudal lord of only a small area in north central France, a compact holding, but greatly inferior to that of many of the other French nobles. But, as feudal king, he was the titular overlord of every noble who had any possessions within an area generally conceded to be that of "France." His position was one not only of prestige, but of some power. As the titular head of the state, he was the natural leader in a crusade, and thus sometimes commanded French contingents made up of men who were not his actual vassals. Lords who died without leaving male heirs often entrusted the wardship of heiresses to the kings. Some kings married their wards thus acquired, but in any case could choose their husbands. If the lords had no heirs at all then their lands escheated to the crown. When lords wished to commend themselves to a superior in exchange for protection the king seemed to many to be a suitable protector. Finally, the Capetian kings had a very fair amount of ecclesiastical patronage in their hands, and the French clergy on the whole favored a monarchy over feudal decentralization. They were continually urging the kings to establish and maintain justice beyond their mere feudal domains, and were willing to give such aid as they could.

The early Capetians, very sensibly in view of their position, rigidly refused foreign adventures in which their vassals were gaining glory and even kingdoms. They stayed at home looking after their affairs;

and they had the very great advantage that, from 987 to 1328, eldest son succeeded eldest son in the monarchy, thus establishing a certain sanctity for the line and making extremely unlikely any disputed succession, since there could be no occasion for dispute. The French kings, unlike the German and the English, thus appeared from the beginning to be marked out by God as rulers. The Archbishop of Rheims consecrated them as kings with sacred oil, but there was no occasion to submit the choice to a body of electors or to a national assembly. Moreover, most of these kings reigned for a considerable number of years; this meant that there would be no minority period under a regency, a situation which frequently caused trouble in England, since it gave various factions the chance to quarrel over the control of the child.

The first thing to do was to establish some kind of administration. The French kings used the old Germanic custom of appointing household officials and giving them charge of various departments connected with the management of their feudal estates. But for a long time they did not even have control over these appointments, which tended to pass from father to son, like the old "mayors of the palace." However, the king also gave appointments to clergymen, who were barred by celibacy from handing down such offices. And as the kings from the twelfth century onward managed to establish some order in their own territories, a task in which some of the earlier kings had had indifferent success, so they were able to obtain control of their official appointments and began to appoint commoners who were more susceptible to royal control.

Louis VI, the Fat (1108–1137) was the first French king who really fully controlled his own poor territories, and he began to extend his jurisdiction beyond them, summoning to his court occasional vassals who only owed him allegiance as king and sometimes succeeding in enforcing his will. His son Louis VII married Eleanor of Aquitaine, adding for a time territories far greater than his own to the kingdom. This marriage was the direct result of his prestige as king, since the lady's father had asked Louis to look after her when he died. But Louis divorced her after the Second Crusade, and she married Henry II of England, who thus became a landholder far more powerful than the French king, possessing not only England but two thirds of France, though he was still supposed to do homage to the French king for his lands.

Louis had little success in dealing with Henry, though he lost nothing. But his successor Philip Augustus was able to use shrewd diplomacy and occasional military campaigns to take almost the whole of Henry's lands from his sons. John, the younger brother of Henry's heir Richard I, as long as he was not king, intrigued with Philip Augustus against his brother. Philip returned from the Holy Land whither he had gone with Richard on the Third Crusade, leaving Richard there. He found that John was quite amenable to a few bribes in the form of Richard's French possessions. When Richard was taken prisoner and held to ransom by the emperor, John continued to enjoy Philip's support; but when Richard at last was freed and rushed back to France to put an end to Philip's depredations, for a few years Philip could barely hold his own. Then, fortunately for him, Richard was killed in France and John came to the English throne (1199). Of course he was no longer willing to play with Philip, but Philip had acquired another card, a better heir to the throne than either Richard or John, though he had been too young to be considered at the time of Richard's accession. This was Prince Arthur of Brittany.

Philip proceeded to espouse this young man's claim, and called John to his French feudal court to defend himself against charges brought by Arthur, who as lord of Brittany was also a vassal of the French king. John refused to come, and we have already seen how Philip was able to gain the support of the French nobility with promises of loot and lands from the English possessions in France, and how with their aid and some useful support from the pope he succeeded in conquering the bulk of John's possessions. Some more were added by his son Louis VIII, and recognition of the conquests in return for the cession of Aquitaine to England was agreed to by Louis IX in 1259. Meanwhile, as we have also seen, much of southern France was given to Philip and his successors through the Albigensian Crusade. Philip also by the battle of Bouvines (1214) defeated not only the English and the Germans but also the Count of Flanders, who now became his vassal.

THE MACHINERY OF GOVERNMENT IN THE TIME OF PHILIP AUGUSTUS

The French king, unlike the English, had no ancient customary rights to enforce, nor had he hedged his barons with restrictions on their independence like William the Conqueror of England, for his vassals owed a more direct obedience, more easily enforceable, to their own suzerains. So the kings had to concentrate their attention on trying to make their own domains at least subservient to themselves, and within this domain they did provide an administration far superior to those of other ordinary feudal lords, and which was capable of being extended as soon as the domain itself was enlarged. The earliest official was the *prévôt*, who looked after the king's interests in matters of justice and finance. As prévôts were paid by the grant of fiefs, their offices became hereditary, and it was not possible to do much to improve their administration until the king was in a position to pay them in money, and appoint and dismiss them at will. This reform was largely the work of Philip Augustus, who, by the help of his new feudal possessions, was able to find for the first time enough money for royal needs. He appointed *baillis* to watch the *prévôts*. These new officials at once became the chief instruments of royal policy. Their instructions were to support not only the king's feudal prerogatives but also as many of his kingly ones as they could, including within their jurisdiction as much of the king's nonfeudal territory as possible, and extending his influence in areas where he was not the feudal suzerain. This was done especially through listening to complaints against the local administrations of justice and trying to substitute an appeal to the king's justice instead of to the feudal court.

The king himself made effective use of his power of summoning his vassals, direct and titular, to his court for advice and assistance, accustoming them to regard themselves as his real vassals, and, as we have seen, he led them against the English possessions in France at a profit to themselves as well as to him. But one of his greatest titles to fame was his recognition of the importance of the towns, which were as prosperous as any in Europe in the thirteenth century. Philip was entirely willing to grant them charters giving them freedom to organize local internal government, in exchange for suitable amounts of money. The towns recognized the value to themselves of having an efficient king rather than an irresponsible feudal nobility as their protector. So they provided him not only with money but with soldiery, and in many cases guaranteed to undertake their own defense. Philip also appointed townsmen to high positions in his government.

But it was, on the whole, the conquests of Philip that made all the other successes possible. He had the nucleus of an administration which took care of very small territories; when the territories were enlarged he increased the number of his officials and maintained the same organs of government, adding only a few new officials, such as seneschals. All the officials had to be watched carefully by each king, as it was not easy to control them.

CONTINUED GROWTH OF POWER OF
CAPETIAN KINGS

Louis IX and full exploitation of feudal powers

Perhaps as early as Philip Augustus the officials of the king sometimes, in committee, tried cases under feudal law in which the king's interests were involved. This committee of the king's council ultimately developed

St. Louis IX, King of France. From a Moralized Bible *(French), 1226–1234.* (COURTESY THE PIERPONT MORGAN LIBRARY. Ms. 240, folio 8)

into the Parlement of Paris, the chief law court of the realm. Another committee looked into the receipts of money that came into the king's treasury to see that the *baillis* and seneschals were doing their duty. But by the time of Louis IX (1226–1270) the king was asserting successfully his prerogative of administering justice for the entire kingdom of France, and not only for his feudal vassals. The king had always in theory been supposed to be the protector of all and the maintainer of peace. He and his lawyers now asserted that many cases tried locally by feudal nobles came within his jurisdiction. By decree Louis forbade feudal warfare, and tried to persuade contenders in disputes that might have led to war to come to his courts, either to himself, for he often gave personal judgments, or to the Parlement of Paris, which was under his control; and he forbade also, following the example of the Church, all recourse to trial by ordeal and combat. He did not trouble, as a rule, to obtain the consent of his vassals to his decrees, as had been the previous custom; but since he was everywhere revered as a saintly person—he was later formally canonized as a saint—this addition to royal authority was generally accepted, and on several occasions he obtained the signatures of a representative selection of vassals. Louis, finding that the communal government of the towns given charters by Philip Augustus too often failed to work well because of internal quarrels between merchants and other burghers, suspended many charters and renewed them only when the towns could show that they deserved them. He made the towns have their public accounts audited by his officers, and introduced officials of his own such as mayors, which for centuries were royal and not local appointees.

Philip IV (the Fair, 1285–1314)

Centralization of public finance—importance—It should be understood that the French kings as yet had no right to tax, and though occasionally they attempted taxes for special purposes, such as crusades, there was always such an outcry that the attempts were abandoned immediately. Philip and the able corps of lawyers who formed his body of advisers recognized the importance of money in any centralized administration, and set themselves determinedly to find new sources of royal income, which was used for the purpose of enlarging the realm and controlling the feudal nobility by an increasing use of mercenary rather than feudal troops. On the towns he laid increased customs duties, forced loans, and sales taxes. He assessed the nobles highly for the privilege of avoiding military service, he expropriated the Templars, hitherto the king's bankers, and, as we have seen, he succeeded in taxing the French clergy. All accounts were carefully scrutinized by a special accounting department staffed by salaried officials.

The bureaucracy—Philip reorganized the official organs of state into what will hereafter be called the king's council, which had an inner group consulted on special occasions. The latter remained the chief advisory body to the crown until the Revolution. The Parlement of Paris under the king's direction became a real law court composed of trained lawyers. One branch was given the task of listening to requests that the king rather than any other court render justice. The Parlement of Paris also assumed jurisdiction over local courts, transferring their cases when necessary to itself.

It may be mentioned that this council, made up so largely of lawyers trained in the Roman law, was something new at this early period, and was found to be extremely effective in enhancing the king's authority. Looked at with suspicion by the feudal nobility, which in France throughout history remained an aristocratic military caste and made no effort to control the civil administration or even to cooperate with it, these lawyers had only one duty and one aim—to aid the monarchy which had appointed and could dismiss them. Paid in money and not in lands, they never became part of the aristocracy; even in later times when lawyers and assistants to the king were ennobled, they became a separate nobility, known as the nobility of the robe rather than of the sword. Moreover they were, in the time of Philip IV, laymen and not clergymen, and thus could be independent even in dealing with the Church. As the power of the monarchy grew, so must their own power with it; while if the monarchy's power declined they personally would lose any authority they possessed. They therefore took every opportunity to exalt the power of the monarchy over any competitor that threatened it, and, being thoroughly educated men, took the lead even in appeals to public opinion. It was the king's counselors in particular who dominated the great appeal to national unity presented by the quarrel with Pope Boniface VIII, which has already been discussed from a papal point of view in an earlier chapter.

The States-General—For the calling of the States-General in 1302 by Philip IV was essentially an appeal to public opinion, and was intended by the lawyers who dominated it to be precisely this, presenting a complete contrast with the English Parliaments of the same period, which were called by the English kings in response to pressure by the barons and taxpayers, and diminished rather than increased the absolute authority of the monarchy. In later times the States-General was called for the purpose of gaining consent to new taxes, and, since these could be refused, a refusal could have been a step toward limiting the monarchy. But Pierre Flotte, doctor of laws in the University of Montpellier, the royal chancellor, at the assembly of 1302 devoted almost his entire address to the iniquities of the pope who, according to him, was trying to submit the French monarchy to dictation by a foreign power. One pamphleteer, engaged in laying the groundwork of public opinion for the royal defiance of the pope, had even gone so far as to accuse Boniface of having said that he would "rather be a dog than a Frenchman."

The representation in the States-General called by Philip IV was substantially similar to that of the English Parliaments. The first estate, the clergy; the second estate, the nobility; and the third estate, the remainder, especially representatives of the towns, was the same as in England, though there was nothing in France to correspond with the crucial group in England, the knights of the shire who gave leadership to the bourgeoisie without being dominated by their special urban interests. In Philip's assembly his policy had virtually unanimous support because the quarrel was so well calculated to appeal to all. No one was anxious to see France dominated by an authoritarian and grasping papacy. Bishops, monks, and friars were as favorable to the king's position as were lords, bourgeoisie, and university professors. But if the king had called them, as later kings were compelled to call them, for the purpose of extracting funds from them, there would have been no such impressive unanimity. However, the precedent had been set for an assembly of all classes of the realm dominated by the king and his council; and we should note in passing that the sentiment of nationality must have been growing if the well-informed and able lawyers who knew what they wanted found it worth while to couch their appeals in patriotic vein as the sentiment most likely to command the gesture of unanimity which they needed.

The end of the Capetians

After the death of Philip the Fair in 1314 the feudal lords made a determined effort to regain some of their power lost to the encroachments of the monarchy, so that Philip's successors were forced to make a few concessions, defining limits of the king's power within the feudal system; and one lawyer was dismissed who was particularly hated because he had unduly enriched himself. But Louis X, who reigned only two years, left no son to succeed him. Not since the tenth century had the throne failed to pass from father to son. He was succeeded by each of his brothers in succession, none of whom left any male heir. The last of the Capetian kings designated his cousin Philip of Valois, son of the brother of Philip the Fair, as king and he was accepted by the French nobility and duly assumed the crown. But Edward III, king of England, whose mother was the daughter of Philip the Fair, asserted that the French throne could descend through daughters in default of sons, as had been accepted by this time in England. This was the excuse for the Hundred Years' War, which has been dealt with from the English point of view in the first part of this chapter.

THE HUNDRED YEARS' WAR

The first phase to the Treaty of Brétigny (1360)

In a very real sense the end of the Capetian monarchy in France marks the close of the consolidation of the French kingdom as much as the reign of Edward I in England marks the greatest power of the later medieval English monarchy. Thereafter both monarchies lost power to the as yet undefeated forces of feudalism, while the two countries fought with each other and with the feudal nobility. But France had developed no constitutional counterbalance to the crown and at the end of the period of medieval disintegration absolutism was re-established in a modern form with relatively few changes from the monarchy of Philip IV, while in England the institution of Parliament had grown throughout the period of disintegration, and remained still potentially strong even during the period of absolutism that followed it. During the Hundred Years' War for a brief period it seemed that the French monarchy would be brought under control by the same forces that limited it in England; but the chance was missed and it never recurred again. Fundamentally it was the failure of the nobility to accept any social responsibilities and its insistence on remaining a privileged and irresponsible group harking back to a long-outmoded military tradition that handed absolute power back to the monarchy; the bourgeoisie found it impossible to cooperate with the lords, and made few attempts at effective action on their own. Preferring an orderly absolute monarchy to a disorderly and irresponsible feudalism, they were willing to pay the price exacted of them right down to the Revolution in 1789. When for a few years in the middle of the seventeenth century the nobles and the bourgeoisie found that it was to their joint interest to control the monarchy, and an opportunity presented itself in the form of the minority of a king under a grasping and detested chancellor, they could agree neither on a program of reform nor on the means for accomplishing it. The *Fronde,* the name of their party of opposition, petered out, and the absolute monarchy was established more firmly than ever under Louis XIV.

The period of the Hundred Years' War therefore presents a picture of gloom relieved only by individual heroism and the appealing figure of the Maid of Orléans.

The consolidation of the national state which followed was carried out by force and diplomacy and did not really become permanent until the end of the sixteenth century with the accession of Henry IV and the Bourbon dynasty. Nothing really new came out of it; the French nobles learned nothing from their disasters, and far too much of the monarchs' energies had to be spent in combating them. Throughout the sixteenth century the nobility still pursued its own interests, waging war against the monarchs, intriguing for the succession, or trying to gain the ear of the kings. It was, in the last analysis, the failure to make any political and social gains out of the long period of royal weakness and civil war that made France into the politically backward country which had to submit, too late, to the French Revolution—and this, in spite of the fact that for almost the whole period she was the most culturally advanced of any European nation.

We have seen already how the English brought on the Hundred Years' War in defense of trade interests in Flanders and southern France as well as of the English claim to the French throne. We have seen also how the English kings were forced to obtain from the English Parliament the money for fighting the war and had to make concessions accordingly. At the time when national feeling was still in the process of formation it did not seem impossible, even to the English bourgeoisie, that the French and the English thrones should be united under one monarchy, with all the commercial advantages that this would entail; otherwise it seems unlikely that the English Parliament should have given the crown the subsidies which the feudal nobility had refused to John and Henry III when they wished to defend the personal possessions of their family in France. The English therefore always had an advantage in this war in that England itself was in no danger. The war was fought on French soil, and the French kings were for a long time unable to persuade their feudal vassals that the war was any real concern of theirs as long as it was kept away from their own territories. The territory of France, if it had been recognized as something that needed to be defended as a whole, was far more populous and prosperous than England, and there could have been only one result if all classes in the realm had united to defend it against an army that was so far from home. But the English could almost always count on support not only from the feudal possessions of its kings in southern France but from individual lords of varying power, who were theoretically vassals of the French crown but wished to throw off the allegiance and become independent, even if this meant accepting English overlordship instead. And if they could not count on actual allies, then at least they could count on neutrality, which as often worked in their favor.

The first phase of the war was marked by continuous English successes, even though the actual battles were invariably fought against heavy paper odds. The members of the French nobility who formed the bulk of the French king's armies were useless against the English militia. They fought in the old spirit of chivalry, which could hardly be expected to be observed by the English common soldiers. On one famous occasion the English army under Edward III had been drawn up in a well-chosen position in which it was relatively safe from attack by the French cavalry. Philip VI, the French king, sent to Edward to ask him if he would be kind enough to move his army into another position where the rules of chivalric warfare could be better observed. When Edward summarily refused the reasonable request, Philip was badly put out, and regarded the English king as false to the traditions of knighthood. The French chronicler Froissart is entirely at one with the nobility in the matter. If war was not fought any longer within the rules of proper knightly behavior, it was the English fault, and not the fault of the French nobility.

When the French King John was taken prisoner at the battle of Poitiers in 1356, and the heir had to try to struggle along with only the authority of a Dauphin, a real opportunity arose to gain concessions from the Dauphin, who was short of money with which to pursue the war. He was forced to call the States-General—this time, unlike Philip IV, as a suppliant. Not only had France been suffering from the ravages of war, which were serious enough because the English troops did not hesitate to try to live off the country, *their* country as Edward III claimed; the Black Death of the years 1347–1350 decimated many of the towns and killed off perhaps as much as 20 per cent of the whole population. The peasants were hardest hit, the nobles and richer bourgeoisie suffering much less. Moreover, after the battle of Poitiers the enormous numbers of ransoms for the knights who had fallen in their heavy armor and been taken prisoner without even much fighting further impoverished the peasantry, who ultimately had to find the sums required.

The States-General, made up of classes who were already heavily enough burdened by either taxation or ransoms, was in no mood to grant the Dauphin any further sums for the pursuit of the war. It made demands on him, insisting that he account for his expenditures and allow his ministers to be supervised, but it did not present a coherent program to him, and he doubted in fact whether it would even be able to find the money he needed. He therefore refused any demands that would have seriously limited his power, and on several occasions went behind its back and by personal requests to provincial notables was able to obtain enough for current needs. Meanwhile Paris, a city which was many times larger than any other in the country, had organized a private revolution of its own under Étienne Marcel, a merchant prince of the city who seems to have hoped for some kind of bourgeois control of the monarchy, perhaps through helping to put a pretender, one Charles the Bad of Navarre, on the throne. Marcel succeeded in rallying bourgeois and workers in Paris to his side, and welcomed assistance elsewhere wherever it could be found, among the Jacquerie, groups of peasants in Normandy and Picardy and Champagne who had broken loose and were burning and pillaging the castles of their lords; from Charles of Navarre, and finally from the English, with whose Flemish allies Marcel hoped an accord could be reached. Faced with this situation, the States-General and the nobles who largely controlled it realized that they needed the king or the Dauphin to restore order. They voted two important taxes which were easily collectible, a sales tax and a tax on hearths, and ceased to press their demands for control of the monarchy. The Dauphin, thus fortified, was able to suppress both the Parisian revolution and the Jacquerie. He then negotiated a peace with the English (Brétigny, 1360) under which the king of England renounced his claim to the French throne in return for a considerable increase in his French lands and a huge ransom for the French King John, who returned to France for a time, leaving a son as hostage for the fulfillment of the treaty. As the hostage escaped, John considered it his duty to return to captivity in England, which was at this time a far more attractive situation than being king in France.

The failure of the States-General to control the king

It has been contended, probably with some justice, that the decision of the nobles at this time to make common cause with the king against the Jacquerie and some of the bourgeoisie and the granting of important permanent taxes to the king were a crucial failure from which the States-General never recovered. The English barons, working in cooperation with the townsmen and lesser nobility, had presented a united front to the king, and a parliament had resulted, which, though it was sometimes kept in subjection by absolute monarchs, nevertheless did succeed in establishing itself as a regular institution which controlled especially the king's arbitrary power of taxation. The right to wage and declare war remained in the power of the English monarch, but he could not in fact go to war without the consent of the people, since the funds under his personal control were insufficient for the purpose. This

meant that he must call his parliament to obtain financial backing.

The French king, as we have seen, was given taxes in perpetuity for which the English king had to ask his parliament; and in a later section of this chapter we shall see how many more taxes were granted to Charles vii, also in perpetuity, in the last phases of the Hundred Years' War. When the French king wanted more he could call the States-General, and if this failed he could call the lesser provincial estates, and hope to obtain enough to carry on temporarily; while the towns, for lack of support from the nobility, were powerless to resist royal exactions. Thus an instrument which in England was found most potent for exercising control over the monarchs was thrown away by the French nobility at a time when it was perhaps within its grasp.

Whatever truth there may be in this contention, there is no doubt that the States-General was never again able to stand up to the king, and of course it never became a parliament. The history of England has shown that wars provide a wonderful opportunity to force the monarch to grant concessions; yet in France the Hundred Years' War resulted in the consolidation of power in the hands of the French monarchy. Probably the answer to the enigma is to be sought in the different kinds of war waged by the two monarchies. The Hundred Years' War was as much a civil conflict as it was war with a foreigner; and the English War of the Roses, a civil conflict, also resulted in the consolidation of power in the hands of an absolute monarch. It is doubtful whether the States-General could have held any gains it had made in the absence of those valuable local institutions which had been inherited by the English from Anglo-Saxon times, the system of sheriffs and justices and the local courts which actually supervised the collection of taxes agreed upon by Parliament. The French monarchy had too much control over the local institutions in France, as we shall see; while the tradition of royal legislation, a feature of the Roman law operative in France, was probably too strong to allow any gradual evolution of self-government. Even the French Revolution at the end of the eighteenth century did not substantially change the centralized government which France inherited from her medieval kings.

The second phase of the war—Uniting of the French and English crowns

Nevertheless at the Treaty of Brétigny the authority of the French kings was at a low enough ebb. The reigning king himself was a prisoner in England, and more than half of France was in English hands. Though in the later years of the fourteenth century a remarkable soldier, the constable Bertrand du Guesclin, was able to take the initiative in the war and recover much of the land lost to the English, in the second decade of the fifteenth century England was again on the offensive under her young warrior king, Henry v (1413–1422), and after the battle of Agincourt (1415) all northern France fell into his hands. Under the Treaty of Troyes (1420) Henry was recognized as the heir to the French throne, and a marriage was arranged between him and Catherine of Valois, the daughter of the French King Charles vi, who was intermittently insane (as was Henry vi of England, the offspring of this unfortunate marriage). This union was intended to settle forever in favor of England the claims of the English monarchy to the throne of France. The claim of the Dauphin Charles (later Charles vii), whose legitimacy was in doubt, was passed over.

This arrangement was the result of the rise of the House of Burgundy to a position in France equal to or superior to that of the French king himself. It is unnecessary here to go into details concerning the means by which the dukes of this house achieved such a position by war, carefully planned marriages, and the ownership of lands outside the jurisdiction of the French king. But the Burgundian support was crucial to the success of the English, who could not have made much headway against a united France. The dukes of Burgundy had no loyalty to the nation of France, nor, certainly, to her kings. They were looking solely to the advancement of their own house, which for a time seemed best assured by the abasement of the French monarchy.

On the death of the English King Henry v in 1422, the succession of his infant son Henry vi to the thrones of England and France was proclaimed by the English and Burgundians. The allies held northern France, and a considerable portion of the rest of the country. The Dauphin Charles was also proclaimed king by his supporters, but he was lazy and lacked energy, and he was in grave financial difficulties. It is possible that he might never have consolidated his throne against such odds had it not been for the Maid of Orléans, Joan of Arc.

St. Joan of Arc and the end of the Hundred Years' War

It is often the fashion to minimize the importance of Joan of Arc, since the unification of France came after her death, and the policy which she favored, outright war against Burgundians and English, was not the one that was adopted. The policy of attempting to separate the Burgundians from the English, which Charles vii and his advisers, especially Reginald of Chartres, Archbishop of Rheims, followed, was brilliantly successful after her death. Nevertheless, if it had not been for her, Charles would never have been in a position to negotiate with the Burgundians. He was not yet crowned king, and he had as yet no victories to his name. Joan gave him both his first taste of victory, with the consequent return of many vacillating towns and territories to his cause, and she made his doubtful title clear and acceptable by having him crowned publicly at Rheims by the only man competent to perform the ceremony, his one loyal churchman of note, Reginald of Chartres. But, more than this, she never wavered at any time, even while the king she had crowned appeared to have deserted her; she never wavered in her loyalty to him and her certainty that he would expel the English from France. She evoked the idea of France under a legitimate king, the chosen of God, in a way that was really new in her

Portrait of Charles VII, King of France (the Dauphin, later king, to whom Joan of Arc was sent with her famous message). Painted by Fouquet.

time. The great force of patriotism unquestionably brought back many waverers to their allegiance to the throne, and for the first time anti-English feeling became so dominant that even the warring nobles could not altogether neglect it in pursuit of their own private interests. It was Joan who made possible the negotiations with Burgundy that in turn made possible the expulsion of the English, which she had promised to her king, without knowing the means by which it would be accomplished.

St. Joan of Arc was born in a family of fairly well-to-do free farmers in an area that had remained faithful to the king. Her fam-

ily was not, as is sometimes supposed, a family of poor peasants; nor was Joan herself a shepherdess, as was later suggested in order to exalt the miracle of her work, though she did occasionally look after the flocks of her family. She could not read or write and she was not educated. From an early age she heard "voices" telling her she must go to the Dauphin and by her work rescue France from the English, and crown Charles as king. For years she resisted this supernatural advice until the position of the king became so desperate that at last she decided she must obey, and relieve the city of Orléans, which was being besieged by the English and was in danger of falling. Orléans was the strategic key to the whole south of the country; if it fell then it seemed that nothing could save the king and his adherents.

Going to the lord of the local castle she was able by her simple sincerity to persuade him to lend her a horse and attendants, whom she also convinced of her mission. She was led to the presence of the Dauphin, whom she found among his courtiers with no insignia of office by which she could tell that he was the king. She went directly up to him and greeted him as king, saying that she had been sent to his aid. The king was clearly impressed, especially by her recognition of him and of his title, which he had previously had reason to doubt. But he took the precaution of having her examined by a committee of theologians led by Reginald of Chartres, who pronounced that the voices heard by Joan were apparently from heaven and could be trusted. Joan was then fitted out with splendid armor, dressed in male clothes, and a new spirit became visible in the royal forces. The army marched to Orléans, and under Joan's leadership the siege was raised, and the English army retreated. One of the most remarkable consequences of Joan's early campaigns was the superstitious awe engendered in the English troops who began to desert, fearing that they were opposed by a sorceress.

With clear vision Joan saw that what must be done was to establish the Dauphin as king, so that the doubtful and the waverers would return to their allegiance; and this, at the moment, she thought was more valuable even than more military victories. So, against the advice of the military men, she insisted that the Dauphin proceed to Rheims, the city where all the French kings had been crowned, in spite of the fact that much of the territory in between was in the hands of the English or the Burgundians. The venture was successful, the royal party reached Rheims, and Reginald of Chartres performed the ceremony. Joan's work was really done; the great gesture had been made, and it could have been left to the men of politics to complete what she had

begun. But the "voices" continued to urge her on, and she insisted that now more military victories were needed, including the conquest of Paris, which was in the hands of the Burgundians. But here Charles and Reginald would not follow her. They knew that, from a political point of view, there could be no lasting peace unless the Burgundians came over to the support of the French crown and could be persuaded to abandon the English. Joan was now a heroine, the people all clamored for her to be given her way, and many of the troops of the French army wished to follow her. She proceeded, with doubtful or no recognition from the king and the archbishop, to continue to wage war on the English until at last she was captured, sold to the English by her Burgundian captors, who thereupon tried her for heresy under the auspices of the Inquisition.

Charles has often been accused of deserting her. But only two courses were available to him, and he in fact tried them both. He could not match the price the English were prepared to pay for the destruction of her influence, which they feared especially for its effect on their own soldiers. He complained bitterly that she was a prisoner of war and under the rules of war of the time she should be held to ransom; and he tried to raise a sum of money sufficient to tempt the Burgundians who had originally captured her, but could not offer enough. Once she was sold to the English the only thing he could do was to try to rescue her by force; but his forces were insufficient to hope to be able to capture Rouen, where she was ultimately imprisoned, and he was unsuccessful. As soon as the war was over he took steps to see that her good name was restored and her trial declared illegal, though of course this was a political necessity, as he would not wish to owe his crown to the efforts of a sorceress and heretic. It is difficult to see what else he could have done; nor did Joan in her trial think that he had deserted her then. She thought only that he ought to have supported her military efforts before her capture.

The trial was entirely illegal, and always under pressure by the English, who were determined to ensure a verdict of guilty and would not have tolerated any other after they had paid such a high price for the captive. The Bishop of Beauvais, the presiding officer, had few claims to be the proper authority for the purpose. He was personally vindictive against the Maid, having been driven out of his bishopric by troops under her command; he had altogether sold out to the English, and anyone during the trial who suggested that his procedure was in any way irregular and that there was anything to be said on behalf of the defendant was summarily dismissed. Several objectors to the procedure were, in fact, imprisoned by the English. Nevertheless, the authorities wanted a regular conviction, and if possible an admission that her "voices" were inspired by the Devil or had been invented. So the trial lasted for many months while the untutored and illiterate girl gave such astonishing answers that the learned theologians were frequently confounded, and had to fall back upon intimidation. At last, after Joan had been weakened by nearly a year of imprisonment and a long Lenten fast, they showed her the stake to which they had already condemned her, and told her she could be spared it if she would recant. She did so, denying her voices but continuing to insist that the king would expel the English from France all the same; but when she had time to think over what she had done, and had resumed her feminine clothes, she withdrew her recantation, and as a relapsed heretic she was handed over to the English to be burned.[9]

But the policy of Reginald of Chartres, pursued ceaselessly during the trial and afterward, was successful. The Duke of Burgundy was detached from the English alliance, and before his death Charles VII was able indeed to drive out the English, leaving them only Calais out of all the English possessions in France. It was not a spontaneous uprising of French patriotism that worked the miracle. It was patient negotiation, combined with careful attention to the improvement of French finances and of the army, followed by a remarkable series of military victories. But the way had been prepared by the Maid, and it is doubtful whether any of it would have been accomplished without the aid of her "voices."

LOUIS XI AND THE RECONSTITUTION OF ABSOLUTE MONARCHY

The destruction of the Burgundian realm

Charles VII had bought off the dukes of Burgundy, but the price had been heavy. There can be no doubt that the last duke of the line, Charles the Bold, desired to become a king, sever his lands from France, and add more to them from territories that had never belonged to France. For a time he was successful in his efforts, adding to his domain some of the fairest lands of Holland and Flanders, and even negotiating for the title of Holy Roman Emperor. But in the end his designs were foiled by the patient persistence of the new French king, Louis XI (1461–1483), and the latter's judicious use of bribes and diplomacy to foment insurrections in Charles's home territories. At last Charles was killed in battle by the Swiss, who resisted his attempts to add the ever-disputed Alsace-Lorraine to his empire (1477). Louis allowed the Burgundian lands held outside France to go to the duke's daughter Mary, who married a Hapsburg, but he took Burgundy itself and the northern French possessions of the Burgundian dukes, and his son married the heiress of Brittany, which had been lost to France for generations. So France was again united within substantially the boundaries that it has today.

The machinery of absolutism as developed by Charles VII and Louis XI

The secret of French absolutism is to be found in the financial autonomy granted

---

[9] It may be added that in 1456 the papacy had the case retried, and Joan was declared to have been wrongly convicted. She was canonized as a saint in 1919.

by the States-General to the French kings during the Hundred Years' War, and in the efficient organization of an improved bureaucracy to collect the new permanent taxes, devised in part by Charles VII but perfected by Louis XI and his two Valois successors. Until the rise of modern Germany France was always potentially the richest country in Europe, possessed of the finest resources and the hardest working peasantry. When she has been well governed prosperity has always been quick to return, but she has always needed a strong hand at the helm. In a centrally administered kingdom so many possibilities existed for corruption, so many opportunities presented themselves to unwatched officials for personal enrichment that the kings were often ludicrously short of money in a country where ample funds were really available.

The work of Charles VII consisted in obtaining the authorization from the States-General, or the nobility and bourgeoisie, to collect taxes on a permanent basis beyond the simple receipts from the king's property which were all that a feudal king commanded. Charles was granted this in order that he might be enabled to defeat and expel the English. The taxes thus granted, however, were never abandoned by the monarchy, though the fiction was observed that some revenues were temporary and extraordinary, while others were ordinary and regular. The chief tax granted in 1439 was the *taille*, a tax imposed upon all financial and real property throughout the kingdom. A remarkably complex system was inaugurated to collect this tax, which remained the chief tax in France till the Revolution and even afterward. The total amount needed by the crown for each particular year was assessed. This total was then divided by the officials through each unit of government down to the level of the parish, which was assessed for its portion of the whole. On tax collection day in the parish the bells were tolled and the citizens were informed what their contribution was to be. Then they had to elect assessors who determined what the individual share of each must be. Naturally every peasant wished to avoid his tax, and tried to conceal his wealth—a French custom which has persisted to this day—and many were the expedients adopted. But the taille could be collected, even though large parts of the collections found their way into the pockets of the officials through whose hands it passed on the way to the treasury. Louis XI was extremely careful to check all corruption, and in general the best French kings have done their utmost, until the later kings defeated their own objectives by granting excessive numbers of immunities from taxes to favorites.

The aids, or sales taxes, and the customs duties, both interior and those collected at the ports, and the proceeds from royal monopolies, especially the infamous *gabelle*, or salt tax, were given into the hands of tax farmers, who established their own collection posts and bought the whole contract for taxes from the king. The latter was therefore able to command the expected income from these taxes without having to go to the trouble of instituting a system for collecting it himself. This task was thus performed by private enterprise, which helped itself to considerably more profit from the collection than was officially permitted by the kings. The difficulty, however, was the control of the tax farmers, and, again, only the most efficient kings were able to keep them in order. And, with such possibilities for living beyond their means many French kings in later times would persuade the tax farmers to give them several years' income in advance, and thus would be short of income in later years when it might be equally needed.

With the money thus newly available, and with the services of a great financial expert to assist him, Charles VII reorganized the French army. It was officially announced in 1439 that only the king could levy and maintain troops. But he then proceeded to enforce this decree by levying an army of professional troops, with a permanent cavalry of twenty companies, of about six hundred men to a company, including bowmen and lancers. Then a further body of bowmen was organized for the infantry, the soldiers being exempted from the taille (free-archers) in time of peace. They were to be chosen by the king's officials, the *baillis*. They were instructed in the use of firearms and artillery, engaged in periodic maneuvers, and were kept together according to the regions from which they hailed—the ancestors of the modern regiments. In addition to these French soldiers, enormous numbers of mercenaries from all the countries of Europe were added when necessary. But it will be seen that the basis for all this military activity was the ability to collect the taxes to pay for it. If the mercenaries were unpaid they preyed upon the country, if the king could not establish his authority firmly the trained troops might just as easily join a pretender or a feudal lord who promised to pay them. For most of a century, or at least until the death of Francis I in 1547, the French kings were the masters of France through possession of an adequate income and well-paid troops able to maintain the king's peace against any feudal lord, and during this period France had a growing prosperity. When the royal government again failed in the middle of the sixteenth century, feudalism, which had only been held in control, burst forth anew.

The new financial regime called forth thousands of new officials, and it is from this time that a bureaucratic career became the position of honor in France that it remained until very recent times. Louis XI, an indefatigable bureaucrat himself, took very great care of all the appointments that he made, and he watched the behavior of his nominees with the most meticulous attention. He would stand no communal nonsense from the towns and insisted on appointing all the superior officials in them. Every official in the country had to be absolutely loyal to Louis on pain of instant dismissal. Each official felt it to be his duty to enhance the authority of the king, his master, and incidentally his own at the same time. He received a good salary, and there were many valuable perquisites to be obtained from office. Thus it came to be the

custom that the positions were actually purchased by the incumbents; and the kings did not usually dismiss them unless they proved exceptionally inefficient or disloyal. The majority of the officials of whom we know died safely in office, after designating a successor who would have to pay an indemnity to the king for confirmation of his appointment as well as to the departing official who had selected him. When a king died, the officials were all required to receive a confirmation of their title to the office, which assisted the new king over what would otherwise have been financially a difficult time.

But the system worked, for the interests of kings and officials were one. The sufferers were the taxpayers who groaned, but for a long time thought that the comparative efficiency of the government was at least far better than the anarchy and civil war that had preceded it. Under feeble kings the officials paid less to the treasury than under the efficient ones, but they still paid something and the country was administered, and a high degree of stability was ensured. The law courts functioned, administering the king's justice as in the earlier medieval period, and the accounts were audited or at least examined by the central bureaus set up in earlier reigns for the purpose. At the top were the great officials of the king's council, appointed directly by him, usually from the ranks of the Church or the upper bourgeoisie.

When the crown failed in the middle of the sixteenth century the system endured for a while until it too collapsed under the recrudescence of feudal anarchy. But as soon as the centralized government was reestablished by Henry IV in 1589 few indeed were the changes that had to be made. The machinery of the late medieval *ancien régime* was the machinery in all essentials that lasted till the French Revolution of 1789; and by no means all its earlier features were changed even by the Revolution. Almost as much as in England can the structure of modern France be traced back to its medieval antecedents.

► The Spanish national state

SPAIN PREVIOUS TO THE DUAL MONARCHY

Spain was not unified into a national state until the close of the Middle Ages. Details of the process of unification are of little interest in a text of this kind, but a few facts of the consolidation of the kingdoms of Aragon and Castile in the fifteenth century will be summarized, since the whole Iberian peninsula played such an important part in European history in early modern times.

We have already seen how almost the whole of the peninsula fell into Muslim hands, and for centuries Muslim influence and civilization predominated there. Out of the centuries-long warfare for the Christianization of the country and reconquest from the Muslims, by the twelfth century four Christian kingdoms had emerged—Leon, Portugal, Castile, and Aragon. In Granada, the southern tip of the peninsula, a small kingdom of Muslims remained, while in the north there was a Christian kingdom ruled by French feudal princes. This kingdom, called Navarre, occupied the regions immediately north and south of the Pyrenees. During the twelfth century Leon united with Castile, making the new kingdom by far the most powerful in the peninsula, while Aragon in the following century acquired extensive interests in the Mediterranean, especially when Peter III of Aragon married a Hohenstaufen heiress, and in 1282 took Sicily from the French. By the fifteenth century, Aragon had also gained influence in southern Italy, which was ruled by Aragonese princes, and at one time had extensive trade rights as far away as Greece. Meanwhile the kingdom of Portugal remained independent, and turned her attention to the sea, colonizing various islands in the Atlantic and systematically sending out explorers in search of new territories. Castile, at all times the most important land power in the peninsula, acquired with Leon important maritime interests in the Bay of Biscay region and, with the conquest of Seville from the Muslims in the thirteenth century, also gained an outlet to the Mediterranean. In the fifteenth century the Castilian navy was a powerful organization and Castile had an important merchant fleet. Although she is usually regarded as primarily a land power, she was by no means exclusively this, and her navy was in these centuries a force to be reckoned with.

In all the Iberian states there were several important towns remaining over from the Muslim civilization, and representatives of towns, as well as the nobles, exercised some control over royal policies through fairly powerful assemblies known as *Cortes,* organized on the same lines as the French States-General.

FERDINAND AND ISABELLA

In the earlier Middle Ages the Iberian kingdoms constantly warred among themselves, and much energy had to be spent by the rulers in combating the feudal nobility. But in 1469 a decisive change came over the situation when the heirs of Aragon and Castile were secretly married, against the expectations and efforts of many interested parties throughout Europe, especially King Louis XI of France, who would have preferred that Spain remain disunited and never develop into the great power which she potentially was. In due course Ferdinand of Aragon and Isabella of Castile inherited their respective thrones; and though the two countries were not officially amalgamated, and the union was only a personal union of the monarchs, in fact under their joint rule Spain became at last a national entity (1479). When Isabella died before her husband, a number of important Castilians tried to sever their kingdom from Aragon. But the movement quickly collapsed, and the whole kingdom was inherited by the daughter of the two monarchs, who proceeded to marry into the Hapsburg family. The son of Joanna, this first queen of Spain, was Charles V, who was elected Holy Roman Emperor, thus bringing Spain as a great power into the politics of Central Europe.

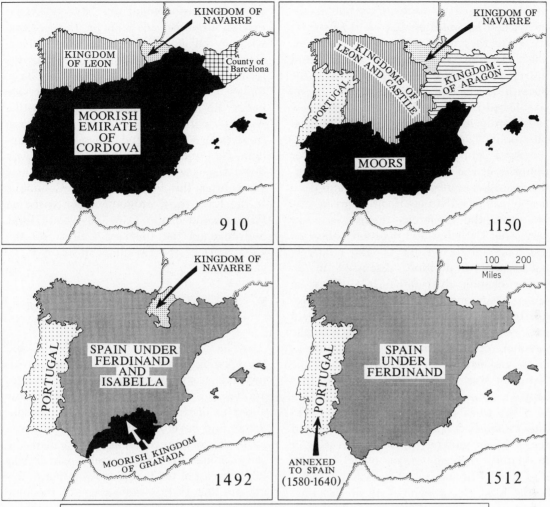

KINGDOM OF NAVARRE
KINGDOM OF LEON
County of Barcelona
MOORISH EMIRATE OF CORDOVA
910

KINGDOM OF NAVARRE
KINGDOMS OF LEON AND CASTILE
PORTUGAL
KINGDOM OF ARAGON
MOORS
1150

KINGDOM OF NAVARRE
PORTUGAL
SPAIN UNDER FERDINAND AND ISABELLA
MOORISH KINGDOM OF GRANADA
1492

0   100   200
Miles
PORTUGAL
SPAIN UNDER FERDINAND
ANNEXED TO SPAIN (1580-1640)
1512

TERRITORIAL UNIFICATION OF SPAIN

Ferdinand and Isabella brought together the commercial experience of Aragon and the great military tradition of Castile, which had been the leader in the wars against the Muslims. At once they proceeded to consolidate the entire peninsula except for Portugal. They drove the French out of that part of Navarre that was south of the Pyrenees, and they drove the Muslims out of Granada in the south, where they had been harmlessly living for centuries, paying regular tribute to the kings of Castile. For good measure Ferdinand and Isabella then expelled the Jews to an estimated number of two hundred thousand. This was an economic as well as a human disaster for the country, as many of these people, skilled in commerce, industry, and agriculture, could hardly be replaced. However, converted Muslims (Moriscos) were permitted to remain for another century, and it was not till the expulsion of these latter in 1609 that the disastrous policy of persecution had its full effect. It is generally conceded that much of Spanish economic backwardness to this day can be traced back to the systematic destruction or expulsion of those classes which had always borne such a large share of the economic activity of the country.

For the suppression of the feudal nobility the monarchs, especially in Castile, won the support of the towns, which, as usual, preferred absolutism to feudal anarchy, and by enlisting picked troops from the towns they were able to make considerable headway. But perhaps the greatest instrument for enforcing absolutism was the Spanish Inquisition, the adaptation of an established and accepted institution for new ends hardly in conformity with its original purpose.

As a "crusading" people, engaged for centuries in war against the Muslim infidels, the Spanish had a horror of heresy, and were deeply attached to militant Christianity. Moreover, the monarchs themselves were very strict Catholics and detested heresy no less than did their subjects. The relatively mild papal Inquisition, discussed in an earlier chapter, had fallen into disuse in Spain. Ferdinand and Isabella therefore requested the papacy to set up a new and more severe Inquisition, no doubt with the intention of subordinating it to the monarchy and using it for political ends. Pope Sixtus IV was reluctant to permit it, but allowed himself to be persuaded, and in 1478 the so-called Spanish Inquisition was duly established. The monarchs were indeed successful in gaining control of it, using it to establish their supremacy over the Spanish Church, driving out of the Church many of the local clergy, who were at this time rather lax in their discipline and observances, and replacing them with rigid disciplinarians. They also used the Inquisition against dissenters and their own personal enemies, and later, of course, against Protestants. They met little opposition from their own subjects who were, on the whole, very religious and very orthodox. As long as the monarchs presented their persecutions under a religious guise they could rely upon popular support.

The result was a reformed Church in Spain which was able in the following century to give much-needed leadership to the Catholic Reformation, made necessary by the initial successes of the Protestants. Spain was thus enabled to become dominant in Europe for a time by the use of religious as well as political and military means. Even so, the Spanish would not have possessed enough resources to maintain this position without the aid of the riches of the New World, discovered at the end of the fifteenth century by the Italian sailor Christopher Columbus, who had taken service under the monarchs of Aragon and Castile. A few years previously, the Portuguese, from their separate and independent kingdom, had succeeded in making their way down the coast of Africa, and in 1498, six years after the first voyage of Columbus to the East, the Portuguese sailor Vasco da Gama rounded the Cape of Good Hope, and reached the town of Calicut on the west coast of the Indian peninsula.

▶ **The national state as the key political institution of modern times**

The discovery of the New World, and the opening up of Asia, is as fitting a dividing line as any between the Middle Ages and the early modern era which we are now about to discuss. Europe had been consolidated into several national states, under a form of government sometimes called the "new monarchy," a monarchy which was fully abreast of the times, and was in a strategic position to take advantage of the new opportunities, economic and political, which were opened up by the new discoveries. The old universal state, which had always been the ideal of the Middle Ages, was now, in reality, gone forever, or at least postponed for an unforeseeable future although, as we shall see, the Holy Roman Empire had not yet fully abandoned its pretensions, and on at least two separate occasions came close to restoring some of its former glories.

The great political fact of the centuries since 1500 has been the rise and growth of the national state, an entity larger than the ancient city-states of Greece and Rome, but smaller than medieval Christendom. These national states have shown themselves capable of taking care of tremendous commercial and industrial expansion, and of ensuring certain basic rights, ultimately including self-government, for their particular nationals. In the process they have fought terrible internecine wars with each other, and they have competed by war and diplomacy for the resources not only of each other, but also of the distant lands which they have subjected to their control. Above all, the national state has shown itself capable of inspiring loyalty in its nationals, a kind of substitute religion which has, to a large extent, taken the place of the universal religion which was the norm of the medieval world. Now, in the present century, the Oriental peoples have done the West the compliment of learning from it, purloining Western nationalism and adapting it to their own purposes.

Thus nationalism remains, possibly the single most potent force in the modern world. An institution which grew out of the needs of men in the Middle Ages has been sanctified as the natural form of government among men, as the Roman Empire was once sanctified by Christians who had grown up beneath its shadow. It remains to be seen whether the national state can survive the trials of the present epoch, or whether, as Toynbee has urged, it is already obsolete and will give way to some other equally "natural" form of government. But it cannot be denied that from the sixteenth to the twentieth century A.D., it was the predominant form of governmental organization, and this, too, we owe to our medieval forebears.

▶ Suggestions for further reading

Books on the English national state are far more plentiful in English than similar works on the French state. But to set the stage, a remarkable novel which deals with the conquest of Britain by Duke William of Normandy will first be recommended: Hope Muntz, *The Golden Warrior, the Story of Harold and William* (New York: Charles Scribner's Sons, 1949). Few historical novels have surpassed this moving account, based on many years' research by the author into all the available documents of the period. It is a living piece of work, written in a language admirably fitting to the subject, without self-conscious archaism, and yet without a false note, even in the language, in the entire volume.

The standard book on English constitutional history, G. B. Adams and R. L. Schuyler, *Constitutional History of England* (New York: Henry Holt & Co., Inc., 1934), is a fine piece of work, containing almost everything that the beginning student needs to know of English constitutional development in the Middle Ages. This should, however, be supplemented for the historical material, by a book such as G. M. Trevelyan, *History of England* (New York: Doubleday & Co., Inc., 1953), a Doubleday Anchor Book. Volume 1 covers the Middle Ages. Other books which may be profitably used to supplement these works for specially important periods are S. Painter, *The Reign of King John* (Baltimore: Johns Hopkins University Press, 1949), and relevant parts of two books in the Pelican History of England series: D. M. Stenton, *English Society in the Early Middle Ages* (2nd ed.; Harmondsworth, Middlesex: Penguin Books, 1952), and A. R. Myers, *England in the Late Middle Ages* (London: Penguin Books, 1952). Any really interested student should also attempt the pioneer work on which almost all later writers base their own studies in constitutional history, a series of lectures given by the great legal historian, F. W. Maitland, *The Constitutional History of England* (Cambridge, England: Cambridge University Press, 1908). The peculiar organization of this work, which does not at first seem easy to grasp, combined with the easy conversational style, permits the reader to glimpse a great mind at work in a field hitherto hardly touched. This fact alone would make the effort of reading the book well worth while.

Several books cover both the French and English national states, since they deal with a time when the relations between them were of the first importance. An attractive study of the reigns of Henry II and his sons, built around the charming figure of Eleanor of Aquitaine, is Amy Kelly, *Eleanor of Aquitaine and the Four Kings* (Cambridge, Mass.: Harvard University Press, 1950), which presents an accurate picture of the times, based on solid research, although the book was intended primarily for popular consumption. S. Painter, *The Rise of Feudal Monarchies* (Ithaca: Cornell University Press, 1951), gives a good deal of useful and necessary information in a short space. But for France, undoubtedly the best work in English is C. Petit-Dutaillis, *Feudal Monarchy in France and England from the 10th to the 13th Century* (tr. E. D. Hunt; London: Kegan Paul & Co., 1936). The writer of this book was probably the greatest expert in the field; he presents material on the French monarchy and its relations with England that can hardly be found elsewhere in English. A very good recent book on the Hundred Years' War, E. Perroy, *The Hundred Years' War* (tr. W. B. Wells; New York: Oxford University Press, 1951), gives a full political history of the relations between England and France during this period and includes a fair-minded estimate of the work and influence of Joan of Arc. The early history of Spain is best studied in Rafael Altamira y Crevea, *History of Spain: From the Beginnings to the Present Day* (tr. Muna Lee; New York: D. Van Nostrand Company, 1949).

VII The Preparation of the Modern World

Niccolo Machiavelli, Secretary of the Republic of Florence until 1512, when he was driven into exile. During his exile he wrote his epoch-making work The Prince, *which has proved to be the primer for all despots since his time, whether they have followed his precepts with or without acknowledgment. This portrait by an unknown contemporary Florentine artist was discovered only recently, and presented to the Italian nation.*

16

The Renaissance

General characteristics of the Renaissance • Why it started in Italy • The Italian humanists: Petrarch and his successors • Individualism, the cult of personality • The Church in the Renaissance • Art and science • Expansion beyond the Alps • Italian influence and native characteristics • Montaigne, Shakespeare, and Erasmus • Art and science

---

► General characteristics of the Renaissance

IN WHAT SENSE WAS IT TRULY A REBIRTH?

Up to this point it has been possible to treat the civilizations of the world as separate entities, and to discuss them individually. Medieval European civilization was the most difficult to treat in this manner, since, as was pointed out on several occasions, that civilization is only the early period of our own Western civilization and cannot therefore be properly distinguished from it. With the period conventionally styled the Renaissance, the procedure hitherto followed finally becomes impossible. There are no landmarks in time to distinguish the Renaissance from the period that preceded it, and though, of course, one may, and indeed must, distinguish the countries in which the familiar features associated with the Renaissance "spirit" first showed themselves and trace this spirit as it gradually spread through Europe, we cannot say that all men in a particular country at a particular time were filled with it. The Renaissance therefore is an abstraction, a term used by historians to indicate a certain kind of activity characteristic of the most culturally advanced peoples of Europe in the early modern period.

Nevertheless the word Renaissance has a very definite meaning. It signifies rebirth. There can be no doubt that the cultural leaders of early modern times, and historians in later centuries who have accepted them at their own valuation, believed that there had indeed been a rebirth of interest in, and excitement about, the world around them and the life of men on earth, and were wont to contrast this interest with the exclusive interest in the other world supposedly characteristic of the Middle Ages. It was believed that this outlook, which may be termed secular as distinct from religious, had prevailed in the halcyon days of the Greek city-state and the Roman Republic and Empire; hence a renewed interest in the works of classical antiquity and a reaction against the religiously oriented work of the Middle Ages. In this sense, therefore, it was not a new birth, but a rebirth.

Modern historians who have been well informed on the achievements of the Middle Ages have tended to depreciate the whole idea of a Renaissance, and speak of it as a "so-called" Renaissance. They can see no essential change, but merely a development of what was there in potentiality in the Middle Ages. They like to point to the continued medieval interests of many early Renaissance figures. Dante's interests, they point out, were primarily those of the Middle Ages, and his *Divine Comedy* rests solidly upon the thinking of Thomas Aquinas; yet Dante is sometimes heralded as a Renaissance man. Petrarch and Boccaccio, both born before Dante's death, are more frequently regarded as Renaissance figures than Dante. What to make of Giotto the painter, undoubtedly a herald of a new style in painting which foreshadows Renaissance painting, but a contemporary of Dante, living in the thirteenth century? Should therefore the term Renaissance be abandoned as totally misleading and corresponding to no essential reality?

Whatever historians may say, the term is firmly embedded in popular belief, and to the author of this book it does embody a real but very intangible change. Although we must give full credit to the Middle Ages for its achievements, which rank among the highest of mankind, they do seem qualitatively different from those of the period that followed. In making his own abstraction, therefore, of what he considers characteristic of the Renaissance spirit, the author relegates some men to the Middle Ages (and has mentioned them in the chapter on medieval culture, e.g., Dante, Boccaccio, and Chaucer) and others, such as Petrarch and Giotto, to the Renaissance. If this appears arbitrary, the reader may be assured that all such allocations are necessarily arbitrary when we deal with abstractions that are created by the mind of man and are not rooted in the very nature of things, thus compelling acceptance by all.

Giuliano de Medici by Raphael

Dirk Berck by Hans Holbein, the Younger

Two portraits of typical Renaissance noblemen who rose to their positions through successful commercial enterprise. Note how the Italian Medici is obviously now a noble, while the northerner looks what he is, a successful bourgeois merchant. (BOTH COURTESY THE METROPOLITAN MUSEUM OF ART)

► chronological chart

Summa Theologica of Thomas Aquinas	1267–1273	Acceptance of Bramante's plans for	
Divine Comedy of Dante	1300–1311	St. Peter's	1503
Giotto's frescoes at Padua	1305	First part of Cervantes' *Don Quixote*	1505
Petrarch crowned poet laureate at		Colet becomes Dean of St. Paul's	1505
Rome	1347	Reign of Henry VIII in England	1509–1547
Decameron of Boccaccio	1353	Erasmus' *In Praise of Folly*	1509
Foundation of Brethren of Common		"School of Athens" and "Disputa" of	
Life at Deventer	ca. 1380	Raphael	1509–1511
Chaucer's *Canterbury Tales*	1388	Leo X, pope	1513–1521
Arrival of Manuel Chrysoloras in Italy	1393	Francis I, King of France	1515–1547
Council of Constance	1414–1418	*The Prince* of Machiavelli	1515
Return of Papacy to Rome	1417	*Utopia* of Thomas More	1516
Opening of humanist school at Mantua		Dispute between Reuchlin and	
by Vittorino de Feltre	1425	Pfefferkorn	1520
Masaccio's "Virgin Enthroned"	1426	Dürer visits the Low Countries	1520–1521
Rule of Cosimo de Medici at Florence	1434–1464	Foundation of Collège de France	1530
Valla's *On the Donation of Constantine*	1440	Rabelais' *Gargantua and Pantagruel*	1532
Nicolas V, pope	1447–1455	"Last Judgment" of Michelangelo	1534–1541
Marsilio Ficino becomes head of		Hans Holbein the Younger painter to	
Platonic Academy at Florence	1458	Henry VIII of England	1536
Rule of Lorenzo de Medici at Florence	1469–1492	*Seven Books on the Structure of the*	
Sixtus IV, pope	1471–1484	*Human Body* by Vesalius	1543
Botticelli's "Birth of Venus"	1485	*On the Revolution of Celestial Bodies*	
Reign of Henry VII in England	1485–1509	by Copernicus	1543
"The Last Supper" of Leonardo da		Foundation of La Pléiade	1553
Vinci	1485–1498	Reign of Elizabeth I of England	1558–1603
Alexander VI, pope	1492–1503	Philibert Delorme publishes manual of	
Maximilian I, Holy Roman Emperor	1493–1519	architecture	1561
Invasion of Italy by Charles VIII	1494	Death of Titian at age of 99	1576
Sebastian Brant's *The Ship of Fools*	1494	*Essays* of Montaigne	1580
Execution of Savonarola in Florence	1498	*Tamburlaine the Great* by Marlowe	1587
Guillaume Budé goes as ambassador		First part of *The Faerie Queene* by	
to Venice	1501	Spenser	1590
Julius II, pope	1503–1513	*King Lear* by Shakespeare	1605

MEDIEVAL CONTRASTS

The Renaissance as an urban phenomenon

Saying that the Renaissance spirit is qualitatively different from the spirit of the Middle Ages is not to be taken to mean that any of the characteristics of the Renaissance to be detailed here were altogether absent in the Middle Ages. But the general spirit of the time, as reflected especially in its intellectual and cultural interests, was different. The Renaissance is above all an urban phenomenon. The medieval nobility had had chivalry as its ideal; its pastimes were rudely physical, not to say rustic. The noble was expected to be a soldier, ready to dash to arms at any moment in defense of his feudal rights or in fulfillment of his feudal obligations. The medieval noble, even in Italy, was rarely literate, and his tastes were certainly not bookish. Many Renaissance leaders sprang from the class of the upper bourgeoisie in the cities; they had wealth and leisure for cultivating literature and the arts.

The Renaissance prince altogether lacked chivalry; he preferred to gain his position by intrigues and the use of paid professional soldiers rather than relying on feudal vassals. Sometimes he was a professional soldier (*condottiero*) himself, who captured his city by force. But, at least as often, he was, like the Medici family in Florence, a skilled political manipulator, capable of using force when necessary and able to pay for it, but preferring to rely upon control of the masses by adopting popular policies which won their support against rival nobles. There can therefore be little doubt that the rise of towns to importance, an achievement of the Middle Ages described in Chapter 14, was an essential prerequisite for the Renaissance.

Interest in this world

Interest in this world was not, of course, absent in the Middle Ages. But the Church had consistently taught that the proper task of men on earth was to seek salvation in the hereafter; and the ordinary man had access to no other teaching. Peculiar individuals such as Emperor Frederic II had been skeptical of Christian teachings, and had even inquired into Muslim alternatives. Yet even he prepared himself for death in the garb of a penitent. The Church, as we have seen, had been losing prestige constantly over the last medieval centuries. But, while it lost its power to impose its policy upon the national states which defied it when royal and national interests were threatened, it had not lost its stranglehold on education; and thus the general Christian teachings, as far as they were known, were still accepted without question. When the city-dwelling nobility of the Renaissance emphasized self-development as being the task of men on earth, and stressed the possibility of the enjoyment of this life rather than its passive endurance in hopes of a better hereafter, and when they imported teachers from Greece who provided an education in the classics which adopted a similar point of view, then those who had access to such education found it possible to free themselves from the bonds of Christian education which had preached a totally different ethos.

Freedom for the individual for self-realization

Similarly, the teachings of the Church that society was static, that each man had his properly appointed place in a particular class, that humanity rather than individual man was important (the contention of the prevailing realist philosophy), that it was sinful to wish to rise above one's station in life, found no echo in the lives of the bourgeois nobility, many of whom had indeed risen from a lower station by their intelligence and industry. It was an undoubted reality in the towns that one could rise to greatness by one's own efforts. Why then pretend that it was not, or say that it was sinful? Such a Church teaching was behind the times except in so far as it could be used to prevent the lower classes from rising and to keep them content with their present lot.

We have seen how the Sophists in ancient Athens in similar circumstances abandoned the polis ideal in favor of the cult of the individual personality. Alcibiades would have felt entirely at home in a Renaissance city; his peculiar talents would certainly have found useful employment, and it is not difficult to imagine that he would have become an effective Renaissance prince. On the other hand the medieval feudal noble could hardly rise far by his own efforts. He was hedged around by too many restrictions. He had to find a suitable heiress to marry, other nobles had to die providentially—even his king could not help him much, however faithful his service to him. He could not simply conquer more land without bringing down upon himself the wrath of his peers. Only by entering the Church could he rise to higher position, and this too was hardly likely to be successful merely as a result of his own efforts. We may say therefore that, in the sense used in an earlier chapter when Sparta and Athens were being contrasted, the society of the Middle Ages outside the towns was a closed society, whereas urban society was potentially open. It has become ever more open from that day to this. It is no accident that in all historical societies the development of demo-

This wonderful Raphael painting, now in the Kaiser Friedrich Museum of Berlin, is usually called "The Holy Family with a Child Saint." The identity of the child on the right is not known. The child on the left is presumably John the Baptist. Painted about 1505.

cratic institutions has always gone hand in hand with the growth of cities and of the middle class which finds in urban life the field for its activity.

THE RENAISSANCE IDEAL—HUMANISM

The consistent ideal of the Renaissance was humanism, which in its widest sense meant the cultivation of the human personality, the regarding of man as the earthly creature he apparently is, and not exclusively as a candidate for salvation. The Greeks in this sense were humanists, as were some of the better-educated Romans such as Cicero, who had been permeated by Greek culture. It was, however, not unnatural for the men of the Renaissance to give humanism a more restricted meaning. They used it to mean especially the cultivation of the classics, or what are called the humanities. When one speaks therefore of the humanists as a class at this period, the reference is particularly to the scholars who cultivated the use of classical Latin and Greek, and sought for ancient manuscripts in these languages.

Nevertheless the term in its wider sense can be made to apply to the works of the Renaissance as a whole. The men of the Renaissance were interested primarily in man as an earthly being. Though most of them would not have denied man's spiritual being nor the fact of salvation, salvation was no longer their primary interest, and they postponed the search for it until they felt the imminence of death. Without denying the teachings of the Church they tended to disregard them; in this sense they may be said to have been the founders of modern secular culture, which also does not deny the teachings of religion so much as it disregards them, except perhaps on Sundays. The Christian humanist, on the other hand—and Christian humanism is a recognized movement in modern times—regards man as a being of spiritual and earthly nature. Any other concept to him would be one-sided. To such a humanist St. Thomas Aquinas remains the greatest humanist of them all, for he gave full recognition to the earthly element in man, but certainly not at the expense of the spiritual.

The greatest artists of the Renaissance, as distinct from the writers, were Christian humanists in the fullest sense. It is impossible to doubt the depth of the faith and certainty of such a man as Raphael of the high Renaissance in Italy. No one without faith, indeed, could have painted such a series of wonderful Madonnas, nor could he have portrayed the love and wisdom of the Jesus child without a profound understanding of and acceptance of Christianity. Yet the Madonnas and children are real human beings, based, no doubt, on real human models; and the technique of painting and composition is unsurpassed. It is impossible to think that Raphael painted such pictures merely because it was the Church that commissioned them. He and others of the greatest painters had an insight into the balance between the earthly and the spiritual that the Renaissance achieved at the height of its maturity—even though there arose no writer of a similar stature and thus no comparable maturity in thought was achieved.

THE RENAISSANCE AS THE GATEWAY TO MODERN TIMES

Essentially the Renaissance is the gateway to modern times, but it suffered from the undue optimism that is the hallmark of immaturity. The humanist writers believed that they had rediscovered the world, and that all that had gone before them was of no account, barbaric, uncouth, rustic. They called medieval architecture Gothic, not as a term of description but as an opprobrious epithet. They turned to antiquity for their architectural models; and though the genius of the best architects of the Renaissance was able to make of Renaissance architecture something nearly new, they were always somewhat constrained by their models: the Parthenon, even in ruins, surpasses all their work. They thought that the men of the Middle Ages had not observed nature, and that they themselves were the first since antiquity to do so. They did not trouble to observe the careful naturalism of the medieval sculptors, a naturalism too complete and too careful, perhaps, but not to be despised. The observations of an Albertus Magnus were more painstaking and accurate—at least till Vesalius (1514–1564)—than anything the Renaissance produced, for it was not a scientific age. The careful reasoning of the scholastics, they despised as being expended on matters of no consequence; such knowledge was valueless in comparison with the joys of life experience.

Since the time of the Renaissance, we have discovered science and allowed it to change our life; we have lost the freshness of Renaissance optimism, and we no longer believe so wholeheartedly in the joys of simple experience. With Freud's theory of the "Oedipus complex" we have returned to a secular variant of original sin; we are riddled with feelings of guilt unknown to a Machiavelli; and we look to all varieties of religion, including psychoanalysis, to save us. But we can still dimly recognize the men and women of the Renaissance as our ancestors, the intellectual founders of the modern world. They are less alien to us than the men of the Middle Ages. Their secular philosophy of life is basically ours. In a quite real sense a new age had dawned. If it was immature, that is to be expected. The bloom of a new world was upon them; the arteries had not yet hardened, and the blood coursed freely in their veins. It was a brief moment in history, comparable in many ways to fifth-century Athens, and perhaps to Old Kingdom Egypt. There has been no such moment since then in the history of Western civilization—a moment of utter self-confidence, free from guilt and introspection. Let us, with our hardened arteries and our passion for undistinguished anonymity, not to be too hard on them.

▶ Why did the Renaissance start in Italy?

It can never be determined with finality why a particular movement started in a particular place. All that the historian can do is to point to the fertility of the soil in which certain ideas may take root—if a seed is planted there.

In northern Italy by the high Middle Ages there was a developed urban life in numerous centers. Long before, as related in an earlier chapter, these towns had freed themselves from the tutelage of feudal nobles whose protection they rarely needed; and the holy Roman emperor, once the Hohenstaufens were no more, made no attempt to assert any authority he may still legally have possessed. Thus these cities by the beginning of the fourteenth century were self-governing, unless they were under the domination of another city like themselves. Other cities in Europe, however, existed with almost as much self-government and almost as much freedom of opportunity for the intelligent and industrious. But the Renaissance did not arise in them, and they did not at once follow the lead given them by the Italians. Perhaps the sense of community was still too strong in these cities for individualism to become their ideal; at no time did individualism run as rampant beyond the Alps as in the Italian cities. Perhaps the solid German or Flemish burgher was more interested in business for its own sake, and preferred to spend all his energies in increasing his business rather than in spending the wealth that it brought him. Such national characteristics are visible and persistent and not easily to be explained. But in any case the northern cities lacked a stimulus that was strong in Italy, the desire of the Italians to emulate and equal the achievements of their own personal ancestors.

Italy had never experienced the full pressure of the barbarian invasions at the end of the Roman Empire. Though Ostrogoths and Lombards ruled much of Italy, Italians —descended directly from the Romans— remained in the majority. So the Renaissance Italians believed themselves to be the direct inheritors of the Romans. Their language was the nearest of the European languages to Latin. It was not difficult for them to learn it, and many of the Latin classics were still easily available, even before the humanists began their search for manuscripts. Moreover, there were far more Roman remains in Italy than elsewhere. Thus it was that the Italians, seeking for new ideals suitable to the new situation, had no further to look for examples of secular living than their own Roman ancestors; and it is not surprising that the first stirrings of the Renaissance spirit found expression in the search for ancient manuscripts and the accumulation of libraries of works in the Latin language—not, of course, medieval Latin, which to a true humanist was a barbarous Germanized hodge-podge, but the stately periods of Cicero and the works of the Augustan Age. For the proper understanding of the Latin classics it was soon recognized that a knowledge of the Greek classics was essential. So to the Greeks of Constantinople the Italians went searching for tutors, and the revival of classical learning was under way.

▶ The Italian humanists

PETRARCH

The founder of Italian humanism was Francesco Petrarcha (commonly known as Petrarch; 1304–1374). A very complex man, he has variously been called the "first modern man" and the "first modern sentimentalist." To both titles he has some claim. It is, in fact, easy to make fun of him if one does not appreciate the age in which he lived, the age of the Avignon papacy, of the Great Schism, and of the Conciliar Movement; the age of the Black Death, in which indeed his beloved Laura lost her life; the age of late, hair-splitting scholasticism. Petrarch wrote satires against the Church, and accepted a living from the same tainted source. He wrote some of the best love lyrics in the Italian tongue, but valued far more highly his often pedantic and uninspired Latin epics, because Latin was the language of his beloved Cicero. He was worried in later life about the salvation of his soul for having loved Laura and addressed to her those exquisite lyrics. He searched for manuscripts, found one of Homer and adored it, but could not bring himself to learn Greek in order to read it. He climbed a minor mountain for the purpose of enjoying nature in the raw and himself expatiating upon that pleasure. He allowed himself to be crowned with laurel as a poet, and accepted with due humility this uncontested title given to him by a self-appointed group of unauthorized donors (at least a modern honorary degree is authorized by some board of trustees!). But when all this is admitted the Italian lyrics and odes remain; the self-advertisement did advertise to all that the profession of letters could lead to fame and was thus worthy of pursuit by others; he did initiate the search for manuscripts, and they were safer in the hands of humanists than in fourteenth-century monasteries. Moreover, there can be little doubt that the humanists appreciated them more than did the monks, and they made them available to others who would appreciate them likewise. And if he abstained from learning Greek himself, it is true that many of his successors followed his exhortations rather than his example.

SUCCESSORS OF PETRARCH

But in a sense Petrarch's life was an archetype of the lives of many of the later humanists in Italy. Many of them were poseurs, very much a self-conscious élite class, writing letters in polished if over-rhetorical Latin to their opposite numbers, advertising their own excellence and eternally quarreling over trifles. As a self-constituted class of learned men they were often, too often perhaps, accepted at their own valuation. They were unable to hinder for long the development of the vernacular, the language of the *Divine Comedy;* but they did succeed in making their contemporaries think of the still developing medieval Latin tongue as something barbarous and unfit for the lips of polite society. Thus they helped to kill off what might have become a real European language common to all the educated. By self-consciously and self-righteously adopting a dead language incapable of natural development they showed themselves as reactionaries rather than innovators.

But by the recovery of the works of antiquity and by making them available outside the monasteries and the Church they did set in motion other trends which did have a future. And many of the humanists did become first-rate scholars and critics. Lorenzo Valla by acute internal criticism showed the famous Donation of Constantine (p. 267) to be a forgery. He and many others edited and improved the texts of the classics, which had often been corrupted by ignorant monkish copyists performing their daily task without vital interest in what they were doing. Poggio Bracciolini was an indefatigable traveler, who spared no expense or pains in tracking down his manuscripts and who was rewarded most greatly by discovering what is still the only extant manuscript of Lucretius, copied in some earlier century by who knows what odd religious man who could bring himself to transcribe those famous words *"Tantum religio potuit suadere malorum."*[1] There was also Niccolo Niccoli, a successful business man who sacrificed every ducat he possessed to build a library which was to be the best in the world, falling at last into bankruptcy from which he was rescued by Cosimo de Medici. Such men are worthy of praise, for it was their work which gave to the centuries to come their taste for the humanities, without which few will deny we should all be the poorer.

For a while Greek studies languished, but enthusiasm for all of antiquity ultimately overcame the natural difficulty of learning a

[1]"To so many evils has religion been able to persuade mankind."

foreign language in adulthood. Manuel Chrysoloras came from Constantinople, and the most eminent humanists sat at his feet; many of the second generation humanists learned Greek well. Amongst these was Marsilio Ficino who founded a Platonic Academy in Florence under the patronage of the Medici, and translated Plato into Italian for the first time, in 1482. Since Aristotle had been adopted by the Church it was to Plato that so many humanists turned their attention, ignorant of how much Platonism already lay concealed in Thomas Aquinas and the earlier Church fathers. But, curiously, though some adopted the suitably pagan philosophy of Plato as it appears in the *Phaedrus*, with its archetypes of heavenly beauty to be pursued by earthly men but never fully attained, others, including Marsilio himself, took over Neoplatonism, the religious philosophy derived from Plato by way of Plotinus, the closest to a religion of all pure philosophies, even though it is the individualist religion of mysticism which seeks a personal experience of God. Though the Academy itself did not produce much fruitful work in the years of its existence, and became immersed in much curious mysticism far removed from Plato, nevertheless its influence was considerable, especially in England where Platonism was always more popular than Aristotelianism, rigidified as it had become in the hands of the later scholastics and the northern universities.

▶ Individualism—the cult of the personality

THE "UNIVERSAL MAN"

Ultimately more important than the much publicized recovery of antiquity was the growth of individualism, the desire for self-realization and self-expression, the development of individual potentialities to their fullest extent. It is difficult to say how much this new cult owed to the rediscovery of antiquity and the Greek spirit. The humanists knew little of the Sophists and their revolution—as indeed we know little today. The philosophy of Aristotle, which gives

strong support to the ideal of self-realization, was almost certainly not understood in this sense. Probably too many of the humanists, who tended to accept the authority of antiquity instead of that of the despised and backward-looking Church, were not well equipped to strike out for themselves in a new direction, though Pico della Mirandola in an *Oration on the Dignity of Man* does give fine expression to the ideal of man's latent powers to create of himself what he will. "Restrained by no narrow bonds, according to thy own free will . . . thou, thy own free maker and molder, mayest fashion thyself in whatever manner thou likest best. . . ." But Pico was a noble, and no ordinary humanist. He aspired to universal knowledge as well as to being a "universal man," like so many of the great men of the Renaissance.

Yet it seems more probable that this ideal was not derived from books, but from the possibility of its fulfillment in the world of the Renaissance. Freed from clerical restrictions, freed from feudal obligations, still ignorant of the vast world of science and the depth of the knowledge of the world that was still to be acquired, the world of Italy seemed to be a good place to live in and develop oneself and win approval in the eyes of men.

THE PRINCE

Machiavelli and Machiavellianism

First let us consider the Renaissance prince. Though the title might descend from father to son, there was certainly nothing static in the princedoms of nothern Italy. Southern Italy for the most part took little share in the Renaissance. The throne of Naples and Sicily, though disputed by the Angevin princes of France, remained for most of the time securely in the hands of the monarchy of Aragon. The kings were often cruel and tyrannical, but they were rarely enlightened. But in northern Italy there was little sacred about a title. A family could hold dominion only while it was prepared to defend its possessions. Sometimes the outgoing despot had only illegitimate offspring to inherit his possessions. The mere fact of this illegitimacy did not deter him from insisting on his son's right of succession, a thought abhorrent to feudal nobles of the past. A soldier of fortune, hired to conquer a city, might keep it for himself after conquest, and could thereafter be turned out only by force. Most of these lords patronized the arts; each wished to have a fine palace designed by the best architect and decorated by the best sculptors and painters. Many patronized scholars and borrowed their glory; some collected books. All these things were conducive to their fame amongst their competitors in other cities; and fame was to them the breath of life. Always insecure in their position, they resorted to all means, fair or foul —not excluding even poison—which could help them to defend their positions at home or win other cities to their control abroad.

One man of genius grew up in this atmosphere. Niccolo Machiavelli (1469–1527) saw that politically Italy was far behind the other European states. When Charles VIII of France invaded Italy in 1494, Machiavelli saw how hopelessly divided the Italians were, how some joined with the invader, others did not resist, and how all failed to work together against him, save in temporary spasmodic alliances for the immediate gain of the city and its despot rather than for any higher end. He had been secretary of the Florentine Republic, one of the most stable of Italian states under the Medici family. In forced retirement he wrote two famous works, the *Prince* and *Discourses on Livy,* which have given rise to controversy ever since. For the *Prince* gives realistic and amoral advice to princes on how to win and hold power, while the *Discourses* show his clear preference for a democratic republic such as he imagined ancient Rome to have been. He had no illusions about the goodness of man; he saw clearly man's weaknesses, his love of power, his greed, and the thin veneer of his morality. Such weaknesses should be used by the prince to obtain and keep his power; it was, in the final analysis, better for men to be well governed by a despot, how-

ever tyrannical, than to be insecure under a feeble republic. With clear eyes he saw the world of Italy around him; it was not his business to change it but to study it and formulate conclusions on the basis of his study. All despots since his day have in a greater or lesser degree accepted his advice, with or without acknowledgment. Machiavellianism as a word has passed into the language as a synonym for political behavior without scruple and without morality.

But Machiavelli was very much a man of his time. The sanctions of the Church and the old morality had passed into disuse. Where is man to find his morality if man is the measure of all things? The problem of Socrates was the problem of the Renaissance also— how does one find the good? Can one say that the safety of the state is the supreme law? If not, what law is higher? It was Machiavelli's task to pose the problem in its most acute form. The Church of his day was represented in Italy by the secular and worldly papacy. He had dealings with Alexander VI, the Borgia who above all popes has gone down in history as the least scrupulous; he visited Julius II, who reconquered and ruled the states of the Church like any other Renaissance despot. Clearly such men could hardly speak for morality. Nor could he prefer the sermons of the Dominican friar Savonarola, who ruled Florence for a few years by his power over the people, won by his thunderings against clerical and noble immorality.

The Prince as patron

What Machiavelli preached in the *Prince,* the princes themselves practiced. But the Medici family was to some degree an exception to this rule. They were not despots of Florence, which remained a republic. They ruled in part by consent, and their strength lay in their unlimited wealth and their diplomatic talents rather than in their military prowess. The Medici had a long history of support for the lower classes in the city of Florence, including the poorer class of business men, and the unenfranchised proletariat, against the big business men who through their power and money controlled most of the Italian states. In the early fifteenth century Giovanni de Medici, the leader of the house that had greatly expanded its fortunes through successful banking, supported a tax which laid the burden mainly upon the rich, including himself, and thereby endeared himself to the lower classes, upon whose support his great son Cosimo relied all his life. Cosimo was once driven out by the aristocracy which controlled the government (an oligarchy with democratic forms known as the *signoria*), but returned when the government in his absence began to lose a war. Thereafter Cosimo ruled Florence effectively as political boss, preferring to keep his own supporters in the government rather than accepting the direct responsibility himself.

He had studied Greek with Chrysoloras, became proficient in both Latin and Greek, and was interested in philosophy and theology. But he is above all known for his sure taste in the arts. As patron of every artist of importance in his day, willing to expend any sums from his vast wealth for what he wanted—and what he wanted was always the best—he is an altogether remarkable figure who could have expressed his manifold talents only in the age of the Renaissance. Efficient and supremely successful in everything he touched, understanding perfectly the

world of his day, and possessed of impeccable artistic taste, he almost overshadows his better known and equally effective grandson Lorenzo the Magnificent, under whose benign management Florence reached the full height of her splendor. Lorenzo added to the talents of his grandfather the ability to express himself in poetry and song in the Italian language. Without such patrons neither humanist scholars nor artists could have thrived. It is to the eternal honor of these early Medici rulers that they were also full participators in the expanding life around them and not parvenu rich with the deplorable taste of the Roman banker of the last days of the republic, that they understood as well as patronized, and that they realized their wealth was not best used for private display but for public adornment. Without such men there would have been no artistic Renaissance, but only a few scholars writing to each other and a few artists working humbly in their garrets.

A word also deserves to be said of the patronage of a very different kind of work carried out by Francesco I of Mantua. Mantua was a relatively small principality, with few resources to spend on art. But Francesco earned undying fame by inviting the leading educator of the day to his court to set up a school for children, based on humanist ideas

A school of the Italian Renaissance period. Note the "progressive" elements, far different from the medieval cathedral school—the open windows, the hand tools, and the animal—and the general informal atmosphere in spite of the notice behind the teacher which calls for silence. (COURTESY NEW YORK PUBLIC LIBRARY)

and the cult of antiquity. This gifted man, Vittorino da Feltre, was given an entirely free hand to put into effect some rather startling ideas. The first pupils of his school were the sons of the local nobility. But he did not confine himself either to the nobility or to the male sex. On the contrary, he thought all classes and both sexes should have the benefit of education, and this education should be neither vocational nor one-sidedly bookish. Greek, Latin, and Italian literature were to be studied as a matter of course, and moral training was not neglected. But in addition physical exercise was required, such as swimming and fencing, and artistic education in such subjects as drawing and music. In short, Vittorino designed his education in part after what was known of the ancient Greek world, but for the clear purpose of preparing his charges for the kind of life most of them would be expected to lead after their schooling was over. Since the school was for resident pupils, and all class distinctions were obliterated by the use of a common dress and common food, it might have been doubted whether even fifteenth-century Italy was yet ready for such innovations. But the fact was that the school prospered and obtained a reputation in Italy second to none. Nobles vied for the privilege of having their children study with Vittorino. His educational ideas spread over Europe likewise, and the English public school is a not too distant descendant of the education first made possible for a chosen few by the prince of Mantua.

▶ The Church in the Renaissance

THE AFTERMATH OF THE GREAT SCHISM

It was not possible for the Church to stand aloof from a movement so all-pervasive as the Renaissance. It might have been possible for a few popes to combat the spirit of the times, to see the dangers of the secular view of life to an institution whose powers were based on the supremacy of the spiritual over the temporal. But, as has been seen, the Church itself had been declining as a spiritual power since the thirteenth century. By laying claim to too much, as in the days of Boniface VIII, it had been forced to submit to humiliation at the hands of the secular powers; it had undergone the "Babylonian Captivity" and the Great Schism, and only with the greatest difficulty had it fought off the Councils. When at last the papacy returned to Rome the city itself was almost desolate, and it required the utmost attention on the part of the popes to consolidate its power even over the Eternal City. And in doing so it had to make use of more than such spiritual sanctions as it could still wield. It had to make use of its temporal powers bequeathed to it long ago in the Donation of Pepin (see p. 267) and added to in succeeding papal reigns. It still officially possessed the suzerainty of the states of the Church, as they were now called, and of the kingdom of Naples in southern Italy. The pope, it is true, was feudal overlord of these territories, but feudalism in northern and central Italy was almost gone. The only way available to a pope to alter this situation was to become a Renaissance prince, and use princely tactics in addition to what could be salvaged of the spiritual sanctions of the Church to secure the absolute dominion of these states in the Renaissance manner, rather than remain as feudal overlord with vague and largely unenforceable privileges.

THE PAPAL PROBLEM—RECONCILIATION OF SPIRITUAL AND TEMPORAL POWER

Such a situation posed the old problem in a new form. How could an institution based on spiritual supremacy act as a temporal power without losing its prestige as a spiritual organization, or could it afford, as it was to be forced to do in a later century, to abandon its temporal position? The choice was made to act as a temporal power; but the choice probably made inevitable the Protestant Reformation, and it is certain that papal financial policies connected with this choice provided the occasion for the Lutheran revolt.

The papacy had one advantage over all secular states. It possessed a source of income denied to them, either money contributed by the faithful in exchange for gifts that only the Church could offer, or money accruing to it from benefices in its gift, now usually shared with the monarchs, as described in an earlier chapter. There was also a considerable income from pilgrims, especially in jubilee years. On the other hand it had one great disadvantage in that the papal office could not run in any particular family. Several popes filled the high office of cardinal with their nephews and other relatives; but, even so, only rarely could they control the election of their successors. Moreover, they were already well advanced in age when they reached the papal chair, and could not act as vigorously as younger men—though some, like Julius II, were hardly inferior, even in this respect, to the greatest of secular princes. But when they decided to act as patrons of art and literature their resources could hardly be equaled. For almost a century, with a few exceptions, they built up Rome, and supported the humanist writers and translators of the classics, beginning with the noted humanist Nicholas v (1447–1455), who invited numerous humanists to Rome, including even Lorenzo Valla, who had recently proved the Donation of Constantine to be a forgery. Nicholas began a great library, though it was dissipated after his death by a pope unsympathetic to humanism. Aeneas Silvius, another noted humanist, was pope from 1458 to 1464 under the title of Pius II, and he was able to set the tide once more in the direction of humanism, a tide which was seldom diverted afterward until the Reformation.

THE POPES AS RENAISSANCE PRINCES

Sixtus IV (1471–1484) in his relatively long period as pope entered boldly and openly into Italian affairs, acting more as the head of the states of the Church than as head of the universal Church itself. Attempting to interfere in Florentine affairs, quarreling with the Medici, and trying to depose Lorenzo the Magnificent from his position as Florentine leader, he was also undoubtedly privy to the murder of Lorenzo's brother and did not scruple to use his spiritual powers likewise for all they were still worth. He was at least partly successful in his schemes, and filled important positions in his principality with his relatives. His reign—and it is ironical that before his elevation to the papal see he had been a Franciscan friar—marks the definite secularization of the papacy. Yet, at the same time, he patronized writers, revived the Vatican library, built the Sistine Chapel and had it decorated by the greatest artists, and he inaugurated a huge building program for the city of Rome. His example, good and bad, was followed by a whole series of popes, culminating in Alexander VI, Julius II, and Leo X, the Medici pope who had to face the Lutheran revolt. Thus the papacy began to lose, for the last time before the Reformation, the spiritual allegiance of Christendom, while the popes sought for glory, fame, power, and wealth as strongly as any secular prince, and while in lands outside Italy the sparks of revolt were kindled which needed only the defiant acts of a Luther to fan them into flame.

▶ **Renaissance art**

ARCHITECTURE—GENERAL CHARACTERISTICS

Contrast with Gothic and debt to antiquity

As we have seen, the great native artistic achievement of medieval Western civilization was the Gothic cathedral. Medieval sculpture and painting, though it has been much admired for the deep religious feeling it embodies, and for the way in which it so clearly fulfilled not only its religious, but its architectural, purpose, cannot be said to have struck out in a new direction. Medieval sculpture was largely a realistic copying of nature, usually with the greatest fidelity. This applies to both the sculptured human figures and their surroundings. Painting, though sometimes stiff and formal when required for religious reasons, since often it had to provide material for religious meditation, became far more free when it was used for illustration, as in so many beautifully illustrated medieval manuscripts. But during the Renaissance, sculpture and painting burst the bonds of tradition altogether and escaped beyond the confines even of their classical models. They also owe little to their medieval forebears. Though their debt to antiquity is heavy, the greatest of the Renaissance sculptors and painters transcend their models. This is especially true of the painters who, of course, had no classical models to follow.

The Gothic cathedral was an original achievement because of the unique way in which the form was determined by the purpose of the whole, so that all details are subordinated to the central theme. Its great technical achievement was the ribbed structure which, again, made possible the unique use of light so necessary for the fulfillment of the religious purpose of the whole. It may be said, therefore, that the structure dominated the building and determined everything else in it. It was far otherwise with the Renaissance building, based on the much more simple structure of Greek and Roman buildings, the simplicity of which has already been noted in the section on Greek classical architecture. Here the structure is of little importance and is largely concealed, whereas in the Gothic cathedral it is forced upon the attention. Simplicity and purity were insisted on by Renaissance architects, and yet the civilization of the Renaissance was neither pure or simple, nor did the builders and their patrons have in mind anything so naïve as a simple dwelling place for a tutelary god or goddess—nor, in truth, did the Romans, whose works were so much more available to Renaissance architects than the works of the Greek originators.

The result was the same as in the case of the Roman imitators. The Renaissance architects, paid by their munificent patrons, at least one of whose motives was competition with their peers in other cities, had to compete; and there were few fields in which competition could be open, except in decoration and size. The Greek style, originated for a particular purpose in ancient Greece, was incapable of any true evolution into something different and truly original. Thus there is a certain monotony in the great public buildings of the Renaissance. Colonnades may be multiplied indefinitely, capitals may become more ornate and lavish; when there is no need for them, they may be inserted as decorations supporting nothing. Renaissance architects had great technical virtuosity, their relatively simple problems were solved with ample ease, and it is certainly possible to admire their work immoderately, especially the work of Bramante. But one cannot help feeling that they were following a dead end and that the coming of the baroque, a style indigenous to Western civilization, allowed the artists of the post-Renaissance period a freedom that was much needed, in spite of the extravagances that were in most artists an inseparable part of this latter style. Since Gothic in the sixteenth century likewise reached its own dead end in the flamboyant Gothic, the way was open for a new style that combined elements of both Gothic and Renaissance, and yet in itself was distinctive and original. This new style, the baroque, will be discussed briefly in Chapter 21.

SCULPTURE—GENERAL CHARACTERISTICS

Influence of Greece and Rome

Medieval sculpture was, as has been said, strongly realistic, except in the portrayal of the human form, whose inherent beauty could not be stressed in that age of contempt for the body and all its attributes. Here, therefore, the recovery of interest in the ancient world acted as a real inspiration to the Renaissance sculptor. We have seen how in the Hellenistic world sculpture added a certain realism to the ideal figures of the classical Hellenic period, and the Romans continued the trend, especially in portrait sculpture. The old market woman, illustrated on page 105, is a typical example. But this realism was lost in the Middle Ages, to be recovered now during the Renaissance. All the conditions were ripe for such a recovery. Much Roman sculpture was available in Italy; there was a revived interest in and appreciation of the human body; and ancient taboos which required that the human form should always be fully clothed lost their urgency. Moreover, patrons were numerous who desired that their own form and features should be perpetuated in bronze or stone as a contribution to their eternal fame. There was also opportunity for sculpture in the great Renaissance churches, which had plenty of space available for all forms of decoration. Funerary sculpture also tended to perpetuate the memory of the deceased.

The transcending of models from the past—Donatello and Michelangelo

Renaissance sculptors early revolted against simple realism; they fully appreciated how the Greeks had striven to represent the ideal form, while retaining a recognizable closeness to the original model. They tried for both anatomical exactness and ideal beauty at the same time, and very many of them achieved outstanding success. Leonardo da Vinci has given us a personal account of his efforts to attain the former, through innumerable drawings and painstaking anatomical observation. We know also how carefully he tried to model a horse for an equestrian statue of his patron so that it should be a truly perfect horse and not only a mount for its rider, and how many times he destroyed his imperfect efforts. But the greatest sculptor of them all, and in the opinion of many the greatest sculptor probably of all time, was Michelangelo Buonarotti (1475–1564), one of the universal geniuses of the Renaissance, as far removed from the artist specialist of our own times as Leonardo da Vinci himself. He was skilled in architecture, painting, and poetry, as well as in sculpture, though always in his own mind primarily a sculptor —as may be agreed by those who have seen his magnificent, but still sculptural, paintings in the Sistine Chapel.

Sculpture had burst its medieval bonds already in the work of Donatello (1386–1466), who performed a service for sculpture similar to that of Giotto and his followers in painting. Donatello shows his own de-velopment clearly, since he executed his first two works in the Gothic manner, only then branching out on his own. But Michelangelo, whatever he owed to Donatello, was always *sui generis,* living in the Renaissance but belonging to all time, hardly influenced in his mature work by any other sculptor, and unthinkably far removed from the Gothic world. If he had lived earlier it is still impossible to imagine Michelangelo helping to carve the portal of Chartres. An individualist to the core, conscious of his own uniqueness and genius, given to towering rages and impatient of all control, he yet had to submit to the whims of his patrons, at least one of whom, Pope Julius II, was as full of furious energy as Michelangelo himself. His technique learned early and fully a part of himself, he could do anything he chose with the utmost virtuosity. Already at the age of twenty-four he had completed a remarkable Pietá, which remained one of his best works. But as he grew older his

Preparatory sketches for a Madonna painting by Leonardo da Vinci. The sketches suggest something of the care used by Leonardo before he undertook the final version of a painting. (COURTESY THE METROPOLITAN MUSEUM OF ART)

The tremendous fresco of the "Last Judgment" by Michelangelo shows Christ as the great Judge. To the left are the elect, held and aided by angels while demons strive to pull them down; to the right are the damned being whirled down to hell by demons. The inspiration for the fresco is certainly the Inferno *of Dante. Although this composition is a fresco, the sculptural quality should be noted, as in all Michelangelo's work. This is seen even more clearly in the details on the opposite page.*

Detail from the "Last Judgment": St. Lawrence, a third-century martyr said to have been roasted on a gridiron for his faithfulness to the Church in the administration of funds.

Detail from the "Last Judgment": Christ and the Virgin Mary.

individual thought began to dominate his work, and into it is incorporated the experience of a life which it is impertinent to call unhappy. In a trivial sense no doubt he was unhappy. But his very greatness derives from his inward understanding of the lot of man, its joys and sorrows, its exaltations and depressions. It was his life experience that alone made it possible for him to create those artistic forms for which humanity will be for ever in his debt.

His great figures, "Day and Night," "Dawn and Sunset," "Moses" and "David" all are eloquent of his understanding of man as individual and universal type; all save the early "David" are inexpressibly sad. When later, at the insistence of Julius and contrary to his own first wishes, he painted the ceiling of the Sistine Chapel—an almost superhuman feat that he accomplished in four years in spite of the complaints of the furiously impatient Julius that the work was going too slowly—he chose the story of Creation. Into this huge fresco he poured all the artist's profound knowledge of man—his body, his soul, and his spirit, as also in the "Last Judgment" executed for a later pope in the evening of his life. During the painting of this last masterpiece he received the deep friendship of one of the most noble of Renaissance women, Vittoria Colonna, accentuating even more deeply his religious perceptions, which culminated after her death in a final sculptured Pietá in which the artist himself appears as Nicodemus helping to lift the dead Christ from Cross (strangely, in tone, reminding the viewer of Van Gogh painting himself as Lazarus risen from the dead at the word of the Master). Yet, such was Michelangelo's energy, even in the last years of a prodigious life, that he was still able to answer the call of another pope to become the chief architect for the still unfinished St. Peter's; and it was his plan, modifying that of Bramante, that was finally carried out after his death. Not unfittingly did the movie which showed the lifework of Michelangelo call him the Titan; few men in history have as much title to the name, for he was a true son of Prometheus.

PAINTING—THE CHIEF GLORY OF THE RENAISSANCE

Giotto as founder of Renaissance painting

Few will dispute that Renaissance painting is the chief of all the Renaissance claims to glory. In many ways it was a new art. Though there had been paintings in the ancient world, as far back in time indeed as Cro-magnon man, and though Egyptians in their traditional way had succeeded superbly in what they undertook, the real problems recognized as such in the modern age had never been solved: how to compose a painting so that it is an artistic and satisfying whole as a picture, how to give the illusion of three dimensions in a two-dimensional medium (the problem of perspective), and how to deal with light and shadow. We have learned only recently how the Greeks handled these problems, and the earlier Cretans, whose work is known to us but not to the men of the Renaissance, showed no awareness of them. The Renaissance painters solved all these problems, and in the opinion of many their work has never been surpassed in the succeeding centuries in spite of (or, conceivably, because of) the manifold technical inventions since their day. Faced therefore with the unalterable fact that they had no models to follow, the Renaissance painters were forced to solve their problems out of their own resources, as the medieval cathedral builders had solved theirs.

The greatest figure in early Renaissance painting to whom all his successors owed a great debt was Giotto, a Florentine artist contemporary with Dante (ca. 1265–1337), to whom indeed Dante himself pays tribute. In Giotto's day all art was still religious, and painting was under the influence of the Byzantine religious tradition. The painted medieval figures are, in their way, impressive, but there is little that is specifically human about them. No medieval Madonna can be imagined as a human mother with a human child. It was not, indeed, the artist's intention to draw any attention to their human nature, but rather to raise the soul of the beholder to meditate upon the mystery of Christ and the Virgin without possible distraction by the earthly beauty of womanhood or the beauty of the world in which they lived. With Giotto we already have a Madonna who is humanly tender, and a child who is a real child. The stiff, hieratic forms of medieval and much of Byzantine art have taken on movement as well as human grace. The subjects and themes of Giotto are still altogether religious, as they were to remain to a large extent throughout the whole of the Italian Renaissance. But Giotto was able to win at least one important secular patron who commissioned a religious work for the benefit of the soul of his dead father, a desire soon to be replaced in the Italian cities with the desire for the perpetuation of the mortal likeness of the patron himself for the benefit of posterity. Giotto did most of his work for the Franciscan Order, and he seems to have been especially sympathetic to St. Francis himself, although his own life activities were hardly in accord with the teachings of the great medieval friar, since he was successful in business, managed business enterprises, and was noted for his wit. Already indeed he fulfilled the Renaissance ideal of versatility to a marked degree. He did not, however, solve the problems of light and perspective, and it is doubtful whether he yet realized that they were problems. But he gave great care to his composition, and his colors were as beautiful as those of many of his great successors.

Successors of Giotto—Masaccio and Botticelli

Amongst the myriads of great and near great painters who succeeded Giotto in Italy only a few can be singled out here, either for their influence or for their supreme achievement. It should be understood that at this time no Italian painter worked in isolation. In the early Renaissance no painter confined himself to painting alone, but worked in sculpture, architecture when opportunity presented itself, but especially in the lesser arts, for the products of which there was constant demand among the

A Madonna fresco by Giotto, in the Church of Santa Cruce at Florence. In spite of the fact that the fresco is almost ruined, the difference can be seen even now between this human portrait and the figures of the Virgin which illustrate Chapter 13.

bourgeoisie. Thus an ambitious painter would apprentice himself at an early age to one of the masters of his craft, and even in his later years he was not inclined to specialize in only one field. One of the results of the system was that any innovation in any of the fields would be quickly known and imitated. Moreover, part of the training consisted in visiting and studying the masterpieces of earlier artists, which were, of course, open to view in the churches and public buildings of the time. Later, when they were housed in private buildings, the owners asked nothing better than to have artists admire their possessions. Michelangelo was a simple apprentice when he caught the eye of Lorenzo the Magnificent, who saw him in the Medicean gardens admiring his statuary. This proved to be the beginning of Michelangelo's career, for Lorenzo shortly afterward asked to see his work and thereafter became his first patron.

A detail from a fresco by Masaccio in the Church of Santa Maria del Carmine at Florence. The detail depicts the moment when the disciples are anxiously awaiting Christ's answer to the question of whether tribute money should be paid to Caesar.

So when a great innovator such as Masaccio (1401–1428?) for the first time succeeded in mastering the problem of perspective and the handling of groups without distortion or overcrowding, all later artists, including Leonardo da Vinci and Michelangelo, learned from his work, even though he himself died before he was thirty and barely had time to create a school of painters. Figures and landscapes were handled by Masaccio in a new manner, and his modified naturalism was imitated by a host of artists and became the prevailing mode. An equally, or perhaps even more highly talented painter, his contemporary Fra Angelico (1357–1455) still looked back to the past, and was not imitated; though of its kind his work has never been equaled for its clear spiritual inspiration, the delicacy of his details, the freshness of his coloring,

and the absolute perfection that he achieved in what he set out to do.

Sandro Botticelli (1444–1510) was, in his day and since his time, one of the most popular of all painters; but critical opinion has not been in agreement as to his real merits. He is certainly important in so far as he was truly a representative of his time, with its taste for antiquity and somewhat precious affection for the old gods of Greece and Rome, combined with an appreciation for Christianity which was as much aesthetic as it was religious. His famous "Venus" and "Spring" are works of great beauty, technically equal to any work of his time, pleasantly fanciful, but in theme hardly inspired. His work suggests the poverty of any inspiration still to be obtained from antique sources in his day. The religious paintings which predominate in his work show greater power of feeling, and it is clear that inspiration from Christianity was far from exhausted in spite of the secular preoccupations of the age. But there is in all Botticelli's work a very clear aesthetic appreciation of the beauty of the human, especially the female form. The models of beauty that he saw in the world around him are all faithfully portrayed, yet with an idealism that was evidently part of his nature. The Botticelli angels are still ideals of purity and grace unequaled by later painters. But in other ways he was so far surpassed by his contemporary Leonardo da Vinci, and his successors Raphael and Michelangelo, that one sometimes feels seriously the lack of any true intellectual content in his work and realizes how necessary this was if art were to advance along its true path, now that the technical problems had been solved and the mind of the Renaissance was reaching its maturity.

The great masters of the high Renaissance—Leonardo, Raphael, Titian

Leonardo da Vinci (1452–1519) was obviously a great painter, almost the greatest. Yet he did not devote himself exclusively, or indeed mainly, to painting. Indeed he painted little, but the few works we have from his brush are all unique masterpieces. His was a life as completely fulfilled as any man's known to us in history. Occupied with scientific observations, filling notebooks with drawings and diagrams, called in as consulting engineer by princes, interested in everything that pertains to man with a restless curiosity that could not be satisfied, and yet a painstaking perfectionist, he is perhaps the most outstanding example of the *uomo universale*, the ideal of Renaissance versatility. As a painter he is renowned for the "Last Supper," a fresco which already in his lifetime, in part because of his own passion for experimentation, was beginning to disappear from the wall on which it had been painted; the "Madonna of the Rocks," a masterpiece of light and shade (*chiaroscuro*) and background in addition to being one of the most beautiful and thoughtful of all

Madonna pictures, and the famous "La Gioconda," or the "Mona Lisa" of the enigmatic smile. The dramatic grouping of the "Last Supper" and the wonderful individuality of each apostle, has made this picture, even in "restored" copies which bear too often little resemblance to the original, one of the best known of all paintings. To achieve this masterpiece Leonardo spent many years meditating upon each apostle, trying to penetrate into the soul of those men who had just heard Christ's prophecy that one of them would betray him. For the "Mona Lisa" we know that he tried for many years to penetrate that famous smile to the soul of the beautiful woman who was his model. It has already been mentioned how many times he modeled the horse for his Milanese equestrian statue. From his drawings and writings we know how carefully he studied human anatomy so that no least element in the human body should be wrong. If he lacked the enormous energy of Michelangelo and too few masterpieces were created by him to make a full comparison, there can yet be no doubt that he stands in the same rank among the very highest of mankind.

Raphael Santi (1483–1520) is often, perhaps usually in this age, denied a place amongst the giants of the high Renaissance. He has been called the "perfect painter," as if this was a disqualification for fame, and it has been pointed out how much he owed to his various masters, features of whose work he incorporated into his own. While greatness is allowed to his Madonnas, and to the "Disputa" and the "School of Athens," what has always seemed to be missing (and somehow culpable) was the great struggle for self-development so marked in Leonardo and Michelangelo. Everything came too easily to him; he had no lack of patrons, for everywhere his services were in demand. There are no records of quarrels with his patrons when his wishes clashed with theirs, if they ever did. No crisis marked his life—and of course he died young, perhaps before he could reach the full maturity of his genius.

These things may be admitted, but their

relevance may be doubted. For what seems so eminently clear is that Raphael, above all other painters, painted from inspiration with absolute certainty, authority, and clarity touched by no other. Every Madonna is so much more than beauty; it portrays truth. Gifted with this inspiration, how should he have to struggle? To view the Madonna with the three children—the soul of love, but without knowledge, manifested in the child in the Madonna's arms, and the child on her left gazing at him full of the utmost wisdom— is to glimpse one of the deepest mysteries of Christianity as Raphael understood it. To view some of the Madonnas with the angels perceived, not as Botticelli perceived them, but as ministering, supersensible beings, is to share Raphael's vision of the heavenly world which is lost to us. These pictures are for the healing and inspiration of mankind, as the medieval picture was solely for his meditation on the mysteries of medieval Christianity as it was then understood. It is sometimes found difficult to distinguish between one Madonna and another. The difference lies in the quality of the inspiration which informs it. It is impossible to look at, say, a Rubens Madonna, after seeing Raphael's, without a sense of sacrilege.

On another level is the "Disputa" (sometimes called the Triumph of Religion), and the "School of Athens," painted on the walls of the Vatican. Here again Raphael, in addition to handling a large scene with the utmost technical perfection, has penetrated to the heart of his subject, one chosen by himself and never imitated. The ancient world of philosophy is shown in the "School of Athens," and the moment of transubstantiation is shown in the "Disputa" (Dispute over the Sacrament). At the top of the "Disputa" is the figure of Christ, with the Virgin and St. John the Baptist on either side, surrounded by Old and New Testament figures; below on earth the assembled Fathers of the Church, bishops, and other personages contemplate the sacred Host, shown on a table in front of them; between heaven and earth is the Holy Dove, descending toward the Host. It seems clear that the fresco represents no dispute, in spite of the animation of the earthly figures, but rather the supreme salvation-giving moment of the Christian ritual. This is contrasted with the salvation through philosophy that was the greatest achievement of the Greeks and which is shown in the "School of Athens."[2]

After the death of Raphael and Michelangelo the high Renaissance in Italy was almost over, save for Venice where Titian worked, until 1576, when he died at the age of almost a hundred. Titian was a master of every technical gift granted to the painter, a superb colorist, and prolific in masterpieces till the very end of his long life. Rich and successful, for most of his life he glorified the Venetian noble and his womenfolk, though in the last years of his life he also turned again to religious subjects and produced a deeply felt Pietá. But by the mid-sixteenth century the work of the Italian Renaissance was done. Its influence had expanded over other lands in ever wider circles. Italy herself, no longer the center of trade after the discovery of the Americas, fell upon evil times. Her prosperity passed away, and her political life, never very orderly, became less secure than ever as she was forced to submit

[2] There has always been difference of opinion about these frescoes, and it is not even certain that the "School of Athens" is correctly named. The central figures appear to be Plato and Aristotle, and the books they are carrying are the *Timaeus* and the *Ethics* respectively. But Hermann Grimm, the nineteenth-century art critic, used to insist that the figure known as Aristotle is really St. Paul, and he claimed that Raphael's other pictures of St. Paul show exactly the features here attributed to "Aristotle." The books, according to Grimm, were inserted later, and not by Raphael, at a time when the original meaning of the painting had been forgotten. If this is indeed the case, then the figure called Plato would likewise not be of the Greek philosopher, but of a contemporary of St. Paul, presumably Dionysius the Areopagite, whom Paul converted to Christianity. In this case the "School of Athens" would itself show the Triumph of Religion and the absorption of Greek philosophy into Christianity, while the "Disputa" would show the spiritualizing of the human being through the act of transubstantiation and the transforming of his thinking through the coming of the Holy Spirit, a more profound understanding of the deed of Christ and one that does not seem beyond the powers of the artist who painted the Madonna with the three children.

The so-called "Disputa" by Raphael, discussed in the text on page 544. Painted on the walls of a room in the Vatican (Camera della Segnatura) it shows God the Father at the top, with Christ below him; and on the earth, the Host (the sacrament of the Eucharist) on the table, with the Latin Fathers of the Church at the right: Saints Jerome, Gregory, Ambrose, and Augustine. The last-named is seated, dictating to a secretary, suggesting the interpretation (given in the footnote in the text) that his thinking has been newly inspired by the Holy Spirit.

to alien and native rulers who cared little for her special talents. The papacy, never fully recovering from the sack of Rome in 1527 by imperial troops, at last found it necessary to reform itself into a truly spiritual institution, but in the process adopted many of the puritanical tendencies of the northern reformers. But in its heyday the Italian Renaissance had taught the rest of Europe an art hardly known before; it had created masterpieces which, with the medieval cathedral, are the chief artistic glory of Western civilization, and it had in the process helped a world still inclined to look within for all knowledge to look out at the earth and the men and women who inhabit it, and find beauty and goodness and joy in them.

▶ Science in the Renaissance

Before leaving the world of the Italian Renaissance and turning our attention to the Renaissance in other countries, a few words should be said about Italian science. It has already been noted in the medieval chapter that the University of Padua continued to study various practical and theoretical problems concerned particularly with motion. This work proceeded during the Renaissance as a kind of backwater from the main stream of life. And we have already noted that out of this milieu came, after all, the foundations of modern science and especially mathematics. Without the work of the still little-known men of the University of Padua and other schools of learning in northern Italy there could have been no Italian Galileo. Most Italian science of the Renaissance period was practical, as in the Middle Ages, arising out of the needs especially of artillerymen. It is now realized that much of the work of Leonardo himself, still by far the greatest scientific name of the Renaissance, was based on work already done by his predecessors and contemporaries with whom he must constantly have been in touch. His curiosity was his own, his incomparable drawings were his own, and his minute and careful observation of plant forms was his own; but his speculations were no more necessarily original with him than those of Roger Bacon in the Middle Ages. But being interested in all things in heaven and earth, he made it his business to find out all that was known about all subjects that came to his attention, and, being a practical genius as well, he pondered how the knowledge available could be put to use, and how certain remarkable theories could be made of practical use. It is a mistake therefore to regard him, any more than Roger Bacon, as a lone genius working in solitude with a mind centuries ahead of his time. His claim to undying fame is already beyond dispute, without adding anything more to it which he does not deserve. So it may be said of the Italian Renaissance that the greatest and most influential minds of the time were not interested in science, except in so far as it could be used for material ends, such as success in warfare, and then only to a very limited degree. The joy of the search for pure knowledge of the world and the universe had not yet communicated itself to the Western mind, which preferred to live in the joys of aesthetic experience. The aphorism of Aristotle that "all men by nature desire to know" was not yet true of the men of the Renaissance, and in this respect they still fell behind the greatest of the Greeks. And though such men as Galileo had a great share in it, on the whole it fell to the northerners to take up the quest for scientific knowledge, which will be studied in the final chapter of this book.

▶ **The expansion of the Renaissance beyond the Alps**

INFLUENCE OF ITALIAN HUMANISM IN THE NORTH

We have already dealt with the question of why the Renaissance started in Italy and suggested a few reasons why it did not arise spontaneously in any other part of Europe. Material and social conditions, we found, were largely different, the peoples of northern Europe were not surrounded by the physical monuments of antiquity, and there was thus no natural stimulus to imitate the achievements of men who had not been their ancestors. Their own native Gothic had not yet exhausted its possibilities for growth. Nevertheless, when travelers from the north visited Italy it was impossible for most of them to refrain from admiring the vital culture of the Italian cities, so different from their own. This was particularly evident when the French King Charles VIII, with his army of twenty thousand, made his triumphal progress through Italy in 1494. However much the French may have despised the Italian inability to unite in defense of the country, they had only admiration for the great artistic and literary achievements of their enemies. And many were inclined to accept the Italian point of view that they themselves, conquerors as they were, were nevertheless cultural barbarians; and instead of merely resenting the fact they determined to remedy the defect by sitting at the feet of as many great Italians as they could persuade to come and live with them. Francis I of France made every effort to persuade artists to come to France, and was successful at last in persuading Leonardo da Vinci himself to come to Amboise for the last years of his life, even though the visit proved to be unfruitful, as far as is known. Henry VIII of England, on the other hand, spent much energy in attempting to persuade such men as Raphael and Titian to come to England, though with no success at all. What would such painters have done in such a provincial atmosphere? But all the Renaissance northern monarchs were able, when they tried, to persuade at least a few second- and third-rate Italians to go to their countries. Such was Italian prestige that any Italian was usually considered far better than the best available local talent.

In the field of scholarship the position was different. Italian humanists searching for manuscripts visited the old monasteries in northern Europe where they were to be found, and sometimes became acquainted with European scholars who knew medieval Latin and were willing to extend their knowledge to the classics, hitherto often imperfectly understood. It was possible to keep in touch with foreign scholars and humanists by correspondence, whereas in the field of art it was necessary to visit the actual works of art and receive visits from living artists. Moreover, though the universities on the whole were strongholds of conservatism, Aristotelianism, and traditional theology throughout the Renaissance, there existed notable exceptions which did not remain aloof from Italian influence. Smaller schools existed which were willing to favor the new humanism. Above all the great school of the Brethren of the Common Life at Deventer (see p. 372), while it retained its original religious orientation, offered studies in classical Latin which inspired many of its pupils to go to Italy and drink at the pure fountain of antiquity. Returning with a knowledge of Latin and Greek and a new enthusiasm, many, such as Rudolf Agricola (1442–1485), returned to their native countries, and in some cases were rewarded with university positions, enabling them to spread more widely what they had acquired.

In general, the new learning made its way slowly but with some sureness, gradually penetrating into the universities which were the main seats of learning in Germany, and into cultivated circles elsewhere. The learning, however, once it had been acquired, was taken far more seriously than in Italy. Northern Europeans continued to learn Greek for its own sake long after the fad had passed in Italy; and the humanities have remained a staple of European education ever since that time. The Renaissance spirit, then, was never the same elsewhere as in Italy. Occasional individuals became, as it were, Italianized; but for the most part, as in all diffusions of culture that we have studied, the native genius of the receiving peoples allowed the new culture to stimulate them to new efforts in keeping with their own culture and traditions, rather than adopting it wholesale. Thus German, Flemish, and French painting retain their own characteristics while making use of Italian technical inventions, and to a lesser degree adopting Italian idealism, which contrasted so strongly with late medieval naturalism. In England, on the contrary, where there was no important native tradition, all that could be done was to invite Italian painters to work in the country, while inferior artists tried to imitate the Italians directly. We shall therefore in this consideration of the expansion of the Renaissance beyond the Alps study the effects on the native tradition, country by country, trying to show what use was made by native writers and artists of the lead offered by Italy. Erasmus, a man of the world and a true European, who can be said to belong to no country though he was born in Holland, will be treated separately, summing up as he does in his own person the whole of European humanism.

Germany—the new learning and its influence

As has already been said, Germany for the most part remained content with the old traditional learning. The nobility continued to indulge its taste for martial exercises and was rarely interested in things of the mind. This condition of course was the result of the very slow decline of feudalism. Though the towns could well have supported a leisure class, prosperous merchants for the most part found their pleasure in growing more prosperous rather than turning to "idle" pursuits such as were the vogue in Italy. Such men as the Fuggers, who had the resources to have patronized writers and artists as lavishly as the Medici—becoming indeed far richer in the sixteenth century than any Italians through investment in the Oriental trade, did not care to spend money in this way. Indeed it is somewhat ironical that Emperor Maximilian I, one of the few German rulers who became interested in humanism and even tried his hand at writing verses himself, was always chronically poor, and had to borrow money from Jacob Fugger for his numerous wars. No doubt some of the proceeds of his loans reached the pockets of humanists, as well as the painter and engraver Albrecht Dürer.

Some of the universities, however, did depart from their traditional ways far enough to support German humanists such as Agricola, and gave them an opportunity to teach. Agricola himself taught for a time at the University of Heidelberg, whose patron, the Elector Palatine, was to some degree favorable to humanism; he knew Latin and Greek well enough to translate some Greek works into Latin, and his influence at the university bore some fruit. John Wimpheling (1450–1528) studied at Heidelberg and became competent in Greek, opening a Latin school in Strassburg in his later years. Wimpheling and his friend Sebastian Brant (1458–1521) not only used their humanism to defend classical learning against their entrenched opponents, but also attacked the morals and general behavior of the clergy. The *Ship of Fools,* an elaborate satire by Brant, won the author a considerable reputation throughout Europe.

Title page of the first (1494) edition of the Ship of Fools, *by Sebastian Brant.* (COURTESY NEW YORK PUBLIC LIBRARY)

But most famous of the early German humanists was John Reuchlin, who became proficient, not only in Latin and Greek but also in Hebrew, which he learned particularly for the purpose of studying the Scriptures in the original, though he was also interested in Jewish mystical writings. He had no difficulty in showing that much of the current interpretation of the Bible had no basis in the original scriptural text. However, he might never have come into the limelight if it had not happened that just at this time a Jew named Pfefferkorn, who had been converted to Christianity, with the ardent support of the old-fashioned University of Cologne had succeeded in obtaining a decree from the Emperor Maximilian that all Hebrew books should be destroyed as representing a danger to the faith. The emperor, however, could not carry out his decree without local support, which was not forthcoming from the archbishop of Mainz, the responsible official. The latter, oddly enough with the approval of Pfefferkorn who thought Reuchlin was on his side, demanded that the latter express his authoritative opinion in the matter. Reuchlin promptly defended the study of Hebrew, claiming that there was nothing in any Hebrew work that attacked the Christian religion. A war of pamphlets ensued, culminating in an anonymous *Letters of Obscure Men,* one of the classic satires of the northern Renaissance, which attacks wittily and vitriolically the old-fashioned theologians who were at the root of the dispute, together with many of the more superstitious customs of the Church. Reuchlin was finally summoned before the inquisitor-general; but though his chief polemic was finally condemned in 1520 by Pope Leo x, there was nothing much that could be done about it by the Church, since by that time the Lutheran revolt had already begun and the papacy had its hands full with far more serious matters.

Thus German humanism, through the gradual improvement of education and the characteristic attacks on old theological methods which took little account of the Bible, contributed to the Reformation; for this reason further consideration will be paid to it in chapter 18, which deals with the Reformation. Although most humanists would have had little desire for such a conclusion to their efforts, their contribution to the Reformation was by no means a small one. There can be little doubt that studious Germans were, for the most part, interested in making use of the classics rather than enjoying them for their own sake; and they certainly had little or no interest in the supposed "way of life" of the ancient world.

Humanism in France

Initial conservatism to the invasion of Italy in 1494—It was far otherwise with France. Humanism came very slowly to France also, and Italian influence even in art was negligible until the expedition of Charles viii to Italy in 1494. But thereafter its influence was deeper than in any other country, and it lasted longer, merging at last almost insensibly into French seventeenth-century classicism. Before 1494 a few Italian humanists had visited France and an occasional French scholar had studied in Italy, but they had made little headway against entrenched custom and opposition. In architecture the French were still well content with their Gothic which had reached its flamboyant stage. Chateaux and private and public buildings as well as churches were built in the Gothic style, with an occasional borrowing from antique models. The monarchy had been too busy consolidating its position, as described in an earlier chapter, to pay attention to frivolities—and in any case it is hard to imagine such a monarch as Louis xi wasting his money on anything so unrewarding as artistic or literary patronage.

Then, suddenly, France was a great power, secure in herself, incomparably the most important monarchy in Europe; and there was time and energy to spare to look for an Italian crown to which kings of France for some years had held the title, though they had been unable to make good their claim against the Aragonese incumbent. The French army of twenty thousand men, making what was little more than a march and a military demonstration, freed Pisa from Florentine domination to the accompaniment of an ovation to the French monarch in the best Italian operatic style, stayed in Florence itself for a few days (and left in exchange for a large sum of money), entered Rome by agreement with Pope Alexander vi, while the Neapolitan monarch, the cause of the whole expedition, simply abdicated, allowing Charles to assume the crown. It was not so easy for him to make his way back, as he was opposed by a hastily constructed league, and the Neapolitan kingdom was soon lost, thus setting in motion a series of wars between France and various Italian states. But the expedition had given the French a glimpse of an utterly different way of life from their own, which they admired exceedingly. Successive expeditions served only to reinforce their admiration, until Francis i (1515–1547) and his sister Marguerite of Navarre (who wrote a book of short stories modeled after Boccaccio in form) gave a lead to the upper classes of France which altered the whole character of French culture, made the sixteenth one of her greatest centuries, and laid the foundation for her undisputed cultural leadership in the seventeenth and eighteenth.

Francis i and the flowering of the French Renaissance—Budé and Rabelais—Probably the most important name in the early French Renaissance is that of Guillaume Budé, who became secretary to Francis and was responsible for much of his patronage of learning, though Francis himself needed no urging to act as patron of the arts, as will be described in a later section. In Budé's youth a few Greek scholars were teaching in France and Budé studied with them, translating Plutarch for the first time into French. As a lawyer he also studied carefully the texts of the Roman law codes and wrote important commentaries on them. Louis xii sent him as ambassador to Venice and the papacy, where he returned more enthusiastic for things Italian than ever. But much more important than his original work was the influence he exercised over Francis i, who not only made his court a center of learning and patronized humanists, but founded the Collège de France, with its teachers paid directly out of the royal treasury, where classical Latin and Greek, Hebrew, and even Arabic were to be taught, as well as practical sciences such as mathematics, medicine, and philosophy. The project was designed, no doubt, to by-pass the conservative Sorbonne, in which it was in part successful.

Budé also persuaded his royal master that there was glory to be won by collecting manuscripts of ancient texts and founding a library at his palace of Fontainebleau, which should contain not only these texts but the finest books printed in Venice. Already before the reign of Francis, French printers had begun to issue Greek texts, but now the royal example handsomely rewarded their enterprise, especially since Marguerite, the king's sister, possessed a court of her own, no less learned than the king's. When the palace of Fontainebleau began to take on its new shape with its troop of Italian artists entrusted with the décor filling the grounds with "classical" statuary, the interest of the ever volatile French people turned as feverishly to the interest in this life and antiquity as ever the Italians had done a century before. It was in this atmosphere that François Rabelais (ca. 1490–1553) began his work, filled with an overwhelming zest for life in all its aspects.

Rabelais did not write for the élite of the court, but for the ordinary bourgeois. "How," he once wrote in a letter to a friend, "can it be that in our wonderful century there are still some people so constructed that they cannot raise their eyes from the hellish darkness of their Gothic age to the bright flame of the sun?" Destined for the priesthood, and studying in a monastery which had been slightly infiltrated by the new humanist learning, escaping from his first monastery when his views were looked upon with disfavor by the authorities, studying further in a second more congenial monastery, he finally quit and became a doctor. Occasionally practicing his profession he preferred to enjoy himself and savor everything that life could offer. Out of this background came the story of the two giants *Gargantua and Pantagruel,* a work unique in all literature, though it may reasonably be called the ancestor of the picaresque novel. Incredibly successful—Rabelais himself had no expectation that it would sell—it appealed to everyman. Part of it is autobiographical, incidents from his own fabulous life. But the most important part is the uproarious satire on monks and their pedantic learning, and on the ascetic ideal for which, as an escaped monk himself, he had nothing but contempt. Gargantua in the story founds a monastery—needless to say, in good Renaissance architecture—which is the exact antithesis of the monastic ideal, where everyone is to be free, where all women were to be young and beautiful, where the only rule to follow was to do as you please and follow your instincts, for they are certain to be good. Here is the natural man of Renaissance France, the unabashed pagan, lacking the refinement of the Italians (or, indeed, of the later French), but far indeed also from the German seriousness which was represented in France by a different sort of humanist, the best example of which was Jacques Lefèvre d'Etaples (1455?–1536).

Influence of humanism on religion—Lefèvre d'Etaples—This man's life was spent in utter devotion to learning, but for the purpose of bringing about a purer Christianity freed from the abuses that defiled the life of his time. Deeply imbued with the mystical Platonism that he found on an early journey to Italy and at the Academy of Florence, after lecturing in Paris for some years, he gradually drew around himself a circle of pupils who thought as he did. One of these, Briçonnet, became later bishop of Meaux, and the circle of students, now reformers, gathered there under Lefèvre's spiritual leadership, where they studied the Biblical texts and tried as far as they could to reform the superstitious and frequently immoral practices of the Church of the day. Lefèvre himself got into trouble with the Sorbonne and the Parlement of Paris by openly criticizing the accepted Vulgate version of the Bible, but as long as Francis was able to protect him, he and the Meaux circle were safe, though once while Francis was a prisoner in Spain the Parlement was supreme, and Lefèvre had to take refuge in Strassburg. Ultimately he was made tutor to the royal children and to the end of his life he remained protected by Marguerite of Navarre, while others of the circle at Meaux had either to recant their views and conform, or go into exile and become Protestants, like Farel, the first leader of the reformed church at Geneva. Thus in France also, one branch of the humanist movement became absorbed within the early Protestant Reformation.

Purification of the French language—La Pléiade—A further contrast to Rabelais in a different direction should also be noticed. Rabelais himself had appealed to the multitude, to bourgeois rich and to the poor, and indeed everyone who could read. But his work was full of crudeness and popular expressions hardly understood by the refined classes. Two poets, Joachim du Bellay (1522–1560) and Pierre de Ronsard (1525–1585), took it upon themselves to steer French literature away from the direction pioneered by Rabelais. Around themselves they gathered a coterie of refined spirits which called itself La Pléiade. Though they had no use for the "Gothic" past, which was for them altogether and irrevocably over, they yet disliked equally the crude effusions of Rabelais. They were, indeed, the first self-conscious literary artists of France. It was their intention, in which they quite largely succeeded, to purge the French language, and especially French poetry, of all crudities, and to write in a pure French. Their poems, especially those of Ronsard, breathe the enjoyment of all the refined pleasures of life. The poets seek for fame and glory—Ronsard's famous answer "I am Ronsard, and that is enough for you" speaks for itself—each searching for perfection in his own way, but within the limits prescribed by art. Though they cannot be described as having achieved all their aims, it is certainly true that La

Pléiade did indeed prepare the way for the classical literature of the next two centuries. Since the sixteenth century the French writer has always been far more conscious of the artistic form of his work, and the place that his particular work fills in the history of French letters, than the writers of any other country. It is probably true to say that these writers of the French Renaissance were the first to recognize and lay down the rules for literature as a form of art.

The individualist writer par excellence—Montaigne—The greatest writer of the French Renaissance, who summed up the whole movement in his person, was Michel de Montaigne (1533–1592), a man of affairs who retired to his country estate in middle life to devote himself to writing. His *Essays*, which are saturated with knowledge of the classics, appeared in 1580. The literature of antiquity is by this time no longer a novelty, but accepted as part of the literary equipment of every educated man. At any moment Montaigne can choose apposite examples from antiquity from his well-stocked mind to illustrate his ideas. His subject is man, and his source of information on this incomparably interesting subject is primarily himself. Detached but observant, gently skeptical but not disillusioned in the modern manner, his essays read today as well as when they were written. He is the supreme example in literature of the enlightened man who withdraws himself by choice from the world for the purpose of observing it more closely and making it possible for him to give it advice from his own ripe wisdom. Whereas his younger contemporary Shakespeare has a greater feeling for the tragedy of life which he expressed in his plays, one feels that Montaigne is not unaware of this element, but that he still believes in the power of reason of the enlightened man to overcome it. He uses self-discipline to avoid being carried away by his own emotion. The few brief words in which he speaks of his loneliness on the death of a friend whom he had loved with all his being suggest that, from choice, he left so much unsaid that was not necessary for the world to know, but that

his personal experience went far deeper than he was willing to say. And his comment on the religious wars raging in his time, that it shows "a great self-love and presumption to consider one's own opinion so highly that it is necessary to destroy public peace and introduce so many evils to establish them" goes right to the heart of the matter from the point of view of the enlightened man. No one may gainsay his comment; and yet has such enlightenment ever triumphed over the forces of unreason, the forces of tragedy and destiny and human wickedness of which Shakespeare was so conscious, and the understanding of which, in the last analysis, gives Shakespeare his superiority over the Sieur de Montaigne?

The new learning in England

Humanism and English bourgeois culture—In England the economic, social, and cultural conditions were not dissimilar to those of France. In the universities of Oxford and Cambridge, however, England had two major institutions of learning separate altogether from the greatest concentration of bourgeois wealth in the capital of London, whereas the University of Paris was centered in the capital itself. France, however, had far more important concentrations of wealth and potential cultural activity than England had outside London. Moreover, it was a constant feature of English life that major political changes took place in England earlier than in France. Thus the English feudal nobility had been largely destroyed by the Wars of the Roses at the close of the Middle Ages, and the position of the monarch was finally established by the end of the fifteenth century, whereas the French Renaissance monarchs, far from solving this problem, maintained a precarious coexistence with the nobility whom it was unable to discipline until the advent of the Bourbons at the end of the Wars of Religion. The Tudor monarchy in England was thus able to establish itself firmly with the aid of the bourgeoisie, while the remnants of the feudal nobility made the best of things, usually set up headquarters in London, and patronized the same kind of culture as the bourgeoisie, while continuing to draw their revenues from their provincial estates. It was also the policy of the crown to draw eminent bourgeois into the royal service, elevating them into the nobility as partial reward. It was this combination of noble and bourgeois patronage, especially in the city of London, that made possible the great Elizabethan age of culture, with relatively minor royal support, unlike in France where royal support was the mainstay of the French Renaissance.

The two great English universities, on the other hand, held almost a monopoly of learning, and nobles and bourgeois studied there, since there was no comparable center in the capital. In the early fifteenth century the faculties were still entrenched in the conservative tradition of learning, but this learning did not have quite such a stronghold as in Paris, its place of origin. Moreover, the system of virtual autonomy for the colleges of the university permitted competition between the colleges, and thus prevented a concerted university policy toward humanism such as prevailed at Paris. Thus when dissatisfied scholars such as William Grocyn (1446?–1519) went abroad to Italy to study and returned to their universities afterward, willing and eager to teach Greek, there was not too much difficulty in finding some college willing to try out something new. So Oxford before the end of the fifteenth century already offered some courses in classical Greek and Latin, and its example was soon followed by Cambridge.

Influence on religion—Henry VII (1485–1509) was too busy consolidating his political position and amassing a fortune, which he did not care to spend, to patronize the new learning, but his son Henry VIII (1509–1547), in the intervals of fighting continental wars and reforming the Church according to his own ideas and needs, did patronize literature and art, though hardly imitating the lavish manner of his contemporary Francis of France. The new learning bore fruit in England as it had in Germany and among the enthusiasts of Meaux. The English humanists became interested in the mysticism of the Platonic Academy of Florence, desiring above all to return to a purer and more individual worship, and to purge the Catholic Church of its superstitious elements and return to the Bible. John Colet (1467?–1519), son of a wealthy London merchant, after studying at Oxford, was appointed Dean of St. Paul's, from whose pulpit he preached reform and the study of the Bible in accordance with the best texts available. He was much influenced by Erasmus, whose close friend he became. When his father died he founded one of the public schools of England, St. Paul's, devoted to the new learning and under secular rather than clerical control. The most famous of these early English humanists was Sir Thomas More (1478–1535), later canonized as a saint, whose *Utopia* was a gentle attack upon the unenlightened social system of the England of his day, on the excessive death penalties, and generally on its rude and backward conditions. Utopia (Greek for nowhere) was a beautiful, well-planned Renaissance city, with hospitals and the best of sanitation, and tolerant toward religion. Implied also in More's work, though not explicitly stated, was the necessity for the reform of the Chuch, as advocated by his Oxford friends, who came to be known as the Oxford Reformers.

Colet died before the Reformation had got under way; Latimer, a Cambridge humanist and bishop, in later life went all the way over to Protestantism and perished at the stake in the reign of Mary; Thomas More, appointed chancellor by Henry VIII, refused to accept his master's repudiation of the pope as head of the Church and died on the scaffold. All these men desired reform but in different ways. Their movement as a reform movement within the Church failed, like that of Meaux, dependent as both movements were on the support of the political power, which adopted different policies at different times according to temporary national interests. It was not until the Reformation had been securely established under the Elizabethan Compromise of 1558–1559 that the people were freed for a season of religious troubles, and the Renaissance came to full fruition in the greatest of ages in English literature. The queen was popular, and herself learned and sympathetic to learning. The bourgeoisie was prosperous and the country strongly nationalistic, secure in its navy and self-confident by reason of its successful defense against the worst that the greatest continental power had been able to do.

Influence on literature—Marlowe and Spenser—Yet Elizabethan England was still far from viewing life in the Italian or French manner. Occasional Renaissance figures such as Christopher Marlowe appear like comets, full of a Rabelaisian zest for life, supremely creative. Marlowe, a poet and dramatist and man of action, died in a tavern brawl at the age of twenty-nine. Other men of action, especially the sea-dogs and explorers of the age, such as Francis Drake and Walter Raleigh, suggest something of the Renaissance spirit and joy in life. But the two greatest poets of the reign, Edmund Spenser (1552?–1599) and William Shakespeare (1564–1616), are more serious. Spenser was a great artist in poetry, one of the greatest artists in the English language. In him classical learning had been fully assimilated, and it is used with the utmost naturalness even in his allegorical poem *The Faerie Queene,* written in honor of and in glorification of Queen Elizabeth, using a medieval form and a medieval theme, with pageants, tournaments, encounters between knights, and much of the paraphernalia of chivalry. His consciousness of form, the extreme care of his writing, and his experimentation with meter are reminiscent of the French school of La Pléiade. The self-conscious artist in words had emerged even in an age where much was rude; and it is not surprising that he was not too greatly appreciated in his own time and received scant reward from Elizabeth—though he was ultimately honored with burial in Westminster Abbey.

The new understanding of man—Shakespeare—With William Shakespeare we reach the culmination of both the Elizabethan Age and English achievement. What

Michelangelo was to Italy, Montaigne to France and Cervantes to Spain in a lesser degree, and Rembrandt to Holland, Shakespeare was to the English, their greatest man of genius, who belongs to the world as much as to his own country. He was not, in the sense of the Renaissance, a "universal man." He devoted his whole genius to poetry and drama. But for the understanding of man and his heights and depths he has had no equal. The work of Shakespeare is unique for its utter objectivity; no one can say that here, or here, is Shakespeare depicting himself (save, intentionally, in the figure of Prospero in the *Tempest*). His men and women live in and for themselves as full-scale human beings, acting out their tragic destiny in the tragedies, good men, moderate men, wicked men and women, but all equally human. Shakespeare was steeped in classical, especially Roman, learning and he used many Roman themes; he imagined for himself the life of Italian Renaissance cities, and laid several of his plays in them. But in everything that he wrote he utterly transformed his sources and made them his own by his genius. In him comes to fruition the Renaissance understanding of man and the many-dimensioned being that man is, rather than the one-sided being perceived by Machiavelli and even to some degree by Montaigne. So today, and for many centuries to come, we may still drink at the well of Shakespeare, knowing that we in Western civilization have not surpassed him, have not learned everything he has to tell us and perhaps never will.

Spain—Lack of a secular culture— Attack on chivalric ideal—Cervantes

Spain has had a history that in many ways has kept her outside the main stream of Western culture. The expulsion of the Muslims from the Peninsula occupied so much of her energy during the Middle Ages and produced such a fervent and militant Christianity that there was little energy left for other pursuits. Thus the medieval spirit, even in accentuated form, long survived its disappearance elsewhere. There were few

Illustration for Don Quixote *by the famous French historical painter, sculptor, and illustrator, Paul Gustave Doré (1833?–1883), showing Don Quixote and Sancho Panza.* (COURTESY NEW YORK PUBLIC LIBRARY)

cities of importance where a secular culture could develop, and most Spanish scholars who became interested in Italian culture or classical letters stayed in Italy, or betook themselves, like the noted humanist Juan Vivès (1492–1540) to more congenial centers elsewhere.

Thus the greatest work of the Spanish Renaissance, fittingly enough, was an all-out attack on the chivalric ideal and on the mind that soaked up the chivalric romances of a culture now long outdated in the rest of Europe. Miguel de Cervantes (1547–1616) had lived an adventurous life, studying and working in Italy, a prisoner of war and slave in North Africa, always afflicted by poverty. The novel on which his reputation is based, the superb *Don Quixote de la Mancha*, has as a hero a chivalrous knight who pursues the fantastic adventures of a medieval knight in ordinary rural Spain of the late sixteenth century. His head is filled with romance, and it is implied that he is insane; it is the task of his down-to-earth squire Sancho Panza to look after him and see that he comes to no harm. Since he is far from successful in protecting his master, the book is full of pathos as well as comedy, and it is clear that the author who chose this strange medium for the expression of his knowledge of life is inferior to few men in his understanding of man, the whole man with his head in the stars and his feet on the earth—and in this he can hardly be compared with any save Shakespeare himself.

Erasmus, the "man of the world"

We have left to the last in this study of humanism the great figure of Desiderius Erasmus (1469?–1536), because in his life and work he typifies and has always typified the ideal humanist, with all his strengths and weaknesses. He was no poet, nor was he a man of action. He was a man of words, and his tool was the pen; probably no pure writer in all history wielded such an influence as he. Occupied much of his life with translating classical works and the Bible into Latin, which was his preferred tongue even for conversation, and acting as editor to a

Portrait of Erasmus by Hans Holbein, the Younger (1523). Original in the Louvre.

Basel publisher, he was never wealthy and had no source of income beyond his work. But every humanist in Europe at least knew of him, and none would not have been proud to make his personal acquaintance. He had been welcomed at courts and private houses in many countries, and his correspondence, by far the most extensive of his day, was valued and quoted by all who received it, and through it he exercised his influence.

Ordained a priest, he spent a great deal of his energy in attacking the abuses of the Church with his satirical pen, especially in his best-known work, *In Praise of Folly.* Luther felt that he should have been a supporter of the German Reformation, for how could Erasmus continue to favor a Church which was in truth all that he said it was? But Erasmus would not join the German, objecting to the violence that was characteristic of Luther's nature. Such passion must lead to the kind of attack on the Church that Erasmus, for all his satirical words, could never have approved. The papacy, on the other hand, sensing the possibility of the powerful support that the humanist could give to it, offered him the hat of a cardinal. As firmly as he had rejected Luther, Erasmus, though old and in poverty, refused the gift.

Enlightened, steeped in antiquity and the Christianity of the New Testament as it appeared to him, Erasmus was the most tolerant of human beings, almost a grotesque figure in his age of violent and passionate men. Gently calling down a plague on both their houses, he remained to the end an independent individualist, with the courage of his tolerant convictions, as impressed by Socrates as by Jesus Christ, and sure that they were both human ideal examples worthy to be followed. If it be asked whether he was born out of his time and would have found himself more at home in another century—or whether indeed such a "liberal" in the truest sense of the word can ever be countenanced by the men of will and passion—one can only answer that there seems to be, for the vast majority of mankind, something immoral in neutrality. In Erasmus' own day he was greatly admired, he had an unequaled reputation, and whatever his contemporaries, Luther or the pope, may have felt, they came to him for assistance. It is doubtful if any liberal has wielded so much influence since his day (for Voltaire, whom Erasmus resembles in so many ways, was in the last analysis a defender at least of his own privileges). Liberalism of the uncompromising kind of Erasmus has always been a luxury. It is perhaps well for his own fame that he did in fact live in the fifteenth and sixteenth centuries; for in 1536, when he died, it was still not entirely necessary to take sides—as long as one lived in the free city of Basel within the Swiss Confederation.

RENAISSANCE ART BEYOND THE ALPS

Flanders

In the late Middle Ages the most flourishing school of painters existed in the Low Countries, especially after the dukes of Burgundy became lords of Flanders in the fourteenth century. The Flemish towns had become wealthy during this period, as we have seen in an earlier chapter, and the burghers could often afford patronage to all forms of art. The subjects in demand were all, however, religious, and most of the works commissioned were for the benefit of the churches. Flemish art of this period, as in the Middle Ages, was strongly realistic, a tendency it always retained. The figures in Flemish painting, as in their illustrated manuscripts, are always executed with the utmost attention to detail, based on the most careful observation. The Pietàs, in accordance with late medieval taste, always picture the extremes of suffering; when the subject calls for the depiction of sorrow, nothing could be more expressive of sorrow than what the Flemish painters provided. Wonderful religious masterpieces exist from this period, especially the deeply thoughtful altarpiece of John Van Eyck at Ghent. Flemish painting never altogether abandoned its realism, though techniques were imported from Italy, and Flemish painters began to understand and use perspective, and psychological penetration appears in the portraits to add to the accuracy of detail. Such men as Antonio Moro (1512–1575) were much influenced by Italian art, but at the same period other great painters such as Peter Breughel (1525–1569) show little Italian influence save in technique.

Germany

In Germany also, the careful attention to detail remained. Albrecht Dürer (1471–1528) visited Italy several times and learned all he could, especially in the treatment of space, touring the Low Countries also for further inspiration. He had difficulty, however, in obtaining commissions for painting, since patrons of art were in short supply, though Maximilian, as ever, within the limits of his resources did what he could. Nevertheless Dürer was able to make a living, doing much of his work in the new art of copper engraving, in which he remains perhaps the greatest master of all time. He drew, painted, engraved, and wrote, being perhaps as near to the Italian *uomo universale* as Germany could produce. Hans Hol-

Woodcut portrait of Albrecht Dürer by one of his school. (COURTESY THE METROPOLITAN MUSEUM OF ART)

bein the Younger (1497–1543) also visited Italy and used Italian techniques after his return to Germany, where he painted a large number of portraits. Driven out of Germany by the religious troubles, he settled in England where he painted the portraits of many notables, especially from the merchant class which was growing in prosperity. His work includes the justly famous portrait of Henry VIII.

Neither in sculpture nor architecture was there much of originality contributed by Germany or the Low Countries until later centuries, though funeral monuments executed for such patrons as the Emperor Maximilian made use of Italian ideas and technique.

England contributed nothing of its own to any of these fields during the period. All the northern countries remained dominated by the Gothic. The fan-vaulting (illustrated on p. 421) in the Henry VII chapel at Westminster dates from the early sixteenth century. While such work as this could still be done, little need for any innovation was likely to be felt in England.

France

In France the Renaissance had a curiously delayed effect. The native French Gothic continued to dominate French architecture in its later flamboyant form until at least the reign of Francis I (1515–1547), and for a long time afterward elements of the Gothic continued to be used, making for a style which is really uniquely French, a kind of combination of Gothic and Renaissance. Italians were imported in great numbers, but as a rule they carried out the decorative work rather than designing the whole structure. In almost all cases—the few exceptions were private buildings designed for individual patrons who wished for an Italian-style building on French soil—the work was done under the direction of French architects. The French architects from the beginning were very anxious not to subordinate themselves to the Italians whose prestige was so great in the rest of Europe, but preferred to use what seemed good to them and reject the rest. However, in the design of the gardens and landscapes around the new buildings evidence of the

"The Virgin and Child with St. Anne," by Dürer. (COURTESY THE METROPOLITAN MUSEUM OF ART)

One of Dürer's superb copper engravings showing St. Eustace, a second-century martyr, who had formerly been a lover of the chase but was converted to Christianity when he saw a stag with a cross between its horns. (COURTESY THE METROPOLITAN MUSEUM OF ART)

classical revival was everywhere to be found in the form of colonnades, mechanical fountains, and pagan gods and goddesses after the Greek and Roman manner.

Not until the seventeenth century did Italy exercise a really important influence on French architecture with the development of the French classical style, to be dealt with briefly in Chapter 21—though even at that period French architects greatly modified Italian concepts to fit their own needs.

Typical of the self-conscious deliberative attitude toward the Italian architectural achievements is the work of the man who was probably the greatest French architect of the sixteenth century, Philibert Delorme (1515–1570). Distinguished as engineer as well as architect, it was through his writings on architecture that he exercised his greatest influence. As a young man he made a grand tour of Italy, spending three years in Rome measuring every monument of antiquity that survived and all the newer works that seemed important. Leaving Italy, he returned to France where he again proceeded to examine Roman antiquities such

as the Pont du Gard. He was engaged as chief architect by the French King Henry II (1547–1559), but on the death of his royal patron was forced for a while by his enemies to retire from the court. He spent his enforced leisure in writing his books on architecture.

Delorme was an empirical scientist, who tried to discover the laws of symmetry by observation and analysis. He used what he had seen to develop his own ideas, and his buildings are distinctly original and French, fitted for the climate and needs of France, although he incorporated in his work much of what he had seen that seemed to be applicable to French conditions. He was always pondering the problem of how the French needs could be met, how French materials could be used instead of Italian marble, whether a French order for architectural columns could be devised, as well as giving much attention to the matter of decoration. He worked closely at times with the French sculptor Jean Goujon (ca. 1510–1566) whose ideas seem to have corresponded with many of his own, and who is noted especially for his wonderful "Diana

"Diana and the Deer." Sculpture by Goujon, now in the Louvre. Formerly the property of Diane de Poitiers, mistress and political adviser of Henry II of France.

and the Deer," now in the Louvre. Delorme greatly disliked decoration for its own sake, and always insisted that the architect must be fully responsible for the ensemble of any work commissioned. He must have the final say even in the decoration. The patron should discuss the whole matter with the architect in advance, and then leave him to carry out the agreed design without further interference. For his clear-sighted understanding of architectural problems and his effort to use reason to establish order and harmony in his work Delorme must be considered a precursor of the great classical age of the succeeding century.

Spain

Spanish painting remained under religious influence and absorbed little if anything from Italy until the advent of the Cretan El Greco in the last quarter of the sixteenth century. Having himself absorbed little but some elements of Italian technique, he can hardly be considered as in any way a Renaissance artist. Spanish architecture, with its native Moorish tradition that was never lost, adopted only a few features from Italian work, principally the Greek-style columns. The massive Escorial at Madrid, built by Philip ii as his seat of government, shows little foreign influence.

SCIENCE IN THE NORTHERN RENAISSANCE

As we have already seen, the humanists cared little for science, from whatever country they hailed. Nevertheless, during the centuries of the Renaissance, a certain amount of progress was made outside Italy, for the most part by practical working men who found from experience that the ancient world, in spite of the authority it enjoyed in the recognized seats of learning, did not possess a monopoly of knowledge, and indeed was often mistaken. Paracelsus (Theophrastus Bombastus von Hohenheim) (1493–1541), was for a long time regarded as a charlatan, largely because of his extreme claims, his self-advertising, and his scurrilous criticism of his predecessors and contemporaries. He is now considered as a

Illustration from the first edition of Vesalius' book on anatomy which appeared in 1543.

good observer and practical physician, with many interesting medical theories, not all of which have been disproved. Ambroise Paré (1517–1590), as surgeon to the French armies, learned much about the treatment of wounds. The Fleming Andreas Vesalius published in 1543 his revolutionary *Seven Books on the Structure of the Human Body*, which founded the modern science of anatomy, and thereafter discoveries in the field of physiology followed rapidly. Some of these will be mentioned in Chapter 22, which is devoted to the rise of modern science. Another Fleming, Girardus Mercator (1512–1594), invented the system of map-making associated with his name. The greatest scientist of his age, however, the Polish astronomer Nicolas Copernicus, although he died in 1543 and can thus be considered as a product of the Renaissance, will not be dealt with here, but will be reserved for the same later chapter, in which the fruits of his original speculation can be considered in conjunction with his own work.

Although, as we have seen, the work of the Renaissance in northern countries shades over into the age of the Reformation, a subject requiring special consideration, and the Reformation could therefore be conveniently taken up at once, it cannot be fully understood without a prior grasp of the new commercial forces in northern Europe that served so much to make the Reformation successful, while all previous efforts at modifying the Catholic religion had proved abortive. We shall therefore devote the next chapter to the age of discovery and the commercial revolution that followed it, taking up in the succeeding chapter the Reformation and the Wars of Religion that usher the European state system into its modern phase, which to a large degree is with us yet.

▶ Suggestions for further reading

The most famous of all studies of the Renaissance is undoubtedly Jakob Burckhardt, *The Civilization of the Renaissance in Italy* (New York: The Modern Library, 1954). The nineteenth century Swiss historian had a method and approach to historical study that was all his own, and in almost all the fields in which he wrote he has continued to exercise an extraordinary influence. In his writings on the Greeks, for instance, he attacked the prevalent viewpoint of his time which was certainly excessively laudatory and far too uncritical of the Greeks. In his work on the Renaissance, on the other hand, he has been attacked as having emphasized altogether unduly the uniqueness and newness of the Renaissance. Even today, however, in spite of scholarly criticisms of Burckhardt, the ordinary man, without being aware of his indebtedness, tends as a matter of course to adopt the Burckhardtian point of view, especially since it was reinforced by the brilliant writing of one of his younger contemporaries, John Addington Symonds, whose seven volumes of essays on the Renaissance, now incorporated

into two, *The Renaissance in Italy* (New York: The Modern Library, 1935), early became a classic.

In this century a reaction has set in against Burckhardt, although it is difficult to point to a book of the stature of either of the two already mentioned which will serve to represent adequately the point of view of the revisionists. Mention may be made of an interesting study, Hiram Haydn, *The Counter-Renaissance* (New York: Charles Scribner's Sons, 1950), which takes somewhat of a middle ground, acknowledging some element of newness in the Renaissance but insisting that it was soon overwhelmed by reaction in the direction of antirationalism and anti-intellectualism. The most useful book to read on the whole subject as a preliminary to further study is Wallace A. Ferguson, *The Renaissance in Historical Thought* (Boston: Houghton Mifflin Company, 1948), which contains extracts from the writings of both the followers of Burckhardt and the revisionists. The extracts and the bibliographies, if followed up, will help the student to make up his own mind on the matter.

Two good books on Renaissance art may be recommended. The first is by Bernard Berenson, a critic and lover of art who has spent most of his life in Italy, and who has written numerous books on specialized areas of Italian art. In later life he summed up his unrivaled knowledge in a relatively short work, *The Italian Painters of the Renaissance* (London: Phaidon Press, 1952). On French art, Penguin Books recently published in their series, the Pelican History of Art, an admirable summary of French art and architecture during two centuries. This series should be carefully distinguished from the ordinary Penguin series. Although inexpensive as art books go, the publisher has not skimped in providing art books of quality in this series. In this book the illustrations are especially well chosen, and the student interested in art is strongly urged to look into it. It is very clear and to the point, highly informative, and is notable for its distinction between the native French artistic tradition and the borrowings from the Italians. (Anthony Blunt, *Art and Architecture in France, 1500–1700* (Baltimore: Penguin Books, Inc., 1954). The notebooks of Leonardo da Vinci should certainly be looked into: Edward McCurdy, ed., *Leonardo da Vinci's Notebooks* (New York: Charles Scribner's Sons, 1910). The editor of the *Notebooks* has also written a very helpful book called *The Mind of Leonardo da Vinci* (New York: Dodd, Mead & Company, Inc.,

1948), which is a clear and well-presented life and work, rather than primarily an attempt to interpret his mind. McCurdy, unlike some others who have written in this field, although greatly admiring his hero and occasionally letting slip some remark which tends to emphasize the uniqueness of the great *uomo universale,* is nevertheless well aware of the debt of Leonardo to his contemporaries and predecessors. J. A. Symonds, *The Life of Michelangelo Buonarroti,* beautifully written like everything by this author, is a classic; but I also like a more recent work, Michele Saponaro, *Michelangelo Buonarroti* (New York: Pellegrini and Cudahy, 1950), although the translation from the Italian leaves something to be desired. It is much shorter than Symonds, is strongly impressionistic but entirely accurate, and contains many new and interesting insights into the great master.

As much as possible of the works of the great humanists should, of course, be read. Erasmus' *In Praise of Folly* is available in an excellent Classics Club edition, Desiderius Erasmus, *In Praise of Folly,* edited and illustrated by Hendrik Willem van Loon (New York: The Classics Club, 1942). Preserved Smith, *Erasmus, a Study of his Ideals and Place in History* (New York: Harper & Brothers, 1923), is a solid and informative book on Erasmus, and I also like a very attractive short biography by Stefan Zweig, *Erasmus of Rotterdam* (New York: The Viking Press, 1934), which emphasizes the real courage always shown by the great humanist in his efforts to maintain his consistently tolerant and liberal position. Another valuable Classics Club edition exists of Montaigne's essays, Michel de Montaigne, *Selected Essays* (New York: The Classics Club, 1943). The translation by Donald M. Frame is excellent.

Finally, if more is needed on the factual material of the Renaissance, Henry S. Lucas, *The Renaissance and the Reformation* (New York: Harper & Brothers, 1934), may be consulted, although the chapters on art are somewhat perfunctory, not too well in accord with the most modern interpretations of Renaissance art and too much interlarded with names. It is, however, a useful work of reference, though recommended with fewer qualifications for its sections on the Reformation than on the Renaissance.

17

The Expansion of Europe and the Commercial Revolution

Trade and industry at the close of the Middle Ages • The Age of Discovery • Motives of the discoverers • Portuguese explorations in the East • Spanish discovery and exploitation of the New World • Voyages of the English, French, and Dutch • The Commercial Revolution—Importance for evolution of national states • Capitalism and mercantilism • Summary: In what sense was it a revolution?

► Trade and industry at the close of the Middle Ages

GRADUAL EMANCIPATION OF MEDIEVAL ECONOMY

In Chapter 14 a fairly extensive account was given of the attitude of the Middle Ages toward trade and industry. It was also shown how through long slow processes medieval economy was gradually freeing itself from the artificial restrictions that had been put upon it in an earlier age, especially by the Church. The Church, it will be remembered, did not approve of profit-seeking, deeming it dangerous for the human soul. It had forbidden the lending of money at interest. Yet ways were found to circumvent its regulations: money was lent at interest by one means or another, and the Church itself borrowed money which it repaid with interest. Industry was supposed to be on a small scale because there were only a few people who, by their position in life, were fitted to consume luxury goods, and necessities could be made

at home in the time left from agricultural pursuits. But, as we have seen in the last chapter, the towns, specializing in trade and industry, had ceased to pay attention to these restrictions. The bourgeoisie, especially in Italy, showed few inhibitions about spending its wealth. The forces making for increased trade and industry were too great for artificial restrictions.

NECESSARY LIMITS ON TRADE

Low consumption in peasant economy

But some restrictions were not artificial. Agriculture was still inefficient, in spite of the growth of a free tenantry toward the close of the Middle Ages. The production of food could not suddenly be increased. Though some of the surplus rural population could be absorbed by the towns, a tremendous rural population still had to live on the land as long as agricultural methods remained so primitive. As the Middle Ages waned, more land was brought into cultivation; but towns could grow only slowly as long as townsmen were dependent on food grown outside their boundaries. Not until better use was made of the land to permit higher yields, and not until partly mechanized agriculture took the place of human and animal labor, thus making a larger labor surplus in the country, could a truly urban civilization develop, as in many, but by no means all, Western countries today.

Thus one absolute limit to the growth of towns was the ability to feed the urban population, and this was not an artificial restriction but a real one. It was not solved, even in principle, in the Middle Ages, and it is not solved everywhere, even today.

Shortage of markets for industry

Urban industry needed markets, and it needed a means for exchanging its products for food and industrial products from other cities. Some industrial products naturally found their way into rural towns, and into the houses of nobles and landowners who possessed surplus food from their manors which they were willing to exchange. But the market for luxuries was really limited. Nobles and rich bourgeois could buy, but peasants could not. Until the monetary income of the peasant could rise, the tiny monetary surplus could purchase only the simplest of urban products. Therefore most of the products of urban industry in the late Middle Ages could be sold only to the inhabitants of other cities, and to a small class of privileged nobles whose income was sufficient, either from their lands or from their villages, to buy them; and of course to the king, who had at his disposal income which, though drawn from many sources, amounted to a very substantial total. Such income until recent times was regarded as being entirely at the king's disposal to spend as he would, and not earmarked for the benefit of those from whom it had been taken. The Church was in a somewhat similar position to the king's, and, as we have seen, during the Renaissance many popes and other churchmen did not refrain from spending money lavishly on what pleased them and suited their tastes.

Thus there were very real limitations on the possibility of selling an increased quantity of industrial goods, and these had no relation to artificial restrictions imposed by political or religious authorities.

ARTIFICIAL RESTRICTIONS ON TRADE AND INDUSTRY

The guilds

The artificial restrictions have already to a large extent been dealt with in Chapter 14. We have already alluded to the restrictions imposed by the Church, which the towns learned to circumvent. The theory of the closed society, that man should live contentedly in the position to which he had been born, was negated in the towns, where opportunity for advancement existed in increasing measure as the centuries wore on. The Church viewpoint ceased to correspond to the reality and was necessarily abandoned in the towns, and more gradually elsewhere. We have seen how the craft guilds tried to restrict manufacture through keeping it within a few hands, but how the trained journeymen broke down this industrial oligarchy when they were excluded from it. The leagues of merchants still controlled a great deal of the trade by the end of the Middle Ages; but we shall see in this chapter how even their monopolies collapsed when faced with the new conditions following the age of discovery.

Feudal restrictions on movement of goods

There were, however, a few serious restrictions which were partly natural and partly artificial. A country like England was a large free trade market, as a result of the centralization of the government in the hands of the king and the relative powerlessness of the English feudal nobles. France and Germany, however, suffered from the multiplicity of authorities who could levy toll upon products passing through their country, thus raising considerably the prices of all goods which used inland transportation. Prices therefore might be too high at the point of

► chronological chart

Voyages of Marco Polo	1271–1295	Founding of Universities of Mexico and Lima	1551
Henry the Navigator begins to patronize Portuguese voyages	1418	Voyage of Chancellor to Moscow and organization of Muscovy Company	1553–1555
Exploration of Madeira by Portuguese	1418–1419	Foundation of St. Augustine, Florida	1565
Discovery of Azores	1427–1431	Reorganization of Peruvian administration by Alvarez de Toledo	1569–1581
Cape Bojador rounded by Gil Eannes	1433	Sack of Antwerp ("Spanish Fury")	1576
Fall of Constantinople to Turks	1453	Voyages of Frobisher in search of northwest passage	1576–1578
Discovery of Cape Verde Islands	1455–1457	Circumnavigation of world by Drake	1577–1580
Death of Prince Henry the Navigator	1460	Union of Crowns of Spain and Portugal	1580
Reign of John II of Portugal	1481–1495	Founding of first colony of Virginia (Roanoke Island) by Walter Raleigh	1584
Norwegian voyage towards North America with Cortereal on board	1486	Defeat of Spanish Armada by English	1588
Diaz rounds Cape of Good Hope	1487–1488	Dutch expedition to East under Cornelis Houtman	1595–1597
Discovery of America by Columbus	1492	Formation of English East India Company	1600
Treaty of Tordesillas	1494	Formation of Dutch East India Company	1602
Treatise of Pacioli explaining double-entry bookkeeping	1494	Founding of Jamestown colony in Virginia	1607
Voyage of Vasco da Gama to India	1497–1499	Founding of Quebec by Champlain	1608
Voyages of Cabot brothers to North America (Cape Breton Island)	1497–1498	Founding of Bank of Amsterdam	1609
Voyages of Amerigo Vespucci to South America (Amazon)	1499–1502	Voyage of *Mayflower* to Cape Cod	1620
Voyage of Cabral to Brazil and India	1500–1501	Formation of Dutch West India Company	1621
Negro slavery introduced to Santo Domingo	1501	French settlements in West Indies	1625–1664
Almeida governor of the Indies	1505–1509	Purchase of Manhattan Island by Dutch	1626
Battle of Diu: victory of Almeida over Muslims	1509	Control of part of Brazil by Dutch Prince Maurice of Nassau	1637
Conquest by Spanish of Jamaica and Puerto Rico	1508–1511	Restoration of Portuguese independence	1640
Albuquerque governor of the Indies	1509–1515	Capture of Malacca by Dutch from Portuguese	1641
Conquest of Malacca by Portuguese	1511	Founding of Montreal by De Maisonneuve	1642
Conquest of Cuba by Spanish	1511	Expulsion of Dutch from Brazil	1654
Ponce de Leon discovers Florida	1512	Financial administration of Colbert	1661–1683
Balboa discovers Pacific Ocean	1513	Founding of French East India Company	1664
Conquest of Mexico by Cortes	1519–1521	Last assembly of Hanseatic League	1669
Voyage of Magellan to Philippines, survivors circumnavigate world	1519–1522	Founding of Bank of England	1694
Colonization of Brazil begun by Martin de Sousa	1530		
Opening of Antwerp Bourse	1531		
Conquest of Peru by Pizarro	1532–1533		
Voyages of Jacques Cartier to North America	1534–1541		
Promulgation of "New Laws" in Peru	1544		
Organization of colony of Brazil by Governor Thomé de Sousa	1549		

sale to make possible a really large market for manufactured goods. The same applied, as we shall see, to luxuries imported from the East over many thousands of miles by primitive methods of transportation. Toward the end of the Middle Ages the Venetians were sending their galleys around Europe by sea to the Hanseatic and other ports of northern Europe, thus increasing their sales by reducing their prices. But the inland towns gained no relief. Always some internal tariffs would raise prices and restrict sales. But the problem of transportation was a real one. It was always expensive in the Middle Ages, and for a long time to come it seriously hindered the sale of goods except those that were scarce, not bulky, and very greatly desired, like spices.

Shortage of medium of exchange

Finally there was the great difficulty of the means of payment for goods. We have seen in Chapter 14 how many ingenious inventions arose in the Middle Ages to make possible large transactions between merchants, how little money was needed for a complicated deal by which goods taken to the north from, say, Venice, could be exchanged for a new cargo to be taken back to Venice for distribution in Italy. But when the goods were in the merchants' hands they still had to be distributed to the final consumers who might have goods to exchange. And there was no exact way of determining the proportion of those goods which equaled the value of what was to be bought. This needed a true money economy, with money in the hands of everyone who was willing to exchange the surplus products of his labor for manufactured goods. In the fifteenth century there simply was not enough money to go round.

We have already spoken of the essential work of the money-changer in determining the equivalent of different kinds of money offered in payment for goods. In the fifteenth century Venetians and Florentines standardized their money and kept an honest coinage which was acceptable everywhere and needed no professional money-changers. This was a considerable advance, but there were far from enough precious metals available to satisfy all the possible purchasers of Europe. Copper was widely used in addition to silver and gold; but it was difficult to standardize, and not everywhere accepted. It was never regarded as in any way equivalent to silver and gold, and it had such a low value that it could not be used for substantial transactions. Silver and gold were regarded as having an *intrinsic* value, quite apart from what could be bought with them.

Today we can do without gold coins, and the value of silver coins bears no relation to the value of the silver that may be in them. Today we use paper money universally because we know that the *credit* of the issuing authority is behind it. If we ceased to trust that we could buy goods with this money—in other words if we ceased to trust the credit of the issuing authority, then we should refuse to accept the paper, or refuse to sell anything of real value in exchange for it. The bill of exchange works on the same principle as paper money and depends on the credit of the drawer. In Germany after World War I there was an uncontrolled inflation of the currency and all trust in the credit of the German government was lost. Such was also the case when kings in early modern times took to depreciating their coinage, making, say, six gold coins with a certain supposed value stamped on them out of as much gold as they should have put into three, and pocketing the profit. The monarchs' credit then ceased to be good, as people no longer trusted them to mark the true gold value on their coins.

It is important to bear this in mind as we come to study the age of discovery and what has been called the commercial revolution that followed it. The influx of new gold and silver from the Americas solved the problem of the shortage of currency for smaller transactions. A great deal of this new gold and silver was lost forever in countries of the Far East which had little use for European exports and would accept nothing but gold and silver. But production of gold and silver continued to grow from other sources, acceptable paper money in time began to take its place, and there has never since been such a shortage as really to hamper trade as it did at the close of the Middle Ages.

► The Age of Discovery

SEARCH FOR ALTERNATIVE ROUTE TO EAST

In the fifteenth century the Italians had a virtual monopoly of the trade with the Far East. This trade had received a considerable stimulus from journeys made in the later Middle Ages to India and China, which were both at that time superior to the West in the quality of the goods they manufactured. This, as mentioned earlier, was no longer true of the Muslim world, but for centuries to come it was true of India and China. The English learned to print cotton by importing Indian cottons, especially calico (an Indian word), and then imitating them. Using improved manufacturing methods in later centuries the English undersold the local Indian industries, which were unable to protect their industry since the English controlled their political life. Porcelain and china from China were likewise regarded as luxuries and imported, then imitated in European countries. In addition the Far East grew many products which could not be grown in the more temperate climate of Europe. In later centuries tea was the product most in demand. But in the Middle Ages what the Europeans desired most were spices—above all, pepper. These articles were not bulky, but there were never enough of them in Europe and the price was always high.

In the thirteenth century after the conquest of almost all Asia except India by Jenghiz and Kublai Khan, a number of friars penetrated into the Mongol domain anxious to convert the Mongols to Christianity, a not impossible feat since the latter were shamanistic and thus prospects for a higher religion. Though they were ultimately converted to Islam, they gave the visiting friars a good reception. Marco Polo, a Venetian merchant, also reached the court of Kublai Khan and lived to return to tell of the great riches of the kingdom, and of the much

safer and easier travel now that the Great Khans enforced peace and good order within their huge empire. But trade remained relatively small for want of a good transportation system, and it remained a monopoly of the Italians who controlled the Near Eastern caravan routes.

Naturally many eyes were cast covetously toward the fabulous East, of which so little was known. It seemed possible that the Mediterranean Sea could be circumvented by sailing round the coast of Africa. But no one knew how far such a journey would be; and it was known that the Muslims controlled the approaches to India. And China, or Cathay, was farther still. It was, of course, well known that the world was round, and that therefore in theory one could sail west and reach Cathay by that method. But no one knew how far it was. To venture into the empty spaces of the Atlantic was a hazardous undertaking with only a mariner's compass to determine direction, an astrolabe to determine latitude, but no way at all to determine longitude without the aid of a perfect chronometer, which was not yet in sight.

PORTUGUESE ENTERPRISE

Prince Henry the Navigator

The little country of Portugal, with a population estimated at barely a million, took the lead in the age of exploration. Fully independent at the end of the fourteenth century and unified under an effective monarchy, possessed of fine harbors facing on the Atlantic but no entry to the Mediterranean, gifted with few natural resources save specialized agricultural products like wine, it was natural that she should turn toward the sea for a living. What was new in European life and characteristic of the modern age was the careful systematic way in which she planned her future and prepared herself for the new age in which she was destined to play such a crucial part. The Spanish may almost be said to have blundered into their discoveries. The great pioneer Christopher Columbus, an Italian, showed Spaniards the way, though he had considerable difficulty in obtaining Spanish backing for his enterprise. Magellan, the great sailor who first circumnavigated the world, was a Portuguese in Spanish employ. But it was the Portuguese, starting with short voyages from which they learned everything possible, using all the inventions of their own and previous ages that might help in navigation, who finally succeeded in the great task of by-passing the Mediterranean and establishing direct trade relations with the Far East.

The man who above all was responsible for this success was Prince Henry the Navigator (1394–1460), third son of the great King John I, who had won Portuguese independence in 1385. In addition to being a prince and a duke, the latter title having been granted him for conspicuous valor against the Moors, he was Grand Master of the Order of Christ, a Portuguese successor to the suppressed Knights Templars. Henry's own motives were unquestionably mixed. With the instincts and training of a Crusader, he was a true child of the Middle Ages and the Iberian Peninsula; yet his methods were new and, as we would regard them, modern. To judge from the instructions issued to his mariners, his primary intention was always to defeat and conquer the Moors in their own stronghold of Africa. He hoped to be able to join forces with a supposed Ethiopian emperor named Prester John, who was believed to be the ruler of a nation of black Christians (the Coptic Church of Ethiopia). But, whatever his prime purpose, he prepared the way for the voyages of discovery by his careful and systematic work in an observatory and school of navigation at Sagres on Cape St. Vincent,

Portrait of Henry the Navigator, a miniature from a fifteenth-century manuscript.

using the nearby port of Lagos as the training ground. The Portuguese had developed the caravel, a three-masted square-rigged sailing ship which was greatly superior to any other ships of the time for long voyages. While Prince Henry was alive success had already attended the enterprise of many of his sailors. The Madeira Islands, the Azores, and the Cape Verde Islands far to the south had been discovered and were in the process of being colonized as steppingstones toward the vaster expeditions being planned.

Sailing down the coast of Africa does not seem to us today to be such a difficult feat, and certainly not as difficult as the long voyage across the Atlantic. But if these voyages had never been undertaken, Columbus could not have made his own; he learned from all sources available to him, and not least from the Portuguese. Venturing ever farther toward the equator, not knowing for certain that the end of Africa would ever be reached, beset with superstitious fears that they would turn black or that the water would boil, and by real fears of the dangers of tropical lands and their inhabitants, these voyagers nevertheless made progress. Cape Bojador was successfully passed, and by the time of Henry's death the Gulf of Guinea had been almost reached.

Resumption of explorations after the death of Henry

Henry's death disrupted further exploration. But the delay was only temporary. King John II (1481–1495) took up the quest again, and poured the meager resources of his kingdom into it, making himself personally familiar with all the geographic knowledge that had been accumulated. In this phase Bartholomew Diaz sailed round the Cape of Good Hope and beyond (1488). He did not reach India; this was to be accomplished after the death of John by Vasco da Gama, who reached Calicut in India, traded successfully, and returned home with a cargo that realized a huge profit (1498). Meanwhile, after the voyage of Diaz and the discovery of America by Columbus (1492), Pope Alexander VI, a Spaniard, had issued a bull demarcating

the respective halves of the world which should belong to the Spanish and Portuguese, and his settlement was agreed to by the rulers of Spain and Portugal, with some changes, in the Treaty of Tordesillas, signed in 1494.[1]

The Portuguese colonial empire

Once the voyage of da Gama had been accomplished, trading activity and crusades against the Muslims could be carried out at the same time. The Muslims were badly organized, and they had lived safely for too long to be able to put up an effective resistance against the numerically far inferior forces of the Portuguese. Two successive governors of "India," Almeida and Albuquerque, sent out by the Portuguese, thoroughly defeated the local Muslims in several sea battles. Two years after the death of the latter governor the Turks were likewise effectively shut off from all commerce with India by sea. Trading posts were organized, intermar-

[1] It may be worth noting at this point that there has been much controversy, which is still far from being settled in Europe, as to whether the Portuguese discovered the American continent before Columbus. It is not unnatural that the Portuguese should be the chief proponents of the theory that they, from their base in the Azores, sailed west and discovered South America. Their historians are almost unanimous in the matter. Although the theory has never obtained much backing in this country, there is some important evidence, especially in the form of ancient Portuguese maps, which tends to support it; and it has appeared curious to many that the Portuguese mariner Cabral was able to sail straight to Brazil (1500) as soon as it was clear that this protruding portion of South America would fall into the Portuguese sphere of occupation under the Treaty of Tordesillas. Cabral, after having made his discovery, at once left Brazil and went to India, which was presumably his principal destination. There can be little doubt that if the Portuguese had made the rest of the world aware that they had already discovered a great new continent, an important part of which would be granted to them under the treaty, the treaty itself would have taken a different form. It is known also that a Portuguese observer accompanied a Norwegian expedition to find the Northwest Passage in 1476, so that the Portuguese must be credited with interest in Atlantic exploration. It is possible that some day the matter may be conclusively settled; meanwhile it will be assumed in this book that Columbus and the Spaniards hold the priority with which they are customarily credited.

Portrait of Vasco da Gama, artist unknown.

riage with the Hindus was encouraged, and several important enclaves were wrested from the inhabitants and remained as Portuguese possessions. One of these, Goa, is still a bone of contention between the young republic of India and the Portuguese, who claim that it is an integral part of Portugal. Colonies in Africa still remain to the Portuguese as relics of their great age of discovery though Brazil was lost in the early nineteenth century. Portugal retained the monopoly granted to her under the Treaty of Tordesillas until 1591 when she lost it to the Dutch.

THE SPANISH DISCOVERIES

The voyage of Columbus

Mention has already been made of the geographic knowledge of the world in the time of Columbus, and of the difficulties of navigation beyond sight of land. But it should not be thought that the existence of the continent of America was altogether un-

known, though the knowledge of it was very thinly diffused, and had become highly uncertain by the time of Columbus. We know now that Norse and Icelanders had already been in America several centuries before Columbus, although there is still a great deal of dispute, often acrimonious, about the extent of their penetration, and whether a famous stone found in Minnesota and a tower in Rhode Island are of Norse origin. From time to time the skeptics have apparently demolished the believers, only to find that their most cherished arguments have failed to convince and have left many of the believers' arguments intact.[2] Whatever the final result of the controversy, it is certainly true that Columbus was not interested in discovering or rediscovering any supposed continent to the west. What he sought was a western route to China and India. Though he paid a visit to Iceland in his earlier years, and might have heard of the North American continent from contacts made in that seafaring country, we know nothing of this from him, nor do we know of his private conversations with the rulers whom he tried to persuade to back his schemes. A sailor who had risen by his own efforts, he first approached the king of Portugal, John II, but was discouraged by that monarch, who was hardly likely to trust such an obvious adventurer, and who could have found crews of his own if he had wished to make the effort. Ferdinand and Isabella of Spain, after long hesitation, finally decided to entrust Columbus with three ships, the *Santa Maria*, the *Pinta*, and the *Niña*, and a crew of some ninety sailors, many of them of very doubtful character. The first landfall was probably in the Bahama Islands, and Cuba and Haiti were discovered soon afterward and taken possession of in behalf of the Castilian crown. The first real settlement in the New

[2] For the present state of the controversy, see Hjalmar Holand, *Explorations in America before Columbus* (New York: Twayne Publishers, 1956), esp. pp. 154–251. Holand makes out a very good case for the "believers." He himself has devoted almost fifty years to research into Norwegian expeditions to America.

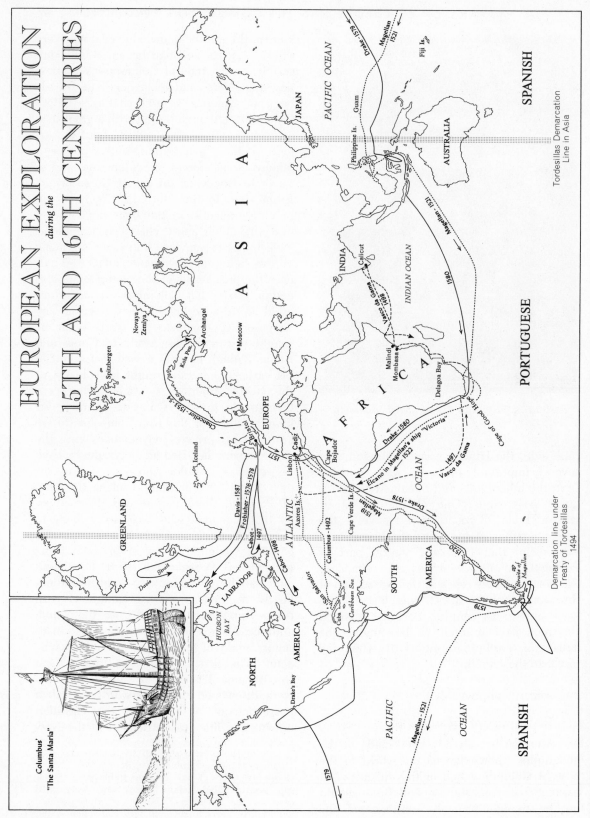

EUROPEAN EXPLORATION
during the
15TH AND 16TH CENTURIES

Columbus' "The Santa Maria"

Tordesillas Demarcation
Line in Asia

Demarcation line under
Treaty of Tordesillas
1494

SPANISH

PORTUGUESE

SPANISH

PACIFIC OCEAN

INDIAN OCEAN

ATLANTIC OCEAN

PACIFIC OCEAN

ASIA

AFRICA

EUROPE

NORTH AMERICA

SOUTH AMERICA

AUSTRALIA

GREENLAND

Iceland

Spitzbergen

Novaya Zemlya

Kola Pen.

Archangel

Moscow

JAPAN

INDIA

Calicut

Philippine Is.

Guam

Fiji Is.

Malindi
Mombasa

Delagoa Bay

Cape of Good Hope

Cape Bojador

Lisbon
Cadiz

Bristol

Azores Is.

Cape Verde Is.

San Salvador

Cuba

Caribbean Sea

HUDSON BAY

LABRADOR

Davis Strait

Drake's Bay

Straits of Magellan

Magellan - 1521
Magellan - 1521
Magellan 1522

Drake - 1579

Drake - 1580

Drake - 1578

Davis - 1587

Frobisher - 1576-1578

Cabot - 1498
Cabot - 1497

Columbus 1492

Chancellor - 1553-54

Vasco da Gama
1498

1497
Vasco da Gama

Elcano in Magellan's ship "Victoria"
1522

1519

1520

1579

1580

1521

572

A model of the Santa Maria, *the flagship of Columbus. It is estimated that this ship was 91 feet in length, with a 26-foot beam.* (COURTESY ADDISON GALLERY OF AMERICAN ART, PHILLIPS ACADEMY, ANDOVER)

World was Hispaniola, the name given by the Spanish to the island now composed of Haiti and the Dominican Republic, and the first Spanish New World capital was Santo Domingo on that island (1504). When resistance was offered by the natives they were conquered by fire and sword, forcing many of them into slavery.

The islands—called the West Indies, thus perpetuating the hopes of the first discoverers—were made almost at once the base for further discoveries on the mainland. Jamaica was conquered in 1509, Cuba entirely subdued by 1514. Expeditions by Ponce de Leon to Florida failed, as he did not possess enough force to put down the natives, and Florida was not won until after

the middle of the sixteenth century. The West Indian islands were exploited for their agricultural rather than mineral products, especially sugar cane which was cultivated by slaves. Meanwhile the mainland was being fully explored and was ultimately conquered.

Amerigo Vespucci, a highly skilled navigator and pilot, an Italian in the service of Spain, explored the mouth of the Amazon as early as 1500 and gave his name to the American continent, a great length of whose southern coasts he had explored. Vasco de Balboa, aided by friendly Indians, made an epic march across the Isthmus of Panama, and discovered and claimed the Pacific Ocean for the Spanish monarch (1513).

Soon after, Ferdinand Magellan, a Portuguese in Spanish service, sailed around Cape Horn and reached the East Indies (1521). Though Magellan himself was killed by hostile natives, the Philippine Islands accrued to the Spanish monarchy as a result of the voyage, and his ship succeeded in returning to Spain, having circumnavigated the globe.

Conquest of Mexico

The epic feats of the Spanish *conquistadores* culminated in the conquests of Mexico and Peru, the most astonishing conquests in the history of the world. In both cases the conquest was made by a very small army of Spaniards, under leadership exactly suited for the purpose, and in both cases the invaders were faced by peoples and armies which so far outnumbered them that they could have utterly destroyed the Spaniards if they had initially possessed the will to resist. The Aztecs in Mexico were the heirs of an ancient civilization (the Mayan) which had achieved great heights in the field of the arts with extremely primitive technical means at their disposal. But the Aztecs were not themselves a very creative people, and their talents had been devoted to the arts of war rather than of peace. Their religion was bloodthirsty, including human sacrifice on a wide scale. War victims were sacrificed constantly to their war god, and they kept their neighboring peoples in a condition of humiliating servitude. It was thus not too difficult for Hernando Cortes, conqueror of Mexico, to obtain allies amongst the other Mexican peoples, once he had persuaded them that he would win or had a reasonable chance of winning, though at the beginning they feared the possible vengeance of the Aztecs so profoundly that the best Cortes could hope for was a benevolent neutrality.

The key to his success proved to be the superstitious fear of Montezuma, the Aztec monarch, that the conquerors from over the sea were destined to prevail, and that it was useless to fight against the gods who had decreed it. Thus his resistance was

Hernando Cortes, from a contemporary engraving.

half-hearted, and he allowed himself to be taken as a hostage by the Spainards, who had penetrated into his capital in November, 1519. After his death—whether at the hands of the Spaniards or of his own people will never be known—the Aztecs drove the Spaniards from the capital city of Tenochtitlán with the loss of a large part of the small Spanish force, in spite of prodigies of valor on the part of the Spaniards. But it had been shown that the Aztecs were not unbeatable. In spite of his defeat, Cortes was able to attract great numbers of Mexicans to his banner for a return to the capital, which was recaptured in 1521.

Conquest of Peru

Francisco Pizarro, **conqueror** of Peru, had an even smaller army than Cortes when he began his expedition of conquest a decade later. But the more pacific civilization of the Incas proved an easier target than the warlike Aztecs. The Inca civilization was a highly complex social organism, ruled by a paternal despotism that could not survive the loss of its leader. The entire Incan Empire had been organized in such a way that everyone worked on a communal basis, there was no unemployment, and probably little real poverty. It was a life very close to nature and dependent upon her. The rulers defended the territory against outsiders and extended their empire as circumstances permitted. But the ordinary man and woman had no share in government, no opportunity of advancement, and no incentive to progress. Faced by the highly individualist Spaniards these people had no chance without leadership, and of this leadership they were deprived in the first days of the war.

Atuahalpa, the Incan ruler, like Montezuma and the Aztecs, had little will to resist, also believing that his country was destined by the gods to fall to warriors from over the sea. He went unarmed with a small band into the Spanish camp and was taken prisoner. Pizarro had him tried on a variety of charges and put him to death in 1533. The people, left without a leader, were lost, and allowed the Spaniards to bring up reinforcements and in part take over the country. Before serious resistance was offered under different leadership, the Spaniards had prevailed.

Characteristics of Spanish colonialism

The motives of the Spaniards in their conquests were mixed. There is no doubt that in Mexico, at least, they were revolted by the cruelty of the Aztec religion. But from the beginning it was always their intention to convert the native peoples to Christianity, and priests accompanied all their expeditions. Once they were in the country, even more potent became their lust for gold, and later for lands. After the first conquests all the precious metals that had been accumulated by the natives were sent back to Spain, thereby encouraging ever more immigrants in search of adventure and fortune. In time almost the whole of South and Central America was conquered, and North America was penetrated. The valor and courage shown by the adventurers can hardly be overestimated. It is also true that large numbers of them did regard the conquest of America as a Christian crusade. But it is also true that few were averse to enriching themselves, and few considered the inevitable hardship that this entailed for their Indian subjects.

The Spanish monarchy, however, especially in the time of Philip II, was far more concerned with the salvation of the Indians and their well-being than most of the men in the conquered lands, though of course it appreciated the gold and silver sent from the Indies, a fifth of which belonged to the crown. But it found the greatest difficulty in keeping such a large territory under royal control, and it had no governmental system available which could ensure real protection for the natives. The position was radically different from that which prevailed later in the North American colonies. There were relatively few Indians in North America. In South America they were always in the majority. There was no self-government in Spain; the regime was always centralized and autocratic. Self-government through democratic institutions would never have been thought of as a possibility by any Spanish monarch or colonial landholder. The colonial government at best could therefore only be paternalistic, depending upon the high-mindedness and integrity of individual governors rather than on "equal protection of the laws."

In the sixteenth century there were many excellent viceroys, who were the direct representatives of the king and held office only for a few years at a time. They were appointed only after exhaustive investigation, and were subject to examination of their acts after they laid down their office. When in office they possessed full authority delegated from the king. Yet their task was difficult, if not impossible. The great number of *mestizos*, for the most part the result of unions between Spanish men and Indian women, were regarded as Spanish rather than Indian; the Indian himself was severely exploited by his conquerors, especially by the new class of large landowners (*encomenderos*), who had in many cases won their domains by their own efforts and did not easily submit to any authority. Desire for gain tended to make them use the Indians as slaves or low-paid laborers, and the paramount power did not have the resources at its disposal to protect them. Governors and individual priests did what they could, while missions set up by the religious orders of the Church sometimes exercised full authority in some areas of the continent, paternally protecting the Indian even though giving him little responsibility for his own welfare and allowing him no share in government.

Typical of the difficulties to be encountered in South America is the case of Bartolomé de las Casas, a missionary who went to the country in its early years. Deeply distressed by the plight of the Indians, he sought the help of the Spanish monarch who promulgated, at his insistence, a series of so-called "New Laws." When the governor was instructed to put the laws into effect he found himself faced by united opposition from the *encomenderos,* who contended the statutes were unworkable, and they were probably right in the existing state of the country. Talk arose of setting up a new and independent state, outside Spanish authority. The laws were repealed and the opposition movement subsided. Thereafter Bartolomé de las Casas devoted his life to doing what he could to relieve the plight of the Indians by individual action.

As in all imperial territories it is not easy to persuade the native inhabitants to work for money when their wants are adequately supplied by comparatively little labor. The Spaniards wanted them to work regularly. The precious metals had to be mined, the raw materials produced. Their only resort was compulsion, tempered by individual kindness and the ministrations of the Church. The problem was never solved, and its continuance built up resentment not only against the system but against the Spanish government which was believed to be responsible for it. This resentment aided the independence movement of a later century against a Spain that was by then long decadent. But for a long time under the system, as we shall see, "Latin America" filled a regular stream of treasure ships which provided the Spanish monarchy with the means for making itself feared and respected in Europe far beyond what it would have been able to accomplish from its own resources, and gave Spain an army that was for a long time superior to any that could be matched against it.

VOYAGES OF ENGLISH, FRENCH, AND DUTCH

The other countries of Europe did not admit the legality or justice of the Treaty of Tordesillas, but in the early sixteenth century they were not strong enough at sea to challenge effectively either the Spanish or Portuguese monopolies. They were thus compelled to explore primarily in the regions not controlled by these countries.

Still looking for a way to China and India, the English made many efforts to find a northwest passage, an effort which was pursued throughout the sixteenth century, naturally without success since the passages which do exist are blocked by ice. A northeastern passage was also attempted, resulting in the discovery of the Archangel route to Russia, and the formation of a company to trade with that country; but no passage to China via the Arctic was found. The English seamen, thwarted by these failures, compensated for them, often with considerable profit, by preying on Spanish shipping and occasionally looting inadequately protected treasure ships. At the end of the century, when Portugal had been incorporated into the Spanish kingdom, and her Spanish masters lost interest in protecting the ancient Portuguese monopoly in the East, the English decided to use the old Portuguese route around the Cape of Good Hope. Since the Dutch had the same idea and were at that time superior to the English in shipping, the latter were not able to win very much of the East for themselves at that time. Later, of course, they were to fall heir to some of the Dutch domain, and to carve out for themselves magnificent territories in

India. These conquests, however, fall outside the scope of this book.

The French also made spasmodic voyages of exploration, and after the discovery of America, fishermen found the Newfoundland waters a profitable source of food for the French market. Jacques Cartier made three important voyages to North America in search of the northwest passage to China, sailed around Newfoundland, and up the St. Lawrence to Montreal. Close to Montreal today one finds the Lachine Rapids, which are a reminder that Cartier believed that only these rapids stood between him and China. For the rest of the century Cartier's explorations and achievements were neglected. His work was not followed up until early in the seventeenth century, Samuel de Champlain rediscovered Montreal, founded Quebec, and laid the foundations of the French possession of Canada, which was disputed with the latecoming English throughout the whole of the next two centuries, ultimately falling to the English in the middle of the eighteenth century.

The Dutch, though they were fine seamen, preferred through the sixteenth century to reap the fruits of the explorations made by others and act as carriers especially for the merchandise brought to Lisbon by the Portuguese, for whose further distribution the Portuguese lacked shipping. Indeed it is certain that from the point of view of strict profits the Dutch prospered far more than any of the other countries, not excepting the Spanish themselves, as will be seen. Holland and Flanders were in the sixteenth century part of the Spanish Hapsburg territories in Europe and did not have full self-government. When Holland turned Protestant and revolted against Spain, the Dutch were excluded from the Lisbon market by the Spanish overlords, and were thus forced to take the initiative in trying to keep the trade by shipping the Oriental products directly to Holland from India and the Far East. By this time the Portuguese were well established in the Far East, especially in the so-called "spice islands" of the Celebes and the Moluccas.

The Dutch during the course of the seventeenth century, working through a state-chartered organization called the Dutch East India Company which had been granted a monopoly of the Eastern trade, succeeded in expelling the Portuguese from all their possessions save a few tiny outposts and trading centers such as Macao and Portuguese Timor. Later they had to yield some of their possessions to the English, but maintained the large bulk of their empire intact until 1949, when the United States of Indonesia was formed as an independent state. A company similar to the Dutch East India Company was also formed to make settlements and trade in the New World (Dutch West India Company). Though not as successful as its Oriental counterpart, it was able to capture some West Indian Islands from the Spanish and obtain a foothold in South America in what is now Surinam. For some twenty years in the seventeenth century the Dutch held part of northern Brazil until they were driven out by the Portuguese, who then founded Rio de Janeiro and thereafter used it as a base for counterattacks which the Dutch were not strong enough to repel.

CONSEQUENCES OF THE EXPLORATIONS

Portugal

The mother countries of the two leading exploring powers did not reap much of really permanent benefit from the explorations which, on the whole, benefited the rest of Europe more than themselves. Portugal was a small country and its resources were far too greatly extended by trying to keep up its empire. Not only were many seamen lost on the voyages and in the East through disease and battle, but the homeland was to a large degree neglected in favor of foreign trade. The Portuguese imported large numbers of Negro slaves from Africa to take care of their neglected agriculture—almost the only case of Negroes being used as slaves in Europe itself. Little effort was made to use the new-found riches to establish industry. The merchants of Lisbon grew rich on the monopoly, and Lisbon became the leading port of Europe for a short time. But the Portuguese were unable to provide ships for distribution of the imported produce, and foreign ships had to be permitted to take the goods away for distribution in Europe. As soon as Lisbon, through the Spanish union of 1580, lost her monopoly of Far Eastern trade, no longer did ships come to Lisbon and the harbor lost almost all its importance. All her prosperity had been bound up with the Oriental trade. When it was lost Portugal possessed a magnificent harbor, but far too little trade to keep it fully occupied, while her home agriculture and even the export trade in wine had been allowed to fall into decay. Portugal has never been an important power in Europe since that day.

Spain

Spain, through the importation of gold and silver, became the leading military power of Europe for a century. Possessed of much greater resources and manpower than Portugal, it was nevertheless not a rich country. Its most important product was wool from the fine Merino sheep. Moreover its social system, which gave excessive power to the noble or grandee and the Church, discouraged industry. Only in Seville and Barcelona was there much industry. As long, however, as the Spanish treasure ships were able to enter Spain freely with their valuable cargo the Spanish monarchs had enough money from the fifth that belonged to them to pay for their unending wars on the continent in which, mainly for dynastic ends rather than for any Spanish national interests, they indulged. The Spanish for a time ruled the Netherlands as a private possession of their kings, and when faced by a revolt on religious and commercial grounds, they determined to suppress it. The resources of Spain, even the resources of New Spain, were insufficient to enable them to carry out the military policy of its monarchs, and long before the end of the sixteenth century the Spaniards were taxed as highly as any other country. Only if a solid industrial base had backed the policy with goods necessary for war could it have been maintained. But, curiously enough, Spain lost much of what industry she had previously possessed through neglect and inflation.

With the influx of money into Spain, that country was the first to feel the effect of rising prices—too much money chasing too few goods. The price level in all Europe rose, but nowhere so steeply as in Spain, where there were few goods to sell in the first place. There was a little febrile prosperity as so often occurs in periods of inflation. But the money was not used as investment capital except to a very small degree. What happened, on the contrary, was that Spain became a fine consuming market for the luxury goods of the rest of Europe, which had to satisfy Spanish demands. In order to do this they had to compete with one another. All countries in that early mercantile age wanted to export as much as they could and import as little. The one great importing market for a while was Spain. Thus the other countries by competition were forced to lower prices, thus forcing the inefficient existing industries in Spain to follow their lead if they hoped to maintain their position. This they were unable to do, in part for want of the commercial spirit that actuated the nations in the north—the Spanish upper classes preferred to fight or live as grandees on their estates—and in part because of the real difficulties issuing from the price inflation. The treasure ships continued to sail, if less frequently. But they were unable to save the Spanish state from sinking into an economic and political decline from which it has scarcely aroused herself to this day.

Germany and Italy

The effect of the discoveries upon the two great medieval trading countries of Italy and Germany was slow, but very sure. Venice, as a great center of capital, was able for a long time to maintain a modicum of prosperity. But most of her slow-moving caravan trade with the East had been lost forever. With the declining prosperity of Venice and Italy the German towns, which had acted as distributors for the Oriental

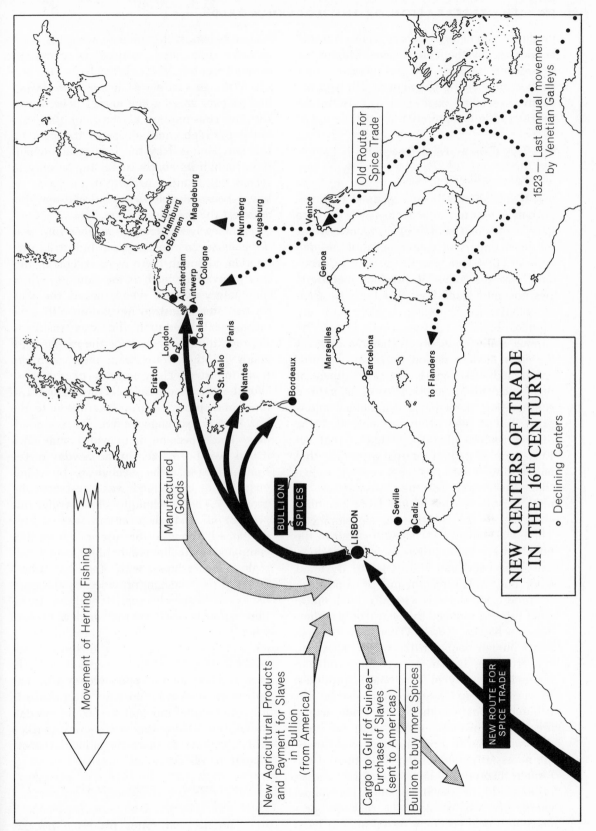

NEW CENTERS OF TRADE
IN THE 16th CENTURY

o Declining Centers

Old Route for
Spice Trade

1523 – Last annual movement
by Venetian Galleys

to Flanders

Lubeck
Hamburg
Bremen
Magdeburg
Nurnberg
Augsburg
Venice
Genoa
Marseilles
Barcelona
Amsterdam
Antwerp
Cologne
London
Calais
Paris
Bristol
St. Malo
Nantes
Bordeaux
Seville
Cadiz
LISBON

BULLION
SPICES

Manufactured
Goods

Movement of Herring Fishing

New Agricultural Products
and Payment for Slaves
in Bullion
(from America)

Cargo to Gulf of Guinea –
Purchase of Slaves
(sent to Americas)

Bullion to buy more Spices

NEW ROUTE FOR
SPICE TRADE

579

products, also entered a slow decline, rapidly accelerated by the Thirty Years' War in the seventeenth century. But this process is best studied in the original map which appears on the preceding page, and will be further considered in Chapter 19.

▶ **The Commercial Revolution**

GENERAL CHARACTERISTICS

It has already been explained how important it was to the economy of Europe to have a sufficient supply of currency. By far the most important consequence of the discoveries, therefore, for the European economy, was the influx of precious metals. It was not until much later that the possession of colonies by European powers had any significant effect on the economies of the various states. The other characteristics of the early modern period were already present in medieval times. Every development of this so-called "revolution" was a natural continuation of medieval commercial enterprise. But it does seem probable that the discoveries provided the "trigger" that set Europe on its path of internal expansion that has continued until this time, with the Industrial Revolution or the introduction of machinery to replace human labor a natural element in the continuous development. There was, however, a *necessary* limit to the possibilities of expansion in a world dominated by hand and animal labor. By hand labor only a limited amount of goods can be produced; there is virtually no limit to what can be produced by the use of machines and mechanical power. There are only so many human beings in the world. They can convert their human energy into only so much in the way of consumable products. By various means these products can be distributed throughout the world. Some people are large consumers, others must be small consumers. But in a pre-machine world there are necessarily more of the latter than of the former; theoretically this need not be the case in a world of machines and mechanical energy. It was no accident that the pre-machine world economy rested upon a basis of an enormous number of low-consuming

human beings, who produced a surplus available for distribution to those who had the power to obtain it for themselves. The pre-machine age saw a vast increase of slavery and an ever-growing number of poor; it was the low consumption of the poor that provided the high consumption of the rich. All this was changed by the Industrial Revolution, though its effects came slowly; only in recent times, and especially in this country, has it been possible to spread consumption amongst the previously poor.

The early modern period, therefore, was not conspicuous for increased industrial production, although there were several important innovations, such as the slow growth of the factory system, which paved the way for the later Industrial Revolution. What the commercial revolution did was vastly to improve the mechanism for the exchange of goods. In other words, trade increased more than industry. The products of the New World were now available throughout Europe, and through Europe were sent to the Far East in exchange for Far Eastern products. Trade became more world wide than it had ever been, even in the heyday of the Roman Empire. The mechanism by which goods were exchanged was constantly improved. The technique for organizing production and distribution was greatly developed through the use of joint-stock companies with limited liability, and large-scale partnerships, with their attendant facilities for financing provided by the great banks and finance houses. All of these institutions could be used for further development when the time called for it. The same banks and companies which had financed trade could later be used to finance industry; the bourses in which it was possible for men with only a small surplus to take their share in financing trade and industry could become in later centuries the great stock markets where millions of shares of industrial stocks change hands every day.

THE MONARCHS AND THE COMMERCIAL REVOLUTION

The national states played a peculiar part in the commercial revolution. On the one hand monarchs lent their protection to commercial ventures and often by the use of their tax monies helped finance them. On the other hand they also served to hinder any real expansion of trade by the manner in which they carried out what they conceived to be their duty toward trade. They granted monopolies to one company at the expense of all its competitors. Only rarely could such a monopoly handle the entire trade of the territory or commodity allotted to it. Thus it tended to skim the cream, and what could have been done by competitive enterprise was never attempted. Thus the monopoly made for insufficient penetration into a market, and it was able to fix prices as high as it wished provided only that the government permitted it. Kings also felt, rather naturally, that the goods of their own countries had to be favored at the expense of all foreigners. Since protection of the goods of its own nationals meant tariffs upon the goods of foreigners, prices again were too high to ensure as large a consumption as could have been obtained. Finally, the merchants had visible wealth which could be taxed for the benefit of the monarch in his dynastic wars and other extravagances. Colbert, the French finance minister in the time of Louis XIV waged an ever-losing battle against his master's military and cultural extravagances. Sometimes, however, the wars were approved by the commercial classes. Nearly all seventeenth-century wars had an important economic motive in addition to the supposed political motive. Navigation laws did protect the shipping interests of a country; if they led to war, perhaps the war would pay for itself by enforcing the laws, or by destroying the capacity of a competitive trading nation for trade and commerce for a long time to come, thus allowing the winner to capture the rival's markets for goods.

THE EVOLUTION OF CAPITALISM

The expansion of credit and banking

Perhaps the most important feature in a capitalist system is the proper provision for credit. It is impossible to carry on much business if money has to exchange hands before goods are delivered; and in international trade almost no business could be carried on at all if foreign money had to be exchanged and accepted before goods could be shipped. We have already seen how in the Middle Ages the bill of exchange was developed. In the early modern period the *endorsing* of a bill of exchange greatly increased its usefulness. The bill could be endorsed over to another man to whom the owner of the bill of exchange owed money, and thus the bill could pass from hand to hand, covering several transactions before the foreign drawer of the bill paid up on his original bill.

The promissory note, also introduced at this time, was the forerunner of the check. A merchant in ordering goods could give a promise to pay a stipulated sum of money on a certain date. If made out to a particular individual then the note could be endorsed to one of his creditors, and, again, many transactions could take place before the promissory note was presented for payment. When made out to bearer, even the endorsement was no longer necessary. If the note was drawn for a certain date in advance, then it could not be presented for payment before that time. Thus grew up the custom of *discounting* such notes in advance for a monetary consideration. Owners of money, if they trusted the credit of the original giver of the note, could then make a profit merely by using his money, without taking part in any commercial transaction whatsoever. This service was especially useful in international transactions in which the banker who had discounted the notes could collect on all at the same time, often through an agent who represented him in the foreign city.

It can readily be seen how banking would grow in such circumstances. There was constant demand for money for all purposes, and anyone who had money could use it with the greatest of ease to make more, either by lending directly, or by its equivalent, the discounting of notes. We have seen earlier how the Bank of Genoa came into existence in the Middle Ages. But there was especially great need for banks in the new centers of trade. Most banking in the Middle Ages had been in the hands of private bankers, usually family affairs or partnerships, and private banking continued an important feature of early modern times. Private banks in the hands of families could often, however, lose money as well as make it. Too often they were called upon by important monarchs whom they were sometimes not in a position to refuse. And monarchs had a tendency to overspend their income in costly wars; then, whether they liked to do so or not, they might repudiate their debts and the bankers could do nothing about it.

The vastly wealthy family bankers in Augsburg, the Fuggers, though they prospered for a long time, were eventually ruined by royal bankruptcies. A need became visible for deposit banks which would act as safe custodians of money owned by companies and individuals, while at the same time they could facilitate transfers of money between merchants who banked with them by simple bookkeeping transactions instead of any physical transfer of funds. But it was essential that these banks should be reliable and safe and should not speculate with the deposits made by their customers, and that they should convert all the strange kinds of money that came into their hands into an acceptable currency. Thus the new banks were closely connected with the governments of the countries in which they were founded. The first of such banks in northern Europe was the Bank of Amsterdam, centered in the greatest commercial city of the time (1609). The Bank of England was not chartered until 1694, but from the beginning it handled all the business of the English government, and adopted very safe and conservative banking policies.

The stock exchange

The wide distribution of goods in these centuries necessitated far better facilities than could be provided by the old-fashioned medieval fairs, although many of these continued to flourish in various centers. A distinctive feature of the six-teenth century was the *bourse*, an exchange for all kinds of commodity transactions. The Antwerp bourse, opened in 1531, was by far the largest attempted up to that time, as befitted the leading commercial city in Europe. Here it was that merchants gathered to buy goods that might not yet be available for delivery in Antwerp, or indeed in Europe. Every European trading country had its representatives there, and financial transactions of all kinds were handled. Goods could be bought at the present prices for future delivery, although by the time they were delivered the price might have increased or decreased. Thus there were additional chances for speculative profit. In Antwerp also commercial insurance developed, originally for a particular shipment through separate negotiation; then, as commerce became safer, it was possible to establish a system of set premiums. Here in Antwerp it also became profitable and possible to commit a very deadly medieval sin, cornering the market by getting together with the few other merchants who dealt in a particular commodity such as pepper and manipulating prices accordingly.

Commercial organization— Partnerships and companies

The development of the medieval company into the true joint-stock company was slow but sure. Organizations for particular adventures such as raiding a Spanish fleet or setting up a colony in America were for a long time far more popular. Profits would be shared as soon as the enterprise was completed, and the capital made available for another well-chosen enterprise. Partnerships, sometimes with more than twenty partners, each sharing in the profits at an agreed rate, were less impersonal than companies, and the profits might well be much higher since there were relatively few persons with an interest. But as time went on, many people preferred to keep their money in a venture which showed signs of being permanently profitable, and a percentage of the proceeds would be returned to them every year as the company continued to do business. Moreover, this system allowed small investors' money to be used, unlike the situation in the partnership where only men of substantial means would be of use to the organization. Some of the companies were "regulated," that is, they were set up for a definite purpose which required government support, such as the exploitation of a royal monopoly. Of such a kind were the Dutch and British East India companies, which paid high dividends for more than a century to their stockholders. The ordinary joint-stock company which appealed to the large and small investor alike depended for its success on the purpose intended, and was obviously more suited to manufacturing industry than to the kind of trade prevalent in the early modern period, so much of whose success depended on privileges granted and sustained by governments. However, toward the end of the seventeenth century the lure of "sucker" money became so great that a great many companies were formed, some for manufacturing purposes and many others for rather nebulous schemes for getting rich quick. The more solid of these prospered, but others were made the vehicle solely, or at least primarily, for manipulation of the stocks on the exchange. The result was a number of severe failures, followed by attempts at government regulation.

AGRICULTURE AND INDUSTRY DURING
THE COMMERCIAL REVOLUTION

As we have seen, during the later Middle Ages the manorial system was breaking down in most parts of Europe and a free peasantry was taking its place, though it continued to pay heavily for the use of its lands to its former masters. However, during the commercial revolution, with the urban population growing and the absolute population of Europe increasing likewise, more efficient production methods were necessary if the urban population was to be fed. Moreover, with the textile industry making its demands for

agricultural raw material, some kind of regular supply had to be secured. With the increase of money and the wider development of a money economy the peasants became accustomed to selling their produce in the open market and paying their landlords no longer with produce but with cash. Thus the incentive grew for producing more, and buying urban products with the cash thus gained. In this way some farms could become profitable commercial enterprises. While Germany retained much of the old feudal system until the French Revolution, with communal land and payments to lords in kind rather than in money, merchants elsewhere were already in the seventeenth century beginning to invest some of their money in the land. The Dutch, in particular, engaged in improving and draining their land, and building the familiar windmills, treating the farms thus improved and reclaimed as capital investments which often indeed showed handsome profits. By the same period the Dutch had also developed a number of systems of crop rotation which improved the yields from the soil and maintained fertility.

The English did not make so many technical improvements as the Dutch, but through many centuries they succeeded in converting the old manorial estates into much more efficient units, especially by the system of *enclosures*. In medieval times there had been common land used by all the peasants in an area, and the prevalent system of farming was in strips, often separated from each other by considerable distances. No less efficient system could have been devised, and well before the Middle Ages were ended enterprising farmers and manorial lords were taking steps to consolidate their holdings. Especially after the royal confiscation of monastery lands, to be mentioned in the next chapter, when merchants and business men bought up the monastic estates, there was a considerable improvement in efficiency. The majesty of the law was used to bring about enclosures. Tenants and small farmers with customary rights were made

OLEVM OLIVARVM.

Decuſſæ oliuæ adhuc acerbæ, ex arbore,   Preſſæq̄, pinguis dant oliui copiam.

The manufacture of olive oil, an early example of what was later to become the "factory system." This old print shows the whole process from the raw material to the finished product.

to prove that they were legal rights also, which they could rarely do. The verdict then went in favor of the owners who enclosed the common land and consolidated the strips, and then frequently turned the land into pasture for sheep. This, of course, resulted in tremendous social dislocation and complaint from the dispossessed tenants who were sometimes able to persuade Parliament to halt the process. Perhaps as frequently, however, the land was merely improved and turned into arable land, on which the peasants could remain as tenant farmers. A surprising result, for those who know present-day England, was that by the end of the seventeenth century England was a net exporter of grain.

The development of urban industry was slow. The guilds were still powerful in

early modern times in most of Europe, and far bigger profits were to be obtained by enterprising business men in trade than in manufacture. Most manufacturing businesses were small, usually comprising nothing more than the family unit. On the whole the organization of production in the colonies of large crops, such as cocoa, tobacco, and sugar, organized under the plantation system and with slave labor, were far more efficient and supplied far more to the European market than the small indigenous industries. Yet some European industries already had factories by the end of the seventeenth century, producing what could not be made in small shops, especially military supplies such as cannon and gunpowder, ships, and products such as paper and iron that entailed too many processes to be handled under

The "domestic system" in the seventeenth century, showing the division of labor within a family. The men have just returned from the fields, and the women are weaving flax for the market. An old French print.

one small roof. Mines were developed continually during this period, especially the coal mines in England, although coal was not used for making steel until the technical difficulties were solved in a later century.

But by far the most important increase in manufactured goods came in the field of textiles, where the system already in vogue in the Middle Ages of "putting out" work in rural homes was very greatly increased. This putting-out system, also known as the "domestic system" was the regular system of manufacture in the textile industry until the nineteenth century, and had not altogether disappeared by the twentieth. The merchant controlled the system, and it was his capital and enterprise that alone made it possible. Thousands of small farmers and townsmen were dependent upon the raw material that was bought by these men, distributed to the homeworker for his share of the work, collected again by the merchants' agents, and then finally finished by another worker, small factory, or sometimes abroad when the country permitted export. The system required capital in the hands of the merchant to finance all the small transactions with individual workers, and required much labor of middlemen besides. But it did succeed in producing very considerable quantities of cloth and finished textiles in all the textile-producing countries of Europe. Not until larger machines were invented that could do the work more quickly than the small machine afforded by the craftsmen, and not until water power took over some of the work done by hand and foot, was the system superseded.

THE COMMERCIAL REVOLUTION AND
THE NATIONAL STATE

Theory and practice of mercantilism

The commercial revolution proved to be of considerable assistance to rulers. There had always been a tendency for the bourgeoisie to join hands with the national governments, as against the nobility whom they regarded with disfavor as privileged parasites, whose private wars could disrupt business for no good purpose. From the monarch's point of view the bourgeois, with his visible wealth, was the obvious source of the sinews of war which he so often needed. In the commercial revolution the monarchs had a new task to perform, protecting the shipping routes and ensuring the safe arrival of the merchant's goods. They were also expected to promote in every way possible the trade interests of their own nationals against the interests of foreigners, even if this involved them in small wars which could be fought at low cost, with ultimate profit for the country and its trade interests.

It is clear that only those countries which had already developed powerful national states, and where a definite concept of national interest had come into existence, could be expected to act on behalf of the commercial interests of the country. Thus, parallel with the growth of a national commercial policy, grew nationalism itself, a force which has not yet by any means expended itself. The national entity may in some respects be considered an artificial creation, but there can be no doubt about the emotional content that has gone into the idea of a nation, *our* particular nation in contrast with all other nations. The monarchs of the early modern period who understood the fact of this emotional content, such as Elizabeth of England, and adopted policies in accordance with it, were far more popular and certainly more successful than those monarchs like Charles v and Philip ii of Spain and Louis xiv of France, who adopted dynastic policies that might—and

often did—run contrary to the commercial interests of the nation. Philip ii certainly overextended his commitments in Europe at the expense of Spain, while Louis xiv's wars, though some were defensible on economic grounds, were too long and expensive to be profitable. England, on the other hand, who after the time of Elizabeth can hardly be said to have fought any wars that did not look to commercial advantage —such exceptions as the minor wars of the Stuarts go to prove the rule, since they were fought by the monarchs and left unsupported by the commercial interests and so had to be quickly liquidated—undoubtedly was assisted to her commanding economic position in the nineteenth century by the policies of governments in earlier centuries.

The policy of supporting national commercial and industrial interests by governmental means may be called mercantilism. It was a practical policy devised piecemeal to fit the needs of the particular country at at a given time. Being developed slowly, it was not based for a long time upon any definite theories. As usual in history, the theory came long after the practice had been in force. The French minister of Louis xiv, Jean Baptiste Colbert, was perhaps the clearest mercantile thinker, as he was undoubtedly the most effective of all mercantile practitioners, so much so that the developed mercantile practice is sometimes called Colbertism. So mercantilism is an abstraction derived from the actual practices of two centuries rather than a clearly thought out theory. It never disappeared altogether. Those countries which had been economically backward in the sixteenth and seventeenth centuries adopted mercantile policies in order to try to bridge the gap and foster home industries, rather than being content with exporting raw materials and receiving finished products in return. Britain and France by the end of the eighteenth century felt that the restrictions of mercantilism were more onerous to them than any advantages they might bring, and thus desired a policy of letting well alone, or laissez faire. But, just at the time when Britain and France were abandoning their mercantile policies, Prussia, hitherto economically backward, felt that she needed a mercantile policy to protect her from competition by Britain and France. In the late nineteenth century the United States, with a developing industry, likewise adopted a mercantile policy (now called economic nationalism, but substantially the same as the older mercantilism, though developed to fit the changing times). By the twentieth century it had become impossible for any country in a world of competing nationalisms to retain a laissez-faire policy and hope to survive.

The fundamental theory behind all mercantilism of the early modern period was that every national entity should strive to export more than it imported and take the difference in gold and silver. This meant that each country should try to achieve what is called a favorable balance of trade, that is, that in the total international account more money should come into the country than left it. We have already noticed that Periclean Athens was well aware of the balance of trade, though it had no theory on the matter. In the simple economy of ancient Athens the money used by Athens from the treasury of the league made up the balance in the form of invisible exports. Now in this modern world it was noticed that shipping, insurance, and other such services meant money in the hands of the country providing them, in addition to the visible exports; thus every effort was made to ensure that goods should be shipped in so far as possible in boats provided by the exporter. Navigation laws were passed to enforce restrictions of foreign shipping, entailing high port duties or even embargoes.

The "bullionist" theory

The monarchs quite naturally regarded the flow of money or bullion into their countries with pleasure, since such money could be used easily in the furtherance of national and dynastic policies and for personal expenditure. It was widely believed that the amount of bullion in a country constituted its real national wealth, contrary to the more modern theory that national productive assets are the only real wealth. It should therefore be understood that behind all the mercantile policies to be described was this so-called "bullionist" theory. But, in addition to this theory, it was also widely believed that the actual amount of foreign trade was limited. Colbert, in particular, gave clear expression to this thought. He calculated that about three quarters of the world's shipping in his day was in the hands of the Dutch, while France had a bare 3 per cent. He reasoned that the French ought to be able to capture some part of this trade. But if so, it must be at the expense of some other country, preferably the Dutch, who could most easily spare it. He did not believe, as has been generally believed since the Industrial Revolution, and more particularly since the days of Henry Ford, that the *total* world trade can be increased and that all nations will benefit from it in some degree. If the French, for instance, doubled their shipping, it would not necessarily mean that the Dutch would have to decrease theirs. Colbert's theory, of course, is not wholly wrong, and was indeed partly true for his time because production increased so slowly; prices, so often controlled by monopolies, could not decrease and, by decreasing, increase consumption. But the importance of the theory lies in the fact that it justified the trade war, it justified restrictive policies against the commerce of other nations, and it played straight into the hands of national monarchs intent on aggrandizing themselves, an aggrandizement which could only be at the expense of other countries, since it was clear that territory, if not wealth, was really limited

National monopolies of colonial trade

Mercantilism naturally took different forms according to the country in which it was practiced. The great colonial countries of Spain and Portugal practiced mercantilism in relation to their colonies. This meant that they tried to keep trade with their colonies exclusively in their own hands by whatever means were available to them. For Portugal this meant maintaining a monopoly of the Far Eastern trade, excluding the ships of all foreign nationals by force, and taking all the produce to the Portuguese port of Lisbon. It could also have meant that the Portuguese would insist on having the goods transported from Lisbon in Portuguese ships. The very intelligent Portuguese monarchy, however, which actually did the trading in the East and owned the whole monopoly itself, realized early that this was not practicable. Clearly the Portuguese had neither enough shipping nor manpower to be able to enforce such a policy. It therefore actually encouraged foreign shipping, especially Dutch, to come to Lisbon and take away the Far Eastern produce in their own boats. At one time, indeed, Portuguese were forbidden to ship it themselves. By such means the Portuguese were able to concentrate their own shipping on protecting the trade routes to the East, and conserve their slender manpower. This policy, it may be confidently asserted, alone made it possible for such a small country to hold such a vast empire for so long. And, incidentally, their adoption of a free-port policy at a time when other countries were rapidly increasing their restrictions certainly made them popular with the European shipping interests, thus perhaps prolonging a monopoly which they might not have been strong enough to defend.

Spain tried to maintain a jealous monopoly of her entire colonial trade. The monarch did not himself trade directly. Local enterprise took all the risks and was able to keep its profits so long as the crown received its stipulated fifth. But only Spanish nationals were permitted to take part in the trade, although, of course, European ingenuity was quite capable of setting up Spanish men of straw in whose name the trading could be done. For a long time immigration from any country but Spain was forbidden into the colonies. Even Spanish

Jews were usually excluded, and sometimes expelled. Nevertheless these restrictions could be circumvented, often with the connivance of the local governor. There was always the temptation to avoid the payment of the royal fifth by means of deals between local officials and foreigners. All gold and silver coming from the colonies had to be sent first to a royal commission set up in the colonies, and thereafter sent to another such commission in Spain. But there were ways of by-passing even such regulations.

It is clear, however, that in the sixteenth century Spanish restrictive policies were successfully carried out, though it is doubtful whether they were of benefit to the mother country. The Spanish navy provided adequate protection for the treasure fleets, and only stragglers could be picked off by buccaneers. Valuable as such a cargo might be for a man like Sir Francis Drake, it represented a very small proportion of the total that reached Spain. Not until well into the seventeenth century did a whole fleet fall into enemy hands, and by that time the greater part of the monetary wealth of

Late sixteenth-century engraving of Sir Francis Drake.

Spanish America had been drained off, and Spain was on the way to becoming a second-rate power. There was much smuggling and much circumvention of regulations, but it was not these that lost Spain her supremacy in Europe; overextension of her resources and an aggressive political policy based on past supremacy were the culprits, to which smuggling by foreigners was a very minor addition.

Holland as the leading commercial power

Before we reach the two chief mercantile powers attention should be drawn to Holland, which in many ways was such a great exception to the European rule of the period. In many respects the position of seventeenth-century Holland is comparable to that of nineteenth-century England. Her practices were neither more nor less ethical than those of England and France, Spain, and Portugal; but conditions were different and favored a less rather than a more restrictive policy except in special circumstances which closely parallel, indeed, the nineteenth-century circumstances of England. Holland possessed a great colonial empire, exploited fully and thoroughly by the Dutch East India Company which enjoyed a monopoly of all East Indian trade. This trade was protected by the powerful Dutch navy. And the company's policies with regard to the inhabitants of the empire were dictated entirely by commercial considerations, including wage fixing, destruction of crops to keep the prices up, and similar practices. No nonsense was tolerated in the empire. Furthermore in Europe the navy made certain that Dutch merchant ships were not molested.[3]

In addition to this natural use, the navy was also permitted to threaten and make small wars upon countries which were unable to resist (such as Denmark) for the purpose of compelling them to lower their restrictions. The Dutch did not seek for monopolies in Europe, because they did not need them; nor did they need restrictive internal policies. The reason for this was that the Dutch, alone of the great European powers, were thoroughly efficient for their day, and in a free competitive field they needed to fear no one. Their ships were the cheapest and most suitable for their task of any in Europe. Built for commercial purposes only, and hardly armed at all (since they were protected by the Dutch navy), the Dutch *fluitschip* was not only sold to other European countries freely but it was sold at a far lower price than that for which the foreign countries could build theirs, even with governmental help. The Dutch had specialized in this type of boat. They imported the necessary materials (in their own ships) and then assembled them into these simple ships by a method very closely approaching that of modern mass production.

The result was that Dutch freight rates were so low that every country in Europe was undersold, and any individual shippers who had the choice would naturally have used the Dutch merchant marine for the purpose. Restrictions against shipping in foreign bottoms could therefore only be enforced with great difficulty. The Dutch of this period had few natural resources of their own; but to compensate for this they made full use of all the raw materials they could import, even on some occasions founding a new industry in competition with the industry of some other country which itself produced the raw material. Such was the case with the Dutch silk industry, which for a time successfully competed with European producers of silk, although it was dependent upon Chinese imports of raw silk to keep its looms busy. The only thing that could prevent Dutch products from making headway in Europe was the artificial restriction placed on their

[3] It is worth noting that the Dutch navy should not be thought of as similar to modern navies, controlled effectively by national governments. The Dutch *stadholder* had difficulty in controlling it; it was, even at best, five semi-independent navies: and armed merchantmen on many occasions performed the tasks ascribed here to the "Dutch navy." Functionally these ships were the Dutch navy; but not necessarily organizationally.

Dutch warships of the midseventeenth century, from an oil painting en gri-saille *by William Van der Velde, who sailed with the Dutch fleet as official painter to record its stirring deeds for posterity.*

commerce by other nations in the form of tariffs, embargoes, navigation laws, and the like. Other nations tried to entice skilled Dutch workers away from Holland to teach them the tricks of their various trades. The Dutch complained, but did not take action. For a long time Holland herself attracted all the persecuted Protestants in Europe, political exiles from absolutist governments, and large numbers of Jews who were not accepted elsewhere and who, if accepted, possessed no rights. The Dutch gave them civil rights, and the Jews responded by greatly increasing the commercial suprem-acy of their adopted country. So Holland, for whatever reasons, prospered greatly even in a mercantile world until toward the end of the seventeenth century she was faced by too much power allied against her, and ultimately by too much competition in the very fields in which she had excelled. Then at last her lack of natural resources told against her, and that lack was decisive. Although her commercial power was never altogether lost, and today she still lives by her industry and commerce, the command-ing position in Europe that she possessed for a short time could never be regained. The palm had passed to the larger coun-tries, England and France.

The Tudor mercantile monarchy in England

Henry VII (1485–1509) has been called the first mercantile king. There can be little doubt that he belonged to the modern age and that above all he understood the value and power of money. He will be further dealt with, from a political point of view, in Chapter 19. Knowing that his power rested upon the support of the rising bour-geoisie he was careful to cater to their interests whenever he could. Early in his reign, for instance, he had two navigation laws passed, forbidding the use of foreign shipping to import French wines and dyes. Henry also sold monopolies widely, mainly because for him there was quick money to be obtained thereby. The monopolies were intended at least as much for the purpose of gaining him some quick money as for any new business that would accrue. The time was too early for a fully fledged mercantile policy. Yet in one field in particular all the English monarchs were interested, and here the monarchy could assist in preventing money from leaving the country unnecessarily. This was the wool trade, for many centuries the staple English industry. The raw material was produced in England, and in medieval times it had been customary to export it as raw wool. But it was also always possible to process the wool before exporting it. Any or all of the many processes in making finished cloth could be carried out at home. And the more manufacturing processes were completed in England, the more money would be kept in the homeland and the less sent abroad. The Tudors were very conscious of the fact that money ought to be kept at home and early they forbade the export of bullion, and placed many restrictions on the export of raw wool and semifinished cloth. When the bourgeoisie reached the seats of power in the mid-seventeenth century raw wool export was prohibited altogether.

The fact that there was a Parliament in England which controlled the purse strings, and could even keep the crown in order and limit its power, ensured that a policy for the benefit of the bourgeoisie would always receive a hearing, and usually win the day even against the crown. Elizabeth had to receive numerous petitions asking that she refrain from granting monopolies which restrained competition. Ultimately the British made definite rules as to what did constitute a monopoly, which became the basis for patent laws in England and elsewhere. Only products which were the result of real invention could be permitted to be exploited by monopolies. Throughout Tudor times the monopoly was used mainly for the purpose of exploration and exploitation of trade with certain areas. When the Stuarts tried to sell new monopolies they were transparently a money-making device for the crown, and were abolished as soon as Parliament had limited the power of the crown.

It was not until the mid-seventeenth century that the English became thoroughgoing mercantilists. By this time they had colonies for which trade policies had to be

The wharf of the German merchants in London in 1641, from an engraving by William Hollar.

devised, inhabited, for the first time, by Europeans rather than merely ruled by Europeans. At this time also the Dutch were very severe competitors whom the English felt they were strong enough to dispossess. So grew up the special colonial policies, the development of which in the following century did so much to embitter relations with the colonies and ultimately to help bring about their independence. But at first the policies, embodied in the navigation laws of Cromwell (1651) and Charles II (1660) bore hard upon foreigners but not upon the colonies themselves, which gained many useful favors from them. They were based upon the understanding that England provided an entrepôt for goods brought from all over the world and reshipped to foreign countries. The profits from this import and export business were small for each individual shipment, but very large in total. From a commercial point of view they constituted a most important invisible export, as did, of course, the profits from shipping itself. So the colonials were permitted to send goods to England only in ships that were either of English or colonial origin, and they were not permitted to sell anywhere else than in England or the colonies.

This blow of course was directed against the Dutch, whose ships were everywhere and played an energetic part in winning new trade with the American colonies. The result was large-scale smuggling, using the Dutch West Indian islands as a base, and the navigation laws could not be fully enforced. Later, tariffs were also placed upon foreign goods, from which the colonial goods were exempted. Thus already there was a kind of imperial preference long before the idea cropped up in late nineteenth-century conferences. No doubt these navigation laws, where they were enforceable, did have some restrictive effect, even in the colonies. But the colonies could evade them, when worth while, without too much difficulty, while the preferred market in England was a reality. It may be added that, contrary to Dutch policy, which was to hire seamen wherever they could be found ready to work for the wages offered, the English navigation laws insisted that only British seamen could command and serve in British ships. In that age, unlike ours, the wages paid were not thereby materially increased, but at least some money was kept at home that might have been spent abroad.

During the late seventeenth and eighteenth centuries England also engaged in an orgy of tariff making. This was not primarily her fault, as it was precipitated by the policies of Colbert in France, whose manufactures, so effectively supported by him, needed at least the home market to themselves. When Colbert issued his tariff in 1667, England naturally retaliated, greatly damaging trade relations with France for a century. Not until it was fully realized how damaging tariffs were to the country whose trade was most efficient were they repealed.

The culmination of mercantile theory and practice in France—Colbertism

French industry, as has been indicated above, was greatly hampered by medieval feudal rights and by a centralizing process which had left many traditional rights substantially unimpaired. Moreover, it had been the customary practice to create monopolies for tax purposes which prevented competition, while the king had no better method of collecting many of his taxes than by setting up internal custom stations in the hands of private enterprise, which had bought the customs duties from the crown. Such arrangements greatly hampered the free flow of commerce in France; nevertheless, France was such a potentially rich country and owned such large and varied resources that there was always a considerable industry, and though the price of the goods exported was necessarily high, they were sold as long as the quality remained high enough. Thus we find that most of the mercantile regulations of the sixteenth century were directed toward ensuring the high quality of French

A seventeenth-century Gobelins silk and wool tapestry showing the coats of arms of France and Navarre, joined when the Bourbon family inherited the throne. (COURTESY THE METROPOLITAN MUSEUM OF ART)

products, a policy to be followed later by Colbert. The kings of the earlier period, very well aware of the possibility of extracting taxes from the bourgeoisie, were highly favorable to industry, and encouraged the founding of new industry, whereas foreign trade did not attract so much of their attention. In the "bullionist" period efforts were made to prevent gold from leaving the country, and even from being sunk into such unproductive items as clothes and jewelry.

When the monarchy was once more established firmly in the hands of the capable Bourbon monarch Henry IV (1589–1610), serious efforts were made to encourage new industry of all kinds, especially luxury products. During his reign the Gobelins tapestry manufacture was converted into an actual state concern. Leading bourgeois were consulted on what industries were needed and what governmental support would be required. Unfortunately for France, in the following reigns so many wars were engaged in that the government had little time and energy to devote to commercial problems. Richelieu, minister under Louis XIII, supported foreign trade by the creation of great companies armed with monopolies, especially for the Canadian fur trade. When Colbert was appointed minister to Louis XIV in 1661, this support was substantial. France was then far behind her competitors in every field, while still remaining potentially the greatest manufacturing country in Europe, and well able to gain a large share of shipping and foreign trade. For twenty-two years Colbert labored to correct this position, and if all his efforts did not meet with equal success, there can be little doubt that he was the real founder of French greatness in the second half of the seventeenth and all of the eighteenth century. And he is always regarded as the mercantilist par excellence.

Colbert's improvement of the French financial system, the partial abolition of internal tariffs, the improved methods of collecting taxes, and the general administrative reforms which allowed Louis XIV to become the greatest monarch in Europe, *Le Roi Soleil*, lie outside the scope of this chapter, in which we are concerned with his mercantile policies. Theorist as well as practical man, Colbert accepted the bullionist theory and was willing to pursue the policies which sprang from it. Recognizing that gold and silver must be brought into the country by some means or another, and the time having long passed when it could be merely stolen, he set to work to improve the French balance of trade—which, as we have seen, must be at the expense of other countries. This necessitated a strong commercial policy, the fostering of industry to provide goods for export, the forcing of these goods into foreign markets, and preventing of unnecessary imports. In addition, as many invisible exports as possible should be won from the entrenched competitors.

Indefatigably he searched for new industries. Anything that could be manufactured elsewhere could certainly be manufactured in France. Only finance was necessary and this could come from the royal purse, which could also attract into France skilled foreign workers. The final products of such industry must also be inspected to see that they conformed to definite standards, as this was essential when no previous supply of good will for French manufactures had been gained. Since not too many workers could be spared from agriculture France must strive to increase her birth rate by giving bounties to large families. When the goods were finally produced, encouragement then must be given to export them, rather than consume them at home—hence export bounties on certain kinds of exports which were competitive in quality but could not sell on quality alone. Finally, to protect home industries and prevent money from leaving the country, there were the famous tariffs, very highly selective, against just those goods that could be manufactured in France.

Goods being now available for export, Colbert used every device to ensure that they should be shipped in the French merchant marine, when one that was worthy of the name should come into existence. Thus he subsidized shipbuilding, and was not too proud to import ships built abroad, though careful to make his subsidies such that they encouraged both processes, without favoring the foreigner so much that no ships would be built at home. He tried to build up a corps of French seamen and prevent them from serving on foreign ships. He taxed all foreign ships entering French ports. Finally, to protect the merchant fleet, he built a navy, which by the end of the century was to be the equal of any in Europe and succeeded in defeating a combined English and Dutch fleet in 1690.

It was fortunate that Colbert was dead when his master Louis XIV, uninterested in the furthering of Colbert's work, which he probably understood only in so far as it provided him with money for wars and the palace of Versailles, revoked the Edict of Nantes, to be described in Chapter 21. This caused the emigration of many thousands of the best artisans in France and the partial ruin of much of the industry which had been so carefully fostered. But most of the rest of Colbert's work remained; and though there are many flaws to be found in it (the dependence of industry upon government aid was to hamper France when it entered the industrial age), it must be said that Colbert exploited to the full the administrative structure that he had inherited. Since all power in France was centered in the monarchy it was only natural that the monarchy should also undertake the support of the trade and industry which provided the sinews for its power. In England the bourgeoisie controlled the government, legislated in its own interests, and it needed no Colbert. In France, where control and legislation were different, perhaps a clearsighted and indefatigable bureaucrat was the only possible substitute.

SUMMARY—HOW FAR WAS THE
COMMERCIAL REVOLUTION REVOLUTIONARY?

The age of exploration and the commercial revolution ushered Europe into the modern age. Though tendencies to be observed already during the Middle Ages came to fruition only in the early modern period, and nothing came into existence that was truly new, the great increase in international commerce and the slower but still substantial increase in manufacture combined to provide an atmosphere in which the machine could be utilized to save labor and produce new goods for consumption. If great inventions such as the steam engine had occurred in the Middle Ages, no possibility would have existed for their proper utilization. In a semifeudal structure, with towns small and rigidly controlled by conservative forces, the goods produced by the machine could neither have been made efficiently nor distributed widely enough to pay for the large capital involved in installing it. Nor, indeed, was

there sufficient accumulation of capital. All these things were provided during the early modern period, and their provision perhaps justifies the name of revolution— as long as we remember that it was an intensification of existing processes, that it only slowly altered society without in any way overthrowing it, and that the real revolution which involved the machine and its full utilization was yet to come, and may be with us for many hundred years yet.

▶ Suggestions for further reading

Two very solid books on the economic history of Europe have already been recommended in the suggestions which follow Chapter 14; Herbert Heaton, *Economic History of Europe* (rev. ed., New York: Harper & Brothers, 1948), and S. B. Clough and C. W. Cole, *Economic History of Europe* (rev. ed., Boston: D. C. Heath and Company, 1947). Heaton's interpretations are very well thought out and easily comprehensible to the student, while Clough and Cole is rather more informative and contains a great deal of information not easily acquired elsewhere. There is also a short Berkshire Study of considerable merit, Lawrence B. Packard, *The Commercial Revolution, 1400– 1776* (New York: Henry Holt and Company, 1927), which explains briefly and clearly the nature of the commercial revolution, and especially the developed mercantilism of the time of Colbert. A specialized but extremely useful study is Earl J. Hamilton, *American Treasure and the Price Revolution in Spain* (Cambridge, Mass.: Harvard University Press, 1934), which provides the raw material on the movement of prices as a consequence of the discoveries, on which all subsequent work in this field has been based.

A readable and extremely effective synthesis on the rise of modern capitalism is provided in Henri Sée, *Modern Capitalism, Its Origin and Evolution* (London: Noel Douglas, 1928). There is a good deal of argument in the book since Sée is presenting a thesis and explanation, but it is very clear and well presented. The book is especially strong on France, usually somewhat neglected in economic studies. Eli F. Heckscher, *Mercantilism* (2 vols., rev. edit., London: George Allen & Unwin, Ltd., 1955) by a Swedish historian, is a very full and scholarly account of mercantilism in all its phases. It is both theoretical and full of information. The author treats of mercantilism in all its phases, bringing the subject up to modern times under such stimulating headings as "Mercantilism as a system of power," and "Mercantilism as a conception of society." It is, however, rather an advanced work for the beginning student, though it is clearly enough written to be comprehensible to anyone who is seriously interested and will take the necessary trouble.

For the Age of Discovery, the best and most reliable as well as the most colorful, primary source for the expedition of Cortes, unique in its field, written by one of his followers, Bernal Diaz del Castillo, is *The Discovery and Conquest of Mexico* (New York: Farrar, Straus and Cudahy, Inc., 1956), translated excellently by A. P. Maudslay. If the reader is interested in the Norse voyages to America before the time of Columbus, he is referred to the book by Holand, mentioned in a footnote in the chapter. Samuel E. Morison's rather specialized work *Portuguese Voyages to America in the Fifteenth Century* (Cambridge, Mass.: Harvard University Press, 1940) which concludes against Portuguese priority, largely on the basis of voyages made by the author himself, still holds the field in this country, and will probably do so until better concrete evidence has been produced than is so far available. Professor Morison also wrote a fine study of Columbus, *Admiral of the Ocean Sea: a Life of Christopher Columbus* (2 vols., Boston: Little, Brown & Company, 1942). The classic William H. Prescott, *History of the Conquest of Mexico and History of the Conquest of Peru* (New York: The Modern Library, 1936) is now seriously out of date in view of later research, but it is still worth reading as one of the finest examples of nineteenth-century American historiography, and a pioneer work in its field.

Out of a long list of books concerned with the settling of Latin America, I recommend as the best I know for its fairness, comprehensiveness, its mastery of significant detail and its broad epic sweep, the whole combined with beautiful writing and considerable understanding and sympathy, John A. Crow, *The Epic of Latin America* (New York: Doubleday and Co., Inc., 1952). The book is free from the moralistic tinge too common in books about the Latin conquests, and it is especially good on the part played by the missionaries of the religious orders; it also explains clearly the nature of Spanish and Portuguese colonization, and wherein it differs from the colonization of North America. The book, however, does not always seem to make clear what is going on in the mother country. It is thus slightly uneven, though the value of the whole is scarcely marred thereby. A fairly brief but clear and well-organized book on explorations in North America is John B. Brebner, *The Explorers of North America, 1492–1806* (New York: The Macmillan Company, 1923). Brebner offers some information about each explorer of note, and by treating the North American continent as a whole he is able to suggest something of the sweep of the colonization movement. A much larger work, well written and interesting, and containing a great deal of information about a relatively little known phase of exploration, is George M. Wrong, *The Rise and Fall of New France* (2 vols., New York: The Macmillan Company, 1928).

If the student is interested in any of the other explorers, there are numerous biographies of the more important ones, none of which will be specially recommended here. The lives of these men were so interesting that if the student has acquired a suitable framework from some of the books suggested above, whichever he chooses he is not likely to go far astray.

18

The Revolt against Medieval Christianity— Reformation and Counter Reformation

The Church at the beginning of the sixteenth century • The Lutheran Reformation • The religious Peace of Augsburg • Calvinism: General characteristics • Influence of Calvinist doctrines • The Reformation in England • Establishment of a national Church • The Catholic Reformation • The Council of Trent • Foundation of the Society of Jesus • Summary: Consequences of the Reformation

---

▶ The Church at the beginning of the sixteenth century

THE PAPACY AS A POLITICAL POWER

We have already had occasion in Chapter 12 to notice the decline of the medieval Church: the difficulties it experienced in dealing with the rising national states, the recrudescence of heresy in the fourteenth and fifteenth centuries—never fully suppressed, not for the Church's lack of will but for its lack of power—and the efforts of secular rulers and foreign prelates to divide the concentrated power of the papacy through the Conciliar Movement. In Chapter 16 we saw the impact of the Renaissance on the Church, its increasing worldliness, and the tendency of the popes to act like Italian secular princes. We saw also the growing demand for reform voiced by the more serious humanists, especially in Germany and France.

At the beginning of the sixteenth century the papacy was still supreme, and Roman Catholic Christianity was still the only form of Christian worship in western Europe. But defense against reformers and heretics had become increasingly difficult in the fifteenth century. The Church, in the eyes of so many observers, was obviously in need of reform, and yet no pope hitherto had arisen who was willing to undertake it, or even seemed to realize the need for it. When Bishop Briçonnet and Lefèvre d'Etaples at Meaux had preached reform in mild and far from inflammatory terms, Lefèvre had been forced to flee and Briçonnet to retract. The Dominican friar Savonarola in Florence had preached with fiery eloquence a puritan gospel. The people had followed him and a revolution had broken out in the city. For a few years Savonarola had been supreme and the city had been purged. But in the end Pope Alexander VI had excommunicated him, and the people, in expectation of a miracle from him which he had refused to attempt, turned away from him. So the papal victory had proved easy after all. Savonarola had been hanged and his body burned (1498), and no one in Rome seemed to think that his movement had been significant. The old policy of suppressing opposition rather than instituting reform was still maintained in a century in which papal power over Christendom no longer depended solely on papal will but on favorable political factors.

Such political factors had hitherto favored the papacy. The policy of sharing Church monies and appointments with secular rulers seemed to have solved the problem of relations with the great European monarchies. After all, Charles VIII's invasion of Italy had done no apparent damage; he had entered Rome, and there was momentary danger; but he had departed peaceably. The year before Luther nailed his ninety-five theses to the church door at Wittenberg a treaty had been signed with Francis I of France (Concordat of Bologna, 1516) under which France had an almost independent Church, with the king head in everything but title. Though the terms were onerous for the papacy, they did at least ensure royal support. To offset its loss of some foreign funds, the Renaissance papacy had set itself to exploit more efficiently its lands in Italy. No pope seems to have imagined that the demand for reform would one day become overwhelming, or that some day secular rulers would arise who would not come to terms and would not be satisfied with a division of the spoils—that heresies which, with secular support, had hitherto always been safely suppressed might one day find themselves supported and not suppressed, favored instead of being exterminated.

DECLINE OF CHURCH IN POPULAR ESTEEM

The weaknesses of a power based on spiritual, not political, sanctions have already been explored in connection with the medieval papacy. But the medieval papacy was able to vanquish the secular powers of the day precisely because it was able from its abundant resources to enlist the services of dedicated reformers (the Franciscans and Dominicans), who enabled it to recover from its political excesses, and because the papacy had not as yet fallen into moral decay. More-

over, in the thirteenth century the idea of a universal religion and a universal empire was still dominant in the minds of men; heretics were everywhere thought to be treasonous to Church and state alike—they were rending the seamless robe of Christ. Now in the sixteenth century the empire was a ghostly relic, national states and minor princes had divided its inheritance, popes had sojourned in France; at one time there had been three papal contenders at the same time, and all three had been deposed by a council. Though there was now one pope in Rome, the papal prestige had grievously decayed. And since the Church was obviously not entitled to the allegiance of Christendom for the moral example it set, it was not surprising that to some earnest souls it appeared to have outgrown its usefulness. Luther in 1517 had no idea of throwing off allegiance to Rome, still less of forming a separate schismatic Church; nevertheless by 1520 it had become clear to him that the Roman Church performed no useful function. An institution that had existed for fifteen hundred years, founded by Christ himself, had suddenly been revealed to him as decadent beyond repair.

▶ The Lutheran reformation

KEY ROLE OF MARTIN LUTHER

The enormity of his thought was probably never fully appreciated by Luther himself. But in the religious strife of the sixteenth century it seems clear that a majority of those who fought on the Catholic side, often fought against their own material interests, as in the case of the southern provinces of the Netherlands. In the early years, at least, they fought not for the theology of the Church which they did not understand, nor for the visible Church as they saw it represented by its clergy—certainly not for its Medici popes—but for the unity of Christendom being destroyed by the Protestants. It was the venerable institution which they had always looked upon as their Mother to which they gave their allegiance, not because it was moral or righteous but because it was familiar. Only with the Council of Trent,

► chronological chart

Council of Constance	1414–1417	Execution of Sir Thomas More	1535
Hussite Wars	1420–1433	Death of Erasmus	1536
Council of Basel	1431–1439	*Institutes of the Christian Religion* by	
Establishment of Spanish Inquisition	1478	Calvin	1536
Alexander vi, pope	1492–1503	Dissolution of English monasteries	1536–1539
Foundation of Oratory of Divine Love	1497	Establishment of Protestant Church in	
Execution of Savonarola	1498	Denmark	1536
In Praise of Folly by Erasmus	1509	Promulgation of Six Articles by	
Leo x, pope	1513–1521	Henry viii	1539
Concordat of Bologna between		Papal recognition of Society of Jesus	1540
Francis i and Papacy	1516	Return of Calvin and Farel to Geneva	1541
Publication of new Greek edition of		Persecution of French Protestants by	
New Testament by Erasmus	1516	Francis i	1545
Indulgence mission of Tetzel in		Council of Trent	1545–1563
Germany	1516	Death of Luther	1546
Ninety-five Theses of Luther	1517	Schmalkaldic War	1546–1547
Reign of Charles v, Holy Roman		Reign of Edward vi of England	1547–1553
Emperor	1519–1556	First English Book of Common Prayer	1549
Beginning of work of Zwingli in Zurich	1519	Julius iii, pope	1550–1555
Excommunication of Luther by Pope		Reign of Mary i of England	1553–1558
Leo x	1520	Paul iv, pope: reform of Roman Curia	1555–1559
Pope grants Henry viii of England		Religious Peace of Augsburg	1555
title "Defender of the Faith"	1521	Martyrdom of Thomas Cranmer,	
Conversion of Ignatius Loyola	1521	Archbishop of Canterbury	1556
Condemnation by Sorbonne of work		Establishment of the Index	1557
of Lefèvre d'Etaples	1521	Death of Calvin	1559
Defiance of Charles v by Luther at		Return of John Knox to Scotland	1559
Diet of Worms	1521	Pius iv, pope	1559–1565
Translation of Bible into French by		Return of Mary Queen of Scots to	
Lefèvre d'Etaples	1523–1530	Scotland	1561
Peasants' War in Germany	1524–1525	Establishment of Anglican Church in	
Foundation of Theatine Order	1524	England	1563
Foundation of Capuchin Order	1525–1528	Duke of Alva appointed governor of	
National Protestant Church established		Netherlands	1567
in Sweden	1527	Escape of Mary Queen of Scots to	
Second Diet of Speyer: prohibition of		England	1568
spread of Lutheranism	1529	Excommunication of Queen Elizabeth	1570
Death of Zwingli in battle of Kappel	1531	Massacre of St. Bartholomew	1572
Marriage of Henry viii of England to		Pacification of Ghent	1576
Anne Boleyn	1533	Jesuit mission to England	1580
Organization of Society of Jesus by		Declaration of independence from	
Ignatius Loyola	1534	Spain by United Provinces	1581
Act of Supremacy (Henry viii)	1534	Execution of Mary Queen of Scots	1587
Paul iii, pope	1534–1549	Edict of Nantes	1598
Anabaptist theocracy at Münster	1534–1535		

and the real and lasting reform of the Church and the clarification of its teachings, did it become possible to reconvert as individuals those who had taken the individualistic path with the Protestants and fallen away.

When Luther first attacked the Church for its sale of indulgences he was not worried about the money thus lost to Germany, nor did he care about the political activity of the papacy. Though he accepted the support of the princes, who did care about these things, and thus was enabled to succeed in his movement where his predecessors had failed, he was no politician, but merely a religious man who could not conceive how a soul could be spared the pains of purgatory by the purchase of an indulgence. From his own experience he drew his belief that man cannot be saved by his own deeds; he can be "justified" only by faith and saved by God's mercy. Already in 1520 he was declaring that every man is his own priest. Why, then, all the paraphernalia of a great Church which claimed that its sacraments were necessary to salvation? He had visited Rome and seen the lack of morality among the higher clergy at the Curia. Disgusted he may have been, but it was not disgust that led him to schism, nor even the need for reform. Erasmus had been disgusted too, and many others.

Luther was led to repudiate the authority of the Church; he did not repudiate authority as such. No one was more willing than he to accept the authority of secular princes in the secular realm. He did not even object to a national Church. But from one conviction he never wavered, and never could waver. Salvation was a gift of God's mercy, and it was personal to each individual man. No other man, much less an institution or its sacraments or rituals, could cleanse any man from his sins. Thus in their essence the ideas of Luther were profoundly individualistic, and it was to individuals in that age that they made their appeal. However medieval in his outlook in so many ways, however far from the enlightened humanism of an Erasmus or a Montaigne and the indi-

vidualism cultivated in the Italian Renaissance, in this one respect he joins them. And Calvin, however much in some respects he diverged from Luther's teachings, and however different his emphasis, in this matter was at one with Luther. Only God could save, as the Catholics would have agreed; but that the Church has no part in the process, either to save or to destroy—and such a belief, if held everywhere, must destroy the Catholic Church—to this belief Luther and Calvin held equally. This fact should never be forgotten, if the inner logic of the process of separation from the Catholic Church which is variously called the Protestant Revolt or the Protestant Reformation is to be grasped.

CONDITIONS IN SIXTEENTH-CENTURY GERMANY FAVORING SUCCESS OF LUTHERAN REFORM

Economic and social conditions— Decline of German prosperity

Only very brief mention was made of Germany in the previous chapter. We have seen in Chapter 15 how Germany failed to become a national state in the Middle Ages, and we shall give an account, in Chapter 19, of the political conditions in Germany that prevented the establishment of a single national state until the nineteenth century. It will be recalled that the shifting of the center of trade to the Atlantic gradually ruined the prosperity of most German cities, especially those which had been dependent upon the trade over the Alps. Since they were unable to establish control over the Baltic Sea and could not reach the Atlantic with their ships, the Hanseatic towns declined slowly for lack of overseas trade.

Outside the towns feudal conditions reigned. The Holy Roman emperor might sometimes be powerful if he happened to control lands outside Germany as well as his native Austria. Otherwise he was only one of many German princes, most of them simple feudal lords who acknowledged a theoretical allegiance to the emperor as suzerain, but were in fact independent. Thus they were able to defy the emperor and refuse to obey either his decrees or the decrees of the imperial diet in which they were represented. The elector Frederic the Wise of Saxony, who constituted himself the protector of Luther, could not be compelled to give up his prisoner except by force; and against imperial force it was always possible to muster allies who objected to the emperor's exercising his theoretical rights. Moreover, the German princes, though proud of their independence, were usually weak, both financially and militarily, since they had too few resources to draw upon. So they looked with extreme disfavor upon the loss of their hard-earned money into the coffers of a foreign power like the papacy, whence it would never return to be spent in Germany.

Opposition of German rulers to papal exactions

The Church extracted money from the faithful in many different ways, and the bulk of the money thus taken found its way over the Alps to Italy, where the popes were in constant need of it for their building programs, especially the building of St. Peter's. In all Europe the Church owned land that was free from taxation by the secular powers, and it claimed ecclesiastical jurisdiction for many offenses that the secular powers felt by right belonged to them. Clergymen were usually not subject to lay courts even for crimes that were civil in nature. All cases heard outside the country naturally cost money which was left in Rome. Income from Church benefices belonged partly to the papacy, the first year's total income (*annates*) belonged wholly to the pope. As if this were not enough, there was a regular scale of charges for various services which could be performed only by the pope, such as the granting of permission to marry within the canonically prohibited degrees. Further charges were made by the local clergy for administering church rites; and though the money for these might at least have been expected to remain in the country, in fact it often did not, since the pope might have

sold the Church office in the first place to the incumbent, and in that case he would have to pay out of the proceeds of his incumbency; thus that money too left the country. Finally there were direct sales to the people, such as the indulgences which, being voluntary in nature, the princes could forbid only at the cost of a quarrel with the clergy.

Germany was in a worse position with regard to Church exactions than the powerful national states which had already, as we have seen, made private arrangements with the papacy to share the spoils. Small German princelings often did not carry much authority within their own states except over their feudal underlings. The great international Church was too big an opponent to tackle. Thus their grievances, frequently presented to the emperor at the diets but rarely heeded by him, were many and serious, and only by acting in unison could they hope to achieve much against the strongly entrenched Church. Such an opportunity, when it was presented in the form of Luther's defiance of the pope on religious grounds, was too good to miss; and when the Lutheran movement finally made possible the control of the religion of each state by its prince, with everything that had been in the hands of the Church now in their own, it is not surprising that they resisted forcibly all attempts to bring them and their subjects back into the Catholic fold.

THE IGNITING SPARK—THE INDULGENCES

The spark that ignited the dry tinder was provided by the entry into Germany of a supersalesman of indulgences named Tetzel, a Dominican friar. The archbishop of Mainz, the chief cleric of Germany, one Albert of Brandenburg, had recently bought his position from the papacy for 30,000 ducats, but was unable to find any ready money within his archdiocese, since it was already heavily in debt. He had borrowed the 30,000 ducats from the banking house of Fugger in Augsburg, which was pressing for payment. So he appealed to the pope for help and the latter obliged, for a further consideration of 10,000 ducats, with Tetzel and his indulgences. As stated earlier, an indulgence was granted only after confession and absolution, and without them was inefficacious. Moreover, the sum of money which obtained the indulgence was in the nature of a penalty for the sin committed, and the indulgence therefore was not, strictly speaking, bought. But the custom had grown up of permitting indulgences to be bought for the dead, so that they might escape the pains of purgatory. Church teachings on purgatory, however, were probably little understood at the time, and in the popular mind no doubt release from purgatory was often confused with salvation. It does not therefore require much imagination to see what could be done with the sale of indulgences by a man like Tetzel. It was said that as soon as the money tinkled in the box one more soul would fly out of purgatory, and it was no doubt hinted that salvation itself could be bought by these means instead of merely the lessening of the time spent in purgatory *if* the soul had already been saved. At all events Tetzel did a thriving business, and though the elector of Saxony forbade the sale of indulgences within his dominions, the faithful of Wittenberg did not have far to go before they were out of his territories and close to the precious "pardons" purveyed by the Dominican.

Now we have seen briefly what Luther thought of salvation, and with what earnest strivings he thought it was to be attained. He was himself very uncertain about purgatory, and thought it doubtful, even if there were such a place, as taught, that the Church knew very much about it or how souls were able to escape its sufferings. What he did know, and that quite for certain, was that the human soul is saved only by God's mercy, and this would necessarily apply to release from the pains of purgatory also. So he composed his famous ninety-five theses, and nailed them up on the church door in Wittenberg where he taught at the newly opened university. He had expected to find opponents ready to refute him and his theses, and he welcomed the chance for a public

disputation on the matter of indulgences. But the furor that greeted his act was altogether beyond what he had imagined. He was suddenly a German hero who had given utterance to what anticlericals of all kinds had been thinking. Repercussions from his provocative act swept him into the leadership of a movement that he had not planned but for which, as it happened, he was the ideal leader.

MARTIN LUTHER—PERSONALITY AND TEACHINGS

It has been suggested already that the key to the understanding of Luther's teachings is to be found in his personality. He was not in any way a profound thinker nor a systematic theologian. The nearest approach to a clear exposition of his theology is to be found in a book called *The Bondage of the Will,* which he was stung into writing by Erasmus, who had explained in a very cogent manner why he thought that God had given free will to man as a gift of his divine grace, and thus that all human works could be good and valued as such by God. To which Luther replied that he would not even wish for free will to be given man, since in this case his own acts would contribute to his salvation, a position he could not accept. Man is utterly wicked; he is saved only by God's mercy. If he does good, it is due to the active working of God within him, and the deeds are thus indirectly performed by God.[1]

Luther's thought was not unconnected with that of his predecessors. These predecessors, however, if one excepts St. Augustine, were not the theologians but the mystics, Tauler and Suso, Eckhart and Ruysbroeck, and others mentioned in Chapter 12. Luther had read their works, and his writing speaks of the comfort some of them had given him in his spiritual struggles. These men in their day had remained within the fold of the Catholic Church, although for their attempts to approach God directly through inner experience it was clear no Church was needed.

[1] See especially Harbison's chapter entitled "Protestant and Catholic," in K. Setton and H. Winkler, ed., *Great Problems in European Civilization* (New York: Prentice-Hall, 1954), pp. 262–265.

But their obvious piety and saintliness could not be denied, and since they caused no trouble to the Church and did not attack it, they could be tolerated and even accepted in spite of the potential danger of their approach. If Luther had been born earlier, and conditions had not driven him into attacks on the Church, he would probably have lived and died an earnest monk seeking his own salvation in his own way and disturbing no one else.

Luther has given us an intimate account of his struggles. He felt convinced of his own sin, and of being utterly unworthy of salvation. None of the aids offered him by the Church could convince him that he was saved. "I was a pious monk," he tells us, "and if ever a monk got to heaven by his monkery, I should certainly have got there. . . . If I had kept on any longer I should have killed myself with vigils, prayers, reading and other work."[2] Not knowing why these things could not help him, his mind ever at work trying to understand, and reading over and over again the epistles of St. Paul, especially the epistle to the Romans, suddenly he had an experience as if he had "entered Paradise through wide open gates," and understood that if in the fullness of faith one casts oneself upon God's mercy, then that mercy is granted and one is saved and healed. It was this faith that had wrought the miracle, and so the idea of "justification by faith" was born. The teaching was to be found in St. Paul, but not with the emphasis that Luther gave to it, to the exclusion of St. Paul's many other teachings on the matter of salvation and how it is attained.

Generalizing therefore from his own experience, Luther concluded that the individual soul is personally saved by God's mercy; if it earnestly seeks to understand, then light will be vouchsafed by God. So to the followers of Luther the Bible contains all the teachings necessary for understanding. The primary duty of the Christian is to study it, and not the later teachings of the fathers of the Church and of the theologians who were

[2] Setton and Winkler, *op. cit.*, p. 251.

but men and did not have the divine inspiration of the Bible. Still less could a pope be permitted to interpret the Scriptures with a binding authority on Christians. It is not surprising, therefore, that as soon as Luther had the time and leisure to undertake the task while in protective custody in the castle of Wartburg, he should have undertaken the translation of the Bible into German, the first great masterpiece in the German tongue.

With an inexorable logic Luther was driven to criticize those other parts of the Church teachings which conflicted with his personal convictions. Having taken the lead, and being a man of the utmost firmness where his convictions were concerned, he remained at the head of the revolt he had started. In all the work of his life we find no effort to temporize; even those acts for which he has been condemned by posterity —his lack of sympathy with the Anabaptists and his antagonism toward the peasant revolts—are entirely consistent with his character and convictions. He was a staunch supporter of the secular power within its own realm and he had the utmost respect for its authority. He was no anarchist, like the early Anabaptists, nor was he in any way sympathetic with democracy. He believed in the necessity for a Church to help bring men to salvation and to express the bond among Christians in common worship, so that, as might be expected, in Lutheran churches emphasis was always given to teaching and congregational singing. He did not accept the possibility of the miraculous transubstantiation of the bread and wine in the Eucharist into the body and blood of Christ by the agency of the officiating priest, but on Biblical authority he was willing to accept the fact of a change by which the body and blood of Christ *join with* the bread and wine (consubstantiation). Again this is a direct intervention of God, and is in no sense a "sacrifice" as in the Roman transubstantiation. The sacraments are in no way efficacious for salvation, but serve to unite Christians in a mystical bond, Christ present with them, as Christ himself taught in saying that "where two or three are gathered together in my name I am in the midst of them."

THE PROGRESS OF THE LUTHERAN REVOLT

Appeal of Luther for princely support

In 1517 Luther posted his theses on the door of the Wittenberg church. They were at the same time printed and sent round to friends in other cities, and distributed there. So widely were they read that the sale of indulgences dropped off alarmingly, and the pope himself took cognizance of the matter, demanding that Luther be investigated by his order and made to retract. This he refused to do, and instead published a sermon in which he emphasized his points more strongly than before. An imperial diet summoned for 1518 took up the matter of Luther, and the cardinal-legate present demanded that Luther be sent to Rome for trial. This demand the emperor refused, since it was contrary to his policy to allow German cases to be tried at Rome. So he called upon Luther to defend himself at Augsburg. Luther appealed to his own elector, Frederic the Wise of Saxony, who supplied him with a safe-conduct, which, unlike that of Hus at Constance, was honored, since the emperor could not afford to offend an influential elector. Again Luther refused to recant, and this time threatened the pope by calling for a council, the one thing which popes had dreaded for a long time as a result of past sad experience. Leo x issued a bull defining indulgences in a sense contrary to that adopted by Luther.

At this point a noted theologian took up the cudgels on behalf of the papal position and called for a debate with Luther, which was held at Leipsig in 1519. This theologian, John Eck, had little difficulty in inveigling Luther into the admission that his position was similar to that of the heretic John Hus, burned at the council of Constance in 1415. Since Luther had appealed to a council, this was to suggest that even a council had erred, and it cut the ground from under his feet. Presumably he would not accept even the verdict of a council if it was to go against his own convictions.

Defiance of papacy— The great pamphlets

Luther now recognized that he had gone too far for forgiveness by the Church, and proceeded to take the offensive in a remarkable series of pamphlets in which he branded the pope as antichrist, gathered together all the grievances he had against the Church that had hitherto been suppressed, and appealed directly to the only source of support he could hope for, the independent princes of Germany. The papacy, he declared in his *Address to the Christian Nobility of the German Nation,* had been taking upon itself the right to do what no human agency can do, setting itself up as intermediary between man and God, and had erected three "walls" which effectively immunized it against opposition. When pressed by the civil authority, the papacy claimed that spiritual authority was superior to civil and thus the civil had no jurisdiction over it, that only the pope could interpret the Scriptures, and that no one but a pope could call a council, and thus not even the united body of Christendom could serve to modify papal absolutism. These pretensions Luther vigorously opposed. All men, he said, belong to the spiritual estate, not only ordained priests. Civil authority has the right and duty to preserve order in the realm, and if priests disturb it, they must be punished like anyone else. With regard to the second "wall," the Scriptures may be interpreted by anyone who possesses the Holy Spirit, not alone by popes who are not conspicuous for their piety, which alone can permit the entry of the Holy Spirit. As for the calling of a council, obviously it is the duty of all Christians to help reform the Church if it needs reform, and civil authorities are the best equipped to do so. If it should happen that the pope and the papal *curia* were most in need of reform, then papal power should not be able to prevent it.

In the other pamphlets of the year 1520 Luther attacked the entire sacramental system of the Church, providing enough ammunition for the all-out revolt against the church that was to come.

Martin Luther and his wife, Katherine Bora, painted by Lucas Cranach, the Elder. Both at the time were in middle life. Katherine Bora had been a nun prior to the Reformation. (1526)

Defiance of the empire— Protection by princes

Meanwhile the old Emperor Maximilian had died in 1519, and after the usual haggling over terms Charles v, grandson of Maximilian, had been elected, the first emperor in more than a hundred years to possess real power, power based not on his imperial crown nor mainly on his Hapsburg possessions in Austria but on his inheritance, through the marital policy of his grandfather, of the newly rich kingdom of Spain and the flourishing commercial territories of the Netherlands. Charles v was a sincere Catholic and hater of heresy, and was prepared to cooperate with the pope in stamping it out, as far as this was consistent with his imperial interests.

In 1520 Pope Leo x condemned the teachings of Luther and ordered them to be burned. Luther retaliated by burning the papal bull, calling it the "execrable bull of Antichrist." Leo then excommunicated Luther, and Charles v, who had just returned from Spain and was now free to deal with him, summoned him to appear at an imperial diet, to which again he came with a safe-conduct extracted from the emperor by the elector Frederic. At this Diet of Worms, where all the princes and many of the towns were represented, by no means all the representatives were against Luther; on the contrary he may even have possessed a majority, since there was great discontent with the Church, and the diet itself had drawn up its own list of grievances. Nevertheless Charles's influence was dominant, and he finally placed Luther under the imperial ban, demanding that he surrender to the government after his safe-conduct had expired. For his part Luther refused to make any retractation, ending his speech with the famous words, "I neither can nor will recant anything, for it is not safe to go against conscience. I can do no other. Here I stand. God help me. Amen."

The elector Frederic, knowing that it was unsafe to leave Luther at large, placed him at once in protective custody in the castle of Wartburg, where, as already mentioned, he spent his time translating the Bible into German, beginning with the New Testament, which he completed there. But he was not left without followers outside the castle who worked constantly, setting up first a reformed Church at Wittenberg, while everywhere arose spontaneous movements to set up new churches, purged of everything in Catholic teaching and practice that was not to be found in the Bible. Luther himself was allowed to return to Wittenberg in 1522 and there joined his followers, writing for many years a stream of pamphlets, on the basis of which more and more communities turned to Lutheranism, or Evangelicalism as it is more properly termed. Most of the earlier churches were formed in the big cities, since the feudal nobility and the princes were hesitant to take steps that might leave them isolated from both the powerful emperor and the Catholic Church, until they were assured that their fellow princes were of the same mind and were willing to pursue the policy to the end.

THE ANABAPTISTS AND LUTHERANISM

Unfortunately for Luther, almost as soon as he had returned he was faced by a movement that no one had foreseen, but was a natural consequence of his conservative revolt against the Church. It is not always possible to contain popular revolts within a

Pope Leo X and his cardinals, a painting by Raphael now in the Pitti Palace in Florence.

Capture of a noble during the Peasants' Revolt in Germany. From an old engraving.

conservative framework, which was what Luther desired. Within Germany, where there was very little prosperity accruing from the commercial revolution, and where ancient feudal aristocratic privileges remained virtually intact in the country, there was very serious unrest latent, and this unrest was by no means principally directed against the Church. Rather the feudal nobility and the upper class burghers were the immediate and visible oppressors. Inspired but far from approved by Luther, a host of evangelical revivalist preachers arose who demanded a new order of society as well as a return to what they believed to be primitive Christianity. Few of these preachers agreed with one another in doctrine, save that the majority disapproved of infant baptism and regarded baptism rather as a symbol of conversion in adulthood; but all agreed in demanding a new order in society, even preaching primitive communism, and sometimes polygamy. They demanded rule by the people and the destruction of the old order of aristocratic privilege. The most important and for a time effective leader of these Anabaptists, as they were called, was one Thomas Munzer who for a brief period established a theocratic state in a city (Mulhouse) of which he and his followers gained control. Throughout northern and central Germany the movement spread, to be followed by an uprising of the peasants against their masters and against the serfdom which was still the customary condition in Germany.

Luther was placed in a difficult position. On the one hand he disapproved of anarchy, yet on the other hand, as a man, he also realized that the radical reformers had some legitimate grievances. When, however, they took to fighting and revolution and committed a number of atrocities, and above all when the peasants took to open warfare, he ceased to give them any support, and, realizing that the movement was endangering his whole church, he called upon the princes to suppress them by meeting violence with counterviolence. Being an entirely immoderate man himself, he used no moderate terms in summoning the aid of the nobility against the "thieving and murderous peasants." Though the nobility had some difficulty in organizing themselves effectively in the absence of the main German army, with Charles v in Italy, they finally did put down the uprisings. The peasants were treated with the utmost savagery by the troops, and the movement collapsed. The result was that serfdom was fastened more heavily than ever upon the unfortunate peasants, and much-needed social reform was indefinitely postponed. The radical communists from the cities were likewise defeated by the armies of the princes and by the established civil powers. At a diet, to which the Lutherans came in 1529 and gave their assent to the measure, Charles v decreed that all Anabaptists should be put to death wherever they were found. The movements went underground, but for the most part they were unable to survive as organized entities, though some were able in a later century to emigrate to America, where their peculiar religious ideas and the societies based on them were tolerated. The Mennonites and Moravian brethren, amongst others, are direct heirs of the sixteenth-century Anabaptists.

LUTHER AND THE HUMANISTS

In the early years of the Reformation, it seemed that a real reform would be carried out, without necessarily a full separation from Rome. It was still believed that the most serious of the Lutheran criticisms of the Catholic Church would be accepted and acted upon. Therefore there was some chance of a compromise, and the majority of the humanist reformers followed Luther. But when he showed himself unwilling to alter his theology in any particular and appeared to believe himself to be as much inspired as any Catholic pope—when, in short, he became dogmatic and authoritarian, then the humanists gradually deserted him. They could not bring themselves to believe in the absolute impotence of the human will and in the absolute uselessness of human works. They also could not comprehend this barbaric German with his violence and willingness to fight for what he believed to be the truth, when on the whole they themselves believed in searching for the truth and allowing others to do the same. In particular Erasmus, who had approved of Luther's original attack on indulgences, refused, as we have seen, to follow him on the matter of human free will. He disapproved of all forms of violence, especially in religious matters, which were, to him, still open to question. But Luther continued to maintain his position, and was backed by far the most powerful forces of the time in his intolerance. Gradually Erasmus and most of the other humanists deserted his cause, and returned

to the Catholic Church of their fathers, believing it was preferable to try to reform the Church from within, even if the chances of success seemed slight, rather than seceding from it altogether and in the process helping to destroy it. Certainly the Renaissance Church had been far more tolerant and humane than the church that was being set up by Luther, and so, necessarily, Erasmus and the humanists felt themselves more at home in it; even if it was not yet prepared to reform, hope need not be abandoned that some day it might be.

LUTHER AND THE SWISS REFORMATION OF ZWINGLI

Highly symptomatic to the humanists was Luther's attitude toward a Swiss reformer who came close to him in so many of his ideas, but yet differed on one point that to the theological mind of the day seemed of supreme importance. Ulrich Zwingli (1484–1531), originally a Catholic priest imbued with humanist ideas and educated at humanist centers of learning, had followed the lead of Luther in Switzerland. At the time, Switzerland was a confederation of cantons under the nominal rule of the emperor, but virtually free and self-governing. Zwingli in the early part of his life had not been especially a religious man, and had probably entered the priesthood for the purpose of furthering his humanist studies. He mildly ridiculed the superstitious practices of the Church as he saw them, including the sale of indulgences, but took no lead in the reform movement until after an inner experience at the age of thirty-five, when he was stricken by the plague and unable to recover from it for some months. As a priest in Zurich and the head of the canton of that name, he suddenly began to preach against Catholicism, and his ideas on justification by faith were similar to those of Luther, though he always claimed they had been arrived at independently. Again, however, it was personal experience of God's mercy and grace that started him off as a reformer and eloquent preacher. Though he never was quite so extreme and dogmatic as Luther on the matter of the utter impotence of the human will, he was basically in agreement with his fellow reformer. Swiss conditions, however, were very different from those of Germany. The town councils had a large measure of self-government, and their composition was in many respects democratic. When therefore Zwingli began to preach in Zurich and demanded that the Catholic mass be abolished, the burghers allowed him to speak before the town council, and throughout his career he gained most of his reforms through open and public disputation in which he vanquished his opponents by fair means. In time he fully converted Zurich, and a number of the other German-speaking cantons followed. Yet when Anabaptists tried to make more radical reforms Zwingli opposed them and ultimately became a persecutor, with the death penalty being inflicted on the radicals. Zurich became a theocratic state under his influence, and though it never was as extreme a theocracy as the later Geneva, and Zwingli never had the absolute power that Calvin enjoyed, puritanism rapidly took the place of the moderate humanism of Zwingli's early life.

The Protestant movement in Switzerland under Zwingli's guidance rapidly became political. Many cantons became Protestant and entered into alliance with Zurich, and some of the southern German states were likewise brought to Zwinglian Protestantism. Then the reformers proceeded to try to convert the so-called Forest cantons, which were solidly Catholic. Zwingli did not hesitate to demand that the force of arms be used. The Catholic cantons appealed to Ferdinand of Austria, brother of Charles v, who had relinquished Austrian rule to him. Ferdinand being too heavily engaged elsewhere, the Protestants were able to compel them to grant toleration to Protestants in their Catholic cantons—a privilege they did not accord to Catholics in their own. But the victory was short lived. Ferdinand at length obliged with an army, and the Catholic cantons took the offensive. Zurich was unable to persuade the Protestant cantons to give aid in time, and thus the small army of Zurich, with which Zwingli himself went along as chaplain, was badly defeated and

Zwingli himself slain (1531). The Protestant cantons, however, were able to maintain the reformed religion after his death, though the Catholic cantons retained their Catholicism also. This religious distinction between the Swiss cantons remains to this day.

If Luther had earnestly supported Zwingli it is possible that there would have been no basic schism in the Protestant churches, though this is doubtful in view of the centrifugal forces let loose through the insistence by all Protestants on the supremacy of Scripture. This can be interpreted in so many different ways that sects emphasizing one aspect or another are always likely to arise, and have not, indeed, ceased to arise even today. But Luther differed from Zwingli in his interpretation of the meaning of the Mass or Eucharist. As we have seen, his theory was consubstantiation, or the actual presence of the body and blood of Christ in the bread and wine. Zwingli adopted a position closer to that of the humanists, that the Eucharist is not efficacious for salvation, as Luther would have agreed, but that it is in fact only symbolic, a remembrance of the Last Supper of Christ on earth. Thus there is no real presence of the body and blood of Christ. Neither reformer would give way on this theological point. To Luther, Zwingli was as much an enemy as the papacy itself, and he never spared his invectives, even when Phillip of Hesse tried to get them to reconcile their views. So when Calvin, following mainly Zwingli rather than Luther, set up his church in Geneva it was without support from the Lutherans, whose churches were confined to Germany and the Scandinavian countries.

THE LUTHERAN STATE CHURCHES OF GERMANY AND SCANDINAVIA

The confession of Augsburg

Having quarreled with the humanists and with Zwingli, Lutheranism, under the leadership of Luther himself, and then of his followers, nonetheless continued to make headway in Germany. It had already achieved too much support from the influential middle classes and nobility for it to be stopped by any except violent means. The Lutherans were well represented in the imperial diets and were able to force toleration and the virtual removal of the imperial ban on Luther himself at the diet of Speyer in 1526, which allowed the German rulers to choose between the two religions; and even at the second diet of Speyer in 1529, when Lutheran princes were forbidden to extend the Lutheran reform further and were made to agree to tolerate Catholicism in their domains, while the Catholics were bound by no such agreement to permit Lutheranism, the Lutherans nevertheless joined the Catholics in refusing to tolerate either Anabaptists or Zwinglians. The diet of 1529 also gave a name to the Lutherans. A number of princes and cities protested against the decree of the diet, and thereafter were given the name of Protestants.

At this point Charles v decided to interfere actively, until this time having had his hands full elsewhere with the Turks and French. Hoping to settle the problem of the Protestants once and for all, he summoned a diet to meet at Augsburg for the express purpose of trying to reconcile the views of Protestants and Catholics and ensure peace in his divided empire. The Protestants produced the confession of Augsburg, drawn up largely by Luther's more moderate follower Melancthon, a man of humanist inclinations, which made far more concessions to the Catholics than Luther approved, but which was offered in hopes of a compromise. Though the Catholics suggested one or two concessions also, the diet voted against the Protestants, who began to arm themselves and enter into an alliance known as the Schmalkaldic League. But again Charles was called away to other things, and the Lutherans were left a little more time to organize and proselytize. They gained several more states to their cause, some by force of arms.

Meanwhile the papacy had been filled by the reforming pope, Paul III, who was willing to try negotiations with the Lutherans, who had still not officially seceded

This portrait of Luther shows the reformer in later life, the year before his death. He has put on weight, and the artist has been so discourteous as to paint his subject in need of a shave! Compare with the earlier portrait by the same artist on page 605.

from the Church. When, however, they demanded recognition of the doctrine of justification by faith, that the Mass was inefficacious for salvation, and that the pope should abandon his claim to be the supreme head of the Church, it was obvious that nothing could be gained and the council was not held. Though more negotiations were started, nothing came of them. Luther continued to the end of his life to attack the pope with the most violent invective. He died in 1546.

War with the empire

War broke out between the Schmalkaldic League and the imperial forces in the same year, though by no means was it a straight fight between Protestant and Catholic, since princely interests sometimes dictated support of the emperor or antagonism to him. But for the most part the Protestant princes remained loyal to the league and fought against Charles. Although, on the whole, Charles was victorious, the cause of Protestantism was very little damaged, and the emperor finally agreed to what is known as the Religious Peace of Augsburg in 1555.

The religious peace of Augsburg— cuius regio, eius religio

This peace established a formula under which the princes and rulers of the free cities of Germany could decide on the religion of their subjects and enforce it. Dissenters, such as Calvinists, Zwinglians, and Anabaptists, however, were forbidden. If any subjects of the princes did not accept the religion of their state they were permitted to emigrate. All lands confiscated from the Church after 1552 must be restored. The principle behind the settlement, known as *cuius regio, eius religio* (a succinct Latin phrase defying literal translation but broadly meaning that the religion of a territory is to be decided by the particular territory), was a natural consequence of the protection given to the Lutherans by the secular powers.

The idea of universal tolerance had hardly been accepted by any in that age. Catholics had always warred against heresy, and in 1555 Lutherans were as willing to persecute heretics as any Catholic. What had happened was that the Catholic Church had been compelled for lack of political power to yield some of its authority to a schismatic Church, but it had in no way changed its views on the necessity of one universal Church, as will be seen by its later efforts to reconvert those who had fallen away into Lutheranism. It gave the princes what they wanted, namely, the control of the new Church, and the use of the possessions formerly belonging to the Catholic Church. It thus greatly increased their absolutism; and while many of them no doubt were convinced Lutherans in religion, the settlement made for no increase of toleration and no freedom from authoritarian dictation in matters of religion for their subjects. But

as a compromise it endured for a considerable time until the Catholics were strong enough to renew their efforts, which culminated in the devastating Thirty Years' War, which will be dealt with in the next chapter.

LUTHERANISM IN NORTHERN AND EASTERN EUROPE

The principle of *cuius regio, eius religio,* rather naturally, proved highly acceptable to rulers in other lands than Germany. In Scandinavia the nobles were powerful and, together with the upper bourgeoisie, were the leaders in turning to the doctrines of the reformers. During the sixteenth century Sweden, under Danish rule since the fourteenth, was in the process of breaking away from Denmark. The Danish king, Christian II, backed by the Catholic hierarchy, refused to turn Protestant, while the Swedish pretender, Gustavus Vasa, early adopted Protestantism as part of his effort to win the crown against Christian. Ultimately Christian's successors, deciding that it was better to free themselves from a dependence on a hierarchy which they could not control, turned Protestant, all their subjects being compelled to follow their lead.

Norway, under the Danish crown, followed suit, while Gustavus Vasa was ultimately able to secure his throne as a Protestant. Finland, under the Swedish crown, did likewise. In Poland, which was by the sixteenth century largely controlled by nobles rather than the king, the Protestant Reformation made many converts among the nobles and bourgeoisie, though hardly at all among the peasants. No Polish king was converted, but the monarchs were compelled by their powerful subjects to grant toleration to Protestants, who, however, could not agree amongst themselves and so were never able to make their power fully felt over the monarchy. In time the Jesuits were invited in by the crown, and were able to reconvert the large majority of the people, so that Poland as a whole was lost to the Reformation and has remained Catholic to this day, with only a small Protestant minority.

In Bohemia, which, with its Hussite tra-

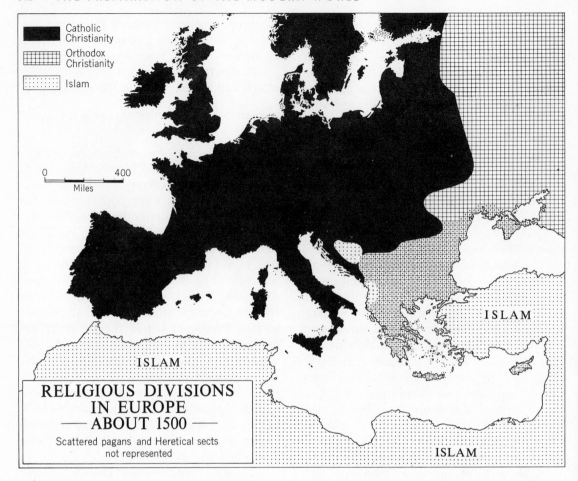

Catholic
Christianity

Orthodox
Christianity

Islam

0   400
Miles

ISLAM

ISLAM

ISLAM

**RELIGIOUS DIVISIONS
IN EUROPE
—— ABOUT 1500 ——**
Scattered pagans and Heretical sects
not represented

dition, was well prepared for the Reformers, there were a large number of separate Protestant sects, again preventing union against the Catholic monarchy. But toleration was granted in 1567 to the Lutherans and Calvinists. Their gains, however, were lost in the following century when Bohemia became part of the Catholic Hapsburg Empire, as will be described in the next chapter.

▶ Calvinism

GENERAL CHARACTERISTICS AND DOCTRINE

In contradistinction to Lutheranism, Calvinism, the second most important branch of Protestantism, owed its success in large measure to its freedom from domination by the existing state. It was far more successful in converting individual men and women than Lutheranism, and no Calvinist country ever was reconverted by the Counter Reformation and the Jesuits. The reason for this is that there was something in the teachings of Calvin that really convinced those who were predisposed to believe; and the conviction led to action. Calvinists as a matter of course were militant; they felt they had a duty to convert, and their self-confidence, self-reliance, and willingness to endure martyrdom if necessary seem to have carried conviction, although the humanists regarded Calvinist doctrine as so manifestly contrary to reason that few were interested. Yet it was logical and convincing once the basic premises were accepted. Moreover, Calvin expounded his teachings in a thoroughly convincing manner, and it was difficult indeed to find flaws in his logic. There were prob-

OFFICIAL RELIGIOUS
DIVISIONS IN EUROPE
— ABOUT 1600 —

Catholicism   Anglicanism
Orthodox   Calvinism
Christianity   Lutheranism
(Religious Minorities not represented)

ably also sound psychological reasons for the acceptance of Calvinism. The convinced Calvinist, by virtue of his very acceptance of Calvinism, became one of the elect, and knew that he was saved. Such a conviction would effectively prevent any later apostasy, for with the loss of his beliefs he would at the same time lose his psychological security. Finally, it may be added that the bourgeois class to which Calvinism essentially appealed has always been inclined to suffer from self-righteousness, considering itself to be the only real producer and worker in the world's economy, and despising the lack of seriousness of the noble and the peasant. Thus,

when it was offered a religion which approved, even glorified, its own natural tendencies, it accepted it with alacrity.

FOUNDATION OF GENEVA AS A THEOCRATIC STATE

John Calvin (1509–1564) was born in northern France and received the education of a theologian in the Catholic Church, though he did not became a priest, and later turned to the study of law. He became prominent through his writing of a book, *Institutes of the Christian Religion,* which in its many editions became the central collection of the teachings of all the Calvinist (Reformed) Churches. It is written in a very clear style, cogent and compelling, and it made Calvin's reputation. It is an altogether astonishing work to have been published only three years after his conversion to Protestantism (1536). Wandering through France and teaching, he was continually made to flee from one place to another until he was invited by William Farel, a former pupil of Lefèvre d'Etaples, to stay in Geneva, where Farel was trying to persuade the town council to turn the city over to Protestantism. Calvin accepted the invitation and for a short time the city let the two reformers have their way. Protestantism was established, but not in accordance with the teachings of Calvin. It inclined toward the system of worship used in the rest of Protestant Switzerland, which had been laid down by Zwingli. Rather than accept this, Farel and Calvin left Geneva after they had apparently instigated a riot. But while Calvin was away in Strassburg, reworking his *Institutes,* the town council in Geneva changed its composition, and, unable to deal with its difficulties, the new council decided to recall Calvin (1541). Thereafter Calvin was the virtual dictator of Geneva which he remodeled as a theocracy, using severe penal laws against all dissenters and those who would have modified his authoritarian regime. He had no hesitation in using all his powers of compulsion to force outward conformance to his numerous edicts, and he broke the back of any incipient opposition by the use of the death penalty.

DOCTRINE OF CALVIN

Justification by faith—"The elect"

In order to understand the kind of society that Calvin was trying to produce in Geneva it is essential to understand his teachings and see wherein they differed from those of Luther. He owed almost all his thought to Luther, and to Luther's own teachers, St. Paul and St. Augustine, but his emphasis was different; and this difference in emphasis was enough to create an entirely different kind of church organization which,

if Calvin's theology be accepted, was strictly logical. Calvin emphasized, above all, the fact that God had chosen certain men, and certain men only, for salvation. These men were *predestined* to be saved before ever they were born, and their good deeds on earth were entirely irrelevant to their salvation. All the rest of mankind was predestined to damnation. Though the chosen person will naturally have faith, this faith itself is the result of God's grace bestowed on him through his having been chosen by God himself (cf. St. Augustine). God's justice would require that every man should be damned, but God's mercy ensures that a certain number will be saved, in order to exhibit his magnanimity (a possible interpretation of St. Paul to the Romans). Thus it may be said that only indirectly is there justification by faith, since faith is the result of God's election or choice; but it was certainly true for Calvin that good works availed not at all, as in Luther. St. Paul, faced with this problem, that if man is justified by faith then there is no reason for good works, had

John Calvin. From an old engraving.

said that a man's faith should be shown by his works. This statement Calvin seized upon and utilized for all it was worth, and in fact based his entire theocratic state upon it.

For, he argued, a man who is saved will naturally do good works, whereas, conversely, a man who does not do good works is obviously damned. So, if any man in Geneva did not do good works this showed he was not a member of the elect, and he must be made to do good by example and rigorous enforcement of the law, lest his wickedness lead other men astray. In spite of his good works a man might be damned, but it was sure that he was damned if he did *not* do them. It was the task of the Church, therefore, not only to provide spiritual sustenance with its ritual and sacraments, but to enforce godly behavior. And if one wished to know just what godly behavior was, the place to look was in the Bible, which was the inspired word of God, revealed by him just for this purpose. Everything not specifically permitted by the Bible was held to be sinful, and it was the task of the ruling body of the Church, which in practice meant Calvin himself during his lifetime, to interpret the Bible and make laws from it. These laws must be enforced with all the means available to the theocratic state. Thus the state, far from being supreme over the Church as in Lutheran lands, actually was the Church. In lands where, unlike at Geneva, the state was distinct from the Church, it was the duty of the elect to try to dictate to the state, and if necessary, even rebel against it for the sake of their own consciences.

Consequences of Calvinist doctrine

The new canon of deadly sins—In Geneva all forms of frivolity and amusement were condemned and forbidden, save the most simple. The Jewish Sabbath became the Calvinist Sunday, set aside for divine service and Bible reading. No gambling or dancing or unnecessary display was permitted. All forms of art were regarded as frivolous and tainted with "popery." If one prospered, one could not spend one's money because there was nothing worth while to

spend it on; the only alternative was to accumulate it. For the first time the bourgeois class, hardworking and thrifty, had a religion which glorified its virtues and did not, like the medieval scholastics, condemn the accumulation of money as avaricious. But in other respects many of the medieval categories of sin were retained; idleness and sensuality were as deadly to Calvin as to any medieval moralist. But, more than this, it was claimed by the Calvinists that God showed his joy in his elect by allowing them to prosper; thus prosperity was an actual *sign* of godliness, that one was indeed a member of the elect. Hence the Puritan belief (not unknown in America) that God is with the rich; that the poor man is poor through his own fault, and God is not with him—poverty being a moral crime as well as a deserved misfortune.

Self-reliance and resistance to tyranny—Incipient democracy—Though Calvin was no democrat, and loathed and persecuted the Anabaptists, most curiously his theological system led indirectly to democracy, while Lutheranism fastened the yoke of the state more firmly on the necks of believers. The Calvinist was taught to obey his conscience and the Bible. If the state gainsaid him, then it was his duty to oppose the state. A secular tyrant would be sure to have the hands of all the Calvinists in his kingdom against him, unless he were visibly one of the godly—in which case he would agree with them. The right to overthrow such tyrants was implicit in Calvinism. More than this, it should be understood that the choice of the elect, those predestined for salvation, was in the hands of God and not man. Thus no hereditary privilege would avail the ungodly man, and no obedience was due him. It was the elect who should dominate and, when possible, rule the state; and the elect might come from any class, but would demonstrate their election by their evident godliness. Thus the elders of the Church who supported Calvin in Geneva, John Knox in Scotland, and the Reformed Church in South Africa, had no prescriptive right to their position. They won it by their good works. So, in a curious sense, there was equality of opportunity, the first prerequisite of democracy, and there can be no doubt that the Puritan tradition deriving from Calvin was vastly efficacious in the New England colonies in building the democratic spirit and the resistance to English tyranny that finally resulted in the Declaration of Independence.

THE "COMMUNITY OF SAINTS" IN GENEVA

Though there was much hidden opposition to Calvin in Geneva, as long as he was alive he retained his power. Those who could not brook his tyranny no doubt emigrated rather than fall into his revengeful hands, for he never forgave an opponent. One of these, a physician named Servetus, who unwarily visited Geneva, he had burned for denying the Trinity. If anyone voiced his opposition publicly, there were numerous laws that could be used against him, and Calvin used them without mercy. In his time all was outward conformity, since he employed spies to see who was breaking the laws, and the elders had to visit all the houses in the city at least once a year to see that the sumptuary laws were being observed. The accounts of the many trials for breaking minor laws suggest that the attempt to change human nature was far from truly successful. But at the same time it should be added that Protestants from all over Europe came to Geneva when expelled from or persecuted in their own countries. These men desired nothing better than to live in a "community of saints" such as Calvin appeared to have in Geneva. Thus they at least were not unhappy there; and they greatly added to the reputation of the Genevan theocracy, which was always willing to lend advice and help to any Calvinists in Europe.

CALVINISM AND PURITANISM—"NOT LACKING IN MORAL GRANDEUR"

When Calvin died, the worst of the theocratic excesses were over and the tyranny in Geneva was relaxed, though it remained a center of Calvinist teachings and the Mecca for all good Calvinists. Calvinists from other countries came there for spiritual sustenance, and from there went out missionaries wherever they were needed. Not all Calvinists were made in the image of Calvin, and the Puritan ideal, as it came to be called in England and America, was not so rigid as his. The ideal Puritan consulted his conscience in all matters, and though he could quote the Bible and read it diligently, he did not take all his precepts from it. He was self-reliant and self-confident, sure of his salvation. He was always tempted to be self-righteous too. He dressed plainly, was sober, chaste, and thrifty, and he worked hard. Usually he was dour and lacking in humor, but not necessarily. In spite of all its shortcomings Puritanism was an ideal, like the Spartan, that was not lacking in a certain moral grandeur. And there can be no doubt that the Puritan was an extremely valuable citizen at a time when there was a need for the accumulation of capital, and, from an economic point of view, when there was not so much need for high consumption of luxuries, especially those imported from the Far East. The modern world owes a great deal to him. Without his self-reliance there might have been no English settlement of America; without his hatred of tyranny there might have been no democracy; and without his thrift there might have been no Industrial Revolution.

CALVINISM IN FRANCE

Persecution of the Huguenots— First wars of religion

As we have seen already, the French monarchy in the Concordat of Bologna (1516) had already made its own arrangements with the papacy. This fundamental fact explains why Protestantism in France was ultimately unsuccessful, although at one time it must have numbered millions of adherents. But the power of the state in the end proved too strong for it, and the state, even though for a few years it was ruled by a Protestant, found that it could not do without the power of the French (Gallican) Church, which had for centuries been a mainstay of the monarchy. The best the

Protestants could win was almost a century of toleration, and this too was lost when the monarchy had become sufficiently powerful and absolute to act on its religious convictions, without troubling about the political and economic consequences.

The history of Protestantism in France is inextricably woven into the political life of the period, because the Protestants, or Huguenots, as they were called in France, belonged not only to the bourgeoisie but to the nobility, who saw in the Protestant movement a chance to restore the feudal anarchy which the French monarchy had with such difficulty been able to get under control in the later Middle Ages. This is not to say that the many Huguenot nobles were not sincere in their religion; only that during the reigns of the last Valois kings there was a great temptation to turn Protestant when it seemed possible that their cause might be successful, that a Protestant might inherit the throne, and that they themselves might become the power behind the throne, as Calvinists everywhere desired. It may be added that Lutheranism as such made little appeal to the French. The fundamental Calvinist book had been written in French as well as in Latin, and the logical nature of Calvinist thought appealed to their minds.

Some of the political story will be told in the next chapter. Here it is enough to say that most of the Protestant converts were made in southern France, where there had been numerous heretics in the Middle Ages. The chief stronghold of Protestantism in later times was in southwestern France and especially in the port of La Rochelle, close to Bordeaux. Francis i, though not personally averse to Protestants except when they rebelled—his sister protected them all her life, though she did not formally become one—found it necessary to have papal support in the later years of his reign, and at papal instigation suppressed all Protestant books and turned Protestants over to the tender mercies of the very conservative Parlements, while the University of Paris attempted to confute their teachings. Parlements and the university were strong bulwarks of orthodox Catholicism during the entire period, as was the city of Paris. Henry ii pursued his father's policy, but sometimes allied himself with Protestants because he needed them in his wars. When Henry ii was accidentally killed in 1559 a considerable number of nobles had turned Protestant and controlled large parts of the country, while the Catholics on the other side were also under arms. Meanwhile the government fell into the hands of Catherine de Medici, widow of Henry ii, who was utterly uninterested in the religious issue and wished merely to make peace between the factions. She was supported by a number of moderates known as the *politiques,* who were usually powerless in face of the violence everywhere prevalent. At one time she and the kings, whom she kept as ineffective as she could, inclined toward the Protestant side, and at another time toward the Catholic. To offset Protestant influence on Charles ix, she arranged the massacre of St. Bartholomew (1572) in which the chief Protestant leaders were murdered, and, probably beyond her expectations, thousands of minor Protestants were massacred throughout France. With the accession of Henry iii (1574–1589) the Catholic League, led by the able Duke of Guise, became the leading power in the land, and civil war raged between the league and the Protestants. The latter were led by the heir presumptive to the throne, Henry of Navarre, whose accession was feared by the Catholics. Henry iii was a virtual prisoner of the league until he had the Duke of Guise murdered, only to be murdered himself shortly afterward.

The Edict of Nantes

This left the Protestant Henry of Navarre as the legitimate king, and there was no pretender of comparable ability. Nevertheless he had to fight for his throne, which he found it impossible to secure unless he abjured his religion. For the sake of peace he decided to become a Catholic, but tried to pacify his former coreligionists by granting them full permission to keep their religion, conceding liberty of worship in all places where it had been practiced for the past two years (Edict of Nantes, 1598). Protestants had the same legal rights as Catholics, and the king left them some two hundred towns over which they had full authority and where they could keep garrisons. Thus was a Protestant state within a state created, but it did succeed in stopping the civil wars, allowing France to recover. In the early seventeenth century Cardinal Richelieu, acting for Louis XIII, succeeded in capturing the fortified towns of the Huguenots, thus unifying the country politically, but he did not disturb their freedom of worship (1628). It remained for Louis XIV to revoke the Edict of Nantes in 1685, causing the exile of those Huguenots who refused to abjure their religion. Being highly skilled and industrious, they were everywhere welcomed by Protestant countries, and their departure greatly weakened France. The Protestant movement in France was dealt a fatal blow, and today the Protestants are a very small minority in that country.

Facsimile of the last page of the Edict of Nantes (1598), the decree of Henry IV giving toleration to the Huguenots by which Henry secured his throne. Henry's signature is in the center.

CALVINISM IN SCOTLAND

The Catholic crown and Protestant people

The Reformation in Scotland can best be considered in connection with France, since Scotland during the sixteenth century until the triumph of Calvinism may be thought of as almost an appendage of the French crown. England, as the stronger neighbor of Scotland, had constantly been trying to annex Scotland or arrange for the union of the two crowns, ever since the Middle Ages, as described in Chapter 15. Scotland, in self-defense, had turned to France for protection, and at the beginning of the sixteenth century a Frenchwoman of the Catholic house of Guise was queen. When her husband James v was defeated by an English invasion and died shortly afterward, Mary of Lorraine became regent for her infant daughter. She arranged in due course for the betrothal of this daughter to the heir to the throne of France. The child grew up to be the famous Mary Queen of Scots.

Thus the Scottish crown was strongly Catholic, but many of the nobles paid as scant attention to the crown as in France, and the large majority turned to the reformed religion, in part because they were antagonistic to the crown. The leader of Scottish reform was, however, not a noble, but a peasant named John Knox, a fiery preacher trained in Geneva, who was able to use Scottish nationalism to overthrow the Catholic Church, ably abetted by the follies of Mary Queen of Scots. Since he was able to convince the burghers of the truths of Calvinism by his preaching, and since the nobles of the Scottish lowlands, whether convinced or not, believed in the overthrow of the French-dominated monarchy, the revolution in Scotland, unlike that in most other countries, was almost bloodless.

John Knox was at one time an English minister during the short reign of Edward vi, when the Protestant reform in England was in full swing, and his visits to Scotland were only periodical until he finally returned in 1559 with a great reputation and following in Scotland amongst the bourgeoisie and some of the artisans of the lowlands. He was able to obtain the support of a number of nobles, who, for political reasons, had banded themselves together as "Lords of the Congregation" to destroy the Catholic Church and its worship throughout Scotland. They had done this when Mary Stuart was betrothed to the French Dauphin. French soldiers were brought into the country by the regent, and civil war appeared imminent. At this point the nobles called upon Elizabeth of England for help, and that astute politician succeeded in making a treaty with the French under which most of the French soldiers withdrew, leaving power in the hands of the Lords of the Congregation and leaving John Knox leader of the popular reform party. Providentially the regent Mary had just died (1560).

Protestant victory—John Knox and Mary Queen of Scots

The result was inevitable. The nobles assembled a Parliament in which not only great nobles but lesser nobles and urban representatives took part, and the Catholic religion was declared abolished. So Scotland was already a Calvinist country when Mary Queen of Scots, after having become queen of France by marriage, only to have her husband die within a year, returned to Scotland to claim her Scottish crown. Though a Catholic, she did not feel an overmastering necessity to try to re-establish Catholicism, provided she was permitted to keep her own religion, which was agreed to, though John Knox was far from approving. But she was always suspect, and when she married Lord Darnley, who, like herself, was close to the English throne, Elizabeth of England, whose title was not recognized by Catholics, naturally became hostile to her as being the possible focus of Catholic plots in England. Mary ruined all her chances by her behavior. When her Italian Catholic secretary (David Rizzio) was murdered she suspected her husband of the crime, and almost certainly connived in the murder of her husband. Then, to set the seal on her folly she married

Mary Queen of Scots, probably painted by François Quesnel, supposedly during her captivity at Fotheringay. If the date of 1586 is accepted and the painting is a true likeness, she must have preserved her famed beauty to the end. In 1586 she was forty-four years old. The painting is now in the Hermitage at Leningrad.

the man who almost certainly had murdered Darnley. This played into the hands of John Knox, who was determined to get rid of Catholicism altogether and to whom a Catholic queen was a standing offense. Mary, unable to rely on any firm support, fled the country to England where she was imprisoned by Elizabeth and later executed after a number of Catholic plots were traced to her.

Meanwhile her infant son, whose father was presumably Lord Darnley, grew up in a country run by Calvinist nobles and elders under different regents until he was of age to assume the crown himself. Then he was able by clever maneuvering to place himself at the head of the Scottish Church, which position he was able to maintain as long as he pursued policies agreeable to the Church

leaders. When, however, he tried to go against these leaders at the end of his reign, and began to write books about the divine right of monarchy, the elders soon showed him that they could oppose him in the name of God, and he was heartily sick of them by the time he inherited the English crown in 1603 on the death of Elizabeth. This man, James vi as king of Scotland and James i as king of England, will be considered in Chapter 20. But his Scottish background should be understood before the reasons for his support of Anglicanism and his dislike of Puritanism can be fully appreciated.

By no means all of Scotland was converted to the new religion, which was mainly a phenomenon of the Lowlands. However, though the Scottish Highland lairds remained Catholic, the government made no effort to suppress them at this time. The united English crown in a later century (1715–1745) was forced to deal with the Highlanders when they supported the restoration of the then Catholic Stuart family to the throne of England and Scotland.

The Scottish National Church

The Scottish Church (or Kirk) was made into a national Church (the Presbyterian) through the Calvinist Reformation. Though it did not altogther control the state, the state as a rule was powerless without its support. The state, in accordance with Calvinist teachings, made many laws regulating the behavior of individuals, as Calvin had done in Geneva. The elders of the Presbyterian Church were undoubtedly the most influential men in the Scottish Parliament. As in Geneva they rose to their position through their godliness rather than through hereditary right. Thus there was a large element of a kind of democracy in Scotland long before any real democracy was established in England. The influence of this Scottish Church in English affairs will be discussed in Chapter 20, since Scottish support was crucial for the success of the Puritan Revolution in England in the seventeenth century.

CALVINISM IN HOLLAND

The early years of Lutheran influence

Calvinism in Holland is so closely bound up with the political struggle for Dutch independence from Spanish rule that it will be dealt with only briefly here, reserving the main account of this struggle for the next chapter. The Low Countries (now Holland and Belgium), had become part of the territories of the Duke of Burgundy in the fifteenth century (see Chapter 15). The Hapsburg family of Austria married into the Burgundian family and the Low Countries thus became a part of that patrimony of Charles v, who became Holy Roman emperor in 1519, as we have seen. The emperor thus had three main territories: Spain, which he acquired through his mother; the Low Countries, through his grandmother; and the Hapsburg domains, through his grandfather, the previous Holy Roman Emperor Maximilian. Born in Ghent, Charles was brought up as a Fleming, and was always regarded by the Low Countries as a native ruler. But as Holy Roman emperor it was his duty to maintain the Catholic religion, and when possible, as we have seen, he tried to carry out this task.

Soon after the Lutheran revolt in Germany, Lutheran ideas began to spread into the Netherlands, especially the northern part, the chief provinces of which were Holland and Zeeland. The people of the Netherlands were, on the whole, better educated than any in Europe of that time. There was no feudalism, and a considerable proportion of the population lived in the commercial towns. They had representative institutions in the form of Estates, and there was an Estates-General which acted as adviser to the monarchy. Thus it was natural for new ideas to spread in the territory, especially since it was one of the leading centers of printing in Europe. In the early years of the Reformation most of the new ideas were either Lutheran or Anabaptist. After Charles had issued his imperial ban on Luther, he naturally had to try to enforce it in the Netherlands, which he controlled. So a special kind of inquisition was set up, over the protests of the members of his council, which proceeded to take action against the Lutherans, setting up a censorship and sending a number of Lutherans to the stake. But the movement continued to grow, and it was difficult to enforce the laws since the Lutherans, for the most part, kept their views to themselves. But when the Anabaptists began to riot, as was their custom, the local authorities were willing to lend their aid to the suppression of these members of the lower classes, who were always subversive of good order. There is no doubt that most local officials resented the efforts of the central authority to intrude on their sphere, and all through the reign of Charles the edicts against heretics were very poorly enforced, except against Anabaptists, in spite of the increasing rigor of the royal decrees against all heretics.

Growth of Calvinism—Revolt against Catholic Spain

The position changed when Philip II inherited his father's crown. Philip was regarded as a Spaniard, and he used the Netherlands mainly as a source of income for his endless wars. From this time onward Calvinism, which began to gain a hold in the Netherlands, especially in the north, from about the time of the accession of Philip in 1556, is hardly to be distinguished from the national feeling against Spain, and Philip made use of the Inquisition, as previously in Spain, for the political purpose of keeping the Netherlands in subjection to him. Calvinism, which preaches the duty of Christians to resist tyranny, provided an ideal means of turning the struggle for independence into a religious war. The leaders of the revolt remained for a long time Catholic and declared that they had no quarrel on the religious issue with Philip. Only when this policy of moderation failed did they embrace Protestantism, so that it became a Protestant revolt also. But during the progress of the war the northern provinces became strongly Calvinist and remained so. The southern provinces cooperated with the north in help-ing to drive out the Spaniards, but did not wish to change their religion. Finally, under the Duke of Parma at the end of Philip's reign, the southern provinces were recon-quered, but the northern ones held out and ultimately gained their independence; the northerners were fully Protestant, while the southerners retained their Catholicism. Prob-ably there was a large emigration of Prot-estants to the north during the last years of the war, as also happened in France, where the Huguenots naturally joined their core-ligionists in the towns allotted to them after the Edict of Nantes. So, even in Cal-vinist countries, the principle of *cuius regio, eius religio* was substantially retained in the sixteenth century, even though in Holland (called the United Provinces after independ-ence) it was no prince that decided the religion but the government of the republic.

▶ The Reformation in England

TRADITIONAL OPPOSITION TO PAPACY

As we have seen in an earlier chapter there was always a considerable amount of anticlericalism in England, in part due to the position of the country for a long time as a fief of the papacy. And there had been no dearth of verbal attacks on the Church in the later Middle Ages. We have seen that John Wyclif, the first translator of the Bible into English, and the intellectual leader of the Lollard heresy, was protected by the king against efforts by the papacy to have him condemned as a heretic. We have seen also how several humanists attacked the vices and immorality of the Church without get-ting into any trouble. It is not surprising, therefore, that the English Reformation came about largely because of opposition to the papacy rather than from any profound con-viction by the people that the reformed teachings were the true ones. This accounts for the ease with which the monarchs were able to make religious changes, and the very considerable similarities in the Anglican religion and Catholicism. Only for a com-paratively short time in the first sixty years

of the seventeenth century was there a strong Calvinist movement in England, based upon real conviction. And the events of that period showed that the Puritan Calvinists were but a small minority in the country, in spite of the fact that they were able through a pecul-iar combination of circumstances to rule the country for eleven years.

HENRY VIII AND THE BREAK WITH ROME

Papal refusal to annul royal marriage

The occasion for the break with Rome was provided by the efforts of King Henry VIII (1509–1547) to have his marriage with the Spanish princess Catherine of Aragon annulled. The Tudor dynasty, of which Henry VIII was the second to occupy the throne, was by no means the closest to the old royal family, and on a strictly heredi-tary basis many persons could have been found to dispute the throne on good legal grounds with the Tudor family. So it was necessary for Henry to have a male heir, to prevent any dispute between rival nobles and perhaps the recrudescence of civil war. But Catherine apparently could give Henry no heir, though she had a daughter, Mary, who could succeed. He pretended also, as grounds for petitioning the pope for an annulment, that he had always had it on his conscience that he had married his deceased brother's wife, in spite of having obtained permission from a previous pope to do so.

Breaking of ties with Rome— Dissolution of monasteries

Cardinal Wolsey, papal legate, arch-bishop of York, and royal chancellor, was by far the most important man in the king-dom after Henry, and his closeness to the papacy should, in Henry's view, have been sufficient for him to win the annulment. Unfortunately for Henry and Wolsey, Cath-erine of Aragon was the aunt of Charles V, the emperor, and the emperor was present in person in Italy and was indeed in substantial control of the papacy at the time. Moreover, it did not fit in with Charles's plans to give

An engraving showing Sir Thomas More, author of Utopia *and Chancellor of England, put to death by Henry VIII for refusing to take the Oath of Supremacy to him as head of the Church of England.*

any help to Wolsey, who was angling for the papacy himself. Finally, Henry had already picked out the woman he wanted to marry, Anne Boleyn, one of the ladies-in-waiting to the queen. Wolsey failed to win the annulment, and was disgraced; Anne was importunate; and Henry decided to throw off the yoke of the papacy and to appoint a subservient churchman to the position of archbishop of Canterbury. This clergyman, Thomas Cranmer, was already a Lutheran and married, and as one of his first acts he announced solemnly that the king had never been rightfully married and was therefore free to marry again. This Henry did, following it up with an insistence that Parliament should declare that no foreign power had jurisdiction over England. At the king's request, Parliament then decreed that there

should be no more payment of annates or other monies to Rome, that it was high treason to question the legality of the king's marriage, and that the king was now supreme head of the Church of England. Prominent persons in the country were made to swear that they recognized the legality of the king's new position. The humanist Sir Thomas More, who had succeeded Wolsey as chancellor, refused to take the oath and was executed.

The next step was the dissolution of the monasteries, and their sale or bestowal into private hands, thus creating a class of persons who had a vested interest in the Reformation. This also was done through the agency of Parliament and a royal commission led by the king's secretary, Thomas Cromwell.

Royal attitude toward Protestants and Catholics

Meanwhile Henry, who still considered himself a Catholic in spite of the changes he had made in the Church, had been given no male heir by his new queen. When Anne fell out of favor also for other reasons Henry had her tried for adultery and beheaded. He thereupon married his third wife Jane Seymour, who did present him with a male heir, though she died in childbirth. Cromwell decided to turn Protestant and began to support the reformers, asking advice from Luther and Melancthon on how to set up an English Lutheran Church. The king took the advice in his own fashion, having the subservient Church promulgate a book of Articles of Faith and Ceremonies, which was substantially Lutheran in tone, though differing from Luther in the matter of salvation, which, according to these articles, was both by faith and good works. Luther's own remarks about King Henry were hardly complimentary, as he regarded him simply as an autocrat who insisted that his subjects believe what he himself happened to find it politic to believe at the moment. In 1539 Henry issued *Six Articles,* which were condemned by the Protestants as quite contrary to their faith, because the articles supported various practices of the Catholic Church such as the celebration of private Masses, and auricular confession. Moreover, they reaffirmed transubstantiation as well as the Real Presence, favored by Luther.

Though Henry considered himself a Catholic to the end of his reign, and in his later years had a number of Protestants executed, he nevertheless retained the married Lutheran Cranmer as archbishop of Canterbury, allowed the more fervent Lutheran bishop Latimer to retire without molestation, and supported the use of the English Bible, newly translated by Tyndale and Coverdale. So, though Protestants railed against him for being too Catholic, and Catholics condemned him for being too Protestant, there can be little doubt that by the end of his reign the ground was well prepared for Protestantism. The council that he provided for the young son, who was not yet of age when Henry died, was dominated by Protestants—a fact that can hardly have escaped Henry's notice.

Edward VI of England by Hans Holbein, the Younger. During the brief reign of Edward, the First Book of Common Prayer was issued, and the Reformation had its first king on the English throne. (COURTESY THE METROPOLITAN MUSEUM OF ART)

GROWTH OF PROTESTANTISM UNDER EDWARD VI

In the reign of Edward VI (1547–1553) the Protestant Reformation made great progress. Probably the bulk of the converts were in the towns, especially in the south, but the support of the royal council and the Lord Protector, followed by that of the young king as he grew to manhood, enabled considerable advances to be made. The First Book of Common Prayer, a new liturgy for use in the churches, was followed by an Act of Uniformity making the use of the new prayer book compulsory. The year before Edward's death, when the council was wholly dominated by Protestants, a Second Book of Common Prayer was introduced and made compulsory, which removed most of the remaining vestiges of the Roman rite and showed marked Calvinist influence. There is great controversy as to how many of the people of England had really been converted to Protestantism by this time. Though it may be regarded as certain that they were not yet in a majority, the probability is that most of the more active and articulate Christians had been converted, especially in the east and

south; but that, if a census had been taken which would have shown the religion of all, including the indifferent, this would have shown a Catholic majority, since it takes an active effort to change one's religion.

CATHOLIC REACTION UNDER MARY I

When Edward died an effort was made by the Duke of Northumberland, leader of Edward's council, to install a Protestant pretender on the throne. But the effort collapsed and the Catholic eldest daughter of Henry VIII by Catherine of Aragon was proclaimed queen (Mary I, 1553–1558). At first she took no drastic steps to restore the old religion, but after her marriage to Philip, son of Charles V, who shortly thereafter became king of Spain, she influenced the choice of a Parliament favorable to Catholicism and proceeded to use all the force of the law to enforce the return of papal supremacy and restoration cf all Catholic teachings and celebrations, though she was unable to persuade Parliament to restore church property that had been confiscated in the time of her father. There was one rebellion early in her reign,

A contemporary engraving showing the burning of two obscure martyrs at Smithfield during the reign of Mary I.

but otherwise the people accepted passively the more than three hundred burnings of heretics, high and low, that were initiated by her. Though she was unpopular with the people, far more unpopular was her Spanish marriage, followed by the effort to make English policies subservient to Spanish interests. In this field she was unable to have her way, and Philip, disgusted, left England and his wife. She died shortly afterward. Thus Elizabeth I, daughter of Anne Boleyn and the last surviving child of Henry VIII, came to the throne (1558–1603).

ELIZABETH I AND THE PROTESTANT
REFORMATION

The "Elizabethan Compromise"

She was at once faced by the religious issue that was clamoring for a settlement. Elizabeth herself was a lukewarm Protestant,

with a penchant for ceremony, and a dislike for extremism in any form. Public opinion had so obviously condemned the burnings during Mary's reign and Mary was so detested for her pro-Spanish policy that it would have been difficult, though not impossible, for Elizabeth to have maintained Catholicism in the country, providing she abjured the persecution. Many and rich favors were available to her if she had joined the Catholic monarchs of the continent, and almost certainly she could have obtained from the pope an arrangement similar to that won by Francis I at the Concordat of Bologna. But there was also to be considered the obvious distaste for papal supremacy which conflicted with English nationalism, together with the great advantages for an absolute monarchy which accrued from rulership over the Church and absolute control of churchmen. Therefore Elizabeth left the matter to Parliament, confident that Parliament would do just what she proposed, with or without her interference.

And so it happened. Parliament decided on a settlement that has since been called the Elizabethan Compromise, though in fact it was not in any real sense a compromise, except that the Anglican Church, established as the Church of England by the settlement, was far closer in most respects to Catholicism than any reformed Church of the time. Elizabeth herself accepted the title of supreme governor of the Church, which was acceptable to the Calvinists in her realm who thought only God could be the head of a Church, and she did not too seriously offend Catholic sensibilities. The Book of Common Prayer of 1552 was restored, with a few minor changes, and another Act of Uniformity was passed. No provisions were made for punishment for heresy, which ceased to be a crime unless it was accompanied by treason. The clergy were required to accept the position of the queen as governor, and only some three per cent refused, as far as can be ascertained. The episcopal system was maintained, and it may have seemed to many that there had been little real change in the religion despite the official establishment of Protestantism. For the early years of Elizabeth's reign very little attempt was made to enforce conformity in beliefs, and even the private celebration of Mass by Catholics was winked at.

Organization of Elizabethan Church

Once Parliament had done its initial work Elizabeth took her position of governor of the Church seriously and refused to allow Parliament to do anything more in the matter of religion except by her special request. Religious matters were settled in the Church assembly, known as Convocation, which was made up exclusively of members of the clergy. This body during the course of Elizabeth's reign, in spite of her right of appointment of bishops, became tinged with Calvinism, and many times the queen had some difficulty in getting her way. The basic beliefs of the Anglican Church were em-

bodied in the Thirty-nine Articles, passed by Convocation by the narrowest of majorities. Thus Elizabeth was faced by opponents of her religious policy both on the right and on the left, and she was forced to steer a very careful course between the two. On the whole, during her lifetime it must be said that she succeeded, though in the last years of her reign only her personal prestige and the uncompromising refusal of the Calvinists to have anything to do with the Catholics, whom they never hesitated to attack in the most vituperative language, managed to save her policy of moderation. The Calvinists were to make life very difficult for her successors.

Catholic efforts at restoration of the old religion

But the most open defiance of the queen came from the Catholics. In 1570 Pope Pius v gave up hope of converting her, and formally pronounced her excommunication. Many English Catholics had gone abroad rather than tolerate Protestantism as the established religion of their country. A special college was opened in Rome to train the most promising of these exiles, and another in Douai in northern France, where a Catholic version of the Bible was prepared in English. Already in the 1570's some of these trainees appeared in England, ready to celebrate Mass and teach the newly reformed Catholic religion. Parliament at once took cognizance of the danger by strengthening the treason laws. Then in 1580 an organized movement was launched by the Jesuits, and a pope is known to have given his approval to a plot to overthrow and even assassinate the English monarch. All these efforts were well known to the queen through spies, and the Protestants and the government were inflamed, not only with religious zeal against the attempted reconquest of their country, but with patriotism. Although the Calvinists kept sniping at the queen and complaining bitterly in pamphlets and sermons against the continuing "popish" customs in the Church—the use of vestments, the episcopal system, the elaborate ritual—and although many times the matter was raised in Parliament contrary to the queen's expressed wishes, they were entirely at one with her in willingness to enforce the treason laws to the letter. The number of Catholics put to death numbered fewer than a hundred, and a few incorrigibly outspoken Calvinists also lost their lives. All, however, were officially condemned for treason, and beheaded or hanged. The execution of Mary Queen of Scots in 1587 put an end to the Catholic plots to place her on the throne, but other plots not connected with religion persisted till the end of Elizabeth's reign.

Rise of Puritanism—Attitude of Elizabeth

The total result of her reign in the field of religion will never be fully known. But it is certain that Catholicism, identified as it was with foreign intervention, suffered a severe blow, and the Jesuit mission, though it may have comforted many Catholics and confirmed them in their faith, badly failed in its main purpose. In the forty-five years of her reign probably the vast majority of former Catholics, including all the lukewarm ones, became converted to the established Church. On the other hand there was a considerable growth of Calvinism, especially amongst the bourgeoisie and lesser landed gentry. These people resented in particular the remnants of "popery" in the Anglican Church and the position of the queen as its governor and real ruler. Being strong in Parliament they wished to use it for the purpose of making reforms in the Church in accordance with their own ideas. They wanted a Christian state like that in Scotland, where the civil power was forced to remain subordinate to the religious power wielded by the Presbyterian Church, and they wanted the government to interfere in the private lives of the people to ensure godly behavior. In England the crown stood squarely in their path. The monarch was governor of the Church, she had in her hands the appointments of the higher clergy, and through a special commission set up for the enforcing of Church discipline, the Court of High Commission, she was able to see that bishops and priests adhered to the Anglican forms and did no proselytizing for Calvinism. She continued to refuse permission to Parliament to discuss matters concerning the Church which she reserved for herself, and when, all the same, on one or two occasions they braved her displeasure and discussed them, she always had the last word with a royal veto of any measure they might pass.

When, therefore, James I, the next king of England, by his folly and pedantry played

A Puritan family. From an engraving in an old psalter dated 1563.

into their hands, the Puritans were able to gain enough support from fellow members of Parliament who did not share their religious convictions to begin a serious movement to make England into a Calvinist state. For a short while this was successful. But this discussion, bound up as it is with political as well as religious issues, will be left for Chapter 20.

▶ The Catholic Reformation or Counter Reformation

SPONTANEOUS MOVEMENTS TOWARD REFORM

As we have already seen, there had been many movements for reform within the Church in all the countries of Christendom. But the papacy in the hands of a number of indifferent and politically minded popes lagged far behind the best Catholic opinion abroad, and for a long time the only method of dealing with Luther and his supporters seemed to be the time-honored method of suppression through the aid of the temporal powers which remained faithful to Catholicism. In its hour of need, however, as had happened in the thirteenth century, two important new religious orders were founded, the Capuchins and the Theatines, to be followed shortly afterward by the Jesuits, the greatest group of proselytizers ever known within the Church. Together these reformers created the atmosphere necessary for the thoroughgoing reform that was so long overdue, and the papacy itself, as in the eleventh century, was taken over by the reformers. This was the foundation for the modern papacy, which has changed little in essentials since that time.

The Capuchins were an offshoot from the Franciscan Order, and were started, characteristically enough, by a friar who had visions directing him to return to the original spirit of St. Francis, but to wear a pointed cowl instead of the rounded cowl of the Franciscans. The movement attracted great numbers of Franciscans who had become disgusted with the part played by their order in secular affairs, together with other dedicated men who wished to engage in chari-

Portrait of a Capuchin monk by Rembrandt.

table and evangelizing work amongst the poor. These Capuchins were of great assistance to the more political work carried out by the Society of Jesus, especially attracting converts by their example.

More important politically, since it was they who took over the papacy and reformed it, were the Theatines, founded in 1524 by Caraffa, then a bishop. These men were specially selected for their outstanding talents and desire for reform. Originally, a company of reformers had met together to discuss and plan reform in Rome under the name of the Oratory of Divine Love. Amongst these men there were many earnest souls who sought for a spiritualization of the Church, notably a young Spaniard named Juan de Valdes. But when Caraffa organized them into the Theatine Order he chose only those who wished for and were willing to work for the practical reform of the Church. Indeed many of Valdes' disciples in later years were persecuted by Caraffa for their heretical views, which too often favored a far less institutionalized religion than that provided by the Catholic Church. It should be understood, therefore, that a Catholic Reformation might well have ultimately taken place without the Protestant Reformation. Thus it is not altogether fair to characterize the Catholic Reformation as a Counter Reformation, if by this term is understood only a reaction against Protestantism.

When Luther's movement began to grow, the Emperor Charles v was most anxious to avoid a split in the Church, which meant a split in his own dominions. There was never any doubt that he must stand with the Catholics, but he first wanted to see whether there was any chance of accommodation with the Lutherans. He therefore used all his influence with the papacy to persuade some pope to call a council for the airing of the points at issue and settling the controversy.

THE REFORMING POPES

Paul III and the first Council of Trent

The first reforming pope was Paul III (1534–1549). He was anxious to reform abuses, and he set up a commission of cardinals to investigate what the abuses were and to make suggestions. But even he was very wary of a council, for no pope could forget how dangerous councils had proved to papal authority in the fourteenth and fifteenth centuries. He much preferred to investigate, and even try to reach some agreement with the Protestants directly. To this end one of the cardinals went over the Alps to confer with Protestant leaders in 1541, but found it impossible to reach any accord over fundamental disagreements in doctrine. This played into the hands of Caraffa who became the most influential cardinal in Rome, backed as he was by his Theatine Order. And Caraffa had not the slightest intention of making any concession whatever in matters of doctrine, though he was entirely willing to reform the Church as thoroughly as would be required. As the

emperor also continued to insist on the council, Paul III finally decided to call one, after making sure that the Italians, appointees of the pope, would be in a sufficient majority to prevent the council from behaving like some of its predecessors. Protestants were invited, but, knowing they would be in a minority and not wishing to associate themselves in any way with the decisions that would be taken, they declined.

This first Council of Trent (1545–1547) was faced with the question of whether it would make any concessions whatever to the Protestant point of view on dogma. Perhaps the most important question of all was whether the Bible should, as Protestants insisted, be regarded as the sole authority in matters of faith, or whether Church tradition was equally authoritative. And what translation of the Bible should be used? It was decided by the council that Church tradition had an equal authority on the grounds that the Holy Spirit was always present in the Church and that therefore it could not err. And, in spite of the weight of criticism offered by the humanists in a century of learning, it was decided that the Vulgate version of the Bible as translated by St. Jerome in the fourth century was inspired also by the Holy Spirit and so was authoritative. Although the representatives of the emperor, who was himself unable to be present, tried to postpone discussion of the doctrine of justification by faith, in hopes that some concessions would be made to the Protestant position and thus halt the schism, the council, after considerable altercation, decided that the seven sacraments of the Church were necessary to salvation, a decision hardly likely to attract the Lutherans back to the fold. After two years there had been very little attempt to reform any but minor abuses, and after the plague broke out and it proved impossible to transfer the council elsewhere, it was adjourned.

Julius III and Paul IV

The next pope, Julius III (1550–1555), still under pressure from the emperor, agreed to reconvene the council at Trent, and some progress was made in defining the Eucharist and the sacrament of penance. The council was adjourned, however, when Trent suddenly became a place of danger, as war had broken out between the emperor and France.

Meanwhile the Inquisition, which had been dormant in Italy for a considerable time, was set up anew by Paul III, and its activities were defined carefully and its personnel strengthened by Julius III. The Society of Jesus had already embarked on its spectacular career. There was now no question that there was to be a reform in earnest, and in May, 1555, the formidable Caraffa himself was elected pope as Paul IV. He called no council during his pontificate but devoted himself to the cause of the reform of the clergy in Italy with unflagging zeal. Most of his cardinals were appointed solely for the purpose of carrying out the reform. The Inquisition was made more powerful and all-embracing, and given the task also of enforcing certain kinds of discipline within the clergy itself. If a priest took money for dispensing the sacraments he could now be cited before the Holy Office, instead of being disciplined by his ordinary clerical superior. In 1557 Paul IV set up the Index of Forbidden Books, later to be administered by a group of clergy known as the Congregation of the Index, which exists today and still provides lists of books which good Catholics may not read.

THE WORK OF THE COUNCIL OF TRENT

Refusal to compromise with Protestants

When Paul IV died in 1559 the old Renaissance papacy was gone forever. Though few of the later popes matched Paul IV in reforming zeal it was now unthinkable that the reform should stop, and the cardinals agreed on a reformer of somewhat milder temper, who took the name of Pius IV (1559–1565). He reconvened the Council of Trent, which in the space of one year completed its work with the redefinition of Catholic dogma which has remained authoritative to this day. Substantially the Church had made no retreat of any kind. The old teachings, hallowed in the Middle Ages, remained,

but were now greatly clarified, and the old latitudinarianism so noticeable in the time of St. Thomas Aquinas was banished forever. Catholic dogma is as clear and rational, having regard to its premises, as the logical teachings of Calvin. Out of this Council of Trent came the so-called Tridentine Catechism, which was widely distributed as a means of teaching Catholics the truths of their religion, and in this it performed a function similar to that of the catechisms adopted by the Protestant churches for the education of their young.

In brief, the third session of the Council of Trent decided in the same sense as the first. The various divergences of doctrine insisted on by Luther were all condemned and any persons holding them were anathema (cursed). Belief in purgatory was retained; the worship of saints and the use of images and relics were permitted and approved. Justification only by faith was condemned and the sacraments were declared to be necessary to salvation. Only the Church was permitted to interpret the Bible, and Church traditions were to be considered as authoritative as the Bible itself.

Restatement of Church doctrine

It should be understood that, from the point of view of the Church, nothing else was possible than this refusal to countenance any change in the basic teachings of the Church as they had been handed down by tradition; for this would have been to admit that in the past the Church had sometimes been mistaken. But the whole contention of the Church had always been that it had been founded by Christ, that the authority of Peter, the first bishop of Rome, chosen by Christ himself for the founding of the Church, had been transmitted in a direct line through the whole series of popes. Even during the Great Schism there had only been one pope at a time who had been canonically elected. At all times the Holy Spirit had been working through the Church and thus in matters of faith and practice any decrees made by the pope in his capacity of supreme head of the Church had been dictated by the Holy Spirit working through him. Thus it was impossible for him to be in error, although the actual infallibility of the pope as a dogma to be held by all Catholics was not proclaimed until 1870.

The popes and the Church were entirely willing to admit that in other respects the popes had not lived exemplary lives, and that the clergy had often been corrupt and worldly. These were sins committed as men, and in no way invalidated the sacraments they had administered during their priesthood, as the lives of the popes had not invalidated any pronouncements they had made in their capacity as pope. So the position adopted at the Council of Trent was entirely logical and in keeping with the basic religious position of the Church; it is not possible to think that it could have given way to the Protestants in any matter on which popes had already pronounced. There was thus no room for compromise, as there still is not. The Church might welcome back the schismatic Protestant Churches into its fold; but necessarily it would have to be on terms set by the Church in all that concerns doctrine and practices.

It is worth while summing up the answers given by the Church at the Council of Trent and during the movement of reform, to see how well calculated they were to do exactly what was asked of them. If this is understood, the triumphant reconversion of so many countries by the Jesuits will not appear quite so remarkable. As against the Protestant doctrines the Church reaffirmed its traditional beliefs in a clear and cogent manner. In the Tridentine Catechism these beliefs were made available to all the clergy, and through the clergy to all Catholics. The clergy in the future were to be trained in special seminaries, one of which must be set up by each bishop in his diocese. Thus in the future there would be no excuse for ignorance on the part of either priest or layman as to what were the beliefs to which he subscribed.

Index and Inquisition

To prevent the Catholic from learning of alternative doctrines he was forbidden to read any heretical books, or books regarded as dangerous to faith or morals. The permanent Congregation of the Index was to see that the list was kept up to date. Though the books, of course, were still printed in Protestant countries, Catholic governments, especially the Spanish, instituted strict searches at the ports to see that no forbidden literature was imported, and in Catholic countries the forbidden books could not be sold openly.

Finally, if any still persisted in heresy, the Inquisition could and did deal with them, as long as the secular powers supported it. Thus heresy was to be driven back, while the missionary forces went forth to try to reconquer those who had fallen away. By far the most influential of these missionaries were the members of the Society of Jesus, popularly called the Jesuits.

THE SOCIETY OF JESUS

Life and teaching of St. Ignatius Loyola

The Society of Jesus was in origin an entirely independent order, as were so many orders in the Church. The particular task that it undertook in the sixteenth and following centuries was dictated by the needs of the time, but its origin resembled many of the orders, notably the thirteenth-century Dominicans and Franciscans, in that it was founded by a man who felt himself called by God as the leader of a chosen band to carry out a particular task with the utmost devotion. Pope Paul III, like his predecessor Innocent III, was somewhat suspicious of such an excess of devotion, but finally confirmed the Society of Jesus in 1540, thus starting it on its remarkable way, and like the orders of the thirteenth century, once it had started it received every support from the papacy, to the jealousy of the older and less vital orders.

The founder of the Jesuits, Ignatius Loyola, was a Spaniard who had in early life been a soldier, and his order always retained the impress of his essentially military genius. Seriously wounded in a campaign and permanently crippled by inefficient surgery, knowing that his life as a soldier was over, he abandoned the chivalrous romances

St. Ignatius Loyola, founder of the Society of Jesus, from an old print.

his imagination told him that there was a need for such soldiers in the religious struggles that were rending the Christian world.

It can readily be seen how such a spirit could very easily have taken the other side, and how natural it was that he should have been called before the Spanish Inquisition three times to answer for his opinions; and it is not difficult to understand the suspicions of orthodox churchmen when they came in contact with him. His temperament and aristocratic upbringing would have made it difficult to work with Calvinists; but there is much that is similar in the dedication, self-reliance, and tenacity shown by Loyola and the best of the Calvinists. Martyrdom would have held no terrors for him. His indomitable will led him, already in his thirties, to master foreign languages and theology, even though he had to "go to school with boys," and submit to the discipline imposed on boys in that age. And at last he was able to gather around himself a few dedicated spirits like himself and found the Company or Society of Jesus.

Work and influence of the Jesuits

All the members of the society had to go through as much as they could stand of a rigorous training similar to that undergone by its founder, who wrote in the *Spiritual Exercises* the details of the training, the ascetic practices, the special meditations, and the prayers. The novitiate was long and in the early years only a comparatively small number, mostly Spaniards like Loyola himself, passed fully through it, to become "professed" members of the society. At this point they took the Four Vows, the fourth of which was absolute obedience in mind and will to their superiors. And the society as a whole took a vow of absolute obedience to the pope.

It is impossible to overestimate the value for the Catholic Church, in the process of reforming itself, of having at its disposal such a band of devoted helpers. Once the Church had accepted them they were showered with aid and privileges. Naturally the Catholic rulers viewed them with some

on which he had hitherto been nurtured when a Bible was put into his hands.

There followed a period of struggle comparable to that of Luther. Loyola also felt convinced of his damnation for the enormity of his sins. After trying every method he could think of for mortifying and humiliating himself, he at last received comfort and illumination, and recognized, like Luther, that he had been freed by the mercy of God. But, not being a theologian, this experience did not lead him to heretical doctrines, still less to the thought of salvation outside the Church. When the severe asceticism to which he had subjected himself yielded its fruit in the form of visions, described by Loyola with the utmost concreteness in his *Spiritual Exercises*, he concluded that the discipline of the will, which had led in his case to a mystical experience of God, was the true path to be followed by the devoted Christian. But he did not stop there. Being a soldier, and still having to an extreme degree the soldier's spirit of selfless devotion to a cause,

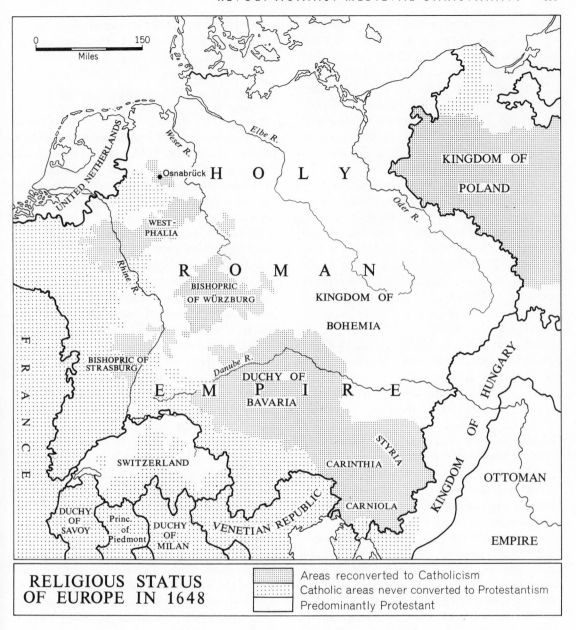

RELIGIOUS STATUS
OF EUROPE IN 1648

Areas reconverted to Catholicism
Catholic areas never converted to Protestantism
Predominantly Protestant

dismay, for here was an instrument for the recovery of the papal domination which had been thrown off with such difficulty in the previous centuries. Protestant rulers, of course, could only regard them as dangerous enemies. But the Jesuits preached amongst the people and lower clergy as well as amongst the more influential, dispelling their ignorance and inspiring a new spirit of devotion. A catechism was drawn up by a Dutch Jesuit St. Peter Canisius and widely

used for the education of children, and key persons in every country were encouraged to use Jesuits as their confessors.

It was widely said that they used the secrets of the confessional to gain power and influence over individuals, and that they used the powers of absolution entrusted to them as priests to frighten or cajole penitent souls into political actions approved by the Jesuits. It was said that they were masters of casuistry, able to argue that sins considered mortal were not really so; that they were willing to condone any crime; and not only were their own consciences elastic but they promoted the elasticity of the consciences of others provided it served their political ends. Certainly they intrigued with rulers, going straight to the most influential persons, knowing well enough the power of rulers to coerce their subjects. Because no special habit was prescribed for them, no one even knew who they were; since they were unknown all sorts of conspiracies were attributed to them. Unfavorable events, easily explicable by other means, were almost invariably laid at their door in Protestant countries. The "Jesuit menace" was as firmly believed in the sixteenth and seventeenth centuries as ever the "Communist menace" in the twentieth century.

It may be added that by setting up schools and colleges and providing the best education available in their day and taking no money for their services, they prepared the way for the future. With a proper education they believed that their students would be forever afterward immune from heresy. And of course this too was held against them by their enemies.

Through the Jesuits' many-pronged attack—on the rulers through their consciences and the confessional, through political intrigue when necessary, through their near monopoly of education, and through their well-organized missionary activities— they, with a reformed Church behind them, were the chief instrument in rolling back the tide of Protestantism. Between them and the Inquisition all incipient Protestantism in Spain and Italy was stamped out. South Germany, Hungary, Poland, Austria, and Belgium all returned to the faith of their fathers, although by the mid-sixteenth century Protestantism might well have been thought likely to conquer, even in these countries. And though in the eighteenth century ruler after ruler expelled them from their states, and for a short time the society itself was dissolved by the papacy, by then their work had been done. The tide of Protestant reform had been turned. It was

never to know again the success it had won in the century in which Luther and Calvin had worked.

▶ Summary—Consequences of the Reformation

It is not easy to summarize the effects of the Protestant Reformation, not all of which were to be observed in the century of its introduction. In the economic realm the rising and ever-growing bourgeoisie found in Calvinism a religious teaching which justified the bourgeois virtues of thrift and hard work for profit, needed for the full development of capitalism.

In the political realm the national state was glorified by Lutheranism; princes gained power and prestige through their new control of a national Church. The papacy, even in Catholic countries, lost ground as a political force, since Catholic rulers, while remaining Catholic in religion, assumed many of the powers which accrued to Protestant rulers through the Reformation. As an international political organization the papacy was virtually dead by the end of the sixteenth century, though its religious reform prepared the ground for a new kind of papacy, working indirectly through its reformed clergy and moral example rather than directly by political interference with secular powers.

In the cultural field literacy greatly increased through the Bible reading required by the Protestants. The new Protestant universities, such as the Dutch University of Leiden and the Jesuit schools and colleges in Catholic countries provided a more modern education than that provided hitherto in a haphazard way by the Church. The Protestant contempt for most forms of art as "popery" put a halt to the religious pictures so characteristic of the Renaissance, while the new plain Protestant churches had no use for the elaborate architecture of the Gothic or Renaissance styles. Even the papacy in its reformed period no longer acted as patron of the arts, and indeed moved far toward the Protestant viewpoint on the lack of necessity for earthly display.

Finally, it may be added that the age of the Reformation was as intolerant as any age in history, and the intolerance was not confined to one side. However, indirectly, the persecutions of the age and the insistence on cruelly punishing men and women for their religious opinions led to a feeling of surfeit in later centuries, and to the thought that in a field where nothing can be proved and all is a matter of opinion, a man may hold whatever opinions he wishes, as long as they do not lead to the subversion of good order.

And, though Calvin himself may hardly have been a democrat, within Calvinism, as we have seen, there were the seeds of democracy. These could not flower in the age of the Reformation itself, but had to wait until all men were in fact more nearly equal than they were in the sixteenth and seventeenth centuries.

▶ ## Suggestions for further reading

One of the difficulties inseparable from the study of the Protestant Reformation is that the subject can only with great difficulty be handled without the intrusion of some kind of religious bias. A famous book by a lifelong student of the Reformation is Preserved Smith, *The Age of the Reformation* (New York: Henry Holt and Company, Inc., 1920). There can be no doubt that Preserved Smith knew the Reformation thoroughly, and his work is a mine of information, well organized under countries, and containing a great deal of important historical material which needs to be known by the student studying the religious reform. The book is extremely readable, even dramatic; but on every page the author's Protestant sympathies are apparent, and a reader without such sympathies might well find the book unpalatable, even though it is always couched in temperate language. It is therefore perhaps safer for most students to obtain an accurate knowledge of the period from such a text as Harold Grimm, *The Reformation Era* (New York: The Macmillan Company, 1954) which is very fair-minded and comprehensive but remains basically a textbook.

A Berkshire study, George Mosse, *The Reformation* (New York: Henry Holt and Company, 1953) is a brief and concise study, which,

like most of the series in which it appears, gives a clear picture of the subject in a minimum of space and is also relatively free from bias. The second half of Henry S. Lucas, *The Renaissance and the Reformation* (New York: Harper & Brothers, 1934) is shorter than Grimm, and though distinguished by no graces of style, is nevertheless readable and well organized around the progress of the Reformation in the different European countries, and gives an adequate explanation of the conditions within which the Reformation operated.

The Catholic Reformation, or Counter Reformation, is in general not so well covered in easily available literature. A solid work in this field is Beresford Kidd, *The Counter-Reformation, 1550–1600* (London: Society for the Promotion of Christian Knowledge, 1937), which has no discernible bias, but is presented in a rather formidable and not very interesting manner, though it contains most of the relevant facts. An excellent introduction to the whole subject is provided in an edition of the *Letters of Obscure Men* referred to in Chapter 16 as one of the important polemics put out by the humanists. This is Francis G. Stokes, ed., *Epistolae obscurorum virorum* (London: Chatto & Windus, 1909). The book contains the Latin text with an English rendering and the historical introduction just mentioned, which succeeds in connecting the work of the humanists with that of the reformers in an easily comprehensible manner.

Biographies of the leaders of the Reformation and Counter Reformation are numerous. Most of them are marred to some degree by bias in favor of or against the persons studied, and the purpose of the writers has been to convince rather than necessarily to enlighten. One of the best of these which makes a good effort at objectivity is written by a distinguished historian of the Church, who has also written a general account of the Reformation which is brief but an effective synthesis. The latter book is Roland Bainton, *The Reformation of the 16th Century* (Boston: The Beacon Press, 1952), and the Lutheran biography is called *Here I Stand: A Life of Martin Luther* (New York: Abingdon Press, Inc., 1950). Both of Bainton's books, incidentally, are beautifully produced and decorated with excellent woodcuts. It seems that no one has ever been able with full success to make John Calvin into a sympathetic character, and his biographers have difficulty in making him stand out as a person, in the way Luther stands out even in inferior and biased biographies. The student is urged to try Georgia E. Harkness, *John Calvin: the Man and his Ethics* (New York: Henry Holt and Company, 1931), by a student of ethics and professor of philosophy who has made a notable effort to present both Calvin's life and teachings in a clear and objective manner. The teachings are very carefully considered and the way in which they flow from his theology is clearly explained. James Mac-Kinnon, *Calvin and the Reformation* (London: Longmans, Green & Co., 1936) is devoted more to Calvin's work, but if read in conjunction with Harkness, will give a well-rounded picture of the Calvinist reform and effectively distinguish Calvinism from the more conservative Lutheranism. The standard life of Ignatius Loyola is Paul van Dyke, *Ignatius Loyola, the Founder of the Jesuits* (New York: Charles Scribner's Sons, 1927) which contains many quotations from the *Spiritual Exercises,* and presents a very clear picture of the founder of the Society of Jesus, as well as material on the order itself.

Preserved Smith, *The Life and Letters of Martin Luther* (Boston: Houghton Mifflin Company, 1911) may be recommended especially for the light thrown on Luther's character by his correspondence. Luther's most important polemical works are printed in Henry Wace and C. A. Buchheim, eds., *Luther's Primary Works* (London: Hodder and Stoughton, 1896). Calvin's fundamental ideas may be found in John Calvin, *Institutes of the Christian Religion* (tr., John Allen, 6th American edition, Philadelphia: Presbyterian Board of Christian Education, 1930). This book is well worth more than a casual glance, since Calvin's methods of argument and the logical nature of his thought may be illustrated on almost every page. If the material in Van Dyke is not sufficient for the student on the teachings of Ignatius Loyola, *The Spiritual Exercises of St. Ignatius* (tr., Louis J. Puhl, Westminster, Md.: Newman Press, 1951) may be consulted. Finally, attention should be drawn to the excellent chapter entitled "Protestant and Catholic" by E. Harris Harbison in Kenneth Setton and Henry Winkler, *Great Problems in European Civilization* (Englewood Cliffs, N. J.: Prentice-Hall, Inc., 1954) which contains an admirable selection of the writings of the leading reformers and their opponents, classified under various topics on which there was difference of opinion. Many of these selections were translated by the author and not previously available in English, in spite of their obvious importance.

For the Max Weber thesis briefly referred to in the text, that the success of Protestantism reflected the interest of the bourgeois class in having a religion suited to its commercial ideals, the pioneer work was Max Weber, *The Protestant Ethic and the Spirit of Capitalism* (revised and enlarged edition, New York: Charles Scribner's Sons, 1930). For most English readers, however, the thesis is more satisfactorily and more eloquently expounded in Richard Tawney, *Religion and the Rise of Capitalism* (New York: The New American Library, a Mentor Book, 1953), in which the author states the thesis clearly and defends it in a convincing, if one-sided manner. A curious offspring of these two books may be studied, though it is hoped with caution, in Erich Fromm, *Escape from Freedom* (New York: Rinehart & Company, Inc., 1941), Chapter 3, "Freedom during the Reformation." The author, a noted psychoanalyst, writing in a very positive and convinced manner, tries to show in this book how the Reformation, in the hands of its original leaders, was a reversion to authoritarianism, and represents an effort to escape from the individualism implicit in the Renaissance and from the freedom which should have been accepted as an outcome of the latter. The rest of the book is devoted to an exposition of the consequences of this fact in modern history. It is an interesting sidelight, and though few will accept it in its entirety, it is a stimulus to further thought on the matter.

Finally, attention should be drawn to a book on the Anabaptists which is well written and extremely interesting, though the reader should be warned that the author, who was a prominent Socialist in his day, is writing to a particular thesis. But his book, Ernest B. Bax, *Rise and Fall of the Anabaptists* (New York: The Macmillan Company, 1903) does contain a great deal of information on the ramifications of the Anabaptist movement in all the countries where it penetrated, and this information is not easily available elsewhere. Anabaptism was a social movement at least as much as it was a religious movement, and the Socialist interpretation by Bax is as valid, perhaps more valid, than any other.

19

The Evolution of National States
during the Early Modern Period

*Political concepts of the modern world • Contrast between medieval and
modern concepts • The Turkish menace • The Holy Roman Empire under
Charles V and his successors • The Thirty Years' War • Scandinavia, Brandenburg-Prussia, Poland, and Russia • Philip II and the rise of the Dutch Republic
• France and England in the sixteenth century*

► Political concepts of the modern world

THE MEDIEVAL CONCEPT—CHURCH AND EMPIRE

In the last three chapters we have considered three important factors in the preparation of the modern world. In isolating such
factors as an aid to understanding the whole,
we referred necessarily to the political systems under which the changes were wrought.
There will thus be some overlapping of subject matter in this chapter, which attempts
to draw the strands together into a coherent
whole.

From Chapter 15, in which the development of national states in the Middle Ages
was studied, the general principles under
which medieval governments operated may
have been grasped. But in order to clarify
the contrasts between governmental theory
and practice in the Middle Ages and the
early modern period, these principles will
be more directly summarized here. In some
respects, as will be observed, governmental
theory in recent centuries has returned to the
best thought of the Middle Ages and modi-

fied it, rather than adopting wholeheartedly
the theory of the absolute rights of the monarch, deriving from Renaissance and early
modern thought—even if governmental practice in modern times has too often tended
to follow the precepts of the Renaissance
thinker Machiavelli.

The most important and tenacious
thought in the early Middle Ages held that
there ought to be both a spiritual and earthly
government for all Christendom—the first
in the hands of the Church, headed by the
pope, and the second in the hands of the
emperor, whose government was termed
Holy because the emperor derived his right
to rule from God, and Roman because it
was regarded as a successor to the Roman
Empire, which had in fact exercised an imperial sway over the greater part of what
was to become Christendom. But, as we have
seen, the emperor was never able to wield
the authority that theoretically belonged to
him, while a serious struggle had developed
between the rival pretensions of Church and
emperor, since the former demanded obedience from the emperor in realms which the

► chronological chart

The Holy Roman Empire

Reign of Maximilian I	1493–1519
Reign of Charles V	1519–1556
Victory of Charles V over Francis I of France at battle of Pavia	1525
Sack of Rome by Charles's troops	1527
Turkish siege of Vienna	1529
Schmalkaldic War	1546–1547
Religious Peace of Augsburg	1555
Abdication of Charles V	1556
Reign of Ferdinand I	1556–1564
Peace of Cateau-Cambrésis	1559
Formation of Protestant (Evangelical) Union	1608
Formation of Catholic League	1609
Issue of *Letters of Majesty* by Emperor Rudolf II	1609
Reign of Matthias	1612–1619
Defenestration of Prague	1618
Thirty Years' War	1618–1648
Reign of Ferdinand II	1619–1637
Frederick V (the Winter King) accepts throne of Bohemia	1619
Battle of the White Mountain	1620
Transfer of Palatine electoral vote to Maximilian of Bavaria	1623
Entry of Christian IV of Denmark into the war	1625
Siege of Stralsund by Wallenstein	1628
Issue of *Edict of Restitution* of Church lands by Ferdinand	1629
Treaty of Lübeck—retirement of Christian from war	1629
Dismissal of Wallenstein	1630
Entry of Gustavus II Adolphus into war	1630
Victory of Gustavus Adolphus at Breitenfeld	1631
Restoration of Wallenstein to command	1631
Battle of Lützen—death of Gustavus Adolphus	1632
Assassination of Wallenstein	1634
Battle of Nördlingen—victory of imperialists	1634
Peace of Prague	1635
Reign of Ferdinand III	1637–1657

The Holy Roman Empire (cont'd)

Accession of Frederick William, the Great Elector, of Brandenburg-Prussia	1640
Entry of French into the war	1639
Peace of Westphalia	1648

Sweden

Union of Kalmar (three Scandinavian crowns)	1387
Massacre of Stockholm—execution of Swedish national leaders	1520
Gustavus I Vasa, king of Sweden	1523–1560
Hanseatic trade monopoly ended	1537
Reign of Eric XIV	1560–1568
Reign of Sigismund III (also king of Poland 1587–1632)	1592–1599
Treaty of Teusina—acquisition of Livonia	1595
Deposition of Sigismund III	1599
Swedish intervention in Russian "Time of Troubles"	1604–1613
Reign of Gustavus II Adolphus	1611–1632
Treaty of Stolbovo—acquisition of Karelia and Ingria	1617
Wars with Poland—occupation of all Livonia	1621–1629
Intervention of Gustavus II in Thirty Years' War	1630–1632
Death of Gustavus at battle of Lützen	1632
Reign of Christina—rule by Chancellor Oxenstierna	1632–1654
Peace of Westphalia	1648
Reign of Charles X	1654–1660
First Northern War	1655–1660
Peace of Oliva	1660
Reign of Charles XII	1697–1718

(For Swedish participation in Great Northern War see chronological chart for Chapter 21.)

Denmark and Norway

Union of Kalmar	1387
Reign of Christian II	1513–1523
Separation of Sweden under Gustavus Vasa	1520

Denmark and Norway (cont'd)

Reign of Christian III	1534–1558
Establishment of Danish national Protestant Church	1536
Reign of Christian IV	1588–1648
Wars with Sweden	1611–1613, 1643–1645
Intervention of Christian IV in Thirty Years' War	1625–1629
Reign of Frederick III	1648–1670
Peace with Sweden	1660

Brandenburg — Prussia

Union of Brandenburg and Prussia by inheritance	1618
Rule of Frederick William, the Great Elector	1640–1688
Frederick III, elector of Brandenburg, assumes title of king	1701

Poland — Lithuania

Reign of Sigismund II—last of Jagiellon monarchs	1548–1572
Union of Lublin	1569
Election of Henry of Valois to kingship (Henry III of France)	1573
Stephen Batory defeats Russia in Livonian Wars	1579–1582
Intervention of Poland in Russian "Time of Troubles" under Sigismund III	1609–1618
Renunciation of claim to Russian throne by Vladislav IV	1634
Wars with Sweden	1655–1660
Peace of Oliva	1660
Reign of John III Sobieski	1674–1696
Raising of siege of Vienna by John III	1683
Expulsion of Augustus II from Polish throne by Charles XII of Sweden	1704
Restoration of Augustus II after battle of Poltava	1709

Russia

Reign of Ivan III (the Great)	1462–1505
Reign of Ivan IV (the Terrible)	1533–1584
Assumption of personal power and title of Tsar by Ivan	1547
Convocation of first *zemsky sobor*	1549
Conflict with boyars and formation of *oprichnina*	1564

Russia (cont'd)

Formation of Russian patriarchate	1589
"Time of Troubles"—conflicts over succession	1604–1613
Election of Michael Romanov as tsar	1613

Spain

Reign of Charles I of Spain (Charles V of the Empire)	1516–1556
Capture of Francis I of France at battle of Pavia	1525
Wars with France	1521–1529, 1535–1538, 1542–1544, 1551–1559
Reign of Philip II	1556–1598
Treaty of Cateau-Cambrésis with France	1559
Beginning of struggle in Netherlands	1567
Victory of Don John of Austria (natural brother of Philip) against Turks	1571
Succession of Philip to Portuguese throne	1580
Defeat of Spanish Armada by English	1588
Intervention of Philip in efforts to exclude Henry IV from French throne	1589–1598
Reign of Philip III	1598–1621
Reign of Philip IV	1621–1665
Independence of Portuguese crown	1640
Peace of the Pyrenees	1659

Spanish Netherlands

Netherlands pass to rule of Philip II of Spain	1556
Governorship of Margaret of Parma	1559–1567
Governorship of duke of Alva	1567–1573
Sack of Antwerp and Pacification of Ghent	1576
Governorship of Alexander Farnese, duke of Parma	1578–1592
Proclamation of independence of northern provinces	1581
Assassination of William the Silent	1584
Twelve Years truce between Spain and United Provinces	1609–1621
Resumption of war	1621
Recognition of independence of United Provinces at peace of Westphalia	1648

France

Reign of Francis I	1515–1547
Wars with Spain and empire (See under Spain)	
Peace of Cateau-Cambrésis	1559
Religious wars	1562–1598
Massacre of St. Bartholomew	1572
Formation of Holy League (the Guises)	1576
Henry of Navarre becomes heir apparent to throne	1584
War of the three Henrys	1585–1589
Assassination of Duke of Guise and King Henry III	1589
Reign of Henry IV	1589–1610
Abjuration of Protestantism by Henry IV	1593
Edict of Nantes and end of civil and religious wars	1598

France (cont'd)

Assassination of Henry IV	1610

England

Reign of Henry VII	1485–1509
Establishment of Court of Star Chamber	1487
Rebellions of Perkin Warbeck	1488–1499
Reign of Henry VIII	1509–1547
Chancellorship of Cardinal Wolsey	1515–1529
Act of Supremacy—Henry head of the Church of England	1534
Dissolution of monasteries	1536–1539
Religious changes in succeeding reigns (See chart for Chapter 18)	
Reign of Elizabeth I	1558–1603
Renunciation of claims to Calais, last French territory in English possession	1564
Defeat of Spanish Armada	1588

latter deemed to be secular. This conflict of jurisdiction doomed the medieval empire, though the Holy Roman Empire continued to exist as an institution, shorn of its universal pretensions and usually with less power than an ordinary national state. It was, however, universally accepted that the emperor's power was not absolute, and that he, like any other ruler, had to rule in accordance with established customs and justice.

ROLE OF NATIONAL MONARCH—MEDIEVAL
THEORY AND PRACTICE

In the later Middle Ages a new institution began to gain ground—a national state, and medieval political theorists who were employed by national monarchs naturally attempted to transfer to their masters the attributes hitherto reserved to the emperor. The Church theory, on the other hand, remained basically that of St. Thomas Aquinas, who held, following Stoic thought as developed in Roman law, that there was a natural equality of man because men are

all endowed with the same reason and all are made in the image of God. Hence all men are entitled equally to justice. Rulers therefore, in medieval theory, were bound to administer equal justice in relation to their subjects. There is a natural law, to be discovered by the thinking mind, which rulers must obey, since they derive their power from God and are Christian kings. Implied in this theory is a peculiar contradiction, that on the one hand it would appear that there should be a "natural" right to oppose a tyrant, while on the other hand a rebellion against a monarch who had been sanctified by God could be held to be a revolt against God himself—a problem that, as we shall see, was to become very important in the seventeenth century, when Calvinists, in particular, were claiming this very right of rebellion. It was, of course, understood in medieval thought that the Church had the duty to remind a monarch of his obligations, and certain popes had even attempted to depose monarchs and release their subjects from their allegiance when the obligations were not kept.

No medieval thinker would have dared to question the fact of natural law, which was hallowed by the tradition of more than a thousand years, which had been implied in St. Paul, and accepted by all the Christian fathers as well as by pagan philosophers like Cicero. Moreover, the belief that a monarch had to obey the dictates of natural law was strongly fortified by the customs and practices developed by the national states. The feudal monarch, in fact, was hedged around by innumerable restrictions on his freedom of action. This especially applied to the English king, whose subjects had the *right* to sit in Parliament and be consulted on matters that affected them. The king could not by unilateral action abrogate these customary rights and legislate by decree; nor could the fundamental laws of the realm be changed except by consent, and agreement by the representatives of the people who sat in Parliament. Where there was no statute applicable, then the common laws of the realm prevailed. King John in 1215 had been forced to admit the limitation on his powers when he agreed to Magna Carta. Parliament was to cross swords with Charles I in the seventeenth century and ultimately behead him because he wished to act like an efficient "modern" monarch and rule without the consent of his Lords and Commons; and it was no accident that it was the conservative guardians of the common law who took the lead in the struggle.

The French monarchy was in a similar position. The French king too was bound by the customs of his realm, and feudal nobles fought for the right to retain their privileges in innumerable civil wars. But during the Hundred Years' War they had allowed some of their rights to fall into royal hands which did not wish and could not be compelled to release them; hence in the sixteenth-century civil wars the powers of nobles and king were fairly evenly matched, and France was able to emerge as an absolute monarchy. The Tudor monarchy in England was never absolute and only managed to give that appearance by the tactful behavior of the monarchs in never forcing a showdown. In Spain likewise, the king's power was supposedly limited by the Cortes, which did in fact exercise considerable power and maintain the customary rights of the nobles and people until Ferdinand inherited the crown of Aragon in 1479 and Isabella, his wife, inherited the crown of Castile in 1474. The power of the Cortes in the separate kingdoms of Aragon and Castile was greatly weakened when the two thrones were occupied by a married couple, ruling the two kingdoms jointly.

The medieval theory, therefore, in the matter of the limitation of the power of kings did correspond to the facts of the age. And no medieval monarch would ever have denied that he had a moral responsibility to his people. He held his position by the grace of God, he was anointed in a religious ceremony, and at death he was a Christian man like anyone else, hoping for salvation. He might have a quarrel with his clergy or the papacy, but it would be a political quarrel, usually a result of political claims by the Church; and unless he had political grounds for supporting heretics, he would certainly consider it his duty to suppress heresy as severely as any pope or inquisitor as rebellion against the whole concept on which his throne rested.

THE RENAISSANCE DESPOT—POWER WITHOUT MORAL RESPONSIBILITY

With the coming of the Renaissance the medieval concept of the position of the ruler radically changed. Naturally it was the practice that changed first, and theory followed haltingly behind. Too many Renaissance despots knew that they had acquired their princedoms by their own individual efforts; and though they might wish the Church to sanctify their achievements and position, it was an ex post facto sanctification, a recognition of the accomplished fact. Moreover, they were, as individuals, proud that they had won their position, rather than humbly grateful for having inherited it. And having won it, there was no reason why they should not exploit it to the utmost of their ability. No natural rights of their subjects could possibly be binding on them, for they had never accepted such rights. If the subjects claimed them, then let them fight it out; and if the subjects won, then they had won their rights on the only battlefield that mattered, the battlefield of force matched against force. Machiavelli was the supreme exponent of this point of view. He provided the prince with instruction in the techniques of acquiring and keeping power, and every despot in Europe read his books to learn. So began the period of realistic politics. Too often the Church used the same techniques, thereby losing the right to remind princes that there were higher powers in the world than they, that earthly government is bestowed by God and that it carries responsibilities with it.

CONCEPT OF BALANCE OF POWER—DYNASTIC AND NATIONAL INTERESTS

This is not to say that all monarchs of the early modern period were ready to admit that their policies had no moral justification, and, as we shall see, religious reasons provided an attractive cloak for expansionist policies. Most of the innumerable wars of the sixteenth and early seventeenth centuries which we shall discuss in this chapter were, however, private wars initiated by monarchs who merely wished to increase their glory and the glory of their families by adding territories to their hereditary domains. Of course they had legal excuses satisfactory to themselves, and legal excuses can quickly become moral excuses in the minds of experienced politicians. Such were the wars of Francis I and of Charles V, though it may be admitted that Charles V was usually on the defensive and forced into them, due to the fact that he was the chief possessor of the time. Diplomacy in the sixteenth century largely consisted in arranging for matrimonial alliances which could add territories to one ruling house at the expense of another, and in arranging for alliances in such a way that one side would obtain military advantage in a war at the expense of another.

Francis I had no hesitation in allying himself with the infidel Turkish sultan, nor had the Catholic Charles V or the Cardinal Richelieu in allying themselves with Protestants when it suited their political needs. In a later age the system was to be dignified by the name of the "balance of power." And indeed when the national spirit was further developed and the concept of national interests had some validity, the balance of power was taken into serious consideration by diplomats and their masters, since its main purpose was to stop wars or see that they were fought with the sides as equally matched as possible. But in the sixteenth century, alliances were made with no such end in view, still less with any conception of national, as distinct from dynastic interests. Nothing would have been further from the thought of Francis I than the consideration of the needs of his people, which were almost certain to require that the wars be halted. But it should be added that the boundaries of European countries were by no means fixed as yet. Mary Tudor of England said that when she died the word "Calais" would be found written on her heart because she had lost it in warfare; whereas we today could only consider the possession of such an outpost by England as unnatural, because the inhabitants regard themselves as French, speak the French language, the city is contiguous with other French lands, and the people are in every way as French as the people of Paris.

GROWTH OF PRINCIPLE OF NATIONALITY— INCIPIENT NATIONALISM

In the sixteenth century while the monarchs were seeking their own ends and the ends of their families, the idea of the nation-state was gradually growing. As we have already seen, the idea that a monarch should be a native of the country that he ruled, and conversely that a people were entitled to be ruled by a native prince was not altogether absent in medieval times. Patriotism and xenophobia undoubtedly played their part in the final success of

France in the Hundred Years' War. The spirit grew mightily in England during the Tudor rule, especially under Elizabeth, who, perhaps the first of all European monarchs, understood the concept of national interest and tried to direct all her policies in accordance with the concept. The brilliant success of her long reign and the position of power and dignity to which she raised her small country, were in large measure due to the single-mindedness of her policies. She was, as she said, "married to England"; and one does not have to look far into Shakespeare to see how deeply he was filled with patriotism and love for "this precious stone set in the silver sea . . . this blessed plot, this earth, this realm, this England." Henry IV (1589–1610) was the first king of France to have such a concept, as he was almost the last, for later kings, especially Louis XIV, reverted to the dynastic policies still prevalent in the rest of Europe, which almost succeeded in ruining their country.

CONFUSION OF POLITICAL AND RELIGIOUS ISSUES—THE REFORMATION

Into this world of incipient nationalism were suddenly thrust the problems involved in an issue which was basically irrelevant to the main one—the schism in the Church caused by the Protestant Reformation. The real problem was to develop a form of government in the national states which would take care of national interests while protecting the rights of individuals in those states, help states which were not yet national to become so, and prevent them from destroying each other by attempting to expand their borders in a limited territory. If all the states had continued to hold the same religious beliefs as in the Middle Ages, all that would have been necessary would have been to reform the Church and inhibit its interferences in political life—in short have the Church behave more or less as it does now. But the unreformed Church with its hierarchy was a made-to-order political instrument for use by monarchs in the sixteenth and seventeenth centuries, and

many of them coveted the chance to adapt it to their own ends for the purpose of increasing their power. So they had a strong motive for setting up their own national Church which, again, had little to do with the interests or wishes of their subjects, who were rarely consulted in the matter. Thus the Reformation, as we have seen, was used by most monarchs simply for the purposes of their power politics; while even the Catholic monarchs who did feel deeply about the schism, and felt it their duty toward God to restore the old faith by force of arms if necessary, frequently did so because by so doing they gained the political support of the papacy and the Jesuits. It is therefore not surprising that all the so-called "Wars of Religion" became something else rather rapidly, and played their part in settling or aggravating the real political problems that have been mentioned. The Dutch were helped by their Calvinism to gain independence for their country, as their opponent retained Belgium because Belgium wished to stay Catholic. But the Dutch would have been willing to let Philip of Spain rule them if he had not interfered with their religion, thus driving them to rebellion. The German princes did not unite into a German nation until the nineteenth century largely because of religious difference; and the princes themselves used their national Lutheran Church as an aid to their particularism, or local independence. Sweden used the religious issue to try to build a Baltic empire, and she did gain national independence by expelling a Catholic monarch.

So the political and religious issues became inextricably confused, and any uniform national development became impossible. And behind the confusion there was the ever-present question of what was the duty owed by the people to their monarch, and vice versa. Was there a right to rebellion if the king did not look to national interests, did not consult the wishes of the people, or changed their religion? If indeed he held his position from God, then it was sin as well as treason to rebel against him. If he suppressed the religion of the majority of his subjects, could he claim that he held his position from God, however legitimate he might be according to the laws of heredity? Was the medieval theory correct that men owed unlimited obedience to their rulers, although in medieval times it had always been understood that the king accepted responsibility as well as power? Was there an exception to Christ's injunction to "render unto Caesar the things which are Caesar's and unto God the things that are God's" if Caesar did not rule justly and in accordance with the interests of his subjects?

Martin Luther had been very definite in the matter. Passive obedience was the duty of all subjects to their monarchs in all circumstances. Calvin himself, as a ruler of a state, personally held the same view, although not entirely consistently in all his writings. But not the Calvinists who followed him. John Knox was extremely explicit on the matter when questioned by his sovereign, Mary Queen of Scots. She had no right whatever to establish a Church contrary to the will of her people. When she replied that he must then think she ought to obey him, he insisted, as a good Calvinist, that God was the only true ruler of the country, and he himself was only an unworthy instrument. So naturally Calvinist theorists were led to preach the right of rebellion against tyrants, and to them all rulers were tyrants who did not accept the right of the Calvinist Church to have an important say in the government. Bodin in France, as a good lawyer, allowed that the king had the right to make laws, but pleaded for the traditional idea of natural law, and believed that the king should act in accordance with it. He was not explicit on what should be done if the king did not recognize natural law. That these theories were important in that age may be shown by the undoubted fact that Calvinists indeed rebelled and helped to change the state system of Europe, while the German Lutheran princes maintained their hold on their subjects until the nineteenth century, and even then the princedoms were absorbed into a larger system rather

than being overthrown by internal rebellions.

GOVERNMENT BY CONSENT OF THE PEOPLE —ALTHUSIUS AND GROTIUS

It was left to the Dutchmen Althusius and Grotius, both mild Calvinists, to bring forth the concepts that prevailed in the following centuries. Althusius, having observed the United Provinces of the Netherlands, believed that all power resided with the people, though through their leaders they might yield it to a sovereign for the purpose of carrying out their wishes (an early form of the Social Contract, to be considered in a later chapter). If these wishes were not carried out, power naturally reverted to the people, and state notables were entitled to take it from the unworthy sovereign. Grotius revived the medieval and Stoic theory of natural law, which may be discovered by right reason which resides in all human hearts. It is dictated only indirectly by God, since of course God, the author of nature, put reason itself in human hearts; but in fact God may be disregarded since evil is evil and even God cannot make it good. Thus Grotius explicitly abandoned the earlier Calvinist idea that God's word as given in the Bible is the only law, and went back to the medieval and pagan notion of a natural law binding on all peoples and therefore usable in the international relations in which Grotius was so vitally interested. It was not surprising that these thoughts should have come forth from Holland where the Dutch had indeed expelled their hereditary monarch in favor of a confederation of provinces—as much because he was ruining their trade through his taxation as because he persecuted their religion. And since not all countries were Calvinist and could not therefore be expected to accept the Bible as a complete rule for everyday life, in international relations—so important for a trading country—some more universal law must surely operate.

With Althusius and Grotius we are in the modern world. Hobbes with his materialism and his variant of the Social Contract, Locke with his theory of the natural rights that all governments must protect, merely appended extensive footnotes to their work. These men will be considered in Chapter 20, but the Dutch theorists should be remembered as the men who pointed the way out of the international anarchy of the sixteenth century and did it in the country which overcame the anarchy first, and moved forward into the modern world with a governmental system not unlike a true democracy.

► European state system in the sixteenth century

NATIONAL STATES AT THE CLOSE OF
THE MIDDLE AGES

In studying the evolution of the national state in early modern times it is important to keep in mind the European state system as it had developed by 1914 before the modern revolutionary forces burst upon it. These forces are still in the process of altering it and will certainly never restore it to the form it had in 1914. It will also be instructive to note the changes that were made in 1919 when the number of states reached its maximum. Although this later period will not be studied in this book, which ends with 1715, comparative maps are provided, since it should be understood that the evolution of the European state system of the twentieth century was the result of a long process, in which the wars of the sixteenth and seventeenth centuries played an important role. The rulers during these centuries did not know what would come from their work, nor indeed that modern national states with their accompanying nationalism would be a by-product of it. Least of all could they have imagined that the ideology developed from the national states would become a powerful world force in the twentieth century. Their interest and motives were not ours. They fought for their religion or for the interests of their families, or simply to gain personal power, glory, and prestige. In this chapter, therefore, we shall stress as far as possible the evolutionary aspect of the struggle, the decline of the universal Holy Roman Empire, the new states that arose and be-

came permanent, and the further development of the medieval national states. In the sixteenth century England, France, and Spain developed strong monarchies centered around the king. In seventeenth-century England (to which a separate chapter will be devoted in view of the importance of the development as a model for later democracies) the English monarchy was limited by action of the people and became a constitutional monarchy, with the crown gradually becoming a figurehead by the nineteenth and twentieth centuries.

THE NON-CHRISTIAN STATE—THE "TURKISH
MENACE"

Before coming to the Christian states a few words should be said about the Muslim power in eastern Europe of which the Christian states were well aware, a power which could never be far from their calculations. For the best part of three centuries the French monarchs were in alliance with the Ottoman Empire, although the alliance did not often mean military aid from one to the other. The purpose of the alliance, in French eyes, was of course to weaken the power of the Hapsburgs, their traditional enemies, whose eastern territories touched the borders of the Ottoman Empire.

We have already noted in Chapter 8 the decisive defeat inflicted on the Hungarians and their allies by the Turks at the battle of Mohacs in 1526. The Ottoman sultan, Suleiman the Magnificent, already possessed Egypt and most of the North African coastal lands, won by his father. Suleiman, after completing the conquest of the Balkans and defeating the Hungarians, moved forward into Austria and laid siege to Vienna (1529), but was unsuccessful, contenting himself with annexing most of Hungary. After Suleiman's death the peculiar governmental system of the Ottoman Empire began to weaken Ottoman power. The sultans delegated a great deal of power to their grand viziers and local potentates, whom they seldom trusted, frequently putting them to death for minor offenses or for none. They themselves were too often the victims of harem politics,

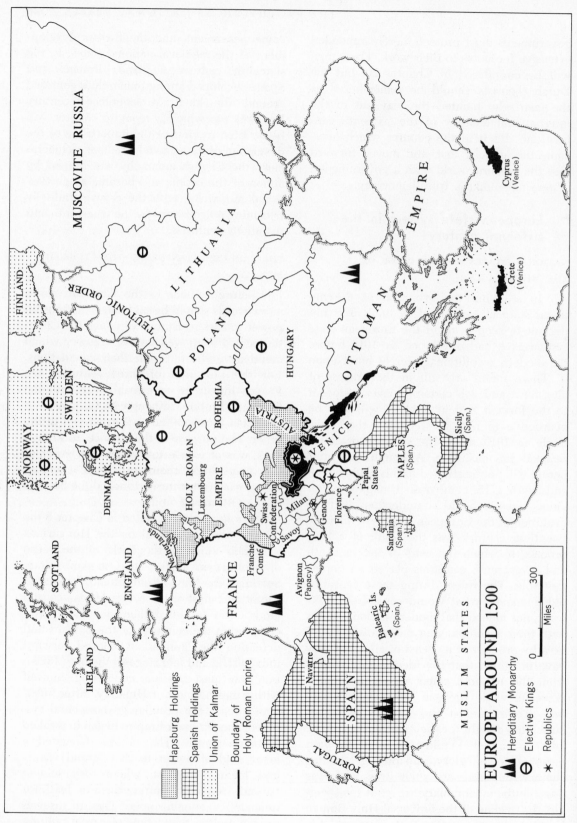

MUSCOVITE RUSSIA

FINLAND

NORWAY

SWEDEN

TEUTONIC ORDER

LITHUANIA

POLAND

OTTOMAN EMPIRE

Cyprus (Venice)

Crete (Venice)

SCOTLAND

IRELAND

ENGLAND

DENMARK

HOLY ROMAN EMPIRE

Luxembourg

Netherlands

BOHEMIA

AUSTRIA

HUNGARY

VENICE

NAPLES (Span.)

Sicily (Span.)

Spanish Netherlands

FRANCE

Swiss Confederation

Franche Comté

Savoy

Milan

Genoa

Florence

Papal States

Sardinia (Span.)

Avignon (Papacy)

Navarre

SPAIN

Balearic Is. (Span.)

PORTUGAL

MUSLIM STATES

EUROPE AROUND 1500

Hapsburg Holdings

Spanish Holdings

Union of Kalmar

Boundary of Holy Roman Empire

▲▲▲ Hereditary Monarchy

⊕ Elective Kings

★ Republics

Miles

0   300

EUROPE IN 1914
0   300
Miles

EUROPE AFTER
WORLD WAR I
World War I Losses

by Germany
by Austria Hungary
by Bulgaria
by Russia
0   500
Miles

estimated them until they learned that they could be beaten, and that what success the Turks had was largely due to Christian difficulties in mustering sufficient troops to fight against them in the prevailing state of discord in Europe.

The naval victory of Lepanto, won by Don John of Austria on behalf of the Hapsburgs and Venetians in 1571, destroyed the Turkish reputation for invincibility as well as saved the Mediterranean from falling into Muslim control. For the next century the Turks expanded little, until in the 1680's a huge force was assembled for European conquest under the grand vizier Mustafa. This army, aided by some Hungarian rebels, laid siege to Vienna again but was unable to capture it (1683), the Polish king, for once a native Pole, managing to relieve the city at a very dangerous moment. The Christian counterattack recovered Hungary and hastened the decline of Turkish power which culminated in the nineteenth century when Turkey was the "sick man of Europe."

But the ever-present Turkish menace, however much overestimated it may have been, was a constant calculation in the military plans of the Christian powers. Charles v and his brother Ferdinand, who looked after his eastern Hapsburg possessions during his reign, had a real menace to meet in the form of the sultan Suleiman. If they had not remained alert the Turks in the early sixteenth century would indeed have penetrated into central Europe, with incalculable consequences for Western civilization.

THE HOLY ROMAN EMPIRE

Charles V, Hapsburg leader of Europe

Reference has already been made in Chapter 12 to the Golden Bull of 1356 which stated officially how the emperor was to be chosen. Under this bull there were to be seven electors. Of these, three were archbishops (Mainz, Trier, and Cologne) while three were German princes, the count palatine, the duke of Saxony, and the margrave of Brandenburg. The seventh was the king of Bohemia who might or might not be

the Muslim system of polygamy making it difficult to determine who was the rightful heir to the throne, without a civil war or at least a series of assassinations. But when the Muslims went to war, Christians trembled, since the armies that the Turks could muster were considerable, and supposed by many Christians to have supernatural aid from the nether regions at their disposal. Moreover, the Turks were in the habit of enslaving Christians and making them serve in their armed forces, a custom offensive to Christian sensibilities. So the Christians usually over-

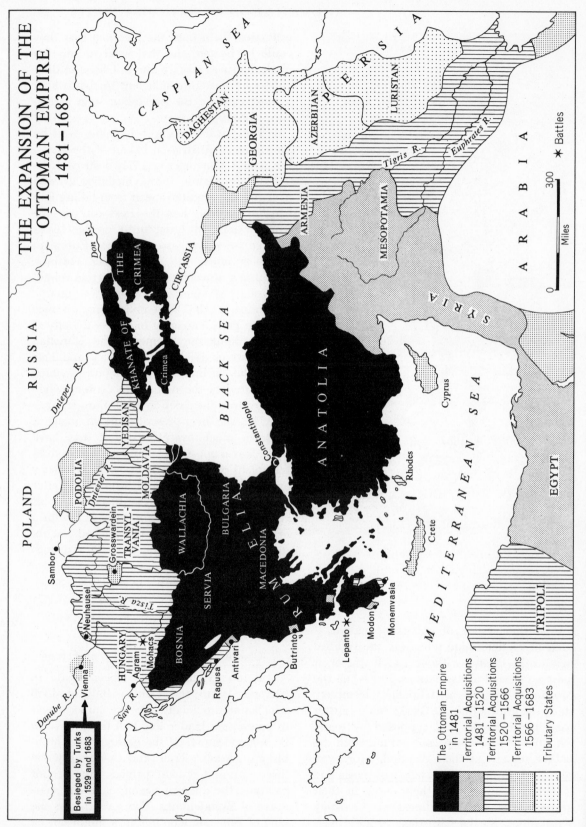

THE EXPANSION OF THE
OTTOMAN EMPIRE
1481–1683

★ Battles

CASPIAN SEA

RUSSIA

POLAND

PERSIA

DAGHESTAN

GEORGIA

AZERBIJAN

LURISTAN

ARABIA

Tigris R.

Euphrates R.

300

0

Miles

ARMENIA

MESOPOTAMIA

CIRCASSIA

Don R.

THE
CRIMEA

KHANATE OF

Crimea

BLACK SEA

ANATOLIA

SYRIA

Dnieper R.

Sambor

PODOLIA

YEDISAN

Dniester R.

MOLDAVIA

Constantinople

Cyprus

Rhodes

EGYPT

Grosswardein

TRANSYL-
VANIA

WALLACHIA

BULGARIA

R
U
M
E
L
I
A

Crete

MEDITERRANEAN SEA

TRIPOLI

Tisza R.

Neuhausel

Vienna

HUNGARY

Agram

Mohacs

SERVIA

MACEDONIA

Rhodes

Monemvasia

Danube R.

Save R.

BOSNIA

Ragusa

Antivari

Butrinto

Lepanto

Modon

Besieged by Turks
in 1529 and 1683

The Ottoman Empire
in 1481

Territorial Acquisitions
1481–1520

Territorial Acquisitions
1520–1566

Territorial Acquisitions
1566–1683

Tributary States

Portrait of the Emperor Charles V by an unknown sixteenth-century Venetian artist. (COURTESY THE METROPOLITAN MUSEUM OF ART)

the fact that he should have desired the title at all suggests forcibly both the prestige attached to the title and Henry's personal ambition, as distinct from his feeling of responsibility to his people, who could scarcely have been benefited by their monarch's efforts to fulfill the duties attached to the imperial position.

The electors, however, made the obvious choice, though not without having pocketed bribes from all the contenders. They selected Charles i of Spain, the head of the Hapsburg family, whose ancestors had held the throne since 1438. He was to spend the rest of his life trying to hold together his vast dominions, and finally abdicated, worn out by his labors.

Charles was no ordinary German prince or archduke. He possessed the family archduchy of Austria as did all previous Hapsburg emperors. But his grandfather Maximilian i, whom we have already had occasion to observe as a monarch influenced by the Renaissance, had made very careful matrimonial arrangements for his family which now were to bear fruit for Charles v, who inherited all the scattered territories whose rulers had lacked male heirs. Maximilian himself had married Mary of Burgundy, the heiress of those Burgundian territories which had not fallen to France after her father Charles the Bold had been killed in battle.[1] These territories were considerable and included Flanders and Artois, Franche-Comté (the county of Burgundy), Luxemburg, and the Netherlands. These fell to the son of this marriage, Philip the Handsome, on the death of Mary in 1482 as a result of a fall from her horse. Although Maximilian had to fight the French to establish the claim for his son, he was ultimately successful, losing only a few minor territories to the French in exchange for the recognition of his claim.

Philip the Handsome married Joanna, daughter of Ferdinand and Isabella of Spain, and became king of Castile, which had passed to Joanna on the death of Isabella, although the effective rule had remained in

a German prince, since he also was elected. These men remained electors until 1623 when the first change was made among the personnel of the electors as will be explained later in the chapter. Thereafter there were several changes, which need not concern us here.

By virtue of their position as electors these princes gained considerable prestige within Germany. They formed one of the colleges in the imperial diet, while the other princes sat in another college apart from them. Moreover, since the position of emperor was often sought by rich and important monarchs, their votes could command considerable sums of money from the contenders. In 1519, after the death of Emperor Maximilian i, the three most important monarchs in Europe sought the title: Charles i (usually known as Charles v, since he was the fifth emperor of that name) of Spain and the Netherlands and several minor territories, Francis i of France, and Henry viii of England. What would have happened to England if Henry had won is difficult to imagine, but

[1] Supra, p. 513.

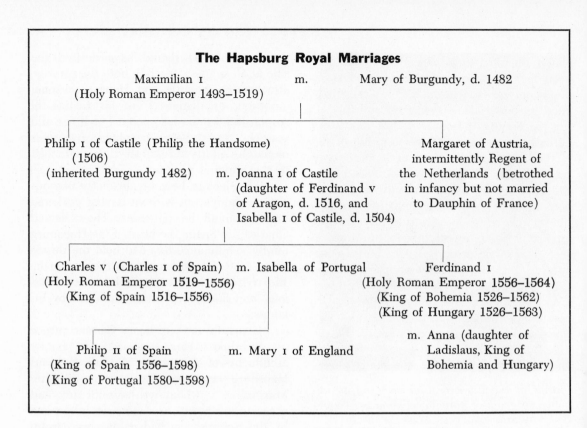

The Hapsburg Royal Marriages

Maximilian I   m.   Mary of Burgundy, d. 1482
(Holy Roman Emperor 1493–1519)

Philip I of Castile (Philip the Handsome)   Margaret of Austria,
    (1506)   intermittently Regent of
    (inherited Burgundy 1482)   m. Joanna I of Castile   the Netherlands (betrothed
                                  (daughter of Ferdinand V   in infancy but not married
                                  of Aragon, d. 1516, and   to Dauphin of France)
                                  Isabella I of Castile, d. 1504)

Charles V (Charles I of Spain)   m. Isabella of Portugal   Ferdinand I
(Holy Roman Emperor 1519–1556)   (Holy Roman Emperor 1556–1564)
 (King of Spain 1516–1556)   (King of Bohemia 1526–1562)
                                                   (King of Hungary 1526–1563)

                                             m. Anna (daughter of
    Philip II of Spain   m. Mary I of England   Ladislaus, King of
 (King of Spain 1556–1598)   Bohemia and Hungary)
(King of Portugal 1580–1598)

the hands of Ferdinand. However, Philip died the same year that he assumed the throne. Joanna, already far advanced in insanity, became totally insane shortly afterward. But, on the death of her father Ferdinand, her elder son Charles inherited Ferdinand's kingdom of Aragon, together with the Aragonian possessions in Italy, comprising the kingdom of Naples, Sicily, and Sardinia. He also inherited the Spanish colonial empire which had been won under the joint rule of Ferdinand and Isabella though officially it was the possession of the latter as queen of Castile and Léon (1516). Finally, Maximilian died in 1519, leaving his hereditary Hapsburg possessions to Charles, and as we have seen, the electors also chose Charles as emperor.

Spain and the Netherlands under Hapsburg rule

Spain was far from happy to find itself with a Flemish ruler who could not speak Spanish, and who, at the beginning of his reign, passed over his Spanish subjects in favor of trusted Flemish counselors. Moreover, his religious appointments were looked upon with disfavor, and the Spanish were very much afraid that he would open the colonial trade to foreigners. After a serious revolt which flared up as soon as Charles became emperor, which took on the aspect of a struggle between the nobles and the cities, Charles mended his ways and granted the demands of his Spanish subjects, agreeing also to take a bride suggested by the Cortes. This was Isabella of Portugal, through whom Philip II was in later years to claim the throne of Portugal. So Spain was pacified, and though Charles used Spanish resources from the New World and Spanish manpower to assist him in his many wars in central Europe, and thus contributed to the ultimate decline of the country, the Spanish were reasonably content with him, especially since his son Philip was brought up as a Spaniard.

The Netherlanders were also reasonably content with their monarch. First of all, he was a Fleming, and his first language was French. They therefore looked upon him as one of their own, who had, as it were, made good by being elected emperor and inheriting the Spanish possessions. But difficulties naturally arose as to the relationship of the Netherlands with the empire. Some parts of the Burgundian territories had belonged to the empire while others had not. The matter was finally settled by making the "Burgundian circle" as a separate district of the empire, with representation in the imperial diet. This circle comprised all Charles's possessions in the Low Countries. Ruling through regents from his eastern patrimony, Charles made no attempt to interfere with traditional Netherlandish liberties, and well understood that the people's prosperity enabled him to fight his wars. Nevertheless, though the regents did a good deal for the Netherlands in the way of improvement of administration, the people resented them as foreigners. We have already noted Charles's efforts to suppress heresy in the Netherlands, a policy which was popular as long as it was confined to suppression of Anabaptists, and, when it was directed against Lutherans, was simply not enforced by the independent nobles and cities. So Charles was able to complete his reign without serious trouble from the Netherlands, though, as we shall see, with the rise of Calvinism and the accession of a king who was thoroughly Spanish and had no understanding for his Low Country possessions, his reign could be seen as only a calm before the storm which was to sweep away foreign rule from the north and replace it with native rule under the first near-democracy of Europe.

The reality behind the imperial title

Though the outlying kingdoms of his patrimony were useful to him (even the Italian kingdoms, ruled by viceroys, were made to contribute money, from the payment of which the Church was largely exempt), Charles always regarded himself as first and foremost the Holy Roman Emperor of the German Nation, its official title since the fifteenth century. As such he was the natural protector of Christendom against the Turkish menace, and the natural protector of Catholicism against the Protestant schismatics. Yet his imperial heritage, outside the archduchy of Austria, gave him little real power. The empire was a heterogeneous collection of territories, all with their individual rights which they had possessed for centuries and had no intention of giving up. These rights were known as the "German liberties," and, though they accrued only to nobles and leading burghers of the free cities, popular opinion so far as it could make itself felt, clung tenaciously to them. Maximilian I had tried to make the constitution of the empire workable, by using the diet (a kind of imperial parliament made up of representatives from the various components in the empire) to decree an imperial taxation and to maintain an imperial peace. But both peace and taxation had to be enforced by the component units, and these were reluctant either to part with cash or keep any peace if it appeared that advantage was to be gained by war. Charles V gave his diets other work to do, such as laying the ban of the empire on Martin Luther. But we have seen how one of the imperial princes, an elector, protected him against the emperor with complete success for a number of years, and until Charles was willing to fight a war against the Protestant princes. Charles, who knew that he would be away from Germany for much of his reign looking after his other possessions, set up a council of regents to act for him. This provided him with an administrative body, but its powers were limited. So the imperial title remained, as it had been for generations, little more than an empty name, and though it conferred prestige upon Charles beyond what he would have gained from his ancestral possessions, on the whole it probably weakened his power more than it strengthened it. And it certainly gave him serious responsibilities.

Conflict with France

Worse than this, however, his possession of the title succeeded in terrifying all the rest of Europe, and particularly France. In

This exquisite likeness of Francis I, the first French Renaissance monarch and the perennial foe of Charles V, was executed on Limousin enamel. (COURTESY THE METROPOLITAN MUSEUM OF ART)

which prevailed in northern Italy to obtain allies there; and it was a satisfactory diversion. Francis, however, was severely defeated at the battle of Pavia and taken prisoner (1525). He was kept in Spain by the emperor until he was willing to sign a treaty granting the duchy of Burgundy to his enemy, and permitting the traitor Constable Bourbon to take his French lands and to do homage to the emperor for them. As soon as Francis reached France, as can hardly have been surprising to the emperor, he repudiated the treaty signed under duress, on the grounds that he was not permitted by the French people to alienate lands from France and had sworn long before not to do so, and that if such lands were alienated it could only be by the express permission of the people voiced through their *estates*.[2] The estates were then duly called and refused their permission as expected. As war broke out again Francis tried to build up a league against the emperor, but it was not very effective, and once more he had to sign a treaty under which he was allowed to keep Burgundy; as Constable Bourbon had died in Italy the troublesome question of his territories did not arise.

But Francis had not finished with Charles. Though Charles's troops (who were mostly Lutherans and disapproved of Rome) had shocked Europe by sacking Rome in 1527, a deed disowned by the emperor, he still remained the virtual controller of northern Italy, and Francis was determined to diminish his power and prevent him from attacking southern France to gain some territories that had previously belonged to the empire. This time there was so much fear of Charles that a substantial league could be built, in which, to the scandal of Christian Europe, the pope joined, while the Turks were also in the alliance. To make matters worse the Schmalkaldic League of Lutheran princes was also in it. The Turks sent a fleet into Toulon, and amused themselves by turn-

Charles's reign people spoke of a "universal monarchy," a thought which by now was horrible to Europeans. Hence combinations were constantly formed against him, lest his rule become really universal in Europe. Francis I of France feared for his own possessions, especially those that had belonged to the French crown less than half a century. When one of his greatest nobles, the Constable Bourbon of France, after long negotiations with Charles, threw off his allegiance to his French suzerain and offered it to the emperor, Francis naturally seized his lands, as their loss would have meant an excision in the soil of France. And Charles wanted the duchy of Burgundy, which had been lost to Louis XI, and was separated from the rest of the Burgundian possessions which effectively now did belong to Charles. So Francis and Charles became embroiled in war, and Francis began to pursue the policy of his fathers: he invaded Italy and stirred up trouble there, in lands which theoretically belonged to the empire—lands to which France could lay some claim. The important thing was that it was always possible in the state of anarchy and constant petty wars

[2] The French word is *états*, more nearly *states* than *estates*; *estates* is used in this chapter as being less likely to lead to confusion, in view of the alternative meaning of the word "state."

ing a large house into a mosque, but otherwise did not achieve much. Charles appealed to the Schmalkaldic League to remember they were Germans, and a few did. He himself invaded Provence in southern France, and at last again a peace was patched up, under which Francis gave up his claims to various parts of the empire and to the throne of Naples. Shortly afterward Francis died (1547).

It was, however not so easy for any French monarch to resign the possession of northern Italy and especially Milan, for which the French had fought hard in the years just before Charles's accession, and where they had set up in several places, notably Turin, quite efficient administrations. So the new French king resumed the wars and was able to take from the emperor the bishoprics of Metz, Toul, and Verdun, in Lorraine. These bishoprics had been disputed for centuries and thereafter were to remain with France. The French king again attacked Italy. Charles had abdicated before the war ended. It was finally brought to a close by Philip II who made peace with the French king Henry II in 1559 on the basis of a withdrawal by France from Italy. The Italian territory fell into the hands of the Spanish monarchy, but Henry was left free to deal as he desired with the Huguenots in France.

Thus for Charles, the wars had lost him part of Lorraine but secured the remainder of his possessions. France was moving closer to her present boundaries; her subsequent history will be dealt with in a later section.

Abdication of Charles V—Excessive burden of empire

We have seen already how Charles was forced sporadically to deal with the German Lutherans, and it will now be apparent why he could give little of his time and energy to Luther. It will be appreciated also why he had to compromise with the Lutherans in spite of the fact that he defeated the Schmalkaldic League the only time he was able to fight with it directly. The religious peace of Augsburg of 1555 was the result of Charles's constant preoccupations elsewhere at least as much as of the resistance of the Lutheran princes, who were also looking after their temporal interests, even changing sides occasionally when prudence dictated.

Worn out by the burdens he had carried so long, Charles, who had in the last years of his reign increasingly left the affairs of his archduchy in the hands of his brother Ferdinand, resigned them altogether to him, together with his German interests, with the justified expectation that in due course he would be elected emperor. He was already "king of the Romans" a customary title for the next heir. Charles's Spanish possessions and the Netherlands were left to his son Philip of Spain. When finally Charles abdicated and went into a monastery his wishes

Detail of an engraved illustration of the Sack of Rome by the troops of Charles V, executed by the contemporary painter Martin van Heemskerck.

were carried out. Ferdinand became Holy Roman emperor, while Philip became king of Spain, inheriting the Low Countries which were thus severed from the empire until 1713, when they were returned to the eastern Hapsburgs by the treaty of Utrecht.

CENTRAL AND EASTERN EUROPE FOLLOWING THE DEATH OF CHARLES V (1558)

Ferdinand I, inheritor of eastern Hapsburg possessions

The new emperor Ferdinand had lost some of the excessive responsibilities and burdens that his brother had had to carry. Indeed, in the last years of his brother's reign he had had to bear the brunt of the fighting in Germany, and it was he at least as much as Charles who was responsible for the peace of Augsburg with the Lutherans. He had also had to bear the brunt of the fighting against the invading Turks, though he did not gain much beyond the raising of the actual siege of Vienna. He obtained the title of king of Hungary, but his possession of Hungary was limited to a northwestern strip, and even for this he and his successors had to pay a regular sum of money to the sultan.

So Ferdinand and his successors for the rest of the century concentrated on their own domains, which were still extensive. They could do little with Germany after the religious peace. The settlement, as everyone knew, was a compromise, and the religious issue had by no means died down. It was further complicated by the fact that in 1555 there had been few Calvinists in the country, and the peace made no provision for them. Yet a number of the German princes and cities, especially the important electorate of the Rhineland (Palatine), became Calvinist. Ferdinand had invited in the Jesuits to see what they could do in the way of reconverting the schismatic Germans, and they made considerable progress in south Germany. There was much exchange of population among the states, especially when a prince changed his religion and his subjects had to change also or emigrate.

Furthermore, there was trouble over Church lands. The date of 1552 had been inserted into the peace as the year before which lands must have been sequestrated from the Church, if the permanent possession by the new owners was to be legal. And if Catholic princes decided to become Lutheran, then they were supposed to restore the lands they had been administering to the Church. Both these provisions were constantly violated, since there was no paramount power to enforce them. The titular emperor was helpless.

Finally, as we have seen in Chapter 17, there was a serious decline in German trade due to the transferring of most overseas trade to the Atlantic. Moreover, under the new mercantile policies adopted by the powerful national states, monarchs were expected to protect the trade of their nationals and to make treaties with foreign powers. The Germans, possessing no navy and divided into hundreds of petty states, were unable to protect their trade, and no one could speak for Germans as a whole in possible negotiations with non-German powers. The emperor, even if the Germans had accepted his jurisdiction, could, as ruler only of a land power, have done little for them. So, with trade declining, and the peasantry sinking deeper into serfdom since their abortive rebellion in the early days of Lutheranism, while the rulers quarreled with one another over religious matters, it is not surprising that the emperors left their German titular subjects to their fate, until in the early seventeenth century an opportunity presented itself to make a supreme effort to unite the country into a whole.

The kingdom of Bohemia

In the territories bordering on the Austrian homeland where their control was stronger, the emperors were by no means idle. Perhaps the most important of these territories, since it provided a large portion of imperial revenue, was the ancient and honorable kingdom of Bohemia, which comprised several smaller territories united under the Bohemian crown. This crown was elective, although in practice it had for a long time been hereditary within the Hapsburg family, and held jointly with the imperial title. The king of Bohemia was an elector of the empire, and possession of the Bohemian throne therefore gave the ruler a vote in the electoral diet, which the archduke of Austria, the head of the Hapsburg family, did not otherwise possess. The greater part of the Bohemian population was strongly Protestant, although the Protestants were seriously divided amongst themselves. Not only were there Lutherans and Calvinists, but also native sects descended from the warring religious groups of the fifteenth century, described in Chapter 12. Ferdinand I, as already mentioned, had invited the Jesuits into the country to help convert them, but without much visible success. He had also tried to take away some of the privileges of self-government that they had long exercised through their diet. Imperial policy towards Bohemia was thus compounded of political and religious elements. The Catholic Hapsburg emperors disliked Bohemian political and religious independence, and as long as the Bohemian diet was allowed to choose the king, it was never certain that the throne would remain in Hapsburg hands. Finally there may have been some ethnic dislike of the Bohemian people, since they were not Germans but Czechs, a Slavic people, with a different language from their Austrian and Hapsburg masters.

Bohemian independence made some headway against the empire during the reigns of the successors of Ferdinand I. In order to ensure their election, these emperors had been compelled to agree to freedom of worship for Protestants, and thus retard the progress of the Counter Reformation which they were energetically promoting in the rest of their dominions. They had guaranteed this freedom of worship in a formal Letter of Majesty, and even agreed to permit the establishment of a group of Defenders of the Letter of Majesty to see that it was maintained. Nevertheless the Catholic Emperors, under the constant prodding of the Jesuits, had not given up hope of converting or forcing their Protestant subjects back into the Catholic fold, and frequently attempted to encroach upon the rights they had been forced to grant. Above all they wished to make sure that the crown of Bohemia should never fall into the hands of Protestants. Naturally this was a real danger, since the nobles in the Bohemian diet were largely Protestant, and were restrained from electing Protestants only from fear of the consequences. Bohemia was not in a position to defend herself alone against Hapsburg might, which would undoubtedly be turned against her should she decide to bestow her crown on a non-Catholic.

Background of the Thirty Years' War

Problem of Bohemian succession—The old and feeble Emperor Matthias (1612–1619) was very well aware of the difficulties likely to ensue after his death. In his mind there was only one possible candidate for both the Bohemian throne and the imperial title, Ferdinand, Archduke of Styria, a Hapsburg province. Ferdinand was a strong Catholic, greatly influenced by the Jesuits, and quite determined to advance the Counter Reformation in all his dominions. Yet, if he were to succeed to the throne of Bohemia, it was essential that the Bohemian Protestants should be either maneuvered or coerced into accepting him. If he were to succeed to the empire, the Protestant electors would also have to be made to accept him by similar means.

The electoral college for the empire was at this time also divided in religious affiliation. The electors, as has already been noted, were seven in number. Three were archbishops, and therefore could be relied upon to vote for a Catholic emperor. But the three German princes in the college were all Protestants, the elector of Saxony a Lutheran, and the elector palatine and the elector of Brandenburg Calvinists; although, to complicate the matter further, the latter elector had a Lutheran wife, while his older son and heir was Calvinist and his second son a Lutheran! Thus there were three Catholics and three Protestants, and the seventh elector was the king of Bohemia, not yet elected, who might be either a Protestant or a Catholic, whose vote might well be decisive.

To complete the complications in Germany two further items should be taken into consideration. The Calvinist princes were jealous of the Lutherans, and vice versa, and in individual cases might prefer a Catholic ruler to a Protestant of a different persuasion, provided that the Catholic ruler did not attempt religious coercion. It was therefore difficult to secure agreement between the Protestant princes, who thus relinquished much of their bargaining strength to the Catholics who knew what they wanted, at least in matters of religion. Finally, the most militarily powerful of the German states outside the Hapsburg domains was Bavaria, a south German territory ruled by its Duke Maximilian, who was a Catholic and leader of a Catholic league of German states devoted to the principles of the Counter Reformation. This league, which was effectively dominated by Maximilian, had a well-trained army under a competent general, Johann Tilly, while its opposite number, the Evangelical union, formed by some of the Protestant states for eventual military defense against the rising tide of the Counter Reformation, was bedeviled by internal disputes between Calvinists and Lutherans and never became the effective force that the Catholic league became in the hands of Maximilian. But Maximilian was not an elector. He coveted an electorate, and won one during the Thirty Years' War. His bargaining position therefore rested on his domination of the Catholic league and its army rather than on his direct influence in the electoral college.

When the Emperor Matthias, feeling his death approaching, demanded in 1617 that the Bohemian diet should elect Ferdinand of Styria to their throne, the Bohemians were faced with a difficult, if not impossible, task. On the one hand they greatly feared the anti-Protestantism of Ferdinand and his Jesuit advisers. On the other hand there seemed no other suitable candidate on the horizon, who could lead them in the war against the Hapsburgs that seemed certain

to follow a choice outside the Hapsburg family. There seemed no German prince capable of rising above the religious feuds of the time, and uniting Germany against the Hapsburgs, and no native prince or noble who could gain support sufficient to offset Hapsburg might in Austria, which would almost certainly be supported by the great Spanish army controlled by the Hapsburg rulers of Spain. Looking back now from the vantage point of more than three centuries upon the situation in 1617, it would seem that only two possibilities were open which might have saved Bohemia from the fate which threatened the country and did in fact engulf it. If there had been an outstanding Bohemian native prince of known ability, acceptable as a Protestant to his own people and able to enlist the support of the Protestant German princes against any attempt by the Hapsburgs to upset the Bohemian election by force—a prince who made it clear that he had no intention of standing for election as emperor, then it is possible that such a man might have succeeded in averting the imminent Thirty Years' War. He would have presented no threat to the Germans, and the emperor might have acquiesced. The second possibility would have been to choose a Catholic king of Bohemia outside the Hapsburg family, who could also be elected emperor. Such a man must then have been willing to sign and enforce the Letter of Majesty, and to have allied himself with the German princes rather than with the Hapsburg ruler of Austria. Such an alliance might have preserved the balance of power in Germany. Spanish and Austrian Hapsburgs in military alliance would not have possessed preponderant force against such a coalition, in view of the large Spanish commitments outside central Europe.

A candidate meeting these qualifications would have had to possess outstanding abilities, both in politics and in war, if he were to ensure respect from his fiercely competitive fellow rulers. It is possible that Maximilian of Bavaria could have filled the role of the tolerant Catholic ruler. But there was no native Bohemian of the necessary rank and prestige in 1617. Count Thurn led the rebellion but he was only a knight. Wallenstein had not yet risen to prominence; and though he may have had the necessary abilities, it is doubtful if he had the character required, as he certainly did not have the rank which would have made him acceptable.

Danger presented to Europe by union of Spain and empire—It was clear to all the European rulers that the Bohemian situation was an explosive one. But Bohemia was far from being the only danger spot on the continent. The Spanish Hapsburgs still yearned for the restoration of their lost provinces of the northern Netherlands which had been independent since 1581 and were predominantly, though not exclusively, Calvinist. They had an excellent base of operations in the southern Netherlands, which had remained Catholic and under Spanish rule. The Spanish army, especially its infantry, was still incomparably the best in Europe; and though the Spain of Philip III and Philip IV was far from what it had been in the sixteenth century, the galleons from Peru still provided the Spanish with more money than any other European country had at its disposal in 1617, though France was soon to outstrip them. The Spanish monarchs, in spite of the crying need for money at home, were still willing to pour it out in foreign adventures. They had a treaty with the Dutch which was due to expire in 1621, and everyone expected that its end would be the signal for a renewal of the war. In 1617 the Spanish were already building up an army for the projected invasion.

This situation affected the position in central Europe in various ways. The Spanish Hapsburgs naturally looked for help in their adventures to their relatives in Austria and the empire. The general understanding between the two branches of the family was that Spain would provide money while the empire would provide troops for their joint operations. The money sent by the Spaniards, in view of the strength of the potentially hostile English and Dutch navies, had to be sent by the long route through Spanish possessions in northern Italy, and thence through the dangerous Val Telline into Austria. The Val Telline was usually controlled by the fierce and dangerous Swiss mountaineers of the canton des Grisons. It was a consistent French policy to save France from encirclement by the Hapsburgs by helping the Swiss to control this strategic valley or controlling it themselves, while nibbling at the Hapsburg possessions in northern Italy. Thus France was potentially an enemy of the imperial Hapsburgs because she wished to cut off important supplies from the emperor, while she was anxious to prevent the Spanish Hapsburgs from becoming too powerful in the Netherlands to her north.

The Spanish menace effectively prevented Bohemia from receiving any important aid from the Dutch, who were heavily occupied not only by preparations for defense against the Spanish invasion but by internal quarrels over the power exercised by the stadholders of the House of Orange. Although sympathetic to the Protestant cause, they could ill afford even financial aid, and all military aid was excluded until the Spanish menace had been dealt with.

Other foreign interests involved in Thirty Years' War—Further complications in the extremely complex picture of Europe on the outbreak of the Thirty Years' War should finally be mentioned. England was not wholly separated from German politics, for Elizabeth, the daughter of James I of England, was married to the Calvinist elector palatine. Denmark and Sweden, whose Lutheran monarchs coveted German territories on the Baltic, were far from uninterested. Denmark was joined to Germany by land and possessed the dukedom of Holstein, well into territory that could be considered German, and was legally a part of the empire. Sweden in the early sixteenth century was engaged in an expansion throughout the whole Baltic area at the expense mostly of Poland, but also of some of the German states. She was quite willing to add to her empire whatever northern Germanic territories she could acquire. Finally, to the east of the Hapsburg dominions, was Gabriel Bethlen, prince of Transylvania.

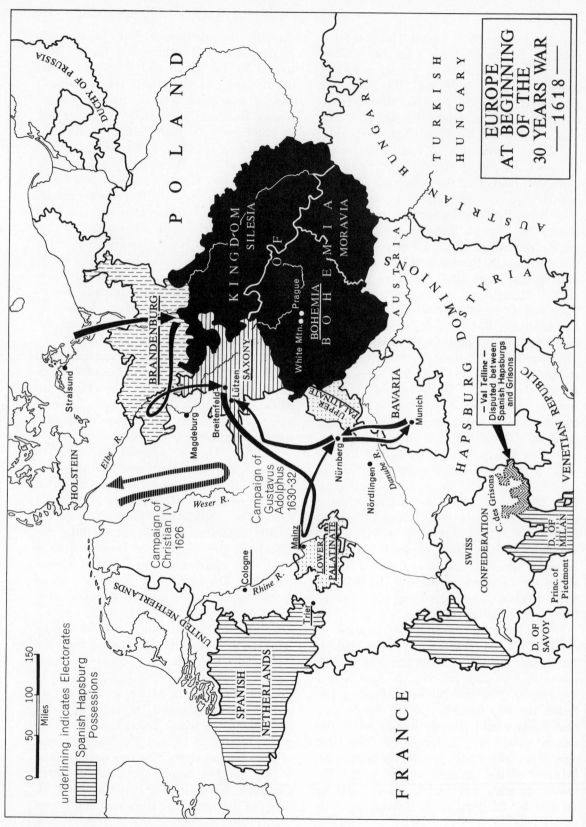

EUROPE
AT BEGINNING
OF THE
30 YEARS WAR
— 1618 —

POLAND

DUCHY OF PRUSSIA

TURKISH HUNGARY

AUSTRIAN HUNGARY

KINGDOM

SILESIA

OF

BOHEMIA

MORAVIA

Prague

White Mtn.

AUSTRIA

STYRIA

HAPSBURG DOMINIONS

BRANDENBURG

SAXONY

Lützen

Breitenfeld

Magdeburg

Stralsund

HOLSTEIN

Elbe R.

Weser R.

UPPER PALATINATE

BAVARIA

Munich

Nürnberg

Nördlingen

Danube R.

Campaign of
Christian IV
1626

Campaign of
Gustavus
Adolphus
1630-32

UNITED NETHERLANDS

Cologne

Rhine R.

Mainz

LOWER PALATINATE

Trier

SPANISH
NETHERLANDS

FRANCE

SWISS
CONFEDERATION

C. des Grisons

— Val Telline —
Disputed between
Spanish Hapsburgs
and Grisons

D. OF
MILAN

VENETIAN REPUBLIC

Princ. of
Piedmont

D. OF
SAVOY

underlining indicates Electorates

Spanish Hapsburg
Possessions

Miles

0   50   100   150

He was a Calvinist prince, with a consistent policy of trying to weaken Hapsburg power in Austria and Hungary, ready at all times to ally himself and his small army with any power that seemed to offer any assistance in his long term aims, though not above allying himself with the emperor when circumstances dictated it. Though in the course of the war Bethlen gave much military aid to the Protestant powers, his influence was too small for such aid ever to prove decisive.

THE THIRTY YEARS' WAR (1618–1648)

The first stage—Acceptance of Bohemian throne by elector palatine

The Bohemian diet, finding itself without any alternative, at last decided to submit to the inevitable and chose Ferdinand of Styria as king, in exchange for the usual formal acceptance of the Letter of Majesty. He soon showed, however, that the acceptance was only formal, at least in the opinion of the Bohemian Protestant nobles. Ferdinand proceeded to favor Catholics and discriminate against Protestants, and to interfere with the religious observances of the Protestants, especially the Calvinists. This so incensed the Protestants of Prague that they threw two royal commissioners out of a window (Defenestration of Prague, 1618). Though they emerged not greatly hurt from a dunghill on which they had fallen, it was a gross insult to Ferdinand, and offered him the opportunity to take serious punitive measures against the Bohemians. Since force would in any case be needed to carry out his steadfast policy of reconverting the Bohemians to Catholicism, the "defenestration" provided a good excuse. The Bohemians continued their rebellion by formally deposing Ferdinand, while looking around once more for another king who would be a Protestant and could help them. Meanwhile the old Emperor Matthias died, and Ferdinand became the leading candidate for the imperial title, indeed the only man who was willing and anxious to assume such a dangerous position. Faced with a possibly united vote of the Protestant electors against him, it was essential to keep the Bohemian vote. So, naturally, he refused to be deposed and declared the deposition illegal and invalid.

The German princes played for time, trying to win concessions from the probable new emperor. Lutherans and Maximilian of Bavaria, the Catholic, feared the extension of Hapsburg power, and the possible loss of their "German liberties" to an autocrat backed by military might. Protestants feared for their religion, especially the Calvinists whose religion had never been recognized as permissible in the peace of Augsburg of 1555. All Protestant princes feared that a powerful emperor, obeying the instructions of his Jesuit backers, would try to restore to the Catholic Church lands which had belonged to it before the peace of Augsburg. Yet, in spite of the fears shared by all German rulers, some of them also had hopes of adding to their territories by careful and judicious use of their power and influence in a situation which was as fluid as it appeared to be in 1618. Lutheran princes would not have been averse to aggrandizement at the expense of Catholics or Calvinists, nor Catholics at the expense of any Protestants. It was not too difficult for a princely conscience to confuse religious zeal with political ambition. Yet the princes prided themselves on their common Germanic heritage. Probably none of them would have submitted to the Spanish outsiders if it had ever become clear that such was to be the result of their intrigues. It was Germany herself that was ultimately to pay the price for the pusillanimity of the German seventeenth-century princes, not only in the terrible devastation wreaked on her lands in the Thirty Years' War, but in her distorted political development and retarded national growth from which the world has continued to suffer in the twentieth century.

When the Bohemian diet chose Frederick, the Calvinist elector palatine, as king of Bohemia in the place of the deposed Ferdinand, and the elector, after long consideration, decided to accept the dangerous gift, he could look for no support from the

German princes save from other Calvinists; and these were too weak to give him much aid. Their union gave a little financial support but nothing else, as did the Dutch. The English king, who for domestic reasons could not afford a war and was profoundly pacifist in temperament, allowed a handful of troops to join his son-in-law. So Frederick was left with little but his own forces at his disposal, the promised aid of the Bohemians, and what armies he could rent on credit. Moreover, a campaign in eastern Europe would leave his territories on the Rhine exposed to an attack from the Spanish, or from Maximilian of Bavaria if he joined the Catholic Hapsburg, as his Jesuit advisers would probably urge him.

Defeat of Bohemia—Subjugation by Ferdinand

Armies at this time were, for the most part, actually rented from their generals. They fought for pay as a regular profession, and were loyal to their general as long as he could pay them. They were all polyglot bodies, made up of professional soldiers from every country of Europe. If they were not fed they revolted and lived off the country they occupied. They expected to be allowed, like the soldiers of the Roman Republic, to take booty in order to make up for any deficiencies in food and pay. The Thirty Years' War was almost entirely a war between mercenaries of this kind. The single exception of importance was the first Swedish army of Gustavus Adolphus, which was mainly composed of individuals who followed their great leader from patriotic and religious feeling. The truly national army was still a long way in the future.

The details of the war need not detain us long. At first Frederick was successful, because he was able to hire a large army which was for the moment unemployed.

Portraits of Frederick V, Elector Palatine, known as Frederick the Winter King, and his wife Elizabeth, daughter of James I of England. Frederick's acceptance of the crown of Bohemia touched off the Thirty Years' War. Portraits by Anthony van Dyck.

But for want of a better alternative the princes decided to elect Ferdinand emperor, as Ferdinand II. This greatly increased Ferdinand's legal authority and prestige. When Maximilian of Bavaria at last decided for him and against Frederick, in exchange for a promise of the electoral vote of the Palatinate, and threw his army under the efficient general Johann Tilly into the fray, Frederick's cause was quickly lost. The German princes either remained neutral or actively sided with the emperor. The Bohemians were crushingly defeated at the battle of the White Mountain in 1620, and their country was incorporated into the Hapsburg dominions, where they remained until 1919. Frederick and his wife and family went into exile. No prince had defended the integrity of the elector's own Palatinate. Ferdinand and the Spanish army, ably abetted by the predatory Maximilian, dispossessed Frederick of his ancestral lands, and, too late, the Protestants realized that Ferdinand now held the whip hand over them and it would go hard with their religion if they did not make a stand, even now, at this late hour.

Wallenstein and the northern kings

In fact the bulk of what aid did come from the Protestants came from King Christian IV of Denmark and Holstein, against whom Ferdinand called in the aid of the greatest of the organizers of mercenaries thrown up by the war, one Count Waldstein, or Wallenstein. This man drove out the Danes, and became so powerful in Europe that he was virtually independent of control by his nominal employer and allies. Ferdinand now believed he was strong enough to enforce the restoration of Church lands and the forcible reconversion of the Protestants. The German princes were helpless against the emperor and Wallenstein.

But another foreign champion of Protestantism was on the way, and when Wallenstein and the Catholic German allies of the emperor began to enforce the Edict of Restitution, under which lands which had belonged to the Catholic Church in 1552 were to be restored, this champion, King

Gustavus Adolphus of Sweden, would no longer be destitute of allies. Richelieu, now in charge of French policy, and seriously worried about the union of the two Hapsburg empires, and the Spanish invasion of the Netherlands, which had taken place as expected, was willing to give Gustavus a regular subsidy. Faced with this new threat, and peremptorily called upon by the Spanish for aid in their Dutch war which was not going favorably, Ferdinand was willing to make some concessions in exchange for German support. He dismissed the unpopular Wallenstein as a temporary measure, hoping he could do without him, and to a slight degree modified enforcement of the Edict of Restitution.

Gustavus Adolphus, with his fine victorious army, struck consternation into the imperial and Bavarian troops, whom he defeated in several important battles. A brilliant if over reckless military leader, with a trained army fresh from victories in Poland, known as the "Lion of the North" and devoutly Protestant, he seemed likely to change the whole face of Europe and overthrow the imperial policy. The only recourse was to recall Wallenstein and trust that he could raise an army able to resist the Swedes and their Protestant allies. Wallenstein, who had been waiting for the summons and was able to dictate the terms of his return, did raise an army, but he did not defeat the Swedes. However, in the imperial defeat of Lützen (1632) Gustavus was killed; and though the Swedes fought on under a succession of capable generals the tide turned slowly in favor of the emperor and the latter was able to sign a favorable peace with the German princes at Prague in 1635. He gained advantages for the Hapsburgs at the cost of abandoning the Edict of Restitution, and the German princes, for the most part, were satisfied.

Intervention of France and the end of the war

Neither the French paymasters nor the Swedish fighters were satisfied. Sweden desired a portion of Pomerania in northern

Engraving of the city of Magdeburg, made before the city was utterly destroyed after a long siege in the Thirty Years' War.

Germany which was coveted by the elector of Brandenburg, and other concessions in the Baltic. France desired to break Spanish power in the Netherlands and win a Rhine frontier if possible. She wished to put an end for ever to the danger of encirclement by the two Hapsburg powers. So this time she decided to enter the war actively. Her inexperienced army, led by equally inexperienced generals, was at first unsuccessful, and France herself was invaded. But in time the generals Condé and Turenne gained their experience, and the native French army was always potentially superior to most of the mercenary armies against whom they fought. Wallenstein was murdered, almost certainly at the instigation of Ferdinand, who had no further use for a general who so openly and even rebelliously pursued his own aims. Before the war was over, while it was becoming clear that the unexhausted French would turn the tide of battle against the Hapsburgs, Calvinist Brandenburg and other German princedoms began to aid the anti-Hapsburg forces or else withdrew into discreet neutrality.

For several years a peace conference met at Osnabruck and Münster to try to put an end to the war, while the armies that were still fighting maneuvered and fought to put pressure on the negotiators. But at last, in 1648, the peace of Westphalia was signed with the new Hapsburg Emperor Ferdinand III; and though the Franco-Spanish War dragged on eleven years longer, at last it too was over and the peace of the Pyrenees signed in 1659.

The last stage of the war had been almost entirely a war fought on German soil by French and Swedish troops and mercenaries hired by the French. Not until 1641 did the new elector of Brandenburg, Frederick William (the "Great Elector"), reverse the neutralist position of his father and take an active stand in opposition to the emperor, and by his leadership encourage other Protestant princes to follow him. All through the war the Germans had seen their lands ravaged by mercenary troops, but the last phase was probably the worst of all. It is claimed that the loss of population and the desperate condition of the peasantry after

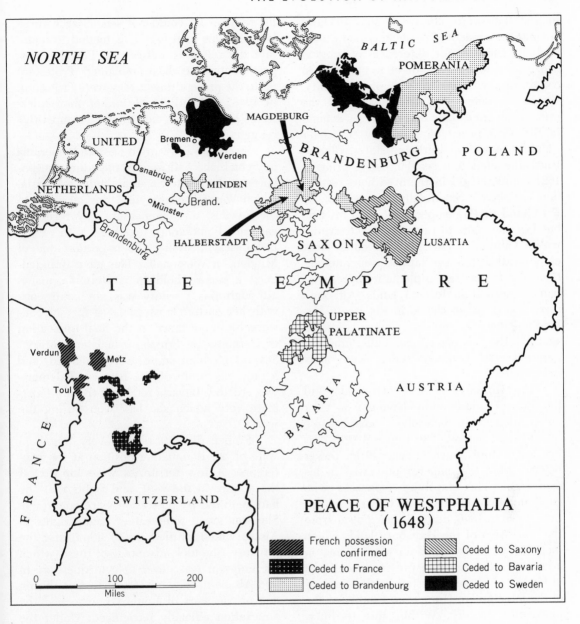

NORTH SEA

BALTIC SEA

POMERANIA

MAGDEBURG

Bremen
Verden

BRANDENBURG

POLAND

UNITED

Osnabrück

MINDEN

NETHERLANDS

Münster

Brand.

Brandenburg

HALBERSTADT

SAXONY

LUSATIA

THE   EMPIRE

UPPER
PALATINATE

Verdun   Metz

Toul

AUSTRIA

BAVARIA

FRANCE

SWITZERLAND

0   100   200
Miles

PEACE OF WESTPHALIA
(1648)

French possession
confirmed

Ceded to Saxony

Ceded to France

Ceded to Bavaria

Ceded to Brandenburg

Ceded to Sweden

the war has been exaggerated; but there can be no doubt at all that the destruction was very great indeed and that the population decreased by many millions at a time when the other countries of Europe were making slow but permanent gains in wealth and population. Save for tiny pockets no part of Germany had been spared; and though German industriousness was to make up the loss with exemplary speed, Germany as a whole had fallen far behind her contem-

poraries and did not catch up with them again until the late nineteenth century.

The Peace of Westphalia

Since the terms of the peace of Westphalia were to fix substantially the boundaries of European countries until the French Revolution and the conquests of Napoleon, and since it is the first of the truly European peace treaties, it deserves an analysis here, both of the terms and the principles involved, such as they were. The treaty shows clearly how far the concept of nationality had grown by 1648, and how far differences of religion had ceased to be a factor of importance in comparison with the principle of nationality.

In Germany the treaty extended the principle of *cuius regio eius religio,* as defined in the 1555 peace of Augsburg, to cover Calvinist as well as Lutheran states. Church lands alienated into secular hands prior to 1624 could remain in them without restitution, as had been finally agreed to by Ferdinand II. The emperor retained his title but lost the right to raise taxes and armies within Germany. The German states were each entitled to negotiate as separate entities and to maintain diplomatic representation as needed in foreign lands. Although there was a vague clause in the treaty forbidding them to make alliances directed against the emperor, for all practical purposes the German states were now independent.

The United Provinces (Holland) and the Swiss Confederation, having won their independence for themselves, now became independent in law. The imperial title thus for the future carried very little power beyond what the emperor possessed in his own right. The Hapsburg monarchs who continued to be elected, with only one exception, down to 1806, derived their power from the possession of the Hapsburg lands which included now the kingdom of Bohemia in addition to the Austrian provinces and part of Hungary. These lands formed the nucleus of the later Austro-Hungarian Empire of the nineteenth century. Within this territory, composed as it was of a nucleus of Germans, with Slavs in Bohemia and Magyars in Hungary, the principle of nationality had made no headway. The emperors possessed supreme power in these territories, and used it mainly to reconvert their subjects to Catholicism. Here the Catholic Reformation in its militant phase had its last successes.

In the remainder of Germany the Catholics had one success at the peace of Westphalia. Protestantism was held in check by the provision that if the ruler changed his religion he could not secularize Church lands for his own use. This tended to maintain the religious status quo. For the most part Protestants have remained Protestant up to the present time if they were Protestant in 1648, and individuals rather than rulers have been converted to the competitive religion.

Sweden was awarded western Pomerania for which she had fought, including the important city of Stettin. Brandenburg-Prussia, which was forced to yield this territory to the Swedes, was compensated by receiving eastern Pomerania together with some bishoprics, including the important one of Minden, in Westphalia. This gave Brandenburg a secure hold in western Germany, although this territory was not contiguous with her eastern possessions—a fact of considerable importance in the final unification of Germany by Prussia, in a later century.[3] Several German states were enlarged, and a new electorate of the Rhenish Palatinate was created, Bavaria retaining the old Palatinate vote which she had won during the war.

France did not receive very much, in spite of her dominating position at the conference. A few territories were lopped off the empire in the west, and rights that she had acquired by possession were confirmed. She was given some rather vague rights in Alsace which entitled her to administer the territory. She took advantage of these, which the emperor was never able to question, to add Alsace to the kingdom of France during one of the wars of Louis XIV, who had the annexation officially recognized. Under the subsequent peace of the Pyrenees, signed in 1659, France received some sections of Flanders, while rounding out her borders satisfactorily at the natural boundary line of the Pyrenees.

At the peace of Westphalia some problems that had been plaguing Europe for a long time were finally settled. It was clear that there was to be no "universal monarchy"

[3] Brandenburg already had inherited the west German duchy of Cleves, but her possession had been hotly disputed for many years.

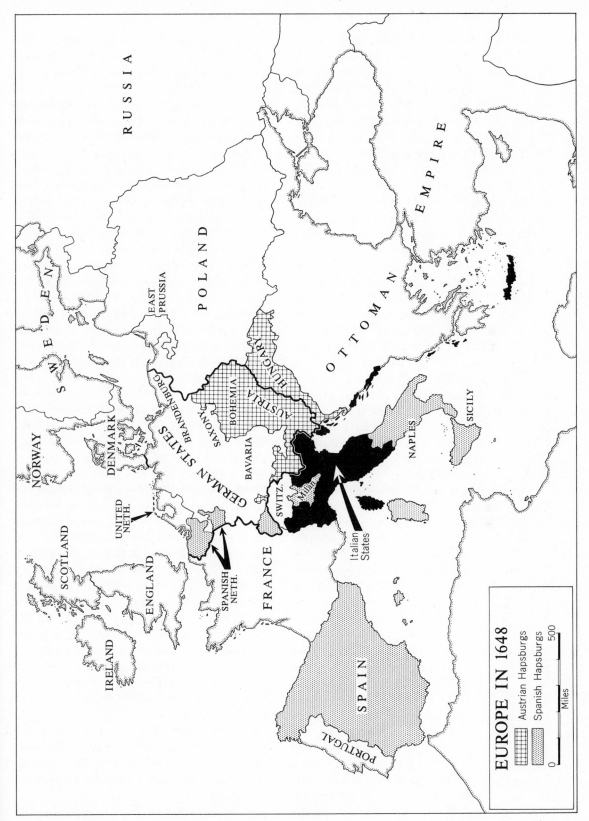

EUROPE IN 1648

Austrian Hapsburgs

Spanish Hapsburgs

0   500

Miles

RUSSIA

SWEDEN

NORWAY

SCOTLAND

IRELAND

ENGLAND

DENMARK

POLAND

EAST PRUSSIA

BRANDENBURG

GERMAN STATES

SAXONY

BOHEMIA

HUNGARY

AUSTRIA

BAVARIA

SWITZ.

Milan

UNITED NETH.

SPANISH NETH.

FRANCE

SPAIN

PORTUGAL

OTTOMAN EMPIRE

Italian States

NAPLES

SICILY

under the Holy Roman Empire. If there was to be any such monarchy in the future it would have to be won by force of arms by one power or another, against which the other foreign states in Europe could band themselves if they desired. The juridical basis for such an empire had disappeared. The future of Germany appeared to be that she was not to unite as a national state for the forseeable future. Particularism had proved too strong; and it may be mentioned in passing that while Germany did not unite at this time, and, unfortunately for the peace of Europe, did unite only by "blood and iron" later, the disunity was not necessarily so bad for the German people of that age. The small princes, devoted to their independence, developed a kind of paternalism toward their states, and many of them were able to recover fairly quickly from the war. The tiny courts of the princes became in some cases centers of culture in the eighteenth century. Goethe, Schiller, Mozart, Bach, Beethoven, and Leibniz were all products of these states; and in particular Goethe's universal genius could hardly have found a suitable field of expression in any of the great national states.

Flanders remained a disputed territory. Most of it remained in Spanish hands at the end of the war, but French ambitions to absorb a part of it were undiminished. Her northern boundaries were not yet fixed, but her southern boundaries were settled in 1659. Spain still ruled much of Italy, and the possession of the Spanish throne by the Hapsburgs represented a continuing danger to other European powers. But declining Spain and the remaining imperial Hapsburg territories were not powerful enough together to present much of a danger to the great national states. Moreover, Portugal, which had for sixty years been ruled by the Spanish Hapsburgs, freed herself in 1640 during the Thirty Years' War, and again became independent under the House of Braganza. The peace of Westphalia recognized this situation legally. Holland and Switzerland were, as already mentioned, now legally recognized as national and independent states.

The phase of European history during which one European power was subject to another was moving toward its end, though the monarchs themselves did not cease trying. At the end of the seventeenth century the great Spanish inheritance was partly dismembered, the southern Netherlands falling to the indestructible Hapsburg family while Spain, after the dismemberment, under a Bourbon family related to the French monarchy, ruled the Spanish possessions in Italy, surviving even the heavy-handed interference of Napoleon. The Hapsburgs survived into the twentieth century as rulers of Czech Bohemia and Magyar Hungary (though the latter was a personal union of the two crowns). But much had been achieved, and there can be little question that the political, economic, cultural, and intellectual leadership of Europe had passed to the national states rather than to the decaying empires.

SWEDEN

We have referred briefly to the important intervention of Sweden in the Thirty Years' War. It remains to say a few words about the new Swedish national state. At the beginning of the sixteenth century Sweden was under the Danish crown, but had resented the fact and was only looking for an opportunity to cast off the Danish yoke. The opportunity presented itself during the Reformation when a Danish Catholic king murdered a large number of Swedish nobles. Thereafter the nobles met and chose Gustavus I Vasa as king (1523–1560) with the enthusiastic support of the Swedish peasantry, who followed him in a war of independence against Denmark. During his long reign a Lutheran national Church was established, and Gustavus consolidated his authority over the whole country, having to crush various revolts during the process, especially from the Catholic clergy and Catholics who refused to accept Lutheranism. He founded Sweden as a modern state, and established the throne as hereditary within his family.

In the reign of his successor Eric, the conquest of Livonia was begun, with the intention of extending Swedish territories in

EXPANSION OF
SWEDEN
to the
TREATY OF OLIVA
— 1 6 6 0 —

the Baltic. Finland, always a Swedish rather than Danish appendage, followed Sweden in the break from Denmark. Eric's brother John, however, married a Polish princess, whose son inherited the Swedish crown. The Swedes refused to tolerate his Catholic religion and deposed him in favor of Charles IX. This involved Charles and his successors in long wars with Poland which lasted for some sixty years. Charles was succeeded by his son Gustavus II known as Adolphus, whom we have noticed already as the Lion of the North, the great Protestant leader in the Thirty Years' War. But before he entered this war he consolidated his position at home, suppressed the feudal nobility, and prepared a most efficient war machine, with the best artillery in Europe and the most highly trained army. With this army he gained several successes at the expense of Poland, and, aided by French diplomacy, was able to win a number of Baltic ports and to make a temporary peace. Then, fortified by a considerable subsidy from Richelieu, the French minister who wished to support the tottering Protestant cause against the Hapsburg emperor, he entered the war, only to die on the battlefield, as already related. Though his ministers, ruling for the infant Queen Christina, continued the war they did not meet much success until the French declared their entry into the war. Then they shared in the successes and, as we have seen, were able to add western Pomerania to their possessions at the peace of Westphalia.

During the period of the wars Count Oxenstierna was the virtual ruler of the country. A financial genius and able administrator, he was able to make Sweden into one of the most efficient states in Europe. He did not enter wars lightly and advised against Gustavus' entry into the Thirty Years' War. But he did plan and execute a small war with Denmark (1643–1645) which added several Danish provinces to Sweden, where they remained after the ensuing peace. Charles x (1654–1660) spent almost all his reign fighting, mostly against the Poles and the Danes, though he also carried out a campaign in Russia. On his sudden death in 1660 the peace of Oliva was signed with the Poles, who recognized Swedish possession of northern Livonia, while the treaty of Copenhagen recognized finally Swedish possession of the provinces taken from Denmark. Thus Sweden in 1660 had become a fully developed national state with considerable territories around the Baltic Sea. These territories, however, as we shall see in Chapter 21, she was unable to keep, but was able to retain the frontiers which she continues to possess today.

DENMARK AND NORWAY

When Sweden seceded from the Scandinavian union in the early sixteenth century Norway, a poor and backward country, remained united with Denmark. Sweden made no attempt to break up this union, although in one of her wars with Denmark she sheared off a couple of Norwegian provinces. But Denmark, as we have seen, continued

to contest Scandinavian supremacy with Sweden, not losing it definitively until 1660. Christian III (1534–1559) established Lutheranism in Denmark and Norway in 1536, and threw off the last vestiges of Hanseatic control of her sea trade. Christian IV (1588–1648) who, as we have seen, was worsted in the Thirty Years' War, spent his time more fruitfully at home except when he was drawn into warfare with Sweden which cost him several provinces. His state during his long reign was consolidated into an effective national unity, while his immediate successors finally put an end to the rebellions of the turbulent Danish nobility, and created what was close to being an absolutist monarchy. Thereafter Denmark played but a small part in European affairs, though again becoming involved in wars with the expanding power of Sweden, which fortunately cost her no territory. She lost Norway at the Congress of Vienna, as a punishment for having sided with Napoleon.

BRANDENBURG-PRUSSIA

The double title is given to this territory because until 1618 they were two separate entities, although both were ruled by princes of the house of Hohenzollern. The Margrave of Brandenburg was one of the electors of the Holy Roman Empire, and his lands were not of special importance. The duchy of Prussia (or what is now East Prussia) has been noticed in an earlier chapter as having been Christianized by the Teutonic Knights. In the early fifteenth century the Grand Master of the Teutonic Knights, Albert of Brandenburg, secularized his territory, which became a fief of the Polish crown. In 1618 Brandenburg and Prussia were united by inheritance, and thereafter the new state of Prussia began its meteoric rise. The basic work was done by Frederick William, known as the Great Elector, who ruled the electorate from 1640 to 1688. The rise of Prussia is a very special case of a national state arising from unpromising beginnings through a carefully planned policy of its extremely able rulers. Since much of this work was done in the eighteenth century and therefore falls outside the scope of this book, only the general outlines of the policy and the work of the Great Elector will be given here.

Prussia, as we may now call it, possessed a few territories in western Germany which still belonged officially to the Holy Roman Empire, but like other German territories was practically free after the peace of Westphalia. These states made contributions to the Prussian army but otherwise there was little contact between the divided lands. Frederick took some part in the Thirty Years' War, and was able to gain some territory in the treaty, but it was, like the rest of East Prussia, a poor and barren territory. Nor was Brandenburg itself much better. Moreover, the whole of Brandenburg and Prussia together was almost surrounded by the ramshackle kingdom of Poland. It was therefore the elector's task to rid himself of Polish suzerainty, and if possible at some later time, when he was strong enough, take western Pomerania for himself and so unify his territories in the east.

The policy the elector adopted—and it remained a continuing Prussian policy—was to build an efficient army which could be used for defense and diplomacy, but, if possible, never for fighting, as he could not in such a poor territory afford any appreciable losses. His diplomacy was simple enough —threaten the use of the army and thus obtain whatever he wanted. And force his poor state somehow to pay for the army. He and his successors centralized the state, developed a professional corps of administrators, and put as many as possible of the lesser nobility into uniform as officers. Thus arose the famous *Junker,* or professional military class, made up of landowners. To pay for this extravagance the elector and his successors continually kept a paternal eye on everything in their state, setting up industries out of state funds when necessary, doing on a tiny scale what Colbert was doing for France.

By the end of the century the policy had proved so successful that Polish suzerainty had been thrown off, and the elector was about to become king. The state had a sound

little army perfectly trained, ready for exercising pressure. The Hapsburg emperor needed the use of his army, and the price was the kingship, the only king outside the ancient kingdom of Bohemia within the Holy Roman Empire. In 1701 Frederick I, son of the Great Elector, became king of Prussia. His grandson Frederick the Great was to become one of the mightiest rulers in Europe, but none of the greatness would have been possible had it not been for the peculiar institution of Prussia, the army, the support of which was the prime purpose of the regimentation of the state. The army has been sometimes called more of a state than Prussia itself.

POLAND

We have already briefly noted in Chapter 8 the conditions in medieval Poland which heralded its subsequent sad fate as a tempting morsel to be gobbled up by the predatory powers on all sides of it. Essentially the failure was political. In the sixteenth century Poland-Lithuania, united fully by the Union of Lublin in 1569, possessed a territory which in size rivaled the Holy Roman Empire. It had a few important cities and centers of culture which traded with the West, and a small middle class amongst which could be distinguished considerable numbers of Jews who had been welcomed there when expelled from other countries. But the huge sprawling territory, made up of peoples who spoke many different languages, was far too large to be governed effectively in the early modern period. Power fell into the hands of nobles and landed gentry who were able to make life impossible for any monarch, however personally capable he might be. This class was not a tiny minority as in some other states, since there was no wide social gap between nobility and gentry; but their power was based upon the ownership of land. Poland was thus in essence a feudal country at a time when the rest of Europe was emerging from feudalism, and increasing numbers of the peasants were in fact reduced to serfdom, following a process we have considered elsewhere in this book, in countries where local landowners were permitted to wield effective power.

The governmental institutions characteristic of irresponsible decentralized rule were conspicuous in Poland. There were large numbers of regional diets composed of nobles and gentry which were naturally controlled by the more powerful nobles, and there was a central diet which carried irresponsibility to an extreme, even for a feudal state. Any member of the diet had a free veto on the action of the diet. It was thus to be expected that since no central action was probable, local groups had the right to join together for various purposes and to take up arms, including the forcing through of their program vetoed at the diet. It goes without saying that no king could hope to function effectively in this atmosphere, nor did the Polish magnates often agree to the exercise of royal authority by one of their number, in case he might use it as kings of France and Holy Roman emperors had used it to increase their power. Moreover, the nobles took advantage of the Reformation to weaken the one support that monarchies had found in other states; large numbers of them accepted Lutheranism and other Protestant sects, and as a consequence were able to expropriate Church lands. It was therefore probably a matter of indifference to them when the Jesuits reconverted most of Poland to Catholicism in the following century. The lands stayed secularized.

This effective control of the country by the nobility and gentry did not prevent Poland from trying to keep her territories intact, and even expanding when possible; for the nobility, like all feudal lords, had no objection to fighting, and were even willing to follow the leadership of their elected kings for this purpose. They engaged in long wars with Sweden and Russia over the possession of Livonia, and they maintained their suzerainty over Prussia until the latter became too well unified and too powerful to submit to it any longer (under the Great Elector, 1660). But in the late seventeenth century they lost the eastern Ukraine to Russia, and though a native king, Jan Sobies-

ki, gained undying glory by rescuing Vienna from the last Turkish invasion, it did neither him nor his country any good. At the opening of the eighteenth century Poland, with too much territory too loosely controlled, ruled by a class that spoke much of liberty but was not prepared to yield any of it for the sake of unity, was ripe for partition among the greater and more unified powers around her. She did not recover her independence till 1919.

RUSSIA

Political and social conditions in the sixteenth century

The creation of the modern Russian state is, in many respects, the work of Peter the Great (1682–1725). But the preparatory work which laid the foundations on which he could build was done by a succession of rulers in the sixteenth and seventeenth centuries. In this chapter we shall study the nature of Russian society in the sixteenth century and especially the work of Ivan IV (1533–1584), which was to culminate in the partial modernization of Russia and the opening of Peter's "windows on the West" at the turn of the eighteenth century. The Romanov dynasty will be left to Chapter 21.

The duchy of Moscow, as has already been indicated in Chapter 8, had become the leading power in Russia in the fifteenth century, largely because it had been recognized as the responsible authority by the Mongol overlords who had conquered most of the country in the thirteenth century. The regular tribute money paid to the Mongols was collected by the duke and taken in person by him to the Mongol headquarters at Sarai in southeast Russia. In return the duke was recognized as an authoritative chief by his superiors. When Ivan III achieved independence from the Mongols he thus retained his old authority and gained the additional prestige which naturally accrued to him from his victory over the foreign invader.

But this did not mean that the princes and nobles (boyars) of Russia in any way accepted his right to rule with authority over them. On the contrary, they regarded

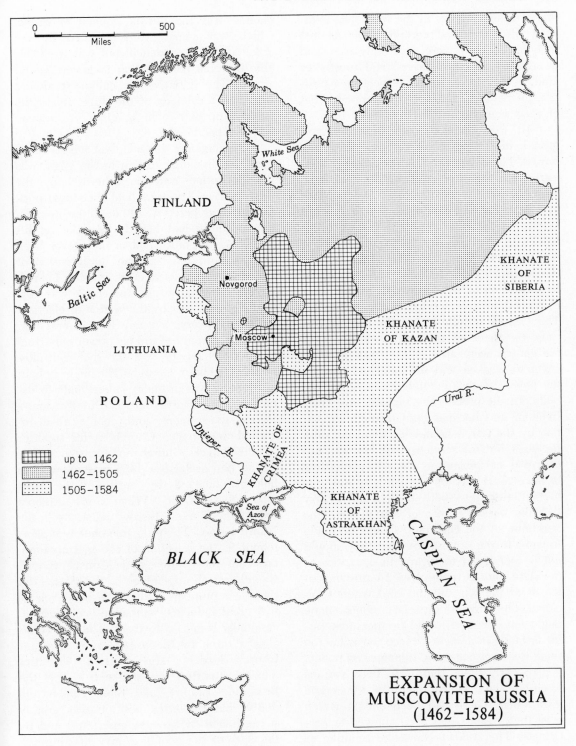

EXPANSION OF
MUSCOVITE RUSSIA
(1462–1584)

themselves as entirely independent, possessing ancient traditional rights which they
were willing to defend against any encroachment by the duke of Moscow. When they

finally decided to accept the suzerainty of
the duke, this in no way implied that he
had any absolute authority over them. In
this respect their position was analogous to

that of feudal vassals in the west. The peasantry also possessed certain rights against their lords. They were personally free, and owed only specified taxes, paid mostly in kind, to their lords; in this respect their position in medieval times was superior to that of their counterparts in the West.

All this changed with the continued growth of the power of the duke over the boyars. The means used by the dukes (called tsars from the time of Ivan IV) was, in a broad sense, the development and support of a new class of landowners who did not belong to the old nobility, who were ennobled, if at all, by the tsar, and held their lands directly from him. These lands they held only for their lifetimes, and they could be passed on to their sons only if the latter continued to give service to the monarchs. This class is usually called the gentry. The tsars, by virtue of the hold they had over the gentry, were able to use them to good effect to weaken and ultimately to destroy the power of the old hereditary boyar nobility. In the process the peasants lost their freedom and became serfs through legislation by the tsar, who needed them not only for taxes but for service in his armies, and thus was as anxious as their local masters to have them stay on the land. It was also to the interest of both boyars and gentry that the peasants, who of course were the backbone of the economy, should be made to work to the utmost and that they should not be permitted to escape their service to the state and to themselves. In this the interests of the tsar and the landowners coincided. The tiny middle class, which alone might have wished to aid the peasants (as, for instance in ancient Greece), was far too small to exercise any real influence on policy.

In early times there had been various assemblies, and the rudiments of democratic institutions. There had been one in which even the peasants had been allowed to participate. The ancient Hanseatic republic of Novgorod had possessed several institutions which might have grown toward democracy. But with the conquest and sack of Novgorod by Ivan III these disappeared. All that remained was the boyars' council or *duma,* which was sometimes summoned by the duke when he needed it, but was itself unable to force participation in governmental affairs. The initiative for calling it always rested in the hands of the duke unless the latter happened to be a minor or in some way incapacitated.

Over against this incipient feudal structure, not dissimilar to that in the West, was the Byzantine tradition inherited by the duke or tsar. The tsars held their own position by strict heredity. Although traditionally the assembly had hailed the duke on his accession, the office had in fact never been elective, and the tsar had no intention of allowing it to become elective, as in Poland, where, as we have seen, the crown was kept virtually impotent by the system of election. On the contrary, like any Roman emperor, he believed that he held his power only from God. Moreover, he was the real controller of the Orthodox Church. The metropolitan of Moscow was in theory subordinate to the patriarch in Constantinople. But Russians—clergy, government, and people alike—regarded the Russian Church as far superior to the Greek Church in Constantinople, whose patriarch after 1453 was allowed to hold his office only by courtesy of the Turks who ruled his city. When Constantinople fell to the Turks, Moscow called itself the "Third Rome." The tsar's influence was paramount in the selection of the metropolitan, and thus the Church, as in Constantinople, was almost an appendage of the state, even though a number of distinguished prelates had great influence wth some tsars and occasionally stood up to them. The tsar could always force the deposition of recalcitrant Church leaders. This Russian "Caesaropapism" was thus very similar to that of the Byzantine Empire, and there can be no doubt that the tsar's position was greatly strengthened by his religious status, and by the duty of the people to give him implicit obedience as preached by the Church.

With an independent and autocratic tsar believing in his Byzantine heritage and right to rule as an undisputed autocrat, and backed by the whole force of Russian religion—and on the other side an old nobility, with an independence of several centuries' standing, suspicious of all attempts by the tsar to increase his power—the stage was clearly set for a struggle between these two competitive centers of power. It came in the reign of Ivan IV, known as the Dread or Terrible; but the ground had been well prepared during the long reigns of his father and grandfather. They had added much to the domain of the duchy of Moscow, and in the process had reduced the power of the old independent lords while gaining the allegiance of new landowners, who owed their position to the conquest made with their aid by the dukes.

The reign of Ivan IV (1533–1584)

When Ivan's father Vassily III died the new monarch was a young child. The necessary regency gave the boyars a chance to exercise some authority. But they used the opportunity mainly in fighting and intriguing against each other for the control of the regent, Ivan's mother, to the detriment of good government. The experience of this period no doubt greatly influenced Ivan against boyar rule. At the age of sixteen he declared himself of age, and announced that he intended to assume the burden of personal rule with the title of tsar. The divided boyars accepted the position, and Ivan proceeded to institute a series of reforms.

The real government was carried on by the tsar, with the aid of an efficient council of personally chosen advisers. But he called together fairly frequently a kind of national assembly, known as the *zemsky sobor,* in which were represented the boyars and gentry, together with a number of merchants and other members of the middle class. Ivan asked advice of this assembly, and allowed it to debate and decide matters of policy. It should be understood, however, that the initiative for calling the *sobor* rested with himself, and without Ivan it could not function. He also determined its composition. In line with this policy of spreading responsibility among the better-qualified persons

in his country he allowed local officials and tax collectors to be elected, instead of using noble governors selected by himself. In all these reforms his purpose was to ensure for himself competent and loyal officials rather than make use of nobles who held their positions by virtue of their birth and whose loyalty to him was doubtful.

As a help toward his consistent plan for dispossessing the hereditary nobility of its power, he organized a fairly large body of permanent troops which he stationed either near Moscow or in key positions in the country (the *streltsy*), and organized on a more efficient basis a corps of officers who were given lands which they could not pass on to their sons. These men, dependent upon himself, belonged to the gentry rather than the boyar class. The zemsky sobor gave formal approval to the changes, in spite of the fact that boyars were included in this body. The boyars, however, would hardly have been likely to have approved these changes, had they known what use would be made of them.

When Ivan had been some thirty years on the throne, a boyar general went over to the side of the enemy during a war. Ivan used this as an excuse to put into effect measures against the whole boyar class. He was aided in this by the outright defiance of the boyar in question who claimed that all boyars were entitled to transfer their allegiance to any authority they wished. This was a part of their traditional rights. Ivan, on the other hand, took the position that the tsar was an autocrat to whom all owed allegiance, who could not be questioned, and who held his power only from God. He proceeded to organize a picked body of men called the *oprichnina*, who were subject only to himself. This was an élite corps of armed guards, wearing a distinctive uniform, and living apart under the tsar's special protection. The oprichnina, naturally, did not contain more than a handful of boyars. It was made up almost entirely of the lower gentry with a sprinkling of foreigners. On Ivan's orders the oprichnina instituted a reign of terror, which was for ever afterward to be associated with his name. Innumerable atrocities were committed, and almost open war was waged upon the boyars. Members of the corps were, in many instances, permitted to keep the estates of the boyars whom they had killed. Finally the terror was called off, but it had done its work. The tsar had broken the power of the boyar aristocracy for good, though certain boyar families were still able to cause difficulties for the monarchy during the ensuing period known as the "time of troubles."

"The time of troubles"

Ivan the Terrible died in 1584. Since he had, probably unintentionally, killed his son and heir during a quarrel, he was succeeded by his younger son Theodore (1584–1598) who was feeble-minded and incapable of ruling. Throughout his whole reign of fourteen years there was a regency, controlled first by one noble and then by another. These men claimed to rule on behalf of Theodore, or later on behalf of his youngest brother Dmitri, the last surviving heir of the line of Rurik, who was almost certainly already dead, either by murder or suicide during the regency. Finally the leaders of two noble families ruled in their own names. Throughout the period, therefore, civil war was incessant, and the Poles took the opportunity to try to control the Russian throne through their nominees, so that war with Poland, as also during much of Ivan's reign, was added to the domestic troubles of the period. During the "time of troubles" the Russians acquired a hatred of domestic anarchy and foreign intervention which has survived, one might say, to the present.

At last the nobles and gentry and merchants decided that it was time for a halt to be called to the anarchy. A zemsky sobor was called in 1613 for the purpose of choosing a tsar from a new family, since there were few who now believed that the unfortunate Dmitri had survived. The assembly chose Michael Romanov, a youth of sixteen, whom some boyars no doubt believed they could control. As it happened, Michael succeeded in consolidating the position of his dynasty by reviving some of the institutions

of Ivan IV, and it continued on the throne till 1917. The work of the Romanovs, especially Peter the Great, grandson of Michael, will be taken up again in Chapter 21.

THE IBERIAN PENINSULA

Greatness and decline of Portugal

We have already considered at some length the history of Portugal in the early modern period. Portugal had become an independent national state before the close of the Middle Ages, and gained great power and glory by her voyages of discovery and subsequent exploitation of the Eastern trade. But her population was too small and her native resources too few to permit her to hold the Eastern trade against the more powerful states of England and Holland. Too many men were lost in the East, and Negroes had to be imported to take care of home agriculture. Finally, a half-mad king, Sebastian (1557–1578), insisted on making an attempt to conquer North Africa for the Christian faith and was killed in battle. His brother Henry who succeeded him reigned for only two years, leaving no heir of the old house of Aviz, save Philip II, king of Spain, whose mother Isabella of Portugal had married the Emperor Charles V. Thus the crown of Portugal fell into Spanish hands, and, although Philip had to make good his claim by force of arms, he became king ultimately, and thus Spain and Portugal were united under a common crown. In 1640, when Spanish monarchy was on the decline Portugal made a successful bid to rid herself of Spanish domination and the family of Braganza was given the crown. Though Spain tried to recover it, she was unsuccessful, and thereafter Portugal was an independent national state, supported by an alliance with England, but no longer able to play any effective part in the affairs of Europe.

Spain at the opening of the sixteenth century

We have already seen how Spain became a national state under the dual monarchy of Ferdinand of Aragon and Isabella of Castile in the late fifteenth century. These monarchs were the first to establish an effective bureaucracy in Spain, though much of their success was due to the conquest of Granada and the expulsion of the Jews, which appears to have generated a national feeling very strongly connected with the peculiar Spanish reverence for their religion. The monarchs had established the Spanish Inquisition in 1478, as a tool for increasing their own power at least as much as for the maintenance of the true religion free of all heretical taint. During this reign also the Spanish Church was thoroughly purged of its worst moral offenses so prevalent elsewhere in Europe, mainly under the leadership of Cardinal Ximenes (or Jiminez), a learned and effective cleric who was made archbishop of Toledo, and who also founded the University of Alcala, one of the best in Europe. Spain, therefore, at the death of Ferdinand was already in a position to exercise the leadership of Catholic Europe against the coming Protestant Reformation, a task which was gladly accepted by his Most Catholic Majesty Philip II when he was handed his throne by his father the Emperor Charles V (1556).

The reign of Philip II (1556–1598)

Character and policy—Spain, of course, was by no means confined to its share of the Iberian Peninsula. We have already had occasion to speak of the large European possessions inherited by Philip, which included southern Italy; Sicily and Sardinia, the duchy of Milan; the Netherlands and Franche-Comté, part of his Burgundian inheritance; and the large portion of the New World that had fallen to Spanish arms. And while Charles V had had to spend most of his life defending his huge empire, Philip II who reigned forty-two years (1556–1598) had appreciably gained strength by losing his Germanic heritage to his uncle Ferdinand. Nevertheless, in spite of the tremendous sources of income and power at Philip's disposal, it was not easy for him to maintain his position in face of the other powers in Europe who coveted his possessions. He squandered his resources by constantly ex-

tending his commitments instead of endeavoring to contract them, as from our unassailable vantage point we can see that he ought to have done. In any view of his reign we can hardly call him a successful king, considering the resources he commanded and the use to which they might have been put. But he was undoubtedly feared and hated, if rarely loved; and he was by all odds the most redoubtable monarch of his day. If he had been a child of the Renaissance this would have contented him.

But he was no child of the Renaissance. On the contrary, he was a child of the Catholic Reformation, a far different spirit; and his greatest desire was to destroy the Protestant Reformation and all its works, a task which proved beyond his powers, though he had some hand in containing it. His policies lost him the richest territory in his possession, the United Provinces of Holland. And though he married Mary Tudor of England, which might have given him or his offspring a crown, he was so unpopular in England through his excessively Catholic policies that the English were a thorn in his side all during his reign. And he could not stop a Protestant monarch from ascending the throne of France, though he may have been in part instrumental in persuading that monarch to change his religion and to turn Catholic for the sake of peace in his realm.

Charles V, his father, though born a Fleming, had found Spain very difficult to deal with in his early years. As time went on, however, and Charles became more Spanish in feeling, the Spanish accepted him, and appreciated the fact that Philip had been brought up as a Spaniard and not as a German or Dutchman. And it can hardly be denied that Philip's policies, although not forced upon him by the Spanish, were, in the main, popular with his subjects. Charles had built up a useful machine for administration. Philip, himself an indefatigable bureaucrat, improved and perfected this machine.

He was the first European monarch to appreciate the value of paper work in the management of a kingdom and empire. He loved to write notes and memoranda. Having built himself a huge palace for his govern-

This absurd painting is said to have been done by Titian under protest. A minor artist named Sanchez Coello had executed a sketch, showing Philip II of Spain offering his infant son to heaven, which so pleased the monarch that he determined to have the final painting done by the greatest artist of his time, who was, of course, Titian. The latter suggested that Coello should complete the job but Philip was adamant, so Titian obliged, with the result shown above. The coloring is excellent in the original, but the unnatural position of the angel and the way in which Philip is apparently prepared to give his son a push suggest Titian's distaste for the whole project. The captive Muslim at the bottom left appears to have no relation to the rest of the painting. Philip presumably wanted value for his money and felt it necessary to include a reference to his half-brother's victory over the Turks, whether it had any relevance or not.

ment, he used to closet himself with papers and ministers for days at a time. Every little detail of his kingdom he required to know about, preferably in the form of written memoranda. Then, faced with a mountain of details, like other bureaucrats since his day, he could not make up his mind what to do. And there was no "buck" to pass. He had to make up his mind to do something; then, when it went wrong, he suffered agonies of remorse and renewed indecision. Violent at one moment and conciliatory at another, no one could predict or rely on his apparent policies, because he might change them at any moment. The probability is that he had never thought them through, and never predicted for himself the results of his actions; hence he was constantly surprised and upset. Officials and generals who were unsuccessful could find themselves forgiven when they expected disgrace; but it was very dangerous to answer him back. He could burn heretics without compunction, and yet write charming letters to his own immediate family. If he had not been born to a position of power and greatness he would probably have made an inoffensive secretary, as long as he was not given too much responsibility and no power of hiring and firing. Placed as he was at the head of the greatest empire of his day, his virtues rarely were allowed to show themselves. Their only achievement was the centralized governmental administration, which was a dubious blessing to the country and more dubious still for the Spanish colonial domain that he inherited. The defects of his virtues, along with his vices and his blindnesses, left a trail of destruction behind him and prepared the way for the ruin of his own country. Neither Spain nor Spanish America would be what they are today if Philip had not worn the crown of Spain during the second half of the sixteenth century.

It might have been expected that Philip would have had at his disposal plenty of money, and not been troubled with financial difficulties, in spite of his wars. But the bullion that came from the Indies, important though it was, and yielding to the king one fifth of the entire treasure, was far from enough to pay for such expensive luxuries as constant wars. It is true that Philip could hardly have managed without this source of income; but it is also true that frequently the expectation of the arrival of the ships was as good as money to him. He borrowed heavily on the expectation, having therefore to pay interest to his bankers, which ate into the proceeds of the voyages. Only through rigid economy in other matters, and by very heavy taxation of all his subjects who had any income or property, could he find enough money to pay his troops, and even then it was notorious in Europe how irregularly the pay arrived for them.

Early in his reign Philip had won several important victories in France and could certainly have captured Paris. But even while he was winning his victories he was suing for peace, and the peace he was so anxious for and finally signed was far from being as advantageous for him as he could have made it, if he had not known that his troops were on the point of mutiny for lack of pay. His Netherlandish subjects were the best source, obviously. But they were also very loath to pay any taxes that Philip imposed. They were accustomed to agree to taxation through their estates. Furthermore, they did not approve of the way he was spending his money, especially when the Dutch became Protestant; but Catholics and Protestants alike did not hesitate to drag their feet when the tax collectors were after them.

Italy, on which Philip bestowed almost no care, was heavily ground down by taxation enforced through the royal viceroys. Southern Italy in particular suffered for centuries through Spanish taxation. Philip did not hesitate to tax even the Spanish homeland; but here he was met with opposition from the Church and nobility who were unaccustomed to such impositions. Philip therefore imposed, and collected, a 10 per cent sales tax. However, the measures that should have gone with it, Philip was far too little of an economist to understand. The industry that might have been supported by him was allowed to languish and to be ruined by inflation; the grandees and the Church were left relatively immune.

A mercantile policy was adopted, as was customary in his day, with regard to the Spanish Indies, and various unsuccessful efforts were made to keep money from leaving the country, contrary to the obvious economic facts of life. Nevertheless, the policy, like everything else undertaken by Philip, was unintelligent and improperly thought out. One only has to consider Cardinal Richelieu, who was no economic genius but at least an efficient administrator, able to bribe Swedish kings with huge annual subsidies to fight his wars for him. Or consider Colbert, able to pay for his royal master's wars and the Palace of Versailles and still not unbalance his budget too severely. One can then appreciate the difference between these French ministers' national policy, and Philip's poor efforts to scrounge money from his subjects for whom his government did so little. And the difference is not only that between the sixteenth and seventeenth centuries.

Wars of Philip II—France, Turkey, Portugal—Philip's earliest wars were fought against France, which under Henry II was militantly anxious to shear off a few of Philip's outlying possessions. This phase was finished, after Philip had won several victories, by the Treaty of Cateau-Cambrésis in 1559. The French monarch agreed to keep out of Italy, where so much French blood had been uselessly spilt in the previous sixty years. In the north of France he was allowed to administer the Lorraine bishoprics, which were later to be fully incorporated into the French kingdom. Savoy was allowed to return to its duke, who had fought on the Spanish side. So, on the whole, though the treaty was regarded as a triumph for Spain, France lost little thereby that she was capable of keeping, while Philip had merely asserted his inherited hegemony over what he should have been able to possess in peace.

The remainder of Philip's wars with France were religious in nature. Philip desired that France should remain Catholic at all costs, and he was willing to back the Catholic forces with his armies. France, as

we shall see, was rent by civil wars from the death of Henry II till after the accession of Henry IV of Bourbon (1559 to 1598). Philip supported Catherine de Medici, the regent of France, as long as she supported the Catholics; after that he supported the Guise family. He did not withdraw and make peace until he was forced to, even after Henry IV had ascended the French throne and turned Catholic. Though he did put in a claim to the French throne at this time, clearly the war that he fought was for no material Spanish or even his own dynastic interests, but was inspired by his mission to eradicate Protestant influence wherever it could be found. One of the greatest joys of his reign was the French massacre of Protestants on the feast of St. Bartholomew in 1572. He was reported to have laughed on that auspicious occasion.

Against the infidels his half-brother John of Austria won a great naval battle (Lepanto, 1571), using an allied fleet of which perhaps the greater part was Spanish. And, as we have seen, Philip won the crown of Portugal in 1580. These successes, however, were far more than counterbalanced by his two most serious failures—against the two Protestant countries of England and Holland. There, his efforts were uniformly unsuccessful, except in so far as it may be called a success that he kept the Catholic provinces of Flanders in his possession, by the choice of their inhabitants, who could have driven Spanish influence from the whole territory if they had been willing to become Protestant and join the north.

Alliance with England and its failure—Spanish armada—First Philip married the English queen Mary, even before he had inherited his realm of Spain. The marriage was unfruitful, and though Philip persuaded Mary to send an army to France, contrary to the interests and wishes of the English, the venture met with no success and the English lost Calais into the bargain, their last mainland possession in France. Philip was extraordinarily unpopular with the English although he did his best, on the whole, not to make himself personally offensive. But the people blamed Philip in part for the persecution of Protestants that disfigured Mary's reign, although he is reported to have tried to restrain her, rather than to encourage her. When Mary died Philip tried to marry Elizabeth, although she was a Protestant. He probably had hopes of converting her, as he certainly had hopes of converting her subjects by any means available to him. Elizabeth played hard to get, a policy she pursued all her life, and Philip lost patience, thinking, quite correctly, that she was playing a game with him. When the Pope excommunicated her and finally deposed her, Philip regarded himself as one of the leading instruments of God for the purpose of carrying out the papal mandate, and he did his best with intrigue to support the various plots against her life by Catholics and Jesuits. Meanwhile the English seadogs were amusing and enriching themselves picking off occasional treasure ships, and Philip was so careless on one occasion as to let Sir Francis Drake with his light ships penetrate into the port of Cadiz and, as the saying was, "singe the king's beard." The last straw was when Elizabeth sent fairly substantial help as well as money to the rebellious Netherlanders. Then Philip made up his mind that the "she-devil" must be taught a real lesson. So he outfitted the famous Spanish Armada.

Unfortunately, when it came time to send the expedition, Philip, an armchair strategist as well as a bureaucrat, wrote out all his orders in advance as to how the expedition was to be conducted, and its leader, the duke of Medina Sidonia, knowing his master's fury if he did not obey instructions to the letter, made a persistent attempt to carry them out,[4] even though conditions were not what the monarch had figured they would be. As it happened, he saved his skin if not his reputation by this policy, since he was forgiven by the monarch even in defeat. The plan was to land a huge army at a channel port and not to fight the war out at sea. The

The Spanish flagship of the Armada, the San Martin, *commanded by the Duke of Medina Sidonia. The ship returned to Spain safely with its commander, though badly damaged by storms and the English navy.*

duke was also to be joined by further troops from the Netherlands who were to be conveyed across the channel by their leader, the duke of Parma.

Unfortunately, the English fleet gave battle, in spite of greatly inferior numbers, as soon as the armada entered the channel, and the duke of Medina Sidonia did not put into Plymouth and land there, which might well have been possible. It would have saved him from the terrible losses he sustained from the fast and easily maneuverable English ships which harassed him as he ploughed eastward. Philip had not ordered it that way. And the duke of Parma, trying to embark his troops in the Netherlands, found it impossible, since the Dutch pressed everything that would float into service and the famous Sea Beggars did not allow even a platoon to reach England. The result was inevitable. The fleet was badly cut up going up the channel, and winds and storms did the rest. The whole armada was destroyed

[4] Philip's principal pastime was playing chess. The chess addict will have no difficulty in imagining the kind of game Philip must have played, even though no records exist which will confirm our hypothesis.

save for a few ships that managed to make their way back to Spain. They inflicted almost no damage on their enemies.

Philip, however, expensive though the loss was, bore it with fortitude, and did not desist from his other military adventures; nor did he make peace with Elizabeth. The defeat did not destroy Spanish naval power as yet, though it greatly increased the English prestige. The treasure ships continued to reach Spain from the Indies, protected by Spanish naval convoys. In truth the armada was a special venture, and primarily intended as a transportation project for the Spanish troops. Philip had not planned to defeat the English by sea but had in mind, rather, a two-pronged large-scale invasion, and the conquest of England would have thus been achieved by the incomparable Spanish soldiery on land.

The rebellion of the Dutch and the rise of the Dutch Republic

Philip and the Reformation in Netherlands—Philip's most costly and spectacular failure was in the Netherlands. Since from this failure a new national state arose, a special section will be devoted to it. Charles v, as we have seen, treated his subjects in the Netherlands with some consideration, although he did his best to extirpate heresy by decrees and the use of what machinery already existed in the country that he could control. His policy, however, cannot be considered successful, although the Anabaptists were suppressed without too much difficulty. The early Netherlandish sentiment had been toward Lutheranism, which did not advocate rising against secular authority, but rather recommended passive obedience. It was not, therefore, until Calvinism took hold in the north that any considerable sentiment grew for independence under a Protestant Church. But at all times Calvinism was aided by a strong national sentiment and by perhaps even stronger anti-Spanish feeling.

When Philip inherited his Dutch possessions he was regarded by the people of the Low Countries as a foreigner, and the worst was expected of him. Charles v had

William of Orange (William the Silent), leader of the Dutch rebellion against the Spanish monarchy, was assassinated in 1584 when independence was almost accomplished. An early engraving from a portrait by Cornelius Vischer.

taxed the people heavily, since the Low Countries were one of his best sources of income, and the people were anxious to have the tax burden lightened. When Philip called the Estates-General to obtain a subsidy they insisted that he take his army out of the country, which he finally promised to do. After various shifts had failed, he kept his promise. But at the same time he left as a member of the council of state which acted for him, a Cardinal, Granvelle by name, who was a determined foe of heretics and ready to use all measures to suppress them. He corresponded with Philip above the head of Philip's half-sister, who was the official regent and was the virtual ruler of the country. Obtaining permission from the pope to set up new bishoprics, he proceeded to use them for the purpose of dealing more efficiently with the heretics. The Calvinists in the northern Netherlands began to organize, while many thousands emigrated to

England. Some of the Dutch nobility joined them. Others, notably the national leader William of Orange, known as William the Silent, who was still at this time a Catholic, began to think seriously of a national revolt, especially when Philip, to damage Elizabeth of England, forbade all English imports into the Low Countries.

War for Dutch independence—William the Silent—The Calvinists provided the provocation for open warfare by engaging in outbursts of iconoclasm, destroying churches and all forms of "popish idolatry." This was more than Philip could stand, and he sent into the Netherlands the able but ruthless soldier, the Duke of Alva, with an army of some ten thousand Spaniards. This army of occupation proceeded to execute with the utmost thoroughness all edicts against heretics and rebels, including some of the highest nobility. Against Alva's army the patriots, led by Orange, could do little, while Philip forced new and heavy taxes upon the country to pay for the war. All that could be done that was really effective was to prey upon Spanish shipping, a task performed by the so-called Sea Beggars, a terrifying force of highly skilled seamen led by William's brother Louis of Nassau. Meanwhile Alva took town after town, which the miserably paid Spanish soldiery treated like conquered cities. In some towns all the inhabitants were put to death. But at last Philip relieved him of his command, and though his successor took up the struggle again, the Dutch discovered a way to stop the Spanish from

The *"Spanish Fury" at Antwerp in 1576. Antwerp was completely destroyed by the unpaid Spanish soldiery after the resignation of their leader, the Duke of Alva. The artist is unknown, but the engraving is probably contemporary with the event.*

UNITED PROVINCES
OF THE NETHERLANDS
AT THE
UNION OF UTRECHT
—1579—

0   50
Miles

Joined
United
Netherlands
in 1581

FRIESLAND   GRONINGEN

DRENTHE

OVERYSSEL

HOLLAND

Amsterdam

Leyden

UTRECHT   GELDERLAND

ZEELAND

Breda

Antwerp

Calais   Dunkirk   Ghent

SPANISH   NETHERLANDS

Meuse R.

Rhine R.

Somme R.

Amiens

Luxemburg

F R A N C E

taking their northern cities. They opened the dikes and let the water in, whereupon the Beggars who controlled the sea routes could sail into the cities and push back the Spanish troops. The northern provinces of Holland and Zeeland were now virtually independent.

By this time the sentiments of all Netherlanders were substantially the same. At all costs the Spanish must be driven out. No longer was it a question of Catholics taking the Spanish side while the Protestants aimed for independence. When the Spanish army, temporarily without a leader through the death of the governor, sacked Antwerp in 1576, one of the greatest and most prosperous cities in Europe, dealing it a blow from which it never recovered, the Estates-General of the whole Netherlands united and signed the Pacification of Ghent, under which they undertook jointly to drive out the foreigner.

At this point Philip tried a policy of reconciliation. He sent out his half-brother Don John of Austria to see what could be done, and he even withdrew the army. At this point it might have been possible to arrange a compromise on the basis of toleration for both religions, and indeed William of Orange proposed this to the now supreme Estates-General of the whole Netherlands. But, though the southern Catholics agreed, the Calvinists would have none of it, and the war broke out again, with large numbers of outrages committed on both sides, especially by the lowest classes who had been converted to Calvinism, their fathers having been Anabaptists. So William decided that he would fight for independence for the northern Protestants, who, meeting together in their estates, deposed Philip. The latter now appointed a new and efficient general Alexander Farnese, duke of Parma, as governor. The pacification of the country was begun from the south, and the southern provinces remained Catholic and under the rule of Spain. The northern provinces, in spite of the assassination of William of Orange in 1584, fought off the duke with the ever-present aid of the sea and some support from Elizabeth of England, and proclaimed a republic. Thus the United Provinces were born (1581) and, as we have seen, their independence was formally recognized at the peace of Westphalia in 1648.

Establishment of Dutch independence —United Provinces—The seven provinces of the north continued to wield considerable power in the country for the next century, although the House of Orange, by virtue of its services in the war of independence, retained a privileged position, with its leader the stadtholder of Holland, the largest and most important of the provinces. But he was very far from being an absolute ruler, and the new country was rather a kind of bourgeois democracy, with the people represented in the Estates of the provinces and in the Estates-General. It was this governmental system that gave rise to the theory of government propounded by Althusius, whose views were briefly considered at the beginning of this chapter. Throughout the seventeenth century the United Provinces, in spite of their small population, was one of the leading powers of Europe, with the bulk of the trade in the East in their hands, wrested from the feeble grasp of Portugal whose interests the Spanish monarchy felt itself unable to protect. Not until Louis xiv in the later part of the seventeenth century warred against them, were the Provinces forced out of their role as a great power; and even then their decline was slow; and in spite of being overrun by the armies of Napoleon, they were able to make the transition to a small but relatively prosperous state by virtue of their hard work, thrift, and genius for making the best use of their scanty natural resources.

FRANCE

Conflict of crown, nobility, and Huguenots

Much of the history of France during this period has already been covered in the course of earlier chapters, since France was at the center of all European events, from few of which could she hold aloof. We have seen how the French national state was consolidated under Louis xi in the late Middle Ages, and we have seen the effect of the Renaissance upon France, her interference in Italian affairs, and her constant Italian wars concluded only by the treaty of Cateau-Cambrésis in 1559. Her internal system was hardly changed from the time of Louis xi, which was discussed in some detail in Chapter 15, and the constant wars waged by her kings prevented any real prosperity. As soon as there was any peace, however, then prosperity soon was recovered. The peasantry continued to work hard and fruitfully, but the great advantage that France possessed in her position, climate, resources, and comparatively large population had never yet been fully exploited. Once the early Bourbon monarchs gave some peace and stability to the country, she rapidly forged ahead of all the other European countries and maintained an undisputed ascendancy over Europe for almost two centuries.

In the sixteenth century, after the long reign of Francis I, who managed to keep the nobility under effective control and waged enough foreign wars to keep them occupied, France was plagued with religious dissension and weak rulers. After the death of Henry II in 1559 until the consolidation of his power by Henry IV in the last decade of the century there was civil war in progress almost the entire time. The nobility, in spite of the efforts of the medieval kings of France, were still turbulent, and still had not accepted the fact that they had a master. At that time, they had all been feudal lords with merely a nominal allegiance to the throne for so many centuries. They were accustomed to having private armies and using them. If the king gave them suitable cause to fight against him, they did not regard it as treason. They built castles at will and exercised local authority. Some of them, like the constable of Bourbon in the reign of Francis I, whose treason we have already noted, regarded it as no crime to take their ancestral possessions out of the French realm and offer them to the Holy Roman Empire. To such a lord it was merely a matter of changing a local master who appeared to be able to defend his possessions for a more distant one who would not interfere. Only a knowledge of the way in which the French kingdom had been built up and consolidated can explain why it was that the nobles so frequently rebelled. They had never really accepted the monarchy as a power which was entitled to coerce them; they preferred to regard themselves as independent lords or princes, willing to do honor to the king as their superior in rank and social prestige, but not as in any way their master to whom they owed obedience.

The issue of religion was extremely important, especially for the participants who were below the rank of the nobles. However, the civil wars can best be understood as the effort by various noble families to control the king and use what power he had in their own interests. Catherine de Medici, on the other hand, who ruled the country on behalf of three different sons for most of the period, was interested in ruling the country through the monarchy, but was not powerful enough at any time to suppress the whole nobility. She therefore had to try to play off one party of nobles against the other, with the undoubted hope that they would destroy one another as the English baronage had destroyed itself during the Wars of the Roses. The religious issue was a nuisance to her, since it could not be controlled at all, and involved far more of her subjects than would have been occupied in a struggle between rival nobles. Sometimes she favored Protestants and sometimes Catholics; it remained her intention to see that her sons ruled, of course with her assistance. To do this it was necessary to keep around her at least a nucleus of faithful servants who for various motives wanted peace and the cessation of the civil wars. This group, known as the *Politiques,* were indifferent in matters of religion, or at least kept their religious views subordinate to what they conceived of as the needs of the country.

The events of the civil wars have already been dealt with in part and need not concern us much here. Many of the leading nobles became Protestant and used the religious issue to gain support in the towns. This brought about the Catholic League, led by the family of Guise, who were ardent Catholics and possessed many able military leaders. Both Huguenots and Catholics hired foreign troops and organized their own peasants to fight, and it was entirely clear, especially after the massacre of St. Bartholomew in 1572, that no side possessed a sufficient preponderance of power to exterminate the other or to drive out the other's religion. The famous massacre was only an incident in the wars, costly though it was to the Huguenots. The immediate reason for the massacre was the ascendancy of the leading

Huguenot, Admiral Coligny, over the king, Charles IX. Catherine de Medici was afraid either that the king would turn Protestant himself or that she would lose her influence over him or both. With great difficulty she persuaded Charles to agree to the massacre but agree he did. Though many thousands of Huguenots were killed, including Coligny, the event only made the survivors more furious and little was gained for the Catholics.

Accession of Henry IV—Edict of Nantes

At last, when the Spanish monarch had already sent troops into France to support the Guises, the head of the Guise family was murdered at the instigation of the king Henry III, and a Guise supporter promptly revenged him by murdering the king. This double event brought to the throne Henry

of Bourbon, king of Navarre, a small kingdom in the south of France. He was a Protestant. This was what the Guise family had been fearing for years, and they had no pretender who had the slightest chance of being accepted by the majority of the people. But they continued to fight, with Spanish support, until Henry renounced his religion for the sake of the peace of his kingdom. Opposition gradually collapsed. It had been centered in the city of Paris with its Parlement and university and a fanatically Catholic population, which had resisted the best siege tactics Henry had been able to bring to bear. Peace was made with Spain, and Henry issued the Edict of Nantes (1598), granting to the Huguenots a number of fortified cities, freedom of public worship wherever Protestant religion had previously been accepted, and freedom of private wor-

Contemporary painting, by Gilles van Coninxloo, of Henry IV of France at the siege of Chartres. The character of the swashbuckling Henry has been perfectly caught by the artist, who died three years before Henry did and who must have known him from life.

ship for everyone. Special provision was made for Protestant judges, and even subsidies were granted for Protestant schools.

Administration of Henry IV— Re-establishment of law and order

This statesmanlike act, bitterly resented by the Catholic diehards, was the beginning of the recovery of France. Henry set to work to try to heal the wounds inflicted by the civil wars. He chose as his minister of finance a dour Protestant who was created duke of Sully and was given a free hand in reforming the royal finances and the tax system; though Henry regularly visited him while he was doing his accounts, and, according to his minister, made numerous intelligent suggestions. As much by his free and open personality and his thorough understanding of his people as by the financial acumen of Sully, France suddenly became the prosperous land that she always could have been. The nobles were for the present completely subdued, while the towns prospered; and the peasantry, at last able to exercise their special talents without fear of having their land fought over and their crops stolen, appreciative of Henry's pledge to pursue a policy which would allow a "chicken in every pot," worked hard and made Henry into their ideal king—and he is so regarded to this day.

For the rest, Henry was no great innovator. The trappings of the *ancien régime* of France were maintained, along with its officials who purchased their posts and were paid out of the proceeds; with its tax system under which private enterprise collected the taxes and remitted the proceeds to the king after subtraction of its percentage; and with its collectors of direct land taxes who also took their share, since it was far too difficult to institute any choice. But the administration was greatly improved, and Sully was able to put aside more than a million livres every year against probable future wars. Royal officials, superprefects known as *intendants,* also made their appearance in this reign, charged with the task of looking after the king's interests in the provinces. Sully

meanwhile used some of his hard-earned money to improve roads, and insisted that local landowners do their share of road and bridge repairing. Another minister, Barthélemy De Laffemas, preached a mercantile theory long before Colbert, and was able to set up a number of new industries and entice skilled artisans from abroad. But the great blessing of the reign was peace. The prosperity that followed it and left a surplus even in the royal treasury owed little, perhaps, to an improvement in institutions. Yet France was once again, at the death of Henry IV—murdered by a Catholic fanatic in 1610—a strong national state. The work of Richelieu in the following reign, in making France powerful abroad as well as at home, owed much to the patient labor of Henry and Sully.

The work of Richelieu and his successor Mazarin laid the essential foundations for the ascendancy of France in the reign of Louis XIV. This, however, will be studied in the chapter devoted to that ascendancy.

THE TUDOR MONARCHY IN ENGLAND

The Tudor form of government

As we have seen, Henry VII of the Tudor family, who became king of England in 1485 after his victory over the Yorkists at the battle of Bosworth, was far from being the nearest heir to the throne. Nor did even his marriage to Elizabeth of York, the nearest princess to the throne on the Yorkist side, make his claim any more valid, though a son by this marriage might have improved this son's claim. Henry owed his crown to his victory and to his acceptance as king by Parliament. This latter gave him any legitimacy as monarch that he had, while of course his victory made that acceptance something it would have been difficult to withhold.

During the course of his reign Henry began to modernize the monarchy. However, he did not fundamentally change the form of the medieval monarchy, which remained substantially what it had been before the deposition of Richard II and the Wars of the Roses. England remained a national state ruled by a king, whose powers were limited by safeguards that had existed from the very foundation of the monarchy as a feudal kingdom under William the Conqueror. In this section therefore we do not have to follow the process by which a monarch took full control of a state, developing it into a national entity, but rather to examine the modernization process, and the Tudor kings' use of the powers, traditionally theirs, to make a more efficient system of government.

It is a complete misnomer to speak of Tudor absolutism except in the limited sense that the monarchs acted as if they were absolute, with almost complete impunity. But the safeguards remained nonetheless, and the Tudors did not attempt to tamper with them. The English crown was the executive, and it used to the full the powers which accrued to the executive in those days and in large measure still do. If we are to compare it with our own system in the United States, we should have to say that in Tudor times the executive controlled the judiciary, because their separate fields of competence had not yet been determined and the king was, in theory, still the supreme judge. But the executive did not control the legislative. The legislative, on the other hand, had not yet acquired the measure of control over the executive that it has in the United States, since the legislative power did not have to make all appropriations for the work of the executive, but only special appropriations. Though it might criticize the executive, it did not possess the power of coercing it unless special appropriations were suddenly to become necessary, as in the case of war. The position remained the same through the reigns of the first two Stuarts in the seventeenth century. But Parliament was able to take advantage of the involvement of Charles I in a war for which he needed special appropriations to curb his executive powers; having done this to its own satisfaction, it then began to interfere with the king's policy in regions hitherto considered to belong to the executive. Rather than submit to this

Charles chose the alternative of civil war. As a result of the war, which he lost, the relative positions of the executive and legislative powers were substantially altered, while the judiciary became virtually independent.

Since constitutional monarchy as a form of government and the republican democracy that arose from it were the result of English experience, in any study of the heritage of the past this achievement must be given its due. While the other countries of Europe were trying to establish a government which could function effectively, the English, having already achieved that, were now engaged in a pioneering second phase— how to have an effective government that would also ensure individual liberties and participation in the government by the governed. Now, in this twentieth century, the legatees of this form of government are faced with the question of how effective this form is in an industrial world. May it not be that the efficiency of an oligarchy which does all the thinking and planning for its subjects and does not welcome the participation of the ignorant, is to be preferred to the muddle and waste inseparable from such participation? Will the Republic of India, which has adopted the form developed by the English, or the People's Government of China, with a government modeled on the Russian oligarchy, prove better fitted for giving leadership to those countries which have great tasks to perform in the coming centuries and need effective government as much as the states of Europe in the sixteenth and seventeenth centuries?

Relations of Tudor monarchy with Parliament

Henry VII (1485–1509), then, faced with a task which he appears to have fully understood, moved cautiously. He recognized that it was essential to establish his rule by dealing effectively with any trouble from pretenders to his throne, and with the feudal nobles who would support them. To meet this challenge he was well aware that he had the solid support of the growing bourgeoisie, and the landed gentry who were not noble and had no feudal heritage. With these two classes, who were represented in the House of Commons, he knew that he would have to work; thus it would be necessary to use the institutions he had inherited. The key to success therefore lay in avoiding excessive appeals to the pockets of this class, while at the same time accumulating enough money in his own hands to take care of sudden emergencies. He must not be compelled to ask for special appropriations at any time when he could not afford to do without them if they were refused.

If he did not need money, he did not have to call Parliament except for legislation. Without new legislation he could rule perfectly comfortably by administrative decree, by virtue of the powers which he already possessed that were inherent in his office. So he, and all the Tudors, only called Parliament for legislation when they were sure of its passage. The purpose of having them legislate at all was to obtain the consent of the people as expressed through their representatives, and thus increase its moral weight. And if Parliament presented petitions, as was its right, the mere presentation could do him no harm. The petitions might have merit, in which case they could be given serious consideration. If the king did not wish to accept them he could not be forced to do so.

The Tudors did not use their Parliaments to govern. The king himself governed, with the advice of his appointed council. In Tudor times this council was not greatly different from a modern Cabinet, especially the United States Cabinet. The king presided over it, and expected to be kept informed, and major issues were referred to him for decision. The council had no powers whatever save those which the king delegated to it. If council members were inefficient they could of course be dismissed at a moment's notice. Already the Tudors had secretaries of state for various specialized tasks, in addition to the treasurer and chancellor inherited from medieval times. The principal secretary of state was the king's

chief servant, and was already frequently called the king's chief minister. He was closest to the monarch, and was entrusted with the most important work, especially that of informing Parliament what legislation or what money the king required in a particular session. The council had committees which investigated and made recommendations to the king, and were sometimes empowered to act on their own. Such a committee was the Court of Star Chamber, set up by Parliament in 1487 at the king's request, though this was by no means the only committee that functioned as a court for special kinds of cases. Members of the council, authorized by the king, saw that the king's will was made known to his subjects, and took steps to see that he was obeyed, and to the members of the council the people made petitions to be conveyed to the ear of the king. In the countryside the king had local officials called justices of the peace. They were known as the Tudor "maids of all work," since more and more duties were laid upon them: administering justice in minor cases, fixing the wages of laborers, and administering the poor laws. Thus the government functioned in accordance with the king's will.

Independent of the king only remained Parliament, which was called when needed, and the common law courts which administered the laws that had been passed by Parliamentary statute, and the customary, largely unwritten law built up by precedent. The judges of these courts, appointed by the king, were independent only up to a point. And the point was crucial, for they held office only at the king's pleasure. When in the reign of James I some of them ceased to give pleasure to the king and were dismissed, the judges and Parliament fought for the right of judges to hold office during good behavior and won. And so during good behavior they hold office today.

Reign of Henry VII

If the principles of Tudor government are understood the details need not greatly concern us. Henry VII was early faced with several important rebellions. He put them down without too much difficulty and executed very few of the participants, since he preferred to break their power with heavy fines that not only impoverished them, but filled his treasury. He also had Parliament pass a law forbidding the lords to maintain private retainers who could at their will become private armies, endangering the peace of the realm (Statute of Livery and Maintenance). This law could be enforced through the Court of Star Chamber, established by Parliament as we have seen. The court, contrary to public opinion which usually knows only of the abuse of the court by the Stuarts, was not an instrument of tyranny when it was set up, although obviously it could be lent to that purpose. The local courts at the time were intimidated by the great nobles and no convictions could be secured against them. By transferring jurisdiction to the council, with the authority of the king behind it, convictions could now be secured, and for a long time the court was very popular with the people. The traditional legal safeguards, however, did not have to be observed; torture was permitted; and evidence against one's self was especially the object of the whole process, as in inquisitorial trials by the Church. When the court was abolished by the Long Parliament in 1641 it had long outlived its usefulness.

To fill his treasury Henry used all the methods available to him in this early commercial age. He asked for gifts from merchants which they felt it wise to grant (benevolences). He compelled loans which were supposed to be repaid with interest, though it cannot be said that the expectation of repayment was the first consideration for the creditor. He made regulations calling for fines when royal land had been encroached upon, and compelled some restitution. He granted monopolies for manufacture of a particular product, or for trade in a particular area. But the neatest trick of all—if it was a trick, which we shall never know—was the profitable use to which he put the desire of Parliament for a war with France. Henry did not approve of wars, since they might

deliver him into the hands of Parliament, and in any case he had no particular quarrel with Charles VIII of France. Nevertheless he accepted Parliament's proffered subsidy, equipped an army, and landed in France. Without fighting a battle he allowed himself to be bought off for a large sum by the French king. Thus Henry pocketed both the Parliamentary subsidy and the French king's bribe, all for the cost of equipping and transporting an army to France which was never called upon to fight. Henry died the richest monarch in Europe and left his young son Henry VIII a full treasury along with a policy for dealing with Parliament that avoided trouble, allowing the monarch a wonderfully free hand in spite of all constitutional safeguards.

Reign of Henry VIII

Henry VIII (1509–1547) had little or no understanding of finance, and probably despised his father's parsimony. He was a typical Renaissance monarch, anxious for glory, supremely egotistic, and without moral scruple. But he did understand and even improve upon Henry VII's use of Parliament, and he made as much use of his council as ever his father did. He was an excellent judge of character, and knew very well the kind of person he needed for a particular purpose. Unfortunately for his ministers, he could not be content with merely dismissing them when their policy failed to meet with his approval; he insisted also on beheading them. In the early part of his reign he left governmental matters to his chancellor, the papal legate, Cardinal Wolsey. Wolsey fell from power when Henry wished for an annulment of his marriage and Wolsey could not obtain it for him. On his way to the king for almost certain execution, Wolsey died, and Thomas Cromwell became Henry's chief secretary.

The purpose for which Cromwell was to be used was the nationalization of the Church, which was carried out by means of the Reformation Parliament. Henry thus made use of Parliament to demonstrate to all that the English people were behind his policy. It was not necessary to pack the Parliament. All that had to be done was for Cromwell to manage it, informing the members what was the king's will, and drum up some national feeling against the Roman foreigner. There is no doubt the people felt very badly about the casting off of Catherine of Aragon, and the raising of Anne Boleyn to the throne, but when the matter was put the way it was, they acquiesced. Then came the turn of the monasteries, handled first by a crown commission, which investigated the state of the monasteries and made recommendations that they, or a large number of them, should be dispossessed. Thereupon Parliament proceeded to dispossess them. Henry's father would have made sure to use them for the benefit of the crown, and probably would have kept many of them as crown possessions. But Henry VIII sold them in a buyer's market, and he was soon short of

money again. This time he debased the currency.

Anne Boleyn, after she had borne Elizabeth but no son, was beheaded for various crimes, including adultery. As a special favor typical of Henry, the queen's uncle presided over the special court constituted to try her. The third wife, Jane Seymour, died in childbirth, but not before she had presented Henry with a male heir. The fourth marriage was for dynastic reasons, as the unbeautiful bride brought the duchy of Cleves to her husband. Henry thought it a bad joke, and Cromwell, who had now completed his work —or almost—was beheaded, but not before he had been created Earl of Essex and given one last important chore to perform for the king in Parliament. The moment the chore was completed Cromwell lost his life. The fifth wife, to complete the record—Anne of Cleves having been given her freedom by

Portrait of Henry VIII of England by Hans Holbein, the Younger.

an annulment on the grounds that the marriage had never been consummated—was young Catherine Howard, who was not enamored of the aging and tyrannical monarch, and almost certainly was guilty of the adultery with which she was charged. She too was beheaded. Catherine Parr comforted Henry in his old age and survived him.

Before he died Henry persuaded Parliament to pass an act allowing him to regulate the succession, thus admitting Parliament's competence in such a matter. Obviously if Henry had never legally been married to his first queen Catherine, then Catherine's daughter Mary must be illegitimate. If he had not been legally married to Anne Boleyn—and he could not have been if the marriage to Catherine was legal—then Elizabeth, Anne's daughter, must be illegitimate. Jane Seymour's son Edward was in any case legitimate, since Henry's two previous wives were both dead at the time of his marriage. Parliament had already declared both the daughters illegitimate at different times, after the annulment of Catherine's marriage, and after the execution of Anne Boleyn. So Parliament gave up the struggle and delegated the authority to the king to choose his own successors. He declared both daughters to be legitimate and capable of succeeding to the throne if Edward, who was to come to the throne first, died without leaving any progeny, as seemed probable, for he was a very sick lad and did not seem likely to grow to manhood. Henry tried also to bequeath the throne after Elizabeth to the heirs of his younger sister Mary rather than to his older sister Margaret, who was married to the king of Scotland. When Elizabeth died, however, it was the latter's grandson who in fact inherited the throne. For the rest, Henry named the whole council for his son, including the uncle of the young man, who became at once the chief council member and was made duke of Somerset and Lord Protector of the realm.

Edward VI and Mary I

With the king sickly and a minor, everything depended upon the ability of the Protector to keep his council together and, as the king grew up, to maintain his personal influence over him. But Somerset was unable to fulfill this role. Parliament was called frequently to enact measures to help the economy, which was languishing; its measures were of a class nature, and peasants revolted. The feudal nobility was encouraged to come out of its semi-retirement where the two first Tudor rulers had placed it. Somerset lost his support in the council, and his place was taken by the earl of Warwick who had gained influence over the king. Warwick became the duke of Northumberland, and Somerset was tried by the nobility for treason and felony. He had tried to be merciful to the rebellious peasantry, which was sufficient to cause a conviction for felony and his execution. Parliament during this reign passed measures establishing Protestantism, for Somerset and Northumberland were at one in this. But Edward's short life was drawing to a close, and Mary Tudor was the heir, a Catholic. As the king was dying Northumberland planned a last coup to put Lady Jane Grey on the throne to which she had some claim if both Mary and Elizabeth were illegitimate. The coup was unsuccessful, and Mary became queen (1553–1558).

We have already dealt with as much of Mary's reign as is necessary. Her policy was dictated by her religion and her marriage to Philip of Spain. At home she was able to find two Parliaments willing to work with her, and after Archbishop Cranmer had been burned for heresy a good Catholic was made archbishop. Parliament probably was in a state of reaction against the excesses of Edward's reign, and was also against the Protestantism, which may well not have been held by a majority of the people. For her third Parliament Mary used influence to secure men of a "wise, grave and catholic sort," and the Parliament that she gained passed the reunion with Rome. It may be added here that the method by which the crown could exercise more than influence in Parliamentary elections was by creating new boroughs. It was impossible for the monarch to make new counties since land was limited, but boroughs could be created anywhere in the country. Naturally the crown would choose to make new boroughs in areas where it believed it had support. In Edward's, Mary's, and Elizabeth's reigns this right was freely used, and the size of the House of Commons was increased in these three reigns alone by 129 members. More will be heard of this practice in the seventeenth century.

The reign of Elizabeth I—Problems postponed for successors

Mary was succeeded by Elizabeth (1558–1603). We have already described the religious settlement effected by this astute queen, which, as in the case of her father's nationalization of the Church, was accomplished by Parliament at the queen's suggestion. We have also dealt with English mercantile policy and relations with Spain, which culminated in the defeat of the Spanish Armada. It remains therefore only to tell in some more detail of Elizabeth's relations with her Parliaments. She used the council as her grandfather and father had done, save that she trusted her ministers; and her greatest, Lord Burghley, was chief secretary for almost her whole reign, surviving into the reign of her successor. Elizabeth did not call Parliament very often in her long reign. She rarely needed it for legislation, and tried to be as economical in her wars as possible, only going to war when it was clear to her that Parliament wanted it. Her subsidies to Protestants abroad were notably meager. She was a true granddaughter of Henry VII. But Parliament was extremely interested in keeping the throne out of the hands of foreigners and, when called into session, earnestly besought her to take to herself a husband and to beget an heir. But Elizabeth had a more delicate task to perform than Parliament ever understood. She was trying to use the fact that she was still marriageable in her relations with foreign powers, and Parliament's flat-footed meddling produced a number of tart retorts from the queen.

Elizabeth also refused to abate any part of what she considered the prerogatives of the crown. This in particular applied to the

William Cecil, Lord Burghley, Chancellor of England throughout the reign of Elizabeth, who was responsible for much of the success of Elizabeth's policy and the power and prosperity of England during her reign. Portrait by Marius Geeraerts, the Elder.

discussions Parliament insisted on having, and the petitions it insisted on presenting with regard to Church policy. Elizabeth was supreme governor of the Church, and this, to her, meant that all matters pertaining to the Church were to be settled by her as governor, working through the court of high commission, authorized by the act of supremacy that made her governor. For internal matters the Church convocation should be used. Religious matters were therefore no affair of Parliament. This was not the opinion of the Calvinists or Puritans in Parliament who railed against "popery," and used the utmost freedom of speech against the queen. When Elizabeth imprisoned one for speaking out in this manner in Parliament, and Parliament complained that this infringed upon traditional English liberties, Elizabeth promptly withdrew. This was typical of her policy. She knew exactly how far she could go, and if she recognized that

Parliament was really adamant in a matter on which it was traditionally entitled to speak, she gave way with the utmost graciousness. In the matter of monopolies, which Parliament complained were damaging to business, she even agreed to the Parliamentary point of view in such a manner as to suggest that she would have refrained from granting them of her own accord. This Elizabethan policy was undoubtedly all that prevented open struggle over religion, which was thus postponed for the reign of her successor. If she had lived another few years it is doubtful whether even she could have held back the tide of Puritanism.

So the storm clouds gathered for her successor, but Elizabeth herself died, beloved of her people, the first monarch who had at all times put the interests of England as she pereceived them above any personal interests. Her policy, in an age when religious wars raged on the continent and when absolutism was ascendant everywhere but in Holland, held her people together, avoided civil war, raised her country to a prestige as yet unequaled, and yet maintained intact the ancient liberties of the people. This was no mean achievement in the sixteenth century.

▶ **Suggestions for further reading**

No attempt will be made here to offer a detailed list of histories of all the countries with which this chapter has tried to deal. What seems to the author to be most needed is mention of at least one reliable history for each country which can be used to supplement the material given in the text, especially on the political developments with which the chapter has been concerned. However, before coming to the specialized histories, mention should be made of a very fine study by Cicely Wedgwood entitled *The Thirty Years' War* (New Haven: Yale University Press, 1939). This book is extraordinarily successful in achieving an almost impossible task, the compression within a manageable compass of the events not only of the Thirty Years' War itself, but of the relations between the various smaller German states and the Holy Roman Empire. There is a background of the position of the empire at the time of Charles V, followed by a full account of its evolution and the struggle within the empire that resulted in the war. The role of all the protagonists is described, and the motives and political aims of each of the German princelings, as well as of the empire, are elucidated in an altogether admirable manner. Considering the difficulties of the subject, this is a remarkable achievement, and the fact that the book is also readable is an unexpected bonus.

For the purpose of clarifying some of the material in this chapter, William McElwee, *The Reign of Charles V, 1516–1558* (London: Macmillan & Co., Ltd., 1936) is useful, dealing as it does with the political and religious developments of the reign of Charles, to the exclusion of social and economic affairs and without too much attempt at serious biography. It remains a good introduction to the subject. For the Spain of Philip II there is a huge work written by William Walsh, *Philip II* (New York: Sheed & Ward, Inc., 1937), which contains a mass of information on European events of the sixteenth century in which Philip played his part. The judgments should be taken cautiously. It is a considerable understatement to say that they are not widely accepted, but the book does contain a great deal of factual material intermingled with the odd judgments, and it is written in a highly readable, if overpicturesque manner. On the other hand Cicely Wedgwood's long and attractive biography *William the Silent, William of Nassau, Prince of Orange* (New Haven: Yale University Press, 1944) is bitterly critical of Philip and, though her opinion would undoubtedly represent the Dutch point of view, it is far from being all that should be said of Philip. William, on the other hand, is presented with the utmost sympathy, and his role in the Dutch revolt is, if anything, somewhat overestimated, although Miss Wedgwood is able to produce evidence for all that she says. The famous old classic in three volumes by the nineteenth-century American historian Motley, full of vim and fire and much prejudice but vastly entertaining still, beautifully written and generally accurate as history, is just as sympathetic to William about whom Motley has coined a number of undying phrases. John Lothrop Motley, *Rise of the Dutch Republic* (London: J. M. Dent & Sons, Ltd., Everyman's Library, 1909). Preserved Smith's *Age of the Reformation,* referred to at the close of the previous chapter, also contains a vigorous account of the Dutch rebellion.

For Germany before the rise of Prussia, Geoffrey Barraclough, *The Origins of Modern Germany* (Oxford: Basil Blackwell & Mott, Ltd., 1946), a rather brief but well thought out treatment, should be consulted, while the work of the

Great Elector is handled clearly and effectively in Ferdinand Schevill, *The Great Elector* (Chicago: The University of Chicago Press, 1947). For Sweden, the work by a patriotic expatriate, Andrew A. Stomberg, *A History of Sweden* (New York: The Macmillan Company, 1931) has long held the field in this country, although it has a patriotic slant and is somewhat over-detailed for ordinary consumption. It is possible that a new work by a noted Swedish historian recently translated, Ingvar Andersson, *A History of Sweden* (London: Weidenfeld and Nicholson, 1956) may take its place as the standard work on the subject.

There are no adequate histories of Denmark in English, though an effort was made a few years ago to provide one. John Danstrup, *A History of Denmark* (Copenhagen: Wivel, 1948) is brief, but will provide some supplementary information and is available in most libraries. For Poland, the works by Roucek and Halecki referred to at the end of Chapter 8 may be consulted. They are as good for the period covered by this chapter as they were for the earlier history. On Russia the student is referred forward to Chapter 21 where a number of histories of Russia are discussed.

There is somewhat of a dearth of good books in English on sixteenth-century France. J. E. Neale, *The Age of Catherine de Medici* (London: Jonathan Cape, Ltd., 1943), a series of four lectures given by the noted historian of Queen Elizabeth, is very fair but rather too brief. An interesting study of the part played by an anachronistic feudal lord which throws much light on the period is to be found in F. C. Palm, *Politics and Religion in Sixteenth Century France* (Boston: Ginn & Company, 1927). There is a biography of Henry IV which contains a good deal of useful information on the period, but is rather better on the reconstruction carried out by Henry than on the conditions that led up to it (Quentin Hurst, *Henry of Navarre* (New York: Appleton-Century-Crofts, Inc., 1938). In this field, however, my preference is for a new biography by Maurice Andrieux, *Henri IV* (Paris: Artheme Fayard, 1955) which may soon be available in English.

For England under the Tudors a pleasant, informative and reliable work appears in the Pelican history of England series, S. T. Bindoff, *Tudor England* (Harmondsworth, Middlesex: Penguin Books, 1950), while the first half of Vol. II of the Anchor edition of George M. Trevelyan, *History of England* (Garden City, N. Y.: Doubleday Anchor Books, 1953) is, as always with this author, selective, but valuable as far as it goes. For the more advanced student the series the Oxford History of England is always reliable, if somewhat full for the beginner. The books in this series for this period are: J. D. Mackie, *The Earlier Tudors, 1485–1558* (Oxford: The Clarendon Press, rev. edit., 1952) and J. B. Black, *The Reign of Elizabeth, 1558–1603* (Oxford: The Clarendon Press, 1936). J. E. Neale, *Queen Elizabeth* (New York: Harcourt, Brace and Company, Inc., 1934) is an excellent study written by perhaps the most eminent specialist on this reign. Special attention should also be drawn to two books by G. R. Elton, *The Tudor Revolution in Government* (Cambridge, Eng.: Cambridge University Press, 1953) and *England under the Tudors* (New York: G. P. Putnam's Sons, 1955). These books are not easy reading, but they represent the best modern evaluation of the Tudor system, and will be helpful to those who wish to understand the strengths and weaknesses of Tudor absolutism and how it was overthrown, as is to be discussed in the next chapter. For other books on the constitutional developments in England during the period the reader is referred forward to the suggestions following Chapter 20 on the Puritan Revolution.

VIII Approach of the Modern World to 1715

The Tryal of the King.

The Army having purg'd the House of Commons and left none but their own Creatures to sit there, appointed a Committee for ye Kings Tryal wch began 20 Jan 1648, on which day 67 Commissioners were present and when Genl. Fairfax's Name was called over, his Lady cryed out He has more Wit than to be here, and when he was Indited in the Name of all the good People of England she also Cryed out, no nor one hundred part of them, his Gold Head dropt from his Cane, this day without any visible cause, on the 2d 70 Commissioners were present, as were 71 on the 3d day, and 66 on the 4th when Bradshaw pronounced the Sentence.

Seventeenth-century engraving of the trial of Charles I. As the royalist engraver was at pains to point out, only a small minority of the House of Commons was willing to condemn the king, for which act several paid with their lives upon the restoration of Charles II. (COURTESY NEW YORK PUBLIC LIBRARY)

20

The Puritan Revolution in England and the Establishment of the Constitutional Monarchy

The divine right of kings • Reigns of James I and Charles I • The Civil War and the establishment of the Commonwealth and Protectorate • The Restoration under Charles II • James II and the Glorious Revolution • The constitutional monarchy and the beginnings of cabinet government • Summary: Limited constitutional government

---

► The "divine right" of kings

PROBLEMS PRESENTED BY ABSOLUTE MONARCHY

In many ways absolute monarchy is the most natural form of government, as it has in historical times been by far the most prevalent. Athenian democracy survived for more than two centuries, but fell to the Macedonian monarchy when it had become clear that the city-state was too small a political unit to survive in a warring world. The Roman Republic, though it had democratic forms, was essentially an oligarchy, and proved itself unable to manage an empire under political forms suitable only for a city-state. It too was replaced by one-man rule. There had been several oligarchical republics in Renaissance Italy, some, such as Venice, ruling appreciable territories outside the home state. But these exceptions to the general rule of absolute monarchy are few, and it is significant that both oligarchies and democracies had been found practicable only in relatively small political units. By the opening of the seventeenth century no country had yet discovered a means by which a large political unit could be ruled save by a strong executive in whose hands were concentrated all the powers of the state. The Pharaoh of ancient Egypt, the Assyrian warlord, the great king of Persia, the emperor of Rome—all these had been absolute monarchs, concentrating all authority in their own hands, and ruling through advisers chosen by them and responsible to them, who possessed no authority themselves save what was delegated to them by the monarch.

The dangers of absolute monarchy to us seem obvious. The monarch may be inefficient or tyrannous, he may be irresponsible or negligent; yet there is no way of removing him save by assassination or civil war. And if he is removed by violence his place must be taken by someone who has no *right* to rule, and thus the field becomes wide open for competition. So, in almost all historical states, the principle of hereditary monarchy

697

► chronological chart

James VI (James I of England) becomes king of Scotland	1567
True Law of Divine Monarchy by James I	1589
Reign of James I of England	1603–1625
Hampton Court Conference	1604
Gunpowder Plot	1605
Bate's case	1606
Dissolution of Parliament and personal rule by James	1611
Addled Parliament summoned and dismissed	1614
Dismissal of Coke as Chief Justice	1616
Intervention of James in Thirty Years' War	1621
Mission of Charles, Prince of Wales, and Buckingham to Spain	1623
Summoning of last Parliament of James	1624
Reign of Charles I	1625–1649
Marriage of Charles to Henrietta Maria of France	1625
Failure of expedition to relieve French Protestants	1627–1628
Petition of Right	1628
Assassination of Buckingham	1628
Dissolution of Parliament and beginning of Charles's personal rule	1629
Laud appointed archbishop of Canterbury	1633
Introduction of Book of Common Prayer into Scotland	1637
Invasion of England by Scots	1639
Short Parliament April to May	1640
Summoning of Long Parliament November	1640
Execution of Strafford by bill of attainder	1641
Grand Remonstrance	1641

Civil wars	1641–1649
Execution of Laud by bill of attainder	1645
Battle of Naseby	1645
Execution of Charles I	1649
Commonwealth and Protectorate	1649–1660
Leviathan of Thomas Hobbes	1651
Dissolution of Rump Parliament	1653
Barebones Parliament summoned and dismissed	1653
Instrument of Government— Cromwell becomes Protector	1653
Humble Petition and Advice	1656
Death of Cromwell	1658
Restoration of Charles II	1660
Clarendon Code	1661–1665
Conversion of James, Duke of York, to Catholicism	1668
Treaty of Dover	1670
Test Act	1673
Marriage of Mary, daughter of James, duke of York, to William of Orange	1677
Popish Plot	1678
Personal rule of Charles II without Parliament	1681–1685
Rye House Plot	1683
Reign of James II	1685–1689
Monmouth Rebellion	1685
Declaration of Indulgence	1687
Birth of heir to throne	1688
Invasion of William of Orange and flight of James II	1688
Reign of William III	1689–1702
Bill of Rights	1689
Defeat of James II in Ireland at Battle of the Boyne by William	1690
Act of Settlement	1701
Reign of Anne	1702–1714
Union of England and Scotland	1707
Accession of George I, Elector of Hanover, to English throne	1714

has been accepted as the only one which can ensure a peaceful succession; and if the hereditary monarch has proved to be incompetent his rule has nevertheless been endured in the certainty that even kings are mortal and the next reign may prove to be better.

Yet the thought is persistent, and becomes more persistent as we move toward modern times, that at least the more competent and influential of the monarch's subjects should have some share in the rule, or, if nothing else, should be able to exercise some check on the possible irresponsibility of the monarch. But the institutions through which such a check could be exercised were never devised in the ancient world, and arose only through much trial and error in the modern. Even now, few would claim that they are really satisfactory in any country, though they are far more satisfactory in some than in others. In the Middle Ages the feudal monarch did not really rule. Government in a feudal state was almost entirely local, though the king, as we have seen, constantly strove to increase his power to the end that it might eventually become absolute, and thus convert the feudal state into an absolute monarchy. When, as in the Holy Roman Empire or in Bohemia or Poland, the kingship was elective, the noble electors were careful to see that the man they elected should be kept as weak as they could make him. Such states, therefore, remained to a large degree feudal and virtually anarchic. The nobles retained the power they had inherited, based on their local authority, but the price was high. Their states lacked any government worthy of the name, and they were doomed to fall, like Poland, to any truly efficient government that decided to concentrate its forces against them.

IMPORTANCE OF PURITAN REVOLUTION

The importance, therefore, of the Puritan Revolution in England, and the constitutional monarchy that followed it, can hardly be exaggerated, for it offered a solution to the problem of how monarchy can be shared, how the people can keep a check on the actions of their monarch and yet avoid anarchy—how, in short, democratic government is possible, with or without a monarch. The English kept their monarch and made him by the twentieth century into a figurehead. The Americans understood better the logical implications of the Puritan Revolution and built a republic based on the principle, already developed by the Puritan radicals in the seventeenth century, that all power derives from the people, and all legitimate government must command the assent of the governed. But both these peoples devised governmental institutions which do work, and other Western peoples have followed their example to a greater or lesser degree. The *ideas* behind these governments have also prevailed in the Western world, to such an extent that at the end of World War I almost no one would have failed to pay at least lip service to them; and though not all Western countries have been able to provide institutions which give adequate expression to these ideas, few people in these countries would be willing to give up trying and revert of their own free will to the older tradition of absolute monarchy.

THEORISTS OF ABSOLUTISM

James I, King of England and Scotland

Only in England was there any effective check on absolutism, at the beginning of the seventeenth century; and under Tudor rule this check had not appeared very effective. Therefore it would have been altogether surprising if James I, who had ruled Scotland, which was a virtual theocracy (a different form of absolutism and not a sharing of power between ruler and people), had not believed in absolutism as a divinely willed form of government. It would have been no less astonishing if he had been willing to concede in principle that government depended upon the consent of the people, still less that it was shared between king and people and that the people were entitled to limit his absolutism. It was so obviously necessary that power should be concentrated in responsible and effective hands, that for him it was hardly necessary to argue the matter. But he was interested in explaining, to anyone who would listen, why the existing institution of hereditary monarchy was ideal for the purpose, and, being so ideal, why it must have come about as the result of God's will. And, after all, it was God who provided the rulers with progeny to inherit the throne, so that on the basis of the evidence, the right to rule was essentially of divine origin. There is nothing at all illogical or inconsistent in James's thought, as expressed in his book *The True Law of Free Monarchies*, and throughout his English reign he never deviated from it, either in theory or attempted practice. And probably almost all the political thinkers in Europe who lived under hereditary monarchs would have agreed with everything that he said.

Thomas Hobbes—The *Leviathan*

The English political thinker Thomas Hobbes, who wrote his *Leviathan* during the reign of Charles I, and published it after the latter's execution, appreciated exactly why there must be concentration of power, and he made use of an important myth to sustain his view. At some time, Hobbes explained, the people banded together and chose one man to whom they yielded all the rights they possessed in exchange for the essentials of government which they could not do without, especially for protection. This Social Contract was not reciprocal, in Hobbes's view, but unilateral. The people had forever yielded up their rights in exchange for protection, but the monarch had agreed to nothing, save that he would protect them. Thus in Hobbes's thought any strong government capable of providing protection had earned the right to rule by this very power of protecting. It was possible to defend Cromwell's government or the government of Charles I; but since the latter had proved ineffective and had in fact been overthrown, the right passed to Cromwell and his army, who could do what Charles had been unable to do. Without such a Social Contract the life of man would be, as it had been in primitive times before monarchy, "solitary, poor, nasty, brutish, and short." Hobbes recognized no indefeasible right of any particular monarch or any particular family to rule; his sole criterion was the effectiveness of the rule. But he assumes the necessity for an absolutist form of government, and he bases this necessity upon the nature of man in society, which, in Hobbes's view, does not change, since man is exclusively actuated by self-interest.

THEORY OF CONSTITUTIONAL LIMITED MONARCHY—JOHN LOCKE

A monarch, then, could be as tyrannous as he wished, provided he did his duty by affording protection to his subjects. The people had no rights against him, as they had yielded them to their monarch. If he were not tyrannous, the reason would be solely that he did not conceive tyranny to be in his own interests; for he, like everyone else, was actuated by self-interest. The theory of John Locke after the Glorious Revolution of 1688 that monarchs owe certain rights to the people, and if he does not grant them, he may be overthrown, would have seemed an invitation to anarchy to Hobbes. Yet it is the latter view that prevailed, because the Glorious Revolution was successful, and needed a theoretical justification. At the beginning of the century few, if any, thinkers would have been bold or imaginative enough to put forward such a theory as that of Locke. Yet the men who fought the Stuart monarchs were gradually forced, as they fought, to justify their resistance, and the idea gradually came to them, out of their own experience and understanding of why they were fighting, that absolute monarchs must be compelled to recognize their responsibilities. They needed more than protection from him. They needed certain basic liberties, even though they were not prepared as yet to extend these basic liberties to all. So, when John Locke wrote, there was nothing startling in what he said. It was what the Puritans had been thinking for a long time. All that he did was provide a variant of the Hobbes myth, by acknowledging the fact of the Social Contract, but claiming that the Contract involved mutual obligations, under which both sides were obligated equally. The monarch was entitled to expect that the people would act as loyal subjects and perform their duties. If they did not he was entitled to use force against them. But, on the other side, the people also had the right of rebellion and the right to choose another monarch who was ready to perform his side of the contract. The long list of the crimes of George III which appears in the

Declaration of Independence is merely intended to provide the evidence that George had not performed his side of the bargain, and to justify the rebellion of the American colonists whose fundamental rights had not been respected.

LIMITED MONARCHY—THE "WAVE OF THE FUTURE"

It should not therefore be thought that the Puritan Revolution was in any way a planned revolution. It began with the attempt on the part of the Puritans to change the king's religious policies through the use of the main institution that they controlled, and the one actual power that they possessed of forcing the king to come to Parliament for money in emergencies. But it was supported by many who were not Puritans and were quite content with the religion as established under the Elizabethan Compromise. These men wished to see a monarchy limited as it had been when it was a feudal kingdom in the Middle Ages, a concept of the monarchy which was now seriously out of date. The Stuart monarchs, like other absolute monarchs in Europe, wished to be modern and efficient and unhampered by ignorant and irresponsible subjects. The French and Spanish monarchs had long ago disposed of their opposition. Their feudal nobility, with bourgeois aid, had been taught their place, and the bourgeoisie had been quite content to let the kings run their governments without interference from them. But the English conservatives wished to limit the monarchy and even share the government. This, in the view of the monarchs, was a backward step, a return to the near-anarchical conditions of feudal times. It was certainly no "wave of the future."

Yet it did prove to be the wave of the future, because in the process of trying to recover rights which they believed the king had filched from them and that they had once possessed, the English actually succeeded in devising new forms for a truly limited government, based ultimately not only on popular consent but on popular participation, although for a long time it was only the influential classes that either consented or participated. And in the process the monarchy disappeared as an effective institution and became merely a symbol, possessing, as Edward VII in the early twentieth century explained, not even an opinion of his own but only the opinion of his ministers. It may be safely said that no one in the early seventeenth century could have predicted such an outcome to the struggle. Yet it was inherent in the logic of the events as they unfolded; and though the outcome might have been different if different personalities had been involved, if the first two Stuarts had been wiser men and if Parliamentary leadership had been more pliable and less determined, the historian can only note that these were the persons involved, and that this is the way it did happen—and because of this democracy and its institutions came into being in Western civilization.

▶ The reign of James I

UNDERLYING REASONS FOR CONFLICT

It has already been noted in the last chapter how the Tudor monarchs had been able to deal with their Parliaments and with the rising bourgeoisie. And we have noted how at the end of the long reign of Elizabeth tension was already rising. Complaints were made of the queen's use of monopolies, and of her dictatorial attitude with regard to the Church. And it was suggested that even had Elizabeth lived, Puritan intransigence would sooner or later have forced a showdown on religion. We have seen how the Tudors used their Parliaments—how, while apparently keeping them subservient by managing them, they nevertheless did make use of them for their own purposes, incidentally adding to their prestige and providing them with precedents on the basis of which they could demand an increased share of government as due to them by right. By fighting for them, even against Elizabeth, Parliament had already secured the recognition of certain privileges. Though Elizabeth had objected to debates on certain subjects in the House of Commons, she had been unable to prevent them. When she tried to punish members for exercise of what they regarded as a necessary privilege, they had never recognized her right to do so. They consistently maintained that they could debate any subject they wished, and they could not be held to account for the exercise of freedom of speech within the House. How, they argued, could they give advice if they did not hear many points of view? The Stuarts were to hear much more of this argument, but consistently they replied that the House of Commons had the right to give advice only when asked for it, not on its own initiative. The king's council was an advice-giving body, selected by the king himself. He did not desire advice from persons elected by his subjects unless he asked for it, as he sometimes did when he thought their advice would be worth listening to, in view of their local knowledge.

Members of Parliament therefore wished not only to give advice, but to make sure that it was taken. By custom they had made the laws. In Tudor times they made only such laws as the king asked for; now they wished to make laws whether or not they were asked to do so. If the king did not like them, then he could refuse to pass them. But in such a case he could not expect too much consideration from them next time he came to them for money. They wished the king to execute the laws he and they had made, and if he did not they wished to be able to insist that he should do so. If they could not do anything directly to the king, at least they wished to hold his ministers responsible for the execution or nonexecution of the laws and be able to punish them if they did not do their duty. They wished that the laws they had made should be properly enforced in the law courts, that judges should be neither corrupt nor unduly influenced by the king. But above all, probably what they desired most was that the king should at least listen to them and treat them with respect, as both having knowledge, and as being vitally interested in his acts as monarch, by which they and all the people were affected. But the first two Stuarts, at least, were not willing to grant them so much. They themselves knew what was best, and it was the duty of the Parliament merely to support the king's policy and behave as loyal and subservient subjects. Everywhere in the debates of this period one can sense the frustration of these good bourgeois and gentry at the way the kings treated them, lecturing them on their duties as subjects, using heavy-handed methods to enforce compliance with their wishes, sending members to prison for "speaking their conscience freely," assuming that they had the monopoly of wisdom.

CHARACTER OF JAMES I

James I was a well-intentioned man, and when he came to the English throne he had the reputation of having been a successful king in Scotland. He could never bring himself to admit that he had anything to learn. He understood thoroughly the theory of absolutism, and he was well aware how by shrewd manipulation of the forces opposing him he had been able to secure a position in Scotland that was close to a Tudor absolutism. But he had also learned how difficult it was to deal with Calvinists, how obstinate they could be in matters affecting their consciences, and how insistent they could be in getting their own way, which was, in their view, also God's way. He did not like the Scottish Church system, which was difficult for the monarch to control. He greatly preferred the English system, with the king the official governor of the Church, and the bishops as his executive assistants, appointed by him and unlikely to contest his views and policies.

Rule of the Church by the godly rather than by the monarch was derogatory to royal dignity, and it had been only with great difficulty that James had succeeded in Scotland in assuring his ascendancy over the Scottish Kirk, in rather exceptional circumstances not likely to recur elsewhere. He does not seem to have been an especially religious man, although he was passionately interested in theology and passionately argumentative. But he liked the Anglican Church for political reasons, and he was prepared to enjoy its headship.

Not without ability, especially a certain canny shrewdness that kept him from the worst excesses into which his son fell, and which was to cost the latter his life, James was nevertheless totally unsuited to be the monarch of the England of his day. Living in his abstractions, learned from books, and logical to a fault, he yet had no knowledge whatsoever of people. Not only did he fail to possess even the slightest modicum of tact, but he chose advisers on grounds which had nothing to do with their ability, and retained them in important positions even when their incompetence had been long demonstrated. An ungainly and unattractive man himself, he liked to have handsome men around him and showered favors on them. He had a very good understanding of the needs of his new country, yet was for personal reasons unable to make it accept-

able to his people. Above everything else towered his belief in his own infallibility and his own right to rule as seemed best to him, without check or hindrance from those he believed to be his inferiors. And it was this monumental self-esteem that drew forth the opposition in his realm which had never risen against Elizabeth in spite of her own predilection for autocracy, and was to prepare a revolution and the destruction of his dynasty.

THE CROWN AND THE COURTS

On his triumphal procession toward his capital James gave a foretaste of the kind of rule he was to exercise in England. A thief had been captured by his guard and James was asked what was to be done with him.

James I of England was personally extravagant, dressed richly, and spent much money on his favorites. But he could never compensate for his lack of personal dignity and his ungainly appearance, in this respect such a contrast to his Tudor predecessors. This portrait by an unknown artist of the Italian school suggests why.

The new monarch ordered his immediate execution. In England this was not a royal prerogative. He could pardon in certain circumstances, but he could not convict. For that there were courts. But James throughout his life believed that the courts were there for his use, and not for the purposes of ensuring justice for his subjects. He looked upon all the courts as branches of the executive, because he had the right to appoint and dismiss judges, and some of the courts (known as prerogative courts) had indeed been set up by the monarchy with or without Parliamentary consent, for the purpose of enforcing administrative decrees. We have already noted the Court of Star Chamber and the Court of High Commission. The Council of the North and the Council of Wales exercised the king's authority in these sectors of the country, while the king in his private capacity as feudal monarch possessed also his personal courts, such as the Court of Wards and Liveries, whose task was to ensure the proper payment of his remaining feudal dues. But there were three courts which were not prerogative courts, and not controlled by the king—the Court of Exchequer, the Court of Common Pleas and the Court of the King's Bench. In these courts the judges were supposed to be independent and to administer the law. The judges of these courts regarded themselves as serving the interests of justice rather than the interests of the king, and they administered the statute law made by king and Parliament. When there was no statute law that was clearly applicable, then the judges used precedents. The so-called "common-law courts" were one of the protections enjoyed by the citizen against the king; and though the people themselves may not have appreciated the fact, the judges did. From the ranks of the judges and common lawyers came what was perhaps the most formidable opposition the Stuart kings faced. These men wanted no part of modernism. They wanted all the ancient liberties (whether or not they had really existed) preserved. They are the ancestors of those who speak about the government by laws and not by men. The king had his position in the constitution as the

executive, and he had certain well-defined rights and duties. But he was not supreme, and not above the law; though he could not be punished, his ministers could be punished for obeying him. Even the king, according to the common lawyers, must live within the law.

James, it need hardly be said, did not agree with this concept; and it is more than doubtful whether the common lawyers did indeed have history behind them. When therefore he found that the judges gave opinions against him, in his heavy handed way he dismissed them, thus succeeding in intimidating some and influencing their opinions. One, Sir Edward Coke, amongst others, refused to be intimidated. Dismissed by James from his position as chief justice of the King's Bench, he retaliated by having himself elected to Parliament and leading from that vantage point the opposition to the king. And ultimately not only did the revolution abolish all the prerogative courts, but under the Act of Settlement of 1701 the justices forever afterward could not be dismissed, and only with the greatest difficulty could they be removed by both Houses of Parliament acting together.

JAMES AND THE CALVINISTS

Still on his way to London, James was presented with a petition signed by a substantial number of Calvinist ministers. These worthies complained of the increasing Catholicism of the English Church, the numerous "popish" customs, such as the use of ceremonial vestments, and a service not far different from the Catholic high Mass. They objected also to the Episcopal system carried over from the Catholic Church, and especially complained of the fact that far too many bishops did not attend to their dioceses, and that the custom of plural benefices had not been abolished. James graciously agreed to hold a conference on the matter, looking forward perhaps with some relish to his first duty as governor of the Church, and to a good argument with Calvinist divines in which he could lay down the law, certain of being obeyed—a pleasant contrast with his Scottish experience.

But the Hampton Court Conference, held the next year, was a horrible failure. The Puritans were not suitably subservient. They spoke their minds with considerable freedom, especially on the matter of the bishops. Some even went so far as to demand their abolition, when all James had been ready to do was reform a few abuses. James lost his temper at being resisted in this manner, without a proper regard for his majesty, and gave vent to the famous statement "No bishop, no king." If the king had no loyal servants within the Church to enforce discipline, there would be an intolerable freedom in the land, so that the very crown would totter. James also told his audience that if they did not conform he would "harry them out of the land." Many of them indeed did emigrate to Holland at the time, whence in due course some went to America. Others were to leave England directly during the reign, including those who sailed on the *Mayflower,* to found a community more to their liking, where the Church would rule the state in accordance with God's will.

Interference with parliamentary prerogatives

In 1604, likewise, James made his first mistake with his first Parliament. Parliament claimed that it had the absolute right to decide who could sit in the House of Commons. An outlaw had been elected to the House, as had also a man who had been imprisoned for debt. A court had declared that the former was not eligible to take his seat, and the king insisted that he should not. The House declared that it alone was competent to decide on the matter, and sent a so-called "Form of Apology" to James in which it set forth in no uncertain language that the right was an ancient one, confirmed by all the king's predecessors, and adding for good measure that it was the custom of monarchs to increase their power by every means at hand, while the few rights of subjects are seldom permitted to grow at all. James, of course, asserted that subjects held their rights only by grace of the king. His position

The conspirators in the Gunpowder Plot (1605), from a print published immediately after the discovery.

was clear enough, and from the point of view of the historical development of Parliament it is not at all clear that he was not right. However, the matter was not worth quarreling over yet, and he let the affair of the debtor and the outlaw drop.

In the following year (1605), a famous plot (the "Gunpowder Plot") was discovered, celebrated for centuries by displays of fireworks. Since James at Hampton Court had refused to permit more than a few minor changes in the Anglican Church, and had insisted on full compliance with the Act of Uniformity of his predecessor, both Puritans and Catholics were alarmed, the latter especially, because they had been led to believe that their worship would be at least tacitly tolerated. But when a number were fined for "recusancy" (refusal to attend services of the Church of England), a group of Catholics devised a harebrained plot to blow up both Houses of Parliament when they were in session. Rather naturally, however, some of the conspirators had Catholic friends who would be blown up in the holocaust, and desired to warn them. One of the men so warned betrayed the plot to the government, and the incendiary was taken as he made his preparations in a cellar. Thereafter James must have recognized that only the convinced Anglicans were on his side, and the laws against all who did not conform to the Church of England worship were ever more strictly enforced.

Increase of taxation without parliamentary consent

In spite of his tactlessness James might never have got into trouble with his Parliaments if he had not been compelled to hurt the men of property also in their pockets. When he came to the throne there was no money in the treasury but an unpaid debt of some £400,000, mainly the result of Elizabeth's wars in Ireland toward the end of her reign. James was not an economical man, and his court expenses were high. Moreover, prices had been constantly rising for the previous hundred years, and the king's fixed revenues from his lands, fees, and other regu-

lar royal income were no longer enough to pay his expenses. So he looked around for new sources of income. He could always try to obtain subsidies from Parliament, but since this entailed questioning and perhaps statements of grievances, James was reluctant to use this source if it could be avoided. His first Parliament had resulted in the Form of Apology, and he could conveniently do without more of the same.

So he decided to raise the customs duties on imported currants. As was customary, Parliament had already granted the king the customs duties (tonnage and poundage) for life, but, in the opinion of Parliament, granting the right did not involve the right to change the rate of duty. A merchant named Bate refused to pay the duty and was haled into the exchequer court (one not controlled directly by the king). Here the judges ruled against him, giving it as their opinion that the king, by virtue of his right to take action for the common good, was permitted to raise the rate of duty for the purpose; and clearly his purpose was indeed on this occasion to provide for the common good. Delighted at the news, which confirmed what he had always thought about the monarchy, James proceeded to raise the duties on large numbers of other commodities. Parliament, which happened to be in session, grumbled, but did not do anything definite. It was, indeed, in the opinion of many, quite possible that the judges were right, and that the king did have the power they attributed to him. But they remembered it against the king later, and constantly in the later years of the reign were to bring up the matter of what they called "impositions."

Since the first Parliament of James continued in session for many years, it felt that it could not look with equanimity upon the personal extravagances of the monarch, which members felt were wasting the people's hard-earned money. When the members began to complain of such things the king finally dissolved Parliament and tried to do without further parliamentary subsidies (1611), relying upon the increased income from customs duties to tide him over.

Attempts to by-pass Parliament— Extraparliamentary exactions

But his financial difficulties became worse, and he had to call Parliament again in 1614; and Parliament insisted on discussing grievances, especially the impositions, before they would vote him any money. Thereupon the king dissolved this Parliament (the Addled Parliament) before it had passed a single measure. He also sent four members to the Tower to be imprisoned. Determined now to do without a Parliament at all, James resorted to the time-honored measures of obtaining money already discussed in Chapter 19, under the reign of Henry vii, with a few extra embellishments. He invited loans from cities and individuals, and he sold monopolies. A confirmed pacifist, he could hardly hope to turn the neat trick of Henry vii and threaten to go to war and obtain bribes from his potential enemies, but he insisted that all who had sufficient property to become knights should purchase this honor or be fined for not doing so, and he invented a new title, baronet, also for sale, at a higher price. But these shifts did not help him much, especially when he was faced by the necessity for a foreign war.

Conflict over foreign policy

The Thirty Years' War could hardly leave James or his people altogether indifferent, for James's daughter was married to Frederick the Winter King, whose expulsion from Bohemia, already dealt with, was the signal for the outbreak of the war. The English people regarded it as an attempt by the Catholic powers to suppress Protestantism on the continent of Europe, and the English Protestants, including of course the Calvinists who were highly influential in Parliament, wanted the king to go to war on behalf of Protestantism, or if not for God's cause, at least for the sake of his dispossessed daughter. But James did not want to call Parliament, since he had a good idea that it would, after seven years away from Westminster, complain bitterly of his impositions and monopolies. Apparently he would rather abandon his daughter and the Protestant cause than call Parliament.

Circumstances, however, forced his hand. The war on the continent was going too unfavorably for even James's patience to endure. When Spanish troops invaded the Palatinate, the home territory of his daughter and her husband, he decided to call Parliament, with every expectation that it would at least grant him enough money for the war for which the Calvinists were clamoring (1621). Parliament gave him far too little for his needs, since the members were entirely incompetent to judge what the needs really were and James did not explain the matter properly. Indeed Parliament even tried to suggest a different strategy from the one envisaged by James, thus undoubtedly interfering with what had always been a prerogative of the executive. The king, as it happened, had a very remarkable plan for winning the war, also without too great a cost. He was planning a marriage with the Infanta of Spain for his son Charles, thinking that this marriage might prevent the Spanish Hapsburgs from aiding the Austrian Hapsburgs in Europe, thereby giving the Protestants a chance of winning by themselves. Parliament naturally did not understand such tortuous thinking, and on principle objected to Spanish marriages. So, being in session, the members one after another complained bitterly of the royal policy, bringing down upon themselves a severe admonition from James not to meddle in "deep matters of state." Parliament remonstrated, and James, not to be outdone, had the pages of the Parliamentary record which contained the remonstration torn out. Whereupon he dissolved Parliament, but not before having some of the members arrested and imprisoned, thus denying them their cherished freedom of speech.

So now James at the end of 1621 had a war on his hands, a Spanish marriage to be negotiated, and an empty treasury. Meanwhile, it should be mentioned, Parliament had rediscovered a further medieval weapon. In the intervals of quarreling with the king about foreign policy, it had struck a blow against monopolies without directly touching the king at the time. The House of Commons had impeached a monopoly holder before the House of Lords, and followed this with an impeachment of the Lord Chancellor himself, one of the king's servants who had executed faithfully the king's commands, but had in the process enriched himself. This was Lord Bacon. The House of Lords found him guilty and the king had no grounds for interference. The evidence was convincing, but the precedent was established for attacking a minister of the crown for his public acts.

Unable to go to war effectively in Europe with such a small subsidy as he had received, James decided to stake everything on the success of his Spanish negotiations, which were encouraged by the Spanish ambassador in England, who of course desired to prevent England from interfering on the continent. Charles and the king's reigning favorite, the duke of Buckingham, paid a visit to Spain, but they were brusquely rejected, the Infanta going into a convent rather than submitting to marriage with a heretic. Charles and Buckingham returned to England in a fury. James at once reversed his policy and tried to arrange an alliance with France, at the same time negotiating a treaty with the Dutch. As a result of this *volte-face* he felt fairly confident that Parliament, which had always wanted war with Spain, would agree to pay for it. He therefore summoned his last Parliament in 1624, and managed to obtain almost half of what he had asked for, in exchange for his signature on an act forbidding monopolies except for patents on new inventions. The same Parliament also impeached the king's treasurer for malfeasance in office and obtained a conviction. James died the following year after having dissolved Parliament, leaving his son Charles to call another one if he needed it.

SUMMARY OF REIGN OF JAMES—PROBLEMS UNSOLVED BUT ROYAL POSITION MAINTAINED

James had been able to keep his country out of war for almost the whole of his reign, but at the cost of a very considerable loss in English prestige, which had never been so low on the continent as when he refused to aid his son-in-law and his coreligionists. In his struggles with Parliament he had not been too severely worsted. He had secured the right to increase customs duties but at the cost of having to forego monopolies. He had maintained the Anglican religion and the laws against Catholics and dissenters, but at the cost of a considerable emigration to Holland and America. Parliament had set a precedent for impeaching the king's ministers, but since the ministers had in fact been guilty and given a fair trial, James could not have defended them with propriety. Though he may have had suspicions as to where the process would lead, he could not have known for certain that Parliament in the reign of his successor would impeach ministers for doing what they had been instructed to do by the king, and without any malfeasance. The House had debated more or less as it wished when called into session, and the king's gesture of imprisoning members for their freedom of speech had remained an empty gesture, as had his tearing out of the parliamentary record. In his own view James had never given way on a matter of principle, he had maintained his position that Parliament had no rights but only privileges granted by the crown.

So it must be admitted that James had held up the tide of resistance as long as he reigned. But he had neither suppressed nor in any way tamed the Puritans in Parliament, who had in fact through resistance to James learned more of what they really wanted, and realized that it was in essence a constitutional struggle. Already by the accession of Charles I it is certain that many parliamentary leaders had understood the implications of what they were doing, and they had understood and appreciated the tactics they could use to bring about their ends. All this knowledge was to bear fruit in the reign of Charles, when what had begun as a mere struggle for certain fundamental rights and a share in certain functions of government was to end in a revolution which cost the life of Charles, and in an experiment in republican government unique in English history.

▶ The reign of Charles I

THE FIRST PHASE—ATTEMPTED RULE
WITH PARLIAMENT

Conditions at beginning of Charles's reign—Failure of Spanish war

Charles I was as rigid and autocratic as his father, but a good deal less competent. His ability to antagonize his parliamentary opponents without having in all probability any such intention amounted to genius. He was also extremely unlucky, although his ill luck was greatly aggravated by his incompetence. He always gave the impression of deceit so that no one trusted him, although it is quite likely that he had no intention of deceiving but merely thought he was playing his cards close to his chest. There can be little doubt that, as contemporaries said, the best thing in his life was his manner of leaving it, which was done with dignity, honor, and with a proper sense of kingly pride.

When he came to the throne, as we have seen, he was already saddled with a war, for which he was convinced Parliament would be willing to pay since it was against the traditional enemy, Spain. To further the war, for which he himself was extremely anxious since he had a personal humiliation to avenge, he carried out his father's plans and married Henrietta Maria, sister of the king of France. This was an offense to Parliament, which feared the worst from a Catholic wife. And Parliament, as it happened, was far more interested in the dangers to be apprehended from "popery" than in the Spanish War. Moreover, it was also anxious to take advantage of the new reign to redress some of the grievances which it had been unable to persuade James to do anything about. So when Charles called his first

Charles I and his French wife, Henrietta Maria, with their family. Portrait by Anthony van Dyck.

Parliament it was not in a mood to please the king. The majority in the House of Commons wanted Charles to enforce the laws against Catholics and relax those against Calvinists; and it was very much afraid that the king would be influenced by his young wife, a fear that was later to prove well founded.

This first Parliament provided Charles with about a quarter of the sums he asked for the prosecution of the war. It was willing to grant him customs duties but, contrary to all precedent, it significantly offered them only for one year, with the implied threat that the grant would not be renewed in the event that the duties were raised by the king's prerogative. It objected to having the incompetent duke of Buckingham in charge of the armed forces; it objected to Charles's first ecclesiastical appointments which were all of High Churchmen, little better than papists in the eyes of the Puritans. Charles therefore dissolved his first Parliament and determined to do what he could without it, and with the small subsidy that he had been granted. An expedition, fitted out on credit, was sent to Cadiz but failed ignominiously. The English ships refused to fight Protestants in France as their king had agreed they should do. And meanwhile there was still an army on the continent, raised by James I, that somehow had to be paid, useless though it was. So Charles was forced to summon his second Parliament in 1626.

Refusal of Parliament to provide war subsidies

This time Parliament insisted on making an inquiry into the fiasco of Cadiz, and on impeaching Buckingham whom it blamed for the failure, and it would make no grants until it had been satisfied. Furthermore, since the king had not accepted the one year's grant of customs duties, it complained that the duties which he had continued to collect in spite of his lack of authorization were illegal. Charles was furious, but somewhat mollified when the House of Lords failed to convict Buckingham, who had,

after all, only carried out the quite legal, if ill-advised, orders of the king. To settle the matter finally he had Buckingham formally acquitted by the prerogative Court of Star Chamber. Then he threw into prison two of the parliamentary leaders in the attack. At this, Parliament refused to consider the matter of a subsidy, and Charles yielded. Then it refused the subsidy and was dissolved.

Charles, however, still needed money, and his foolish foreign policy had allowed the country to drift into a war with France as well as with Spain, details of which need not be entered into here. He could think of nothing better than forced loans, and of imprisonment of those who refused to pay. He collected customs duties "illegally." He forced the maritime counties to fit out fleets at their own expense. But he did not have a bureaucracy at his disposal competent to collect the loans, which he planned evidently as regular substitutes for the tax monies that had been refused him. The men imprisoned for failure to pay raised the question as to whether the king had the right to imprison without stating charges based on the law; and though the judges sustained the monarchy, very little money was collected.

The result was only to harden the opinion of the influential classes against the king. When the king declared martial law, and billeted raw levies in private houses, they realized something of what it would mean if the king's power were left uncontrolled. The methods were certain to make the next Parliament called by the king more intransigent than ever. And the king could not avoid calling one, for he could not do without money when at war with France. But it was reasonably certain that Parliament would demand redress of what were now very serious grievances before it was ready to offer any subsidies. It wanted to bind the king in the future not to commit any of the acts of which they complained. So the Petition of Right was drawn up under the inspiration of Sir Edward Coke, assented to by both Houses, and presented to the king.

The Petition of Right (1628)

It was, however, impossible to make a law which would forbid the practices complained of. These were executive matters. The king had to be persuaded not to perform some acts which it was impossible to prevent him from doing except by the exercise of such pressure as Parliament was applying now. As in Magna Carta, therefore, the king had to be bound by a promise, which was in the last analysis unenforceable, though the king's attention could always be drawn to the fact that he had made such a promise. Courts of law, however, could not enforce it. Nevertheless, the Petition of Right of 1628 was accepted by the king with the customary formula given in answer to a petition "Let right be done." Under this, the monarch bound himself not to "make any loan, benevolence, tax or suchlike charge" without the consent of Parliament; not to molest anyone for refusing to pay an illegal tax; not to imprison any freeman without charge; and not to billet soldiers and punish by martial law. It was an important statement of principle, which made quite clear for all future time where the taxing authority in the country rested. For the rest, it was only a restatement of what had already been the custom for hundreds of years, as the Parliament did not forbear to point out, although recent monarchs had constantly breached it. And Charles now did promise to refrain from certain acts that belonged to the royal prerogative; in this sense it was a reduction of his prerogative powers and a stage in the victory of Parliament over royal authority.

Parliament, after receiving word that the king had accepted the Petition of Right, at last voted a fairly substantial sum of money, though far from enough to cover his expenses and debts. It then proceeded to remonstrate against the illegal collection of customs duties and was adjourned. Called again the next spring, it took cognizance of the fact that the king appeared still to be collecting illegal taxes and imprisoning men who did not pay them, contrary to the recent Petition of Right. Then, instead of voting more money, Parliament began to debate the condition of the Church and to pass resolutions against the continued use of "popish" practices. Three resolutions, one on religion and two on taxation, were prepared by Sir John Eliot, a Puritan leader. The king sent instructions that Parliament was to be again adjourned, but the Speaker was not allowed to speak the necessary words. Two strong men held him down while the resolutions were passed. Then Parliament voted its own adjournment. The king had been deliberately disobeyed, and a number of members were sent to the Tower, Eliot dying there rather than admitting the king's right to taxation by prerogative power. Charles dissolved Parliament, declaring that he would never call it again. Thus began the eleven years of personal rule, called by its opponents the eleven years' tyranny.

THE SECOND PHASE—PERSONAL RULE OF CHARLES

Attempt of Charles to rule without Parliament

The only way in which it was possible for Charles to rule without calling Parliament was to make himself independent of all financial aid and live exclusively on the resources available to him in his personal capacity as monarch, plus whatever he could collect through using to the full all means available to him as chief executive. He could control his prerogative courts, and he could hope to control the common-law courts through intimidation of the judges. He controlled the customs houses, and there was no difficulty in collecting customs duties. But he could not be sure of controlling local authorities such as justices of the peace, since these were, as a rule, members of Parliament also, and would probably resist. He had also to contract his expenditure, as it would be clearly impossible to raise the large sums of money necessary for extraordinary expenditure. Obviously he must keep out of war.

It was therefore a trial of strength between Charles and the taxpayers, to see

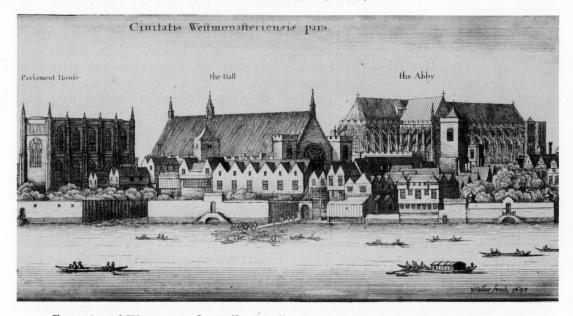

Engraving of Westminster by William Hollar dated 1649, the year of the execution of Charles I. The House of Commons met in Parliament House, the House of Lords in Westminster Hall.

whether the latter would resist, and if so whether they would submit to intimidation by the courts. It was quite possible that he might win this struggle if the people gradually grew accustomed to paying taxes voluntarily to the king, and permitted him to decree what should be paid rather than pay only what had been agreed to by Parliament. It should be emphasized that the king did not have at his disposal any system like that of the French whereby representatives of the central authority could collect taxes directly, as described in an earlier chapter, nor was there such a body as the private enterprise collectors who collected taxes on a commission basis, remitting a portion to the monarch, such as had existed under the Roman Republic and still existed in France. Charles had no large body of government officials at his disposal. The entire English system had been based, as are modern systems, on the voluntary payment of taxes calculated according to property valuation, with the courts in the background to enforce payment if it was not made voluntarily. It was English resistance to paying it in any

other way, plus the fact that Charles allowed himself to drift into war, that caused the failure of his effort at absolutism. Even the resistance might in time have been broken had he been able to avoid war; as it was, the resistance had not yet been broken in eleven years, and the war with the Scots ultimately doomed him to failure before he had time to overcome the resistance.

Charles and his advisers, however, made a very good attempt, and in fact succeeded in putting the royal finances in better order than they had been since the beginning of the century. There was no foreign policy worthy of the name, and all the military commitments made in the first years of the reign were liquidated. Administration was greatly improved and the yield from feudal dues which belonged to the king in his private capacity was more than doubled. Heavy fines were inflicted for encroachment on royal lands; the king's right of wardship over minors was strictly enforced through a special court; the usual recourse was made to forced loans; the crown jewels were pawned; and ever more monopolies were

An Antient View of St. James's, Westminster Abbey & Hall. &c. from the Village of Charing, now Charing Cross.
1 St. James's Palace   3 Westminster Abbey   6 Fields near St. James's Park.
2 A Public House at the Village of Charing,   4 Westminster Hall   7 A Conduit supposed standing
   now Charing Cross.   5 A Wall belonging to the Palace, now Pall Mall.   where St. James now is.

This engraving of the Houses of Parliament, also by William Hollar, shows the rural setting which is not apparent in the previous picture. William Hollar was a Czech refugee from the Thirty Years' War who worked in England for many years after the failure of the Bohemian revolution against the House of Hapsburg.

sold. For the most part these exactions did not drive the merchants to open resistance in spite of the fact that Parliament in its last session had resolved that any who paid taxes not authorized by it were to be regarded as enemies of the country. Parliament, now prorogued indefinitely, held no terrors for them, while the king's power was close to them, and there was no doubt at all that he could punish severely any who refused.

The case for the king—The strong executive and weak legislature

It should be understood that few Englishmen had yet accepted the thought that they were engaged in a revolution. They had been accustomed to obeying the king, and taxation in any case fell largely upon the shoulders of the educated and influential few. For the common man, the authoritarian regime of Charles was probably far from unacceptable. There was less corruption than usual. The king's representatives, as an incidental part of their work, actually forced better observance of such legislation as

helped the poor, as for instance the famous Poor Law of Elizabeth, which provided for outdoor relief paid for by the local parish. It was the minority of the bourgeoisie who were affected by the exactions, who recognized the dangers of arbitrary government, and who desired a share in deciding how the money they provided should be spent. They composed the hard core of the opposition; and since they had been deprived of a privileged platform where they could state their grievances, they now were forced to resist as individuals, and this, as always, proved difficult in the face of the power wielded by the king. It should also be added that it was not entirely certain, except in the minds of the resisting minority, that the king was not in the right. In the past, kings had raised money by executive decree; the Petition of Right was not clearly binding on the king; and in any case Charles made every effort to avoid breaking the actual letter of the Petition, though his entire behavior was, of course, contrary to its spirit. There was much difference of opinion on the actual extent of the king's powers and it should not therefore be thought that all the judges who gave decisions in his favor were actually intimidated into doing so.

New taxes—Ship money and resistance to its payment

But with all Charles's efforts the income still was not enough, and he wished to be able to play at least some part in the affairs of the continent, if only by offering his services in exchange for important considerations. This necessitated at least a navy, and there were thousands of seamen available with experience who could man the ships if they were built. So Charles decided on a new tax, or rather an old tax in a new form, which would help build a navy and provide some surplus money. Seaport towns in the past had made direct financial contributions to a navy, although it had not been done in recent years. When Charles revived this tax and called for it to be paid in money, there was some protest, but the tax was generally paid. But when he decided that inland towns as well as seaports should pay it there was a storm of protest, although, as Charles reasoned, the navy was a protection for the whole country and not only for the seaports. One wealthy landowner, a member of previous Parliaments, refused to pay and made a test case out of the matter. The case was brought to the common-law Court of the Exchequer where it was decided by a majority of only seven to five that the taxation was legal. But the case of John Hampden caused a great stir amongst the possessing classes, and crystallized opposition to the king. The latter, nevertheless, fortified by the decision, proceeded with his collection, and in fact spent the greater part of the money on equipping a fleet. The Court of Star Chamber was now made to deal with recalcitrants, and the regime became for the first time close to a real tyranny, with a royal court punishing offenders and permitted to use inquisitorial methods and torture, as had been the custom in this court in the past.

The king's servants—Laud and Strafford

In another direction the regime had been gathering opposition to itself through the activities of Archbishop Laud, who had become primate of England in 1633. Laud was a High Churchman, hardly to be distinguished in Calvinist eyes from a Catholic. Freed from any criticism by Parliament, he had been enforcing the laws for compulsory worship in the Anglican form, had been purging the Church of all dissenting views, forbidding sermons in the Calvinist manner, and, it seemed, openly favoring all those Catholic practices to which the Puritans most objected. There can be no doubt that many Puritans thought that his intention was ultimately to restore Catholicism, and they blamed the influence of the Catholic queen for the activities of Laud. Thousands of Puritans, now really unable to practice their form of worship in England, emigrated to America. Those who remained had to submit to persecution and heavy fines and imprisonment enforced by the busy archbishop through the Court of High Commission and the Star Chamber. Meanwhile the laws against Catholics were hardly enforced at all.

Another of the king's servants had also won a remarkable degree of unpopularity. This was Thomas Wentworth, Earl of Strafford, who had been a parliamentary leader at the time of the Petition of Right, but had left Parliament for the side of the king when he began to fear that parliamentary policy would lead to a revolution. Made head of the branch of the king's council in the north, he began to execute with considerable efficiency the king's policy in that region, everywhere upholding the king's prerogative and suppressing all opposition. Sent over to Ireland, he began to enforce stringently all decrees against Puritans in Ulster, which was populated largely by Scottish Calvinists who had migrated there. In the south, then as now, the population was Catholic, but greatly resented the subsidiary position of Ireland and its domination by

England. So even here Strafford had little support; and though he did pacify the country by means that he called "thorough," he was cordially detested by all parties save the few who benefited by the undoubted improvement in law and order; while Parliament regarded him naturally as a renegade, on whom it was determined to revenge itself if ever it got a chance.

Quarrel with the Scots

The step that was to lead Charles to the scaffold was probably taken without much thought of the consequences; or if it was ever properly considered, then Charles and his advisers had an egregious lapse of judgment. Laud decided that the Scottish Kirk should be made to conform to Anglican religious practice, and for the purpose, as a first step, introduced the English Book of Common Prayer, with very slight variations. This, he decreed, must be used in all Scottish churches hereafter, and the order carried with it the threat of all the instruments for enforcement used so freely by the archbishop in England.

The Scots were outraged. It was true that Charles was also king of Scotland in his own right, but the Scots did not regard themselves as under the rule of England, and especially not in ecclesiastical matters. A large body of Scots thereupon swore to a Solemn League and Covenant never to submit to English domination in ecclesiastical matters and flew to arms. They invited back from the continent a number of experienced and efficient military leaders, who had been engaged in professional fighting on behalf of foreign potentates. This army swept up to the English border which was poorly defended, and Charles had a war on his hands with the traditional enemy of England (1639). He had no army at his disposal for England's defense. He tried to raise an army by all the old methods, including levy, that had not been used for hundreds of years. But the army thus raised was helpless against the fanatically determined Scots, who demanded that the general assembly of the Scottish Kirk should be recognized as supreme over the bishops, thus virtually making the Presbyterian Church of Scotland an independent body. Rather than agree to this, which implied the failure of his entire ecclesiastical program in Scotland, Charles decided to call a Parliament. In taking this step, on the advice of Strafford, he probably thought that the English would be willing to fight the Scots on patriotic grounds as they had always been willing to in the past.

THE LONG PARLIAMENT AND THE CIVIL WAR

Charles's need for Parliament

Charles had failed to consider what the eleven years' tyranny had done to the propertied classes whose votes elected the members of Parliament. If there had been an election on the basis of manhood suffrage it might have been found that more of the people were for Charles than against him. But the members of Parliament elected under the propertied franchise were precisely those who had resented Charles's behavior in the matter of taxation, and it included an actual majority of non-Anglicans, although the Puritans themselves, as will be described later, were split into parties also. This majority actually favored the Scots because of their religion. So they were in no mood to grant any supplies at all for the war, and certainly not before their many grievances had been attended to. The most they were prepared to do was grant some small supplies for the purpose of making peace with the Scots.

Charles evidently had no idea of the precariousness of his position. As if he had been able to do without the aid of Parliament, which in fact he had only summoned because he was *in extremis,* he insisted that supply must precede the presentation of grievances. And though he persuaded the House of Lords to agree to this, the House of Commons naturally refused, and in a rage Charles dissolved Parliament (Short Parliament, April–May, 1640). His only proffered concession was to give up ship money, hardly a bare minimum in the eyes of Parliament, whose leadership was becoming frankly revolutionary.

Strafford now became the king's adviser, and suggested the use of his "thorough" methods by hanging aldermen of the city of London if necessary. Money was demanded from the city, and all other means that could be thought of were used. But the king was helpless; there was no more money to be had beyond what could be taken by force. An army of a sort was raised, of which Strafford took command. It was hopelessly defeated by the experienced and united Scottish army which swept over the border and occupied the northern counties of Northumberland and Durham. When the king sued for peace he was met by a demand for a continued occupation of these counties, and a heavy indemnity to pay for Scottish military expenses. There was no alternative but to call Parliament again; and this time the king had few supporters left, even the convinced Anglicans objecting to his arbitrary measures and despising his feebleness. Moreover, Parliament was extremely well led by John Pym, a Puritan who knew exactly what he wanted and was not to be swayed from his resolve even by offers of royal appointments. Thus, in November, 1640, the Long Parliament met, the most famous in English history. It was not to be officially dissolved until the Restoration under Charles II in 1660.

Work of the Long Parliament— Dismantling of apparatus of absolutism

The attack on the king was to be twofold. All the king's instruments of tyranny were to be taken away from him, and Parliament was to be a permanent body controlling the executive; and the ministers of the king were to be held responsible for the acts of their royal master and made punishable by Parliament, not even by the courts. This policy could now be successful because Parliament had at its disposal not only its usual money power, but could rely upon the support of the Scottish army in the north, which would effectively prevent the king from using his police powers except in a very limited way. The Scottish army, with Parliamentary support, could march on London without meeting any opposition worthy of the name. Since the king was at their mercy, the leaders of the House of Commons had no need even to consider the question of supply. They proposed to settle the Scottish War themselves in whatever manner seemed fitting to them. In fact, the only recourse of the king at the time would have been to undertake the trial of a civil war, which he was bound to lose in view of the presence of a Scottish army on English soil. He was forced either to submit to the English Parliament or to the Scottish army. And since these two were in sympathy with one another this was no true alternative. He preferred, therefore, to submit to all the demands of Parliament, trying to save for himself what he could, and hoping that the tide would turn in his favor through the leaders of Parliament falling out amongst themselves. This in fact did happen, and when the civil war came Charles had some chance of succeeding.

In a session of unprecedented activity Parliament dismantled the entire apparatus of tyranny. The prerogative courts were abolished, leaving only the common-law courts to function, although the matter of the appointment of common-law judges was not settled at this time. The powers of the king's council were drastically reduced and all its branches abolished. Strafford and Laud were impeached on the grounds that they had subverted "the fundamental laws of the realm" and thus were guilty of treason. But it was not found possible to convince the House of Lords that carrying out the commands of the king was treason, and at length they were put to death by bills of attainder (a special law passed by both houses and signed by the king, but against which no defense could be offered nor did any crime have to be proved). The king had no recourse but to sign the bill against Strafford. Laud was not put to death till 1643, by which time the civil war was in progress and the king's signature was unnecessary.

Parliament ensured its own existence by passing a Triennial Act, providing for a meeting at least once in three years. If the king did not call it, then writs for an election could be issued without his signature. After being called, it could not be prorogued or dissolved without its own consent within fifty days of its meeting. Each Parliament, however, would only last three years, though the Long Parliament itself, by another statute, could not be dissolved or prorogued save by its own consent. By other acts the king was forbidden by clear statute to collect customs duties without the consent of Parliament, and various other methods of raising money that had been used by the Tudors and Stuarts were abolished. All these bills were duly signed by the king, while the Scottish army remained threatening in the north and various mobs in London were calling for the king's blood. Then Parliament decided to accept the terms of the Scots without troubling to negotiate. The Scottish Kirk was to be virtually independent, and its general assembly was to be supreme over the bishops, as asked for in the previous year.

A satire on the religious differences between the Puritan sects at the time of the Civil War. The satire appears on playing cards in use among the Cavaliers.

Dissensions in Parliament over religion— Anglicans, Presbyterians, Independents

Now, however, with the ecclesiastical question up for discussion, the first signs of a rift in Parliament occurred. In order to understand the nature of this rift the religious variations among members must be considered. On the one side, what one might call the right wing, there were the Anglicans, stronger in the country than in Parliament, especially among the nobility and gentry. In the center were the Presbyterian Calvinists, who were in sympathy with the Scots and wished to establish a Presbyterian form of Church, under which the ecclesiastical authority was exercised by presbyters, or elders of the Church. Such a Church, as in Scotland, should be a state Church and have the power to enforce Calvinist discipline. On the left, however, were the independents, who believed in something far more resembling democracy in Church affairs, with each congregation of worshipers entitled to choose its own ministers and have full permission to worship as they wished, without any interference from the state. The local parish and its church would be entrusted with the disciplining of its own members. This latter group, not approving of a state Church, were on the whole republicans, and wished to abolish the monarchy altogether in favor of a rule by the godly, but not by an established Church. Oliver Cromwell was an independent, while John Pym, who was to die in 1643 leaving the Presbyterians without any leader of stature, was a Presbyterian, although a moderate one. Further over to the left were large numbers of more radical sects, similar to that of the Anabaptists in Europe; but these were barely represented in Parliament, though they were to exercise considerable influence in the army during the rule of Cromwell.

By the end of 1641 there could be no doubt that numbers of moderate Presbyterians, as well as the Anglicans, thought that enough had been demanded of the king and anything more would amount to a revolution. His absolutist apparatus had been dismantled, Parliament was now in control of all that it had fought for, and, short of abolishing the office of the crown as the executive of the country, no more could be asked. But others wished to make further progress and force the disestablishment of the Anglican Church. A number of Presbyterian and independent leaders therefore drew up what they called a "Grand Remonstrance" which, after recounting the misdeeds of the king, demanded what amounted to the abolition of the episcopal system in the Church and approval by Parliament of the appointment of the king's ministers. This resolution passed the House of Commons by a very small majority, giving the king some hope that the tide of revolution was over, and that he could rely on a substantial support even in Parliament. But he made a foolish and undignified mistake in tactics when he attempted to arrest five members of the Commons for their part in the Grand Remonstrance, acting on no authority that he possessed. To show the ineptitude of his action it is only necessary to examine the official grounds for his action. He wanted to have the five men impeached in front of the House of Lords for treason and "attempting to subvert the fundamental laws and inviting the Scots to invade the kingdom of England." The king, of course, had no right to impeach. If he believed he had a case against the men and could prove it, they could have been tried in the common-law court of the King's Bench.

The Civil War

The first phase—Ascendancy of Presbyterians—Of course the five members had news of the king's intention and were not there when he appeared in person to arrest them in the House. Nor would the city of London give them up. War was now certain. A serious rebellion had broken out in Ireland and considerable numbers of Protestants had been murdered. But Parliament had no intention of allowing the king to have an army which it suspected would be used against Parliament itself, and it wished to appoint its own commanders and itself conduct the war in Ireland. The king refused to sign a bill authorizing Parliament to appoint commanders; but Parliament went ahead and appointed them anyway, claiming that its act had the "stamp of the royal authority, although His Majesty, seduced by evil counsel, do in his own person oppose or interrupt the same." Following this up with Nineteen Propositions which virtually transferred all authority in the kingdom to Parliament, leaving the king himself almost nothing but the executing of parliamentary decisions, Parliament began to prepare for the inevitable. The king, of course, refused to accept the Propositions, and Parliament appointed a Committee of Safety and proceeded to recruit an army, while Charles himself raised his standard at Nottingham.

In the two civil wars that followed, Parliament from the beginning had a considerable advantage. The parliamentary supporters, known as Roundheads, had the almost solid support of the city of London—its propertied inhabitants along with a great many of the common people who had objected to the religious policy of Laud. Moreover, the fleet, although built up by Charles's efforts, deserted at once to the Roundheads. Charles had most of his support in the north and west, while east and south were on the Roundhead side. In Parliament itself about three hundred members voted for war against the king, far more than had agreed to the Grand Remonstrance, presumably because the moderate Anglicans feared that if the king won, the constitutional reforms of the Long Parliament would be undone. Only a very few combatants actually took part in the wars, most of the population preferring to remain neutral.

There are two distinct stages of the war, or, if it be preferred, two separate civil wars. Probably the war would have been indecisive if it had not been for the intervention of the Scots, who were brought over to the Roundhead side by the acceptance by Parliament of the Scottish Solemn League and Covenant, which meant the establishment

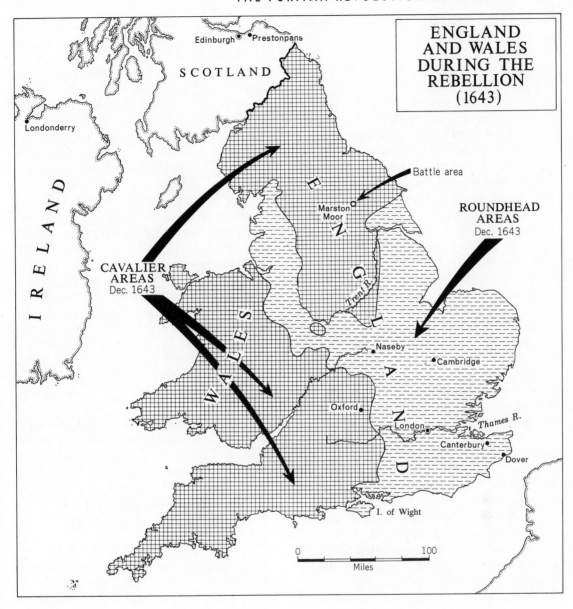

ENGLAND
AND WALES
DURING THE
REBELLION
(1643)

of the Presbyterian Church of Scotland in England instead of the Anglican establishment. This move alienated the Anglicans, who for the most part joined the king's side (Cavaliers) thereafter and left Parliament. But the independents accepted it for the moment, and the Scottish army invaded England from the north. Meanwhile Oliver Cromwell, a member of Parliament and an independent, was organizing a force of cavalry called the "Ironsides," which was to prove the decisive factor in the war, although as yet Cromwell himself was far from the supreme command of the Roundhead forces.

After the royalist forces had been defeated at Marston Moor by the Scots and Cromwell's Ironsides, quarrels ensued among the Roundhead commanders, resulting in the formation of a "New Model Army" with new commanders, Cromwell now being second in command to the moderate Presbyterian Thomas Fairfax. This army won the most important battle of the war at Naseby in 1645, and Charles was forced to take refuge with the Scots, who sold his person to Parliament, thereby putting an end to the first civil war. It was at this point that the serious differences among the various groups in the Roundhead camp became apparent.

The second phase—Ascendancy of Cromwell and execution of Charles—Cromwell and his New Model Army were for the most part made up of radicals both in religion and politics. They went to battle singing hymns, and they were convinced that they were the body of the elect. Though Cromwell himself was a relatively moderate man, he was gradually becoming converted to republicanism and he had no desire to see either the king restored, or the Presbyterian Church established in England, though he had perforce agreed to the arrangement for the sake of Scottish military support. Now, however, he believed that his army was a match for the Scottish and Cavaliers together and he was under constant pressure from his troops to resume the war and depose the king. Parliament, on the other hand, controlled by Presbyterians, was entirely content with the war as it had gone so far and wished to disband the army, especially when Charles, under pressure, also accepted the establishment of Presbyterianism as the national religion for a trial period.

Cromwell and his army acted, and in a sudden foray captured the king from the ill-guarded place where Parliament had confined him. Then the army leaders proceeded to negotiate with the king, Cromwell and the upper classes in his army apparently still unable to visualize any alternative to keeping the king on the throne. The radicals, meanwhile, drew up a remarkable republican document (the "Agreement of the People") full of extreme democratic ideas, calling for a republic. This document was later to be submitted to Parliament after the execution of the king.

Charles, although in the hands of Cromwell, did not cease to negotiate. His only considerable source of support was now the Scots and the Presbyterians in Parliament. He had agreed to pay their price, and the Scots indeed proved willing to make another invasion. At the right moment the king escaped and Cromwell was faced with a second civil war, this time with the support only of his army, since Scots, king, and Parliament had now agreed together. But the Scots delayed too long in their invasion, the Cavaliers had no effective army, and Parliament did not act. The result was the decisive battle of Preston in 1648. Cromwell lost hope of using the king in any way and finally went over to the ideas of the republicans, while one of his colonels went down to Westminster and purged the House of Commons of all Presbyterians, leaving only a "rump" of a few independents. This Parliament, called the Rump Parliament, decided to have the king tried on the grounds that he had "wickedly designed to erect and uphold in himself an unlimited and tyrannical power to rule according to his will, and to overthrow the rights and liberties of the people."

In due course the king, who refused to plead or recognize the jurisdiction of the court, was condemned to death, and he was executed early in 1649.

► The Commonwealth and Protectorate (1649–1660)

PROBLEMS FACING THE COMMONWEALTH

It was, in the last analysis, the New Model Army that had won the victory, and the regime that followed was in essence an army dictatorship. General Fairfax, who had been Cromwell's superior, refused to take part in the condemnation of the king. Cromwell was in reality the sole dictator, with his only civilian support the Rump Parliament, which, being made up of convinced Calvinists, could not be relied on for support and was, of course, completely unrepresentative. In his own army also there were many varying degrees of religious and political opinion. An extreme radical group called the Levellers possessed a great deal of support among the rank and file, while there

Portrait engraving of Oliver Cromwell by Peeter Huybrechts (Flemish school, 1614–1660).

The thorn in Cromwell's side was his own people, and his total inability to find any substitute form of government for his military dictatorship, which he, at least as much as anyone else, desired to end, provided that what he conceived to be the necessary policy for the country to follow would be adopted by some other body than himself and his generals. But the truth was that Cromwell did in fact represent only a minority of the people; any government that he administered must be a minority government, and a true civilian free government would not follow his policies in civil affairs. No one was *loyal* to Cromwell in the sense that one was loyal to the monarchy and the person who happened to sit on the throne. He was obeyed because he possessed preponderant force, and he was followed by inviduals who approved of what he was doing. Not all the efforts he made to bolster the legitimacy of his position by written constitutions and laws could alter the fact that in truth his rule was not legitimate, whether power emananted from the crown or from the people.

CROMWELL'S ATTEMPTS TO SECURE CONSTITUTIONAL GOVERNMENT

The domestic history of his rule therefore is of his many attempts to find a governmental form to satisfy his needs and legitimize his tenure of office. Surviving the civil war was the Rump Parliament, which proceeded at once to appoint a 41-member Council of State, which, of course, was dominated by Cromwell. But the Rump itself, made up of very independent-minded Calvinists who disagreed with Cromwell on many matters and could not agree among themselves, was far from a subservient body. On the other hand, agreement from the Rump was by no means necessary for Cromwell's government (called at this time a commonwealth), since Parliament during the civil war had greatly tightened the procedure for tax collecting and this machinery was now safely in Cromwell's hands as long as he controlled the army. When the Rump in 1653 began to argue interminably and do nothing

were even some communist groups, such as the Diggers, who looked for an altogether new form of society.

Cromwell himself was in a difficult, if not impossible position. He had no right to power beyond the fact that he had usurped it with the aid of the army. In so far as simple action was demanded of him he was extremely successful. He had little difficulty in putting down efforts of Charles, the heir to the throne (later to become Charles II), to regain his throne with the aid of the Scots or Irish. He suppressed rebellion in Ireland with such severity that his campaign is remembered to this day as the "curse of Cromwell." Abroad he made himself respected, and England again became the great power she had not been since the days of Elizabeth. He was even able to defeat the redoubtable Dutch navy at sea. As long as Cromwell lived, European monarchs, however much they might despise his origin and abhor the regicide by which he came to the throne, were forced to treat with him as an equal.

A contemporary satire on Cromwell's dismissal of the Rump Parliament in 1653. Cromwell's famous words on this occasion were "Begone, you rogues, you have sat long enough."

that Cromwell wanted, he dissolved it. When it refused to accept its dissolution, he expelled it by force of arms.

The next experiment was to have a nominated Parliament, chosen by a number of Calvinist ministers, a real attempt to set up a government of the godly. But these men were theorists out of touch with the needs of the country and anxious also to reform the nation in accordance with scriptural teachings. This Parliament also (usually known as Barebone's Parliament, after the name of the first member on its list, one Praisegod Barebone) was sent home by Cromwell. It was followed by the first written English constitution, known as the Instrument of Government. Under this instrument Cromwell was appointed Protector (the period, 1653–1660 being therefore called the Protectorate), aided by a Council of State and a Parliament chosen from among property holders, with a high property qualification for the electors also. This Parliament had real powers, in theory, and the Protector had only a suspensory veto on legislation so long as the legislation was not contrary to the Instrument of Government. Religious toleration was granted except to those who believed in either "Popery or Prelacy" (Catholics and High Church Episcopalians).

But now Parliament desired Cromwell to disband his army and refused to pay it. This he could not permit as long as his

power rested on the army. Moreover, it debated interminably about the constitution itself and how it could be amended. Two successive Parliaments were finally sent home, having helped the Protector not at all to legitimize his government and make it work. Since indeed rebellions occurred, fomented by the radical democrats, the government was finally turned over to a number of major generals who enforced law and order, maintained a severe censorship, and managed to get the taxes collected necessary for Cromwell's continental wars. But they could hardly be regarded as a permanent institution.

Finally, accepting a Humble Petition and Advice, Cromwell became almost the equivalent of king. He had the right to nominate his successor, and a new upper House was created to be chosen by the Protector. Unfortunately for himself, rivalry developed between the two bodies of legislators, and, since most of his best friends and supporters were in the upper House, no business was done, and the Commons refused to vote supplies for the Protector. He thereupon dissolved it and ruled for his last year without any Parliament. He died in the fall of 1658.

DEATH OF CROMWELL AND RESTORATION OF CHARLES II

With Cromwell's death it became at once clear to all, if it had not been before, that his power had rested exclusively on his ability to control the army. The generals did not wish to give their allegiance to Cromwell's son, who had been nominated as his successor, nor did this son Richard wish to assume the arduous responsibilities of his father. A general named Lambert overthrew Richard Cromwell's government and decided to call the ancient Rump Parliament back into session, but could no more make it behave than his predecessor. The country was therefore in a state of anarchy, with no Parliament, and a conspiratorial group of generals and radicals unable even to maintain law and order. At this stage it had become apparent that the only remedy was the return of Charles II to the throne. The move was planned by a parliamentary general named Monck, who had always supported Cromwell and would have supported his son if Richard had been at all anxious to keep the power wished upon him by his father. Monck marched on London, which made no resistance, and arranged for the summoning of a new "Convention Parliament," whose acts were later to be legalized by the king. This Parliament naturally invited the king back. Charles for his part issued the Declaration of Breda, promising "liberty to tender consciences" and a general pardon to all but the actual regicides. For the rest, Parliament should decide. So the Restoration was accomplished and Charles became king in fact as well as in name on May 29, 1660.

Portrait of Charles II by an unknown Dutch artist of the seventeenth century.

▶ The restoration under Charles II (1660–1685)

CHARACTER, STRATEGY, AND TACTICS
OF CHARLES II

When Charles II was restored to his throne conditions not unlike those of the first period of the Long Parliament were restored with him. Charles, who was a much more intelligent ruler than any others of his family who occupied the throne, and had learned, perhaps to excess, some of the diplomatic arts, understood perfectly well that he could only keep his throne by recognizing the power of Parliament. He had no less desire than his father and grandfather to reign as an absolute monarch, but if he were indeed to become absolute it could be only through careful manipulation of Parliament and all other powers at his disposal, and not by direct assault. Affable and pleasure-loving, he yet concealed a good deal of political wisdom under his mask of bonhomie. He was to prove by far the most successful of the Stuart kings, though his foreign policy resulted in loss of prestige for England, and even though he humiliated the English monarchy by becoming the pensioner of France, by which means alone he was able to avoid submission to Parliament.

It is difficult to do justice in a short space to the many convolutions of Charles's policy, and equally difficult to disentangle the elements of consistent strategy that he employed amid a wealth of frequently contradictory tactics. It seems certain that he had been converted to Catholicism during his exile, though he concealed the fact until his deathbed. His consistent policy was to try to obtain toleration for Catholics. He also was determined to keep his dynasty on the throne in the person of his brother, who disclosed publicly his Catholicism well before the reign was over. For these two ends he was prepared to go to any lengths, even to selling out his country's interests and engaging in wars from which the country could obtain no benefits. He had no objection whatever to hoodwinking Parliament when opportunity presented itself for the furtherance of his personal and dynastic policies. Clearly he regarded Parliament as a necessary nuisance rather than as a possible partner in government; but he preferred to manage it rather than to intimidate it, recognizing that it was unlikely that he could succeed in the latter enterprise.

THE CAVALIER PARLIAMENT

Measures to control Puritanism—The Clarendon Code

The so-called Convention Parliament that had invited Charles to return had, of course, no legal status, not having been summoned by the king. Charles, therefore, called another election as soon as opportunity presented itself, and the new Parliament proceeded to legalize the acts of its predecessor, so that everything was now in good legal order. All legislation up to the time of the civil war was regarded as being in full effect, except what had been passed by the Long Parliament without the king's signature. It was just assumed by both king and Parliament that this was the case, and the new Parliament merely took up its task as if there had been an unfortunate intermission during which neither king nor legal Parliament had functioned.

The new Cavalier Parliament, which was to last for eighteen years, was at the beginning very strongly Anglican. All Puritans, even the moderate ones such as the Presbyterians, were considered tarred with Cromwell's brush, and the people had had their fill of Puritan rule. Even the city electors seem to have voted for good royalists or Anglicans. Neither Charles nor his chief minister Lord Clarendon made any attempt to prevent this Parliament from doing as it

wished about the Puritans, save that all were agreed that reprisals were to be few. Even the lands confiscated by the Puritan regime from Catholic and Anglican owners who had refused to obey the laws against the practice of their religion were, for the most part, left in the hands of their new owners. The Anglican Church, however, was restored as the established Church of England, with its episcopal system, and severe laws were passed against all dissenters (sometimes called nonconformists). These laws, embodied in the so-called Clarendon Code—though Clarendon himself had desired less severe penalties for dissenters—were passed with enthusiasm by Parliament. They succeeded almost in destroying Presbyterianism since this form of Calvinism required a Church government. It was a competitor of the Anglican Church for supremacy in the state, and could not survive without its organization, which was completely destroyed by the Clarendon Code. On the other hand the Puritan sects, though persecuted, could survive, since these required no central organization. Most of the former Presbyterians probably joined the Anglican established Church, where they acted as a kind of opposition within the Church to the tendencies toward Catholic ritual that remained in it (Low Churchmen).

Relations with Cavalier Parliament

Early in his reign Charles thought that he could exempt or "dispense" individuals from the operation of the laws against Catholics and dissenters. Parliament, even this Cavalier Parliament so favorable in other respects to the restored monarch, would not tolerate this, and Charles had to withdraw the first Declaration of Indulgence that he had issued. From that time onward, especially after he had married a Catholic queen, many members of Parliament suspected him of secret Catholic sympathies, even though Charles had been careful, and always was careful in his reign, to extend his toleration to Puritan dissenters and Catholics alike. The Cavalier Parliament continued to sit. No new elections were called for, since the Parliament repealed the Triennial Act of the Long

Parliament, but by-elections on the death or retirement of members materially altered its political complexion, while the king's policy itself served to alienate many of his supporters. But one thing Parliament would not do, however much the king desired it. It would never vote him enough money to enable him to carry out an effective foreign policy, still less to keep an effective army in being. It gave him many new taxes, in exchange for relinquishing the last rights of the king as feudal suzerain, but Charles remained chronically starved for funds throughout his reign until the very last years. Thus Parliament was able to keep its whip hand over him, as it had over his father.

Attempted toleration for Catholics— Role of Louis XIV

In 1670 Charles signed with Louis XIV of France a secret, and then a public, treaty of Dover. He had been intermittently at war with the Dutch for several years but had recently made peace. But now Louis XIV, in pursuit of his policy for French aggrandizement, which will be dealt with in more detail in the next chapter, wanted Charles to join him in a new war against the Dutch, with the country to be virtually partitioned between England and France, though England was to have only the most meager portion. Had the plan succeeded, as it nearly did, France would have controlled western Europe, and could easily have threatened England far more seriously than the Dutch could ever have done. Under the terms of the treaty Charles was to declare himself a Roman Catholic, as well as inveigle Parliament into a war with the Dutch. The scheme, with Louis XIV playing a part in it, was flagrantly contrary to English interests, and would destroy the balance of power in Europe. All Charles was to receive besides his small portion of Holland, which was in any case untenable, was a subsidy from the French king, and not a very large one. Nevertheless Charles declared war, as was still his prerogative, but followed it with a Declaration of Indulgence to Catholics and dissenters. Parliament retorted furiously with a Test Act, which the king was forced to sign,

since otherwise he would have had no funds to pursue his war (1673). Under this act oaths were required of all office-holders denying the belief in transubstantiation, which no good Catholic could do, and communion had to be taken according to the Anglican rites. Puritans were not of course affected by this act, but there were already severe enough laws in force against them. One result of the Test Act was that it was disclosed that the king's brother, James, duke of York, was a Catholic; and James was the heir to the throne. The Portuguese queen had not produced any children, and although Charles had many illegitimate offspring they could not succeed to the throne.

From this time onward not only was it strongly suspected that Charles was a secret Catholic and intended at some time to try to convert the Anglican Church to Catholicism, but that James was committed to such a policy if ever he inherited the throne. Thus arose a substantial party with the avowed aim of excluding James from the throne and bestowing the succession elsewhere. On the other hand, there were now, besides the queen, many avowed Catholics close to the king, even if they could no longer hold civil or military office under the crown. It was suspected likewise that there were thousands of Jesuits in disguise, all of whom favored the policy of His Most Catholic Majesty of France.[1] High Church Anglicans continued to favor the king and especially his bishops and other high clergy, and preached regularly from their pulpits a doctrine hardly to be distinguished from the Divine Right of Kings. In its new form this doctrine stated that it was the duty of the subject to pay absolute obedience to the monarch, however tyrannous he might become.

PARTY POLITICS—WHIGS AND TORIES— THE "POPISH PLOT"

In this climate of opinion the Whig and Tory parties were formed, the Tories being strongly associated with High Anglicanism, and the doctrine of passive obedience, while

[1]In actual fact Louis XIV was not generally well disposed to Jesuits; he regarded them as instruments of papal not royal policy.

Anthony Ashley Cooper, first Earl of Shaftesbury, Whig leader in the reign of Charles II, supporter of Titus Oates; later forced into exile by Charles after the tide had turned against Oates. Portrait from the seventeenth-century studio of J. Greenhill.

Titus Oates, the "discoverer" of the Popish Plot. Convicted of perjury under James II and flogged and tortured, he was later freed and pensioned by William III for his political services to William's Whig supporters, although his stories of the Plot were undoubtedly fabricated. Artist unknown.

the Low Church Anglicans and dissenters favored the opposite party, the Whigs, an outgrowth of the Green Ribbon Club, pledged to the exclusion of James from the throne. Both parties now made serious efforts to influence the electorate to vote for their candidates, and a seat in the House of Commons now appeared to be more desirable than in previous times, especially since the government-backed Tory Party began to dispense patronage on a large scale in exchange for political support, as well as offering actual bribes for voting their way in Parliament.

But the political tide was running with the Whigs. Charles's foreign policy was hopelessly unsuccessful. It was more than suspected that he was receiving financial help from France whose king was the archenemy of all Protestants. A former counselor of

Charles, the earl of Shaftesbury, an exceedingly astute political leader, was responsible for the outpouring of thousands of "exclusionist" pamphlets. James, duke of York, urged the king to call a new Parliament, since the old Cavalier Parliament still in session was now controlled by Whigs, at least in the matter of excluding James from the throne.

It was at this point that the infamous "Popish Plot" burst on a credulous public. Two clerical informers—one of them Titus Oates, an impostor—stated that they had information of a Catholic plot against the throne, masterminded by the Jesuits with the support of English Catholics in high places. The king questioned them, discovered that they had no real evidence, and dismissed them. But the Whigs took up the case and exploited it to the full. Amid an atmosphere of frantic hysteria juries convicted anyone denounced by Oates; names rolled out of his mouth, and good Tories of impeccable loyalty and Anglicanism were condemned to death. Oates grew bolder and bolder, and Charles was unable or unwilling to help the victims until the queen herself was denounced and accused of treason before the House of Commons. Then Charles moved and at last dissolved the Cavalier Parliament.

The Whigs had no objection. Still exploiting the Popish Plot even though it was by now clear to all fair-minded persons that there was no further evidence available, in spite of Oates's endless list of names, the Whigs in three successive Parliaments rolled up large majorities. Each time they proceeded at once to the Exclusion Bill to exclude James from the throne and to ensure a Protestant succession, James's daughter having been brought up a Protestant and married to the Protestant prince of Orange, who was himself a grandson of Charles I through his mother. By the third Parliament the climate of opinion had begun to change. Moderate persons thought the persecution of Catholics had gone far enough, and that bloodshed should be halted. It was the opportunity for which Charles had been waiting. Louis XIV, who naturally feared the results of William's accession to the throne, was ready to subsidize English neutrality, and did not require that Charles enter the war actively on his side. So, no longer needing funds from Parliament, he could safely rule without it. And he was assured of the continued support of the Tories, who had only royal power to protect them from the dominant Whigs. In 1681 he triumphantly dissolved his third Parliament, openly boasting that he would call it no more.

RULE WITHOUT PARLIAMENT—TRIUMPH
OF CHARLES

Charles II made good use of his freedom from Parliament. The Whigs, who had overplayed their hand and lost much of their popular support, no longer had Parliament at their disposal, and they found themselves in grave difficulties. Many of them fled the country, while Charles, supported by a sol-

idly Tory council, proceeded to do his best to see that the Whigs would never have a majority in Parliament again. He achieved his ends by the use of some very effective legal tactics. His law officers began to investigate, especially in Whig strongholds, by what right electors were exercising their right to vote. If they could not prove by legal documents that they were entitled to do so, they were disfranchised. The king also canceled many borough charters, claiming that he was legally entitled to cancel them since they had been granted by his predecessors as a revocable privilege. Even the city of London, the chief Whig stronghold, was finally compelled to submit, and before Charles died in 1685 he had indeed made the country safe for Tories, as it should have proved, for good. There was no chance whatever of any further Whig majority in Parliament. It should also be added that, to make matters doubly sure, a Whig plot, real or fancied, had also been discovered during these years, under which the king and his brother were to be murdered (Rye House Plot). The plot, needless to say, implicated several important Whig leaders, two of the most prominent of whom were executed. Thus James, for whose sake all this had been accomplished, inherited in 1685 a throne whose security was greater than that of any previous Stuart. He could rely on a Tory party which owed everything to the crown, a Church which had preached in season and out of season the duty of nonresistance to the crown, and a subsidy from France which might well have been continued for many years if necessary, although with a Tory majority assured perhaps even a Parliament could have been called safely.

▶ The reign of James II (1685–1689)

THE MONMOUTH REBELLION AND
ITS AFTERMATH

James, however, threw everything away in his three short years of rule. A stubborn Catholic, determined to re-establish Catholicism by all means at his disposal, obviously without understanding of or sympathy for Charles's subtle maneuverings, he managed to antagonize every group in the country of importance, so that when William of Orange landed in England no one, or almost no one, stood to defend him. He could not understand that no substantial body of opinion would tolerate the restoration of Catholicism, not even the Tories of the extreme right, and there were far too few actual Catholics left, after more than a century of Protestantism of one form or another as the established religion.

The reign started mildly enough. James called a Parliament under the new electoral arrangements of his brother, and was rewarded by having a body to deal with in which there were barely forty Whigs. The Parliament voted him a fairly substantial income for life, and there was no sign of the tumult to come as James solemnly promised to maintain the Anglican establishment, though he himself had private Mass cele-

brated for him at home. While Parliament was still sitting, two rebellions broke out, both in the Puritan interest, but evidently not concerted. One was suppressed easily, but the other, led by the duke of Monmouth, illegitimate son of Charles II, required the use of an army, which was authorized by Parliament and paid for out of taxes. Its English adherents for the most part belonged to the laboring and farming classes of the west, who were strongly Puritan.

But it was the aftermath of the Monmouth rebellion that shocked the people. Not only did James fail to disband his army of some 30,000 men but a terrible vengeance was taken on the rebels. Gibbets were lined up along the roads of the west country, and on them were hanged poor Puritan farmers and workers condemned to death by the activity of Judge Jeffreys and his Bloody

Portrait of James II by James Riley, now in the National Portrait Gallery of London.

Assize. Then Jeffreys was promoted Lord Chancellor.

Fortified by his army, James then proceeded with his plan for the re-establishment of Catholicism. He claimed the right to dispense with the law, and obtained a legal opinion from a packed court, which, by a vote of eleven to one, affirmed this right. Thus James began to break the Test Act openly, and issued a Declaration of Indulgence to Catholics and dissenters alike, making a transparent appeal to the latter to join with the right wing in crushing the center of solid Anglicans. Parliament, after objecting to the declaration, was dissolved. But James was not short of money, and he had nothing further to hope for from Parliament, unless he could obtain a Parliament that was willing to repeal the Test Act. He made efforts in the country to find out whether such a Parliament could be elected, but found few supporters anywhere. There was no doubt at all that the Catholic religion could be reimposed only by force, against the will of the majority. James did not hesitate to follow this course.

ATTEMPTED RESTORATION OF CATHOLICISM

It should be understood that public opinion in England at this time had been crystallized against Catholicism largely by the acts of Louis XIV and especially by his revocation of the Edict of Nantes in 1685, and the persecution of the Huguenots that followed it. Thousands of Huguenots perished, while many thousands more were driven into exile. Moreover, Louis was engaged in a war against all the Protestant countries of importance in Europe and appeared to be winning, though the coalition against him led by William of Orange (whose wife Mary, it will be remembered, was the daughter of James and the next heir to the English throne) was holding its own for the moment. Thus all non-Catholic Englishmen with few exceptions and even a substantial number of Catholics opposed James's policy. What Pope Innocent XI desired was toleration for Catholics and the repeal of the Test Act. Even he was in

opposition to the policy of Louis XIV and in fact was in William's coalition. In England, only the principle of nonresistance to the king, which had been preached so long by the Anglican clergy, kept the English loyal during the years of James's efforts to re-establish the Catholic Church.

In 1686 James began to replace the officers of his army by Catholics and occasional dissenters. But there were few enough to go round. He did the same thing in the army rank and file. There were just too few Catholics, and James was driven to import Irish Catholics, regarded with abhorrence by the English as uncouth savages. This caused disunion and sometimes mutiny in what had been a fine army at the time of the Monmouth rebellion. The next step was to place Catholics in the ranks of the clergy itself. A new court, similar to the old illegal Court of High Commission (the Court of Commissioners for Ecclesiastical Causes), was set up to deal with clergy who refused to conform. Finally, in 1687, a new Declaration of Indulgence was issued which all the clergy were ordered to read from their pulpits. When a number of them, including the aged archbishop of Canterbury, refused and remonstrated in writing, the king ordered them tried for seditious libel.

THE GLORIOUS REVOLUTION—FLIGHT OF JAMES

It had been clear for a long time that the king could be opposed only by armed force, against which he still had his army, which was in the process of being catholicized. Early in the reign a number of opponents of the king had sounded out William of Orange, but the latter had not judged the time to be ripe. Opposition in England took a few years to crystallize, and James was constantly playing into his hands. Tories still feared that the Whigs would come to power if James were deposed, and many of them still felt strongly about resistance to the king. The king as yet had no male heir, and when he died the throne would be inherited by Mary of Orange and her husband William, both Protestants. But James was now married to a Catholic, and she was expecting a

Contemporary print showing the embarkation of William of Orange, later William III, for England. William was able to take the crown from James II without the use of this fleet, since James fell into despair when deserted by his own troops and fled abroad.

child. If it should prove to be a boy, then the country could look forward to a long line of Catholics on the throne.

On June 10, 1688, the queen was delivered of a boy. Ten days later the trial of the bishops for seditious libel ended in an acquittal amid tremendous popular demonstrations. At this point a group of seven men—four Whigs and three Tories, including Danby, the leader and founder of the Tory party, who was instrumental in swinging his party to the side of Orange—waited upon William and Mary in Holland and formally invited them to take the English throne. All they asked was toleration in matters of religion, and conformity to the laws of the realm, including, of course, the acceptance of the role of Parliament as it had been established during this century of revolution. After long hesitation William accepted. He needed English support in his wars with Louis at least as much as the English needed him, and he was able to raise a fairly substantial force which might have held its own against James's by now seriously divided army. As it happened, he hardly needed it. At the last moment James lost his nerve.

William landed in the west. James heard that his army had greeted William's arrival with joy, and he stayed to hear no more. With his wife and child he escaped to Ireland and then to France, leaving England to his supplanter without any bloodshed. Thus was the Glorious Revolution accomplished. A Parliament summoned without the consent of King James, again calling itself a convention Parliament, was ready to welcome the new monarch and, if it so desired, invite Mary or William or both to assume the throne. After much discussion it was decided that the throne was now vacant by the "abdication" of James (who protested from his safe haven that he had done no such thing) and offered the crown to William and Mary jointly. By their acceptance they tacitly acknowledged that Parliament had the right to determine the succession, and thus a new constitutional principle was established. Parliamentary supremacy, fought for with varying success throughout the century, was now secured, and John Locke's treatises on civil government, which had been in manuscript for some twenty years, were now published. The king had broken the Social Contract between him and his people by claiming to dispense with the laws, and he was now justly dethroned. He was succeeded by a monarch who promised to observe the fundamental laws of the realm and who was willing to incorporate his agreement in a statute which became known as the Bill of Rights.

► The constitutional monarchy and the beginnings of cabinet government

THE BILL OF RIGHTS

It may be said that the Bill of Rights is the nearest approach the English possess to a written constitution, although in fact most of the clauses are devoted to statements of certain practices which were henceforth considered to be illegal. These were, for the most part, acts of which James had been guilty, such as pretending to be able to suspend or "dispense with the laws," setting up a prerogative court for the trial of ecclesiastical offenses, levying money without parliamentary authority, and maintaining a standing army without authority in time of peace. The other clauses, several of which were later incorporated into the United States Constitution, concerned the right of subjects to bear arms, to petition the king, to speak freely in Parliament, and to have free elections. No part of the English Bill of Rights has ever been repealed, and its acceptance for almost three centuries makes it exceedingly unlikely that it ever will be, although in theory Parliament could still repeal or change it.

The Bill of Rights was quickly followed in the same year (1689) with an Act of Toleration, under which full liberty of worship was permitted, though the Test Act remained in force until a quarter way through the nineteenth century, thus preventing Catholics from holding office under the crown. Under the Act of Settlement of 1701, since William and Mary had no direct heirs, and Anne, Mary's sister, the next heir to the throne, had no children, Parliament decided to regulate the succession to ensure that no Catholic came to the throne in spite of the number of Catholics who could lay claim to it by strict heredity—to say nothing of James II's son the Old Pretender who was to make an effort in 1715 to obtain the throne by force of arms. Parliament decided on Sophia, electress of Hanover, and her heirs. She was descended from James I and his daughter Elizabeth, who had married Frederick the Winter King of Bohemia. This was a very remote hereditary claim to the throne. Nevertheless George I, elector of Hanover, did succeed to the English throne on the death of Anne, and he and his line were always well aware that they owed their crown to Parliament and ruled "by consent of the people." It may be added that in the same Act of Settlement the independence of the English judiciary was finally established, the High Court judges to hold office during good behavior instead of during His Majesty's pleasure as in the time of the Stuarts.

THE BEGINNINGS OF CABINET GOVERNMENT

In the reign of William and his successor Anne the first tentative steps were taken to establish the form of government that was later to be known as cabinet government. It was not a planned development but arose from actual practice of the monarchs in dealing with a Parliament which had established its supremacy over them. The king, though forbidden many things, was still the chief executive, and he still initiated policy with the aid of his advisers, the privy council. He possessed a veto, he could dissolve Parliament and call for new elections, though he was compelled by statute to call Parliament and dissolve it at least once in three years. He had the full choice of all his ministers, who were responsible to him and could be dismissed only by him, though Parliament could impeach them after they had committed acts which might reasonably be expected to secure convictions in the House of Lords.

Throughout almost all William's reign the country was at war with Louis XIV, and William's prime interest was in securing supplies for the war. It turned out in practice that the Whig Party was more ready to vote supplies when it had the majority in the Parliament, since the Tories who were mostly landowners suffered from the war; while many Whig merchants prospered by it, and especially by the new financial arrangements under which the crown could borrow at high rates of interest from the financiers and from the newly established Bank of England. Such loans were sought after by the commercial interests represented by the Whig Party. William personally was inclined to dislike the Whigs. But he could not feel very friendly to the Tories either, since many of them were suspected, and indeed guilty, of clandestine negotiations for the return of James II, who waited at Calais for many years in the expectation of an invitation from these dissident Tories (Jacobites). Nevertheless, William needed to have some majority in Parliament which could give him the supplies he needed, and thus, after experimenting with coalition privy councils which contained men of whom he approved, he found it simpler in later years to choose men of whom he might not approve, but who could obtain what he needed from Parliament. Anne, even more than William, did not conceal her Tory preferences; yet on several occasions she had to choose Whig ministers, or risk having Parliament refuse her the necessary supplies.

Gradually the leading ministers of the privy council (a much larger body than the "ministry," which was composed only of men responsible for the functioning of various branches of the executive) was converted into something not unlike a modern cabinet. Some of the councilors were ministers, and these formed the cabinet or ministry, while others were merely friends of the king who could be consulted on occasion but who held no special responsibilities in the government. These ministers had to be chosen because they could work in harness with the chief minister, and the whole ministry had to be able to work in harness with Parliament. The only way of achieving this was to have them belong to the majority party in Parliament. In Hanoverian times this became the invariable custom. When George III attempted to rule through a cabinet which

did not hold a majority, he found himself unable to govern for long.

Parliament did not understand for a long time what was happening. When it did, it suddenly discovered that there was no further need for impeachment of the king's ministers. If Parliament merely voted against the majority party, government by it would be impossible and the ministers would have to resign. Thus the king would change them as a matter of course. The king also found that he no longer needed his veto—Anne was the last monarch to exercise it. If Parliament passed laws of which he disapproved he could dissolve it without using the veto. But if the country in the ensuing elections backed up the party whose bill had been objected to, the king would have to give way. Thus the right of dissolution became the equivalent of a suspensory veto. This is still the way in which the English discover the will of the country in legislative matters, though now it is the cabinet which must advise the dissolution.

▶ **Summary—Limited constitutional government**

Through revolution and adjustment, the seventeenth century in England thus saw the establishment of a truly limited monarchy. The king and his ministers remained the executive, subject to a very real control by the legislative power, with an independent judiciary to enforce the laws of the realm by which, it was acknowledged, the whole people including the monarch were bound. Though there were still laws on the books against dissenters and Catholics, and the Church of England was the only established Church, a substantial measure of toleration for individual religious opinion had been attained. As yet there was no democracy, though democratic forms were retained which had been originally the work of the old limited medieval monarchy. Parliament, instead of being allowed to fall into disuse as in Spain and France, had successfully asserted its rights; though the propertied franchise had to be abolished and the distribution of parliamentary seats according to population had to be won before there could be any measure of true democracy. Throughout the first half of the eighteenth century Parliament fell into the hands of a permanent Whig majority, and both parties held up electoral reform until 1832. But the institutions were there by the beginning of the eighteenth century, and these institutions have required only minor reforms to enable them to function even today.

Britain had no further major constitutional changes—and no more revolutions, for none were necessary. Development has been continuous, but only development and not radical change. And in process of time the example set by England was adopted because it seemed that in England constitutional problems had really been solved. A position had even been found for the monarch, largely honorific. So when thrones were tottering in the nineteenth century and monarchs were faced with abdication followed by a republic, or with accepting the honorable position of a constitutional monarch, many opted for the English system and survived.

Both democracy of the American type and constitutional monarchy of the Scandinavian type have stemmed from the English example, almost fully worked out during the Puritan Revolution. It was no mean achievement for the Puritans, who most certainly did not know what they were doing for posterity.

▶ ## Suggestions for further reading

This chapter has dealt with the Puritan Revolution at considerable length. It should not therefore be necessary to read also various shorter accounts in books dealing with English constitutional development. Nevertheless two brief accounts will be recommended here for the admirable way in which they sum up, without the detail felt to be necessary in this chapter, the general principles involved and the consequences of the struggle for later times. These are: Sidney A. Burrell's chapter "Absolutism and Constitutionalism" in *Chapters in Western Civilization* (2nd edit., Vol. 1 (New York: Columbia

University Press), edited by the Contemporary Civilization Staff of Columbia College, and the long Chapter 3 of S. B. Chrimes, *English Constitutional History* (London: Oxford University Press, Home University Library, 1948), called "Developments in the 16th and 17th centuries." Chrimes is one of the foremost scholars in the field of English government and administration, and this is, to my knowledge, the only work in which he has attempted to explain briefly to a general audience the fruit of a lifetime's research and scholarship.

The chapters on the Stuarts in George B. Adams, *Constitutional History of England*, revised by R. L. Schuyler (New York: Henry Holt and Company, Inc., 1936) are a classic exposition of the constitutional development of the period and are much fuller than the present text, although along the same lines. Another classic treatment, excellent in every respect and highly readable, written in a clear narrative style without excessive technical material, is Joseph R. Tanner, *English Constitutional Conflicts of the Seventeenth Century* (Cambridge, Eng.: Cambridge University Press, 1928, reprinted 1952). The reader, however, should be warned that these two older books do not take as much account as is warranted of the "modern" aspects of the absolute rule of Charles I, and should therefore be supplemented by the chapter in Chrimes. Finally, mention should be made of what is probably the best textbook treatment of the subject, in Marshall Knappen, *Constitutional and Legal History of England* (New York: Harcourt, Brace and Company, Inc., 1942), which has the merit of being entirely up to date in interpretation, and though not easily readable as straight narrative, is well organized under topics and admits of ready and easy reference. Pages 307–454 cover the Puritan period.

The Oxford histories, Godfrey Davies, *The Early Stuarts, 1603–1660*, and George N. Clark, *The Later Stuarts, 1660–1714* (Oxford: The Clarendon Press, 1952, 1949), contain a great deal of information, also on the social and economic history of the time. The Commonwealth and Protectorate may perhaps best be studied in the first-mentioned of these works, but an old work, Charles H. Firth, *Oliver Cromwell and the Rule of the Puritans in England* (Boston: Houghton Mifflin Company, 1934, originally published 1900), is still accurate and very readable, Firth having been one of the greatest Cromwellian scholars of his day. An interesting biography of the Protector by a great admirer is John Buchan, *Oliver Cromwell* (Boston: Houghton Mifflin Company, 1934) but on the whole, the vast majority of the works on Cromwell, including Firth, are perhaps excessively laudatory. A suitable antidote may be found in a thorough-going study of the Commonwealth period by a noted early Marxist, Eduard Bernstein, *Cromwell and Communism* (London: George Allen & Unwin, Ltd., 1930), which deals effectively with the social and economic history of the time. The extreme democratic movements of the time may be studied in T. C. Pease, *The Leveller Movement* (Washington: The American Historical Association, 1916) as well as in Bernstein's work just referred to.

David Ogg, *England in the Reign of Charles II* (2 vols., Oxford: The Clarendon Press, 1934) is a very full account of this reign, though not all of it will be found equally valuable by the student. George M. Trevelyan, *The English Revolution, 1688–1689* (London: Oxford University Press, Home University Library, 1938) is a very readable brief account by one of the finest living writers of English historical prose. The same author's work, *England under the Stuarts,* which originally appeared in 1904, though it was reprinted with revisions in 1925 (New York: G. P. Putnam's Sons, 1925) was not greatly changed and remains English history written from the Whig point of view. Though somewhat out of date in interpretation, it contains, as always in Trevelyan's works, a considerable amount of social material rarely used at the time of the original writing.

Among the primary sources for the period there is the standard Samuel R. Gardiner, *Constitutional Documents of the Puritan Revolution* (3rd edit., Oxford: The Clarendon Press, 1906),

still of great interest and not excessively long, which does not, indeed, require too much skipping; also a more modern selection by a great scholar in the field, A. Browning, ed., *English Historical Documents,* Vol. 8 (London: Eyre and Spottiswoode, 1953). Not all the documents in Browning's book are relevant to the subject of this chapter, but the student should have no difficulty in determining those which are, and all are of high interest. There is also much primary material in William Haller, *The Rise of Puritanism* (New York: Columbia University Press, 1938) an excellent work which is, however, difficult to read straight through, but should be culled at leisure. The same author's *Liberty and Reformation in the Puritan Revolution* (New York: Columbia University Press, 1955), much more readable, is a very fine work, representing the fruit of a lifetime's study of the Puritan Revolution, especially of its religious side, by a professor of English whose major field of interest was England of the seventeenth century. The information this book contains is hardly to be found elsewhere.

John Locke's *Second Treatise on Civil Government,* in which the philosopher draws conclusions on the proper form of government from his own experience, should be read in any edition available (one such edition is referred to in the suggestions following Chapter 22). This book by a prominent Whig was of course most influential in America in the following century. Hobbes' *Leviathan,* written to justify absolutism, should be read in conjunction with it. Finally, once more, G. H. Sabine, *A History of Political Theory* (New York: Henry Holt and Company, Inc., 1937) will be recommended for the study of the political thought of the period. Chapters 22 to 25 cover the period of the Puritan Revolution.

21

French and Russian Absolutism
in the Seventeenth Century

Contrast between English constitutionalism and continental absolutism • Development of absolutism in France • The Age of Richelieu and Mazarin • The Frondes • Reign of Louis XIV • The economic foundations of French absolutism • Expansion of France under Louis XIV • Ascendancy of French culture • Russian absolutism • Reigns of Michael and Alexis Romanov • Peter the Great and the modernization of Russia

► Contrast between English constitutionalism and continental absolutism

In the previous chapter we examined the manner in which the apparent absolutism of the Tudor monarchy of England was weakened, and finally transmuted to constitutional monarchy. Our study made clear that it was the continued existence of representative institutions in England that made resistance to the king possible without the necessity of a truly violent revolution. It is true that one monarch was executed, there were a few years of civil war, and then another monarch was expelled and forced to abdicate. But such happenings were very mild in comparison with those of most historical revolutions. Moreover, the kingship was not abolished. The English monarchs continued to reign after the revolution, though with much-reduced powers, and it could be said with some justice that all that

the revolution accomplished was a change in the balance of power between king and Parliament.

Constitutional development in Europe has, for the most part, followed the English pattern. During the nineteenth century most monarchs who had at one time enjoyed virtually absolute powers were constrained to yield much of their power to representative institutions similar to the English Parliament. If they had attempted thereafter to abuse what powers remained to them, there is no doubt that they would have been shorn even of these by their subjects, and without the necessity for any further violent revolutions once the initial one had been completed. Effective power had fallen into the hands of the people and their institutions, and monarchs existed simply because the people preferred retaining them to establishing republics.

But two European monarchies became so absolute in the seventeenth century that

► chronological chart

France

Reign of Louis XIII	1610–1643
Ascendancy of Concini	1610–1617
Meeting of States-General	1614
Assassination of Concini	1617
Ascendancy of Luynes	1617–1621
Richelieu, chief minister of Louis XIII	1624–1643
French settlements in West Indies	1625–1664
Capture of La Rochelle from Huguenots	1628
Peace of Alais with Huguenots	1629
Subsidy treaty of Richelieu with Gustavus Adolphus	1630
Final exile of Marie de Medici	1630
Founding of Académie Française	1635
Le Cid by Corneille	1637
Entry of France in Thirty Years' War	1639
Nicholas Poussin painter to Louis XIII	1640–1643
Deaths of Louis XIII and Richelieu	1643
Reign of Louis XIV	1643–1715
Battle of Rocroy—victory of Condé over Spanish	1643
Ascendancy of Mazarin	1643–1661
Frondes	1648–1653
Peace of Westphalia	1648
Provincial Letters of Pascal	1656
Peace of Pyrenees with Spain	1659
Death of Mazarin and assumption of personal rule by Louis	1661
Building of Versailles	1661–1682
Financial administration of Colbert	1662–1683
Founding of French East India Company	1664
Tartuffe of Molière	1664
War of Devolution	1667–1668
Treaty of Aix-la-Chapelle	1668
Fables of La Fontaine	1668–1694
Dutch War	1672–1678
L'art poétique of Boileau	1674
Phèdre of Racine	1677
Treaties of Nijmegen	1678–1679
Explorations and colonization by La Salle in North America	1679–1689
Chambers of Reunion	1680–1683
Marriage of Louis to Madame de Maintenon	1684
Revocation of Edict of Nantes	1685
War of League of Augsburg	1688–1697

French naval victory of Beachy Head	1690
French naval defeat of La Hogue	1692
French naval victory of Lagos	1693
Treaty of Ryswick	1697
Negotiations for division of Spanish inheritance	1698–1700
Settlement of French colony of Louisiana	1699–1702
Death of Charles II of Spain	1700
War of Spanish Succession	1701–1714
Battle of Blenheim	1704
Suppression of Port-Royal by papal bull	1704
Battle of Malplaquet	1709
Peace of Utrecht	1713
Treaties of Rastatt and Baden with Emperor	1714
Death of Louis XIV	1715

Russia

Reign of Michael Romanov	1613–1645
Treaty of Stolbovo with Sweden	1617
Treaty of Polianov with Poland	1634
Pioneers reach Pacific	1637
Reign of Alexis	1645–1676
Promulgation of new law code	1649
Beginning of ecclesiastical reform by Nikon	1667
Peasant revolt of Stenka Razin	1670–1671
Ivan V and Peter I co-tsars—regency of Sophia	1682–1689
Personal rule of Peter the Great	1689–1725
Expeditions against and capture of Azov	1695–1696
European journey of Peter	1697–1698
Revolt and suppression of *streltsy*	1698
Great Northern War	1700–1721
Battle of Narva—defeat of Russians	1700
Charles XII of Sweden at war with Poland and Saxony	1701–1708
Foundation of St. Petersburg	1703
Battle of Poltava—decisive victory of Russians over Swedes	1709
Exile of Charles XII in Turkey	1709–1713
Turkish War	1710–1711
Establishment of the Senate by Peter	1711
Peace of Nystadt with Sweden	1721
Death of Peter the Great	1725

really violent revolutions were needed before they could be overthrown and the monarchs forced to share or yield their power to the people. A case could certainly be made for the theory that the French Revolution at the end of the eighteenth century, and the Russian Revolution in the early part of the twentieth, were as violent as they were largely because they had been so long delayed. Moreover, the absolute monarchs resisted all change and orderly constitutional development to such an extent that moderate reformers in France and Russia could make little headway, and found their position undermined by extremists who had no objection to violence, and who indeed believed it to be the only efficacious method available to them. Even in England it is worth noting that the moderate Presbyterians who desired to keep Charles I on his throne were forced by the stubbornness and duplicity of the king to give way to the less moderate independents, who put the king to death.

In this chapter we shall study the absolute monarchies of France and Russia as they existed in the seventeenth century, and try to see what it was in them that made them so long-lived and resistant to change. From this study it may be easier to understand the nature of the later French and Russian Revolutions. The French monarchy reached its height both in power and prestige in the seventeenth century, and in so doing increased the prestige of absolute monarchy as an institution; at the same time, French culture of this age became the pattern for all the Western nations, including Russia. Therefore rather more attention will be given in this chapter to French culture as a whole than is possible to give to any other country within the limits of this book. On the other hand, the Russian monarchy, which was at this time only in its formative stages, does not require a similar treatment, and will therefore be handled more briefly, with attention given only to the nature of the monarchy itself, and to the means by which that monarchy was able to establish its supremacy in the country.

▶ ## The development of absolutism in France

THE AGE OF RICHELIEU AND MAZARIN— PREPARATION FOR THE "SUN KING"

The rise of Cardinal Richelieu

We have already considered in Chapter 19 the history of France up to the murder of Henry IV, the first Bourbon monarch (1610), and we considered briefly the efforts made by Henry and his chief minister Sully to unify the French state after the long and ruinous civil wars. Unfortunately Henry's murder entailed another regency, since his son and heir Louis XIII (1610–1643) was a child of eight when Henry died. The regency was assumed by his mother Marie de Medici, who had few of the abilities of her remarkable family. When she began to rule through foreign favorites, in the customary manner of foreign queens, she at once excited the opposition of the French nobility, which had been forced to remain quiescent during the strong reign of Henry IV.

Irresponsible as ever, a number of nobles, led by Prince Condé, revolted in 1615 against Concini, Marie's Italian favorite, but Condé was bought off. Two years later Louis XIII himself had Concini murdered, in resentment over his influence on Marie. Marie herself thus fell from power, and Louis ruled through a favorite of his own, the duke of Luynes, against whom Marie organized several revolts which were led by her partisans among the nobility. Meanwhile the money that the frugal Sully had left in the treasury had been squandered, and in 1614 Marie and Concini had even been forced to call the States-General, which met but refused to vote any funds.

These events follow so closely the pattern of the French monarchy as it had existed in the latter half of the sixteenth century that it might well have seemed to a contemporary Frenchman that Henry IV's work had all been lost. And since Louis XIII was a melancholy man, incompetent to rule personally, and temperamentally submissive to any stronger character who happened to

Cardinal Richelieu, by the Flemish painter Philippe de Champaigne. (COURTESY THE TRUSTEES OF THE NATIONAL GALLERY, LONDON)

be in his vicinity and was personally acceptable to him, the future of the French monarchy must have appeared dark indeed. A long reign was in prospect, during which the king would rule through favorites; the nobility, as usual, would please themselves; while the country would get on as best it could in the customary condition of semi-anarchy.

But, as it happened, a strong man had emerged during the troubles, who knew what he wanted, and was one of the most perfect masters of political strategy that has yet been known in Western civilization. Armand de Richelieu, a young French bishop, whose small see of Luçon was far too restricted a field for his talents, had come to the attention of Marie de Medici at the meeting of the States-General in 1614. He had been brought into the king's council at her suggestion. After the murder of Concini, Richelieu naturally lost his position as minister and councilor, had to retire to his bishopric and even go into exile for a

short period. But he continued to support Marie, and at last was rewarded by reconciling her with her son in 1622. In the same year Richelieu was created cardinal.

By 1624 it had become obvious to the king that Richelieu was a man of remarkable ability, unlike previous favorites whom he had loved but who had not been competent to hold their positions. So, bowing to the inevitable, he made him chief minister. A few years later Richelieu was able to persuade the king to banish his mother from the court, and thereafter Richelieu was the undisputed ruler of the country, for as long as he could retain the support of his master.

This support he in fact retained as long as he lived, in spite of many efforts by the nobles to unseat him. Louis was not, as is too often supposed, a monarch who lacked interest in the affairs of his country. He insisted on being informed at all times of the policies of his minister, and though, as far as we know, he never withheld his approval, he made Richelieu understand that

○ Pockets of Huguenot concentration
● Important Huguenot military strongholds

KINGDOM OF FRANCE

Valognes
Rouen
Caen
Domfront
Rennes
Laval
Nantes
Saumur
Thouars
Châtellerault
St. Maixent
Niort
La Rochelle
St. Jean d'Angély
Taillebourg
Royan
Jarnac
Montendre
Mussidan
Turenne
Bordeaux
Bergerac
Ste. Foy
Capdenac
Lyons
Grenoble
Castets
Monflanquin
Marvejols
Privas
Die
Embrun
Casteljaloux
Clairac
Castelsagrat
Rouergue
Gap
Nérac
Nègrepelisse
Millau
Alais
Montauban
Uxés
Mauvezin
Realmont
Nîmes
Orthez
Toulouse
Castres
Montpellier
Pau
Maxamet
Mauléon
Nay
Marseilles
Osse
Foix

RELIGIOUS SITUATION IN FRANCE
AFTER THE EDICT OF NANTES (1598)

0   50   100
Miles

such approval was always necessary. He recognized, of course, that Richelieu, in working for the aggrandizement of the monarchy, incidentally improved his own position. In actual fact the interests of king and minister were identical. Thus the reign presents a unique picture of a legitimate monarch willingly delegating his authority to a single minister whom he grew to trust; while that minister, relying on the king's support, in fact ruled the country in the king's name.[1] The result was that in the next

[1] A parallel case is that of the German Emperor William I, who enjoyed a similar relationship with Bismarck as long as he lived.

reign Louis XIV, who desired to be a real king himself, found that the entire apparatus of absolutism was at his disposal.

Suppression of Huguenots

Richelieu's domestic policy in his eighteen years of rule was entirely consistent and logical. Before France could be a great nation abroad, she must be secure at home. To be secure at home she must have a strong monarchy. The threats to this strong monarchy were two—the nobles and the Huguenots. In combination they could ruin the country, as they had during the religious wars of the sixteenth century. Many of the

*Engraving by Jacques Callot of the Siege of La Rochelle under the direction of Riche-
lieu. After a long siege the Huguenot citadel finally fell in 1628.*

nobles were, indeed, still Protestant, and thus were the natural leaders of the Huguenots. But it was also possible for Catholic nobles to make use of the Huguenots on occasion, when their political interests appeared to coincide. And the privileged position of the Huguenots under the Edict of Nantes, under which they were permitted to retain their own strongholds, was a standing temptation to rebellion.

So Richelieu struck at the Huguenots. Few cardinals of the Catholic Church have cared less about the religion of their supporters than Richelieu. In later years he was to support the German Protestant princes and the Protestant king of Sweden against the Catholic Holy Roman emperor. But he objected very strongly to the anomalous position of the Huguenots in France, as being a state within a state; though, as the sequel showed, he had no objection to tolerating their Protestant religious worship.

The most important independent Huguenot stronghold was La Rochelle, a port city in southwestern France which would be difficult to capture if it received aid from the English Protestants, as seemed likely. Hence Richelieu's efforts to marry Henrietta Maria, sister of Louis XIII, to Charles I, the new king of England. When this had been secured, the alliance with England seemed safe in spite of the Protestantism of the English monarch. Unfortunately for Richelieu's plans Henrietta had some ideas of her own, in keeping with her youth but not helpful to French policy. She was unwilling to submit herself dutifully to her young and autocratic husband, who treated her in an insulting manner, which infuriated her royal brother and endangered Richelieu's carefully laid plans. However, Charles handled the matter expeditiously, aided perhaps by a careful reading of Shakespeare,[2] and thereafter Henrietta adapted herself and became a faithful instrument of French policy. Though in later years her influence undoubtedly confirmed Charles in the religious policy which ended in his exe-

cution, at this time she was able to win the benevolent neutrality of Charles toward France at a time when it was most needed. While Charles was estranged from his wife, Buckingham, his favorite, made an effort to relieve La Rochelle but was unsuccessful. After a difficult siege the stronghold was captured in 1628, and the following year the Huguenots submitted and signed the treaty of Alais. They lost all their special political privileges and their right to private armies. But they retained the religious privileges granted them under the Edict of Nantes. Thereafter they were peaceful and industrious subjects until Louis XIV, as will be seen, revoked the Edict of Nantes altogether in 1685.

Growth of centralization—The intendants—Undermining and suppression of the nobility

Though Richelieu was prepared to curb the nobility by all means available to him, it was clear to him that the task hitherto performed by the nobles must now be performed by the king's servants, thus undermining the position of the nobles rather than directly attacking it. So many tasks had been carried out in the provinces by nobles, more or less independently, that it was essential to replace them in these tasks by men who were dependent upon the king for their positions. So Richelieu modernized and improved the system of intendants that he had inherited. He appointed nobles to this position very rarely indeed. Instead he gave the intendants full power to speak and act in the king's name, appointing one for each of the various centers of administrative jurisdiction (généralités). They were made responsible for the maintenance of local law and order, for the collection of taxes, and for promulgating and enforcing the king's decrees. If they were not absolutely loyal to royal policy they could be and were dismissed. But since their whole power emanated from the king, and not from ancient traditional feudal customs, it was natural that they should remain loyal and obediently carry out the monarch's will.

[2] See *Taming of the Shrew, passim!*

The system of intendants may fruitfully be contrasted with the English system of the justices of the peace, who, as we have seen, held their position because of their local influence, frequently sat in Parliament, and could form the nucleus of opposition to the crown if circumstances dictated it. Although the king officially appointed them, he could only with great difficulty dismiss them, since, as a rule, no one would be available to take their place. The French intendants, on the contrary, were the very instrument of centralization, and thus were naturally opposed by the nobles who believed themselves entitled by birth and ownership of land to exercise any authority in the provinces that the king delegated. The growing power of the intendants under Richelieu was undoubtedly the basic motive for the numerous noble rebellions in the reign of Louis XIII and during the minority of Louis XIV, although the nobles themselves would hardly have admitted it.

But they did know that they were extremely jealous of the power of Richelieu over the king, which they seemed helpless to lessen; and their temper was not improved by the extreme haughtiness of the cardinal, who was well aware of his position of strength. Indeed, it is not impossible that, like Henry VII of England before him, Richelieu actually encouraged the rebellions with the intention of teaching the nobles who was master. It is certain that he was kept extremely well informed of all the potential conspiracies, and none presented him with any real difficulty. After each conspiracy a few nobles were executed, a considerable number of castles were pulled down, and the king's power was a little stronger than it had been before. The final rebellion of the Fronde in the time of Mazarin, after the death of Richelieu, was doomed to failure from the start, in spite of the fact that Mazarin was much weaker than Richelieu, since by this time all the real strength of the nobles had been undermined.

The rebellions centered around Gaston d'Orléans, the brother of the king, with whom the nobles wished to replace him, believing that he was amenable to their influence, as Louis XIII patently was not. Unfortunately for them Gaston was a shiftless and treacherous character, not without military ability, but utterly unable to match himself with the king and Richelieu. Driven into exile several times when one or another of the rebellions collapsed, he made little effort to save the lives of the nobles who had been implicated, and always made his peace with his brother until the next rebellion broke out. Thus it was not difficult for Richelieu to watch him and to crush his rebellions. During this reign all private war was prohibited. All private castles were commanded to be pulled down unless they held military value for the king. The rebellions provided the excuse for carrying out these orders, especially since many of the nobles rebelled for the very reason that they had been ordered to pull down their castles. Today one may still see the ruins of many of the castles destroyed in the reign of Louis XIII (see especially the picture page 292); indeed, if one sees a ruined castle that obviously is a few centuries old it is almost possible to predict to within a few years the date of its destruction.

Foreign policy of Richelieu— Aggrandizement of France

Meanwhile, Richelieu had been pursuing a consistent foreign policy designed to attain the ends he had in mind. Most important of all these ends, in his view, was the weakening of the power of the Hapsburgs, Spanish and Austrian, and above all preventing them from uniting. France had remained neutral at the outbreak of the Thirty Years' War (1618), but under Luynes this neutrality had not been a planned one, nor had Luynes ever appreciated for what reasons it was a good policy. He had felt above all that the interests of the French lay on the side of weakening the Hapsburg power, but he had also looked upon the war, as so many of course did, as a war of religion, in which it was unthinkable for Catholic France to take the Protestant side. Unthinkable or not, for Richelieu this was the only possible policy in French interests; but, also for religious reasons, it was in the initial years unwise for France to support the Protestants openly—not until the war had clearly become a political war with religious interests subordinate, and if possible not until the Hapsburg power had already been so seriously weakened by the war that it would be possible for France to intervene decisively with fresh force.

This policy Richelieu adopted with a virtuosity that can hardly be overestimated. Stationing skilled diplomats in every center of power in Europe, he read their reports with the utmost care, thinking out exactly what the interests of his policy demanded, and issuing instructions accordingly. He

was willing to expend considerable sums of money to save himself from the necessity of using his army, but willing also to use this army if necessary. Thus he held the chief trumps and knew it. Gustavus Adolphus was in his pay, as were many of the Lutheran and Calvinist princes. When the war was halted by the peace of Prague, and only the Swedes were dissatisfied, it was to Count Oxenstierna, the Swedish chancellor, that his diplomats went, and persuaded him that now the French would seriously intervene on his side. And so it happened. Although the French army was inexperienced and often outclassed by the veteran Spanish troops, and suffered many defeats during the early years of the campaign, nevertheless it con-

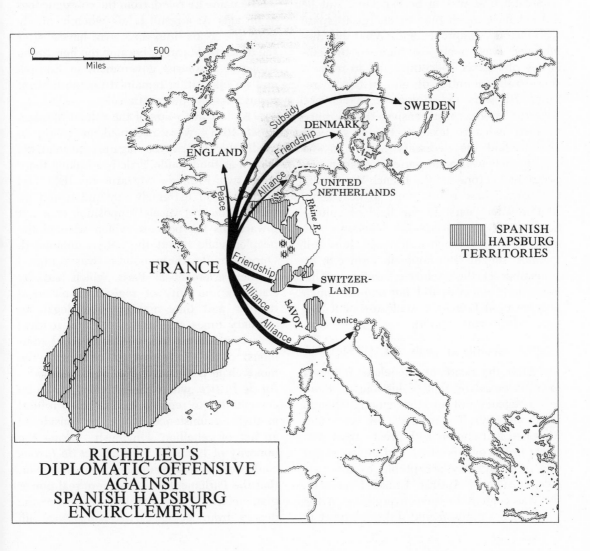

RICHELIEU'S
DIPLOMATIC OFFENSIVE
AGAINST
SPANISH HAPSBURG
ENCIRCLEMENT

stantly increased both in size and efficiency till the Hapsburgs were weakened beyond repair. The result, as we have seen, was the treaty of Westphalia and, eleven years later, the treaty of the Pyrenees. And even though Richelieu was dead and it was Mazarin who was responsible for the treaties, the real triumph was Richelieu's, and he it was who had made possible the potentially dominant power of France in Europe, symbolized by these treaties, to be exploited later in the century by Louis xiv. France had now the Pyrenees as the boundary with Spain, though the northern boundary was still far from settled, as we shall see from the efforts of Louis xiv to extend it.

In economic policy Richelieu was a mercantilist, as was to be expected. But he did not have much time or energy to spare for economic improvement. What he did, however, was greatly to improve the efficiency of the tax collecting, and to make a considerable number of administrative reforms. His wars and diplomatic maneuvers, however, were so expensive that France groaned under his taxation, though she was able to find the necessary money in the end. Richelieu also supported Canadian exploration and founded the French West India Company. These efforts were to bear some fruit in later years. In the field of culture he founded the *Académie Française,* the most noted of French academies; it is still the most sought-after honor in France to be a member of the exclusive academy. This institution, however, did not acquire much prestige until Louis xiv made use of it and gave it full royal support.

The minority of Louis XIV (1643–1661)

After the death of Richelieu, followed soon afterward by that of his master, there was a regency but no interregnum. Though Louis xiv himself was only four years old, Richelieu had chosen with great care a successor for his own position, and this successor was in every way acceptable to the new regent, Anne of Austria. Unlike Louis xiii, she was content to leave everything in the hands of her minister and did not expect to be consulted on policy. The result was that this minister, Jules Mazarin, cardinal without ever having been a priest, an Italian who had been naturalized as a Frenchman, was absolute in a manner that Richelieu had never been. In spite of several glaring shortcomings, especially a penchant for nepotism and a desire for wealth for himself and his family, he was an extremely able man, and thoroughly versed in the policies of his late master. Thus he was enabled to put the capstone on the work of Richelieu in the Hapsburg and Spanish treaties; and though his policies excited the enmity of all classes in the state, their inability to find an alternative policy on which they could get together saved Mazarin and the young monarch, in whose name he ruled, from the consequences of his acts. As a result Louis, when he finally took the reins into his own hands after the death of Mazarin, became the heir to the strongest absolutist government in Europe, and no opposition remained on the horizon to his personal autocratic rule.

Almost five years of the rule of Mazarin (1648–1653) were occupied in trying to quell the last revolt against absolutism, known as the Fronde. Strictly speaking there were two Frondes. Mazarin by 1648 had made himself extremely unpopular, and, as was customary, special opposition was felt toward his tax policies, which affected the people, while it left the nobles untouched. Opposition to these policies was centered in the Parlement of Paris, which had, by tradition, the duty of registering all royal decrees and thus making them legal. In ordinary times a refusal to register a royal decree would be followed by a royal summons to the Parlement to meet with the monarch in a special formal session called a *Lit de Justice,* where the members would be commanded to register it. Continued refusal in such circumstances would be considered an act of rebellion. Obviously, during the minority of Louis xiv no such *Lit de Justice* could be called. This did not mean, however, that the Parlement had any more real power than before. It was helpless to prevent the decree from being carried out, since all executive power was concentrated in the hands of Mazarin. But in an access of sudden emotion, fanned by the plaudits of the Paris mob which cried out for violent action, Parlement, for a brief moment, did give its support to an uprising, which was serious enough to compel Mazarin and his young master to seek safety outside Paris. But no effort had been made to enlist the support of the army, which might well have been willing, under the leadership of the Great Condé (to be distinguished from Henry of Condé, leader of a previous rebellion in 1615) to aid any revolt against Mazarin. As it happened, some army contingents did join in the rebellion, though far too few to turn the scale in favor of the rebels, while the Great Condé, for the moment, remained loyal.

The divided rebels were therefore quelled without any difficulty, and Mazarin and Louis returned to Paris. But Condé was nursing his own grievances against the cardinal, and was apparently preparing a military coup. Mazarin, however, struck first and arrested him, whereupon a rebellion broke out in earnest, supported by a considerable number of the nobility and the other leading French military man of the day, Marshal Turenne, who was at that time a Protestant and may have joined the rebels for religious reasons. On this occasion the Parlement held aloof, wanting no part of a movement led by the nobility, and only a few of the Parisian workers joined it. Mazarin again went into exile and the nobles liberated Condé, who went off to Spain to bring in a Spanish army.

The course of the rebellion was confused. Noblewomen rode about the streets of Paris on fiery chargers, changing sides and loves according to temporary inclination. No one had any clear idea what to do, whether Louis XIV should be replaced by another prince of the blood, or whether he should be brought back on the promise to dismiss Mazarin. All were united in detestation of the cardinal but in nothing else. Finally Marshal Turenne switched to the side of the government, taking with him

the only remaining effective armed force in France. The last of the rebellion was stamped out, though Condé, who had become Spanish commander in chief, had to be defeated in several pitched battles before he was subdued. Mazarin returned to Paris and thereafter was secure until his death in 1661. Louis XIV, who up to that year had been content to let Mazarin rule, declared that henceforth he would be the ruler himself. He was then twenty-two years of age.

The Frondes have been dealt with at this length not because they were important in themselves, but because the form taken by the revolts and their complete irrelevance to the situation, their unplanned nature, and their utter abortiveness demonstrate so clearly why the French people submitted to absolutism, and why there were no more revolts throughout the reign of Louis XIV. There was only one bond of unity between the discontented groups—hatred of Mazarin. Parlement was a legal body without power to do more than issue protests. The peasants and urban populace, whose grievances were considerable and deserved attention, could do nothing without leadership. The nobles refused to admit that their day was over. They had neither plan nor program save the re-establishment of feudal ascendancy over the king and the restoration of their traditional "liberties," which were being encroached upon by a bankrupt government and a foreign upstart who could not apparently put an end to the continuous war and ensure the departure of the ever-threatening Spanish army. The nobles did not even make a serious effort to gain the person of the young king to bend him to their will, as other nobles in the previous century had tried. It would have been entirely impossible for them to have governed the country except through the institutions of the absolute monarchy which were being used by Mazarin. The whole futile revolt has been called by an eminent French historian (Lavisse) a "cruel parody" of what was being done seriously in England at the same time, and one can hardly disagree with him.

The English had alternative institutions

of government which the English rebels could and did use. They permanently broke the power of the monarch and made it subservient to their own. The French people, on the other hand, forced to realize by the failure of the Fronde the hopeless irresponsibility of the nobles, naturally turned to the only form of government that could guarantee them the law and order and protection they needed. From this time onward they recognized that there was no alternative. No one saw this more clearly than the youthful king Louis XIV, who was able to say not so many years later that he himself *was* the state, which by that time had become strictly true. Without the king and the institution of absolute monarchy there was no true *state*, but only disorderly and irresponsible centers of local power. Under Louis XIV there was a true state, the center of which was the monarch, who referred to himself as the Sun King—a Copernican idea very much in keeping with the growing scientific thought of the age. Around the monarch, in his own country, revolved the planets, dependent upon him for their reflected light; and, as Louis was to grow to believe, around France were to revolve all the other countries of Europe, shining likewise by reflected light from the great central French throne occupied by himself.

THE REIGN OF LOUIS XIV (1643–1715)

The king and government of France— The "Sun King"

Louis XIV himself was at all times in his reign the center of his government. He presided over meetings of his council, he made all appointments. His decrees were registered by the Parlement of Paris as a matter of course, since, as we have seen, if the Parlement resisted, he had the last word always at his disposal. Louis was one of the hardest workers of all kings in history. He was neither especially able nor attractive, yet he had a very high sense of his own dignity; he looked the part of a king and played it to perfection. As an autocrat he was not an unreasonable or arbitrary one, though in his later years he performed many arbitrary acts which he had been persuaded were for the good of his kingdom or dynasty. He regarded himself as so far above ordinary men that there was no need to take vengeance on any of them or to allow himself to be ruffled by their feeble opposition. He was content with banishing from his august presence courtiers who offended him; to the old rebels of the Fronde he was gracious and forgiving; as soon as it was politically safe to do so he extended his royal pardon to them.

Since there was no real competitor for his power in the realm of France, and France herself was so strong that she was able to fight any wars engaged in by Louis almost entirely outside her own borders, Louis rather naturally had an extremely exalted opinion of himself, and there can be no doubt that he genuinely believed in the divine right of kings as applied to himself. In this belief he was ably seconded by his great Bishop Bossuet, who also believed in the theory and was able to preach and write convincingly on it, making excellent use of scriptural authority. To illustrate his semi-divine position as effectively as possible, Louis surrounded himself with the most elaborate system of etiquette ever devised in the Western world, an etiquette scarcely to be paralleled even in Constantinople. Yet there is a striking difference between Byzantine ceremonial and the ceremonial of the court of Versailles which bespeaks the significant difference between the Germanic and Eastern heritages.

In the Oriental court of Constantinople and its Russian successor the monarch was so high above all others that even his nearest companions could be, and were, regarded as little better than slaves, who might be expected to kiss the emperor's foot or even the ground in front of his foot. The monarch had absolute power even over his viziers or chief ministers, a power of which he frequently availed himself. From his subjects could come no complaint at such arbitrary treatment, and Roman law, as we have seen, emanated from the really absolute power of the monarch ("What pleases the emperor has the force of law"). In the countries with a Roman heritage, menial tasks were performed only by slaves. But in countries with a Germanic background the companions of the monarch had always sought to perform tasks for their master, and the performance raised them in prestige, not lowered them. The household was the center of the king's government, and officers of the household were the most important personages in the realm.

Thus Louis carried this ancient tradition to its furthest extension. Every act that he performed had to be according to a solemn ritual that appears in this democratic age and country to be somewhat ridiculous, if we do not stop to consider how important, even in America, is the household of the President, and how influential are the men in his immediate entourage. When Louis arose in the morning the great nobles regarded it as an honor to be present at the ceremony (the *lever*) and as a grave dishonor if they were excluded. Each noble had a particular task assigned to him, such as holding the sleeve of his master's shirt while the royal hand was thrust into it. More ceremonies accompanied every necessary act of the king's life. Only a monarch of the greatest hardihood could stand such a strain, and Louis' successors were not men enough for the job. Louis presided over all his council meetings and made it his business to know everything that

A ceremonial audience given by Louis XIV. The engraving is dated 1672 and represents an audience which took place on 26 August, 1670, with the counselors all mentioned by name.

The Chateau of Versailles and the grounds; from a seventeenth-century French painting.

was being done in his name as far as he possibly could. He was determined that the life of France should indeed revolve around him, as in theory it should. Only a man of great application and remarkable physical endurance could have solemnly gone through the palace ritual every day of his reign—but Louis achieved it, and the rest of Europe did its best, outside England, to imitate it. It was perhaps fortunate that a sense of the ridiculous was not included amongst Louis' more sterling qualities; or if he possessed it no one during a long reign was ever allowed to suspect it.

For the proper diffusion of the light radiated by the Sun King, the largest palace in the world was built, to the sorrow of the financial minister Colbert, but to the undoubted glorification of the monarch, not only in France but in every country of Europe. This palace, which may still be seen today by the curious, and is still admired by some, was able to accomodate some ten thousand persons. It was not only the court of the king but also the working quarters of the royal household and the seat of government. As a monument it was more functional,

therefore, than the Pyramids, and far more attractive to Western eyes; and in Louis' time it was a hive of activity.

The exterior is built in the style of the late French Renaissance, and resembles in some respects St. Peter's in Rome for the magnificence of its layout and symmetry. The gardens, tended by scores of highly expert gardeners, were geometrical, in accordance with the growing French taste for order and reasonableness. The hedges were clipped and formal; nothing was permitted to be out of place, and the long walks of the great park were designed with the greatest care and regard for the particular kind of vista desired by the designers, the greatest of whom, responsible for the whole, was Le Nôtre. Some of this has been spoiled by later efforts at "improvement," especially those of Louis Philippe, a postrevolutionary monarch. Nevertheless the great park of Versailles, with its statues and its fountains, must have been a great marvel in its day. But, even while Louis reigned, the interior was discovered to be damp and uncomfortable to live in. It was made endurable only by the magnificence of the great salons, and especially the enormous hall of mirrors, the contemplation of which may in some degree have compensated for the boredom and material discomfort unavoidably attached to the task of being a good courtier, or even, be it said, a good king.

Louis XIV was in no sense an innovator in government. His greatest claim to fame as a ruler attaches to his ability to make the best use of what he had inherited as his governmental structure, and to his selection of ministers to do his will. He ruled through several councils of state, which gradually developed almost into modern specialized departments. These councils were kept very small, and the councilors met with the king frequently to concert policy. From the councils went forth instructions to the king's servants in the provinces, primarily the intendants, who had in some of the larger *généralités* a few assistants. The king also had a high court, which in many ways acted like the English Court of Star Chamber; the latter, it will be remembered, was also a part of the king's council. It dealt with special royal cases and in some respects acted as the equivalent of a court of appeal, in which the king's justice prevailed over any local decision.

Fully subject to the king for the first time in French history was the new army, previously recruited almost entirely by private enterprise, through officers who had received the king's commission to recruit and train troops. The same system was maintained, but now the officers were closely checked to see whether they really had the troops under their command that they claimed, and they were now equipped from royal warehouses and arsenals. Thus the nobility could no longer use their retainers as private armies, for without proper equipment they could not hope to stand against the royal hosts. So the old armies fell into disuse. A real minister of war was responsible for the training of the army, and new practices of drill and training were adopted. The French military system was undoubtedly responsible for the successes of Louis in his wars, often against numerically superior

forces which had no unified training and only slightly unified command. For communication the ministers of Louis organized an efficient postal system. This also had previously been handled by many different organizations with many tolls to pay before a letter reached its destination. Now the contract was let out, but to only one semi-official corporation. Letters were carried for a single charge, with any customs surtaxes to be paid at the destination.

The efficient centralization of the government did not mean that at once all the liberties of the French subjects of the crown were lost. Indeed, for the most part, they were not lost at all, since the king in all probability would never interfere with them. By far the larger number of official positions were still bought and paid for. They were regarded as property to be bequeathed to one's family after death. The holders did not earn any regular salary, as indeed even the ministers of the crown who were directly employed by the king did not. They obtained their incomes from the exercise of their functions, as for instance when fines were assessed and paid. Naturally there was a definite value in such positions, and the incomes could be calculated, so that to regard them as valuable property was hardly inaccurate. The officials would have fought bitterly against the monarch if he had in any way tried to deprive them of their jobs, which were indeed in many cases far from sinecures. Louis' administration preferred to take away occasional tasks from these men and give them to the intendants and their staff.

The Parlements had a long and distinguished history. Men bought their positions in these also, and they held great prestige. They carried out a great deal of the legal work of the country. It would have been folly to dispossess them, nevertheless the administration liked to have a superior court which in cases of special concern could quash the verdicts of the Parlements. The States-General was never called during the reign of Louis, as he had other means of obtaining money, and, though he might never have been plagued with the usual grievances, it was better not to incur the danger. The provincial Estates, however, where they existed, were summoned by the intendants and asked to vote sums of money voluntarily. They usually did so without voicing any grievances.

Thus the absolutism of Louis, though in theory complete, in practice was modified considerably by ancient vested interests which it was not worth while disturbing. The nobility was almost entirely exempt from taxation, and Louis frequently handed out immunities to his favorites, again to the distress of his finance minister, who was looking for ways to persuade the nobles to make some contribution to the expenses of government. In the vast number of legal cases ancient precedents were followed and administered, not by royal appointees but by men who had bought or inherited their positions and knew what the ancient customs of the kingdom were. In this respect they were similar to the English common lawyers, and were at least as much devoted to ancient tradition. So the monarchy was to a large degree only superficially modernized. Not until the eighteenth century did the vested rights of the ancient institutions come up against the royal power when the latter was compelled by circumstances to try to improve the administration and modernize it. Then the Parlements and other relics of the Middle Ages resisted fiercely every effort to improve them, to such an extent that the lethargic king Louis xv merely gave up in despair, with the famous if apocryphal remark "After me, the deluge."

In the age of Louis xiv everything seemed good under the façade. The tremendous efforts of Colbert to improve the sources of income of the people and thus increase the base for taxation were to a large degree successful. When the king wished to exercise power there was no one who effectively said him nay. And it should be understood that his absolutism was not based on the army as in modern dictatorships, although the army was used to suppress a number of minor uprisings, especially amongst the peasantry,

and to aid in collecting taxes and keeping order. There can, however, be little doubt that the government really did rest upon the consent of the various classes of the people. Generally speaking the peasants were content as long as the monarch was Catholic and legitimate. The bourgeoisie had not yet become politically conscious as in England, and respected any government that could provide protection after the long civil wars and did not conspicuously mismanage the state. The nobles had had their teeth drawn by Richelieu. Most of them were content to exchange their position of independence for one of dependence on the crown, which in turn was willing to keep them as courtiers and pay them pensions. It was a poor substitute, but in the reign of Louis xiv the moral decay of the noble class was not yet as visible as it became in the reigns of his successors.

Religious policy of Louis

Relations with the papacy—Ever since the Concordat of Bologna in the reign of Francis i the French Church had been virtually controlled by the king, and the French clergy was at all times a willing instrument for the furtherance of royal policy. Nevertheless much had happened since the time of Francis i, and the Counter Reformation papacy was anxious to recover the ground lost in the previous centuries to the national states, in which policy it had met considerable success in other countries than France. But Louis was determined to yield nothing of his absolute powers, nor share them with the pope, however willing he might be to execute papal policy of which he approved. He had no intention of losing his hold on the French clergy, and in this he was, of course, backed by the clergy who were his own appointees. He was willing to grant the pope authority in the field of faith and morals but nothing more. Goaded by the papacy he even went so far as to declare in 1682, in a document drawn up by Bishop Bossuet, that the pope even in this field should be willing to submit himself to a general council. This was an old doctrine which had made popes shudder in earlier times, and which they had fought hard to prevent the emperor from asserting at the time of the Lutheran revolt. But apparently Louis had used it only to maintain his hold on the clergy. He had threatened the pope in the best military manner in order to lessen papal demands, and then refrained from pressing the point. At all events Louis had not yielded the "Gallican liberties" by the time of his death.

In dealing, however, with Protestantism and other beliefs that smacked of heresy, Louis was severe—more severe, indeed, in the persecution of Huguenots than the papacy itself approved. Pope Innocent XI asked him to stay his hand and did not even approve of the revocation of the Edict of Nantes. Louis regarded heresy in much the same way as a medieval monarch, as a kind of treason not only to the Church but to the state. Though he is said to have missed daily Mass only once in his life, he appears to have had no particular knowledge of his religion; but he approved of uniformity of worship as being a means of unifying the people. He had no toleration whatever for subjects who disagreed with him in religion any more than in anything else. After all, he ruled by divine right and divine inspiration.

The Jansenists—The most troublesome group to the Church and to Louis were the Jansenists, who possessed a large monastery at Port-Royal, and conducted a number of schools in competition with the numerous Jesuit foundations. The Jansenists, named after a certain Cornelius Jansen, one-time professor at Louvain and bishop of Ypres, were in doctrine not very far from the Calvinists, believing in a modified form of predestination and staying extremely close to the teachings of St. Augustine as they interpreted them. In morality they were distinctly puritan. It was extremely difficult to attack them, since they gained a great deal of support from the austere moral lives that they lived and their evident sincerity, and they were quite content to remain within the Church. Politics also became strongly interwoven with any action taken against them

since their implacable enemies were the Jesuits, and the latter, as instruments of papal policy against the Gallican Church, were highly unpopular with the king and the ordinary clergy. So the center of Port-Royal was closed once early in the reign of Louis, since he suspected the Jansenists of sympathy with the Frondeurs, and it was clear that their emphasis on predestination was too close to Calvinism. Later in the century, after the pope had accepted a milder interpretation of their doctrine, it was reopened, only to be suppressed again when Père Quesnel published a French New Testament with Jansenist commentary. Finally the teachings were condemned by the papacy in the early eighteenth century.

Jansenism nevertheless left a very strong mark on French thought and literature in the age of Louis XIV. Many of the greatest writers had spent time and studied at Port-Royal, and there can be no question that the drama of Racine in particular was marked by the strong morality of Port-Royal. But most important in its day was the famous *Provincial Letters* of Blaise Pascal, the mathematician and religious thinker, who attacked the Jesuits for the laxity of their morality and for the way in which they used the confessional and made fine distinctions on the kind of sins that were permissible and mortal. For Pascal, as for the Protestants, sin was not something to be explained away or condoned. He introduced into the *Letters* a clownish Jesuit who agreed with everyone who argued with him, contradicting himself and adapting himself with infinite flexibility to the needs of his audience. The *Letters* were an immediate success. All literate France read them and laughed at them, while the Jesuits fumed; and the French Gallican clergy used the occasion to join in the attack on the Jesuits, their traditional enemies. Bishop Bossuet accused them of "putting cushions under the elbows of sinners and looking for coverlets for their passions." The Jesuits, always adaptable, conformed, and reformed themselves, and became thereafter pillars of respectable morality. Another group of persons was also condemned for heretical

Portrait of Blaise Pascal, author of the Provincial Letters *and noted scientist and mathematician. He was a sympathizer with Jansenism and connected with Port-Royal. The portrait used to be attributed to Quesnel, but François Quesnel could not have painted it. It may have been executed by another of the Quesnel family, many of whom were artists. It is certainly seventeenth-century French.*

opinions—the Quietists, who believed in a form of mysticism which in its logical conclusions required no Church. Several Quietist leaders were thrown into prison and their works destroyed after the papacy had condemned their founder and leader Molinos.

The Huguenots—Revocation of Edict of Nantes—But, important though Jansenism was as a reform movement within the Church, far more important in its effects on France was the exodus of the Huguenots after the revocation of the Edict of Nantes. The revocation was undoubtedly due in the main to the efforts of the clergy. Every year for decades, whenever the clergy met to vote taxes to the king, they petitioned him for the revocation or forced conversion of the remaining Huguenots, who must have numbered in the early part of Louis' reign at least a million, concentrated in a few impor-

tant centers, especially in Languedoc and Normandy. As a rule the Huguenots were peaceful citizens; they had taken no part in the Fronde. But they were still a standing reproach to the Catholic clergy who were entirely unable to convert them.

At last Louis took action, in the sense demanded by the clergy, by making use of some of his military powers to force conversion. It was his right to station troops in private houses for purposes of war. Someone suggested to him that he quarter his roughest troops in Huguenot homes until they were converted. By the use of this and other methods of pressure, a fairly substantial number of them did in fact decide to embrace the Catholic religion, and in 1685 it was represented to Louis by his councilors and clergy, and by his dour and pious mistress Madame de Maintenon whom he later married, that the bulk of Huguenots had been converted. All that was necessary now was to revoke the "temporary measure" which had granted them toleration and had been adopted only for political reasons. So Louis, either believing or wishing to believe them, and sure that he was striking a blow for the true religion, revoked the Edict of Nantes.

It might have been possible for the Huguenots to emigrate, but this was not permitted, as French policy was strongly against all emigration except to French lands overseas, and it was known that much of French prosperity would depart with them as well as the trade secrets and skills that they had acquired. The French army was therefore stationed at the frontiers to prevent their escape, and when they returned they were forcibly converted to Catholicism. Hundreds of thousands nevertheless succeeded in leaving, without their possessions but determined not to abandon their religion. What was France's loss was the gain of every Protestant country. Over forty thousand were welcomed in Brandenburg-Prussia alone, bringing an industry to that backward state that altogether changed the character of the economy. England and Holland and the German Protestant princes all opened their doors, as did even the Dutch in South Africa and the American colonies.

The French economy can be said never to have fully recovered from the expulsion of the Huguenots. It was without question the most senseless of all Louis' acts and the most damaging to his country. Whole industries had been in the hands of Huguenots, and the industries just ceased to exist after the expulsion, while it took the remaining Catholics many decades to rebuild the industries which had been ruined by the departure of so many skilled workers. On the other hand every country which welcomed these seventeenth-century "displaced persons" profited by it, and were enabled to compete better with the French industry which had been growing so quickly up to that time. It was fortunate indeed for Colbert that he had been in his grave two years when the edict was revoked—for it is sure that at that stage of his reign Louis would not have listened to him.

The economic foundations of French absolutism

We have already dealt in the chapter on the commercial revolution and mercantilism with the work of the great French finance minister Jean-Baptiste Colbert, who was a faithful servant of Louis until his death in 1683. We have seen by what means Colbert built up French industry, completing the work of his great predecessors of the reign of Henry IV. It was Colbert's belief that France should be the greatest industrial country of Europe and should have a very fair proportion of European trade. It would then be possible to provide the king with enough money for his uses without having to raise the rate of taxation, and without having to fall back constantly upon the peasants who were taxed heavily enough. Agriculture could and must be improved, especially by the use of new agricultural methods already in use in Holland; but the main source of income must be the towns, of which there were more in France than in any other country, while impediments to trade within the country should be lessened

and the collection of the taxes greatly improved by superior administration.

None of Colbert's predecessors had put all these policies into effect at the same time, and the result was astonishing. France became by far the richest country in Europe, surpassing even the United Provinces (Holland), which no doubt had a greater wealth per capita, but which with a far smaller population could not equal France in national income. A great effort was made to get rid of the numerous hindrances to trade, such as excessive customs barriers, and interference by the nobility with the free flow of traffic. The greater part of the country for the first time became a customs-free area, within which trade could flow freely. A canal was dug from the Bay of Biscay to the Mediterranean. This huge engineering project vastly improved the flow of trade between the different areas of France, while the roads, which had been improving throughout the century, were now made into the best in Europe.

France is a potentially rich country. Her lands are the most fertile in Europe, and her people are amongst the most thrifty and industrious. But, with rare exceptions in her history, she has been ill served by her governments, which have either been too extravagant, or unable to provide effective internal security. For a brief while under Colbert she was better served than at almost any other time in her history. This resulted in prosperity, even for the peasant, for a time, while the bourgeoisie flourished for considerably longer. And Louis was able to build Versailles and carry out his wars. If he overextended himself at the end and had to use the worst methods of his predecessors and contemporaries to raise money for the constant wars, it was assuredly not the fault of Colbert, who had been long dead and who, if he had lived, might have just possibly counteracted the influence of Louvois, the militant war minister. But it is doubtful. Louis approved of the wars which added to his glory and power; there is no reason to believe that he regarded Colbert as anything but a useful instrument to help him win his

EXPANSION OF
FRENCH FRONTIERS (1667–1697)

French acquisitions – 1668 (Treaty of Aix-la-Chapelle)
French acquisitions – 1678 - 1679 (Treaty of Nijmegen)
French acquisitions – 1697 (Treaty of Ryswick)

0   50   100
Miles

wars, or that he really understood anything of his great minister's work.

The Wars of Louis XIV

Disturbance of the balance of power— The idea of the balance of power has been briefly noticed in an earlier chapter. We have seen how the French under Richelieu had struggled hard and effectively to prevent the union of the Spanish and Austrian Hapsburgs, which union would have put them within striking distance of dominating Europe. Charles v, as we have seen, achieved a similar position by means of Hapsburg

marriage alliances in the sixteenth century. The French king Francis i had been forced to spend almost all his life in fighting Charles, while Richelieu in the next century had spent considerable blood and treasure in trying to prevent a military union between the two Hapsburg powers by way of Italy. Now, however, in the time of Louis xiv, with the Hapsburg power broken by the treaties of Westphalia and the Pyrenees, France herself was close to being in a position to dominate Europe and too strong to be defeated by any but a very strong combination of powers. Thus all the rulers who understood, however vaguely, the concept of the balance of power, could not help but regard France as the natural enemy.

The situation during the entire personal reign of Louis XIV was greatly complicated by the fact that on the throne of Spain was a mentally unbalanced and impotent king who was certain never to produce an heir and who might die at any moment, leaving the huge Spanish possessions in the Netherlands, Italy, and America to some other ruler. Austria was not so far fallen into decay that the Hapsburg emperor, with the Spanish Empire under his control, could not recover his former power; while the danger to Europe from French rule over the Spanish Empire was even more obvious. Both France and Austria, as we shall see, possessed princes who might be considered legitimate heirs for the Spanish inheritance.

England did not feel herself especially threatened by the early wars in which Louis engaged. Her interests were different from those of her continental contemporaries. She was anxious not to see the Spanish Netherlands (Belgium) in French hands, but she was also engaged in a constant trade rivalry with the Dutch. Thus for different reasons it was possible to fight against either the Dutch or the French, but she had to have a good sense of timing to know which was the right enemy to fight at a given moment, while it was also possible to be neutral as long as the French made no attempt to take the Spanish Netherlands. But the Dutch were constantly threatened by the French. A rich and prosperous country, but without great reserves of soldiers, was obviously a standing invitation to an enemy; and though she expected to be able to hold her own against most navies that could be brought against her, she simply did not have enough troops to defend her by land without alliances. When we consider that she was a Protestant country with a Catholic country to her immediate south and a militantly Catholic country beyond that, her reasons for feeling insecure are easily understood.

On the other hand, in fairness to Louis, it should be remembered that the northern French frontier was not as yet fixed and accepted. The Spanish Netherlands had no particular reason to belong to Spain, which was a decadent country with nothing left but a strong military tradition, and there were various imperial towns and duchies on the borders of France which had obviously little chance of remaining independent during the current expansion of national states and the incessant rivalry between them. Franche-Comté (Burgundy) was not yet in France, nor was much of what is today northern France. Alsace and Lorraine were partly under French control but far from definitively incorporated within her boundaries. The only defensible natural frontier for France was the Rhine, but to obtain this, much of the Spanish Netherlands would have to be incorporated. There was still no national German state. The Holy Roman Empire's natural interests were in Austria, and it seemed no doubt unreasonable in a day of growing national states for this international power to own scattered territories far from its true homeland, even though these territories now enjoyed substantial independence. Much of Louis' fighting should therefore be considered in the light of the need for a defensible northern frontier and for the incorporation within France—which was capable of administering them—of all the small independent territories that, if not taken, would only fall to some other power with no more right to them than France.

War of Devolution—The first effort was the so-called War of Devolution (1667–1668). According to the custom of the time the French had some semblance of a right to the territories which they invaded. The legal excuses were always exploited to the full in hopes of some kind of settlement without fighting, but seldom was fighting avoided for long. Louis was married to a Spanish princess who had renounced all her personal rights to the Spanish Netherlands when she married him. But the Spanish, being short of money, had not paid the dowry promised. Louis and his diplomats therefore concluded that this broke the original marriage contract, so the territories could go to him. Moreover, they claimed, they were due to fall to him because his wife was the daughter of the Spanish king's first wife, while the heir to the Spanish throne was a son of his father's second marriage. The legal complications having taken some time, and naturally having achieved nothing beyond furnishing Louis with an adequate pretext for war, he duly invaded the Spanish Netherlands and conquered Franche-Comté, only to be met by a strong alliance of the Dutch, the English (who could not have fought very effectively in it) and the Swedes. So Louis gracefully withdrew, and returned Franche-Comté, but was allowed to keep a few important towns now in northern France.

The Dutch War—The second war is usually known as the Dutch War (1672–1678). This time Louis had purchased the neutrality of the English king Charles II, and the Swedish king had also been persuaded not to enter the war in exchange for a few financial concessions. This time, therefore, the Dutch were isolated, while Spain, the titular owner of the disputed Spanish Netherlands, was unable to play any effective part in defending them. Only when Louis had overrun the Spanish Netherlands and invaded Holland did the other powers awake to the danger and forge a new alliance. Meanwhile the Dutch themselves, under William of Orange, who had just been brought to power in a sudden revolution, drove back the invader by the time-honored method of cutting the dikes. Again Louis made peace in 1678–1679 (Treaty of Nijmegen), and this time he received from Spain Franche-Comté and a few more Flemish towns.

Franche-Comté, which had hitherto enjoyed all but complete independence under the Spanish crown, with its own Parlement at Dôle, was quickly integrated into the French administrative system, with a new capital at Besançon, to which the old Parlement was transferred. This point is mentioned to illustrate the general policy followed by the French at this time, which cannot be shown to have been merely in the interests of the ruling Bourbon dynasty, but aimed at making a larger and more effective national state under centralized control. This old territory of Franche-Comté has, of course, been part of France since that time, and once French centralized administration was established there after the cession by Spain, it did indeed become really French territory, and there was no chance of its ever being returned to an independent status or to foreign rule. Thus the policy of conquest and the policy of centralization marched parallel; the one was designed to take, while the other was a means of holding what had been taken and making it an integral part of France.

It is also true that concessions might have been extorted from Holland by the treaty, since Holland had suffered many military reverses. However, Louis was content with the weakening of Dutch military and to some extent naval power which had come about as a result of the war and, since Dutch territory did not touch French territory as yet at any point, no territorial concessions were demanded. It seems clear, however, that at this time all the other European countries had come to recognize the menace of French power, and William of Orange in particular believed that France was aiming to establish a hegemony over Europe—the old fear of a "universal monarchy." On the other hand the French merely thought that the national state of France should be extended to include as much contiguous territory as could be acquired, especially to the north and east. No evidence has ever been discovered that any French statesmen of this age planned to establish a "universal monarchy" under French domination; but it is entirely understandable that foreign countries who had to withstand French aggression, or who saw that the balance of power was greatly in favor of France, should plan to make the unintended hegemony impossible. Herein, of course, lies the danger to peace inherent in all concepts of "balance of power," in that the country which through its growth and power becomes a potential menace to its neighbors cannot be permitted to keep such power, even though it never intends to use it. For just such a reason more than two thousand years previously Sparta and her allies had launched a preventive war on Athens. If they had merely waited for an attack which might or might not ever have come, they would have found themselves helpless. Their only chance was to *prevent* the Athenian Empire from growing so powerful that it could have overwhelmed them, as William of Orange now tried to organize an alliance against France which would make her hegemony impossible, should it be attempted.

Further expansion and the War of the League of Augsburg—But first the French gave evidence of a continued aggressive spirit. Again Louis began to expand, using legal means to add new territories to the north and east, with the military threat as far as possible kept in the background. By means of *chambres de réunion,* groups of lawyers whose job it was to find legal grounds for joining various contiguous territories to the French state, Louis advanced into imperial territory, claiming Alsace for France, and occupying its capital of Strasbourg. Luxemburg was also occupied, while the Emperor Leopold I had some difficulty in making any defense since he was at the time trying to hold off the last great Turkish invasion of his Hapsburg home territories. Nevertheless, in 1686 he was able to form the league of Augsburg against further French expansion, to which adhered all the important European states except England; and even England joined later when William of Orange, stadholder of Holland, who was an important figure in the organization of the league, though it was officially an imperial venture, became king of England as William III. At this point the league changed its name to the Grand Alliance, with its avowed purpose being to curb the power and aggressions of the French.

Louis began the war that followed by invading the Rhenish Palatinate with his armies (1688). But it proved beyond his power to defeat the entire Grand Alliance, while, on the other hand, the Grand Alliance could not invade France nor without invasion bring the war to an end.[3] The great navy

built by Colbert for the French won a victory over the English and Dutch navies combined at the battle of Beachy Head in 1690, showing what might have happened had French resources and will been sufficient to keep up a good navy as well as the best army in Europe. But a comparatively minor allied victory at La Hogue in 1692, which the French even disputed as a defeat at all, seriously weakened the French navy, so that, in spite of a few further victories it gave no further serious trouble to the Alliance and was unable to disrupt its lines of communication.

Since neither side could win the war, a peace was arranged at Ryswick (1697) under which Louis gave up almost all of his conquests, but was permitted to keep Alsace and its capital of Strasbourg. Like Franche-Comté, Alsace was permitted to keep its own Parlement, but in other respects it was incorporated into the French national state. However, most of the inhabitants of the territory continued to speak their German dialect, although learning to speak French also. The territory was later in constant dispute between the new national state of Germany, which in the seventeenth century could of course have had no claims to it, and France. It was part of the German Empire from the Franco-Prussian War till 1918.

The War of the Spanish Succession—Meanwhile Charles II, king of Spain (known as Charles the Sufferer), who had not been expected to attain adulthood but had somehow managed to survive, was now at last sinking toward his grave, and the question of the Spanish succession, that had been in the minds of European statesmen throughout the reign of Louis XIV, would clearly soon have to be resolved. If the Spanish monarchy could be added to the French, then not only would the great overseas Spanish Empire be added to French possessions but the boundary line of the Pyrenees would disappear. Louis and his successors would rule a vast contiguous territory including the whole of the Iberian peninsula. The balance of power in Europe would be destroyed for ever, and the smaller states could simply be gobbled up at leisure. On the other hand, if the

[3] The position of the Germans in Western Europe, 1914–1918, provides an instructive parallel.

Spanish territories could be joined to those of the empire, then the latter, which would then possess the Spanish Netherlands, would be as large as in the days of Charles v. The empire seemed at the moment to be less dangerous than the France of Louis xiv, but there was no saying whether it might not recover its sixteenth-century power. The only chance for the survival of the small nations was that the Spanish throne be kept away from both the Bourbon and Hapsburg families, or, if that could not be done, have it accepted that the new Spanish monarch could never occupy the throne of either France or the empire at the same time.

Before the death of Charles II efforts had been made to settle the matter among the emperor, Louis, and the other interested powers in the hopes of avoiding a new war. Agreement was reached first on the succession of Joseph Ferdinand, the elector of Bavaria, but under this agreement the Spanish territories outside the homeland would have been divided amongst other claimants. Charles the Sufferer refused to agree and named Joseph as the sole heir. Then, unexpectedly, Joseph died, and the succession was wide open again. The two principal claimants, both with a hereditary claim about equally good, were the archduke Charles, son of the emperor, and Philip, grandson of Louis xiv. Both Charles and Philip were the nearest heirs to their respective crowns, so that in either case there was the danger of uniting the Spanish crown with one or other of the two most important European rulers. The Dutch and French agreed to allowing (1700) the Spanish dominions to fall to the archduke Charles if France were allowed to be compensated by taking many of the old Spanish possessions in central Europe and Italy. But the emperor would not agree, since he still hoped to obtain the whole Spanish Empire intact. At this moment Charles the Sufferer again entered the picture by leaving in his will the whole Spanish Empire intact to Philip of France; in the event of his refusal the whole territory should go to Charles. Having accomplished this, the Spanish monarch at last died.

The temptation proved to be too much for Louis. Philip, his grandson, could now, under the terms of the late king's will, at once inherit the Spanish Empire; and when Philip inherited the French throne in due course, the boundary of France would be extended to the Mediterranean at the Straits of Gibraltar, and to Holland on the north by the incorporation of the Spanish Netherlands. This was so much more than would have been obtained by the proposed partition treaty of 1700 that Louis decided to accept the inheritance, thereby making a new war certain, since the empire, the Dutch, and, almost certainly, England would not accept it. By this time England, under the influence of the recent continental wars under her king William III, had now almost completely accepted the thesis that the Spanish Netherlands (Belgium) could never be permitted to be in the hands of France or the strongest European power—a policy which persisted until 1914 and after, largely causing the early entry of Great Britain into World War I.

The emperor was the natural leader of the new alliance, since he had been the chief loser by the will. He was joined by the Dutch and the English as well as some of the German princes, especially the prince of Prussia who was allowed to become king in exchange for his support. France had been seriously weakened by the Dutch War, and her navy was almost abandoned. She was in no position to fight against such a formidable alliance with any real hopes of success. When the alliance found two superb generals to lead its armies, the English Marlborough and Prince Eugene of Savoy, the French began to lose land battles in spite of the superiority of the French engineers, French methods of training, and the national and patriotic spirit of the French army.

By 1709 France was completely exhausted and had been invaded by the victorious allies. Louis sued for peace, but was offered such severe terms that he preferred to make one final effort rather than accept them. He appealed directly to the people, imploring them to provide him with new

HITHER POMERANIA
to Prussia - 1720

BREMEN-
VERDEN
to Hanover
1719

SPANISH
NETHERLANDS
to Austria-1714

Rhine R.

Elbe R.

Oder R.

Danube R.

MILAN
to Austria-1718

Milan

Banat

Little
Wallachia

SERBIA

to Austria-1718

1714

SPAIN
to House of
Bourbon

to England
1713
Minorca

to Austria
1714

NAPLES

Gibraltar
to England -1713

SARDINIA
to Austria -1714
to Savoy -1720

SICILY
to Savoy -1714
to Austria -1720

MOREA
to Turkey
1718

EUROPEAN TREATY
ADJUSTMENTS
1713 — 1720

0   400
Miles

soldiers and dig deep to find the necessary money to continue the war. The people responded with an extraordinary effort, and in 1711 the whole complexion of the war was altered by the death of the emperor and the accession of his son Charles, who would presumably have succeeded to the Spanish inheritance if the allies had won the war, and if Philip had been driven from the throne of Spain. The English, fearful of the disturbance of the balance of power, whether by Hapsburg or Bourbon victory, withdrew from the war and tried to make a separate peace. Only the emperor continued to fight, until at last all parties agreed to the peace of Utrecht (1713) and ancillary treaties signed by the emperor.

The Peace of Utrecht—Under the terms of the peace Philip was allowed to keep his Spanish throne on condition that it never be united with the throne of France. The Spanish Netherlands went to the emperor, and in future were called the Austrian Netherlands. The emperor also was granted some of the Spanish possessions in Italy. The Dutch were granted permission to fortify the boundaries between Holland and the new Austrian Netherlands. England was allowed to keep the fortress of Gibraltar captured during the war, and she gained a number of other concessions from Spain, while a number of French possessions in eastern America passed also to England. The duke of Savoy who had fought on the winning side became king of Sardinia as an indirect consequence of the peace, a fact that was to prove important in the unification of Italy by the Sardinian monarch in the nineteenth century.

The peace of Utrecht, which with certain minor changes affecting mostly eastern Europe determined the balance of power for the eighteenth century, put an end to French expansion, for the wars of the Spanish succession had proved that for the time there could be no further expansion without facing inevitable defeat. What had been gained in the earlier wars of Louis was not lost, but France was now to be forced to be content with what she had. Moreover, the Hapsburg Empire was now strong enough to act as an effective counterbalance to French expansionism should it ever again be revived. England had become a permanent factor to be reckoned with in the European power system, and it seemed clear that she could be relied upon if ever the Austrian Netherlands were to be again threatened by France. So the world settled down again into a period of peace, under the unquestioned cultural, but no longer political, leadership of France.

Colonial policy of Louis XIV

Before coming to the culture of France in the so-called Classical Age, a few words should be added on Louis' colonial policy and French colonial rivalry with the English. For well over a century France and England were almost continuously at war in the colonial territories. Whenever a great war between the two countries was in progress in Europe, the colonists of both nations eagerly resumed the struggle. In 1660 there were only some twenty-five hundred Frenchmen in the whole of the American mainland, and they were, of course, far outnumbered by the English immigrants. Twenty years later, as a consequence of the vigorous policy of Louis and Colbert, there were over twelve thousand. But the American mainland was not the chief colonial interest of either the French government or the French capitalists. In the French West Indies it was possible to make vast fortunes in the production of tropical products, especially sugar. So in these islands there were both more French immigrants and more invested capital than on the

mainland of America. The plantations, of course, were worked by Negro slaves, though the proportion of slaves to freemen was much lower in French territory than in English.

In eastern America the French owned Acadia (Nova Scotia) and Newfoundland. But far to the west of the English settlements in America they had also conquered a wide swath of American territory, including much of what is today French-speaking Canada. This included the valley of the Mississippi, which had been explored from Canada and Hudson Bay long before the Americans from the Atlantic coast states had penetrated so far inland. This territory was consolidated during the reign of Louis XIV by expeditions down the great river, culminating in the settlement of New Orleans a few years after Louis' death.

It was Colbert's policy both to encourage and finance emigration to America. After an experiment with private and then regulated companies, such as the West India Company, the government itself assumed full responsibility for the administration of the conquered territories. The French West Indies, which had been captured from Spain and disputed with England, were governed by the French monarchy from 1674. Thereafter some of the islands changed hands through the treaties which concluded wars between France and England in Europe. Nova Scotia, for instance, went to France after Louis' first war (1667, treaty of Bréda) and then had to be given to the English at the treaty of Utrecht. Newfoundland also was ceded by the latter treaty. But Canada and the Mississippi valley remained French at the death of Louis XIV, and it required the eighteenth-century wars before these territories also fell into English or American hands.

In East India again Colbert was the leading proponent of empire. He founded the French East India Company in 1664, and a number of strategic islands were captured. Coming into the field as late as they did and not moving into the Far East rivalry was again mostly with the English. After the Dutch War (treaty of Nijmegen, 1679) the

French lost all the posts on the mainland of India that the company had organized for trade and defense. Nevertheless the two posts that they retained, Surat and Pondichéry, were used as bases for expansion in the eighteenth century, and the struggle between the English and French for control of the lucrative trade of India became serious during that period. It should be added that the French at no time were willing and able to put forth efforts comparable to those of the English to conquer or retain their empire. Possessed of a flourishing and almost self-sufficient homeland, France had no essential need to be served by the possession of empire as had the English, with their increasing population and shortage of natural resources, and their need for exporting manufactured goods. For the same reason the possession of a navy was something of a luxury for the French, whereas it was a necessity for the English with their all-important trade routes to protect. The French capitalists with mercantile interests in North America and more particularly in the West Indies, represented but a small minority in the country. Thus it was more for prestige and to protect the interests of a few that France tried to maintain her overseas empire; and when the French monarch, as in the time of Louis XIV, was especially jealous of his prestige, then the interests of king and capitalists converged. It might have been a different story if the French bourgeoisie had controlled the king and could initiate policy as the English merchants could in certain circumstances control English imperial policy through Parliament.

THE ASCENDANCY OF FRENCH CULTURE

L'esprit classique

We have discussed in an earlier chapter the ascendancy of Italian culture during the Renaissance, and tried to distinguish the specifically Italian Renaissance spirit from that spirit as it was taken over and developed in other countries. It must have been clear from that chapter how different the *quality* of the Italian original contributions was from the work of any of their imitators abroad. Only when, as in Montaigne or Shakespeare, the Italian influence had been completely assimilated by the individual man of genius, and subordinated to his own French or English inheritance, did new works of real genius emerge.

In the seventeenth and eighteenth centuries the torch had passed to France. It cannot be said how much French influence in Europe owed to the cultural achievements of the French as a people, and how much to the prestige of the court of Louis XIV. But it may be surmised that far more was due to the former than to the latter, since French cultural prestige was at least as high in the eighteenth century when French political life had fallen on evil times. However it may be explained, there can be no doubt that French manners and customs (including cooking), to some extent French art, and above all French literature, were imitated everywhere in Europe.

The French language was learned by every educated man as his second tongue. In many foreign courts French was spoken in preference to the mother tongue, and no foreigner could consider himself a cultivated man until he had spent a considerable time in France. Yet in many fields the French still borrowed from Italy. The baroque was an Italian art style, used for the decoration of the interior of the palace of Versailles. Italian music, especially the opera, was far ahead of anything to be found in France; and indeed Louis XIV had to import Lulli from Italy to head the French Royal Academy of Music. What the French did achieve in the classical period of the seventeenth century was to modify all that they received, convert it into the French mode, and impose what they called *l'esprit classique* on what they imported, while producing great works of genius from their own native talent which were, of course, infused with this spirit.

The French classical spirit can best be described as the attempt to discipline natural vigor by the human reason. The effort may sometimes appear to impose too rigid a form upon material unsuited for the imposition of arbitrary rules, and requiring more exuberant expression. But when reason, within the artist himself, has already imposed its discipline, and from the fusion of reason and emotion emerges the finished work of art, with the form and content inseparable from one another so that the reader or viewer says at once that no other was possible, then the work may be said to be in tune with the classical spirit. This spirit was therefore an ideal and very far indeed from being expressed in all the works of the seventeenth century.

It is clear therefore that, appearing as it must in only a few men of genius, it cannot be imitated without first undergoing the travail of self-discipline. Foreign imitators of the French too often studied French form and imitated that, with the result that form and content do not fuse. They must fuse within the man of genius himself, and not all kinds of content can be compressed within a given form. The observance of the "three unities" of Aristotle (time, place, and action) became a fetish, and infraction of the rules became little less than a crime; while grammarians who did not understand the efforts of their greatest, Vaugelas, to assist writers in acceptable usage, regarded his precepts as unbreakable laws which could not be transgressed—thus helping to rigidify a living tongue and prepare the way for the later romantic reaction.

The work of the French classical period is thus often imperfectly understood. Because critics like Nicolas Boileau examined what was being done by his contemporaries and tried to derive canons of good form from it, he was permitted to become a pundit. Yet he was by all criteria one of the finest critics who ever lived, and was in his day regarded as an oracle. But his reputation really rested on his sureness of taste. He could recognize a work of genius when he saw it, and posterity has amply supported his judgments. No one was more severe than he on writers who did not measure up to his standards— writers who, it may be said, were nevertheless read and valued, as always, by the

reading public who did not share Boileau's taste, though they probably did not receive, nor need, pensions from the king.

But the men who did win Boileau's admiration, and the admiration of those arbiters of taste who thought like him, have actually survived to the present day, and are still appreciated, read, and performed by the French, and sometimes in foreign countries also. Of their particular kind it may be safely said that the best writers of the French seventeenth century have never been surpassed; but in all their works the form and content were fused; in all, the human reason is triumphant. Discipline has been imposed upon the material through self-discipline in the human being.

French classical drama

French drama before Louis XIV had scarcely a theater to call its own, and there can be no doubt that the hope of a performance at Versailles did encourage French dramatists, although a Parisian performance was possible also during the reign of Louis. Pierre Corneille (1600–1684) received a pension from the king, but did his best work in the age of Richelieu and Mazarin. His tragedy, though in a sense more powerful than that of his successor Jean Racine (1639–1699) idealizes his human beings, perhaps to excess, in this imitating the older Greek tragedy. His figures are painted as human idealism would have them rather than as human realism and respect for truth would see them. His heroes are more than life size; they must always undergo hardship before they win love; they renounce early joys for the sake of their ideals. The best plays of Corneille are noble and inspiring, and order and clarity are already present; though in some of his later works idealism, as so often, descends to preaching, and melodrama and pathos take the place of tragedy.

Order, clarity, and truth are never absent from the work of Racine, nor from that of Molière (1622–1673), who was perhaps the greatest of the world's writers of comedy. Both writers, unlike Corneille, were realists. Racine, with tenderness and com-

An engraving of Jean Baptiste Molière done by Pollet in 1833 from a contemporary portrait.

passion and profound psychological insight, records the lives of men and women, whereas Molière, sometimes savagely satirical, usually overlays his satire with gentle wit and humor. In Molière's greatest comedy, *Tartuffe,* he points inexorably to the fact that man is but man, limited by his humanity, and unable to transcend his limitations through a superimposed idealism, in spite of all his efforts of will to make himself other than he is. Such efforts transform the character of Orgon from a mild and respectable natural goodness into its very opposite; whereas Racine in *Phèdre* perceives the tragedy of passion which cannot be overcome by reason or will and must lead inevitably to disaster. It is instructive indeed to contrast Racine's treatment of this theme and Euripides' in his *Hippolytus,* and thus perceive the differences between human reason as it was understood by the French Racine and the Greek Euripides, how it may operate within man, and to contrast likewise the views of the two men on the realm to be ascribed to divine authority in the world.

French literature of the classic age

In a different branch of literature the *Characters* of La Bruyère, with their close observation of man, are unsurpassed in their field by any writer, living or dead. La Bruyère began where the Greek Theophrastus finished—and indeed the first book of his *Characters* is a translation of Theophrastus. La Rochefoucauld observed the foibles and weaknesses of men, and expressed them with a brilliant clarity in his *Maxims.* Perhaps greater than either of these two, because he attempted more, is La Fontaine, whose *Fables* of animals make their points with an unexampled pungency. In all of these writers one feels that no other form could have been used so effectively—as in yet another genre few letters have ever been written to equal those of Madame de Sevigné, still read and still translated for their exquisite urbanity and concealed artistry.

These are the greats of classical French literature, and all in their different ways truly express *l'esprit classique.* There were other great writers in foreign countries during this period, such as Milton or Dryden in England. Milton may have been a greater man of genius than any of the French writers of the day. But not even in his sonnets can it be suggested that the particular French combination of form and content was fused so perfectly, nor can one suggest for a moment that reason, in the French sense, dominated his work or dictated its content or form.

French art—Baroque tempered by classicism

In the field of art the baroque style was dominant in Italy and necessarily had its effects in France. At one time baroque was regarded, especially by followers of the influential German neoclassicists of the end of the eighteenth century, as a late decadent form of Italian Renaissance art—as flamboyant Gothic is a late decadent form of Gothic, and as even Hellenistic art is sometimes considered decadent classical Hellenic art. The elements of theatricality and extravagance undoubtedly present in baroque— much of the Versailles design and execution is in this style—tend to support this view. But it has also been argued convincingly by

"Blind Orion" by Nicolas Poussin. (COURTESY THE METROPOLITAN MUSEUM OF ART)

"Sunrise" by Claude Lorrain or Gellée. (COURTESY THE METROPOLITAN MUSEUM OF ART)

modern art historians and critics that baroque is the characteristic expression of what Spengler calls the "Faustian soul" of Western civilization, which yearns for the infinite, is dynamic and vital, and is not at all "classical" in the usual sense of that word. In baroque there is far more life and movement than in neoclassical art—a new and original use of space and groupings. Above all there is a tension, such a tension as has always been characteristic of life in Western civilization, which looks both outward and inward and is unable to reconcile the contradiction or explain the relationship between the outer and the inner. To such a view the French *esprit classique* itself is fundamentally baroque, an attempt, never fully successful, to discipline its exuberant vitality and its profound exploration of the heights and the depths. To such a view, also, Corneille is the baroque dramatist par excellence, Milton the baroque poet, and Rembrandt the greatest of the baroque painters.

Nicholas Poussin (1593–1665) and Claude Gellée (or Lorrain, 1600–1682) were the two greatest painters of the reign of Louis xiv, and were long regarded as the two chief exponents of classicism in painting. But it is pointed out by the art historians that Poussin was certainly influenced by the many years he spent in Rome, the center of baroque at the time. He not only painted a number of magnificent battle scenes, but even in his famed landscapes there is an idealization characteristic of baroque, and a kind of tension which communicates itself to the beholder, in spite of the way in which Poussin has undoubtedly succeeded in establishing order and harmony in his often huge canvases. The luminous landscapes of Gellée have sometimes been considered to reflect nothing of the still turbulent age in which he was living, but their ideal quality is claimed for the baroque, as is also their sense of unity. What must certainly be said, however, is that in both Poussin and Gellée the mind has indeed triumphed over the emotions, and what is shown in the paintings is the result of a conscious effort to attain an inner serenity, even though baroque exuberance and vitality may lie not far below.

It is not too easy to say how much of the artistic excellence of France during the period was due to the monarch. In spite of Louis' efforts to be dignified, one cannot help feeling that vulgarity lurks only just beneath the surface, as in the overdecoration of the interior of Versailles. Louis himself was no artist and it is doubtful if he even had good taste. Who indeed knows what the man beneath the planned appearance really was? He certainly was willing to take credit for the cultural achievements of his age, and he was perfectly willing to spend money to enhance the prestige of his court, including the possible ennui of sitting through a few command performances of distinguished playwrights approved by Boileau.

It is difficult to find much good to say of the court itself, with its tame nobles cavorting in the park and exercising themselves and their beasts amid the artificial canals, fountains, and carefully prepared hunting grounds, then returning to the palace to perform their solemn ritual in the king's bedchamber. This was the part of court life for which Louis himself was responsible, and though it had its political uses, it is not one of the great achievements of the French classical age. Louis, however, may be justly credited with not having spoiled its major achievements; this in itself is perhaps something of an achievement for such an autocratic, intolerant, and self-satisfied monarch.

▶ Russian absolutism

THE REIGNS OF MICHAEL AND ALEXIS (1613–1676)

Strengthening of the royal power

If France was the country where legal absolutism limited by ancient Germanic liberties and traditions flourished most strongly, a different type of absolutism, unmodified by the ancient native traditions of liberty, grew to fruition in seventeenth-century Russia. We have already noted in Chapter 19 the development of this absolutism in the sixteenth century, and the manner in which Tsar Ivan iv was able to crush the power of the boyars by setting up machinery that gave him command of enough force to free him from dependence on the doubtful loyalty of nobles. We have also noted how the boyars were for a time able to control the crown during the regency and "time of troubles" that followed the death of Ivan. Finally we saw how the national assembly, or *zemsky sobor,* wearying of the anarchy and war of the "time of troubles" finally chose a boyar named Michael Romanov as tsar. Though Michael at this time (1613) was only a youth of sixteen, and the surviving boyars may well have hoped to be able to control him, on being chosen tsar he was compelled by the logic of his position to desert his former class, and he continued the antiboyar policy of his predecessors.

Michael (1613–1645) and Alexis his son (1645–1676), who ruled for the greater part of the seventeenth century, were, like the tsars of the sixteenth century, engaged in foreign wars for the greater part of their reigns. This fact strengthened their positions as autocrats, since the armies, as had been perceived during the "time of troubles," required a unified command and loyalty to the state, best represented in the person of the tsar. The power of the boyars dwindled away to nothing, while the star of the gentry, tied to the monarch, was constantly in the ascendant. The wars were duly settled, though at heavy cost in money and territory, to the advantage of Poland and Sweden, the principal enemies.

Encouragement of foreign advisers

But the tsars and their ministers came to recognize during these reigns that Russia, for all her size and population, was so backward in military technique that she must learn from the West, if ever she were to become the power she was capable of becoming, and exercise the power and influence to which her size and population entitled her. During the seventeenth century encouragement was given to foreign merchants to settle in Moscow and other cities, where they were given a status and privileges that enabled them to become largely independent of the tsarist government. Foreign officers

were hired in considerable numbers to train the Russian armies. Nevertheless native Russians remained jealous and distrustful of the foreigners and especially resented the implication that they were superior to themselves. The average uneducated Russian did not wish to be educated, especially by foreigners, nor did he admit the backwardness of his countrymen. Russians resented the fact that foreigners, when in royal employ, received far better salaries than themselves. Unlike the tsar, they did not recognize that monetary inducements were necessary to persuade foreigners to come to live in such a primitive and uncivilized place as Moscow—and indeed they would hardly have been willing to admit that Moscow was uncivilized and primitive. As they had not seen other European cities, Moscow to them was the very center of civilization.

The peasantry and the Cossacks

Michael and his son Alexis for a time kept on fairly good terms with the surviving boyars, gentry, and merchants, though they had no intention of granting them any real power. The *zemsky sobor* was called until the middle of the century for the purpose of giving advice and ratifying legislation. It could be relied upon for such tasks, since the tsars were genuinely anxious to relieve the disabilities of the small middle class and promote their efficiency, while the bulk of the legislation was directed toward the degrading of the peasantry, a purpose approved by the dominant gentry. During this period the peasants gradually sank to the position of serfs or even slaves. They were tied to the land and to their immediate masters, their taxes and compulsory service were increased. Stringent laws were passed against runaway serfs, who could be bought and sold by their masters like chattels, even without any transfer of land ownership. The rule of the time may thus best be characterized as a rule by monarch and gentry, based on the complete subjection and near slavery of the peasant class on which the whole government and economy were based. It is not therefore surprising that peasant uprisings were common, culminating in the great revolt led by the Cossack Stenka Razin in 1670, which was suppressed only with difficulty by the tsar.

During much of the century the nomad warriors called the Cossacks were troublesome to the Russian monarchs. The bulk of these men, who were called by the name of the region where they lived, were in the territories to the south and southeast of Russia which was nominally ruled by the Poles. Others, however, were congregated in Russia itself, and for several centuries carried out a remarkable series of expeditions which finally led them as far as the Pacific. These Cossacks were willing to submit to the nominal suzerainty of the tsar of Russia, in exchange for what in the earlier centuries amounted to virtual independence. But those who remained in the Polish or Russian Ukraine resented the power of the Polish monarchs and the Russian tsars, and constantly rebelled against their authority, playing one side against the other in the numerous wars between Russia and Poland. Ultimately most of them were absorbed into the growing Russian state, but in the peasant rebellions individual Cossacks frequently supplied leadership to the peasants, and their lands acted as a magnet to peasants trying to escape the burdens of their servitude in their homeland.

Schism in the Orthodox Church—The "Old Believers"

The second half of the seventeenth century saw a severe struggle develop within the Church. In 1589 the metropolitan of Moscow had been permitted by his fellow leaders of the Orthodox Church to assume the title of patriarch, which gave him full authority over the Russian Church, although, as before, his appointment had to be approved, if not actually made, by the tsar. In this struggle the strong-minded patriarch Nikon had the backing of tsar Alexis, a devoted and pious son of the Church, until he went too far with his reforms and innovations and threatened to disrupt the unity and peace of the state. Then he was degraded and banished, but the reforms were maintained in a form only slightly modified from that originally suggested by Nikon. The struggle, however, gave Peter the Great an opportunity to abolish the patriarchate and put the Church more completely under the control of the state, directed by a synod, whose head was a layman appointed by the tsar.

The schism within the Church arose out of the divergence between the religious customs of the Russian and the parent Greek Orthodox Church. Variations in ritual and doctrine had arisen in the centuries during which the Churches had had little contact with one another. Nikon came to the conclusion that the Greeks and not the Russians were correct, and determined to use all his authority as patriarch to restore Russian practices to their pristine purity. He probably did not imagine in advance what a furor he would arouse; he must have underestimated the fanatical conservatism of the Russian believer and of the lesser clergy. An incipient national feeling was aroused. The "Old Believers," as the conservatives were called, were utterly confident that everything Russian was superior to everything Greek, and that everything old and hallowed by long tradition was superior to everything new. Vast numbers were willing to submit to every form of persecution rather than alter their beliefs or ritual in any respect, however minor in our eyes. The Old Believers persisted right up to the Russian Revolution of the twentieth century, even though diminished in numbers by the persecutions of Church and state.

Summary—Foundations of absolutism of Peter the Great

During the reigns of Michael and Alexis the more technically efficient foreign nations presented a constant threat to the integrity of Russia, especially Poland and Sweden. Alexis therefore made it part of his task to encourage foreigners to settle in the country, and tried hard to improve the army. Though the *streltsy* or palace guard remained officered by Russian nobles and gentry, and all landowners, whether gentry or old nobles, still had to recruit most of the army from their estates, the army by the time of the death of Alexis may be considered as a willing tool in the hands of the tsars. In spite of some foreign training it was not as yet very efficient, as was to be shown in the early wars of Peter the Great. But in the main it may be said that the early Romanovs had done their work well, and thoroughly prepared the ground for the work of Peter. The peasantry were thoroughly cowed, and in any case lacked leadership for any concerted resistance to the tsar; the boyars and gentry were largely indistinguishable and both were by now tied to the crown and dependent upon it; the merchants were accustomed to providing financial resources to assist the tsar in his wars, while the monarch mainly used for his administration royal appointees and went regularly for advice only to such men as he wished. The Church had had to lean heavily upon the authority of the tsar to suppress the schism within its ranks. The *zemsky sobor* was rarely called and represented no alternative source of authority. The greatest need now was for more efficient administration and government. This Peter the Great was to provide in full measure.

THE REIGN OF PETER THE GREAT (1682–1725)

Government and administration— Emphasis on efficiency

At the death of Tsar Alexis, the heir was a sickly youth named Theodore, son of Alexis' first wife. His second wife, however, had borne him a son named Peter who was obviously of entirely different caliber. Theodore was allowed to become tsar, but died after six years (1682), leaving a younger brother Ivan, also a weak youth, and Peter to dispute the throne. The patriarch and the people of Moscow—the *zemsky sobor* was no longer of enough importance to warrant consultation—decided that Peter should be tsar, to the discomfort of Sophia, the able sister of Theodore and Ivan, who wished to rule in the name of her incompetent brother. The determined young woman enlisted the help of the streltsy and was in fact able to rule for a period until Peter took the govern-

ment into his own hands with the aid of an opposition party in the streltsy. Thereafter his rule was undisputed.

Peter was a man of extraordinary capacity and energy, ruthless and efficient, driving all his servants to the utmost and himself doing more than any of them. He was also flexible and intelligent. But above all he was an improviser and opportunist of genius, with an unequaled capacity for quick decision. His willingness to acquire knowledge wherever it was to be won made him into the real founder of modern Russia.

He recognized at once through defeats suffered at the hands of Western powers that Russia was so backward that she could not hope to catch up with the West by the slow processes of natural growth. The West must be pillaged for its ideas which, in the West, had been developed over long periods of time. These ideas must then be put to use in Russia by all the means available to an autocrat. Leaving the government in the hands of subordinates, he set out himself with an embassy, traveling incognito to all the countries in Europe from which he hoped to learn. He examined their techniques, especially those likely to be of use to him in his wars; he examined their machines, for the understanding of which he had a natural talent that he used to the full. He hired foreign technicians whose task it would be to train the Russians while for the moment he used the technicians themselves to modernize the country for immediate practical purposes. By such processes he built himself an army and navy which were able to defeat the great power of Sweden, and force the Swedes to a humiliating peace which greatly enlarged the Russian state and gave it access to the Baltic.

For many years Peter was occupied with his army and the war with Sweden. During this period he laid a heavy hand upon his people for the purpose of recruiting enough troops and training them in modern warfare. No longer was it left to the landowners to enlist their serfs in the army. Imperial governors and agents recruited them; and though there were many desertions, punished by fearful penalties, the armies were finally raised and they won their victories. The officer class was made entirely dependent on the tsar. All nobles had been liable for military service in the past. Now, however, they lost all hereditary right to promotion. They were to hold rank entirely in accordance with their ability. A man not previously a noble was ennobled at once on receiving his commission from the tsar. Such recruits into the officer class were, as a rule, members of the gentry rather than boyars, so that the distinction between the old nobility and the new was lost altogether. All were thus bound to the tsar, dependent entirely upon him.

Everyone in the country was by law made liable for state service. The tsar could even force his people to go to school and learn what he considered necessary. Many were even compelled to go abroad to study. State service in Peter's eyes meant not only service in the army but service in industry if necessary. Important industries were started under the spur of the tsar, always with the expressed intention of somehow, by forced growth, catching up with the West.

Peter set up several new institutions for the purpose of increasing efficiency. Regulations were drafted by a professional body called the Senate, completely under the control of the tsar, who kept watch over them to see that they were not idle. He set up various specialized departments of state, some of which included foreigners. These departments had collective rather than individual responsibility. No one in the state was ever permitted much degree of initiative if Peter could prevent it. He was himself the source of all initiative and authority, and he made every effort to supervise the work of his servants as well as issuing instructions. For the purpose of checking up on the work of his servants he set up a system of spies and informers to see that corruption was stamped out. Endless laws were passed to try to prevent it, but they had no more success than such laws usually have. Opportunities for corruption were numerous, for vast numbers of indirect taxes were imposed, as well as a poll tax, based on a census taken by the tsar with his usual pitiless efficiency.

The whole effectiveness of the system depended upon the ability of the tsar. Though special tasks were distributed locally throughout the country, responsibility was not really shared. At its basis was force rather than consent. Peter was hated as few men have ever been, though he could not but command respect and obedience. Peasants and religious men called him the antichrist, and he was regarded by them with a superstitious awe. Nevertheless, in spite of constant small and hopeless revolts there was never any widespread organized revolt against him, and he cannot be regarded except as a highly successful monarch who achieved the ends he set for himself, with very few failures debited against him.

Contrasts and comparison with French and Byzantine absolutism

The reader will appreciate the similarity of the system of Peter the Great to that of the later Roman and Byzantine empires. The incentive was the same. By all means the army had to be built up and made capable of resistance to invasion and, if possible, of expansion into new areas. The state had the first call on the services of every man; compulsion would be used when found to be necessary. Governmental institutions would be changed by the ruler in every case to fit the needs of the state. The Russia of Peter the Great was as nearly a totalitarian state in the modern sense as any known until the twentieth century.

It will also be evident from this brief account in how many respects Russian absolutism contrasted with the absolutism of Louis xiv, whose state by no extension of the word can be considered "totalitarian." Though there was in Russia no doubt a widespread element of consent, this consent, such as it was, rested on a semireligious veneration for the person of the tsar, whose word was law and who ruled by divine right. He was not too unlike the ruler of the theories of Hobbes, or at least more like him than any other monarch of the time. But there is also in the Russian tsar an element of the divine ruler of ancient Egypt as well as of the late Roman or Byzantine emperor.

PETER'S "WINDOWS" ON THE BALTIC

■ PETER'S GAINS ON THE BALTIC AT SWEDEN'S EXPENSE TREATY OF NYSTADT (1721)

Problem of the succession

The great problem of the succession, always a difficulty in autocratic states, as we frequently have had occasion to notice, was solved by Peter late in his life when his son showed signs of rebellion and conservatism. Since this could obviously not be tolerated, he had this son put to death, and declared that the tsar alone could determine the succession by nomination. However, as Peter himself did not perform this important duty, the throne was disputed amongst his successors much as before, as it might well

have been disputed even if he had named his successor. But his decree shows at least that he was aware of the problem that had troubled Augustus and many others since Augustus' time. In fact the Russian monarchy remained hereditary, modified only by the customary assassinations.

Wars with Charles XII of Sweden

When Peter became king the great power in the Baltic world was, as we have seen, the kingdom of Sweden, whose throne was still in the Vasa family, noted for its military prowess. The Black Sea was in Turkish hands and the smaller Caspian Sea in Persian hands. In his early years Peter wrested some concessions from the Persians, but the Caspian Sea had no useful outlet. What he needed was what he called "a window on the West." First he tried conclusions with the Turks on the Black Sea, seeking to wrest the port of Azov from them. Unsuccessful in 1695, he built a navy during the winter on the river above Azov, returned the next year, and captured the port. Later in his reign, he had, however, to give it back to the Turks. So at last he came to concentrate his efforts on the destruction of Swedish power in the Baltic; and here there were many allies available, all anxious to chop off some of the extensive Swedish domains.

The opportunity seemed to present itself when the Swedish throne was inherited by Charles XII, who was but a boy of fifteen with no military experience. But as it happened, Charles was one of the greatest warriors hitherto produced by the West,

although his talents appear to have been confined to the military sphere. Charles, faced by an alliance of the Danes, Poles, and Russians, struck a lightning blow at Denmark, and within two weeks had forced her out of the war. He turned on Peter, whom he defeated with the greatest of ease in spite of the fact that the Russian army was five times the size of the Swedish (battle of Narva, 1700). Then he turned on Poland, and forced the German monarch of Poland off the throne in favor of his own candidate.

But Peter, as we have seen, had learned his lesson, even though it had been expensive. He knew that his army was in no position to defend itself against the highly trained and disciplined Swedish forces. He therefore put into effect, in the time available to him before the renewal of the Swedish attack, the reorganization of the army and the home front already discussed. He also developed a new strategy to deal with the momentarily expected invasion.

The terrible Swedish monarch, still only

Portrait of Peter the Great attributed to Aert de Gelder, now in the Rijksmuseum at Amsterdam.

twenty-six years old, finally invaded Russia in 1708, but Peter adopted the tactics used later by Alexander I and then by Stalin, scorching the earth so that the Swedes could obtain no supplies, and harassing the army by sudden raids on the flanks. Thus Charles was drawn deeper into Russia and was unable to capture his original objective of Moscow. In 1709, after a terrible winter that had been more than usually cold, he tried a campaign in the south, but was held up by the strongly fortified fortress of Poltava. Here the Russians gained a complete victory, destroying almost the whole Swedish army. Charles himself was fortunate to escape to Turkey with his life. In Turkey he stirred up the Turks to declare war on Russia. But as soon as the Turks had retaken Azov they were willing to make peace, and Charles found himself an unwelcome guest in Constantinople. After various adventures he returned to Sweden, and was killed shortly

afterward. The war dragged on for a while under his successor but was finally settled at the peace of Nystadt in 1721. The gains made by Peter were enormous, and Sweden thereafter rapidly declined to the status of a second-class power. Russia had gained Estonia, Livonia, the Karelian Isthmus, Ingria, and the important fortress of Viborg.

St. Petersburg—"Window on the West"

Meanwhile Peter, before the second Russian campaign of Charles XII, had begun to build his new capital of St. Petersburg in territory just wrested from the Swedes. And Charles had made no attempt to recapture it, preferring to try conclusions with the Russian army in which case the infant St. Petersburg would presumably fall safely into his hands. Since, as it happened, the Russians won, Peter was able to continue his building program unmolested.

The city was designed by Italian and

Equestrian portrait of Charles XII of Sweden, the young conqueror who was finally defeated by Peter the Great. Portrait by a member of the Swedish eighteenth-century school of painters. (COURTESY THE OWNER, DR. ERNST FREDRICK WERNER ALEXANDERSON, AND FRICK ART REFERENCE LIBRARY)

French architects, and built without any regard whatever for the human lives lost in its construction. It is by far the most Western of Russian cities, and from the beginning it was regarded with detestation by a large majority of the Russian people. It was no whim that decided the victorious Bolsheviks to transfer the capital to Moscow when tsardom at last fell in the twentieth century, for St. Petersburg was a monument both to Peter's power and to his westernizing policy. Filled with factories, docks, and military supply centers, and protected by a nearby fortress at Kronstadt, it was from the beginning thronged with foreigners and under foreign influence. Nobles were expected to build their town houses there, and themselves in time tended to become westernized; sometimes they even used their native language as second to French.

St. Petersburg was a true window on the West, the window that Peter had always desired. But St. Petersburg was not Russia, just as Peter's absolutism was not French. It has remained for us in the twentieth century—when Russia has become the greatest of the European powers, with a window to the West and a window to the East—to learn how the West and the East are to be reconciled if the world is to escape destruction through their enmity.

▶ Suggestions for further reading

It is probably safe to say that French history and particularly French culture have only in rare cases been adequately dealt with by English-speaking historians. The material covered in this chapter is therefore much better studied in any of a number of French histories, especially in such a large-scale work as the history of France by Ernest Lavisse and his collaborators. French Classicism is indigenous to France and is unlike the classical period anywhere else, and it seems to be difficult for other peoples to appreciate it in the manner of the French themselves. One of the best books on French classicism, Henri Peyre, *Le classicisme français,* has never even been translated into English. There is, however, one work which comes close to being really satisfying by a Franco-American, Albert Guérard, *The Life*

and Death of an Ideal: France in the Classical Age (New York: G. Braziller, 1956), which is slightly uneven, but does succeed in explaining the ideal of classicism and relating the events of the age of Louis xiv to the ideal. Two books by Germans in the historical series, the Rise of Modern Europe, edited by William Langer, have some valuable insights into seventeenth-century France: Carl J. Friedrich, *The Age of the Baroque, 1610–1660* and Frederick L. Nussbaum, *The Triumph of Science and Reason, 1660–1685* (New York: Harper & Brothers, 1952, 1953). The former, by a man noted for his work in the history of art, has an especially good summation of modern theories about the baroque in art and life.

On the historical material of the period, David Ogg, *Europe in the Seventeenth Century* (2nd edit., London: A. & C. Black, Ltd., 1931), is a clear and useful work dealing with the countries of Europe separately and relating each to the other. Cicely Wedgwood has another useful little work on Richelieu, C. V. Wedgwood, *Richelieu and the French Monarchy* (New York: The Macmillan Company, 1950), specially written for the casual reader, obviously based on a good deal of learning, but in my view, in places rather severely oversimplified for the serious student. Paul Doolin, *The Fronde* (Cambridge, Mass.: Harvard University Press, 1935) is a short scholarly work, but makes the Fronde rather clearer and more purposeful than it seems to have been to its participants.

There are two good short books on the age of Louis xiv, one in the Home University Library, David Ogg, *Louis XIV* (London: Oxford University Press, 1956), and the other in the Berkshire series, L. B. Packard, *The Age of Louis XIV* (New York: Henry Holt and Company, Inc., 1929). A curiosity worth mentioning by Voltaire, *The Age of Louis XIV* (London: J. M. Dent & Sons, Ltd., Everyman's Library, 1951) is available in English, but should be treated with extreme caution as history, though it is most satisfactory as entertainment, which was certainly Voltaire's primary intention. Voltaire is more interested in the foibles and idiosyncrasies of the monarch and his court than he was in recounting the mere facts of interest to historians. He even includes a long disquisition on the manners and customs of the Chinese in order to point out the obvious cultural superiority of the heathen Chinese to the French barbarian Christians of the seventeenth century.

An excellent politico-economic history which casts a useful sidelight on the governmental system of France during the whole ancien régime, although it is a comparison between the French and English systems, is John Ulric Nef, *Industry and Government in France and England, 1540–1640* (Philadelphia: American Philosophical Society, 1940).

Mention was made in an earlier chapter of G. Vernadsky, *A History of Russia* (4th edit., Completely revised, New Haven: Yale University Press, 1954), as the standard book for the study of Russian history. For the period under study in this chapter Vernadsky, in my view, lacks something of the clarity visible in most of his book. It is clear that he thoroughly understands the material but he overestimates the ability of the reader to absorb and understand such a severely compressed account in a period and civilization of which he is likely to know very little in advance. Thus the work becomes rather too technical and in places confusing. Much simpler and clearer are both of the two following works, neither of which devote a great deal of space to the period covered by this chapter and Chapter 19, but do bring out clearly the facts needed to understand the complicated structure of local and feudal rights upon which the absolutist structure was superimposed. These are: Anatole G. Mazour, *Russia, Past and Present* (New York: D. Van Nostrand Company, Inc., 1951) and Sidney S. Harcave, *Russia, a History* (Philadelphia: J. B. Lippincott Company, 1952). By far the best history of Russia, however, is V. O. Kliuchevsky, *A History of Russia* (5 vols., London: J. M. Dent & Sons, Ltd., 1911–1931), but it is very long and detailed for the beginning student, though in no way difficult to read. Volumes 2 through 4 are devoted to the period discussed in Chapters 19 and 21 of this text, with Volume 4 spent entirely on the work of Peter the Great. Best known in America is Bernard Pares, *A History of Russia*, a condensed version of which once appeared in a Mentor edition, but reissued recently in its complete form with an introduction by Richard Pares (New York: Alfred A. Knopf, 1953). The book is well written, interesting, and generally accurate although it was written by a lover of Russia rather than a professional historian. It contains much information not easily available elsewhere and has a great deal of interesting and occasionally colorful detail. Nevertheless it is not a book to be recommended unreservedly, for it is not strong on analysis, and the descriptions of Russian institutions are occasionally confusing and were perhaps confusing even to its author. It can well be read in conjunction with either Mazour or Harcave, which are rather bare in just those things provided by Pares.

Finally, mention should be made of a very interesting study by a Marxist who was evidently really convinced by the official ideology, but was always a fine, indeed brilliant, historian. The facts chosen to stress are not those found in ordinary histories, but do not become any the less true for that. The book, therefore, is well worth reading, or at least worth examining carefully, though it should hardly be read by itself. This is Mikhail N. Pokrovsky, *History of Russia from the Earliest Times to the Rise of Commercial Capitalism* (New York: International Publishers, 1931). It is well translated by J. D. Clarkson and M. R. Griffiths.

22

The Rise of the Scientific Outlook

Contrast between medieval and modern outlook on the world • Growth of idea of world-machine: From Copernicus to Newton • Descartes and Cartesianism: Dichotomy between mind and matter • The progress of empirical science • Consequences of the Scientific Revolution • Summary: The importance and permanence of the Scientific Revolution

---

▶ **The modern view of the world—Contrast with medieval outlook**

In this final chapter there remains to be considered a development in the realm of the human mind that may prove to be the most important of all the contributions of Western civilization to world history. Its effects, direct and indirect, upon the lives of all people in the world have already been profound and entirely beyond calculation. Already it has made possible the complete extinction of life on our planet and it may have put an end to large-scale wars through mutual fear of reprisals. In advanced countries it has made abundance for the first time into a problem, raising the question of how mankind can use leisure creatively, in a manner worthy of human potentialities and human dignity. It has made possible the world-wide abolition of poverty; and it has altered and will continue to alter in a radical manner all those established forms of government which evolved in earlier ages and which have been studied in this book.

Essentially this development may be expressed in one sentence. Modern man has emancipated himself from the world of nature, and no longer looks upon it as a world to be admired and reverenced, but to be manipulated for his use. And the world of nature has shown itself to be amenable to such manipulation, while the gods have not, as yet, intervened, as the Greeks believed they would, to chastise the *hybris* of man in an effective and unchallengeable manner.

This development is new in the history of mankind. There had been science in ancient times; Hellenistic science, indeed, had been far more objective than any science that followed, and had few preconceptions such as those which vitiated too much of medieval science. But the Greek search was exclusively for knowledge as something worthy to be sought for its own sake. "All men by nature desire to know," Aristotle had said, thus giving expression to the Greek view that man as a thinking being should develop his powers of thought by exercising it on the world of nature. But, though modern science was pioneered by men who sought only to know and to understand, it was seen by publicists of science, foremost amongst them Francis, Lord Bacon of Verulam (1561–1626), that this knowledge could and should be made useful for mankind. This was the crucial step that differentiates modern from Greek science, to perceive that scientific knowledge is an instrument to bend nature to human purposes—that knowledge, in short, is power. This it is that has led to the modern world as we know it.

To be able to use the world of nature, it is necessary that knowledge of it be exact and accurate. This knowledge must be independent of man's subjective feelings. In ordinary conversation one may speak of something as being hot or cold, light or heavy; but the expression is scientifically meaningless, since all that such a remark states is that to our sense perception the object has such or such a quality. Almost all ancient and medieval science was based on such qualitative descriptions, with which nothing can be done.

Modern science is based upon the quantitative, upon the ability to weigh and measure exactly. Its descriptions are objective; we do not have different opinions about weights and measurements. All men will agree on the matter, and the reference will be to some objective standard. If the heat of an object is raised or lowered then it will, subjectively, be more hot or more cold to the sense of touch. But the information is useless unless the degree of added or lowered heat can be measured and repeated at will. Exact measurements can make the heat subject to control. Ancient and medieval science looked upon the qualities of objects as residing in some way in them. Aristotle spoke of potentiality and actuality; he speculated about what a thing could become because of its potentialities. Modern science has found this to be irrelevant, and has relegated such descriptions to the realm of the philosopher. What the scientist wishes to do is to determine what causes the change in nature, and his concept of cause is what it is that he can apply which will repeat the change, or what it is without which the change will not take place. This requires the measurement of the change by objective criteria—not merely observing it through the fallible human senses.

Traditional medieval science had reached a dead end. Nothing more could be gained by it except more observations and more aesthetic appreciation of the marvels of the universe. Somehow the world must be made amenable to more exact methods of observation. *How* change took place must be perceived rather than simply saying that it did take place, thereby showing that it could take place, and there must be a good reason for it—which was essentially the medieval method. And the good reason, for most medieval men, was to be found in the purpose of the change, that, in some way or another, good was served by it. Or, in Aristotelian terms, efficient causes for phenomena must take the place of final and formal causes.

The great scientists of the early modern period built, of course, upon the work of their predecessors. Observations in all fields were available to them; and in some centers of study, such as the Italian University of Padua, discontent had been expressed regarding the traditional theories which did not seem to fit the observed facts. But when great men such as Kepler (1571–1630), Galileo (1564–1642), Descartes (1596–1650), and Newton (1642–1727) used their new mathematical tools to explain the *how* of the universe, they were well aware of the significance of what they were doing. All recognized that they had stumbled upon a new method which was radically different from those used by their predecessors. The world, to them, seemed to be opening up its secrets; and all used their imaginations to speculate upon what would be revealed to them next, and what a tremendous field of study had suddenly become manifest to them —first the world, and then the whole universe, all comprehensible to man if the right method were used. The world was capable of being understood and not only admired; and, as Bacon insisted, if it could be understood, the knowledge could be turned to the uses of man.

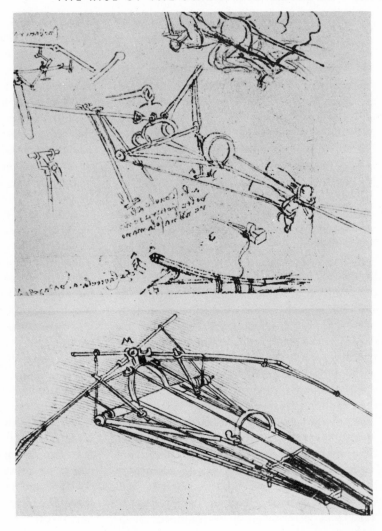

Leonardo da Vinci (1452–1519) was interested in everything that pertained to man and his world. Though he is not known to have made any inventions himself, he was well aware of what was being done in his time, and he speculated endlessly on the great possibilities that would some day be realized from the development of science and technology. These two pictures represent Leonardo's design for a flying machine as it appears in his notebooks, and a model constructed by Dr. Roberto Guatelli for the International Business Machines Corporation. (BOTH PICTURES COURTESY OF INTERNATIONAL BUSINESS MACHINES CORPORATION)

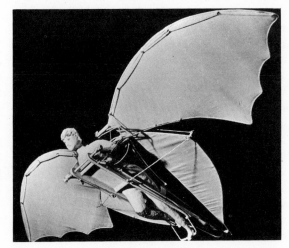

► **Trial and error versus exact mathematical knowledge**

There can be little doubt that practical needs already felt in the Middle Ages acted as a stimulus to study. The gunner working with the new artillery could not be satisfied with the weapons at his disposal, nor could the navigator be happy with his instruments. It was possible to go on trying indefinitely to improve the explosive material at the gunner's disposal by mere trial and error, possible even to improve gun sights and see at what angle the gun should be pointed for maximum effect. Such experiments could be tested at once. But still the gunner would not know *why* his experiment had been successful. And progress would be extraordinarily slow while each minor change was put into operation and its effects observed by experience. On the other hand, if the angle of the trajectory could be measured accurately, if, without trial and error and without experiment, it could be known in advance how far a cannon ball would carry for a particular kind of gun with a particular explosive charge, then all that would be needed would be to make the necessary calculations *in advance,* and then construct a gun according to the specifications indicated, and see whether it would perform as predicted. Trial and error would be reduced to a minimum.

For centuries, of course, from the time, indeed, of Cro-magnon man and his bow and arrow, there had been trial and error, and the results had been transmitted by practical men to future generations. Cro-magnon man did not feel the need for a theory of motion. He knew from experience how far his arrow would carry when sped from his bow. Nor, no doubt, did the late medieval gunner know anything about Aristotelian theories of motion, and would have cared nothing for them if he had known. But the time was at hand when the university scholars were to feel the need for observing how guns actually worked in order to test their theories of motion, and ceased to be content with studying and teaching the theories they had received from their predecessors and taken on trust: while outstanding individuals such as Leonardo da Vinci (1452–1519), one of whose fanciful "inventions" is illustrated on another page, studied the science of their day when called upon to give their attention to the improvement of artillery and succeeded in making notable progress in this science.

It was an important moment in the history of the world when it was perceived by men of learning that their theories had to conform to the facts of the practical world or be abandoned. This truth was only slowly accepted by the medieval scientist and scholar, accustomed to taking his facts on authority, whether they were facts of science or facts of religion. The customary method was to hold the received theory as true; then, if some discrepancy were discovered, to explain the discrepancy *away.* This was called "saving the phenomena." Only slowly did men come to recognize that the Greeks, on whose scientific theories all their own theories were based, had themselves observed the phenomena and devised theories to fit them. If they had observed faultily then the theories based on their observations would necessarily collapse with them.

The recognition of the relation between theory and fact was the beginning of the partnership between the scientist and the engineer which is the basis of modern scientific progress. The scientist plans an experiment in little, which the engineer will later carry out on a large scale, when the results of the scientific experiments have been confirmed by constant repetition. Thus trial and error as a method disappeared from fields where there is a substantial body of approved theory and where planned experiments are possible. Only in fields such as medicine and some branches of biology, where theory is primitive and experiment difficult, does trial and error survive as an acceptable method. Its disappearance is due to the triumph of the mathematical and quantitative method of studying the universe which first arose in early modern times.

► **The growth of the idea of the world machine**

MOTION IN THE WORLD

Early theories of motion

One of the first things to be noticed about the world as visible phenomenon is the prevalence of movement in it. Everything is observed either at rest or in motion. For practical purposes, such as those of the gunner, knowledge of the way in which movement takes place, how movement is to be calculated, is clearly essential. The monk contemplating the heavens is also aware of the fact that the heavenly bodies appear to move. Why should they move? the medieval and ancient scientist asked. Why should they not stand still? What purpose did the movement fulfill?

It was one of the most fundamental assumptions of the ancient and medieval world that a "natural" condition of an object was to be at rest; only if some force were applied was this natural inertia disturbed. Some force was therefore needed to explain the movement of the heavenly bodies, comparable with the force which it was believed was needed to explain the movement of earthly objects. It was believed that all motion was communicated from one body to another, and a hypothesis had been handed down from the classical world, and elaborated by medieval thinkers, to the effect that the movement of the heavenly bodies was to be accounted for by communicated motion from a postulated prime mover, which was identified by Aristotle and Aquinas as God. Each of the known planets had its orbit of movement, which had to be imagined as actual crystalline translucent spheres, which received their motion from the next contiguous sphere, the whole receiving motion from the *primum mobile,* the dwelling place of God, eloquently described by Dante. Only the earth was at rest, in the lowest place in the universe, unless one accepted hell as a definite place, in which case it was lower even than the earth. The

earth was not an exalted place, but the lowest—and low was used in a qualitative sense as well as merely descriptive. It was not like one of the perfect unchangeable planets wheeling around it in a perfect circular movement, but was a corrupt, changing, degenerate body, corrupted indeed by the sin of Adam, and only made capable of redemption by the deed of Christ. If the difficulty of accepting the Copernican theory of the position of the earth in the hierarchy of planets is to be fully appreciated, it is essential to understand how closely this conception of the motionless earth was bound up with the prevalent theory of motion.

It was, then, the nature of all movement to cease as soon as the motion communicated to it ceased. At that moment all objects sought their "natural" place. Not all objects, however, fell to the earth, because the earth was not the natural resting place of all things. On the contrary, only two of the four elements tended toward the earth—water and earth. It was a property (quality) of all earthly and watery objects to tend toward the earth where, having found their natural resting place, they rested. This quality was called "gravity" or heaviness, while fire and air possessed "levity" or lightness, and tended upward.

It was, of course, recognized that objects could be diverted from their natural position by the exercise of an "unnatural" force. Thus a cannon ball could be fired from a gun, and as long as the initial force was acting upon it, it could be propelled away from its natural direction which, since the cannon ball is earthly and metallic, would be downward. On the other hand as soon as the force ceased to act, the cannon ball would drop straight to its natural resting place, the earth. If the force tailed off and did not cease at once it could gradually drop toward the earth, moving on a little and tending downward a little, in the curve that observation showed it did take. The theory of communicated motion, however, had great difficulty in explaining the phenomenon, since there seemed no reason why the motion should ever cease to be communicated, and why the cannon ball should not sail on forever. The theory required a medium through which the motion had to be communicated. If this were the air particles which pushed the cannon ball on its way, air particles would always be available to communicate the motion. But manifestly cannon balls did not sail on forever; and although the theory had been accepted as true without question for hundreds of years, a number of scientists at the University of Paris in the late Middle Ages did come to believe that the phenomena were not "saved" or explained by the theory. It seemed to them that in some way the explosion that set off the movement gave an "impetus" to it, which was in time expended, enabling the cannon ball to seek its last resting place. Though this theory raised as many problems as it solved, it was significant as showing that the late medieval mind was indeed beginning to inquire into the theories of motion received from Aristotle, and to modify them when needed by the phenomena.

The medieval theory of impetus

But perhaps the most disturbing phenomenon that urgently demanded explanation was acceleration. Impetus, the large send-off, as it were, from the gun, could account for acceleration and deceleration in the firing of a projectile. But how account for the acceleration of an object dropped from a height toward the earth? There seemed to be no new motion communicated to it on the way. As long as it was not observed that there was such an acceleration, then naturally the problem did not arise. But when the acceleration was noticed by, amongst others, Aristotelian scientists at the University of Padua, then it became obvious that it could be in no way due to the initial force. One could throw a ball downward toward the earth from a tower, but the impetus thus given quickly expended itself, while the acceleration followed the same pattern as if there had been no initial impetus at all. It might be thought that a ball seeking its natural resting place might

go faster as it neared its goal (like a horse seeking its feed pail), but the inquiring minds at Padua during the Renaissance were not content with this simple explanation. It is true that the learned Paduan scholars for a long time preferred to describe the phenomenon of acceleration rather than explain it, using ever more difficult terms for it, thus exciting the derision of such humanists as Erasmus. Was it uniformly difform, difformly uniform, or even uniformly uniformly difform?—did it take place in accordance with regular and discoverable laws, did it take place in spurts, did it tail off?

The idea of "laws" of motion— Galileo—The world subject to law

From this kind of speculation, however, it is not too great a leap to the thought that the answer could only be found by making accurate measurements, seeing how fast the ball actually. moved when falling toward the earth, and then considering what were the possible hypotheses to explain it. Nevertheless, it was a crucial step to decide that the movement could not be *random*, that it must fall according to definite laws. The ball could not fall as it liked; if it were deflected from its course, as for instance if the wind caught it, then the wind movement must also be measurable, and the amount of deflection calculated. In the absence of such deflection the acceleration must be in proportion either to its weight, the distance, or the time traveled.

Galileo, who studied at the University of Padua, was well aware of what his predecessors and contemporaries had done. But it is his distinctive achievement that he saw so clearly the nature of the problem, recognized that the necessary mathematics had to be worked out, and realized that a theory would have to be devised which could be proved true by experiment. When he built his inclined plane, and measured the time which was occupied by the falling of the ball, and discovered that the acceleration was in proportion to the time during which the ball had fallen, then he discovered a valid law, which could be put into mathematical form as a universal phenomenon applicable to all falling bodies. But even more important than this achievement was the *discovery*, now no longer a mere assumption, that there were real *laws* of motion from which one could predict, thus establishing the fact of mechanical laws that required no unverifiable assumptions such as "natural place" or "inherent tendencies."

From this it was no huge leap to the thought of Descartes (1596–1650) that the world itself was a vast machine; of Hobbes (1588–1679) that the human being himself is a machine, with his sensations governed, like the world, by laws of motion; of the eighteenth-century physiocrats that there are economic laws that may be discovered, in every way analogous to mechanical laws; of Newton that not only is the world a machine, but the heavens themselves are all obedient to the laws of universal gravitation. So the stage was set for the eighteenth-century belief that it was the proper task of scientific man to discover the laws applicable in each special field of inquiry, and for the nineteenth- and twentieth-century understanding that, as long as the laws are grasped, the world can be manipulated to suit man's convenience.

MOTION IN THE UNIVERSE

The Copernican theory

It has already been mentioned that the traditional medieval theory to account for the movements of the planets called for motion communicated from the First Mover. This idea stemmed from Aristotle. But the accepted astronomy of the Middle Ages was taken not from Aristotle but from the work of Claudius Ptolemy, an Alexandrian astronomer of the second century A.D., whose work had been known since the thirteenth century in the medieval world. Since it was obvious to Ptolemy that the planets did not move in simple concentric circles around the earth, he, following earlier Hellenistic scientists, especially Hipparchus, had devised a system which was highly complex, but accounted for the fact that sometimes certain planets

appeared to be moving in a retrograde direction. The large concentric circles (called deferents) were there, but they did not correspond to the actual movements of the planets. The planets themselves moved in smaller circles (epicycles) whose centers were on the deferents.[1] Thus it was assumed that the larger spheres circled the earth, carrying along the planets which were moving in their epicycles along with them. To account for such phenomena as the precession of the equinoxes, new additional hypotheses had to be made and more epicycles added, until there were some eighty epicycles. The details of the Ptolemaic scheme need not concern us; but the important thing to be understood is that, cumbrous though the scheme was, it did satisfactorily explain almost all the phenomena that could be observed, or had been observed, by the naked eye until the time of Tycho Brahe (1546–1601). It was possible to predict by using the scheme, and that was all that could be asked of it at the time. There were some substantially accurate astronomical tables available, based on the Ptolemaic system. It took great hardihood to question it in view of the fact that it undoubtedly "saved" what phenomena there were in a most satisfactory manner.

But Nicolas Copernicus, a Polish astronomer and mathematician (1473–1543) was offended by the cumbrous nature of the system. He wondered why the universe had to follow such a strange and intricate system of movements. Were there *really* eighty epicycles, or was this only a device to account for the observed movements, an intellectually contrived device but not necessarily true in actual fact? As a mathematician rather than an observer himself, he asked himself whether there might not be a simpler explanation of the phenomena which was more readily believable than the cumbrous monstrosity of Ptolemy and Hipparchus. So, according to his own account, he began reading the works of the Hellenistic scien-

[1] The illustration on page 387 from a medieval textbook gives a graphic picture of the Ptolemaic system.

Nicolas Copernicus, from an old engraving.

clear that the earth would appear to circle around the sun. So Copernicus was prepared to discount earthly prejudice and imagine that the earth moved around the sun as Aristarchus had suggested. If the earth and the other planets moved round the sun, and it was the sun that was stationary and not the earth, what would the consequences be? Would it simplify the cumbrous scheme of Ptolemy? In working out the consequences Copernicus discovered that the number of epicycles would be reduced to thirty-four. Therefore the hypothesis was justified in that it provided a more elegant solution of the problem.

But it was still not very elegant. The epicycles could not be abandoned. They remained, fewer in number but still undoubtedly necessary. For Copernicus was unable to abandon, as did later astronomers, the idea of circular movement as the most perfect of all movements and therefore fitted to the heavenly incorruptible worlds. It is difficult for us now to appreciate the hold this idea of circular movement had upon medieval men. It seemed quite obvious to them that if a body were to return in due time to its starting point, then it must observe the most economical manner of reaching it—and this could only be a circle. All other movement was unnatural and irregular, and could not be expected of the "perfect" heavenly bodies. Thus in the work of Copernicus, in spite of his mathematical genius and the courage with which he undertook to put forward a proposition that appeared to be contrary to observation and entailed many strange and inexplicable features, as well as being contrary to traditional opinion, there remains the preference for the qualitative and aesthetic judgment that we have noted as characteristically medieval. The heavens were perfect. They moved in perfect circles, and were incorruptible and not subject to change. When Kepler, a greater mathematician, who had access to a huge collection of observations not available to Copernicus, sought to discover the "harmonies" in the universe, he found himself forced to abandon the circular movement in favor

tists and those who had written about them, and discovered that these ancients had not all been of the same mind. On the contrary there were divergent opinions even in Alexandria. One opinion, that of Aristarchus, had held that the sun was the center of the universe rather than the earth; but it had given rise to so many difficulties that he had obtained few adherents to his theory. It seemed to Copernicus, as to all mathematicians, that the Ptolemaic solution was inelegant: it could not be the simplest explanation. And for him, as for all mathematicians, the simplest explanation was necessarily the best, unless it could be definitely disproved.

It is impossible, of course, to say from observation whether the sun moves around the earth or the earth moves around the sun. From the earth it looks as if it is the sun that moves around the earth, but the least thought will show that this is an earthly prejudice, and one cannot say that it is true. If one imagines one's self upon the sun, then it is of what was demanded by his mathematical calculations. He was coerced by the evident facts, rather than keeping his a priori assumptions held on aesthetic grounds—and in this showed himself to be a true scientist. With Copernicus the scientific spirit is stirring; with Kepler it has settled on the path which modern science had to follow if it were to be a method for truly understanding the world.

Opponents and supporters of the Copernican theory

It should not be thought that the objections to the Copernican hypothesis were primarily religious. Objection to the idea that the earth moved did not spring from churchmen until a much later date. The objections in the sixteenth century subsequent to the death of Copernicus in 1543 were based at least as much on properly scientific ground as on the natural conservatism of scholars. Under the Copernican theory the stars would have to be much farther from the earth than anyone was willing to admit possible, and the universe would have to be much larger than hitherto imagined. It was thought that if the earth moved, when it seemed to be so solidly at rest, objects would fly off the earth; and pieces of the earth itself would fly off into space. If objects were dropped from a height then they ought not to fall directly to the ground as they obviously did, but should land some distance from where they had been dropped. Some mathematicians were inclined to approve of the theory; but to those who accepted the Aristotelian physics it seemed especially difficult to accept the idea of the sluggish earth moving itself around for no reason that Copernicus could explain, except that a sphere "naturally" tends to turn in a circular movement, while the light crystalline heavens, airy and weightless, could be moved almost by a breath communicated from the *primum mobile*. The acceptance of the theory therefore had to wait until far better evidence could be produced for its truth, a theory of motion totally different from that of Aristotle, and an abandonment of qualitative distinctions between heavenly and earthly matter. These were not fully to be provided until the time of Isaac Newton at the end of the seventeenth century.

One Copernican enthusiast, however, should be mentioned, since it was he who in large part brought down the wrath of the Church upon the theory. This was Giordano Bruno (1548–1600), a mystical philosopher rather than a scientist, who was fascinated by the panorama of the heavenly bodies wheeling in infinite space, each perhaps inhabited, each believing itself to be the center of the universe, when really there is no center. Man is but a tiny drop in the infinite universe; the sun itself is only one of millions of suns. How ridiculous, mused Bruno, to imagine that the world is made for man, that man on the tiny planet of earth can be the special care of God the Creator of the universe, that the act of redemption by the death and resurrection of the only Son of God should be enacted on this tiny planet, so insignificant in the total universe. Perhaps, he speculated, the same act of redemption is even now being performed on other planets for other creatures of God. Or perhaps God himself is really in all things; perhaps he is not personal but is manifest in every form of life.

It is not surprising that the Church found itself in disagreement with this pantheistic philosophy which made nonsense of its teachings. Though Bruno had committed many offenses against the Church, for any one of which he might have been condemned to death, and it cannot be said with certainty that he was a martyr of science, there is no doubt that he was condemned by the Inquisition to be burned as a heretic, and was put to death in 1600. His teachings can hardly have endeared the Copernican theory to the Church, since such heresies could sprout from it. But it remains true that it was not until many years later that Galileo was forced to recant his belief that the earth moved, and that for several years after the condemnation of Bruno, Galileo was supported by the pope, who apparently found nothing contrary to Scripture in his theory.

And though the Congregation of the Index existed by the middle of the sixteenth century, the treatises of Copernicus were not put on the index of forbidden books until after the quarrel of Galileo with the pope, which will be briefly dealt with later in the chapter.

Tycho Brahe—Provision of adequate empirical data

Three years after the death of Copernicus, the man was born who, through his observations, was to provide enough material for the acceptance of the Copernican theory by the vast majority of seventeenth-century astronomers. Without such observations it was not possible to make astronomy into the empirical science that Kepler always thought it to be; nor would the discrepancies in the Ptolemaic system ever have become so clear. The Ptolemaic system worked fairly well and "saved" most of the phenomena known to Copernicus. But it could not save enough of the phenomena observed by Tycho Brahe (1546–1601) to be satisfying to the generation of astronomers which followed him. Brahe was a Danish astronomer who built an observatory for the primary purpose of observing the movements of the heavenly bodies at all times and all seasons of the year. Thus it became possible for later workers to confirm their mathematical calculations, while at the same time they were provided with enough material for them to discover the mechanical laws according to which the planets moved. By pure mathematics Kepler could never have arrived at his laws, nor would it ever have occurred to him to imagine that the planets move in elliptical orbits; and if he had, he would not have been able to prove it with the data available to Copernicus. Thus the work of the indefatigable observer was shown by the work of Tycho Brahe to occupy a crucial position in the history of science, even though Brahe himself did not accept the Copernican theory, preferring an intermediate position between Ptolemy and Copernicus. From his observations he concluded that the sun moved around the earth, while the other planets moved around the sun.

Johannes Kepler—The three laws of planetary motion

In many ways the work of Johannes Kepler (1571–1630) is the most interesting of these early modern astronomers to study, because he occupies a position midway between the medieval and the modern outlook, and represents in his own person the change from an aesthetic appreciation of the universe to a passion for understanding the mechanism that underlies it. On the other hand he had not the smallest interest in making use of the knowledge that he acquired; his sole delight was in discovering what he called the "harmonies of the universe," and the discovery in itself satisfied him fully. There was nothing of the engineer or technician in his make-up.

From his early youth he had access to all the work of Tycho Brahe, some of which he edited; and he recognized at once what a field of exploration lay open to him with the aid of the huge mass of observations accumulated by his teacher and predecessor. He also possessed a thorough training in the mathematics of his day which enabled him to discover some of the fundamental "laws" of the universe and express them in mathematical (geometrical) form. From the beginning, like Copernicus, he assumed that the universe was subject to mathematical interpretation and that the simplest explanation of the mechanism must be true. Indeed, he even went so far as to insist that the universe is made in the way that it is because it is mathematically harmonious. The universe had to be made in this manner by God because God, as Plato had said, always "geometrizes." The harmony in the universe is there because it is an expression of the Divine Mind. The human mind has been made by God to comprehend the world of mathematics and to understand quantities, as distinct from qualities; and it is the task of this human mind to discover, as it were, the mind of God in the harmonies of the divinely created universe. The harmony is basic and fundamental, and it is in a real sense the *cause* of the universe being the way it is.

Feeling in this way about the universe, it was natural for Kepler to prefer the Copernican system to the disorderly system of Ptolemy with its excrescences such as equants and epicycles. But Kepler also had a great aesthetic enthusiasm for the glorious sun, so much more glorious than the wretched corruptible earth; and it therefore seemed only to be expected of God that the planets should be made to revolve about their most exalted member, rather than about their least exalted. So, from the beginning, Kepler assumed that the main tenet of the Copernican theory was true. What was necessary for him was to show from the observations of Brahe that it was true, and to reveal the manner of its working. He did not, like Newton, feel called upon to explain why the planets moved as they did. He did not use the new laws of motion being enunciated by his contemporary Galileo, with whom he was in correspondence. In all his work his chief desire was to show the mathematical harmonies to be observed in planetary motion, but not to explain them. They are just there—a picture of the mathematical harmony in the mind of God. Thus one "harmony" is as interesting to him as another. An entirely useless and only vaguely approximate discovery was more aesthetically satisfying to him than his famous three laws which provided Newton with the basis for his laws of gravitation. But Kepler never cheated. He had, as he thought, discovered a magnificent harmony concerning the orbit of Mars that he was on the point of publishing, when he found a discrepancy of eight minutes between his theoretically constructed orbit and the actual orbit as observed by Brahe. So, in a properly scientific manner, having after long effort failed to explain the discrepancy and "save" Brahe's phenomenon, he abandoned the theory.

For a long time he refused to abandon the circular movement that had spoiled the system of Copernicus. Yet try as he would, he could not get rid of the offending epicycles without abandoning circular movement. At last he began to try other forms of movement until he hit upon elliptical movement. And suddenly the problem was solved, and the way lay open for Newton to show that the movement *had* to be elliptical as a consequence of the universal laws of gravitation.

Kepler became known to history, not for the many harmonies that he discovered, but for the three *laws* that bear his name, which he would never have selected himself as his title to fame. The first law states that the orbit of each planet is an ellipse, with the center of the sun one of its foci. The second law states that the line joining the center of each planet with the center of the sun (radius vector) moves over equal areas of the ellipse in equal times, while the third states that the square of the time required for the completion of the planet's journey around the sun (period of the planet) is proportional to the cube of its mean distance from the sun. If Isaac Newton had had to work out these laws for himself and had not been able to use them as formulated by Kepler, he might not have reached his law of gravitation; but having formulated the law of gravitation, Newton then found it possible to deduce the laws of Kepler from it.

Galileo and the telescope

When Tycho Brahe had completed his work almost all the useful observations to be made with the then known instruments had been made. But the key advance, made already in Kepler's lifetime, that was to open up the observational field of astronomy beyond anything Brahe had imagined, was of course the telescope. This was probably invented in Holland by an obscure maker of spectacles and optical instruments who made no use of the invention. But the principles involved in making it became known to Galileo Galilei (1564–1642) whose imaginative mind and mechanical skill immediately seized upon the idea, and he succeeded in making a telescope which magnified distant objects more than thirty times. Thereafter, for the rest of his life, he continued to make telescopes, although astronomical observation was but one of his own many interests.

By means of the telescope he was able to explode a number of erroneous Aristotelian notions, which naturally excited much

Portrait of Galileo in his old age by Justus Sus-termans. The old astronomer, mathematician, and physicist is holding a telescope of his own invention.

opposition against himself in some university circles, as well as later within the Church. He was, for instance, able to observe the satellites of Jupiter, which demonstrated plainly that not all heavenly objects circled the earth. The planets, and especially the moon, were now seen to be in no way perfect or unchangeable, but like everything else, subject to change and "corruption." The moon, he declared, had a rough mountainous surface and seemed in no way to differ from the earth as far as its physical constitution was concerned. And even the glorious sun itself was found to undergo change; it was possible to observe "spots" on its surface. It was not, of course, possible to *prove* the Copernican theory by observation, but what Galileo had done was to show that many of the objections made to it by Aristotelian conservatives were quite invalid, and as time went on less and less was to be said for it. Not until Newton was the Copernican theory fully accepted by scientists and philosophers, and not until 1835 was the work of Copernicus removed from the Catholic Index.

Clerical opponents of Galileo

Galileo himself had a difficult time with the Church. As we have seen, Giordano Bruno was burned for heresy in 1600, and at least a part of his heresy was his deductions from the Copernican system. It is possible that Galileo himself might never have incurred the displeasure of the papacy, since, in general, the Catholic Church did not adhere to the literal interpretation of Biblical texts which was prevalent among Protestants of the seventeenth century; and the Bible in any case had not been extremely specific on the matter. But Galileo was an extremely choleric character, who did not suffer fools gladly. He was constantly under attack from university professors who continued to adhere to Aristotelian teachings which Galileo, quite correctly in many cases, believed he had fully disproved. Yet the professors went on repeating their errors, finally rousing Galileo to such wrath that he published a highly sarcastic work entitled *A Dialogue on the Two Chief Systems of the World* (1632), in which one of the characters is presented as something of a buffoon because he defends the Ptolemaic and Aristotelian systems. This book infuriated Pope Urban VIII, who was persuaded by the Aristotelians that Simplicio in the *Dialogue* was intended to be himself. Galileo was summoned before the Inquisition and made to recant. Thereafter he was imprisoned for a time, but then allowed his personal freedom under close supervision. On the whole it seems probable that the Church objected more to Galileo's discovery that the heavens were corruptible and subject to change than to his insistence that the earth moved. The movement of the earth was of no special interest to the Church. The earth was known to be a body of no special consequence as a planet and it held no exalted position in the universe, whether it moved or not. But the heavens were in every way different from the earth, and God had his dwelling place in their far distances. It was both heretical and extremely derogatory to heavenly dignity to claim that the heavens could be in any way similar to the lowly earth.

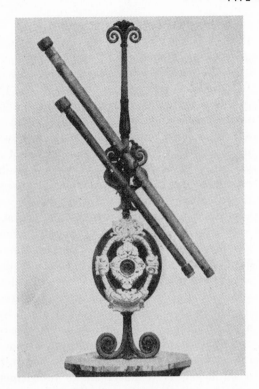

Two of Galileo's telescopes, preserved in Florence.

Galileo's last invention after he became blind: a pendulum made from details dictated just before his death.

Before the work of Newton was possible two further advances were necessary, which need not detain us long here. The other work of Descartes will be handled in a later section of this chapter; it need only be mentioned here that Descartes' great mathematical contribution of analytical geometry provided a tool for the mathematical representation of the geometry of the universe, and enabled mathematical problems to be solved without the geometrical constructions that had previously been necessary. Christian Huyghens (1629–1695), a Dutch mathematician and physicist, in a work published in 1673, showed that a force in a spherical body must act as if all force were concentrated in its center. It is not, however, certain that Newton had not solved this problem before Huyghens, though he had not published his results. It is, of course, a key concept for the mathematical demonstration of universal gravitation.

Newton—The law of universal gravitation

Sir Isaac Newton (1642–1727), working on the discoveries of his predecessors, especially Kepler in the field of pure astronomy and Galileo in the field of physics, crowned the edifice of astronomy that had been in the process of being constructed since Copernicus. Galileo had left the theory of motion in an unfinished condition. He had seen that motion must conform to definite mechanical laws and through theory and experiment had suggested the lines on which these laws must be framed. But some of his observations had been faulty—he never did discover the true speed of falling bodies—and his laws had not been properly formulated. Newton, after considerable thought and experimentation, was able to give the correct laws which hold good for what is now called Newtonian space (to be distinguished from the new concept of space-time associated with the name of Einstein). These laws are: that every body perseveres in its state of rest or uniform motion in a straight line, except in so far as it is compelled to change that state by forces imposed from without; change of motion is proportional to the moving force impressed, and takes place in the direction of the straight line in which such force is impressed: reaction is always equal and opposite to action.

Descartes had provided Newton with a tool the importance of which can hardly be overestimated, in the form of analytical geometry. But another tool was also needed to give a proper mathematical representation of a force, something which changes movement and is not merely an algebraic picture of a geometrical fact. This he provided for himself by the invention of calculus, although it had been invented, apparently quite independently, by Leibniz (1646–1716) in Germany. Knowing then how movement takes place and able to represent it in effective algebraic form, Newton was now able to arrive at and prove his universal gravitational theory.

It is said (by Voltaire) that Newton first gave full attention to the problem of gravity by wondering idly from how far an apple would fall to the earth. Would it fall to the earth if it were originally as high as the moon? It was already known—Newton himself had deduced it from Kepler's third planetary law, as he himself tells us—that a force decreases as the square of the distance increases, and that the force needed to keep the planets in their orbits could be calculated with some exactness. The question then came as to whether it was possible to use the knowledge of the gravitational pull of the earth to find whether the earth attracted the moon in such a way as to deflect it from its orbit by an observable amount. In other words, if he could calculate from his knowledge of planetary movements and earthly gravitational pull that the moon, subject to the same pull, would be deflected by a certain amount, and if he could then show that the moon did indeed move from its

orbit by this particular amount, then his theory would be proved, and universal gravitation established.

Although Newton at the early age of twenty-three was, as he tells us, "in the prime of my age for invention, and minded mathematics and philosophy more than at any time since," and had already perceived the essentials of his theory, he could not as yet prove it. He especially needed to be certain of the truth contained in Huyghens' theory mentioned above. But in 1685 he was persuaded to return to his calculations and was now able to prove in a manner which has never been disputed that the sun, moon, earth, and the planets could indeed be taken as massive points for the purposes of calculation, whatever their actual size; and from this he was able to demonstrate that the moon was indeed deflected from its orbit by exactly the amount calculated in advance. From this he was then able to demonstrate why the observed movement of the planets must be elliptical, through the influence of gravitation. All this was written up in his epoch-making book *Principia Mathematica* in 1687.

The universe as a machine—The scientific method

So, for the first time, a great scientific synthesis was created which showed that all the known heavenly bodies followed exact laws. The universe, from the time of Newton onward, was thus assumed to be a mechanism which worked in accordance with exact and determinable laws capable of being expressed mathematically. The far-reaching effects of this new concept in other fields than mechanics and astronomy will be dealt with in a later section of this chapter. Meanwhile, it may be noted from the above description of his work that Newton also made use of what has since come to be called *the scientific method*. A problem needs to be solved. The scientist brings to bear on it, in his mind, all the previous work known on the subject, including of course its mathematics. Then deductions are made from the material, in the form "if such and such is

the case, then such and such will follow."
At a certain point observation is necessary
to see if such and such does in fact follow.
This observation may be in the form of a
planned experiment, or, as in the case of
Newton, or of the confirmation of Einstein's
hypothesis in 1919, attention may be focused
on some event in the heavens. If the result
is found to conform to the prediction ("then
such and such will follow"), the theory is
presumed to be true, unless and until later
deductions are shown to be unconfirmed by
experiment, thus calling for some modification in the theory. It will be seen that in
this method both theoretical considerations
and experimentation have their part; but it
is a definite part. Trial and error had been
finally discredited as a method.

It may be added that the work of Newton was in part made possible by the gradual
development of the community of science.
In the seventeenth century scientists were no
longer condemned to work in isolation from
others working on similar problems. Not only
were the universities beginning to throw off
the shackles of scholasticism and Aristotelianism, and welcoming men who could teach
the new science, but a number of academies
were founded for the sole purpose of the
advancement of science. Galileo had belonged to the *Accademia dei Lincei,* a
Roman scientific center founded in the
early seventeenth century, while Richelieu
founded the French *Académie des sciences,*
which, however, became really effective only
when Louis xiv gave it his patronage, at the
instigation of Colbert. The most important
of all was, perhaps, the English Royal
Society, founded in 1645, which soon began
to publish *Proceedings,* and arrange for the
printing of scientific papers. The French
published regularly from 1665 a *Journal des
savants.* This was a good beginning; but for
the most part scientists still largely informed
one another of their work through correspondence, giving rise to such disputes as
that between Leibniz and Newton on the
priority in the invention of calculus. Newton
also, as we have seen, does not seem to have
had access to Huyghens' important work in

time to use it. He therefore claimed independent discovery, while admitting that the
Dutchman probably made his discovery
first.

▶ Descartes and Cartesianism

DICHOTOMY BETWEEN MIND AND MATTER

We have traced in some detail the
development of astronomy from Copernicus
to Newton with two purposes in mind. One
was to illustrate the development of science
and scientific method during a century and
a half. The second was to examine how the
concept of a world machine ruled by mechanical laws expressed in mathematical
terms came to replace the older concept of
a world ruled by final rather than efficient
causation, a world in which one looked for
purposes (the why), rather than try to
discover the means by which things took
place (the how). Implied in the work of
many of these men, especially Galileo and
Newton, was both a new method for discovering the truth and the reduction of man
himself to the position of an onlooker, whose
natural perceptions through his senses had
no relevance to real truth, and were indeed
certain to be faulty. Aristotle's world conception had rested upon the validity of sense
perceptions and common sense. His ideas
of potentiality and actuality had been based
essentially on his concept of the human being
as a growing and developing being moving
toward his fulfillment, and this perception
he had transferred into the world, looking
for potentiality and actuality in everything.
As in all the ancient world conceptions man
had been a microcosm, a picture of the great
macrocosm without. Even the stars were
connected with man, and the planets ruled
his various bodily organs. But in the new
world that was being unfolded by the astronomers and the physicists man had no place,
and the study of man was entirely irrelevant
for the study of the universe. Man's puny
purposes could no longer be used as analo-
gies for the purposes of the world and the
universe; indeed the world did not seem to
be going anywhere; it had no purpose at all,

but was just there to be studied. It was a static universe, built like a clock or any other mechanism. Movement went on indefinitely in accordance with inexorable and unchangeable laws. No force was needed, no communicated motion. No being had to make an effort to make it go; it went of itself.

The scientist and philosopher who perceived these facts most clearly in the seventeenth century was René Descartes (1596–1650), and since his influence rivaled even that of Newton in the seventeenth and eighteenth centuries, and since his method became the accepted one in so many fields of inquiry that he had not touched himself, an effort should be made to understand his outlook and the facts and ideas on which it was based. At an early age Descartes studied mathematics and before he was twenty-five he knew as much mathematics as anyone in the world of his day could teach him. He remained throughout his life primarily a mathematician; although he turned his mathematics to the study of physical phenomena, he was not really interested in the phenomena in themselves, and he experimented only when it was absolutely necessary to confirm a theory.

René Descartes. A small portrait study by Franz Hals, the Elder, which gives the impression of a rapid work done from the life.

THE MATHEMATICAL METHOD OF UNDERSTANDING THE UNIVERSE

At the age of twenty-three he tells us that he had a vision, an intense mystical experience which revealed to him that mathematics was the sole key for understanding the universe. This vision led him to concentrate his attention on the expression of all the truths of the universe in mathematical terms. As he was above all things a geometer, and since the world as perceived was geometrical, what was needed was to express the geometrical facts in a shorthand form in which the numbers, and the letters which represented numbers, could be used instead of the actual figures to be perceived in the universe. It is possible to construct an equation $(ax + by + c = 0)$ which will be true for *all* straight lines. The physical straight line has never been seen and never will be, but this does not alter the truth of the equation. There is a full correspondence between the equation and the ideal straight line, and it was obvious to Descartes that everything in the outer world could be expressed in his algebraic formulas. Even motion itself, he reasoned, ought to be observable as a dimension of matter, although he did not pursue this line of thought far enough to make it acceptable to fellow thinkers; and he himself was to say that with only extension (best considered as matter in space according to some kind of configuration) and motion he could create a universe.

To Descartes, observing and thinking about the world, the one essential factor in all phenomena was that they could be measured. Objects may be lighter or darker, smoother or rougher. Such differences are merely qualitative and it is meaningless to talk about them unless one says by how much they are lighter or darker. And in the end one must come down to the fact that the explanation will involve matter in motion. No object in the world has any inherent qualities. He will not even admit the existence of gravity as inherent in objects. Gravity is to be explained as part of motion which creates vortices in which planets and earthly bodies alike are carried around in accordance with the laws of motion, on an impalpable material that Descartes calls prime matter or ether. So Descartes explicitly rejected the Copernican theory in favor of a theory of vortices, although he could find no experimental evidence for them, and their existence in fact was shown by Newton to be contrary to Kepler's laws.

The world was therefore regarded by Descartes as a highly complicated machine. There was nothing in it which did not obey mathematical laws, and nothing in it that was not ultimately to be reduced to extension and motion. How then can we account for the fact that man does perceive qualities and qualitative differences between objects? How is color to be accounted for as an experience, even if the mind does know that it is ultimately merely matter in motion?

EPISTEMOLOGICAL IMPLICATIONS—WHAT DOES MAN REALLY KNOW?

Here Descartes was forced to face the great unsolved problem. Galileo had already shown that the evidence of the senses could not be trusted, as in the fact that the senses suggest that the sun moves round the earth while reason tells us that the earth moves round the sun. And Galileo had been ready to differentiate between real and primary qualities which actually did exist in the objects, and secondary qualities which were not real and could not be demonstrated and therefore might be quite false. Descartes goes all the way and says that the secondary qualities perceived by the senses exist in man himself, and not in the objects; only those qualities which are susceptible to mathematical treatment are, in fact, real. There is a causal relationship between the objects and the observer; certain kinds of matter in motion will give the impression to the observer that they are white or blue or hard or soft.

Descartes offers the example of a sword which cuts the skin. The person whose skin is cut experiences pain, but he does not experience the primary qualities of the sword, namely its motion or configuration. This person, with his mind and his thinking and his feeling, is altogether cut off from the real world, a different being altogether, unextended in space and without motion. The realm of thought is on one side of the abyss, and the real extended world on the other. And yet it is the extended world that causes sensation in the thinking being, and the thinking being who alone can know the reality of the world, and its extension and motion. How to bridge that gap has been the most outstanding problem in philosophy since the time of Descartes. Platonic and Aristotelian answers did not solve the problem, for in the ancient world it had never been posed in this uncompromising manner. In a world of common sense ruled by the naïve man it would never have been broached, for the naïve man thinks what he sees and experiences is real, and is induced by the objects, which are just as they appear to be. But Descartes had come to the conclusion, through his thinking mind, that the world was not as it appears to be, but, on the contrary, what the mind *knows* it to be. Such knowledge is superior to the defective evidence of the senses.

CARTESIAN METHODOLOGY—"CLEAR AND DISTINCT IDEAS"

So Descartes wrote his famous and influential little preface to his mathematical works which he called a *Discourse on Method*. In this work he explains how he came to the conclusion from experience that evidence from the senses is untrustworthy, so that he had to decide for himself what then could be trusted. And he proceeded to doubt methodically all that he had been taught and all that he had learned, and was able successfully to doubt everything away. But one residual core of consciousness remained. He could not doubt that he was doubting, that he was thinking. So he made his fundamental statement, the first thing which could not be doubted: *"Cogito, ergo sum"*—I think, therefore I am. Someone must be thinking, and it must therefore be himself; he existed. And he came to ponder other things that could not be doubted, finding in his mind that the idea of God was there; so, like Anselm before him, using an ontological argument, he came to the conclusion that God had put that idea in his mind, therefore God existed. Proceeding further he came to the conclusion that there were other ideas in his mind, clear and distinct ideas, as he called them, which could not be doubted, certain truths that were of a mathematical nature. It surely was not possible to doubt the axioms of geometry, that two things equal to the same thing are equal to one another. And he concluded that he had now found a true method, the method of methodic and purposeful doubt. Everything which is not clear and distinct in the mind is not true, and everything that is clear and distinct must be true. He was back where he started. The equation for the straight line is true, even though the straight line is not to be found in nature. Thought and reasoning alone can give truth and certitude. That two and two make four is a necessity of the human mind. It corresponds to the facts in the world of extension, but it is not derived from them.

His method, like that of the scholastics, is deductive in nature. The basic axioms which cannot be doubted, the clear and distinct ideas, are the primary data. From the existence of God it was possible to deduce facts about God and the created world which likewise could not be doubted, even though not all would necessarily agree with the particular deductions made by Descartes, and might attribute his choice of deductions to personal predilection rather than to strict logic. As the social and economic philosophers who followed his method chose their axioms in a somewhat arbitrary manner and then drew conclusions from them which pleased them, so did other philosophers dispute Descartes' axioms and their conclu-

sions. But the method itself was to prove extraordinarily enticing in all forms of inquiry, social as well as physical. When John Locke declared the basic axiom of human psychology to be that the mind at birth is a *tabula rasa*, an empty slate, and offered as a necessary deduction the omnipotence of environment, he was thinking like a true Cartesian. And when Thomas Jefferson declared that all men have been endowed by the Creator with certain "unalienable" rights, he was again stating an axiom derived not from experience but from the rational mind, stating a proposition which could not be doubted, a clear and distinct idea.

▶ **The progress of empirical science**

FRANCIS BACON AND THE SEARCH FOR FACTS—
THE INDUCTIVE METHOD

"One method of delivery alone remains to us; which is simply this: we must lead men to the particulars themselves, and their series and order; while men on their side must force themselves for awhile to lay their notions by and begin to familiarize themselves with facts."[2]

We have already had occasion to notice Francis Bacon as a scientific publicist (like his medieval namesake) calling for an advancement in useful learning, using the world of nature for the benefit of man. An influential man of affairs, and lord chancellor of England until convicted for taking bribes, Bacon was also by avocation a student of science, and a thinker rather than an experimenter (again like the medieval Roger). He was a severe and penetrating critic of the science of his own and earlier ages, but, unlike most critics, he also strove to construct and lay down the lines on which he believed science should progress. Though some men, especially in England, were influenced by him in their own work in the seventeenth century, it was not until the eighteenth that he really came into his own. The shadow of Descartes hovered over almost all the seventeenth.

[2] Francis Bacon, *Novum Organum*, Aphorism 36.

Bacon attacked the Aristotelian system and helped to give it the *coup de grâce*. But it was already crumbling in his time under the impact of Galileo and the theoretical physicists and astronomers. More interesting to us is his attack on the mathematical science of his own day. He complained that it was not useful, nor verified by experiment, and grossly premature. He never tires of criticizing the excessive generality of the conclusions of the physicists. Certainly, he says, the Copernican system is mathematically consistent and maybe it is true. But does it fit all the known and observable facts? Is it not an "anticipation of nature," a premature hypothesis? He himself, as he admits, has offered far more hypotheses than are justifiable, because it is the fashionable thing to do and he would be thought a coward if he did not. The mathematical method, he says, while it offers explanations which the mind may accept, is singularly useless; it

Sir Francis, later Lord Bacon, philosopher of science and Lord Chancellor of England. Portrait by Paul van Somer.

cannot be used for the benefit of man. On the whole it is almost as much "contentious learning" as the Aristotelian system. And thousands of inconvenient facts can be offered by any observer which suggest that its findings are not even true.

What Bacon suggests, therefore, is what he thinks of as a totally new method, and the only one that offers knowledge that is both true and useful. This is the method that he calls induction—the observation of the particular facts and the derivation of general laws from the facts. Keep the hypotheses to a minimum, and let the facts suggest the hypotheses. This is what is now called the "natural history" method of inquiry, and it has a recognized place in science when suitably modified. It is not improbable that Bacon was right, given the state of science of his own day. His method, when so little of the physical phenomena of the world was actually known and when more careful observation of *how* things behaved was essential—Bacon was at least as anxious to eliminate the Aristotelian *why* as any contemporary physicist—was likely to lead not only to more useful knowledge but actually to more correct knowledge. He was perhaps inclined to minimize too much the importance of the hypothesis as a guide for the proper choice and planning of experiments, and he has been laughed at for the triviality of the experiments he sometimes suggested. It is also true that he did not appreciate the tremendous urge for understanding of the *whole* that inspired such a man as Descartes. He was not a metaphysician, interested in ultimates; he was content that science should move on a less exalted plane, and understand thoroughly the small particulars rather than the large generalities. Both, of course, are necessary for the true progress of science. And it is perhaps as well that both were followed in this great age of the beginning of modern science; and though very few men of Bacon's time, even among the empiricists, were willing to eschew theory altogether, there is a recognizable school of scientific workers who can be considered Baconian in spirit. It is to the work of one

of the most eminent of these that the next section of this chapter will be devoted.

THE ADVANCE OF MEDICINE AND ANATOMY

Traditional theories of Galen

For obvious reasons medical science has from the earliest times been, of all sciences, the most hedged around by superstitions and preconceived notions. Thus any advances in human physiology have always been made in the teeth of entrenched opposition, both from conservative medical men and theorists of all kinds, devoted to their own point of view, their preconceptions derived from religious, astrological and other irrelevant fields of inquiry. Medieval medical science, however, was dependent upon the teachings of the second century A.D. Greek doctor Galen to a degree that can hardly be comprehended now, and his theories absolutely dominated the entire field of medical inquiry. Platonists and Pythagoreans at least provided some competition for Aristotle in the field of physical theory, but Galen had the medical field to himself. It was known that Galen had carried out dissections and that his own writings were a synthesis of all earlier Greek thought with a number of important contributions of his own. But it remains difficult for us to comprehend why he was regarded as such an indisputable authority, even in an age given to reliance upon authority of the past. Theoretical medical instruction even at universities like Padua, modern in other respects, was largely a commentary on Galen; and such experiments as were carried out were devised largely as illustrations of his theories rather than as efforts to discover new information.

Galen, of course, had been occupied with the question of how the human being is nourished as a result of the intake of food, and it was obvious to him that in some manner the blood performed this service. Through his dissections of human beings and animals he had carefully examined the heart and perceived that the arteries and veins contained different kinds of blood. He had then arrived at his theory, based in part on observation, a theory which for over fifteen hundred years had been believed to account for the facts which he wished to explain. The liver, he said, was the source of blood. Through the liver's activity part of the blood is filled with "natural spirits" and then carried through the veins to the rest of the body, thus nourishing it. But the rest of the blood flows through the veins to the heart, where it seeps from right to left through the septum which divides the heart in two. Here it is mixed with air which comes from the lungs, adding to itself new "spirits" which are known as "vital spirits." This superior form of blood now ebbs and flows through the body by means of the arteries, thus enabling the organs of the body to perform their proper functions. The arterial blood which flows to the brain there generates "animal spirits," which spirits, now unmixed with blood, flow along the nerves to enable the human being to carry out movements. Thus venous blood flows from the liver to the heart, and arterial blood to the rest of the body, with an ebb and flow movement from the heart.

Vesalius, founder of modern anatomy

It will be noticed at once that the various "spirits" are hypotheses which cannot ever be expected to be verified by experiment. They must be accepted on faith. But there are two physiological facts which Galen assumes; these had not been observed but were capable of being observed if they were indeed present. Blood was assumed to be able to seep through the nonporous septum, and air was assumed to be capable of being pumped from the lungs to the heart in spite of the presence of blood in the passage through which the air must pass. The Flemish anatomist Andreas Vesalius (1514–1564), already briefly mentioned, who performed many dissections and founded modern descriptive anatomy, hit upon the key difficulty of blood seepage through the septum, but, still obsessed with Galen's general theory and unwilling to abandon all its consequences, merely contented himself with

stating that it showed the wonderful power of God that he could make the blood flow through a septum that was not porous. Probably he did not believe that God did perform this miracle, but, unwilling to abandon the rest of the Galenic theory, he did not wish, or did not dare, to go further than merely cast doubts upon the matter of the septum; and indeed he was already criticized severely enough by his contemporaries and had to resign his professorship at Padua and go into private practice as a physician.

Vesalius had not recognized the second difficulty, but it had occurred to Leonardo da Vinci many years before his time to see whether he could indeed force air into the heart by means of a pump. He was unsuccessful, but it is likely that his experiment was not generally known in university circles. This particular difficulty, in any case, was cleared up shortly after the death of Vesalius when the pulmonary circulation was discovered. Through further research at Padua the valves of the veins were found, though again their function was improperly explained. Everyone, it seemed, wished somehow to retain the Galenic theory in spite of the by now really indisputable disproof of all that could be experimentally disproved.

William Harvey and the circulation of the blood

Physiology was in this state when William Harvey (1578–1657) studied at the University of Padua, returning later to practice in England as royal physician. His key work *Exercitatio de Motu Cordis et Sanguinis,* published in 1628, is a classic of clear scientific exposition. He explains how he looked at the facts available and engaged in "repeated vivisections" and dissections, looking for more important and crucial facts. And, without any question of a doubt, the facts appeared to reveal two things with the utmost clarity, that there was only one kind of blood, and that it circulated. How, he asked, could the liver produce so much blood, when it was visible that the heart threw out as much blood in an hour as the weight of a man? Following the progress

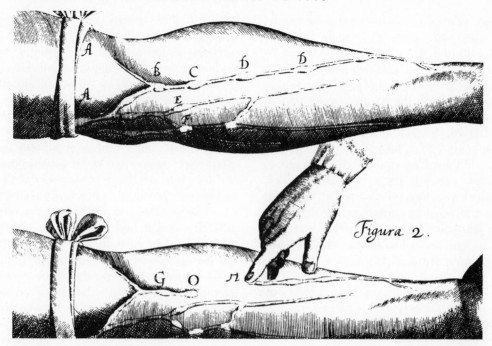

Illustration from the first edition of William Harvey's fundamental work on the circulation of the blood (1628). The pictures show the location of the arterial and venous pathways for the blood in the human arm.

of the blood, Harvey suddenly saw each separate fact fall into place, and the revolution in physiology was completed. Thereafter the discovery of lacteal and lymphatic vessels was not long delayed, and Malpighi, with the aid of the newly invented microscope, published in 1661 his discovery of the capillary system, and thereafter the picture was complete.

No speculations or hypotheses beyond the minimum had been needed; the readiness to believe the evidence and abandon previous erroneous theory had indeed been required and found to be difficult of achievement. But it had at last been done. The circulation of the blood had been seen to be a simple mechanical process requiring no knowledge of the laws of motion or mathematics. And from the beginning it was "useful" knowledge. The Baconian method had been justified, though he did not live to see it; nor probably did Harvey know that he was following it.

Robert Boyle, the father of chemistry— Criticism of Cartesianism

The second figure whom we shall study here was a convinced Baconian who had yet read and been much impressed by the philosophy of Descartes. Robert Boyle (1627–1691) is, of course, known as the father of chemistry and the author of Boyle's Law. His book, *The Sceptical Chemist,* showed by careful reasoning and descriptions of experiments he had made that the old theory of the four elements, or the alternative theory of some of the alchemists that salt, sulphur, and mercury were the "true principles of things," were neither of them tenable in the light of experimental knowledge. He preferred to distinguish real substances which could not be considered compounds of other substances as being what he called "elements" or "principles." He pointed out that the supposed element fire had different effects according to the degree of heat of the fire, and that it did not always resolve compounds into their constituent parts. In all this he was one of the great pioneers of chemistry; but it is rather for his scientific thought that he will be considered here, representing, as he does, a continuing trend of thought which is neither exclusively empirical nor exclusively theoretical and mathematical. Clearly a religious man and a believing Christian, Boyle was not willing to abandon God as a Final Cause or the first Efficient Cause; and yet he felt the strength of the Cartesian thought that the world is a great machine, and he could not find anything in his experiments that would prove the contrary. He was also unwilling to leave man out of the picture as completely as Descartes. Obviously, as he says, "there are de facto in the world certain sensible and rational beings called men," and these beings perceive the secondary qualities. This is a fact and cannot be neglected in building a total theory.

Boyle accepts the Cartesian viewpoint that the primary qualities of all things are to be understood by mathematics, so far as that understanding goes. The world is a mechanism, and sensible objects can be reduced in the mind to atoms in motion (an idea that had recently come to the fore again through the work of Gassendi, who revived with modifications the atomic ideas held in the ancient world). Nevertheless, though the mind knows this, the actual diversity of sense phenomena must be taken as a fact also; even local motion itself is diverse. Boyle agrees that, according to what human reasoning can tell us, the diversity of phenomena is in fact due to the configuration of their constituent corpuscles. So much for what the human mind can tell us. But though the ultimate reality may be as agreed, the task of the scientist is to examine the diversity and account for it, working with experiments and induction in the Baconian manner. It is not always useful and necessary to deal with the primary causes, which lie behind the secondary causes, but rather to investigate the secondary causes and

come to some useful results. Only by such methods had he been able to reach useful conclusions in the field of chemistry.

With regard to Descartes' argument that the secondary qualities cannot be known to have a definite existence apart from the person perceiving them, Boyle was ready to agree that the body itself belongs to the mechanical world, and is thus, like everything else, merely matter in motion, moving according to mechanical laws. But the human being also has a soul, not to be thought of as existing in any particular place, not extended in space and not subject to mechanical laws nor to be explained by them. "I see no necessity," he says "that intelligibility to a human understanding should be necessary to the truth or existence of a thing, any more than that visibility to a human eye should be necessary to the existence of an atom, or of a corpuscle of air, or of the effluviums of a loadstone."[3] The laws of mathematics as expounded by Descartes and acceptable to the human mind are acceptable in their proper sphere. But in the field of the unextended in which nothing could be discovered by mathematical means, Boyle is willing to accept the teachings of the Christian religion, and is ready to accept the fact that God created the world and man and is still interested in the activities of man and active in the world. God could also create and possibly has created other worlds, serving other purposes for other beings than man. Unlike Descartes, Boyle makes no attempt to prove the existence of God.

So Boyle, faced with the Cartesian dualism, agrees with Descartes' fundamental proposition that there is a dichotomy between man and the world; but, unlike Descartes, he does not find this to be an insurmountable problem, because he is not willing to push his thought to its logical extremes. God is the author and first efficient cause of the world, and everything that

[3] Quoted by E. A. Burtt, *The Metaphysical Foundations of Modern Science* (Garden City, N. Y.: Doubleday & Company, Inc., Anchor Books, 1955, p. 186).

happens in it is by his "general concourse." It is a fact that man perceives the world and that the secondary qualities are known to him through his senses. The fact does not have to be explained since man is obviously capable of such perception. Man knows with his mind that behind the secondary qualities are primary qualities, matter and motion, and this happens to be intelligible to him through his mathematical mind. But all things do not have to be intelligible to him; the mathematical mind cannot perceive an entity which has no extension and does not occupy space, such as the human soul. In this field it is good, says Boyle, to admit our ignorance and rely upon faith.

St. Thomas Aquinas would not have felt himself out of place in this thought. Again the world is to be understood by reason, and what lies beyond reason is in the realm of faith. All that science had added was a more profound and ever-increasing knowledge of the phenomena. There was no reason why this should induce religious skepticism or a thoroughgoing materialism.

▶ Consequences of the Scientific Revolution

THE SEARCH FOR A "NATURAL" RELIGION

But the trend of the times was against Boyle and those who thought as he did. Most of the intellectual consequences of the new scientific thought are to be discerned in the eighteenth rather than the seventeenth century and so lie beyond the scope of this book. The Christian religion began to appear to many as a kind of excrescence upon true scientific thought. It certainly was not a clear and distinct idea in the Cartesian sense. Thinkers began to consider whether God himself was a reasonable idea. At first, with Newton, many of the thinkers believed that a First Cause was necessary—some super-clockmaker who made the clock in the first place and then left it to its own devices. Newton himself inclined to the idea that once in a while the clock had to be repaired by the clockmaker. But in any case all men for a time seemed to agree that the mechanism of the world which was seen to be so

perfectly regulated needed some explanation. Why should it be there in the first place? So the argument from design, which Thomas Aquinas had relegated to fifth place among the proofs for the existence of God, became the most popular. The men who held this idea were called Deists, although there were several different kinds of deism. Some thinkers, like Boyle, were inclined to accept the fact of revelation, that God had revealed to men through the Scriptures various things about the world, and the Scriptures were believed to be true because they were attested to by miracles. This brought up the pertinent question as to how miracles were attested, a matter dealt with by David Hume in a devastating manner.

The question of the future life naturally came up for criticism. Was it reasonable, was it a clear and distinct idea? It fitted in with man's ideas of justice, everyone was agreed. But did this prove that it was really so? Having created the human soul, why should God destroy it? Why did Christ come to earth? Was it reasonable that he should redeem the world by his death and resurrection? Surely this proposition at least could be accepted only on faith and not on reason. Well, said some, it was certainly necessary for human beings to have a good example set them and it would be only reasonable of God to send his son, a perfect man, as a perfect example, and to explain to man how God wished to be worshiped. For Voltaire it seemed necessary that there should be a God as a judge and enforcer of morality, especially for the lower classes, who otherwise would never behave themselves.

It is not necessary here to go into all these ideas, still less to attach names to the thinkers who put them forward. What had happened was that suddenly man was faced with a world which he believed he could understand, that was simply a mechanism, that might always have existed and so needed not even a First Cause to explain. The world would go on just as well if man were not there. Under Cartesian thought he was nothing but an onlooker, no longer a part in the world process, no longer a microcosmic picture of the great macrocosm that was the universe. But one thing man did possess—his power of reasoning, and this had unlocked for him the keys to the mechanical functioning of the universe. Descartes had shown that the human mind really knew, it was not deceived, while the senses could always be deceived. In his *Discourse on Method* he had told how that idea which is clear and distinct and cannot be doubted must be true, like the mathematical axioms. Descartes himself had not doubted the existence of God, which to him was truly the most clear and distinct of ideas. But it was not necessary for his successors to follow him in this, especially since logicians were quick to point out the logical fallacy of his ontological argument for the existence of God.

Moreover, even if the existence of God were to be admitted by those who felt it necessary to accept a First Cause, what about all the other strange and "unreasonable" things in the Christian religion? So those who held to religion in the post-Cartesian and post-Newtonian epoch held to it largely on faith and could not give really reasonable arguments to support their position. Reason proved itself, at least reason as the eighteenth century thought of it, completely incompetent in this realm. For every argument in favor of any religion a counterargument could be produced, until finally hope for a universally acceptable religion, based on reasonable propositions acceptable to all, was tacitly abandoned.

STUDY OF SOCIETY BY MATHEMATICAL METHOD —"SOCIAL PHYSICS"

Sensationalism of Thomas Hobbes

But in realms other than religion the Cartesian-Newtonian revolution held out tremendous possibilities, above all in the study of man and society. The method had been suggested by Descartes. Seek out the clear and distinct ideas in every field that cannot be doubted. Then draw out by deduction all the consequences of the ideas, which will therefore, as in mathematics, be as true as the original axiom. Search for a "social physics," a science as accurate and convincing as physics itself.

But before coming to the Cartesians attention should first be paid to Thomas Hobbes, whom we have already met as a political scientist, who did his work before much of the work of Descartes was published and before Newton was born. Hobbes was a student rather of Galileo, and when in later life he came to know the work of Descartes he severely criticized him. From Galileo he accepted the idea of a mechanical universe, ruled by laws of motion. For Hobbes the only reality was material, and the human being was a part of the material reality; everything in the universe, including man, consisted of matter in motion, and matter was, in the last analysis, particles. Being a nominalist in the most extreme form he would not admit the existence of any abstract idea at all. Triangles exist only as bodies; if we have the idea of a triangle in our mind it is simply because we have seen one and we can now re-imagine it. All we are doing in reality is becoming aware of the matter in motion in our mind, this matter being what Hobbes calls "the stuff of knowledge."

In Hobbes's scheme there is no need for a Cartesian dualism, since everything in the mind and outside it is equally particles in motion. Sense images are motions in the brain, while reason is the grouping and regrouping of the particles of sense, in a particular manner. How we become aware of this organic motion within us Hobbes, however, does not explain, so that the problem of how one knows that one is thinking, the primary awareness of a Self, which Descartes did recognize, feeling that it had to be explained, is never dealt with. The secondary qualities of objects, he recognized, were not really in them but in the perceiving being; but this caused him no trouble since even within this perceiving being there was only matter in motion. The primary qualities residing in the objects were to be reduced to particles which have diverse effects upon the human being, in accordance with their particular form of motion, thus *causing* in him certain other forms of motion which are to be distinguished from the real primary qualities. Thus the particular configuration of the matter without, and its form of motion, affect the perceiving human being always in a particular way, thus enabling him to say to himself that something is light, noisy, or of a certain color.

In developing his theory which is usually called "sensationalism" and is, of course, based on an extreme form of mechanical materialism, Hobbes goes on to classify different kinds of bodies (natural, human, and artificial) and different kinds of motion, such as "natural" motion when bodies are left to themselves, and "compound" motion when bodies are influenced by other bodies. In this way, when dealing with the human body he can speak of the "natural" motion of his body as being sense, memory, and imagination, while "compound" motion is reasoning. But it is all determined in a perfectly mechanical manner, and it is the geographical closeness of certain impressions (particles of knowledge) in the mind that causes even such remarkable human abilities as imagination and reasoning. A necessary logical consequence of the scheme would be that it would be possible by self-observation to discover what all men think, since similar sense impressions received into the mind would result in similar imaginations and similar reasoning.

John Locke—The mind as blank slate

This latter thought foreshadows the very influential psychological ideas of John Locke (1632–1704) who was also notable for his contributions to political science. By the time Locke was working and writing his *Essay on the Human Understanding* (1690) it had become the fashion to search for clear and distinct ideas which could not be doubted, and to work by strict deduction from valid premises. Voltaire, indeed, was to remark later that for a nonmathematician Locke had a perfect command of the mathematical method. "No one has proved better than he that one can have the geometrical spirit without the aid of geometry." The first proceeding, of course, was to examine the object, in this case man. One should come to some truth that could not be doubted, and then proceed to draw from

this and other truths all the consequences that could be drawn by strict logic. Locke also, as did many of the psychological thinkers of the eighteenth century, proceeded to make further deductions as to the nature of the society demanded by such a being as the man whose nature he had analyzed. The method, of course, is the exact reverse of the painstaking methods of modern sociologists who carefully study what actually does go on in society, rather than make deductions from the nature of man.

We have already briefly mentioned the most famous dictum of Locke, that the mind of man at birth is a *tabula rasa,* a blank slate. With this, of course, Hobbes would have agreed. As Hobbes had said (and Aristotle indeed before him), "there is no conception in a man's mind, which hath not at first been begotten upon the organs of sense." Locke then goes on to make his natural first deduction, that the mind is furnished entirely by experience, from which comes all our knowledge. All the materials which make possible human understanding are provided by observation, or through the internal reflections of the mind working upon the data thus supplied. It will be noticed that Locke has retreated somewhat from the extreme position taken by Hobbes that there is not really a reflecting self, but only mechanical causation in the mind. But, though this is a clear and distinct idea with him, and therefore primary, Locke does not feel it necessary to explain how it can come about that there is a reflecting self at all.

Other thinkers who followed in the eighteenth century accepted this self but tried to determine the manner of human thinking. Thus the thought implicit in both Hobbes and Locke that there are associations of ideas derived causally from sense perceptions becomes the leading thought in psychology. Clearly to be derived from Locke is also the practical conclusion, so vehemently insisted on in the eighteenth century, that education is the greatest necessity for man, even though not all would have gone so far as one educational propagandist who declared that with a proper education there could be thirty million Newtons and thirty million Shakespeares (Charles Fourier). Why not? If there are no innate ideas, and no inherent potentialities peculiar to the person, if environment is all that molds the human being, then surely it would follow that in theory the same environment would produce the same genius. It can hardly be denied that, practicable or not, the conclusion follows from the premises.

Political and economic thought of John Locke—Natural rights

Locke was hardly less influential in his political and economic thought. We have noted already his political thought, and his version of the Social Contract. But it should be noted here again how his political thought itself was conditioned by the search for absolute truths which could not be doubted. He came to the conclusion that there were three inalienable "natural" rights to which man was entitled. Since he could not say that these were social rights agreed to by the society, as this would take away their absolute character, he stated that they were inalienable and he claimed that they had been granted by God. These rights, in his view, were life, liberty, and property. If the government did not grant these God-given rights, then it was the right, even the obligation, of the people to see that they were granted, if necessary by revolution. Locke also claimed that it was right for everyone to pursue an enlightened self-interest, or happiness, since he perceived from his examination of society the unalterable truth, the clear and distinct idea, that all men in fact were motivated by self-interest. So the right to property in the American Declaration of Independence was metamorphosed into the "unalienable" right to the pursuit of happiness.

▶ Summary—The importance and permanence of the Scientific Revolution

We ought not to criticize too sharply the somewhat simple ideas of these seventeenth and eighteenth century men. Most of them believed in a universe about which

before very long everything would be known, as from the time of Newton it was believed that everything of importance in physics was already known. As Pope said:

> "Nature and Nature's laws lay hid in night:
> God said, Let Newton be! and all was Light."

The tremendous empirical work of the later centuries had yet to be embarked upon in full seriousness. A few facts were known, and at once the mind of that age leaped to speedy generalizations and speedy conclusions. It was much more pleasant to speculate than to do hard and unrewarding research. If Locke altogether neglected the possible effects of heredity it was because no one had as yet done any research into the subject. If the nature of the atom was altogether different from what Galileo and Gassendi had imagined it to be, these men had not the tools as yet to discover what the atom really was, still less the elementary particles of which it was composed. What these men did was very considerable. They directed attention to subjects that had seldom been seriously considered before, and they abandoned the old prejudices that had stood in the way of new knowledge. The social scientists such as John Locke believed that society could and should be changed, and they came to believe in education as one of the principal means for the attainment of this end.

For the first time since antiquity there was a widespread desire for new knowledge in every field, and scientists became aware of what other scientists were doing, thus stimulating invention and new hypotheses. It was now possible for new knowledge to be incorporated within the total framework of science, and inventions could be used as soon as they were devised, for they had been invented to fill a particular need. And with the perfection of the Newtonian method for increasing knowledge, the use of hypothesis and planned experimentation to prove it, a tool had been invented which might prevent forever the constant production of unverifiable a priori ideas that could never be shown in practice to be of use.

Nineteenth- and twentieth-century science has only followed in the footsteps of the age we have been discussing, which was called by Whitehead the Century of Genius. Old physical theories have been abandoned, in a few cases to be replaced by new and more adequate ones. Refinements have been added to Newtonian physics as in the Einsteinian theories, but the basis still stands as true for the world described and studied by Newton. The subatomic world has been opened up and put to use, a world which these pioneers could hardly have imagined with the information available to them. And a fashionable biological theory in the form of nineteenth-century Darwinism has replaced the overmechanistic Newtonian-Cartesian theories which had been too quickly applied in fields where they were not applicable. And all this science, developed in the few countries of Western Europe, has been spread over the whole world so that it is now studied by all who desire to partake of its benefits.

Certainly the seventeenth and eighteenth centuries were new ages of faith—faith that the universe was intelligible and would soon yield all its secrets to inquisitive man. We now believe that the process will take far longer than the pioneers imagined, yet the dream has not faded, though we should perhaps be wise to remember the famous words of the greatest pioneer of them all, Newton himself. "I do not know what I may appear to the world; but to myself I seem to have been only like a boy playing on the seashore, and diverting myself in now and then finding a smoother pebble or a prettier shell than ordinary, whilst the great ocean of truth lay undiscovered before me."

▶ Suggestions for further reading

The emphasis given in this chapter to the new attitude toward physical phenomena characteristic of modern times is supported by three important books which are recommended for study. These are E. A. Burtt, *The Metaphysical Foundations of Modern Science* (2nd edit., Garden City, N.Y., Doubleday & Company, Anchor Books, 1955). This work, which first appeared in 1924 and was revised in 1932, was a pioneer study of the type of thinking engaged in by the early modern scientists, and it is still unsurpassed for the close thinking given to the subject and the selection of apt quotations from the writings of the men studied. John Herman Randall Jr., in *The Making of the Modern Mind* (2nd edit., Boston: Houghton Mifflin Company, 1940), after studying the medieval attitude toward life, goes on to take in a wide range of material in the field of early modern thought. The scientific Chapters 9–11 are fairly well done, though in places they may be found a little confusing to the student. The thread of the argument cannot be followed as well in Randall as in the much more difficult Burtt, whom Randall uses. Where this book especially excels, however, is in the subsequent Chapters 12–15, where the author discusses the effects of the new scientific viewpoint on religious, political, social, and economic thinking of the seventeenth and eighteenth centuries. This material is difficult to find elsewhere, and nowhere, as far as I am aware, has it been gathered together as effectively as here. Herbert Butterfield in *The Origins of Modern Science* (New York: The Macmillan Company, 1951) selects a few outstanding problems studied by early modern scientists and in an extremely interesting manner discusses how these problems came to be solved. For lucidity and readableness it would be difficult to surpass this work in its field.

The early chapters of F. C. S. Northrop, *The Logic of Science and the Humanities* (New York: The Macmillan Company, 1947) study the various possible scientific methods and the problems that arise from them, making a valuable comparison between the methods. The early chapters also of Alfred N. Whitehead, *Science and the Modern World* (New York: New American Library, a Mentor Book, 1954) should be read since they stress the importance of seventeenth-century science as the preparation for the modern world. The later chapters, however, are very difficult for the beginning student.

Among the standard histories of science which provide the essential facts, probably the best is William C. Dampier, *A History of Science and its Relations with Philosophy and Religion* (4th edit., revised and enlarged, New York: The Macmillan Company, 1949). The chapters on seventeenth-century science are not, however, among the best in the book, which becomes progressively better as modern times are approached. But there is plenty of useful information which will fill out the interpretative material to be found in the other books recommended.

The best anthology of primary sources known to the author is Holmes Boynton, *The Beginnings of Modern Science* (New York: The Classics Club, 1948), an altogether invaluable work which contains a large number of crucially important selections from all the important scientists of the early modern period, continuing into the eighteenth century. Amongst the scientists themselves Descartes, *Discourse on Method*, a short, admirably lucid, and of course altogether unique work, should not be missed, and can be read in any English edition, although for those with even an elementary knowledge of French the original, which is written in clear and simple French, might be attempted with profit. Since Galileo himself wrote with humor, wit and clarity, his works are still very much readable and are constantly being retranslated even in our day, two appearing in the same year in sumptuous editions recently. One of these is Galileo Galilei, *Dialogue Concerning the Two Chief World Systems* (tr. Stillman Drake, Berkeley, Calif.: University of California Press, 1953). The other is *Dialogue on the Great World Systems in the Salusbury Translation* ed., G. de Santillana (Chicago: The University of Chicago Press, 1953), and there seems little to choose between them. This is the most important work of Galileo to read since it contains the arguments that brought him into trouble with the Inquisition. The third great scientist, Isaac Newton, did not write his works to be read by any except the specialist. The *Principia* is of course available in English, but it is not recommended for the beginning student unless he has a considerable background in mathematics and physics, much fortitude, and a great interest in the subject.

Finally, mention should be made of an excellent edition of John Locke's writings on politics and education which will illustrate his method of combined rationalism and empiricism referred to in the text: John Locke, *On Politics and Education* (New York: The Classics Club, 1947). This edition contains the *Second Treatise on Civil Government* in its entirety.

Appendix

Major Rulers and Regimes

The Papacy

Alexander vi, 1492–1503
Pius iii, 1503
Julius ii, 1503–1513
Leo x, 1513–1521
Adrian vi, 1522–1523
Clement vii, 1523–1534
Paul iii, 1534–1549
Julius iii, 1550–1555
Marcellus ii, 1555
Paul iv, 1555–1559
Pius iv, 1559–1565
Pius v, 1566–1572
Gregory xiii, 1572–1585
Sixtus v, 1585–1590
Urban vii, 1590
Gregory xiv, 1590–1591
Innocent ix, 1591
Clement viii, 1592–1605
Leo xi, 1605
Paul v, 1605–1621
Gregory xv, 1621–1623
Urban viii, 1623–1644
Innocent x, 1644–1655
Alexander vii, 1655–1667
Clement ix, 1667–1669
Clement x, 1670–1676
Innocent xi, 1676–1689
Alexander viii, 1689–1691
Innocent xii, 1691–1700
Clement xi, 1700–1721

Holy Roman Empire

Maximilian i, 1493–1519
Charles v, 1519–1556
Ferdinand i, 1556–1564
Maximilian ii, 1564–1576
Rudolph ii, 1576–1612
Matthias, 1612–1619
Ferdinand ii, 1619–1637
Ferdinand iii, 1637–1657
Leopold i, 1658–1705
Joseph i, 1705–1711
Charles vi, 1711–1740

Austria

Maximilian i, 1493–1519
Charles i, 1519–1520;
    Holy Roman Emperor as
    Charles v, 1519–1556
Ferdinand i, 1556–1564
Maximilian ii, 1564–1576
Rudolph ii, 1576–1612
Matthias, 1612–1619
Ferdinand ii, 1619–1637
Ferdinand iii, 1637–1657
Leopold i, 1658–1705
Joseph i, 1705–1711
Charles ii; Charles vi as Holy
    Roman Emperor, 1711–1740

Spain

Ferdinand and Isabella, king
    and queen, 1479–1504
Ferdinand, 1504–1516
Charles i, 1516–1556; Holy
    Roman Emperor as Charles v,
    1519–1556
Philip ii, 1556–1598
Philip iii, 1598–1621
Philip iv, 1621–1665
Charles ii, 1665–1700
Philip v, 1700–1746

France

Louis xi, 1461–1483
Charles viii, 1483–1498
Louis xii, 1498–1515
Francis i, 1515–1547
Henry ii, 1547–1559
Francis ii, 1559–1560
Charles ix, 1560–1574
Henry iii, 1574–1589
Henry iv, 1589–1610
Louis xiii, 1610–1643
Louis xiv, 1643–1715

in the Modern Period

Great Britain (England before 1707)

Henry VII, 1485–1509
Henry VIII, 1509–1547
Edward VI, 1547–1553
Mary I, 1553–1558
Elizabeth I, 1558–1603
James I, 1603–1625 (James VI of Scotland)
Charles I, 1625–1649
The Commonwealth and Protectorate under Cromwell, 1649–1658; under Cromwell's successors, 1658–1660
Charles II, 1660–1685
James II, 1685–1688
William III and Mary II, 1689–1694
William III, 1694–1702
Anne, 1702–1714
George I, 1714–1727

Russia

Ivan III, tsar, 1462–1505
Basil IV, 1505–1533
Ivan IV, 1533–1584
Theodore I, 1584–1598
Boris Godunov, 1598–1605
Michael, 1613–1645
Alexis, 1645–1676
Theodore II, 1676–1682
Ivan V and Peter I, 1682–1689
Peter I, 1689–1725

Brandenburg-Prussia

Frederick William, 1640–1688
Frederick III, 1688–1701; Frederick I, king of Prussia, 1701–1713
Frederick William I, 1713–1740

Sweden

Gustavus I, 1523–1560
Eric XIV, 1560–1568
John III, 1568–1592
Sigismund, 1592–1604
Charles IX, 1604–1611
Gustavus II, 1611–1632
Christina, 1632–1654
Charles X, 1654–1660
Charles XI, 1660–1697
Charles XII, 1697–1718

Index

► pronunciation key

This Pronunciation Key is reprinted from *The American College Dictionary*, edited by Clarence L. Barnhart, with the permission of Random House, Inc., publishers. Copyright, 1947, Random House, Inc. Most of the pronunciations given in the Index are taken from *The American College Dictionary*.

The symbol ('), as in **moth·er** (mŭ*th*'er), is used to mark primary stress; the syllable preceding it is pronounced with greater prominence than the other syllables in the word. The symbol ('), as in **grand·moth·er** (grănd'mŭ*th*'er), is used to mark secondary stress; a syllable marked for secondary stress is pronounced with less prominence than the one marked (') but with more prominence than those bearing no stress mark at all.

ă	act, bat	l	low, all			ŭ	up, love
ā	able, cape	m	my, him			ū	use, cute
â	air, dare	n	now, on			û	urge, burn
ä	art, calm	ng	sing, England				
						v	voice, live
b	back. rub	ŏ	box, hot			w	west, away
ch	chief, beach	ō	over, no			y	yes, young
d	do, bed	ô	order, ball			z	zeal, lazy, those
		oi	oil, joy			zh	vision, measure
ĕ	ebb, set	o͞o	book, put				
ē	equal, bee	o͞o	ooze, rule			ə	occurs only in un-
		ou	out, loud				accented sylla-
							bles and indicates
f	fit, puff	p	page, stop				the sound of
g	give, beg	r	read, cry				a *in* alone
h	hit, heart	s	see, miss				e *in* system
		sh	shoe, push				i *in* easily
ĭ	if, big	t	ten, bit				o *in* gallop
ī	ice, bite	th	thin, path				u *in* circus
		th	that, other				
j	just, edge						
k	kept, make						

Foreign Sounds

à   as in French *ami* [a vowel intermediate in quality between the ă of *cat* and the ä of *calm*, but closer to the former]

KH   as in German *ach;* Scottish *loch* [a consonant made by bringing the tongue into the position for *k*, as in *key, coo*, while pronouncing a strong *h*]

N   [a symbol used to indicate nasalized vowels as in *bon*. There are four such vowels in French, found in *un bon vin blanc* (oeN bôN văN bläN)]

œ   as in French *feu;* German *schön* [a vowel made with the lips rounded in position for ō as in *over*, while trying to say ā as in *able*]

Y   as in French *tu;* German *über* [a vowel made with the lips rounded in position for o͞o as in *ooze*, while trying to ē as in *easy*]

Index

(NOTE: Page references to illustrations are given in bold face; page references to maps are given in italics.)

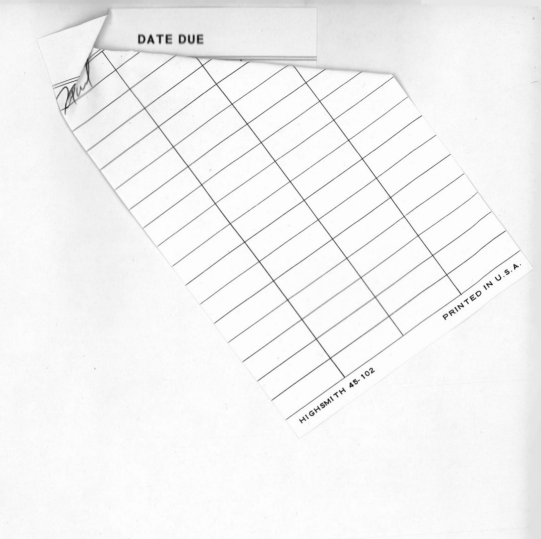

DATE DUE

HIGHSMITH 45-102

PRINTED IN U.S.A.

EUROPE IN 1360

showing
Famous Cathedrals — Leading Universities

NORWAY

SCOTLAND
Elgin
Glasgow

IRELAND

NORTH
SEA

DENMAR
Roskilde
Ratzeb

Durham
York
ENGLAND
Lincoln
Lichfield
Peterboro
Gloucester
Oxford
Cambridge
12th C.
1209
Wells
London
Winchester
Calais
Ponthieu

ATLANTIC

OCEAN

Utrecht
Münster
Antwerp
Hildesheim
Brunswick
Mag
Bruges
Cologne
Elbe R.
Rouen
Coutances
Caen
Amiens
Paris
12th C.
HOLY
RO
Trier
Mainz
Rheims
Metz
1379
Erfurt
Bamburg
Heidelberg
Rhine
1385
Le Mans
Angers
13th C.
Chartres
Strasburg
Rati
Loire R.
Orléans
ca. 1231
Poitiers
Bourges
Autun
Freiburg
Basel
EMPIR
Duchy of
KINGDOM
Angoulême
OF
Lausanne
BAY OF
Aquitaine
FRANCE
Geneva
BISCAY
Grenoble
Brescia
1339
Milan
Vicenza
Santiago di Compostella
Lugo
Leon
Garonne R.
Toulouse
1229
Albi
1248
Padua
1204
Venice
1222
Genoa
Piacenza
Po R.
Bologna
Valladolid
1213
Navarre
Perpignan
1349
C. of
Provence
Reggio
1188
Florence
11th C.
Salamanca
1230
Saragossa
Lerida
Montpellier
12th C.
CORSICA
1343 Pisa
1246 Siena
Arezzo
1215
PORTUGAL
Burgos
Coimbra
1290
CASTILE
Toledo
Tagus R.
ARAGON
Ebro R.
Barcelona
Tarragona
Papal States
Guadiana R.
Valencia
Rome
1303
SARDINIA
Seville
1254
Balearic Islands
TYRRHENIAN SE
GRANADA
MEDITERRANEAN
Naples
1224
Monreale
Pale
SICI